BEYOND CAPITAL

By the same author:

MARX'S THEORY OF ALIENATION
THE WORK OF SARTRE: SEARCH FOR FREEDOM
PHILOSOPHY, IDEOLOGY AND SOCIAL SCIENCE
THE POWER OF IDEOLOGY

BEYOND CAPITAL

Towards a Theory of Transition

István Mészáros
Professor Emeritus, University of Sussex

First published in 1995
by The Merlin Press
10 Malden Road
London NW5 3HR

UK ISBN 085036 432 9
US ISBN 085345 881 2

This edition published in the U.S. by
Monthly Review Press
122 West 27 Street
New York
NY 10001

Library of Congress Cataloging-in-Publication Data

Mészáros, István, 1930–
        Beyond capital: toward a theory of transition/by István
        Mészáros.
        p. cm.
        Includes bibliographical references.
        ISBN 0-85345-881-2 (pbk: alk. paper) : $25.00
        1. Marxian economics. 2. Dialectical materialism.
3. Postmodernism.
HB97.5.M39 1995
335.4'1—dc20
                                                                95–41551
                                                                CIP

Printed in Finland by WSOY

To Donatella

CONTENTS

'By a dialectical advance, *subjective self-seeking* turns into *mediation* of the particular through the universal, with the result that each man in earning, producing, and enjoying on his own account is *eo ipso* producing and earning for the enjoyment of everyone else. The *compulsion* which brings this about is rooted in the *complex interdependence* of each on all, and it now presents itself to each as the *universal permanent capital.*'

Hegel

'The historic task of bourgeois society is the establishment of the *world market,* at least in its basic outlines, and a mode of production that rests on its basis. Since the world is round, it seems that this has been accomplished with the colonization of California and Australia and with the annexation of China and Japan. For us the difficult question is this: the revolution on the Continent is imminent and its character will be at once socialist; will it not be *necessarily crushed* in this *little corner of the world,* since on a much larger terrain the development of bourgeois society is still *in the ascendant.*'

Marx

Preface

THE 'little corner of the world' of which Marx spoke in 1858 is no longer a little corner: the severe problems of the capital system's increasing saturation cast their shadow everywhere. For capital's historical ascendancy is by now consummated also on that 'much larger terrain' whose disconcerting existence Marx had to acknowledge in his letter to Engels (8th October 1858). Today we live in a world firmly held under the rule of capital, in an age of unfulfilled promises and bitterly disappointed expectations, defied for the time being only by stubborn hope.

To many people the present state of affairs seems to be fundamentally unalterable, corresponding to Hegel's characterization of thinking and acting as right and proper — or 'rational' in his sense — only in submission to the requirements of *universal permanent capital*. Moreover, this impression of fateful unalterability seems to be reinforced by the fact that one of the most often repeated political slogans offered by our decision makers as the justification of their actions is: *'there is no alternative.'* Such wisdom continues to be uttered without any concern for how bleak it would be if this proposition were really true. It is much easier to resign oneself to the finality of the predicament asserted in this blindly deterministic political slogan of our times — without even attempting to assess, let alone question, its grievous implications — than to devise the necessary challenge to it.

Curiously, however, the politicians who never tire of repeating that there is no alternative to the existing order of affairs do not hesitate to describe at the same time their own trade as 'the art of the possible'. They refuse to notice the blatant contradiction between the traditional self-justification of politics, as the socially beneficial 'art of the possible', and the uncritically advocated resignation to the rule of capital to which, in their view — claimed to be the only rationally tenable view 'in the real world' — there cannot be an alternative. For what on earth could be the meaning of politics as the 'pursuit of the socially commendable *possible*' if the viability of any alternative to the imperatives of the ruling order is apriori excluded as worse than hopeless because *impossible?*

To be sure, the fact that so many decision makers — in the East and West alike — embrace the idea that there can be no alternative to the prevailing determinations cannot be considered simply a corrigible personal aberration of those who advocate it. On the contrary, this bleak idea emanates from the present stage of development of the global capital system as such, with all its paralyzing interdependencies and objectively narrowing margins of action. For in the ascending phase of development of commodity society a whole range of meaningful alternatives could be contemplated (and successfully implemented) in the interest of profitable capital accumulation and expansion by the dominant (as a rule also empire-building) capitalist countries.

Things have drastically changed in this respect. For the age of globally saturated *monopoly capital* cannot tolerate, as far as the essentials and not the marginal trimmings are concerned, the practice of parliamentary political pluralism that once upon a time could provide the self-justification of reformist socialdemocratic strategies.

Not surprisingly, therefore, the recent demise of the parties of the left is not confined to the ignominious disintegration of the former (Stalinist) communist parties, in the East and West alike. In this regard it is far more significant (and paradoxically also hopeful) that the century-old socialdemocratic promise of instituting socialism 'little by little' has conclusively demonstrated its illusory character with the — by now quite unashamedly explicit — abandonment of the original social and political aspirations of the movement. It is significant and hopeful, despite everything, because the precarious condition of democratic politics today — all too obvious in the unholy consensus concerning the wisdom of 'there is no alternative' and its direct practical consequences, as exemplified for instance by the authoritarian legislative measures already experienced by the trades unions — can only be redressed by a radical extra-parliamentary mass movement. A movement which cannot arise without the working class being shaken out of the earlier successfully institutionalized illusion of establishing 'socialism little by little' within the confines of self-reforming capitalism.

THE self-serving slogan of 'there is no alternative' is often coupled with an equally tendentious clause of self-justification which proclaims that '*in the real world*' there can be no alternative to the advocated course of action (or inaction). This proposition is supposed to be a self-evident truth, automatically exempting all those who continue to assert it from inconveniencing themselves with the burden of proof.

Yet, the moment we ask the question, what sort of 'real world' are they talking about, it becomes clear that it is an utterly fictitious one. For the structural defects and explosive *antagonisms* of the world in which we actually happen to live are apologetically denied or blindly disregarded by those who expect us to believe that in the 'real world' there is no alternative to the meek acceptance of the conditions necessary for the trouble-free functioning of the global capital system.

In the name of reason, common sense, and 'real politics' we are invited to resign ourselves to the existing state of affairs, no matter how destructive its antagonisms. For within the parameters of the established order — eternalized as the rational framework of the fundamentally unalterable 'real world', with 'human nature' and its corresponding ideal reproductive instrumentality: the 'market mechanism', etc. — no solutions can be envisaged to the ubiquitous contradictions.

Thus we are expected to pretend to ourselves that classes and class contradictions no longer exist or no longer matter. Accordingly, the only viable course of action in the thus postulated 'real world' is supposed to be to ignore, or to 'explain away' the evidence of structural instability provided by our own eyes, wishfully sweeping under an imaginary carpet the chronic problems and crisis symptoms of growing severity with which our social order confronts us every day.

As things stand today, the ideologists of the established order do not believe any longer even in the earlier popularized notion of changing their order 'little by little'. With the end of the ascending phase of capitalism no real change can be considered legitimate; neither by major structural intervention nor indeed 'little by little'.

If it is true, as they say, that *'there is no alternative'* to the structural determinations of the capital system in the *'real world'*, in that case the very idea of *causal interventions* — no matter how little or large — must be condemned as an absurdity. The only change admissible within such a vision of the world belongs to the type which concerns itself with some strictly limited negative *effects* but leaves their *causal foundation* — the given system of metabolic control — completely unaffected.

Yet, if there is an approach that truly deserves to be called a total absurdity in the realm of social reform, it is not the advocacy of major structural change but precisely the kind of apologetic wishful thinking which *divorces the effects from their causes*. This is why the 'war on poverty', announced with reforming zeal so many times, especially in the twentieth century, is always lost, given the causal framework — the poverty-producing exploitative structural imperatives — of the capital system.

The attempt at divorcing effects from their causes goes hand in hand with the equally fallacious practice of claiming the status of a *rule* for the *exception*. This is how it can be pretended that the misery and chronic underdevelopment that necessarily arise from the neo-colonial domination and exploitation of the overwhelming majority of humankind by a mere handful of capitalistically developed countries — hardly more than the G7 — do not matter at all. For, as the self-serving legend goes, thanks to the (never realized) *'modernization'* of the rest of the world, the population of every country will one fine day enjoy the great benefits of the 'free enterprise system'.

The fact that the rapacious exploitation of the human and material resources of our planet for the benefit of a few capitalist countries happens to be a *non-generalizable* condition is wantonly disregarded. Instead, the universal viability of emulating the development of the 'advanced capitalist' countries is predicated, ignoring that neither the advantages of the imperialist past, nor the immense profits derived on a continuing basis from keeping the 'Third World' in structural dependency can be 'universally diffused', so as to produce the anticipated happy results through 'modernization' and 'free-marketization'. Not to mention the fact that even if the history of imperialism could be re-written in a sense diametrically opposed to the way it actually unfolded, coupled with the fictitious reversal of the existing power relations of domination and dependency in favour of the underdeveloped countries, the general adoption of the rapacious utilization of our planet's limited resources — enormouly damaging already, although at present practised only by the privileged tiny minority — would make the whole system instantly collapse. It is enough to think in this respect of the wild discrepancy between the size of the U.S. population — less than 5 *percent* of the world population — and its 25 *percent* consumption of total available energy resources. It takes no great imagination to figure out what would happen if the 95 percent adopted the same consumption pattern, trying to squeeze *nineteen times* 25 percent out of the remaining 75 percent.

To hide the vacuity of the promised corrective solutions is the convenient ideological function of turning the strictly *exceptional* conditions of the privileged few into the *universal rule*. Only in an utterly fictitious world in which effects can be divorced from, and even diametrically opposed to, their causes can such an approach be considered feasible and sound. This is why these two fallacies — the first that stipulates the possibility of manipulating effects in and by themselves as divorced from their causes, and the second the universalization of ungeneralizable exceptions — are so closely tied together in the ruling 'pragmatic' ideology. An ideology which finds its ultimate self-justification and satisfaction in its claim to depict the order of 'the real world' to which 'there can be no alternative'.

MARGARET Thatcher earned the nickname TINA — an acronym for 'There Is No Alternative' — for denying with monotonous regularity the possibility of alternatives. In her footsteps Mikhail Gorbachev, too, went on repeating the same wisdom on countless occasions. Ironically, though, Mrs Thatcher had to find out that there *had* to be an alternative to her, when the Tory party forcibly removed her from office. At that point she sighed: 'It's a funny old world!' But she refused to let us into the secret whether in her view that 'funny old world' still qualified for the all-absolving status of 'the real world'.

Nor did Party Secretary and President Gorbachev fare any better than Mrs Thatcher when he lost not only his office, but the entire state system which he once ruled and tried to convert into a capitalist market society, in the name of 'there is no alternative'. But his was a much more complicated case than that of his British counterpart. For it is perfectly understandable why someone like Margaret Thatcher should wholeheartedly embrace and 'internalize' as right and proper — i.e. as not only *de facto* but also *de jure* — the ever narrowing margin of action left open by the imperatives of the capitalist order. People like Baroness Thatcher put their mouth where their money is.

However, all this should be very different on the opposite side of the social divide. Once people who claim to be socialist adopt the wisdom of 'there is no alternative' as the justification of the policies pursued, they cease to have anything whatsoever to do with socialism. For the socialist project was defined right from the beginning as the alternative to the established social order. It is therefore not in the least surprising that during the years of his office, in the aftermath of his conversion to the philosophy of 'there is no alternative', Mikhail Gorbachev should have abandoned even the vaguest references to socialism. He ended up — in his resignation speech — wishing for the future, in a complete social vacuum, 'democracy and prosperity'. Given the disastrous legacy which he had left behind, his good wishes must have sounded particularly hollow to his starving fellow countrymen.

But be it as it may, the devotion of our political leaders to carrying out the imperatives of the capital system does not remove its structural deficiencies and potentially explosive antagonisms. Contrary to the laboriously cultivated mythology of the ruling order, the perilous contradictions are *intrinsic* and not *external* to it. This is why the world is a much more unstable place today — after the capitulation of the old 'external enemy' and the short-lived triumphalist celebration of the 'end of the cold war' — than ever before.

In the light of recent developments, bringing with them not only the fragorous collapse of the unreformable Stalinist Soviet system (and of its formerly dependent territories in Eastern Europe) but also the undermining of the wishful edifices built in the capitalist West on the Soviet Union's collapse, only a fool can believe that we can now march undisturbed towards the liberal-capitalist millennium. In truth, however, the existing order demonstrates its untenability not only through the growing socioeconomic 'dysfunctions' arising from the daily imposition of its inhumanities on the 'unfortunate' thousands of millions. It does so also through the spectacular deflation of the most cherished illusions regarding the irreversible socioeconomic stabilizing power of the capitalistically advanced world's victory over yesterday's enemy.

The awareness of this untenability helps to sustain the hope for a fundamental structural change, despite all the setbacks and bitter disappointments experienced in the recent past. Filling holes by digging bigger and bigger holes — which happens to be the preferred way of solving problems at the present stage of development — cannot be continued indefinitely. Finding a way out of the maze of the global capital system's contradictions through a sustainable transition to a very different social order is therefore more imperative today than ever before, in view of the ever more threatening instability.

INEVITABLY, the historical challenge for instituting a viable alternative to the given order also calls for a major reassessment of the socialist strategic framework and the conditions of its realization, in the light of twentieth century developments and disappointments. We badly need a socialist theory of transition not simply as an antidote to the absurd theorizations of 'the end of history' and the concomitant premature burial of socialism. In its own, positive terms, a theory of transition is needed in order to reexamine the conceptual framework of socialist theory, worked out originally in relation to the European 'little corner of the world'.

In contrast to the objective potentialities of capitalist development as confined to the limited European setting, the severe problems arising from the global consolidation of an immensely powerful system — which successfully unfolded through capital's historical ascendancy during the last century and a half, assuming a 'hybrid' form, in contrast to its 'classical' variety with regard to the operation of the law of value — have far-reaching implications for the necessary reformulation of the original socialist strategies of emancipation. The bewildering transformations and reversals which we have witnessed in our century can only be made intelligible if reassessed within this broader framework of the global capital system, as it came to dominate the world in its dynamic and contradictory historical reality. The same goes for the possibility of carrying out a fundamental structural change in a genuine socialist direction: it must be made feasible and convincing in terms of the historical dynamics of the selfsame 'actually existing' global capital system to which the socialist mode of control, through the self-management of the associated producers, is meant to provide the much needed alternative.

Beyond the false stability of the global 'Potemkin Village', erected from the wishful images of the 'New World Order,' it is not too difficult to point to crisis symptoms that foreshadow the breakdown of the established socioeconomic and political order. However, in and by itself the profound structural crisis of the capital system is very far from being enough to inspire confidence in a successful outcome. The pieces must be picked up and put together in due course in a positive way. And not even the gravest crises or the most severe breakdowns are of much help by themselves in that respect.

It is always incomparably easier to say 'no' than to draw even the bare outlines of a positive alternative to the negated object. Only on the basis of a coherent strategic view of the overall social complex can even a partial negation of the existent be considered plausible and legitimate. For, the alternative advanced — whether explicitly or by implication — by any serious negation of the given conditions must be sustainable within its own framework of a social whole, if it is to have any hope of success against the 'incorporating' power of the potentially always 'hybrid' established world into which the forces of a critique want to make an inroad.

The point of the socialist project, as originally conceived, was precisely to counterpose such a strategic overall alternative to the existent, and not to remedy, in an integrable way, some of its most glaring defects. For the latter could only facilitate — as indeed varieties of reformism did — the continued operation of capital's mode of metabolic control within the new 'hybrid' system, notwithstanding its crisis.

As time went by, the socialist political adversaries of commodity society became hopelessly fragmented by the rewards which the ruling order could offer, and the capital system as such successfully adapted itself to all partial criticism coming from the socialdemocratic parties, undermining at the same time the original socialist vision as a strategic alternative. The ruling ideology — understandably from its own standpoint — declared that 'Wholism' was the ideological enemy, assured in the knowledge that even the sharpest partial criticism becomes quite impotent if its totalizing framework of intelligibility (and potential legitimacy) is categorically ruled 'out of court', with the help of the exorcizing pseudo-philosophical swearword of 'Wholism' (or of its several equivalents).

Thus, the positive approval of the overall framework and command structure of capital became the absolute premiss of all legitimate political discourse in the capitalist countries, and was willingly accepted as the common frame of reference by the socialdemocratic/labourite interlocutors. At the same time, and notwithstanding its verbal radicalism, the Stalinist system closely mirrored capital's command structure in its own way, liquidating, together with countless militants who tried to remain faithful to the originally envisaged quest for emancipation, even the memory of the genuine socialist objectives.

Understandably, therefore, these two principal practical perversions of the international working class movement, emanating from very different sociohistorical circumstances, fatefully undermined all belief in the viability of the socialist alternative with which they were for a long time falsely identified. In reality, far from being coherent and comprehensive socialist negations of the established order, they both represented *the line of least resistance* under their specific historical conditions, accommodating themselves as modes of social control to the inner demands of the incorrigibly hierarchical capital system.

Thus, on the one hand, the failure of the socialdemocratic strategy (given its willing acceptance of the constraints imposed by the parameters of 'self-reforming capitalism') had to take the form of totally abandoning in the end the once held socialist aims. And on the other hand, all efforts at 'restructuring' the Stalinist system, from Khrushchev's 'de-Stalinization' to Gorbachev's 'perestroika' — brought about when running society by means of artificial states of emergency and the corresponding labour camps became both economically and politically untenable — had to founder, because the hierarchical command structure of the postrevolutionary social order, with its authoritarian political extraction of surplus-labour (which should have been, instead, the object of a sustained attack) was always retained by the would-be reformers. They could not contemplate restructuring the established structure except by preserving its overall character as a hierarchical structure, since they themselves occupied, as if it was their birth-right, the top echelons. And through their self-contradictory enterprise of *'restructuring' without changing the structure itself* as the embodiment of the hierarchical social division of labour — just like social democracy wanted to *reform capitalism without altering its capitalist substance* — they condemned the Soviet system to staggering from one crisis to another.

The 'crisis of Marxism', of which a great deal has been written in the last decades, denoted in fact the crisis and almost complete disintegration of the political movements which once professed their allegiance to the Marxian conception of socialism. The clamorous historical failure of the two principal movements — social democracy and the Stalinistically metamorphosed Bolshevik tradition — opened the floodgates to all kinds of triumphalist propaganda which celebrated the death of the socialist idea as such. The negative effects of such propaganda cannot be countered simply by identifying the material vested interests which underpin the anti-socialist celebrations. For what happened did not happen without weighty historical causes. The world of capital is in fact very different today to what it used to be at the time when the modern socialist movement embarked on its journey in the first half of the nineteenth century. Without a serious scrutiny of the intervening decades of development — concerned with the strategic theoretical framework of the socialist alternative as much as with its radically changed organizational requirements — the socialist project cannot renew itself. This is the challenge which all socialists have to face in the foreseeable future.

THE present volume is meant as a contribution to the task of theoretical reassessment and clarification. As already mentioned in the Preface to the third edition of *Marx's Theory of Alienation,* in 1971, the whole project emerged from the analysis of Marx's critique of alienation, set against the claim advanced both in the East and in the West (and in the West particularly in the United States, by people like Daniel Bell) that Marx's concern with emancipation from the rule of capital belonged to the nineteenth century, since not only classes and class antagonisms but all aspects of alienation had been successfully and irrevocably overcome. Having directly experienced Stalinist rule and the bloody suppression of the 1956 uprising in Hungary by the Red Army (applauded, to their indelible shame, by the Communist parties in the West), it became clear to me not only that the proclaimed end of alienation in the East was a fairy-tale, but also that the actually existing Soviet system had nothing whatsoever to do with socialism.

Likewise, direct experience of life in the West after 1956 made it amply clear that capitalist alienation continued to impose quite unmitigated hardship and inhumanities on the overwhelming majority of the people in the 'Free World', and especially on that part of it which the apologists of commodity society preferred to call the 'Third World', so as to be able to ascribe blame to the countries concerned for the grave problems of their so-called 'underdevelopment', and not to a certain kind of *capitalist development:* one pursued in total subordination to, and structural dependency from, the 'First World'.

Moreover, a closer look at the internal power structure of even the capitalistically most advanced countries revealed that — notwithstanding the relative privileges of their working people, as compared to the conditions of countless millions in the former colonial territories — they have preserved fundamentally unaltered the exploitative class relations of the alienating capital system. For, despite all theoretical obfuscation, the deciding issue, applying to all grades and categories of workers everywhere, was and remains the *structural subordination of labour to capital,* and not the relatively higher standard of living of working people in the privileged capitalist countries. Such relative privileges can easily disappear in the midst of a major crisis and escalating unemployment, the sort we are experiencing today. The class position of no matter how varying groups of people is defined by their *location in the command structure of capital,* and not by secondary sociological characteristics, like 'life-style'. As regards their necessarily subordinate location in the command structure of capital, there is no difference between the workers of the most 'underdeveloped' countries and their counterparts in the most privileged capitalist societies. A worker in the U.S. or in Great Britain may own a handful of *non-voting shares* in a private company, but the Robert Maxwells of this world, protected by the legal loopholes of the capitalist state, can rob him or her with the greatest ease even of their hard earned *pension funds,* * as we have found out after the curious death of Maxwell, subjecting them to the conditions of grave existential insecurity, totally at the mercy of the alien power — capital — to which, as the nasty tale devised to frighten the children goes, 'there can be no alternative'.

All this pointed towards the conclusion that the original socialist project, if complemented by the evidence of the changed historical circumstances, retains its validity for the present and the future. However, in the light of disheartening historical and personal experience, it was necessary to acknowledge that one could only remain a socialist *despite* and not *because of* the Soviet Union, in contrast to the way in which many people in the West tried to preserve their left-wing convictions by proxy, abstracting from the conditions of their own countries and fictionalizing at the same time the reality of their proclaimed model.

Given this difference in perspective, the recent collapse of the Soviet system could not come as a great surprise; if anything, it was to be expected after the

---

* The true extent of such practices may one day make Maxwell's deed — a paltry £350 million theft — pale to insignificance. For it has been reported that 'To cover some cash shortages General Motors has dipped into its $15 billion pension fund, as it can under American law. But now *$8.9 billion of the money set aside for pensioners is unfunded.*' (Andrew Lorenz and John Durie, 'GM makes final attempt to avert financial crash', *The Sunday Times,* 1 November 1992, Section 3, p.9.) Thus fraudulence is not marginal or exceptional but belongs to the normality of the capital system.

shock of 1956 and the failure of de-Stalinization thereafter. (The reader can find comments on the permanence of alienation and on the insurmountable antagonisms characteristic of the unstable Soviet type system not only in *Marx's Theory of Alienation* — written between 1959-1969 and published in 1970 — but also in Part Four of *Beyond Capital,* written between 1970 and 1990.) But the importance of the socialist project is infinitely greater than the former Soviet Union. It was conceived, as a way of overcoming the power of capital, a very long time before the Soviet Union came into being, and it will remain with us, in a form suitable to the altered historical circumstances, long after the nightmare of Stalinism is completely forgotten. For the challenge of going 'Beyond Capital', through the establishment of a genuine socialist order, concerns the whole of humanity.

THE title of the present volume — *Beyond Capital* — must be understood in three senses:

- 1. The central meaning of the expression 'beyond capital', as intended by Marx himself when he undertook the monumental task of writing his *Capital.* In this sense it means going beyond *capital as such* and not merely *beyond capitalism.* (For a brief summary of this issue see pp.911-14, 938–40 and 980–82 of the present volume, and for a detailed discussion Chapters 2, 4, 5, 17, and 20.)
- 2. Beyond the *published* version of Marx's *Capital,* including its posthumously printed second and third volumes, as well as the *Grundrisse* and the *Theories of Surplus Value.* For, the whole project to which Marx dedicated his life remained not simply *unfinished,* but — according to the plan briefly sketched by its author in his letters and prefaces — reached only the completion of its early stages, and therefore could not adequately reflect his recorded intentions.
- 3. Beyond the Marxian project itself as it could be articulated under the circumstances of commodity society's global ascendancy in the nineteenth century, when the possibilities of adjustment for capital as a 'hybrid' system of control — which became fully visible only in the twentieth century — were as yet hidden from theoretical scrutiny.

The contents of *Beyond Capital* may be summed up as follows.

Parts One and Two, constituting the first half of the book, deal with *The Uncontrollability of Capital and Its Critique,* and the second half surveys the problems of *Confronting the Structural Crisis of Capital.*

Part One — The Shadow of Uncontrollability — brings into focus the vital reasons for going *beyond capital,* and indeed the inescapable necessity of doing so in the interest of human survival. As a point of departure the Hegelian idealization of 'universal permanent capital' — the outstanding philosophical conception and monumental rationalization of the bourgeois order — is contrasted with the actual completion of capital's historical ascendancy in the form of a not only uncontrollable but also ultimately destructive and self-destructive global system. The salient features of *Capital's Order of Social Metabolic Reproduction,* foreshadowing from the outset its uncontrollability, are discussed in Chapter 2. This is followed up in Chapter 3 with an analysis of the major theories dedicated to finding *Solutions to the Uncontrollability of Capital — from Capital's Standpoint*. Chapters 4 and 5 consider the all-important question of limits, setting out from the way in which causality and time must be treated in this system, followed by a detailed assessment of *The Vicious Circle of Capital's Second Order Mediations* (as well as a critique of its apologists, like Hayek), and conclude with an analysis of the *Relative and Absolute Limits of the Capital System* as a unique — in human history quite exceptional — mode of social metabolic reproduction. Here, in Chapter 5, four issues of particularly great importance are singled out, each of them constituting the focal point of some major contradictions: (1) the antagonism between globally self-asserting transnational capital and national states, remaining irreconcilable despite the more than willing facilitating efforts of capital's personifications in the political domain to make palatable the push for 'globalization' under the hegemony of less than a handful of 'global players'; (2) the catastrophic impact of the productive practices of 'advanced' capital on the environment, tending toward the complete destruction of the most basic conditions of social metabolic reproduction; (3) the total inability of the capital system — including its post-capitalist varieties — to meet the irrepressible challenge of women's liberation, of substantive equality, exposing thereby the vacuity of the traditional way of dealing with the problem of inequality through hollow formal/legal concessions and under the hypocritical rhetorics of 'equal opportunity'; and (4) the cancer of chronic unemployment devastating the social body even in the capitalistically most advanced countries, making a mockery of the post-Second World War article of faith of the liberal/conservative/labour consensus which proclaimed — and claimed the realization of — 'full employment in a free society'.

Part Two is concerned with the *Historical Legacy of the Socialist Critique*. Here the way of proceeding cannot be a straightforward historical account of the socialist theoretical legacy. For the severe problems confronting socialists today did not arise from general theoretical and political concerns. They have erupted from the painful historical experience — the practical appearance and disastrous collapse of an attempt to gain a major foothold for a postcapitalist order in the twentieth century — in relation to which all those who argued in favour of instituting a viable socialist alternative to the rule of capital always had to define their own, widely differing and even sharply conflicting, positions. In this sense, against the background of actual economic and social developments marked by the dramatic implosion of the Soviet system, today — more than ever before — it is impossible to consider the future prospects of socialism without a radical critical reassessment of the relevant historical experience. This is why our point of departure must be the way in which the socialist movement founded by Marx and Engels produced a new historical landmark with the outbreak and temporary survival of the Russian Revolution. The latter inevitably redefined, in tangible practical terms, the originally envisaged perspective of socialist transformation. As a result, the earlier seen theoretical and political negation of capitalism had to be complemented by proving the viability of the postrevolutionary order in positive socioeconomic terms. But even before the first major steps could be taken in that direction, the Russian revolution was raised —

through the successful defence of the conquered state power against Western capitalist intervention — to the status of a model, despite the enormous sociohistorical constraints of the actual situation. The radical wing of the socialist movement tried to come to terms with this circumstance, as we must now in a very different way with the grave implications of the collapse. To reassess these problems in their proper historical perspective, Chapters 6–10 — dealing with *The Challenge of Material and Institutional Mediations in the Orbit of the Russian Revolution* — analyse Lukács's *History and Class Consciousness* as a representative theoretical work conceived in response to the October revolution: a work which offered in its heightened terms of reference rather idealized prospects of development for the socialist movement as a whole. Lukács's volume of essays, on the basis of the author's personal involvement in the revolutionary events in Hungary in 1918-19 as Minister of Education and Culture, as well as in the international socialist movement afterwards, provided a direct theorization of the challenge represented by the Russian revolution. *History and Class Consciousness* (published in 1923) offered a striking philosophical generalization of the historical achievements of October 1917 and turned into positive assets the monumental difficulties with which the 'revolution at the weakest link of the chain' had to struggle. This is how Lukács's work had acquired its representative character and legendary influence. Also, in the midst of the profound intellectual crisis caused by the conflagration of the first world war and its socially explosive aftermath, *History and Class Consciousness* tried to build a bridge between the Hegelian conceptualization of the global capital system and Marx's socialist vision, for the benefit of all those intellectuals who were willing to acknowledge the crisis itself but were unable to respond in positive terms to the Marxian diagnosis and solutions. In Chapters 6-10 *History and Class Consciousness* is situated within the framework of its author's subsequent theoretical development. Through the latter it transpires that under the growing constraints imposed by the bleak reality of 'actually existing socialism' of which Trotsky offered the most devastating critique, the necessary — but under the conditions of Stalinism (including its phase of failed de-Stalinization) not feasible — material and institutional mediations of the socialist ideal had to disappear completely from the great Hungarian philosopher's horizon, removing even the limited extent to which they were present at the time of writing *History and Class Consciousness*. The intellectual roots of Lukács's final position, which tried to derive the much needed alternative to the given order from a noble but wholly abstract direct appeal to the individuals' moral consciousness, can be traced back to his outstanding early work, *History and Class Consciousness*, even if they were later greatly accentuated as a result of the blocked development of the postrevolutionary Soviet system and of its East European transplants. The way in which many disappointed intellectuals who once shared Lukács's position — whether brought up in the tradition of Frankfurt 'critical theory' or in the Western communist parties — in recent years turned against the idea of socialism altogether, underlines the need for basing socialist expectations on a much surer material footing.

The second half of *Part Two* deals with the problems of *Radical Break and Transition in the Marxian Heritage*. Following on from the challenge implicit in Lukács's representative intellectual trajectory, it considers the major difficulties that must be faced by any attempt at elaborating a socialist theory of transition. This is done by going back to the origins of the socialist movement and examining in some detail Marx's own vision in the light of subsequent historical developments. After the discussion of the way in which the Marxian theory was conceived and directly or indirectly affected by the objects of its negation — especially by Liberal theory and the Hegelian vision of world historical development — Chapters 11-13 explore the actual response of the bourgeoisie to the emerging international working class movement, analyzing capital's ability to adjust its mode of control to the changed sociohistorical conditions. The problems of the state loom large in this respect, since the temporarily viable *displacement* (often misconceived as the permanent *overcoming*) of the capital system's inner contradictions goes hand in hand with a fundamental change from 'laissez-faire' capitalism to ever greater reliance on direct state intervention in economic affairs, even if ideological mystification continues to glorify the practically non-existent 'free market', the make-believe 'freedom from state interference', and the virtues of boundless individualism. Marx's unavoidable theoretical difficulties — manifest in the temporal ambiguities of the developments envisaged by him and in the absence of the necessary institutional mediations between the rejected capital system and the advocated alternative — are explained in the context of these historical transformations, concerned both with the direction taken by the working class movement as a mass movement (criticized by Marx with regard to the German socialdemocratic 'Gotha Programme') and with the dynamic possibilities of expansion opened up for capital by the new imperialist phase of development, in tune with the system's at the time far from exhausted 'global ascendancy'.

Part Three — Structural Crisis of the Capital System — sets out from the sombre fact that all three major forms of twentieth century development — monopolistic private capital accumulation and expansion, 'Third World modernization', and Soviet type 'planned economy' — have glaringly failed to fulfil their promises. Fifty years of 'modernization' have left the 'Third World' in a condition worse than ever before; the Soviet system has experienced a most dramatic collapse, without any prospect of stabilizing itself by joining the club of 'advanced capitalism', since even the successful restoration of a most 'underdeveloped' form of *dependent capitalism* presents the splintering system with forbidding difficulties; and the privileged few countries of 'advanced capitalism' are going through recessions (and even 'double-dip recessions') at ever shortening intervals. Moreover, for several of them (including Britain and, most seriously for the survival of the capital system as a whole, the U.S.) such recessions are linked to a veritable *black hole* of insoluble indebtedness, euphemistically described by the defenders of the established order as 'the debt overhang'. Since the dominance of Western 'advanced capitalism' is now overwhelming, the inherent limits of economically regulated surplus-extraction practised within that system are of a crucial importance as regards future developments of the global order. As a way out of the intensifying contradictions, the decreasing rate of utilization under 'advanced capitalism' demonstrates its limited viability and ultimate untenability, even when the massive resources of the state are mobilized in the service of the military/industrial complex. For it tends to activate one of the untranscendable structural limits of the capital system: the profit-seeking destruction of the planet's unrenewable resources. Furthermore, this way of managing the decreasing rate of utilization, even today (despite all talk about the 'New World Order') still in conjunction with an enormous military/industrial complex directly sustained by the state, continues to waste human and material resources on a prohibitive scale, in the name of 'military preparedness' against the no longer even identifiable, let alone credible, enemy; thus putting into relief again and again the fact that the real reasons behind such practices are primarily *economic* and not *military*. Under the new historical circumstances crises, too, unfold in a very different way. At the time of capital's global ascendancy, crises erupted in the form of 'great thunderstorms' (Marx), followed by relatively long *expansionary* phases. The new pattern, with the end of the age of capital's historical ascendancy, is the growing frequency of *recessionary* phases tending towards a *depressed continuum*. And given the globally intertwined character of the self-enclosed capital system — which makes all talk about 'the open society' sound utterly farcical, if not altogether obscene — the great challenge, without which the crisis of development cannot be overcome, is this: how to break the vicious circle of the reciprocally paralyzing 'macrocosm' and constitutive cells of the system.

Chapters 17–20 consider the structural parameters of capital in the light of 20th century historical transformations, contrasting them with the defining characteristics of the socialist alternative. They also investigate the reasons for the catastrophic failure of the Soviet type system, together with all attempts at reforming it, including Gorbachev's so-called 'perestroika', undertaken without (and indeed against) the people. The continued rule of capital in the Soviet type system, under a politically very different form, is identified as principally responsible for such failures. Postrevolutionary developments, consolidated under Stalin, followed *the line of least resistance* in relation to the inherited socioeconomic structures, thus remaining trapped within the boundaries of the capital system. They continued to exploit and oppress the working people under a most *hierarchical division of labour* which operated a politically enforced extraction of surplus-labour at the highest practicable rate. The positive alternative, contrasting with this tragic historical experience, as well as with the illusions of solving the grave structural problems of postrevolutionary societies through capitalist marketization, is provided by the orienting principles of the socialist *communal* (and in no way abstract collectivist) production and consumption system. Quality-oriented regulation of the labour process by the associated producers, in place of the political or economic superimposition of predetermined, and mechanistically quantified, production and consumption targets; the institution of socialist accountancy and genuine planning *from below,* instead of fictitious pseudo-plans imposed on society *from above,* which are bound to remain unrealizable because of the insuperably *adversarial* character of such systems; mediating the members of society through the *planned exchange of activities,* in place of the arbitary political direction and distribution of both labour-power and goods in the Soviet type postcapitalist capital system, or of the fetishistic *exchange of commodities* under capitalism; motivating the individual producers through a self-determined system of material and moral incentives, instead of ruling them by ruthlessly enforced Stakhanovite norms or by the tyranny of the market;

making meaningful and actually possible the voluntary assumption of responsibility by the members of society through the exercise of their powers of decision making, in place of the *institutionalized irresponsibility* that marks and vitiates *all* varieties of the capital system: these are the main operative principles of the socialist alternative. The need for their implementation arises not from abstract theoretical considerations but from the deepening structural crisis of the global capital system.

Part Four: Essays on Related Issues. Part Four contains six essays, several of them published in English here for the first time. They were written in the same period as the rest of *Beyond Capital* but all before the clamorous collapse of the Soviet system. The reasons for including them in the present study are twofold. First, to incorporate a great deal of relevant material and avoid unnecessary repetition. And second, in order to show that confronting the contradictions and the necessary failure of 'actually existing socialism' — not in hindsight, for, as these essays testify, they have been visible for decades — does not have to mean the abandonment of the socialist perspective.

PART ONE

THE SHADOW OF UNCONTROLLABILITY

Primeval rat spreads plague among us:
thought not thought through to the end.
It gnaws into everything we cooked
and runs from one man into the other.
This is why the drunkard ignores
that drowning his mood in champagne
he is gulping down the empty broth
of the horrified poor.

And since reason fails to press
fertile rights from the nations
new infamy rises up to set
against one another the races.
Oppression croaks in squadrons,
it lands on living heart, as on carrion —
and misery dribbles all over the world,
as saliva on the face of idiots.

Attila József

CHAPTER ONE

BREAKING THE SPELL OF 'UNIVERSAL PERMANENT CAPITAL'

1.1 Beyond the Hegelian legacy

1.1.1

THE Hegelian legacy represented a challenging problem for the socialist movement both in a positive and in a negative sense. It was necessary to come to terms with it by appropriating its great achievements, on the one hand, and by subjecting to a radical critique its capital-eternalizing mystifications on the other. The reasons for focusing attention on Hegel's work in the course of articulating the Marxian conception were threefold.

First, the major political and philosophical debates of the period of Marx's intellectual formation, the 1840s, made it quite unavoidable. For they saw the conservative-inspired exhumation of the old and most reactionary Schelling by the Prussian government, intended as a bulwark against the dangerous radicalizing influence of Hegel on the younger generation of intellectuals. Tellingly, both Marx and Kierkegaard attended the old Schelling's anti-Hegelian lectures at Berlin University in 1841: the opening of a decade of pre-revolutionary and revolutionary confrontations. And just as tellingly, the two young philosophers drew diametrically opposite conclusions from such lectures as regards the path which they had set themselves to follow. The dominant — and politically most relevant — philosophical discourse of the period made it necessary to side with or to go against Hegel. However, from the first moment of entering these debates Marx introduced some major qualifications. For at the same time when he expressed his fundamental reservations *vis-à-vis* Hegel and his followers he also tried to preserve and enhance the radicalizing intent of the 'young Hegelians'. In this way he defined the emancipatory aim of philosophy as not just exploring to the full the critical potential of Hegel's own approach, but as a historically arising necessity to go well beyond what could be accommodated within the (no matter how generously stretched) confines of the Hegelian system.

The second reason — applying equally to the later socialist theoreticians who have taken their inspiration from Marx's most important works, *Capital* and the *Grundrisse*, which (contrary to ill-informed claims) happened to be considerably more rather than less positive towards Hegel than the young Marx's *Critique of the Hegelian Philosophy of Right* — was the necessity to rescue Hegel's achievements later on from the attempts by the intellectual representatives of his own class to bury them forever and to treat their author as 'a dead dog', as Marx and Engels complained on more than one occasion. To undertake such a defence was not simply an intellectual matter. For after the revolutions of 1848/1849 the radicalizing potential of Hegel's philosophy had become a great embarrassment even to those members of the liberal bourgeoisie who earlier thought to be able to back up their own reforming zeal with arguments derived from the work of the great German philosopher. This is how both the *dialectical methodology* and the *historical conception* of Hegel's 'objective idealism' had been abandoned in favour of a grotesquely flattened, utterly subjectivist, and often even explicitly anti-historical neo-Kantian orientation.

Moreover, the latter orientation was adopted not only by the leading intellectual representatives of the bourgeoisie but also by the reformist wing of the socialist movement. Indeed, through Edward Bernstein and his followers neo-Kantian varieties of positivism and neo-positivism became so diffused in party circles that they constituted the tame orthodoxy of the socialdemocratic Second International from the second decade of the 20th century all the way to its final extinction. Hegel's philosophy was originally conceived under the historical circumstances of great social conflicts, and — despite the conservative accommodations of their originator in his later years — it could never lose the marks of a dynamic age of transition. Indeed it was the permanence of such marks that made the Hegelian philosophy amenable to a variety of radical interpretations, including the most striking and comprehensive one of them, embodied in Marxian socialism. Once, however, integration into the established socioeconomic order, with its corresponding state system, had been adopted by the party leadership as the horizon of socialdemocratic critique, there could be no room left in it for a genuine historical conception. For who knows what surprises the — by its very nature totalizing and not 'piecemeal' — dynamics of actual historical development might have had in store by setting into motion the 'cunning of reason' theorized by Hegel. Nor could there be, of course, any room in it for the dialectical method which had to envisage not only the *possibility* but also the *necessity* of *qualitative changes* in terms of which revolutionary transformations could be rationally anticipated and worked for, in contrast to the gradualist and mechanical/quantitative 'economic determinism' of the Second International.

It might look surprising, even incomprehensible, that by the mid 1920s the Stalinist bureaucrats of the Third International adopted the same negative line of approach to Hegel's legacy, thereby becoming bed-fellows of Bernsteinian reformist social democracy, despite their rhetorical differences. They used the label 'Hegelian' only as a term of abuse with the help of which they could excommunicate the thinkers who tried to stress the vital importance of objective dialectics also in a socialist society, and thus dared to depart from the newly instituted Comintern orthodoxy. In truth, however, there was nothing really surprising in this unholy ideological convergence. For the common denominator between the two orientations was that, in the same way as in the view of reformist social democracy, also for Stalin and his followers history had already done its job as far as the system within which they operated was concerned. It was absolutely out of the question to envisage qualitative changes and radical transformations. The task of the individuals was defined as their 'positive' integration into the established socioeconomic and political order (hence the cult of the 'positive hero'), allowing them to produce partial improvements by following with devotion the party hierarchy already in possession of the Truth. This elitist talking down to the masses was much the same as the way in which

Bernstein in his patronizing treatment of the working classes assigned to them the neo-Kantian-inspired duty of dedicated 'self-improvement' under the 'advanced' socialdemocratic leadership — in his view the embodiment and ultimate measure of what ought to be emulated.

The third reason was the most important both for Marx personally and for the revolutionary socialist project in general. It concerned the substantive ground from which the affinities between Hegel's and Marx's theories have arisen under determinate historical circumstances. Naturally, this meant that the relationship had to be qualified in tangible historical terms. But such a qualification could not obliterate, not even weaken, the significance of objectively grounded affinities. The revealing circumstance that after the bourgeois revolutions of 1848/1849 Hegel had become a great embarrassment to his own class, could only underline the importance of this substantive connection. For Hegel's attempt to bring the historical dynamic to an arbitrary closure in his own writings in the focal point of capital's eternalized present, under European colonial supremacy (as we shall see in Sections 1.2 and 1.3) could not alter the fact that he grasped history in the first place as an inexorable objective movement, with a compelling logic of its own which could not be tamed by wishful subjective design and corresponding voluntaristic intervention.

Just like Adam Smith, Hegel adopted capital's vantage point, incorporating with great sensitivity the main tenets of Smith's political economy into his own magisterial philosophical conception. But Hegel was, precisely in his intellectually most important formative years, also a contemporary to the 1789 French Revolution as well as to all those historically quite unprecedented — for the first time ever in a meaningful sense global — upheavals which followed from it. Thus he could not help assigning to the dialectically defined category of *contradiction* a place of central importance in his system, even if the social relationships embodied in that category were treated by him in an extremely abstract and idealist way, attenuating thereby their explosive implications for capital's mode of social metabolic reproduction. We shall see in several chapters below how the perceived antagonisms of the objective historical dynamics were weakened and even completely done away with by Hegel in his idealist reconciliatory syntheses. What must be stressed here is the importance of the fact that the recognition of objective historical antagonisms was present at all in a philosophy conceived from the vantage point of capital at a certain stage of historical development.

Hegel's theory was articulated in a historical moment when, in the aftermath of the French revolution, the outstanding intellectual representatives of the bourgeoisie in the ascendant were trying to come to terms with the uncomfortable fact that the 'Third Estate', far from being homogeneous, was deeply divided by conflicting class interests. They acknowledged this fact at a time when they still genuinely believed, or at least hoped, that the identified diverging class interests could be reconciled under some universally beneficial force or 'principle'. However, after the revolutions of 1848/49 even the distant memory of such hope, together with the terms in which its realization had been theorized — in Hegel's case with reference to the postulated overcoming of selfish class interests, through the agency of the 'universal class' of selfless civil servants, who were supposed to counter-balance in the idealized state the unalterably self-seeking determinations of 'civil society' — had to be banished for good from legitimate philosophical discourse. Even the gratuitous Hegelian postulate of the 'universal class' was considered far too much, because unwittingly it conceded the presence of some structural defects in the established social order. This is why Hegel in the end had to become a 'dead dog' for his own class and the historical vision pioneered by him had to be abandoned altogether.

Thus, in the controversies surrounding Hegel the fundamental issue at stake was not the intellectual significance of the great German philosopher but the nature of the objective historical dynamics itself which made it possible for the bourgeoisie to bring into life one day Hegel's monumental achievements, and necessary in another historical moment for the same class to destroy its own creation. Yet if a class, for reasons of its changing role in society, turned its back to its own history, that could not make the historical process itself of which any particular class's history is an organic part — but only a part — cease to exist. Socialist defence of the Hegelian legacy in a historically qualified sense therefore meant focusing attention on the objective dialectic of the historical process as such: its *continuities in discontinuity* and *discontinuities in continuity*. Hegel's insights could be, and had to be, preserved because they have arisen from that objective *continuity* of antagonistic class relations which the socialist project was attempting to master in its own way. At the same time, the limiting horizon of Hegel's vision — the class-determined ahistorical 'conclusion' of his historical syllogism: the eternalized social metabolic order of capital — had to be subjected to a radical critique, as an unavoidable but by no means forever overbearing objective practical premiss of the new historical reasoning. This had to be done in order to bring to the fore the real target to aim at — the necessary *discontinuity* of radical structural change, to be achieved by overcoming the relations of hierarchy and domination beyond capital's objective historical ascendancy — without which the socialist project could not succeed.

1.1.2

DESPITE many of Hegel's particular propositions taken by themselves, it would be quite wrong to call *optimistic* the Hegelian system as a whole. Already Voltaire treated with great sarcasm, in his philosophical novel *Candide,* the proponents of unqualified optimism, even though the illusions of the Enlightenment, which predicated the successful removal of the encountered problems by the irresistible power of Reason, had set their limits also to his horizon. By the time Hegel started to write, it was no longer possible to maintain the same belief in Reason as a 'faculty' possessed by the individuals. In fact Hegel sharply criticized his great predecessor, Kant, for his inclination to do away with major philosophical difficulties by pulling faculties out of his 'faculty bag'. Thus in his own philosophy Hegel gave a radically new — supra-individual — meaning to the category of Reason.

As mentioned above, what made a fundamental difference in this respect, excluding the possibility of a straight optimistic view of human affairs in the conception of a great thinker, was the fact that Hegel was a contemporary to the French Revolution and its turbulent aftermath. He followed with keen interest the elemental upheavals in France and all over Europe in the midst of the Napoleonic wars. At the time of completing *The Phenomenology of Mind* he resided at Jena and witnessed Napoleon's victory in the surrounding hills, commenting that he saw the 'World Spirit' carrying out its design on horse-back. Even more importantly, he also witnessed, with considerable foreboding, the emergence of the working class as an independent social and political force which began to act, however tentatively, on its own behalf, and no longer only as a subordinate part of the 'Third Estate'.

Nevertheless, even though Hegel avoided the traps of *uncritical optimism*, he produced a system of *'uncritical positivism'* (Marx) with regard to the bourgeois order. His message was that no matter how it all might look to the individuals themselves — who were described by him even in their capacity as 'world historical individuals' (like his great contemporary, Napoleon) as *tools* in the hands of Reason/World Spirit, and on that account as merely destined to carry out unconsciously the *World Spirit's design* while pursuing more or less blindly their own limited aims — we have *arrived* at the final historical stage beyond which it would be inconceivable even to attempt to go without self-contradiction. For what had been accomplished was not the outcome of a limited human enterprise but the — from the very beginning anticipated — journey of the World Spirit's self-realization, culminating at the plane of human endeavour in the final order of *'universal permanent capital'*.

Thus the contrast with Marx's approach to the ongoing historical developments could not have been greater. For the adoption of the standpoint of capital by Hegel as the absolute, insurmountable horizon and culmination of human history and of its conceivable institutions, with the 'Germanic' capitalist state — the embodiment of Hegel's 'principle of the North' — at its apex, carried with it the great dialectician's 'uncritical positivism' towards the established order. An apologetic standpoint that ultimately prevailed in Hegel's system, notwithstanding the resignation[1] with which he depicted the role of philosophy in relation to the unalterable developments brought to their conclusion by the World Spirit. The adoption of this standpont by Hegel inevitably also meant a blind attitude towards capital's *destructive* dimension as a system of control.

This is where Marx had to part company with Hegel. For he viewed capital not as an unalterable *termination* of the historical process but as a *dynamic movement* which even with its apparently irresistible *global expansionary logic* had to be considered transient. It is therefore ironical, not to say preposterous, that Marx should be accused of being a 'starry-eyed optimist' and a 'naive believer' in a benevolent 'human nature', and (according to Hayek and others) in the illusions conjured up by the vision of 'the Noble Savage'. For, against all kinds of uncritical positivism, including those which projected it, like Hegel's philosophy, with contemplative resignation, Marx was precisely the first to size up the devastating implications of capital's unrestrainable drive for self-expansion. Far from pomising a necessarily positive outcome, this is how he expressed the *mortal danger* inseparable from the ongoing developments in one of his earliest writings:

> In the development of productive forces there comes a stage when productive forces and means of intercourse are brought into being which under the existing relations only cause mischief, and are no longer productive but *destructive* forces. ... These productive forces receive under the system of private property a one-sided development only, and for the majority they become destructive forces. Thus things have now come to such a pass that the individuals must appropriate the existing totality

of productive forces, not only to achieve self-activity, but, also, *merely to safeguard their very existence*.[2]

When Marx wrote these lines, in 1845, the destructive forces identified by him were still very far from being fully developed. His numerous works, bearing the subtitle of 'Critique of Political Economy', were looking for a countervailing power through which capital's destructive self-expansionary logic could be brought to a halt and the social individuals, through their own *'self-activity'*, freed from that *'alien force'* which not only controlled them but ultimately threatened the very existence of humanity.

The destructive forces of capital's production order are in our age no longer just threatening potentialities but ubiquitous realities. Today the 'normal' functioning and continued expansion of the capital system are inseparable from the unrestrained exercise of the 'one-sidedly developed productive/destructive forces' which dominate our life, no matter how catastrophic their already visible impact and the — even by far from socialist environmentalists acknowledged — dangers for the future.

Thus, despite all historical setbacks and relapses which tend to reinforce 'uncritical positivism', the task of breaking the spell of Hegel's 'universal permanent capital' remains on the historical agenda. Indeed, what makes the situation today particularly acute, in contrast to Marx's lifetime, is that the present-day articulation of capital as a global system, in the shape of its accumulated repressive forces and paralyzing interdependencies, confronts us with the *spectre of total uncontrollability*.

1.2 *The first global conception — on the premiss of 'the end of history'*

1.2.1

THE development of historical consciousness is centred around three fundamental sets of problems:

(1) the determination of the historical *agency*;

(2) the perception of change not merely as lapse of time, but as a movement that possesses an intrinsically *cumulative* character, hence implying some sort of advancement and development;

(3) the implicit or conscious opposition between universality and particularity, with a view to achieving a *synthesis* of the two in order to explain historically relevant events in terms of their broader significance which, of necessity, transcends their immediate historical specificity.

Naturally, all three are essential for a genuine historical conception. This is why it is by no means sufficient to state in generic terms that 'man is the agent of history' if, either, the nature of historical change itself is not adequately grasped, or the complex dialectical relationship between particularity and universality is violated with regard to the subject of historical action. Likewise, the concept of human advancement as such, taken in isolation from the other two dimensions of historical theory, is easily reconcilable with a thoroughly ahistorical explanation if the supra-human agency of 'Divine Providence' is assumed as the moving force behind the unfolding changes.

In this sense, Aristotle's complaint against historical writing — ranking historiography known to him well below poetry and tragedy, in view of its 'less philosophical'[3] character — is fully justified. Not because the original meaning of the Greek term of history — derived from 'istor', i.e. 'eye-witness' — indicates the danger of too great a reliance on the limited standpoint of particular individuals who themselves participate in, and hence have some vested interest also in reporting, the events in question in an unavoidably biassed way. The issue was even more intractable than that. It concerned the very nature of the historian's enterprise itself as manifest in the apparently insoluble contradiction between the particularistic point of departure and evidence as displayed in the chronicled actions, and the generic 'teaching' or conclusion one was supposed to derive from them. In other words, it was the inability of the historians of Antiquity to master the dialectical complexities of particularity and universality which carried with it the necessary consequence of remaining trapped at the level of anecdotal particularism. And since it was, of course, inadmissible to leave things at that, the 'non-philosophical' and anecdotal *particularism* of ancient historiography had to be directly turned into *moralizing universality,* so as to claim the reader's attention on account of its asserted general significance.

On the other hand, the historiography of the Middle Ages violated the dialectic of particularity and universality in a contrasting way, setting out from quite different premises and determinations in relation to which the 'eye-witness' of ancient history completely lost its relevance. The representative systems of the Middle Ages were characterized by the radical *obliteration* of the life-like vitality of actual historical particularity. Instead, they superimposed on the chronicled events and personalities alike the *abstract universality* of a religiously preconceived 'philosophy of history' in which everything had to be directly subordinated to the postulated work of Divine Providence, as positive or negative instances — that is, *illustrative exemplifications* — of such Providence. Thus, according to Saint Augustine, the author of the greatest religiously inspired philosophy of history, 'in the torrential stream of human history, two currents meet and mix: the current of evil which flows from Adam and that of good which comes from God'.[4]

The universalizing tendency of capital enabled modern philosophers to interpret the problems of historical change in a very different way. Nevertheless, the first global conception of history, attempting to synthesise the historical dynamics in its entirety as a process of 'self-development', appeared only in Hegel's philosophy. Well beyond even his greatest predecessors in the field, like Vico and Kánt, Hegel offered an account of actual historical events and transformations in terms of the underlying necessities of an unfolding *world history* and its realization of freedom.

To the extent to which it was compatible with his social standpoint — but only to that extent, — Hegel's philosophy made the most coherent attempt at satisfying all three criteria of a genuine historical conception mentioned above. He tried to make history intelligible in relation to an agency which *had* to strive forward on the road of the unfolding 'world history' leading to the modern 'Germanic State'. In the same spirit, historical time for Hegel was neither the succession of anecdotal events speaking only for themselves, nor the concatenation of repetitive cycles, but the time of a relentless forward movement in the course of realizing the idea of freedom. And thirdly, he offered an explanation in terms of the dialectic of particular and universal, in that his concept of historical agency was neither a limited particularity, nor 'Divine Providence' in its directly religious sense — which clouded even the progressive historical visions of Vico and Kant — but identifiable subjects, from chronicled nations and peoples to 'world historical individuals', like Alexander the Great, Julius Caesar, Luther, and Napoleon.

However, just like the great English and Scottish political economists, Hegel identified himself with the standpoint of capital, with all its inescapable limitations. Accordingly, he could not conceptualize history as *irrepressibly open*. For the ideological determinants of his position stipulated the necessity of reconciliation with the present and thereby the arbitrary *closure* of the historical dynamics in the framework of capitalist 'civil society' and its state formation. History could be treated as open and objectively unfolding all the way down to the present, but its shutters had to be pulled down in the direction of a radically different future.

The ideological need for justifying such closure of history led Hegel to the identification of *'rationality'* with *'actuality'* from which the equation of actuality and *positivity* could be derived and brought into harmony with unavoidable resignation. Thus, despite his original intentions, the characteristic quasi-theological teleology of capitalistic 'civil society', in its circular reciprocity with the bourgeois state, asserted itself as the ultimate reconciliatory frame of reference — and 'point of rest' — of the Hegelian system. Not surprisingly, therefore, we were told by Hegel that

> In the history of the World, only those peoples can come under our notice which form a state. For it must be understood that this latter is the realization of Freedom, i.e. of the *absolute final aim*, and that it exists *for its own sake*. It must further be understood that all the worth which the human being possesses — all spiritual reality, he possesses only through the State. ... For Truth is the Unity of the universal and subjective Will; and the *Universal* is to be found in the State, in its laws, its universal and rational arrangements. *The State is the Divine Idea as it exists on Earth*.[5]

And since this idealized State subsumed under itself, despite its contradictions, the world of 'civil society', the whole construct could be uncritically eternalized in the name of the 'Divine Idea', so as to rationalize and legitimate as absolutely insurmountable capital's established social metabolic order.

1.2.2

WHEN Kant accepted without reservation both the category and the social horizons of Adam Smith's 'commercial spirit', the socioeconomic order which the classics of political economy — from the standpoint of capital — expressed was as yet not fully articulated. However, by the time Hegel wrote his *Philosophy of History* and *Philosophy of Right*, well after the conclusion of the Napoleonic wars and the consolidation of the new social order, the antagonisms of 'civil society' and its political state were too much in evidence to be able to reassert Kant's Enlightenment illusions and moral postulates, like the reign of 'eternal peace'. In fact the latter was greeted with sardonic laughter by Hegel himself. Thus, the determination of the state's behaviour through the material interests of 'civil society' had to be acknowledged for what it appeared to be from the standpoint of political economy itself. As Hegel put it:

A state through its subjects has *widespread connexions and many-sided interests*, and these may be readily and considerably injured; but it remains *inherently indeterminable* which of these injuries is to be regarded as a specific breach of treaty or as an injury to the honour and autonomy of the state.[6]

Thus not an abstract moral imperative but the principle of 'inherent indeterminacy' ruled in Hegel's account of the unfolding changes and conflicts. But even his greater sense of realism with regard to the existing state of affairs could not extricate Hegel from the blind alley of his apologetic social and political assumptions. The main reason why by both Kant and Hegel the law which determined the course of ongoing historical developments had to be conceptualized as the mystery of a quasi-theological teleology was because they took for granted the permanence of 'civil society', in all its contradictoriness, as the necessary premiss of all further explanation.

The uneasy coalescence of the multifarious constituents of the historical process was described by Hegel with graphic imagery:

> It is as particular entities that states enter into relations with one another. Hence their relations are on the largest scale a maelstrom of external contingency and the inner particularity of passions, private interests and selfish ends, abilities and virtues, vices, force, and wrong. All these whirl together, and in their vortex the ethical whole itself, the autonomy of the state, is exposed to contingency. The principles of the national minds are wholly restricted on account of their particularity, for it is in this particularity that, as existent individuals, they have their objective actuality and their self-consciousness.[7]

At the same time, the 'world mind' was postulated by Hegel as the resolution of the manifold actual contradictions without questioning, however, the social world of 'civil society' in the slightest. Particular states, nations and individuals were described as 'the *unconscious tools* and organs of the world mind at work within them',[8] and the 'individuals as subjects' were characterized as the '*living instruments* of what is in substance the deed of the world mind and they are therefore directly at one with that deed though it is *concealed* from them and is *not their aim and object*'.[9]

In this way, again, a profound insight was inextricably combined with an apologetic mystification. On the one hand, Hegel recognized that there is an inherent lawfulness in the historical process which necessarily transcends the limited and self-oriented aspirations of particular individuals. Accordingly, the objective character of historical determinations was grasped the only way feasible from the standpoint of capital and its 'civil society': as the paradoxically conscious/unconscious set of individual interactions effectively overruled by the totalizing 'cunning of Reason'. On the other hand, however, the stipulated historical law, as depicted not only by Hegel but in the entire bourgeois philosophical tradition, had to be ascribed to a force — be it Vico's 'providence', Adam Smith's 'hidden hand', Kant's providential 'plan of nature', or Hegel's 'cunning of Reason' — which asserted itself and imposed its own aims *over against* the intentions, desires, ideas and conscious designs of human beings. For envisaging the possibility of a real *collective subject* as the — materially identifiable and socially efficacious — historical agent was radically incompatible with the eternalized standpoint of 'civil society'. This is why there could be no *trans*-individual historical agency in such conceptions. Only a *supra*-individual (and consequently also *supra-human*) agency was compatible with the standpoint of capital — and the corresponding 'standpoint of political economy', — postulating thereby the rather mysterious resolution of the manifold contradictions of fragmented 'civil society' without altering their material ground. In other words, the projected Hegelian solution envisaged no significant change in actually existing and inherently conflict-torn 'civil society' itself.

Thus despite Hegel's major advances in detail over his predecessors, we were offered in his philosophy of history the finality of the 'Germanic realm', which was said to represent the 'absolute turning point'. For he claimed that in that realm the world mind 'grasps the principle of the unity of the divine nature and the human, the reconciliation of objective truth and freedom as the truth and freedom appearing within self-consciousness and subjectivity, a reconciliation with the fulfilment of which the principle of the north, the principle of the Germanic peoples, has been entrusted'.[10]

Hegel hailed the developments under the 'principle of the Germanic peoples' — including the empire-building English, animated, in his view, by the 'commercial spirit' — as the 'reconciliation and resolution of all contradiction', and he summed up his claims with regard to what was in the process of being accomplished in the following terms:

> The *realm of fact* has discarded its barbarity and unrighteous caprice, while the *realm of truth* has abandoned the world of beyond and its arbitrary force, so that the *true reconciliation* which discloses the *state as the image and actuality of reason* has become objective. In the state, self-consciousness finds in an organic development the actuality of its substantive knowing and willing.[11]

Hegel often protested against the intrusion of 'ought' into philosophy. In truth, though, what could have been more blatantly the 'ought' of wishful thinking than his own way of making historical development culminate in the modern state defined as the image and actuality of reason?

1.3 Hegel's 'universal permanent capital': false mediation of self-seeking individuality and abstract universality

1.3.1
THE term 'globalization' has recently become a buzz-word. As to what kind of 'globalization' is feasible under the rule of capital, this question is carefully avoided. It is much easier to assume, instead, that globalization by its very nature is unproblematical, indeed a necessarily positive development that brings commendable results to all concerned. That the process of globalization, as we in fact know it, asserts itself through the strengthening of capital's most dynamic centres of domination (and exploitation), bringing in its wake growing inequality and extreme hardship for the overwhelming majority of people, all this is best left outside the framework of legitimate questioning. For the answers of a critical scrutiny might conflict with the policies pursued by the dominant capitalist powers and their willing collaborators in the 'Third World'. Yet, through the ongoing and allegedly most beneficial globalization the 'underdeveloped countries' are offered nothing but the perpetuation of the differential rate of exploitation. This is well illustrated by the figures acknowledged even

by the London *Economist* according to which in the newly established U.S. factories in the northern border region of Mexico the workers earn no more than 7 *percent* of the income of the American labour force doing the same job in California.[12]

All the same, the question of global development is undoubtedly a matter of great importance and has been in theoretical discussions for well over a century and a half. It was none other than Hegel who called attention to it in a most powerful way, even if in an idealist form, in his closely interconnected works: *The Philosophy of History* and *The Philosophy of Right*.

In *The Philosophy of History*, after surveying the course of world historical development and after defining its essence as 'the Ideal necessity of *transition*',[13] Hegel curiously concluded that 'The History of the World travels from East to West, for *Europe is absolutely the end of history*'.[14] No more transition, then, since we have arrived at 'absolutely the end of history', whereafter only marginal adjustments could be envisaged within the finally attained order of the World Spirit. Saying this was for Hegel not a matter of challengeable historical contingency but the very *'destiny of Reason'* itself. This is how he defined the issue:

> The inquiry into the essential destiny of Reason — as far as it is considered in reference to the World — is identical with the question what is the *ultimate design* of the World? And the expression implies that the design is *destined to be realized*.[15]

Thus the 'absolutely unalterable' European colonial domination of the world had to be declared to be nothing less than the very 'destiny of Reason'. It was therefore just too bad for the Mexican workers that this lofty design of the 'World Spirit' assigned to them a forever subordinate and pauperized position in the great scheme of things. There was nothing that could be done about that without violating the requirements of Reason itself. And nothing could be considered more reprehensible than that.

Naturally, this was Hegel's way of saying: *'There is no alternative!'* The question, though, is: are we really destined to live forever under the spell of capital's global system glorified in its Hegelian conceptualization, resigned — as he advised us to be in his poetic reference to 'the owl of Minerva [that] spreads its wings only with the falling of the dusk'[16] — to the tyrannical exploitative order of his World Spirit?

Paradoxically, Hegel's answer had bleak implications for every member of the lower classes. For if the relatively advantaged working people, situated on the 'absolutely final' historical stage of colonially dominant Europe, thought that their destiny was not an extremely problematical one, to be endured in terms of Hegel's *'understanding the rationality of the actual and reconciling/resigning themselves to it'*,[17] they had to be greatly disappointed by the German philosopher. For this is how he described the *internal* order of — in its external relations highly privileged — Europe in *The Philosophy of Right*:

> By a dialectical advance, *subjective self-seeking* turns into *mediation* of the particular through the universal, with the result that each man in earning, producing, and enjoying on his own account is *eo ipso* producing and earning for the enjoyment of everyone else. The *compulsion* which brings this about is rooted in the *complex interdependence* of each on *all*, and it now presents itself to *each* as the *universal permanent capital*.[18]

Thus the 'essential destiny of Reason' and the 'ultimate design of the World' turned out to be in the Hegelian system the prosaic world of 'universal permanent capital' (i.e. a certain way of producing and distributing wealth) which operates through the ruthless *compulsion* imposed on every single individual by 'the complex interdependence of each on all' in the name of the 'rationality of the actual' and the 'realization of Freedom'.

1.3.2

NATURALLY, the centre-pillar of this conception — namely the assertion of 'the complex interdependence of *each on all*' — was an ideological mystification: a way of closing the circle of commodity society from which there could be no escape. For if it was really true that the *compulsion* inseparable from the nature of — far from *universal* and by no means necessarily *permanent* — capital was the result of the complex interdependence of *individuals as individuals*, in that case nothing could be done about it. In order to alter that condition it would be necessary to invent a world radically different from the one in which we happen to live.

In truth, however, the 'dialectical advance' which rationalizes and legitimates the Hegelian apologetic conclusion is a pseudo-dialectic. For the self-seeking *particular* cannot be mediated with Hegel's *universal*, because the latter only exists as a self-serving conceptual fiction. True universality in our actually existing world cannot emerge without overcoming the antagonistic contradictions of the *capital/labour* relationship into which the particular individuals are inserted and by which they are dominated.

In Hegel this problem is resolved — or, rather, bypassed — with the help of a double fiction. First, with the help of the abstract logical postulate which directly links the particular to the (non-existent) universal and idealistically stipulates that 'each man in earning, producing, and enjoying on his own account is *eo ipso* producing and earning for the enjoyment of *everyone else*'. And second, with the help of a mystifying shift through which he overturns the meaning of compulsion. For, having completely invented both his terms of reference — i.e. harmoniously reciprocal-enjoyment-producing 'eo ipso' particularity on the one hand, and mysteriously conflict-removing universality on the other, — and having equated 'universal permanent capital' with the apriori determination of the individuals' interdependence among themselves, he eliminates *compulsion* from where it actually resides: i.e. in the *productive and distributive imperatives that emanate from capital itself as a historically specific mode of social metabolic control*. In this way it is obfuscated that capital is a historically created (and historically transcendable) *property relationship* — the *alienated means of production embodied in private or state property* — which is counterposed to the individual producers and rules them. As a result of the Hegelian shift, compulsion is conveniently transmuted from oppressive historical reality into a timeless *virtue* on the ground of the indisputable and ontologically unalterable condition that the human race is made of particular individuals. What disappears in this kind of 'dialectical advance' is the objective reality of antagonistic social classes and the unceremonious subsumption of all individuals under one or the other of them. A subsumption that imposes a type of compulsion which they all must obey in the real world not simply as *particular* individuals but as particular *class individuals*.

To be sure, the productive relationship between the particular working subjects (as actually existing social individuals) must be mediated in every conceivable form of society. Without it the 'aggregative totality' of the individuals who are active at any particular time in history could never coalesce into a sustainable social whole. Indeed, the historical specificity of the given form of mediation through which the individuals are linked together, by means of the historically given intermediary groupings and their institutional corollaries, into a more or less closely intertwined societal whole, happens to be of seminal importance. For it is precisely this — practically inescapable — mediatory specificity of the individuals' reproductive interrelations that ultimately defines the fundamental character of the various, historically contrasting, modes of societal intercourse.

The point is that — not because of unalterable ontological determinations but as a result of the historically generated and changeable division of labour which continues to prevail under all conceivable forms of the rule of capital — the individuals are mediated among themselves and combined into an *antagonistically structured* social whole through the established system of production and exchange. This system is ruled by the imperative of ever-expanding exchange value to which everything else — from the most basic as well as the most intimate needs of the individuals, to the various material and cultural productive activities in which they engage — must be strictly subordinated. It is the unmentionable ideological taboo of the actually existing forms and structures of iniquitous material and institutional mediation under the capital system which makes Hegel pursue the postulate of the direct mediation of particular individuality through a fictitious abstract universality, so as to squeeze out of it with miraculous dexterity 'universal permanent capital' as a totally dehistorized entity.

1.3.3

THE great ideological mystification consists in the Hegelian misrepresentation of *compulsion* as the *necessary 'give and take'* of individuals engaged in 'eo ipso' *mutually beneficial* 'production, earning and enjoyment', on the basis of *full reciprocity*. Yet, on closer inspection we find the total absence of reciprocity. To take a characteristic example, whereas the inventor of 'junk bonds' (a Wall Street 'financial wizard' called Michael Milken) was earning in a year the sum equivalent to the salaries of 78,000 American workers[19] (and when one calculates the corresponding Mexican figure, the sums involved must be expressed in the income of well over one million workers in the relatively privileged new American industrial enterprises of northern Mexico, not to mention the rest of the country), and Milken 'earned' such astronomical sums for totally parasitic and, as it turned out, quite unlawful activities, without producing anything at all. Thus, instead of reciprocity and symmetry we find in reality a *structurally safeguarded exploitative hierarchy*. The real question under the antagonistically structured capital system is: which class of individuals actually produces the 'wealth of the nation' and which one appropriates the benefits of such production; or, in more precise terms, which class of individuals must be confined to the subordinate function of *execution* and which particular individuals — as 'personifications of capital' in Marx's terms — exercise the function of *control*.

The Hegelian construct offers the unsurpassable model of liberal philosophical conceptions. For the underlying ideological need consists in the idealization of the existing relations of structural domination in such a way that their explosive antagonisms should be removed. In order to be made tenable, and indeed unquestionable, the transient historical conditions of self-seeking particularity must be turned into *absolute permanence*. This is accomplished *by definition,* postulating both the unalterable ubiquitousness of self-seeking particularity — in other words, the obliteration of its historical ground and specificity, subsuming under it every single individual, under all conceivable conditions also in the future — and, with even more obvious ideological intent, the universally beneficial character of the interactions of strictly self-seeking particularities within the framework of 'universal permanent capital'. Unlike some of his intellectual predecessors and 20th century descendants, Hegel does not lump all this together simply under the category of 'human nature'. His solution is much more ingenious than that. For the way in which he defines his terms of reference, he not only preserves the bourgeois substance — self-seeking particularity — of capital's social order but also stipulates the harmonious reconciliation of all its antagonistic constituents to the benefit of all. Thus he elevates the eternalized image of this social metabolic order to the plane of rationally uncontestable rightfulness.

In one of his early works Hegel castigates his philosophical predecessors for smuggling into the presuppositions of their arguments the desired conclusions. He rightly criticizes their procedure whereby

> After the fiction of the state of nature has served its purpose, that state is abandoned because of its ill consequences; this simply means that the *desired outcome is presupposed*, the outcome namely of an *harmonization* of what, as chaos, is in conflict with the good or whatever goal must be reached.[20]

However, even if Hegel is not guilty of indulging in the same *specific* presuppositions, his general procedure is the same, with regard to both method and ideological substance. For he, too, presupposes the necessary '*chaos*' of self-seeking individuality, with its 'ill consequences', as the inescapable condition of human interaction, so as to be able to derive from it the desired '*harmonization*' of the whole complex through the stipulated 'dialectical advance', which is supposed to emerge from the — rather mysterious — 'mediation of subjective self-seeking' with the purely assumed 'universal'.

1.3.4

INCORPORATING classical political economy into his system as the science which extracts from the endless mass of details the underlying 'principles', Hegel produces an account of both the division of labour and inequality. He conflates means of *production* with means of *subsistence*, as well as *work* with socially divided and *hierarchically controlled labour*. At the same time, significantly, *utility* (or use-value as manifest in the inherent 'purposefulness' of goods produced for the gratification of needs) and *exchange-value* ('the demand for equality of satisfaction with others'[21]) are also conflated in the Hegelian conception. In the same spirit, the characteristics of the capitalist division of labour are deduced from the idea of 'the abstracting process which effects the subdivision of needs and means',[22] in full harmony with the self-realizing universality of the World Spirit, removing thereby the pernicious dimensions and implications of the capitalist labour process. Accordingly, in Hegel's account 'this abstraction of one man's skill and means of production from another's completes and makes necessary everywhere the dependence of men on one another and their *reciprocal* relation in the satisfaction of their other needs'.[23] From this Hegel can conveniently deduce in the next paragraph the just mentioned 'dialectical advance' which mediates self-seeking particularity with the assumed universal and transforms compulsion emanating from capital into a forever valid virtue. It is by no means surprising, therefore, that the iniquitous capitalist exchange relationship is justified on the ground of the same reasoning, asserting that

> The *infinitely complex,* criss-cross, movements of *reciprocal production and exchange,* and the equally *infinite* multiplicity of means therein employed, become crystallized, owing to the *universal* inherent in their content, and distinguished into general groups. As a result, the entire complex is built up into particular systems of needs, means, and types of work relative to these needs, modes of satisfaction and of theoretical and practical education, i.e. into systems, to one or other of which individuals are assigned — in other words, into *class divisions.*[24]

Thus, the Hegelian deduction, with its arbitrarily and tendentiously stipulated 'infinite complexity' (enthusiastically adopted by all twentieth century apologists of the capital system and of its allegedly insurmountable 'modernity') and with its imaginary 'mediation', turns out to be the rationalization of an antagonistic structural relationship. Knowing that he is on dubious ground when he defends at all cost the established order of things, Hegel tries to confer the status of the highest rationality on it. Indeed, he dismisses in no uncertain terms all those who actually do, or even just might, question the postulated absolute rationality of the state of affairs described by him. He tells them that their critical arguments remain foolishly imprisoned at the inferior level of the Understanding (Verstand), unable to reach the lofty domain of Reason itself (Vernunft). For, in his view

> Men are made *unequal by nature,* where inequality is in its element, and in civil society the right of particularity is so far from annulling this natural inequality that it produces it *out of mind* and raises it to an inequality of skill and wealth, and even to one of *moral and intellectual* attainment. To oppose to this right a demand for equality is a *folly of the Understanding* which takes as real and rational its abstract equality and its 'ought-to-be'.[25]

As to what might take us beyond the philosophically inadmissible limitations of mere Understanding, is revealed in the concluding sentence of the last quoted paragraph. According to this 'it is *reason,* immanent in the restless system of human needs, which articulates the sphere of particularity into an *organic whole* with different members'.[26] Naturally, this 'organic whole' happens to correspond to the Hegelian ideal of capitalist class society. Thus we are offered in the name of *Vernunft* proper the most peculiar conception of both 'mediation' and 'universality'. Indeed Hegel's concepts of 'mediation' and 'universality' could not be more peculiar and problematical than they are in that together they produce the claimed ideality of *permanent class divisions,* solidified and eternalized as the *organic whole* (another gratuitous but most convenient assumption, in the age-old spirit of Menenius Agrippa). At the same time, the notion of class antagonism remains a strictly forbidden concept (which is seemingly justified by the assumption projecting the 'organic' character of the given structural order). For conflict as such must remain at the level of self-seeking individuality, in bourgeois 'civil society', so that the whole edifice embodying 'the principle of the North' should be erected upon it.

1.3.5

HOWEVER, the edifice thus erected is built upside-down, using the same procedure castigated in others by Hegel himself, as we have seen above. It is built by fallaciously *assuming* the division of labour, in a neutral/technical sense, as the sufficient determining ground of a sociohistorical specificity — the desired and through the adopted philosophical procedure by Hegel eternalized conclusion — instead of demonstrating the determinate character of a *certain type* of hierarchical social division of labour (which must be spirited far away from scrutiny, in the interest of the absolute permanence of the ruling capital system). Another of the main supporting pillars of Hegel's idealized edifice is constructed by *assuming* in the same fallacious way the *generic* institution of exchange — i.e. the mere fact that mediatory exchange of one sort or another must take place in the course of social production and distribution — as the sufficient and self-evident explanatory ground of capital's *historically unique* exchange relation.

Thus, since the question of capital's *origin* is circularly avoided not only by Hegel but by all defenders of 'civil society' — in other words, the exploitative dimension of capital's *genesis* from the 'appropriation of alien labour', in permanent *antithesis* to labour, is pushed out of focus, — the inherently *contradictory* and ultimately explosive character of the capital system as a whole remains conveniently hidden from sight. For the bourgeois conceptualizations of the labour process, predicating the absolute viability of the given conditions of wealth production, cannot be disturbed by the thought of the historical dynamics and objective antagonisms of the capital/labour relationship.

It is by no means accidental that no philosophical system conceived from the incorrigibly distorting standpoint of capital — not even the greatest — can offer a coherent concept of mediation. Idealizing the established order as the 'rationality of the actual', and assuming its contradictory constituents as the necessary premises and conclusions of all rational discourse, amount to an insurmountable obstacle in this respect.

Capital's second order mediations — i.e. alienated means of production and their 'personifications'; money; production for exchange; varieties of capital's state formation in their global context; the world market — superimpose themselves in reality itself on the social individuals' essential productive activity and primary mediation among themselves. Only a radical critical scrutiny of this historically specific system of second order mediations could show a way out of its fetishistic conceptual maze. By contrast, however, the uncritical acceptance of the given, historically contingent but powerfully effective, system as the absolute reproductive horizon of human life in general makes impossible the understanding of the real nature of mediation. For the prevailing second order mediations obliterate the proper awareness of the primary mediatory relationships and present themselves in their 'eternal presentness' (Hegel) as the necessary point of departure which is simultaneously also the unsurpassable end-point. Indeed, they produce a complete *inversion* of the actual relationship as a result of which the primary order is degraded, and the alienated second order mediations usurp its place, with potentially most dangerous consequences for the survival of humanity, as we shall see in Chapters 4 and 5.

This is why in the last analysis the Hegelian 'dialectical circle' and 'circle of circles' (to use his own words) — which assume and idealize the unalterability of capital's social metabolic order — cannot produce a dialectical conception of mediation, despite the great German philosopher's explicit aim to do so. Quite the contrary, the 'dialectical advance' asserted by Hegel must remain a conceptual fiction. For the *structurally prejudged particularism* of the capital system, notwithstanding Hegel's universalistic claims, is absolutely inimical to true universality that might arise from the actual productive self-mediation of the social individuals in their metabolic interchange with nature in a radically different kind of society: one regulated by socialist accountancy and a corresponding mode of social metabolic control.

The fact that Hegel as a philosophical genius can perceive and criticize the fallacies committed by his predecessors, and then — as if nothing had happened — go on repeatedly committing them himself, shows that what is at stake here is not the intrusion of more or less easily avoidable 'logical fallacies'. The stubborn persistence of unjustifiable assumptions which circularly anticipate the desired conclusions demonstrates that *social necessities* are at work in all such conceptualizations of bourgeois 'civil society'. For even the greatest philosophical genius is hopelessly constrained by the narrow path imposed upon him by the adoption of capital's standpoint, and must pay a heavy price for his vain attempt at reconciling and harmonizing the inner antagonisms of the established system within the confines of which he visualizes 'absolutely the end of history'.

1.4 Encircled revolution at the 'weakest link of the chain' and its representative theorization in HISTORY AND CLASS CONSCIOUSNESS

1.4.1

MAJOR historic upheavals — like the English and French revolutions — are always dense with tragedies. The Russian revolution of October 1917 is no exception to the rule. Inevitably, the fact that such a revolution — which aimed at initiating the necessary transition from the reign of capital to a new historic order — had erupted in the closing stages of a disastrous global conflagration 'at the weakest link of the chain', could only aggravate matters beyond even the worst expectations.

Today it is fashionable to try to rewrite history by squeezing it into the mould of recent developments, as if the Russian revolution had never happened. This kind of self-serving 'historiography' inside or outside the former Soviet Union is now often attempted by precisely those who in the past were the worst apologists of Stalin's Russia. They and their newly acquired sponsors refuse to acknowledge that historic events of this magnitude cannot be wishfully undone in order to suit the political contingencies of the day. For the echoes of such elemental historic upheavals continue to reverberate across centuries; the more so in fact the longer their intrinsic contradictions are not faced up to in the course of subsequent social and political practice. In this sense, the French

Revolution of 1789 had left a contradictory legacy. For while it overthrew the old feudal order, it had also set into motion a multifaceted historical development, with its positive and negative concatenations and still persisting challenges. It was the latter which no less than two hundred years later, at the official bicentenary celebrations, induced the ruling class of France under Mitterrand's 'socialist' presidency to attempt to refashion the haunting memory of 1789, so as to bury it forever in the interest of its own eternal rule. A vain exercise indeed! For two hundred years are far too short a time to smooth over the mountain-ranges brought to the fore by a great historic earthquake and wipe out its traces successfully from living memory.

In the same way, the undeniable failure of not only Soviet type 'socialism' under Stalin but also of all the half-hearted later efforts of 'de-Stalinization' — which aimed to remove some effects of the system's contradictions while preserving its substance — could not undo the historic challenge of the 1917 revolution itself. For only the most subservient and foolish apologists of the established order can maintain that this revolution occurred without deep-seated socioeconomic and political causes. In truth it unfolded in the midst of a massive crisis of the global capital system and affected — for better or worse — the rest of the world for a long time to come. The subsequent stabilization of Western capitalism, of which the historic failure of the Soviet system itself was already an integral part well before the collapse of 'perestroika', cannot alter these interconnections. Nor can it wish out of existence the profound structural contradictions of the Soviet and Western capital systems, no matter how much effort is invested by the interested parties in retrospective refashioning of history with the help of 'counter-factual conditionals'.

Today the need to come to terms with the historical experience and legacy of the Russian revolution by putting its contradictions in perspective in the light of twentieth century developments is greater than ever before, precisely because of the dramatic collapse of the so-called 'societies of actually existing socialism'. Lukács's seminal work — *History and Class Consciousness,* explored in detail in Part Two of the present study — offers an important point of reference for a critical examination of the relevant issues, both in terms of the historical context of its origin and in relation to subsequent political and intellectual developments within the international socialist movement.

The influence of this work, published in 1923, was legendary right from the time of its publication all the way to 1968, and even thereafter, for as long as the 'moment' of 1968 lasted. In part this was due to its condemnation by the Comintern immediately after it appeared. But there was much more to it than that. For although *History and Class Consciousness* was by no means the greatest intellectual achievement of its author, it was certainly his most representative. In fact the speedy condemnation of *History and Class Consciousness* by the Comintern only underlined in its own sinister way the representative significance of this work.

History and Class Consciousness was conceived in the aftermath of the Council Republic's defeat in Hungary. Lukács actively participated in the 1919 Council Republic, first as Minister of Education and Culture, and in the final weeks of this shortlived revolution as the Political Commissar of an army division. After the military defeat he moved to the West, where the ebbing away of the revolutionary wave brought similar, even if not quite as extensive and dramatic, defeats for socialists, particularly in Germany. The major theoretical problems discussed by Lukács in *History and Class Consciousness* were all tackled by him from this perspective, and thus met with a most favourable echo in Western revolutionary circles whose aspirations were likewise crushed by the 'force of circumstance'.

Western socialists found themselves in great affinity with the spirit of *History and Class Consciousness* in that this work categorically refused to submit to the temptations of pessimism, no matter how tragic the prevailing circumstances. As we shall see in Part Two, the sharp emphasis on *method* as the deciding factor in what should constitute genuine Marxism had a great deal to do with the book's appeal. For it could be used as a way of overturning the painful evidence of the overwhelmingly negative relation of forces at the time. But also in other respects, the key philosophical categories scrutinized in *History and Class Consciousness* — particularly the Hegelian problematic of the 'identical Subject/Object' — aimed at providing historical reassurance under conditions when everything seemed to point in the opposite direction. Even the bad news coming from Russia in great abundance could be assessed within the discourse of *History and Class Consciousness* in a hopeful and reassuring way. The representativeness of Lukács as the author of *History and Class Consciousness* was inseparably connected with this shared predicament and aspirations. He provided the defiant theorization of a perspective which both acknowledged the tragic character of the recently suffered historical defeats and, in contrast to many intellectuals at the time, passionately refused to accept the verdict of the present as the final judgement on the subject.

1.4.2

IN relation to the representative character of *History and Class Consciousness* it must be stressed that the determinants of the conception articulated in it were manifold. The correlations through which this work acquired its significance could be summed up, reiterating also the relevant historical connections mentioned above, as follows:

(1) the theoretical embodiment of the problems arising from the fact that the first large-scale socialist revolution broke out at the 'weakest link of the chain' and had to face the prospect of 'lifting itself up by its own bootstraps' because of the extreme backwardness of its socioeconomic framework; in official literature 'the weakest link' was canonized and given compulsory positive connotations; *History and Class Consciousness* offered a much more differentiated view (hence its speedy condemnation by the Moscow party authorities), attempting to suggest a way out of the constraints and contradictions of any postrevolutionary order through the practical implementation of the philosophical categories elaborated in it;

(2) Lukács's active participation as a leading figure in a failed revolutionary experience and the resonance of the latter with other failed attempts in the West; the implicit and in parts also explicit aim of *History and Class Consciousness* was a searching examination of what could guarantee success against the extremely unfavourable relation of forces;

(3) the terms in which, in the light of the Hungarian failed experience, the

evaluation of the causes of the failure could pinpoint at a very early stage certain trends — for instance with regard to the 'bureaucratization' of the Party, even if Lukács identified them only in an 'Aesopic language', by attributing the criticized negative traits and contradictions to the 'party of the old type' — which became ever more prominent in the course of the successful 'Stalinization' of the international working class movement; the widespread influence of this work was clearly visible in the writings of the revolutionary intellectuals who suffered from the inexorably advancing negative trends within the movement itself, including Karl Korsch and Antonio Gramsci;

(4) the class of bourgeois intellectuals who changed sides under the impact of the Russian revolution, like Lukács himself, brought with it its own agenda and objectives, calling for a specific line of theoretical mediation to which all those who could in principle contemplate the same move might respond; this dimension of the work later generated responses in the key of a mythical 'Western Marxism' (pushed into the centre of philosophical debates in 1955 by Merleau-Ponty's *Adventures of the Dialectic)*, but, as we shall see in Chapter 8, the praise heaped upon *History and Class Consciousness* in this way was meant only as a 'funeral oration' for Marx and Marxism in general, without any real connection with either Lukács's original concerns or with the severe problems facing those who were looking for answers within Marxian horizons; a funeral oration which was simultaneously also an attempt of the social group represented by Merleau-Ponty to disengage itself from its earlier commitments;

(5) a more fundamental dimension of the problems mentioned in point (4) concerned the whole of the bourgeoisie, as Lukács saw the class from which he made his own escape towards the end of 1917; the final year and the immediate aftermath of the war was the juncture where the roads divided and separated Lukács not only from Max Weber (up until then his intellectual soul-mate and close friend) and from Thomas Mann — both of them enthusiastic supporters of German chauvinism and its war aims during the first world war, in contrast to Lukács who condemned the whole imperialist venture without reservation, — but later also from some major figures of the Frankfurt School, like Adorno and Horkheimer, characterized by the old Lukács as those who are pleased to inhabit 'Grand Hotel Abyss' and enjoy its contemplative thrill; the problem the old Lukács was talking about concerned the change in the position and attitude of the whole class in the intervening period: the move of the bourgeoisie from a position reflecting a *'crise de conscience'* — i.e. a crisis of both consciousness (theoretical orientation) and conscience, including the admission of some sort of guilt, which brought with it a 'guilty conscience', or at least a modicum of awareness regarding its own role in perpetuating social injustice — to one wholly *without conscience:* a generalized 'bad faith' (not only in Sartre's sense but even in its meaning as 'bordering on cynicism'), rather than the more ambiguous and potentially still somewhat open 'false consciousness' (in Lukács's sense) of an earlier age, visible especially immediately after the disastrous world war and the ensuing revolutions; this change in class attitude towards social injustice brought with it later an obvious retreat into the smug self-complacency of the so-called 'radical right', fully in tune with the ever narrowing margin of feasible alternatives within the socioeconomic premisses of the global capital system.

A corollary of all this was the *tragic* character of the Hungarian philosopher's enterprise, both in a broader historical sense and in personal terms. Historically in that:

(a) certain *objective possibilities* failed to materialize and the revolution 'at the weakest link of the chain' remained not only isolated but subsequently also succeeded in consolidating its worst contradictions and greatest weaknesses as a monstrous compulsory ideal, imposing thereby a mill-stone on all socialist revolutionary attempts everywhere;

(b) a similarly negative change gravely affected socialists in the capitalistically advanced countries in that their adversaries adjusted their strategies to the changed circumstances and maximized the benefits which they could derive from the contradictions of the authoritarian and economically backward Soviet system. They successfully disarmed their own working classes for the time being partly through the deterrent example of the 'societies of actually existing socialism', and partly through the (however unwitting) complicity of the Western labour movement in the imposition of the massive burden of the *differential rate of exploitation* on the rest of the world.

In personal terms Lukács's tragedy was that his *appeal* — to the 'responsibility of the intellectuals' (an important and constantly recurring theme in Lukács's writing throughout his life, and for a long time also a major source of his success) lost the *subject* to which it could be addressed as a *collective* entity. By contrast, as we shall see in Chapter 10, Lukács ended up in his final works with the only discourse remaining open to the author defeated by the tragic changes that have taken place in the field of economics and politics: a direct moral appeal to the *individual's moral consciousness,* representing for Lukács the last stand after being forced off the rails of his lifelong search for a no longer 'false-conscious' but morally conscious and responsible *trans-individual* subject.

1.4.3

A quotation from one of Lukács's greatest works — *The Young Hegel* — provides the key to understanding his inner motivations not only at the time of writing *History and Class Consciousness,* but also much later. It also helps to explain some of the prominent features of the mature Lukács's development, above all his alleged 'aesthetic conservatism'. He was often condemned by his critics for siding with Goethe and Balzac — and also with Thomas Mann who was praised by the Hungarian philosopher as the outstanding twentieth century representative of the *positive alternative* to the perspective of despair, analysed by Lukács in his reflections on Hegel — and for favourably contrasting such authors with the disconcerting world view of the 'avant-garde' and its defenders. As the quotation below from *The Young Hegel* makes it amply clear, the judgement favouring Goethe, Hegel, Balzac, and Thomas Mann was by no means a matter of aesthetic taste for Lukács, conservative or not. It concerned the tragic vision he had of the ongoing social and historical developments, which he tried to convey in all his principal writings, including *History and Class Consciousness.* This is how he formulated the stark alternative facing humanity in a work written in emigration in the Soviet Union, in defiance of the official Stalin/Zhdanov line on Hegel as the 'representative of extreme conservative reaction against the French Revolution':

Ricardo and Balzac were no socialists, indeed they were declared opponents of socialism. But both Ricardo's objective economic analysis and Balzac's literary mimesis of the world of capitalism point to the necessity of a new world no less vividly than Fourier's satirical criticism of capitalism. Goethe and Hegel stand on the threshold of the last great and tragic blossoming of bourgeois ideology. *Wilhelm Meister* and *Faust, The Phenomenology of Mind* and the *Encyclopaedia* form one part of the monumental achievement in which the last creative energies of the bourgeoisie are gathered together to give intellectual or literary expression to their own *tragically contradictory* situation. In the works of Goethe and Hegel the reflection of the heroic period of the bourgeois age is even more clearly visible than in Balzac, for whom the age appears as no more than a glorious prelude to the final and terrible victory of the prose of the capitalist epoch.[27]

A few pages further on Lukács spelled out the tragic implications of Hegel's predicament as shared by the other great figures of his class:

The hard core of Hegel's conception of 'tragedy in the realm of the ethical' is that he is wholeheartedly in agreement with Adam Smith's view that the development of the material forces of production is progressive and necessary, even in respect to culture... He is as forceful as Smith and Ricardo in his strictures on the complaints of the Romantics about the modern world and he heaps scorn on their sentimentality which fixes on particulars while ignoring the overall situation. But at the same time, he also sees — and this brings him closer to the interests and preoccupations of Balzac and Fourier — that the type of man produced by this material advance in and through capitalism is the practical negation of everything great, significant and sublime that humanity had created in the course of its history up to then. The contradiction of two necessarily connected phenomena, the indissoluble bond between progress and the debasement of mankind, the purchase of progress at the cost of that debasement — that is the heart of the 'tragedy in the realm of the ethical'. Thus Hegel articulates one of the great contradictions of capitalist society, and with certain reservations, of all class societies.[28]

And this is how Lukács in the end connected the Hegelian vision of 'tragedy in the realm of the ethical' with the socialist imperative, and within that with his own predicament, as well as with the necessary appeal to the 'responsibility of the intellectuals' arising from the conceptualization of the alternatives that in his view must be faced in the contemporary world:

... it would be superficial to urge that Hegel would have been all the greater if he had never taken up the concept of 'reconciliation'. For the real, dialectical analysis of human progress and its contradictions can only be undertaken from a point of view dominated by a belief in the ultimate victory of progress, despite all the contradictions. Only the perspective of a classless society can provide a view of the *tragedies to be encountered en route* without succumbing to the temptations of a *pessimistic romanticism*. For this reason we must place Fourier's social criticism higher than Hegel's. If this perspective is not available to a thinker — and we have seen that it could not be available to Hegel — then there are only two possibilities open to anyone who has a clear view of the contradictions. Either he will hold fast to the contradictions, in which case he will end up as a romantic pessimist. Or he will *keep his faith, despite everything,* that progress is inevitable, *however many tragedies lie along the road.* ... Only because of Hegel's love of reality and his profound commitment to it could the concrete richness of the Hegelian dialectic come into being. And if his system culminates in 'reconciliation', this only shows that, as long as the horizon of class society is closed off, human progress even in the realm of the mind, of philosophy, is compelled to take detours through the labyrinth of what Engels called 'false consciousness'.[29]

Thus the moral and intellectual attitude advocated by Lukács was not chosen and commended on the basis of aesthetic criteria at all. In Hungary, where Lukács had his intellectual formation, the role of literature for centuries consisted in direct intervention in the most fundamental social and political matters and, fittingly, the revolution of 1848-49 against Habsburg domination was initiated on March 15 (still today the most important day in the national calendar) by the great poet, Sándor Petöfi reciting his poem 'Rise Hungarian' on the steps of the National Museum. In the same tradition, the young Lukács's idol (who never ceased to be the object of his veneration), the poet Endre Ady, said it loud and clear in his artistic credo:

> I did not come to be an artist
> but to be everything!
> The Master was I, the poem
> embellished servant only.

As far as Lukács himself was concerned, his chosen path was moral and political, and an intensely public and crusading one at that. He was *forced* into the domain of aesthetic theory and literary criticism after being defeated in 1929 by Stalin's underlings as a politician. And even then, he wanted to continue to proclaim the originally chosen moral and political message, using the medium of literary analysis and aesthetics — like Ady used poetry as his 'embellished servant' — in the service of human emancipation, accepting a predicament that went with 'tragedy in the realm of the ethical'. He continued to appeal to the example of Goethe and Hegel, as well as of Balzac and Thomas Mann, because he wanted to make people avoid the pitfalls of 'romantic pessimism'.

Lukács's approach — including the so-called 'Olympian' way of distancing himself, in the key of Goethe and Hegel, from the conflicts of the day after being forced to retreat from the field of politics — was representative of many bourgeois intellectuals who embraced the socialist cause like him. Their change of perspective was triggered off by the Russian revolution and they refused to break with it, at times notwithstanding the cost of their own personal tragedies. Lukács himself was imprisoned for some time in Stalin's Russia and he had to face more than once in his life the danger of being arrested in Hungary, including the months of his captivity after the Hungarian uprising of 1956. He could face such adversity with fortitude, because he fully shared what he asserted about Hegel: 'a belief in the ultimate victory of progress, despite all the contradictions', even if it meant for the foreseeable future 'tragedy in the realm of the ethical'.

However, the question remains: to what extent did the determinations of 'false consciousness' identified by the author of *History and Class Consciousness* and *The Young Hegel* affect his own predicament, when the anticipated and endorsed historical attempt to break out of the 'closed horizon of class society' followed a *blocked path* — the fatefully *blocked development* of the Soviet system. For under such conditions, in the absence of a clear recognition that all those decades of sacrifice and 'tragedy in the realm of the ethical' could only produce a derailed development, 'keeping one's faith, however many tragedies lie along the road' amounted, no matter how unwittingly, to an uncritical attitude towards the major contradictions of the system that retained the rule of capital in another form: through the alienated state control of the means of production and the concomitant politically enforced extraction of surplus-labour. Inevitably, remaining faithful, 'despite all the contradictions', to the perspective of *History and Class Consciousness* and *The Young Hegel* could not escape the charge of 'false consciousness', in the sense attributed by Lukács himself to Hegel, as against 'bad faith' with which his detractors tried to indict him.

Another difficult question concerns the historical disappearance of the original appellee of Lukács's moral exhortations: the bourgeois intellectuals willing to embrace the socialist cause. Could the profound structural crisis of the global capital system produce a significant reversal in the future in this respect? Be that as it may, the 'return to the fold' of the bourgeois intelligentsia brought with it a major problem for the working class movement everywhere. For a most uncomforting fact that must be faced is that Lenin's thesis of 'importing class consciousness into the working class from outside', through the agency of bourgeois intellectuals — a thesis embraced by Lukács, not surprisingly, to the very end — proved to be historically unviable in the course of twentieth century developments. Marx's original formulations — talking about the necessity of developing 'communist *mass* consciousness' — envisaged a very different solution. In this way, by indicating the strategic necessity of mass orientation and action in terms of which the socialist project was originally conceived as the measure of its viability or failure, the Marxian definition of the way ahead offers a hopeful pointer for the much needed reorientation of the movement. But only a pointer. For in the light of the intervening historical experience the difficulties of radically rearticulating the socialist movement as a viable *mass movement* cannot be overstated.

1.4.4

DESPITE all its mystifications, in the Hegelian system 'capital' was viewed at times not simply as some material entity (like 'capital assets') but as a *relationship*. However, Hegel depicted this relationship as:

(1) *absolutely inescapable;*

(2) a *benevolent compulsion;* and as

(3) of necessity ruled by a *supra-individual subject,* in view of the isolated individualistic constituents — the self-seeking individuals — from which the totalizing complex of 'civil society' was supposed to be made up.

Hegel's conception of the 'identical Subject-Object' was a necessary corollary of all this. For the only cohesive determination which he could offer in order to bring under control civil society's (in his own terms *infinite*) centrifugal forces — within the confines of a system conceived from the standpoint of capital — was the pseudo-mediation accomplished by the 'cunning of Reason' subsuming all individuals under itself. The identical Subject-Object as the true historical agency had to realise its own design, producing and perpetuating through the chosen instrumentality of particular individuals its own — already established — order beyond which there could be nothing rationally conceivable.

Lukács adopted as his philosophical point of departure the Hegelian conception. This was the point of contact through which he wanted to mediate his new-found socialist message to all those who still viewed the world through the spectacles of classical bourgeois philosophy. Understandably, in view of the given circumstances of revolutionary and postrevolutionary turmoil, the question of historical agency was at the forefront of Lukács's concerns in *History and Class Consciousness*. To convey the intended message, he had to reject not only Hegel's fairy-tale of benevolent compulsion but also the German philosopher's vision of absolute inescapability from the determinations of 'civil society'. At the same time, Lukács also had to try to turn Hegel's *supra*-individual subject into a *trans*-individual collective subject fully in control of its own destiny, without which the envisaged overcoming of 'tragedy in the realm of the ethical' would not be convincing. Curiously, however, Lukács thought that he could find a satisfactory solution to the relevant theoretical and practical issues in terms of his own version of the 'identical Subject-Object of history'.

In the 1967 Preface to *History and Class Consciousness* Lukács admitted that his efforts amounted only to *'out-Hegeling Hegel'*.[30] This was a generously correct diagnosis. For as a result of the incorrigible 'substitutionism' characteristic of *History and Class Consciousness,* Lukács's identical Subject-Object turned out to be a totally abstract and *Sollen*-like (i.e. 'ought-ridden') — even if secular — *supra-individual* entity: the Party, writ large, and hypostatized as the carrier of a *moral imperative*.

In truth the Hegelian problematic of identical Subject-Object — as a hierarchy-reproducing conception — could not be more alien to the socialist mode of social metabolic control. As we shall see in Chapter 19, the Marxian counter-image and criteria of viability to the rule of capital concerned the establishment of proper material and institutional mediations among individuals in the framework of a highly productive communal system, and not the invention of a new supra-individual subject. For the socialist project had to aim at the *restitution* of the alienated powers of social metabolic control to the associated producers, in the sharpest possible contrast to the ever-increasing and in the end totally petrified as well as violently superimposed *substitutionism* with which they were confronted under the Stalinist system.

The real tragedy (and not only 'in the realm of the ethical') was that under the circumstances of revolutions defeated everywhere except in Russia — which inevitably also meant the isolation of the only surviving revolution — the historical conditions for successfully developing in the required material and institutional terms the socialist mode of metabolic alternative to the rule of capital as a *global* enterprise had been cruelly denied. The door became wide open not only for the restabilization of the badly shaken capital system in the West but also for the emergence of a new form of 'personification of capital' in postrevolutionary Russia. The latter could operate a forced rate of surplus-labour extraction in the name of the revolution and for the declared purpose of the necessary 'socialist accumulation', justifying itself by its promise to overtake before long the leading capitalist countries in per capita pig iron, steel, and coal production as the measure of socialist success. As to the command structure of this new kind of social metabolic control, the Party had to remain at its apex as the regulator of the politically enforced extraction of surplus-labour, together with all of its cultural/ideological corollaries. Thereby the state was reinforced and more than ever centralized in the form of the Party-State, instead of embarking on the road to its 'withering away', as envisaged in the original socialist project.

Lukács's representative theorization of the postrevolutionary situation in

History and Class Consciousness had arisen from the new historical circumstances and constraints. His work by no means anticipated, let alone positively identified itself with, the subsequently prevailing Stalinist solutions. Quite the contrary, *History and Class Consciousness* presented an idealized picture of the possibilities inherent in the ongoing developments. In fact Lukács tried to devise solutions which were meant to prevail not only over against the suffocating material inertia but, for him more importantly, also against the dangers of political derailment and bureaucratization — the firmly rejected ways of the 'party of the old type' — by defining the Party's *raison d'être* in terms of a strict moral mandate.

Nevertheless, Lukács's identical Subject-Object — the proletariat, with its 'standpoint of totality' — in the end turned out to be not the class of workers but the Party. For the class as such was said to be captive of its 'psychological consciousness', as opposed to its 'ascribed' or 'imputed consciousness' without which in his view the revolution could not succeed. The substitutionism of *History and Class Consciousness* necessarily followed from this diagnosis. Lukács's dilemma — shared by many intellectuals who were at the time sympathetic to the revolution — thus became: how to demonstrate the inevitable victory of socialism despite the forbidding weaknesses of the 'weakest link' and despite the ideological inertia dominant among the workers. The difficulties arising from the latter were underlined by the author of *History and Class Consciousness* by repeatedly highlighting the negative consequences of the successful manipulation of the proletariat's 'psychological consciousness' by the reformist parties of the Second International.[31]

As we shall see in Part Two, Lukács produced a guarantee of socialist victory in philosophical/methodological and ideological terms. The category of 'identical Subject-Object' was an essential part of his solution. For by the very definition of its nature Lukács's 'identical Subject-Object of history' could offer an *aprioristic guarantee* of success, in the same way as in the Hegelian philosophy it was quite inconceivable to envisage other than total success for the enterprise of the identical Subject-Object, the self-realizing World Spirit. The only proviso stipulated by Lukács as the necessary condition of success was a *moral* one, by insisting that the Party had to *deserve* the role historically assigned to it by fighting for the trust of the working class and truly earning it, which disqualified much of what he could see around himself in his own struggles against some high ranking Hungarian and Comintern party figures.

But well beyond the aprioristic character of the identical Subject-Object, put by Lukács to the service of turning into strength the weaknesses of the 'weakest link', he needed Hegel for other reasons as well. He saw in Hegel the ultimate possibilities as well as the insurmountable limits of the classical bourgeois philosophical tradition. As against the latter, Lukács considered the intellectually viable adoption of 'the standpoint of totality' by socialist thinkers — a possibility which in his view had to be denied even to Hegel, not to mention his predecessors and successors, by the objective logic of history itself — as the proof of socialist victory not only in the domain of philosophy but in the fundamental social confrontation between capital and labour in general. At the same time, the dilemma with regard to the 'psychological consciousness' of the working class was also resolved by Lukács in intellectual/ideological terms: by projecting the successful ideological 'work of consciousness upon consciousness'. This work had to be envisaged through the agency of the Party, defined by Lukács both as 'the visible and organized incarnation of class consciousness'[32] and as 'the ethics of the proletariat'.[33] This kind of characterization of the Party was offered not as an end in itself but as a potential way of confronting the historical challenge. For in Lukács's view as expressed in *History and Class Consciousness* the alternative that had to be faced was stark but simple. Provided that the Party, in full consciousness of its historic mission, could live up to the requirements of its moral mandate, a way would be found to overcome 'the ideological crisis of the proletariat'. Otherwise humanity was bound to precipitate into barbarism.

Thus the Marxian concern with the objective conditions of the necessary social/metabolic alternative to capital was abandoned in favour of a heightened theoretical/ideological discourse. At the same time, the supra-individual agency of history was brought back by Lukács through the back door in the shape of the Party, and it was characterized by him as *'the concrete mediation between man and history'*.[34] Thus the author of *History and Class Consciousness* offered not only an aprioristic guarantee of success but also bypassed the need for indicating, in no matter how incomplete terms, the necessary material and institutional mediations which could in due course overcome at least in principle the constraints and contradictions of the postrevolutionary Soviet system.

1.4.5

LUKÁCS'S solution to the great burden of the *present* could only be abstract theoretical, in the same mould in which he postulated 'theoretical victory' over classical bourgeois philosophy as the guarantor of socialist victory over the bourgeois order. This is how he argued the point about the right way of seeing the present, paradoxically giving the last word to none other than Hegel himself:

> As long as man concentrates his interest contemplatively upon the past or future, both ossify into an alien existence. And between the subject and the object lies the unbridgeable 'pernicious chasm' of the present. Man must be able to *comprehend the present* as a becoming. ... Only he who is willing and whose mission it is to create the future can *see the present* in its concrete truth. As Hegel says: 'Truth is not to treat objects as alien'.[35]

'Comprehending the present as becoming' and 'seeing it' in the light of a correct understanding of its 'processual' character — thanks to the work of consciousness upon consciousness — thus became the idealized solution to the growing contradictions of the present. In this way, however, the spell of Hegel's 'universal permanent capital' could not be broken. On the contrary, the whole enterprise of *History and Class Consciousness* had to remain within the limits of some key categories of the Hegelian system.

Nevertheless, Lukács's magisterial undertaking acquired its representative significance not *despite* but precisely *through* and *together with* its limitations. For the Hungarian philosopher's problematical conception of materially sustainable historical development and of the role of conscious political intervention in it was not simply his own. The nature of the revolution 'at the weakest link of the chain' had a great deal to do with it. He had in front of him the evidence of a successful revolution — the only surviving one — and he was looking for ways to *generalize* what he identified as its reassuring conditions of success, vis-à-vis the materially more advanced world of the capitalist West where he and his fellow socialists had to suffer defeats. Thus it was not enough to assert, repeatedly and with passion, that defeat was 'the necessary prelude to victory'.[36] The material weakness itself had to be turned into a revolutionary asset. Accordingly, Lukács proclaimed that 'the *undeveloped* character of Russia ... gave the Russian proletariat the chance to resolve the ideological crisis with greater dispatch',[37] promising an easier ride also in the future on the ground of the claimed historic asset: 'the more feeble influence exerted by capitalist modes of thought and feeling in Russia upon the proletariat'.[38] Thus Lukács — fully in accord with his conscious aim — succeeded in avoiding the pitfalls of 'romantic pessimism'. Ironically and tragically, however, under the prevailing circumstances he could only do so by casting some of his most cherished hopes in the mould of a 'romantic optimism'.

To be fair, though, given the ebbing away of the revolutionary wave in Europe and the material backwardness of Russia, the Marxian programme of overcoming in socioeconomic terms the rule of capital as the globally dominant metabolic mode of control could not be on the historical agenda at the time of writing *History and Class Consciousness* either in Russia or anywhere else. Besides, the long years of the civil war and of its painful aftermath shifted attention even more strongly to the political plane. 'Making a virtue out of misery' — under the impact of the 'force of circumstance' — meant that the real target of socialist transformations: the necessity to go *beyond capital*, practically disappeared from the horizon. Its place was taken by an orientation centred on *politics*, ignoring or disregarding Marx's insistence that the revolution had to be *economic and social*, as opposed to the necessarily limited and constrained margin of action which any *political* revolution could provide. This brought with it that capital's productive achievements and structures had to be taken for granted as directly usable, defining thereby the principal task of socialist strategy as the speediest possible overtaking of the leading capitalist countries, and finding positive words even for the most intensive exploitative practices of *Taylorism*. This is how the fateful weaknesses of the weakest link came to dominance not only in post-revolutionary Russia but in the international socialist movement as a whole.

Naturally, Lukács did not identify himself consciously with every aspect of this development. Nevertheless he wholeheartedly embraced its central characteristics. The philosophical/ideological solution he offered to the perceived problems in *History and Class Consciousness* was complemented by an exclusively *political* orientation in practical terms, hopelessly restricting thereby the Marxian concept of transformatory social practice. Again, this was done in the service of demonstrating the strength of the weakest link. The details of these problems must be left to Part Two, especially to Chapters 8 and 9. But to conclude this section it is necessary to mention very briefly the meaning Lukács conferred upon the political revolution which 'expropriated the expropriators', the capitalists. He celebrated in it not simply the first step on the road to a potential socialist transformation but altogether the abolition of the opposition 'between past and present'. And he went on postulating that through the political act of 'taking the domination of labour out of the hands of the capitalist'[39] the emancipation of labour is effectively accomplished, leaving only the task of 'socialization' — defined in terms of making the proletariat 'become conscious of the changed inner relation of labour to its objectified forms (the relation of present to the past)'[40] — to the future. This is how the 'encircled revolution at the weakest link of the chain' had found its representative theorization in *History and Class Consciousness.*

1.5 Marx's unexplored alternative perspective: from the 'little corner of the world' to the consummation of capital's 'global ascendancy'

1.5.1

MARX had no need for 'out-Hegeling Hegel'. His primary focus was not an underdeveloped and devastated country struggling with the task of 'primitive accumulation', but the classic form of capitalist development which produced the self-confident theorization of its own 'natural' ways and absolute rightfulness in the writings of classical Political Economy: Marx's principal theoretical target. Similarly, with regard to the revolutionary agency, what Marx had in mind was not a small and in a civil war even decimated working class but the forcefully ascending industrial proletariat of the dominant capitalist countries. Given his primary focus — the 'Critique of Political Economy', rendered explicit in the subtitles of *all* of Marx's main works — the complications that had to be faced in the absence of a strong industrial proletariat could only be marginal to his concerns. And even when they entered Marx's horizon, in the last few years of his life, they did not bring major theoretical reassessment with them. The idea of a substitute agency, in whatever form, was anathema to Marx. When its prospect assumed a tangible organizational form in Europe, at the time of the adoption of the German *Gotha Programme,* he vehemently protested against it. Marx clearly realized that 'substitutionism' could only bring disaster to the socialist movement.

For all these reasons, Marx's relationship to Hegel could be quite unproblematical. He gave the great German philosopher his due, as the pathbreaker of dialectical thought, but did not hesitate to dismiss at the same time his 'identical Subject-Object' as conceptual mythology. In Marx's view what vitiated Hegel's philosophy was not simply its idealism but the fact that he shared the 'standpoint of Political Economy', which meant a totally uncritical stance towards capital as the metabolic control of society. And since Marx adopted the 'standpoint of labour' in his attempt to spell out a radical alternative to the given structural order, his conception of history had to be diametrically opposed to that of Hegel.

To be sure, Marx's concept of capital as a dynamically developing and all-encompassing historical order was linked in its origin to the Hegelian conception of 'world history': the domain of the World Spirit's irrepressible self-activity. However, to Hegel's grand idealist view of the ideally unfolding world history the Marxian approach counterposed a set of tangible, empirically identifiable events and developments, concerned with real individuals in their actually existing institutional setting. This is how Marx formulated his materialist counter-image explicitly against the Hegelian conception:

> The further the separate spheres, which act on one another, extend in the course of this development and the more the original isolation of the separate nationalities is destroyed by the advanced mode of production, by intercourse and by the natural

division of labour between various nations arising as a result, the more *history becomes world history*. Thus, for instance, if in England a machine is invented which deprives countless workers of bread in India and China, and overturns the whole form of existence of these empires, this invention becomes a *world-historical fact*. ... From this it follows that this transformation of history into world history is by no means a mere abstract act on the part of 'self-consciousness', the world spirit, or of any other metaphysical spectre, but a quite material, empirically verifiable act, an act the proof of which every individual furnishes as he comes and goes, eats, drinks and clothes himself. In history up to the present it is certainly likewise an empirical fact that separate individuals have, with the broadening of their activity into *world-historical activity,* become more and more enslaved under *a power alien to them* (a pressure which they have conceived of as a dirty trick on the part of the so-called world spirit, etc.), a power which has become more and more enormous and, in the last instance, turns out to be the *world market*.[41]

Naturally, this view of world history, conceived as the universal diffusion of the most advanced mode of production in the framework of a fully developed world market — i.e. as a process of actual 'becoming', characterized by clearly identifiable productive and consumptive activities within their well defined structural and institutional parameters — carried with it a corresponding vision of the way out of the destructive antagonisms of the prevailing social order. For it envisaged, as the necessary preconditions of its realization, on the one hand, the highest possible level of productivity — which in its turn implied the necessary transcendence of the given local and national barriers and contradictions, as well as the all-round beneficial integration and co-operative rationalization of material and intellectual production on a global scale. And, on the other hand, it anticipated, as the necessary corollary to the global character of the identified task, the concerted action of the industrially most powerful nations, so as to bring about the new — in its objective mode of functioning 'universal' and in its spirit consciously internationalist — social order. To quote Marx again:

this development of productive forces (which at the same time implies the actual empirical existence of men in their *world-historical,* instead of local, being) is an absolutely necessary practical premiss, because without it privation, want is merely made general, and with want the struggle for necessities would begin again, and all the old filthy business would necessarily be restored; and furthermore, because only with this *universal development* of productive forces is a *universal intercourse* between men established, which on the one side produces *in all nations* simultaneously the phenomenon of the 'propertyless' mass (universal competition), making *each nation dependent on the revolutions of the others,* and finally puts *world-historical, empirically universal individuals* in place of local ones. ... Empirically, communism is only possible as the *act of the dominant peoples 'all at once' and simultaneously,* which presupposes the *universal* development of the productive forces and the *world intercourse* bound up with them.[42]

This way of approaching matters demonstrated not only the superiority of the materialist conception of history to its idealist counterparts, including the Hegelian vision, but also the great difficulties that went with the adoption of the Marxian method. For as far as idealist philosophies were concerned, the burden of material proof in relation to the practical realization of historical trends — grasped in the objective circumstances of actually living individuals who pursued their aims within the network of complex social determinations — did not and could not really exist. Operating within the idealist conceptual framework enabled Hegel to substitute for the required material proofs the conveniently malleable and ultimately circular abstractions of 'self-alienating' World Spirit which reached its ultimate 'self-realization' in the untranscendable world order of capitalist 'civil society' and its 'ethical State'.

Marx's difficulties, by contrast, were inseparable from the adoption of the materialist orienting principles and the corresponding historical and dialectical method. The problematical aspect of the vision displayed in the last two quotations was not its relevance to the new historical epoch as a whole but its relation to the actual state of affairs in the greater part of the world at the time of its conception.

1.5.2

TWO fundamental issues are at stake here. The first concerns the necessity of *transition,* and the second the *global historical framework* in which a successful transition to the advocated socialist order might be accomplished.

Hegel depicted capital as *frozen permanence,* in conjunction with his definition of universality as 'the modern'. Likewise, the freedom Hegel was concerned with, in the postulated 'realization of freedom' through world history, was only the 'idea of freedom'. According to Hegel everything was governed by its 'principle', and 'the principle of the modern world' was said to be 'thought and the universal'.[43] The problems of world history were thus resolved through the definition of a set of interlocking concepts, within the domain of self-anticipating and necessarily self-realizing World Spirit. In this way the structurally prejudged and historically frozen particularism of capital could be elevated to the ideal status of timeless universality and rationally unchallengeable permanence. Since in Hegel's view we have already reached the historical stage of the World Spirit's full adequacy with itself, the question of transition to a different historical order could not conceivably arise.

In contrast to Hegel, Marx treated the capital system as *necessarily transient.* Notwithstanding the historical advancement embodied in capital's mode of functioning as regards productivity when compared to the past (which happened to be more than generously acknowledged by Marx), he considered its social metabolic viability as confined to a strictly limited historical phase that had to be left behind by the radical intervention of the socialist project. For the innermost structural determinations of the capital system — based on a set of mediatory relations articulated for the domination of labour, in the service of the necessary extraction of surplus-labour — were irremediably *antagonistic* and ultimately not only destructive but also *self*-destructive.

The socialist project, as conceived by Marx, envisaged the qualitative redimensioning of this *antagonistic structure* of actual mediations which Hegel, in tune with his social standpoint and despite his greatness as a thinker, had to envelope in a mystical fog. Once the actual terms of reference of the historically given forms and institutions of social mediation were identified in the Marxian way, laying bare their incurably antagonistic inner determinations, it became also clear that *partial remedies* could not rectify the capital system's fundamental structural inequalities and material, political, and cultural antagonisms.

Thus the socialist enterprise had to be defined as a radical *alternative* to the social metabolic mode of control of the capital system as a whole. For the latter could not function in any other way than in the form of imposing itself as the *radical alienation of control* from the individuals. Consequently no tinkering with some partial defects through the medium of accommodatory reforms — the path vainly pursued for more than a century and recently altogether abandoned by the socialdemocratic movement — could face up to this challenge.

If it wanted to achieve anything at all, the socialist project had to define itself as the *restitution* of the historically alienated function of control to the social body — the 'associated producers' — under *all* its aspects. In other words, the socialist project had to be realised as a *qualitatively different mode of social metabolic control:* one constituted by the individuals in such a way that it should not be *alienable* from them. To be successful in this respect, it had to be a mode of control capable of regulating the material and intellectual productive functions of the individuals' mediatory interchanges among themselves and with nature not *from above* — the only way in which the *supra-individual* 'hidden hand' could assert its far from benevolent power, by usurping the *inter-individual* powers of decision making — but arising from the *broadest social base.*

So long as capital remains *globally dominant,* its 'transitoriness' (emphasised by Marx) is bound to remain latent only. For no matter how problematical in its innermost constitution, under the conditions of its global domination the false appearance of the capital system's unalterable permanence can mark out the horizon of everyday life relatively undisturbed in commodity society.

THIS is where the Marxian conception must be contrasted with his own unexplored alternative perspective. For actual historical developments since the time of Marx's death have themselves produced some painful qualifications in this respect.

In the second passage quoted from *The German Ideology,* in Section 1.5.1 above, Marx twice referred to the category of *simultaneity* in attempting to explain the nature of the ongoing developments. First, he indicated that the universal development of the productive forces under the rule of capital brings with it not only 'universal intercourse' within the framework of the world market but also *'in all nations simultaneously* the phenomenon of the "propertyless" mass (universal competition)'. And second, as a corollary to the first, he stressed that 'communism is only possible as the act of the *dominant peoples* "all at once" and *simultaneously'.* As to the terrain on which the 'dominant peoples' were expected to act simultaneously, Marx had in mind Europe.

So long as the object of analysis is the classic type of capitalist development, without the complications introduced into it by 'uneven development', the criteria enumerated by Marx remain valid. Competition, if universally extended, would undoubtedly produce 'propertyless mass', simultaneously as well as at a fairly uniform rate, in all nations. From such a predicament it would also follow that when the contradictions of the system mature and the situation becomes untenable to the 'propertyless mass', simultaneous action is likely to follow in defence of the workers' interests against the ubiquitous and more or less uniform stranglehold of capital. Moreover, due to unabatable competition within the framework of a properly functioning world market, there can be no significant ways of alleviating the contradictions of the system in its drive towards saturation and eventual breakdown. The predicated simultaneous action of the 'dominant peoples' is more than plausible under such circumstances.

Once, however, the differential conditions of growing advantage and disadvantage among capitalistically developing nations are added to this picture, the situation changes beyond recognition. Indeed it does so not only on the side of capital but — however temporarily — also in relation to labour. As regards capital, *imperialist* expansion on the one hand, and *monopolistic* developments on the other, give a new lease of life to the capital system, markedly delaying the time of its saturation. They confer enormous advantage on the dominant socioeconomic forces as sustained in every possible way, internally as well as abroad, by the capitalist state. Thus competition, although quite impossible to eliminate, becomes a rather problematical notion within the framework of an imperialist complex. Many of the contradictions of the industrial competitive system are transferred to the plane of inter-state rivalry, with potentially ruinous consequences, as two world wars testify. At the same time, due to monopolistic developments, the rules of competition can be twisted and turned to the advantage of the dominant economic forces. The consequences are twofold. First, the powerful monopolies acquire major privileges within the framework of the world market. And second, the concentration and centralization of capital is greatly facilitated, in accordance with the interests of the dominant monopolies, oligopolies and cartels.

Also with regard to labour the changes are quite significant. For now from the margin of the differential advantage — yielding *differential rates of profit* and super-profit — a certain portion can be allocated to the 'metropolitan' labour force. This is how the *differential rate of exploitation* — without which the required highly favourable differential rates of profit would not be feasible — becomes an integral part of the global capital system, rendering also in this respect problematical the idea of simultaneous action by the working classes of the 'dominant peoples' for the — however temporary — duration of the conditions described above.

1.5.3

OF course, Marx was no contemporary to these developments. The full impact of the emerging capitalist empires both at home and in their inter-state relations was during his lifetime far from visible. Also, monopolistic transformations in the economy were hardly on the horizon as yet, let alone could they render evident their full potential for restructuring the capital system as a whole. It would be therefore quite absurd to blame Marx for not offering solutions to problems which only much later coalesced into tangible historical challenges for the socialist movement.

However, there was a point in time when Marx hinted at the possibility of an alternative sociohistorical perspective as compared to the one normally advocated by him. This alternative perspective was mentioned in a passage of a little known letter by Marx to Engels to which I repeatedly tried to draw attention for many years. It reads like this:

> The historic task of bourgeois society is the establishment of the *world market*, at least in its basic outlines, and a mode of production that rests on its basis. Since the world

is round, it seems that this has been accomplished with the colonization of California and Australia and with the annexation of China and Japan. For us the difficult question is this: the revolution on the Continent is imminent and its character will be at once socialist; will it not be *necessarily crushed* in this *little corner of the world,* since on a much larger terrain the development of bourgeois society is still *in the ascendant.*[44]

Obviously it was not a matter of indifference whether the inner antagonisms of classically developed capital exploded within the limited European domain — blowing thereby the system's operational framework itself apart — or a way of displacing the accumulated contradictions could be found through the continued ascendancy of the bourgeois order in by far the greater part of the world. It was true that on a round planet earth after the colonization of California and Australia as well as the annexation of China and Japan there remained no more continents to be discovered by capital for colonization and annexation. But it was true only in the sense of the planet's 'extensive totality'. As far as the 'intensive totality' of the already discovered and annexed vast territories were concerned, the capital system was very far from reaching the limits of its productive expansion and accumulation. Indeed, not only in the newly colonized and annexed areas, not even only in the countries conquered by the dominant imperialist powers during the entire historical phase of colonial/imperial expansion, but *everywhere,* including the most privileged 'metropolitan' countries, the hidden continents of labour's ever-intensifying exploitation were yet to be fully discovered and put to the benefit of capital's social metabolic order. To use an analogy, the big difference in this respect was the same as the sharp contrast between *absolute* and *relative* surplus value. If capital could rely as its vehicle of expansion only on absolute surplus value, or on the geographically limited size of the planet, its life-span would be, to be sure, most dramatically curtailed. For a day has only twenty four hours in it, just as the round planet has an incomparably more limited size than the 'intensive totality' of exploitation and the corresponding magnitude of capital accumulation, squeezed or 'pumped out' of labour through the good services of relative surplus value.

Marx could only hope that positive developments for the prospects of socialism would come to fruition through a major — non-isolated — social revolution in Europe, accomplished by the working classes of the 'dominant peoples', so as to block in that way the road to capital's indefinite historical ascendancy on the existing, and by Marx readily acknowledged, 'much larger terrain'. In fact he added in the same letter to Engels that 'One cannot deny that bourgeois society lives its second 16th century which, I hope, will take it into the grave, just as the first one brought it into life'.

As we all know, the hope expressed in the last sentence had been bitterly disappointed. Nevertheless, Marx remained faithful to his original perspective. This he did despite the fact that the social revolution anticipated by him — the Paris Commune of 1871 — was indeed crushed in the European 'little corner of the world', due to a considerable degree also to the fact that it remained an isolated event, and the ascendancy of bourgeois society continued thereafter without great hindrance. Too much tied Marx to the perspective in which his work was originally articulated, and too little was as yet visible from the new trends of — imperialistic and monopolistic — development to enable him to make a major shift to an alternative perspective, in the spirit intimated in his letter to Engels.

Today, by contrast, it is necessary to face the relevant problems for two main reasons. First, because no socialist can seriously entertain the idea that the capital system can be historically superseded so long as the ascendancy of the bourgeois order can assert itself on the global terrain. This means that the much needed reassessment of all socialist strategies, in different parts of our planet, must take on board the disturbing and negative dimension of this ascendancy, both in interpreting the historical past and in the assessment of the future. For a failure to give due weight to the forces that sustain the capital system as a whole leads either to the naive expectations of 'catastrophism' or to defeatist disenchantment and the total abandonment of the socialist perspective, as witnessed in the recent past.

The second reason is equally important. For the positive aspect of Marx's unexplored historical dilemma is that the ascendancy itself is limited by the ultimately final terrain which can be — and up until now successfully has been — brought into the framework of capital expansion and accumulation. In other words, the historical ascendancy even on the global terrain — and even when considered in its intensive totality — is *historical only*. It is necessarily confined to the limitations of capital's genuine productive potentialities and remains subject to the ineradicable inner antagonisms of this system of social metabolic reproduction in its entirety.

Given the obvious global nature of the historical transformations experienced since Marx's days, no one could confine any longer the prospects of fundamental social upheavals to a 'little corner of the world'. There are not, and absolutely there cannot be any more 'little corners', let alone 'socialism in one country', no matter how large or vast in population that country might be. Nothing could underline this simple truth more strongly than the dramatic implosion of the Soviet system.

AS mentioned before, capital's historical ascendancy in its broad outlines has been brought to its conclusion. Significantly, this process could unfold only in a most contradictory form, storing up enormous problems for the time ahead of us. As a result of the slanted global development accomplished in the last hundred years, under the domination of a handful of capitalistically advanced countries, the terms of Marx's original equation have fundamentally changed. The way in which this process has been brought to its conclusion pronounces a very severe judgement on it. For the consummation of the capital system's global ascendancy, despite five centuries of expansion and accumulation, carried with it the condemnation of the overwhelming majority of humankind to a hand-to-mouth existence.

There are, of course, those who can see nothing wrong with the existing state of affairs. Heads of governments — like John Major in England — declare with smug self-complacency that 'capitalism works'. They refuse to entertain the questions: for whom? (certainly not for 90 percent of the world's population) and for how long?

Curiously, though, when they have to defend themselves on account of their miserably failed policies and constantly broken promises, they can only repeat like a broken record that the problems which forced them 'off the rails' are not of their own making but shared by every 'industrial economy' (a euphemism for capitalist countries), from Japan to Germany and from the United States to France, not to mention Italy and all the other members of the European Economic Community. Thus they refuse to see the blatant contradiction between their self-confident declaration of faith that 'capitalism works' and the forced admission that after all it doesn't (a conclusion which they never explicitly draw, although it stares them in the face).

In the course of the last century capital has certainly invaded and subdued every corner of our planet, little and large alike. However, it proved quite incapable of solving the grave problems which people must confront in their everyday life all over the world. If anything, the penetration of capital into every single corner of the 'underdeveloped' world only aggravated these problems. It promised 'modernization', but after many decades of loudly trumpeted intervention it only delivered intensified poverty, chronic indebtedness, insoluble inflation, and crippling structural dependency. So much so in fact that it is now highly embarrassing to remind the ideologists of the capital system that not so long ago they nailed their flags to the mast of 'modernization'.

Things have significantly changed in the last few decades, as compared to the expansionary past. The displacement of capital's inner contradictions could work with relative ease during the phase of the system's historical ascendancy. It was possible to deal under such conditions with many problems by sweeping them under the carpet of unfulfilled promises, like modernization in the 'Third World' and ever greater prosperity and social advancement in the 'metropolitan' countries, predicated on the expectation of producing an endlessly growing cake. However, the consummation of capital's historical ascendancy radically alters the situation. It is then not only no longer possible to make plausible new sets of vacuous promises but the old promises too must be wiped out of memory, and some real gains of the working classes in the privileged capitalist countries must be 'rolled back' in the interest of the survival of the ruling socioeconomic and political order.

This is where we stand today. The triumphalist celebrations of a few years ago now sound very hollow indeed. The slanted development of the last century brought no solutions on the model of 'mobile property's civilized victory' (Marx), in that it simply multiplied the privileges of the few and the misery of the many. However, a radically new condition has emerged in the course of the last few decades, gravely affecting the prospects of development in the future. For what is particularly grave today from the point of view of the capital system is that even the privileges of the few cannot be sustained any longer on the backs of the many, in sharp contrast to the past. As a result, the system as a whole is being rendered quite unstable, even if it will take some time before the full implications of this systemic instability transpire, calling for structural remedies in place of manipulative postponement.

Thus Marx's alternative perspective is coming into its own only in our own times. Not so long ago the accumulated problems could be ignored or minimized by indulging in self-complacent talk about more or less easily manageable 'dysfunctions'. However, when even the privileges of the small minority are unsustainable despite the ever-intensified exploitation of the overwhelming majority, such talk must sound problematical even to its formerly most uncritical practitioners. In fact the same people who still yesterday wanted us to be satisfied with their explanatory discourse on merely 'technical difficulties' and 'temporary dysfunctions', recently started to talk about 'shared problems' and the need for a 'common effort' for solving them, within the confines of the established order, confessing at times their bewilderment as to what seems to be happening everywhere. What baffles them more than anything else is that the collapse of the Soviet system not only removed their favourite self-justifying *alibi* but, to make things worse, failed to deliver the hoped for beneficial results to their own side. For the expected revitalization of the Western capital system through its 'victory' over the East, and the concomitant 'natural' and happy marketization of the postrevolutionary part of the world stubbornly failed to materialize. The ideologists of 'advanced capitalism' liked to think of the Soviet system as the diametrical opposite of their own. They had to be awakened to the disconcerting truth that it was only the obverse side of the same coin.

It is a sobering fact that the carpet which could successfully hide for far too long even the gravest problems swept under it is becoming very difficult to walk on. Indeed, it is a matter of great importance that the wantonly ignored problems affecting the very survival of humanity must now be faced under circumstances when the capital system as a whole had entered its *structural crisis*.

CHAPTER TWO

CAPITAL'S ORDER OF SOCIAL METABOLIC REPRODUCTION

2.1 Structural defects of control in the capital system

2.1.1

IN earlier phases of historical development many negative aspects and tendencies of the capital system could be ignored with relative safety, as indeed they were, except by some far-sighted socialists, like Marx himself, as we have seen in a passage quoted on page 6, written by him as far back as 1845. In the last few decades, by contrast, protest movements — notably the various shades of environmentalism — emerged from a very different social setting, even with far from socialist value orientation. These movements attempted to gain a foothold in the field of politics in several capitalist countries through the agency of reform-oriented Green parties. They appealed to individuals concerned about the ongoing environmental destruction, leaving undefined the underlying socioeconomic causes, as well as their class connotations. This they did precisely in order to broaden their own electoral appeal, in the hope of successfully intervening in the reform process for the purpose of reversing the identified dangerous trends. The fact that within a relatively short space of time all such parties became marginalized, despite their spectacular initial successes almost everywhere, underlines that the causes manifesting in environmental destruction are much more deep-seated than it was assumed by the leaders of these programmatically non-class oriented reform movements, including the people who imagined that they could institute a viable alternative to the socialist project by inviting its adherents to move 'From Red to Green'.[45]

No matter how important — indeed literally vital — as a 'single issue' around which varieties of the Green movement tried to articulate their reform programmes, so as to make an inroad into the power structure and decision making processes of the established order, the incontestable imperative of environmental protection turned out to be quite intractable on account of the corresponding necessary restraints which its implementation would have to mean to the prevailing production processes. The capital system proved to be unreformable even under its most obviously destructive aspect.

Today the difficulty is not only that the dangers inseparable from the ongoing development are much greater than ever before, inasmuch as the global capital system had reached its contradictory zenith of maturation and saturation. The dangers now extend over the whole planet, and consequently the urgency of doing something about them before it is too late happens to be particularly acute. To aggravate the situation, everything is further complicated by the fact that it is not feasible to find partial solutions to the problems that must be faced. Thus no 'single issue' can be realistically considered a 'single issue'. If nothing else, this circumstance has been forcefully highlighted by the disconcerting marginalization of the Green movement on the success of which so much hope has been placed in recent times, even among former socialists.

In the past up to a few decades ago it was possible to squeeze out of capital what appeared to be significant concessions — such as relative gains for the socialist movement (which later turned out to be *reversible* both as legislative measures for working class action and as gradually improving standard of living), obtained through the *defensive organizations* of labour: its trades unions and parliamentary parties. These gains could be conceded by capital so long as they could be *assimilated* and *integrated* by the system as a whole and turned to its productive advantage in the course of its self-expansion. Today, by contrast, confronting even partial issues with any hope of success implies the necessity of challenging the *capital system as such*. For in our own historical epoch, when productive self-expansion is no longer a readily available way out of the accumulating difficulties and contradictions (hence the purely wishful thinking of getting rid of the black hole of indebtedness by 'growing out of it'), the global capital system *of necessity* frustrates all attempts at interfering even to a minimal extent with its structural parameters.

In this respect the obstacles to be overcome are actually *shared* by labour — that is, labour as the radical alternative to capital's social metabolic order — and the 'single issue' movements. For the historic failure of social democracy clearly underlined that only integrable demands can gain legitimacy under the rule of capital. Environmentalism by its very nature — just like the great historic cause of women's liberation — is *non-integrable*. Consequently no such cause will for the capital system conveniently fade away, irrespective of how many setbacks and defeats the politically organized forms of 'single issue' movements might have to suffer in the foreseeable future.

However, historically/epochally defined non-integrability, no matter how important for the future, cannot guarantee success on its own. Switching the allegiance of disappointed socialists from the working class to so-called 'new social movements' (praised now *in opposition* to, and by discarding altogether the emancipatory potential of, labour) must be considered, therefore, far too premature and naive. Single issue movements, even if they fight for non-integrable causes, can be picked off and marginalized one by one, because they cannot lay claim to representing a coherent and comprehensive alternative to the given order as a mode of social metabolic control and system of societal reproduction. This is what makes focusing on the socialist emancipatory potential of labour more important today than ever before. For labour is not only non-integrable (in contrast to some historically specific political manifestations of labour, like reformist social democracy, which may be rightly characterized as integrable and indeed in the last few decades also completely integrated), but — precisely as the only feasible *structural alternative* to capital — can provide the comprehensive strategic framework within which all 'single issue' emancipatory movements can successfully make their common cause for the survival of humanity.

2.1.2

TO understand the nature and strength of the prevailing structural constraints, it is necessary to compare the established order of social metabolic control with its historical antecedents. For, contrary to the self-serving mythology of its ideologists, the capital system's mode of operation is the *exception* and not the *rule* as far as the productive interchange of human beings with nature and among themselves is concerned.

What must be stressed first of all is that capital is not a 'material entity' — let alone a rationally controllable 'mechanism', as the apologists of the allegedly neutral 'market mechanism' (to be happily embraced by 'market socialism') tried to make us believe, as we shall see in Part Three — but an *ultimately uncontrollable mode of social metabolic control.* The main reason why this system must escape a meaningful degree of human control is precisely because it itself emerged in the course of history as a most powerful — indeed up to the present time by far *the* most powerful — *'totalizing'* framework of control into which everything else, including human beings, must be fitted, and prove thereby their 'productive viability', or perish if they fail to do so. One cannot think of a more inexorably all-engulfing — and in that important sense *'totalitarian'* — system of control than the globally dominant capital system. For the latter blindly subjects to the same imperatives health care no less than commerce, education no less than agriculture, art no less than manufacturing industry, ruthlessly superimposing its own criteria of viability on everything, from the smallest units of its 'micro-cosm' to the most gigantic transnational enterprises, and from the most intimate personal relations to the most complex decision making processes of industry-wide monopolies, favouring always the strong against the weak. Ironically (and rather absurdly), however, in the opinion of its propagandists this system is supposed to be inherently *democratic,* indeed the paradigm foundation of all conceivable democracy. This is why the Editors and Leader writers of the London *Economist* can commit to paper in all seriousness the proposition according to which:

> There is *no alternative* to the free market as the way to organize economic life. The spread of *free market economics* should gradually lead to *multi-party democracy,* because people who have *free economic choice* tend to insist on having *free political choice* too.[46]

Unemployment for countless millions, among many other blessings of 'free market economics', thus belongs to the category of 'free economic choice', out of which in due course the fruits of 'free political choice' — 'multi-party democracy', no less, (and certainly no more) — will arise. And then, of course, we shall all live happily ever after.

In actuality, though, the capital system is the first one in history which constitutes itself as an unexceptionable and irresistible totalizer, no matter how repressive the imposition of its totalizing function must be whenever and wherever it encounters resistance.

To be sure, this characteristic makes the system more dynamic than all the earlier modes of social metabolic control put together. But the price that must be paid for this incommensurable totalizing dynamism is, paradoxically, the *loss of control* over the decision making processes. This applies not only to the workers, in whose case the loss of control — whether in paid employment or out of it — is quite obvious (even if *The Economist,* viewing the world from the dizzy height of cloud cuckoo land, can characterize his or her predicament under the category of 'free economic choice'[47]), but even to the richest capitalists. For no matter how many controlling shares the latter might be able to boast in the company or companies which they legally own as particular individuals, their power of control within the framework of the capital system as a whole is quite negligible. They must obey the objective imperatives of the system as a whole just like everyone else, or suffer the consequences and go out of business. Adam Smith had no illusions whatsoever in this regard when he chose to describe the real controlling power of the system as *'the invisible hand'*. The more the objective determinations of capital's global metabolic order asserted themselves in the course of history, the more obviously the notion of the 'caring capitalist' in charge of the economic processes turned out to be nothing but a fantasy of socialdemocratic leaders.

As a historically specific mode of social metabolic control the capital system, of necessity, articulates and consolidates itself also as a unique *command structure*. The life chances of the individuals under this system are determined according to where the social groups to which they belong are actually *situated in the hierarchical command structure of capital*. Moreover, given the unique modality of its socioeconomic metabolism, coupled with its — in all history so far not even remotely matched — totalizing character, a formerly quite unimaginable correlation must be established in this system between *economics* and *politics*. We shall consider in Section 2.2 the nature of this relationship and discuss its implications at greater length in subsequent chapters. Let it be simply mentioned here in passing that the immensely powerful — and equally totalizing — modern state arises on the ground of this all-engulfing socioeconomic metabolism, irreplaceably *complementing* (and not simply serving) the latter in some vital respects. It is therefore by no means accidental that the Soviet type post-capitalist capital system could not take even an infinitesimal step towards the 'withering away of the state' (quite the contrary), despite the fact that to do so was from the very beginning, and for very good reasons indeed, one of the seminal orienting principles and essential practical concerns of the Marxian socialist movement.

2.1.3

CAPITAL is a mode of control above all else, *prior* to itself being — in a rather superficial sense — controlled by the private capitalists (or later by the officials of the Soviet type state). The dangerous illusions of overcoming or subduing the power of capital through the legal/political expropriation of the private capitalists arise from disregarding the real nature of the controller/controlled relationship. For as a social metabolic mode of control capital, *of necessity,* always retains its *primacy* over the *personnel* through which its *juridical embodiment* can be manifest in different forms at different times in history. Accordingly, if critics of the Soviet system simply complain about 'bureaucratization', they miss their intended target by an astronomical distance. For even the complete replacement of the 'bureaucratic personnel' would leave the edifice of the post-capitalist capital system standing, just like the invention of the 'caring capitalist', if by some miracle it were feasible at all, would not alter in the slightest the utterly dehumanizing character of the 'advanced capitalist' capital system.

As mentioned in the last paragraph of Section 2.1.2, in order to be able to function as a totalizing mode of social metabolic control, the capital system must have its historically unique, and to its major functions appropriate, command structure. Consequently, in the interest of the realization of the adopted fundamental metabolic objectives, society as a whole must be subjected — in all its productive and distributive functions — to the innermost requirements of capital's structurally limited (even if within such limits significantly adjustable) mode of control.

Under one of its principal aspects this process of subjection takes the form of dividing society into all-embracing but to one another on objective grounds irreconcilably opposed *social classes,* and of instituting the modern state as the likewise all-comprehensive form of *political control* under the other principal aspect. And since society would fall apart if this duality could not be firmly consolidated under some *common denominator,* an elaborate system of *hierarchical social division of labour* must be *superimposed* on the *functional/technical* (and later highly integrated technological) division of labour as the uneasy cementing force of the — in its deepest underlying tendency disruptively centrifugal — overall complex.

This superimposition of the hierarchical social division of labour as a most problematical — indeed ultimately explosive — cementing force of society is an unavoidable necessity. It arises from the insurmountable condition whereby under the rule of capital society must be *antagonistically structured* in a specific way, since the *productive* and *controlling* functions of the labour process must be radically divorced from one another and assigned to different classes of individuals. Quite simply, the capital system — whose *raison d'être* is the maximal extraction of surplus-labour from the producers in whatever form might be compatible with its structural limits — could not possibly fulfil its social metabolic functions in any other way. By contrast, not even the feudal order has to institute this kind of radical divorce between material production and control. For no matter how complete is the serf's political bondage, depriving him of the personal freedom to choose the land on which he labours, he remains none the less in possession of the working tools and retains not formal but substantive control over much of the production process itself.

As an equally unavoidable necessity, under the capital system the hierarchical social division of labour must be not just superimposed, as a deteminate power relationship, on the functional/technical aspects of the labour process. It must be also misrepresented as the absolutely unchallengeable ideological justification and buttressing pillar of the established order of things. To this end the two distinctly different categories of 'division of labour' must be *conflated,* so as to be able to characterize the historically contingent and forcibly imposed condition of hierarchy and subordination as the unalterable dictate of *'nature itself',* whereby structurally enforced inequality can be reconciled with the mythology of 'equality and freedom' — 'free economic choice' and 'free political choice' in *The Economist's* parlance — and also sanctified as nothing less than the dictate of Reason as such. Significantly, even in Hegel's idealist system in which — perfectly in tune with the value orientation of all idealist philosophical systems — the category of nature is assigned an inferior position, direct appeals to the authority of nature are nevertheless made without the slightest hesitation and fear of inconsistency in the ideologically most telling contexts, justifying socially created and enforced inequality in the name of 'natural inequality', as we have seen above.[48]

With regard to its innermost determination the capital system is *expansion-oriented* and *accumulation-driven*. Such a determination constitutes both a formerly unimaginable dynamism and a fateful deficiency. In this sense, as a system of social metabolic control capital is quite irresistible for as long as it can successfully extract and accumulate surplus-labour— whether in directly economic or in primarily political form — in the course of the given society's *expanded reproduction*. Once, however, this dynamic process of expansion and accumulation gets stuck (for whatever reason), the consequences must be quite devastating. For even under the 'normality' of relatively limited cyclic disturbances and blockages the destruction that goes with the ensuing socioeconomic and political crises can be enormous, as the annals of the twentieth century reveal it, including two world wars (not to mention countless smaller conflagrations). It is therefore not too difficult to imagine the implications of a *systemic,* truly *structural* crisis; i.e. one that affects the global capital system not simply under one of its aspects — the financial/monetary one, for instance — but in all its fundamental dimensions, questioning its viability altogether as a social reproductive system.

Under the conditions of capital's structural crisis its destructive constituents come to the fore with a vengeance, activating the spectre of total uncontrollability in a form that foreshadows self-destruction both for this unique social reproductive system itself and for humanity in general. As we shall see in Chapter 3, capital was *never* amenable to proper and durable *control* or rational self-restraint. For it was compatible only with limited adjustments, and even those only for as long as it could continue to pursue in one form or another the dynamics of self-expansion and the process of accumulation. Such adjustments consisted in side-stepping, as it were, the encountered obstacles and resistances when capital was unable to frontally demolish them.

This characteristic of uncontrollability was in fact one of the most important factors that secured capital's irresistible advancement and ultimate victory, which it had to accomplish despite the earlier mentioned fact that capital's mode of metabolic control constituted the *exception* and not the rule in history. After all, capital at first appeared as a strictly *subordinate* force in the course of historical development. And worse still, on account of necessarily subordinating '*use-value*' — that is, production for human need — to the requirements of self-expansion and accumulation, capital in all of its forms had to overcome also the odium of being considered for a long time the most 'unnatural' way of controlling the production of wealth. According to the ideological confrontations of medieval times, capital was fatefully implicated in 'mortal sin' in more ways than one, and therefore had to be outlawed as 'heretic' by the highest religious authorities: the Papacy and its Synods. It could not become the dominant force of the social metabolic process before sweeping out of the way the absolute — and religiously sanctified — prohibition on 'usury' (contested under the category of 'profit upon alienation', which really meant: retaining control over the monetary/financial capital of the age, in the interest of the accumulation process, and at the same time securing profit by lending money) and winning the battle over the 'alienability of land' (again, the subject of absolute and religiously sanctified prohibition under the feudal system) without which the emergence of capitalist agriculture — a vital condition for the triumph of the capital system in general

— would have been quite inconceivable.[49]

Thanks to a very large extent to its uncontrollability, capital succeeded in overcoming all odds — no matter how powerful materially and how absolutized in terms of the prevailing value system of society — against itself, elevating its mode of metabolic control to the power of absolute dominance as a fully extended global system. However, it is one thing to overcome and subdue problematical (even obscurantist) constraints and obstacles, and quite another to institute the positive principles of sustainable social development, guided by the criteria of humanly fulfilling objectives, as opposed to the blind pursuit of capital's self-expansion. Thus the implications of the selfsame power of uncontrollability which in its time secured the victory of the capital system are far from reassuring today when the need for restraints is conceded — at least in the form of the elusive desideratum of 'self-regulation' — even by the system's most uncritical defenders.

2.1.4

THE basic units of earlier forms of social metabolic control were characterized by a high degree of *self-sufficiency* with regard to the relationship between material production and its control. This applies not only to primitive tribal communities but also to the household economy of ancient slave-owning societies as well as to the feudal system of the Middle Ages. By the time this self-sufficiency breaks down and progressively gives way to broader metabolic/reproductive connections and determinations we are already witnessing the victorious advancement of capital's mode of control, bringing with it in due course also the universal diffusion of alienation and reification.

What is particularly important in the present context is that the switch from the conditions expressed by the medieval proverb *'nulle terre sans maître'* (no land without its master) to *'l'argent n'a pas de maître'* (money has no master) represents a veritable sea change. For it indicates a process of *radical overturning* which finds its ultimate consummation in the fully developed capital system.

Some elements of the latter can be identified — at least in embryonic form — many centuries earlier. Thus money, quite unlike land in its fixed relationship to the feudal lord, not only has no permanent master but cannot be confined even in principle to artificial boundaries as regards its potential circulation. Similarly, mercantile capital's confinement to limited territories can only be temporary and artificially enforced. Consequently it is destined to be swept away sooner or later.

In this way a specific mode of social metabolic control emerges out of such fundamentally unrestrainable and fetishism-producing constituents. One which cannot possibly recognize boundaries (not even its own insurmountable structural limits), no matter how devastating the consequences when the outer limits of the system's productive potentialities are reached. For — in the sharpest possible contrast to earlier forms of highly self-sufficient socioeconomic reproductive 'microcosms' — the economic units of the capital system are neither *in need of,* nor *capable of,* self-sufficiency. This is why in the shape of capital for the first time ever in history human beings have to confront a mode of social metabolic control which *can* and *must* constitute itself — in order to reach its fully developed form — as a *global* system, demolishing all obstacles that stand in the way.

Capital as a historically specific value-producing potential cannot be actualized and 'realized' (and through its 'realization' simultaneously also reproduced in an extended form) without entering the domain of *circulation*. The relationship between *production* and *consumption* is thus radically redefined within its framework in such a way that the much needed unity of the two becomes insuperably problematical, bringing with it as time goes by also the necessity of crises in one form or another. This vulnerability to the vicissitudes of circulation is a crucial determination to which no 'household economy' of antiquity, nor indeed of the feudal Middle Ages — let alone the socioeconomic reproductive units of primitive communism and of the ancient communal towns to which Marx refers in some of his main works[50] — must submit, since they are primarily oriented towards the production and direct consumption of use-value.

The consequences of this liberation from the shackles of self-sufficiency are, of course, highly favourable as far as the dynamic of capital expansion is concerned. Indeed without it the capital system could not be described at all as expansion-oriented and accumulation-driven (or the other way round when considered from the standpoint of its individual 'personifications'). For at any particular point in history the prevailing conditions of self-sufficiency (or their absence) obviously also circumscribe the given reproductive system's drive and capacity for expansion.

By ridding itself of the subjective and objective constraints of self-sufficiency capital becomes the most dynamic and the most effective *extractor of surplus-labour* in history. Moreover, this removal of the subjective and objective constraints of self-sufficiency is brought about in an utterly reified form, with all the mystifications inherent in the notion of 'free contractual labour'. For the latter seemingly absolves capital from the burden of enforced domination, in contrast to slavery and serfdom, since 'wage slavery' is *internalized* by the working subjects and does not have to be imposed and constantly reimposed on them *externally* in the form of direct political domination, except in situations of major crises. Thus capital as a system of metabolic control becomes by far the most efficient and flexible machinery of surplus-labour extraction, and not merely up to the present. Indeed, it can be cogently argued that capital's 'pumping power'[51] for extracting surplus-labour does not know *boundaries* (though it has *structural limits* which the personifications of capital refuse, and must refuse, to acknowledge) and thus whatever is conceivable as the quantitative extension of surplus-labour-extracting power in general can be rightly considered to correspond to the very nature of capital, i.e. to be fully in tune with its inner determinations. In other words capital drives relentlessly through all the obstacles and boundaries which it is historically confronted with, adopting even the most surprising and baffling — apparently with its character discordant and operationally 'hybrid' — forms of control if conditions demand it. This is in fact how the capital system constantly redefines and extends its own *relative limits*, pursuing its course under the changing circumstances precisely in order to maintain the highest possible degree of surplus-labour extraction which constitutes its historic *raison d'être* and actual mode of functioning. Besides, capital's historically successful mode of surplus-labour extraction — because it works and so long as it works — can also set itself up as the *absolute measure* of 'economic efficiency' (which many people who considered themselves socialists would not dare to challenge, promising therefore *more* of what the adversary could deliver as the legitimatory ground of their own position; and through this kind of dependency on the object of their negation — as well as through their failure to subject to a searching critical enquiry the far from unproblematical relationship between 'scarcity and abundance' — they contributed to the grave distortion of the original meaning of socialism).[52] Indeed, by setting itself up as the absolute measure of all attainable and admissible achievements capital can also successfully hide the truth that only a *certain type* of benefit can be derived — and even that always at the expense of the producers — from capital's mode of 'efficient' surplus-labour extraction.[53] Only when the *absolute limits* of capital's innermost structural determinations are brought into play, only then can we speak of a crisis emanating from the *faltering efficiency* and frightening *insufficiency* of surplus-labour extraction itself, with far-reaching implications for the survival prospects of the capital system as such.

In this respect we can identify a trend in our own days which must be disconcerting even to the most enthusiastic defenders of the capital system. For it involves the complete overturning of the terms in which they defined their claims to legitimacy in the recent past as representing 'the interest of all'. The trend in question is the ongoing metamorphosis of 'advanced capitalism' from its postwar stage epitomized by the 'welfare state' (with its ideology of 'universal welfare benefits' and the concomitant rejection of 'means-testing') to its new reality of 'targeting welfare': the present-day jargon for means-testing, with its cynical pretences to 'economic efficiency' and 'rationality', and embraced even by the former socialdemocratic adversary under the slogan of 'new realism'. Naturally, no one in his or her right mind is supposed to raise doubts about the viability of the capital system itself even on this score. All the same, no matter how strong might be the strangle-hold of ideological mystification, it cannot wipe out the uncomfortable fact that the transformation of advanced capitalism from a condition in which it could boast about its 'welfare state', to one in which it has to target — even in the richest countries — *soup-kitchens* and other meagre benefits *'for the deserving poor'*, is highly revealing about the faltering efficiency and by now chronic insufficiency of the once unquestionably successful mode of surplus-labour extraction at the present stage of development: a stage which threatens to deprive the capital system in general of its historic *raison d'être*.

2.1.5

THE great productivity-enhancing dimension of the process of liberation from the constraints of self-sufficiency in the course of history is quite undeniable. But there is another side as well to this incontrovertible accomplishment of capital. It is the earlier mentioned inevitable loss of control over the social reproductive system as a whole, even if that loss remains hidden from sight for a long historical stage of development, thanks to the displacement of capital's contradictions during its strong expansionary phase.

In the history of the capital system the ever-intensifying imperative of expansion is itself a paradoxical manifestation of this loss of control in that it helps to postpone the 'day of reckoning' for as long as the all-encroaching expansion process can be sustained. But precisely on account of this paradoxical interrelationship, blocking the road of undisturbed expansion (as a result of the consummation of capital's historical ascendancy), and through this blockage undermining the simultaneous displacement of the system's inner antagonisms, is bound to reactivate and multiply the harmful effects of the formerly accomplished problem-solving expansion as well. For the newly arising problems and contradictions on the scale of the attained magnitude of the over-extended global capital system *of necessity* call for a corresponding magnitude of displacing expansion, presenting us thereby with the spectre of *total uncontrollability* in the absence of the required gigantic expansionary displacement. Thus even the relatively limited problems of the past, as for instance the procurement and servicing of state debt, now assume cosmic proportions. This is why today only those who believe in miracles can seriously entertain the idea that the literally astronomical sums of dollars and pounds sterling — as well as liras, pesos, pesetas, French francs, Deutschmarks, roubles, escudos, Bolivares, cruzeiros, etc. — sucked into the black hole of global indebtedness, will one fine day reemerge from it, with compound interest, as unlimited amounts of available healthy credit, so as to enable the system to meet its boundless self-expansionary needs to the end of time.

No matter how hard it is tried, the loss of control at the root of these problems cannot be remedied on a sustainable basis by the radical separation of production and control and the superimposition of a separate agency — the 'personifications of capital' in one form or another — on the social agency of production: labour. And precisely because the successful exercise of control over the particular production units — in the form of 'tyranny in the workshops' exercised through the private 'entrepreneur', or the manager, or the Stalinist party secretary, or the state factory director, etc. — is far from sufficient for securing the viability of the capital system as a whole, other ways must be attempted to remedy the *structural* defects of control.

In the capital system these structural defects are visible from the outset in that the new microcosms of which it is made up are internally fractured in more ways than one.

- First, *production* and its *control* are radically severed from, and indeed diametrically opposed to, one another.
- Second, in the same spirit, arising from the same determinations, *production* and *consumption* acquire an extremely problematical independence and separate existence, so that in the end the most absurdly manipulated and wasteful 'overconsumption' in some quarters[54] can find its gruesome corollary in the most inhuman denial of the elementary needs of countless millions.
- And third, the new microcosms of the capital system are combined into some sort of manageable whole in such a way that total social capital should be *able* to enter — since it *must* — the *global* domain of *circulation* (or, to be more precise, so that it should be able to create *circulation as a global enterprise* out of its own *internally fractured* units) in an attempt to overcome the contradiction between *production* and *circulation*. In this way the necessity of *domination* and *subordination* prevails not only *inside* the particular microcosms — through the agency of the individual 'personifications of capital' — but also *across* their boundaries, transcending not only all regional barriers but also all national frontiers. This is how the total labour force of humanity becomes

subjected — with the greatest imaginable iniquities, in conformity to the historically at any particular time prevailing power relations — to the alienating imperatives of the global capital system.

In all three instances mentioned above the deep-seated structural defect of control can be pinpointed in the *absence of unity*. Moreover, any attempt at creating or superimposing unity of some sort on the internally fractured social reproductive structures in question is bound to be problematical and remain strictly temporary. For the irremediable character of the missing unity is due to the fact that the fracture itself assumes the form of *social antagonisms*. In other words, it manifests itself through fundamental conflicts of interest between hegemonic alternative social forces.

Thus the social antagonisms in question must be fought out with greater or less intensity as the specific historical circumstances permit, undoubtedly favouring capital against labour during the long period of its historical ascendancy. However, even when capital gains the upper hand in the confrontations, the antagonisms cannot be eliminated — notwithstanding the full arsenal of wishful thinking activated in the interest of such an outcome by the ruling ideology — precisely because they are *structural*. For in all three instances we are concerned with capital's vital and therefore irreplaceable *structures*, and not with — by capital itself transcendable — limited historical contingencies. Consequently the antagonisms emanating from these structures are necessarily reproduced under *all* historical circumstances covering capital's epoch, whatever might be the prevailing relation of forces at any particular point in time.

2.2 Capital's remedial imperatives and the state

2.2.1

REMEDIAL action is accomplished — to a degree feasible within the framework of the capital system — through the formation of the immensely bloated and in strictly economic terms wastefully bureaucratized modern state.

To be sure, such a remedial structure should appear highly questionable from the standpoint of capital itself as the efficiency-predicating economic entity *par excellence*. (Idle criticism to this effect is in fact a constantly recurring theme of some brands of bourgeois economic and political theory, advocating — in vain — the 'necessary discipline of good house-keeping'.) It is all the more revealing, therefore, that the modern state should emerge with the same inexorability which characterizes the triumphant diffusion of capital's economic structures, complementing the latter as the *totalizing political command structure of capital*. Such a relentless unfolding of capital's closely intertwined structures in all spheres is essential for establishing the qualified viability of this unique mode of social metabolic control for its entire historical life-span.

The formation of the modern state is an absolute requirement both for securing and for safeguarding on a permanent basis the productive accomplishments of the system. Capital's coming to dominance in the realm of material production and the development of totalizing political practices in the form of the modern state go hand in hand together. It is, therefore, by no means accidental that the end of capital's historical ascendancy in the twentieth century should coincide with the crisis of the modern state in all its forms, from liberal democratic state formations to extreme authoritarian capitalist states (like Hitler's Germany or Pinochet's Miltonfriedmannized Chile), and from post-colonial regimes to Soviet type postcapitalist states. Understandably, the now unfolding structural crisis of capital deeply affects all state institutions and corresponding organizational practices. Indeed, this crisis brings with it the crisis of politics in general, under all its aspects, and not only under those directly concerned with the ideological legitimation of any particular state system.

The modern state is brought into being in its specific historical modality above all in order to be able to exercise *comprehensive control* over the unruly centrifugal forces emanating from the separate productive units of capital as an antagonistically structured social reproductive system. As mentioned before, the dictum: 'l'argent n'a pas de maître' signals the *radical overturning* of what went on before. For by superseding the ruling principle of the feudal reproductive system a new type of socioeconomic microcosm comes into being, characterized by great mobility and dynamism. But the successful unfolding of this dynamism can only take place through a 'Faustian pact with the devil', so to speak, without any guarantee whatsoever that in due course a benevolent god might come to the rescue and outwit Mephistopheles when he claims his rightful prize.[55]

The modern state constitutes the only feasible remedial structure which is compatible with the structural parameters of capital as a mode of social metabolic control. It is brought into play in order to rectify — again it must be emphasised: only to the extent to which the much needed remedial action can be accommodated within capital's ultimate social metabolic limits — the absence of unity in all three respects referred to in the last section.

2.2.2

IN relation to the first, the missing ingredient of unity is 'smuggled in', so to speak, by courtesy of the state that legally safeguards the established relation of forces. Thanks to such safeguard the various 'personifications of capital' can dominate (with ruthless efficacy) society's labour force, imposing on it at the same time the illusion of a 'freely entered' (and at times even constitutionally fictionalized) relationship between equals.

Thus, as regards the possibility of managing the structural separation and antagonism of *production and control,* the legal framework of the modern state is an absolute requirement of the successful exercise of tyranny in the workshops. This is on account of its ability to sanction and protect the alienated material and means of production (i.e. property radically divorced from the producers) and its personifications, the (by capital strictly mandated) individual controllers of the economic reproduction process. Without its legal framework even the smallest 'microcosms' of the — antagonistically structured — capital system would be internally torn by constant strife, nullifying thereby its potential economic efficiency.

Under another aspect of the same fracture between production and control, the machinery of the modern state is likewise an absolute requirement of the capital system. It is needed in order to be able to avoid the repeated disruptions which would arise by the absence of a forcefully regulated — that is: legally prejudged and sanctified — transmission of property from one generation to the next while perpetuating the alienation of control from the producers. And under yet another aspect, equally important is — in view of the far from harmonious interrelations of the particular microcosms — the necessity of direct or indirect political and legal interventions in the constantly regenerated conflicts of the particular socioeconomic units. This type of remedial intervention takes place in accordance with the changing dynamics of capital expansion and accumulation, facilitating the prevalence of the potentially most powerful elements and tendencies all the way to the formation of giant transnational corporations and industry-wide monopolies.

Naturally, bourgeois theorists, including some of the greatest, like Max Weber, love to idealize and depict all these relations upside down.[56] This predilection, however, cannot alter the fact that the highly bureaucratized modern state, together with its complex legal/political machinery, arises from the absolute material need of capital's social metabolic order, and then in its turn — in the form of a dialectical reciprocity — becomes a vital precondition for the subsequent articulation of the whole complex. That is to say, the state asserts itself as a necessary prerequisite for the continued functioning of the capital system, both within its microcosms and in the interactions of the particular production units among themselves, powerfully affecting everything from the most immediate local interchanges to those at the most mediated and comprehensive level.

2.2.3

AS to the second complex of problems under consideration, the fracture between *production and consumption* characteristic of the capital system does indeed remove some major constraints of the past so completely that the controllers of the new socioeconomic order can embrace the belief that 'the sky is the limit'. The possibility of formerly unimaginable and in its own terms of reference limitless expansion — due to the earlier mentioned fact that the dominance of use-value characteristic of self-sufficient reproductive systems is historically left behind — by its very nature is destined to hit the buffers sooner or later. For the unrestrainable capital expansion of the last few centuries is opened up not simply in response to very real needs but also by generating imaginary or artificial appetites — to which, in principle, there cannot be any limit, other than the breakdown of the engine itself which continues to generate them on an ever-increasing and ever more destructive scale — through the independent mode of existence and self-assertive power of consumption.

To be sure, the ideological need of the established order prevails by producing mystifying rationalizations which aim at hiding the profound *iniquities* of the given structural relations also in the sphere of consumption. Everything must be misrepresented in order to provide the impression of cohesion and unity, projecting the image of a sound and rationally manageable order. To this effect the social relations depicted by Hobbes as *'bellum omnium contra omnes'* — with its objective tendency to let the weak be devoured by the powerful — become idealized as universally beneficial *'healthy competition'*. Also, in the service of the same objectives, the actual conditions of a structurally prejudged and even legally safeguarded exclusion of the overwhelming majority of society from the possibility of controlling the socioeconomic reproduction process — including, of course, the criteria for regulating distribution and consumption — are fictionalized as individual 'consumer sovereignty'. Since, however, the structural antagonism of production and control is inextricable from the microcosms of the capital system, the combination of the particular socioeconomic units into a comprehensive productive and distributive framework must exhibit the same characteristics of fracture as found in the smaller socioeconomic units: a problem of quite fundamental importance which must be addressed somehow. Consequently, notwithstanding the constant pressure for ideological rationalization, it becomes necessary to come to terms with the actually existing state of affairs in a way compatible with the structural requirements of the established order, acknowledging certain characteristics of the given socioeconomic conditions without admitting their potentially explosive implications.

Thus, although the proclaimed 'supremacy of the customer' in the name of 'consumer sovereignty' is a self-serving fiction, just like the notion of the claimed 'healthy competition' within the framework of an idealized market is, the fact cannot be denied that the worker's role is not exhausted in being a *producer* only. Understandably, bourgeois ideology likes to depict the capitalist as 'the producer' (or 'the producer of wealth') and speak of the consumer/customer as a mysterious independent entity, so that the real producer of wealth — the worker — should disappear from the relevant social equations and his or her share in the total social product should be rightfully declared to be 'most generous' even when outrageously low. However, the effectiveness of this kind of blatant apologetics is confined strictly to the sphere of ideology. For the underlying major socioeconomic issues cannot be satisfactorily resolved by simply spiriting away labour from the domain of practical policy. In that domain it must be recognized through the application of appropriate practical measures that the worker as *consumer* plays a role of major — even if in the course of history considerably varying — importance in the healthy functioning of the capital system. His or her role varies according to capital's more or less stretched stage of development, which in fact means a tendency to gain in its impact on the reproduction process. Thus it must be *practically* acknowledged, in the interest of the established socioeconomic order itself, that the worker-customer-consumer's role happens to be of much greater importance in the twentieth century than in Victorian times, no matter how strong the yearning might be in some quarters to turn the clock back and reimpose on labour some idealized Victorian values as well as, of course, the corresponding material constraints.

In all these matters the totalizing role of the modern state is vital. It must always adjust its regulatory functions in tune with the changing dynamics of the socioeconomic reproduction process by politically complementing and reinforcing capital's domination against the forces that might dare to challenge the gross iniquities of distribution and consumption. Furthermore, the state must also assume the important function of direct purchaser/consumer on an ever-increasing scale. In this capacity it must cater both for some real needs of the social whole (from education to health care and from the building and maintenance of the so-called 'infrastructure' to the provision of social security services) as well as for the satisfaction of largely 'artificial appetites' (like feeding not only the vast bureaucratic machinery of its own administrative and law-enforcing system but also the immensely wasteful, yet to capital directly beneficial, military-industrial complex), — alleviating thereby, even if by no means forever, some of the worst complications and contradictions which arise from the fracture of production and consumption.

Admittedly, the totalizing intervention and remedial action of the state cannot produce genuine *unity* on this plane, because the separation and opposition of production and consumption, together with the radical alienation of control from the producers, belongs to the innermost structural determinations of the capital system as such, and therefore it constitutes a necessary prerequisite for its continued reproduction. Nevertheless, the remedial action undertaken by the state on this score is of paramount importance. The material reproductive processes of capital's social metabolism, and the political framework and command structure of its mode of control, reciprocally sustain one another for as long as the unavoidable waste that goes with this unique symbiotic relationship does not become prohibitive from the point of view of social productivity itself. In other words, the outer limits of reconstituting and managing in this unique way the problematical correlation of production and consumption on the fractured ground of capital's social metabolic order are determined by the extent to which the modern state can actively contribute to the system's irrepressible need for capital expansion and accumulation, as opposed to becoming a materially unsustainable burden on it.

2.2.4

WITH regard to the third principal aspect which we are concerned with — the need for creating circulation as a global enterprise out of the internally fractured structures of the capital system, or in other words the pursuit of some kind of unity between *production and circulation* — the active role of the modern state is equally great if not greater. By focusing attention on it, in conjunction with the various functions which the state is called upon to fulfil in the domain of consumption, in the first place within its own national boundaries, it transpires that all these relations are not only 'infected with contingency',[57] as Hegel had once put it, but simultaneously also with insoluble contradictions.

One of the most obvious and ultimately most intractable contradictions is that historically the capital system's political command structure and overall remedial framework is articulated in the form of *national states,* although as a mode of social metabolic control and reproduction (with its imperative of global circulation) this system cannot conceivably be confined to such limits. We must return to the far-reaching implications of this problem in Sections 2.3.2 and 5.1. What needs to be underlined in the present context is that the only way the state can attempt to resolve this contradiction is by instituting a system of 'double book-keeping': a considerably higher standard of living for labour — coupled with liberal democracy — at home (that is, in the 'metropolitan' or 'core' countries of the global capital system) and maximally exploitative as well as ruthlessly authoritarian (and whenever needed even openly dictatorial) rule, exercised directly or by proxy, in the 'underdeveloped periphery'.

Thus the nowadays much idealized 'globalization' (a trend emanating from the nature of capital from the very beginning) in reality means: the necessary unfolding of an international system of domination and subordination. On the plane of totalizing politics it corresponds to the establishment of a hierarchy of more or less powerful national states which enjoy — or suffer — the position assigned to them by the prevailing (but from time to time of necessity violently contested) relation of forces in the global pecking order of capital. It must be also stressed that the relatively easy operation of such 'double book-keeping' is by no means destined to remain a permanent feature of capital's global order. Indeed, its duration is confined to the conditions of the system's historical ascendancy, when undisturbed capital expansion and accumulation can provide the required profit margin for operating a relatively favourable rate of exploitation for labour in the 'metropolitan' countries, as compared to the conditions of existence of the labour force in the rest of the world.

Two — complementary — trends of development are highly significant in this respect. First, we have witnessed in the last few decades, in the form of a *downward spiral* affecting labour's standard of living in the capitalistically most advanced countries, a certain *equalization in the differential rate of exploitation*;[58] a trend which is bound to assert itself as a downward spiral for labour in the 'core' countries also in the foreseeable future. Second, parallel to this levelling tendency in the differential rate of exploitation we could also see the emergence of its necessary political corollary, in the form of a *growing authoritarianism* in formerly liberal 'metropolitan' states, and a perfectly understandable general disenchantment with 'democratic politics' which is deeply implicated in the authoritarian turn of political control in capitalistically advanced countries.

The state as the totalizing agency for creating global circulation out of capital's internally fractured socioeconomic units must behave rather differently in its international actions from the way in which it does on the plane of internal policy making. In the latter domain it must watch — to the extent to which this is compatible with the changing dynamics of capital accumulation — that the inexorable tendency of concentration and centralization of capital should not prematurely destroy too many still viable (even if, as compared to their bigger brothers and sisters, less efficient) production units, since failure to do so would unfavourably affect the combined strength of total *national* capital under the circumstances. This is why some genuine *anti-monopolistic* legal measures must be introduced if internal conditions demand and overall conditions permit. Nevertheless, the same measures are unceremoniously swept aside the moment the changed interests of combined national capital so decree, making all belief in the state — the political command structure of the capital system — as the guardian of 'healthy competition' against monopoly in general not just naive but utterly self-contradictory.

On the international plane, by contrast, the national state of the capital system has no interest whatsoever in restraining the boundless monopolistic drive of its dominant economic units. Quite the contrary. For in the domain of international competition the stronger and the less restrained is the politically (if needed also militarily) supported economic enterprise, the more likely it is to succeed against its actually given or potential rivals. This is why the relationship between the state and the relevant economic enterprises in this field is primarily characterized by the state quite unashamedly assuming the role of the facilitator of as monopolistic as possible capital expansion abroad. The ways and means of this facilitating role are, of course, altered with the change in the internal and external relation of forces due to the changing historical circumstances. But the monopolistic orienting principles of all states which occupy a dominant position in capital's global pecking order remain the same, despite the ideas of 'free trade', 'fair competition', etc., which were at first genuinely believed (by people like Adam Smith) but later turned into cynical camouflage or the object of ritualistic lip service only. The state of the capital system must assert with all means at its disposal the monopolistic interests of its national capital — if need be through the imposition of 'gunboat diplomacy' — *vis-à-vis* all rival states involved in competition for the markets needed for capital-expansion and accumulation. This is the case with regard to the most varied political practices, from early modern colonialism (with the role assigned in it to monopolistic trading companies)[59] to full blown imperialism as well as to the post-colonial 'disengagement from empire' by securing new forms of neo-colonial domination, not to mention the aggressive neo-imperialist aspirations and practices of the U.S. and its subservient allies in the recently decreed 'New World Order'.

However, even though the interests of particular national capitals can be distinguished from, and in the case of the dominant states to a large extent also protected against, encroachment by other national capitals, such a protection cannot remove the antagonisms of *total social capital,* i.e. the inner structural determination of capital as a *global* controlling force. This is because in the capital system all 'harmonization' can only take the form of a strictly temporary *balancing* — and not the proper *resolution* — of conflict. It is by no means accidental, therefore, that in bourgeois social and political theory we find the glorification of the concept of 'balance of powers' as the unsurpassable ideal, when in fact at any given time it can only amount to the imposition/acceptance of the prevailing relation of forces, envisaging at the same time its overturning when circumstances permit. The axiom of *bellum omnium contra omnes* is the unsurpassable *modus operandi* of the capital system. For as a system of social metabolic control it is *antagonistically structured* from the smallest to the most comprehensive socioeconomic and political units. Moreover, the capital system — as indeed all conceivable forms of global social metabolic control, including the socialist — is subject to the absolute law of *uneven development* which prevails under the rule of capital in an ultimately destructive form, because of its antagonistic inner structuring principle.[60] Thus, to envisage the genuine and sustainable resolution of the capital system's antagonisms at the global level it would be necessary first to believe in the fairy tale of eliminating forever the law of uneven development from human affairs. This is why the 'New World Order' is either an absurd fantasy or a cynical camouflage designed to project the hegemonic interests of the preponderant capitalist powers as the morally commendable and universally beneficial aspiration of mankind. Nothing would be resolved here by setting up a 'World Government' — and the state system corresponding to it — even if it were feasible at all. For no global system can be other than explosive and ultimately self-destructive if it is antagonistically structured all the way to its inner core. In other words: it cannot help being unstable and ultimately explosive if, as an all-embracing system of social metabolic control, it is constituted from microcosms torn by internal antagonism, due to irreconcilable conflicts of interest centred on the radical separation and alienation of control from the producers. For the absolutely insoluble contradiction between production and control is bound to assert itself in all spheres and at all levels of social reproductive interchange, including of course its metamorphosis into the contradiction between production and consumption as well as that between production and circulation.

THE chances of success of the socialist alternative are determined by its ability (or failure) to face up to all three contradictions — between production and control, production and consumption, and production and circulation — by instituting an internally harmonizable social reproductive microcosm. This is what even the greatest figures of bourgeois philosophy — viewing the world from the standpoint of capital in the ascendant (or, in Marx's words, 'from the standpoint of political economy') — could not contemplate, since they had to take the internally fractured microcosm of the capital system absolutely for granted. They offered, instead, remedies which either bypassed the problems at stake, by assuming the power of Reason as the generic and apriori solution to all conceivable difficulties and contradictions, or devised special and on the whole greatly idealized schemes through which suitable answers *ought to be* found to the identified disturbing historical contingencies. Let it suffice to refer here only to Adam Smith, Kant, Fichte and Hegel.

Smith's notion of *'the hidden hand'* continues to exercise its influence to our own days, projecting a wishful remedy to the acknowledged conflicts and contradictions on the plane of an ideal *'ought to be'*. Kant borrowed Adam Smith's idea of the *'commercial spirit'* on the basis of which he envisaged the permanent solution of all destructive conflicts and international conflagrations by the establishment of a universalistic state system which would implement — as beyond doubt it should be able to implement, since in Kant's philosophy *'ought implies can'* — the 'moral politics' of the coming *'perpetual peace'*. Fichte, by contrast, advocated the equally utopian *'closed commercial state'* ('der geschlossene Handelsstaat', with its reliance on the strict principles of autarchy) as the ideal solution to the explosive constraints and contradictions of the prevailing order. It was Hegel who offered the most realistic account of these matters when he admitted that contingency rules in the international relations of national states, summarily dismissing at the same time Kant's ideal solution by saying that 'corruption in nations would be the product of prolonged, let alone "perpetual" peace.'[61] But even Hegel's account is peppered with many instances of 'ought to be', not to mention the fact that the ideal apex of his entire system is the 'Germanic state' (which, as mentioned above, in Hegel's conception is by no means nationalistically German, as his critics claimed, but includes the embodiment of the 'commercial spirit' in the state of the English colonizers), culminating with the assertion of 'the *true reconciliation* which discloses the state as the image and actuality of reason'.[62]

Thus in all the above hypostatizations of the state as the remedy of the acknowledged defects and contradictions — whether we think of Kant's ideal postulate of the state as the agency of 'perpetual peace', or of Fichte's self-reliant 'closed commercial state', or indeed of Hegel's projected 'true reconciliation' as the state embodying the 'image and actuality of reason' — the solutions we are offered amount only to the advocacy of some unrealizable ideal. It could not be otherwise since the antagonistically structured microcosms of the capital system — with its ineradicable *bellum omnium contra omnes*, manifest in the threefold contradiction between production and control, production and consumption, and production and circulation — are never really questioned. They are merely subsumed under the ideality of the state and declared thereby to represent no longer any danger of disruption or explosion thanks to the attained ideality of one form or another of 'true reconciliation'.

In actuality, however, the explosive antagonisms of the system as a whole persist for as long as its internally torn microcosms are not radically altered. For in the antagonistically fractured capital system the constantly regenerated conflicts and contradictions must be fought out at all levels, with a tendency to move from lower levels of conflict to higher ones parallel to the growing integration of capital's social metabolic order into a fully developed global system. The ultimate logic of this fighting out of conflicts to their conclusion at ever higher levels and with growing intensity is: 'unlimited war if the "normal" methods of subjection and domination fail', as demonstrated with painful clarity by two world wars in the twentieth century. Thus the hypostatized institution of 'perpetual peace' on the material ground of capital's internally fractured microcosms cannot be other than pure wishful thinking.

Nevertheless in our own days the global capital system must come to terms with a new structural contradiction, superimposed on all of its constituent parts by post-Second World War historical developments and by a fundamental change in the technology of warfare. The latter carries with it the imposition of peace to the extent of ruling out not partial wars (of which there can be, as indeed there are, since there *must* be in capital's conflict-torn domain, many) but another *all-out war*, in view of the inevitable annihilation of humankind implied by such a war. As a result the explosive antagonisms of the system as a whole are aggravated, instead of being altogether eliminated in conformity to the Kantian dream. For the uncomfortable fact is that through the constraints of peace forced upon it the capital system has been *decapitated* as regards its previously available *ultimate sanction* of violently prevailing over the otherwise uncontrollable adversary. To manage its affairs in a sustainable way without such ultimate sanction the capital system would have to be qualitatively different — in its innermost structural constitution — from what it actually is and can be. Thus, as capital attains the highest level of globalization through the consummation of its historical ascendancy, the socioeconomic microcosms of which it is made up reveal their awesome secret of being *ultimately responsible* for all destructiveness, in the sharpest possible contrast to their idealizations from Adam Smith and Kant all the way down to the various Hayeks and 'market socialists' of the twentieth century. Thus it becomes unavoidable to confront the disturbing truth that the constitutive microcosms themselves must be the subject of radical scrutiny if we want to find a way of overcoming the incorrigible destructiveness of capital's social metabolic order. This is the challenge directly arising from the contradiction between *production and circulation* brought to its highest intensity through capital's fully completed global enterprise.

2.2.5

AS we can see in relation to all three principal aspects of capital's structurally defective control discussed in the last three sections, the modern state as the only feasible remedial framework comes into being not *after* the articulation of the fundamental socioeconomic forms, nor as more or less directly *determined* by the latter. There can be no question of a *uni-directional determination* of the modern state by an independent material base.For capital's socioeconomic base and its state formations are totally inconceivable separately. Thus it is right and proper to speak of 'correspondence' and 'homology' only in relation to capital's basic *structures,* as historically constituted (which itself implies a time limit), but not of the particular metabolic functions of one structure corresponding to the direct structural determinations and requirements of the other. Such functions may in fact forcefully contradict one another as their underlying structures are subsequently stretched in the course of the capital system's necessary expansion and adaptive transformation. The 'homology of structures' paradoxically arises in the first place from a *structural diversity of functions* fulfilled by the different metabolic organs (including the state) in the historically unfolding — quite unique form of — hierarchical social division of labour. This structural diversity of functions produces the most problematical division between 'civil society' and the political state on the common ground of the capital system as a whole of which the basic structures (or metabolic organs) are constitutive parts. But despite the common ground of their constitutive interdependence, the structural relationship of capital's metabolic organs is full of contradictions. If that were not the case, the socialist emancipatory enterprise would be condemned to futility. For the always successfully prevailing homology of all basic structures and functions, fully corresponding to the material imperatives of capital's order of social metabolic control, would produce a veritable 'iron cage' for all times — including the global phase of capital's development, with its grave national and international antagonisms — from which there could be absolutely no escape, in accord with the projections of people like Max Weber, Hayek and Talcott Parsons.

We must return to some of these problems in the context of the socialist critique of the state formation itself — i.e. not simply the capitalist state — in Parts Two and Three. Here only a few remarks are in order, concerning the material ground and the overall limits within which the vital remedial functions of the historically evolved state formation must be undertaken under the capital system.

As mentioned before, capital is a unique mode of social metabolic control, and as such — quite understandably — it is incapable of functioning without an adequate command structure. Consequently, in this all-important sense capital *is* a specific historical type and articulation of command structure. Moreover, the relationship between the socioeconomic reproductive units — i.e. capital's social metabolic microcosms — and the political dimension of this system cannot be one-sidedly dominant from either direction, in contrast to the feudal system, for instance. Under feudalism the political factor could assume a dominant position — to the point of conferring on the feudal lord the power of even executing his serfs if he so wished (and was blind enough to do so, since his own material existence depended on the tribute which he could extract from them on a continuing basis) — precisely because (and for as long as) the principle of the lord's 'political supremacy' was sustainable in its own terms. The *formal boundlessness* of arbitrary feudal power could be maintained because the prevailing mode of political control was in fact *substantively constrained* by the way in which it was actually constituted. For it was restricted — in two directions — by the very nature of the feudal system itself:

- (1) it was essentially *local* in its exercise, in accord with the relatively high degree of self-sufficiency of the dominant social metabolic units, and
- (2) it had to leave the basic control functions of the economic reproduction process itself to the producers.

Thus the power of the political was *external supervisory* rather than *internal reproductive*. It could persist for only as long as the feudal system's basic metabolic units themselves remained *internally cohesive and restrained* under both aspects just mentioned, which circumscribed in a very real sense the exercise of feudal supervisory power itself. Paradoxically, therefore, it was the extension of feudal political power — from being locally constrained — in the direction of the *substantively absolute* on the one hand (through the development of absolute monarchy, in France for instance), and the intrusion of disruptive capitalistic constituents into the formerly to a very large extent self-sufficient reproductive structures on the other, which together helped to destroy this social metabolic system at the *peak* of its political power.[63]

By contrast the capital system historically evolved from *unrestrainable* but far from self-sufficient constituents. The structural defects of control which we have seen above necessitated the establishment of specific control structures capable of *complementing* — at the appropriate level of comprehensiveness — the material reproductive constituents, in accordance with the totalizing need and changing expansionary dynamics of the capital system. This is how the modern state as the comprehensive political command structure of capital was brought into being, becoming as integral a part of the 'material base' of the system as the socioeconomic reproductive units themselves.

With regard to the question of *temporality*, the unfolding interrelationship between the direct material reproductive structures and the state is characterized by the category of *simultaneity* and not by those of 'before' and 'after'. The latter can only become subordinate moments of the dialectic of simultaneity as the constituent parts of capital's mode of social metabolic control evolve in the course of global development, following their inner logic of expansion and accumulation. In the same way, in relation to the question of 'determinations' we can properly talk only of *co-determinations*. In other words, the dynamics of development must be characterized not under the category of *'as a result of'* but in terms of *'in conjunction with'* whenever we want to make intelligible the changes in capital's social metabolic control arising from the dialectical reciprocity between its socioeconomic and political command structures.

Thus, it would be quite misleading to describe the state itself as a superstructure. Since the state constitutes the totalizing political command structure of capital — which is absolutely vital for the material sustainability of the whole system — it cannot be reduced to superstructural status. Rather, the state itself as a comprehensive command structure has *its own superstructure* — appropriately referred to by Marx as 'the legal and political superstructure', — just as the direct material reproductive structures themselves have their own superstructural dimensions. (For instance the theories and practices of 'public relations' and 'industrial relations', or those of so-called 'scientific management', originated in the capitalist enterprise of Frederic Winslow Taylor.) Similarly, it is quite futile to waste time on trying to make intelligible the specificity of the state in terms of the category of *'autonomy'* (especially when that notion is stretched to mean 'independence'), or on its denial. The state as the comprehensive political command structure of capital cannot have autonomy, in any sense whatsoever, from the capital system, since it happens to be inextricably one with the latter. At the same time, the state is very far from being *reducible* to the determinations directly emanating from capital's economic functions. For the historically given state contributes in a crucial way to the determination — in the earlier mentioned sense of *co-determination* — of the direct economic functions, circumscribing or extending the feasibility of some as against others. Moreover, also the 'ideological superstructure' — which should not be confused or simply equated with 'the legal and political superstructure', let alone with the state itself — cannot be made intelligible unless it is understood as *irreducible* to direct material/economic determinations, even though in this respect, too, the frequently attempted attribution of a fictitious autonomy (in the idealistically overstretched sense of independence) must be firmly resisted. Besides, the question of 'autonomy', in a properly defined sense, is relevant not only to the assessment of the relationship between ideology and the economy, ideology and the state, 'base and superstructure', etc. It is essential also for understanding the complex relationship between various sections of capital directly involved in the economic reproduction process as they come to prominence — at different times and with varying relative weight — in the course of historical development.

The question of 'legal and political superstructure' of which Marx speaks can only be made intelligible in terms of the modern state's massive materiality and necessary articulation as a fundamental command structure *sui generis*. The common ground of determination of all vital practices within the framework of the capital system, from the direct economic reproductive to the most mediated state regulatory functions, is the expansion-oriented structural imperative of the system to which the diverse social agencies active under the rule of capital must conform. Otherwise this unique system of metabolic control could not survive, let alone secure the global domination which it had achieved in the course of historical development.

The necessary material condition for successfully asserting the expansion-oriented structural imperative of capital is the continued extraction of surplus-labour under one form or another, in accordance with the changing historical circumstances. However, due to the *centrifugal* determination of capital's economic reproductive constituents, irrespective of how small or large they might be (all the way to the giant quasi-monopolistic transnational corporations), they are incapable of realizing on their own capital's structural imperative, in that the *cohesive* determination vital to the constitution and sustainable functioning of a social metabolic system is missing from them. It is this missing cohesive ordering principle of the basic economic constituents which is conceptualized, even by the greatest thinkers who view the world from capital's standpoint, as the mysterious 'invisible hand' of Adam Smith and the 'cunning of Reason' of Hegel. This is how the mythology of the *market* as not only the *sufficient* but even the *ideal overall regulator* of the social metabolic process arises. Later on this view is carried to the extreme, reaching its climax in the grotesquely apologetic theories of the twentieth century in the form of the ideology of 'rolling back the boundaries of the state' when the actually unfolding transformations point in the opposite direction. Yet, the greatly varying role of the market in different phases of development of the capital system, from its phase of limited local interchanges to that of the fully completed *world market,* is totally incomprehensible without relating it to the other side of the same equation: the likewise changing dynamics of the state as capital's totalizing political command structure.

Thus, to consider the direct economic reproductive units of the capital system as the 'material basis' on which the 'superstructure of the state' arises is a self-contradictory simplification, which leads to hypostatizing a group of all-powerful 'captains of industry' — the crudely determined mechanical expressions of the material base — as effective controllers of the established order. And worse than that, this conception is not only mechanical reductionist but also fails to explain how a totalizing and cohesion-producing 'superstructure' could arise on the basis of its total absence from the 'economic base'. Indeed, instead of a plausible explanation of the functioning of the capital system, it offers only the mystery of an 'active superstructure' arising on a structurally vital material absence so as to successfully remedy the defects of the whole system, when it itself is supposed to be directly determined by the material basis. If all this was only a matter of self-consuming academic arguments, it could be safely ignored. Unfortunately it is not. For the mechanical interpretation of the relationship between capital's 'material base' and its 'legal and political superstructure' can be — and actually has been — translated under the circumstances of postrevolutionary societies into its self-delusory obverse, according to which the voluntaristic political control of the postcapitalist order, after the transfer of property ownership to the 'socialist state', represents the proper supersession of capital's material ground.

In truth, however, the modern state belongs to the materiality of the capital system, embodying the necessary cohesive dimension of its expansion-oriented and surplus-labour-extracting structural imperative. This is what characterizes all known forms of the state articulated within the framework of capital's social metabolic order. And precisely because the economic reproductive units of the system are incorrigibly centrifugal in character — which happens to be for a long time in history an integral part of the unparalleled dynamism of capital, even if at a certain stage of development it becomes most problematical and potentially destructive, — the cohesive dimension of the overall social metabolism must be constituted as a *separate* totalizing political command structure. Indeed, as a proof of the substantive materiality of the modern state, we find that in its capacity as the totalizing political command structure of capital it is no less concerned with securing the conditions of surplus-labour extraction than the direct economic reproductive units themselves, though, naturally, it has to bring its contribution to the successful outcome in its own way. None the less, the structuring principle of the modern state, in all its forms — including the postcapitalist varieties — is its vital role in securing and safeguarding the overall conditions of surplus-labour extraction.

As an integral part of the material basis of capital's comprehensive system, the state must articulate its legal and political superstructure in accordance with its inherent structural determinations and necessary functions. Its legal/political superstructure can assume parliamentarian, or Bonapartist, or indeed Soviet type post-capitalist forms, as well as a great many others, as the specific historical circumstances require it. Moreover, even within the framework of the same socioeconomic formation — e.g. the capitalist — it can switch from fulfilling its functions in a, say, liberal-democratic legal/political institutional network to adopting an openly dictatorial form of legislation and political rule; and it can move in this respect backwards and forwards. In relation to these problems it is enough to think of Germany before, under and after Hitler, or of the changes from Allende's Chile to the establishment of the Pinochet regime and the 'restoration of democracy' in that country while leaving Pinochet and his allies in control of the military. This kind of switch would be inconceivable if the state as such was simply a 'superstructure'. For both in Germany and in Chile the capitalist material ground remained structurally the same throughout the historically experienced transformations, backwards and forwards, of the respective legal and political superstructures. It was the major crisis of the overall social complex in the countries concerned (of which the states in question were a weighty material constituent), together with their international ramifications (where, again, the materiality of the respective states was of seminal importance), which had to lead to such developments.

2.2.6

THE articulation of capital's comprehensive political command structure in the form of the modern state represents both an adequate *match* and a complete *mismatch* to the basic socioeconomic metabolic structures.

In its own — totalizing — way the state exhibits the same structural/hierarchical division of labour as the economic reproductive units. In this way the state is literally vital for keeping under control (even if by no means for removing altogether) the antagonisms that constantly arise from the disruptive duality of the socioeconomic and the political decision making processes without which the capital system could not properly function. By making tenable — for as long as it remains historically tenable — the metabolic practice of assigning 'free labour' to the fulfilment of strictly economic functions in an unchallengeably subservient capacity, the state is the perfect match to the inner requirements of this antagonistically structured system of social metabolic control. As the overall guarantor of capital's incorrigibly authoritarian mode of reproduction (its 'tyranny in the workshops' not only under capitalism but also under the Soviet type capital system), the state reinforces both the duality of production and control, and the structural/hierarchical division of labour of which the state itself is a most obvious manifestation.

The *unrestrainability* of capital's constitutive principles determines the limits of viability of this historically unique system of metabolic control both in positive and in negative terms. Positively, the capital system can drive forward for as long as its internally unrestrainable productive structures find resources and outlets for expansion and accumulation. And negatively, a structural crisis sets in when the established order of socioeconomic reproduction collides with the obstacles made by its own dualistic articulation, so that the threefold contradiction between production and control, production and consumption, and production and circulation cannot be any more reconciled, let alone used as powerful engines in the vital expansion and accumulation process.

The key remedial role of the state is defined in relation to the same imperative of unrestrainability. What is important to stress here is that the positive potentialities of capital's unrestrainable dynamics cannot be realized if the basic reproductive units are taken in isolation, abstracted from their sociopolitical setting. For although the inner drive of the productive microcosms is irrepressible, its character is totally indeterminate — i.e. it could also be utterly destructive and self-destructive by itself. This is why Hobbes wants to impose *Leviathan* as the necessary corrective — in the form of a politically absolute controlling power — on his world of *bellum omnium contra omnes*. To make the productive potentiality of capital's unrestrainable drive prevail, the manifold interacting reproductive units must be turned into a *coherent system* whose overall defining principle and orienting objective is the highest practicable extraction of surplus-labour. (In this respect it does not matter at all whether the extraction of surplus labour is regulated economically or politically, or indeed by any feasible combination and proportionality of the two.) Without an adequate — firmly surplus-labour-extraction oriented — totalizing command structure the given units of capital do not constitute a *system,* but only a more or less haphazard and unsustainable aggregate of economic entities exposed to the dangers of slanted development or outright political suppression. (This is why some promising capitalistic beginnings are halted and even completely reversed in certain countries in the course of European historical development. Post-Renaissance Italy offers a striking example in this respect.)

Without the emergence of the modern state, capital's spontaneous mode of metabolic control cannot turn itself into a system with clearly identifiable — dynamically surplus-labour producing and extracting, as well as properly integrated and sustainable — socioeconomic microcosms. The particular socioeconomic reproductive units of capital taken separately are not only *not capable* of spontaneous co-ordination and totalization but *diametrically opposed* to it if allowed to follow their disruptive course, in accord with the centrifugal structural determination of their nature mentioned above. It is, paradoxically, this complete 'absence' or 'lack' of a positively grounded cohesion in capital's constitutive socioeconomic microcosms — due above all to their divorce from use-value and spontaneously manifest human need — which calls into existence the political dimension of capital's social metabolic control in the form of the modern state.

The articulation of the state, in conjunction with capital's innermost metabolic imperatives, simultaneously means the transformation of the disruptive centrifugal forces into an unrestrained system of productive units; one in possession of a viable command structure both inside the given reproductive microcosms and across their boundaries. Unrestrained — for the duration of its historical ascendancy — because the command structure itself is geared to maximizing the dynamic potentialities of the material reproductive microcosms themselves, whatever their implications and possible consequences on a longer time-scale. Thus there is no need at all for the Hobbesian *Leviathan* as long as the expansionary dynamics can be maintained. Indeed, John Stuart Mill and others — rather naively — dream about the permanence of their idealized liberal state even when they contemplate the arrival of the 'stationary state of wealth'[64] and the controls that must be 'accepted' by society on account of the unavoidable constraints of the economy. Naively, because only for so long need one not fear the devastating consequences arising from capital's disruptively centrifugal social metabolic units as the available resources and outlets for accumulation give sufficient scope for 'resolving' the conflicts of the contending forces by constantly *raising the stakes*, like the imaginary roulette player whose 'unbeatable method' of doubling his stake after every lost round is matched by an inexhaustible purse. Thus the showdown among the dominant players can be postponed by making the scale of the required operations ever greater, allowing at the same time the system as a whole 'to grow out of the experienced difficulties and dysfunctions' (as we are now supposed to do not only with regard to the astronomical global indebtedness but, self-contradictorily, also in relation to the faltering process of accumulation itself). This is how the meaning of the Hobbesian *bellum omnium contra omnes* is redefined in a manageable way in the capital system, *on the assumption that there shall be no limits to global expansion*. A redefinition which remains tenable for as long as the simple truth does not assert itself with peremptory finality that there can be no such thing as an inexhaustible purse.

It would be quite mistaken, however, to simply equate the state on its own with the capital system's command structure. Capital is a historically specific mode of social metabolic control which must have its appropriate command structure in all spheres and at all levels, because it cannot tolerate anything at all above itself. One of the principal reasons why the Soviet system had to collapse was that the *political command structure of its state formation greatly overreached itself*. It vainly tried to *substitute itself for the socioeconomic command structure* of the postrevolutionary capital system in its entirety, voluntaristically assuming the *political regulation of all productive and distributive functions* for which it was quite unsuitable. I argued in *The Power of Ideology* well before the failure of Gorbachev's 'perestroika' and the catastrophic implosion of the Soviet system that

> The capitalist state is quite incapable of assuming the substantive reproductive functions of the material regulatory structures, except to a minimal extent in an extreme situation of emergency. But neither is it expected to do so under normal circumstances. In view of its intrinsic constitution, the state could not control the labour process even if its resources were multiplied by a hundredfold, given the *ubiquitousness* of the particular productive structures which would have to be brought under its necessarily limited power of control. Tragically, in this respect, the failure of postcapitalist societies in the sphere of production must be attributed to a very large extent to their attempt to assign such metabolic controlling functions to a centralized political state, when in reality *the state as such* is not suitable to the realization of the task that involves, one way or another, the everyday life-activity of each individual. (p.421.)

What is at issue here is that capital as such is itself *its own* command structure of which the political dimension is an *integral part,* even if by no means a *subordinate* part. Here, again, we can see the practical manifestation of a dialectical reciprocity.

The modern state — as the comprehensive political command structure of capital — is both the necessary *prerequisite* for the transformation of capital's at first fragmented units into a *viable system,* and the *overall framework* for the full articulation and maintenance of the latter as a *global system.* In this fundamental sense the state — on account of its constitutive and permanently sustaining role — must be understood as an integral part of capital's material ground itself. For it contributes in a substantive way not only to the formation and consolidation of all of the major reproductive structures of society but also to their continued functioning.

However, the close interrelationship holds also when viewed from the other side. For the modern state itself is quite inconceivable without capital as its social metabolic foundation. This makes the material reproductive structures of the capital system the necessary condition not only for the original constitution but also for the continued survival (and appropriate historical transformations) of the modern state in all its dimensions. These reproductive structures extend their impact over everything, from the strictly material/repressive instruments and juridical institutions of the state all the way to the most mediated ideological and political theorizations of its *raison d'être* and claimed legitimacy.

It is on account of this reciprocal determination that we must speak of a close match between the social metabolic ground of the capital system on the one hand, and the modern state as the totalizing political command structure of the established productive and reproductive order on the other. For socialists this is a most uncomfortable and challenging reciprocity. It puts into relief the sobering fact that any intervention in the political domain — even when it envisages the radical overthrow of the capitalist state — can have only a very limited impact in the realization of the socialist project. And the other way round, the corollary of the same sobering fact is that, precisely because socialists have to confront the power of *capital's self-sustaining reciprocity* under its fundamental dimensions, it should be never forgotten or ignored — although the tragedy of seventy years of Soviet experience is that it had been wilfully ignored — that there can be no chance of overcoming the power of capital without remaining faithful to the Marxian concern with the 'withering away' of the state.

2.3 Mismatch between capital's material reproductive structures and its state formation

2.3.1

YET the vicious circle of this reciprocity need not be forever overpowering. For, as mentioned above, we can also identify a major *structural mismatch* between the modern state and capital's socioeconomic reproductive structures: a mismatch which happens to be most relevant for assessing the prospects of future developments. It concerns in the first place the human agency — the social subject — of control in relation to the ever-extending scale of the capital system's operation.

As a mode of social metabolic control the capital system is unique in history also in the sense that it is, properly speaking, a *subjectless* system of control. For the objective determinations and imperatives of capital must always prevail over against the subjective wishes — not to mention the potential critical reservations — of the controlling *personnel* which is called upon to translate those imperatives into practical directives. This is why the personnel at the top echelons of capital's command structure — whether we think of private capitalists or party bureaucrats — can only be considered 'personifications of capital', irrespective of how enthusiastically they may or may not wish to carry out capital's dictates as particular individuals. In this sense, through the strict determination of their margin of action by capital, the human agents as 'controllers' of the system are in fact themselves being on the whole *controlled,* and therefore in the last analysis no self-determining human agency can be said to be in control of the system.

This peculiar mode of *subjectless control* in which the controller is actually controlled by the fetishistic requirements of the capital system as such is unavoidable, because of the radical separation of *production and control* at the heart of this system. Once, however, the function of control takes on a separate existence, due to the imperative to subdue and keep permanently under subjection the producers, despite their formal status of 'free labour', the *particular* controllers of capital's reproductive microcosms must be subjected to the control of the *system* itself, since failure to do so would destroy its cohesion as a viable reproductive system. The stakes involved in making capital's mode of social metabolic control work are far too great to let the 'personifications of capital' be really in control of the command structure and assess their own task in terms of possible major alternatives. Moreover, these stakes not only are great but are also getting progressively greater, as the system moves from the small and fragmented productive units of early capitalistic developments to the giant transnational corporations of its full global articulation. But as the scale of the operations expands in the course of the ongoing integration of the production units, the difficulties of securing the rule of capital over labour through a subjectless command structure grow with it.

The capital system is based on the alienation of control from the producers. In this process of alienation, capital degrades the real subject of social reproduction, labour, to the condition of a reified objectivity — a mere 'material factor of production', — thereby overturning, not just in theory but in palpable social practice, the real subject/object relationship. However, the trouble for capital is that the 'material factor of production' cannot cease to be the real subject of production. To perform its productive functions, with the consciousness demanded of it by the production process as such — without which capital itself would cease to exist — labour must be made to acknowledge another subject above itself, even if in reality the latter is only a pseudo-subject. To this effect capital needs its personifications in order to mediate (and impose) its objective imperatives as consciously executable commands on the potentially most recalcitrant real subject of the production process. (Fantasies about the coming of totally automated and worker-free capitalist production process are generated as an imaginary elimination of this problem.)

The state's role in relation to this contradiction is of the greatest importance, in that it provides the ultimate guarantee that the producers' recalcitrance and potential rebellion does not get out of hand. Inasmuch as that guarantee can be effective — partly in the form of political/legal deterrent and partly as the alleviator of the worst consequences of the poverty-producing socioeconomic mechanism through the resources of the social security system — the modern state and capital's social metabolic reproductive order match one another.

Nevertheless, the alienation of control and the antagonisms generated by it belong to the very nature of capital. Thus recalcitrance is reproduced on a daily basis through the normal operations of the system, and neither the mystifying efforts at establishing ideal 'industrial relations' — through 'human engineering' and 'scientific management', or by inducing the workers to buy a few shares and thereby become 'co-owners' of, or 'co-partners' in the management of, 'people's capitalism', etc. — nor the deterrent guarantee of the state against potential political rebellion can remove for good labour's emancipatory (self-controlling) aspirations. In the end this issue is decided by the feasibility (or not) of such self-controlling social metabolic order, grounded on labour's hegemonic alternative to capital's subjectless authoritarian control order. The idea of 'perpetual peace' between capital and labour, no matter how diligently it might be promoted at all times, turns out to be no more realistic than Kant's dream about 'perpetual peace' between national states which was supposed to emanate from the capitalist 'commercial spirit', of all things.

Indeed, there is a most important dimension of the ongoing socioeconomic developments with regard to the question of control which escapes the combined ability of capital's personifications inside the production units and the potential intervention of the state in its own sphere as the totalizing political command structure of the system. In this regard we find a major and objectively intensifying contradiction between the material imperatives of capital and its capacity to maintain its control where it matters most: over the production process itself.

The ground of this contradiction is the tendency for a growing *socialization of production* on capital's global terrain. This process objectively transfers certain potentialities of control to the producers — even if within the framework of the established social metabolic order in a negative sense only — by opening up some possibilities for making the uncontrollability of the capital system more acute. It will be necessary to say more about this problem in Chapter 5. The point to stress here concerns the structural mismatch between the material reproductive structures of capital and its state formation. For the state — notwithstanding its great repressive force — is totally powerless to remedy the situation, no matter how authoritarian its attempted intervention might be. There can be no conceivable political remedial action in this regard on capital's socioeconomic foundation. The complications and irrepressible contradictions due to the growing socialization of production affect the inner core of capital as a reproductive system. They arise, paradoxically, from the greatest asset of the capital system: a process of dynamic productive advancement which capital cannot possibly renounce without undermining its own productive power and concomitant legitimacy. This is why the structural mismatch here referred to is bound to remain with us for as long as the capital system itself.

Indeed, it is worth remembering — a reminder which happens to be also a pointer towards the future — that one of the principal contradictions which made the Soviet capital system implode was that it heavily relied on its state formation for the wished for but unachievable remedial action in this respect. It mobilized the Soviet state for forcefully *enhancing* the socialization of production — in order to be able to maximize politically the extraction of surplus labour — and at the same time tried to repress, with all means at its disposal, as if nothing had happened since 1917, the consequences necessarily arising from the increased socialization for the potential emancipation of labour. Thus, instead of remedying the productive defects of the postcapitalist Soviet capital system through a politically forced rate of production, it ended up with a highly *forced rate of socialization of production* which could not be sustained both on account of its structural failure to control recalcitrant labour, and the low level of productivity going with it. The implosion of the Soviet system occurred under the unmanageable weight of such contradictions.

2.3.2

UNDER another vital aspect the structural mismatch is identifiable in the contradictory relationship between the totalizing mandate of the state and its ability to deliver. For the state is successful in fulfilling its role only if it can enhance the productive potential inherent in the *unrestrainability* of the particular reproductive units inasmuch as they constitute a *system*. In other words, what is ultimately at stake here is not simply the effectiveness of the support provided by the state for this or that particular fraction of capital under its jurisdiction. Rather, it is the ability to secure the advancement of the 'whole' in the changing dynamics of accumulation and expansion. In effect the preferential support that can be given by any particular state to its dominant sections of capital — to the point of facilitating extreme monopolistic developments — is part of the logic of sustaining the advancement of the given 'whole' (which in practice means: the total national capital of the state in question), subject to the necessity to conform to the structural limits of the capital system as such.

This is where a major contradiction comes to the fore. For in the capital system — the way in which it has been historically constituted — the 'whole' forcefully sustained by the state cannot embrace the totality of capital's globally existent socioeconomic reproductive units. It goes without saying, the emergence and consolidation of *national capitals* is a historically accomplished fact. Likewise, there can be no doubt about the reality of the — often disastrously conflictual — interactions of national states. But this also means that national capitals, in all their known forms of articulation, are inextricably intertwined with *national states* and rely on the latter for their support, be they imperialistically dominant or, on the contrary, subjected to the domination of other national capitals and respective states.

'Global capital', by contrast, is *devoid of its proper state formation,* notwithstanding the fact that the capital system asserts its power — in an extremely contradictory form — as a *global system.* Thus *'the state of the capital system'* demonstrates its inability to carry the objective logic of capital's unrestrainability to its conclusion. A multiplicity of modern states were constituted on the material ground of the capital system as it historically evolved, from early capitalist state formations to the colonial, Bonapartist, liberal bourgeois, imperialist, fascist, etc. states. All such varieties of the modern state belong to the category of 'capitalist states'. On the other hand, a variety of post-capitalist states were also constituted on capital's materially — in a somewhat altered form — persisting ground in postrevolutionary societies, from the Soviet state to the so-called 'People's Democracies'. Moreover, new variations are not just theoretically feasible in the future but already identifiable in our own days, in particular since the implosion of the former Soviet system. For the states emerging from the ruins of the latter could not be simply qualified as 'capitalist states', at least not to date. Whether or not they will be so describable in the future, depends on how successful the now ongoing efforts at the restoration of capitalism will eventually turn out to be. Those who in the past used to characterize the Soviet Union as a 'state capitalist' society should now have second thoughts, in the light of what has actually happened in the recent past. For even today, more than ten years after Gorbachev started the job of capitalist restoration as newly promoted Party Secretary, the former Stalinist leaders of the Soviet Union still encounter immense difficulties in their efforts to complete that process. Despite the fashionable but utterly vacuous talk about 'conservatives' and 'reformers', their difficulties certainly do not arise from want of really trying. For today's 'conservatives' are yesterday's 'reformers', and their equally tainted successors — the various Yeltsins who even a few moments ago were celebrated with unqualified enthusiasm in the Western capitalist press — are accused (by *The Economist,* no less) of 'acts of gross irresponsibility'.[65] In truth, however, what is being clearly demonstrated through the failure of full-scale capitalist restoration so far in Russia (as well as in other former Soviet republics) is that attempts at overturning a social reproductive system through political intervention, at no matter how high a level, are unable to scratch even the surface of the problem when the social metabolic ground of the capital system itself (in this case that of the postcapitalist Soviet capital system) puts up the real obstacle to the envisaged transformations.

It is not feasible to restore even the *capitalist state* by political change alone, let alone to institute the capitalist 'market economy' without introducing quite fundamental changes (together with their massive *material* prerequisites) in the social metabolic order of postrevolutionary societies with regard to the profoundly altered — primarily political and not economic — mode of regulating the extraction of surplus labour that prevailed under seventy years of Soviet power. The bait of Western capitalist 'economic aid' can help, at most, only with the job of political restoration, as it did so far, but it is quite laughable in terms of the required monumental social metabolic change. Such aid is dispensed on the model of the long established practice of 'aid to underdeveloped countries', with political strings attached with unvarnished cynicism and total disregard for the humiliation that must be swallowed by 'the recipients of aid'. Thus *The Economist* does not hesitate to openly advocate the use of the 'big stick of economic sanctions', thundering (in the same Leader in which it censured Yeltsin before he dissolved parliament and ordered a tank regiment to fire on its building as well as the people in it, and thereby conclusively proved his good credentials in accord with Western 'democratic expectations') that *'no more aid should be forthcoming'*[66] until the Russian President falls into line, expiates his 'gross irresponsibility', sacks 'the board of the central bank', 'throws his weight' behind their favourite flavour of the month, 'the reformist finance minister Boris Fyodorov', etc.

What is, however, forgotten or ignored in all such approaches to 'aid' is that the so-called 'Third World' countries were subordinate but integral parts of *capitalist* empires before they tried to embark — as it turned out, with very little success — on the road of post-colonial 'modernization'. Thus — quite unlike Russia, where the issue at stake is a major change from a post-capitalist political extraction of surplus labour back to its former capitalist economic mode of surplus-value extraction — post-colonial countries did not have to make any effort at all in order to become a dependent part of the global capitalist system, since they were fully dependent on it from the outset. They did not have to struggle for the restoration of capitalism, since they already had it — in no matter how 'underdeveloped' a form — the moment the potentially damaging impact of the 'wind of change' was conceded (in Macmillan's famous speech) by their former imperialist masters, so that the latter should be able to manage the new forms of 'neo-capitalist' and 'neo-colonial' domination. In the countries of the Soviet Union — precisely because they were under the rule of capital in one of its *postcapitalist* varieties — very different conditions prevailed (and to a significant extent still prevail). This is why even a *hundredfold* greater Western capitalist 'economic aid' (whose magnitude, as repeatedly promised but never actually delivered to Gorbachev and Yeltsin, is laughable even by comparison to what would be needed in order to turn Albania into a prosperous capitalist country) would remain utterly trivial in relation to the real size of the problem as measured on the scale of the required social metabolic change.

Particular states of the capital system — both in their capitalist and postcapitalist varieties — assert (some with greater others with rather less success) the interests of their national capitals. In complete contrast, '*the state of the capital system as such*' remains to the present day a Kantian 'regulative idea' only, without any sign of its future realization being discernible even as a faint historical trend. And this is by no means surprising. For the actualization of this 'regulative idea' would presuppose the successful overcoming of all the major internal antagonisms of global capital's contending constituents.

Thus the state's inability to deliver in full what is ultimately required by the totalizing inner determination of the capital system represents a major problem for the future. The seriousness of this problem is illustrated by the fact that even the capitalist state of the most privileged hegemonic power — the United States today — must fail in its attempt to carry out the mandate for maximizing the *global unrestrainability* of capital as such and impose itself as the unchallengeable commanding state of the global capital system. Of necessity it remains *nationally restrained* in its enterprise both politically and economically — and its hegemonic power position is potentially threatened as a result of the changing relation of forces at the level of the international socioeconomic interchanges and confrontations — no matter how dominant it might be as an imperialist power.

This inability to take the interest of the capital system to its ultimate logical conclusion is due to the structural mismatch between the imperatives emanating from capital's social metabolic process, and the state as the comprehensive political command structure of the system. For the state cannot be truly comprehensive and totalizing to the degree to which it 'ought to be', since in our own days it is no longer in accord even with the already attained level of social metabolic integration, let alone with that required for extricating the global order from its growing difficulties and contradictions. As of today, there is no evidence whatsoever that this profound structural mismatch can be remedied by the formation of a *global state system* capable of successfully eliminating the actual and potential antagonisms of the established global metabolic order. The attempted substitute solutions of the past — in the form of two global wars initiated for the sake of redrawing the lines of the prevailing hegemonic power relations — speak only of disaster in this respect.

The capital system is an irrepressibly expansion-oriented mode of social metabolic control. Given the innermost determination of its nature, the material reproductive and the political functions must be radically separated in it — producing thereby the modern state as the *structure of alienation par excellence* — just as production and control must be radically divorced in it. But 'expansion' in this system can only mean *capital-expansion* to which everything else must be subordinated, and not the development of positive human aspirations and the co-ordinated provision of the means for their satisfaction. This is why in the capital system the wholly fetishistic criteria of expansion must impose themselves on society also in the form of the radical separation and alienation of the power of decision making from *everyone* — including the 'personifications of capital' whose 'freedom' consists in imposing on others capital's imperatives — at all levels of societal reproduction, from the domain of material production to the highest levels of politics. For once the objectives of social existence are defined by capital in its own way, ruthlessly subordinating all human values and aspirations to the pursuit of capital-expansion, there can be no room for *decision making* other than one strictly concerned with finding the *instruments* best suited for reaching the *predetermined goal*.

But even if one is willing to disregard the desolate character of human action being confined to such a narrow margin of fetishistic material pursuit, the prospects of development are very far from being cheerful in the longer run. For as an irrepressibly expansion-oriented mode of social metabolic control, the capital system can either sustain its accumulation-driven course of development or sooner or later it *implodes,* like the postcapitalist Soviet capital system did. There was not — nor could there be — any way of overthrowing from outside the Soviet capital system without risking the annihilation of humankind by means of a global nuclear war. To give a helping hand to Gorbachev and friends (with whom even Margaret Thatcher and company could 'do business'), thereby facilitating the eventual implosion of the system, was a much better bet. In the same way today there can be no question of 'overthrowing from outside' the capital system as such, for it has no 'outside'. And now, to the great chagrin of all the apologists of capital, the mythical 'outside enemy' — Ronald Reagan's 'evil empire' — has also disappeared. But even in its present-day more or less absolute dominance the capital system is far from being immune to threats of instability. The danger to it does not come from the mythical 'enemy within', which was as dear to Reagan's and Thatcher's heart as the 'enemy without', in the shape of the 'evil empire'. It resides, rather, in the prospects of capital-expansion and accumulation one day driving to a complete halt. For John Stuart Mill's 'stationary state' — which he expected to be materially sustainable and politically liberal/democratic on capital's expansion-oriented and accumulation-driven ground — is nothing but a self-contradiction and a daydream to which in reality only the absolute nightmare of global authoritarianism can correspond. A form of authoritarianism compared to which Hitler's Nazi Germany would shine as a model of democracy.

CHAPTER THREE

SOLUTIONS TO THE UNCONTROLLABILITY OF CAPITAL AS SEEN FROM CAPITAL'S STANDPOINT

3.1 *The answers of classical Political Economy*

3.1.1

CONTRARY to widespread belief, popularized by the legitimate fears of green movements, the shadow of uncontrollability is not a new phenomenon. Although undoubtedly it has become much darker in the twentieth century, this shadow certainly did not arise in recent decades with the dangers of the nuclear age on the one hand and the frightening impact of large scale industrial and agricultural pollution on the other. Rather, it was inseparable from capital as a mode of social metabolic control ever since it succeeded in consolidating itself into a coherent reproductive system, with the triumph of generalized commodity production.

A system of control which takes the unalterability of its own structural parameters for granted cannot escape the fateful contradiction of absolutizing the relative, and at the same time decreeing the *permanence* of what can only be *transient* in actuality. In order to proceed in a different way, it would be necessary to address causes as causes — instead of treating the encountered problems as manipulatable effects of the sacrosanct causal order — so as to intervene in a desirable and tenable fashion on the plane of the underlying causes themselves. For the latter sooner or later are bound to reproduce the temporarily adjusted and for a while successfully managed negative effects with a vengeance.

The meaning of the socialist project can in fact be none other than its conscious corrective intervention in — and in due course fundamental restructuring of — the causal determinations of the established social reproductive order. This is why socialists, to have any hope of success at all, must negate *capital* itself — as unalterable *causa sui* — and not simply one or another of its historically contingent variants, as for instance the now dominant global *capitalist* system. Indeed, the socialist project represents humanity's crying need for addressing causes as causes in the established mode of social metabolic control, in order to eradicate capital's by now all too visible and ever more preponderant destructive tendencies, before it becomes too late.

The only mode of social reproductive control which qualifies for being socialist is the one that refuses to submit the legitimate aspirations of the individuals to the fetishistic imperatives of a structurally predetermined causal order. In other words, it is a mode of social metabolic reproduction which is truly *open* with regard to the *future* in that the determination of its *causal framework itself* remains always subject to alteration by the self-managing members of society. A mode of social metabolic control that can be structurally

72

altered by the individuals, in the light of their consciously chosen ends, in place of superimposing on them, as it happens today, a reified and narrow range of ends directly emanating from capital's preexistent causal network: an allegedly unalterable causality operating over above the heads of the individuals. By contrast, even the greatest thinkers who perceived and theorized the world from the vantage point of capital, as did the author of the *Wealth of Nations,* had to champion the self-serving illusion of the system's permanence not only as *de facto* but also as *de jure,* i.e. as one *rightfully* destined to continue its rule to the end of time. They justified such position by arguing that the social order with which they identified themselves represented *'the natural system of perfect liberty and justice'*[67] and, therefore, could not conceivably be in need of major, let alone of fundamental structural changes.

The fateful uncontrollability of the capital system never posed a problem to all those who, given their social standpoint, could not consider it as a *transient* mode of control. Even when they were willing to admit that the very idea of control was somewhat problematical in their cherished system (inasmuch as they were forced to postulate the viability of 'control without an identifiable controller or controllers'), they ran away from the difficulties implicit in that admission by presenting — at first naively, but as time went by and the crisis of control became too obvious to be deniable, less and less innocently — an idealized picture.

To be sure, the terms in which the acknowledged absence of control has been 'remedied' in all such theorizations of the capital system were changed in order to suit the circumstances, but the *idealization* of the claimed remedy — circularly anticipated in the tendentious diagnosis of the encountered problem itself — remained their common method, from Adam Smith to the present. To show these correlations, it should suffice here to discuss three representative varieties of assessing the absence of control over the last two centuries, all of them formulated in the spirit of taking back in the end the original admission and denying that the acknowledged defect might be considered a defect after all. After surveying as the first in the historical order Adam Smith's solution, the second typical approach which we must briefly look at is that of the various 'marginal utility' theories, wedded to belief in the controlling power of the innovating 'entrepreneur' on condition that he translates into sound business strategies the demands emanating from the 'utility-maximizing' consumers. And finally, the third typical attempt at addressing and at the same time apologetically 'resolving' the dilemmas of control inseparable from the capital system is centred around the quasi-mythical concept of the 'manager', from the 1930s on through Burnham's 'managerial revolution' (1940) and Talcott Parsons' eager rejoinder in the 1950s all the way to Galbraith's fictitious 'technostructure' which promises to all would-be believers no less than the final elimination of the socialist challenge thanks to the claimed 'convergence' of all feasible forms of efficient socioeconomic reproduction under the corporatist order.

3.1.2

THE first way of identifying and at once spiriting away the problem goes back to the founding father of classical political economy, Adam Smith. Even today

Smith's postulate that the limited and selfish actions of particular capitalists necessarily produce a most beneficial overall result remains the model of all those who continue to glorify the unsurpassable virtues of the capital system. This is how the great representative of Scottish Enlightenment formulates his line of argument:

> As every individual *endeavours as much as he can* both to employ his capital in the support of domestic industry, and so to direct that industry that its produce may be of the greatest value, every individual necessarily labours to render the annual revenue of the society as great as he can. He generally, indeed, neither intends to promote the public interest, nor knows how much he is promoting it. By preferring the support of domestic to that of foreign industry, he intends only his own security; and by directing that industry in such a manner as its produce may be of the greatest value, he intends only his own gain, and he is in this, as in many other cases, *led by an invisible hand to promote an end which was no part of his intention.* ... By pursuing his own interest he frequently *promotes that of the society more effectually than when he really intends to promote it.* ... What is the species of domestic industry which his capital can employ, and of which the produce is likely to be of the greatest value, every individual, it is evident, can, in his local situation, judge much better than any statesman or lawgiver can do for him. The statesman, who should attempt to direct private people in what manner they ought to employ their capitals, would not only load himself with a most unnecessary attention, but assume an authority which could safely be trusted, not only to no single person, but to no council or senate whatever, and which would nowhere be so dangerous as in the hands of a man who had folly and presumption enough to fancy himself fit to exercise it.[68]

As we can see, Adam Smith at first admits that the individual capitalist can only '*endeavour* as much as he can' in order to render the wealth of his society 'as great as he can'. Yet by the time we reach the end of the quoted passage he declares that it would be a '*dangerous folly*' to imagine that the order of things idealized by him as 'the natural system of perfect liberty and justice' would be amenable to improvement by any other type of decision making authority, be that vested in an individual or in some collective body. Understandably, for declaring the self-evidence of such a conclusion not the progressive followers of the Enlightenment but the most extreme conservatives remained grateful to Smith ever since. Thus, to take one particularly reactionary example, Margaret Thatcher's guru and Nobel Prize winner Companion of Honour (1984), Friedrich August Hayek wrote that 'The nineteenth-century enthusiast who claimed that the *Wealth of Nations* was in importance second only to the Bible has often been ridiculed; but he may not have exaggerated so much'.[69] Never worrying about self-contradiction, Hayek also asserted that Adam Smith's notion of the 'invisible hand' was 'the first *scientific* description'[70] of the market processes, after accusing him in an earlier chapter — on account of the same idea — of remaining captive of '*animism*'.[71]

Naturally, compared to the irrationality — indeed the sheer mysticism — of the kind of 'marginal utility theory' championed by Hayek and his ideological companions, Adam Smith's concept of the 'invisible hand' represents a great scientific achievement. However, that does not make it either scientific or plausible. For, as Smith had to admit to himself half-way through his reasoning quoted above, the intensity of the individual capitalist's endeavour is no guarantee whatsoever of success either for himself or for society at large, and therefore the system could not function without 'the invisible hand'. Today the great Scottish thinker would be completely at a loss in that he would also have to admit that one of the main pillars of his explanatory edifice — the argument about favouring enterprise in domestic as against foreign industry, justified in terms of the capitalist's self-evidently rational motivation with regard to his own security — has been utterly demolished by the dominance of the giant transnational corporations in the global capital system. Also, he would have to abandon his idealization of the capitalist's eminent qualifications for his 'local situation' under the circumstances of — nowadays in an opposite sense idealized — 'globalization' of the economy. For the latter makes Adam Smith's reliance on the allegedly well understood structures of the 'local situation' as the guarantors of success extremely naive, if not altogether meaningless, since in reality grave troubles are generated by the system's vital imperative to subsume all 'local situations' under the immense monopolistic units of the dominant capitalist countries which confront one another with their conflicting interests in the world economy. Nor would Smith be able to claim anything even remotely approaching general acceptance for his *perfectly self-evident maxim* according to which *consumption is the sole end and purpose of all production*[72] at a time when in fact all kinds of subterfuges — including direct state policy devices — must be invented by the personifications of capital not only to ram down the throats of the individual consumers quite unwanted commodities but, more importantly, in order to be able to justify the most wasteful imaginable allocation of resources for the benefit of the military-industrial complex in a world of crying need.

The mysterious benevolent 'invisible hand' would be today hopelessly out of business in terms of Adam Smith's scheme of things, since his kind of capitalist, inasmuch as he exists at all, is by now relegated to a role of almost negligible importance. Consequently it could not be claimed, even if we accept the relevance of Smith's metaphor as a theoretical gap-filling metaphor for his own times, that it is the 'invisible hand' which guides today the dominant corporations and thereby orders the general state of affairs in a universally beneficial way. In fact already the early propounders of 'marginal utility theory', in the 1870s, had to shift the emphasis from the individual capitalist to the individual *consumer* as the all-important 'subject' of their 'subjective revolution'. And today, apart from the fictitious notions of 'consumer sovereignty', explanations as to how the dominant economic units of the capital system are being controlled stand in sharp contrast to Adam Smith's explanatory postulate, as we shall see below in Section 3.3 in relation to the third typical way of theorizing the problem of control from capital's vantage point.

Adam Smith's projection of the 'invisible hand' as the guiding force of his individual capitalists is tantamount to admitting that the reproductive system idealized by him is *uncontrollable*. To counter all possible misgivings on this score, this great thinker must also assume that the mysterious 'invisible hand' is generously *benevolent* both towards the particular capitalists and towards society as a whole. Moreover, the 'invisible hand' is supposed to act — while guiding the capitalist agents — also as the magnanimous harmonizer of all possible conflicts of interest, including that between *production and consumption*. Thus the contradiction between *production and control* — the central defect of the capital system — cannot conceivably arise, since the supreme benevolent hand is postulated as the real controller which by definition cannot possibly fail in its all-round beneficial control. But suppose that the 'invisible hand' is not always, or not in every respect, so benevolent. This thought appears for a moment as a menace to Adam Smith when he writes:

> The progress of the *enormous debts* which at present oppress, and will in the long run *probably ruin, all the great nations of Europe,* has been pretty uniform.[73]

However, he cannot concede that the correctly identified danger would call for at least a partial reconsideration of his general scheme.There can be no corrections made to the latter because it fulfils the required dual function of focusing on the difficulties of control — so that it should be possible to argue in favour of remedial action in *particular* contexts, on the plane of the effects and consequences — and at the same time to make them disappear in terms of the characterization of the system as a whole. For the perception and acknowledgement by a great thinker that the individual capitalist controlling 'subjects' of his idealized system can only constitute a *pseudo-subject,* in that they need a mysteriously invisible but benevolent guiding force behind them to be successful at all, must be immediately undone when the implications are considered from capital's vantage point. Because of the radical separation of production and control under the rule of capital there can be no alternative to asserting the objective imperatives of the capital system through the intermediary agency of such pseudo-subject, making the incorrigible and uncontrollable determinations of capital — as *causa sui* — prevail over above the heads of all individuals, including the 'personifications of capital'. And precisely because the capital system cannot operate in any other way, identifying oneself with capital's vantage point, as Adam Smith does, precludes the possibility of seeking solutions without taking for granted the structural framework of the system — with its objectively imposed uncontrollability — as 'natural' and 'perfect'.

It is the vantage point of capital which necessarily defeats even a great thinker like Adam Smith. The orienting principles of the system imposed upon Smith make him — and many others who follow in his footsteps — look for answers where they cannot be found. Their discourse is confined to attempting to understand the operational parameters of the capital system in terms of the *intentions* and *motivations* of the controlling personnel. (This approach persists from Adam Smith to the present day, embracing all varieties of 'marginalists' — from the originators of 'marginal utility theory' to its recent academic popularisers — and from Max Weber and Keynes to believers in one form or another of the 'managerial revolution' all the way to the most enthusiastic apologists of the capital system, like Hayek.) In truth, however, it is not the subjective 'intention' or 'motivation to accumulate' of the individual capitalists that decides the issue but capital's *objective imperative of expansion.* For without successfully pursuing its process of *expanded* reproduction the capital system would — sooner or later but with absolute certainty — collapse. As far as the 'subjective intentions' and motivations are concerned, the individual personifications of capital *'must intend',* so to speak, the ends delineated by the expansionary determinations of the system itself, and not simply their own 'selfish ends' as particular individuals. Without forcefully asserting over all 'personal intentions' and 'motivations' this mindless primacy of the expansionary imperative the rule of capital could not be sustained even in the shortest of short runs.

The capital system in its innermost determination is absolutely *expansion-oriented* — that is to say, it is oriented in that way from its own, objective vantage point — and *accumulation-driven,* in terms of the necessary *instrumentality* of its projected objective. It is the selfsame correlation that appears (and must appear) from the subjective standpoint of capital's particular personifications exactly the other way round — i.e. they must picture their system as *accumulation-oriented* and *expansion-driven.* 'Expansion' comes into their field of vision in a negative way, most strongly under the circumstances of its damaging absence, rather than as the most substantive and positive determination of the system which they serve. It is under the conditions of economic disturbances and failures that they are forced to acknowledge the importance of the systemic parameters and — forgetting or brushing aside altogether Adam Smith's strictures concerning politics and 'dangerous' as well as 'foolish' politicians — make a 'u-turn' by pleading for government intervention to secure general economic expansion. For they must realize that without the continued expansion of the economy at large they themselves as individuals at the top echelon of their particular business enterprises cannot accumulate either on their own behalf or for their firms. At the same time, though, they picture themselves and their own drive for accumulation as the crucial *determinant* of the given production order, although in actuality they fulfil a fundamentally *instrumental* function in the successful operation of the system — in other words they act as *'determined determinants'* in it — however vital, indeed irreplaceable is their instrumental function in view of the fact that the established mode of social metabolic control is totally inconceivable without the personifications of capital being hierarchically superimposed on labour. In any case, the notion of 'accumulation' itself is in need of demystification. For the accumulated funds cannot be freely disposed of by capital's personifications as they please. Far from it. In one sense (in their direct links to the particular capitalists) they are subordinate moments of the system's expansion; and in another sense (when abstracted from that link and considered as an organic whole) the 'accumulation of capital' is synonymous with expansion. 'Intentions' and 'motivations' are practically determined accordingly. For accumulated capital is dead capital — i.e. no capital at all but the useless hoarding of the miser — unless it is *realized* as capital by way of constantly re-entering in an expanded form the overall process of production and circulation. If this were not so, the capitalist — the 'rational miser' in Marx's words — would degenerate into a plain miser: 'a capitalist gone mad'.[74] But there is no danger of that happening on a significant scale; it happens sporadically whereby the 'capitalist gone mad' inevitably ceases to be an operative 'rational capitalist'. The overwhelming bulk of accumulating capital is 'predestined' by systemic determinations for reinvestment without which the realization and expansion process would be terminated, carrying with it capital — and of course all of its given and potential personifications — into the historical grave.[75]

The important point here is that the capital system remains uncontrollable precisely because the objective structural relationship between conscious intention and objective expansionary requirement cannot be *reversed* within the parameters of this particular social metabolic system in favour of truly controlling intentions (i.e. intentions that would make expansion itself subject to the test of positively justifying qualifications). There can be no room for consciously carried out — that is to say, truly autonomous — operative intentions within the structural framework of capital because the imperatives and strictly *instrumental* demands of the system as a whole must be imposed on and *internalized by* the personifications of capital as 'their intentions' and 'their motivations'. Any attempted departure from the required instrumentality results in necessarily frustrated and nullified — i.e. utterly Quixotic — intentions. The system follows (and ruthlessly asserts over all individuals, including its 'controlling' personifications) its own 'iron determinations', no matter how grave their implications even for human survival, and even in the not so long run. But of course this cannot be admitted by those who view and theorize the world from capital's vantage point. This is why Adam Smith's profound diagnosis of a fateful defect in the capital system — its uncontrollability by human agency — had to be coupled with a *mythical reassurance* concerning its nonetheless continued (indeed 'natural' and 'permanent') viability. And this is why Hegel — in Adam Smith's footsteps — had to characterize even the 'world historical individuals' as mere *tools* in the hands of the mythical 'World Spirit': the only being with a not self-deceiving relationship between consciousness and action.

To envisage the control of the social metabolism not by the mysterious 'invisible hand', or by its 'universalized' Hegelian reformulation for the whole of world history, but by a conscious and self-determining human agency, — one capable of acting in such a way that its intentions are not a perverse and self-deceiving camouflage for the summarily imposed instrumentality of a fetishistic reproductive order, — it is necessary to step outside the structural framework of capital and abandon its material determining ground which is amenable only to the constitution of an uncontrollable mode of control. This is precisely what gives meaning to the socialist project.[76]

3.2 *'Marginal Utility' and neo-classical Economics*

3.2.1

DESPITE Adam Smith's reassuring words on the benevolent control of the capitalist order by the 'hidden hand', the latter failed to live up to expectations. Instead, crises of growing severity became an undeniable feature of Smith's 'natural system of perfect liberty and justice', compelling its defenders to offer some sort of explanation implying also a remedy.

Given the new circumstances, a simple declaration of faith in the 'hidden hand' successfully guiding the actions of the individual capitalists in their 'local situations' was not enough. A different way of assessing the issue of control had to be found; partly because the dominant units of business enterprise were becoming ever larger (and, of course, inextricably intertwined with far from local connections); and partly because it had to be acknowledged that the 'trade cycles' which were assuming most damaging proportions had to be at least accounted for — in full agreement with the imperatives of the system — without which the reassuring message would no longer be credible at all. This is how the second typical theorization of the dilemmas of control and uncontrollability mentioned in Section 3.1.1 came into being out of a partial awareness of the crisis symptoms. Characteristically, however, also the representatives of the new approach refused to acknowledge the causes of the identified difficulties. They preferred to address themselves to the symptoms only, reinterpreting the earlier accounts of the established mode of social metabolic reproduction in such a way that it should not query in the least the uncritically assumed belief of the classics of bourgeois political economy in the naturalness and absolute permanence of the capital system.

W. Stanley Jevons, one of the pioneers of this new approach — which became celebrated as the 'marginalist revolution' or the 'subjective revolution' — insisted that a rigorous scientific method, with a proper mathematical apparatus, should be applied to the encountered problems. The fact that his trend-setting book — *The Theory of Political Economy* — appeared in the midst of a major international crisis and the year of the Paris Commune, 1871, is of course a coincidence. It is also a mere coincidence that the most influential English economist who offered the fruits of the same 'revolution', Alfred Marshall, was pursuing his research project in Berlin at the same time when Bismarck's Prussian troups were besieging Paris, and thereby massively contributing to the eruption of the Paris Commune. What was, however, anything but coincidence was the increasing frequency and intensity of crises over decades, until a new imperialist expansion relieved tension in the European 'little corner of the world' and gave a new lease of life to capital in the dominant imperialist countries. After all, Stanley Jevons himself had to interrupt his University studies and seek employment in Australia for five years — until he could save enough money to resume his studies — because his formerly wealthy iron merchant father's business had suffered bankruptcy as a result of a serious economic crisis.

As a matter of fact, the spectre of crises haunted Jevons to the end of his life. As a very young man he expressed his concern in a letter to his brother Herbert, in April 1861 (i.e. more than two years before receiving his M.A. at University College, London) in these terms:

> Whether commercial revolutions be or be not as necessary and inevitable as are the flux and efflux of the tide, forms a curious and doubtful question. Certain it is that they make their appearance in the ordinary course of affairs, if not at periods exactly regular, at least in cycles of which it is not difficult to determine the average extent. Difficult though it be accurately to determine the principles which regulate them, they are usually found preceded by symptoms and followed by results bearing an analogy, if not a resemblance to each other. A close attention to them on the part of our *business men* would go far towards the dissemination of that sound information *respecting the laws of trade, which would greatly mitigate the severity of commercial revulsions.*[77]

Indeed, fifteen years later, in a lecture on 'The Future of Political Economy' — occasioned by the centenary celebrations of Adam Smith's *Wealth of Nations* held at the Political Economy Club in 1876 — he insisted that

> We need a science of the money market and of commercial fluctuations, which shall inquire why the world is all activity for a few years, and then all inactivity; why, in short, there are such tides in the affairs of men.[78]

Yet, the successful elaboration and application of Jevons's 'science of money and of economic fluctuations' remained an elusive dream ever since, despite all efforts expended on it and despite all honours — including quite a few Nobel Prizes — lavished upon its propounders. Nevertheless the illusion rooted in wishful thinking persisted ever since that such a science — capable of eliminating the much deplored 'commercial fluctuations' and periodic crises or in Jevons's term 'revulsions' — was feasible within capital's structural parameters, provided that 'rigorous quantitative methods' (encapsulated in mathematical formulas) were adopted by its representatives; as indeed they were fairly quickly, constituting a distinguishing feature of the new orthodoxy. Even Alfred Marshall, who was very anxious to retain the popular accessibility of his writings in order to be able to influence businessmen, happily accepted Edgeworth's characterization of his work as 'bearing under the garb of literature *the armour of mathematics*'.[79]

However, instead of the postulated remedy touching the causal ground of the system, only the effects were tackled, often with overbearing mathematical and statistical apparatus, producing most problematical results even in the opinion of those who were expecting solutions from the same formalized science of money. Thus many years later, in 1936, Keynes had to sound more than a word of caution against sanguine expectations, appealing to ordinary discourse and common sense as the necessary correctives to mathematical zeal. He argued that

> in ordinary discourse, where we are not blindly manipulating but know all the time what we are doing and what the words mean, we can keep 'at the back of our heads' the necessary reserves and qualifications and the adjustments which we shall have to make later on, in a way in which we cannot keep complicated partial differentials 'at the back' of several pages of algebra which assume that they all vanish. Too large a proportion of recent 'mathematical' economics are mere concoctions, as imprecise as the initial assumptions they rest on, which allow the author to lose sight of the complexities and interdependencies of the real world in a maze of pretentious and unhelpful symptoms.[80]

But the roots of the problem reaching back in its mathematicized form to the 1860s and 1870s were much deeper for any appeal to the guidance of common sense and ordinary discourse to rectify. It is true, as Keynes stated, that in the late 1860s 'the notion of applying mathematical methods was in the air'.[81] But something of much greater import — the deeply felt concern, if not alarm, of capital's personifications about the growing socialist labour movement — was also in the air. The various theories of 'marginal utility' — from the English and Swiss versions to the Austrian variations — were conceived to a large extent as an antidote in this respect. Wesley C. Mitchell rightly stressed in his lectures delivered in 1918 at Columbia University that

> No one can read the Austrian writers, whose general scheme was similar to Jevons's, without feeling that they are interested in developing the concept of the maximizing of utility largely because they thought it answered Marx's socialistic critique of modern economic organization. It seemed at least at first blush, to show that, so long as interference with competition is repressed, theoretically the best possible organization of society results when everyone is left perfectly free to make his own decisions. ... One of the interesting and rather ironical developments of the generation after Jevons was that this line of economic theorizing which the Austrians used in answer to Marx was adopted by the Fabian socialists as their basic economic doctrine, and a new scheme of socialism, very different in character from Marx's, was erected on its foundation.[82]

The economists who embraced the main tenets of marginal utility theory politically ranged from Francis Ysidro Edgeworth's extreme conservative position, stretched to the point of obscurantist insanity[83] — and to be fair to

Edgeworth, there was a touch of lunacy in the remedial conceptions of all of them, including Jevons, who wanted to explain 'scientifically' what he called 'commercial revulsions' by statistically linking them to sun-spots (by which standard the sun must have been excessively, nay perversely spotty in recent decades; but who in his or her right mind would wish to quarrel with the sun?) — to varieties of paternalism towards labour, prominent among the Fabians. The neo-classical paternalist Marshall, for instance, despite his reputation as a careful and most scrupulous scientific thinker,[84] was nonetheless perfectly happy to dismiss Marx in the most summary fashion — by means of grotesque caricaturistic misrepresentations — in order to be able to do away at the same time with the notions of *surplus labour* and *exploitation*.[85] Indeed, after patting Marx on the back for his 'sympathies with suffering', he did not hesitate to indulge even in playing up to the philistine academic gallery, sneering that Marx's arguments were 'shrouded by mysterious Hegelian phrases',[86] although (as we know from Keynes's account, based on Mrs Marshall's biographic sketch of her late husband) when Marshall himself was 'living in Berlin in the winter of 1870-71, during the Franco-German war, Hegel's *Philosophy of History* greatly influenced him'.[87]

The big difference in the second half of the 19th century with regard to 'commercial revulsions' and crises was that the established production and political order was increasingly being challenged by the organized socialist movement which dared to put forward the 'extra-economic' proposition that economic crises are not due to cyclic extra-terrestrial disturbances, nor to the unalterable determinations of 'human nature', but to the fundamental structural defects of the capital system.

Understandably, the personifications of capital had to do something about that challenge, since they could not expect an automatic solution from their earlier adopted *deus ex machina:* the much revered 'invisible hand'. Whether conservative or paternalistic, they had to offer explanations and justifications which could at least appear to respond to the demands arising from the labour movement. Even the extreme reactionary Edgeworth was suggesting that 'The whole creation groans and yearns, desiderating *a principle of arbitration, an end of strifes.*'[88] It is true that Edgeworth was somewhat special in that his 'principle' turned out to be the most naked apologetics for the privileges of the ruling classes, backed up by pseudo-scientific humbug which justified the entrepreneur's superior social position and corresponding wealth with Darwinian verbiage and utilitarian camouflage by saying that 'a more highly nervous organization required on the average a higher minimum of means to get up to the zero of utility'.[89] Nevertheless, the substance of the teaching of his ideological comrades in arms was the same as regards their 'principles' of grossly iniquitous distribution and its claimed 'scientific' justification. For they all wanted to spirit away even the possibility of considering the relationship between wages and profits, surplus-labour and surplus-value, the fact and the potential remedy of exploitation. And to do this with a view to proclaiming — no longer in theoretically and politically contestable Political Economy but more and more in the rationally unchallengeable 'science of Economics' — the 'end of strifes'.

Shifting the emphasis from Adam Smith's individual capitalist decision makers to the utility-maximizing consumers in general — whose demands are, of course, soundly interpreted and realized by the capitalist entrepreneurs — served the same purpose. For if it was true, as Jevons argued, that 'value depends entirely on the final degree of utility'[90] — a proposition shared in one form or another by all variants of 'marginal utility theory' — in that case rationality itself prescribed that all claims of the workers had to be assessed in terms of, and in subordination to, purchaser/consumer demand, removing thereby the possibility of contesting in strife-bound class terms the structural determination of the system. What a pity that the claimed link between sun-spots and 'commercial revulsions' could not be really established, despite the fact that Jevons twice modified his 'scientific' economic statistics in order to fit the (for his scheme most unfortunately) revised astrophysical sun-spot data; and despite the fact that he introduced the notion of 'normal cycles' — a methodological procedure of arbitrary definitions and assumptions widely adopted by later apologists so as to be able to prove what could not be sustained by any other way — in order to exclude the stubborn cycles that refused to fit into his neat and convenient preconception. For success in this respect would have demonstrated how absurd all those socialists were who were looking for explanations and remedy not in the sky but on earth by focusing attention on the monstrous iniquities and contradictions of the established socioeconomic order.

3.2.2

HOWEVER, notwithstanding the hypotheses and reassurances of the new economists who adopted the faith of marginal utility theory, the deplored 'commercial revulsions' and crises — with their concomitant strifes and class struggles — not only did not fade away but tended to grow in severity. At the same time the persistent challenge of the organized labour movement — not only in France (despite the bloody suppression of the Paris Commune) but in Germany, Russia, Austria/Hungary, Italy, and England as well, to mention only the European 'little corner of the world' — made it much more rational from the vantage point of capital to adopt the strategy of *co-option* in place of confrontation. The concern about social conflict was constantly voiced by Alfred Marshall — probably the most enlightened of the caring paternalists — who argued in an essay written shortly after the 1905 Russian revolution that

> In Germany the dominion of bureaucracy has combined with other causes to develop a bitter class hatred, and occasionally to make social order depend on the willingness of soldiers to fire on citizens; and the case is, of course, much worse in the even more bureaucratic Russia. But under collectivism there would be no appeal from the all-pervading bureaucratic discipline. ...collectivism is a grave menace to the maintenance even of our present moderate rate of progress.[91]

And Marshall combined his categorical rejection of collectivism with an idealized picture of both the capitalist 'rich man' — who not only fully understands but also generously implements the teachings of the compassionate marginalist creed — and the socioeconomic order of which the Marshallian rich man was supposed to be an exemplary representative. According to this picture, in Marshall's slowly but inexorably unfolding Utopia

> The rich man would further co-operate with the State, even more strenuously than he does now, in relieving the suffering of those who are weak and ailing through no

fault of their own, and to whom a shilling may yield more real benefit than he could get from spending many additional pounds. ... Under such conditions the people generally would be so well nurtured and so truly educated that the land would be pleasant to live in. Wages in it would be high by the hour, but labour would not be dear. Capital would therefore not be very anxious to emigrate from it, even if rather heavy taxes were put on it for public ends: the wealthy would love to live in it; and thus true Socialism, based on chivalry, would rise above the fear that no country can move faster than others lest it should be bereft of capital. National Socialism of this sort might be full of individuality and elasticity. There would be no need for those iron bonds of mechanical symmetry which Marx postulated as necessary for his 'International' projects.[92]

Thus, characteristically, preaching the virtues of conflict-avoidance with an appeal to the fairy-tale conditions of the coming capitalist 'chivalry' could be happily wedded to a militant anti-socialism, misrepresenting Marx, again, as a crude mechanical thinker. At the same time Marshall also had to maintain that the idealized capitalist socioeconomic order contained within it the true Socialist system, in its 'National Socialist' variety. After all, he was not only a 'friend of labour' and of the British Co-operative movement (at one time even the President of the latter), but also a good English imperialist who — while strongly condemning German and Russian bureaucracy, as well as too much state involvement in general — could believe and argue in all seriousness that 'The chivalry which has made many administrators in India, Egypt, and elsewhere, devote themselves to the interests of the peoples under their rule is an instance of the way in which British unconventional elastic methods of administration give scope for free, fine enterprise in the service of the State'.[93] Surely this must have pleased national imperialists from all classes, including the 'moderate' and 'realistic' Fabian labourite 'National Socialists'. The curious thing was only that Marshall imagined that he could combine without incon- sistency his militant strictures against the unreality of radical socialists — like: 'in recent years we have suffered much from schemes that claim to be practical, and yet are based on no thorough study of economic realities'[94] — with the total unreality of his own idealization of both capitalism in general and of its British imperialist variety in particular.

But, of course, he was not alone in all this. The 'economic realities' which he proclaimed to be the necessary premisses of rational economic discourse were the imperatives of the capital system to which all social reform strategy had to conform. Marshall was far from unique in defining the only legitimate form of 'collective action by the working classes' as 'employing their own means, not indeed suddenly to *revolutionize*, but *gradually* to raise their own material and moral condition'.[95] Reformism surfaced in the radical socialist movement in the late 1860s and early 1870s, and Marx's 1875 *Critique of the Gotha Programme* clearly sounded the alarm in this respect. However, his critical intervention proved to be in vain in that the emerging Socialdemocratic parties in the dominant capitalist countries moved in the direction of reformist participation in their national Parliaments.

This tendency was both reflected and actively influenced by marginalist economic theory, not only in England — mainly through the agency of the Fabians — but all over Europe. 'Co-option' was 'in the air' both before and —

with greater intensity — after the Paris Commune. Indeed it was so much preferable to confrontation in the view of capital's personifications that no less a prominent figure than 'Iron Chancellor' Bismarck himself wanted — by 'scheming with Lassalle', as Marx and Engels complained at the time[96] — to entice the 'Red Doctor' Karl Marx to return home in order to suitably manage the German working class on behalf of national-imperialistically aspiring German capital. (The repeal of Bismarck's anti-Socialist Law in due course was fully consistent with the Iron Chancellor's national imperialist design and the role assigned to the working classes in it.) Understandably, Marshall treated Lassalle with much greater sympathy than Marx, praising him for his rejection of the 'iron law of wages' while crudely ascribing adherence of it to Marx. As to the theoretical formation of the leading light of German 'evolutionary socialism', Edward Bernstein (who later became also Max Weber's favourite socialist), he derived much inspiration not only from the Swiss and Austrian variety of marginal utility theory but also from its British versions during his long stay in England.

This is how the organized socialist movement — in the new imperialist expansionary phase of dominant European capital, and in tune with the specific form of division between economics and politics in the capital system — became fatefully split between labour's 'industrial arm' and its 'political arm', from which later the split and antagonism between revolutionary and 'evolutionary'/reformist socialism inevitably also followed. Capital, the extra-parliamentary force *par excellence,* could exercise political power as a matter of course through the capitalist state — i.e. its own political command structure of which Parliament is only a part, and by no means the decisive one. By contrast, the 'economic arm' of labour (the trades unions) were confined to the strictly limited economic domain, and labour's 'political arm' (the reformist socialdemocratic parties) to the bourgeois self-serving rules of the parliamentary game, — established a long time before the working class was allowed to participate in political legislation in a structurally entrapped and therefore necessarily subordinate position. In this way 'evolutionary socialism' condemned itself to 'evolving' absolutely nowhere beyond the 'practicable' and by capital in its own favour predetermined 'economic realities'.[97]

But despite all of capital's successes and labour's self-paralyzing accommodations the uncontrollability of the system itself could not be remedied. Instead of gradually progressing towards Alfred Marshall's (according to him 'in the course of being accomplished') Utopia of capitalist chivalry — a condition which was supposed to secure higher and higher achievements thanks to the happily paid high taxes of risk-taking entrepreneurs and to the proper education of the working classes for appreciating 'economic reality' and for accepting their moral and political obligations implicit in it — the antagonistic contradictions of capitalist society already in Marshall's lifetime erupted in the form of a most devastating imperialist conflagration, co-involving the entire world (for the first time ever) in the 'Great War' lasting four long years. As to the postulated National Socialist solution, defined as the harmonious fusion of chivalrous businessmen with the 'rational' sections of the working class — people who would hold the conviction that it was possible to 'rise above the fear that no country can move faster than the others' without trampling upon the others in order to avoid becoming 'bereft of capital' — this strategy, far from leading to a state 'full of individuality and elasticity', resulted in the monstrous inhumanities of Hitler's national and global adventure. Besides, such a grave turn of events in Germany and elsewhere did not come about without the active complicity, for several years, of powerful sections of foreign capital, nurturing its own 'International project' to liquidate forever through Hitler's and Mussolini's agency Marx's 'mechanical International' socialist project.

3.2.3

ECONOMISTS viewing the world from capital's vantage point cannot simply ignore the structural uncontrollability of their cherished system, no matter how much they might wish to do away with the underlying contradictions. Depending on the given stage of historical development, the difficulties of control are more or less prominent in their conceptualizations, but no one can completely avoid them.

Adam Smith, writing in the age of capital's dynamic historical ascendancy and the dawn of its global expansion — that is, at a time when his own fight against mercantilist protectionism represented a real progress — could well content himself with brief references to the 'invisible hand' as not only the evidence for but also the benevolent solution of the system's uncontrollability by the individual capitalists. No such straightforward solution was awailable to his late 19th and early 20th century successors when, in sharp contrast to Adam Smith's age, the second half of the 18th century, all further territorial expansion of the capital system had been terminated in the form of the rival imperialist carve-up of the entire planet, and of necessity the prospect of major systemic crises entered the horizon. John Stuart Mill's 'stationary state' already foreshadowed some of the dangers implicit in the coming closure not only territorially — which could be in principle reopened through the 'zero-sum game' of imperialist wars in favour of the victors and at the expense of the defeated — but in terms of the constraints imposed in the future on the productive expansion of the capital system as a whole. Significantly, therefore, in the 'new economics' of Mill's successors all the dark shadows had to be removed; and the 'stationary state' had to be turned into a pillar of apologetic economic wisdom through its transformation into an openly admitted 'convenient' technical device in terms of which all of the arbitrarily adopted *assumptions* of 'scientific economics' could be proclaimed to correspond to the *'normal'* state of affairs.

In Adam Smith's scheme of things the 'invisible' hand fully solved the identified problem and thereby assigned to the individual capitalists the satisfactory operational control of their part in the system. Thus there was no reason for Smith to indulge in inventing a bewildering network of assumptions through which the dominant but by labour contested values of the capital system could be readily justified. Under the new circumstances, however, responsibility for the system's actual mode of operation — and, of course, for its potential defects and crises — had to be spread as wide as possible in order to deflect and neutralize criticism. To quote Joan Robinson, according to Mill's successors

Each employer of factors [of production] seeks to minimize the cost of his product and to maximize his own return, each particle of a factor seeks the employment that maximizes its income and each consumer plans his consumption to maximize utility.

There is one equilibrium position in which each individual is doing the best for himself, so that no one has any incentive to move. (For groups to combine to better themselves collectively is strictly against the rules.) In this position each individual is receiving an income governed by the marginal productivity of the type of factor that he provides, and marginal productivity is governed by scarcity relatively to demand. Here 'capital' is a factor like all the rest, and the distinction between work and property has disappeared from view. Setting the whole thing out in algebra is a great help. The symmetrical relations between x and y seem smooth and amiable, entirely free from the associations of acrimony which are apt to be suggested by the relations between 'capital' and 'labour'; and the apparent rationality of the system of distribution of the product between the factors of production conceals the arbitrary nature of the distribution of factors between the chaps.[98]

Thus the concept of 'sovereign subject' which is supposed to 'plan' the 'normal' functioning of the socioeconomic metabolism and to which responsibility for the encountered economic problems and 'dysfunctions' could be legitimately ascribed embraced in equal measure the totality of individuals in society. Accordingly, the very idea of contesting the system as such in collective terms could be ruled out of court as utterly irrational. For in the neatly streamlined accounts of 'marginal utility theory' all such contestations must have been based on a total misunderstanding of the 'factors of production' as well as of their constituent parts or 'particles' which were predestined to define in the interest of all the nature of the established order of production and distribution. At the same time, the use of algebra and suitable diagrams not only removed the real actors — capital and labour — from the historical stage but also created the semblance of great scientific rigour in dealing with the subject matter of 'Economics' supplying the best possible tools for the healthy functioning of the system.

Naturally, there could be no question of challenging the individual capitalist's ideal suitability to fulfil the functions assigned to him in this scheme. For, as Marshall argued, 'no fairly good substitute has been found, or seems likely to be found, for the bracing fresh air which a *strong man with a chivalrous yearning for leadership* draws into his lungs when he sets out on *a business experiment at his own risk*'.[99] Indeed, remaining wedded to the idealization of the individual capitalist, Marshall insisted that 'If he [the businessman] is working at his own risk, he can put forth his energies with perfect freedom. But if he is a servant of bureaucracy, he cannot be certain of freedom'. Accordingly, Marshall passed utterly negative judgement on the control structure not only of the 'industrial undertakings of Governments' but also of *very large joint-stock companies*':[100] an attitude radically reversed at the next stage of trying to control capital's inherent uncontrollability, as we shall see in Section 3.3 of the present study. The courageously risk-taking and innovative businessman/entrepreneur remained for Mill's successors the proper intermediary figure who would perfectly facilitate for the totality of individual consumers the maximization and harmonization of their interests, acting without interference from the freedom-denying bureaucratic forces.

As mentioned above, Edgeworth characterized Marshall — and through the writings of the latter what he himself considered the essential feature and the most important achievement of the new economics in general — as 'bearing under the garb of literature the armour of mathematics'. In truth, however, such a claim was by no means justified. For the 'mathematical armour' was in fact no armour at all; it would be much more appropriate to call it 'mathematical garb'. The real armour was something else, providing a consciously produced defensive shield against the socialist critics of the capital system. Indeed, given the *conceptual structure* of the new economics — and not its *mathematical garb* which gave it the appearance of 'hard-headed' and 'tough-minded' scientific rigour — the defensive shield of the so-called 'subjective revolution' had to be considered in its own terms of reference quite impregnable.

Here it is important to remember the link of marginal utility theory to one of its forefathers, utilitarianism. For in the new economics the key orienting principle of *'equilibrium'* is inextricably tied to the notion of the individuals' *'utility maximization'*. Everything else is built around these two principles which are never *established*, but always *assumed*. They reciprocally and quasi-axiomatically support one another, constituting thereby the real armour of the theory. According to the believers in the 'subjective revolution', the irrepressible drive of the — by their 'human nature' so determined — individuals for maximizing their utilities brings about the happy economic condition of equilibrium; and by the same token, economic equilibrium itself is the required condition under which the maximization of the utilities of all individuals predestined for the purpose of selfish utility-maximization can be — and for good measure actually is being — accomplished.

This impregnable circular reasoning provides the theoretical framework in which assumptions can run riot, enabling the economists concerned to derive the desired conclusions from the earlier enunciated 'assumptions' and 'suppositions', without any need to subject them to the test of actuality. (This is how we are offered explanations in terms of 'general equilibrium', 'perfect competition', 'competitive equilibrium', 'perfect freedom of exchange', etc., etc.) If discrepancies and anomalies appear for some reason, that can be also quite easily remedied by the attribute of 'normal' as the convenient qualifier and help to put the derailed carriage back on the rails, or, with better apologetic foresight, to prevent it from being derailed by the intrusion of reality. 'Normal' is whatever needs to be defined in that way in order to fit the requirements of the theory. Indeed the category of 'normality' is used in great abundance, from Stanley Jevons (as we have seen earlier with reference to his 'corrective' to his own sun-spots theory of periodic crises) to everybody else, including Marshall who uses it hundreds of times as an obliging self-referential escape-clause in his *Principles of Economics* and in his other writings.[101]

When it comes to the concept of utility, the ubiquitous individualistic assumptions conveniently remove the potentially most embarrassing question in relation to the real world — as opposed to the tendentiously assumed 'economic realities', — namely: 'whose utility' are we talking about. For if it is stipulated from the outset that the maximization of utilities is a strictly individual matter — and therefore the ongoing process of maximization adequately covers all individuals who are themselves responsible for pursuing their own strategies in the best possible way for themselves, and thereby indirectly also for all — in that case the most problematical and disturbing reality of *actually existing power relations* into which the individuals are inserted completely disappears from sight. Not surprisingly, therefore, the concept of 'power relations' is conspicuous in the writings of all the marginalist economists by its absence. They are happy to depict their own world of 'economic realities' in strictly individualistic terms when in the actually observable world the ever-intensifying tendency of *monopolistic* transformations — with all its brute force for nullifying the decision making power of the individuals, including even that of the idealized 'risk-taking and innovative entrepreneurs' — is staring them in the eye.

A great deal has been written about the so-called 'naturalistic fallacy' concerning 'pleasure' and the 'desirable' in utilitarian discourse. However, the real fallacy of utilitarian philosophy — fully embraced in one form or another by the representatives of marginal utility theory — is to talk about *'the greatest happiness of the greatest number'* in *capitalist* society. For the suggestion that anything even remotely approaching the greatest happiness of the greatest number of human beings can be achieved under the rule of capital, without even examining let alone radically changing the established power relations, constitutes a monumental vacuous assumption, whatever the subjective intentions of the major utilitarian philosophers behind it. Marginal utility theory, instead of acting in this respect as a corrective to Bentham and Mill, makes everything worse by asserting not only that it is possible to maximize every individual's utility within the established framework of production and distribution, but also that the desired maximization is actually being accomplished in the 'normal' processes of self-equilibrating capitalist economy. People who deny the reality of such a happy state of affairs are dismissed even by the enlightened paternalist Alfred Marshall by saying that 'they nearly always divert energies from sober work for the public good, and are thus mischievous in the long run'.[102]

In this way even the indirect acknowledgement of capital's uncontrollability does not last very long. Admitting that the controlling power of the businessman/entrepreneur cannot account for the functioning of the system, let alone guarantee the satisfaction of the wants generated under capitalism, does not lead to a badly needed critical examination. On the contrary, the broadest possible extension of the notion of the controlling subject (done in such a way that it fictitiously embraces the totality of individuals) — which is another way of saying that no identifiable subject is really in control, other than what Hegel characterized with the notion of 'bad infinity' — is used for the most apologetic purpose. For with the help of this extension and individualistic harmonization of all 'legitimate' claims the actually existing class subjects of the system — capital and labour — are fictitiously 'transcended' towards 'bad infinity', thereby simply *assuming out of existence* the problems and antagonistic contradictions of the established socioeconomic order. The mathematical and 'scientific' garb in which this conceptual framework of *assuming out of existence the dilemmas of control* is dressed up well serves the purpose of removing the temptation of contesting the various tenets of the 'subjective revolution' and 'marginalist revolution' in other than the purely self-referential 'rational' terms of the theory, far away from actual substantive social — not to say class — issues.

If in the end the problem of uncontrollability is still contemplated by some of the marginalist and 'neo-classical' economists, it is done in a characteristic way. Edgeworth, for instance, refers to what he calls the *'controlless core'* of human affairs in his discussion of utilitarian theory.[103] However, his purpose is not the

investigation of the objective social relations and identifiable economic determinations of the given system of production and distribution, with a view to
finding some remedy to uncontrollability, but, on the contrary, an attempt to
freeze and turn into an unalterable absolute the identified defect. For in his view
the ineradicable core of controllessness is a characteristic of *human nature* itself.
To counteract its consequences 'It would have to be first shown that the interest
of all is the interest of each, an *illusion* to which the ambiguous language of Mill,
and perhaps Bentham, may have lent some countenance'.[104]

Comparing Marshall with Jevons as originators of the new 'scientific economics' Keynes wrote in his celebratory essay published in the *Memorials of Alfred
Marshall* volume:

> Jevons saw the kettle boil and cried out with the delighted voice of a child; Marshall
> too had seen the kettle boil and sat down silently to build an engine.[105]

Perhaps so — even though the judgement seems rather harsh on Jevons — but
to what effect? For Marshall himself was in his later years somewhat dissatisfied
with his own steam engine. He wrote, accordingly, that 'The Mecca of the
economist is *economic biology* rather than *economic dynamics*'.[106] And, without
intending to, in the same article he also revealed the secret of why the economists
of his own liking could never reach their Mecca. He proclaimed that 'The chief
difficulties of economic science now arise *rather from the good than from the evil
fortunes of mankind*'.[107] This he did at a time when the overwhelming majority
of humankind lived — as it does today, almost one hundred years after
Marshall's sanguine diagnosis — in the most abject poverty. Thus, just like
Keynes himself[108] who ten years later criticized Marshall for very different
reasons, the representatives of the new 'scientific economics' could not see
anything wrong with totally divorcing in their theoretical considerations the
conditions of the privileged imperialistic countries in which they lived from those
of the 'wretched of the earth' at the receiving end of their system. It was not
the insufficiency of statistical data, as Marshall claimed, that had to prevent
them from reaching the Mecca of their claimed scientific anticipations even in
a thousand years. Rather, their necessary failure was due to the fact that they
could formulate their diagnoses and solutions in such conveniently separate
compartments, against the painfully obvious evidence of a hierarchically structured and globally intertwined world.

The actually existing capital system took no notice of the wishful thinking
and corresponding remedies of control advocated by the marginalist and neo-
classical believers in its steady progress towards the happy 'solution of mankind's
economic problem', as Keynes went on promising it even in 1930, disregarding
the sobering evidence of a grave world economic crisis. Instead, capital continued inexorably on its own uncontrollable course of development which became
theorized by its faithful defenders at the next stage under the promising label
of yet another 'revolution'.

The newfound answer to the structural deficiencies of control was no longer
called 'the marginalist revolution' and 'the subjective revolution' — although,
of course, in the new theory the old claims to scientific rigour and sound
evaluation of the 'economic realities' remained as strong as in the writings of
the neo-classical predecessors — but 'the managerial revolution'. By adopting
such orientation, the new conception of how to gain control over the encoun-

tered 'dysfunctions' — of which there were far too many in evidence in the period of the great world crisis of 1929-33, when the first theories of 'the managerial revolution' were articulated in some detail — abandoned the earlier idealized notion of the risk-taking and innovative businessman/entrepreneur as the pivot of the capital system. The remedial powers ascribed to the managers in the new approach constituted the third typical way of addressing and by the same stroke happily resolving the stubborn problem of uncontrollability. This is what we must now consider.

3.3 From the 'Managerial Revolution' to postulating 'technostructure convergence'

3.3.1

ONE of the main characteristics of the many 'revolutions' in the field of economic theory — to which the 'Keynesian revolution' and the 'monetarist revolution' must be also added, not to mention the subsequent use of the 'second industrial revolution', the 'green revolution', the 'information revolution', etc. for deflecting criticism from the capital system — is the curious insistence on the necessity and absolute virtue of *gradualism*. We have seen how Marshall combined his neo-classical 'scientific revolution' with the firmest possible prescription that social and economic changes should never be envisaged as potentially revolutionizing the established state of affairs. They had to be conceived, instead, as a way of slowly and gradually improving the standard of living in the spirit of his utopian vision, so as to be able to run society on capital's permanent material ground — i.e strictly within the existing parameters of the system — with the enlightened generosity of his 'chivalrous' risk-taking entrepreneurs. And even if the other claimants to the exalted status of 'initiators of revolution in Economics' did not share his illusions about capitalist 'chivalry' and 'National Socialism', none the less they all sided with the *absolute imperative of gradualism*, without entertaining doubts even for a moment over the logical consistency of their position. Evidently their heart-felt belief in militant anti-socialism — which made Keynes aggressively state that 'the class war will find me on the side of the educated bourgeoisie'[109] — was more than enough to completely satisfy them on that score. In this way they could go on proclaiming with boundless intellectual self-assurance that the one and only rational meaning of 'theoretical revolution' in their field was to erect and defend the barriers of capital-eternalizing gradualism against all socialist-inspired — and not only the Marxian — strategies of actual social and political revolutions. The expropriation of the term 'revolution' was most useful, and became intellectually respectable, precisely with regard to what Keynes openly admitted to be his 'class war'.

Naturally, many of the marginalist and neo-classical tenets of Economics remained almost completely unaltered in the celebrated economic textbooks of the new phase, including in a prominent place the apologetic use of 'utility-maximization' and the concomitant justification of the established order of production and distribution with reference to the mythical 'consumer' set against the worker. However, such theoretical overlaps do not concern us in the present context where the issue is the altered theorization of capitalist control under the new circumstances.

In the economic and sociological literature a famous book published in 1932 by Berle and Means is counted as the first landmark of the new orientation.[110] However, Paul Sweezy made the necessary corrective when he wrote that

> If I were asked to date the beginning of a distinctively bourgeois theory of the capitalist system as it has taken shape in the twentieth century, I think I would cite Schumpeter's article, 'The Instability of Capitalism', which appeared in the *Economic Journal* in September 1928. There we not only find the giant corporation or trust as a characteristic feature of the system; even more important, this economic unit, so foreign to the whole corpus of classical and neoclassical theory, provides the basis for new and important theoretical propositions. It will be recalled that in the Schumpeterian theory as set forth in *The Theory of Economic Development,* innovation is the function of the individual entrepreneur and that it is from the activity of innovating entrepreneurs that all the dynamic features of the system are directly or indirectly derived. ... In 'The Instability of Capitalism', however, Schumpeter places the innovative function no longer in the individual entrepreneur but in the big corporation. At the same time innovation is reduced to a routine carried out by teams of specialists educated and trained for their jobs. In the Schumpeterian scheme of things, these are absolutely basic changes destined to produce equally basic changes in capitalism's *modus operandi.*[111]

Understandably, it was very difficult for economists who theorized the social world from the vantage point and in the interest of capital to give up the idea of the entrepreneur/innovator. For the abundant benefits claimed to arise from the exercise of such a role for society as a whole provided the much needed justification for the capitalist expropriation of surplus-value (called 'reward', or 'interest', etc., while always denying, of course, the fact of exploitation), i.e. for the practicably most intensive extraction of surplus-labour and its conversion into profit on which the normal functioning of the system was based. This may explain why it took such a long time even to attempt to come to grips with the change in capital's control structure, despite the fact that the inexorable growth of 'very large joint-stock companies' — as Marshall called them — was clearly in evidence already in the last quarter of the 19th century, and the allegedly 'obsolete' Marx recognized their growing significance at the time of their first appearance. It was much easier and ideologically most convenient to quixotically dismiss them, as Marshall did on account of their 'bureaucratism'. Equally, it was in general much easier to treat for as long as possible the new — unmistakably corporatist — structures of production and control more as 'aberrations' and 'exceptions'. For the admission that they were about to become the *rule* was bound to wreak havoc with the long-established and far from scientific legitimatory theories of the capitalist order. In fact in the aftermath of the grave world economic crisis of 1929-33 and the continued depression lasting for almost another decade, and relieved only when the economy had to be put on an emergency footing well after the outbreak of the second world war — when, that is, it had to be acknowledged that the new 'economic realities' were not only given but also *dominant,* instead of being considered reversible exceptions and aberrations — the old type of ideologically well established legitimation could not be maintained any longer. It had to give way to the depersonalized blanket justification according to which the ruling order was preferable to all possible alternatives because it was the *'most efficient'* and the only one capable of *'delivering the goods'*.

This line of argument was much weaker for justifying the permanence of a deeply iniquitous system than the earlier one, exposing itself also to the danger of being attacked in case of failure in efficiency and in the event of faltering with regard to the promise of 'delivering the goods'. For in favour of the entrepreneur's expropriation of surplus value (or his 'preferential share in the surplus product') it could be argued that he deserved it on account of 'risk-taking' and the pursued objective of 'innovation', irrespective of how well or how badly he succeeded in his business ventures. Failures could be considered partial and 'immediately punished' (in the same way as the successes were said to be 'properly rewarded'), and therefore could not affect negatively the legitimacy of the system as a whole even under the conditions of major 'commercial revulsions', as Jevons called the periodic crises. All this changed for the worse when 'delivering the goods' had to become the legitimatory ground of the capitalist order. Not surprisingly, therefore, in due course the new legitimatory claims of private capitalism had to be strengthened again by inventing a fictitious but allegedly quite inextricable link between 'freedom and democracy' (or 'free political choice') on the one hand, and 'free economic choice in a market society' on the other, as we have seen in Section 2.1.2 with reference to the fashionable editorial sermon of the London *Economist*. Without this intrusion of a substantially *political* justification into the system — that is, without the adoption of a most peculiar crutch as an important part of the new ideological arsenal of private capitalism — the claimed legitimacy would have been very shaky indeed. For corporatist 'planning' and scientific/technological mastery fell far short of proving their great 'efficiency', and (with an alarming tendency for getting worse rather than resolving the no longer deniable problems by maintaining the earlier pattern of growth) they failed to 'deliver the goods' to countless millions of unemployed people even in the most privileged 'advanced capitalist' countries. Thus, whereas the enthusiastic apologists of the new managerial phase — Talcott Parsons, for instance, as we shall see in a moment — hailed the corporatist developments as the right and proper separation of politics and economics and as the earlier not even imaginable flourishing of economics in its finally attained purity and 'emancipation from politics', the 'economic realities' themselves moved in the opposite direction. They did this not just through the appearance of symbiotic economico/political formations, like the military-industrial complex, but even more so through the necessary failure of a system in which such direct state-subsidy-dependent formations had to be assigned a vital role, storing up great problems for the future.

Another major complication of the new developments concerned the 'subjectless subject' of the capital system. For in the course of twentieth century transformations the 'innovative entrepreneur' had been pushed to the periphery of the system from its strategic core, and the much resented 'very large bureaucratic joint-stock companies' of Alfred Marshall — in the form of immensely powerful monopolistic corporations — came to occupy the centre stage of capital's rule over society. In this way the circle stretching from Adam Smith's individual capitalist (who was supposed to be ideally competent for his 'local situation') through the 'buccaneering entrepreneur' and 'captain of industry' (who conquered and kept firmly under his personal supervision a much vaster terrain) to the corporate manager and 'expert' (mandated to carry out strictly defined tasks in the interest of the giant company which he served) had been irretrievably closed. And through this change of form of the supervisory personnel it became also palpably obvious (to all those, that is, who did not have a vested interest in blinding themselves even to the obvious) that the individual capitalists and managers were only the 'personifications of capital', exercising control in any particular form on its behalf and readily assuming a very different form whenever the altered historical conditions of capital's by conscious human agency uncontrollable mode of social metabolic control so decreed.

To be sure, it could never be admitted that — notwithstanding all theoretical and practical mystification — the real subject of the social reproductive metabolism under the rule of capital remains labour and not the personifications of capital in whatever shape or form. Even when it was asserted — whether under the title of the 'Managerial Revolution' (apologetically celebrated by the ex-communist James Burnham[112] who belonged to what Merleau-Ponty castigated as 'the league of abandoned hope, a brotherhood of renegades'[113]) or in even sharper contrast to the older varieties of control under Galbraith's conceptualization of the allegedly omniscient and omnipotent *technostructure* — that the established order of production and distribution was run by *structural determinations,* rather than by personal initiative, this was done with an apologetic intent, unmindful of the enormity and perilous implications of what had been acknowledged.

The pernicious marginalization of human rationality and personal responsibility in the course of capital's historical unfolding repeatedly underlined the system's uncontrollability. Yet after every belatedly acknowledged change in the control structure of capital the problematical character of the underlying process whereby enormous shifts occur without prior human design was never queried by the defenders of the system. Quite the contrary, the accomplished facts were always presented as change for the better, indeed as the best possible state of affairs destined to endure — and rightfully so — forever in the future, and maybe even thereafter. It could never be admitted that the ultimate logic of such blind, uncontrollable transformations which periodically had to be recognized (and of course after every forced recognition immediately celebrated) as the ultimate 'revolution' in economic affairs may be in fact the destruction of humanity, and therefore some meaningful alternative to the prevailing trends should be contemplated.

However, no viable alternative to capital's social metabolic order could be invented out of some ideal desiderata. It could only be constituted on the existing material ground of society by the repressed real subject of the given system of socioeconomic reproduction, labour, through the necessary mediations which could overcome the rule of capital over the producers. But precisely because the only actually feasible alternative to capital's uncontrollable mode of control had to centre on labour — and not on the various utopian postulates of bourgeois economic theory, like Adam Smith's benevolent 'hidden hand', or Alfred Marshall's National Socialism-instituting 'chivalrous capitalists', or Galbraith's 'convergence-producing' and universally beneficial 'technostructure', etc. — the thought of such an alternative could never be entertained by the people who tried to theorize (and eulogize) the yet again happy solution of the established system's structural uncontrollability.

3.3.2

THE *aprioristic* rejection of the socialist alternative — as managed by the real subject of production — carried with it the necessity of explaining everything in terms suitable to be used against the real or potential socialist adversary. There were some noble exceptions, like Schumpeter himself, who in the light of the historically unfolding evidence tried to reassess matters in a different way, expressing a more positive attitude towards the possibility of socialistic changes in the future. However, the rule remained the kind of militant anti-socialism which we have encountered above more than once already, vitiating not only the solutions offered to the identified problems but even the diagnosis of particular historical situations. For the claimed happy outcome of the new developments had to be described in such a way that it could be directly turned into yet another final refutation of any need for the socialist alternative.

Thus Talcott Parsons eagerly adopted the Berle & Means thesis on 'the separation of ownership and control'[114] in order to be able to proclaim that the socialist critique of the property relations of the established order no longer applied (if ever it did[115]), because 'many large corporations had come under the effective control of career "managers" whose personal ownership of securities in the firm was only of nominal significance as an instrument of control'.[116] Presumably, then, the no longer capitalistic 'career managers' of the Parsonian fairy tale bought giant packs of jelly babies with their 'only nominally significant securities' and chivalrously distributed them among the needy children of the 'deserving poor'. But be that as it may, the socialist critique did not concern the smaller or larger number of shares owned by the individual personifications of capital — be they 'buccaneering entrepreneurs' or 'humble career managers' — but the structural subordination of labour to capital (and precisely that was, as indeed also remains, the non-fetishistic meaning of the established property relations and the focus of its socialist critique) of which nothing whatsoever had changed through the celebrated 'managerial revolution'. In other words, the issue was — and still is — the permanence of *class* domination and dependency, and not the relative change of form in one or another constituent part of capital's ruling personnel within its substantively unaltered hierarchical command structure; a change of form made necessary by the ongoing centralization and concentration of capital which could not remove but only intensify the inner antagonisms of the capital system.

According to Talcott Parsons 'Schumpeter despaired of the future of free enterprise or capitalism, and posited the inevitability of socialism'.[117] But, in Parsons' view, his fear was based on a failure to understand the meaning of the momentous changes taking place in the twentieth century. To quote from *Economy and Society:*

> Schumpeter failed to appreciate the importance of the third possibility. Contrary to much previous opinion we feel that 'classical capitalism', characterized by the dominance of the role of ownership in the productive process, is *not a case of full 'emancipation' of the economy from 'political' control,* but rather a particular mode of such control. ... [But the modern type of economy] is neither capitalism in the classical

(and, we think, Marxist) sense nor socialism... The development of 'big government', such a conspicuous phenomenon of modern society, is, therefore, by no means incompatible in principle with the continuing growth of a non-socialist economy. ... We suggest, therefore, that the kinship-property combination typical of classical capitalism was, in the nature of the case, a temporary and unstable one. Both economic and political differentiation were *destined,* unless social developments stopped altogether, to proceed toward 'bureaucratization', toward differentiation between economy and polity and between ownership and control[118].

Thus we were assured that there was absolutely no need to be worried about the ongoing transformations, let alone to entertain the idea of a possible crisis leading to the breakdown of the capitalist social order. For the 'third possibility' apparently ignored by Schumpeter — who theorized the problem of corporatist developments well before Berle and Means, even if not to the liking of Talcott Parsons — provided the guarantee for the undisturbed future course of development of the no longer capitalist 'modern type of economy'. Moreover, we were also assured that this kind of felicitous development did not just come about as a matter of contingent historical transformation, but was *destined* to be realized (god only knows why and how) if there was to be any social development at all.

The fact that everything so reassuringly described in *Economy and Society* rested on the *counter-factual* proposition that what was being accomplished represented the 'full "emancipation" of the economy from "political" control' — when in fact the magnitude of the capitalist state's direct and indirect involvement in the 'modern type of economy' had never been even remotely comparable to its newly reached and ever-extending size, and by no means only in the multifaceted domain of the military-industrial complex (which made the Parsonian diagnosis of the situation fundamentally false) — and that 'bureaucratization' (rather deprecated by Alfred Marshall: the neo-classical theoretical backbone of *Economy and Society*) was very much a part of the optimistically described process, all this was handled with a self-assuring apologetic touch. For against all possible critical objections, suitable definitions and redefinitions of the key terms could be always provided — a vice adopted by Parsons from his idol, Max Weber — as foreshadowed in the last quoted passage by the curious inverted commas around the terms 'emancipation', 'political' and 'bureaucratization', in the same way as in the passage quoted in note 115 we found them around 'the new economy', 'exploitation of labour', and 'capitalistic control'. Thus the economy could and also could not be emancipated from political control, whichever way the cause of apology in a particular context would stipulate it; and 'bureaucratization' could and also could not be taking place in 'the new type of economy', depending on how well or how badly its presence would reflect on the 'inescapably differentiated' (hence soundly bureaucratized) or 'consumer-sovereignty-securing' (hence not really bureaucratic but ideally marketized) free and democratic society. In the same way, there could be absolutely no question of economic recessions and crises thanks to 'the great output of new products to a high-wage consuming public', nor indeed of social conflict directed at the *ruling class*. For the idea of an objectionable 'ruling class' was introduced — again in inverted commas, which turned it even retrospectively into a 'not really objectionable' quasi-ruling class only — at the point of its soothing disappearance, just like the concepts of 'exploitation of labour' and 'capitalistic control' were treated at an earlier point. To quote Parsons:

> For a brief historical moment American capitalism appeared to be creating a new Schumpeterian 'ruling class' of family dynasties founded by the 'captains of industry'. But this moment passed early in the present century, and the trend since then is clear — the *occupational* manager, not the lineage-based owner, is the key figure in the American economic structure.[119]

And all this was presented as if the 'occupational manager' did not belong to the actually existing ruling class (without mystifying inverted commas), occupying in fact a key position at the top echelon of capital's command structure even if he happened to be a batchelor sworn not to start a new lineage. This is how the ongoing socioeconomic changes — which clearly manifested capital's uncontrollability even by its most devoted personifications — were taken on board by the ideologists of the system only for the purpose of deriving ammunition from them against socialists, in the service of the most transparent apologetics of the established order.

3.3.3

ELEVEN years after the publication of the Parsonian tale of *Economy and Society*, John Kenneth Galbraith, in a book entitled *The New Industrial State* tried to improve on the earlier theorizations of the 'modern type of economy' by bringing his readers up to date with regard to the transformations recently accomplished, or in the process of being accomplished, in his view under the pressure of technology. He did not content himself with an account covering only the Western capitalistically advanced countries but offered what he claimed to be a universal theoretical explanation of the 'converging industrial structure' of East and West, allegedly arising from the irresistible demands of their progressively shared 'technostructure'. To quote a key passage:

> In the industrial enterprise, power rests with those who make decisions. In the *mature enterprise,* this power has passed, *inevitably and irrevocably,* from the individual to the group. That is because only the group has the information that decision requires. Though the constitution of the corporation places power in the hands of the owners, the *imperatives of technology and planning* remove it to the *technostructure.* Since *technology and planning* are what accord power to the technostructure, the latter will have power wherever these are a feature of the production process. Its power will not be peculiar to what, in the cadenzas of ideology, is called the free enterprise or capitalist system. If the intervention of private authority, in the form of owners, must be prevented in the private firm, so must the intervention of public authority in the public firm. ...As a further consequence, puzzlement over capitalism without control by the capitalist will be matched by puzzlement over socialism without control by the society.[120]

This approach, with its assertion of the 'inevitability and irrevocability' of technology's impact on the New Industrial State, represented yet another version of *technological determinism,* as Sweezy rightly stressed.[121] The great convenience of this approach, centred upon the notion of 'technostructure', was that — analogously to the sun-spots of Jevons — everything under the sun could be aprioristically rejected or approved in its name. Thus the crude determinist theory built on Galbraith's idealization of the 'technostructure' could be used not only to attempt to deliver the knock-out blow to the original socialist project — dimissed as 'ancient and impractical' on page 109 of the book

— but also to embrace as positive the 'inevitable and irrevocable' industrial practices of both the capitalist West and the allegedy converging Soviet system. In this way the fiction of 'capitalism without control by the capitalist' was turned into a most peculiar form of legitimation of the Soviet type 'socialism without control by the society'.

Despite the studiously striking terminological differences Galbraith's theory was a version of the 'managerial revolution', contrasting what the author called 'the Mature Corporation' with the 'Entrepreneurial Corporation'[122] — both with capital letters. And it was strange that Galbraith should think that this terminological innovation represented a theoretical advance. For whereas both 'entrepreneurial' and 'managerial' denoted something specific and identifiable, 'mature' (or 'Mature') sounded rather vacuous by contrast. Its only rational meaning in the context to which it was applied consisted in the arbitrary postulate of the absolute permanence of the finally attained mature type of industrial enterprise. For the author of *The New Industrial State* could be the last one to concede that after 'maturity' might come senility. Thus the apologetic intent of the otherwise vacuous term — exactly as we find it in the writings of Walt Rostow with whom Galbraith used to brainstorm in President Kennedy's select Brains Trust — was meant to underline that the problem of control had been happily solved and it would make no sense at all to ask what other forms might emerge in the future. Divergent forms of business enterprise presented no problem. In the time-honoured tradition of arbitrary assertions and circular definitions they could be handled with the help of a *tautology,* by saying that the big firms — the small ones did not count — which could not be accommodated within the framework of the new category 'have yet to reach *full maturity* of organization'.[123]

Just like in the Parsonian account, also in Galbraith's New Industrial State the fiction was maintained that 'The men who now run the large corporations own no appreciable share of the enterprise'.[124] Their multi-million dollar annual salaries, mysterious bonuses and preferential share options obviously counted for 'no appreciable share' — the jelly baby syndrome, again. And worse still was in store for these poor men. For according to Galbraith's humorous assertion 'those who hold high formal rank in an organization — the President of General Motors or General Electric — exercise only modest powers of substantive decision'.[125] One could only wonder in amazement, why on earth they do it?! Moreover, this account of the incomprehensibly selfless motivation and behaviour of the top personnel — while everybody else was supposed to be incurably 'selfish by nature' — was coupled with the suggestion that capitalist control had given way through 'the loss of power by stockholders' and 'the dwindling magnetism of the banker' to its happy alternative in the form of 'the increasingly energetic search for industrial talent, the new prestige of education and educators'.[126]

Naturally, all this was done in the interest of making the fact of capitalist *class domination* disappear. And if despite all of Galbraith's idealizing claims it had to be admitted that the top echelon of capital's command structure was confined to an extremely narrow circle — indeed the 'mutual beneficial society' of a self-appointing vicious circle — even such an uncomfortable fact was not allowed to disturb the bucolic technostructural picture. The give-away circumstance of capital's effectively prevailing vicious circle had to be transfigured into something perfectly understandable and acceptable — the manifestation of a universal but quite innocuous human frailty. This was accomplished with the help of a frivolous witticism according to which the men who (without an appreciable share in the 'fully Mature Enterprise' and with very modest powers of substantive decision making) run the large technostructural corporations are in fact 'selected not by the stockholders but, in the common case, by a Board of Directors which *narcissistically* they selected themselves'.[127]

By the time Galbraith's book was published the Parsonian illusions about the 'full emancipation of economics from politics' could no longer be voiced, let alone seriously believed. Thus it was conceded that under the new circumstances it is a commonplace that the relation of the state to the economy has changed. The services of Federal, state and local governments now account for between a fifth and a quarter of all economic activity. In 1929 it was about eight percent.[128] But, again, this was done with a totally uncritical attitude towards the existent. The fact that 'there is a *close fusion of the industrial system with the state*'[129] gave no cause for concern to Galbraith. On the contrary, he not only took its allegedly unproblematical character for granted but went further than that and prophesied with eager approval that 'the mature corporation, as it develops, becomes part of the larger administrative complex associated with the state. In time the line between the two will disappear'.[130]

Indeed, the wishfully apologetic characterization was not confined to the capitalistic West but embraced Brezhnev's Soviet system as well. For the author of *The New Industrial State* insisted that 'convergence between the two ostensibly different sytems occurs at all fundamental points.'[131] The arguments about this fictitious convergence centred upon the proposition that both systems operate on the basis of '*planning*'. But as a matter of fact neither of the two systems could have anything even remotely resembling genuine and viable planning. In the Soviet system the term was usurped for a system of *arbitrary central directives* which turned out to be unrealizable and fatally flawed for a multiplicity of reasons, in a prominent place among them the necessary failure of the forced political extraction of surplus-labour foundering on the recalcitrance of an unmotivated, indeed in many respects hostile labour force. As to the 'planning' practised in the Western capitalist system of Mature Enterprise — i.e. in plain language the giant monopolistic transnational corporation — it could be at best *partial* and even in that respect subject to the potentially disastrous consequences of 'commercial revulsions' and periodic crises.

In Galbraith's own account such 'planning' was in fact no more than pure wishful thinking on the one hand, or utter fallacy on the other. In the first category we find repeated assertions to the effect that 'planning *must* replace the market,'[132] without the slightest attempt to demonstrate how such a desideratum could be accomplished within the framework of capitalist society. Instead, the shaky postulate of the 'technostructure' served the purpose of making us believe that it has already been accomplished. The same assertion of successfully accomplished fact was made by fallaciously equating 'need', or 'must be done', with 'existing state of affairs' or 'has been done'. Thus we were presented with a list of necessarily interconnected factors — 'advanced technology, the associated use of capital, and the resulting *need for planning*'[133] — out of which we were expected to conclude that, like the other two (factually existing) members of the triad, the 'need for planning' attained the same status. Indeed the next paragraph on the same page opened with a sentence which took the facticity of planning for granted by saying that 'complexity enters with planning and is endemic thereto', whereafter the concepts of 'complexity' and 'planning' were used to circularly reinforce one another. In the end the only non-fallacious meaning of 'planning' in *The New Industrial State* was equated with the monopolistic cornering of that portion of the market which could be cornered in that way, by talking about 'that organized part of the economy in which a developed technostructure is able to *protect its profits by planning.*'[134] But this use was very far indeed from deserving the name of planning.

Combining the technological determinism of the 'technostructure' with Galbraith's postulate of 'planning' was still not enough to add up to a sustainable picture. This is why the author of *The New Industrial State* had to introduce another — equally fallacious — postulate in order to fill in the massive gaps: the state required *and capable* of solving all the remaining problems of control in the West and East alike. The argument ran like this:

> Convergence begins with modern large-scale production, with heavy *requirements* of capital, sophisticated technology and, as a prime consequence, elaborate organization. These *require control* of prices and, so far as possible, of what is bought at those prices. This is to say that planning *must* replace the market. In the Soviet-type economies, the control of prices is a *function of the state.* ... Large-scale organization also *requires autonomy.* The intrusion of an external and uninformed will is damaging. In the non-Soviet system this means *excluding the capitalist from effective control.* But the *same imperative* operates in the socialist economy. There the business firm seeks to minimize or *exclude control by the bureaucracy.* ... The industrial system has no inherent capacity for regulating total demand — for ensuring a supply of purchasing power sufficient to acquire what it produces. So it *relies on the state* for this. At full employment there is no mechanism for holding prices and wages stable. This stabilization too is a *function of the state.* The Soviet-type systems also make a careful calculation of the income that is being provided in relation to the value of the goods available for purchase.[135]

Here, again, 'requirements' and 'imperatives' were equated with fallaciously assumed abilities and achievements. The earlier quoted propositions about the necessary 'close fusion of the industrial system with the state' and about the subsequent total disappearance of the line between the 'mature corporation' and the administrative system of the state were the corollaries gratuitously guaranteeing a successful outcome. Yet, actuality refused to conform to the 'converging' technostructural 'ideal types'. For the Soviet-type system could no more 'exclude control by the bureaucracy' than the 'mature corporation' could 'exclude the capitalist from effective power'. In any case it should have been obvious to the author that it does not follow at all that just because you wish it, or 'require' it even as a matter of dramatic 'imperative', the state will be able to *deliver* what you require of it. Nor could it make much sense trying to eulogize the inescapable autonomy of the technostructural system — in the age of similarly idealized 'globalization' — with one breath and stipulate the state's even more inescapable intervention with the other. Equally, it was naively self-complacent, to put it mildly, to fantasise about the ideal setup in terms of *full employment* when the objective structural imperatives — and not the wishfully proclaimed pseudo-imperatives or 'requirements' — of 'the industrial state' (East and West alike) made impossible the reconciliation of 'productive capital-expansion' with providing work for all. It was always *inconceivable* to squeeze full employment — *ex pumice aquam* — from the global capital system. Even in the most privileged 'advanced capitalist' part of it full employement was available only for a brief historical moment, during the postwar years of expansion; by the time Galbraith's book was written the inexorable rise of unemployment had put a truly irrevocable end to the Keynesian (and by Beveridge propagandized) 'Full Employment in a Free Society' even in the dominant imperialist countries, but the author of *The New Industrial State* took no notice of it. At the same time — as always — the people in the overwhelming majority of the countries constituting the deeply iniquitous capitalist world continued to suffer the indignities and inhumanities of not marginal but *massive* unemployment. As to the Soviet-type system, its brief historical moment of full employment covered only the period of intense industrialization and postwar reconstruction, running into grave difficulties thereafter, trying to conceal them with its ultimately quite untenable *structural underemployment,* with the concomitant disastrously low level of productivity which greatly contributed to the system's implosion and collapse. These were the painfully obvious gaps between the 'requirements' to which the state as such was supposed to adequately respond, and the sobering actual ability of the respective states of the allegedly converging technostructural systems to live up to Galbraith's expectations.

3.3.4

THE main point of this kind of reasoning was to confront the reader and make him accept the brutal alternative 'between *success without social control and social control without success*'.[136] In other words, the 'alternative' meant that there could be *no alternative,* since no one in their right mind could renounce the possibility of success. The reasoning on which this pernicious conclusion was based consisted, again, in a series of unsustained proclamations. It went as follows:

> The misfortune of democratic socialism has been the misfortune of the capitalist. When the latter could no longer control, democratic socialism was no longer an alternative. The technical complexity and planning and associated scale of operations, that took power from the capitalist entrepreneur and lodged it with the technostructure, removed it also from the reach of social control.[137]

These 'arguments' fell flat already on account of the totally vacuous claim concerning the 'misfortune of the capitalist', the poor dear to whom the destiny of democratic socialism was supposed to be anchored. Nor could Galbraith's equally vacuous notion of 'planning' which we have seen above — in its circular relationship to 'complexity' — help sustain the concluding pseudo-alternative between success and social control. As to the allegedly unquestionable virtues of the proper vast scale of operations in the age of the technostructure, every self-respecting bourgeois economist was preaching the *'economy of scale'* at the time when *The New Industrial State* became a bestseller, not only Professor Galbraith. They were doing it with the same religious fervour with which they now pontificate about the *'diseconomy of scale'*. But devotion to an unsustainable belief does not make it acceptable just because the correlation hypostatized in it is maintained one day in one sense and, when the cause of apologetics so demands, in its diametrical opposite sense.

In any case, Galbraith's boundlessly self-confident assertions about what constituted *success* could not fare well at all. For the same smugness with which he dismissed the need for, and the possibility of realizing, the socialist project characterized also his positive approval of the dominant structures and practices of the capitalist system, from the 'Mature Enterprise' to the state as the facilitator of the ongoing monopolistic transformations. He noted that the share of the giant corporations which rely on massive state funds for their 'healthy' functioning was on the increase, but he could see absolutely no complications, let alone the danger of a serious economic crisis arising from such a trend. With a quite astonishing sense of unreality he simply assumed that the state had a bottomless purse eternally at the disposal of the military industrial complex.[138] This is why he could declare with dogmatic finality that *'big corporations do not lose money'.*[139] The powerless Presidents of IBM, General Motors, Ford, et al., — who were indeed most powerless not as regards making decisions in their 'Mature Enterprises' but in controlling the uncontrollability of the capital system, ending up with multi-billion dollar annual losses in recent and not so recent years — must have derived tremendous reassurance from knowing that they have accomplished the impossible. And Professor Galbraith was so carried away with his own dream of the boundless possibilities of the New Industrial State that he eulogized its Mature Corporations in poetic language. For, according to him

> No grant of feudal privilege has ever equalled, for effortless return, that of the grandparent who bought and endowed his descendants with a thousand shares of General Motors or General Electric. The beneficiaries of this foresight have become and remain rich by no exercise of effort or intelligence beyond the decision to do nothing, embracing as it did the decision not to sell.[140]

Thus the workers sacked in massive numbers all over the world — including the U.S. and other capitalistically advanced countries — by the Boards of near-bankrupt IBM, General Motors, et al., need not worry. Nor should the workers still remaining in employment whose pension funds are raided or 'borrowed' by the management of their near-bankrupt firms — like General Motors — look forward to the future with the slightest anxiety. Not to mention the grandchildren who inherited the legendary thousand shares. For, obviously, all these troubles belong strictly to the realm of impossibility.

Alas, Professor Galbraith's track-record of confident predictions did not fare any better with regard to the converging technostructural cousin, the Soviet-type system either. For this is how the author of *The New Industrial State* depicted the Soviet trends of development and the future arising from them:

> Decentralization in the Soviet-type economies involves not a return to the market but a shift of some planning functions from the state to the firm. This reflects, in turn, the need of the technostructure of the Soviet firm to have more of the instruments of successful operation under its own authority. It thus contributes to its autonomy. There is no tendency for the Soviet and the Western systems to convergence by the return of the former to the market. Both have outgrown that. There is measurable convergence to the same form of planning.[141]

As a Hungarian adage puts it, Professor Galbraith was pointing his gun at the bull's head and hit the cow's udder. And this was by no means accidental. For his aprioristic scheme of 'technostructural planning' made the bullet fly in the wrong direction. Nor could the author of *The New Industrial State* claim that nothing whatsoever of what later happened could be perceived even as a faint trend at the time of the book's publication. In fact debates raged in the U.S.S.R. at the time of his writing *The New Industrial State,* centred around the issue of how best to adopt the 'market mechanism'. They greatly intensified afterwards — not only in Russia but also in Hungary, Czechoslovakia, Poland, and elsewhere — culminating in the end in Gorbachev's 'perestroika'. The last quoted passage showed not only that Galbraith was aware of such debates but, even more so, that he chose to evaluate them in a certain way, in accordance with his ideas of technological determinism and technostructural predestination. The way things actually turned out provided a resounding rebuff to his theorization of capital's newfound control attempts also in this respect.

3.3.5

THE desolate technostructural utopia of *The New Industrial State* postulated the permanence of 'capitalism without the capitalist', together with the impossibility of social control in the name of 'success', dismissing at the same time with boundless self-confidence the 'ancient' socialist project as an utterly quixotic enterprise. As it happened, neither the author's theoretical predictions, nor indeed the actual performance of the Mature Enterprise which they eulogized proved to be a great success.

Moral justification for Galbraith's vision of how the fusion of the technostructure with the state solves the problem of capital's uncontrollability was offered in two steps. The first appealed to the absolute inescapability of technological determinism, dragging into the picture for good measure even the hypostatized nature of 'modern man'. It went like this:

> It is part of the vanity of modern man that he can decide the character of his economic system. His area of decision is, in fact, exceedingly small. He could, conceivably, decide whether or not he wishes to have a high level of industrialization. Thereafter the imperatives of organization, technology and planning operate similarly, and we have seen to a broadly similar result, on all societies. Given the decision to have modern industry, much of what happens is inevitable and the same.[142]

Thus complicitous resignation to the inhumanities of the existent could be turned even into a virtue by elevating the men of superior insight — that is, insight into the inevitability of the claimed unalterable — above the futile 'vanity of modern man'.

The second step offered the apology of the given system on different grounds. It asserted that

> There is little doubt as to the ability of the industrial system to serve man's needs. As we have seen, it is able to manage them only because *it serves them abundantly.* It requires a mechanism for making men want what it provides. But this mechanism would not work — wants would not be subject to *manipulation* — had not these wants been *dulled by sufficiency.*[143]

In this way even the wasteful and grossly iniquitous system of distribution, with its concomitant manipulation of the 'wants' of those who were acknowledged to count, could be justified in the name of great 'abundance' and the 'dulling effect of sufficiency'. But everything in this way of approaching the problem was assessed hopelessly out of proportion. The fact that the overwhelming majority of the world population did not participate in the ruling social metabolic order's self-justificatory 'abundance' counted for naught. The size and the predicament of the overwhelming majority was misrepresented by a casual half-sentence at the foot of the page from which the last quotation was taken. It stated that the system of dulling sufficiency excludes only 'the *unqualified* and the *unfortunate* from its beneficence'. That the number of these 'unqualified' and 'unfortunate' was approaching at the time of writing *The New Industrial State* — not to mention today — the figure of one hundred million people even in the most privileged capitalist countries, had to be kept under silence. Perhaps more important still, the fact that the condition of being 'unqualified' and 'unfortunate' did not rain out of the sky but was *produced* by the given socioeconomic system itself, *dis*qualifying[144] and turning into 'unfortunate' the people who were considered 'superfluous' to the requirements of capital-expansion and accumulation, this fact too had to be swept aside by the terms carefully chosen by the author to characterize them in the interest of social apology.

Thus Galbraith's way of solving capital's uncontrollability reproduced the same old pattern, despite the terminological differences. Just as in the past, the terms in which it was admitted that the system behaved in a way very different from what was earlier expected of it, only served to assert the very moment of uttering the admission, that none the less, everything was proceeding as it really ought to do, even if the 'vanity of modern man' might disagree. The structural antagonisms of the capital system were 'explained away', so that everything could be considered safe in carrying on from now on forever in the selfsame form which under the given circumstances could be observed as dominant.

Adam Smith's 'invisible hand' was used by its originator and his followers as *deus ex machina* which would provide the much needed services of the missing totalizer. John Kenneth Galbraith thought that he could do away with that benevolent mystery by offering his *machina without deus* in the form of the 'technostructure'. But in the end the latter turned out to be quite unsuitable for the elusive task of totalization. Thus the author of *The New Industrial State* was forced to bring back *deus ex machina* into the newly proclaimed healthy framework of the Mature Enterprise via the back door, in order to give some plausibility to his own solutions. He did this through the wishful characterization of the *state*, postulating that it could readily fulfil the many 'requirements' and 'imperatives' with which the benevolent state had to be burdened. This is how the third typical way of addressing the problem of capital's inherent uncontrollability had to end, culminating in the same sort of postulates which characterized all of its predecessors. And no wonder. For by all thinkers who shared the standpoint of capital the social antagonisms of the system had to be avoided, or minimized, or even transfigured into happy circumstances and virtues while leaving their explosive potential deeply hidden from view.

CHAPTER FOUR

CAUSALITY, TIME, AND FORMS OF MEDIATION

4.1 Causality and time under capital's 'causa sui'

4.1.1

THE most problematical aspect of the capital system, notwithstanding its incommensurable power as a mode of social metabolic control, is its total inability to *address causes as causes,* no matter how serious their implications in the longer run. This is not a transient — historically surmountable — but an irremediable structural dimension of the expansion-oriented capital system which in its necessary remedial actions must seek solutions to all problems and contradictions generated within its framework by adjustments made strictly at the level of *effects* and *consequences.*

Relative limits of the system are those which can be overcome by progressively expanding the margin and productive efficiency of the — within the given framework feasible and pursued type of — socioeconomic action, minimizing thereby for the time being the harmful effects which arise from, and are containable by, capital's fundamental causal framework. Approaching the absolute limits of capital, by contrast, calls unavoidably into play the causal framework itself. Consequently, going successfully beyond them would necessitate the adoption of reproductive strategies which sooner or later would undermine altogether the viability of the capital system as such. It is not surprising, therefore, that this system of social reproduction must at all cost confine its remedial efforts to the structurally compatible partial modification of the effects and consequences of its given mode of operation, taking their causal foundation — even under the circumstances of the most severe crises — absolutely for granted.

In relation to capital's mode of social metabolic control — which cannot contemplate the possibility of a future unless the projected future is envisaged as a direct extension of past and present determinations — there cannot be any such thing as 'the longer run'. The apologists of capital are fond of quoting the Keynesian wisdom according to which 'in the long run we are all dead', as if that kind of frivolous dismissal of concern with the future could settle the matter. The truth, however, is that because of its *necessary nihilation of the future* the capital system is locked into the vicious circle of the short run, although its ideologists try to misrepresent such vice as an unsurpassable virtue. This is the reason why capital is incompatible with any meaningful attempt at comprehensive *planning,* even when the need for it is quite overwhelming in the troubled relations of global capitalist enterprises. And this is why also the Soviet type capital system, belying all of its explicit claims to the establishment of a socialist planned economy, could only produce a gruesome caricature of planning. For metamorphosing the private capitalist personifications of capital into their variants as Soviet bureaucrats could introduce changes only on the plane of *manipulatable effects,* leaving their historically long established causal foundations unaltered.

The reason why capital is structurally incapable of addressing causes as causes — in contrast to treating all newly arising challenges and complications as more or less successfully manipulatable effects — is because it happens to be *its own causal foundation:* a veritable unholy *'causa sui'.* Anything that might aspire at socioeconomic legitimacy and viability must be accommodated within its predetermined structural framework. For as a mode of social metabolic control capital cannot tolerate the intrusion of any principle of socioeconomic regulation that might constrain its expansion-oriented dynamics. Indeed, expansion as such is not simply a *relative* — to a greater or lesser extent commendable, and in that light under certain circumstances freely adopted whereas under others consciously rejected — *economic* function but an *absolutely necessary* way of displacing the capital system's emerging problems and contradictions, in accord with the imperative of avoiding like plague their underlying causes. The self-propelling causal foundations of the system cannot be questioned under any circumstance. If troubles appear in it, they must be treated as temporary 'dysfunctions', to be remedied by reasserting with ever greater rigour the imperative of expanded reproduction. It is for this reason that there can be *no alternative* to the pursuit of expansion — at all cost — in all varieties of the capital system.

So long as the scope for unobstructed expansion is objectively present, the process of displacing the system's contradictions can go on unhindered. When things do not go well, i.e., when there is a failure in economic growth and corresponding advancement, the difficulties are diagnosed in terms of the circular proposition which runs away from the underlying causes and highlights only their consequences by saying that 'there is not enough growth'. Dealing with problems in this perverse circular way, constantly repeating even at times of major recessions that 'everything is in place' for healthy expansion, creates the illusion that capital's mode of social metabolic control is in no need of fundamental change. Legitimate change must be always envisaged as limited alteration and improvement of what is already given. Change must be brought about by innovation undertaken strictly at the *instrumental* level, which is supposed to make it self-evidently beneficial. Since, however, the necessary historical qualifying conditions and implications of continued expansion are systematically disregarded or brushed aside as irrelevant, the assumption of the permanence and unquestionable viability of capital's *causa sui* is utterly fallacious.

But here, again, the issue is not the intrusion of a logical fallacy into theory. Rather, it is the unsustainable overturning of actually existing practical relations. For the perverse corollary of the *absolutized relative* (i.e. the limited historical) conditions required by capital's expanded reproduction process — the gratuitously assumed availability forever of both the resources and the scope needed for successful capital expansion — is the irresponsible *relativization of the absolute* constraints (as, for instance, the wilful ignorance of the dangers involved in the ongoing dissipation of the planet's unrenewable resources). Instead of dangerously tampering with them, such constraints should be recognized as necessary limiting conditions in any finite system, including all feasible varieties of the capital system, unless one is willing to play Russian roulette with the survival of humanity. Since, however, the acceptance of constraints of this kind would inevitably call for a major change in capital's fundamental causal framework — in that the postulated imperative of expansion would have to be qualified and justified, instead of being used as the allegedly self-evident ground of all conceivable justification, thus itself in absolutely no need of justification — there can be 'no alternative' to the relativization of the absolute, no matter how irresponsible.

4.1.2

THE unalterable *temporality* of capital is *a posteriori* and *retrospective*. There can be no future ahead in a meaningful sense of the term, since the only admissible 'future' has already arrived in the form of the existing parameters of the established order well before the question of 'what is to be done' is allowed to be raised.

Given its fundamental structural determinations to which everything under the sun must conform, capital's mode of operation can only be *reactive* and *retroactive*, even when the defenders of the system speak — quite inappropriately — of its beneficial 'restructuring'. In reality nothing is allowed to create a genuine opening. The impact of unexpected historical events — as they arise, for instance, from a major crisis — sooner or later must be compressed back into the structurally preexistent mould, making *restoration* an integral part of the normal dynamics of the capital system.

Everything that *can be* in a sense already *has been*. Thus, when the virtues of 'privatization' are exalted it is not considered right and proper to ask the question: what problems have led in the first place to the newly deplored condition of nationalization which must now be reversed in order to establish the 'future' of the *status quo ante?* For in the course of the adopted socioeconomic and political transformations nothing is supposed to change in such a way as to put at stake capital's structural parameters. 'Nationalization' of private capitalist enterprises, whenever introduced, is treated simply as a temporary response to a crisis, to be contained within the overall determinations of capital as a mode of control, without affecting in any way whatsoever the fundamental *command structure* of the system itself.

As a result, on the face of it major but in actuality quite marginal economic changes amount only to some limited rescue-operation to sections of bankrupt capital, precisely because the structural framework and command structure of the system itself remains unaltered. This is why the process of nationalization can just as easily be reversed once certain adjustments to the original crisis symptoms are made, permitting thereby the continuation of what went on before. Inevitably, therefore, all talk about 'conquering the commanding heights of the mixed economy' as a way of establishing in the fullness of time a socialist order — predicated for almost a century by the leaders of the socialdemocratic labour movement — reveals its total vacuity in the light of these structural and temporal determinations which *apriori negate* the future possibilities of time.

Similarly — even if in a somewhat more surprising setting — the Soviet type postrevolutionary order, operating within the structural parameters of the capital system, makes no attempt at fundamentally altering the inherited hierarchical command structure of *domination over labour*. Instead of embarking on the difficult road of instituting a socialist labour process — within the framework of *open temporality* that connects the present with a genuinely unfolding future — by creating the conditions of meaningful *self-management*, it responds to the grave crisis of the first world war and of its painful aftermath by changing the *commanding personnel* only, and even that by no means consistently. Rather, it changes the hereditary legal entitlement — the automatic property rights — of the ruling personnel but leaves the new type of personifications of capital in authoritarian control of the inherited hierarchical labour process. By doing so, however, some fundamental determinations of the old social metabolic control remain in force from which in due course also the demand for the restoration of the legal entitlement to private property can arise, as indeed it did in the form of Gorbachev's 'perestroika' (another instance of utterly misusing the notion of 'restructuring'). It is therefore by no means accidental nor surprising that the loudest British crusader for privatization, Prime Minister Margaret Thatcher, and the Soviet politician, Mikhail Gorbachev, who proclaimed the 'full equality of all types of property' — i.e. in plain language the restoration of capitalist private property sanctioned by the Party — should have so quickly and enthusiastically embraced one another as bosom friends. Such developments are not only possible but quite unavoidable for as long as the paralyzing restoratory temporality of capital prevails and the past — with its deadening inertia — continues to dominate the present, destroying the chances of a qualitatively different future order.

In terms of capital's unavoidably reactive and retroactive temporality change is admissible only if it can be absorbed or assimilated within the structurally already given network of determinations. Whatever cannot be handled in that way must be done away with altogether. This is why genuine *qualitative* changes are unacceptable — corresponding to the spirit of the French axiom: *'plus ça change, plus c'est la même chose'* — since they would endanger the cohesion of the given structural order. *Quantity* rules absolute in the capital system, in accordance with its retroactive temporality.

This concords well also with the requirement of *expansion* which is of necessity conceived in strictly quantitative terms. There cannot be a way of defining expansion itself within the framework of the capital system in other than purely quantitative fashion, projecting it as the straightforward extension of the existent. It must be visualized as *more of the same thing as seen before* — even when the prospects of securing the advocated 'more' appear to be most problematical, not to say absurd. For the absurdity of the unquestionable 'more' (including Stalin's advocacy of pig-iron production bigger than in the U.S. as the criterion of reaching the highest stage of communism) is the only language understood by the system, and under no circumstance the orienting force of something *qualitatively different* which should arise from long ignored human need.

The same goes for the consideration of *cost,* which must be always assessed in a mechanically quantifiable way. As a result, the idea that the advocated expansion might bring with it *prohibitive costs* not in readily quantifiable financial terms but on the plane of *qualitative* considerations — i.e. that under certain conditions the pursuit of 'economic efficiency' and 'profitable expansion' might indeed result in irreversible damage to the elementary conditions of a sustainable societal reproduction process — is inadmissible by the necessary mode of operation of the capital system.

This is how the innermost causal determinations of capital confine the system's feasible corrective actions to the effects and structurally assimilable consequences, in conformity to the nature of capital as unalterable *causa sui*. But in doing so they also project the shadow of total uncontrollability when the perverse overturning of the relationship between the relative and the absolute — by treating the historically produced and limited *relative* (that is, capital's structural order) as the *untranscendable absolute,* and the *absolute* conditions of social metabolic reproduction and human survival as *readily manipulatable relative* — cannot be maintained any longer.

4.2 *The vicious circle of capital's second order mediations*

4.2.1

THE capital system's second order mediations constitute a vicious circle from which apparently there can be no escape. For they interpose themselves — as ultimately destructive 'mediations of primary mediation' — between human beings and the vital conditions of their reproduction, nature.

Thanks to the preponderance of the capital system's second order mediations it becomes obfuscated that the conditions of societal reproduction can only be secured under all circumstances through the necessary intermediary of productive activity which — not only in our own age but for as long as humanity survives — is inseparable from highly organized *industrial* productive activity. Tellingly, however, the apologists of the established mode of social metabolic reproduction continue to fantasise about our allegedly *'post-industrial* society', perversely dismissing the absolute conditions of human survival as a historical anachronism in order to be able to misrepresent capital's historically generated and ever more problematical second order mediations as absolute and historically insurmountable.

The claimed 'evidence' put forward in support of such theories is the ongoing transfer of the 'smoke-stack industries' from the privileged 'metropolitan' areas of the capitalist West to the 'underdeveloped periphery'. As if the atmosphere — which remains as polluted as ever (if not more so) despite such contemptuous discriminatory treatment of the 'Third World' — could be safely and permanently cordoned off in convenient portions by a new Chinese wall extending all the way to the moon; and as if the now and then hypocritically deplored productive practices of the 'smoke-stack industries' did not arise in the first place — and would not of necessity continue to arise within the given reproductive framework — from the profit-seeking determinations of the globally intertwined economy (mostly to the benefit of the dominant 'metropolitan' countries) of the ruling social metabolic order.

The second order mediations of the capital system can be summed up as follows:

- the *nuclear family,* articulated as the 'microcosm' of society which, in addition to its role in reproducing the species, partakes in all reproductive relations of the social 'macrocosm', including the necessary mediation of the laws of the state to all individuals, thus vital also to the reproduction of the state;

- alienated means of production and their 'personifications' through which capital acquires 'iron will' and tough consciousness, strictly mandated for imposing on everyone conformity to the dehumanizing objective requirements of the given social metabolic order;

- money assuming a multiplicity of mystifying and ever more dominant forms in the course of historical development, from the worship of the golden calf already at the time of Moses and from the stalls of the money-changers in the Temple of Jerusalem at the time of Jesus (figuratively depicted yet very real practices which were passionately castigated — but on the evidence of actual history utterly in vain — by the moral code of the Judeo-Christian tradition), through the usurer's chest and the necessarily limited undertaking of early merchant capital all the way to the global stranglehold of the present-day international monetary system;

- fetishistic production objectives, submitting in one form or another the satisfaction of human needs (and the corresponding provision of use-values) to the blind imperatives of capital expansion and accumulation;

- labour structurally divorced from the possibility of control both in capitalist societies, where it must function as wage labour coerced and exploited by economic compulsion, and under the post-capitalist rule of capital over the politically dominated labour force;

- varieties of capital's state formation in their global setting, where they confront one another (at times even with the most violent means, dragging humankind to the brink of self-destruction) as self-oriented national states; and

- the uncontrollable *world market* within the framework of which the participants, protected by their respective national states to a degree feasible by the prevailing power relations, must accommodate themselves to the precarious conditions of economic co-existence while endeavouring to procure the highest practicable advantage to themselves by outwitting their competing counterparts, inevitably sowing thereby the seeds of ever more destructive conflicts.

In relation to the way in which all these constituents of the established mode of social metabolic control are linked together we can only talk of a vicious circle. For the particular second order mediations reciprocally sustain one another, making impossible to counter the alienating and paralyzing force of any one of them taken in isolation while leaving intact the immense self-regenerative and self-imposing power of the system as a whole. On the basis of painful historical evidence the disconcerting truth of the matter is that the capital system succeeds in imposing itself on partial emancipatory efforts aimed at limited specific targets through the structural interconnections of its constituent parts. Accordingly, what must be confronted and overcome by the adversaries of the established, incorrigibly discriminatory, order of social metabolic reproduction is not only capital's positively self-sustaining force of surplus-labour-extraction but also the devastating negative power — the apparently forbidding inertia — of its circular linkages.

This is why the real target of radical socialist transformation must be the capital system as such, *with all of its second order mediations,* and not simply the legal expropriation of the private capitalist personifications of capital. For the act of legal expropriation can be nullified with relative ease not only by the change of the traditional private capitalist form of personifications of capital into one of its historically feasible postcapitalist varieties, as seen for instance in Soviet type societies. More than that, the disconcerting fact also remains that whatever might be instituted at one historical conjuncture by legislative means can be reversed and completely undone by suitable legislative measures under changed historical circumstances. Thus the legally enacted 'expropriation of the expropriators' on which so much hope had been placed, especially at the early stages in the history of the international socialist movement, can be suitably 'rolled back' in postcapitalist societies also by openly reasserting in due course, when circumstances permit, the restoratory logic of private capitalism mentioned in Section 4.1.2. This is indeed what has been attempted already in Gorbachev's Russia, and more or less successfully accomplished during the last seven years — after a brief moment of projecting, totally in vain, the imaginary remedy of so-called 'market socialism' — in the formerly Soviet dominated countries of postwar Eastern Europe.

4.2.2

THE defenders of capital like to depict the existing order as some sort of divine predestination to which there could be no civilized alternative. Many of them arbitrarily project the capitalist exchange relations back to the dawn of history, eliminating in that way both their contingency and historical transcendability in order to be able to idealize (or at least to excuse) even their most destructive aspects.

In truth, however, European explorers as late as the eighteenth century were struck in the newly discovered parts of the world by the total absence of the possessive value system which they took for granted in their own countries. Indeed, the most radical and far-sighted thinker of the French Enlightenment, Diderot — the same philosopher who insisted that 'if the day-worker is miserable, the nation is miserable'[145] — offered a profound critique of capitalist alienation by favourably contrasting the way of living of the formerly unknown tribes of some Pacific islands to that of his own country. He was in this respect more uncompromising than even his best contemporaries, including Rousseau. In an imaginative commentary on a community discovered by a famous French explorer, captain Bougainville, Diderot indicated as basic contradictions of the socioeconomic system dominant in Europe 'the distinction of *yours* and *mine*' ('distinction du *tien* et du *mien*'), the opposition between 'one's own particular utility and the general good' ('ton utilité particulière et le bien général'), and the subordination of the 'general good to one's own particular good' ('le bien général au bien particulier').[146] And he went even further, emphasising that under the prevailing conditions these contradictions result in the production of *'superfluous wants'* ('besoins superflus'), *'imaginary goods'* ('biens imaginaires') and *'artificial needs'* ('besoins factices').[147] Thus he formulated his critique in almost the same terms as those used by Marx almost a century later in describing the 'artificial needs and imaginary appetites' produced under the alienating rule of capital.

The idealization of capitalist exchange relations became a rule somewhat after Diderot and other great figures of the Enlightenment had formulated their theories. It entered the horizon in the aftermath of the successful diffusion and consolidation of the system of 'satanic mills', bringing with it the acceptance by bourgeois political economists that alienation and dehumanization were a price 'well worth paying' in exchange for capitalist advancement, no matter how miserable the life-chances of Diderot's day-worker might be. And later still even the memory of the once sincerely entertained dilemma itself of having to opt for the production of capitalist wealth, notwithstanding the misery and dehumanization that went with it, had been altogether wiped out from the consciousness of the capital system's ideologists. For the latter could unashamedly celebrate in the name of their fictitious 'post-industrial society' the transfer of the 'smoke-stack industries' and other 'satanic enterprises' of advanced capitalism to the 'Third World'. They callously disregarded the necessary consequences — as, for instance, the mass tragedy at Bhopal in 'underdeveloped' India caused by the criminally sub-standard safety measures and productive practices of 'advanced' U. S. Union Carbide — of such 'transfers of technology', imposed as a matter of routine on the 'underdeveloped' countries concerned, on the iniquitous ground of their *structural dependency* within the framework of the global capital system.

No matter how it might be dressed up by the ruling ideology, also in this regard the system asserted (and continues to assert) its power as an interdependent and hierarchically structured totality, making a gruesome mockery of all belief in finding a way out of the blind alley of structural dependency through the good offices of 'Third World modernization' and a generous 'transfer of technology'. In reality the vicious circle of capital's second order mediations saw to it that all such expectations should come to naught, if not much worse than that, as it happened in Bhopal as well as in countless other parts of the destructively affected former colonial dependencies. Just as the same vicious circle made it sure, in a different setting, that the wishful thinking of 'market socialism' — loudly promoted by the postrevolutionary personifications of capital for the duration of shedding, with blinding speed, their postcapitalist political skin, in order to be able to secure for themselves the financially rather more lucrative private capitalist economic attire — should actually end in economically enforced 'wage slavery' and tears for the masses of the people in Eastern Europe.

Naturally, the capital system did not arise from some mythical predestination, nor indeed out of the positive determinations and self-fulfilling requirements of so-called 'human nature'. In fact the latter happens to be as a rule circularly defined by the philosophers and political economists who adopt the standpoint of capital. They depict the world in terms of the value-imposing characteristics of the capitalist socioeconomic system, which in its turn is supposed to have been 'naturally' derived from 'egotistic human nature' itself. Yet, no matter how powerful might be the influence of the ideologies which postulate capital's origin and continued domination in such terms, neither the beginning nor the forceful persistence of this mode of social metabolic control can be made intelligible on the ground of an arbitrarily postulated and historically insurmountable natural necessity, not to mention the mythology of humanity's predestination to an inescapably capitalist existence. And even if we consider human nature with its objectively given characteristics, as opposed to the just mentioned circular determination of capitalist values by a tendentiously projected 'human nature' and vice versa, even that would be of no help to those who try to hypostatize the ahistorical origin and absolute permanence of the capital system on its basis. For real human nature is itself inherently historical and thus by no means suitable for arbitrarily freezing the dynamics of actual socioeconomic development so as to suit the convenience of capital's mode of social metabolic reproduction.

History, it goes without saying even if it is often tendentiously ignored, does not deserve its name unless it is conceived as open-ended in both directions, towards the past no less than in the direction of the future. Significantly, those who want to close off the irrepressible dynamics of historical development towards the future end up with the necessity of doing the same thing also in the direction of the past, otherwise they would not be able to complete the required ideological circle. And this is true by no means only of minor theories conceived from the standpoint of capital but also of the outstanding representatives of this approach, like Hegel. For the monumental scheme of the German philosopher — the consciously pursued task of gaining the necessary insight into what he unambiguously calls 'the true *Theodicaea,* the justification of God in History'[148] — claims to put before the reader the grand design of the World Spirit's timelessly self-anticipating self-realization. It is telling, however, that this grand apriori design which must be closed off towards the future culminates in the Hegelian philosophy of history at a stage that happens to be none other than the dominance of capitalist and imperialist Europe, described as 'absolutely the end of history'. And since the historical movement must be closed off also in the direction of the past in order to remain perversely consistent to its ideological ground of future-denying determination, the claimed *'true Theodicaea'* as a whole must be depicted by Hegel as a supra-historical process of disclosing — as we have seen in Chapter One above — the 'eternally present'. The present of the World Spirit which 'always has been', and can only be properly understood if it is mirrored, in the words of Hegel himself, by the philosophical embodiment of the 'dialectical circle'.

4.2.3

WHAT is really at stake in these matters is the *nature of capital,* and not the actual or fictitious characteristics of 'human nature', nor indeed 'the justification of God in History'..

This issue is not only extremely complicated, since the historical aspects of capital's mode of social metabolic control are inextricably intertwined with its transhistorical dimension, creating thereby the illusion that capital as such stands above history. Also, it happens to be of the greatest — for human survival literally vital — practical importance. For, obviously, it is quite impossible to gain control over the alienating, dehumanizing and destructive determinations of capital, which proved to be uncontrollable throughout history, without understanding its nature.

According to Marx *'The nature of capital remains the same in its developed as in its undeveloped form.'*[149] This is by no means intended to suggest that capital can escape the constraints and limitations of history, including the historical delimitation of its life-span. To make these problems intelligible it is necessary to situate them not in a class-determined Hegelian 'dialectical circle' but within the framework of an objectively grounded dialectical social ontology, which should not be confused with the traditional theological or metaphysical varieties of ontology. For the sameness of capital in both its undeveloped and developed form applies only to its innermost nature and not to its historically always adapted mode and form of existence.

The socially dominating role of capital throughout the whole of modern history is self-evident. However, what requires explanation is how is it possible that under certain conditions a given 'nature' (the nature of capital) should unfold and realize itself — in accordance with its objective nature, with its inherent potentialities and limitations — by successfully following (despite even the sharpest antagonisms with the people negatively affected by its mode of functioning) its own inner laws of development, from its undeveloped form to its form of maturity.

In this sense, what is required is to understand the objective dialectic of *contingency* and *necessity,* as well as of the *historical* and the *transhistorical* in the context of the capital system's mode of operation. For these are the categorial parameters that help to identify the relative and absolute *limits* within which the always historically adjusted power of capital can assert itself *transhistorically,* across many centuries. Subject to such categorial and structural determinations capital, as a mode of social metabolic control, can successfully assert over all human beings the operational laws emanating from its nature, irrespective of how well or ill disposed they might be towards their impact under determinate historical circumstances.

The unalterable nature of capital — which is the same thing as its objective structural determination — makes it

- (1) eminently suitable to the realization of *certain types* of objectives within the systemic framework of its *second order* mediations and
- (2) totally and *powerfully inimical* to undertaking all those types which cannot fit into the established network of second order mediations, no matter how vital the human interests at their roots might be.

This is what circumscribes capital's historical viability for fulfilling the functions of a viable social reproduction process (1) in positive and (2) in negative terms.

One of the examples given by Marx to illustrate the sameness of capital's nature in its developed and undeveloped forms concerns the relationship between creditor and debtor. He writes:

In the code which the influence of the slave-owners, shortly before the outbreak of the American Civil War, imposed on the territory of New Mexico, it is said that the labourer, inasmuch as the capitalist has bought its labour power, 'is his (the capitalist's) money'. The same view was current among the Roman patricians. The money they had advanced to the plebeian debtor had been transformed *via* the means of subsistence into the flesh and blood of the debtor. This 'flesh and blood' were, therefore, 'their money'. Hence, the Shylock-law of the Ten Tables, Linguet's hypothesis that the patrician creditors, from time to time prepared, beyond the Tiber, banquets of debtors' flesh, may remain as undecided as that of Daumer on the Christian Eucharist.[150]

The point is that capital must assert its absolute domination over all human beings, even in the most inhuman form if they fail to conform to its interests and its drive for accumulation. This is what makes the 'Shylock-law' by no means an aberration or an exception but the 'rational' rule in the course of capital's metamorphoses from its undeveloped to its developed forms. Indeed, if we compare the monstrous inhumanities of the capital system in the twentieth century, accomplished on an earlier quite inconceivable mass scale — from the horrors of the first global imperialist war of 1914-18 through the Nazi Holocaust and Stalin's labour camps all the way to the atom bombs of Hiroshima and Nagasaki — the limited 'artisanal' approach of a Shakespearean Shylock pales to insignificance. For the historical adjustment of capital to the new circumstances of mass extermination did not change capital's nature in the least. By adopting a *de-personalized* variety of the original 'Shylock-law', to suit the changed circumstances, capital was able to impose on humanity the inhumanities dictated by its nature on an incommensurably larger scale than ever before, conveniently exempting at the same time its own personifications from blame and responsibility. Doing this, capital only changed its earlier mode and means of operation, utilizing to the full the available technology and instruments of destruction against the challenges which it had to overcome in accordance with its nature.

Characteristically, from the standpoint of capital even the most problematical forms of historical development must be depicted with 'uncritical positivism'. Indeed, this must be done even by the greatest thinkers who conceptualize the world from capital's necessarily short-circuited standpoint, including Hegel. It comes, therefore, as no surprise that the idealist rationalization of the material contingencies, and thereby their curious elevation to the lofty plane of 'ideal necessity', should impose its negative consequences at all levels of the Hegelian philosophy. Even the most palpable material processes must be turned upside down and twisted around, in the interest of social apologetics. Accordingly, they must be derived in their material facticity from the absolutely unquestionable, let alone objectionable, self-determination of the Idea itself, in accordance with the ideally stipulated 'principle' and 'category' of the historical period to which the developments in question belong.

As an example we may think of the way in which even the technology of modern warfare is idealized by Hegel. He achieves this idealization by 'deducing' modern warfare from what in his view must be at the apex of the philosophically most commendable determinations: 'thought and the universal'. This is how Hegel confronts his readers with a most peculiar philosophical deduction:

> The principle of the modern world — thought and the universal — has *given courage a higher form,* because its display now seems to be more mechanical, the act not of this particular person, but of a member of a whole. Moreover, it seems to be turned not against single persons, but against a hostile *group,* and hence *personal bravery* appears *impersonal.* It is *for this reason* that *thought had invented the gun,* and the invention of this weapon, which has changed the purely personal form of bravery into a more abstract one, is no accident.[151]

In this way, through its direct derivation from 'the principle of the modern world', the material contingency of ever more powerful modern warfare, rooted in globally expanding capitalist technology, acquires not only its 'ideal necessity'.

It is simultaneously also set above all conceivable criticism in virtue of its full adequacy — 'the rationality of the actual' — to that principle. And since courage as 'intrinsic worth' is inextricably linked by Hegel to the 'absolute, final end, the sovereignty of the state',[152] the apologetic circle of history reaching its culmination in the Germanic 'civilizing' state of the capital system, with its ruthlessly efficacious modern warfare 'invented by thought' for the sake of realizing, in a suitable 'impersonal' form the 'image and actuality of reason', is fully closed.

Yet, despite the intellectual greatness of its originator, the thought that the mass destruction of human beings — just because it is directed against groups and not particular individuals, as if the destroyed groups of people could be simply constructed as abstract 'numbers of a whole', instead of being human persons under all feasible circumstances — should be considered a 'higher form of courage' and an 'abstract form of bravery' directly emanating from the superior reason of inventive World Spirit, is worse than absurd. For capital's power of overturning everything — by removing their human anchorage through the universalization of fetishistic commodity production — is mirrored here in philosophy by turning human values upside down, in the name of 'thought and the universal'. Thus it becomes possible perversely to equate the most extreme form of *cowardice* — as practised in recent wars, whereby the technologically superior combatant, with no risk to himself, makes so-called 'smart bombs' rain out of the sky on his 'underdeveloped' enemy — with the highest form of *courage and bravery*. With the help of this kind of reasoning it becomes possible to accept, and indeed to philosophically glorify, the fateful and potentially catastrophic idea that *higher abstraction* and its correspondingly developed technology amount to a *higher form of courage and morality*. This is a fateful and indeed potentially catastrophic idea. For the ultimate logic of the underlying actual trend in modern warfare, arising from the liquidation of all human frame of reference through the universal triumph of capitalist reification and of the concomitant impersonal logic of the capital system, in complete defiance of human need and reason, is not 'impersonal bravery' but the truly impersonal destruction of humankind in its entirety: Holocaust and Hiroshima combined on a global scale.

To be sure, in its own terms of reference it is understandable that even the most destructive contradictions of the capital system, protected by its network of second order mediations, should be rationalized, excused, and often even idealized from the 'standpoint of political economy', i.e. the vantage point of capital. For once the prevailing order of things is taken for granted as corresponding with 'full adequacy' to the 'rationality of the actual', every conceivable problem is bound to be envisaged, by the same token, as in its own time and place of necessity fully resolved, and every discrepancy or difficulty properly remedied as a matter of course; in Adam Smith's vision by the benevolent 'invisible hand', and in the Hegelian conception by the equally forthcoming 'List der Vernunft', the 'cunning of Reason'. In the prosaic reality of the actually existing capital system, however, the problems and contradictions that must be faced assert themselves in a far from benevolent and reassuring way. For the established system of second order mediations not only controls the human agents of history on the ground of the objective imperatives of capital's self-expansion. For good measure, it also mystifies them with regard to their motivations as 'free agents' as well as in relation to the perceived margin of their actions.

The second order mediations of the capital system through which the vital functions of social metabolic reproduction must be carried on constitute a most bewildering network into which the particular human individuals are inserted. As members of a social group they are located at some predetermined point in the command structure of capital well before they have the chance to learn even the first words in their family environment. Despite the misleading discourse of the ruling ideology about 'social mobility', they may escape from their 'born into' location, in the small minority of cases, only as isolated individuals, — perhaps by betraying at the same time their class allegiances. The thoroughly apologetic character of the discourse on 'social mobility' (highly promoted on account of its soothing and pacifying functions) is revealed by the simple fact that all such individual escapes put together, over centuries, did not alter in the slightest the exploitative surplus-labour-extracting *command structure of capital*. Let alone could they make the established social order itself democratic and 'classless', as cynical politicians and their ever-obliging speech-writers continue to claim.

Moreover, the respective national states of all individuals are themselves also located at determinate — structurally more or less favoured — points in the international pecking order of capital, greatly at the disadvantage of the 'have-nots' of the less powerful countries (amounting in fact to the overwhelming majority of humankind). This makes the preaching of 'individual social mobility' as a way of alleviating, and in due course happily resolving, the global system's iniquities and contradictions blatantly mystifying in its intent and self-deluding in its impact on all those who expect their emancipation from it. Besides, even in terms of actual class mobility, the situation is by no means better. For capital is spontaneously and necessarily mobile in its pursuit of profit maximization, and can be readily transferred from one country to another under the circumstances of favourable profit expectations in our own days with the speed of light. By contrast the international 'mobility of labour' encounters immense practical obstacles and prohibitive material costs, since it must be always strictly subordinated to the imperative of profitable capital accumulation. Not to mention the fact that the consciously pursued practice of the workers' miseducation and ideological mystification, exercised in the interest of their national capital, erects mountain-size obstacles to the development of labour's international consciousness.

And worst of all, because of the perverse mediation of the essential socioeconomic reproductive functions through the alienated objectification of living labour as capital — superimposed on labour in a reified form, confounding the category of always necessary means and material of production with capital as such, in its independence from and indeed hostile opposition to labour, — the historically generated and likewise historically changeable human power relations appear as purely material entities, unalterable in their essential constitution. Thus the ground is firmly established for the broadest diffusion of belief in the convenient wisdom of 'there is no alternative' to which every 'rational individual' is expected to subscribe and, in practical terms, also to unreservedly conform. This is how the vicious circle of capital's second order mediations adds insult to injury, reinforcing thereby the established system's objective power of structural domination over labour through the 'internalizing' mystification of the individuals' allegedly 'free and voluntary' acceptance of all the dictates which emanate from capital's unalterable nature and necessary mode of operation.

4.2.4

THE constitution of the capital system is identical to the emergence of its second order mediations. Indeed, capital as such is nothing but a dynamic, all-engulfing and dominating mode and means of reproductive mediation, articulated as a historically specific set of structures and institutionally embedded as well as safeguarded social practices. It is a clearly identifiable system of mediations which in its properly developed form strictly subordinates all social reproductive functions — from gender and family relations to material production and even to the creation of works of art — to the absolute requirement of capital expansion, i.e. of its own continued expansion and expanded reproduction as a system of social metabolic mediation.

The process of constitution of this system of mediation is, of course, full of social and historical contingencies, as we have seen above in Section 4.2.2., with reference to Diderot's reflections on the 18th century discovery of very different types of social metabolic reproduction which happened to be quite unaffected by the *'meum and tuum'* of European possessive individualism. Nevertheless, in the course of European developments the impact of the contingent material reproductive factors — favouring in a variety of fields the appearance of embryonic forms of socioeconomic interchange in affinity with capital's mode of metabolic control — becomes *cumulative* through the spontaneous repetition of the practices required for successful exchange.

Naturally, the more such factors and reproductive practices coalesce through their *cumulative repetition,* the more they tend to constitute a powerful *system* and reinforce one another. In this way they simultaneously also intensify the combined impact of the emerging system as a whole, thanks to the intricate interchanges and ever more reciprocally complementary functioning of its constituent parts. Thus the original contingencies are progressively pushed into the background and leave their place to ever more entrenched overall *necessity.* For once the second order mediations are articulated and consolidated as a coherent *system,* it becomes practically impossible to eliminate one or another of its specific mediatory structures and functions in isolation, or to introduce into the firmly established system structurally new and rival factors which would run diametrically counter to its complex network of mutually reinforcing constituents.

Under such circumstances and determinations only an alternative all-embracing structural/systemic change is feasible with any hope of lasting success. This raises the immensely challenging problems of transition from the established mode of social metabolic reproduction, with its historically specific system of second order mediations, to a qualitatively different social order. It is therefore neither accidental, nor a form of 'utopianism', that the Marxian radical negation of the rule of capital should envisage the breakdown of the established system of reproductive mediations as a whole to which the socialist project must provide a comprehensive structural alternative.

However, formulating the issue in this way does not mean that the severe problems of transition out of the projected impasse and breakdown of the given social metabolic order to something positively sustainable can be dispensed with. Quite the contrary. For the avoidance of the difficulties of transition from the capital system to a socialist form of metabolic control, and a failure to theorize the general orienting principles and the viable practical measures of the required transitional mode of social reproductive interchange, can only strengthen the nowadays all too prevalent belief in the historical untranscendability of the established order, no matter how profound might be its structural crisis.

4.3 Eternalization of the historically contingent: the Fatal Conceit of Hayek's capital-apologetics

4.3.1

THE historical specificity of capital's second order mediations can only be understood if their *transhistorical* dimension — i.e. the relative continuity of their successful reproduction across centuries — is not confounded with their far-distant but in their socioeconomic substance very different historical antecedents.

This is all the more important in view of the fact that the apologists of the capital system, like Baroness Margaret Thatcher's Companion of Honour F. A. von Hayek, project the capitalistic exchange relations back to the earliest phase of human history, so as to be able to *eternalize* the existing socioeconomic system's specific mode of expanded reproduction, based on the rule of capital, with 'the extended economic order' as such.

The crusading anti-socialist character of such pseudo-scientific and totally ahistorical theories becomes obvious when we are told that the capitalist system corresponds to 'the spontaneous extended order created by a competitive market'[153] and that

> The dispute between the market order and socialism is not less than a matter of survival. To follow socialist morality would destroy much of present humankind and impoverish much of the rest. ... we are constrained to preserve capitalism because of its superior capacity to utilize dispersed knowledge [Capitalism is] an irreplaceable economic order.[154]

In this kind of theory, operating with empty analogies arbitrarily plucked from the biological sciences, proverbial darkness descends upon the earth in the interest of capital-eternalization, making all cows not only look black but obliterating at the same time also their differences from other living creatures. We are of course permanently trapped by Hayek's 'uncritical positivism' once we accept, in the light of the stipulated darkness, that the only colour that can legitimately exist — in the spirit of Henry Ford's decree that the customer can choose any colour for his car, provided that it is black — must be the darkest shade of black, otherwise human survival would be in mortal danger from the conceited socialists (who 'would destroy much of present humankind'). For by consenting to his frame of thought — which equates all possibility of socioeconomic expansion with its capitalist variety — we are also expected to 'rationally' subscribe to the utterly irrational proposition according to which the now ruling 'extended order' arose from unintentionally conforming to certain traditional and largely *moral* practices, many of which men tend to dislike, whose significance they usually fail to understand, whose validity they cannot prove[155] .

The suicidal upside-down logic of Hayek's capital-apologetics knows absolutely no limits. According to this logic capital is the origin of labour, not vice-versa, deserving therefore not only boundless intellectual veneration but also the highest moral approval. In Hayek's words 'If we ask what men most owe to the moral practices of those who are called capitalists the answer is: their very lives.'[156] Yet, the ungrateful labourers thus created and kept in existence by the generous men who are called capitalists do not recoil from biting the hand that feeds them, instead of 'submitting to the impersonal discipline'[157] required for successfully operating the best of all possible worlds, capital's 'extended economic order'. For 'Although these folk may *feel* exploited ['feel' underlined by Hayek], and politicians may arouse and play on these feelings to gain power, most of the Western proletariat, and most of the millions of the developing world, owe their existence to opportunities that advanced countries have created for them.'[158] Indeed their ungratefulness also carries with it the most deplorable, self-defeating irrationality because as a result 'capitalism is sometimes prevented from providing all it might for those who wish to take advantage of it by monopolies of organized groups of workers, "unions", which create an artificial scarcity of their kind of work by preventing those willing to do such work for a lower wage from doing so.'[159]

In truth, however, the guilt of irrationality does not reside in the labourers' attempts to defend themselves, with rather limited success, against capital's interminable cost-cutting drive. On the contrary, it is Hayek's glorification of the 'irreplaceable' capital system — with its vicious circle of second order mediations — which makes the sun-spots theory of economic crises formulated by Jevons appear the paradigm of rationality.

The one and only acceptable form of rationality, according to Hayek, is the anarchy of the market, 'precipitated in prices',[160] which must be treated as the absolute frame of reference of all economic, social, and political activity. Naturally, the 'free market' idealized by the author of *The Fatal Conceit* nowhere exists. Not even in relation to his own, by capitalist vested interests highly publicized, *Fatal Conceit*. For on the one hand the author curtly dismisses 'intellectuals in general' for their 'reluctance to relinquish control of their own products in a market order.'[161] On the other hand, however, he is the last person to allow the market to be the judge of the economic viability of his own books. Instead, this High Priest of the 'free market' of the capitalist 'extended order' barricades himself behind the richly armoured battallions of the most reactionary propaganda organizations of the so-called 'free enterprise' system, from The Heritage Foundation, Washington DC, and from the Institute of Economic Affairs, London, to the Swedish Free Enterprise Foundation, Stockholm; all acting as generous financial sponsors for publishing his Collected Works: a practice which Hayek and his friends and wealthy promoters on the 'Radical Right' would no doubt condemn with the greatest ideological indignation if it took place on the Left. Like capitalists in general who think that *others* should conform to the 'rules of the game', whereas they themselves break the rules whenever they can get away with it, Hayek and his militant right wing friends unashamedly bend the material conditions of the 'free market' in his favour, loudly demanding at the same time that intellectuals — and especially socialist intellectuals — should 'relinquish control of their own products in a market order'. Thus one set of rules is supposed to be appropriate for Margaret Thatcher's Companion of Honour and a very different one for his adversaries. The non-existence of the idealized 'free market' is of no consequence for Hayek and his sponsors. Singing its praises serves the purpose of the anti-socialist crusade, and nothing else. Nobody is expected or allowed to question the validity of the adopted procedures, least of all the socialist critics. For all feasible forms of the socialist alternative are condemned as 'constructivist rationalism', exempting in the same breath the second order mediations of the capital system itself from all rational scrutiny.

Hayek's defence of the established network of reproductive mediations is done not by rational arguments but *by circular definitions*. For rationality as such is apriori ruled out of court in the name of the unfathomable 'mysteries' of the 'extended economic order', the validity of which, according to the propounder of *The Fatal Conceit,* no one can nor should even attempt to prove. Thus, whereas Stanley Jevons at least wanted to retain a causal framework of explanation in his attempt to make intelligible, and in due course to counteract, capitalist crises, even if he failed to identify their real causes, Hayek's pseudo-scientific apologetics is most eager to do away with causal explanations altogether. Accordingly, he insists that 'The creation of wealth ... cannot be explained by a chain of cause and effect'.[162] And he proclaims the peremptory finality of this arbitary position in order to be able to disqualify others from querying on rationally contestable grounds the viability of capital's crisis-prone second order mediations.

If anyone raises the question how such a peculiar theory might be justified, another authoritarian circle is offered in answer by fallaciously retorting that 'The issue of justification is indeed a red herring'.[163] This is the basis on which we are invited to subscribe to the Popperian wisdom that 'we never know what we are talking about'.[164] People who think that it is a legitimate purpose of rational economic investigation to try and remedy the identified problems of the given social reproductive system are curtly dismissed by the author of *The Fatal Conceit* as suffering from 'the delusion that macro-economics is both viable and useful'.[165]

Given the advocacy of such an irrational position it is not surprising that the nature of economic theory should be defined by Hayek in identically vacuous and irrational terms by proclaiming that 'The curious task of economics is to demonstrate to men how little they really know about what they imagine they can design.'[166] At the same time we find that not only the Marxian approach but virtually the whole of philosophy, as well as social, political, psychological, and sociological theory (and even the greater part of economic theory, with the notable exception of the 'marginal revolution' and its claimed anticipators, like Adam Smith) — starting with the views of Plato and Aristotle, following with Thomas Aquinas, Descartes, Rousseau, Hegel, Comte, James and John Stuart Mill, and extending all the way to Einstein, Max Born, G.E. Moore, E.M. Forster, Keynes, Freud, Bertrand Russell, Karl Polányi, Monod, Piaget, and many others — are dismissed in the most summary fashion as 'errors' and fatally flawed misconceptions. For good measure, not only 'market-reluctant intellectuals' but the educational system in general is severely censured on the ground that it actively prevents people from seeing the light of day in the spirit of Hayek's propositions. According to Hayek his tenets, alas, 'are highly abstract, and are particularly hard to grasp for those schooled in the mechanistic, scientistic, constructivist canons of rationality that dominate our educational systems'.[167] And all this is done in a book whose author has the nerve to prattle about the 'Fatal Conceit' of *other people.*

And yet, the theoretical core of Hayek's eternalization of the 'extended economic order' is by no means 'highly abstract and particularly difficult to grasp'. Rather, it happens to be built around a perfectly straightforward tautology. For all it states is the incontestable but singularly unilluminating fact that the large numbers of people in existence today could not materially survive if the economy necessary for their material survival did not make it possible for them to survive. But, of course, this proposition totally ignores the countless millions who had (and still have) to suffer, and even to perish, under the conditions of capital's 'extended order', just as it says absolutely nothing about its sustainability — or not, as the case might be — in the future. Instead, what the author of *The Fatal Conceit* concludes from his core assertion, with the authority of a customary Hayekian fallacious *ex cathedra* decree, is the glorification of the tyranny and structurally enforced iniquitousness of hierarchical capitalist market relations, which we must in his view accept unless we are in favour of the extinction of humanity. For we are told that what Hayek calls 'distributive justice' is

> irreconcilable with a competitive market order, and with growth or even mainte-
> nance of population and of wealth. ... Mankind could neither have reached nor could
> now maintain its present numbers without an inequality that is neither determined
> by, nor reconcilable with, any deliberate moral judgements. Effort of course will
> improve individual chances, but it alone cannot secure results. The envy of those who
> have tried just as hard, although fully understandable, works against the common
> interest. Thus, if the common interest is really our interest, we must not give in to
> this very human instinctual trait, but instead *allow the market process to determine the
> reward.* Nobody can ascertain, save through the market, the size of an individual's
> contribution to the overall product.[168]

Naturally, could these words be meant seriously at all, Hayek should have declined the wealthy reactionary sponsorship of his own books, the politically motivated award of his Nobel Prize, and the equally political reward of Companion of Honour received from Margaret Thatcher: none of them 'determined by the market process'. The real meaning of Hayek's decree is quite different. It is formulated from the power position, and in the interest of, the ruling order which rewards with Nobel Prizes and other high honours — totally unconstrained by market processes — its deserving sons and daughters (many more sons than daughters, of course). The 'competitive' norms of 'free market' economics are meant to constrain and keep permanently in their position of structural subordination those who find themselves at the receiving end of the 'extended economic order', i.e. the overwhelming majority of humankind. At the same time, even the aspiring petty bourgeois individuals who fall for the conservative propaganda tenet according to which 'effort brings result', provided that they 'try hard enough', must be admonished not to allow 'envy' to make them entertain doubts about the ideality of the given 'irreplaceable economic order'. And even less should they allow themselves to be tempted through such doubts to bite the hand that feeds them, as labour is supposed to have done by forming 'monopolistic unions' to protect its 'unjustly high wages', at the expense of those who would do the job for even lower wages. For the 'common interest' — now suddenly we are confronted with the notion of 'common interest' which we must adopt as an unchallengeable value, whereas in other parts of Hayek's *Fatal Conceit* we are told that there can be no such thing as a rational discourse on morality and values — is the unquestioning acceptance of the permanent subjugation of by far the greatest part of humanity to the rule of capital.

4.3.2

SINCE the market idealized by Hayek is acknowledged to be anarchic in character, history must be re-written backwards, to fit the same picture. Thus capitalistic developments are explained like this: 'of the revival of European civilization during the later Middle Ages it could be said that the expansion of capitalism — and European civilization — owes its origin and *raison d'être* to *political anarchy*.'[169] A similarly absurd proposition 'explains' the collapse of the Roman Empire, by projecting upon it another one of Hayek's pet dogmas — this time against 'state interference' — according to which the decline and collapse came about 'only after central administration in Rome increasingly displaced free endeavour.'[170] As if the establishment of the Roman Empire in the first place had nothing whatsoever to do with the deplored interfering practices of its 'central administration'.

In the same vein, although in this case by reversing the historical order, rather primitive monetary relations are quixotically projected forward, as an ideal for the future, by postulating that 'the market economy might well be better able to develop its potentialities if *government monopoly of money were abolished*',[171] because such monopoly 'makes competitive experimentation impossible'.[172] In an age when the 'government monopoly of money' exercised by *national* states is under threat — not from some local Linen Banks, or by some minor Building Societies intent on releasing their own brands of paper money, but by the contradictory transnational development of capital, in the European Union as much as in other parts of the world — Hayek's plea for 'local experimentation' with money, to be adopted while uncritically retaining the structural framework of capital's 'extended economic order' itself, speaks volumes about the soundness of his way of defending the system's second order mediations.

The orienting force of Hayek's capital apologetics is his pathological hatred of the socialist project. Since Marx is critical of reification and the fetishism of money, for Hayek they must be hailed as a good thing, and consequently 'mysterious money and the financial institutions based on it' must be exempt from all criticism.[173] The distorting lens of this hatred, encapsulated in yet another circular 'argument', turns even Aristotle into a deplorable socialist, on the ground that in the ever more wasteful 'extended economic order' of capital

Concern for profit is just what makes possible the more effective use of resources. ...
The high-minded socialist slogan, 'Production for use, not for profit', which we find

in one form or another from Aristotle to Bertrand Russell, from Albert Einstein to Archbishop Camara of Brazil (and often, since Aristotle, with the addition that these profits are made 'at the expense of others'), betrays ignorance of how productive capacity is multiplied by different individuals.[174]

The trouble with this reasoning is not only its circularity: the arbitrary assumption of what should at least be attempted to be proved — i.e. that 'Concern for profit is just what makes possible the more effective use of resources' — from which the fallacious conclusion is then triumphantly derived that Aristotle and other socialists are ignorant of Hayek's totally unestablished 'truth'. Worse than that, Hayek blinds himself — as he has to, in the interest of capital-apologetics — to the really obvious aspect of his own proposition. Namely, that the 'more effective use of resources' of which he speaks, as linked to 'concern for profit', is strictly confined to the kind of production which is amenable to the production of profit, in terms of which its viability is assessed and approved, or — in the event of failing to meet the stipulated criteria of profitability — ruthlessly rejected. It is indeed rejected quite unmindful (or deliberately ignorant) of the suffering, and even of the most reckless destruction of the conditions of sustainable social metabolic reproduction, caused by the necessary pursuit of such course of action.

This takes us to the most problematical aspect of Hayek's approach even in its own terms of reference: its inability to assume a critical stance even towards the most destructive dimensions of the capital system. For 'growth' must have, by definition, a positive connotation in his theory, since he wants to prove on a quasi-axiomatic ground the superiority of capital's second order mediations over all feasible socialist alternative. Thus the destructive consequences of capitalist growth are ignored, and concern with the darkening shadow of growth under any one of its aspects connected with the known tendencies of the given 'extended order', even when such concern is expressed by his own ideological comrades in arms, is dismissed as quite irrelevant. Thus Hayek states disapprovingly that 'Even a sensible philosopher [meaning: an adherent of the 'Radical Right'] like A.G.N. Flew praised Julian Huxley for recognizing early, "before this was even as widely admitted as it now is, that human fertility represents the number one threat to the present and future welfare of the human race".' And Hayek immediately adds: 'I have been contending that socialism constitutes a threat to the present and future welfare of the human race, in the sense that neither socialism nor any other known substitute for the market order could sustain the current population of the world.'[175] However, in the subsequent argument all we are offered is a gratuitous wishful thinking, expressed in terms of 'we may hope' and 'I suspect':

> We may hope and expect that once the remaining reservoir of people who are now entering the extended order is exhausted, the growth of their numbers, which distresses people so much, will gradually recede. ... I suspect that the problem is already diminishing: that the population growth rate is now approaching, or has already reached, its maximum, and will not increase much further but will decline.[176]

To be sure, the frequently voiced danger of 'population explosion' is tendentiously presented by those who identify themselves with the standpoint of capital, since they must look for solutions compatible with — and preferably even capable of extending — the system's structural limits. It will be necessary to consider this problem in Section 5.4. For as a historical challenge facing us today — even if as an undeniable challenge it happens to be of a very different nature from the usual neo-Malthusian diagnoses of an anticipated 'population explosion' — it has in fact much graver implications for the viability of the capital system than what could be handled through a generic biological 'population control' either of the traditional savage kind, asserting itself in the form of mass starvation and other calamities, or by means of a more sophisticated variety of population containment, administered in tune with the requirements of lucrative 'high technology'. In the present context the relevant point is that Hayek's *Fatal Conceit* bluntly refuses to take seriously the problem itself whose existence is admitted even by his closest ideological allies. For if he had to concede that something might be amiss on this important plane of the capitalist reproduction process, that would undermine his idealization of the 'extended economic order', together with his concept of 'growth' crudely equated with capital accumulation, which is uncritically advocated by Hayek even if it can only be accomplished through the violation of the elementary needs of countless millions.

In Hayek's capital-apologetic equations things are very simple. For according to him 'without the rich — without those who accumulated capital — those poor who could exist at all would be very much poorer indeed'.[177] Thus, as regards the people 'who live on the peripheries ... however painful for them this process may be, they too, or they especially, benefit from the division of labour formed by the practices of the business classes',[178] 'even if it means inhabiting for a time [sic!] shanty towns at the periphery'.[179] And, of course, the traditional savagery of letting the final word of judgement be pronounced by the presence or absence of *profitable capital accumulation* — to which absolutely no alternative must be contemplated for a moment — is advocated in matters affecting the size of the population, arguing with boundless hypocrisy in the name of *moral* rectitude that

> a moral conflict may indeed arise if materially advanced countries continue to assist and indeed even to subsidize the growth of populations [in underdeveloped regions] ... With any attempt to maintain populations beyond the volume at which *accumulated capital* could still be currently reproduced, the number that could be maintained *would diminish.* Unless we *interfere,* only such populations will increase further as can feed themselves.[180]

After all that, Hayek's line of argument, not surprisingly, must end on a callously self-complacent note, by saying that 'In any case, there is no danger whatever that, in any foreseeable future with which we can be concerned, the population of the world as a whole will outgrow its raw material resources, and every reason to assume that *inherent forces* will stop such a process long before that could happen.'[181] This is how the idealization of the capital system's second order mediations is carried to its extreme, offering unqualified reassurance over the absolute viability and eternal endurance of the one and only 'natural' economic order.

4.3.3

SINGING in this way the praises of the established structures and mode of social metabolic control must have been sweet music to the governments of the dominant capitalist countries in the late 1970s and throughout the 1980s. This was both understandable and revealing. Understandable, because after the onset of the capital system's global structural crisis in the early 1970s the policy makers of the G7 countries needed the loudest possible reassurance — even against the doubts at times entertained by their own better judgement — that despite the accumulating and even by the official government economists no longer deniable crisis symptoms their socioeconomic system was immune to serious troubles; and Hayek's long neglected theories, culminating in the summation of his *Fatal Conceit,* perfectly matched that need. At the same time, the adoption of Hayek's line of approach by the governments of the capitalis-tically advanced countries was also most revealing. For it required a major switch — at least in ideology and anti-labour political legislative measures, even if, tellingly, not in state-sponsored deficit-financing economic practice — from their uniform Keynesian orientation in the postwar decades of untroubled capital expansion.

Such switches between the two, on the plane of ideological rhetorics sharply contrasting but in socioeconomic substance thoroughly complementary, policy approaches clearly marked the limited margin of manoeuvre of the Western capital system. For Keynesianism could never really amount to more than the 'go phase' of monetarism; just like the latter, notwithstanding all its widely publicized claims to economic purity, coupled with its self-contradictory oppo-sition to 'state interference', could never even dream about offering other than a peculiar equivalent to the 'stop phase' of Keynesianism. Indeed, Hayek's fatally conceited wishful thinking needed state intervention in economic matters on a considerably larger scale — in the form of crusading 'Radical Right' state policies, pursued with authoritarian enthusiasm, even if with very little actually sustainable economic efficacy, by Prime Minister Margaret Thatcher and other heads of government in the same mould — in order to acquire even the slightest degree of plausibility. What people like Hayek liked to forget was that the formation of the modern state was absolutely vital for the full articulation and global triumph of the capital system. Indeed, they wanted us to disregard this inconvenient truth in order to induce us into sharing their enthusiasm for the panacea of the 'marginal revolution', as well as their unqualified belief in the causally inexplicable but nonetheless in their view natural and for humanity absolutely final 'extended economic order'. We were supposed to ignore that the modern state, with all its linkages to all the other parts of the system, in virtue of its objective constitution as the comprehensive political command structure of the established mode of social metabolic reproduction, was as important a member of capital's second order mediations as all of its 'purely economic' mechanisms and institutions put together, including the greatly idealized but in its commended form nowhere really existent market of 'market society'.

At the time when Gorbachev was rewarded with the Nobel Prize, one of his former friends and closest collaborators, Gerasimov, wryly commented that, alas, he did not receive the Nobel Prize for Economics. But what if he did? For Hayek — just like Milton Friedman and other advocates of the same kind of wisdom — were anointed with the holy oil of the Nobel Prize decidedly for their economic theories which were ignored during the long decades of the dominant

Keynesian panacea. Naturally, this was done in the hope that their official elevation to the exalted intellectual status of Nobel Prize for Economics, and thereby the consecration of a new capitalist orthodoxy (duly embraced by the governments of the most powerful Western countries) would bring about the much needed miracles for the successful reproduction of the expansionary conditions experienced during the years of Keynes-inspired German, Italian, French, Japanese, etc. 'miracles'. However, such wishful expectations did not fare any better than those attached to Gorbachev's reforms. Indeed, judging by the evidence of postwar history all the way to our own troubled times, no matter how often the two approaches might be switched around, or even run concurrently in the future by well disposed state policy makers, neither the possible varieties of Keynesianism, nor the Hayek/Friedman types of economic orientation have a better chance of solving the manifold problems and contradictions of the 'extended economic order' in the capitalistically advanced West than Gorbachev's ill-fated perestroika could remedy the structural antagonisms and failures of the Soviet type capital system in the East.

4.4 Productive limits of the capital-relation

4.4.1

THE power of capital is exercised — as a veritable stranglehold in our own age — through the closely interwoven network of its second order mediations. The latter had arisen out of specific historical contingencies over many centuries. They were welded together in the course of the consolidation of the system as a whole, producing thereby an immense systemic power of discrimination in favour of capital's progressively unfolding mode of reproductive interchange and against all rival possibilities of social metabolic control. This is how capital became in the course of its successful historical constitution by far the most powerful surplus-extractor (or 'pump', according to Marx) known to humankind. Indeed, it acquired thereby also the self-evident justification for its mode of operation. This kind of justification could be maintained for as long as the ever-intensified practice of surplus-extraction itself — not for the pursuit of human gratification but in the interest of capital's enlarged reproduction — could hide its ultimate destructiveness.

The complete misrepresentation of capital's *trans*-historical dimension as absolute permanence by the defenders of the system could only work by either eulogizing the always positive character of the 'extended economic order' as such, or by hiding its growing wastefulness (making itself felt already at a relatively early historical stage) as well as its threatening destructiveness as time went by. Only when the imperative of a radically different mode of social metabolic reproduction appeared on the historical horizon, against the background of the established socioeconomic order's visible destructiveness, only then became possible to submit to 'practical criticism' the earlier assumed self-evident rationality and unalterable permanence of capital's second order mediations. In Hegel's philosophy, conceived from the standpoint of bourgeois political economy, the whole system of second order mediations was frozen into the idealized and totally dehistorized structure of modern 'civil society' and its 'ethical state', constructing thereby an eternalized social order on the basis of historical movement being peremptorily terminated — as 'absolutely the end of history' — in the focal point of the present.

Hegel's approach was by far the most ingenious way of dealing with the system's contradictions. For the accumulating evidence of dramatic historical transformations could not be simply ignored or denied. It had to be subsumed under the structural limits of capital's second order mediations, redefining thereby the meaning of all legitimately feasible dynamism. All movement that lay outside such structural framework had to be apriori rejected as an outrage; as nothing but the envy and resentment of the 'rabble', manifesting in irrational and destructive actions against the not only *de facto* but also *de jure* existent. This is how in the greatest bourgeois philosophical system the historical contingency of capital's second order mediations acquired not only its absolute, *supra*-historical necessity, and corresponding eternalization in the direction of the future, but also its likewise absolute *moral* justification. It was celebrated by Hegel as the ideal embodiment of the World Spirit's necessary self-realization. A self-realization which had to assume the form of the forever interlocking and ethically sanctioned relationship between 'civil society' and 'the state disclosed as the image and actuality of reason'. This is the way in which turbulent history, more evident than ever in the aftermath of the French revolution and the Napoleonic wars, could be terminated — as it had to be from the self-eternalizing standpoint of capital — precisely when the tendentially all-engulfing historical dynamism of the system could not be left out of account. And such a paradoxical ending of history — whereby change could be both affirmed with 'uncritical positivism' and rejected with categorical apriorism — could only be devised by making all legitimate movement strictly *internal* to the peculiar 'rationality' of the capital system itself, in agreement with the main tenets of classical political economy. In other words, the termination of history could be envisaged only by locking all movement into the capitalistically constraining and ultimately most irrational margins of operation and expandability of the already established second order mediations, theorized by Hegel under the dual structures of bourgeois civil society and the modern state.

Understandably, in the light of the system's emerging destructiveness and growing antagonisms, this kind of tendentious 'rationalization of actuality' had to be challenged by its critics by forcefully stressing the given reproductive order's inherently historical character and *'transitoriness,'* as Marx tried to do in all of his major works subtitled *'A Critique of Political Economy'.* And just as understandably, in the heat of the critique levelled against the necessarily self-eternalizing standpoint of capital, adopted with the same 'uncritical positivism' by the great English and Scottish political economists as by Hegel in their footsteps, the accent had to be laid on the system's *transitoriness,* at the expense of investigating its immense *staying power* which had emanated — and even in our own times still emanates — from the *vicious circle* of its second order mediations. For a century and a half after Marx's reflections on the subject, the capital system continues to assert its power — and by no means only in the theories of its apologists, but ubiquitously, in the everyday life of the individuals — as an apparently unchallengeable permanence. It prevails by controlling all aspects of social metabolic reproduction and distribution in a way to which, despite the system's contradictions and destructiveness, there seems to be no practically viable alternative.

The undeniable fact that the closely interwoven network of capital's second order mediations had been *historically constituted* does not in and by itself affect the argument in favour of those who stress the necessity of a radical alternative. Indeed, the fact that the particular second order mediations mutually reinforced one another, as well as the system as a whole, in the course of their historical constitution can be put to the use of the more sophisticated forms of apologetics: the kinds that accept and even welcome the efficacy of historical determinations all the way to the formation of the existing structural order, and deny it only in the direction of a qualitatively different future.

What requires proof in this respect — concerning a qualitatively different future — is that the historically constituted and still unfolding ontology of labour, in its fundamental meaning of both agency and activity of social metabolic reproduction, can sustain itself with a higher degree of productivity when freed from the strait-jacket of the established mode of expanded surplus-extraction than when its movement is constrained by the latter's perverse imperative of capital-accumulation. In other words, the alternative to capital's necessarily *external* and *adversarial* mode of controlling the labour process (which can be misrepresented as internal and positive only by the system's uncritical defenders) is the radical reconstitution of both the labour process and of its social agency, labour, on the basis of *internal* and consciously adopted *consensual/coope-rative* determinations. This proof may only be anticipated in its broadest outlines on the plane of theory: by indicating in *positive* terms its conditions of possibility and realization, and in *negative* terms the unsustainable destructive tendencies of the existing order which point in the direction of its necessary breakdown. But the crucial part of the proof in question must be the actual reconstitution of labour itself not simply as the antagonist of capital but as the sovereign creative agent of the labour process. An agency capable of securing the chosen — in contrast to the now by means of the structural/hierarchical social division of labour from the outside imposed — conditions of expanded reproduction without the crutches of capital. This is the real meaning of the Marxian *practical critique* of capital's political economy, concerned with the necessity to go beyond capital and of its now everywhere dominant, apparently permanent, network of second order mediations.

4.4.2

THE critique of capital's 'satanic mills' appeared in history parallel to the establishment of those mills themselves, in the course of the up until then by far the most dynamic phase of the capital system's development. However, for the lasting success of the Marxian enterprise of 'practical critique' even the most passionate denunciation of the 'satanic mills' could not be considered nearly enough. For the more than understandable and justifiable temptation to engage in such denunciations could not provide the proper measure of the force which had to be not only negatively overcome but also positively substituted for in the course of labour's necessary self-emancipation. Indeed, the most disconcerting aspect of the socialist 'practical critique' was that the second order mediations of capital could not be negatively overcome without positively substituting for them at the same time the required structural alternatives. For the capital system could regain its power — even if temporarily subdued under conditions of major historical crises and emergencies — in the event that the vital social metabolic functions of its closely interconnected mediatory network failed to be embodied in alternative forms of effective functioning: forms capable of overcoming the contradiction of having to cripple the producer as the price to be paid for the success in reducing the material costs of production. This is why the passion and compassion of moral denunciation evident in the writings of the great utopian socialists, coupled with the noble but idealistic conception of the enlightened 'educator' of mankind who comes to the rescue, had to be also subjected to a searching critique. A critique that emphasised the need for fundamentally restructuring the objective conditions themselves which inevitably also 'educate the educators'.

Thus, to have any hope of success at all against the structurally incorrigible destructive tendencies of capital, it was not enough to pinpoint its obvious — by no means structurally untranscendable but historically arising and within the limitations of the system also historically surmountable — weaknesses, as for instance the ruthless exploitation of child labour at the time. Rather, it was necessary to recognize the full power of the capital system in existence, acknowledging its — no matter how problematical — historical advancement over all previous modes of social metabolic reproduction. This is why already in his *Economic and Philosophical Manuscripts of 1844* Marx was talking about *'movable property's civilized victory'*,[182] stressing also that 'Precisely in the fact that division of labour and exchange are embodiments of private property lies the twofold proof, on the one hand, that human life required private property for its realization, and on the other hand that it now requires the supersession of private property.'[183]

The same considerations were reiterated by Marx in the published volumes of *Capital* as well as in their earlier versions. Thus, in his *Economic Manuscripts of 1861-63,* talking about the capitalist process of reification and 'the inversion of the subject into the object and vice versa', he insisted that

Looked at *historically* this inversion appears as the point of entry necessary in order to enforce, at the expense of the majority, the creation of wealth as such, i.e. the ruthless powers of social labour, which alone can form the material basis for a free human society. It is necessary to pass through this antagonistic form, just as man had first to shape his spiritual forces in a religious form, as powers independent of him. It is the *alienation process* of his own labour. To that extent, the worker here stands higher than the capitalist from the outset, in that the latter is rooted in that alienation process, and finds in it his absolute satisfaction, whereas the worker, as its victim, stands from the outset in a relation of rebellion towards it and perceives it as a process of enslavement. To the extent that the production process is at the same time a real labour process, and the capitalist has to perform the function of *supervision* and *direction* in actual production, his activity in fact obtains thereby a specific, manifold content. But the *labour process* itself only appears as a *means* to the *valorisation process,* just as the use value of the product only appears as the vehicle of its exchange value. The self-valorisation of capital — the creation of surplus value — is therefore the determining, dominating, and overmastering purpose of the capitalist, the absolute driving force and content of his action, in fact only the rationalized drive and purpose of the hoarder. This is an utterly miserable and abstract content, which makes the capitalist appear as just as much under the yoke of the capital-relation as is the worker at the opposite extreme, even if from a different angle.[184]

Thus, what in the end decided the issue was: how long could the second order mediations of the historically established *capital-relation* fulfil their *productive* functions, notwithstanding the fact that they were exercised in an inhuman form, 'at the expense of the majority'. For 'the *productivity* of capital consists, first of all, even when it is only the formal subsumption of labour under capital that is being considered, in the *compulsion to perform surplus labour;* to work beyond the individual's immediate needs. The capitalist mode of production shares this compulsion with previous modes of production, but exerts it, carries it out, in a manner more favourable to production.'[185] Moreover, capital is also productive 'as absorbing within itself and appropriating the productive powers of social labour, and the social powers of production in general'.[186] This consideration is very important because through the full unfolding of the capital-relation there develops 'a great continuity and intensity of labour and a greater economy in the employment of the conditions of labour, in that every effort is made to ensure that the product only represents *socially necessary labour time* (or, RATHER, less than that). This applies both with regard to the living labour employed to produce the product, and with regard to the *objectified* labour which, as the value of the means of production employed, enters as a constituent element into the value of the product.'[187]

However, these — historically positive — aspects of the established mode of social metabolic reproduction constitute only one side of the coin. The obverse side is that the system of production based on the capital-relation is full of antagonisms. For one thing, both the particular capitalists and the individual workers function in it only as *personifications* of capital and labour, and have to suffer the consequences of the domination and subordination implicit in the relationship between the particular personifications and what is being personified. Thus the law of value, for instance, which regulates the production of surplus value 'appears as inflicted by the capitalists upon each other and upon the workers — hence it in fact appears as a law of capital operating against both capital and labour.'[188] Naturally, labour — both in general and in its particular personifications — is deeply affected by its structural subordination to capital in every respect. This is an antagonistic relationship of the highest intensity, with its necessary impact on the productive potentialities and limitations of the capital system as a whole. Moreover, contradictions spring up also in places where they might be least expected, arising even from the positive accomplishments of the capital-relation. For production within the framework of capital's second order mediations

> is not limited by any predetermining or predetermined barriers set by needs. (Its antagonistic character implies *barriers to production*, which it wants to go beyond. Hence crises, overproduction, etc.) This is one side, one distinction from the earlier mode of production; the positive side, IF YOU LIKE. The other side is the negative, or antagonistic one: *production* in opposition to, and without concerning itself about, the *producer*. The real producer as mere means of production, objective wealth as an end in itself. And therefore the development of this objective wealth in opposition to, and at the cost of, the human individual.[189]

Marx never entered into a detailed discussion of the intermediary historical stages and corresponding forms of metabolic interchange linking the capital-relation to the social order anticipated by him. The socioeconomic constraints of his age and the standpoint he adopted in relation to them made that impossible for him. Nevertheless, he based his critical anticipations on the two solid pillars of (1) the realistic assessment of the historical achievements and immense practical force of the capital system, and (2) the identification of the structural antagonisms which tended to undermine it as a viable system of social metabolic reproduction or 'social life process'. Resting his arguments on these two pillars, he concluded the line of thought distancing and indeed diametrically opposing himself to the classics of political economy by saying that through the articulation of the capital-relation

A complete revolution takes place. On the one hand it creates, for the first time, the *real conditions for the domination of capital over labour,* complementing them, giving them an appropriate form, and on the other hand, in the productive powers of labour developed by it in opposition to the worker, in the conditions of production and relations of communication, it creates the real conditions for a new mode of production, *superseding the antagonistic form* of the capitalist mode of production, and thus lays the *material basis* for a *newly shaped social life process* and therewith a new social formation.

This is an essentially different conception from that of the bourgeois political economists, themselves imprisoned in capitalist preconceptions, who are admittedly able to see how production is carried on *within* the capital-relation, but not how this *relation* is itself produced, and how at the same time the material conditions for its dissolution are produced within it, thereby removing its *historical justification* as a *necessary form* of economic development, of the production of social wealth.[190]

It goes without saying, the loss of capital's erstwhile historical justification as the form necessary for continued economic development is by itself still at an astronomical distance from the establishment of a 'newly shaped social life process'. For the present embodiment of the capital-relation in an economically advanced material basis is no more than a mere *potentiality* for the creation of the projected new, radically different, mode of control of social metabolic reproduction. As such, the new mode of reproductive interchange appears only on the positive outer horizon of a comprehensive social transformatory practice. Its anticipated objectives become attainable only on condition that this trans-formatory practice succeeds (and to the degree to which it does succeed) in positively substituting itself, through the articulation and operation of its 'newly shaped' first order mediations of reproduction,[191] for the established capital system's *oppressive actuality.*

Thus, the important question concerns the transformation of *potentiality* into *actuality*. This task cannot be accomplished without radically restructuring the ever more destructive 'material basis' and 'material conditions' of the ubiquitous capital system — which created 'for the first time, the real conditions for the domination of capital over labour' — into a framework of social metabolic exchange usable by the individuals for securing their own ends. In other words, the task in question can only mean: securing *consciously chosen* ends by the social individuals and fulfilling themselves *as individuals* — and not as particular personifications of capital or labour[192] — in the process. And to do so instead of being resigned, as they are forced to be today, to the service of a system which lays down the imperatives of production for its own sake as an unchallengeable 'end in itself', ruthlessly enforcing them through the vicious circle of its second order mediations, despite the undeniable wastefulness and growing destructiveness of its mode of control. Naturally, to move to the alternative mode of social metabolic reproduction anticipated by Marx requires a *qualitative* change, with far-reaching implications also for the inheritable 'material basis' and 'material conditions'. For in their existing modality they are quite incompatible with socialist aspirations.

To bring about the required qualitative change calls for the establishment of appropriate forms and instruments of mediatory interchanges, so as to make the given material conditions first usable for the positive purposes of a 'newly shaped social life process'. Today, more than ever before, meeting the challenge of this laborious qualitative transformation must constitute the vital orienting principle of the socialist project. For notwithstanding the productive achievements of the capital system in the intervening historical period — or, rather, precisely because of their self-serving perversity — the existing material conditions are even less directly usable for the realization of socialist aspirations today than they were in Marx's lifetime. Indeed, the deeply embedded second order mediations of the established mode of social metabolic reproduction categorically rule out the possibility of shortcuts to the realization of the originally anticipated socialist objectives.

4.5 *Alienated articulation of primary social reproductive mediation and the positive alternative*

4.5.1
THE emergence and domination of capital's second order mediations cannot be properly appreciated without relating them to their far-reaching historical antecedents. This is important for two principal reasons. First, because all those who adopt the standpoint of capital tend to obliterate their historical specificities, so as to be able to assert the unqualified validity and structural unalterability of the established order of social metabolic control, as seen in the writings of all bourgeois political economists and philosophers, from Adam Smith and Kant through Hegel and the 19th century propounders of the 'marginal revolution' in economics all the way to the apologists of capital in our own days, like Hayek. The second reason is even more important for a socialist critique of the capital system. It concerns the other extreme in these matters, i.e. the neglect of the profound historical roots of the now globally dominant mode of socioeconomic reproduction. Adopting such stance results in a fateful underestimation of the magnitude of the task facing socialists. For by concentrating on some rather limited characteristics of the relatively short *capitalist* phase of historical development — and in particular on those aspects of its property relations which can be directly affected by the overthrow of the capitalist state and the legal/political expropriation of private property — the immense regenerative/restoratory power of the prevailing mode of social metabolic reproduction, asserted through the vicious circle of its second order mediations, is completely lost sight of. As a result, the original socialist objectives become ever more elusive, and the inherited metabolic structures continue to dominate society as before. In-

deed, the crippling power of the fundamentally unaltered second order mediations is compounded by the centrally cultivated false belief that a radically different mode of societal reproduction is being operated in postrevolutionary societies. The new mode of societal reproduction is supposed to function on the basis of the truly democratic and consciously planned decisions of all individuals, although they are in actuality as much at the mercy of the 'power of things' as they were in the past. For society is administered by the new type of 'personifications of capital', the party bureaucrats of the postcapitalist capital system, whose primary function is to impose on the new type of 'personifications of labour' (the 'socialist workers' from whom the extraction of surplus-labour is not economically controlled) the imperatives of a reified and fatefully alienating system of social metabolic reproduction.

We can identify in historical terms three sets of determinations which remain embodied, as if they were 'geological' or 'archaeological layers', in the structural make-up of the capital system. Chronologically the most recent of them belongs to the *capitalist* phase of development, extending over the last four centuries only. The middle layer, by contrast, embraces a much longer time scale. It covers in fact many centuries during which some particular second order mediations of capital gradually emerge and become consolidated, as for instance do early monetary and merchant capital. However, these forms of social metabolic mediation can only add up to what Marx calls 'the *formal subsumption* of labour under capital', in contrast to its *'real subsumption'* under the historically specific conditions of capitalism, as we shall see in Chapter 17. And the earliest phase of development relevant to the understanding of capital's historical constitution produces those forms of domination which are by no means characteristic of the capital system's mode of operation but, none the less, are later reproduced in it in a form appropriate to its overall trend of unfolding. Thus the hierarchical/structural *division of labour,* assuming in due course a variety of forms of *class domination,* historically precedes even the most embryonic manifestations of capital's mode of controlling the social metabolic process. Nevertheless, through capital's second order mediations the earlier established hierarchical social division of labour assumes a historically specific form; such that it can fully exploit and put to the use of capital-accumulation at first the *formal* subsumption of labour under capital, on the basis of which ever more powerful capital is then enabled to proceed to labour's incomparably more productive/profitable *real subsumption* under itself, bringing with it the global triumph of the fully developed capital system, in the form of universally diffused commodity production. And the same goes for all the other historically preceding forms of domination. They become subsumed under, or incorporated into, the specific second order mediations of the capital system, from the family to the controlling structures of the labour process, and from the various institutions of discriminatory exchange to the overall political framework of domination of very different types of societies.

It cannot be stressed enough that although the long drawn out process of constitution of capital's second order mediations is *cumulative,* it is by no means *uniform.* Thus, to take an important example, the consolidation of the nuclear family — accomplished in tune with the necessity of *flexible property relations* appropriate to the conditions of universal alienability and reification, as well as to the essential requirement of successfully reproducing a *mobile labour force* without which the *capitalist* phase of development of the capital system could not possibly function — is a much later historical phenomenon than the appearance of dynamic monetary exchange relations. Likewise, the earliest forms of commodity production, even if they happen to be (as in the first place obviously they must be) very limited in extent, precede by many centuries the formation of the modern state, which in its turn is absolutely vital to the full articulation of the global capital system.

All the same, through the cumulative impact of the unfolding process of subsuming under the specific requirements of capital's mode of control the earlier forms of social metabolic mediation, the various constituents of social reproductive interchange coalesce into a powerful and coherent new system. This is possible only through a comprehensive *qualitative redimensioning* of capital's historical antecedents, contrary to the eternalizing apologetics of bourgeois thought conceived from the standpoint of the already developed capital system.

4.5.2

THE salient features of this qualitative redimensioning of the earlier forms and structures of reproductive mediation may be summed up as follows:

- the dominant tendency of capital's second order mediations is *economic* in a twofold sense:

(1) it moves progressively away from the earlier — primarily *political* — control of the social reproduction process, instituting in its place a set of primarily economic modes and instruments of reproductive interchange by orienting itself towards the universal prevalence of the 'cash nexus', in accordance with the earlier mentioned principle of *l'argent n'a pas de maître*, 'money has no master'; and

(2) 'economizing'

(a) with the *means and material* used up in the process of production;

(b) with the ever more productive *methods* required for running an efficient labour process by developing knowledge (natural science, etc.) in a form most appropriate to the expansion and profit-oriented objectives of the capital system;

(c) with the *quantity of labour* required for a determinate quantity of products, reducing to an absolute minimum socially necessary labour time in a number of different ways, including the perfection of the technological division of labour (inside the productive enterprise) as well as the social division of labour between them (in society at large);

(d) with the actual and potential expenditure of productive resources needlessly wasted on *interruptions* in production, by securing a degree of *continuity* in production which — even if still very far from its full potential, attainable only in a non-antagonistic framework of production — used to be totally inconceivable in earlier systems of social metabolic reproduction;

(e) with the efforts needlessly expended — or, considered in another way, with the potentially available productive energies wasted because not activated — by relying on *isolated* productive practices, superseding the limitations of the latter by bringing into play the latent power of what Marx calls 'the animal spirit' through performing productive tasks 'in common', and thereby putting to a productive use — without any cost whatsoever to capital itself — the positive power emanating from the ever-increasing socialization of production; and

(f) with the available — and parallel to the productive advancement of the capital system greatly increased — population, earlier wasted as useless and counter-productive 'surplus population' (and 'controlled' through the most inhuman methods, by hanging hundreds of thousands of 'vagabonds' in England alone during the historical phase of 'primitive capital accumulation'), put to productive use by successfully expanding capital both in employment and as the profitable economy-enhancing 'industrial reserve army';

• the new mode of control is characterized by a high degree of *homogenization* of the forms and institutions of societal interchange, under the dominance of the *economic* principle in both senses mentioned above, with favourable consequences for the overall cohesion of the social reproductive system and the relatively easy controllability of the individuals. On the one hand, in accordance with the first sense the successfully instituted — primarily economic — modes and instruments of reproductive interchange effectively circumscribe the life-activity of individuals (and, of course, they do so also with the highest feasible degree of economic compulsion of 'free labour', as a result of which failure to conform to such compulsion can only be attempted 'on the pain of death' imposed not through the state executioner but through the impersonal agency of starvation). And, on the other hand, the second sense provides the most powerful ideological justification for 'rationally accepting' the given system as the 'best of all possible worlds', functioning 'to the benefit of all' (and, according to Hayek, as we have seen above, functioning 'best of all to the benefit of the proletarians'). By contrast, earlier forms of social reproductive interchange had to control the individuals through *external* means and institutions of norm-enforcement, from political violence to the sanctions of the Church, etc. The highly homogenized reproductive practices of the capital system, as originally constituted, set out to achieve such control by *internal/consensual* means. Hence the central importance — indeed the ideality and unquestioned authority — of the market both in rationalizing ideology and in spontaneous socioeconomic practice;

• the successful pursuit of *expansion* and *accumulation* is the fundamental aim of economic activity, on the assumption that only 'the sky is the limit', both in strictly natural/material terms and in relation to the human resources required for securing the ever-expanded reproduction of the system. Accordingly, the uncritical axiomatic character of the assumption that all obstacles can — since they must — be overcome by enhancing productivity and by endlessly increasing the size of the required, favourably problem-solving, operations of the dominant economic enterprises; and

• the institution and perfection of *formal equality* and *substantive inequality* belong to the normal mode of operation of the capital system. This is fully in tune with the trend of homogenization under the dominant economic principle, serving the need for the supply of a mobile and expanding labour force and for the removal of artificial obstacles — as, for instance, the feudal non-alienability of land and the prohibition on interest-bearing capital, condemned as 'sinful usury' — from the path of successful economic development, and in general terms the viability of contracts. The discriminatory economic structures of 'civil society' — with the necessary subordination of labour built into its economic constituents — are quite sufficient to take care of the need for *substantive inequality* vital to the operation of the system. By contrast, modes of social metabolic reproduction in which the individuals are externally/politically controlled must maintain their iniquitous character also on the formal/legal plane, as shown by the type of domination exercised under slavery or under the formally institutionalized privileges and prohibitions of the feudal system.

All these trends are clearly in evidence during the ascending phase of capital's historical development, securing thereby the dominance of its second order mediations. However, it is important to note that the twentieth century, and especially the last few decades of it, has produced a significant reversal in all of the trends here referred to, including the earlier prevalent, legally safeguarded, movement towards the institution of formal equality. For the limits of formal equality in the capital system are always set in subordination to the requirements of substantive — structurally, through the changing material power relations enforced — inequality. Thus, liberal labour legislation in favour of the trades unions is unthinkable without the benefits it affords to sections of capital which would be negatively affected in their competitive position by 'unscrupulous employers' and 'cowboy operators'. This is, of course, a historically changing condition, rendered anachronistic by the altered power relations between sections of ever more concentrated and centralized capital. It is therefore understandable that in England, at an earlier phase of development, none other than Sir Winston Churchill — the same politician who later, in 1926, was indefatigable in his efforts to suppress first the coal-miners' strike and then the General strike — was most active in initiating 'enlightened labour legislation', precisely in order to deny the fruits of 'unfair advantage' to so-called 'bad employers'. In contrast, his Conservative descendants today (with a most revealing degree of complicity not only by the Liberal but also by the Labour Party) introduced law after law into the statute books in order to castrate the trades union movement. The same goes both for the enactment and the subsequent curtailment or non-enforcement of the once reasonably effective legal safeguards embodied in anti-monopoly legislation. At the time of their original introduction the sponsors of anti-monopoly laws insisted, in the name of parliamentary authority, on the formal equality of capital's competing units. The situation is very different today. The obvious weakening of such laws in recent times to the point of utter meaninglessness is the result of the ongoing monopolistic developments in the material base of contemporary capitalist society which objectively/structurally favour the giant corporations. The potential impact of these changes cannot be exaggerated. For the reversal of the trends which in their time promoted the dynamic expansion of the now globally dominant system of social metabolic control has very serious implications for the future viability of capital's second order mediations.

4.5.3

THE defenders of capital cannot acknowledge the historical character and limits of the established mode and structures of reproductive mediation. In their eagerness to eternalize the capital system as one to which there can be no alternative, they try to characterize a highly specific mode of socioeconomic interchange, based on the historically constituted rule of capital, as if it was in its substance timeless and possessed an absolutely unquestionable, universal validity. Nothing illustrates this better than Hayek's category of 'the extended economic order'. For even with regard to the most remote past, 'time' appears on its horizon only as a mechanical quantitative notion — the inexplicable but wholly commendable 'extension' in the quantity of material reproduction, which in Hayek's view equals 'civilization'. Only a madman, opting for the liquidation of humanity, could question the necessity of maintaining *'the* extended economic order', whose 'extension', according to Hayek, constitutes its absolute justification forever in the future. Naturally, in the course of such reasoning all of the specific — positive or negative but always qualitatively significant — defining characteristics of capital's mode of 'extended reproduction' disappear from the picture, in the interest of eternalizing apologetics. The *primary* social metabolic functions without which humanity could not possibly survive even in the most ideal form of society — from the biological reproduction of the individuals to the regulation of the conditions of economic and cultural reproduction — are crudely equated with their capitalist varieties, no matter how problematical the latter might be. Even the *qualitative redimensioning* of the specific second order mediations of the historically earlier forms of hierarchical domination and subordination is ignored or obliterated, reaching the desired conclusions of capital-eternalizing apologetics on the basis of the telling assumption that domination as such is 'natural' and insurmountable. From this position only a short step is needed, of course, to Hayek's earlier quoted absurd assertion according to which the poor owe their very existence and 'well being' to the rich, and they should be eternally grateful for it.

The other extreme mentioned earlier which we must distance ourselves from, neglects the 'layers' of social metabolic reproduction for very different reasons. In its desire to make shortcuts to the anticipated new historical order it postulates that by the political intervention of 'expropriating the expropriators', and thereby putting an end to the capitalist form of exploitation, the socialist goal of emancipation can be realized. In this firmly but one-sidedly anti-capitalist conception 'capital' is simply equated with *capitalism.* Thus the historical unfolding and the strength of the capital system is unrealistically confined to its phase characterized by the *'real subsumption* of labour under capital'; a position which fails to confront the difficult issues of how such a 'real subsumption' became possible in the first place, and how it can continue to sustain itself despite its explosive contradictions. This way of assessing the historical parameters of the socialist project is problematical in two major respects.

First, the fact is fatefully ignored that in the course of capital's complex historical development, through the successful qualitative redimensioning of the hierarchical second order mediations of the reproductive systems which preceded the capitalist mode of social metabolic control by thousands of years — a process which worked partly by incorporating modes of interchange characteristic of the earliest forms of capital, but not of capitalism, and partly those which had nothing to do with capital's specificities even in its most embryonic form, but asserted themselves none the less through modes of hierarchy and domination — a most powerful and coherent system of metabolic control is constituted. One which cannot be historically superseded without devising viable alternatives to the manifold reproductive functions fulfilled in it through the *formal* as well as *real subsumption* of labour deeply embedded in the various layers of domination and subordination of the capital system. This means that in view of the fact that capital's mode of social metabolic control is historically constituted as a closely interconnected whole, through the *homogenizing* redimensioning of its historical antecedents, *none* of its vital second order mediations can be simply incorporated into the socialist alternative. *There can be no 'pick and choose'* in this respect, contrary to what so-called 'market socialists' imagined in the former Soviet Union and in Eastern Europe before the dramatic implosion of the Soviet system under Gorbachev and Yeltsin brought to them a rude awakening.

The second respect which must be kept in mind is even more important. It concerns the inherently *positive* side of socialist aspirations, in contrast to the necessary but by no means sufficient negation of labour's formal and real subsumption under capital.

The positive side in question happens to be more important because without successfully establishing the conditions of its realization the socialist project cannot prove its viability even as the radical negation of the established order, no matter how genuine is its concern with the ultimate destructiveness of uncontrollable capital-accumulation and the subjection of human need to the imperatives of ever-expanding exchange value. The point is that it is relatively easy to say *no* not only to the capitalist way of controlling the social individuals but in principle also to capital in general, considered with all of its historical roots and ramifications, including its postcapitalist metamorphoses painfully experienced in the twentieth century.

THE positive side of the socialist project cannot be articulated without confronting the problems of *primary* social metabolic mediation. To put it in another way, the positive dimension of the socialist alternative cannot be turned into reality without finding a rationally controllable and humanly rewarding equivalent to all those vital functions of individual and social reproduction which must be fulfilled — in one form or another — by all conceivable systems of productive mediatory interchange.

In this sense, we must be aware of the necessary implications of two unalterable defining characteristics:

(1) human beings are a *part* of nature who must satisfy their elementary needs through a constant interchange with nature, and

(2) they are constituted in such a way that they cannot survive as individuals of the species to which they belong — the uniquely 'interventionist' species of the natural world — on the basis of an *unmediated* interchange with nature (as animals do), regulated by instinctual behaviour directly determined by nature, however complex such instinctual behaviour might be.

As a result of these fundamental ontological conditions and determinations, human individuals must always fulfil the inescapable material and cultural requirements of their survival through the necessary *primary functions of mediation* among themselves and with nature at large. This means securing and safeguarding the objective conditions of their productive reproduction under circumstances which inevitably and progressively change under the impact of their own intervention through productive activity — the uniquely human ontology of labour — in the original order of nature. To do so is possible only by fully involving every facet of human productive — and indeed through the complex dialectics of labour and history self-productive — reproduction.

Thus, there can be no escape from the imperative to establish fundamental structural relationships through which the vital functions of *primary mediation* can be carried on for as long as humankind is to survive. Indeed, paradoxically, what greatly strengthens the vicious circle of capital's second order mediations is that its historically evolved principal forms discussed in Section 4.2.1, are all linked, even if in an alienated way, to some primary or first order mediation of essential productive/reproductive activity: a fact ignored by socialists at their peril.

The essential forms of primary mediation embrace the relations within the framework of which both the individuals of the human species and the progressively more complex and intertwined material and moral/intellectual/cultural conditions of their life-activity are reproduced in accordance with the available, and cumulatively enlarged, sociohistorical margin of action. They include:

- the necessary, more or less spontaneous, regulation of biological reproductive activity and the size of the sustainable population, in conjunction with the available resources;
- the regulation of the labour process through which the given community's necessary interchange with nature can produce the goods required for human gratification, as well as the appropriate working tools, productive enterprises, and knowledge by means of which the reproductive process itself can be maintained and improved;
- the establishment of suitable exchange relations under which the historically changing needs of human beings can be linked together for the purpose of optimizing the available natural and productive — including the culturally productive — resources;
- the organization, co-ordination and control of the multiplicity of activities through which the material and cultural requirements of the successful social metabolic reproduction process of progressively more complex human communities can be secured and safeguarded;
- the rational allocation of the available material and human resources, fighting against the tyranny of scarcity through the economic (in its sense of economizing) utilization of the given society's ways and means of reproduction, as far as feasible on the basis of the attained level of productivity and within the confines of the established socioeconomic structures; and
- the enactment and administration of the rules and regulations of the given society as a whole, in conjunction with the other primary mediatory functions and determinations.

As we can see, none of these primary mediatory imperatives in and by itself calls for the establishment of structural hierarchies of domination and subordination as the necessary framework of social metabolic reproduction. The oppressive determinations of hierarchical modes of reproductive control arise from other roots in the course of history. For, inevitably, the second order mediations of the historically specific social reproductive systems deeply affect the realization of all of the primary mediatory functions.

Thus, through capital's second order mediations every one of the primary forms is altered almost beyond recognition, so as to suit the self-expansionary needs of a fetishistic and alienating system of social metabolic control which must subordinate absolutely everything to the imperative of capital-accumulation. This is why, for instance, the single-mindedly pursued aim of reducing the material and living labour 'costs of production' in the capital system, and the concomitant fight against scarcity, show tremendous achievements on one plane, only in order to nullify them completely on another through the creation of the most absurd 'artificial appetites' and scarcities, which serve nothing but the ever more wasteful reproduction of this 'extended economic order'. Equally, to take another of the primary mediatory requirements — the enactment and administration of the rules laid down for comprehensive societal interchange, — we find their characteristic distortion. For the necessary practices concerned with both the enactment and the administration of those rules summarily exclude the overwhelming majority of individuals, because they occupy the bottom layers in the command structure of capital both in 'civil society' and in the political state. They are allowed to 'participate',[193] even in the best of cases, only in the most superficial sense of once in four or five years exercising their 'political power' for the purpose of abdicating their 'democratic rights', legitimating thereby capital's structurally prejudged and enforced system of formal equality and substantive inequality mentioned above. Thus the primary mediatory functions of societal rule-enactment and administration — which could be in principle exercised in a substantively democratic way by all and to the benefit of all — assume the alienated form of the modern political state. The mandate of the state is to impose on the individuals the imperatives of the extended reproduction of the capital system in its own way, in conformity to its objective constitution and structural determination as the comprehensive political command structure of capital.

But even so, as regards the unavoidable primary functions of social reproductive mediation there can be no question of a romantic nostalgia for some idealized 'natural state' or 'original condition'. For none of them could be considered to be primary in a straightforward chronological sense. In all feasible modes of social metabolic reproduction they do not constitute a *historically* primary layer but a *structural* one. As such, they must be always reshaped in accordance with the sociohistorical specificities of the reproductive order in which they continue to exercise their functions — as *transhistorical* determinations — within the objective dialectic of 'continuity in discontinuity' and vice versa.

Naturally, just as there could be no idealized 'original natural state' directly corresponding to the primary mediations to which one could return, in the same way there can be no question of escaping the structural determination of the transhistorically persistent mediatory necessities. But precisely for this reason, it makes a world of difference whether the structurally inescapable primary mediatory functions are reshaped under the prevailing historical circumstances — always in the form of specific second order mediations — as conducive to human self-realization or, on the contrary, as destructively opposed to it.

It is impossible to move from the vicious circle of capital's second order mediations either to the romanticized world of a more or less idyllic 'original state' which, in the old tales of religion and philosophy, preceded the 'fall' of alienation, or to a no-man's land made up entirely from the structural parameters of — likewise idealized — primary mediation. Like it or not, the latter can only exist in and through the second order mediations of historically changing social orders. Accordingly, the meaning of the socialist project — in contrast to capital's mode of reproduction which puts the levers of control beyond the individuals' reach even in the words of its honourable idealizers, from Adam Smith's 'invisible hand' to Hegel's 'cunning of Reason' — is the establishment of a coherent set of practically viable second order mediations rationally controlled not by some mysterious impersonal entity, like the 'World Spirit' and its variants, nor by a mythical 'collective', but by the real individuals.

Given their unavoidable links to the sociohistorical conditions which preceded them — conditions transcendable only in the threefold sense of the good old German term of 'Aufhebung' (i.e. 'surpassing', 'preservation', and 'raising to a higher level') — no one could seriously maintain that the second order mediations of the socialist reproduction process, especially in its early stages of development, could be free from even severely limiting constraints. Nevertheless, there is a major difference in that the socialist project aims at progressively reducing the power of such objective constraints, rather than making a virtue out of their permanence, as the defenders of the capital system do, in the name of an idealized market and other reified structures of domination.

In this sense, the socialist alternative defines itself as a set of practices which fulfil the primary mediatory functions of social metabolic reproduction on a rationally constituted and — in accordance with historically changing human needs — alterable structural basis, without subjecting the individuals, that is, to the 'power of things'. Indeed, the viability of going *beyond capital* hinges on this cardinal issue. For in the light of historical experience it is painfully obvious that, whatever the difficulties on the way, there can be no lasting success even in the much more limited objective of opposing capitalism without substituting for the vicious circle of capital's interlocking second order mediations a sustainable positive alternative. This calls for the institution of forms and structures of metabolic control through which the social individuals — involved in their necessary interchange both among themselves and with nature, in harmony with the requirements of the primary mediatory functions of human existence — can give meaning to the possibilities of 'enlarged reproduction'. Not in the sense of submitting themselves to the tyranny of a fetishistic 'extended economic order' but by enlarging their own creative powers as social individuals.

CHAPTER FIVE

THE ACTIVATION OF CAPITAL'S ABSOLUTE LIMITS

EVERY system of social metabolic reproduction has its intrinsic or absolute limits which cannot be transcended without changing the prevailing mode of control into a qualitatively different one. When such limits are reached in the course of historical development, it becomes imperative to transform the established order's structural parameters — or, in other words, its objective 'practical premisses' — which normally circumscribe the overall margin of adjustment of the reproductive practices feasible under the circumstances. To do so means subjecting to a fundamental critical scrutiny nothing less than the historically given society's most basic practical orienting principles and their instrumental/institutional corollaries. For under the circumstances of the unavoidable radical change they turn — from being the valid presuppositions and the apparently insurmountable structural framework of all theoretical as well as practical critique — into absolutely paralyzing constraints.

In principle the transformatory practical critique should not constitute a prohibitive problem even in our own historical period, irrespective of how far-reaching and complex the required adjustments might have to be. After all it is a matter of vital concern to human beings to secure 'the rule of society over wealth', in the universalizable, potentially all-embracing sense of their economy, concerned with the economy of life and the proper relationship between invested effort and achievement. The trouble is, though, that such an aim could not be in sharper contradiction to 'the rule of wealth over society' prevailing of necessity under the capital system. For the latter is imposed on the social individuals in the name of the highly selective/exclusive — and in that way most tendentiously perverted — sense of an extremely problematical 'economy', which must be run for the benefit of the ruling minority despite its crying wastefulness. Thus the frequently advanced argument of 'insurmountable complexity' — from Max Weber to Hayek and to their present-day followers — is only used to lend the semblance of rational justification to the absolute permanence of an ultimately unsustainable socioeconomic order. Accordingly, the meaning given to 'complexity' by all those who hide their real concerns and vested interests behind that notion is not that instituting the necessary qualitative changes might indeed be very difficult, calling for the concerted and dedicated efforts of everyone, but that embarking on such an enterprise should not be even contemplated, let alone practically attempted at all.

Yet, the truth of the matter is that the claimed 'insurmountable complexities' which must be faced today arise not from the apriori requirements of any 'extended economic order' but from the problematical structural presuppositions of the capital system itself. For precisely because this system of social metabolic control is *antagonistically structured* — from its smallest constitutive

142

cells or 'microcosms' to its most comprehensive global units of economic and political interchange — the practical premises of its mode of continued operation must be set so as to secure the permanent subordination of labour to capital. Any attempt to modify that structural subordination must count as an absolute taboo, hence the self-evident proof of 'insurmountable complexity'. Indeed, the more the changing historical circumstances themselves point in the direction of a necessary change in the antagonistic, ever more wasteful and irrational structural premises of the capital system, the more categorically the pre-existent operative imperatives must be enforced and the more narrowly the margin of acceptable adjustments must be set. This is why in the last few decades the dictum of *'there is no alternative'* to the prevailing material dictates had become the unchallengeable axiom of the capital system all over the world.

Maintaining the stability of a system built upon a whole range of explosive structural antagonisms is quite unthinkable without the superimposition of artificial layers of complexity whose primary function is the perpetuation of the ruling order and the postponement of 'the moment of truth'. Since, however, the activation of the absolute limits of capital as a viable reproductive system appeared on our historical horizon, engaging with the question of how to overcome the destructive structural presuppositions of the established mode of social metabolic control cannot be avoided much longer.

To be sure, the deeply entrenched interests of capital and of its 'personifications' militate against all serious consideration of this question. For capital cannot function without enforcing as firmly as ever (even in the most authoritarian fashion if need be) its practical presuppositions and structural antagonisms. If it was not for that, the rational assessment of the historically unfolding dangers to the very conditions of human survival would be by itself a great help in tilting the balance in favour of the necessary changes. However, rational arguments on their own are utterly powerless for overcoming enmity to change when the fundamental practical premises of the materially dominant party are at stake. The rationalizations of 'insurmountable complexity' and of its telling corollaries, backed up by the material might of the established order, cannot be persuasively counteracted even by the best rational arguments unless the latter are also fully supported by a practically viable alternative material force. A force capable of substituting its new orienting principles, together with their organizing and productive embodiments, for the ruling practical presuppositions of the given social order which demonstrate their historical anachronism every day by the increasingly intolerant appeal of capital's personifications to the wisdom of 'there is no alternative'. For, revealingly, in our own days (in the spirit of that wisdom) even the limited defensive organs of the labour movement — its traditional parliamentary parties and trades unions — must be rendered totally ineffective either by integrating the top echelons of their leadership within the framework of an unholy consensus, or by openly mobilizing the oppressive legal devices and the direct material repressive force of the 'democratic state' against the formerly tolerated activities of organized labour.

Thus, given the oppressive structural premises of the capital system, the Marxian socialist project could not confine itself to a theoretical demonstration of the necessity to pursue a rationally sustainable course of social metabolic reproduction. It could not do so despite the fact that in historical terms the most important single aspect of the socialist enterprise happens to be to make it possible — by eliminating class antagonisms and the fateful impact of vested interests inseparable from the capital system's antagonistic structure — that the periodically unavoidable structural changes of social development be rationally introduced as a matter of course by the individuals who are fully empowered to exercise control over their life-activity. The theoretical demonstration of the rational course of fully co-operative — i.e. socialist/communitarian — action required for the realization of this end had to be complemented by the *material* articulation of its truth. This is why Marx had to insist that 'The weapon of criticism cannot replace criticism by weapons, material force must be overthrown by material force; ... *It is not enough for thought to strive for realization, reality must itself strive towards thought.*'[194] At the same time he also indicated the way out of the dilemma implicit in this line of approach by stressing that 'theory also becomes a material force as soon as it has gripped the masses. ...Theory can be realized in a people *only insofar as it is the realization of the needs of that people.*'[195]

Laying down these criteria, while realistic in the overall assessment of what had to be done, made the socialist discourse doubly difficult. For, on the one hand, it had to demonstrate with scientific rigour the validity of its rational 'weapon of criticism' by fully taking into account the strength of its adversary both in general theoretical and in historical/practical terms. And, on the other hand, unlike the conceptions of even the most noble utopian socialists — for whom 'future history resolves itself into the propaganda and the practical carrying out of their social plans. ... For, in their eyes, how can people, when once they understand their system, fail to see in it the best possible plan of the best possible state of society?'[196] — it had to rest its case on the ability or failure of radical socialist theory to 'grip the masses', and to do so by no means on account of its invention of 'the best possible plan of the best possible state of society'. Marx knew very well that there could be no such thing because all actual accomplishments carried within them the seeds of their necessary future transcendence. And he also knew that lasting success for the socialist project could only be envisaged on the ground that the aspirations expressed in it corresponded to the real needs of the people.

Despite the defeats of the historical left, or, rather, more than ever precisely in view of them, the criteria of historically sustainable success originally laid down by Marx — according to which 'It *is not enough for thought to strive for realization, reality must itself strive towards thought'* because 'Theory can be realized in a people only insofar as it is the realization of the needs of that people' — remain valid both as regards the strategy to be followed and for a proper assessment of the failures of the past.

In relation to the latter, it is painfully obvious that the social changes imposed in the name of the socialist project — especially under the slogan of 'socialism in a single country' — were tragically distant from the 'realization of the needs of the people'. But even the original Marxian socialist project had to suffer the constraints of its time. For the crisis of capital perceived by Marx in the mid 19th century in the 'European little corner of the world' failed to become for a long time a general crisis. Instead, the continued historical ascendancy of the bourgeois order on the 'much larger terrain' of the rest of the world dissipated for an entire historical period even the relatively limited European crisis. As a result, the socialist movement itself as first articulated by Marx and his intellectual and political comrades in arms could not help being fatefully premature. *The Marxian theory was striving as it could at the time of its conception towards its realization, but reality itself refused to strive towards it in a way hoped for and stiputated by its originator.*

Today the situation is radically different. In a significant sense it is even the diametrical opposite of what used to be the case in Marx's lifetime. For although the deepening structural crisis of capital means that 'reality is beginning to move towards thought', it seems that as a result of the defeats and failures of the socialist movement (especially in the recent past) thought itself — together with the necessary material and organizational forces without which even the most valid thought cannot 'grip the masses' and become effective material force — refuses to move towards reality and 'strive for realization'. In the meantime the needs of the people remain frustrated and denied as ever before.

However, despite the major defeats of the past the deciding issue is that the end of capital's historical ascendancy in our own age — through the extension of its domination even to the most distant and formerly isolated pockets of the planet — has brought with it the activation of the absolute limits of this system of social metabolic control. Given the relationship of capital's mode of societal reproduction to *causality* and *time* discussed at the beginning of Chapter 4, the margin of displacing the system's contradictions becomes ever narrower and its pretences to the unchallengeable status of *causa sui* palpably absurd, notwithstanding the once unimaginable destructive power at the disposal of its personifications. For through the exercise of such power capital can destroy humankind in general — as indeed it seems to be bent on doing just that (and with it, to be sure, also its own system of control) — but not selectively its historical antagonist.

WHILE we must be aware of the activation of capital's absolute limits in order to remain constantly alert to its destructive implications, it is also necessary to introduce here some qualifications, so as to avoid possible misunderstandings and the illusions of false opitimism with regard to the way out of the crisis.

First, on the hopeful side it must be stressed that the term 'absolute limits' does not imply anything in and by itself absolutely untranscendable, as the apologists of the ruling 'extended economic order' try to make us believe in order to submit to the wisdom of 'there is no alternative'. The limits in question are absolute for the capital system only, due to the innermost structural determinations of its mode of social metabolic control.

The second — far less reassuring — necessary qualification is that we should not imagine that capital's relentless drive to transcend its boundaries will suddenly come to a halt, on the basis of a rational insight that now the system as such has reached its absolute limits. On the contrary, what is most likely is that every attempt will be made to cope with the intensifying contradictions by trying to enlarge the capital system's margin of manoeuvre within its own structural confines. Since, however, the causal foundations responsible for the activation of the absolute limits of this mode of control cannot be addressed within such confines, let alone properly remedied, corrective action in relation to some of the most explosive problems of the troublesome social metabolic process is bound to be pursued by other ways. It will be done by manipulating the encountered obstacles and stretching to the extreme the given forms and mechanisms of reproductive interchange on the plane of their now even by the 'captains of industry' deplored limiting effects.

In view of the fact that the most intractable of the global capital system's contradictions is the one between the internal unrestrainability of its economic constituents and the now inescapable necessity of introducing major restraints, any hope for finding a way out of this vicious circle under the circumstances marked by the activation of capital's absolute limits must be vested in the political dimension of the system. Thus, in the light of recent legislative measures which already point in this direction, there can be no doubt that the full power of the state will be activated to serve the end of squaring capital's vicious circle, even if it means subjecting all potential dissent to extreme authoritarian constraints. Equally there can be no doubt that whether or not such a remedial action (in conformity to the global capital system's structural limits) will be successfully pursued, despite its obvious authoritarian character and destructiveness, will depend on the working class's ability or failure to radically rearticulate the socialist movement as a truly international enterprise.

In any event, what makes matters particularly serious is the fact that the far-reaching issues themselves which confront humankind at the present stage of historical development cannot be avoided either by the ruling capital system or by any alternative to it. Although, as a matter of historical contingency, they have arisen from the activation of capital's absolute limits, they cannot be conveniently bypassed, nor their gravity wished out of existence. On the contrary, they remain the overriding requirement of all-embracing remedial action in the reproductive practices of humankind for as long as the vicious circle of capital's present-day historical contingency is not irretrievably consigned to the past. Indeed, paradoxically, the ability to meet in a sustainable way the absolute historical challenge that had arisen from the perverse historical contingencies and contradictions of the capital system constitutes the measure of viability of *any* social metabolic alternative to the ruling order. Consequently, the struggle to overcome the threatening absolute limits of the capital system is bound to determine the historical agenda for the foreseeable future.

The intractable contradiction between capital's unrestrainability and the now historically unavoidable necessity of fundamental restraints highlights a great problem for the future. For through the dynamism of its unrestrainability capital in the past could secure great productive advancement and thereby move in the direction of potentially satisfying human needs and aspirations. The fact that in the course of historical development the original unrestrainable dynamism had turned against the elementary conditions of human survival, through the activation of capital's absolute limits, does not mean that the positive cause of continued productive advancement itself — the necessary precondition for fulfilling legitimate human aspirations — can be wilfully abandoned.

Understandably, however, under the present conditions of crisis all kinds of false alternatives are put forward by the defenders of the capital system. Thus, to take a prominent example, the advocates of corrective measures assembled under the flag of 'The Limits to Growth'[197] argue that the pursuit of growth as such ought to be abandoned in favour of a fictitious 'global equilibrium [in which} population and capital are essentially stable'.[198] Naturally, they recommend this solution without submitting to serious criticism the socioeconomic system itself which is guilty of producing the symptoms quixotically castigated by them.[199] Yet, contrary to the false dichotomy of 'growth or no growth', the historical challenge of having to struggle against the catastrophic implications of capital's absolute limits consists precisely in the need to find viable solutions to every one of the contradictions manifest in them by a successful qualitative practical redefinition of the meaning of productive advancement, in place of the capital system's fetishistic quantity-oriented way of treating the problems of growth. A *qualitative redefinition* which would embrace the whole of humankind on the basis of *substantive equality,* instead of continuing to exclude the overwhelming majority of human beings from the fruits of productive advancement, as before, throughout the long stretch of capital's historical ascendancy. Characteristically, though, all concern with equality happens to be dismissed by the inspirer of the computerized pseudo-scientific model-mongering that permeates the kind of literature epitomized by *The Limits to Growth* as 'the shiboleth of equality'.[200] However, irrespective of the diligence with which this spirit is applied and the fanfare with which its circular conclusions from arbitrary assumptions are greeted under the pretences of sound academic quantification, no amount of such elitistic insult and demagoguery can deflect attention from the grave issues brought to the fore by the structural crisis of the capital system.

THE four issues chosen for discussion below do not stand for isolated characteristics. Far from it. For every one of them happens to be the focal point of a set of major contradictions. As such they prove to be insurmountable precisely because in conjunction with one another they greatly intensify the disruptive power of each as well as the overall impact of the particular sets in question taken as a whole.

Thus the irreconcilable structural antagonism between global capital — which happens to be unrestrainably transnational in its objective tendency — and the necessarily constraining national states is inseparable from at least three fundamental contradictions: those between (1) *monopoly* and *competition;* (2) ever-increasing *socialization* of the labour process and the *discriminatory/preferential appropriation* of its products (by varieties of capital's personifications, from private capitalists to self-perpetuating collective bureaucracies); and (3) the unstoppably growing *international division of labour* and the irrepressible drive of the unevenly developing and therefore necessarily shifting preponderant powers of the global capital system (in the post-Second World War period primarily the U.S.) for *hegemonic domination.*

Similarly, the problems discussed in Section 5.2 are not confined to loudly trumpeted but conveniently limited environmental issues, like the hypocritical concern in official circles with the 'ozone hole' (which should bring brisk business and maximal profits to some transnational chemical companies, like the British ICI, for their promoted 'ozone-friendly alternative to the guilty CFC gases'). As we shall see, they embrace all vital aspects of the social metabolic conditions of reproduction, from the wasteful allocation of resources (be they renewable or non-renewable) to accumulating poison in all fields for the detriment of many generations to come; and doing so not only in the form of the most irresponsible bequest of the atomic legacy for the future (in the field of both weaponry and power plants) but also as regards chemical pollution of all kinds, including those in the domain of agriculture. Moreover, as far as agricultural production is concerned, condemning countless millions world-wide literally to starvation goes hand in hand with the most absurd protectionist 'common agricultural policies', devised for securing profitably institutionalized waste irrespective of its immediate and long-term consequences. Any attempt to deal with the reluctantly acknowledged problems must be conducted under the prohibitive weight of the fundamental laws and structural antagonisms of the system. Thus the 'corrective measures' envisaged within the framework of big international jamborees — like the 1992 gathering in Rio de Janeiro — amount to absolutely nothing,[201] since they must be subordinated to the perpetuation of the established global power relations and vested interests. Causality and time must be treated as a plaything of the dominant capitalistic interests, no matter how acute the dangers. Thus the future tense is callously and irresponsibly confined to the narrowest horizon of immediate profit expectations. At the same time, the causal dimension of even the most vital conditions of human survival is perilously brushed aside. For only the reactive and retroactive manipulation of symptoms and effects is compatible with the continuing rule of capital's *causa sui*.

In the same way, as regards the quite elementary and politically irrepressible demand for the liberation of women, a number of major issues coalesce in it and — as a permanent reminder of the unfulfilled and unfulfillable promises of the capital system as such — turn the great historic cause of women's emancipation into a *non-integrable* challenge to the rule of capital. For there can be no way of satisfying the demand for women's emancipation — which surfaced a very long time ago, but acquired its urgency in a historic period coinciding with the structural crisis of capital — without a *substantive* change in the established social relations of inequality. In this sense, the women's movement that at first appeared to be limited in scope reaches in fact as a historic challenge well beyond the boundaries of its immediate demands. Indeed it cannot help questioning the core of the ruling system of social metabolic reproduction no matter by what ruses the established order might try to derail its multifaceted manifestations. For by the very nature of its objectives it cannot be placated by formal/legal 'concessions', whether at the level of parliamentary voting rights or at that of the grotesquely publicised opening up of the privileged membership of the Stock Exchange to the token bourgeois woman. Moreover, by focusing attention on the *non-integrable substantive nature* of the matter pursued, the demand for women's emancipation also haunts the bourgeois order with its own past, bringing to the fore the total betrayal of the original ethos on the basis of which that order gained its ascendancy. Thus, the demand for women's emancipation offers a powerful reminder that 'Liberty, Equality and Fraternity' were once upon a time not empty words or cynical mystifications to divert attention from their actually existing opposite. Rather, they were the passionately pursued objectives of a class — the progressive bourgeoisie still sharing a substantive common cause with labour within the framework of the 'Third Estate' — which later had to empty, and later still had to dismiss with contempt as 'shiboleths', its own former beliefs and aspirations in order to justify even the most crying iniquities and inhumanities of the rule of capital in the social order. The great trouble with the cause of women's emancipation for the ruling order is not only that it cannot be satisfied at all in the form of ultimately vacuous formal/legal devices. What makes it equally if not more undigestible is that it cannot be characterized and dismissed as the gratuitous 'envy' of the 'hard earned position of the wealth creators by undeserving labour'. In this way the mystifying condemnation of concern with substantive equality — its equation with 'unjust class aspirations' — by the ruling ideology falls by the wayside. Thus the challenge of women's emancipation inevitably reopens the painful questions of what went wrong with the once sincerely held aspirations of human emancipation, and — in the light of not getting anywhere with the substantive demands for equality — why it all had to go wrong on the ground of the unfolding capital system. Furthermore, to make matters worse, it is now impossible to run away from the uncomfortable questions of 'what' and 'why' by curtly dismissing this new historic challenge — one which could not and cannot be substantively tackled within the structural framework of any known or imaginable class society — as yet another 'shiboleth of equality'. Consequently, just when the personifications of capital became confident that they had succeeded in permanently laying the ghost of socialism and with it the spectre of class emancipation to rest — claiming at the same time with typical self-contradiction both that we live in a 'classless society' (and the like), and that the 'shiboleth of equality' is the manifestation of 'class envy and class greed' — they had to be greatly disappointed. For they are now confronted not only by the demand for women's emancipation, but also by its inherent linkages to the necessary emancipation of human beings in general — both in strictly class terms within the capitalistically advanced countries and in the iniquitous relations of the latter to the super-exploited masses of the so-called 'Third World' — from the rule of capital which always asserts itself as an incurably hierarchical system of domination and subordination. Thus in a paradoxical and most unexpected form — since the class of women cuts across all social class boundaries — the demand for women's emancipation proves to be a 'heel of Achilles' to capital: by demonstrating the total incompatibility of substantive equality with the capital system under historical conditions when the issue as such will not fade away, nor can it be violently repressed (unlike class militancy often in the past), nor indeed can it be emptied of its content and 'realized' in the form of vacuous formal criteria.

Finally, the issue of chronic unemployment brings into play the contradictions and antagonisms of the global capital system in the potentially most explosive form. For all measures devised to cure the profound structural defect of growing unemployment tend to aggravate the situation, instead of alleviating the problem. To be sure, it would be a miracle if it could be otherwise, since all of the practical premises and causal determinants of the system must be taken for given and unalterable. Ruthlessly enforcing the structural subordination of labour to capital even in the 'liberal democratic' countries (recently with more openly anti-labour laws) and pretending at the same time that it does not exist in this best one of all actually feasible worlds is the typical way of dealing with the difficulties. Thus large-scale state intervention at all levels and in all matters with direct or indirect bearing on the continued rule of capital over labour — made more than ever necessary by the deepening structural crisis of the system — goes hand in hand with the most cynical ideological mystification concerning the one and only viable form of socioeconomic reproduction, the idealized 'market society' and the 'equal opportunities' which such a society is supposed to offer to all individuals. The reality, though, is that even in the most privileged part of the capital system the most serious social disease of mass unemployment had assumed chronic proportions, with no end in sight to the worsening trend. Thus in capitalistically advanced Europe alone there are well over 20 million unemployed people, and at least another 16 million in other 'advanced capitalist countries'. All these menacing figures are recorded in the form of greatly understated if not cynically falsified official figures in terms of which in Britain, for instance, *16 hours* of work per week (often associated with the most miserable remuneration, offering to millions of workers £2 per hour, i.e. the princely sum of $3 at 1994 currency values) counts as 'full employment', and many categories of actually unemployed people are arbitrarily excluded, under one pretext or another, from the unemployment statistics. The remedy to the ensuing deficiencies and 'dysfunctions' due to chronic unemployment in all countries under the rule of capital is envisaged, in strict conformity to the ultimately self-contradictory causal parameters of the capital system, in terms of 'increased labour discipline' and 'greater efficiency', resulting in fact in the depression of wage levels, in the growing casualization of the labour force even in the capitalistically most advanced countries, and in an overall increase in unemployment. The much idealized strategy of 'globalization' — in truth yet another name for the continued enforcement of the most iniquitous socioeconomic power relations between the capitalistically advanced and the 'underdeveloped' or 'Third World' countries of the global capital system — aggravate the problems of chronic unemployment also in the 'metropolitan' or 'core' countries, accelerating the earlier mentioned trend for the equalization of the differential rate of exploitation. Taming or repressing the labour force — with the active cooperation of its political and trades union leadership — in the name of labour discipline, increased productivity, market efficiency, and international competitiveness, is of no real solution in this respect, despite the *partial* advantages that can be *temporarily* derived from it for one section or another of competing capital. For in its overall effect such measures are not able to counter the trend towards global recession — and in due course depression — for the simple reason that it is impossible to squeeze 'growing purchasing power' (required for a 'healthy expansion') from the shrinking wages and the deteriorating standard of living of the labour force. Despite all efforts and resources of capitalist economic theory and state intervention nobody succeeded in solving this particular contradiction — not even the single-minded and ruthless representatives of the 'Radical Right' in business and government — nor indeed are they ever going to be able to do so. Thanks to its total monopoly of the material and means of production capital can subject the labour force to its imperatives — but only within limits now being approached as a historical trend. This is why the absurdity of the price that must be paid for the permanence of the prevailing conditions cannot be forever hidden beneath the mystifications of the idealized 'market society'. The point is that in order to extricate itself from the difficulties of profitable expansion and accumulation globally competing capital tends to reduce to a profitable minimum 'necessary labour time' (or the 'labour cost of production'), thereby inevitably tending to transfom the workers into an increasingly *super-*

fluous labour force. But by doing so capital simultaneously also undermines the vital conditions of its own expanded reproduction. As we shall see in Section 5.4, neither the intensification of the rate of exploitation, nor the efforts to solve the problem by 'globalization' and by the creation of ever greater monopolies can show a way out from this vicious circle. Thus the conditions necessary for securing and safeguarding the proper functioning of the system — a system of control *par excellence* or nothing — tend to escape from capital's control, raising the spectre of destructive uncontrollability in the absence of a socialist alternative. The contradiction here at work is therefore a truly explosive one. This is what confers a real meaning on the self-serving concern of capital's personifications with the problem of 'population explosion'. As such it has a twofold meaning. On the one hand it indicates the unmanageable multiplication of the 'superfluous labour force' of society, and on the other it points to the accumulation of the unstable explosive charge that inevitably goes with such developments.

IN relation to all four sets of issues we are here concerned with, two further points must be briefly made. First, that these absolute limits of the capital system activated under the present circumstances are not separate from but tendentially inherent from the very outset in the law of value. In this sense they correspond in fact to the 'maturation' or full assertion of the law of value under conditions marked by the closure of the progressive phase of capital's historical ascendancy. And *vice versa*, the progressive phase of capital's historical ascendancy can be said to come to its closure precisely because the global capital system as such reaches the absolute limits beyond which the law of value cannot be accommodated within its structural confines.

The second point is closely related to this circumstance. For once upon a time — as a matter of fact not that long ago — all four sets of determinations have been positive constituents of capital's dynamic expansion and historical advancement; from the symbiotic relationship of capital with its national states to the forcefully self-sustaining use to which the system could put its characteristic (even if always problematical) way of dealing with the issues of equality and emancipation, and from mastering the forces of nature in the interest of its own productive development thoroughly unhindered by sobering external or internal limits (which would question its domination of nature) to the earlier quite unimaginable expanded reproduction not only of its own material assets and conditions of metabolic interchange and control but also the prodigious growth of the truly productive and within capital's parameters profitably sustainable labour force.

By contrast, the forbidding problem for the not too distant future is not simply that the type of dynamic expansionary relationships manifest in the past under all four sets of determination here at issue cannot be positively sustained any longer. It is much worse than that. For under the now unfolding conditions of historical development all four sets of interacting forces represent not just an *absence* (which would be bad enough even by itself) but an *active hindrance* to undisturbed capital accumulation and to the future functioning of the global capital system. Accordingly, the threat of uncontrollability casts a very long shadow over all of the objective and subjective aspects of capital's historically unique mode of controlling humanity's continued social metabolic reproduction.

5.1 Transnational capital and national states

5.1.1

THE contradiction between the fundamental trend of expansionary transnational economic development and the constraints imposed on it by the historically created national states always presented a very difficult problem to the thinkers who tried to come to terms with it from the standpoint of capital. The explosions manifesting in the form of national conflicts were often attributed by them — in the good old tradition of ascribing the troubles, with conveniently prefabricated evasion, to the 'controlless core of human nature', as we have seen above — to the 'irrationality' of 'unruly' (often also labelled and summarily dismissed as 'inferior') people, looking thereby for remedies where they could not be found. Indeed, the solutions in this domain were envisaged as a rule either in the form of pure wishful thinking — in the remote past capable of assuming noble forms, like Kant's advocacy of 'perpetual peace' — or through unvarnished appeals to the necessity of repressive force, including the pursuit of major wars. The latter ranged from Hegel's theorization of the nation state and Clausewitz's definition of war as 'the continuation of politics by other means' all the way to the formulation of racist mythologies of domination and to the most naked apologetics of imperialism. What was common both to the Kantian type of wishful thinking and the more realistic advocacy of force was the failure to confront the antagonistic nature not of that mythical 'controlless core of human nature' but of capital's transnationally expansionary trend itself which was (and still is) *bound* to reproduce the conflicts on an ever greater scale, with increasing severity. Those who are today naive enough to believe, under the guidance of public opinion formers like the London *Economist,* that our age shows the triumph of universally beneficial 'free economic choice', coupled with generous helpings of 'free political choice' and the concomitant universal diffusion of 'democracy', thereby consigning to the past not only imperialism but all attempts to resolve fundamental economic and political antagonisms by force, are bound to suffer a rude awakening.

The main reason behind the unrealistic way of dealing with these problems even in the more realistic approaches is that the deep-seated causal determinants of the conflicting interests inseparable from capital's mode of control cannot be acknowledged to exist without endangering the traditional legitimation of the system itself. Consequently, whenever the antagonisms become too sharp to be manageable by 'consensual' means, the normal democratic pretences must be brushed aside in the interest of preserving the established relation of forces in the global capital system, so as to secure the continued subjection and domination of the 'unruly' peoples by the most undemocratic means. Significantly, this type of solution is pursued or advocated not only by openly authoritarian figures, but also by politicians with explicit claims to 'democratic credentials'. For the latter do not hesitate to argue — quite absurdly — that their commended course of denying the 'democratic option' of autonomy and self-determination to 'unruly' peoples must be pursued for the noble purpose of preserving the democratic values and achievements of the United States and the countries of Western Europe. Thus, in a recent book, the 'Senior Democratic Senator' of the U.S., Daniel Patrick Moynihan, insists that 'It will be necessary for the United States and the democracies of Western Europe to reconsider ... the idea that democracy is a universal option for all nations.'[202] According to this 'realistic' approach the 'democratic option', with all the economic and political privileges claimed to be rightfully assigned to it, must be preserved to the United States and its close associates, the so-called 'advanced capitalist democracies'. By contrast the peoples who stand in the way of perpetuating the established relation of forces in the international order must be disqualified — and kept under firm control by those who have the power to enforce such control by unceremoniously depriving them of the right to self-determination — on account of their alleged irrational predilection to create 'ethnic pandemonium'.

In the same spirit the self-proclaimed champion of liberal values, the arch-conservative Friedrich von Hayek, thunders not only against the socially caring Liberals and Conservatives who in his view joined the socialists in the advanced capitalist countries on 'The Road to Serfdom'.[203] He is equally censorious against all those who have the temerity to raise their voice in favour of the oppressed in the 'Third World', painting the spectre that

> 'liberation theology' may fuse with *nationalism* to produce a *powerful new religion* with disastrous consequences for people already in dire economic straits.[204]

It is of course a complete *non-sequitur* that a 'powerful new religion' must bring in its wake 'disastrous consequences'. After all, the once upon a time 'powerful new religion' of protestantism was said to have brought into existence and to its position of absolute triumph the wonderful world of capitalism, according to a no lesser figure than Max Weber. Apparently, then, only religions pressing for the liberation and emancipation of the oppressed must be aprioristically disqualified. Equally, it is difficult to see what the people referred to by Hayek have got to lose by fighting for self-determination and liberation, with the help of socially conscious religion, if they are already 'in dire straits'. What is, though, amply clear, both in Hayek's tirades against liberation theology and nationalism, and in Moynihan's denial of the 'democratic option of self-determination' to the countries considered unworthy of it by the American Democratic Senator, is that our critics of 'Third World nationalism' must resort to the automatically condemnatory accusation of incurable irrationality — 'religion' in one case and 'ethnic pandemonium' in the other — in order to be able to exempt by the same stroke the causal foundations of their idealized, by definition rational and superior but in reality uncontrollably antagonism-producing, system from the much needed critical scrutiny.

In any case, this way of idealizing capitalism and simultaneously condemning nationalism is utterly self-contradictory, not just hypocritical. For the dominant capitalist countries always asserted (and continue to assert) their vital economic interests as combative national entities, notwithstanding all rhetorics and mystification to the contrary. Their most powerful companies which established themselves and continue to operate all over the world are 'multinational' only in name. In reality they are *transnational* corporations which could not sustain themselves on their own. As Harry Magdoff forcefully stressed, 'It is important to keep in mind that almost all the multinationals are in fact national organizations operating on a global scale. We are in no way denying that capitalism is, and has from its very beginning been, a world system, or that this system has been further integrated by the multinationals. But just as it is essential to understand, and analyze, capitalism as a world system, it is equally necessary to recognize that each capitalist firm relates to the world system through, and must eventually rely on, the nation state.'[205] The term 'multinational' is frequently used as a complete misnomer, hiding the real issue of domination of the local economies — in tune with the innermost determinations and antagonisms of the global capital system — by the capitalist enterprises of a more powerful nation. As a rule the dominant capitalist nations enforce their interests with all means at their disposal, peacefully for as long as they can, but resorting to war if there is no other way of doing so. This relationship between twentieth century capitalism and its dominant economic units is frequently misconceived even by leading figures of the parliamentary left who criticize in vague terms the external form and not the substance. Thus in their critique of the 'multinationals' they often naively envisage that the advocated legislative restraints of their limited national parliaments could and would put matters right. In truth, however, the accusing finger should be pointed firmly at the growing contradictions of the contemporary capital system as such, with its iniquitous international power relations and hierarchies, and not at some 'politically interfering multinational companies', however big. This makes the possibility of a lasting solution incomparably more difficult than the enactment of restraining legislative measures against specific transnational companies. For the remedy must be applied to some crucial leverage of the system as a whole, with its overall relation of forces, if the envisaged legislative intervention is not to be nullified by the latter's structural interdeterminations. To quote Magdoff again:

... the growth of the multinational corporations is merely the latest emanation of the restless accumulation of capital and the innate drift towards greater concentration and centralization of capital. ... whatever success government policies do have comes from maintaining or restoring the health of the economy via promoting the power of the giant firms, for without the prosperity of these firms the economy can only go downhill. The basic reasons for the impotence of governments to maintain their economies on an even keel are to be found in the limits and contradictions of monopoly capitalism. In other words, the problems arise not from the evils of the multinationals or the presumed diminution of the sovereignty of the advanced industrial nation states; the problems are inherent in the nature of a capitalist society.[206]

The representatives of the most powerful sections of capital understand that they are not in a position to dispense with the protection afforded to their vital interests by their national states. At times they are even willing to spell out this fact in their policy recommendations for the future. As a characteristic example we may think of a recent book, written by Robert B. Reich, President Clinton's Labour Secretary and a former Harvard Professor.[207] As it befits a leading politician of the dominant imperialist country, the author of this book has no illusions about giving up the national centre and defence of 'multinational' capitalist power for the sake of fantasy-notions of neutral and universally beneficial globalization. Given the character of the global socioeconomic relations under the rule of capital and the antagonisms generated within their framework, not surprisingly Reich's 'Blueprint for the Future' — echoing the title of Adam Smith's *Wealth of Nations* but shifting the stress to the necessity of integrating *'The Work of Nations'* on a planetary scale — *reflects* the conflicting constituents of the system without acknowledging their contradictions. For he cannot admit that the trends described may be problematical and ultimately even explosive. He prefers to present them side by side, as if they could constitute a harmonious whole. On the one hand, he insists that in the coming century there will be no national products or corporations, not even national industries and economies, and thus he argues for the inescapability of 'globalization'. On the other hand, however, he also commends the adoption of *'positive economic nationalism'*[208] by his country, and anticipates practising it in a form which would reconcile the demands and interests of the national centre championed by the Democratic Labour Secretary of the U.S. with those of the rest of the world. How this wishful reconciliation could be in the first place brought about and thereafter managed on a continuing basis, remains a complete mystery. All the more so if we bear in mind the existing — still *growing* rather than diminishing — inequalities and the structural domination of the weaker economies by the 'advanced capitalist' countries within the framework of the prevailing power relations. The possibility of a solution is postulated by Reich on the premise of the fictitious elimination (again by some sort of a miracle) of the so-called big business/labour relationship which is gratuitously assumed to be the cause of the existing difficulties.[209]

To assume, as Robert Reich and others do, that the existing power relations of domination and dependency could be made permanent, let alone further enhanced to the projected degree in favour of the leading imperialist country, the U.S., is totally unrealistic, no matter how much naked force is deployed by the present beneficiaries. For the deep-seated antagonisms generated by structural domination cannot be dissipated by trying to exorcize 'irrational Third World nationalism' as the devil's work. As a distinguished Filipino historian and political figure, Renato Constantino stressed in *Le Monde*:

> Nationalism remains today an imperative for the peoples of the South. It is a *protection* in that it allows to assert one's sovereign rights, and it is a framework to *defend oneself* against the practices of the North for dominance. Nationalism does not mean withdrawal into oneself: it has to be open; but for that it must presuppose a new world order which — in contrast to what we see today — does not consist in the hegemony of a super-power and its allies, without respect for the young nations.[210]

Moreover, the established global capital system of structural hierarchies reveals its ultimate untenability not only through its necessarily contested domination of the 'Third World'. Serious antagonisms exist also among the dominant capitalist powers, and they are bound to intensify in the foreseeable future. This is so not only because the envisaged 'positive economic nationalism' of the U.S. is already generating far from compliant responses in Western Europe, Japan and Canada, but also because major differences of interest produce less and less manageable conflicts even among the members of the long established European Community (now optimistically renamed 'European Union'). Thus it would require much more than the wishful projection of 'friendly reconciliation' of the colliding economic interests, or even the extension of Senator Moynihan's category of 'ethnic pandemonium' to Europe as a whole, to conjure up a viable solution in this respect.

5.1.2

THE postulate of 'reconciliation' is by no means new in bourgeois theory. At the roots of it we find the irreconcilable contradictions of *'sovereignty'* as conceived from the standpoint of capital, reflecting the mismatch between the system's material reproductive structures and its state formation discussed in Chapter 2. This is so irrespective of the intellectual stature of those who try to produce the promised 'reconciliation'. Even the greatest positive theorization of the bourgeois state — Hegel's *Philosophy of Right* — cannot show a way out of the maze of the underlying contradictions. For on the one hand Hegel puts into relief the *individuality* of the state, insisting that this untranscendable individuality 'manifests itself as a relation to other states, *each* of which is autonomous *vis-à-vis* the others. This autonomy ... is the most fundamental freedom which a people possesses as well as its highest dignity.'[211] Consequently, in Hegel's view, 'The *nation state* is mind in its substantive rationality and immediate actuality and is therefore the *absolute power* on earth. It follows that every state is sovereign and autonomous against its neighbours. It is entitled in the first place and *without qualification* to be sovereign from their point of view, i.e. to be recognized by them as sovereign.'[212] But he must immediately add — in order to create the necessary escape clause for the perpetuation of the most iniquitous power relations among national states — that 'this title is purely formal... and *recognition is conditional* on the neighbouring *state's judgement and will.*'[213] Thus, what was supposed to be 'absolute and without qualification' becomes conditional and qualified as wholly dependent on the arbitrary 'judgement and will' of the more powerful 'neighbouring state'. The latter, as a rule, refuses to confer on its weaker neighbour the originally postulated 'recognition of absolute sovereignty and autonomy' and takes by the force of arms or by the threat of force whatever it is powerful enough to grab.

Naturally, the system of inter-state relations erected on such foundations is extremely shaky, even in Hegel's eyes, although he is not in the least disturbed by the dangers implicit in it. This is how he characterizes the situation:

> The fundamental proposition of international law ... is that treaties, as the ground of obligation between states, ought to be kept. But since the sovereignty of a state is the principle of its relations to others, states are to that extent *in a state of nature in relation to each other.* Their rights are actualized only in their particular wills and not in a universal will with constitutional powers over them. This universal proviso of international law therefore does not go beyond an ought-to-be, and what really happens is that international relations in accordance with treaty alternate with the *severance* of these relations.[214]

What is extremely problematical here is not the description of the existing state of affairs — and the concomitant inescapability of wars — but the postulate of the tenability, and indeed of the absolute permanence of such precarious state of affairs. The class interest behind this kind of conceptualization of the final stage of historical development, with its 'reconciliation' of the contradictions under the domination of the imperialistic 'Germanic state' — the embodiment of the 'principle of the north' — is obvious enough. For Hegel speaks under the heading of *'The Germanic Realm'* — i.e. for him the culmination of world history — of 'the reconciliation of objective truth and freedom as the truth and freedom appearing within self-consciousness and subjectivity, a reconciliation with the fulfilment of which the principle of the north, the principle of the Germanic peoples, has been entrusted.'[215] The fact that the 'principle of the north' turns out to be the domination of the peoples of the South by the preponderant 'advanced capitalist countries' of the North cannot be of the slightest concern in the theorizations of the state from capital's vantage point, with their necessary vision of 'reconciliation' as the absolute permanence of the established structural hierarchies. The contradictions and antagonisms of the capital system are preserved in all such conceptions, offering only the vacuity of verbal 'reconciliation'.

However, no matter how ingenious the envisaged schemes of 'reconciliation', they are sooner or later inevitably shattered even in their own terms of reference. In this sense, Hegel's postulate of the absolute permanence of the capital system's inter-state relations, which he admits to 'remain infected with contingency',[216] is founded on two false premisses. The *first* — briefly touched upon in Section 4.2.3 — is his glorification of modern warfare as directly corresponding to the ultimate stage of the Idea's development. In this respect it simply cannot occur to Hegel, given his categorical defence of the 'rationality of the actual', that the glorified modern principle of 'thought and the universal' might (let alone will) produce types of weaponry capable of destroying humanity, thereby terminating 'World History' instead of 'realizing the Idea' in the form of the perfect reconciliation of the contradictions. Theorizing the world from the vantage point of capital makes it impossible — not only for Hegel but for all those who adopt such a standpoint — to see the inseparable *destructive* side of the system's *productive* advancement in its dynamic unfolding. This failure hopelessly vitiates even the correct description of historically specific but by no means absolutizable states of affairs, like the contradictory operation of bourgeois sovereignty and autonomy acknowledged in *The Philosophy of Right*.

The *second* false premiss is equally grave in its implications for the permanence of the postulated 'reconciliation'. It asserts that

> in civil society individuals are *reciprocally interdependent* in the most numerous respects, while autonomous states are principally wholes whose needs are met *within their own borders*.[217]

This is, of course, a complete illusion, in view of the unconstrainable expansionary tendency of the capital system under all of its major aspects from the outset. However, it is not a personal and in principle corrigible, but a system-dependent *necessary* illusion. It arises from the need to justify the given system of social metabolic reproduction in which the contradictory reciprocities and interdependencies of the 'microcosms' reverberate with ever greater intensity across the whole of capital's 'macrocosm'. Thus the state formation of the capital system is by no means less affected by potentially explosive reciprocities and interdependencies than its 'civil society'. If anything, it is even more so affected. In Hegel, and in bourgeois thought in general, the false opposition between 'civil society' and the state serves the purpose of idealizing 'reconciliation' and the imaginary — in reality at best only temporary — 'resolution' of the acknowledged contradictions and antagonisms. In such scheme of things the state is, by definition, destined to overcome through its institutions and system of laws the contradictions of civil society, no matter how intense, leaving them at the same time totally intact in their 'proper sphere' of operation, namely in 'civil society' itself.

Given the structural mismatch between capital's material reproductive structures and its state formation, it would require a world-shaking miracle to achieve the anticipated outcome. This is why bourgeois theory in all its forms must simply assume the existence of the ideally corrective powers of the state even when on the face of it some ideologists of capital explicitly argue in favour of the 'withdrawal' of the state from economic affairs. For whether they lobby on Keynesian lines for expansionary deficit financing, or in favour of 'creating favourable conditions for business' through monetary restraint and the curtailment of public expenditure, they find their common denominator in the explicit or implicit admission that without the 'appropriate' intervention of the state the material reproductive structures of the established system could not produce the advocated results. Even the notion of 'rolling back the boundaries of state activity' asssumes — as it happens quite wishfully and arbitrarily — at least the state's *ability* of doing so.

Yet the uncomfortable truth of the matter is that even through massive state intervention the projected 'reconciliation' and 'resolution' of the contradictions cannot be accomplished, due to the structural deficiencies of the system and the ensuing activation of capital's absolute limits at the present stage of historical development. Hegel's false premises on which his rationalizing legitimation of the capital system's destructive antagonisms were built are no longer credible today to anyone. Even in Hegel's lifetime 'reconciliation' could only be envisaged on the assumption (1) that unlike 'civil society', the state as such does not suffer from structural antagonisms and cleavages, and therefore it is eminently suitable for resolving the contradictions of 'civil society'; and (2) that the ultimate and perfectly workable/acceptable sanction of the system whose parts are combined into a coherent whole by the state, with its untranscendable individuality, is the fighting out of the conflicts and the defeat of the adversary in a war, however large-scale. These class-apologetic but in their own time and place necessary illusions of the great German philosopher by now have lost all semblance of rationality. The consummation of capital's historical ascendancy through its penetration even into the most remote corners of the planet has brought with it the qualitative redefinition of the fundamental relations of social metabolic interchange, activating the system's absolute limits in a way aggravated by the *urgency of time*. This makes it impossible to hide any longer capital's limits and contradictions under the cloak of timeless 'reconciliation', to be brought about by the more or less idealized national state.

5.1.3

FAR from 'meeting their needs within their borders', as Hegel imagined, even the largest 'autonomous states' — including the Chinese, with a population of well over 1200 million people — find their autonomy significantly curtailed by the objective condition that they cannot satisfy their needs without entering outside their borders into a multiplicity of important material reproductive relations, with their inescapable political corollaries, over which they can have only a strictly limited control, no matter how powerful they might be in military terms. As a result, problems of varying severity and intensity are bound to arise which must be accommodated — since on account of their mutually exclusive claims they cannot be 'resolved' — within the structural determinations and confines of the global capital system. Thus, it would be utterly naive (to put it mildly) to believe that the proclamation of high-sounding principles could happily overcome, in the sense of the frequently postulated but never realized 'reconciliation', the always regenerated tensions and conflicts of this system. All the more since the twentieth century has witnessed not only the Nazi type eruption of the capital system's antagonisms, but also the more recent attempts — under the pretext of 'protecting democracy' from the dangers of *ethnic pandemonium'* — to disqualify the weaker economic powers even from the formal entitlement to defend their elementary interests.

In order to devise 'principled' justification for the existing forms of discrimination, all kinds of theories are invented by capital's political propagandists who are quite undeterred by having to use blatantly false assertions and self-contradictions as the building blocks of such 'theories'. Thus the editors of *The Economist* — in a Leader entitled 'Tribal feeling' — pontificate in a tone of 9 carat plastic indignation:

> Look around the world and, from Serbia to Canada, from Turkey to Sri Lanka, the tribes are asserting themselves. What is more, they are often doing so with the blessing, if not the encouragement, of those who used to trumpet universal values. ... it often seems bad form to suggest the Quebecker, say, that he is also Canadian, to a Tamil that he is Sri Lankan or to a Kurd that he is Turkish.[218]

The curious assertion that the grievances of *French Canadians* could be solved by subsuming them under the name of 'Canadian Quebeckers', and that the Kurds are really Turkish, is one of the worst jokes invented for decades even by *The Economist's* standard. But there is more to come. For the problem of dissenting minorities is falsely ascribed, just a couple of lines further on in the same article, to the past evils of communism, saying that 'Often these minorities have suffered years of discrimination and are only now, with the spread of democracy, getting the chance to air their grievances.' How on earth this assertion might apply to the list of 'tribalists' given a few lines earlier, with the apparent exception of 'Serbia', remains a complete mystery. But even the assertion regarding 'Serbia' is totally contradicted half a page later in the same Leader, when *The Economist* changes horses and admits that 'Yugoslavia exploded *despite* the minority rights that were proclaimed, and indeed *respected, in communist days.*'

The construction of such 'theories' from false assertions and blatant self-contradictions arises from the pathetic explanatory framework adopted, of necessity, by the apologists of the capital system. For they cannot even hint at the real causes of the identified troubles, and therefore are forced to dream up all kinds of pseudo-causes in order to come to terms with the baffling fact that antagonisms continue to erupt all over the world, despite the earlier proclaimed trouble-free 'New World Order' and the happy ending of history with the absolute triumph of 'liberal democracy'. Raymond Aron, a leading ideologist of Western capitalism, used to predict that growing prosperity, bringing with it 'a more middle class mode of life',[219] would inevitably result in the return of the Soviet Union to the fold. As we all know, nothing of the kind had happened.

None the less, the often enough refuted primitive schematism of 'democracy and growing prosperity' — which claims to make intelligible not only past developments but, more importantly for the self-reassurance of the system, also the possible (and admissible) causality of future changes — persists unaffected. Whenever even the most cursory glance at the facts sharply contradicts the favourite pseudo-causal 'explanation', the term 'exception' comes to the rescue to provide the required escape-clause. Thus we are told in another article of *The Economist* dedicated to the disturbing problem of ethnic conflicts that

> With a few exceptions, such as Northern Ireland and the Basque country, the old religious and ethnic tensions of Europe's western parts succumbed long ago to the *soothing effects of democracy and growing prosperity.* The same may eventually happen in Central and Eastern Europe.[220]

But then, again, it may also not happen, which would have to turn the 'few exceptions' — of which quite a few more could be found even in Western Europe, from ethnically polarized Belgium to parts of Italy — into the metaphysical category of permanent 'fault lines' recently supplied by Professor Huntington, eager to match the wisdom and success of his idea of 'strategic hamlets' in Vietnam. In any case, no attempt is made, nor must be made, to try and explain the causes behind the apparently self-illuminating 'exceptions', however few or many. How much more 'democracy and growing prosperity' is required to make the stubborn 'tribalist' French Canadians see the light of reason and recognize that even in Ontario they are really Canadian Quebeckers, like the Kurds are Turks, we shall never know, nor should we pry into. For the topical point of the whole exercise requiring the change of horses half-way through the article is to discredit those who press for *minority rights,* including the advocates of equal rights for *disabled* people curtly dismissed in *The Economist's* principal New Year Leader quoted above. According to the editors of *The Economist,* 'Rights are for *individuals,* not *groups*'. If concessions must be made 'to the aggrieved minorities', they must be made 'on the understanding, maybe in a sunset clause' that they cannot be allowed to last.

'Abolish minority and group rights' — including trades union protection and the old law which once secured the *minimum wage*[221] for the most disadvantaged section of the working class — is the proper rational approach to these matters according to the editors of *The Economist,* who enthusiastically shift the goalpost whenever required to match and further enhance the changed conditions of capital's continued rule. In this spirit, since for the transnational operations of capital the traditionally established national public holidays are considered to be 'economically damaging', the Leader writers of *The Economist* put forward what they call, not in jest but in all seriousness, the 'liberal solution', i.e. that '*Public holidays should be abolished.*'[222] They even show for a moment the colour of their teeth when they say that as a result of such a liberal measure 'Britain's unloved bank holiday in May would disappear',[223] burying thereby the day of workers' solidarity long respected not only in England but in the international labour movement everywhere.

The advocacy of abolishing minority and group rights on the ground of class-conscious rationalization that 'rights are for individuals, not groups' — as if the individuals who suffer from the most iniquitous system of discrimination were not members of hierarchically subordinated and exploited groups —

coupled with a most hypocritical appeal to the individuals' 'common humanity', both reflects the present stage of development of the transnationally intertwined global capital system, and tries to facilitate its course of further unfolding through the removal of 'unnecessary legal constraints', enacted at an earlier stage of development by the selfsame 'liberal democracies' which now are expected to mend their ways. At the same time, the talk about 'rights for individuals, not for groups' has the convenience — carefully camouflaged under *The Economist's* unctuous pseudo-humanitarian concern — that the established *power relations* of labour's structural subordination to capital are left completely untouched. For no amount of rights conferred on particular individuals could make an iota of difference in this respect. We are told that

> In the long run, rights must be based on what people have in common — their membership of the human race — not on genes or accidents of birth that tribalists will always use to divide them.[224]

Naturally, objection to 'accidents of birth' should in no way apply either to the privileged 'North' or across the globe to the truly 'tribalist' owners and controllers of the means of production, the 'personifications of capital'. Besides, talking about the 'long run' is a safe bet. Not so much because in the celebrated words of a former idol, John Maynard Keynes, 'in the long run we are all dead', but because the 'long run' is blocked off with brutal effectiveness by the actuality of capital's rule. For the division of people into antagonistically opposed groups and classes is not the evil deed of national minority 'tribalists' but the necessary condition of maintaining the control of social metabolic reproduction under the capital system. And when the imperatives of transnational operations call for less division, putting into relief the activation of capital's absolute limits in the form of the greatly heightened contradiction between growing division and stipulated but unrealizable unity, it would take much more than *The Economist's* abstract appeal to the individuals' 'common membership of the human race' to find a proper solution.

5.1.4

AS mentioned on page 144 above, the structural antagonism between transnationally expanding capital and national states is inseparable from the deep-seated contradictions between (1) monopoly and competition, (2) the increasing socialization of production and the discriminatory appropriation of its products, and (3) the growing international division of labour and the drive of the strongest national powers for hegemonic domination of the global system. Inevitably, therefore, attempts to overcome the structural antagonisms of capital must embrace all these dimensions without exception.

With regard to *monopoly and competition* the drive towards the establishment and consolidation of monopolistic corporations has been more and more pronounced in the 20th century. As Baran and Sweezy had stressed in their seminal work:

> Monopoly capitalism is a system made up of giant corporations. This is not to say that there are no other elements in the system or that it is useful to study monopoly capitalism by abstracting from everything except giant corporations. ... One must, however, be careful not to fall into the trap of assuming that Big Business and smaller business are qualitatively equal or of coordinate importance for the *modus operandi* of

the system. The dominant element, the prime mover, is Big Business organized in giant corporations. These corporations are *profit maximizers and capital accumulators.* ... Overall, monopoly capitalism is as *unplanned as its competitive predecessor.* The big corporations relate to each other, to consumers, to labour, to smaller business primarily through the market. The way the system works is still the unintended outcome of the self-regarding actions of the numerous units that compose it.[225]

In this sense, although monopolistic developments in the dominant capitalist countries helped to counteract, for the time being and within well marked limits, some aspects of the law of value, they could by no means overcome the law itself. The best they could hope for was and remains the 'postponement of the moment of truth', despite the massively used facilitating role of the state in the 20th century — through a variety of its materially supporting and legally/politically helpful 'white-washing' institutions and 'watchdog' bodies, including the so-called 'Monopolies and Mergers Commission' in Britain (whose primary function is the hypocritical rationalization and legitimation of the newly created monopolies under the pretext of anti-monopoly regulation) and its equivalents elsewhere. As the young Engels pointed out in 1843 in his brilliant 'Outline of a Critique of Political Economy', which exercised a major impact on Marx in his first engagement with the subject:

> The opposite of competition is monopoly. Monopoly was the war-cry of the mercantilists; competition the battle-cry of the liberal economists. It is easy to see that this antithesis is a quite hollow antithesis. ... Competition is based on self-interest, and self-interest in turn breeds monopoly. In short, competition passes over into monopoly. On the other hand, monopoly cannot stem the tide of competition — indeed, it itself breeds competition; ... The contradiction of competition is that each cannot but desire the monopoly, whilst the whole as such is bound to lose by monopoly and must therefore remove it. Moreover, competition already presupposes monopoly — namely, the monopoly of property (and here the hypocrisy of the liberals comes once more to light); ... What a pitiful half-measure, therefore, to attack the small monopolies, and to leave untouched the basic monopoly. ... The law of competition is that demand and supply always strive to complement each other, and therefore never do so. The two sides are torn apart again and transformed into flat opposition. Supply always follows close on demand without ever quite covering it. It is either too big or too small, never corresponding to demand; because in this unconscious condition of mankind no one knows how big supply and demand is. ... What are we to think of a law which can only assert itself through periodic crises? It is just a natural law based on the unconsciousness of the participants.[226]

The apologetic theories postulating in the 20th century the realization of 'planning' in the capital system all claimed, in one way or another, that they have solved the contradictions arising from the 'unconscious condition of mankind' put into relief by Engels. In reality the contradictions in question have become greatly aggravated in the course of 20th century developments, with the global expansion and monopolistic transformation of capital. True, by extending to the ultimate limits the scale of capital's operations all over the planet, it was possible to displace some specific contradictions which threatened to cause explosions inside the walls of their earlier confinement, such as the 'little corner of the world, Europe' — so described by Marx prior to the great imperialist expansion from the last third of the 19th century onwards. Parallel to the temporarily contradiction-displacing great imperialist expansion, however, domination-seeking competition and the clash of antagonistic interests, too, assumed ever greater scale and intensity. It resulted within a few decades not only in the devastating inhumanities of two World Wars — as well as of countless smaller ones — but also in the totally 'unplanned' (or, rather, planned the only way in which monopolistic big corporations are capable of 'planning', with wishful one-sidedness) and decidedly unforeseen but potentially cata-strophic climax of all such developments by taking humankind to the brink of self-annihilation.

The idea that the harmoniously coordinated diffusion of 'scientifically plan-ned and managed' monopolies and quasi-monopolies all over the world, in the form of universally beneficial 'globalization', could show a way out of this set of antagonisms, remedying thereby 'the unconscious condition of mankind' de-plored by socialists, is just as absurd as the projection that a few monopolies of a hegemonically dominant state could permanently control the capital system as a whole. The struggle for hegemonic domination mentioned on page 144 makes the first a cynical camouflage of their real design by the dominant powers, and the objective constitution of the global capital system in the form of necessarily self-oriented national states makes the second a complete unreality. Hegel was right in stressing the untranscendable *'individuality'* of national states. He was only naive to imagine that the violent resolution of the antago-nisms inseparable from this condition — the fighting out of the irreconcilable conflicts in a war of 'life or death' — can be indefinitely pursued.

The impossibility to either make *competition* happily prevail, through the instrumentality of the mythical 'free market', or to achieve the unchallengeable dominance of *monopoly,* thanks to the permanent cornering of all important domains of both production and distribution, puts into relief the insoluble contradictions of the capital system both on the plane of the material reproduc-tive structures and in the field of politics. The 'individuality' stressed with the customary 'uncritical positivism' by Hegel imposes its ultimately insurmount-able negative limits even on the biggest of the giant monopolistic (or quasi-monopolistic) corporations, as well as on the most powerful national states. There can be no way out of these structurally limiting constraints on capital's material ground: 'infected with contingency' and suffering from incurable instability. For capital's material productive structures cannot be reproduced, on the required expanded scale, without the perpetuation of the — by its very nature unstable — capital/labour antagonism.

The inexorable trend towards the ever greater socialization of production, inseparable from the likewise increasing international division and combination of labour under the dominance of the giant transnational enterprises, are integral parts of the attempts to overcome these structural constraints and to displace at the same time the system's contradictions. This is why the actual and potential recalcitrance of 'national minorities' must be condemned and subdued with all means at the disposal of the dominant powers. The pseudo-humanitarian preaching of *The Economist* which wants to deny 'group rights' to so-called 'national minorities' belongs to the more Quixotic end of the spectrum, in that it tries to put forward 'rational arguments' — however class-ideologically transparent and even self-contradictory — in favour of such denial. The 'realists', on the other hand, talk about their absolutely necessary 'positive economic nationalism', or indeed of the need to treat with ruthlessly authoritarian methods the countries summarily dismissed under the label of 'ethnic pandemonium'. At the same time, they provide the generous budgets for the Pentagon's 'non-lethal weapons research', unashamedly targeted against 'international disturbances' deemed to be caused by national and ethnic minorities.[227]

The trouble is, though, that from the standpoint of globally expansionary transnational capital *even the largest country,* with its potentially constraining powers, is an *intolerable 'national minority'.* Monopolies in the past could be established with arguable rationality inside the borders of effectively controllable national territories, as well as in the colonies once upon a time firmly held under their rule by a handful of imperial powers. Today, by contrast, the idea of universally prevailing monopolies which could assert their interests within the framework of a fully integrated global economy, lacks all rationality. The absurdity of this idea nowadays arises from the circumstance that in a globally integrated economy, enduring monopolistic developments would have to be secured on a ground quite impossible even to imagine, let alone realize. For, by the very nature of the — competing and mutually exclusive — undertakings which drive towards the establishment of comprehensive monopoly, the larger the scale of operations the greater the intensity of confrontations. The historically experienced difference between local wars and World Wars well illustrates the nature of these escalating determinations. Thus the ultimate logic of global monopolistic developments would call for the possibility of not even a mere handful but *one* monopoly controlling everything, everywhere, in the absence of a feasible harmonious institutional framework of 'consensually' divided monopolism (an absurdity in itself), or, in view of the impossibility of turning into reality the latter, a compensatory controlling power exercised by naked — and in the end mutually destructive — force on the required global scale. Not to ignore the fact that a successfully working global monopolism would also have to invent a totally compliant labour force, understood in the sense of one which happily accepts being ruled everywhere by the dominant global hegemonic power. The unreality of such invention puts also the feasibility of the envisaged 'positive economic nationalism' — meant to be imposed with or without consent on the rest of the world by the international 'super-power' — under a most uncomfortable question mark.

Thus under the now unfolding conditions the earlier successfully working practice of displacing the capital system's contradictions through global expansionary development becomes extremely problematical. As mentioned before, in the past many grave problems could be postponed by extending the scale of the system's encroachment over all formerly uncontrolled territories, at the same time raising the stakes among the principal powers involved. But now there is nowhere else to go to secure the required expansionary displacement on an adequate scale. Moreover, Hegel's 'decapitated sovereignty' — which in our times deprives the system of its ultimate sanction of enforcing the dominant interests by war — frustrates not only the strictly transient, sooner or later inevitably overthrown, hegemonic solutions. To make matters worse, at the same time it reactivates the internal antagonisms of the particular countries which could once be placated, in Hegel's candidly cynical admission, by national engagement in war.

In the meantime the concentration and centralization of capital goes on 'with the inexorability of a natural law based on the unconsciousness of the participants'. However, troubles seem to multiply even in this respect, contradicting the hopes attached to the long period of transnational expansion and undisturbed 'globalization'. Thus a short time ago the propagandists of capital, at the Quixotic end of the spectrum, started to raise their voice in admonition over against the *'diseconomy of scale'* — after decades of preaching the absolute virtue and unsurpassable advantages of the *'economy of scale'*, — since they have been frightened by the disastrous performance of some of the biggest transnational corporations. This is how they were delivering their new sermon, giving it a meaning diametrically opposed to their celebratory sermons of yesterday:

> The humbling of big firms has only just began. ... As these trends accelerate, the crucial question facing managers of large companies will be not how their firms can grow bigger still, but whether they can survive without shrinking. In 1993 'big' no longer means, as it once did, 'successful'; before long it is likely to mean 'failing'.[228]

Naturally, the personifications of capital in charge of big firms pay no attention to sermons which invite them to mend their ways. They do not see any need for change just because their giant corporations have been losing monumental magnitudes of money. For the time being they can grow money even on asphalt, or legally embezzle it from the pension funds of their workers, as General Motors did. They prefer to get out of the trouble of massive losses by following 'the line of least resistance', in accord with capital's actually unfolding trend of development towards ever greater concentration and centralization. Not surprisingly, therefore, we read one year later in another influential journal that

> Full globalization is being attempted by multinationals in other industries, such as Unilever and Nestlé in consumer products, but nobody has yet succeeded in bringing it off. 'This is definitely Trotman's baby,'[229] said one American source. 'He has a vision of the future which says that, to be a global winner, Ford must be a truly global corporation.' According to Trotman, who told *The Sunday Times* in October 1993, 'As automotive competition becomes more global as we get into the next century, the pressure to find *scale economies* will become greater and greater. If, instead of making two engines at 500,000 units each, you can make one engine at 1m units then the costs are much lower. Ultimately there will be a handful of global players and the rest will either not be there or they will be struggling along.'
>
> Trotman and his colleagues have concluded that full globalization is the only way to beat competitors such as the Japanese and, in Europe, Ford's arch-rival General Motors, which retains a cost advantage over Ford. Ford also believes it needs globalization to capitalise on fast-emerging markets in the Far East and Latin America.[230]

Thus the real trend of development is towards greater, rather than less, concentration and centralization, with unavoidably sharpening propects for quasi-monopolistic confrontation, totally unmindful of the dangerous consequences for the future. Yet — given the 'natural law based on the unconsciousness of the participants' under which the corporate 'planners' and 'captains of industry' operate, confidently anticipating with Trotman that 'ultimately there will be a handful of global players and the rest will either not be there or they will be struggling along' — the prospects are far from rosy even for Trotman's 'handful of global players'. It is much more realistic to visualize them as mountain-size dinosaurs locked into ever-renewed struggles 'for life or death' until they all perish, than to imagine that they will harmoniously sit around the boardroom table and share out in a brotherly spirit the loot which they can squeeze out, in perpetuity, from a totally compliant labour force all over the world. Besides, to envisage that all national states will become happy facilitators for the 'handful of global players', in the same way as their particular national states provide their services to the giant transnational corporations today, accepting without much ado, if any, the ravages to their own economies and dominant business interests, and indeed successfully compelling at the same time their national labour force to accept the consequences of such developments for their ever-worsening prospects of employment, in the interest of the flourishing 'handful of global players', — to envisage all this can be done only by assuming that even the narrow margin of rationality compatible with the 'natural law based on the unconsciousness of the participants', the partial rationality of self-interest, had completely disappeared (or will disappear by the time required by the wishful anticipations of the Ford Chairman) from the countries at the receiving end of the advocated transnational globalization.

5.1.5

THE structural mismatch between global capital's material reproductive structures and its totalizing political command structure — the various national states, with their untranscendable 'individuality' — can only foreshadow the sharpening of antagonisms and the necessity of major confrontations, in complete contrast to the wishful anticipations of even the temporarily most favoured sections of capital. As we have seen above, 'the state of the capital system as such' remains to the present day a Kantian 'regulative idea' only, despite all efforts dedicated in the post-Second World War period to realize it in the form of an international network of economic and political institutions — from the World Bank and the International Monetary Fund to the OECD, GATT, and the United Nations — under the more or less veiled dominance of the United States. Global capital is today as before devoid of its proper state formation because the dominant material reproductive units of the system cannot get rid of *their* 'individuality'. Indeed, they cannot get rid of a necessarily 'combative individuality' (combative in the same sense in which the state must be capable of and ready to engage in combat; in other words, the concept of 'individuality' glorified by Hegel is in reality exhausted in the ability to confront, in order to defeat, the adversary) because they have to operate in an inherently conflictual situation everywhere, given the untranscendable structural antagonisms of the capital system, from its smallest reproductive 'microcosms' to its most gigantic productive and distributive enterprises.

Thus the 'individuality' in question is an unalterable *negative* determination which cannot be filled with positive content. In this sense, on the plane of material reproduction we find a multiplicity of capitals opposed to one another and, more importantly, to groups of labour under their control, and all of them driving — inexorably, and by their very nature unrestrainably — towards overall domination both at home and beyond their national boundaries. At the same time, on the totalizing political plane, the state of the capital system is articulated as a multiplicity of national states opposed to one another (and, of course, to the national labour force under their 'constitutional' control) as particular 'sovereign states'. The negative determination of capital — in the singular or in the plural — cannot be turned into a positive one, because capital is *parasitic* on labour which it must structurally dominate and exploit. This means that capital is *nothing* without labour, since it could not sustain itself for a moment on its own account, without labour, making thereby capital's negative determination — in terms of its dependency on labour — *absolute* and *permanent*. Likewise, the state formation of the capital system is quite unthinkable if it does not reproduce, in its own way, the selfsame multiplicity of untranscendable negative determinations, articulating through its totalizing political command structure — in an inverted hierarchical form, matching the structural hierarchy of the material reproductive process — capital's absolute dependency on labour.

In this sense, to talk about the 'sovereignty of the state' as the negative boundary which divides all states from, and opposes them to, other states, is intellectually coherent, however problematical it must be in other respects, on the plane of actual inter-state power relations. But to expect the state of the capital system to turn itself into a positive formation, so as to be able to subsume and 'reconcile' under itself the contradictions of national states, in the form of a 'World Government' or a Kantian 'League of Nations', is to ask for the impossible. For the 'state' of the capital system — existing in the form of particular national states — is *nothing* without its actual or potential opposition to other states, just like capital is nothing without its opposition to, and negative self-determination by, labour. To think of the state as the political instrumentality of positive (self-sustaining) determinations, means envisaging the restitution of its alienated controlling functions to the social body, and thereby the necessary 'withering away' of the state. As things stand under the rule of capital, negativity prevails and asserts itself with ruthless efficacy on the material reproductive and the political plane, both internally and through the conflictual inter-state relations. However, the absolute limits of the capital system are activated when the sharpening antagonisms of the global material and political interchanges would call for genuine positive solutions, but capital's deeply entrenched mode of social metabolic control is structurally incapable of providing them. For it must drive blindly forward, on its own 'line of least resistance' — under the law of ever-increasing concentration and centralization — towards the domination of a 'handful of global players' both internally and internationally, brushing aside all concern with the explosive dangers of such developments.

Apart from 'revolution', 'sovereignty' is the most abused concept in bourgeois political discourse. In the world of actually existing power relations, it means the righteous justification for the big powers (in Hegel's terms 'the world historical nations') to trample upon the sovereignty — the theoretically inviolable right to autonomy and self-determination — of the smaller nations, using whatever pretext may suit the convenience of the powerful, from the wholly invented 'Tonkin Gulf incident' against North Vietnam to the envisaged quelling of 'ethnic pandemonium'. Thus the principled defence of the sovereignty of smaller nations must be an integral part of the attempted emancipation from the rule of capital in the realm of inter-state relations. Given the existing system of domination and subordination, intensified by the pressure of transnational capital to assert its interests over all aspirations to national autonomy and self-determination, the struggle of the oppressed for their long denied sovereignty is an unavoidable step in the process of transition towards a qualitatively different social metabolic order. It cannot help being negative — the rejection and negation of a more powerful state's interference — and *defensive,* in its opposition to being assigned an inferior position in the international pecking order of the capital system, as Constantino rightly stressed.

The positive alternative to the rule of capital cannot be defensive. For all defensive positions suffer from being ultimately unstable, in that even the best defences can be overrun under concentrated fire, given the suitably changed relation of forces in favour of the adversary. Thus the defence of national sovereignty and the right to self-determination cannot be the last word in these matters, although most certainly it happens to be the necessary first step. For defending oneself from the abuses of big capital still leaves the incorrigible abusiveness of the capital system as such — manifest in its unalterable structural domination and exploitation of labour — totally intact, making thereby strictly temporary and endangered all defensive success. The fate of the great majority of post-Second World War liberation struggles against colonial rule under the leadership of the national bourgeoisie graphically illustrates these difficulties. For they only succeeded in replacing the rule of capital formerly exercised under direct colonial/imperial administration by one or another of its 'neo-colonial' and 'neo-capitalist' versions of structural dependency, despite the immense sacrifices of the people involved in the anti-colonial wars.

5.1.6

THE antagonism between globally expansionary transnational capital and national states — indicating in a most acute form the activation of an absolute limit of the capital system — cannot be overcome by the defensive posture and organizational forms of the historical left. To be successful in this respect needs the forces of genuine *internationalism,* without which the deeply iniquitous global dynamics of transnational developments cannot be even temporarily countered, let alone positively replaced by a self-sustaining new mode of social metabolic interchange on the required global scale. The socialist movement, ever since its Marxian beginnings, had conscious international aspirations. However, their practical embodiments in the form of the traditional parties and trades unions of the labour movement — inserted into the established material reproductive as well as political structures of the capital system, expecting from an increasing share in capital expansion the realization of their hopelessly defensive objectives — proved to be quite inadequate to the task.

The internationalism in question cannot be simply an *organizational* aspiration and determination. For thinking of it in such terms — which proved to be the principal cause of many a failure in the past — would still leave it negatively and defensively defined, and as a result confined to countering capital's perverse globalism, in dependency from the latter. It has to be articulated as a *strategy* for the establishment of an alternative international social reproductive order, instituted and managed on the basis of a genuine equality of its manifold constituents. An equality defined in *substantive positive* terms, in contrast to the unavoidable negativity and defensiveness of even the most obviously justified struggle for national sovereignty, which can only be conquered out of the available margins of capital's historically prevailing determinations and constraints.

Positive internationalism cannot be accommodated within the margins of even the most favourable global capital expansion, let alone at a time when the increasing antagonism between transnational capital and national states is to a large extent due to the narrowing of those margins. All theories of 'reconciliation' of inter-state conflicts within the framework of the capital system — even the noblest ones, like Kant's vision of 'perpetual peace' on the ground of Adam Smith's idealized 'commercial spirit' — came to naught in the past; and they had to. For they never questioned (quite the contrary, as a rule they explicitly glorified) the profoundly iniquitous structuring principle of the material reproductive structures themselves which were ultimately responsible for the constantly reproduced antagonisms. This was always, and remains today, the crux of the matter. Accordingly, the strategy of positive internationalism means replacing the iniquitous — and insuperably conflictual — structuring principle of capital's reproductive 'microcosms' by a fully cooperative alternative. The destructive drive of transnational capital cannot be even alleviated, let alone positively overcome, at the international level only. For the continued existence of the antagonistic 'microcosms', and their subsumption under larger and larger structures of the same conflictual type, necessarily reproduces the temporarily placated conflicts sooner or later. Thus positive internationalism defines itself as the strategy to go beyond capital as a mode of social metabolic control by helping to articulate and comprehensively coordinate a non-hierarchical form of decision making at the material reproductive as well as the cultural/political plane. One in which the vital controlling functions of social metabolic reproduction — expropriated to themselves in the existing order by those who occupy the top echelons in the command structure of capital, in business as much as in the domain of political relations — can be positively 'devolved' to the members of the 'microcosms', and the activities of the latter can be appropriately coordinated all the way to embrace the most comprehensive levels, because they are not torn apart by irreconcilable antagonisms.

We shall consider these problems in some detail in Part Three, especially in Chapters 14, 19, and 20. The point to stress here is that so long as 'activity is not *voluntarily* divided',[231] but regulated, instead, by some kind of 'natural' process, in the overall framework of international competition and confrontation, there must be in existence social structures capable of imposing on the individuals a structural/hierarchical (not merely functional) division of labour. (The fundamental structures of such an enforced structural/hierarchical division of labour are, of course, the antagonistically competing social classes.) And conversely, the potentially most destructive antagonisms are always reproduced on the broadest international plane because capital cannot operate the vital reproductive 'microcosms' of the social metabolism without submitting them to its strict vertical/hierarchical structuring principle of control.

Naturally, the same correlation remains valid for the positive alternative as well. In this sense, the necessary condition for the genuine resolution (and not temporary postponement and manipulation) of conflicts, through socialist internationalism, is the adoption of a truly democratic/cooperative structuring principle in the social reproductive microcosms themselves, on the basis of which the positive self-management and 'lateral coordination' of the associated producers on a global scale (as opposed to their now prevailing vertical subordination to an alien controlling force) first becomes possible. This is what Marx must have meant when he anticipated the conscious self-realization of the social agency as a being 'for-itself'.[232]

5.2 Destruction of the conditions of social metabolic reproduction

5.2.1

WE have seen in Section 5.1 that in the course of its historical development the capital system greatly *overreached* itself with regard to one of its most important dimensions which directly affects the relationship between its material reproductive and political command structure at the most comprehensive level. The irreconcilable contradiction between the rival national states of the capital system and the problematical drive of its most powerful economic units — the giant corporations — towards transnational monopolism is the clear manifestation of this overreaching.

The pursuit of monopolistic aspirations was 'natural' to merchant capital. Understandably, therefore, from its standpoint the state was expected to secure the triumph of such aspirations with all means at its disposal. However, to do so beyond a very limited historical phase had meant not simply hindering but directly contradicting the inner dynamics of the system's articulation as a globally intertwined mode of social metabolic reproduction, under the domination of *industrial* capital. Thus the early monopolistic constraints of merchant capital had to be swept away through a more developed phase of socioeconomic development. The very different monopolism that went with the unfolding of imperialism in the 19th and 20th centuries could not turn the clock back and recreate the relatively unproblematical monopolism of merchant capital, notwithstanding the fact that *finance* capital forcefully asserted itself under the new circumstances. For neither the domination of the global system by a few monopolies, nor restraining the inner dynamics of capital's further unfolding could be considered realistic options. Instead, humanity had to experience the intensification of the system's antagonisms and their explosion in two global wars — not to mention the foretaste, at Hiroshima and Nagasaki, of a total catastrophe in the event of a third one — without getting one inch nearer to a tenable solution.

The irrepressible drive of capital to articulate and consolidate its material reproductive structures in the form of a fully integrated global system on the one hand, and its inability to match the tendency toward economic integration by a correspondingly integrated global state (or 'World Government') on the other, graphically illustrate both the fact that the system overreached itself and the untenability of such a state of affairs. There is 'nowhere else to go' on this planet even in the limited sense of taking over the possessions of the rival capitalist powers (the way in which the last time in the history of imperial rivalry the U.S. succeeded in gaining effective control over the former British and French Empires after the Second World War), and yet the constraining boundaries of the existing national states cannot be tolerated. They must be declared intolerable not by any particular state, but by the imperatives of the established mode of social metabolic reproduction, which make the problem much worse. For there can be no defence against the explosive antagonisms of capital's social reproductive 'macrocosm' while remaining within its hopelessly divisive productive and distributive framework.

The full articulation of the capital system has brought with it challenges which cannot be faced without replacing the frequently heard abstract appeals to the idea of the individuals' 'common humanity' by its effective realization in a viable social reproductive practice. Since, however, both the 'microcosms' and the 'macrocosm' of the system — inseparable from its exploitative antagonisms — must be taken absolutely for granted as the best of all conceivable modes of social metabolic interchange, only the emptiest kind of preaching the 'common humanity' of isolated individuals against the evil deeds of the 'tribalists' can be offered by the apologists of capital, as we have seen above in the absurd sermons of *The Economist*. At the same time, though, the full development and transnational encroachment of the established reproductive 'macrocosm' has activated one of capital's absolute limits in the form of the system *overreaching* itself. For it is now compelled to undertake, in order to secure its permanent global domination, the unchallengeable control of what it cannot subdue even with the most authoritarian forms of rule invented in the twentieth century. Inevitably, thus, the overreaching in question assumes the form of an insoluble contradiction, bringing with it a veritable stalemate. Accordingly, under the unfolding historical conditions capital fails to articulate and regulate in the required way its totalizing political command structure: the ultimate guarantee for the viability of its — in and by themselves dangerously centrifugal — material reproductive structures.

POTENTIALLY fatal overreaching itself is the hallmark of capital's relationship also to the elementary conditions of social metabolic reproduction, in the absolutely inescapable interchange of humankind with nature. Neither the fantasies about the 'post-industrial society' — in which 'informatica' is supposed to replace the 'smoke stack industries', while the 'symbolic analysts' are expected to become, with equally magic cleanliness, the new dominant force — nor the various strategies conceived and commended from the vantage point of capital as the proper way of 'limiting growth' can alleviate this grave condition. For, as a rule, self-complacency characterizes the various 'post-industrial' fantasies, and in the case of the would-be 'growth limiters' the question of limits is tendentiously misconceived.

It is misconceived in order to be able to ascribe responsibility for the perceived troubles and growing dangers to the powerless individuals — said to be unwilling to accept the constraining limits — while leaving, of course, the causal ground and overall framework of the capital system untouched. Thus, true to form, the authors sponsored by the prominent capitalist opinion-forming venture, 'The Club of Rome', define 'the human predicament' and the task facing it as the necessity to stabilize and preserve 'the interlocking sectors of the population-capital system',[233] equating the need to secure the elementary conditions of the social metabolism with the perpetuation of the rule of capital. This kind of approach envisages the limits of the capital system to remain the inescapable limits of our social reproductive horizon forever. Accordingly it insists that the remedy lies in consciously accepting the encountered limits and 'learning to live with them',[234] instead of 'fighting against limits',[235] as our 'culture' conditioned us to do in the past. What is conveniently forgotten in all such diagnoses of 'the human predicament'[236] is that 'fighting against limits' belongs to the innermost nature of capital — the very thing they want to perpetuate.

In this way not only is the responsibility for the deepening crisis falsely ascribed to the 'self-interested individuals' — who are represented as incurably selfish by nature, yet, in the usual self-contradictory fashion, expected to be able to conform to the enlightening discourse of capital's spokesmen — but the vital matter of objective limits on which so much hinges is utterly misrepresented. The overbearing material determinations and imperatives which drive forward capital itself are *minimized* and replaced by superficial psychological drives of the individuals, transforming thereby a multifaceted issue of extreme severity into a largely rhetorical neo-Malthusian discourse over the need for 'population control'. This monotonously one-variable strategy is advocated in order to preserve as given — even if in the future in an unrealistically stationary form — the 'interlocking sectors of the population-capital system'. The advocates of neo-Malthusian solutions cannot understand, or refuse to admit, that the diagnosed disasters appeared on the horizon not because the individuals are accustomed to 'fight against limits', instead of 'learning to live with them', but, on the contrary, because *capital as such is absolutely incapable of limiting itself,* irrespective of the consequences even for the total destruction of humanity. For

> capital is the endless and limitless drive to go beyond its limiting barrier. Every boundary *{Grenze}* is and has to be a barrier *{Schranke}* for it. Else it would cease to be capital — money as self-reproductive. If ever it perceived a certain boundary not as a barrier, but became comfortable within it as a boundary, it would itself have *declined from exchange-value to use-value,* from the *general* form of wealth to a *specific, substantial* mode of the same. Capital as such creates a specific surplus-value because it cannot create an infinite one all at once; but it is the *constant movement to create more of the same.* The *quantitative boundary* of the surplus-value appears to it as a mere natural barrier, as a necessity which it constantly tries to violate and beyond which it constantly seeks to go. *The barrier appears as an accident which has to be conquered.*[237]

Thus, the discourse championing the necessity to 'live within the given limits' completely misses its target. For the individuals, on the one hand, who accept (as they are expected to do) the framework of the capital system as their ultimate reproductive horizon are by the same token condemning themselves to total powerlessness to remedy the situation. At the same time, on the other hand, capital — as the established mode of social metabolic control — would have to be not only *different* from, but *diametrically opposed* to what it can and must be, in order to be able to depart from its necessarily pursued disastrous course of development, and 'restrain itself' in order to function 'within rational limits'. For it would have to 'decline from exchange-value to use-value, from the general form of wealth to a specific, substantial form of the same', which it cannot conceivably do without ceasing to be capital: i.e. the alienated and reified mode of control of the social metabolic process capable of pursuing its inexorable course of self-expansion (quite uninhibited by the consequences) precisely because it broke away from the constraints of use-value and human need.

Not surprisingly, therefore, the question of limits can only be raised at the level of mystifying rhetorics by the advocates of 'zero growth and global equilibrium'. They pay no attention whatever to the real 'population explosion' under the capital system, which we must consider in the last section of this chapter. Tellingly, however, they try to frighten the individuals that unless they restrain themselves in their habits of procreation the world population is doomed, because 'perhaps even the *seventh billion* may arrive before the year 2000, less than 30 years from now.'[238] It is a very good measure of the soundness of such self-proclaimed scientific projections that less than 5 years from the fateful date we are nowhere near the numbers we were threatened with. The truth of the matter is, of course, that the individuals should not be invited to 'accept the given limits', since they are anyway *forced* to do so under the rule of capital. On the contrary, their vital need is to struggle as hard as they can against the incorrigible destructive limits of capital before it becomes too late. Needless to say, addressing the question of limits in this contrasting way cannot be accommodated within the discourse of the defenders of the capital system.

5.2.2
THE universalizing tendency of capital has been an irresistible — and in many ways also beneficial — force for a very long time in history. This is why some classics of bourgeois philosophy could conceptualize — with some justification — 'radical evil' as instrumental to the creation of good. Characteristically, though, seeing the world from the standpoint of capital they had to omit the necessary *historical* qualifications. For capital, considered in itself, is neither good nor evil but 'indeterminate' with regard to human values. However, its 'indeterminacy' in the abstract, which makes it compatible with positive advancement under favourable historical circumstances, turns into the most devastating destructiveness when the objective conditions, linked to human aspirations, begin to resist its inexorable self-expansionary drive.

The universalizing tendency of capital which had brought us to the point where we stand today emanated from its 'endless and limitless drive to go beyond its limiting barrier', whatever the latter may have been, from natural obstacles to cultural and national boundaries. Moreover, the same universalizing tendency was inseparable from the necessity to displace the system's inner antagonisms through the constant enlargement of its scale of operations.

It is in the nature of capital that it cannot recognize any measure by which it could be restrained, no matter how weighty the encountered obstacles might be in their material implications, and no matter how urgent — even to the point of extreme emergency — with regard to their time scale. For the very notion of 'restraint' is synonymous with *crisis* in the conceptual framework of the capital system. Neither the degradation of nature nor the pain of social devastation carries any meaning at all for its system of social metabolic control when set against the absolute imperative of self-reproduction on an ever-extended scale. This is why in the course of historical development capital not simply *happened* to fatefully overreach itself on every plane — even in its relationship to the basic conditions of social metabolic reproduction — but sooner or later was *bound* to do so.

External obstacles could never bring capital's limitless drive to a halt, and both nature and human beings could only be considered external 'factors of production' in terms of capital's self-expansionary logic. To exercise a limiting impact, the constraining power had to be *internal* to the logic of capital. Beyond a certain point the productively advancing and *universalizing tendency* of capital itself had to become an ultimately untenable *universal encroachment* and running out of any further domain to encroach upon in order to subdue. This is how, paradoxically, 'more' started to mean *less*, and 'universal control' (assuming the form of antagonistic 'globalization') started to foreshadow the dangers of a complete loss of control. This came about by capital itself creating world wide a thoroughly unstable situation which calls for comprehensive coordination (and, of course, consensual planning to make it possible) when the capital system by its very nature is diametrically opposed to such requirements. This is why the negative outcome — whereby 'more' is beginning to mean less and the 'control' of the entire world under the rule of capital brings with it the profound crisis of control — did not just happen, leaving open the possibility of reversing the situation, but had to happen with the irreversibility of a Greek tragedy. For it was only a matter of time before capital — in its irrepressible drive to go beyond the encountered limits — had to overreach itself by contradicting its inner logic, thereby colliding with the insurmountable structural limits of its own mode of social metabolic control.

This is how the chickens produced by displacing the system's contradictions through the constant enlargement of scale — on the model of the imaginary roulette player and his bottomless purse mentioned above — are beginning to come home to roost. For today it is impossible to think of anything at all concerning the elementary conditions of social metabolic reproduction which is not lethally threatened by the way in which capital relates to them — the only way in which it can. This is true not only of humanity's energy requirements, or of the management of the planet's mineral resources and chemical potentials, but of every facet of the global agriculture, including the devastation caused by large scale de-forestation, and even the most irresponsible way of dealing with the element without which no human being can survive: water itself. In Victorian times, when some localities were turned into fashionable health resorts, some cynical entrepreneurs produced bottled air with the name of the health Spa on the flasks, to be released in the bedrooms of the credulous wealthy people when they returned home. Today, if capital could corner the planet's atmosphere and thus deprive the individuals of their now spontaneously practised 'unsophisticated' mode of breathing, it would certainly devise a global bottling plant and ration the produce to its pleasure, with total authoritarianism, thereby prolonging its own life-span indefinitely. Perhaps in some futurologist think-tanks capital's apologists are already busy working on such project, as they certainly are now engaged, generously sponsored, on 'non-lethal weapons research' targeted against smaller nationalities. However, it is very doubtful indeed, whether the 'full-scale production phase' of capital's all-important air-bottling plant can be reached fast enough to rescue the system — and humankind — from the explosion of its devastating antagonisms.

In the absence of miraculous solutions, capital's arbitrarily self-asserting attitude to the objective determinations of causality and time in the end inevitably brings a bitter harvest, at the expense of humanity. For all those who continue to postulate that 'science and technology' will resolve the now no longer deniable grave deficiencies and destructive tendencies of the established reproductive order, as 'they always did in the past', are deceiving themselves if they really believe what they say. They ignore both the *prohibitive scale* on which the problems continue to accumulate and would have to be resolved, within the constraints of the actually available or realistically extendable productive resources (as opposed to fictitious projections of boundlessly multiplying resources plucked out of the sky, so as to hypostatize the permanent viability of 'growing out of the constraints'), and the *time limits* due to the great urgency of time, inescapably imposed on everyone by the objective character of the ongoing developments. For a sobering comparison in this respect it is enough to contrast the absurd projections based on the tenuous success of moon-shots at the time of President Kennedy's crusade — when an infinity of resources at the disposal of the 'Free World' was gratuitously assumed, from which it could be deduced with equal soundness that 'the sky is the limit' — with the present-day reality of NASA cut down in size beyond recognition as well as the space programmes of other countries.

In the period of capital's historical ascendancy the system's ability to brush aside the spontaneous causality and rhythm of nature — which circumscribed and 'hemmed in' the given forms of human gratification — brought with it a tremendous increase in productive powers, thanks to the development of social knowledge and the invention of the tools and practices required to translate it into emancipatory potentiality. Since, however, these developments had to take place in an alienated form, under the rule of a reified objectivity — capital — determining the course to follow and the limits to transgress, the potentially emancipatory reproductive interchange of humankind with nature had to turn into its opposite. For the scope of *practicable* science and technology had to be strictly subordinated to the absolute requirements of capital-expansion and accumulation. This is why they always had to be used with extreme selectivity, in accord with the only principle of selectivity available to capital even in the historically known forms of postcapitalist systems. Thus even the already existing forms of scientific knowledge which could to some extent counter the degradation of the natural environment must be left unrealized, because they would interfere with the imperative of mindless capital expansion; not to mention the refusal to pursue the necessary scientific and technological projects which could, if funded on the required monumental scale, redress the worsening state of affairs in this respect. Science and technology can only be pursued in the service of productive development if they directly contribute to capital-expansion and help to displace the system's internal antagonisms. Nobody should be surprised, therefore, that under such determinations the role of science and technology must be degraded to 'positively' enhancing global pollution and the accumulation of destructiveness on the scale prescribed by capital's perverse logic, instead of acting in the opposite direction, as in principle (but today in principle only) they could.

In the same way, on another plane, the advancement of the powers of agricultural production did not bring with it the eradication of famine and malnutrition. For doing so would, again, contradict the imperative of 'rational' capital expansion. 'Sentimental' considerations concerning the health — and even the mere survival — of human beings cannot possibly be allowed to disturb or disrupt the 'market-oriented' system's 'hard-headed decision making processes'. The spontaneous rhythm and recalcitrance of nature are no longer credible excuses for justifying the living conditions of countless millions who had to perish in misery in the last few decades, and so continue to perish today.

The priorities that must be pursued, in the interest of capital-expansion and accumulation are fatefully biased against those who are condemned to famine and malnutrition, mostly in the 'Third World' countries. But it is by no means simply the case that the rest of the world population has nothing to fear in this regard in the future. The productive and distributive practices of the capital system in the field of agriculture — from the irresponsible but highly profitable use of chemicals which accumulate as poisonous residues in the soil to the destruction of water tables, and to large scale interference with global weather cycles in vital regions of the planet, by exploiting and destroying the resources of rain forests, etc. — do not promise much good to come for anybody. Thanks to science and technology in their alienated subservience to profitable global marketing strategies, in our times exotic fruits are made available all year round — for those, that is, who can afford to buy them, and not for those who produce them under the rule of a handful of transnational corporations. But all this happens against the background of the highly irresponsible productive practices we all watch powerless. The costs involved are nothing short of endangering — in the interest of short-sighted profit maximization only — tomorrow's potato harvests and rice crops for all. Besides, already today the 'advanced productive practices' pursued endanger even the meagre staple food of those who are compelled to labour for 'exportable cash crops', and have to go hungry for the sake of maintaining the health of a crippling 'globalized' economy.

By now the most irresponsible tampering with the causality of nature is the rule and the pursuit of genuinely emancipatory productive projects the rare exception. Resources are allocated on a prodigious scale to totally wasteful and inherently dangerous military projects, ruthlessly brushing aside rival claims that emanate from frustrated human need. Nothing is altered in this respect with the end of the cold war and the proclamation of the 'New World Order'. For as long as renewable or non-renewable resources are at the disposal of the system, they continue to be generously allocated to senseless but suitably wasteful military projects. This is so even under the circumstances of recession, when drastic cuts must be made in basic social, health, and educational services. Indeed as a rule nothing seems to be large enough to still the appetite of the military/industrial complex in this respect. Thus, to take only one example of which there are many, we learn that the cost of the so-called 'Eurofighter 2000' — the four nation aircraft project of Britain, Germany, Italy and Spain — has reached the £43 billion figure (i.e. $66 billion at today's currency values). 'When the aircraft was conceived in the mid-1980s, its total cost was budgeted at £21 billion.'[239] The originally 'planned' figure — by which is meant the fraudulent calculation devised by the personifications of capital to push such projects through, with the help of 'three line whips', in their respective national Parliaments — escalated, as it always does, never departing in a *downward* direction from the 'scientific' cost estimates.In the bargain, the 'Eurofighter was now not expected to enter service until December 2000 — two years later than planned.'[240] By that time, with a bit of luck, the anticipated costs may double yet again. Thus the pretence of 'planning' amounts to nothing more than the cynical and deceitful manipulation of public opinion, allegedly in the strictly enforced interest of the 'sovereign consumers' and 'taxpayers' — in truth the exploited and ignored producers — who in the end have to foot the bill. This is the meaning left today of 'rational calculation' glorified by Max Weber and other apologists of the supposedly unalterable and safely eternalizable capitalist 'market society', with its 'iron cage' made to them thoroughly acceptable by the grotesquely postulated 'virtuoso skills' of the 'good bureaucracy', which in their view is serving with proper dedication the capitalist order in the interest of all.

As to the way in which the capital system tramples upon time — fully matching its disastrous tampering with the objective determinations of causality — in the vain belief that it can always get away with it, one should go no further than to remind oneself of the atomic legacy. For even if one is willing to entertain the idea that nuclear disasters will never happen, despite the accumulated tens of thousands of nuclear weapons (and nothing in sight to control and ultimately eliminate them by removing the causes for their existence), not even the greatest credulity can minimize the weight of the atomic legacy itself. For that legacy means that capital is blindly imposing on countless generations — extending in time over *thousands* of years — the burden of having to cope sooner or later, as a matter of absolute certainty, with totally unpredictable forces and complications. Thus even humanity's distant future must be perilously mortgaged because the capital system as such must always pursue its own course of action within the narrowest of time scale, ignoring the consequences even if they foreshadow the destruction of the elementary conditions of social metabolic reproduction.

5.2.3

THE consummation of capital's historical ascendancy intensifies, to the point of rupture, one of the basic contradictions of the system: that between ever-increasing socialization of production (tending towards full globalization) and its restrictive hierarchical control by the different types of personification of capital. Capital's fateful overreaching itself on the plane of the elementary conditions of social metabolic reproduction is the unavoidable consequence of this contradiction.

To be sure, in the course of historical development the continued expansion of the scale of operations helps to displace this contradiction for a long time, by releasing the pressure of 'bottlenecks' on capital-expansion through opening up new supply routes of material and human resources, as well as by creating the consumption needs required to keep the ever-enlarging reproductive system sustaining itself. However, beyond a certain point the further enlargement of scale, and the encroachment over the totality of renewable and non-renewable resources that goes with it is not only of no help but, on the contrary, deepens the underlying problems and ultimately becomes counter-productive. This is what must be understood by the activation of the absolute limit of capital with regard to the way it treats the elementary conditions of social metabolic reproduction.

To understand the gravity of this problem we must bear in mind that what goes sour here is what used to constitute perhaps capital's greatest achievement during the phase of its historical ascendancy. To quote Marx:

> If we speak of necessary labour time, then the particular separate branches of labour appear as necessary. Where exchange value is the basis, this reciprocal necessity is mediated through exchange … This necessity is itself subject to changes, because *needs are produced* just as are products and the different kinds of work skills. Increases and decreases do take place within the limits set by these needs and necessary labours. The greater the extent to which *historic needs* — needs created by production itself, *social needs* — needs which are themselves *the offspring of social production and intercourse,* are posited as necessary, *the higher the level to which real wealth has become developed.* … it is because of this, that what previously appeared as *luxury is now necessary* … This pulling away of the *natural ground* from the foundations of every industry, and this *transfer of its conditions of production outside itself,* into a general context — hence the transformation of what was previously *superfluous* into what is *necessary,* as a historically created necessity — is the tendency of capital. The general foundation of all industries comes to be general exchange itself, the world market, and hence the totality of the activities, intercourse, needs, etc. of which it is made up. Luxury is the opposite of the naturally necessary. Necessary needs are those of the individual himself reduced to a natural subject. The development of industry suspends this natural necessity as well as this former luxury — in bourgeois society, it is true, it does so only *in antithetical form,* in that it itself only posits another specific social standard as necessary, opposite luxury.[241]

Obviously, then, great productive advances are made by the capital system through the historical creation of social needs and the transfer of the conditions of production in every industry *outside* it, into the general context, transcending the original constraints — in that 'natural necessity is suspended' — thanks to the productive impact of an immensely enlarged range of needs and wants brought together in general exchange through the intermediary of the world market. But it is equally obvious that the achievements are made at a heavy, indeed potentially quite prohibitive, cost in more than one respect.

- In the first place, the transfer of the conditions of production *outside* every industry, into the global context, makes the *control* of production (and comprehensive social metabolic reproduction) on the basis of capital's given and feasible operative principles not just difficult but ultimately quite impossible to maintain. Since the objective and subjective conditions of production are situated 'outside', requiring the interchange of the totality of activities, needs, etc. in the framework of global intercourse, they are necessarily *beyond the reach* of any particular enterprise, no matter how gigantic or transnationally monopolistic. Even if we multiply, in our imagination, General Motors or Ford a hundredfold, they would still remain small fry in this respect. Thus control in reality is nightmarishly everywhere and nowhere, even if the Alex Trotmans of this world continue to fantasise about resolving the problem by making sure that their own companies are among the anticipated 'handful of global players', thanks to their ability to impose on others the cost corresponding to the advantages they themselves derive from the mindlessly advocated limitless 'economy of scale'.

The inherent logic of the capital system makes this contradiction progressively worse, instead of helping to resolve it. For the only way to improve the chances of control for the particular enterprises within the logic of capital —

which makes capital-expansion as such the absolute requirement — is to make their own scale of operation constantly bigger, no matter how destructive might be in global terms the consequences of the rapacious utilization of the available resources (for which the particular firms can have neither a measure nor any concern). Securing their relative advantage is both feasible and actively pursued (for as long as the absolute limits are not fully activated) on the basis of enhancing the partial rationality and efficacy of their specific operations — by mass production destined for a global market, by cornering the greatest possible share of that market, etc. — in conformity to the absolute imperative of capital-expansion which applies to *all* of them. This is what drives forward not only the particular firms but, equally, the capital system in general, bringing with it at first the displacement of its contradictions, but in due course inevitably their frightful intensification. For capital's *partial* rationality — and it must be stressed that, due to its antagonistic inner structuring principle, capital is capable of partial rationality only, for the same reasons which make capital's 'for-itself' a mystifying camouflage for its untranscendable 'in-itself' in the sense discussed in note 232 — i.e. the necessary expansionary drive of both the particular firms and the system as a whole, irrespective of the devastating consequences, directly contradicts the elementary and literally vital considerations of *rational restraint* and the corresponding *rational control* of global material and human resources.

Thus *the more successful* the particular firms are (as they must be in order to survive and prosper) in their own terms of reference — dictated by the inner logic and 'rationality' of the system as a whole, imposing on them the fetishistic demands of 'economic efficiency' — *the worse* it must be for the survival prospects of humankind under the prevailing conditions. The fault does not lie with the particular 'offending' enterprises (which could be, in principle, taken to task by the state which claims to watch over and defend the 'general interest'). It emanates from the nature of the established reproductive system of which the particular enterprises are an integral part. Hence the hypocritical unreality of political declarations of faith which envisage remedying the destructive consequences of pollution, for instance, by 'making the polluter pay'.

The capital system's blind expansionary drive is incorrigible because it cannot renounce its own nature and adopt productive practices compatible with the necessity of rational restraint on a global scale. Practising comprehensive rational restraint by capital would in fact amount to repressing the most dynamic aspect of its mode of functioning, and thereby to committing suicide as a historically unique system of social metabolic control. This is one of the main reasons why the idea of a globally rational and consensually restraining 'World Government' on the basis of the capital system — which is necessarily *partial* to the core in its only feasible form of rationality — is a blatant contradiction in terms. Thus the transfer of the conditions of production and social reproduction outside the particular enterprises and industries carries with it that when this process is historically completed, capital as a system of control irreversibly overreaches itself. It cannot revert to a previous — less globally integrated and expanded — condition; nor can it move forward in its restless global expansionary drive on the required scale.

The blockage of further domains over which capital could extend its rule and to which it could 'export' its contradictions activates the absolute limits and the concomitant structural crisis of the system. As a result, the ultimately unavoidable necessity of securing the sustainable management of the conditions of production and social metabolic reproduction in their proper global context reveals itself as being irremediably *beyond capital's reach,* no matter how far and how perilously the system overreaches itself. This is how the inherent structural uncontrollability of capital (right from the beginning) as a mode of control completes its circle — in the form of a truly vicious circle. The circle is completed by making *absolutely necessary* the rational control of the global system (at an appropriately *global* level at which it alone could be sustainably controlled) which it had historically created, and *impossible* its control even in a more limited context, on the plane of the necessarily 'misbehaving' and 'transgressing' particular national firms and transnational enterprises. It is inconceivable to escape from this vicious circle without radically overcoming the fundamental determinations of the capital system itself.

- The second major aspect of these developments, which must be dearly paid for, concerns the 'pulling away of the natural ground from the foundations of every industry' and the transformation of 'luxury' into necessity both for the individuals and for their given system of social metabolic reproduction. The positive, potentially universal emancipatory side of this process constitutes the greatest historical achievement of the capital system. However, it is accomplished by breaking not only with the original natural constraints but also by breaking loose from all humanly meaningful measure and standard, substituting for them, as the only measure, the success or failure in capital-expansion. Thus it comes to pass that not only genuine needs are historically created. For *'anything goes'* is adopted as the orienting principle of production (and value judgement in general), qualified only by the implicit proviso that whatever is practised should contribute to capital-expansion.

With this the possibility — indeed the necessity — of pursuing quite arbitrary and manipulative 'solutions' to the newly arising problems and contradictions of social and economic life is opened up. The negative consequences are visible in relation to both the consuming individuals and the productive system itself. With regard to the individuals, the production and manipulation of *'artificial appetites'* dominates, since 'demand management' must be subordinated to the imperatives of self-expanding exchange-value. If the real needs of the individuals can be accommodated within the confines of the latter in a way advantageous to the system, — with its need for mass produced goods to be diffused with maximum efficacy on the global market, — they may be met or at least considered legitimate; if not, they must be frustrated and obliterated by whatever can be produced in conformity to the imperative of capital-expansion. The rapacious utilization of the renewable and non-renewable resources and the corresponding waste on a monumental scale is the necessary corollary of this alienated way of relating to individual human need. As regards the impact of the same development on the productive system itself, we find that the historically created range of needs (and goods matching them, no matter how artificial) are incorporated into a *highly stretched* reproductive framework, with increasing difficulty in securing the required *continuity* of production as well as capital's necessary 'realization' and 'valorization' on an ever-expanding scale.

Through the development of the productive forces in their subodination to the one and only criterion of capital-expansion, the strictly natural progressively recedes and a new set of determinations takes its place. Thus the removal of newly generated and structurally incorporated (diffused, generalized) 'luxuries' from the existing framework of production would carry with it the collapse of the entire production system. For so long as the given production process follows its own determinations in multiplying wealth as divorced from conscious human design, the products of such alienated and reifying production process must be superimposed on the individuals as 'their appetites', in the interest of the ruling reproductive system, irrespective of the consequences in the longer run. As a result, the 'pulling away of the natural ground from the foundations of every industry' brings with it not a liberation from necessity but the ruthless imposition and universal diffusion of a new kind of necessity, acting on the broadest possible scale, endangering not simply the highly stretched capital system but the very survival of humanity.

- The third vital aspect concerns the contradiction between the inherently social character of the historically created needs — 'the offspring of social production and intercourse' — and the hierarchical/discriminatory control of both production and distribution. Inevitably, this contradiction results in a crippling distortion of what could be an emancipatory and richly fulfilling process, on condition that the structuring principle of the established reproductive system is not antagonistic.

The incorrigible distortion is manifest not only in the deeply iniquitous appropriation of the fruits of productive advancement by the personifications of capital to themselves. Also, genuine social needs and social modes of gratification cannot spontaneously arise, let alone be consciously created, because the necessarily pursued strategy of maximizing the chances of capital-accumulation must overrule everything. For this reason the human agency of consumption must be fragmented to the smallest possible unit — the isolated individual — in that such units are the most easily manipulated and dominated, as well as the likeliest to supply the maximum demand for capital's wares. 'Nuclear' family relations must be adjusted in the same sense, narrowed down ultimately to the one-generation basic unit and the transformation of the offspring into 'sovereign consumers' at the earliest possible opportunity, coupled with ever higher divorce rates acting in the same direction, especially in 'advanced capitalist' countries. For it is no longer possible to consider simply 'the monogamous family as the economic unit of society',[242] with its 'indissolubility of marriage'[243] (for a long time in the past in one way or another imposed upon it), as sufficient in its own sphere for the continued health of the capitalist economy. The expanded reproduction of capital must be secured by whatever means and at all cost, 'harmonizing' in this perverse sense the pursued production targets and the basic units of consumption.

To take in this regard only one (but rather important) example, we may think of the motor car which represents the second largest expenditure for everyone who can afford to buy their houses or flats, and the largest for all those who cannot. It is quite revealing here that the so-called 'family car' belongs to the ante-diluvian demand structure of highly stretched 'advanced capitalism'. For in order to maintain the senseless multiplication of motor cars — and the corresponding neglect or even wilful destruction of public transport services — the system had to devise the absurd marketing strategy of the two or even 'three car family'. The continued 'healthy expansion' of capital's productive order needs such practices despite the immense amount of material and labour resources wastefully locked up in every single motor car, and despite the devastating impact of this grotesquely inefficient form of transport (promoted by a system which takes pride in its own claimed 'efficiency') both in using up unrenewable energy and chemical resources and in poisoning on a mind-boggling scale the natural environment. One shudders to think of the potential impact of the almighty traffic jams in a 'fully automobilized' China or India which the mindless mythology of capitalist 'modernization' used to project as the proper course of development for these countries. But in reality far less extensive increases in car numbers present quite frightening prospects. Thus in Britain it is anticipated that the already vast numbers of motor cars — over 25 million in a country with 55 million people — will *double* within 20 years, although the average speed of the car in large city centres now hardly reaches walking pace, not to mention the concomitant poisonous emissions which have been amply proved to damage public health, especially that of children.

The proposed governmental solution is, typically, nothing but tampering with the effects while leaving intact their causes emanating from the dominant capitalist interests. Accordingly, electronic measuring and recording devices are going to be installed on all main roads, so as to be able to send heavy bills to those who enter the big city perimeters, with the purpose of deterring the less well off (that is, the great majority of motorists) from doing so. The 'ideal' to follow, already loudly trumpeted by the authorities, is this: 'use your car strictly on unavoidable journeys'. Such advice, and the material deterrent measure associated with it, must be set against the background of the absurdly low rate of private motor car utilization as things stand today, amounting to *less than 1 percent* of its potential use. The ultimate logic of this kind of 'solution' — dictated by the way in which capital must manipulate the social needs generated within its framework — is to persuade or compel the 'sovereign consumer' simply to *purchase* at regular intervals the goods on offer, and leave them totally unused until they 'self-destruct'.

In any case, the contradiction between social production/social needs and the hierarchical/discriminatory control of both production and consumption cannot be attenuated, even if the mad logic of capital's 'rational calculation' is not carried to its extreme. Quantitative expansion is the criterion by which the health of the system is measured, and therefore all considerations of *quality* — in relation to any social need whatsoever, including the more and more endangered health of the children — must be ruthlessly brushed aside in subordination to the need for capital's expanded self-reproduction. If there is no other — more palatable and ideologically safer — way to do it, social needs must be not only manipulated (either with subtlety or with transparent crudity) but even repressed with the help of authoritarian legislation and taxation. There can be no hope for changing this state of affairs. For humanly fulfilling social needs and the conditions of their realization could not be produced without radically changing the antagonistic structuring principle of the system and its inescapably hierarchical/discriminatory mode of control. Marx's words in our last quote from the *Grundrisse* laid the emphasis on the positive potentiality of the ongoing developments, indicating the negative side with the briefest reference to their 'antithetical form'. As we have seen, in the course of the last century and a half the negative side gained overwhelming dominance, to the point of confronting humankind with the prospects of being precipitated into barbarism if capital's destructive processes — directly affecting by now the elementary conditions of social metabolic reproduction — are not brought under conscious control in the not too distant future.

The wishful postulate that sooner or later we shall be able to find appropriate remedial measures against the identified destructive processes within the parameters of the capital system itself is at best naive, and often much worse than that. For it is not possible to introduce the required comprehensive rationality and properly planned allocation of material and human resources into this system while adhering to its operative principles and necessary practical premisses. The point of departure and the end point in the ruling social metabolic order are the 'personifications of capital' who must translate into executable commands capital's objective imperatives of expanded self-reproduction with reference to the projected advancement of their *limited* enterprises, no matter how big in size. This remains the case even if for the sake of argument we grant the operational viability of a world made up by Trotman's 'handful of big players'. Accordingly, the battle for comprehensive rationality and genuine economizing restraint is necessarily lost by the environmentally concerned people even before it has begun if their target does not involve the radical change of the structural parameters of the capital system itself. The fact that in the form of the threat to destroy the fundamental conditions of social metabolic reproduction one of capital's absolute limits is being activated is in no way encouraging by itself. For everything depends on the success or failure to complement in the foreseeable future the now gravely distorted but inescapably social conditions of global reproduction by an inherently social — in other words: comprehensively cooperative and in its internal constitution truly communal — mode of production and control at all levels and in all domains of the social reproductive process.

ONE last point must be made in this context, concerning the legacy of the ruling order. It has been too often assumed in the past — and despite all evidence to the contrary even in the recent past — that the highly advanced productive practices of capital can provide the material basis for a socialist reproductive order, promising the fruits of *abundance* for all and the irreversible elimination of *scarcity*.

In Marx's lifetime, before the incorrigible destructiveness of the ongoing developments fully unfolded, there may have been some ground for believing in such an outcome. But even then, it was a questionable belief which had to be forcefully qualified by focusing attention on the countervailing forces and tendencies inherent in capital's mode of operation. Regrettably, however, before the end of the century it became an often repeated but totally unsubstantiated part of the socialdemocratic creed, mesmerizing also its left wing, that 'bourgeois

society carries in all fields the seeds for the socialist transformation of society'.[244]
The only thing to be criticized was that the fruits of the established reproductive
process were provided by bourgeois society on a restricted basis, 'only for its
elect',[245] anticipating therefore the remedy in the form of a large quantitative
increase in the scale of capitalist production under the new, socialdemocratically
managed, political circumstances. Setting out from such false premisses it could
be optimistically postulated that

> The revolutionary transformation that fundamentally changes all aspects of human
> life and especially the position of women is proceeding before our very eyes. It is only
> a question of *time,* when society will take up this transformation on a large scale,
> when the process will be accelerated and extended to all domains, so that all without
> exception are able to enjoy its innumerable and manifold advantages.[246]

Today — one hundred years after this prognostication of the future course of
events was offered by one of the most radical of German left wing social
democrats, August Bebel — in the light of the actually prevailing state of affairs
it would be a dangerous illusion to believe that the capital system could even in
one single field 'carry the seeds for the socialist transformation of society',
preparing thereby the ground for the elimination of scarcity and the creation of
abundance to the benefit of all, let alone that it could do that in all of them. For
the way in which capital's reproductive system has been articulated and brought
to its perverse 'perfection' in the course of the last century — with its structurally
embodied and safeguarded wastefulness and crippling distortion even of the
most basic human needs — makes its accomplishments and highly stretched
mode of operation extremely problematical, if not altogether counter-productive in many respects.

Thus, without a radical restructuring of every single domain and dimension
of the established reproductive order (which must be inherited by all feasible
forms of socialism), the new kinds of perverse necessities created by the alienated
needs of capital's expanded self-reproduction indicated above cannot be overcome. On the contrary, as things stand today the prospects are much less
promising than in Marx's lifetime, since the tyranny of artificially produced
necessity has been extended by capital to vast formerly untouched domains.

Contrary to the way in which many people on the left imagine, technology
and science cannot be considered viable antidotes in this respect. Those who
believe that they actually are tend to project idealized pictures of allegedly
available technical means and unrealized scientific knowledge as the material
foundations of a socialist future of abundance. This may sound good political
rhetorics — the understandably outraged condemnation of existing failures —
but it is very far from being well founded theory. For the sobering truth is that
actually existing science and technology are themselves deeply embedded in the
prevailing productive determinations through which capital imposes on society
the necessary conditions of its precarious existence today. In other words, science
and technology are not well trained and fully energized reserve players sitting
on the side benches, anxiously waiting for the call of enlightened socialist team
managers in order to turn the game around. For in their actual mode of
articulation and functioning they are thoroughly implicated in a type of development which is *simultaneously* productive and destructive. This condition
cannot be remedied by wishfully separating the productive from the destructive

side in order to pursue only the first. Science and technology cannot be extricated from their extremely problematical present-day predicament by any 'thought-experiment', however well-intentioned — according to which they would only participate in productive ventures and refuse to have anything to do with the destructive dimension of those ventures — but only by being radically reconstituted as forms of social practice. Nor should the fact be forgotten that the immense material (and human) resources required for translating scientific and technological projections — on the envisaged scale — into reality cannot be simply taken for granted in the form of limitless abundance, hypostatized as directly springing from the creative forces of science and technology, as Pallas Athene once emerged fully armed from the head of Zeus. To do so would only beg the question by unproblematically assuming what cannot be assumed without violating logic. On the contrary, such resources — which are in actuality nowhere in sight now — could be produced only on a radically different socioeconomic basis, beyond the incorrigible wastefulness of capital at its now attained level of development.

Moreover, the transformation of the alleged technical means from their today perhaps selectively (strictly in a few privileged countries) feasible scale to the *global scale* needed for the optimistically hypostatized positive solution of our problems is not simply a matter of *quantity,* as the social democrats of the Second International (even of Bebel's kind) and others in their footsteps imagined when they projected the universally beneficial effects of capitalist production once it was practised on a *'large scale'*. Under conditions ruled by the orienting principles of capital it is very tempting to look for answers to the perceived absence of material sufficiency by simply anticipating quantitative improvements in the amounts produced, or to advocate the exact opposite when the negative consequences of blindly pursued capital-expansion become far too obvious to be able to ignore any longer. But such answers often exhaust themselves in false dichotomies, like 'growth versus no-growth' and 'economy of scale versus diseconomy of scale'. The truth of the matter is that the real abuse in the socioeconomic domain is not the *diseconomy of scale.* What we are here concerned with is the *wasteful utilization of human and material resources,* that is, in other words, the unforgivable *diseconomy of wasted resources,* which can apply (and under the rule of capital indeed it does) to *any scale,* from the smallest to the most extensive. To be sure, within the framework of the capital system the ever-increasing scale is a most aggravating condition. Inevitably, therefore, science and technology in the service of mass production under capital's rule are themselves mass producers of unaffordable waste. But large scale in and by itself is not the *cause* of the problems; nor could indeed its simple reversal (if it were achievable at all, which of course it is not) offer a way out of them. Ignoring this simple truth can only lead to chasing mirages like 'small is beautiful' which — if taken seriously — would be good only for condemning humankind to the self-induced misery that goes with the adoption of Quixotic productive practices.

In contrast, the globally diffused realization of socialist objectives on the proper scale is inconceivable without the *dialectic of quantity and quality* in the whole complex of social reproductive relations into which science and technology are integrated. Even in the physical sciences there is a *qualitative* barrier that must be overcome — with apparently quite prohibitive difficulties — before the move can be made from experimental nuclear fusion technology, achieved on a minute scale, to full-scale fusion energy production. How much greater must be the difficulties when science and technology do not spontaneously offer the *solution* to the encountered thorny issues but are themselves part of the *problem to be overcome!* For in their present-day articulation they are structurally subordinated to the reproductive imperatives of the capital system which could not possibly impose its wasteful and destructive practices on humankind without their most active role in the process. To think of science and technology today in any other way is to substitute in imagination for actually existing science and technology a form of both, as already existent, which in fact would first have to be — and could only be — created within the framework of a socialist social metabolic order; and to do this in order to be able to go on to argue, quite fallaciously, that the positive emancipatory forces of such science and technology are already at our disposal and could here and now felicitously constitute the productive basis of a socialist reproductive order.

Far from the projected technologically secured abundance, the future can now promise — in the event of a failure to *qualitatively break* with the ruling reproductive practices, and among them with the prevailing practices of science and technology — nothing but the permanent domination of one form or another of scarcity over humanity. Without constantly reminding ourselves of this disconcerting truth we cannot even begin the difficult task of elaborating a socialist agenda in tune with the needs of our own historical predicament.

The vicious circle of artificially created and imposed scarcity can only be broken through the *qualitative* reorientation of productive practices towards a major improvement in the now disastrously low rate of utilization of goods, services and productive capacity (both material/instrumental and human) into which society's resources must be channelled, and the practical redefinition of science and technology in the service of these emancipatory objectives. In this respect, too, it is inconceivable to accomplish the required reorientation and redefinition within the structural constraints of the capital system. For the task requires both a comprehensively rational planning of all material and human resources — of which capital is quite incapable for reasons mentioned above — and a radically different way of regulating social interchange among the individuals, by the individuals themselves, on the basis of which genuine planning first becomes possible at all. This is what puts science and technology in perspective as *yet to be produced* parts of a feasible emancipatory solution, warning us not to confuse an *abstract potentiality* — which can remain forever a totally unrealized potentiality without the successful qualitative reorientation of society's productive practices and mode of living — with an already given *actuality,* when even the conditions of converting *abstract* into *concrete* potentiality in the relevant fields are missing. Furthermore, also in this context we must remember that we do not have a leisurely time scale for the necessary conversion of potentiality into actuality. It has to take place under the aggravating condition of the great urgency of time.

Once upon a time the defenders of the capital system could praise with some justification its power of *'productive destruction'* as inseparable from the positive dynamics of advancement. This way of seeing matters was well in line with the constant extension of capital's scale of operations, truly in the form of 'productive destruction'. The successful encroachment of capital over everything that could be encroached upon — that is, before the system had to overreach itself in the way we have already seen — made the notion of 'productive destruction' tenable, even if progressively more problematical as the scale itself increased. For the destruction involved could be generously written off as a necessary part of the 'costs of production' and expanded reproduction, while the constant extension of capital's scale of operations had brought with it the displacement of the system's contradictions as an additional benefit. However, things have changed for much the worse with the consummation of capital's historical ascendancy and the activation of the system's absolute limits. For in the absence of further possibilities of encroachment on the required scale, the *destructive* constituent of the overall 'cost of production' — to be met within progressively constraining limits — becomes more and more *disproportionate* and ultimately quite *prohibitive*. We have historically moved from capital's reproductive practices of '*productive* destruction' to a stage where the predominant feature is increasingly and incurably that of *destructive* production.

It is not too difficult to see — even if the personifications of capital find it impossible to admit — that no system of social metabolic reproduction can indefinitely survive on that basis.

5.3 Women's liberation: the challenge of substantive equality

5.3.1

AS we have seen in Section 4.5.3, the economically sustainable regulation of humanity's biological reproduction is a crucial primary mediatory function of the social metabolic process. Accordingly, the historically changing articulation of the human relationships involved is of the greatest importance.

The regulatory processes we are here concerned with are inextricable from a whole network of dialectical relationships. Inevitably, their embodiments in historically specific and institutionally reinforced forms of human interchange are deeply affected by the fundamental structural characteristics of the overall social complex. But, of course, in their turn they themselves just as deeply affect the continued articulation of the social metabolic process in its entirety. If, therefore, the alienating imperatives of the established system of economic reproduction call for a discriminatory and hierarchical social control, in tune with the antagonistic structuring principle of society and the corresponding mode of managing the labour process, the comprehensive 'macrocosm' of this kind must find its equivalent at all levels of human interchange, even in the smallest reproductive and consumptive 'micro-structures' or 'microcosms' customarily theorized under the name of the 'family'. And conversely, so long as the vital relationship between women and men is not freely and spontaneously regulated by the individuals themselves within their *autonomous* (but, of course, by no means from society *independent*) 'microcosms' of the historically given interpersonal universe, on the basis of *substantive equality* between the people concerned — i.e., without the imposition of the aprioristic socioeconomic dictates of the ruling social metabolic order on them, — there can be no question of emancipating society from the crippling impact of alienation which prevents the self-realization of the individuals as particular social beings. As Marx puts it in one of his early writings:

> The direct, natural, and necessary relation of *person to person* is the relation of man to woman. ... From this relationship one can therefore judge man's whole level of development. ... In this relationship is revealed, too, the extent to which man's need has become a *human* need; the extent to which, therefore, the *other person* has become for him a need — the extent to which he in his *individual existence* is at the same time a *social being*.[247]

Judging by the way in which the known forms of socially established interpersonal relationship between women and men could be characterized — using the criterion of the humanly fulfilling free determination of their lives by autonomous persons interacting on the basis of substantive equality, — the 'whole level of development' achieved in the course of history is not much higher today than it used to be thousands of years ago, despite all advancement in productivity. As to the gains obtained during the long historical period of capital's ascendancy, they do not go beyond the level of *formal* equality. Indeed, as we shall see in Section 5.3.2, even the relative achievements in enlarging the scope of formal equality — made necessary by the capital system's productive practices of surplus-labour extraction from 'free labour' within the framework of 'contractual equality' — were in the theories of great philosophers like Kant and Hegel, and not only in those of capital's callous apologists like Hayek and his followers, coupled with forceful polemics against demands for substantive equality, often peremptorily disqualifying such demands on the ground that they allegedly committed the ultimate sin of logic and violated the proper requirements of *rationality itself.*

It would be a miracle if the capital system's 'microcosms' could be ordered in accordance with the principle of substantive equality. For this system as a whole cannot maintain itself in existence without successfully reproducing on a continuing basis the historically specific *power relations* whereby the function of control is radically separated from, and in an authoritarian fashion *superimposed* upon, the labour force by the personifications of capital even in the postcapitalist varieties of the capital system. Social complexes always operate on the basis of dialectical reciprocities. However, all such reciprocities have their objectively predominant '*übergreifendes Moment*' which cannot be wished out of existence or fictitiously modified in order to suit the convenience of social apologetics. In this important sense of a dialectically predominant '*übergreifendes Moment*', the substantively always *hierarchical* — even if in its form historically changeable — *command structure* of capital is the necessary *consequence* of the incorrigible determination of the capital system as a system of *antagonistic power relations* in which the power of control is totally divorced from the producers and is ruthlessly superimposed on them. The actually existing varieties of discriminatory hierarchy are not the 'original cause' of the functioning of the capital system as the exercise of antagonistic power relations in the form of the authoritarian subordination of production to alienated control (which constitutes the *trans*historical determination of all conceivable metamorphoses of social metabolic control on capital's material basis, notwithstanding all talk of 'democracy'). For if the specific iniquitous command structure were the cause of the structural antagonisms, that could be in principle reformed by an enlightened modification of the established command structure itself while remaining within the overall reproductive framework. Thus, nothing could be a more absurd violation of logic than the reversal of the actually existing causal relations, so as to be able to envisage the system's ability to introduce all desirable improvements into its 'macrocosm' on the unalterable premiss of maintaining the material power relations of labour's *structural subordination* to capital as necessarily enforced through the system's unavoidably hierarchical (and therefore in any meaningful sense absolutely unreformable) command structure. But that is precisely what we find in all claims to either already well established, or about to be instituted, equality — including the ritualistic appeal to the notion of 'equality of opportunity' — as postulated by the defenders of the capital system in their idealizations of 'modern industrial society' and socially caring 'market society'.

By the same token, to envisage the articulation and sustainable internal functioning of the capital system's 'microcosms' on the basis of substantive equality is not less problematical. For to do so would require either to assume the existence of a totally different — harmonious — comprehensive socioeconomic 'macrocosm', or to postulate the mysterious transformation of the hypostatized truly *egalitarian 'micro-structures'* into an *antagonistic whole*. Indeed the latter would bring with it the additional complication of having to explain how it is possible to secure the *simultaneous* reproduction of the antagonistic whole and its antagonism-free constituent parts. Isolated couples may be able to (and undoubtedly do) order their personal relationships on a truly egalitarian basis. There are in existence in contemporary society even utopian enclaves of communally interacting groups of people who can lay claim to being involved in humanly fulfilling and non-hierarchical interpersonal relations and a way of bringing up children in forms very different from the nuclear family and its splinters. But neither type of personal relations can become historically dominant within the framework of capital's social metabolic control. For under the prevailing circumstances the *'übergreifendes Moment'* is that the reproductive 'microcosms' must be able to cohere in a comprehensive whole which cannot conceivably function on the basis of substantive equality. The smallest reproductive 'microcosms' must deliver without failing their share in the exercise of the overall social metabolic functions which include not only the biological reproduction of the species and the orderly transmission of property from one generation to the other. It is no less important in this respect their key role in the reproduction of the *value system* of the established social reproductive order which happens to be — and cannot help being — *totally inimical* to the principle of substantive equality. By concentrating too much on the property-transmission aspect of the family and the legal system linked to it, even Engels tends to paint a highly idealized picture of the proletarian household, discovering non-existent equality in it. He writes that

Sex love in the relationship with a woman becomes and can only become the real rule among the oppressed classes, which means today among the proletariat — whether this relationship is officially sanctioned or not. But here all the foundations of typical monogamy are cleared away. Here there is no property, for the preservation and inheritance of which monogamy and male supremacy were established; hence there is no incentive to make this male supremacy effective. What is more, there are no means of making it so. Bourgeois law, which protects this supremacy, exists only for the possessing class and their dealings with the proletarians. The law costs money and, on account of the worker's poverty, it has no validity for his relation to his wife. Here quite other personal and social conditions decide. And now that large-scale industry has taken the wife out of the home onto the labour market and into the factory, and made her often the breadwinner of the family, no basis for any kind of male supremacy is left in the proletarian household, except, perhaps, for something of the brutality toward women that has spread since the introduction of monogamy. The proletarian family is therefore no longer monogamous in the strict sense, even where there is passionate love and firmest loyalty on both sides and maybe all the blessings of religious and civil authority. Here, therefore, the eternal attendants of monogamy, hetaerism and adultery, play only an almost vanishing part. The wife has in fact regained the right to dissolve the marriage, and if two people cannot get on with one another, they prefer to separate. In short, proletarian marriage is monogamous in the etymological sense of the word, but not at all in its historical sense.[248]

The trouble is that several of the characteristics here attributed by Engels to the proletarian family could be extended to family types of other social classes, as indeed they were in the course of the 20th century, without removing thereby the extremely problematical character of the nuclear family itself as constituted under the rule of capital. Moreover, the proletarian family is very far from embodying the ideal of egalitarian relations either between the parents or with regard to the upbringing and value orientation of the children. After the second World War German expatriate intellectuals in the U.S. tried to show their gratitude to their host country by explaining 'The Authoritarian Personality' (and the rise of Hitler) in terms of the traditional German family's subservient attitude toward political authority. The real problem of authoritarianism was, in truth, much more intractable than that, and consequently much less obligingly soluble through the adoption of the more or less explicitly idealized Anglo-Saxon family patterns. For the whole issue should have been related to the unquestioning attitude of the individuals brought up in the established family types to the authority of *capital*, and not merely to one of capital's specific political forms of control.

The most important aspect of the family for the maintenance of the rule of capital over society is the perpetuation — and *internalization* — of the deeply iniquitous *value system* which cannot possibly allow the challenge of the authority of capital in determining what may be considered an acceptable course of action by the individuals, if they want to qualify as *normal* individuals, as opposed to being disqualified for their 'deviant behaviour'. This is why we encounter everywhere the '*I know my place in society*' syndrome of internalized subservience, in Anglo-Saxon countries no less than in Germany or in former Soviet Russia, and in proletarian families as a rule no less than in their bourgeois and petty bourgeois counterparts. To have a family type which would make possible for the younger generation to think of their future role in life in terms of an alternative — genuinely egalitarian — system of values, thereby cultivating the spirit of potential rebelliousness toward the existing forms of subordination, would be an absolute outrage from the standpoint of capital.

Thus, given the established conditions of hierarchy and domination, the historic cause of women's emancipation cannot be successfully pursued without asserting the demand for *substantive equality* in direct challenge to the authority of capital, which prevails not only in the all-embracing 'macrocosm' of society but equally in the constitutive 'microcosms' of the nuclear family. For the latter cannot help being authoritarian to the core on account of the social reproductive functions assigned to it within a system of metabolic control ruled by capital, determining the orientation of the particular individuals through its unexceptionable value system. The authoritarianism in question is not simply a matter of the more or less hierarchical personal relationships among the members of the particular families. More than that, it concerns the absolute imperative to deliver what is expected from the historically evolved family type, enforced through the necessary structural subordination of the specific reproductive 'microcosms' to the tyrannical requirements of the overall reproduction process. Substantive equality within the family would be feasible only if it could reverberate across the whole of the existing social 'macrocosm', which obviously it cannot. This is the fundamental reason why the dominant family type must be structured in a way which happens to be fittingly authoritarian and hierarchical. Failing to conform to the general structural imperatives of the established mode of control — by successfully asserting in the ubiquitous 'microcosms' of society the validity and self-realizing power of human interchanges based on substantive equality — the family would directly contradict both the ethos and the effective material/human requirements of securing the stability of capital's hierarchical system of production and social reproduction, undermining its very conditions of survival.

The far-reaching implications of the direct challenge to capital's authority by the cause of women's emancipation can be appreciated by bearing in mind that the established value system could not conceivably prevail under the conditions of the present, and even less could it be transmitted to — and internalized by — successive generations of individuals, without the most active involvement of the hierarchically functioning nuclear family, articulated fully in tune with the antagonistic structuring principle of the capital system. In fact the family is both enmeshed with, and occupies a key position in relation to, the other institutions in the service of reproducing the dominant value system, including the churches and the formal educational institutions of society. So much so, in fact, that when there are major difficulties and disturbances in the overall reproduction process, manifest in a dramatic way also at the level of the general value system — as, for instance, the ever-increasing crime wave in contemporary society — the spokesmen of capital in politics and in business try to heap the burden of responsibility for the growing failures and 'dysfunctions' on the family, preaching from all available pulpits the need for returning to 'traditional family values' and to 'basic values'. At times they even attempt to enshrine such need in — rather Quixotic — legislative form, trying to make the parents responsible (in the form of punitive financial sanctions) for the 'anti-social behaviour' of their children. (Yet another characteristic example of trying to solve problems by fiddling with effects and consequences, because of the incorrigible failure to address the underlying causes.)

All this is indicative of a profound crisis affecting the whole process of reproduction of capital's value system, foreshadowing conflicts and confrontations of which the struggle for women's emancipation — with its irrepressible demand for meaningful equality — is a crucially important constituent. And since capital's mode of operation in all domains and at all levels of societal intercourse is totally incompatible with the necessary practical assertion of substantive equality, the cause of women's emancipation is bound to remain *non-integrable* and ultimately irresistible, no matter how many temporary defeats might yet have to be suffered by those who fight for it.

5.3.2

THE mass entrance of women into the labour force in the course of the 20th century, to the highly significant extent of constituting by now its majority in the capitalistically advanced countries, did not bring with it the emancipation of women at all. Instead, it tended to generalize over the labour force as a whole the imposition of lower wages which women always had to put up with; just as the legislative 'concession' to women over the demand for equal treatment concerning the age of retirement had resulted in raising it to the male norm of 65 years, instead of lowering the time of male retirement to 60, as used to be customary for women in the past. It has been forcefully argued in relation to recent trends of development that

> Throughout the OECD countries low-wage jobs are performed by women, minorities, and immigrants. Both objectively and intentionally, this situation is *lowering the general wage level* of all these economies. And the growth of women in the work force has paralleled the growth of service work in the economy. Some 60-85 percent of the employed women in the OECD states are in the services. As inflation increased and real wages began to fall, two earners maintained family income and the growth of credit sustained consumption beyond income by nearly one-fifth. In the United States the percentage of women in the labour force jumped from 36.5 percent in 1960 to 54.0 percent in 1985, the chief growth being among married women between twenty-five and thirty-four, whose participation rose from 28 percent to 65 percent. In over 50 percent of the families with children, both parents work, including nearly half of all women with children under six years. The gap between the wages of men and women declined after 1978, but *falling wages for male workers* were the origin of the change. Yet, despite more than one income earner, *household spending power fell in the 1980s,* and in 1986 it was below that of 1979, and continued to fall in 1987. The new factories in high-tech and service industries in Europe also moved toward the greater use of part-time, migrant, and women workers. This trend became their means to restructure the economy and increase employment.[249]

Thus, even the relative achievements of the past — made possible by the capital system's dynamic expansion at the time of its historical ascendancy — must be taken back to a not negligible extent when the accumulation process encounters major difficulties. Inevitably, therefore, also the earlier expected improvement in the condition of women within the margins of the established order becomes unrealizable with the shrinking of capital's margin of manoeuvre. That divisiveness within the feminist movement itself becomes more pronounced under these conditions, as compared to the 1960s and '70s, is well understandable. For, due to the shrinking of the margins, much depends on whether or not the advocated strategies of how to secure advancement in women's emancipation are willing to question the *structural limits* set by the parameters of the capital system as such. In other words, it becomes necessary to confront the question of *what kind of equality* is feasible for the individuals in general and for women in particular on the material ground of a social metabolic order of reproduction controlled by capital, in contrast to debating how the resources available within capital's shrinking margins should be redistributed under the present circumstances. For the structural limits of any social reproductive system as a rule determine also its principles and mode of distribution.

As Baran and Sweezy stressed it, 'The egalitarianism of capitalist ideology is one of its strengths, not to be lightly discarded. People are taught from earliest childhood and by all conceivable means that everyone has an *equal opportunity,* and that the inequalities which stare them in the face are the result not of unjust institutions but of their superior or inferior natural endowments.'[250] Accordingly, safeguarding the maintenance of blatant inequality and privileges in education, for instance, 'must be sought indirectly, by providing amply for that part of the educational system which serves the oligarchy while financially starving that part which serves the lower-middle and the working classes. This ensures the inequality of education so vitally necessary to buttress the general inequality which is the heart and core of the whole system.'[251] In this way it is possible to maintain the mythology of equality — at least in the form of the proclaimed 'equality of opportunity' — and perpetuate in the actually existing order under the rule of capital its diametrical opposite.

Although there has been a significant change in the ideological rationalization and legitimation of the established order in the course of its full articulation and consolidation, bringing with it in the end the practice of paying only cynical lip-service to the originally proclaimed ideals of 'freedom and equality' — and to 'fraternity' not even that, — the contradictory attitude to the principle of equality can be traced back a very long way in the past. As one of the greatest philosophers of bourgeois Enlightenment, Kant, acknowledged it without any need for cynical camouflage:

> The *general equality* of men as subjects in a state coexists quite readily with the *greatest inequality* in degrees of the possessions men have... Hence the general equality of men also coexists with *great inequality of specific rights* of which there may be many. Thus it follows that the welfare of one man may depend to a very great extent on the will of another man, just as the poor are dependent on the rich and the one who is *dependent* must *obey* the other as a *child* obeys his parents and the *wife* her husband or again, just as one man has command over another, as one man serves and another pays, etc. Nevertheless, all subjects are equal to each other before the law which, as a pronouncement of the general will, can only be one. This law concerns the *form* and not the *matter* of the object regarding which I may possess a right. For no man can coerce another [under constitutional government] except through publicly-known law and through its executor, the head of the state, and by this same law every man may resist to the same degree. ... In other words, no one can make an agreement or other legal transaction to the effect that he has no rights but only duties. By such a contract he would deprive himself of the *right to make a contract,* and thus the contract would nullify itself.[252]

These words were written after the French Revolution, in 1793, reflecting in Kant's general approach the shying away of the bourgeoisie from the revolutionary implications of their original creed. Rights had to be defined in strictly *formal* terms, absolutizing the 'right to make a contract' and making at the same time equally absolute a far from only formal consideration: the acceptance of the established state order, by arguing that 'all instigation to rebellion is the worst and most punishable crime in a commonwealth. The prohibition of rebellion is absolute.'[253] In the same way, the iniquitous order of domination and dependency had to be absolutized in substance (or 'matter'), despite all talk of confining the discourse to 'formal equality'. Feudal privileges had to be rejected in the name of the same 'free contractual society' of the bourgeoisie — in an age before the inexorable trend toward the concentration and centralization of capital became undeniable by the enthusiastic supporters of the system — on the ground that the descendants of large estate owners 'would always remain large estate owners under feudalism without there being any possibility that the estates would be *sold or divided by inheritance* and thus made useful for more people.'[254] At the same time, the substantive privileges of exploitative domination which went with 'contractually' acquired and enlarged private property had to be uncritically defended, idealizing them by shifting the argument from the field of *material substance* to that of *formal political relations,* justifying the most iniquitous actual power relations by postulating that in the political domain 'artisans and great or small property-owners are *all equal*' in virtue of the fact that 'each is entitled to *only one vote*.'[255]

Within such a framework of ideological rationalization and legitimation of the bourgeois order — in which *women,* just like *children,* could not qualify for citizenship and the right to vote, on the ground that they were 'not their own masters'[256] — everything had to be tendentiously defined. The guiding thread of the definitions was to fit the requirements of a system operated on the basis of 'equality' reduced to the *right to sell* (by means of a 'free contract') one's *'property,* under which we may include any art, craft or science'.[257] Like Rousseau before him, Kant was convinced that the just socioeconomic order was one in which 'all have something and none too much';[258] hence his approval of the sale or division by inheritance of the large landed estates. But since the 'something' for sale by the overwhelming majority of people was only their labour power, as against the exploitative and repressive power derived from the vast amounts of wealth owned by the few, this contradiction had to be faced somehow. It was 'resolved' by Kant and his ideological soul-mates by radically separating 'the *form* of the law' from its *'matter',* so as to be able to maintain in the name of *apriori rationality* that the 'general equality of men' *de jure* (i.e. as a matter of unchallengeable right and justice) can 'coexist quite readily with the greatest inequality in degrees of the possessions men have'. According to this highly tendentious view, therefore, anybody who might have dared to raise the question of equality with reference to the existing differences in material wealth and corresponding power would have automatically banished himself (not to mention herself) from the domain of rational discourse. And that was not all. For the ideological interests asserted by Kant and others in his footsteps through the explicit dualistic separation of the form of the law from its matter were further reinforced by another dualism — proclaimed again in the name of apriori rationality — by sharply opposing the law as such to human aspirations to happiness, insisting that all this is 'so willed by *pure apriori legislative reason* which has no regard for empirical purposes such as are comprised under the general name of *happiness.*'[259]

Thus — under the threat of excommunication from the domain of reason — 'equality' and 'justice' had to be divorced from substance ('matter') and happiness, in conformity to the requirements of bourgeois legality in the service of the material power relations of the capital system, removing thereby the possibility to claim rational justification for the grievances of the people at the receiving end of the existing structural hierarchy. Hegel, too, who criticized Kant on many issues, did not hesitate to relegate all those who tried to raise the question of equality in substantive terms to the inferior realm of the 'mere understanding' (Verstand), excluding them with disdain from the domain of reason (Vernunft), as we have seen above. In general, only such reforms and improvements could be contemplated by the bourgeois philosophical tradition which could be accommodated within the confines of legal formalism prejudged in favour of the ruling order.

Characteristically, the same considerations of vacuous legality which regulated the 'contractual equality' of labour were applied also to the grievances of women. As Engels stressed it:

> Our jurists, of course, find that progress in legislation is leaving women with no further ground of complaint. Modern civilized systems of law increasingly acknowledge first, that for a marriage to be legal it must be a contract freely entered into by both partners, and secondly, that also in the married state both partners must stand on a common footing of equal rights and duties. If both these demands are consistently carried out, say the jurists, women have all they can ask. This typically legalist method of argument is exactly the same as that which the radical republican bourgeois uses to put the proletarian in his place. The labour contract is to be freely entered into by both partners. But it is considered to be freely entered into as soon as the law makes both parties *equal on paper*. The power conferred on the one party by the difference of class position, the pressure thereby brought to bear on the other party — the real economic position of both — that is not the law's business. Again, for the duration of the labour contract, both parties are to have equal rights in so far as one or the other does not expressly surrender them. That economic relations compel the worker to surrender even the last semblance of equal rights — here again, that is no concern of the law.[260]

In this way, the stipulative determination of the terms in which remedies could be sought within the confines of the profoundly iniquitous established system, the struggle for emancipation in every domain had to be frustrated. True, in the 19th and 20th centuries advances could be actually made over the issue of women's emancipation, in comparison to Kant's time, so long as they could be accommodated within the well marked limits of purely formal/legal concessions, like the much celebrated victory of the Suffragettes, or the removal of some discriminatory legislation against women. However, these changes did not significantly affect the material power relations of structural inequality, just as the election of Socialdemocratic and Labour governments did not emancipate labour in the slightest from the rule of capital.

5.3.3

IN Kant's solution of the problem of how to regulate the position of women in society there was in fact not only the open (and still honest) assertion of self-confident patriarchy but also a perverse consistency. He denied equal status to women not because of some morbid personal aversion to women. They had to be assigned a subordinate position in the Kantian scheme of things because the demands for the genuine emancipation of women could not conceivably be satisfied through legalistic formal concessions. To be meaningful at all, the adopted concessions and ensuing changes had to be substantive. However, the command structure of capital always was — and forever remains — totally incompatible with the idea of conceding substantive equality in decision making to anyone, even to the individual 'personifications of capital' who must operate strictly under its material dictates. In this sense, whether or not women have the right to vote, they must be excluded from real power of decision making because of their crucial role in reproducing the family, which must be brought in line with the absolute imperatives and authoritarian dictates of capital. This must be the case because in its turn the family occupies a vitally important position in the reproduction of the capital system as such, being its irreplaceable reproductive and consumptive 'microcosm'. In the same way, labour could not conceivably acquire substantive equality, even if Labour and Socialdemocratic members of Parliament learned to stand permanently on their head — towards which they succeeded in making great progress, even if towards nothing else — because of the absolute necessity to maintain labour in permanent structural subordination to capital as the 'Master' (in the Kantian sense) of the given social metabolic order. For, as Kant put it with self-serving, but nonetheless perversely sustainable, consistency:

> the people have no lawful judgement as to how the constitution should be adminis-
> tered. For if one assumes that the people have such a power of judgement and have
> exercised it contrary to that of the real head of the state, who is to decide which one
> is right? Neither can do so, being judge in his own cause. Therefore there would have
> to be a head above the head of the state to decide between the people and the head
> of the state, which is self-contradictory.[261]

To share a position of equality with capital, while maintaining labour's necessary subordination in the socioeconomic reproductive process, is an obvious contradiction in terms. To resolve it in reality, and not in legal/political fiction, one would need a radically different way of organizing and controlling the social metabolic process. But then, of course, the whole question of 'equality with capital' — or 'equal partnership between government, business and labour' in the mystifying pretences of socialdemocratic governments and their dubious partners — would become a totally redundant preoccupation.

Naturally, Kant could not imagine an alternative socioeconomic order, organized and controlled on the basis of co-operatively shared tasks, in the spirit of substantive equality, although he was a contemporary of François Babeuf: a revolutionary beheaded in 1797 precisely for championing that cause. For Kant the axiom had to be: 'the Master commands and the subjects obey', consistently in all formations made necessary and possible by humankind's 'asocial sociability',[262] from the household to the all-embracing political state. In his view of what may be considered workable decision-making, everything had to conform to a rigorous hierarchical pattern, with someone clearly identifiable at its apex. In economics — where 'one man has command over another' — the decision maker had to be the owner of a given private property, large or small; in the family, the male Master of the family; and in the constitutional state, the totally unchallengeable head of the state. No matter how questionable on *substantive* grounds, this way of dealing with the problem was much more consistent than the later efforts of 'Utilitarians' who exhausted themselves in vacuous, and often towards the masses of the people even outrageously offensive, pronouncements — like John Stuart Mill's pretentious 'principle' of happiness according to which 'better a Socrates dissatisfied than a pig satisfied', on the basis of which he tried to justify (directly contradicting Kant) the proposed allocation of multiple votes to the intellectually superior people; or Edgeworth's male chauvinist and aristocratic/racist 'theories' concerning the most iniquitous but in his view right and proper distribution of 'utilities and happiness', as we have seen in Section 3.2.1.

Kant thought that the principle of 'equality before the law' — by which he meant the abolition of politically fixed feudal privileges, which happened to be a truly radical proposition for his age — would solve the remaining problems. Moreover, he was honest enough to admit that the bourgeois regulation of property relations to which he subscribed 'may cause a *considerable inequality of wealth* among members of the commonwealth'.[263] He found his way out of this difficulty on the one hand thanks to an unqualified belief in the benevolent power of the market (which he fully shared with, and indeed borrowed from, Adam Smith), and on the other by consigning considerations of happiness to a separate realm, arguing that 'material things do not concern the *personality* and can be *acquired* as property and *disposed of* again',[264] unlike the landed estates inextricably tied to their owners by the denounced feudal privileges. In this way, by divorcing the form of the law from its content and, on the same line of approach, by assigning concern with happiness to a separate realm, in his view justifiably out of the reach of legislative reason, Kant also provided the model of founding 'equality' on largely imaginary and materially nullifiable formal/legal 'justice'.

Later rationalizations of capital's social metabolic order — especially in the 20th century — lost even the relative justification of the Kantian illusions, which could be maintained in the 18th century in view of the still far from fully developed character of the capital system. As time went by, however, the market totally failed to live up to the hopes attached to it by Adam Smith and Kant, who both visualized it as the benevolent agency acting in the direction of a just and more equitable social order in the longer run, through the potentially (but as it turned out not really) equalizing tendency of 'universal saleability'. At the same time, even the postulated 'equality before the law' turned out to be utterly hollow, thanks to the ability of exploitative great wealth to buy preferential services (including the services of the law) in actual social practice. For the personifications of capital, accumulating wealth, could grab 'utility' and 'happiness' to themselves in the most iniquitous imaginable way. Indeed, often enough they could get away literally with murder thanks to their institutionally safeguarded privileged position (even if not of the anachronistic feudal type), demonstrating thereby with a vengeance that one can divorce the form of the law from its matter or content — in the service of an allegedly equitable 'universalization' — only in pure legal fiction. Thus, against this painfully conclusive historical background, to defend the established order in the name of the idealized 'Rule of Law', using the once sincerely held Enlightenment illusions about formal equality for justifying the most crying inequalities of the existent, as if nothing had effectively countered those illusions in the course of the last two centuries, could only be done by the most unashamed apologists of capital. Understandably, therefore, where in the 18th century genuine human concerns had set the tone, even if combined with the illusions of the age, now we find naked hypocrisy verging on cynicism.

A particularly telling example in this respect is Margaret Thatcher's Companion of Honour, Friedrich von Hayek. His mode of arguing is characterized by arbitrary declarations and assumptions — for instance, concerning the 'impartiality of the state'[265], — coupled with Nobel Prize-winning tautologies. Thus we are told in his bestselling *Road to Serfdom* that 'It was men's submission to the impersonal forces of the market that in the past has *made possible* the growth of a civilization which *without this could not have developed*'.[266] Likewise, Hayek declares that 'the Rule of Law, in the sense of the rule of formal law' is the only safeguard against 'arbitrary government'. Having thus *assumed* with class-apologetic arbitariness the necessary relationship between 'the rule of *formal* law' and 'non-arbitrary government', thereby aprioristically excluding substantive justice from the domain of legislative reason, Hayek concludes a few lines further on with an equally arbitrary — and utterly tautological — declaration according to which 'a substantive ideal of distributive justice must lead to the destruction of the Rule of Law.'[267] In the same way, Hayek's apriori ideological preconception produces the unsustained axioms that 'planning leads to dictatorship'[268] and that 'the more the state "plans" the more difficult planning becomes for the individual'.[269] However, later in the book he contradicts his own lament about the difficulties of individual planning by happily embracing the idea that 'A complex civilization like ours is necessarily based on the individual adjusting himself to changes whose cause and nature he cannot understand'.[270] In this way we are left not only with a blatant contradiction between the idealization of 'individual planning' under capitalism and its effective denial by the market, but also with a grotesque notion of what the submissive individual is supposed to accept as the ultimate conquest of our 'complex civilization'. Indeed, we are told — curiously in the name of freedom — that unquestioning submission by all individuals to the tyranny of the market is the ultimate virtue. For

> unless this complex society is to be destroyed, the only alternative to submission to the impersonal and seemingly irrational forces of the market is submission to an equally uncontrollable and therefore arbitrary power of other men.[271]

Evidently, Hayek cannot admit the possibility and legitimacy of envisaging an alternative to the rule of capital, to which in his view everybody must submit; least of all if it means taking control by the individuals over their own life-activity through consciously organized — i.e. genuinely planned — forms of productive social interchange, managed on the basis of their own decisions as opposed to preexisting (and in Hayek's view even in principle incomprehensible) material dictates. What remains a complete mystery in Hayek's approach is: why should one prefer his kind of *uncontrollability and submission* to what he quite demagogically projects as the *only* alternative? Just because what he commends is 'impersonal' and 'seemingly irrational'? After all, when he characterizes the system in such terms, everything is presented upside-down. For the capital system is not 'seemingly irrational' but thoroughly and irremediably *irrational;* and it is not 'impersonal' in its real nature but only *seemingly* impersonal. That is, it happens to be impersonal only because of the historically prevailing *fetishism of commodity,* which makes a definite type of relation between men — under capital's mode of social metabolic control — assume in their eyes 'the fantastic form of a relation between things', so that 'their own social action takes the form of the action of objects which rule the producers instead of being ruled by them'.[272] The point is that the stranglehold of this 'fantastic form' to which we are forever supposed to submit can be practically challenged by exposing and fighting the established class relations of domination and structural subordination at the roots of the mystifying impersonality of commodity fetishism, which Hayek is anxious to obfuscate in his fallacious capital-apologetic writings. Here, again, the contrast with Kant could not be greater. For the great German philosopher confessed his sympathy for *philosophical utopianism,* which hopes for a state of perpetual peace based on a league of peoples as a world republic, and the *theological utopianism,* which expects the complete moral regeneration of the entire human race'.[273] And Kant made his own contribution to both, in his reflections on 'Perpetual Peace' and on 'Religion within the Limits of Reason Alone', in order to rescue them from being 'universally ridiculed as day-dreaming'.[274] In Hayek's view, however, such efforts must be indeed condemned as idle day-dreaming, if not much worse. For we already live in the best of all possible worlds. Thus, the question of improving on the existent order, whose 'nature we cannot understand', cannot legitimately arise. The duty of men and women alike, according to Hayek, is to cheerfully 'submit' to the dictates of our 'complex civilization', and to fight tooth and nail those who refuse to accept the necessity of submission as the permanent 'human condition'.

5.3.4

IN this way we witness the complete degradation of an approach which happened to be very problematical — and in fact already questioned — even in the age of partially forgivable Enlightenment illusions. It was questioned not only by Babeuf, who so passionately believed in a radically different idea of equality and justice that he was prepared to die for it, but also by Diderot before him, who insisted — as we have seen in Section 4.2.2 above — that 'if the day worker is miserable, the nation is miserable'. But however problematical were Kant's ideas on the relationship between equality, happiness, and 'the personality', he never tried to pretend that the beneficiaries of material inequality should not be considered privileged, even if, to be sure, not *morally* advantaged. The shameless denial of even the most palpably undeniable link between privilege and material inequality became prominent only within a conceptual framework in which actual relations had to be presented upside-down, deliberately shifting the ground of arguments in the interest of the crudest form of anti-socialist propaganda masquerading as theory.

To take a typical example, Hayek categorically excludes all considerations of 'substantive equality' and 'substantive justice' from the domain of legitimate discussion, offering as the only type of proper law the general obligation to 'drive on the left- or on the right-hand side of the road so long as we all do the same' — even 'if we feel it to be unjust'.[275] Why on earth any of us should feel that this type of formal administrative law might be unjust, when it applies without exception to all in a rationally uncontested (and uncontestable) field, remains a mystery. However, the apologetic intent behind it is clear enough. Indeed, Hayek's purpose is to camouflage *repressive substantive law* — enacted and unceremoniously enforced as the political dimension of capital's tyrannical rule — as if it belonged to the same category as the coercibly enforceable but in fact rationally uncontested (even when in practice by some individuals violated) formal administrative rules. For a few lines further down the page the example given to illustrate legitimate coercive state action, in contrast to what would have to be considered in Hayek's view a thoroughly reprehensible 'inactivity' of the state, is to intervene against *'strike pickets':* an action which by no stretch of even the most disingenuous imagination could be subsumed under the category of uncontested (and rightfully uncontestable) formal administrative rules. Thus, revealing the class-apologetic ideological intent behind this kind of theorization, in the case directly affecting organized labour the qualification that comes into play, thanks to the author's sleight of hand, is that state coercion is right and proper even if the people concerned 'feel it to be unjust'.

Hayek's main argument concerning privilege and inequality is by no means less problematical. It goes like this:

> The conflict between *formal justice and formal equality before the law* on the one hand, and the attempts to realize various ideals of *substantive justice and equality* on the other, also accounts for the widespread confusion about the concept of 'privilege' and its consequent abuse. To mention only the most important instance of this abuse — the application of the term privilege to property as such. It would indeed be privilege if, for example, as has sometimes been the case in the past, landed property were reserved to members of the nobility. ... But to call private property as such which all *can* acquire under the *same rules,* a privilege, because only *some succeed* in acquiring it, is depriving the word privilege of its meaning.[276]

Thus, in the world in which we happen to live *privilege* does not exist at all, only 'privilege' in inverted commas. Those who maintain the opposite are participants in 'the widespread confusion', violating the concept of privilege (which belongs to the feudal past); and worse still, they are also *abusers* of reason, above all because they dare to question the discriminatory power of substantive/material privilege emanating from the structural domination of capitalist private property. And the stipulated reason why the innumerable 'confused' people and 'abusers' of reason should be excluded from rational discourse is because those who — as a matter of existing material relations — are excluded from private property *can* acquire it 'under the same rules', even if they do not succeed in doing so.

Naturally, beneath this 'rational argument' we find concealed, again, Hayek's customary class-apologetic tautology. For first he arbitrarily asserts that raising the question of *susbstantive* equality and justice must be condemned as the manifestation of a 'widespread confusion', because considerations of equality and justice *must be* confined strictly to *formal* rules, and then he 'logically concludes' that, in virtue of the *same formal rules* under which private property *can* be acquired by everyone, in principle, everything is right and proper in this world of ours in which there is no room for privilege, thanks to the ideal operation of the state's formal rules (which, incidentally, is also a total fiction, even if in the present context it is of secondary importance). The vital question, whether the 'can' invoked by Hayek is *effective or utterly vacuous*[277] under the actually existing capital system, must remain in his eyes an absolute taboo. Those who might have the temerity of raising it would be banished by the author of *The Road to Serfdom* from the realm of rational discourse with the peremptory finality of the same axiomatic tautology which he uses here against the alleged 'abusers' of reason, who are said to be guilty of 'depriving the word privilege of its meaning'.

What is typical of all such defences of the capital system is the self-serving evasion of the question of *material power relations*. Through this evasion even the substantively most iniquitous and exploitative forms of domination and subordination can be misrepresented as being fully in accord with the requirements of the 'Rule of Law' and the absence of arbitrariness. We are told that 'it is not the source but the limitation of power which prevents it from being arbitrary.'[278] But in this postulate both the *source* and the *limitation* of state legislative power are fictitiously divorced from the material ground and interests which they serve, as if the idealized 'non-arbitrary' political power could be self-sustaining and self-limiting. To be sure, the political power of capital's state formations is not arbitrary but strictly mandated by the material structural determinations of the established social metabolic system of control. The arbitrariness concerns in part the irrationality of the ultimately uncontrollable 'realization process', which affects even the most privileged 'personifications of capital', and in part the ruthless subjection of the great masses of the people to the structural imperatives of a fetishistic and tyrannical mode of socioeconomic reproduction to which 'there can be no alternative'. In other words, what is arbitrary in relation to the individuals is the categorical exclusion of alternatives to the capital system's absolute material dictates, and not the translation of those dictates into fixed rules of historically specific state legislation. Thus, to argue that the Rule of Law is 'the legal embodiment of *freedom*',[279] on the fictitious ground that the Rule of Law properly restricts itself 'to the kind of *general* rules known as *formal* rules',[280] is a complete misrepresentation not only of the relationship between state legislation and capital's material ground — the non-formal but absolutely real limiting force of political legislative and executive practices, — but also of the nature of political laws and rules themselves. For the apologetically idealized 'known rules of the game'[281] (said to secure the freedom of the individual) are not only 'general and formal', applying in accordance with the approved formal principle of equality to every particular person (in the spirit of Hayek's favourite illustrative examples, taken from the Highway Code and the general adoption of 'weights and measures'). They are also *substantive* as well as *discriminatory*. In the latter capacity they are directed not simply against the interests of a limited number of *particular* individuals (as Hayek's ritualistic references to the ideality of 'the liberal creed',[282] in its vacuous contrast to the substantive orientation of 'the collectivist creed', would have it), but against *classes* of structurally disadvantaged people, as exemplified by the Liberal State's thoroughly substantive and repressive anti-trades union legislation, against strike pickets, for instance.

This kind of reasoning — which is typical of the callous defence of material inequality under the pretences of doing so in the name of the Rule of Law — operates with the arbitrary assertion of a whole series of false equations. Thus, the Rule of Law is said to equal the rule of *formal* law; the two together are said to equal the absence of *privileges;* and the three together are supposed to equal and *safeguard 'equality* before the law which is the opposite of arbitrary government'.[283] As we have seen, no single element of this series of apologetic equations is tenable, let alone could they be considered to amount to the only rationally justifiable position. In fact the purpose of the whole exercise is to make people accept two — totally unjustifiable — substantive propositions. First, that all concern with equality should be strictly confined to the question of 'equality before the law'. And second, in view of the fact that no advance can be made toward substantive equality within the framework of the advocated apriori constraints of the first proposition, it must be also accepted that it is right and proper (i.e. rational and fully justifiable) — and indeed that it should remain so in our view forever, unless we are willing to take upon ourselves the odium of favouring 'arbitrary government' and the demise of 'the legal embodiment of freedom' — that absolutely no one (and least of all any public authority, whatever its electoral mandate) should act in order to change the prevailing relations of substantive inequality. For, according to Hayek, 'formal equality before the law is in conflict, and in fact *incompatible, with any activity of the government deliberately aiming at material or substantive equality of different people'*.[284]

In truth the long disputed question of equality and emancipation cannot be seriously tackled without addressing ourselves to both of its substantive dimensions. The first is linked to the problems of substantive law and the direct or indirect legislative obstacles erected in the course of history against the potential realization of substantive equality, and the second concerns what must go well beyond the powers of straightforward legal redress.

The formalistic theories of capital's apologists are formulated in order to deny the undeniable, namely that such substantive legislative obstacles do — or indeed conceivably even might — exist within the framework of the liberal state. But this is by no means their most important function. For their approach is primarily concerned with the *aprioristic disqualification* of whatever cannot be accommodated within the confines of their favoured material and legal order. Thus the main point of their defence of the Rule of Law, and of the pretended confinement of the latter to 'formal rules', is to circumscribe the field of legitimate action in such a way — applying the stipulated formal criteria as much to the emancipation of women as to the material and substantive equality of working people in terms of their potential powers of decision making — that it should be absolutely unrealizable. In the first place, they restrict the possibility of advancement to the act of voting, and then they nullify even that by conveniently disqualifying the potential emancipatory outcome of the vote itself. For even if the people concerned all voted into power a government with a mandate to institute substantive equality and real — not materially impotent formal/legal — emancipation, the government in question would not be allowed to violate the taboo of substantive inequality, as we have seen in the penultimate paragraph.

However, the obstacles to equality and emancipation do not end there. What is of even greater concern is precisely what lies at the material ground of all legislative practices in this respect. For the forces countering the demand for substantive equality have successfully reasserted themselves — despite all advances in the legal domain, as far as the cause of women's emancipation is concerned — under all of the modern state formations known to us, including their postcapitalist varieties.

5.3.5
THE demand for substantive equality kept surfacing in history with particular intensity in periods of structural crisis, when, on the one hand, the established order was breaking up under the pressure of its internal contradictions and could no longer fulfil its vital social metabolic functions and, on the other hand, the new order of class rule destined to take the place of the old was as yet far from fully articulated. Thus, neither the old system nor the emerging alternative had the power to rule out — with the *internalized authority* of oppressive apriorism — the possibility of realizing the age-old aspiration to free human interchanges from the tyranny of ubiquitous structural hierarchy. Significantly, countless egalitarian systems of belief originated under the conditions of such relative social vacuum 'between two worlds'. Indeed, they often even assumed the form of organized confrontations, from slave revolts to peasant uprisings, and from the numerous sporadic upheavals of the anabaptists to the conspiracy of Babeuf's 'Society of Equals', all the way down to the radical militancy and sacrifice of the early working class movement against uneven odds in the first half of the 19th century. The fact that in the course of history the militant egalitarian movements were as a rule suppressed in blood by the constantly realigned forces of exploitation and oppression cannot diminish their importance. For they testified — again and again — to the ineradicability of an idea, whatever the forces lined up against it, whose time was frequently foreshadowed in history even if not yet come.

The demand for women's emancipation conferred a new dimension on such age-old historic confrontations pressing for substantive equality. The fact that women had to share a subordinate position in every social class without exception made it undeniable even by the most extreme forces of conservatism that their demand for equality could not be ascribed to 'particularistic class envy' and dismissed as such. This circumstance made it also obvious that the 'empowerment of women' in any meaningful sense of the term was inconceivable if the structural framework of class hierarchy and domination was retained as the organizing principle of the social metabolic order. For even if all commanding positions in capitalistic business and politics were legislatively preserved for women — which of course for a multiplicity of reasons, including in a prominent place the established family structure, they could not be, hence the operation of hypocritically inflated tokenism — that would still leave their incomparably greater number of sisters in a position of abject subordination and powerlessness. There could be no 'special space' found for the emancipation of women within the framework of the given socioeconomic order. This is why the 'empowerment of women' had to mean the empowerment of all human beings or nothing, calling thereby for the establishment of an alternative — radically different — social metabolic order of production and reproduction, embracing both the comprehensive framework and the constitutive 'microstructures' of society.

In this way the irrepressible demand for women's emancipation inevitably also focused attention on the early promise and self-definition and the subsequent tragic derailment of the socialist movement. For the derailment took the form of a fateful shift — both by socialdemocratic reformism and post-capitalist state management in the societies of 'actually existing socialism' — from the strategy of instituting an *alternative* to capital's social order to the acceptance of short-lived partial improvements that could be accommodated by the capital system itself.

The contrast in this respect with the Marxian vision becomes clear when we recall that, referring to the proletariat, Marx spoke of 'the formation of a class with radical chains, a class *in* civil society which is not a class *of* civil society, an estate which is the dissolution of all estates, a sphere which has a universal character by its universal suffering and claims no *particular* right because no particular wrong but wrong generally is perpetrated against it; which does not stand in any one-sided antithesis to the *consequences* but to the *premises* of the state; a sphere which cannot emancipate itself without emancipating all other spheres of society'.[285] Thus the class of labour was seen by Marx as a class not in the traditional sense. For traditional classes, aiming at one form or another of class domination, were in his view 'classes *of* civil society' in that they could fulfil their self-serving objectives in the existing hierarchical civil society. The class of labour, by contrast, could not realize its aims in the form of *particularistic* interests, nor could it conceivably become a privileged class over against the producing class, namely itself.

However, the possibility of derailing labour's emancipation by the historically given economic and political organizations of labour becoming entangled in the pursuit of particularistic interests could not be excluded.

First, because the class of labour — unlike women who form an integral part of every single class — occupied a determinate space in the social spectrum, opposite their class adversary: capital and its changing 'personifications'. In this sense, as 'class against class', labour had historically specific aspirations and grievances which could be treated in relative terms, on the model of acquiring (through the increase in labour's productivity) a quantitatively larger *piece* of cake, even if by no means a proportionately larger *slice* of the available cake as compared to the share appropriated by capital. The illusions and mystifications of reformism could be successfully based on this fundamental ambiguity — to which, again, there could be no equivalent in the domain of women's emancipation which by its very nature calls for a *qualitatively* different social order. Adopting this ambiguity as its strategic frame of reference, socialdemocratic reformism could falsely promise the realization of socialist objectives through the gradual extension of limited quantitative improvements in the workers' standard of living (by means of self-deluding and never even under Labour and socialdemocratic governments consistently attempted 'progressive taxation'), when in reality capital always remained in complete control both of the social reproduction process and the distribution of the 'wealth of nation' produced by labour.

Second, the socioeconomic circumstances for a relatively long historical period were quite unfavourable to the realization of the perspectives advocated and anticipated by Marx. For as long as the historical ascendancy of capital could continue undisturbed on the global terrain, there had to be room in effective material terms also for the pursuit of particularistic interests in the labour movements of the relatively privileged countries. Even though the original strategic objectives of socialists had to be shelved while pursuing such limited and in the long run even on their limited scale unsustainable interests, nevertheless for the time being some measurable gains could be obtained from capital's expanding margin of profit for the leading sections of the working classes in the economically most dynamic — as it happened: imperialistically dominant — capitalist countries, modifying thereby the formerly valid dictum of the *Communist Manifesto* according to which all that proletarians could lose were only their chains.

The historic moment of reformist social-democracy had arisen from such developments. Already at the time of Marx's *Critique of the Gotha Programme*, and much more so by the end of the 19th century under the slogan of Bernstein's *'Evolutionary Socialism'*, the socialdemocratic movement adopted the strategy of striving for partial privileges within capital's reproductive framework. In this way it actively contributed to the revitalization of the capitalist adversary, instead of advancing its own cause for an alternative social order. For, inevitably, the acceptance of partial improvements conceded by the adversary from its operational margins of profitable capital-expansion carried a very high price for labour. It had to mean the meek acceptance of the authority of capital in how to determine what may or may not be considered legitimate claims and the proper share of labour in the available social wealth. Thus it was by no means surprising that in socialdemocratic discourse the question of substantive human equality became watered down to the point of meaninglessness, ritualistically reiterated at party conferences in the form of the vacuous and even self-contradictory rhetorics of 'fairness' (of all things *vis-à-vis* capital, by asking even the *minimum wage* in a *'sensible* measure' and at a *'sensible* pace' from it, in the new jargon of Labour leaders) and 'equality of opportunity' dutifully and subserviently counterposed to 'equality of outcome'.

This way of dealing with the stubbornly resurfacing demand for genuine equality was vacuous and self-contradictory because it had left the structural edifice of exploitative class society totally unaffected even as a project, not to mention effective achievement. For, once the established socioeconomic system was taken for granted as the necessary framework of legitimate claims and aspirations, everything had to be 'realistically' assessed on the premises of capital's continued viability and for almost a whole century of socialdemocratic day-dreaming gratuitously assumed 'reformability'. This is how it came about that the idea of equality had to be strictly subordinated to considerations of 'fairness' and 'justice', adopting as the proper measure of both 'fairness' and 'justice' whatever capital was able and willing to concede from its fluctuating margins of profitability.

The rationality of such a discourse which postulated the realization of 'equality' and 'fairness' (not to mention socialism) on the absolutely unchallengeable practical premiss of capital's unalterably hierachical and exploitative social order, could only be characterized with Kant's damning dictum: *ex pumice acquam*, i.e. 'water to be made from pumice stone'. The fact that in our own days, with the global consummation of capital's historic ascendancy, the socialdemocratic movement had to abandon even its limited reformist aims and embrace capital's 'dynamic market economy' without reservations, more or less openly transforming itself thereby everywhere into a version of bourgeois liberalism, signals the end of a road which constituted a blind alley to emancipatory aspirations from the very beginning.

It is gratifying in this respect, as well as reassuring for the future, that the derailing rhetorics of 'fairness' — which in the past invariably meant knocking on doors that could not be opened — plays no appreciable role in the discourse on women's emancipation. As we shall see below, here the question of what is to be done about the existing *power relations* cannot be avoided when raising the question of equality, nor can it be watered down to the vague notion of 'equality of opportunity' against the evidence of its obvious practical negation by the established social order. Imploring a profoundly iniquitous system of social metabolic reproduction — based on the pernicious hierarchical division of labour — to grant 'equal opportunity' to women (or, for that matter, to labour) when it is *structurally incapable* of doing so, makes utter mockery of the very idea of emancipation. For the vital precondition of substantive equality is to confront with radical criticism the question of the established system's necessary mode of functioning and its corresponding command structure which apriori exclude any hope of meaningful equality. Substantive equality must be categorically excluded because of the way in which the social division of labour is constituted in the existing order, going back a very long way in the past. This is what must be reversed. As Marx puts it:

> The division of labour in which all these contradictions are implicit, and which in its turn is based on the natural division of labour in the family and the separation of society into individual families opposed to one another, simultaneously implies the distribution, and indeed the *unequal* distribution, both quantitative and qualitative, of labour and its products, hence property, the nucleus, the first form of which lies in the family, where wife and children are the slaves of the husband. This latent slavery in the family, though still very crude, is the first form of property, but even at this stage it corresponds perfectly to the definition of modern economists, who call it the power of disposing of the labour-power of others.[286]

The apparently intractable problem here is that all internal transformations of the family in the course of history took place within the broad framework of the necessarily iniquitous hierarchical/social division of labour and had to incorporate its overall requirements, at no matter how advanced a level of civilization. Thus the prevailing power relations had to be constantly reconstituted everywhere — including the 'nucleus' of the always given form of 'both quantitatively and qualitatively unequal distribution' of the historically established social productive forces and their products — in such a way that the smallest constitutive cells and their most comprehensive linkages should always remain structurally enmeshed and inextricably intertwined with one another as reciprocally conditioning productive and reproductive structures. Only in this way was it possible to maintain the dominance and continuity of the existing order, securing the reproduction of not just the individual members of society but the overall framework itself in which all reproductive functions are carried on, namely the established system of division of labour. We must recall in this context the crucial role assigned to the family in the perpetuation of both the discriminatory property relations and the corresponding — on one side of the social divide self-righteously domineering and on the other suitably submissive — value system of the ruling social order. Even the historically most recent and 'sophisticated' forms of society's reproductive and distributive 'nucleus', located in the family, could not escape — no matter how enlightened and egalitarian

in intention the personal attitude of its individual members towards one another
— the dehumanizing imperatives of being subservient, consciously or unconsciously, to the values emanating from, and securing the undisturbed operation
of, the ubiquitous structural/hierarchical division of labour. This is why the
fundamental constitutive principles and the effective material power relations
of the latter had to be directly confronted if the historic cause of women's
emancipation was to be carried beyond the frustrating unreality of formal
'equality of opportunity' which leads absolutely nowhere.

5.3.6

THE critique of the established material power relations could not content itself
with the indictment of the glaring iniquities of private capitalist exploitation
and domination. For the record of postcapitalist societies is far from promising
in this respect. As Margaret Randall stressed it in a striking book:

> Neither the capitalist societies that so falsely promise equality nor the socialist
> societies that promised equality and more have really taken on the challenge of
> feminism. We know how capitalism coopts every liberating concept, turning it into
> a slogan used to sell us what we do not need, where illusions of freedom replace the
> real thing. I now wonder if socialism's failure to make room for a feminist agenda
> — indeed, to embrace that agenda as it indigenously surfaces in each history and
> culture — is one of the reasons why socialism as a system could not survive.[287]

> It was the same refrain throughout the socialist world: once economic equality was
> achieved, the rest would follow. This *rest* was rarely if ever named. If you demanded
> space for a discussion of feminism, or encouraged an analysis based on the retrieval
> of women's history, women's culture, and women's experience, you would most likely
> be dubbed a 'bourgeois feminist' — divisive, or worse, counterrevolutionary.[288]

The failure of postcapitalist societies with regard to women's emancipation is
all the more telling since they explicitly promised at some point in their history
to remedy the acknowledged grave iniquities. However, in the end the existing
power relations directly affecting women were not significantly altered. Instead,
they vainly tried to cover up their failure with postcapitalist versions of tokenism. To quote the same author:

> Power remains a major problem. When, year after year, only a few token women are
> elected to positions of political power, socialism seems to defeat its purpose: that of
> creating a more just society for all people. The process of women acquiring political
> power in the Soviet Union and most of Eastern Europe was particularly slow, so slow
> as to remain ludicrous; it was more successful in Vietnam, Nicaragua, and Cuba. But
> nowhere in the socialist world has women representation at the highest levels grown
> beyond tokenism, and more to the point, women with a feminist vision have
> systematically been denied positions of power.[289]

The record of postcapitalist societies in promoting women to key positions of
political decision making is deplorable even by comparision to capitalist countries. For in the latter a not negligible number of women were allowed to occupy
the highest — Prime Ministerial — political office, from Indhira Gandhi and
Margaret Thatcher to Mrs Bandaranaike, to name only a few. By contrast in
postcapitalist countries there were none, and even in the ruling Party Politburos
women were as rare as the white raven in nature, despite the officially proclaimed
policy of 'full equality'. But, of course, this did not mean at all that in capitalist
countries the conquest of the highest political office by some women amounted

to more than tokenism. The differences in this respect were only the manifestation of different kinds and uses of tokenism. Besides, even if by some miracle all of the top positions of political decision making could be occupied by women in postcapitalist societies, that would not make those societies any more socialist and the people — including women — any more emancipated in them.

The striking differences in the occupancy of high political office we have witnessed in the twentieth century can be explained in terms of the significantly different way in which surplus-labour is extracted in the two systems. Under private capitalism (whether 'advanced' or 'underdeveloped'), the successfully prevailing *economic* extraction of surplus-labour (in the form of the capitalist appropriation and accumulation of surplus-value), for as long as it can successfully prevail, assigns very different functions to politics and to direct political decision making than under the postcapitalist varieties of the capital system. In the latter the control of surplus-labour extraction is — for better or worse — in the domain of politics, and the Soviet type 'personifications of capital' cannot fulfil their functions without being directly involved in highly centralized forms of political decision making, involving huge stakes and potentially far-reaching consequences all the time. In private capitalist systems, by contrast, the primary role of politics is to be the *facilitator* (and in due course also the legal codifier) of *spontaneously unfolding* changes, rather than their *initiator*. Thus the people in charge of the various capitalist political organs appropriately decline to assume responsibility for both the occurring and the adversarially advocated changes, using the frequently heard sentences that 'the government's role is no more than to create a favourable climate for business' and that 'governments cannot do this or that'.

Thus, given the economically secured extraction of surplus-labour and the corresponding mode of political decision making under the private capitalist order of social metabolic reproduction, there can be absolutely no room in it for the feminist agenda of substantive equality which would require a radical restructuring of both the constitutive cells and the overall structural framework of the established system. No one in their right mind could even dream about instituting such changes through the political machinery of the capitalist order, in no matter how high an office, without exposing themselves to the danger of being labelled female Don Quixotes. There is no danger of introducing the feminist agenda even by surprise in capitalist systems, since there can be no room at all for it in the strictly circumscribed framework of political decision making destined to the role of facilitating the most efficient economic extraction of surplus-labour. Thus it is by no means accidental that the Indhira Gandhis, Margaret Thatchers and Mrs Bandaranaikes of this world — and the last one despite her original radical left credentials — did not advance in the slightest the cause of women's emancipation; if anything, quite the opposite.

The situation is very different in the postcapitalist systems of social metabolic reproduction and political decision making. For, in virtue of their key position in securing the required continuity of surplus-labour extraction, they can initiate wholesale changes in the ongoing reproduction process through direct political intervention. Thus the determination of the political personnel is of a very different order here, in that its potential orientation is *in principle* much more open than under capitalism. For notwithstanding the mythology of the 'open society' (propagandized by its authoritarian enemies like Hayek and Popper), under capitalism the objectives and mechanisms of 'market society' remain untouchable taboos, strictly delineating the mandate and the unquestioning orientation of the political personnel who cannot and would not contemplate seriously interfering with the established economic extraction of surplus-labour; not even in its socialdemocratic embodiment. This difference in potential openness in the two systems creates *in principle* also a space for introducing elements of the feminist agenda, as indeed the shortlived postrevolutionary attempts testify to it in Russia.

However, the potential openness cannot be actualized on a lasting basis under the postcapitalist rule of capital, since the hierarchically managed extraction of surplus-labour reasserts itself as the crucial determining characteristic of the social metabolism also under the changed circumstances.Thus the whole question of political mandate must be suitably redefined, nullifying the possibility of both *'representation'* (characteristic of the capitalist parliamentary setup, with the totally unquestioning mandate of the representatives towards the established economic mode of surplus-labour extraction and capital accumulation) and *'delegation'*, which used to characterize much of the socialist literature on the subject. An absolutely unquestionable, depersonalized political authority — the Party of the Party-state — must be superimposed over the individual political personnel under the postcapitalist rule of capital, articulated in the form of the strictest hierarchical command structure, oriented towards the maximal politically regulated extraction of surplus-labour.

This is what apriori excludes all possibility of 'making room for the feminist agenda'. Given the significantly different role of politics in the two systems, under capitalism women may be safely allowed to occupy at times even the highest political position, whereas under postcapitalist conditions they must be unceremoniously excluded from it. Under the postcapitalist system, therefore, even the limited attempts of women to establish a new type of family relation in furtherance of their age-old aspirations, which spontaneously surfaced in the immediate postrevolutionary years, must be liquidated. For inasmuch as the politically secured and safeguarded maximal extraction of surplus-labour remains the vital orienting principle of the social metabolism, with its necessarily hierarchical command structure, the question of women's emancipation, with its demand for substantive equality — and by implication: for a radical restructuring of the established social order, from its smallest constitutive cells to its most comprehensive coordinating organs — cannot be entertained for a moment. Any attempt to critically examine the established power relations from the standpoint of women's emancipation, in order to remedy the long established iniquities, must be curtly dismissed. The question of equality must be confined to what is compatible with the prevailing hierarchical social division of labour, enforcing and perpetuating with all political means at the system's disposal the subordination of labour.

Women in terms of such criteria can become fully equal members of the consciously expanded labour force, entering on that account some formerly forbidden territories. But under no circumstances can they be allowed to question the established division of labour and their own role in the inherited family structure. In postcapitalist societies women in general may be genuinely emancipated to the degree of entering any profession. Indeed, they can do this as a rule under the same conditions of financial remuneration as their male colleagues. Moreover, their conditions as working mothers may even be considerably improved with nursery and Kindergarten facilities, so that they should more easily and more quickly return to the full-time labour force. But what has been aptly called the 'second shift' for women, starting after they return home from their place of work, could only underline the problematical character of all such achievements, including the peculiar 'political tokenism' practised in these societies, which could do nothing about altering the established relation of forces and the subordinate role of women in the structurally subordinated labour force. All it could do was to put sharply into relief that the historic cause of women's emancipation could not be advanced without challenging the rule of capital in all its forms.

5.3.7

IT is most revealing in this respect that intellectuals in capitalistically advanced countries who considered themselves democratic socialists could find themselves singing in unison with Stalinist authoritarianism precisely on the question of equality. Thus the Fabian socialist Bernard Shaw spoke with enthusiasm about the Soviet Party leader's public denunciation of 'the politicians with whom Stalin lost patience when he derided them as *Equality Merchants*'.[290]And Shaw did not stop there but went on to justify the Stalinist ideology and practices of subordinating the labour force to a ruthlessly oppressive hierarchical division of labour by conjuring up the image of a fictitious 'natural order' in production and distribution. He wanted to see it controlled by the so-called 'pioneering superior persons' who would and should in no way be challenged by the 'conservative average persons' and 'the relatively backward inferior persons' of society. In this way Shaw projected a social order which was supposed to be fully in tune with 'human nature' and the ideals of 'democratic Socialism'. These were his words:

> In the U.S.S.R. it was found impossible to increase production, or even maintain it, until piece-work and payment by results was established in spite of the Equality Merchants. When democratic Socialism has achieved sufficiency of means, equality of opportunity, and national intermarriageability for everybody, with *production kept in its natural order* from necessities to luxuries, and the courts of justice unbiased by mercenary barristers, its work will be done; ... it will still be *human nature* with all its enterprises, ambitions and emulations in full swing, and with its *pioneering superior persons, conservative average persons, and relatively backward inferiors in their natural places,* all fully fed, educated up to the top of their capacity, and intermarriageable. Equality can go no farther.[291]

It is hard to believe at first sight that a man of G. B. Shaw's intelligence could sink to such a level of mindless prejudice, dressed up in the pseudo-democratic garb of eugenic nonsense. As if the structurally enforced hierarchy of the capital system had anything whatsoever to do with the claimed biologically grounded 'backwardness of inferior persons' that could and should be remedied — and even that only to the point of justifying and codifying the 'democratic Socialist' hierarchy and its 'natural order' in the name of the postulated eternal 'conservatism' and the unalterable 'relative backwardness' of the masses of the people

— by the adoption of the grotesque Fabian eugenic recipe of 'national inter-marriageablity'. Still, what makes the formulation of such views by relatively progressive intellectuals like Bernard Shaw quite believable, however sad, is that he shares the abhorrence of substantive equality with all those who cannot envisage any alternative to the capital system and its incurably hierarchical and dehumanizing social division of labour. And since the practical operational presuppositions of the existing order are in this way taken for granted, even declared to be 'natural' on the ground of the fallacious equation of the specific historical limits of capital with timeless absolute unalterability, nothing remains beyond the fantasy-world of so-called 'equality of opportunity' to be miracu-lously squeezed out of the allegedly not only *de facto* but also *de jure* unchangeable hierarchy of the system. Thus, in place of the self-emancipatory activity of a real social agency Bernard Shaw can offer in his vision of 'democratic Socialism' only the 'enterprises, ambitions and emulations' of a ludicrously personified generic 'human nature' schizophrenically split into 'superior' and 'inferior' personalities. The subservient attitude shown by him towards Stalin's far from only verbal assault on the castigated 'Equality Merchants' demonstrates that the most diverse personifications of capital — not only in their unashamedly self-con-scious bourgeois variety but also in their Soviet type as well as Fabian 'democratic Socialist' embodiments — find their common denominator precisely in the categorical rejection of substantive equality.

Lip-service paid to 'equality of opportunity', in its linkage to 'fairness' and 'justice', serves an apologetic purpose. For, by eliminating substantive equality from the range of legitimate aspirations, the structural hierarchies of the capital system are strengthened as the necessary provider of the vacuously promised 'opportunities', hailed at the same time on account of the claimed 'fairness' and 'justice' in making 'equality of opportunity' possible. That the prodigious advancement in productivity in the last two or three centuries, under the rule of capital, failed to turn into achievements any of the promises need not worry the apologists. For they can always retort that people have only themselves to blame for not taking advantage of the 'opportunities'. Thus women have absolutely nothing to complain about, given the abundance of 'equal opportu-nities' at their disposal, especially in the last century.

Obfuscation of what is really at stake is most prominent in the arsenal of the apologists of inequality. One of the favourite ploys is to use differences in artistic talent as the hypocritical justification — and with reference to nature also eternalization — of the historically established exploitative social hierarchy. As if the musical genius of Mozart could not be imagined without the crippling and humiliating social hierarchies to which he was subjected and under the hardship of which he had to perish as a young man at the peak of his artistic creativity *despite* his genius. Another well rehearsed apologetic ploy is to claim that the socialist aim of substantive equality means 'levelling down', which would in this view make impossible the appearance and free activity of the Mozarts. As if the history of the triumphant capital system in the last few centuries could even remotely match its own claim to 'levelling up', not to mention the ability to demonstrate a complete *non-sequitur*, i.e. the necessary causal relationship between the flourishing of artistic excellence and the system in which the personifications of capital must enforce everywhere the material imperatives of their social metabolic order and dominate to that end, in one way or another, all intellectual and artistic activity.

Preaching the virtues of a society in which 'equality of opportunity' was claimed to be more than a hypocritical lip-service would be deplorable even if the record of actual achievements was just standing still, rather than taking steps towards substantive equality — the only possible sense of the whole enterprise — not to mention moving in the opposite direction. However, the statistics of even the capitalistically most advanced countries reveal a most depressing picture. Thus an official government report in Britain — greatly understating the severity of the situation by manipulating the figures and arbitrarily excluding certain categories from the survey, just like it was done in the 33 times 'refined' and 'improved' (i.e. tendentiously falsified) way of calculating unemployment figures — had to concede that

> The gap between rich and poor has widened ... The income of the poorest 10 percent of the population dropped 17 percent between 1979 and 1991, while the income of the wealthiest 10 percent rose 62 percent. ... The figures, in the latest *Households Below Average Income* report, show that the number of people living below the European poverty line, that is with an income less than half of the average, rose from 5 million in 1979 to 13.9 million in 1991-92. Another 400,000 people had gone below the poverty line since the last report, 200,000 of them children. In 1979, 1.4 million children lived below the poverty line, rising to 3.9 million in 1990-91 and 4.1 million a year later. In cash terms, the average income of the poorest 10 percent of the population was down from £74 [$110] to £61 [$91] a week. The figures are based on data from the Government's Family Expenditure Survey.[292]

At the same time, the 'Radical Right' Adam Smith Institute of London keeps publishing one pamphlet after the other concerned with the quickest way of consigning to the past the once loudly advertised social security measures of the 'Welfare State', including not only unemployment and invalidity benefits but even old age pensions and universal health care entitlement. True to form, the public opinion manipulators of the bourgeois press (and in a prominent place among them the London *Times*) quickly join their 'Radical Right' colleagues and start sermonizing — with sonorously titled editorials like 'Rational Rationing'[293] — about the intellectual and moral commendability of 'rationing' (i.e. discriminatorily withdrawing from those who cannot afford private insurance) health care even in situations when life is at stake. Naturally, this rationalization and legitimation of the brutal constraints arising from the structural crisis of capital are presented in a typical package of unctious hypocrisy, embellished with expressions like 'excellence', 'flexibility' and 'freedom', as illustrated by the quotation below from the same editorial article:

> Elderly people may discreetly be denied life-saving surgery and complex treatment such as kidney dialysis. The health service reforms of the last three years have made the culture of clinical practice more transparent. Not every patient can be given the treatment which he or she desires: that is a fact which must now be confronted. ... From this difficult debate, international and local guidelines are likely to emerge. But the essence of rationing must remain professional excellence and the increased devolution of responsibility to individual doctors. There should be more fund-holding; those GPs that already fundhold should be given even greater flexibility. Sensible rationing will not be achieved through bureaucracy or over-regulation but by giving doctors the freedom to make painful decisions without fear or shame.

It is the height of hypocrisy characteristic of the system that the real choices which must be made — and indeed in a most authoritarian fashion already have been made — are hidden from inspection by covering the bitter food with the sickly sweet 'Generaltunken'[294] of non-existent democratic 'transparency', fictitious 'devolution of responsibility' (without power), by centrally imposed and highly paid bureaucratic Area Trust Authority Managers and by their corruptly appointed cronies in the deteriorating National Health Service callously overruled 'professional excellence', and for transparent capital-apologetic purposes pretended 'individual freedom'. For the real issue is not the individual doctors' 'devolved responsibility and freedom' to condemn to death not only elderly but also middle aged and often even young people by denying them medically available life-saving treatment. It is the decision taken by the personifications of capital in politics and in business — in the interest of continued capital-expansion — over the allocation of society's material and intellectual resources, denying the legitimacy of literally vital, life-saving and life-enhancing, need in favour of the wasteful and destructive domains of capital's self-reproduction, clearly exemplified by the astronomical sums invested in armaments. In other words, the intractable issue is the total absence of *social accountancy* under the rule of capital, bringing with it the system's *uncontrollability* and the mystifying diversion of responsibility from where it belongs to the shoulders of helpless individuals — in this case doctors, who in their overwhelming majority protest in vain and who cannot really assume its burden. It requires no great mathematical skills to calculate how many thousands of lives could be saved by using for the purchase of kidney dialysis machines the billions of pounds allocated to a totally wasteful single item on the military budget, the Trident nuclear submarine project. Instances of this kind could be easily multiplied. However, the apologetic editorial wisdom of the London *Times* over 'Rational Rationing' is devised for the sole purpose of diverting attention from the truly rational but systematically frustrated and nullified *real choices*. This is done in order to be able to exempt the personifications of capital from their obvious responsibility in these matters and for ordering doctors to take upon themselves 'the freedom to make painful choices'. Choices which should never even be contemplated, let alone imposed by an 'advanced' society on many thousands of its needlessly dying individual members whose 'equality of opportunity' does not reach far enough.

In truth, any talk of 'equal opportunity' under the prevailing circumstances is a mockery of the real state of affairs. As we have seen above, the editorial article of *The Times* was projecting into the future a 'difficult debate' from which 'international and local guidelines are likely to emerge'. As a matter of fact the 'future guidelines' were already imposed by the authoritarian British Conservative government well before the *Times* leader was published. The editorial quoted above was complicitously 'wise after the event' despite its pretended anticipatory wisdom. For, as has been revealed recently, under government instruction already last winter doctors decided not to vaccinate against flu many elderly patients in care homes, and a considerable number of them died when the virus struck.

The deaths angered Southampton community health council. Ken Woods, its chief officer said: 'Once you legitimise the idea that you can withhold treatment on the grounds that someone's quality of life is not worth a £5 vaccination you are on a dangerous path. It's doctors playing God.'[295]

In reality the responsibility for 'playing God' lies with government; doctors only obey its guidelines. The day after the revelation, 'Critics attacked the "euthanasia" policy which has been introduced with no public debate. Tessa Jowell, a Labour member of the Commons health select committee, called it "a sinister development". Peggy Norris, a retired GP and chairman of Alert, the anti-euthanasia group, said withholding flu vaccine treatment was scandalous discrimination. As specialists in care of the elderly prepared to select candidates to receive the jab this week, the Department of Health said guidelines leave it up to doctors to decide who should get it, and whether relatives should be consulted.'[296] This is how the 'freedom to make painful choices' must be exercised under long existing political guidelines. As to the coming year,

> The £33.5m flu vaccine programme provides enough doses for 5.5m vulnerable adults and young children, yet there are at least 10m elderly people at risk of a fatal attack of the disease. This creates a moral difficulty keenly felt by psychiatrists and physicians caring for the elderly.[297]

This means that already in the current year well over one half of the elderly, most of them poor, are deprived of the flu vaccine and thereby many of them exposed to life-threatening danger. It seems then that it is only a matter of time (and not that far away) before doctors, in the spirit of the advocated 'Rational Rationing', are burdened with the so-called 'increased devolution of responsibility', together with 'even greater flexibility' and a conveniently targeted 'freedom', for the purpose of administering compulsory euthanasia to the 'undeserving poor'. Indeed, in the interest of greater economic efficiency they will be instructed not to consult even their closest relatives, presenting such policies to the public with customary hypocrisy and cynicism as the democratic recognition of 'professional excellence'. This is how one side of the 'equal opportunity' equation is shaping up for the future of the overwhelming majority of the people. For once they are old and cease to be directly exploitable members of the labour force, their lives are worth — as the chief officer of the Southampton community health council fears it — much less than the £5 flu vaccine apiece that would have to be wasted on them.

The other side of the 'equal opportunity' equation is shown in an Insight Report published on the same page of the newspaper from which the article on 'Doctors let elderly die by denying flu vaccine' is quoted above. The report concerns a man who according to the paper three times failed the exam for the qualification of an Accountant, and yet mysteriously has become a multi-millionaire. The man in question is Mark Thatcher, the son of Hayek's Companion of Honour, Baroness Margaret Thatcher. The Insight Report carries the title 'Revealed: Mark Thatcher's secret profit from £20 billion arms deal' and it offers most uncomfortable reading not only for the Thatcher family but for all members of the governing Conservative Party. For it reminds them that there is a strict rule according to which 'ministers will want to see that no conflict arises nor appears to arise between their private interests and their public duties. No minister or public servant should accept gifts, hospitality or services which would, or might appear to, place him or her under an obligation. The same principle applies if gifts are offered to a member of their family.'[298] Yet, despite the so-called 'witch's warning' — delivered by Sir Clive Whitmore, then Permanent Secretary at the Ministry of Defence and former private secretary to Margaret Thatcher — about the 'potentially disastrous consequences of her son's involvement' as a beneficiary in the lucrative arms deal, a warning brushed aside by the Prime Minister who boasted about 'batting for Britain', Mark Thatcher became £12 million ($18 million) richer as a reward for his dubious services. As the Insight Report goes on:

> The transcripts [of tape-recorded conversations] and corroborating evidence from sources close to the deal, solve the mystery of how Thatcher first made his fortune. It has never been satisfactorily explained how the Old Harrovian [former Public School boy], a thrice failed accountant and would-be racing driver, rapidly went from modest means when his mother became prime minister in 1979 to multi-millionaire status a few years later.

> For some British officials, Thatcher's involvement was ethically wrong. 'Thatcher was an opportunist on a gravy train, scooping whatever money he could from these deals', said a former British Aerospace executive who had a central role. 'He touted his name and position in relation to Margaret Thatcher.'[299]

This is then the share of a Mark Thatcher from the available storehouse of 'equal opportunity'. Absurd and in the just quoted view 'ethically wrong' though it all might be, perhaps one should not be too hard on the poor, three times failed accountant, multi-millionaire. For he shares the predicament of getting much for nothing with all those who, in virtue of their position (or even just their fathers' or mothers' position) in the command structure of capital receive not only a life-long but in capitalist countries even a hereditary Season Ticket for free rides on the gravy train. The fact that Margaret Thatcher in her resignation Honours List gave a Hereditary Peerage to her husband and merely a Life Peerage to herself, must be seen in its proper light. For perish the thought that such a deed could be anything other than the selfless concern of an ordinary grandmother to secure no more than 'equal opportunity' for the future of her grandson. Strangely, though, according to an October 1994 opinion poll, 61 percent of British people, including a large portion of Conservative voters, are convinced that the Conservative Party in office is characterized by 'sleaze and corruption'.

Still, for us the meaning of the examples quoted above is fairly obvious. They are, for sure, contrasting enough. They appear on one single page of one single newspaper, on one single day when the other newspapers of the country supply many other examples. Not to mention the countless number of reportable cases which are not reported or are simply but elegantly 'explained away'. In any case, our examples also show how slender are the margins from which the space for the emancipation of women must be carved out, confining efforts directed towards it to an uphill struggle against the odds of — constantly nullified — 'equality of opportunity'. As a recent report of the United Nations revealed on 17th October 1994: the day meant to open the year 'for the eradication of world poverty' (a most likely prospect indeed!), women represent today no less than 70 *percent* of the world's poor. It would be a miracle if it could be otherwise under the prevailing practices of 'equal opportunity'. For under the rule of capital in any one of its varieties — and not only today but for as long as the imperatives of this system continue to determine the forms and limits of social metabolic reproduction — the 'equality of women' cannot amount to more than tokenism.

5.3.8

SINCE the promise of 'equal of opportunity' is used as a mystifying diversion by the ruling ideology, remaining to all those who aspire at it so elusive as to appear an altogether unrealizable dream, the temptation is great to turn one's back to the whole question of equality and settle for relative advantages for more or less limited sections of the people in structurally subordinate position, be they male or female. And that is precisely what the ideological ruse of the vacuous 'equality of opportunity' is meant to achieve by promising advancement towards a desired condition whose realization it simultaneously denies by apriori excluding the possibility of an equitable social order.

However, despite the mystifications involved, it is by no means a matter of indifference, not even of minor importance, that the ruling order cannot assert its domination over the hierarchically subjected masses of the people without constantly resorting to the false promise of equality of sorts, even if in the bastardized and preempted form of 'equality of opportunity'. The self-legitimation of the capital system — based on the notion of contracts freely entered by equal parties, without which the very idea of the assumed contract would be null and void — cannot conceivably be maintained if the personifications of capital openly declared that they must and do indeed deny equality to the structurally subordinate masses of the population, male or female, in any meaningful sense of the term.

Moreover, the self-expansion of capital makes it necessary to progressively bring into the labour process formerly marginal or non-participating groups of people, and potentially the entire population — including, of course, virtually all women. This kind of change in the labour process carries with it, in one way or another, the significant (even if for a variety of reasons necessarily iniquitous) extension of the consuming circle, altering in a corresponding sense also the family structure as well as the role and relative importance of the younger and older generations in the overall process of socioeconomic reproduction and capital realization. Thus the earlier mentioned and by socialdemocratic and liberal parties politically encouraged illusion of 'upward equalization' — postulated on the ground of the 'growing cake' (an illusion cultivated for as long as the cake grows and even beyond), despite clear evidence all the time that the proportionate *slice* of the cake conceded to labour is not only not growing but shrinking — is further complicated by changes in the labour process directly linked to the extension of the consuming circle. For even if the cause of structural equalization is not advanced by a fraction of an inch by the relative extension of the consuming circle, and even if there are major inequalities as regards the benefits made available to labour in different countries according to their position in the global framework and pecking order of capital (as we shall see in Chapters 15 and 16), nevertheless the underlying process brings with it for important sections of the labour force the improvement of their standard of living during the expansionary phase of capital's historical development.

Naturally, this is a process full of contradictions, as everywhere where the imperatives of the capital system set the rules. The contradictions are manifest not only in the massive differences between groups of labour in any particular country and globally; equally important is that the capital system itself becomes dependent on a process — the expansion of the consuming circle — which cannot be maintained indefinitely, activating thereby in due course a potentially most explosive contradiction between capital and labour. For even if there can be no question of *'upward equalization'*, which would modify the structure of the capital system, there is most decidedly a *downward equalization* directly affecting the labour force even of the capitalistically most advanced countries. This is the necessary concomitant of the appearance of major disturbances in the process of capital expansion and accumulation, witnessed in the last two decades, assuming the form of a dangerous *tendency for the equalization of the differential rate of exploitation* mentioned above.

Another vitally important dimension of the problem we are concerned with is the worsening position of women as a result of the changes in the family structure through the imperatives of capital, directly linked to the necessary extension of the consuming circle. The contradictions are clear enough also in this domain, in that on the one hand capital's undisturbed reproduction process badly needs the changes that have taken place (and seem to continue unabated) in the field of consumption, but at the same time, on the other hand, the system is exposed to the dangers and disturbances arising from the growing instability of the 'nuclear family'. In other words, the rule of capital is both dependent on the continuity of such changes and is bound to be weakened by them. It is significant in this respect that according to a recently published report — called 'Diverse Living Arrangements of Children' — of the U.S. Census Bureau, in 1991 only fractionally more than one half of all children lived in 'nuclear families' in the United States: 50.8 percent, to be precise. (By now the figure must be well under one half, if the trend quoted in the Report was maintained between 1991 and 1994.) Thus in 1991 nearly half of American children, outside the 'nuclear family', lived

> in some other family arrangement: with single parents, step-parents, half-siblings, and so on. This is a big change. Not long ago, a Census official found, in a separate study, that the number of children in 'nuclear' families was 57 percent in 1980. In 1970, it had been 66 percent.[300]

Naturally, the lion's share of the problems and complications for such changes must be placed on the shoulders of women. Indeed, the burden imposed on women by the capital system for maintaining the nuclear family is getting heavier, and their position in the poverty spectrum is shifting constantly for the worse, instead of being alleviated, as the rhetorics of 'equal opportunity for women' and 'the elimination of all gender discrimination' would have it. The disturbing fact highlighted by the United Nations that in 1994 women constituted 70 percent of the world's poor is therefore not in the least surprising. Indeed, given the causal determinations behind these figures, the situation of women is bound to get worse in the foreseeable future. On the basis of the current trends the appalling figure put into relief by the United Nations is likely to reach 75 *percent* within a decade, amounting to a horrendous 3 *to* 1 *ratio* compared to men among the world's poor.

All this sharply underlines what should not but in fact does need underlining, because of the ruse of the ruling ideology and the broadly diffused mystifications of 'equal opportunity'; namely that without *fundamental changes* in the mode of societal reproduction one cannot make even the first steps towards the genuine emancipation of women, well beyond the rhetorics of the ruling ideology and the occasional legal gestures that remain unsustained by adequate material processes and remedies. For without the establishment and consolidation of a mode of social metabolic reproduction based on *substantive equality* even the most sincere legal efforts aimed at 'women's emancipation' are bound to be devoid of elementary material guarantees, amounting therefore at best only to a declaration of faith. What cannot be stressed enough is that only a communal form of social production and interchange can extricate women from their structurally subordinate position and provide the material bases of substantive equality.

The magnitude of the difficulties to be overcome in this respect can be gauged if we remind ourselves of the way in which the production process had been constituted for a very long time, well before the emergence and triumph of capitalism. Accordingly, the radical transformation required for making possible the successful functioning of a social metabolic process based on substantive equality involves overcoming the negative force of the hierarchical discriminatory structures and the corresponding interpersonal relations of 'individual economy' first established thousands of years ago.

The capital system constituted itself on the foundations of the alienating discriminatory structures and second order mediations of 'individual economy' established long before, and, of course, forcefully adapted them to its own purposes and reproductive requirements. Parallel to such developments partly before and partly under the advancing capital system, the question of how to overcome in a radical way the alienating and dehumanizing division of labour inseparable from the reproductive processes of 'individual economy' and private property had also been repeatedly raised. Indeed, the formulation of alternative visions of organizing the reproductive interchanges of individuals in society go back a very long way in the past, as a multiplicity of utopian schemes testify. However, the objectives of these radical critical negations of the individual economy wedded to private property could not be successfully pursued before the full unfolding of the capital system itself, due to the precarious material conditions to which they linked their critique of the established order. As Marx had put it:

> In all previous periods, the abolition [Aufhebung] of individual economy, which is inseparable from the abolition of private property, was impossible for the simple reason that the material conditions required were not present. The setting up of a communal domestic economy presupposed the development of machinery, the use of natural forces and of many other productive forces — e.g., of water supplies, gas lighting, steam heating, etc., the suppression [Aufhebung] of town and country. Without these conditions a communal economy would not in itself form a new productive force; it would lack material basis and rest on a purely theoretical foundation, in other words, it would be a mere freak and would amount to nothing more than a monastic economy. ... That the supersession of individual economy is inseparable from the supersession of the family is self-evident.[301]

The way in which these matters — concerning the 'individual economy' and the basic consumptive units of society: the contemporary 'nuclear family' — are intertwined under the existing conditions constitutes a vicious circle. As always, the capital system asserts itself also in this regard in the form of insoluble contradictions. On the one hand, the economic processes of capitalist industrialization bring *within sight* (but due to the very nature of capital hopelessly *out of reach*) material conditions of a sustainable communal economy, and thereby advance, at least in principle, one aspect of the individual economy/family correlation — through the development of a concentrated and highly centralized mode of production. However, capital fails even to scratch the surface of the other vital precondition of a truly viable social metabolism: the aspect which concerns the necessary restructuring of the consumption units of society in a communal direction, which would make feasible the progressive elimination of the immense waste characteristic of the present system. Not even a tentative small step can be taken within the confines of the established mode of production and social metabolic reproduction towards that end. For capital has a vested interest in doing the exact opposite of what would be required. It must fragment the units of consumption to the extreme and modify the family structure accordingly, in the interest of maintaining its own ever more wasteful 'realization' process, at whatever cost, even if it is bound to prove absolutely forbidding in the longer run. Thus in the course of capital's historical development some positive potentialities also for the emancipation of women are activated — but only to be nullified again under the weight of the system's contradictions.

It is a matter of great importance that the relationship of capital also to women is characterized by overreaching itself. This is similar to what we have seen in Sections 5.1 and 5.2, concerning the contradiction between globally developing transnational capital and national states on the one hand, and the imperatives emanating from capital's objective logic and leading to the destruction of the basic conditions of social metabolic reproduction on the other.

This overreaching itself by capital in relation to women takes the form of bringing into the labour force ever-increasing numbers of women, under the inexorable expansionary drive of the system: a change which cannot be brought to completion without raising the question of women's equality, removing some formerly existing barriers and taboos in the process. However, this move — arising from capital's necessary drive for profitable expansion and not from the slightest inclination to enlightened emancipatory concern towards women — misfires in due course. Not only because women must accept a disproportionate share of the most insecure and worst paid jobs in the labour market and the predicament of representing 70 percent of the world's poor. Also, the move misfires because the demands that are — and must to an increasing degree be — placed upon women, in virtue of their crucial role in the nuclear family, are more and more difficult to satisfy in their broader social setting, contributing thereby to whatever 'social dysfunctions' may be linked to the growing instability of the family, from the concerns of the earlier quoted U.S. Census Bureau Report on societal 'Nuclear fission' to the broad diffusion of an apparently uncontrollable drug culture, an ever-worsening juvenile crime rate, etc. What is worse from the standpoint of the capital system's social stability is that we witness the operation of a vicious circle. For the greater the condemned 'social dysfunctions' the greater the demands and the burden imposed on women as the pivot of the nuclear family, and the greater the burdens the less they are able to cope with them, in addition to their breadwinner role, their 'second shift' after work, and the like. Another important aspect of capital's overreaching itself in its relation to women is that the earlier indicated fragmentation and reduction of the nuclear family to its innermost nuclear core (to which also the ever-increasing divorce rate bears witness), as the 'microcosm' and basic consumptive unit of society, tend to contribute not only to the further instability of the family itself, under enormous strains at a time of deepening structural crisis, but carry in their turn serious negative repercussions for the whole system.

5.3.9

ALL talk about 'fairness' and 'justice' as the foundations of 'equality' puts the cart before the horse even when genuinely meant, and not as cynical camouflage for the effective negation of even the most elementary conditions of equality. Defining the issues at stake in terms of 'equality of opportunity' plays into the hands of those who are keen to prevent any change to the prevailing material power relations and corresponding structurally enforced hierarchies, dangling the unrealizable promise of 'equal opportunity' before the critics of social inequality as the unreachable carrot before the donkey. For the promise of 'fairness' and 'justice' in a world ruled by capital can only constitute mystifying *alibis* for the permanence of *substantive inequality*.

In fact the precondition of moving in the direction of a justifiable social order is to change the now prevailing reversed order between justice and equality. For the only possible way of really founding justice itself and thus removing it from the realm of ideological mystification and cynical manipulation is by making substantive equality the effective regulatory principle of all human relations. It cannot be done the other way round, even if the 'ideal legislators' — who would try to institute the 'fairness' of 'equal opportunity' — became purple in the face by the pressure of their accumulated good intentions. In other words, only substantive equality can be the foundation of meaningful justice, but no amount of legally proclaimed justice — even if it were practicable at all, which of course it is not — could produce genuine equality.

The capital/labour relationship is by its very nature the tangible embodiment of insurmountable structural hierarchy and substantive inequality. Thus the capital system as such, in its necessary constitution, cannot be other than the perpetuation of *fundamental injustice*. Inevitably, therefore, all attempts at reconciling this system with the principles of justice and equality prove to be absurd. They can only amount to what a Hungarian expression calls 'making cast-iron wheels from fire-wood'. The practitioners of this craft, in order to conjure up the vision of their cast-iron wheels, must proceed by decree, stipulating that nothing but purely *formal* criteria are relevant, thereby apriori ruling out all substantive considerations (including the material differences between wood and iron), so that in the end they should be able to assert that '*equality of outcome*' (i.e. meaningful equality) is a matter of no importance whatsoever. They are willing to retain *formal equality* for two reasons. First, because it is essential for the mysterious (or rather: conveniently mystifying) craft of making cast-iron wheels from fire-wood, precluding at the same time by decree the possibility of questioning — on pain of exposing oneself to accusations of 'irrationality' and 'category mistake' — the incurable iniquitousness of the capital/labour relationship itself, which admittedly belongs to the 'category' of 'material contingency', even if in a practically eternalized form. And second, because legally enforceable formal equality has its uses in regulating some aspects of the relationship between particular units of capital, without conflicting with the substantive processes of the concentration and centralization of capital. The never realizable 'equality of opportunity' set against 'equality of outcome' is in its ideological efficacy arguably the most important product of the venerable craft of making cast-iron wheels from fire-wood, reducing substance to 'pure form' and transforming structurally enforced discriminatory hierarchy, with all its obvious inequalities, into 'fairness' and 'justice'. The same magic craft is used by the ·British Labour Party's 'Justice Commission' for the purpose of producing from worm-infected capitalist fire-wood the cast-iron wheels of 'modernized socialist fairness and justice', on the basis of which social security expenditure can be cut to the bone by a future Labour government, in the name of the 'fair and realistic targeting' of the 'deserving poor'.

However, socialists knew it for a very long time that in all relationships in which the question of inequality is involved, including that of women, the real stakes are always defined in terms of actually existing needs and substance. As Babeuf — right in the turmoil following the French revolution — had formulated the criteria by which these matters had to be assessed, refuting by the terms of evaluation which he adopted both utilitarian elitism and mechanistic quantification:

> Equality must be measured by the *capacity* of the worker and the *need* of the consumer, not by the intensity of the labour and the quantity of things consumed. A man endowed with a certain degree of strength, when he lifts a weight of ten pounds, labours as much as another man with five times the strength when he lifts fifty pounds. He who, to satisfy a burning thirst, swallows a pitcher of water, enjoys no more than his comrade who, but slightly thirsty, sips a cupful. The aim of the communism in question is *equality of pains and pleasures,* not of *consumable things* and workers' *tasks*.[302]

No one seriously concerned with the question of equality in human relations could object to these criteria which put also the connection between equality and fairness/justice in perspective, insisting on redefining and refounding the latter by acknowledging the priority of substantive equality directly arising from actual human need. It is significant in this regard that with the challenge of women's liberation centred on the question of substantive equality a great historical cause is set into motion which cannot find outlets for its realization within the confines of the capital system. For the cause of women's equality and emancipation involves the most important substantive processes and institutions of the entire social metabolic order.

It is equally significant that ever since the appearance of the more militant forms of the movement pressing for women's equality the response from even the relatively progressive bourgeois intellectuals was, well in keeping with the general attitude of the system's defenders, to try to confine their demands and evaluate the feasible achievements in terms of *formal* criteria, in the good old tradition of making cast-iron wheels from fire-wood. This is how the radical Fabian socialist H.G. Wells — who even fancied himself as a champion of women's liberation — argued the case in a famous work:

> In the excited days of feminine emancipation at the close of the last century there was much talk of the changes and marvels that would happen when this ceased to

be a 'man-made' world. Women were to come into their own, and all things would be the better for it. As a matter of fact, the *enfranchisement of women,* the opening of every possible profession to them, such legislation as the British Sex Disqualification (Removal) Act of 1919 mean that women were not coming to anything of their own, they were merely giving up their own — or, if you will, escaping from it.[303]

The level of feminine achievement is often high, higher than that of second-rate men, but in none of the open fields, except domestic fiction, can it be claimed that any women have yet displayed qualities and initiatives to put them on a level with the best men ... In literature, in art, in the scientific laboratory, they have had a fair field and considerable favour. They suffer under no handicap. But so far none has displayed structural power or breadth, depth and steadfastness of conception, to compare with the best work of men. They have produced no illuminating scientific generalizations.[304]

And Wells is not contented with minimizing the achievements of women against all substantive discriminatory odds, using as the ground for his judgement the formal criteria that women have been 'enfranchized' and through the removal of 'Sex Disqualification' by a 1919 Act of Parliament 'every possible profession has been opened' to them. After demonstrating in this blind patronizing way his total incomprehension of what is required for making substantive equality possible, presumptiously preserving the domain of 'first-rate achievements' forever to men, and using the red herring of isolated 'best work' in art and science as the legitimatory ground for denying equality with men to more than half of humankind, Wells goes on to offer the prospect of eternal 'ancillary' status to women, embellished — on the ancient but apparently unsurpassable model of Menenius Agrippa's talk to the rebellious masses assembled on the hills of Rome — with the rhetorics of 'service' done 'honourably and willingly'. This is how the Wellsian sermon sounds:

> Women have played the part of a *social mortar.* They seem able to accept more readily and with a greater simplicity, and they conserve more faithfully. In the more subtly moralized, highly educated and scientifically ruled world society of the future, that world-society which is the sole alternative to human disaster, such a matrix function will be even more vitally necessary. That, rather than the *star parts* in the future, may be *the general destiny of women.* They will continue to mother, nurse, assist, protect, comfort, reward and hold mankind together. Hitherto the role of woman has been decorative or ancillary. And to-day it seems to be still decorative and ancillary. Less frankly decorative, perhaps, and more honourably and willingly ancillary. Her recent gains in freedom have widened her choice of what she shall adorn or serve, but they have released no new initiatives in human affairs. This may not be pleasing to the enthusiastic feminist of the late *fin-de-siècle* school, but the facts are so. In a world in which the motive of service seems destined to become the dominant social motive, there is nothing in what we have brought forward here that any woman need deplore.[305]

What is curiously — and conveniently — forgotten in the idealization of 'social mortar' as the 'general destiny of women' is that by its very nature and 'ancillary' function mortar is destined to be squeezed between bricks and stones. It remains ignored and neglected all the time unless through rain or otherwise caused erosion some emergency arises. Then attention can be focused on mortar again, but strictly for the duration of the emergency, in that the building blocks — in the view of H.G. Wells rightfully performing the 'star parts', be they no brighter than bricks or stones — must be serviced again and properly repointed by the ancillary brigade.

THERE is a beautiful and moving early 18th century Hungarian folk ballad which tells us what to make of 'social mortar' as the continuing 'destiny of women'. Its title is *Kömíves Kelemenné*[306] and narrates the tragic story of Mrs Kelemen, the Mistress of Master stone-mason Kelemen's household.

Her husband and eleven other stone masons, lured by the 'rich price of bushels of silver and gold', contract to build the high fortress of Déva, but fail in their efforts because
> what they build till noon, crumbles by the evening,
> what they build till evening, falls down by the morning.

To remedy their failure, they make the law to which they all solemnly resolve to submit: that the first wife to arrive shall be burned, and her ashes shall be mixed into the lime, so as to make indestructible mortar with which they can erect the high fortress.

As it happens, Mrs Kelemen is the first one to set out toward Déva in her fine carriage, drawn by four fine bay horses. Half-way through the journey her coachman pleads with her to let him turn back, saying that in his dream he had a dark premonition, seeing her little boy fall and perish in the deep well at the centre of their courtyard. The Mistress silences him with words against which there can be no appeal:
> 'carry on coachman, the carriage is not yours,
> the horses are not yours, drive them fast forward!'

As they approach Déva, stone-mason Kelemen recognizes them from a distance, praying to God to strike with lightning the road on the spot right in front of them, so that the frightened horses should turn back or, failing that, to break the legs of all four horses, so that they should not reach him and his fellow builders, but all in vain. Mrs Kelemen arrives and the twelve stone-masons tell her in soothing words the harsh fate which she cannot avoid. She calls them 'twelve murderers', including her husband among them, insisting that they must wait until she goes home and returns again, so that she can 'say farewell to my women friends and to my beautiful little boy'.

On her return they burn her and use her ashes for making the strong mortar, and thus they succeed in erecting the high fortress of Déva, duly receiving the contracted 'rich price of bushels of silver and gold' for it. When the fortress is completed and Master stone-mason Kelemen returns home, his son keeps asking him about his absent mother. After lying evasions, in the end the father has to tell the son that his mother is built into the stone fortress of Déva. The son in his despair goes to the mountain-top fortress and cries out three times:
> 'Mother, sweet mother, talk to me once more!'

His mother answers and this is how the folk ballad ends:
> 'I cannot talk to you! the stone wall weighs me down.
> I am walled in and buried under these heavy stones.'
> Her heart broke then, the earth parted with it,
> the boy fell into its depth and was buried in it.

There are some lessons to be learned from the heart-breaking story of this folk-ballad which speaks of 'mortar woman' in a very different but infinitely more realistic way than H.G. Wells's patronizing romantic fairy tale, written in a spirit shared by all those who use the excuse of *formal* equality for the effective denial of *substantive equality.* The lessons are implicit both in the suffering of Mrs Kelemen, cruelly imposed on her with the active involvement of her co-legis-lating husband, and in the tragic fate of mother and child that speaks not of the 'general destiny of women' but of the far from reassuring destiny of humanity if the lessons continue to be ignored. However, on the evidence of the role played under the rule of capital even by Master stone-mason Kelemen, who must obey the foundation of all formal or explicit law enacted under the system, i.e. the ultimate law of being driven by the need for 'bushels of silver and gold', despite his love for his wife, there can be no hope that the personifications of capital — male or female — will take the slightest notice of the lessons.

5.4 *Chronic unemployment: the real meaning of 'population explosion'*

5.4.1
THE dubious distinction for raising alarm about the prospects of 'population explosion' belongs to the Reverend T.R. Malthus, even if he did not use the term itself. Nevertheless, in his *Essay on the Principle of Population as it Affects the Future Improvement of Society, with Remarks on the Speculations of Mr. Godwin, M. Condorcet, and Other Writers,* first published anonymously way back in 1798 and in greatly enlarged editions later on, he laid the foundations of an extreme conservative and alarmist way of approaching the problem of population increase. In the interest of class apologetics he abstracted the ongoing trends of development from their social determinants, attempting to treat the inherently *historical* issues of why and how populations change under a disaster-predicating mechanical 'natural law'. Thus the contrast with socialist assessments of the issues involved could not have been greater. This is how Marx characterized the Malthusian approach:

> [Malthus] regards overpopulation as being of the same kind in all the different historic phases of economic development; he does not understand their *specific* difference, and hence stupidly reduces these very complicated and varying relations to a single relation, two equations, in which the *natural* reproduction of humanity appears on the one side, and the *natural* reproduction of edible plants (or means of subsistence) on the other, as two *natural series,* the former geometric and the latter arithmetic in progression. In this way he transforms the historically distinct relation into an *abstract numerical* relation, which he has fished purely out of thin air, and which rests neither on natural nor on historical laws. There is allegedly a natural difference between the reproduction of mankind and e.g. grain. This baboon thereby implies that the increase of humanity is a purely natural process, which requires external restraints, checks, to prevent from proceeding in geometrical progression. ... He transforms the *immanent, historically changing* limits of the human reproduction process into *outer barriers* and the outer barriers to natural reproduction into imma-nent limits or *natural laws* of reproduction.[307]

The Malthusian transubstantiation of the historically specific into a timeless pseudo-natural determination ended up completely *inverting* the relationship between immanent limits and outer barriers. This served the ideological purpose of exempting the historically established (and therefore in principle historically changeable) socioeconomic system from any conceivable blame in the matter about which the alarm was raised by the anonymous Reverend himself. At the same time he anticipated 'corrective solutions' — in the name of a pretended 'natural law' — which would not only suit the convenience of the existing order of social metabolic reproduction but also reinforce its claims to fully justifiable absolute permanance. It deserved absolute permanence on account of its ability to manage the 'natural law' without altering itself as a social system, articulated through the structural parameters of iniquitously distributed private property and corresponding class domination. Thus, in tune with the underlying conservative ideological intent, the Malthusian pseudo-natural law of population increase — projected to assert itself 'in a geometrical ratio',[308] and described by the author of the *Essay on the Principle of Population* also as 'the effect of one great cause intimately united with *the very nature of man*' whose specificity was curiously seen in its inescapable subsumption under the generic 'constant tendency in *all animated life* to increase beyond the nourishment prepared for it'[309] — could be suitably complemented by Malthus with the pseudo-natural order of structurally unchangeable capitalist society. In this spirit he could pontificate that

> The *structure of society*, in its great features, will probably always remain *unchanged*. We have every reason to believe that it will always consist of a *class of proprietors* and a *class of labourers*.[310]

As Malthus himself acknowledged it, his *Essay* was conceived as a counter-blast against William Godwin's libertarian and utopian socialistic projection of an alternative social order, oriented towards the establishment of genuine equality and the corresponding relations for regulating social interchanges. The 'natural law' behind Malthus's 'principle of population' was supposed to provide an apriori refutation of all such ideas. The established system of structural domination, with its iniquitous property relations represented for Malthus the best of all possible worlds. The apologetic aim of his theory was to provide the rational justification — which in his view should be visible and convincing also to the class of labourers and to the paupers — for the legitimacy and validity of the established order. All improvements had to be envisaged strictly *within* the allegedly eternal structural parameters of this order.

Against the historical background of the French Revolution and the fear of major upheavals which it caused in the ruling classes all over Europe, Malthus painted 'a picture still more appalling to the imagination' than 'the Euthanasia foretold by Hume'[311] in these terms:

> If *political discontents* were blended with the cries of *hunger*, and a *revolution* were to take place by the instrumentality of a mob clamouring for want of food, the consequences would be unceasing change and unceasing carnage.[312]

Malthus then postulated that if the 'structure of society' corresponding to his vision of 'the natural order' were properly understood by all concerned, rich and poor alike, there would be no danger of political discontents and revolutions. He curtly dismissed Thomas Paine's ideas concerning the Rights of Man as 'great mischief': the result of their propounder being 'totally unacquainted with the structure of society'.[313] At the same time he insisted that a human being 'neither does nor can possess a right to subsistence when his labour will not fairly purchase it' (exempting, of course, from such considerations 'the country gentlemen and the men of property'[314]), cynically adding that 'he who ceased to have the *power* ceased to have the *right*'.[315] Thus, according to the Reverend Malthus, 'the inference which Mr. Paine and others have drawn against governments from the unhappiness of the people is palpably unfair'.[316] For what appear to be social and political injustices are nothing of the kind, in that they really arise from the 'principle of population', i.e. from the catastrophic increase in the numbers of people in need of subsistence.

Countering the 'mischiefous' and 'unfair' views of 'Mr. Paine and others', Malthus spelled out his 'rational' message with the partially regained confidence of those who believed that the worst of the revolutionary danger was over, even if the adoption of gradual reforms which could be accommodated within the structural parameters of the established order remained advisable. Arguing in his inimitable way, by fusing the roles of the conservative zealot and the unctuously sermonizing parson, Malthus claimed to provide the basis on which — fully matching the 'daily enlargement of physical science' — also the advancement of 'the science of moral and political philosophy'[317] can be secured. This is how the author of the *Essay on the Principle of Population* summed up the most important aspects of his own 'scientific' achievements:

> That the principal and permanent cause of poverty has little or no direct relation to forms of government, or the unequal division of property; and that, as the rich do not in reality possess the power of finding employment and maintenance for the poor, the poor cannot, in the nature of things, possess the right to demand them; are important truths flowing from the principle of population, which, when properly explained, would by no means be above the most ordinary comprehensions. And it is evident that every man in the lower classes of society who became acquainted with these truths, would be disposed to bear the distresses in which he might be involved with more patience; would feel less discontent and irritation at the government and the higher classes of society, on account of his poverty; would be on all occasions less disposed to insubordination and turbulence; and if he received assistance, either from any public institution or from the hand of private charity, he would receive it with more thankfulness, and more justly appreciate its value.
>
> If these truths were by degrees more generally known (which in the course of time does not seem to be improbable from the natural effects of the mutual interchange of opinions), the lower classes of people, as a body, would become more peaceable and orderly, would be less inclined to tumultuous proceedings in seasons of scarcity, and would at all times be less influenced by inflammatory and seditious publications, from knowing how little the price of labour and the means of supporting a family depend upon a revolution. The mere knowledge of these truths, even if they did not operate sufficiently to produce any marked change in the prudential habits of the poor with regard to marriage, would still have a most beneficial effect on their conduct in a political light; and undoubtedly, one of the most valuable of these effects would be the power that would result to the higher and middle classes of society, of gradually improving their governments, without the apprehension of those revolutionary excesses, the fear of which, at present, threatens to deprive Europe even of that degree of liberty which she had before experienced to be practicable, and the salutary effects of which she had long enjoyed.[318]

Thus the claimed scientific achievements of the *Essay on the Principle of Population* amounted in fact to a naked apologetic and confidence-boosting exercise for which the intellectual and political spokesmen of the 'men of property' never ceased to honour and emulate its author ever since. Moreover, even the evidence claimed by Malthus for the political soundness of his own theory on account of its unquestionable acceptance by 'every man in the lower classes of society' was no less 'fished purely out of thin air' — the thin air of conservative wishful thinking — as its 'scientific' supporting pillar: the postulated 'natural law' of population growth by geometrical progression, as opposed to the fatefully limited 'arithmetical progression' feasible in producing the necessary means of subsistence. He thought that by confronting and frightening people with the implications of his magic formula, no matter how absurd, even 'the most ordinary comprehensions' will be won over and forget all their troubles, or at least cease to direct their complaints against the custodians of the existing order. He preferred to disregard the really evident difference between the actual conditions of living and the material as well as political interests of 'the country gentlemen and men of property' — who responded with understandable eagerness and enthusiasm to his views — and 'the lower classes of society', in order to be able to claim, as the principal political merit of his enterprise, that the class-bridging universal acceptance of his 'self-evident truths' was irresistible.

The absurdity of Malthus's formulas should have been clear enough even at the time of the first publication of his *Essay* because he projected that

> at the conclusion of the first century, the population [of England alone] would be a hundred and seventy-six millions, and the means of subsistence only equal to the support of fifty-five millions, leaving a population of a hundred and twenty one millions totally unprovided for.[319]

As to the increase in the world's population, Malthus envisaged that by the end of the 20th century it will amount to no less than 256,000 millions, and thus 'the population would be to the means of subsistence 256 to 9; and in three centuries [i.e. by the end of the 21st century] 4096 to 13'.[320] Characteristically, he was looking for remedies — supplying the model for his imitators on the 'Radical Right' today — in his constant advocacy of curtailing and ultimately altogether eliminating social assistance to the needy, arguing that

> by creating an artificial demand by public subscriptions or advances from the government, we evidently prevent the population of the country from adjusting itself gradually to its diminishing resources.[321]

Indeed, in the good old tradition of obscurantist writers who could offer no real evidence to sustain their theories, Malthus frequently used in his discussion of very important matters nothing but counter-factual conditionals as the final judgement which no one could question. Nor were people, of course, expected to question such judgements. For precisely their blanket exemption from all critical scrutiny was the apologetic purpose of the counter-factual methodology much favoured by Malthus, as for instance in the self-serving assertion according to which

> if the poor-laws had never existed in this country, though there might have been a few more instances of very severe distress, the aggregate mass of happiness among the common people would have been much greater than it is at present.[322]

His adversaries who pointed to social improvements implemented after the French revolution which even Malthus could not deny were dismissed by the author of the *Essay on the Principle of Population* in the same way. He responded by peremptorily asserting that had the labouring masses in France after the revolution not lived up to the desiderata following from his 'principle' — like 'a greatly diminished proportion of births' (which only existed in the conservative parson's imagination) — 'the revolution would have done nothing for them'.[323]

Just like his present-day imitators, the opponents of granting the 'minimum wage' to the most abysmally paid workers, Malthus condemned all efforts directed at improving wage levels as 'irrational and ineffectual' because it 'must have the effect of throwing so many out of employment'.[324] Great hypocrite as he was, just like his conservative followers today, Malthus presented his condemnation of beneficial social legislation as if his negative stance was due to his heart bleeding for the working people. He tried to make his critics believe that he was only 'anxious for the happiness of the great mass of the community',[325] because the laws enacted in favour of social assistance

> have lowered very decidedly the wages of the labouring classes, and made their general condition essentially worse than it would have been if these laws had never existed.[326]

In the same way, Malthus constantly thundered against what is nowadays called the *'dependency culture'*, advocating as the only rational and humane solution the strictest condemnation of all those who accepted 'dependent poverty', though, again, doing it by assuming the pose of the bleeding heart:

> Hard as it may appear in individual instances, *dependent poverty* ought to be held *disgraceful*. Such a stimulus ought to be absolutely necessary to promote the happinesss of the great mass of mankind; and every general attempt to weaken this stimulus, however benevolent in intention, will always defeat its own purpose. If men be induced to marry from the mere prospect of parish provision, they are not only unjustly tempted to bring unhappiness and dependence upon themselves and children, but they are tempted, without knowing it, to injure all in the same class with themselves. ... positive institutions [of social assistance], which render dependent poverty so general, weaken that disgrace which for the best and most humane reasons ought to be attached to it.[327]

Calling for the *'stimulus'* of labelling people *'disgraceful'* on account of putting up with the dehumanizing condition of *'dependent poverty'* imposed upon them by the capital system was a typical way of presenting everything upside-down, in the most callous fashion, well in line with the present-day advocacy of a 'return to basic values' and 'proper Victorian values'. Malthus complemented this approach with his own version of 'targeting welfare', by sharply condemning 'systematic and certain relief on which the poor can confidently depend' and advocating that general relief should be replaced by 'discriminate and occasional assistance'.[328]

In the same spirit (which should find deep resonance in all those politicians who speak with great indignation today about 'single mothers getting pregnant in order to be able to jump the housing queues'), Malthus expressed his approval of the precarious housing stock of England at the time, by adding — no doubt only because he was 'anxious about the happiness of the great mass of the community' — that 'one of the most salutary and least pernicious checks to the frequency of early marriages in this country is the difficulty of procuring a cottage'.[329] And he topped it all up by asking for a form of education whereby 'a man acquires that *decent kind of pride* and those *juster habits of thinking* which will prevent him from burdening society with a family of children which he cannot support'.[330]

According to the 'Principle of Population', the properly educated children of the labouring classes 'must defer marriage till they have a fair prospect of being able to maintain a family'.[331] They would also have to recognize that — in accordance with the 'habits of prudence and foresight' and the necessary 'co-operation with the lessons of Nature and Providence'[332] — they must acquire the 'habit of saving' and put their money into the established 'savings-banks', which would 'enable the poor to provide against contingencies themselves'.[333] The labouring poor must learn to put 'restraint upon their inclinations'; they must be taught 'to cultivate habits of economy, and make use of the means afforded them by savings-banks, to lay by their earnings while they are single, in order to furnish a cottage when they marry, and enable them to set out in life with decency and comfort'.[334] Moreover, Malthus expected the members of the labouring classes to save up enough money, for themselves and for their families, not only for periods of sickness and old age but even after death for their widows and children[335] — god only knows how, since in another context he admitted that the wages of workers were too low, when he attacked the existing laws of social assistance on the ground that they greatly depressed wage levels. Those who nowadays advocate the progressive abolition of state pensions and their replacement by some sort of universal private pension scheme, in order to alleviate the deepening fiscal crisis of the capitalist state, are not more likely to find a way out of the maze of the Malthusian self-contradictions than their wishful thinking ancestor.

The whole of the Malthusian theoretical construct was centred around one single proposition. Whatever problem the Reverend Malthus raised or responded to, he immediately resolved by a direct appeal to the claimed 'natural law of population'. If only people listened to the teaching spelled out in the *Essay on the Principle of Population,* all dangers would disappear, without any need to alter the existing social order: 'a society divided into a class of proprietors and a class of labourers, and with self-love for the main-spring of the great machine', fully in agreement with 'the inevitable laws of nature'.[336] All one needed against the manifold negative tendencies was to make corrective adjustments in accordance with Mr. Malthus's single but miraculously all-encompassing 'Principle'. Since the author wanted to maintain that the established social order had arisen 'from the inevitable laws of nature' and must be preserved as such, the fitting and effective corrective to the acknowledged problems could only be another 'inevitable law of nature'. Curiously, however, the latter was supposed to be a 'law of nature' only for the blatantly apologetic purpose of frightening people out of their wits, so that they should permanently accommodate themselves to the given structural constraints of the capitalist order. This way of dealing with the problems was fundamentally the same as what we are offered today in the sermons preaching 'the limits to growth' (produced by no means only by the ideologists of 'The Club of Rome'), threatening us with the fatal consequences of the coming 'population explosion' precisely in order to compel us to 'learn to live with the existing limits'.

In reality, though, both sets of the so-called 'inevitable laws of nature' — the constitution and transformations of society and the growth of the population

— are inherently social, notwithstanding the fact that apologists like Malthus cannot acknowledge their social character even when it stares them in the face; and not even in their own terms of reference.[337] In the end what makes tenable the hope for successfully countering the destructive tendencies of the established system of social metabolic reproduction is precisely the circumstance that what humankind must face and bring under its rational control are not 'inevitable laws of nature' but corrigible social trends of development. In fact the idea propounded by Malthus and adapted to their circumstances and tools of 'demonstration' by his conservative twentieth century followers — i.e. the projection that the devastating impact of 'inevitable laws of nature' can be positively countered by the force of unctuous preaching[338] — is no less absurd than the original Malthusian proposition itself according to which the growth of human population is dictated by a law of nature corresponding to a 'geometrical progression'.

5.4.2

AS we all know, the world population did not reach in the last two centuries the projected figure of 256,000 millions. As a matter of fact it fell short of that target by more than 250,000 millions, and certainly not because of the good work of the advocated Malthusian correctives.

Naturally, this does not mean that the problems that go with population increases can be wilfully neglected under the prevailing system of social metabolic reproduction or under any alternative system. It only means that instead of projecting pseudo-natural causal determinations and correspondingly fictitious remedies — for the sake of preserving the existing, untenable socioeconomic system as 'natural' and rationally unobjectionable — the historically specific social causes must be identified and matched by viable policies and social metabolic practices. Bringing human needs in harmony with consciously managed material and human resources is the necessary requirement of any viable metabolic alternative to the established order. This implies the adoption of appropriate measures also on the plane of population growth, made possible through the radical transformation of both the comprehensive framework and the microstructures of social metabolic reproduction. Without such fundamental structural changes, all talk about achieving 'global equilibrium in which population and capital are essentially stable' is nothing but pie in the sky.

The false definition of the problems and the wishful projection of solutions artificially superimposed on them — whether in the form of Malthusian chastity or of its more recent but just as grotesque abstemious equivalents, to be imposed at the expense of the poor, and all commended after threatening humanity as a whole with one form or another of directly *nature-determined* collapse — are due to the fact that the perverse *internal dynamics* of the system cannot be questioned. Thus the 'solutions' must always follow the line of squaring the circle. It is acknowledged that the threatening problems are *all-embracing,* but this acknowledgement is nullified by the incorrigible constraint that the capital system is structurally incompatible with *comprehensive* planning. As a result, the circle must be self-contradictorily squared by stipulating that the 'all-embracing solution' to the all-embracing threat put into relief consists in the unquestioning *accommodation* of humankind, not temporarily but forever, within the limits in which the threat has arisen, retaining its socioeconomic framework of *causal* determinations while wishing the necessary *consequences* of the underlying causes out of existence by projecting the achievement of 'global equilibrium'. The 'minor complication' that capital is absolutely inimical to 'equilibrium' — which exists only in the most apologetic of capitalist theories, just like 'perfect competition' — obviously cannot be taken on board in strategic approaches in which the necessary failure of the system to cope with the requirements of *comprehensive* planning can be camouflaged as being resolved under the totally gratuitous projection of 'global equilibrium'.

Threatening humankind with reaching the limits of *natural absolutes* is just as absurd as expecting the elimination of *scarcity* from advancement in productivity directly defined in absolute numbers. Both sets of problems can only be meaningfully treated within their socioeconomic and cultural framework. In Haiti the average income of people (in 1994) is the almost unbelievable figure of $70 *per annum;* in the U.S. the car-workers' pay, including benefits, amounts to $50 *per hour.* But who could seriously argue on the ground of such sharply contrasting figures that U.S. capitalism had solved the problems of scarcity, or even that car-workers in the United States never experience economic problems? Given capital's mode of controlling social metabolic reproduction, new forms of waste and scarcity are constantly created (as well as many old ones are recreated), even in the economically most privileged countries, in order to drive forward the system beyond all feasible 'equilibrium', although in comparative Haitian terms the problems of scarcity could be considered resolved through one single week's productive efforts in the U.S. Thus the real race is against socially created and reproduced scarcity; and — due to the rules under which it must be conducted — that race must be lost well before it can begin.

Operating with fetishistically projected absolute figures could be considered utterly meaningless if it was not for their apologetic ideological function. For it is, again, precisely the pretended natural force of absolute magnitudes which helps to legitimate the existing order as limited only by *natural* boundaries, and therefore justifiably exempted from all possible *social* censure and correctives. The projected collision with natural limits is usually coupled with the mythical threat of absolute despotism in the event the recipe of total accommodation to the given limits — i.e. the unalterable rule of an already existent despotism — is not willingly accepted. Malthus, for instance, warned that unless his solutions were followed, the outcome would be 'unceasing change and unceasing carnage, the bloody career of which nothing but the establishement of some *complete absolutism* could arrest'.[339] And he did not hesitate to present the authoritarian substance of his message dressed up, with customary hypocrisy, as the love of freedom, saying that

> As a friend of freedom, and naturally an enemy to large standing armies, it is with
> extreme reluctance that I am compelled to acknowledge that, had it not been for the
> great organized force in the country, the distresses of the people during the late
> scarcities [in 1800 and 1801], encouraged by the extreme folly of many among the
> higher classes, might have driven the mobs to commit the most dreadful outrages,
> and ultimately to involve the country in all the horrors of famine.[340]

The threat of collapse due to alleged natural laws and strictly natural causes is thus adopted as the rationalization of extreme authoritarianism through which the established social order can preserve itself, thanks to the good offices of 'large standing armies' and 'great organized force', all in perfect harmony with the proclaimed values of individual freedom and life in the best of all possible worlds. The cataclysmic referents and tone of such discourse, in all of its old and recent variants, were necessary precisely because *none* of its tenets and claims could be substantiated. It could not help being a discourse simultaneously 'inside-out' and 'upside-down'. It was 'inside-out' because its real subject matter was the defence of the established order whose defects had to be transubstantiated into pretended natural limits and purely natural causes. And it was a discourse 'upside-down' because the remedy of idealistic preaching was presented in it as the force capable of countering the power of natural laws. When the projections and forecasts ran into trouble, the ideological substance of the cataclysmic discourse had to be and could be preserved, as if nothing had happened, by simply *'moving the goal-posts'*. Thus, since the cataclysmic projections made in the 1960s and 1970s for the end of the 20th century are obviously not going to be realized, the new goal-posts of nature-determined catastrophe, in the form of the coming 'population explosion', are now set somewhere around 2020. And no doubt more distant dates will be offered in due course if social conditions permit us to approach the year 2020, which is by no means to be taken for granted.

The trouble is that at the same time when pseudo-emergencies and nature-determined catastrophes are gratuitously projected (and postponed), the really threatening 'population explosion' — the irresistibly unfolding trend of chronic unemployment in all countries — is ignored or completely misrepresented. It is misrepresented as if it was due to purely technological developments and to the underlying scientific discoveries, and thereby again to the appearance of some 'laws of nature'. Thus, since the given structural parameters and limitations of the system under which the material and human productive forces of society must operate (including, of course, the scientific and technological productive forces) are ignored, the only admissible correctives — inasmuch as the growing dangers of instability are recognized or acknowledged at all — are, again, those which can be considered *external* to the actual social dynamics, attempting to fasten down the lid on the pot while stoking up the fire responsible for the increasing pressure. The external correctives take the form either of the usual vacuous preaching — e.g., 'the workers must understand that the time of full employment is over' and 'no one can have a job for life', etc. — or, more realistically and ruthlessly, of the imposition of authoritarian measures in the name of 'empowering the individuals' (to satisfy themselves with part-time jobs) and the 'love of individual freedom' (to be directed against the traditional collective organs for the defence of the interests of working people). In other words, the dual pillars of wisdom of the realists are: (1) *casualize the labour force,* and (2) *criminalize those who protest against it.* For if the capital system cannot cope with the intensifying contradictions, no one should even dream about trying to fight for an alternative. Since capital is structurally incapable of comprehensive planning as a way out from the maze of destructive irrationalities, no one should look for answers in the direction of rationally coordinating the powers of production with human needs. Planning through the democratic agency of the producers, in contrast to the dictates imposed on society from above by the personifications of capital, is absolutely inadmissible and must be disqualified as 'complete absolutism' and 'despotism'. What appear to be actual violations of individual liberty and of the once accepted right to a limited collective self-defence of the working people are in fact done, by the 'true friends of freedom', in the interest of safeguarding the only natural and rationally justifiable socioeconomic order. The alternative is a nature-determined catastrophe which must be avoided at all cost, including the repression — if needed by 'large standing armies' and by a 'great organized force' — of the opponents of the system.

5.4.3

THE 'surplus population' or 'redundant population' in the books of those who sermonized about the dangers of 'population explosion' was supposed to be simply the numeric qualification of 'too many people', set in relation to the available means of subsistence, quantified primarily in terms of food. The reality clearly identifiable in our own days turned out to be radically different. First, it is not characterizable on the ground of an alleged inability of society to provide the necessary agricultural produce to feed the population, under conditions when immense amounts of food are as a matter of fact wasted — and their wastage is even denounced in some competing capitalist circles — in the interest of maximizing profit, within the framework of the European 'common agricultural policy', for instance. And second, the 'exploding population' is not the generic category of 'too many people' but happens to be defined by very precise — and in its implications highly dangerous — social determinations. For the so-called 'surplus-population' today means 'superfluous labour' in ever-increasing extent. Worse than that, this 'surplus-population' cannot be simply deducted from an abstract total number, with positive implications for the amount of food to be consumed by the rest of the population, as the traditional fairy-tales of population increase and of its Malthusian or neo-Malthusian containment envisaged it. The now growing 'surplus' or 'redundant population' is 'surplus to requirements' in a very limited sense only. Like everywhere else under the rule of capital, here too we witness the impact of a contradictory process. For the great masses of people — in practically every field of activity — who continue to be ruthlessly ejected from the labour process and dismissed as 'redundant' by the imperatives of profitable capital-expansion are very far indeed from being superfluous as *consumers* required for securing the continuity of capital's self-valorization and enlarged reproduction.

Naturally, the apologists of the system for many years refused to take any notice of the intensifying contradictions and went on fantasizing about 'full employment in a free society', blindly asserting that we could only speak of 'small pockets of unemployment', and even of that not for long, thanks to the 'political sensitivity' of enlightened 'democratic society'.[341] Indeed, some of the leading economic theorists concluded from their counter-factual wishful premisses that

> The notion of unemployment, as traditionally held, is coming year by year to have less meaning. More and more, the figures on unemployment enumerate those who are unemployable in terms of modern requirements of the industrial system. This incapacity may coexist with acute shortages of more highly qualified talent.[342]

This way of looking at the emerging social trends, through the wrong end of the telescope, was astonishing, in view of the troubled times which saw the publication of the book just quoted. In fact the devastating consequences of the contradictory trend of ejecting vast numbers of working people from the labour process even in the capitalistically most advanced countries have been visible for quite some time. I have argued twenty five years ago that

> the problem is no longer just the plight of unskilled labourers but also that of large numbers of *highly skilled* workers who are now chasing, in addition to the earlier pool of unemployed, the depressingly few available jobs. Also, the trend of 'rationalizing' amputation is no longer confined to the 'peripheral branches of ageing industry' but embraces some of the *most developed* and modernized sectors of production — from ship-building and aviation to electronics, and from engineering to space technology. Thus, we are no longer concerned with the 'normal', and willingly accepted, by-products of 'growth and development' but with their driving to a halt; nor indeed with the peripheral problems of 'pockets of underdevelopment' but with a funda- mental contradiction of the capitalist mode of production as a whole which turns even the latest achievements of 'development', 'rationalization' and 'modernization' into paralyzing burdens of chronic underdevelopment. And, most important of it all, the human agency which finds itself at the receiving end is no longer the socially powerless, apathetic and fragmented multitude of 'underprivileged' people but *all* categories of skilled and unskilled labour: i.e., objectively, the *total labour force* of society.[343]

Characteristically, when the defenders of the system started to admit that the scale of unemployment was somewhat larger than what could be contained in 'small pockets' — and they had to admit it because they wanted to cut the state's financial deficit wrongly attributed to 'draining unemployment benefits' and not to their underlying cause, — they went on postulating that the new phase of 'industrial development' and 'technological revolution' would put everything right in due course, once the new policies of the 'Radical Right' were 'in place', and the 'political environment' as well as the 'economic climate' became truly favourable to dynamic private-entrepreneurial expansion. It took some time before the optimistic prediction of relegating to the past the negative trends of development had to be complemented by its far from reassuring corollary according to which even when the 'new prosperity' emerges, there can be no question of returning to the conditions of 'easy time for labour', on the 'cushion of full employment'.

But even the now rather qualified optimism of the not so long ago boun- dlessly arrogant 'Radical Right' greatly understates the difficulties and the troubles ahead. For

> Throughout Western Europe we are probably moving towards a political confron- tation, with the problem of employment, or rather unemployment, at the heart of the conflict. Understandably so. Within the European Economic Community the share of unemployed is averaging nearly 12 percent and almost double that figure, say, in Spain. And these are official data underestimating the real plight, which has come to stay. For a long period now, the boom years of the cycle do not bring about a clear recovery in employment, they merely interrupt for a while the relentless lengthening of the lines of the jobless. The phenomenon is no longer limited to the young, to the women, to the blue collar workers. It affects the whole population, including the middle classes. This may explain why it now hits the headlines of the

European newspapers.[344]

Troubles now erupt with increasing frequency not in the poorest regions of the world but in the most privileged parts of 'advanced capitalism'. According to *The Sunday Times*, 'anxiety is mounting in government circles that the relentless advance of mass unemployment is creating what one police report described as an "insurrectionary spirit".'[345] Anxiety is now a common-place even in German press organs which in the past could never tire of eulogizing the 'German miracle'. But what is happening now to the 'German Miracle'? The present situation and the prospects for the near future are described in this way:

> With widespread layoffs, a tremor of insecurity has lodged deep in the psyche of most employees. Under the headline 'Who's Next? — Fear for the Job', last week's cover of *Der Spiegel* showed workers falling off a conveyer belt. The future looks bleak indeed. Every major company is shedding staff: 13,000 at Siemens, 20,000 at Thyssen, 43,000 at Mercedes. Even the railways and post office want to lose 100,000 workers. In one survey by the Institute of German Economy, 35 out of 41 companies said they were planning to cut jobs in 1994.
>
> At the start of the year Germany's official unemployment/rate stood at 3.7m, although the real figure is said to be considerably higher. 'What will happen to a society with more people joining the unemployment line?' asked *Der Spiegel*. 'Will the very fabric of society change if too many of its people live off handouts? Will people change?'
>
> Certainly not the men at Ford-Zehlendorf. Even though 600,000 jobs have been lost in engineering since 1991 and more than half of all companies in the key industries are losing money, the German car worker still has a rosy view of his market value.[346]

Thus the greatest worry is that the labour force does not seem to be willing to take the blows on the chin, defying, instead, the superior 'rationality' of joining the endlessly lengthening line of the unemployed, as its 'diminishing market value' would advise it to do.

From every country it now emerges that the official jobless figures are false. The systematic falsification or 'massaging' of the statistics is the preferred way of minimizing the problems: a form of 'whistling in the dark' as the source of self-reassurance. It is practised not only in relation to unemployment statistics but also to minimize the grave consequences that follow from catastrophically rising unemployment. In September 1994 the British Government proclaimed that the crime rate had fallen by 5.5 percent: 'the biggest drop for 40 years'. This was a cynical lie, since everybody knew — and ever-increasing numbers did so from bitter personal experience — that the crime rate had actually gone up, and continues to do so every year. The secret of the striking crime-busting achievement was later revealed, to no one's surprise, through press reports, according to which '*The government's much heralded fall in crime is a myth*. Hundreds of thousands of serious crimes have been quietly dropped from police records as senior officers massage their statistics to meet Home Office efficiency targets. ... *only 57 percent* of nearly *8m* reported crimes in England and Wales were recorded [i.e. 3 million 440,000 are unrecorded] in official statistics. A spokesman said the government could not explain why the proportion of recorded crime was falling. Police chiefs and experts, however, said the practice is the inevitable result of recent Whitehall [i.e. government] *pressure on police to improve crime statistics.*'[347] The 'improvement of statistics', in unemployment and in the related fields, is what the governments of 'democratic societies' are nowadays concerned about, admitting thereby their failure to tackle the underlying causes. The only thing one finds hard to understand, who is it they think they can fool with the fruits of the method favoured before them by Hitler's propaganda chief.

The ideologists of the system unashamedly advocate a return to savage capitalism while talking with unctuous hypocrisy about 'shamefully high unemployment'. Thus we read in a Leader of *The Economist* that

> Europe's long history of shamefully high unemployment shows that its *labour markets are broken, and need to be fixed*. A chief cause — especially of the rising toll of long term unemployment — is *welfare benefits* that are *too generous for too long*, and which place too few demands on recipients to find a new job. ... There is little doubt, for instance, that France's anomalously high rate of unemployment among the young is partly due to the *national minimum wage* — at nearly 50 percent of average earnings (covering roughly 12 percent of wage-earners), this is high by international standards, and must prise many young workers out of the market. In other ways, too, governments must avoid adding to the cost of hiring labour. At present they discourage recruitment by offering *too much 'employment protection' to workers once hired.*[348]

The remedies advocated in this Leader to the worsening unemployment problem are absurd even in its own terms of reference. For not one single shred of evidence is put forward in order to substantiate its *non-sequiturs*. The Leader's claims are sustained by nothing but the wishful thinking that the return to industrial practices fully in tune with repressive 'Victorian values', and the liquidation of 'too generous welfare benefits' can provide the answers to the aggravating problems. The ubiquitousness of rising unemployment — in every country and in all fields and grades of labour — does not seem to induce the Leader writers to test their wishful remedies even against their own data, which expose as grotesque the notion of inventing jobs for all those who are expelled from the labour process at the present stage of development of 'advanced capital' by means of depressing wage levels even below the miserly minimum wage. The data contained in another *Economist* article — according to which 'In 1973 Chrysler employed 152,560 hourly workers; even if the car firm continues to prosper, it is unlikely to employ more than 85,000 by 1995. Ford's workforce plunged from nearly 200,000 in the late 1970s to 99,000 early this year. It is unlikely to increase much, if at all. ... many of the new workers are really stepping into the slots created by those who retire'[349] — has obviously no restraining effect on the fanciful flight of anti-labour wishful thinking. The editors of *The Economist* claim in the same article in which they list the just quoted job losses that 'Car workers are among America's best paid ($50 an hour, including benefits) and most secure manual workers.' Just how 'secure' they are, is indicated by the numbers actually made redundant by Chrysler and Ford in the United States — nearly one half of the workforce in Chrysler's case and more than one half of Ford's labour force — and quoted on the same page by *The Economist*. As to how the destructive impact of such savage cuts could be remedied by eliminating welfare benefits and forcing half of the highest paid manual workers in the motor car industry to 'empower themselves' as individuals to join the lengthening queues of soup-kitchens, in the absence of welfare benefits judged to be 'too generous', remains a complete mystery.

The situation is in fact particularly serious because the 'population explosion' of labour made redundant is creating grave economic and social problems in the most powerful capitalist countries, like the United States: often referred to by capital's apologists as the shining example of how to solve the encountered difficulties. In truth there is nothing to praise in the U.S. as the model of viable solutions. Far from it. The total failure to deal with the plight of the unemployed in the United States is well summed up by Staughton Lynd:

> I have just become possessed by the hypocrisy of the Clinton administration's jobs rhetoric. I believe we are in a period like the early 1960s. You have a Democratic President who makes idealistic and compassionate noises. This guy was elected to create jobs. But in reality, his program is to help corporations cut jobs. The profit-maximizing companies today are downsizing. And the Clinton Administration is pushing 'training' — which means you and I learning each other's jobs, so next year one of us will be gone. The 'jointness' that Secretary of Labour Robert Reich is pushing means, the boss says: 'We are going to lay off 30 percent of you, and the union can decide who'. ... American capitalism no longer has any use for, let's say, 40 percent of the population. These are the descendants of folks who were brought over here in one way or another during the period of capital accumulation. They are now superfluous human beings. They are nothing but a problem for the people who run the society. ... Politicians may run for office promising full employment, but they don't want full employment. They never wanted full employment — even in the period of primitive accumulation in England when Marx wrote, or in that same period in the United States seventy-five years later. *Today, in the period of decaying imperialist capitalism, it is as if the reserve army of labour becomes the whole world.*[350]

Some time ago the prominent apologists of capital basked in the light of reflected glory, claiming that 'Keynes set himself the task of defeating Marx's prognosis about the course of unemployment under capitalism; and he largely succeeded.'[351] Just like in many other respects, the burial of Marx on account of his prognosis of unemployment under the capital system proved to be somewhat premature. As it happened, not Marx but the source of light of reflected glory turned out to be rather ephemeral. For Keynes's enthusiastic followers of yesterday now write Leaders with the title: 'Time to bury Keynes?' and answer their own question with an emphatic yes.[352]

5.4.4

NOT so long ago we were promised that the disappearing manufacturing jobs would be amply compensated for by the great expansion of the 'service industries' and the positive economic impact of all kinds of 'value added jobs' with which the 'third world' recipients of our 'smoke-stack industries' — the lucky beneficiaries of our 'transfer of technology' — could not compete. As it turned out, nothing could be further from the truth. For in the last two years newspaper headlines had to raise alarm about the fact that 'Redundancies focus on the white-collar worker'[353] and that 'Axe falls on 50,000 civil service jobs'.[354]

Curiously, though, when the new 'solutions' are offered, instead of something tangible we are presented with vacuous platitudes like this: 'You also need a labour market that works, one that moves workers displaced from contracting industries into new jobs in expanding ones.'[355] Once upon a time a philosopher called Stirling wrote a massive two volume work on *'The Secret of Hegel'*, which has been aptly characterized by a reviewer saying that the author, after all those pages, had succeeded in keeping the secret to himself. The same thing could be said about the achievement of our Leader writers. For in their countless solemn declamations and recommendations they consistently succeed in guarding the secret: which exactly are the happily expanding industries that now offer the required forty million 'new jobs to the workers already displaced from contracting industries' in the capitalistically most advanced countries, not to mention the many more millions who are bound to follow them.

The pattern of actually visible expansion seems to be in fact fairly clear and far from promising. As reported by *The Economist* itself — but ignored by the editors and Leader writers when they commit to paper their editorial sermons — it is precisely in the most dynamic and resource-rich companies that 'many of the new workers are really stepping into the slots created by those who retire'.[356] The same seems to be true in every capitalistically advanced country, no matter how large or small. Thus, to take a Scandinavian example, *'Dagens Nyheter,* Sweden's leading newspaper, reported that the heads of the fifty biggest Swedish companies do not foresee any significant increase in recruitment of personnel, although they expect substantial and rising profits throughout the 1990s.'[357] Yet, one of the solutions envisaged to the problem of unemployment is more quixotic than the other.

> The solutions range from work-sharing at reduced wages to nebulous and nonsensical programs for investment in small companies and educational programs. No one has explained exactly how small companies are supposed to generate the millions of jobs that the transnational corporations are eliminating, but the Swedish SAP [the Socialdemocratiska Arbetarpartiet, i.e. the Socialdemocratic Workers Party] is repeating the new mantra about small companies and education three times a week.[358]

As Staughton Lynd rightly stressed, the much advertised slogan of 'education' and 'retraining' — without a corresponding, dynamically expanding industrial base, and indeed under the circumstances of contracting capitalist 'rationalization' — 'means you and I learning each other's jobs, so next year one of us will be gone'.

Naturally, the Swedish Socialdemocratic Party is not alone in promising solutions conjured up from such mirages, on the 'basic premiss that the welfare of the working class is dependent on corporate profits'.[359] Having abandoned even their once professed gradualist claims to move towards a socialist transformation of society, all socialdemocratic parties now have nothing better to offer than sustaining capitalist business both with generous economic handouts and through the 'proper' legislative framework — i.e. effective anti-union legislation — which protects employers from working class action. A good example of the twofold subservience of social democracy to capitalist business is provided by none other than *The Economist,* which could hardly be accused of anti-capitalist bias. We read in a major article dedicated to the problems of the motor car industry that

> At the beginning of March Nissan asked the Spanish government and the regional authority in Madrid and Castilla y Leon for Ptas4.6 billion of subsidies to help keep two of its five Spanish plants open. [At the same time] Suzuki ... is demanding Ptas38 billion from the Spanish government in return for keeping open Santana's factory at Linares in Andalucia. Even if it gets the money, Suzuki will lay off more than half of Santana's 2,400 workers. [The threat these Japanese companies can employ in their discussions with the government is that] Labour costs half as much in the Czech Republic as in Spain.

Now that the European car market is in recession, the chief problem of foreign owners has become the rigidity of labour laws. 'You can't fire people fast enough to stop the red ink spreading', says Daniel Jones, a car-industry analyst at Cardiff Business School in Britain. In December the Spanish cabinet introduced reforms that would increase part-time contract and make it easier for firms to hire and fire. Although employers welcomed the measures, many say they came too late.[360]

The fact that Felipe Gonzales, the 'Socialist' Prime Minister of Spain, obliged, is well in line with what is happening in all socialdemocratic parties in, or in the vicinity of, government. The British Labour Party perfectly fits the pattern, as shown in a programmatic speech by its leader prominently reported in the bourgeois press. The speech — delivered before an audience of financial speculators and businessmen in the City of London — was greeted with wholesome approval. And no wonder. For

> Labour last night courted British business by promising to keep the framework of the *Tory trade union laws* and to move cautiously in introducing a *minimum wage*. Tony Blair reassured the City that Labour had broken from its 1970s traditions of 'big government', and would not backtrack on the Conservative trade union and labour relations laws of the 1980s. 'There is acceptance that the basic elements of that legislation — ballots before strikes, for union elections, *restrictions on mass picketing* — are here to stay', he told members of the Per Cent Club. 'The *minimum wage* must be set carefully and introduced only so as to avoid any adverse impact on jobs. A balance must be struck between protecting the employee against abuse and *loading an unrealistic burden on employers.*' He ruled out a return to the high marginal tax rates of the last Labour Government. He also said: 'It is high time to move beyond the situation where Labour's relations with business are about reassurance' ... businessmen are now encouraged to see Labour as *their natural home*. They could *forge a new industrial order*, he said.[361]

Indeed, the editors of *The Economist* could not have written the Labour Leader's speech better. Given the acceptance of the practical premises of the capital system in structural crisis, all talk about resolving the grave social problem of unemployment can only amount to empty rhetorics in socialdemocratic strategies. Even in the once radical Italian trades unions, led by the former Communist and now fully socialdemocratized and renamed 'Party of the Democratic Left', 'recognize that some of the privileges they have acquired over the years will have to go. It was significant that the engineering workers broke with their confrontational tradition and agreed to renew their national contract in July without even a token protest strike. ... Since 1992, wages have declined in real terms [and] the decline in real earnings will continue.'[362] But, of course, no concessions squeezed out of labour by its own parties, trade union leaders and governments can ever be considered large enough or early enough to satisfy capital's appetite, — as the ever-obliging Felipe Gonzales had to find out in Spain. In the same way, in Italy, the concessions made by the labour movement are accepted only as the first step, to be followed by many more. In this respect, too, the goal-posts have to be, and are, constantly moved, as dictated by the deepening crisis.

> The Berlusconi government made the first, albeit timid, steps to *liberalize the labour market* in July. The measures introduce the principle of *temporary employment*... This falls short of an *easy hire-and-fire policy*, and does not address many of the employers' complaints of the *high non-wage cost of employment*. Nevertheless, an environment is emerging in which more *flexible rules* can be applied to employment.[363]

'Flexible rules' mean in Italy, too, the *casualization* of the labour force to the highest practicable degree, in the hope of improving the prospects of profitable capital accumulation while pretending to be concerned with safeguarding jobs and reducing unemployment.

As we shall see in Chapters 17 and 18, these developments, which deeply affect the labour movement and demonstrate the historical failure of the traditional left, were necessary corollaries of the greatly reduced margin of manoeuvre of the capital system as it entered its structural crisis in the 1970s. The organizational forms and corresponding strategies for obtaining *defensive gains* for labour proved to be strictly temporary and in the longer run totally unviable. There was never any chance of instituting socialism by gradual reforms within the framework of the established mode of social metabolic reproduction. What created the illusion of moving in that direction was precisely the feasibility — and for a few decades also the practicability — of defensive gains, made possible by the relatively untroubled global expansionary phase of capital. Under the circumstances of the system's structural crisis, however, even the once partially favourable elements in the historical equation between capital and labour must be overturned in favour of capital. Thus, not only there can be no room now for granting substantive gains to labour — let alone for a progressive expansion of a margin of strategic advancement, once foolishly but euphorically projected as the general adoption of the 'Swedish model', or as the 'conquest of the strategic heights of the mixed economy', etc. — but also many of the past concessions must be clawed back, both in economic terms and in the domain of legislation. This is why the 'Welfare State' is today not only in serious trouble but for all intents and purposes dead.

The limits to this regressive movement, with grave implications for the permanence of chronic unemployment, are not set by the 'political sensitivity of democratic societies', as the apologists of the system postulated in the past, confidently predicting the complete elimination of even 'small pockets of unemployment'. Rather, they are circumscribed by the level of tolerable instability that goes with the economic and political pressures created by the process of capital's unavoidable structural adjustments dangerously unfolding before our eyes — which include in a prominent place the claw-back of much of labour's past gains and the inexorable growth of unemployment — threatening with an implosion of the system not on the 'periphery' but in its most advanced region.

5.4.5

ONE of the most chilling headlines about unemployment in recent years came from China: '268 million Chinese will be out of jobs in a decade'. It concerned economic and social developments about which the Chinese government itself is seriously worried:

> The report from the Chinese labour ministry last week was nothing less than awesome. By the year 2000, it said, there would be 268m people unemployed in China — an apparent 60-fold rise on the present. ... [The report] also carried a warning about the risks of unrest as unemployment multiplies in towns and cities in the next few years. ... Many workers have been effectively laid off, even though they have yet to figure in official unemployment tallies. A classified Chinese government report cited more than 1,000 cases of labour unrest last year, many of which

were sparked by lay-offs and unemployment.[364]
This article also mentioned that the Chinese government is trying to cushion the impact of its own economic policies by keeping for the time being many workers on the payroll, by providing unemployment benefits or a so-called 'lump sum parachute' to others, and by allowing most laid-off workers to retain employer-provided housing and access to medical care.

'To throw them out on the street would be too capitalist for a country like ours', said Shen [a salaried but laid-off doctor interviewed in the article], underscoring the irony of a communist regime that is systematically putting its core constituents out of work. But for how long will the government afford these benefits as the jobless continue their inexorable rise?

The concluding question is no doubt pertinent. However, its corollary, which worries the Chinese government — i.e., for how long are the hundreds of millions of displaced and marginalized workers going to put up with their ever more precarious predicament if the current trend of 'the inexorable rise of the jobless' is not halted and indeed reversed — is even more pertinent.

We must remember here that two or three years before the massive rise in Chinese unemployment became too threatening to ignore, Western liberal newspapers were full of raving articles about the 'Chinese miracle', in the good old tradition of eulogizing those other 'miracles' — from the German and Italian to the Japanese and the Brazilian — which in due course were all deflated. At the same time we must also remember that similarly miraculous developments were predicted for Eastern Europe as a whole when Western 'democratic' economic experts and advisers to Russia, for instance, advocated in all seriousness (however incredible it may sound today), that the government must get rid of no less than *40 million* 'superfluous workers'. The Russian government was urged to enforce such strategy with 'iron determination', totally unmindful of the potential explosions, in order to secure the promised 'new prosperity'. The magic remedy to all problems in the postcapitalist societies wanting to return to the fold was *'shock therapy'*, no matter how many tens of millions — and in the case of China even hundreds of millions — of workers had to be declared 'surplus to requirements'. That the 'shock therapy' turned out to be great shock and very little therapy, favouring only a tiny (and as a rule the most ruthless and corrupt) section of the population while callously exposing the overwhelming majority to extreme hardship, shows that the problems of the present-day capital system, in all its varieties, are so hard that the advocacy of remedying them through the 'economic rationality' of mass unemployment cannot even scratch their surface.

The threat of chronic unemployment was only latent in capital's mode of regulating social metabolic reproduction for long centuries of historical development. The 'reserve army' of labour not only did not represent a fundamental threat to the system for as long as the dynamics of expansion and profitable capital accumulation could be maintained but was, on the contrary, a necessary and welcome element in its continued health. So long as the contradictions and inner antagonisms of the system could be managed through *expansionary displacement,* the periodically worsening levels of unemployment could be considered strictly temporary, to be left behind in due course as surely as day follows night, generating the illusion that the 'natural' system of socioeconomic reproduction had nothing to fear as a system because its adjustments are sooner or later always successfully made by 'natural laws'. After all, did not one of the greatest ever political economists, Adam Smith, assert in a troubled period of history that the 'propensity to exchange and barter is implanted in man by nature'? And did not, in the same spirit, one of the greatest philosophers of all times, Immanuel Kant, assert with absolute reassurance — and indeed right in the middle of the formerly quite unimaginable turmoil of the French revolution and the Napoleonic wars — that the 'Commercial Spirit' is going to put right in the end absolutely everything, bringing to humanity in general nothing less than the absolute blessing of 'perpetual peace'? If these propositions could be considered true, whatever difficulties might under the present conditions or in the future arise would persist only for a limited time. For even the temporarily badly affected and discontented masses of the people would sooner or later recognize — once the new avenues for the expansionary displacement of the socioeconomic antagonisms are opened up, as they must do — that their real interests can only be found in the market place defined by the relationship between capital and labour: the only proper framework in which the masses of labouring people can live in accordance with their 'natural propensity to exchange and barter'.

However, the situation radically changes once the dynamics of expansionary displacement and untroubled capital accumulation suffers a major disruption, bringing with it as time goes by a potentially devastating structural crisis. The violent realignment of the relation of forces through two world wars among the leading capitalist powers in the course of the 20th century clearly demonstrated the magnitude of the stakes in this respect. Thus, when the accumulating contradictions of the system cannot be exported any longer through a suitably massive military confrontation, as experienced in two world wars, nor can they be internally dissipated by mobilizing the material and human resources of society in preparation for a coming war — as we have seen it done not only in the 1930s but also in the post-Second World War period of 'peaceful growth and development', until the ever-increasing burden of continued armaments (rationalized by the 'cold war') started to become prohibitive even to the economically most powerful countries — then mass unemployment begins to cast a truly threatening shadow not just over the socioeconomic life of one country or another, but over the capital system as a whole. For it is one thing to envisage alleviating or removing the negative impact of mass unemployment from a particular country, or even from a number of them — by transferring its burden to some other part of the world through 'improving the competitive position' of the country or countries in question: a traditional text-book remedy about which we hear so much even today. However, it is quite another matter to dream about such a solution when the sickness affects the whole system, setting an obvious limit as to how much one country can successfully 'beggar its neighbour', or even the rest of the world if it happens to be the most powerful hegemonic country, as the United States in the post-Second World War period. Under these circumstances 'population explosion' in the form of *chronic unemployment* is activated as an absolute limit of capital.

War — or the fighting out of conflicts through the clash of antagonistic interests — was in the past not only a necessary constituent but also a safety valve of the capital system. For it helped to realign the relation of forces and create the conditions under which the expansionary dynamics of the system could be renewed for a determinate, even if limited, period. However, the question of *limits* could not be wilfully ignored. Thus, it should not be forgotten that the devastating wars of the 20th century were also responsible for 'breaking the weakest link of the chain' first in Russia, in 1917, and later in China, in the final years of the Second World War, by creating conditions under which the forces led by Mao could eventually triumph over the Kuomintang and its Western imperialist supporters in 1949.

What carries grave implications in this respect for the viability of the capital system is not only the total untenability of continuing to use the safety valve of all-out military collisions, in view of the threat which they represent to the very survival of humankind. It is equally important to bear in mind the sobering fact that the two global wars of the 20th century, despite their immense destructive impact, were unable to provide a commensurate breathing space for undisturbed economic expansion on the basis of peaceful developments. The threat of revanchism in Europe, together with the prospects of a military collision affecting the whole world, appeared on the historical horizon almost immediately after the First World War; and the United States, despite its great economic advantages at the end of the war, could not secure for itself a solid basis for expansion in the 1920s and 1930s. Far from it, as its role in the 'great world economic crisis' demonstrated. As to the aftermath of the Second World War, the period of Western capitalist expansion was inseparable from the fate of the military-industrial complex, with its temporarily irresistible but in its substance destructive and ultimately also self-destructive dynamism. Indeed, the first attempts to make acceptable the prospects of a new war, to be waged against the Soviet regime, were made already during the last year of the war itself; and efforts to this effect became a quasi-official policy-orientation in 1946, with Sir Winston Churchill's Fulton speech on the 'iron curtain'.

Thus the Malthusian proposition that wars are made because there is not 'enough room' for the given 'surplus population' — just like Hitler's rejoinder that there was not enough 'Lebensraum' for the superior German population — demonstrated its complete absurdity also through the impact of 20th century wars. In fact the 'German miracle' unfolded in a 'Lebensraum' much smaller than that of Hitler's Germany, as a result of the boundary changes after the Second World War. As regards the general Malthusian proposition, although the wars of the 20th century — and not only the two global wars but also the countless others — destroyed many millions of people, the world population did not diminish but, on the contrary, increased by several times the number of people destroyed by all of the century's wars put together. Wars were — and short of global ones still are — waged not because 'there is not enough room and food' for the people. Wars are endemic to the capital system because it is *antagonistically structured,* from its smallest constitutive cells to its most comprehensive structures.

The rise and fall of Keynesianism is highly relevant in this context. The main tenets of Keynes's theory were conceived in the 1920s and early 1930s under the conditions of persisting capitalist economic and financial crisis. Other major factors in the Keynesian orientation were the existence and the economic expansion of the Soviet system at the time: the only part of the world which seemed to be immune — thanks to massive state intervention and finance — to the kind of recessionary troubles experienced in the capitalist West. Although Keynes was always extremely critical towards Soviet developments, he nevertheless adopted the principle of state intervention as the necessary corrective to capital's negative tendencies. All the more since Roosevelt's New Deal seemed to point in the same direction.

And yet, the Keynesian recommendations were completely ignored until the last year of the war, i.e. way after the war economy itself had made state intervention in the economy a ubiquitous fact of life. Indeed, the influence of Keynes became marked only in the postwar years of expansion and capital accumulation. It was directly linked to the role which the capitalist state had to assume in relation to the fortunes of the military-industrial complex which provided room for a number of years also for significant welfare state policies and for the liberal and social democratic advocacy of 'full employment'. For the same reasons, however, once the expansionary dynamics built to a large extent on the foundations of the armament industry came to a jerky halt, making it necessary for the political parties of Western parliaments to start looking for new answers to the growing fiscal crisis of the state, Keynes became an embarrassing liability, rather than an asset. The change in perspective of socialdemocratic parties had a great deal to do with that, just as the unfolding crisis was responsible for the turn towards 'Radical Right' solutions in liberal and conservative parties, signalling the end of 'Butskellism' (i.e. the consensus between the Conservative intellectual politician Rab Butler and the Labour leader Hugh Gaitskell) and the arrival of Margaret Thatcher in Britain on the political stage. In due course the same crisis had to bring with it the systematic elimination of all former program commitments to realize socialism through gradual reforms in all European socialdemocratic parties, from Germany to Italy and from France to Britain. For once even the modest welfare commitments compatible with Keynesian ideas had to be replaced by quite savage cuts in all social services, from health and social security provisions to education, the idea of a radical redistribution of wealth in favour of labour had lost all credibility.

Thus the success story on Keynesian lines covered a very brief interlude in the 20th century history of the capital system. The connection between 'full employment' and militaristic production is as a rule ignored or misrepresented not only in relation to Europe but also with regard to the United States. Yet, as Baran and Sweezy stressed it:

The New Deal managed to push government spending up by more than 70 percent, but this was nowhere near enough to bring the economy to a level at which human and material resources were fully employed. Resistance of the oligarchy to further expansion in civilian spending hardened and held with unemployment still well above 15 percent of the labour force. By 1939 it was becoming increasingly clear that liberal reform had sadly failed to rescue United States monopoly capitalism from its own self-destructive tendencies. As Roosevelt's second term approached its end, a profound sense of frustration and uneasiness crept over the country. Then came the war and with it salvation. Government spending soared and unemployment plummeted. At the end of the war, to be sure, arms spending was cut back sharply; but owing to the backlog of civilian demand built up during the war (compounded of supply shortages and a massive accumulation of liquid savings), the downturn associated with this cutback was relatively mild and brief and soon gave way to an inflationary reconversion boom. And the boom was still going strong when the Cold War began in earnest. Military spending reached its postwar low in 1947, turned up in 1948, received a tremendous boost from the Korean War (1950-1953), declined moderately during the next two years, and then in 1956 began the slow climb which continued, with a slight interruption in 1960, into the 1960s. As a percentage of GNP, the variations of military spending have followed a similar pattern, except that there was very little change from 1955 to 1961. ... the difference between the deep stagnation of the 1930s and the relative prosperity of the 1950s is fully accounted for by the vast military outlays of the 1950s. In 1939, for example, 17.2 percent of the labour force was unemployed and about 1.4 percent of the remainder may be presumed to have been employed producing goods and services for the military. A good 18 percent of the labour force, in other words, was either unemployed or dependent for jobs on military spending. In 1961 (like 1939, a year of recovery from cyclical recession), the comparable figures were 6.7 percent unemployed and 9.4 percent dependent on military spending, a total of some 16 percent. It would be possible to elaborate and refine these calculations, but there is no reason to think that doing so would affect the general conclusion: the percentage of the labour force either unemployed or dependent on military spending was much the same in 1961 as in 1939. From which it follows that if the military budget were reduced to 1939 proportions, unemployment would also revert to 1939 proportions.[365]

Naturally, there had to be a price to be paid for running the economy on such an ultimately precarious basis behind the false appearance of rock-solidity and unsurpassable health, presented as the model to be followed by all would-be 'modernizers'. Indeed, the negative balance sheet — running into not billions but quite a few *trillions* of dollars — has not been presented yet to those who shall eventually have to pay for it. Even today, despite all the accumulating problems, the industry for generating the mood of false optimism and 'confidence' is working full blast, trying to mesmerize people into believing that what they actually experience is not happening at all. Contrasting with that, it would be wise to listen to the voice of dissent: 'we are sick and tired of hearing how swell the economy is doing these days. You can hardly open your newspapers or turn on your TV without being regaled with a rash of economic success stories. Forget it. We are in the weakest cyclical recovery from a recession since the Second World War. ... Real wages continue the slide of the last two decades, and the quality of the jobs being created in this recovery has never been worse. In its issue of 10 October *Business Week* ran an uncharacteristically frank commentary by its labour editor under the heading "The U.S. Is Still Cranking Out Lousy Jobs". As to the future, the current upswing is likely to run its course in the next year or so, to be followed by the next downturn. We are reminded of nothing so much as the situation that extended in early 1937, when optimism was rife and the collapse of the summer of that year only a few months away. History doesn't necessarily repeat itself, but it certainly can.'[366]

The question of when and in what form exactly the bill for the unpaid trillions will be presented is not our concern in the present context. What matters here is the underlying tendency for the inexorable rise in unemployment during seven decades, at least, of the 20th century, and the unviability of all efforts directed at resolving in a sustainable way the contradictions which give rise to it. The 'tricks of the trade' once celebrated as the great achievement of the 'Keynesian revolution' turned out to be as relevant to tackling the problems of actually existing society as the conjurer's tricks in the circus. And what makes it worse is that in the case of the U.S. and a handful of other Western countries we are talking not about the allegedly quite understandable and strictly temporary difficulties of 'underdevelopment' and movement towards the uncontestable Western model, but about the most privileged parts of 'advanced capitalism' which were supposed to have left all these problems behind way back in the past, never to allow them to return.

The rising unemployment in the countries of Eastern Europe, the former Soviet Union, and China is significant and most disconcerting to the apologists of capital precisely in this respect. For the adoption of the ideals of 'market society' did not bring to the population of these countries the promised 'new prosperity'. Instead, it exposed them to the dangers of savage capitalism and mass unemployment, thereby generalizing all over the world the condition of chronic unemployment as the most explosive tendency of the capital system.

However, it would be quite wrong to view these societies through rosy spectacles, on account of the absence of openly acknowledged unemployment from their way of managing the intractable contradictions and antagonisms of the postcapitalist capital system. Undoubtedly there was a time in history when the 'break of the weakest links of the chain' — after the Russian and Chinese revolutions — opened up possibilities for a very different kind of development, with a feasible perspective of progressively extricating the postcapitalist societies concerned — through a sustained process of radical restructuring — from the contradictions of the inherited capital system. The potential mobilization of the labour force to this end was at first favoured also by their confrontation with imperialist interventionist forces and by the immense task of reconstruction once they succeeded against the forces of foreign capitalist intervention. The vast expansion of employment opportunities was an obvious corollary of these developments. However, as time went by and the authoritarian constituents of the inherited capital system reasserted themselves in a new form, the labour force became progressively more alienated from the established socioeconomic and political order, instead of being successfully mobilized for the realization of a very different mode of social metabolic reproduction. Thus the prospects of mass unemployment reentered the social horizon as soon as the most basic tasks of reconstruction (i.e. the objectives of an 'extensive' kind of labour process, which could be controlled through the most authoritarian methods, including mass labour camps) were left behind. The constantly eulogized constitutional guarantee of full employment — enacted by Stalin and imitated elsewhere — was a way of pacifying the ruthlessly managed labour force, but it could in no way provide guarantees for an economically viable future. Thus *hidden or latent unemployment* became a prominent feature of these societies, with grave implications for their prospects of development. Yet, this failure appeared as an ideal, as if the societies concerned had truly and permanently succeeded in solving the problem of chronic unemployment. Indeed, there was a time in postwar history — the 1960s, to be precise — when the 'Chinese model' was hailed by some development theorists of the left as the ideal which all postcolonial societies should follow, including in a prominent place India. This is what helps to put the chilling figure of '286 million jobless Chinese by the year 2000' in perspective, even if that perspective is very far from reassuring. It means that in our 'globalized economy' the vicious circle of chronic unemployment is now fully completed, relegating all of the celebrated 'models' of 20th century development — from the 'Swedish model' of social democracy to the 'advanced capitalist' as well as the rival Soviet and Chinese models of securing 'modernization' and resolving the contradictions of chronic underdevelopment and of equally chronic unemployment — to the utterly discredited past. Only the model epitomized by the 'five little tigers' of the Far East remains now, for those who are gullible enough to believe in emulating it as the finally discovered universal panacea.

5.4.6

THE ruthless policies of the 'Radical Right' which gained prominence in the late 1970s, as a response to the emerging structural crisis of capital and to the failure of the postwar Keynesian solutions, did not live up to the expectations of their supporters. Understandably, therefore, bitter disappointment and even gloom is voiced now by some of yesterday's most enthusiastic believers and propagandists of 'Radical Right' solutions. They ask the question, what has brought about what is considered to be a depressing state of affairs, and answer it like this:

> In part we are seeing the deeper effects of the market reforms of the 1980s working themselves out in unexpected ways. The Thatcherite reforms, which, like many others, I supported as a necessary counter-movement to the over-mighty government and stagnant economy of the 1970s, promised opportunity and choice for many who had never possessed them. But the long-term result of these reforms, made all the more profound by the Major government's attack on the professions, has been to speed the *disintegration of the middle-class life* to which Thatcher's most ardent supporters aspired. The reforms have also made the new uncertainties of life harder to endure because the buffers of the welfare state have also been torn up. *The middle class is peering into the abyss.*[367]

That these concerns now hit the headlines of Europen newspapers has indeed a great deal to do, as Singer suggested, with the fact that rising unemployment and falling standard of living deeply affect also the middle classes. As the just quoted article argues,

> For a very large number of people in Britain, the middle-class way of life has already ceased to exist. A decade ago it was assumed that the *working class would slowly disappear* as it fulfilled its aspirations and become *absorbed into an enlarged middle class.* Instead, the *opposite has happened,* with the middle class being overtaken by the chronic uncertainty and worry that has always gone with working class life.[368]

What is here asserted to have been 'assumed a decade ago' — i.e. the happy absorption of the working class into the middle class — was in fact postulated by Max Scheler, as an axiom of anti-Marxist propaganda, before the First World War, and popularized by Karl Mannheim's *Ideology and Utopia* seventy years ago. Thus the non-realization of such perspective, and the now admitted movement in the opposite direction (i.e. the inexorable tendency towards a 'downward equalization' mentioned already), can come as a surprise only to those who profess the same wishful thinking as their long ago deceased predecessors.

What makes the pill particularly bitter is that some of the old ideological tenets and legitimizing principles of the bourgeois order must now be criticized by saying that the policies pursued on their ground lead to the 'disintegration of middle-class life'. It is thus argued that:

Only now is it becoming clear that the *ideology of free trade* obscures the *new realities* in which we live. What is now emerging is that turning the world into a vast single market will *drive wages in Western countries down to Third World levels* ... It is not only Western industrial workers whose wages will be bid down to levels unknown for generations. What is now emerging is that those who work in service industries can expect their jobs to be exported to low-wage countries. [The alternative is a new protectionism.] All the circumstances in which the ordinary people of the West find themselves indicate that this new protectionism is an idea whose time has come. ... By itself, the new protectionism will not remove the threat to the middle-class way of life which new technologies, and the legacy of the freeing up of markets in the 1980s, has created. Without it, however, the middle classes in Britain and through-out the West will watch their way of life crumble away before their eyes, as they drift into the chronic insecurity of a new and permanent poverty.[369]

The 'new realities' are, of course, nothing of the sort, just like the recommended quixotic remedy of 'new protectionism' is as new and as sound as its siblings were one hundred and fifty or even two hundred years ago. And when the rich fountain-head of 'Radical Right' protectionist wisdom, the billionaire Sir James Goldsmith — who was knighted, true to form, by a 'socialist' Labour Government in Britain — sounds the alarm that 'Global free trade *massively enriches* the countries with *cheap labour,* and creates *divisions in society far greater than Marx envisaged',*[370] he demonstrates not only the ignorance of anti-Marxist 'scholar-ship', but also the total incomprehension of the contemporary trends of deve-lopment of the socioeconomic order of which he and his ideological allies, all emitting populist noises in the spirit of the customary Malthusian 'bleeding heart', are obvious beneficiaries.

The difference now, compared to the age of Malthus, is that the 'clerical baboon' — rightly dismissed by Marx as such — has lost his clerical attire. (Not that Malthus ever took his own too seriously; all his life he preferred the job of colonial indoctrinator in the service of the East India Company to service in the Church of which he was a consecrated parson.) None the less, with or without the outward sign of dog collars, the substance of theoretical baboonery remains the same. For exactly as in the days of the celebrated intellectual ancestor, the now deplored trends of development — which are *intrinsic* to the actually existing capital system — are expected to be successfully countered by erecting some artificial *external* barriers against them.

To blame a largely non-existent 'free global trade' for the rising unemploy-ment and the lowering standard of living in the Western industrial heartlands of the capital system — when even the modest GATT agreement, still a long way from being fully implemented, is opposed tooth and nail by the economically and politically well entrenched 'Radical Right' — is quite grotesque. It amounts to the blatant reversal of the chronological order, so as to invent a direct causal connection between 'Third World cheap labour' (suddenly discovering, for cynical propaganda purposes, that it is cheap) and the troubles of Western capitalist societies. As a matter of fact the inexorable rise in unemployment and the concomitant lowering in the labour force's standard of living *preceded by a quarter of a century* the present-day Jeremiads. The latter are often used only for rationalizing and justifying the savage cuts now routinely imposed on the working population by the personifications of capital even in the handful of privileged countries. Moreover, it is also conveniently kept under silence that the principal beneficiaries of cheap labour are not the 'Third World' countries — which in the mythology of 'new protectionism' are supposed to be 'massively enriched' today — but the big Western transnational corporations that dominate their economies. The super-profits which they generate through the exploitation of obscenely cheap local labour are an essential ingredient of the overall health of the dominant transnational corporations, with headquarters in the heartlands of Western capital, and cannot be wished out of the way, without catastrophic consequences not only for the companies concerned but also for their countries, by the quixotic advocacy of *'regional protectionism'*.

THE 'new realities' of which the gloomy tale speaks have been in fact with us now for a very long time. Given the fundamental defining characteristics of the existing mode of social metabolic reproduction, with its necessary expansionary drive, the tendency to the *equalization of the differential rate of exploitation* is bound to affect every branch of industry in every single country, including those at the top of capital's international pecking order. The neocolonial economic domination of the greater part of the world by a few countries may delay for a while the full unfolding of this objective tendency of the system in the privileged countries (and even then only in a most uneven way), but it cannot indefinitely soften, let alone completely nullify, its impact. When Ford Philippines could get away with paying only 30 cents per hour to the local labour force, achieving thereby as an annual return on equity the staggering rate of 121.32 percent, in contrast to its worldwide average of only 11.8 percent (which included, of course, the Philippines-type immense profits in various 'Third World' plants), obviously that helped the Ford Corporation to pay the hourly rate of $7.50 for the same type of work to its labour force in the same year (1971) in Detroit, i.e. 25 times more than in the Philippines. However, to imagine that such practices can be always maintained flies in the face of all evidence, as the serious troubles of all U.S. transnational motor car companies in the last few years — resulting in huge overall losses and in the earlier quoted massive redundancy figures in the United States itself — clearly demonstrated. Thus, to suggest that these contradictions, with all their 'metropolitan' and global ramifications, could be happily resolved or even just alleviated through some form of 'regional protectionism' defies all rationality.

The trouble is that the contradictions — manifesting in such a destructive form even in the most privileged capitalist countries that the extreme conservative defenders of the established order are beginning to raise the alarm about 'chronic insecurity' — are inseparable from the *internal dynamics* of capital. Thus, there can be no real hope of keeping them within artificially devised *external boundaries,* just because doing so would suit some sectional interests, no matter how powerful. All talk about 'regional cohesion and harmony' is bound to remain at the level of wishful thinking, even if the interested parties manage to cobble together for a time some sort of institutional framework to match it. As an absolute limit of the capital system, the contradiction between transnational capital and national states — and even between globally expanding transnational capital and the artificially 'regionalized' concoctions of such states — cannot be wished out of existence, no matter how hard the 'harmonious co-operation of self-interested regions' (a thoroughly fictitious notion at that) is wished along even by a financially most powerful group of capitalists. All the less since the contradictions of the system are compounded as the absolute limits are activated. For in conjunction with the intractable problems arising from the conflicts of interest between transnational capital and national states, the unfolding trend of chronic unemployment under the objective structural imperatives and the necessarily ruthless control of capital all over the world — that is, the assertion of a fundamental antagonism that brings into play another absolute limit of the capital system — can in the end only intensify the internal disruptive tensions of the prevailing mode of social metabolic reproduction on *all* planes and in *all* countries. This is bound to be the case even if at present the widely suffered pain of growing unemployment in capitalistically advanced countries is exploited to set worker against worker and to invent a fictitious communality of interest between capital (said to be 'regionally threatened' by 'massively self-enriching Third World countries') and labour.

Thus the now unfolding 'population explosion' in the form of the rise of chronic unemployment in the capitalistically most advanced countries represents a grave danger for the system in its entirety. For massive unemployment in the past was supposed to affect only the 'backward' and 'underdeveloped' areas of the planet. Indeed, the ideology attached to such a state of affairs could be — and with a cynical twist in ideology tellingly still is — used to reassure labour in the 'advanced' countries of their presumed god-given superiority. However, as a great irony of history, the antagonistic inner dynamic of the capital system now asserts itself — in its inexorable drive to globally reduce *'necessary labour time'* to an optimally profitable minimum — as a humanly devastating trend to turn the working population everywhere into an increasingly *superfluous labour force*.

On the 'Third World periphery' this process was supposed to be both natural and desirable, to be enforced in the interest of the claimed future benefits that would in due course follow, as certainly as day follows night, from capitalist 'development' and 'modernization' also on the 'periphery'. However, when the same devastation begins to prevail in the ideally 'advanced' parts of the social universe, no one can pretend any longer that all is well in this best of all possible worlds. At that point people are subjected to a thoroughly bewildering experience, as if they had to live through the reality of a film projected backwards, of historical time flowing in the reverse order. For what is being brought into their present-day conditions of existence is what they were supposed to have left forever behind in a nightmarish past. Under these conditions even the blind apologists of the system, like Hayek, would find it difficult to sing as originally composed — even before the most grateful, reassurance-seeking audience — their old song. For the hard-to-believe experience is neither cinematographic nor imaginary but painfully real. Indeed, seeing the way in which the intrinsic trends of capital's concentration and centralization — under the imperative of its expanded self-reproduction — unfold, it is not too difficult to realize that the uncontrollable multiplication of the 'superfluous labour force' represents not only an enormous drain on the resources of the system but potentially also a most unstable explosive charge.

What we are witnessing today is a two-pronged attack on the class of labour not only in the 'underdeveloped' parts of the world but,with dangerous implications for the continued viability of the established mode of social metabolic reproduction, also in the capitalistically advanced countries. We witness: (1) in all fields of activity a chronically growing unemployment, even if it is often camouflaged as 'flexible labour practices' — a cynical euphemism for the deliberate policy for the fragmentation and casualization of the labour force and for the maximal manageable exploitation of part-time labour; and (2) a significant reduction in the standard of living even of that part of the working population which is needed by the operational requirements of the productive system in full-time occupations.

At the same time, as a corollary, in all capitalistically advanced countries we are confronted by numerous instances of authoritarian legislation, despite the past traditions and the constantly reiterated present claims to 'democracy'. The authoritarian measures are made necessary by the growing difficulties of managing the deteriorating conditions of socioeconomic life without the direct legislative intervention of the state. They are designed to underpin with the threat of law and, whenever needed, the use of force, the more aggressive posture of capital towards its labour force. Indeed, as the chronicle of labour disputes in the last two decades shows — from the authoritarian suppression of the Air Controllers organization in the United States to the massive state intervention under the Premiership of Margaret Thatcher in the British miners' one-year long strike — these measures are not only legally enacted as 'reserve powers' of the state, for use in situations of major political emergency. They are ruthlessly and almost routinely implemented against the defensive organs of the labour movement in economic disputes, at times with the pretext of fighting against the 'subversion of the state', as we have heard it in Margaret Thatcher's denunciation of the miners as 'the enemy within'.

However, notwithstanding all efforts of economic and political manipulation the problems are getting perceptibly worse, with no solution in sight anywhere on the horizon. Given the highly stretched character of the reproduction process under the conditions of 'advanced capitalism', and the correspondingly greater exposure of living labour to the structural requirement of securing a relatively undisturbed production and realization process, the objective vulnerability of the system to a significant decline in purchasing power, due to a dramatic collapse of full employment, is incomparably greater than in 'underdeveloped' societies where high levels of unemployment represent the 'norm' to be improved by 'modernization'. This vulnerability also means that it would be quite intolerable to the labour force to put up indefinitely with being at the mercy of circumstances; not because of a failure to satisfy some fictitious 'middle class aspirations', but in terms of the existing minimal commitments and obligations without which people simply could not carry on their everyday life, adding thereby the fuse to the accumulating explosives. And given the dominant position of 'advanced capitalism' in the system as a whole, it would be quite impossible to envisage its sustainable functioning in the event of a collapse, for whatever reason, of its inner core.

It is relevant to note here the double-edged character of the contradiction of chronic unemployment. For it tends to produce *social dynamite* within the framework of the capital system, whichever way remedies might be sought. In this sense, considered in itself, ever-increasing unemployment is bound to undermine social stability, bringing with it what are now even in official circles admitted to be its 'undesirable consequences', after many years of denying that the denounced negative trends of development had anything to do with the social cancer of chronic unemployment. They range from an ever-escalating crime rate (especially among the young) to defiantly voiced economic grievances and forms of direct action (e.g. the mass revolt against the 'Poll Tax' which caused the downfall of Prime Minister Thatcher in Britain), carrying the danger of serious social upheavals. On the other hand, what could be a fairly obvious alternative to worsening unemployment — which happens to be at times openly advocated by well meaning would-be reformers — is a definite non-starter.

To be sure, other things being equal, the rational alternative to the unavoidably destabilizing impact of unemployment would be a great reduction in the hours spent at one's place of work, say by half, so as to make itself felt and match the size of the problem by providing employment opportunities for many millions. But, of course, other things are not equal. For adopting this solution under the prevailing conditions of production would ipso facto generate 'leisure' (i.e. free time at the disposal of the individuals), and the instability going with it on a quite unimaginable scale. Thus, even if such a solution could be economically feasible at all within the framework of a profit-maximizing accumulation-oriented system — which, of course, it is not, as the consistent rejection of even very modest trades union demands for the reduction of the required weekly hours of work shows — the pursuit of that course of action would still produce social dynamite in the given, utterly aimless, social order. For under the existing conditions of life the only practicable aim which could aspire at being granted social legitimacy is necessarily and narrowly determined by capital as the controlling force and the absolute orienting principle of social metabolic reproduction.

*

* *

THE shadow of uncontrollability, for reasons discussed above in relation to all four sets of problems concerned with the absolute limits of the capital system, is thus getting darker. Under the conditions of its historical ascendancy capital could manage the internal antagonisms of its mode of control through the dynamics of *expansionary displacement*. Now we have to face not only the age-old antagonisms of the system but also the aggravating condition that the expansionary dynamic of traditional displacement itself has become problematical and ultimately untenable.

This is so not only as regards the contradiction between transnational capital and national states as well as the ever more dangerous encroachment of capital's self-expansionary reproductive imperatives on the natural environment, but also in relation to the absolute structural limits encountered by transforming the traditional 'reserve army of labour' into an exploding 'superfluous labour force' — yet at the same time more than ever necessary to make possible capital's enlarged reproduction — with particularly threatening implications for the whole system emanating from the destabilization of its core. As to the demand for substantive equality to which capital is absolutely inimical, it represents a different but no less serious problem. For the demand asserted itself in the last few decades in an irrepressible form, bringing with it insurmountable complications for the 'nuclear family' — the microcosm of the established order — and thereby some forbidding difficulties in securing the continued reproduction of capital's value system.

As an attempt to gain control over the system's uncontrollability, we are subjected to a trend of *increasingly political* determinations in 20th century economic developments. This means a reversal of the long period of capital's historical ascendancy in which primarily *economic* determinations were dominant in the social metabolic process of reproduction. Postcapitalist transformations of the capital system known to us were an integral part of this reversal of the earlier trend. But they were by no means the only forms of state intervention to fail or show very limited success. Rooseveltian New Deal was very far from resolving the unemployment problem in the United States, as we have seen above, and Keynesian strategies of large-scale state intervention in the economy in the postwar world all came to a sorry end. Moreover, the Radical Right's self-contradictory attempt to 'roll back the boundaries of the state' by means of increased state activity in regulating economic development (even if not of a Keynesian type) — still commended in financial papers[371] — produced no better results. Nevertheless, even if the prospects of success are rather precarious on the basis of all available historical evidence, the trend of major state involvement in the control of socioeconomic processes is likely to continue, and even intensify — perhaps even by temporarily imposing the advocated strategies of 'regional protectionism'. Indeed, what makes this trend of direct political involvement particularly telling is that it must be continued and extended despite its less than reassuring achievements.

Thus the need for a transition to a social order, controllable and consciously controlled by the individuals, as advocated by the socialist project, remains on the historical agenda, despite all failures and disappointments. Naturally, this transition requires an *epochal* shift — a sustained effort to go beyond all forms of structurally entrenched domination — which cannot be envisaged without a radical restructuring of the existing forms and instruments of social metabolic reproduction, in contrast to accommodating the original socialist aims to the paralyzing material constraints of the inherited conditions, as it happened in the past. For the *raison d'être* of the socialist enterprise is to retain awareness of the epochal strategic objectives of transformation even under the most adverse conditions, when the power of inertia pulls in the opposite direction: that of the 'line of least resistance' leading to the revitalization of capital's uncontrollable controlling force.

NOTES TO PART ONE

[1] As Hegel himself puts it in the Preface to *The Philosophy of Right:*
> One word more about giving instruction as to what the world ought to be. Philosophy in any case always comes on the scene too late to give it. As the thought of the world, it appears only when actuality is already there cut and dried after its process of formation has been completed. The teaching of the concept, which is also history's inescapable lesson, is that it is only when *actuality is mature* that the ideal first appears over against the real and that the ideal apprehends this same real world in its substance and builds it up for itself into the shape of the intellectual realm. When philosophy paints its grey in grey, then has a shape of life *grown old.* By philosophy's grey in grey it *cannot be rejuvenated* but only understood. The *owl of Minerva spreads its wings only with the falling of the dusk.* (Hegel's *Philosophy of Right*, Clarendon Press, Oxford, 1942, pp.12-13.)

This resignation, confining the role of philosophy to *contemplation* was inseparable from a conception of history totally uncritical towards capital's social metabolic control and its political state. We can see this very clearly in a passage of Hegel's *Philosophy of History:*
> Philosophy concerns itself only with the glory of the Idea mirroring itself in the History of the World. Philosophy *escapes* from the weary strife of passions that agitate the *surface of society* into the calm region of *contemplation;* that which interests it is the recognition of the process of development which the Idea has passed through in realizing itself — i.e. the *Idea* of Freedom, whose reality is the *consciousness* of freedom and nothing short of it. (Hegel, *The Philosophy of History,* Dover Publications, New York, 1956, p.457.)

[2] Marx and Engels, *Collected Works,* Lawrence & Wishart, London 1975ff, vol. 5, pp.52, 73, 87.
[3] See Aristotle, *Poetics,* Chapters 8 and 9.
[4] Saint Augustine, *City of God,* Image Books, Doubleday & Co., New York, 1958, p.523.
[5] Hegel, *The Philosophy of History,* p.39.
[6] Hegel, *The Philosophy of Right*, p. 214.
[7] *Ibid.,* p. 215.
[8] *Ibid.,* p. 217.
[9] *Ibid.,* p. 218.
[10] *Ibid.,* p. 222.
[11] *Ibid.,* pp. 222-23.
[12] 'Mexico beckons, protectionists quaver', *The Economist,* 20 April 1991, pp.35-6.
[13] Hegel, *The Philosophy of History,* p.78.
[14] *Ibid.,* p.103.
[15] *Ibid.,* p.16.
[16] Hegel, *The Philosophy of Right,* p.13.
[17] *Ibid.,* p.12.
[18] *Ibid.,* pp.129-30. Translation is by T. M. Knox.

Even if by no means always, in this particular paragraph (§199) Knox's version is much preferable to H. B. Nisbet's more recent translation of the same work. (See Hegel, *Elements of the Philosophy of Right,* Cambridge University Press, Cambridge, 1991, p.233.) Knox renders the German term *Vermögen* — which literally means 'wealth' — as 'capital', whereas Nisbet, adopting a word used by Knox for the same German term in another context, translates it as 'resources', in the plural. However, the context makes it clear that Knox in §199 is nearer to Hegel's spirit. For Hegel's reflections on the subject have been greatly influenced by Adam Smith's *Wealth of Nations,* as well as by the writings of Ricardo and other political economists. Indeed, in §200 (which is rather inaccurately translated by Knox) Hegel explicitly refers to capital as *Kapital,* indicating at the same time that the possibility of 'participating in general wealth through one's skill' — i.e. *labour* — is determined by *capital* in his 'civil society'. Moreover, also in §199 Hegel calls the reader's attention to an earlier paragraph (§170) in which he is concerned with *Vermögen* as 'permanent and secure', i.e. with establishing private property on an 'ethical' basis, as vested in the family — in contrast to the ethically unfounded possessions of the 'mere individual' *(der bloss Einzelner),* — thereby attempting to ground the class character of private property on something 'communal' *(ein Gemeinsames),* namely the *family as such,* when of course he could not perform such a conjurer's trick with the help of the *bourgeois* family. Nevertheless, in a note added to the same paragraph he has to admit that although ancient forms of property, considered already permanent, appear 'with the introduction of marriage', the 'ethical' family as the foundation of 'permanent and secure property' is much more recent, reaching the level of its proper determination and the means of its consolidation only in the sphere of civil society *(in der Sphäre der bürgerlichen Gesellschaft).*

It is also highly relevant in this context that in §200, in addition to the capital/labour relationship as the determining ground of one's participation/share in universal permanent capital (or capitalist wealth), Hegel talks only about 'accident' or 'contingency' as determining grounds, mentioning them no less than six times within a few lines. This is a very convenient way of avoiding the question of *genesis* of the depicted capital system. For whatever is not explicitly assumed by Hegel as already given in the form of labour-determining 'unearned principal' (Knox, p.130) or 'basic assets' (Nisbet, p.233), or in German *'eine eigene unmittelbare Grundlage, Kapital'* ('its proper direct ground, capital'): which all boil down to nothing but 'capital assets', he tries to 'explain away' as accidental and contingent, and therefore in his view in no need of further explanation. What is essential, here, is that Hegel's obvious concern in these paragraphs is the modality of *wealth-production and distribution,* i.e. the capital system as an 'ethically grounded' metabolic control of 'civil society', and consequently with full justification eternalizable as an order existing *de jure* and not only *de facto.* (More about this problem in Section 1.3.4.)

[19] I owe this calculation to Daniel Singer.

[20] Hegel, *Natural Law: The Scientific Ways of Treating Natural Law, Its Place in Moral Philosophy, and Its Relation to the Positive Sciences of Law,* University of Pennsylvania Press, 1975, p.65.

[21] Hegel, *The Philosophy of Right,* pp.128-29.

[22] *Ibid.,* p.129.

[23] *Ibid.*

[24] *Ibid.,* pp.129-30.

[25] *Ibid.,* p.130.

[26] *Ibid.*

[27] Lukács, *The Young Hegel: Studies in the Relation between Dialectics and Economics,* The Merlin Press, London, 1975, pp.400-401.

[28] *Ibid.,* p.408.

[29] *Ibid.,* pp.418-19.

[30] Lukács, *History and Class Consciousness,* The Merlin Press, London, 1971, p.xxiii.

[31] As Lukács had put it: 'With the ideology of social democracy the proletariat falls victim to all the antinomies of reification'. *Ibid.,* p.197.

[32] *Ibid.,* p.42.

[33] *Ibid.*

[34] *Ibid.,* p.318.

[35] *Ibid.,* p.204.

[36] *Ibid.,* p.43.

[37] *Ibid.,* p.312.

[38] *Ibid.,* p.340.

[39] *Ibid.,* p.248.

[40] *Ibid.*

[41] MECW, Vol. 5, pp.50-51.

[42] *Ibid.,* p.49.

[43] Hegel, *The Philosophy of Right,* p.212.

[44] Marx, *Letter to Engels,* 8 October 1858.

[45] The title of a book by Rudolf Bahro who once professed socialist views. See in this respect Bahro's earlier book for which he received in 1979 the Isaac Deutscher Memorial Prize: *The Alternative in Eastern Europe,* N.L.B., London, 1978.

[46] *The Economist,* 31 December 1991, p.12.

[47] Apologetics obviously knows no limits in its defence of the indefensible. Since it is now impossible to pretend (without blushing) on the basis of usually recommended indicators that the promised fruits of the capitalist 'market economy' have materialized for the masses of the people in Russia (whose standard of living as a matter of fact greatly deteriorated in the recent past), new criteria must be now invented to 'explain away' the troubles. Thus *The Economist* — relying on a publication by 'a trio of advisers to the Russian Government' ('The Conditions of Life', by Andrei Illarionov, Richard Layard and Peter Ország, Pinter Publications, London, 1993) — offers its readers a veritable gem in an article entitled 'Poverty of numbers' (10-16 July 1993, p.34). Accordingly, although forced to admit that the claimed cheering 'benefits that have improved the standard of living' of ordinary Russians are quite 'impossible to quantify' (minimizing at once this admission by disqualifying in the present context — with the title of their article: 'Poverty of numbers' — the otherwise enthusiastically supported virtues of quantification), the editors of *The Economist* assert that things '*like* the time freed by no longer having to spend an average of 15 hours a week queueing', thanks to the lack of money to buy food with, represent a significant improvement in their standard of living. We are not told what those other things might be which come under the promising category of 'like', but it should not be too difficult to figure out. For, obviously, one should not ignore the much greater quantity of time than 15 hours saved week in week out by not having to cook the food-stuff which they could not purchase in the well stocked new markets. Furthermore, if we add to all these benefits also the time saved by not having to eat the food which they could not buy and cook, not to mention the great further benefits gained by avoiding the medical dangers and aesthetic drawbacks of potential obesity, the standard of living of the average Russian pensioner must be at least as high as that of the Rockefellers. Especially if in the same spirit in which Russian income benefits are now calculated by the 'trio of advisers to the Russian government' and the editors of *The Economist,* we allow the poor Rockefellers to deduct an appropriate amount from their declarable income on account of all that anxiety which they must surely suffer regarding the prospects of their companies in these uncertain times.

[48] Recall in particular Sections 1.2.4 and 1.2.5.

[49] Readers interested in these problems are referred to my book, *Marx's Theory of Alienation,* The Merlin Press, London, 1970, and Harper Torchbooks, New York, 1972.

[50] See for instance Marx, *Capital,* Foreign Languages Publishing House, Moscow, 1958, Vol. 3., p.810.

[51] Marx often refers to capital as a surplus-labour extracting pump. For instance when he argues that 'The specific economic form, in which unpaid surplus-labour is pumped out of direct producers, determines the relationship of rulers and ruled, as it grows

directly out of production itself and, in turn, reacts upon it as a determining element.' *Ibid.*, p.772.

[52] The most extreme, and indeed the most absurd position in this respect was assumed by Stalin and his followers who laid down 'overtaking the U.S. in pig-iron production' as the criterion of reaching the highest stage of socialism, i.e. communism.

[53] The defenders of the capital system, including the so-called 'market socialists', like to conflate the notion of 'economic efficiency' as such with its *limited historical type* that characterises capital's specific mode of social metabolic control. It is precisely the latter, with its grave limitations and ultimate destructiveness, which must be the subject of a radical critique, in place of mindless idealization.

[54] See Chapters 15 and 16 below, concerned with the frightful wastefulness due to the decreasing rate of utilization as a fundamental trend of capitalistic developments, and with the role of the state in trying to cope with its consequences.

[55] As the only possible way out of Faust's self-imposed predicament, Goethe's *Faust* — quite unlike Marlowe's — ends with the divine rescue of the hero. However, far from being starry eyed or blinded by apologetic wishful thinking, Goethe presents this solution in conjunction with a scene of supreme irony. For in the scene in question the dying Faust imagines that the sound reaching him from outside is the echo of a great industrial activity — successful land reclamation from the sea by building monumental canals for the advancement and future happiness of humankind — and thus he becomes convinced that he can now really die a happy man, even though he lost his pact with the devil. In truth, however, the sound he hears is the noise made by the lemurs digging his grave. Needless to say, there are no signs of any divine rescue operation on the horizon today. Only capital's noise of grave-digging is getting louder.

[56] Historically the emergence and consolidation of the legal and political institutions of society run parallel to the conversion of communal appropriation into exclusivistic property. The more extensive the practical impact of the latter on the prevailing modality of social reproduction (especially in the form of fragmented private property), the more pronounced and institutionally articulated the totalizing role of the legal and political superstructure must be. It is therefore by no means accidental that the centralizing and bureaucratically all-invading *capitalist* state — and not a state defined by vague geographic terms as 'the modern Occidental state' (Weber) — acquires its preponderance in the course of the development of generalized commodity production and the practical institution of the property relations in tune with it. Once this connection is omitted, as indeed for ideological reasons it must be in the case of all those who conceptualize these problems from the standpoint of the ruling order, we end up with a mystery as to why the state assumes the character it happens to have under the rule of capital. This is a mystery that becomes a complete mystification when Max Weber tries to unravel it by suggesting that 'it has been the work of jurists to give birth to the modern Occidental state.' (H. H. Gerth and C. Wright Mills, editors, *From Max Weber: Essays in Sociology,* Routledge and Kegan Paul, London, 1948, p.299.)

As we can see, Weber turns everything upside down. For it would be much more correct to say that the objective needs of the modern capitalist state give birth to its class-conscious army of jurists, rather than the other way round, as Weber claims with mechanical one-sidedness. In reality we find also here a dialectical reciprocity, and not a one-sided determination. But it must be also added that it is not possible to make more than tautological sense of such reciprocity unless we recognize — something that Weber cannot do, because of his far from neutral ideological allegiances — that the *übergreifendes Moment* (the constituent of primary import) in this relationship between the ever-more-powerful capitalist state, with all its material needs and determinations, and the 'jurists' happens to be the former.

On this issue and on some related points see my essay: 'Customs, Tradition, Legality:

A Key Problem in the Dialectic of Base and Superstructure', in *Social Theory and Social Criticism: Essays for Tom Bottomore,* ed. by Michael Mulkay and William Outhwaite, Basil Blackwell, Oxford, 1987, pp.53-82.

[57] See Hegel's *Philosophy of Right,* §333.

[58] I argued some time ago that

The objective reality of different *rates of exploitation* — both within a given country and in the world system of monopoly capital — is as unquestionable as the objective differences in the *rates of profit* at any particular time, and the ignorance of such differences can only result in resounding rhetoric, instead of revolutionary strategies. All the same, the reality of the different rates of exploitation and profit does not alter in the least the fundamental law itself: i.e. the growing *equalization* of the differential rates of exploitation as the *global trend* of development of world capital.

To be sure, this law of equalization is a *long-term trend* as far as the global system of capital is concerned. Nevertheless, the modifications of the system as a whole also appear, inevitably already in the short run, as 'disturbances' of a particular economy which happens to be negatively affected by the repercussions of the shifts which necessarily occur within the global framework of total social capital. 'Total social capital' should not be confused with 'total national capital'. When the latter is being affected by a relative weakening of its position within the global system, it will inevitably try to compensate for its losses by increasing its specific rate of exploitation over against the labour force under its control — or else its competitive position is further weakened within the global framework of total social capital. Under the system of capitalist social control there can be no way out from such 'short-term disturbances and dysfunctions' other than the intensification of the specific rates of exploitation, which can only lead, both locally and in global terms, to an explosive intensification of the fundamental social antagonism in the long run. Those who have been talking about the 'integration' of the working class — depicting 'organized capitalism' as a system which succeeded in radically mastering its social contradictions — have hopelessly misidentified the manipulative success of the differential rates of exploitation (which prevailed in the relatively disturbance-free historic phase of postwar reconstruction and expansion) as a basic *structural remedy. (The Necessity of Social Control,* The Merlin Press, London, 1971, pp.58-9.)

In the last twenty five years the long term has become somewhat shorter and we could witness a significant erosion of the differential rate, representing obviously a 'mixed blessing' for labour in the capitalistically advanced countries. For even if the ongoing changes in the countries of the 'periphery' could bring limited improvements to some sections of the local working classes, the overall trend is that of a downward spiral. The standard of living of the working classes even in the most privileged capitalist countries — from the U.S. to Japan and from Canada to Great Britain and Germany — has been clearly deteriorating, in sharp contrast to the 'steady improvement' which used to be taken for granted in the past. As Paul Sweezy and Harry Magdoff wrote recently in the 'Notes from the Editors' about conditions now prevailing in the U.S. :

The real rate of unemployment is around 15 percent of the labour force, and over 20 percent of manufacturing capacity lies idle. At the same time the living standards of the majority of the people are eroding. *(Monthly Review,* vol. 45, No. 2, June 1993.)

[59] It is worth remembering in this context that the trade monopoly of the British East India Company was ended only in 1813, under the pressure of forcefully developing — and by that monopoly badly hindered — British national capitalist interests, and Chinese trade monopoly ended as late as 1833.

[60] To be sure, the law of 'uneven development' must remain in force under all humanly feasible modes of social metabolic control. It would be quite gratuitous to postulate its disappearance under the conditions of even the most developed socialist society. Besides,

there is nothing wrong with that by itself. For 'uneven development' can be instrumental also to positive advancement in productivity. The real concern of socialists is, of course, that the law of uneven development should not exercise its power in a *blind* and *destructive* way, which up to the present time could not be avoided. Uneven development in the capital system is inextricably tied to both blindness and destructiveness. It must impose its power blindly, because of the necessary exclusion of the producers from control. At the same time, there is a dimension of destructiveness in the normal process of development of the capital system, even when historically capital is still in the ascendant. For the weaker socioeconomic units must be devoured through the operation of the 'zero sum game' pursued in the course of the concentration and centralization of capital, although even the greatest figures of bourgeois political economy can only see the positive side of all this, describing the underlying process as unproblematically commendable 'advancement through competition'. Also, destructiveness as belonging to the normality of the capital system is clearly evidenced at times of cyclic crises, manifest in the form of liquidating over-accumulated capital. Moreover, we find it under another aspect in the cancerously growing wastefulness of the system in the 'advanced capitalistic countries', geared to the creation and satisfaction of artificial appetites, often celebrated by capital's apologists — not only in the West but also among the newly converted 'market socialists' — as the self-evident proof of 'advancement through competition'. However, the capital system's destructiveness is by no means exhausted with the uncritically accepted 'costs of advancement'. It assumes much graver forms of manifestation as time goes by. In fact the system's ultimate destructiveness comes to the fore with particular intensity — threatening the very survival of humanity — when the historical ascendancy of capital as a global metabolic order draws to its close. That is the time when on account of the difficulties and contradictions arising from the — necessarily contested — control of *global circulation* 'uneven development' can only bring unmitigated disaster under the capital system.

[61] Hegel *Ibid.,* §324.

[62] *Ibid.,* §360.

[63] We can identify a parallel phenomenon in the relationship between the contemporary state and capital's material reproductive functions: the intrusion of what might be termed *'hybridization'* into the global social metabolic order, which cannot help being most problematical. (Hence the constant but on the whole utterly Quixotic attempts by the 'radical right' to turn the clock back and resuscitate Adam Smith and others in pursuit of capitalistic purity.) The future may well confirm that this intrusive and ultimately disruptive trend of hybrid transformation was one of the principal factors for undermining the capital system at the peak of its power.

[64] See Book IV, Chapter VI. of John Stuart Mill's *Principles of Political Economy, with Some of Their Applications to Social Philosophy.*

[65] 'Yeltsin devalued', *The Economist,* 31 July—6 August 1993, p.16.

[66] *Ibid.,* p.17.

[67] Adam Smith, *An Inquiry into The Nature and Causes of The Wealth of Nations,* ed. by J.R. McCulloch, Adam and Charles Black, Edinburgh, 1863, p.273.

[68] *Ibid.,* pp.199-200.

[69] F.A. Hayek, *The Fatal Conceit: The Errors of Socialism,* Routledge, London 1988, p.146.

[70] *Ibid.,* p.148.

[71] 'until the "subjective revolution" in economic theory of the 1870's [i.e. the formulation of the 'marginal utility theory', I.M.], understanding of human creation was dominated by animism — a conception from which even Adam Smith's "invisible hand" provided only a partial escape'. *Ibid.,* p.108.

[72] Both quotations come from Adam Smith, *Op. cit.,* p.298. The passage from which they are taken reads as follows:

Consumption is the sole end and purpose of all production; and the interest of the producer ought to be attended to only so far as it may be necessary for promoting that of the consumer. The maxim is so perfectly self-evident, that it would be absurd to attempt to prove it.

As we can see, the productive and distributive practices of the capital system in our own days are totally at variance with Adam Smith's account of what is supposed to be the case, as well as with his stipulation of why everything — the way summed up by his maxim — ought to be the case. What would be, therefore, absurd today is not the attempt to submit to critical scrutiny Smith's far from 'perfectly self-evident maxim' but a failure to do so.

[73] Smith, *Ibid.*, p.413.

[74] Marx, *Capital,* Foreign Languages Publishing House, Moscow 1958, vol.1, p.153.

[75] The misrepresentation of objective determinations as 'subjective motives' — and thereby the conflation of the subjective and the objective so that the latter should be imaginarily subsumed under the former — is often coupled with the conflation of use-value with exchange-value, for the sake of a likewise imaginary equation of the latter with the former. This kind of conceptual shift fulfils an apologetic purpose. For with the help of such arbitrarily subsuming conflations the authors in question — from Adam Smith (who stipulates the harmonious relationship between consumption and production in his 'perfectly self-evident maxim' quoted above) to Hayek (who asserts that 'the market turns out to produce a supremely moral result', *op. cit.*, p.119) — can decree not only the 'naturalness' of capitalism but also its full harmony with the proper subjective aspirations of the individuals. Marx's analysis helps to disentangle these relations by stressing that

The simple circulation of commodities — selling in order to buy — is a *means* of carrying out a purpose unconnected with circulation, namely, the *appropriation of use-values, the satisfaction of wants.* The circulation of money as capital is, on the contrary, an *end in itself.* The expansion of value takes place only within this constantly renewed movement. The circulation of capital has therefore *no limits.* As the conscious representative of this movement, the possessor of money becomes a capitalist. His person, or rather his pocket, is the point from which the money starts and to which it returns. The expansion of money, which is the *objective basis or main-spring* of the circulation M—C—M, *becomes his subjective aim,* and it is only in so far as the appropriation of ever more and more *wealth in the abstract* becomes the sole motive of his operations, that he functions as a capitalist, that is, as *capital personified and endowed with consciousness and a will.* Use-values must therefore never be looked upon as the real aim of the capitalist; neither must the profit on any *single transaction.* The *restless never ending process of profit-making* alone is what he aims at.

Marx, *Ibid.*, pp.151-2.

[76] Naturally, such a project can only be conceived as a veritable *sea-change,* with almost forbidding difficulties. For as a project, its object to be realized lies in the *future,* but in order to be realized, it must overcome the deadening inertia of the *past* and the *present.* Before the conquest of power everything seems to be relatively simple compared to the postrevolutionary conditions, since the expectations of the future are in the forefront of attention and the temporality of the socialist project is not split. When the split takes place, it tends to assume a form whereby the present is effectively counterposed to the future and dominates the latter.

It goes without saying, there can be no successful socialist transformation without a dynamic *mediation* between the immediacy of the established order and the unfolding future, because the inherited structures of the hierarchical capital system of necessity continue to dominate the social reproduction process after the revolution. They must be radically restructured, in the course of the unavoidable mediation between present and future, if the socialist project is to have any chance of success at all. Tragically, however, the greater the difficulties of dynamic mediation and restructuring, the more the temporality of the socialist project — *future* in the process of unfolding — tends to be subverted by the inertia of past and present determinations. *States of emergency* are declared, *postponing the future* for an indefinite period ahead when, with any luck, such states of emergency will not be required any longer.

But a 'future postponed' is in fact a future denied and sooner or later completely lost even as a promise. At first some states of emergency are *imposed* on postrevolutionary societies through actual or threatened counter-revolutionary interventions, as in post-1917 Russia or in Mao's China for a number of years, becoming thereby instrumental to the fateful subversion of socialist temporality. Later, however, 'emergencies' become *routinized* and function as a most conveniently prefabricated excuse for all avoidable failures. Thus postrevolutionary societies which undergo a transformation whereby the arbitrary imposition of states of emergency becomes their 'normal' characteristic, indeed a more or less permanent feature of their socioeconomic and political interchanges — as for instance in Stalinist Russia — have *no future* (and no chance of survival in their state of suspended animation) because they have allowed themselves to be dominated again by the decapitated temporality of the capital system. They cannot be considered even 'societies of feasible socialism' — let alone 'societies of actually existing socialism' — because the only 'future' compatible with their decapitated temporality is the *restoratory* temporality of capital, bent on constructing a 'future' as some version of the *status quo ante* (e.g. capitalist 'marketization' and 'privatization').

When the routinized states of emergency (and of course the corresponding forced labour camps, etc.) cannot function any longer, the pressure for restoration — under the devastating impact of the ubiquitously visible failures, set against the lies of 'building socialism' and even of 'building the highest stage of communism' — comes from two directions. First, from the Soviet type personifications of capital who want to secure their permanent rule over labour by re-instituting legal entitlement to hereditary possession of capitalist private property. And second, ironically, it comes also from the masses of the people who continue to suffer the consequences of the failures. Ironically, because the last thing they can really expect from the restoration of capitalist 'market society' is the end of their structural domination by the capital system. Nevertheless they press for a radical change, however uncertain the envisaged conditions, because it is impossible to live in a *permanent state of emergency* leading nowhere, under circumstances when it cannot be hidden any longer by cynical propaganda exercises that the 'future postponed' is in fact the *future betrayed and abandoned*. We must return to these problems in Part Three.

[77] W. Stanley Jevons, Letter to Herbert Jevons, 7 April 1861, quoted in Wesley C. Mitchell, *Types of Economic Theory: From Mercantilism to Institutionalism,* edited by Joseph Dorfman, Augustus M. Kelley, New York 1969, vol. 2, p.16.

[78] W. Stanley Jevons, 'The Future of Political Economy', in Jevons, *The Principles of Economics: A Fragment of a Treatise on the Industrial Mechanics of Society, and Other Essays,* with a Preface by Henry Higgs, Reprints of Economic Classics, Augustus M. Kelley, New York 1965, p.206.

[79] F.Y. Edgeworth, 'Reminiscences', in A.C. Pigou (ed.), *Memorials of Alfred Marshall,* Reprints of Economic Classics, Augustus M. Kelley, New York 1966, p.66. Forty five years earlier, in the original formulation of Edgeworth's judgement over Marshall quoted above the author stated that Marshall's arguments were 'bearing, even under the garb of literature, the arms of mathematics'. (See 'On the Present Crisis in Ireland', in Edgeworth, *Mathematical Psychics: An Essay on the Application of Mathematics to the Moral Sciences,* 1881, Reprints of Economic Classics, Augustus M. Kelley, New York 1967, p.138.) However, the later version seems to be a more fitting comparison.

[80] John Maynard Keynes, *The General Theory of Employment, Interest and Money*, Macmillan, London 1957, pp.297-8.

[81] Keynes, 'Alfred Marshall, 1842-1924', in *Memorials of Alfred Marshall*, p.19.

[82] Wesley C. Mitchell, *op. cit.*, vol. 2, p.77.

[83] Edgeworth was obsessed by the thought that the condition of his native country, Ireland — 'a country convulsed by political conspiracy and economical combination' (i.e. trade unionism, p.127 of *Mathematical Psychics* quoted in note 79) — might spread everywhere, and he tried to devise a 'scientific' antidote in the form of an 'aristocratic utilitarianism' (p.80) which would guarantee 'plural votes conferred not only, as Mill thought, upon sagacity, but also upon capacity for happiness'. (p.81.) And surprise, surprise, Edgeworth's 'scientific' scheme of 'mathematical psychics' turned out to be perfectly in tune with his 'aristocratic utilitarianism', arguing that

> If we suppose that capacity for pleasure is an attribute of skill and talent (a); if we consider that production is an unsymmetrical function of manual and scientific labour (b); we may see a reason deeper than Economics may afford for the larger pay, though often more agreeable work of the aristocracy of skill and talent. The aristocracy of sex is similarly grounded upon the supposed superior capacity of the man for happiness, for the *energeia* of action and contemplation; upon the sentiment —
> Woman is the lesser man, and her passions unto mine
> Are as moonlight unto sunlight and as water unto wine. (p.78.)

For good measure, in addition to ruling class apology and male chauvinism a 'scientific' justification of *racism* is also thrown in by Edgeworth on p.131. And talking about future society, he insists that class domination and subordination must remain forever, justifying it by asserting that 'the existence of a subordinate and less fortunate class does not seem to accuse the bounty of Providence.' (p.79) These are the values sustained with undisguised class consciousness by Edgeworth's highly praised mathematical skills and 'scientific rigour'.

[84] According to Keynes

> Marshall was the first great economist *pur sang* that there ever was, the first who devoted his life to building up the subject as a separate science, standing on its own foundations, with as high standards of scientific accuracy as the physical or biological sciences.

Keynes, 'Alfred Marshall, 1842-1924', *op. cit.*, pp.56-7.

[85] Alfred Marshall, *Principles of Economics*, Macmillan, London 1959, p.487.

[86] *Ibid.*, p.489.

[87] Keynes, *Ibid.*, p.11.

[88] Edgeworth, *Mathematical Psychics*, p.51.

[89] *Ibid..*, p.54. And Edgeworth added on p.57 — as a way of reinforcing the soundness and utilitarian justification of his 'principle' — that 'some individuals may enjoy the advantages not for any amount of means but only for values above a certain amount. This may be the case with the higher orders of evolution.'

[90] W. Stanley Jevons, *The Theory of Political Economy*, Edited with an introduction by R.D. Collison Black, Penguin Books, Harmondsworth 1970, p.187.

[91] Marshall, 'Social Possibilities of Economic Chivalry', in *Memorials of Alfred Marshall*, pp.341-2.

[92] *Ibid.*, pp.345-6.

[93] *Ibid.*, p.343. Some of the Fabian socialists had no difficulty whatsoever with embracing the idea of a 'generously enlightened' (in Marshall's terms 'chivalrous') British Empire. Thus, for instance, Sidney Oliver — a far from untypical Fabian socialist, who for services rendered to the state later earned the title and position of Baron Oliver — could dedicate himself to the cause of British colonial rule throughout his life without any misgivings. After serving in Jamaica as a colonial administrator for eight years he was promoted to

the position of Governor there in 1907, and in 1924 he became the Secretary of State for India in the first Labour Government. People like the Fabian Baron Oliver could never see any contradiction between colonial oppression and exploitation and the idea of socialism. Naturally, the marginalist rejection of the Marxian theory of exploitation, together with Marshall's utopian alternatives, came as manna from heaven to them.

94 *Ibid.,* p.329.

95 Marshall, 'Co-operation', in *Memorials of Alfred Marshall,* p.229.

96 The interested reader can find a discussion of these issues in Chapter 8. of my book, *The Power of Ideology,* Harvester Wheatsheaf, London 1989, and New York University Press, 1989, pp.288-380.

97 We must return to these problems in Chapter 18.

98 Joan Robinson, *Economic Philosophy,* Penguin Books, Harmondsworth 1964, pp.58-59.

99 Marshall, 'Social Possibilities of Economic Chivalry', *op. cit.,* p.333.

100 *Ibid.*

101 In a short article entitled 'A Fair Rate of Wages' Marshall uses the term 'normal' in all sorts of combinations. At first he puts 'normal' between inverted commas, as he should, but then he goes on talking without quotation marks about 'normal earnings', 'normal rate of pay', 'normal conditions of trade', 'normal year' and 'normal rate of profit' within the space of three paragraphs. The apologetic character of this neo-classical diet of assumptions topped up with generous helpings of 'normality' becomes clear when Marshall says that 'It is then assumed as a starting point that the rate [of pay] at that time was a *fair rate,* or in economic phrase that it was the *normal rate.*'
The purpose of the whole exercise is to argue that

> It is the unfairness of bad masters which makes trades unions necessary and gives them their chief force; were there no bad masters, many of the ablest members of trades unions would be glad, not indeed entirely to forgo their organization, but to dispense with those parts of it which are most *combative in spirit.*
> (All quotations from pp.214-5 of *Memorials of Alfred Marshall.*)

Naturally, once the 'combative spirit' of the trades unions is removed, their 'legitimate' role is confined to managing the duty-bound and compliant labour force — which sees the 'fairness' of its 'normal' conditions of production and remuneration — on behalf of 'normally fair' capital. As Marshall puts it:

> *Fairness* requires a similar *moderation* on the part of the employed. ... The men *ought* in fairness to yield something without compelling their employers to fight for it.
> *(Ibid.,* p.217.)

That Alfred Marshall should reason in these terms is understandable. Significantly, however, the Minister who tried to castrate the British trades unions in Harold Wilson's Labour Government, the supposedly 'left wing socialist' Barbara Castle, addressed the issue in exactly the same terms. She published an article entitled *'The Bad Bosses Charter'* (in the *New Statesman,* 16 October 1970) when the Conservative Party took over office under Edward Heath, and enacted her own projected anti-unions laws, prepared by the same Civil Servants both in Wilson's and in Heath's Government. The only difference was that the former Labour Minister called Marshall's 'bad masters' the 'bad bosses'.

102 *Ibid.,* p.327.

103 Edgeworth, *Mathematical Psychics,* p.50.

104 *Ibid.*

105 Keynes, 'Alfred Marshall, 1842-1924', *op. cit.,* p.23.

106 Marshall, 'Mechanical and Biological Analogies in Economics', in *Memorials of Alfred Marshall,* p.318.

107 *Ibid.,* 317.

108 Keynes also fantasised that what he called 'mankind's economic problem' will be solved within one hundred years — i.e. by the year 2030 — to such an extent that the

only remaining issue will be how to manage the great material abundance and the leisure time that will go with it. And characteristically Keynes added that all this will happen 'in the progressive countries', by which of course he meant, just like his teacher Alfred Marshall, the imperialistically dominant countries. Thus Keynes, too, imagined that 'the permanent solution of mankind's economic problem' can take place in a world in which the historically given structural domination of the overwhelming majority of humankind by a handful of privileged capitalist countries can be perpetuated, and that the economic processes built on such a shaky foundation can lead to the happy Utopia of boundless abundance. See his article, 'Economic Possibilities for Our Grandchildren' (1930) in *Essays in Persuasion,* Norton & Co., New York 1963, pp.358-73.

[109] Keynes, 'Am I a Liberal?' (1925), in *Essays in Persuasion,* p.324.

[110] See A. A. Berle Jr. and Gardner Means, *The Modern Corporation and Private Property,* Macmillan, New York 1932. See also A. A. Berle, *The Twentieth-Century Capitalist Revolution,* Harcourt, Brace & World, New York 1954, as well as *Power without Property* (Harcourt, Brace & World, New York 1959) by the same author.

[111] Paul M. Sweezy, 'On the Theory of Monopoly Capitalism', Marshall Lecture delivered at Cambridge University, April 21 and 23, 1971, published in Sweezy, *Modern Capitalism and Other Essays,* Monthly Review Press, New York and London 1972, pp.31-32.

[112] See James Burnham, *The Managerial Revolution,* Indiana University Press, 1940.

[113] Maurice Merleau-Ponty, 'Paranoid Politics' (1948), in *Signs,* Northwestern University Press, Chicago 1964, p.260.

[114] See Talcott Parsons and Neal J. Smelser, *Economy and Society: A Study in the Integration of Economic and Social Theory,* Routledge & Kegan Paul, London 1956, p.253.

Against the obvious apologetic intent of the 'separation of ownership and control' thesis Baran and Sweezy rightly emphasised that a closer look at the changes that have actually taken place reveals that the exact *opposite* of what is being asserted happens to be true. For

> managers are among the biggest owners; and because of the strategic positions they occupy, they function as the protectors and spokesmen for all large-scale property. Far from being a separate class, they constitute in reality the leading echelon of the property-owning class.

Paul A. Baran and Paul M. Sweezy, *Monopoly Capital: An Essay on the American Economic and Social Order,* Monthly Review Press, New York 1966, pp.34-5.

[115] The co-authors of this book (of which, as we are told, Talcott Parsons is the 'Senior Author', hence for the sake of brevity references are given under his name) use a peculiar mode of reasoning in this respect. For at a certain point in the book we are told that thanks to the recent transformations 'The new position is consolidated by its routinization, especially by the great output of new products to a high-wage consuming public; the "new economy" has become independent both of the previous "exploitation of labour" and the previous "capitalistic control".' (*Ibid.,* p.272.) What is most peculiar here is not only the account of the miraculous transformation resulting in the postulated permanent abundance of the 'new economy', but also the fact that the notion of 'exploitation of labour' is introduced as 'previous' only at the moment of its happy disappearance, allegedly forever, from the social horizon. Earlier in the book capital and labour appear as harmoniously complementary 'factors of production', exactly as seen in neo-classical economic theory; labour is referred to as 'the input of human service into the economy in so far as it is contingent on short-term economic sanctions', and capital is treated as 'input of fluid resources into the economy contingent on decisions between productive and consumption uses.' (p.27.)

I have discussed some characteristic features of Parsonian methodology in 'Ideology and Social Science', *The Socialist Register,* 1972, reprinted in my book: *Philosophy, Ideology and Social Science,* Harvester/Wheatsheaf, London 1986, and St. Martins Press, New

York, 1986, in particular pp.21-26 and 41-53.

[116] Parsons and Smelser, *Ibid.*, p.253.

We get a good measure of the claimed *'nominal significance* of personal ownership of securities in the firm' from a news item published in the London *Economist*. It reads as follows:

John Sculley, who last month fled Apple, has been given $72 million-worth of share options by his new employer, Spectrum Information Technologies. A sixth of the options can be exercised this year.

The Economist, 13-19 November 1993, p.7.

In other words, in six years Mr Sculley can be richer, as owner/manager, by $72m-worth of shares in his new company. And all this is supposed to have no bearing whatsoever on the nature of the established socioeconomic order; the latter cannot be considered capitalist any longer, in view of the postulated happy 'separation of ownership and control' in it.

Another good example is supplied by the *Financial Times*. It has been reported in the 'Companies & Markets' section of this London paper that

Mr Peter Wood, the highest paid British company director, is to be given £24m to abandon a pay bonus scheme, which brought him £18.2m this year and has proved an embarrassment to his employer Royal Bank of Scotland. Mr Wood gained the payments, totalling £42.2m, as chief executive of Direct Line, the insurance subsidiary which he founded ... He earned £1.6m in bonus pay in 1991and £6m last year, attracting increasing public attention.

(John Gapper and Richard Lapper, 'One man's direct line to £42m', *Financial Times,* 26 November 1993, p.19.)

Thus Mr Wood became richer by £49.8m — equivalent in 1993 to 75 million U.S. dollars — in just three years. In case people might get worried that the world is in danger of running out of jelly beans, due to such potential purchasing power, they can be reassured by another passage of the same article which reveals that 'Mr Wood will invest £10m in Royal Bank shares, which he will hold for at least five years. This makes him the second largest individual shareholder behind the Moffat family, former owners of the AT Mays travel agency which Royal Bank took over.' Furthermore, 'Mr Wood will invest £1m to buy 40 percent of the equity in a new company [set up by the Royal Bank of Scotland], while Royal Bank will invest £1.5m in equity and a further £22.5m in preference shares. Mr Wood will be non-executive chairman and hold majority voting rights.' It has not been disclosed as yet what other financial vehicles Mr Wood might acquire with the remaining £38.8 millions he gained in the last three years in this world of ours in which the 'separation of ownership and control' has been so obviously and fully accomplished.

[117] Parsons and Smelser, *Ibid.*, p.285.

[118] *Ibid.*, pp.285-9.

[119] *Ibid.*, p.290. The word 'occupational' is italicized by the authors.

[120] John Kenneth Galbraith, *The New Industrial State* (1967), Pelican Books, Harmondsworth 1969, p.106.

[121] Paul M. Sweezy, *op.cit.*, p.35.

[122] Galbraith, *op. cit.*, p.100.

[123] *Ibid.*, p.80.

[124] *Ibid.*, p.14.

A recent financial scandal of massive proportions underlined again that cheating and fraudulence (for which the trusted personifications of capital must be, needless to say, adequately rewarded) belong to the normality of capitalism. As the Business Section of *The Sunday Times* reported:

The scandal surrounding Queens Moat Houses deepened again yesterday when the hotel group's delayed annual report revealed one of the directors received an annual salary of more than £1 million in both 1991 and 1992. The unnamed director, suspected to be Martin Marcus, the former deputy chairman, or even David Hersey, the former finance director, had his 1991 salary boosted to just over £1 million. This was due primarily to a bonus payment of £900,000 which had been omitted from the notes to the company's accounts of the time. The following year he received a pay increase of £170,000, taking that year's package to £1,199,000. ... After an investigation the group has released figures restating the 1991 pre-tax profit of £90.4 million as a £56.3 pre-tax loss [which amounts to a £146 million cheating and false accounting in a single year] and showing a £1 billion deficit in 1992. The annual report confirms that the company paid illegal dividends in 1991, 1992, and 1993 and breached the Companies Act and stock-exchange regulations. ... Marcus has been harshly criticized by advisers and investors for selling 1.1 million of his [clearly 'not appreciable'] Queens Moat shares in February at 57p just before the company entered its closed period, when directors are not allowed to trade. On March 31, the shares were suspended at 47.5p 'pending clarification of its financial position'. The suspension was triggered by a sudden shortfall in the group's 1992 figures which had been expected to show profits of more than £80 million. [I.e. what came to light was a discrepancy of more than £1,080 million for a single year, converting a pretended profit of more than £80 million to a loss of £1 billion. Obviously, annual remuneration amounting to £1 million — or even to £1,199,000 — for people who can produce for the company books such miraculous profit figures against the actual background of massive losses must be considered very modest indeed.]

Rufus Olins, 'Queens Moat director was paid over £1million, Profits were artificially boosted', *The Sunday Times,* 7 November 1993, Section 3, p.1.

In the same issue of *The Sunday Times* the journal's regular city columnist rightly commented on this affair:

Amid the financial carnage laid in Queens Moat's annual report and accounts for 1992, there is one eye-popping piece of information. It appears on page 51, under directors emoluments for 1992, the year when the hotel group lost £1 billion. The crucial word is 'bonus'. Yes, even in a year when the company went bust, shareholders were wiped out, and banks started fretting about how they could retrieve more than £1 billion of loans, Qeeens Moat directors earned bonuses of £1.1 million. The report does not explain how the bonuses were calculated, but whatever the method used, it stretches investors' imagination beyond breaking point to fathom what the payments were for. It makes one wonder what they would have received had the company turned in a profit.

Jeff Randall, 'In the City', *The Sunday Times,* 7 November 1993, Section 3, p.20.

[125] Galbraith, *Ibid.,* p.78.
[126] *Ibid.,* p.67.
[127] *Ibid.,* p.14.
[128] *Ibid.*
[129] *Ibid.,* p.393.
[130] *Ibid.,* p.394.
[131] *Ibid.,* p.392.
[132] *Ibid.,* p.390.
[133] *Ibid.,* p.71.
[134] *Ibid.,* p.91.
[135] *Ibid.,* pp.390-91.

We find the same sort of 'sleight of hand' when Galbraith equates the *need for information* in corporate decision making with *effective power* vested in those who *supply* the required information. This is how he argues the point:

In the industrial enterprise, power rests with those who make decisions. In the mature enterprise, this power has passed, inevitably and irrevocably, from the individual to the group. That is because *only the group has the information that decision requires*. Though the constitution of the corporation places power in the hands of the owners, the imperatives of technology and planning remove it to the technostructure. *(Ibid.,* p.106.)

This line of thought is doubly fallacious. First of all, because it postulates an automatic correlation between the production of information (and those who actually produce it) on the one hand, and power on the other. As if information (or knowledge relevant to making business decisions) could not be bought by those who yield effective power of decision making! In fact the capitalist order not only operates, as a matter of routine, on such a basis, but perfects the *division of labour* through which the products of mental labour can be bought and sold as required under the circumstances. (It is in this respect utterly grotesque to suggest that the 'industrial enterprise' of the 'entrepreneurs' required no information — supplied by other than the entrepreneur himself — before business decisions were made.) And second, because it minimizes the role of — often quite arbitrary — decision making at the very top of the 'mature enterprise'. This kind of apologetic idealization of the contemporary capitalist system — in the name of the fictitious 'technostructure', with its imaginary 'imperatives' and automatically corresponding achievements — would make it impossible for the decision makers to *act against available information* and make their companies bankrupt or bring them to the brink of bankruptcy in the process. No wonder, therefore, that Galbraith has to assert, in tune with his imaginary account of the 'mature enterprise', that 'big corporations do not lose money' (p.90). In truth a great deal of information must be cynically overruled by the real decision makers — and not by some masochistic producers or suppliers of information — before a company like Queens Moat (referred to in note 124) could chalk up a loss of £1 billion for the year 1992, or Galbraith's idealized General Motors the correspondingly much bigger losses.

[136] *Ibid.,* p.112.

[137] *Ibid.,* p.111.

[138] This is a characteristic passage to illustrate Galbraith's optimistic treatment of the subject:

It has been noted, 'the market mechanism is replaced by the administrative mechanism.' ... The foregoing refers to firms which sell most of their output to the government — to Boeing which (at this writing) sells 65 percent of its output to the government; General Dynamics which sells a like percentage; Raytheon which sells 70 percent; Lockheed which sells 81 percent; and Republic Aviation which sells 100 percent. But firms which have a smaller proportion of sales to the government are more dependent on it for the regulation of aggregate demand and not much less so for the stabilization of wages and prices, the underwriting of especially expensive technology and the supply of trained and educated manpower.

Ibid., pp.393-94.

[139] *Ibid.,* p.90. And he went on to say that 'In 1957, a year of mild recession in the United States, not one of the one hundred largest industrial corporations failed to return profit. Only one of the largest two hundred finished the year in the red. Seven years later, in 1964, a prosperous year by general agreement, all of the first hundred again made money; only two among the first two hundred had losses and only seven among the first five hundred. None of the fifty largest merchandising firms — Sears, Roebuck, A & P, Safeway, et. al. — failed to return a profit. And among the fifty largest transportation companies only three railroads, and the momentarily unfortunate Eastern Airlines, failed to make money.' *Ibid.,* pp.90-91.

[140] *Ibid.,* p.395.

[141] *Ibid.*, p.116.

[142] *Ibid.*, pp.396-7.

[143] *Ibid.*, p.397.

[144] On the active part of the prevailing productive practices of the 'advanced capitalist' system for de-skilling, and totally frustrating the creative potential of, the labour force, see Harry Braverman's fine book, *Labour and Monopoly Capital: The Degradation of Work in the Twentieth Century,* Monthly Review Press, New York 1974.

[145] 'si le journalier est miserable la nation est miserable', Diderot's entry on *Journalier* in the *Encyclopédie.*

[146] Diderot, *Supplément au Voyage de Bougainville,* in *Oeuvres Philosophiques,* edited by Paul Vernière, Garnier, Paris 1956, p.482. Diderot's italics.

By contrast to Diderot, Rousseau was anxious to defend himself against accusations that his work could be read as an attack on the sanctity of *'meum et tuum'*, asserting that 'the right of property is the most sacred of all the rights of citizenship, and even more important in some respects than liberty itself'. (Rousseau, *A Discourse on Political Economy,* Everyman edition, p.254.)

[147] Diderot, *Ibid.*, p.468.

[148] Hegel, *The Philosophy of History,* p.457.

[149] Marx, *Capital,* vol. 1, p.288.

[150] *Ibid.*

[151] Hegel, *The Philosophy of Right,* p.212.

[152] *Ibid.*, p.211.

[153] F.A. Hayek, *The Fatal Conceit: The Errors of Socialism,* p.7.

[154] *Ibid.*, pp.7-9.

[155] *Ibid.*, p.6. The word 'moral' is italicized by Hayek.

[156] *Ibid.*, p.130.

[157] *Ibid.*, p.153.

[158] *Ibid.*, p.131. Hayek adds on p.111 that 'the main beneficiaries' of the capital system are 'the members of the proletariat.' One wonders, therefore, why should he protest, on p.74, against 'The fruitless attempt to render a situation just'. If the existing order is indeed as generously in favour of the proletariat as he claims, in that case nothing should be feared by rationally formulated moral contention.

[159] *Ibid.*

[160] *Ibid.*, p.99.

[161] *Ibid.*, p.82.

[162] *Ibid.*, p.99.

[163] *Ibid.*, p.68.

[164] *Ibid.*, p.61. The quotation is from p.27 of Popper's 'Autobiography', in P.A. Schilpp, ed., *The Philosophy of Karl Popper,* La Salle, Open Court, 1974; republished, in a revised version, as *Unended Quest,* Fontana/Collins, London, 1976.

[165] Hayek, *Ibid.*, p.98.

[166] *Ibid.*, p.76.

[167] *Ibid.*, p.88.

[168] *Ibid.*, pp.118-19.

[169] *Ibid.*, p.33.

[170] *Ibid.*, p.32.

[171] *Ibid.*, p.104.

[172] *Ibid.*, p.103.

[173] Thus we are told that 'Prejudice arising from the distrust of the mysterious reaches an even higher pitch when directed at those most abstract institutions of an advanced civilization on which trade depends, which mediate the most general, indirect, remote and unperceived effects of individual action, and which, though indispensable for the

formation of an extended order, tend to veil their guiding mechanisms from probing observation: money and the financial institutions based on it.' *Ibid.*, p.101.

[174] *Ibid.*, p.104.

[175] *Ibid.*, p. 121. The quotation is from p. 60 of A. G. N. Flew's *Evolutionary Ethics,* Macmillan, London, 1967.

[176] Hayek, *Ibid.*, p.128.

[177] *Ibid.*, p.124.

[178] *Ibid.*, p.130.

[179] *Ibid.*, p.134.

[180] *Ibid.*, p.125.

[181] *Ibid.*

[182] Marx, *Economic and Philosophical Manuscripts of 1844,* Lawrence and Wishart, London, 1959, p.91.

[183] *Ibid.*, p.134.

[184] *Economic Manuscripts of 1861-63,* MECW, vol. 34, pp.398-99. Marx's italics.

[185] *Ibid.*, p.122. Marx's italics.

[186] *Ibid.*, p.128.

[187] *Ibid.*, pp.430-31. Marx's emphases.

[188] *Ibid.*, p.460.

[189] *Ibid.*, p.441. Marx's emphases.

[190] *Ibid.*, p.466. Marx's italics in the last paragraph.

[191] We shall consider these problems at length in Chapters 19 and 20. What must be stressed here is the fundamental difference between the conscious mediatory exchange of activities on the basis of a 'newly shaped social life process', and the reified, uncontrollable second order mediations of the now established order of societal reproduction.

[192] As Marx puts it, in the production process 'the commodity owner becomes a capitalist, becomes *capital personified,* and the worker becomes a *mere personification of labour* for capital.' Marx, *Ibid.*, p.399.

[193] During the May 1968 upheavals in Paris one of the posters which appeared on the wall of the Sorbonne read: 'I and You participate, He/She participates, We and You participate, They — profit.' This made the point imaginatively and succinctly, raising at the same time also the demand for putting 'imagination into power'. Alas, however, it would take much more than imagination to dislodge capital from its structurally entrenched and safeguarded position of power.

[194] Marx, 'Contribution to the Critique of Hegel's Philosophy of Law, Introduction', MECW, vol. 3, pp.182-3.

[195] *Ibid.*

[196] Marx and Engels, *Manifesto of the Communist Party,* Marx and Engels, *Selected Works,* vol. 1, p.62.

[197] See the activities of the 'Club of Rome' and in particular their famous publication, *The Limits to Growth: A Report for the Club of Rome Project on the Predicament of Mankind,* written by Donella H. Meadows, Dennis L. Meadows, Jorgen Randers and William W. Behrens III, with a Preface by William Watts, President of Potomac Associates, A Potomac Associates Book, Earth Island Limited, London 1972.

[198] *Ibid.*, p.171.

[199] True to form, also in this book the social dimension of the identified issues is avoided in the name of 'complexity', by insisting that 'the major problems facing mankind are of such complexity and are so interrelated that traditional institutions and policies are no longer able to cope with them'. (pp.9-10.) Ironically, though, the result of adopting this approach in the interest of eternalizing the rule of the capital system as we have seen the globally equilibrating aim stipulated in the report for makind is to make 'population and capital essentially stable') is that the method of computerized modelling

offered to intellectually master the claimed 'complexity and interrelatedness' can yield only self-defeating vacuity. Thus we learn in the concluding section of this 'Report on the Predicament of Mankind' that

> The report presents in straightforward form the alternatives confronting not one nation or people but all nations and all peoples, thereby compelling a reader to raise his sights to the dimensions of *the world problematique*. A drawback of this approach is of course that — given the heterogeneity of world society, national political structures, and levels of development — the conclusions of the study, although valid for our planet as a whole, do not apply in detail to any particular country or region. (p.188.)

A most helpful and reassuring conclusion indeed.

[200] See the interview with Professor Jay Forrester of the Massachusetts Institute of Technology in *Le Monde*, 1 August 1972. See also his book, *World Dynamics*, Wright-Allen Press, Cambridge, Massachusetts, 1971.

[201] Characteristically, even the feeble resolutions of the 1992 Rio de Janeiro Conference — watered down almost to the point of meaninglessness under the pressure of the dominant capitalist powers, primarily the United States whose delegation was headed by President Bush — are used only as an *alibi* for carrying on as before, doing nothing to meet the challenge while pretending to 'fulfil the obligations undertaken'. Thus we may note the shameful hypocrisy with which the British Government tried to justify in 1994 the 17.5 percent Value Added Tax imposed on domestic fuel consumption — hitting above all the poor and the low income pensioners — under the pretence of environmental concern, with reference to the Rio 'summit'. In reality this highly unpopular measure — which cynically turned the Conservative Government Party's solemn electoral pledge of tax-reduction into its diametrical opposite — was imposed in an effort to reduce the £50 billion annual budgetary deficit, without any expectation whatsoever that the increased burden of tax will reduce energy consumption and the negative consequences of continuing energy production with the same, highly polluting, methods.

[202] Daniel P. Moynihan, *Pandaemonium: Ethnicity in International Relations*, Oxford University Press, 1993, pp.168-9.

[203] In the Preface to the 1976 edition of *The Road to Serfdom* Hayek says that he is 'rather proud of the insight which made me dedicate it "To the Socialists of All Parties".' F. A. Hayek, *The Road to Serfdom*, Routledge/ARK edition, London 1986, p.viii.

[204] Hayek, *The Fatal Conceit*, p.138.

[205] Harry Magdoff, *Imperialism: From the Colonial Age to the Present*, Monthly Review Press, New York, 1978, p.183.

[206] *Ibid.*, pp.187-8.

[207] See Robert B. Reich, *The Work of Nations: A Blueprint for the Future*, Simon & Schuster, Hemel Hempstead, 1994.

[208] *Ibid.*, p.311.

[209] Robert Reich introduces the category of 'symbolic analysts' as a major part of the anticipated solution. The 'symbolic analysts' in his scheme of things are supposed to be the new dominant force in the economy. All this sounds familiar. For the function of Reich's 'symbolic analysts' is very similar to that of Galbraith's 'technostructure'. The difference being that Galbraith used to fantasise about universal 'convergence', whereas Reich is singing the praises of unproblematical 'positive economic nationalism', with equal likelihood of a positive outcome.

[210] 'Un entretien avec Renato Constantino', *Le Monde*, 8 February 1994.

The cynical way in which the sovereignty of smaller nations is treated by the dominant powers while paying lip-service to the 'principles of democracy and freedom' is clearly illustrated by the recent controversy over the imposition of U.S. military interests — in the form of 'automatic access rights to American military forces' after the abolition of bases — in the Philippines. The matter is handled under the cloak of secrecy, by saying in Washington that 'Military access agreements are generally classified on the grounds that they might be politically sensitive to the host country'. In the case of the Philippines this secret deal between the Pentagon and President Ramos is clearly against the 'host country's' constitution, repeatedly reaffirmed by its Senate. As an article by a specialist on Philippine affairs comments:

> When U.S. [military] forward deployment took the form of the bases, it served for years as a source of extensive U.S. intervention in Philippine politics, climaxing in Washington's embrace of the dictator Marcos. Could not U.S. support for forward deployment in the form of access lead to similar activity? Indeed, when access currently serves to undermine the Philippine constitution, political intervention of a subversive sort is already apparent.

Daniel B. Schirmer, 'Military Access: The Pentagon versus the Philippine Constitution', *Monthly Review*, vol. 46, no. 2, June 1994, pp. 32 & 35.

[211] Hegel, *The Philosophy of Right*, p.208.

[212] *Ibid.*, p.212.

[213] *Ibid.* Hegel must also acknowledge that the grounds (or pretexts) on which 'recognition' may be withdrawn are quite *arbitrary*, even though he prefers to use the much more palatable expression of 'inherently indeterminable'. As he puts it: 'A state through its subjects has widespread connexions and many-sided interests, and these may be readily and considerably injured; but it remains inherently indeterminable which of these injuries is to be regarded as a specific breach of treaty or as an injury to the honour and autonomy of the state.' And the rationalization and 'justification' for accepting arbitrariness as the ground of breaking international treaties is offered — with a reasoning which borders on complete cynicism characteristic of big imperialist powers — in the next sentence: 'The reason for this is that a state may regard its infinity and honour as at stake in each of its concerns, however minute, and it is all the more inclined to susceptibility to injury the more its strong individuality is impelled as a result of *long domestic peace* to seek and create *a sphere of activity abroad.*' *Ibid.*, p.214.

[214] *Ibid.*, p.213.

[215] *Ibid.*, p.222.

[216] *Ibid.*, p.214.

[217] *Ibid.*, p.213.

[218] 'Tribal feeling', *The Economist*, 25 December 1993-7 January 1994, p.13.

[219] Raymond Aron, *The Industrial Society: Three Essays on Ideology and Development*, Weidenfeld and Nicolson, London 1967, p.121.

[220] 'That other Europe', *The Economist*, 25 December 1993-7 January 1994, p.17.

[221] In this respect the unholy consensus between capital and integrated trades union leadership is highly revealing. This is well illustrated by a characteristic interview given by Paul Gallagher, the new General Secretary of the Amalgamated Engineering and Electrical Union (AEEU) — not so many years ago one of the most radical unions in Britain. In this interview Gallagher rejected the idea that the demand for a minimum wage should be pursued by the labour movement, siding with the Tory Government's repeal of the old minimum wage legislation. He insisted that

> 'The union's policy is to oppose a minimum wage', which he said had 'the potential to destroy the differential of higher paid workers.' And he went on:
> 'It is wrong to try to push John Smith [at the time of the interview the leader of the Labour Party] over this issue. It is *politically dangerous* and I hope that we are not *forced into a corner and have to make a stand.*'

('Unions told not to give Labour lists of demands', *The Independent*, 6 May 1994.)

The particular irony of all this is that the politician responsible for introducing into the statute books the law on a minimum wage in Britain, in 1909, was none other than Sir Winston Churchill. He adopted this measure, of course, in the interest of competing capitals, pressing for 'fairness' against 'unscrupulous employers'. Today all sections of capital are 'unscrupulous', and 'fairness' is defined as labour's acceptance of the dictates of the 'market economy' and of its 'rational demands'. What is most revealing is that now even the traditional trades unions policy-objectives are shelved or altogether abandoned in the interest of parliamentary political opportunism, on the basis of a ludicrous belief that capitulation to capital's dictates will counteract the ongoing trend of de-skilling and casualization of the labour force. Thus, Gallagher concluded his interview by stating that

> 'There is a danger that employers will try and de-skill the job and spread skills around, which will make workers less flexible.'

As if the objective imperatives of global capitalist development could be quixotically wished out of existence by the reassurances of trades union 'reasonableness'.

[222] 'Don't bank on it', *The Economist,* 25 December 1993-7 January 1994, p.16.

[223] *Ibid.*

[224] 'Tribal feeling', *The Economist,* 25 December 1993-7 January 1994, p.14.

[225] Baran and Sweezy, *Monopoly Capital,* pp.52-53.

[226] Engels, 'Outline of a Critique of Political Economy', in the Appendix of Marx, *Economic and Philosophic Manuscripts of 1844,* Lawrence and Wishart, London, 1959, pp.194-5.

It is also relevant to stress here that Marx's admiration for this work by the young Engels is not confined to his own early works. In fact he quotes the passage in which Engels talks about 'a natural law based on the unconsciousness of the individuals' in one of the most important sections of *Capital* (volume 1.), concerned with 'The Fetishism of Commodities and the Secret Thereof'.

[227] To prove that he means business in his firm approach to troublesome smaller nations, U.S. Democratic Senator Daniel Patrick Moynihan — 'the most powerful man in the Senate', as he is often called — in June 1994 threatened North Korea with bombing.

[228] 'The fall of big business', principal Leader of *The Economist,* 10th.-17th. April 1993, p.13.

[229] Alex Trotman is British-born Chairman of the American transnational Ford Corporation.

[230] 'Ford prepares for global revolution', by Andrew Lorenz and Jeff Randall, *The Sunday Times,* 27 March 1994, Section 3, p.1.

[231] *The German Ideology,* p.45.

[232] The interested reader can find a detailed analysis of these problems in my essay on 'Contingent and Necessary Class Consciousness', in *Philosophy, Ideology and Social Science,* pp.57-104. Here I can only briefly touch upon a few points.

In his discussion of the subject Marx makes the distinction between labour being a 'class-in-itself' (that is the 'class as against capital') and a 'class-for-itself', which is defined as 'self-constituting universality', opposed not only to bourgeois particularism but to any particularism at all. For it is inconceivable for labour to emancipate itself by simply reversing the earlier terms of domination and installing itself as the new particularism kept in dominance through the exploitation of its former rulers. Social reproduction could not conceivably function on such a narrow basis.

This categorial distinction had its origin in Hegel who talked about the being 'in-and-for-itself' constituting itself through 'self-mediation' and thus being 'posited for itself as the universal'. (Hegel, *The Science of Logic,* Allen & Unwin, London 1929, Vol. 2, p.480.) Under these criteria the bourgeoisie cannot become a 'class-for-itself'. This is, on the one hand, because it stands in an insuperably antagonistic relation to the proletariat, and therefore the condition of 'self-mediation' stipulated by Hegel is missing. And on the other hand, it cannot 'posit itself as the universal', because it is constituted as a necessarily exclusivistic social force, in the self-contradictory form of 'partiality universalized', i.e. partial self-interest turned into the general organizing principle of society. Accordingly, the bourgeoisie is *particularism par excellence:* i.e. the dominant section of the former 'Third Estate' becoming the 'estate in-and-for-itself' — the principle of the Estates, 'definite and limited privilege', universalized as the governing principle of society and as the expropriation of all privilege for itself (e.g. the conversion of feudal land ownership into capitalistic agriculture) — but a class-in-itself only, not a class-for-itself. The bourgeoisie is a class which acquires its class character by subsuming the various forms of privilege under its own mode of existence, becoming thus a class of the estate type, or a class of all estates, arising out of them and carrying their principle to its logical conclusion.

This means that capital can never overcome its *negativity* and permanent dependency on labour which it must antagonistically oppose (negate) and at the same time dominate. Both in the material structures of capital as a system of social metabolic control, and in the historically specific state formation of this reproductive order, the category of 'in-itself' (their definition 'as against the other', i.e. against the antagonist) absolutely prevails. The 'positive/self-sustaining' ground of their constitution is a *pseudo-positivity:* a structure which secures the domination and exploitation of the antagonist by always reproducing the antagonism. Thus both in the material reproductive structures of capital and in its state formation the categories of 'in-itelf' and 'for-itself' mystifyingly coincide in such a way that the actuality of the particularistic 'in-itself' masquerades as the universally beneficial and universally realizable (cf. 'equality of opportunity', etc.), but in reality in substantive terms absolutely unrealizable, 'for-itself'. This perverse coincidence and camouflage creates the deceptive semblance of positivity despite the unalterable negative substance. At the same time it hides, through the false appearance of 'free' material reproductive, and 'sovereign' political, structures and institutions, its real nature. As a result, the parasitic oppressor and exploiter of productive labour can claim for itself the privileges for being 'the creator of wealth', and for its 'democratic state' that the latter defends and enforces the 'general' or 'universal interest'.

However, all this ceases to be a tenable solution when the absolute limits are reached. For the inherent negativity of even the most gigantic monopolies — 'as against other monopolies' and 'as against labour' both at home and abroad — cannot turn itself into a happily reconciling and universally all-embracing positivity. Nor can the political enforcer and defender of the transnationally expansionary capital interests — the national state — turn itself into a positive universal force. This is why the creation of a 'World Government' must remain an unrealizable dream today and in the future no less than two hundred years ago.

[233] *The Limits to Growth*, p.130. See also *Thinking about the Future: A Critique of The Limits to Growth*, edited by H.S.D. Cole, Christopher Freeman, Marie Jahoda and K.L.R. Pavitt, Chatto & Windus for Sussex University Press, London, 1973.

[234] *The Limits to Growth*, p.150.

[235] *Ibid.*

[236] *Ibid.*p.195.

[237] Marx, *Grundrisse*, pp.334-5.

[238] *The Limits to Growth*, p.149.

[239] Andrew Lorenz, 'Britain vets U.S. rivals to Eurofighter', *The Sunday Times*, 10 July 1994, Section 3, p.1.

[240] *Ibid.*

[241] Marx, *Grundrisse*, pp.527-8.

[242] Engels, *The Origin of the Family, Private Property and the State. In the Light of the Researches by Lewis H. Morgan*, Lawrence & Wishart, London, 1972, p.138.

[243] *Ibid.*, p.145.

[244] August Bebel, *Society of the Future*, Progress Publishers, Moscow, 1971, p.114.

[245] *Ibid.,* p.115.

[246] *Ibid.,* p.116. ('Time' is italicized by Bebel.)

Alas, just like the good old Fabian imperialists, German social democrats (even on the left, like Bebel) could not see anything wrong with the whole concept of 'civilizing colonization' either, projected on the basis of the happily embraced technological determinism of the capital system. They questioned only the adopted means, arguing that when their 'new society' is established

the civilizing mission will be carried out only with friendly means, which will make the civilizers appear to the barbarians and savages not as enemies, but as *benefactors.* Intelligent travellers and scientists have long since learned how successful this approach is.

Ibid., p.127. ('Benefactors' is italicized by Bebel.)

[247] Marx, *Economic and Philosophic Manuscripts of 1844,* pp.100-101.

[248] Engels, *The Origin of the Family,* p.135.

[249] Joyce Kolko, *Restructuring the World Economy,* Pantheon Books, New York, 1988, p.315.

Another recent study pointed out that 'over the past twenty years, many U.S. corporations shifted manufacturing jobs overseas. The creation of this "global assembly line" became a crucial component of the corporate strategy to cut costs. In their new locations, these companies hired woman workers at minimal wages, both in the third world and in such countries as Ireland. Poorly paid as these jobs were, they were attractive to the thousands of women who were moving from impoverished rural villages into the cities in search of a better life for their families. But in the United States, millions of workers lost their jobs as the result of capital flight or corporate downsizing. When workers lose their jobs because their plants or businesses close down or move, or their positions or shifts are abolished, it is called worker *displacement.* Over 5 million workers were displaced between 1979 and 1983, and another 4 million between 1985 and 1989. In both periods, women were slightly less likely to lose their jobs than men of the same racial-ethnic group. ... The overall result was that even though women lost jobs to capital flight and corporate downsizing, they did so at a slower rate than men. In fact, the share of manufacturing jobs going to women rose between 1979 and 1990. Women, in other words, claimed a *growing share of a shrinking pie.'* (Teresa Amott, *Caught in the Crisis: Women and the U.S. Economy Today,* Monthly Review Press, New York, 1993, pp.58-60.)

[250] Baran and Sweezy, *Monopoly Capital,* p.171.

[251] *Ibid.*

[252] Kant, 'Theory and Practice Concerning the Common Saying: This May Be True in Theory But Does Not Apply to Practice', in *The Philosophy of Kant: Immanuel Kant's Moral and Political Writings,* ed. by Carl J. Friedrich, The Modern Library, Random House, New York, 1949, pp.417-18.

[253] *Ibid.,* p.423.

[254] *Ibid.,* p.421.

[255] *Ibid.,* p.420.

In the actually existing capital system the role of parliamentary vote changes according to the changing historical circumstances. Despite the original Enlightenment illusions attached to the all-conquering positive power of 'one person, one vote', there have been (and still there are) many ways of actually disenfranchising the masses of the working people, without taking away from them the right to vote, once conceded. In any, case, it is possible to manipulate also the formal voting system when the material constraints of the established mode of social metabolic reproduction so demand. Characteristically, the long established 'democratic constitutional principle' of 'one person, one vote' is already being challenged, in different ways in different countries, under rising pressure from capital's material base. Thus, for instance:

Lee Kuan Yew, Singapore's elder statesman, is campaigning to amend the principle of one person, one vote, and give parents more power at the ballot box. People between 35 and 60 who are married with children would get an additional vote under the former Prime Minister's plan. He said that the idea was to give more say at the polls to those who have heavier responsibilities. ... In his view, the radical change might be necessary in 15 to 20 years because the population of Singapore is growing old, and could give rise to a huge army of elderly who might be tempted to pressure the government for *welfare support*. By 2030 a quarter of the population will be over 60, compared with about 10 percent now. Eight working people support one of the elderly now, and by then the ratio would be 2.2 to 1.

Kenneth Whitting, 'Lee wants extra vote for parents', *The Times*, 28 July 1994, p.14.

[256] Kant, *Ibid.*

[257] *Ibid.*

[258] Rousseau, *The Social Contract*, Everyman Edition, p.19. But in the same sentence Rousseau also asserted — to be sure, before the French Revolution — with biting radicalism that under the existing order *'equality is only apparent and illusory; it serves only to keep the pauper in his poverty, and the rich man in the position he has usurped.'* By contrast, as we have seen, Kant makes 'the poor depend on the rich', without asking how this dependency came about and how it could be done away with. That in reality the poor produce the wealth of the rich, and thus the dependency in question is depicted upside down, cannot count even in the most enlightened philosophical justifications of the bourgeois universe.

[259] Kant, *Ibid.*, p.416.

[260] Engels, *Ibid.*, pp.135-36.

[261] Kant, *Ibid.*, pp.423-24.

[262] Kant, 'Idea for a Universal History with Cosmopolitan Intent', in volume cited in note 252, p.120.

[263] Kant, 'Theory and Practice ...', p.419.

[264] *Ibid.*

[265] Hayek, *The Road to Serfdom*, p.57.

[266] *Ibid.*, pp.151-52.

[267] *Ibid.*, p.59.

[268] *Ibid.*, p.52.

[269] *Ibid.*, p.57.

[270] *Ibid.*, p.151.

[271] *Ibid.*, p.152.

[272] Marx, Capital, vol. 1, pp.72 & 75.

[273] Kant, 'Religion within the Limits of Reason Alone', in volume cited in note 252, p.382.

[274] *Ibid.*

[275] Hayek, *The Road to Serfdom*, p.60.

[276] *Ibid.*

[277] A measure of the total vacuity of the constantly proclaimed and never even minimally actualized 'can' is the widening of the gap between rich and poor, asserting itself despite all promises of liberalism and traditional social democracy. For a brief history and critique of these developments, from Bernstein to post-Second World War idealizations of the 'welfare state', see Chapter 8 of *The Power of Ideology*.

Recent data only underline the absurdity of ever expecting solutions through 'gradual improvements' within the framework of the capital system, when in fact everything pointed in the direction of sharpening inequality. Even the customary falsification of politically unwelcome figures by governments cannot hide this disconcerting truth.

The gap between rich and poor has widened [in Britain] under Conservative rule with a record one in three living in what Brussels defines as poverty, according to new government figures. The income of the poorest 10 percent of the population dropped 17 percent between 1979 and 1991, while the income of the wealthiest 10 percent rose 62 percent. ... The figures, in the latest *Households Below Average Income* report, show that the number of people living below the European poverty line, that is with an income less than half of the average, rose from 5 million in 1979 to 13.9 million in 1991-92. Another 400,000 people had gone below the poverty line since the last report, 200,000 of them children. In 1979, 1.4 million children lived below the poverty line, rising to 3.9 million in 1990-91 and 4.1 million a year later. ... In cash terms, the average income of the poorest 10 percent of the population was down from £74 to £61 [i.e. $91] a week. ... The figures are based on data from the Government's Family Expenditure Survey.

Jill Sherman, 'Child poverty trebles in 12 years while rich get richer', *The Times,* 15 July 1994, p.4.

[278] Hayek, *Ibid.,* p.53.

[279] *Ibid.,* p.61.

[280] *Ibid.,* p.62.

[281] *Ibid.,* p.54.

[282] *Ibid.,* p.52.

[283] *Ibid.,* p.59.

[284] *Ibid.*

[285] MECW, vol.3, p.186. Translation modified.

[286] MECW, vol.5, p.46

[287] Margaret Randall, *Gathering Rage: The Failure of Twentieth Century Revolutions to Develop a Feminist Agenda,* Monthly Review Press, New York, 1992, p.37.

[288] *Ibid.* p.134.

[289] *Ibid.,* pp.168-69.

[290] George Bernard Shaw, *Everybody's Political What's What?,* Constable and Company, London, 1944, p.56.

[291] *Ibid.,* p.57.

[292] Jill Sherman, 'Child poverty trebles in 12 years while rich get richer', *The Times,* 15 July 1994.

[293] 'Rational Rationing', *The Times,* 29 July 1994.

[294] The 'universal sauce' of tasteless cooking.

[295] 'Doctors let elderly die by denying flu vaccine', *The Sunday Times,* 9 October 1994.

[296] *Ibid.*

[297] *Ibid.*

[298] Marie Colvil and Adrian Levy, 'Revealed: Mark Thatcher's secret profit from £20 billion arms deal', *The Sunday Times,* 9 October 1994.

[299] *Ibid.* The paper also reminds its readers that 'On January 15, 1984, just as officials were putting the finishing touches to the [£20 billion Saudi arms deal] contract, the *Observer* newspaper broke a story detailing how Mark Thatcher had three years earlier allegedly won a contract in Oman for Cementation International on the back of a visit by his mother.' This was another occasion when Hayek's Companion of Honour was 'batting for Britain'.

The Economist joined in the recent controversy with its own revelations. To quote: The tactics used by Mr Thatcher to make his fortune have cause alarm in Whitehall for more than a decade. On at least two occasions in the 1980s, senior officials remonstrated with Mrs Thatcher, delivering a warning that her son's activities were in danger of causing great embarrassment to her government. ... In 1984, senior officials read the riot act directly to Mr Thatcher himself about the dangers of trading on his mother's name. Shortly afterwards, Mr Thatcher moved to the United States and based his business there. Despite this exile, Mr Thatcher's extravagant life-style, with houses in Dallas and London and a travelling butler, has continued to attract attention. Party officials tend to shake their heads in despair at what they see as a mother's blind spot. In 1991 the late Sir Y.K. Pao, a Hong-Kong shipping magnate, was taken aback to receive a fund-raising call from the former prime minister's son on behalf of his mother's newly set-up Thatcher Foundation. 'It's pay-up for Mumsie time', the astonished shipping magnate was reportedly told.

('Mumsie's boy', *The Economist*, October 15th-21st 1994, p.32.)

Reminding knighted Hong-Kong shipping magnates of the cash value of the political patronage dispensed by a prominent member of the Thatcher family while Mrs Thatcher was in office was obviously Mark Thatcher's way of 'batting for Britain', proving once again the prescriptive truth of the old English proverb that 'charity begins at home'.

[300] 'Nuclear fission', *The Economist*, 3 September 1994, p.42.

[301] MECW, vol.5, pp.75-76.

[302] See Philippe Buonarroti, *Conspiration pur l'égalité dite de Babeuf,* Brussels, 1828, p.297.

[303] H.G. Wells, *The Work, Wealth and Happiness of Mankind,* Heinemann, London, 1932, p.557.

[304] *Ibid.,* p.558.

[305] *Ibid.,* pp.561-62.

[306] 'Kömíves Kelemenné', in *Hét évszázad magyar versei,* Szépirodalmi Könyvkiadó, Budapest, 1954, pp.26-28.

[307] Marx, *Grundrisse,* pp.605-607.

[308] T.R. Malthus, *An Essay on the Principle of Population,* Everyman's Library, J.M. Dent & Sons, London, n.d., vol. 1, p.8.

[309] *Ibid.,* p.5.

[310] *Ibid.,* vol. 2, p.262.

[311] *Ibid.,* p.187.

[312] *Ibid.*

[313] *Ibid.,* p.190.

[314] *Ibid.,* p.192

[315] *Ibid.,* p.191.

[316] *Ibid.,* p.193.

[317] *Ibid.*

[318] *Ibid.,* pp.260-61.

[319] *Ibid.,* vol. 1, p.10.

[320] *Ibid.,* p.11.

[321] *Ibid.,* vol. 2, p.242.

[322] *Ibid.,* p.51.

[323] *Ibid.,* pp.68-69.

[324] *Ibid.,* p.65.

[325] *Ibid.,* p.66.

[326] *Ibid.,* p.64.

[327] *Ibid.,* pp.49-50.

[328] Both quotations from *Ibid.,* p.249.

[329] *Ibid.,* p.250.

[330] *Ibid.*

[331] *Ibid.,* p.252.

[332] *Ibid.,* p.242.

[333] *Ibid.,* pp.242-43.

[334] *Ibid.,* p.66.

[335] *Ibid.,* p.50.

[336] Both quotations from *Ibid.,* p.21.

[337] We find a striking example for this blindness on p. 60 of volume 2. In a chapter added to the *Essay* Malthus, confidently expecting the corrective impact of his 'natural law' during the years of recession, wrote that

it will be seen probably, when the next returns of the population are made, that the marriages and births have diminished and the deaths increased in a still greater degree than in 1800 and 1801; and the continuance of this effect to a certain degree for a few years will retard the progress of the population, and combined with the increasing wants of Europe and America from their increasing riches, and the adaptation of the supply of commodities at home to the new distribution of wealth occasioned by the alteration of the circulating medium, will again give life and energy to all our mercantile and agricultural transactions, and restore the labouring classes to full employment and good wages.

However, in a footnote appended in 1825 to this prediction Malthus had to admit that the effect he was anticipating on account of his 'principle of population' did not materialize:

It appeared, by the returns of 1821, that the scarce years of 1817 and 1818 had but a slight effect in diminishing the number of marriages and births, compared with the effect of the great proportion of plentiful years in increasing them; so that the population proceeded with great rapidity during the ten years ending with 1820. But this great increase of the population has prevented the labouring classes from being so fully employed as might have been expected from the prosperity of commerce and agriculture during the last two or three years.

Thus, even through this patched-up and confused account it transpires that the predictive value of Malthus's 'natural law' proved to be nil. But, of course, the author of a 'one-variable' theory could not take on board the various social factors, implicit even in his account, which underlined the need for a very different kind of explanation to be given to what was happening and why the Malthusian anticipations had failed, and indeed had to fail. All he could do, again, was to reiterate the validity of his 'principle', coupled with the arbitrary counter-factual conditional proposition according to which had his expectation been realized (which it had not) then the labouring classes would have been more fully employed and better remunerated (which they were not). The failure of Malthus was not simply a matter of misreading a given historical contingency. It concerned his entire theoretical framework. For the idea (central to the Malthusian system) — that a smaller growth in population is bound to solve the perceived problems, bringing also 'full emloyment and good wages' to the labouring classes (and if it does not, that is only because there is 'a greater than expected increase in population'), under the conditions of the capital system (which must maximize profit in its drive for expansion and accumulation) — is not simply untrue in relation to some passing historical circumstances. It is utterly grotesque as a matter of the necessary structural determination of the established order (at times unwittingly acknowledged by Malthus himself, as we have seen above), notwithstanding the contorted counter-factual conditional propostions of its past and present apologists.

[338] To quote Malthus:

These considerations show that the virtue of *chastity* is not, as some have supposed, a forced produce of artificial society; but that it has the most real and solid foundation in nature and reason; being apparently the only virtuous means of avoiding the vice and misery which result so often from the principle of population. *(Ibid.,* p.161.)

The difficulty of *moral restraint* will perhaps be objected to this doctrine. To him who does not acknowledge the authority of the Christian religion, I have only to say that, after the most careful investigation, this virtue appears to be *absolutely necessary,* in order to avoid certain evils which would otherwise result from the general laws of nature. According to his own principle, it is his duty to pursue the greatest good consistent with these laws. *(Ibid., pp.163-64.)*

As it appears, therefore, that it is in the power of each individual to avoid all the evil consequences to himself and society resulting from the principle of population by the *practice of a virtue* clealy dictated to him by the light of nature, and expressly enjoined in revealed religion. *(Ibid., p.166.)*

To expect the solution of the explosive antagonisms of the capital system through 'moral restraint' and the 'practice of virtue' — and in particular from 'chastity', on account of its mechanical direct link to the 'principle of population' — reveals the total vacuity of the Malthusian apologetics. Just like in the writings of Malthus's present-day descendants, the inherently *social* character of the identified negative problems, in their *historical specificity,* is ignored and replaced by pseudo-natural determinations fictitously complemented by the good work of 'absolutely necessary' virtue. Even the ultimate sanction of capital — war if the other forms of antagonistically asserting the dominant interests fail — is directly attributed in this primitive mechanical discourse to the 'natural' cause of population growth. The latter is said to be directly responsible for 'an insufficieny of room and food' *(Ibid., p.165.)*, just like in Hitler's laments over the insufficiency of 'Lebensraum', to be counteracted by the acceptance of Malthus's 'truth' and the 'absolutely necessary virtue' to impose external constraints upon population increase in conformity to 'the truth', whereafter 'It might be fairly expected that war, that great pest of the human race, would, under such circumstances, soon cease to extend its ravages'. *(Ibid., p.164.)* It is a most peculiar reasoning which can take seriously the idea that, just because wars could and did destroy many people, the people thus destroyed should be characterized as *'redundant population'* *(Ibid., p.165.)* and decreed to be the *cause* of wars, to be counteracted by the virtue of chastity.

[339] *Ibid., p.187.*

[340] *Ibid.*

[341] In this spirit Walt Rostow decreed that 'There is every reason to believe, looking at the sensitivity of the political process to even small pockets of unemployment in modern democratic societies, that the sluggish and timid policies of the 1920s and 1930s with respect to the level of employment will no longer be tolerated in Western societies. And now the technical tricks of that trade — due to the Keynesian revolution — are widely understood. It should not be forgotten that Keynes set himself the task of defeating Marx's prognosis about the course of unemployment under capitalism; and he largely succeeded.' W.W.Rostow, *The Stages of Economic Growth: A Non-Communist Manifesto,* Cambridge University Press, 1960, p.155.

[342] Galbraith, *The New Industrial State,* p.233.

[343] Mészáros, *The Necessity of Social Control,* pp.54-55. See pp.889-90 in the present volume.

[344] Daniel Singer, 'Europe's Crises', *Monthly Review,* vol. 46, No. 3, July-August 1994, p.93.

[345] Tony Allen-Mills, 'French jobs chaos provokes spirit of revolt', *The Sunday Times,* 6 March 1994. The same article reported that 'One riot police commissioner observed: "We are opposed by demonstrators who feel lost. Unlike those of 1968 (the year of the Paris student revolt) they have no hope, whether they are farmers, workers or fishermen." ... Police unions have warned that their men cannot be expected to control politically motivated explosions. Gloom was heightened by yet another report, by the Centre for Study of Revenues and Costs (CERC), which found that 11.7m of the 25m-strong workforce was in a situation of "social and economic fragility". Of these, the CERC concluded, 7m people had jobs but were either having difficulties making ends meet or were poorly integrated in French society. Travelling to Lyon on Friday, Balladur insisted that France had to "invent something other than the economic, social, political and administrative model it has relied on for the last half a century".'

[346] Michael Kallenbach, 'Streik rule rises in jobless Germany', *The Sunday Times*, 6 February 1994.

[347] Ian Burrell and David Leppard, 'Fall in crime a myth as police chiefs massage the figures', *The Sunday Times*, 16 October 1994. On the manipulation of unemployment figures see also Phil Murphy, 'Real unemployment: 10%, 25% or 60% ?', in *Living Marxism*, August 1994, pp.16-18.

[348] 'Jobless Europe', *The Economist*, 26 June 1993, p.19.

[349] 'Virtual jobs in Motown', *The Economist*, 26 March 1994, p.102.

[350] Staughton Lynd, 'Our kind of Marxist: From an interview with Staughton Lynd', *Monthly Review*, vol. 45, No.11, April 1994, pp.47-49.

[351] W.W. Rostow quoted in note 241.

[352] 'Time to bury Keynes?', *The Economist*, 3 July 1993, pp.21-22.

[353] Matthew Lynn, 'Redundancies focus on the white-collar worker', *The Sunday Times*, 20 March 1994.

[354] Andrew Grice and Liz Lightfoot, 'Axe falls on 50,000 civil service jobs', *The Sunday Times*, 10 July 1994.

[355] 'Jobless Europe', *The Economist*, 26 June 1993, p.19.

[356] 'Virtual jobs in Motown,' *The Economist*, 26 March 1994, p.102.

[357] Peter Cohen, 'Sweden: the model that never was', *Monthly Review*, vol. 46, No. 3, July-August 1994, p.56.

[358] *Ibid.*, p.57.

[359] *Ibid.*, p.56.

[360] 'Virtual jobs in Motown', *The Economist*, 26 March 1994, p.107.

[361] Alice Thompson, 'Blair will keep union laws intact', *The Times*, 9 November 1994.

[362] Robert Graham, 'Pragmatism may prevail', *Financial Times*, 25 October 1994.

[363] *Ibid.*

[364] Anthony Kuhn, '268 million Chinese will be out of jobs in a decade', *The Sunday Times*, 21 August 1994.

[365] Baran and Sweezy, *Monopoly Capital*, pp.175-76.

[366] Magdoff and Sweezy, 'Notes from the Editors', *Monthly Review*, vol. 46, No. 6, November 1994.

[367] John Gray, 'Into the abyss?', *The Sunday Times*, 30 October 1994.

[368] *Ibid.*

[369] *Ibid.* See also John Gray's book, *Beyond the New Right*, Routledge, London, 1994

[370] Quoted in 'The new protectionists: In defence of voters' jobs', *The Sunday Times*, 30 October 1994. See also, Sir James Goldsmith, *The Trap*, Macmillan, London, 1994.

[371] See for instance David Lane, 'Rolling back the boundaries of the state', *Financial Times*, 25 October 1994.

PART TWO

HISTORICAL LEGACY OF THE SOCIALIST CRITIQUE 1:

THE CHALLENGE OF MATERIAL AND INSTITUTIONAL MEDIATIONS

IN THE ORBIT OF THE RUSSIAN REVOLUTION

> *'There is no alternative.'*
> Margaret Thatcher

> *'We can do business with Mr Gorbachev.'*
> Margaret Thatcher

> *'There is no alternative.'*
> Mikhail Gorbachev

CHAPTER SIX

THE TRAGEDY OF LUKÁCS
AND THE QUESTION OF ALTERNATIVES

6.1 Accelerating time and belated prophecy

6.1.1

TOWARDS the end of 1988 Hungary witnessed a most unusual publishing event. For as a great novelty of the festive season a 218 pages long volume by Lukács appeared in the popular collection of Magvető Kiadó, priced at just 25 florins, i.e. at under 25 pennies. The name of the popular series: 'Accelerating Time'; and the title of the book: *The Present and Future of Democratization*.

What made this event rather peculiar was the fact that Lukács's book — now celebrated in the party press — was written no less than *twenty years* prior to its publication, between the Spring and Autumn of 1968. Strangely, though, it was billed in the dying days of 1988 as if the writer's ink had just dried on a manuscript concerned with a suddenly emerging issue.

Reading the book today, it comes as no great surprise that at the time of writing his soul-searching study on the imperative to democratize *all* postrevolutionary societies Lukács felt that — in the light of the Russian military intervention in Czechoslovakia in August 1968, which put a tragic end to the hopes associated with the 'Prague Spring' — many things that even in the recent past were kept in the realm of political taboos had to be urgently subjected to public scrutiny.

After completing his work the author, somewhat naively, submitted his manuscript to the party's central committee and asked for permission to publish it. Notwithstanding past disappointments, he continued to nourish the hope (and illusion) that he would be allowed to intervene in an effective way, with his politically quite outspoken study, in the troubled process of redefining the meaning of contemporary socialism. However, under the circumstances of the so-called 'Brezhnev doctrine' — painfully underlined in Prague by the tanks of the Red Army — his request was categorically rejected. In fact *The Present and Future of Democratization* was suppressed for two long decades, despite all rhetorics of reform and reconciliation under the post-1956 regime in Hungary. Lukács's work — passionately pleading for urgent democratization — was unceremoniously brushed aside by the selfsame party hierarchy which at the end of 1988, in the midst of the country's no longer deniable economic and social crisis, seemed to be so anxious to give it political prominence and popular diffusion.

The change of attitude towards *The Present and Future of Democratization* at the end of 1988 reminded all those who followed the events in Hungary in 1956 that, in the aftermath of the twentieth congress of the Soviet party, an allegedly long lost political text by Lukács — the internationally path-breaking *Blum Theses* of 1928-29, denounced by the Stalinist leadership — was 'found' again as a result of Khrushchev's secret speech on the Stalin era. In the midst of the then erupting political turmoil they were suddenly 'discovered' in the Hungarian party's secret archives and were debated in the Summer of 1956 at an important meeting of the Petöfi Circle.[1] In much the same mould, in 1988, measures like the sudden decision to publish *The Present and Future of Democratization* signalled the desire of the Hungarian party to come to terms, in its own half-hearted way, with the demands of 'accelerating time'.

As a hopelessly belated tribute, on the last day of 1988 Lukács's book was reviewed in a full-page article in the central newspaper of the party, *Népszabadság*, under the title: 'Belated Prophecy? György Lukács's Testament'.[2] Moreover, a few months later a member of the Politburo, Rezsö Nyers (who in the meantime had become President of the renamed party) published an article entitled: 'The Present and Future of Restructuring'. In this article Nyers positively embraced not only the title of Lukács's long suppressed book but also declared that

> Of the communist movement I deeply feel as my own from the distant past the line which can be defined through the names of Jenö Landler and György Lukács, and to a certain extent József Révai, a line which then spread and became intensified and, at the Seventh Congress of the Comintern, became the new concept of a Popular Front policy. ... I fully agree with György Lukács, though I did not accept his views for a long time — and when I have to choose a past, I am thinking in Lukács's spirit.[3]

However, such awakening of party leaders in Hungary and elsewhere in East Europe occurred far too late to have a credible impact. Within a few months from the official announcement of the intended reorientation of politics in accordance with the growing demand for democratization, all hope that the 'wind of change' sweeping the region could be contained within the limits sketched out in Lukács's essay on *The Present and Future of Democratization* turned out to be a painfully obvious historical anachronism. 'Accelerating time' — by no means the speciality of the East, no matter how unevenly it tends to assert itself in different periods of history — took a most dramatic turn.

TO be sure, historical time — emanating from the dynamics of social interchanges — cannot possibly flow at a steady pace. Given the greatly varying intensity of social conflicts and determinations, we may experience historical intervals when everything seems to grind to a complete standstill, stubbornly refusing to move for a prolonged period of time. And by the same token, the eruption and intensification of structural conflicts may result in the most unexpected concatenation of apparently unstoppable events, accomplishing within days incomparably more than in decades beforehand.

In this sense, after a period of relative immobility, historical time quickened its pace in the last years of the decade, engulfing in 1989 a much greater part of the planet than East Europe alone. Yet the grave structural problems of the dominant capitalist countries could be pushed out of sight under the circumstances. This could be done despite the fact that the problems in question include not only the astronomical U.S. internal and external debt but also the ubiquitous protectionist practices which carry the danger of a major trade war as the sobering counterpart to the idealized – and in our own times nowhere in the world really existing — 'free market'.

Likewise, the irreconcilable conflict of interest between the capitalistically advanced countries and those of the structurally dependent 'Third World' could not be allowed to disturb the celebratory euphoria. Thus, disregarding the far from trouble-free conditions of the Western world under all its major aspects, the dramatic events of 1989 unfolding in the East could be conveniently used as the justification for painting a rosy, triumphalist picture of the health and future prospects of the capitalist system as such.

6.1.2

BY coincidence the year 1989 happened to be the bicentenary of the French Revolution. However, this year will be remembered as a major landmark in its own terms. For there can be no doubt that even in our most eventful century no single year — ever since the 'ten days that shook the world' in 1917 — produced the same quickening of the pace of historical change as 1989. Indeed, the reverberations of the 1989 earthquakes are likely to be felt not only for a long time to come but everywhere. For major historical events and upheavals cannot be kept in isolated compartments in our globally intertwined contemporary world.

It is no exaggeration to say that with 1989 a long historical phase — the one initiated by the October Revolution of 1917 — came to its end. From now on, whatever might be the future of socialism, it will have to be established on radically new foundations, beyond the tragedies and failures of Soviet type development which became blocked very soon after the conquest of power in Russia by Lenin and his followers.

We must return to this question in the last chapters of the present study. Now the point is to indicate very briefly Lukács's dedication to the cause of socialist transformation over a period of more than fifty years, both as a leading politician for a while and — after his expulsion from the field of direct politics in 1929 — as a profoundly committed intellectual.

The trajectory of Lukács's participation in the international communist movement can only be characterized as a tragic one. It must be considered tragic not simply because the present course of development in the former 'societies of actual socialism' runs directly counter to the ideals he advocated and lived for. Many people share that fate with him. Nor could his tragedy be seen in the same light as that of Rosa Luxemburg, who entered the historical stage with her radical ideas far too early, remaining desperately out of phase with her time, and even with ours. (It is in that sense that, in contrast to Lukács, we can recognize in her fate the tragedy of someone whose time has *not yet* come.[4])

Lukács's tragedy was indeed of a very different kind. It consisted in the politically and intellectually representative internalization of that blocked development from which he expected the actualization of his ideals ever since the outbreak of the October Revolution. Having made his choice in 1917 he could never contemplate assuming a radically critical stance towards it without betraying the principles which had led him to making that choice. Tragically, however, remaining faithful to the perspective adopted when he abandoned, out of profound conviction, the privileged class into which he was born left him in the end virtually no margin of action as a politically committed intellectual.

Lukács's predicament was all the more painful in view of the fact that even the little room that remained from 1928-29 to the end of his life for his active intervention in cultural and political matters was considered far too much to be tolerated by the party bureaucracy. Although he never wavered in his dedication to the cause which he embraced in 1917, party officialdom repeatedly subjected him to fierce attacks and to the indignity of enforced self-criticisms, suppressing for as long as it could the evidence of his vital concerns, not only the *Blum Theses* and *The Present and Future of Democratization* but even his final 'Political Testament'.

It must be stressed in this context that — contrary to all accusations of opportunistic accommodation and privilege-seeking capitulation to Stalinism levelled against him — Lukács's internalization of postrevolutionary experience was a thoroughly authentic one. Far from being the product of a limited political conjuncture, it had deep roots in the Hungarian philosopher's intellectual past, going back to its earliest phases.

Nothing illustrates better the personal authenticity of Lukács's orientation than two of his last interviews which only very recently were allowed to be published. He gave these tape-recorded interviews on the 5th and 15th of January 1971, when he already knew for certain that he had at best only a few months to live, because of the very advanced stage of cancer that ended his life on 4th June of that year. He tried to clarify in these interviews not only his relationship to the party, as its militant for more than five decades, but also the political perspective from which he judged the policies pursued by the leadership and the need to change some of the criticized policies in order to avoid the kind of upheavals witnessed in Poland at the time.

Given the circumstances under which the interviews were conducted, it would be quite absurd to suggest that someone in the proximity of death — of which he was fully aware — should be motivated by the need to adjust his perspective in the interest of personal accommodation and the reward of privileges. Yet, in arguing his case with utter conviction, Lukács continued to subscribe to the legitimacy of the institutionalized — and in effect most paralyzing — division of labour between politicians and intellectuals in post-revolutionary society, stressing several times in the course of the interviews that he was 'no politician' but merely an intellectual concerned with the interest of culture and ideology. Moreover, he responded to all major issues raised in the interviews by spelling out in relation to them essentially the same perspective that animated his writings for decades.

The internalization mentioned above remained as clearly in evidence in the January 1971 interviews as in his writings way back to the early nineteen thirties. Solutions to the identified problems were envisaged *'from within'* the blocked development which he criticized. And all this from a dying man to whom party privileges and favours could have no meaning whatsoever. There had to be much more fundamental reasons for the maintenance of this perspective—no matter how problematical in some respects — than those advanced by Lukács's adversaries and detractors not only in the past, when he was still alive, but even in recent years.

As it happened, despite the willingly accepted limiting constraints which are clearly in evidence in the January 1971 interviews, the critical references to the policies pursued by the Hungarian party proved to be quite inadmissible by the leadership even as late as the end of 1988, when *The Present and Future of Democratization* was greeted as 'György Lukács's Testament'. Indeed, they were considered dangerously 'revisionist' even when the new President of the party insisted, as we have seen above, that he now unreservedly identified himself with Lukács's spirit.

The dying philosopher's interviews — which were made in fact at the request of the party, with the promise of unaltered early publication — had to remain buried in the secret archives for another sixteen months after the end of 1988. They were deemed publishable only after it became obvious that the Hungarian party, whatever its name, had to hand over the reins of power to oppositional political forces, as a consequence of its shattering electoral defeat. This is how we were in the end allowed to read — the second time within two years — 'György Lukács's Political Testament',[5] published in the theoretical organ of the party, *Társadalmi Szemle:* a journal from which Lukács was banished for many years of his life.

6.2 Search for 'autonomous selfhood'

6.2.1
AS mentioned already, the internalization of postrevolutionary developments had deep roots in Lukács's intellectual past. In philosophical terms it had a great deal to do with the way in which he conceived, right from the beginning of his literary career, the individual's conditions of fulfilment in his relationship with supra-individual forces.

This is how the young Lukács spelled out in one of his seminal essays, 'The Metaphysics of Tragedy' (1910), a lifelong preoccupation:

> The miracle of tragedy is a form-creating one; its essence is *selfhood,* just as exclusively as, in mysticism, the essence is self-oblivion. The mystical experience is to suffer the All, the tragic one is to create the All. ... The self stresses its selfhood with an all-exclusive, all-destroying force, but this extreme affirmation imparts a steely hardness and autonomous life to everything it encounters and — arriving at the ultimate peak of pure selfhood — finally cancels itself out. The final tension of selfhood overleaps everything that is merely individual. Its force elevates all things to the status of destiny, but its great struggle with the self-created destiny makes of it something supra-personal, a symbol of some ultimate fate-relationship. In this way the mystical and the tragic modes of experiencing life touch and supplement one another. Both mysteriously combine life and death, *autonomous selfhood and the total dissolving of the self in a higher being.* Surrender is the mystic's way, struggle the tragic man's; the one, at the end of his road, is absorbed into the All, the other shattered against the All.[6]

Understandably, the young Lukács — born into the high bourgeoisie as the son of a very rich and politically powerful banker — could not isolate himself from the individualism dominant in the cultural debates of the age. However, he felt most uneasy about the pitfalls of individualism and tried to conceptualize a viable synthesis between the individual and the supra-individual forces, as well as between the platonically supra-historical/essential/everlasting and the historical principles.

The merits of *true individuality* (which he always wanted to preserve and enhance, even when he could only talk about it in what he called an 'aesopic language') were highlighted by the author of 'The Metaphysics of Tragedy' as follows:

> Tragedy is the becoming-real of the concrete, essential nature of man. Tragedy gives a firm and sure answer to the most delicate question of platonism: the question whether individual things can have idea or essence. Tragedy's answer puts the question the other way round: only that which is individual, only something whose individuality is carried to the uttermost limit, is adequate to its idea — i.e. is really existent. That which is general, that which encompasses all things yet has no colour or form of its own, is too weak in its universality, too empty in its unity, ever to become real. ... The deepest longing of human existence is the metaphysical root of tragedy: the *longing of man for selfhood,* the longing to transform the narrow peak of his existence into a wide plain with the path of his life winding across it, and his meaning into a daily reality.[7]

As to the inescapable historical dimension of human existence, the young Lukács tried to reconcile it with platonic essentialism in this way:

> History appears as a profound symbol of fate — of the regular accidentality of fate, its arbitrariness and tyranny which, in the last analysis, is always just. Tragedy's fight for history is a great war of conquest against life, an attempt to find the *meaning of history* (which is immeasurably far from ordinary life) in life, to extract the meaning of history from life as the true, *concealed sense of life.* A sense of history is always the most living necessity; the irresistible force; the form in which it occurs is the force of gravity of mere happening, the irresistible force within the flow of things. It is the necessity of everything being connected with everything else, the *value-denying necessity;* there is no difference between small and great, meaningful and meaningless, primary and secondary. What is, had to be. Each moment follows the one before, unaffected by aim or purpose.[8]

Thus the meaning of history could only be deciphered according to the young Lukács through the good services of tragedy and its extremely paradoxical 'fight for history'. For only the latter could promise to extract the meaning of history from life itself as the 'concealed sense of life', and doing that against the force of history described as 'value-denying necessity'.

The feasibility of success of such an enterprise was only postulated in 'The Metaphysics of Tragedy'. No indication was given how it could be accomplished in actuality. Indeed, the terms of Lukács's analysis pointed in a direction diametrically opposed to the desired synthesis.

Reminiscent of Max Weber's irrationalist conception of history and its concomitant 'personal demons' (that is, the purely subjective and with one another absolutely irreconcilable valuational guides of the self-oriented subjects), the irrationality of the individuals' pursuit of their truly essential objectives was starkly set against the irrational reality of history. Thus the young Lukács could offer nothing but dichotomies and paradoxes as solutions, and an altogether bleak picture of what the postulated realization of the individuals' longing for the wholeness of life and for the authenticity of selfhood in the end really amounted to:

> History, through its *irrational reality,* forces pure *universality* upon men; it does not allow a man to express his own idea, which at other levels is *just as irrational:* the

contact between them produces something alien to both — to wit, universality. Historical necessity is, after all, the nearest to life of all necessities. But also the furthest from life. The realization of the idea which is possible here is only a roundabout way of achieving its essential realization. (The said triviality of real life is here reproduced at the highest possible level.) But the whole life of the whole man is also a roundabout way of reaching other, higher goals; his deepest personal longing and his struggle to attain what he longs for are merely the *blind tools of a dumb and alien taskmaster*.[9]

But how could one resolve the paradox that what is the nearest to life is also the furthest from it? Could one find meaning in history which did not appear as a mysterious 'force of gravity' asserting itself through the meaningless turmoil of particular 'happenings' and revealing an intelligible order to the individuals only when everything is irretrievably buried in the past? How could the apparently irreconcilable opposition between value and historical actuality be overcome? Was it the unavoidable predicament of humanity that those who reach the height of self-fulfilment and realize 'the longing of man for selfhood' should be 'shattered against the All'? How could one rescue the individuals engaged in their struggle for the wholeness of life — which they are said to be equally longing for — from being dominated by an irrational universality, and from the fate of being debased at the same time to the condition of a blind tool in the hands of an alien taskmaster? Could one envisage mastering history not in abstractly hypostatized, universalistic terms but in such a way that the personality of the individuals involved in the enterprise of authentic self-fulfilment should find genuine outlets for its proper and in the real world sustainable actualization?

These questions could not be formulated and answered by Lukács before *History and Class Consciousness* in which he worked out his famous synthesis of Hegel and Marx and redefined the formerly abstract aspiration for authentic personality in relation to the cause of human emancipation. Nevertheless, the tragic vision of the connection between historical necessity and the struggle for authentic selfhood outlined in 'The Metaphysics of Tragedy' provided the foundation for his conceptualization of these matters when he embraced Marxism at the end of the first world war, and in an important sense — which we shall see in the course of this study — it never left him.

6.2.2

SIGNIFICANTLY, the way in which Lukács turned around 'the most delicate question of platonism' — by boldly asserting that the problem of essence must be subsumed under that of individuality conceived as the only really existent, anticipating thereby a central theme of 20th century existentialism — was in the spirit of the individualistic preoccupations of the age. This happened to be the case notwithstanding the fact that the young Lukács wanted to define his position in relation to the culturally dominant forms of individualism from a critical distance while preserving what he considered to be the valid core of such concerns.

Accordingly, *universality* acquired an extremely negative connotation in his vision, becoming synonymous with what Hegel called *'abstract universality'*. Likewise the idea of *unity*, defined in terms of the all-encompassing 'general', could only have a sharply negative connotation in his conceptual framework. For the universality of the 'general' appeared to the author of 'The Metaphysics of Tragedy' as *'too weak'* and its unity *'too empty'*.

In complete contrast to the rejected abstract universality, 'colour', 'form', and 'concreteness' — in their intricate relationship to the role assigned by the young Lukács to tragedy — occupied the pole of positivity in his conceptual spectrum. In this sense, the 'essential nature of man' had to be characterized by him as *'concrete':* a determination which in its turn could only be made intelligible by the author of *Soul and Form* as arising from the claimed metaphysical power of 'form-creating tragedy'.[10]

However, all this sounded irredeemably mysterious. In fact Lukács made no attempt at all to hide the mysterious character of the identified relations and processes. For one thing, he described as *irrational* not only the sombre reality of tyrannical, universality-imposing history, but even its antipode, the true idea of 'concrete-essential man'. As to the positive force of tragedy, its 'form-creating' intervention, too, had to be called a *'miracle'*.

The fact that Lukács's conception of rationality could contain without inconsistency as its key terms of reference the 'irrational reality of history' (together with the 'just as irrational' attempts by the individuals to pursue against the tyrannical irrationality of history the true idea of man), the 'miracle of tragedy', and the 'mystical experience', spoke for itself, indicating the ultimate untenability of the young philosopher's system. For although the way in which Lukács pursued his quest for viable solutions in 'The Metaphysics of Tragedy' clearly identified some major existential challenges facing the individuals, it simultaneously also introduced an immense tension into what was offered by him as a rational explanatory framework. A framework which wanted to make philosophically intelligible and convincing the author's existential concerns but could not do so without repeatedly appealing to the far from explanatory authority of mystery.

Indeed, 'The Metaphysics of Tragedy' characterized the role of tragedy, as well as the mystical experience itself, by a common problematic. This was their — only on the surface opposite — relationship to what really decided everything in the author's eyes: the ethical absolute of selfhood. Only by conferring upon both tragedy and the mystical experience their substantive common determination could Lukács sustain — reciprocally, through the assertion of their profound communality — the meaning and legitimacy of each taken separately, no matter how sharp and mutually exclusive might have appeared at first sight their differences to the uninitiated observer. This is why in the end his analysis had to culminate in the assertion that both of them 'mysteriously combine life and death, autonomous selfhood and the total dissolving of the self in a *higher being'*.[11]

To be sure, what we were offered by Lukács in 'The Metaphysics of Tragedy' and in the other essays of *Soul and Form* conceived in the same vein was a powerful vision, despite its inherent tensions. Indeed, the power and attractiveness of this vision to all those who shared the author's uneasy individualistic standpoint derived precisely from the way in which its inherent tensions were not hidden from sight by Lukács but appeared openly proclaimed and combined into the tragic vision of a complex and humanly authentic whole. No straightforward intellectual argument could significantly alter the suggestive power of this vision in the eyes of those who shared the social perspective from which Lukács's youthful theoretical synthesis had arisen. To notice the problematic aspects of the latter required the appearance of some motivation for 'stepping outside' the social horizon which animated its search for answers compatible with the limits of this horizon, as in fact it came about for the author a few years later.

Naturally, very different rules apply in this respect to the readers who happen to share a given social standpoint and unquestioningly identify themselves with its theoretical articulations, and to the creative intellectual of stature. For the latter must sooner or later confront the inner tensions of his own vision in order to work out a humanly and intellectually more tenable solution to them. By contrast the non-resolution of the tensions and contradictions identified by the philosopher might in fact provide considerable comfort and reassurance to his readers who spontaneously perceive in their own experience not only the contradictions of their social predicament but also the apparently inescapable inertia that goes with those contradictions.

As far as Lukács was concerned, his constant appeals in a purportedly rational explanatory framework to the miracle of the tragedy and to the corollary idea of the mystical experience was one of the two major — at the time quite insurmountable — tensions which tended to rupture his early system. The other was the absence of the historical dimension from it, notwithstanding all references to a — metaphysically transubstantiated — history.

The unique configuration of the powerfully suggestive and the ultimately untenable elements which one could see in Soul and Form was all the more paradoxical in view of the fact that the mystical constituents of the young Lukács's system had at their roots a clearly identifiable, no matter how unconscious, rational determination. For the objective intent of his theory was not a desire to champion mysticism. Rather, it was to put into relief some major existential problems which, given the absence of the required objective historical parameters from his perspective, Lukács could only highlight at this stage of his intellectual development in the form of a timeless metaphysical discourse. After all, by the time when the young Lukács had articulated his tragic vision in Soul and Form, the pursuit of historical temporality had been more or less openly abandoned by the intellectual spokesmen of the class with which he still identified himself despite his slowly emerging but as yet vague and objectless ethical rebellion.

Thus, the challenge to overcome the ethical impotence of timeless metaphysical discourse carried with it the need to escape from the confines of the selfsame social determinations which produced the abandonment of genuine historical temporality even by the outstanding liberal thinkers of the epoch. This could not be envisaged without a radical valuational shift — i.e. a truly fundamental change — as regards the intellectual's social standpoint from which theoretical syntheses become feasible.

AS things stood at the time of writing 'The Metaphysics of Tragedy', the vagueness and ensuing impotence of Lukács's ethical rebellion could be recognized in the way in which he combined 'form' with 'ethics'. Notwithstanding his 'longing' for genuine and humanly fulfilling solutions — and, significantly, 'longing' was one of the most frequently used categories of the young Lukács's essays — he could only derive from the arbitrarily decreed, merely verbal identity of form and ethics a paralysing and resignatory stalemate, instead of an invitation to committed and effective action in the real world. Thus we were told in *Soul and Form* that

> Form is the highest judge of life ... an ethic; ... The validity and strength of an ethic does not depend on whether or not the ethic is applied. Therefore only a form which has been purified until it has become ethical can, without becoming blind and poverty-stricken as a result of it, *forget the existence of everything problematic and banish it forever from its realm.*[12]

The qualifying aside on not becoming 'blind and poverty-stricken' sounded utterly hollow: yet another unrealizable *fiat,* even if proclaimed with the voice of genuine but impotent concern and not that of bad faith. For an ethic that can forget the existence of everything problematic and banish it forever from its realm inevitably condemns itself not only to being blind and poverty-stricken but also to total irrelevance.

To resign oneself permanently to living within the confines of such a vision — a veritable blind alley if ever there was one — was therefore conceivable only in a world in which nothing happened, but not in the real world. The fact that Lukács acknowledged at least in the form of an aside the contradiction between the objectless and inapplicable ethic which he advocated, and the danger of its blind and poverty-stricken futility, showed that he had already begun to acquire awareness of how untenable in terms of his own objectives the system expounded in *Soul and Form* really was.

The dilemmas and existential challenges identified by Lukács in 'The Metaphysics of Tragedy' — some very real problems, crying out for a break with the constraints of the adopted metaphysical discourse and calling instead for a socially specific and historically rooted assessment of what was at stake, precisely in order to bring to the fore that genuine *concreteness* which the author considered to be synonymous with the *essential* — helped him to choose later a very different intellectual path. They pointed well beyond Lukács's original solutions, although much had to be changed before the more radical questions, which were only implicit in the essays of *Soul and Form,* could be clearly articulated, let alone adequately answered by the Hungarian philosopher.

6.2.3

AS a next major step forward, in *The Theory of the Novel* — written in 1914 and 1915 — Lukács's very problematical ethical rebellion acquired a more tangible and in its intent radical frame of reference, even if for the time being only a 'purely utopian' one according to the retrospective judgement of the author. (It was utopian because 'nothing, even at the level of the most abstract intellection, helped to mediate between subjective attitude and objective reality',[13] as he put it in 1962.)

Nevertheless, by unhesitatingly rejecting — in sharp contrast to his friend Max Weber — the 'great war', and reacting to the turmoil caused by it in the spirit of Fichte's condemnation of the present as *'the age of absolute sinfulness',* Lukács intensified his ethical rebellion in such a way that he could justifiably claim later on that

The Theory of the Novel is not conservative but subversive in nature, even if based on a highly naive and totally unfounded utopianism — the hope that a natural life worthy of man can spring from the disintegration of capitalism and the destruction, seen as identical with that disintegration, of the lifeless and life-denying social and economic categories.[14]

As mentioned earlier, the inner logic of the young Lukács's conceptual framework and the tensions manifest in 'The Metaphysics of Tragedy' tended to break up his system. The intellectual challenge to overcome the tensions of this system in accord with its immanent logic was very important for Lukács's subsequent development. However, the decisive element in this respect was constituted by the irruption of reality, in the form of the global conflagration itself, into his self-referential world of 'pure form' in which 'forgetting the existence of everything problematic' could be contemplated in all seriousness.

The war greatly accelerated the process of Lukács's earth-bound theoretical self-definition, producing in *The Theory of the Novel*

a conception of the world which aimed at a fusion of *'left'* ethics and *'right'* epistemology, ontology, etc. ... a left ethic oriented towards radical revolution coupled with a traditional-conventional exegesis of reality.[15]

Understandably, therefore, the new vision of *The Theory of the Novel* — which marked in Lukács's intellectual reorientation not only a transition from Kant to Hegel but also 'a "Kierkegaardization" of the Hegelian dialectic of history'[16] — could not bring with it the solution of his dilemmas and paradoxes. It could represent no more than a somewhat more viable point of departure for later journeys in his complicated course of intellectual development.

Nevertheless, *The Theory of the Novel* signalled a major advance over *Soul and Form*, even if — because of the unsustainability of its perspective, due to the contradiction between the author's abstract ethical imperatives and his uncritical diagnosis of the fundamental structural parameters of the society against which he wanted to rebel — it had to remain unfinished, soon to be overtaken by the unfolding historical events. But even so, *The Theory of the Novel* constituted a major advance in Lukács's development. For the underlying desire of this work was to enhance the rationality of the author's explanatory framework by combining the ethical and political radicalism he aspired at with an empirically sustainable conception of history: a qualitatively new challenge for the Hungarian philosopher.

It was the possibility of realizing the latter, practically viable synthesis that Lukács saw appearing on the horizon, two years after writing the last few lines of *The Theory of the Novel*, with the outbreak of the October Revolution. He embraced the perspective of purifying fire and radical transformation implicit in the revolution with boundless enthusiasm, since he was convinced that it represented the embodiment of his earlier 'longing' for a way out of the crisis. A way out this time not in the form of the 'pure revelation of purest experience',[17] and not even through the adventures of the Kierkegaardized Hegelian 'World Spirit', but through the conscious intervention of a socially tangible historical agency in the actual historical process.

Naturally, this reorientation could not mean simply turning one's back to one's own past. Many of the important themes articulated by the young Lukács continued to resurface in his subsequent writings; some of them as positively redefined and living concerns, whereas others as negative obstacles, pinpointed by the politically committed intellectual in order to be fought and genuinely superseded. In this sense his lifelong battle against *'irrationalism'*, for instance, was not the detached outsider's unproblematical rejection of a major trend of modern cultural/intellectual development, but an anguished critique that happened to be simultaneously also the author's self-critique. It focussed attention again and again — both in their old and in their constantly re-emerging new forms — on the intellectually most tempting ways in which irrationalistic pseudo-solutions and evasions could be substituted for much needed practical answers: temptations which Lukács himself had experienced, no less than any other intellectual, from the inside.

At a more complex plane, the tragic vision of his early works remained — in a 'transcended/preserved' (aufgehoben) form — the structuring core of Lukács's later writings. As such it greatly contributed to the representative significance of a lifework conceived 'between two worlds' whose author never ceased to struggle with the dilemmas arising from the 'categorical imperative' of socialism and the awesome difficulties of its historical realization.

6.3 From the dilemmas of SOUL AND FORM to the activist vision of HISTORY AND CLASS CONSCIOUSNESS

6.3.1

LUKÁCS'S *History and Class Consciousness* had to be not only a critique of the alienating determinations of capitalist society but, equally, a reassessment of the vision spelled out in his own early writings. For an intellectual of substance cannot simply empty himself with every change of the wind of cultural/political fashion and accommodation. Real intellectual growth cannot be other than an organic — retentively superseding and deepening — process, notwithstanding the qualitative changes that can and must go with the writer's redefinition of his or her relationship to the turbulent dynamics of history. Changing one's position by hopping from one *tabula rasa* to another, without even attempting to justify the abandonment of earlier professed beliefs and the proclamation of newly claimed certainties (which often are just as easily abandoned whenever convenience demands) can add up to nothing but unprincipled vacuity.

Lukács's adoption of the Marxian perspective under the impact of the war and of the ensuing revolutions — not only in Russia but in Hungary as well: a revolution in which he wholeheartedly participated — was authentic and creative. It could not come to theoretical fruition without reformulating the central tenets and preoccupations of his early works in relation to the newly identified historical potentialities.

The postrevolutionary conceptual and axiological shift carried with it in some respects the complete overturning of Lukács's terms of reference as articulated in *Soul and Form* and in *The Theory of the Novel*, although decidedly not the abandonment of their implicit or explicit substantive concerns. Without giving due weight to the organic determination of 'continuity in discontinuity' in Lukács's development it would be quite impossible to understand the perspective expressed in his first Marxian synthesis, *History and Class Consciousness*.

On a crucial issue, concerned with the strategic objective of overcoming the deadly inertia of the given sociohistorical determinations, Lukács both reiterated some elements of his earlier vision (including their positive or negative value-associations) and radically redefined them through the way in which they were now situated in the socially activist totalizing conception of *History and Class Consciousness*. To take one characteristic example, this is how the Hungarian philosopher critically redefined and reintegrated his youthful preoccupation with 'inwardness' and with the 'pure revelation of purest experience' in the centre-piece of *History and Class Consciousness*, his celebrated essay on 'Reification and the Consciousness of the Proletariat':

> ... the union of an *inwardness,* purified to the point of *total abstraction* and stripped of all traces of *flesh and blood,* with a *transcendental philosophy of history* does indeed correspond to the *basic ideological structure of capitalism.*[18]

Through such categorial continuity some of the vital constituents of Lukács's early vision were retained while others had to be rejected. And, of course, even those which were retained in the new synthesis have acquired a qualitatively different meaning by being situated within a very different conceptual network. For in the passage we have just seen Lukács made a major shift from the negative connotation given in 'The Metaphysics of Tragedy' to *history* as such to the historically qualified condemnation of the capitalistically oriented 'transcendental *philosophy* of history'. In other words, the negated target was now character-ized by Lukács as a tendentious philosophical conception that arises not from subjective theoretical mistakes or distortions (which would be in principle cor-rigible), nor indeed from the metaphysically determined defectiveness of history itself (which would be in principle absolutely insurmountable), but—as a mat-ter of man-made and thus humanly alterable necessity — from reflecting the innermost nature and historically concrete articulation of the given social order.

This is how it became possible to retain in *History and Class Consciousness* the value-association of 'abstract universality' and its corollaries with negativity, and that of 'flesh and blood' (or in other contexts: substantive 'wholeness' and 'concreteness' as opposed to inessential and naturalistic 'fragmentariness' and 'immediacy') with positivity. The former, negative set of values was expected to be completely done away with in the course of the ongoing historical transfor-mations, and the latter, positive set, to be actualized through the socially and politically specified historical enterprise advocated by the author.

Moreover, the condemned phenomena were not rejected by Lukács as dis-embodied values and timeless metaphysical existents — as they tended to be in the early essays, particularly in those of *Soul and Form* — but as objective structural determinations 'corresponding to the basic ideological structure of capitalism'. The problems he tried to come to terms with in *Soul and Form* acquired thereby a qualitatively new dimension. For seeking solutions on the plane of 'inwardness', no matter how authentic in its subjective intent and rigorous in its strive for the 'pure revelation of purest experience', could have no validity in Lukács's new perspective. Likewise, the utopian rejection of capital-ism in *The Theory of the Novel* — in the form of his naive dismissal of the social and economic categories in general — had to be radically reexamined in the light of actual historical experience and from the point of view of the advocated, materially feasible, alternatives. Without this kind of investigation of the relationship between the 'basic ideological structure of capitalism' and the most abstract forms of consciousness emanating from the latter there could be in his view no chance of producing a valid critique of the ruling ideology: a task considered by Lukács absolutely vital to the historical enterprise of emancipation.

Thus, according to the author of *History and Class Consciousness*, not only 'inwardness' and 'soul' but also, and indeed most importantly, the category of *'form'* had to be given a demystified, materially grounded meaning. All this had to be done not only in order to make truly intelligible what he called the ideological structure of capitalism but also to irreversibly deprive that structure of its suffocating effectiveness.

6.3.2

THIS complex of problems was spelled out very clearly in a passage of *History and Class Consciousness* in which Lukács's critique of his former close friend, Ernst Bloch, contained also a radical redefinition of his own key categories as originally formulated in *Soul and Form* and in *The Theory of the Novel*. The author of *History and Class Consciousness* summed up his newly acquired position as follows:

> When Ernst Bloch claims that this union of religion with socio-economic revolution [in the revolutionary sects, e.g. Thomas Münzer and his followers] points the way to a deepening of the 'merely economic' outlook of historical materialism, he fails to notice that his deepening simply by-passes the real depth of historical materialism. When he then conceives of economics as a concern with objective things to which *soul and inwardness* are to be opposed, he overlooks the fact that the real social revolution can only mean the restructuring of the *real and concrete* life of man. He does not see that what is known as economics is but the *system of forms* defining this real life. The revolutionary sects were forced to evade this problem because in their historical situation such a restructuring of life and even of the definition of the problem was objectively impossible. But it will not do to fasten upon their weakness, their inability to discover the Archimedean point from which the whole of reality can be overthrown, and their predicament which forces them to aim too high or too low and to see in these things a sign of greater depth.[19]

As we can see, Lukács here adopted — characteristically in his own way — the great Marxian insight that the basic categories of thought are 'forms of being' (*Daseinsformen*) in terms of which the actual historical dynamic of the given socioeconomic complexes, as well as the constitution of their correponding ideological structures and forms of consciouness, can and must be dialectically understood. Inevitably, therefore, the categories of 'soul and inwardness' had to be put in their place in this materially grounded totalizing vision, signalling a radical departure from Lukács's earlier discourse. For the crucial question — how to restructure the *'real and concrete* life of man' — had to be given a new meaning in virtue of the fact that the adopted Marxian synthesising theoretical framework itself conferred a new meaning on the category which sustained all the others in the young Lukács's original conceptual universe, namely the category of *form*.

Through this practically oriented reassessment undertaken in *History and Class Consciousness* Lukács's category of form had lost its formerly mysterious character, in that its meaning became synonymous with an emphatically non-mechanistic conception of economics as the foundation of social being. Understood in that sense, it was the historically qualified *'system of forms'* that had to be considered of central importance — and not the vague generality of form as such, as adopted from Plato's system. For the *historically concrete* system of forms was said to '*define real life*' through the inescapable material intermediary of economics. Consequently, in Lukács's new vision there could be no question of 'restructuring the real and concrete life of man' without adequately mastering the complex network of actual determinations as crystallized in the historically identifiable system of forms. In other words, emancipation could not be envisaged in the realm of 'soul and inwardness' but only through 'the real social revolution' which implied the conscious control of the objectively given 'system of forms' by men in their real life. Thus the notion of 'Archimedean point' — which must be seized in its strategic specificity in order to gain control over the whole — acquired a sociohistorically tangible meaning for Lukács by becoming synonymous with 'the system of forms', conceived not as a set of abstract philosophical categories but as the crucial *Daseinsformen* of contemporary capitalist society.

At the time of writing *Soul and Form* and *The Theory of the Novel* the philosophical conceptions of Lukács and Bloch had a great deal in common. Indeed, in *The Theory of the Novel* Lukács put forward some ideas which a few years later appeared also among the main tenets of expressionism championed by Bloch. All this, however, changed fundamentally with the parting of the ways of the two friends after the October Revolution. Lukács could no longer put up with the constraints which the categories of his early writings imposed upon him; nor could he express his socially specific concerns in terms of the 'left ethics and right epistemology' of *The Theory of the Novel*. Ernst Bloch, by contrast, did not significantly alter his position in these respects.[20] Their major differences, which we have seen in the last quotation from *History and Class Consciousness,* figured prominently in their confrontation over expressionism in the 1930s,[21] setting the tone of polemics against Lukács in German literary and philosophical circles also for the future. Understandably, therefore, Lukács later characterized the debate on expressionism and realism in which he was condemned — with a peculiar kind of argument — for having departed from his youthful affinity with the expressionist approach as 'a somewhat grotesque situation in which Ernst Bloch invoked *The Theory of the Novel* in his polemic against the Marxist Georg Lukács'.[22]

As far as Lukács was concerned the choice was made irrevocable towards the end of 1917. There could be no way back to the world of *Soul and Form,* and not even to the more earth-bound but not much less ahistorical vision of *The Theory of the Novel*. In the turmoil of the unfolding revolutions he committed himself for life not only to the Marxian perspective, but simultaneously also to what he considered to be its only feasible vehicle of realization, the vanguard party. From now on all dilemmas and challenges, first strikingly articulated in the famous early volumes, had to be redefined in the spirit of historical materialism not in the abstract, but as closely tied to the instrumentality of the party. Lukács's tragedy was that the scope of his emancipatory project became more and more frustrated by the demands which the institutional/instrumental inertia of the party went on imposing, in ever greater degree, on the adopted theoretical framework under the prevailing historical circumstances.

6.3.3

THE activist character of Lukács's new vision was evident in the way in which he resolved for himself in a short time after 1917 the ethical concerns expressed in his earlier writings, without abandoning in the slightest his intense moral commitment.

At the time of writing *Soul and Form* he forcefully argued in favour of the necessary purification of form 'until it has become *ethical'*.[23] Yet, as we have seen above, he wanted to keep the 'purified' and at the same time strangely 'ethicized' form far away from 'everything problematic', condemning thereby the whole enterprise to futility.

The new orientation acquired in the closing stages of the war coinciding with the eruption of the Russian revolution offered to Lukács a way out of this impasse. For he could intensify his ethical concerns and link them to clearly identifiable objectives within the framework of the Marxian conception of forms — the forms of historically developing social being. This vision offered to him a solution also to the difficult question of the meaning of the intellectual's work or, as he put it, the 'intellectual leadership of society'. This is how he summed up the issue in 'Tactics and Ethics':

> It is at this point that the epistemological question of the leadership of society arises, which in our view only Marxism has shown itself able to answer. No other social theories have managed even to pose the question unambiguously. The question itself is twofold, even if both parts point in only one direction. First, we have to ask: what must be the nature of the forces moving society and the laws which govern them so that consciousness can grasp them and human will and human objectives can intervene in them significantly? And secondly: what must be the direction and composition of human consciousness so that it can intervene significantly and authoritatively in social development.[24]

Following on from this way of formulating the possibilities of active intervention in the social process, in the next paragraph the seminal orienting principles of Marxian theory were described by Lukács as all directly centred on the role of consciousness,[25] reaching the conclusion that 'Intellectual leadership can only be one thing: the process of *making social development conscious'*.[26] Moreover, the model of consciousness used by Lukács was 'man's *moral knowledge* of himself, e.g. his sense of responsibility, his conscience as contrasted with the knowledge of the natural sciences, where the known object remains eternally alien to the knowing subject for all his knowledge of it'. Thus he could argue that in accordance with this view of consciousness 'the distinction between *subject* and *object* disappears, and with it, therefore, the distinction between theory and practice. Without sacrificing any of its purity, impartiality and truth, *theory becomes action, practice'*.[27]

In the light of his newly assumed position Lukács became convinced that the earlier tension (and indeed contradiction) between 'left ethics' and 'right epistemology' had been fully resolved. Now his activist vision, modelled on moral consciousness, enabled him to talk about 'truth' and the 'system' in a radically different way. By contrast in the past he could only imagine 'longing for the system',[28] admitting at the same time 'the ultimate hopelessness of all longing'.[29] Understandably, therefore, in the essays of *Soul and Form* he reached the conclusion, with great resignation, that 'there is no system anywhere, for it is not possible to live the system'.[30] He counterposed to the system the ideal of essay writing which he described as 'an art form'[31] — an idea rejected with derision by the Marxist Lukács, — embracing the judgement of the older Schlegel on Hemsterhuys that essays were really 'intellectual poems'.[32] And when in the following years, before committing himself to the socialist cause, he dreamed about writing one day a major ethical work and twice embarked on the long journey of producing a systematic aesthetic work,[33] he failed to carry the latter anywhere near to the desired conclusion, abandoning it completely the moment he became politically radicalized. Talking to me in 1956 about his youthful aesthetic system, he dismissed the whole enterprise without the slightest sympathy even for the years of effort invested in it, saying that at that stage of his intellectual and political development all he could produce was 'a monster: a six-legged goat'.

The view of the system expressed in *Soul and Form* was linked to Lukács's conception of truth according to which 'Truth is only subjective — perhaps; but *subjectivity* is quite certainly *truth*'.[34] In a world-view in which Sören Kierkegaard loomed large and into which Hegel could be admitted even a few years later only in a 'Kierkegaardized form', truth could only be subjective and the concept of the system itself utterly problematical. Once, however, Lukács's 'epistemological' terms of reference — which he later unhesitatingly and rightly redefined as *ontological* and not simply epistemological — were specified in the sense we have seen above, as centred on a view of the social world in which 'significant intervention' was both possible and necessary, the Kierkegaardian elitistic rejection of the system (that 'omnibus' on which the 'rabble' — the masses of the people — could, horror of horrors, travel) had to be cast aside. At the same time the Hegelian proposition, constituting the conceptual ground of the system, according to which 'truth is the whole', had to be fully rehabilitated and, with it, Lukács's earlier conception of subjectivity — wedded to a conception of the isolated individual's 'autonomous selfhood' — as the foundation of truth banished from the horizon. It was revised by the Hungarian philosopher by asserting that social development was objective not in a fetishistic/reified sense but in terms of the postulated identity of subject and object and the unity/identity of theory and practice. This is how the idea that 'truth is the whole' could be both embraced by Lukács and redefined as 'the standpoint of totality' vested in the proletariat. Indeed, the Lukácsian 'methodologically necessary principle' of the 'standpoint of totality' was coupled by him with the proposition that the proletariat is the 'identical subject/object of history' through the agency of which 'theory becomes action' and the vital 'world-historical mission' of creating a new social order is actualized.

The ethical dimension of Lukács's view of the historical agency was obvious. When we think of the corollary of the idea of theory becoming action pronounced by Lukács in the same breath — i.e. that 'Decisions, *real decisions, precede the facts*',[35] — it acquires its sense only if we remember that it was formulated by him on the model of his definition of moral consciousness. In the spirit of the latter he argued for the necessity of the intellectual's unreserved commitment to the service of the 'identical subject/object's world-historical mission' (said to be objectively in the process of being realized) as an *ethically valid* course to follow.

For he insisted that *'ethical considerations* inspire in the individual the decision that the necessary historico-philosophical consciousness he possesses can be transformed into correct political action, i.e. component of a *collective will,* and can also determine that action'.[36]

6.4 The continued reassertion of alternatives

6.4.1

THE historical background to all this was the revolution 'at the weakest link of the chain' (Lenin). As we shall see, one of the main reasons why *History and Class Consciousness* made an immediate impact and acquired its representative significance was the way in which the author argued that the weaknesses of the 'weakest link' should be in fact considered a positive asset precisely in relation to the key issue of consciousness. For, as he put it, the absence of a long tradition of workers' movement in Russia, in contrast to the negative impact of the reformism and 'economism' of the Second International in the West, was bound to be conducive to the resolution of the proletariat's 'ideological crisis with greater dispatch'.[37] This perspective was underpinned in Lukács's analysis by an astonishingly voluntaristic assessment of the global relation of forces between capital and labour, arguing that *'capital is no longer anything but an obstacle to production'.*[38] Thus an objective trend of socioeconomic development which even today, almost eighty years later, can be underlined with validity only in its *world-historical* terms of reference, on an *epochal* scale, was characterized by Lukács as an *imminent fact,* although he was at the same time quite sarcastic about 'imminent facts',[39] quoting with unreserved approval Fichte's extreme idealist aphorism that being contradicted by the facts is 'So much the worse for the facts'.[40] The still far from exhausted ascendancy of capital on the global terrain had to be not only minimized but altogether ignored in his discourse, centred on the proletariat's 'ideological crisis' and on the role of the politically committed and morally responsible intellectuals in helping to resolve that crisis.

In his arguments addressed to fellow-intellectuals Lukács insisted that under the unfolding historical circumstances 'the individual's conscience and sense of responsibility are confronted with the postulate that he must act as if on his action or inaction depended the changing of the world's destiny, the approach of which is inevitably helped or hindered by the tactics he is about to adopt. ... Everyone who at the present time opts for communism is therefore obliged to bear the same *individual responsibility* for each and every human being who dies for him in the struggle, as if he himself had killed them all. But all those who ally themselves to the other side, the defence of capitalism, must bear the same individual responsibility for the destruction entailed in the new imperialist revanchist wars which are surely imminent, and for the future oppression of the nationalities and classes. ... He whose decision does not arise from such considerations — no matter how highly developed a creature he may otherwise be — exists in ethical terms at a primitive, unconscious, instinctual level'.[41] In this way individual moral responsibility was directly linked to the fundamental social conflicts of the time, inextricably combining also the idea of individual self-awareness with the advocacy of developing a proper class consciousness. Thus

Lukács insisted that 'For every socialist, morally correct action is related fundamentally to the correct perception of the given historico-philosophical situation,
which in turn is only feasible through the efforts of every individual to *make his
self-consciousness conscious for himself.* The first unavoidable prerequisite for this is
the formation of *class consciousness.* In order for correct action to become an
authentic, correct regulator, class consciousness must raise itself above the level
of the merely given; it must remember its world-historical mission and its sense
of responsibility'.[42]

Responding to the dramatic events in Russia and elsewhere in Europe, including in a prominent place the establishment of the Council Republic in Hungary,
Lukács asked the question: 'has the historical moment already arrived which
leads — or rather leaps — from the state of steady approach [toward realizing
the socialist ideal] to that of true realization?'[43] And he unhesitatingly and
emphatically answered it in the affirmative by saying that: 'the *revolution is here,*
... the time has come for the expropriation of the exploiters'.[44] The fact that the
part of the world where the 'chain was broken' happened to be 'the weakest
link' in the overall framework of capital as a global system, with potentially very
grave implications for the prospects of future development, did not matter and
could not matter in Lukács's almost exclusively ideology-centred discourse. All
that mattered was that it had been broken. Consequently, the political revolution in Russia was greeted by Lukács as a fatal blow to capital in general and as
an irreversible historical break-through to socialism on the soil where it erupted.
From now on, in his view, the only question was: how to spread the revolution
to the rest of the world, resolving at the same time the 'ideological crisis' for
which the lion's share of responsibility had to be ascribed to the reformist parties
of the Second International.

The moving force behind the intellectual work envisaged by Lukács had to
be a profound *ethical* commitment which in his view had to characterize not only
the individuals but, as we shall see below, also the party. He went on repeating
for a number of years — until such views became outlawed as heretic and
dangerous, leading to his expulsion from the field of politics — that the 'mission
of the party was moral' and that the 'intellectual leadership' exercised by the
party (and by the intellectuals who joined it) had to be *deserved* in the proper
ethical sense of the term. And although more or less pronounced voluntaristic
anticipations of a positive outcome to the ongoing struggle continued to play a
role in Lukács's perspective, there was never any sign of a simplistic optimism.
On the contrary, he was always anxious to put into relief the *tragic* dimension
of the dialectic of history and the way it was bound to affect the life-chances of
the individuals.

We have seen in Section 1.4.3 Lukács's praise for the Hegelian vision of
'tragedy in the realm of the ethical'. This theme appeared in one form or another,
without any reference to Hegel, already in his early writings, and it was firmly
reasserted also at the time when he first embraced the Marxian perspective. In
this spirit he wrote in 'Tactics and Ethics' that

> It is not the task of ethics to invent prescriptions for correct action, nor to iron out
> or deny the *insuperable, tragic conflicts of human destiny.* On the contrary: ethical self-
> awareness makes it quite clear that there are situations — tragic situations — in
> which it is impossible to act without burdening oneself with guilt. But at the same

time it teaches us that, even faced with the choice of two ways of incurring guilt, we should still find that there is a standard attaching to correct and incorrect action. This standard we call *sacrifice*. And just as the individual who chooses between two forms of guilt finally makes the *correct choice* when he sacrifices his *inferior self* on the altar of the *higher idea,* so it also takes strength to assess this sacrifice in terms of the *collective action.* In the latter case, however, the idea represents *an imperative of the world-historical situation, a historico-philosophical mission.*[45]

The Marxian perspective had meant for Lukács that the unavoidable 'tragedy in the realm of the ethical' could be linked to a strategy of radical social trans-formation. It had meant to him the promise that the 'tragedies to be encountered *en route* to the classless society' will greatly diminish as the 'individuals make self-consciousness conscious for themselves' and — through the formation of 'imputed class consciousness' — the historical agency becomes conscious of its 'historico-philosophical mission' of enabling humanity to take control of its own destiny, beyond the customary pursuit of particularistic class interests. By implication this had also meant in Lukács's view that the everyday life of the individuals — fragmented, isolated, 'privatized' and dominated by 'reification' under capitalism — will become more and more genuinely social and self-ful-filling, conferring thereby a meaning on the sacrifices which they were inevitably called upon to make 'en route' to the envisaged socialist society, and making the conquest of alienation and reification a rewardingly shared enterprise.

As we shall see in Chapter 10, in this regard the personal tragedy of Lukács as a theoretician was that this vision, as a result of the hopelessly blocked development of postcapitalist societies, had to be turned *inwards.* He was forced by the perverted logic of postrevolutionary transformations to reverse the main thrust of his own quest after 1917, projecting in his final works of synthesis — as a most implausible way for overcoming the social predicament of alienation — the power of the imperative arising from the individuals' moral consciousness to fight their own personal alienation. And although to the end he criticized his old friend, Ernst Bloch, for putting his faith into *Prinzip Hoffnung* — the 'Principle of Hope'[46] — as the key category in terms of which the prospects of human development must be assessed, Lukács himself ended up by assuming a very similar position, despite his protestations.[47] For in his *Ontology of Social Being,* as well as in the fragmentary outlines of his *Ethics,* he was relying — hope without hope — on the postulated power of *'ethics as mediation'.* He asserted its effectiveness in the absence of identifiable social forces and viable political movements engaged in the struggle to break out from the vicious circle of capital's second order mediations. This is how it came about that Lukács's moving concern with 'tragedy in the realm of the ethical' *directly confronting the individual* had to have the last word in his system.

6.4.2

AS we have seen in Section 6.2.1, the young Lukács was looking for a way of combining 'autonomous selfhood and the total dissolving of the self in a *higher being'* as a matter of profound existential choice and authentic commitment. By the time he wrote 'Tactics and Ethics' the earlier mystery had been left behind but the imperative of authentic existential commitment through autonomous choice remained, even if its terms of reference had been redefined. The question was not simply the imperative of making a choice but that of finding the '*correct choice*'. And just like in the past, when the authentic solution was described as combining 'autonomous selfhood and the total dissolving of the self in a *higher being*', also for the 'Marxisant' Lukács the individual had to submerge his 'inferior self' in the 'higher idea', which was inconceivable without an adequate form of '*collective action*'. As to the latter, the criteria of its correctness — on which also the authenticity and validity of the individual's existential commitment depended — had to be defined in objective terms, directly related to the given historical conjuncture and the vital alternatives arising from it, confronting humanity as a whole. This is why Lukács had to talk about the collective action representing 'an imperative of the world-historical situation', made synonymous with 'a historico-philosophical mission'. As to the alternatives themselves, they were described in the most dramatic terms not simply as regards the morally responsible individual — who was expected to sacrifice his narrowly self-oriented 'inferior self' to the 'higher idea' — but also in relation to the historical agency of the envisaged collective action. Thus, as we shall see in Section 7.5.1, Lukács described the 'destiny' of the class whose 'ascribed' or 'imputed' class consciousness he was concerned with — as opposed to its 'psychological consciousness' corresponding in his view to the individual's narrowly self-oriented consciousness of himself — by saying that it would 'either *ignominiously perish* or accomplish its task in full consciousness'.

The high point of Lukács's belief in a tangibly positive outcome was March 21, 1919, when the two Hungarian workers parties — the Socialdemocratic and the Communist — united their organizations during the shortlived Council Republic. Even the usually more cautious Lenin greeted this event with great enthusiasm, writing in a letter addressed to the Hungarian workers that 'You have given the world a still finer example than Soviet Russia, in that you have been able to unite all socialists from the outset on the platform of real proletarian dictatorship'.[48] Lukács, in the same spirit, talked about the the act of unification as follows:

> The parties have ceased to exist — now there is a unified proletariat. That is the decisive theoretical significance of this union. No matter that it calls itself a party — the word party now means something quite new and different. No longer is it a heterogeneous grouping made up of different classes, aiming by all kinds of violent or conformist means to realize some of its aims within class society. Today the party is the means by which the unified will of the unified proletariat expresses itself; it is the executive organ of the will that is developing in the new society from new sources of strength. The crisis of socialism, which found expression in the dialectical antagonisms between the party movements, has come to an end. The proletarian movement has definitely entered upon a new phase, the phase of proletarian power. The most prodigious achievement of the Hungarian proletariat has been to lead the world revolution *conclusively* into this phase. The Russian revolution has demonstrated that the proletariat is capable of seizing power and organizing a new society. The Hungarian revolution has demonstrated that this revolution is possible without fratricidal struggles among the proletariat itself. The world revolution is thereby carried another stage further. And it is to the lasting credit and honour of the Hungarian proletariat that it has been able to draw from within itself the strength and the resources to assume this leading role, to lead, not only its own leaders, but the proletarians of all countries.[49]

This evaluation of events did not mean for Lukács that the necessity of 'tragedy in the realm of the ethical' could be left behind. It meant that great historical achievements were on the horizon, provided that moral consciousness prevailed over the self-consciousness-corrupting temptations of 'immediate interests' or any other form of disorienting 'immediacy', be that in direct material consumption or in the domain of the purportedly most sophisticated forms of philosophical and artistic activity, with their 'cult of immediacy': all forcefully condemned by the Hungarian philosopher throughout his life.

As the revolutionary expectations of a great historical turning point receded from the horizon with the brutal consolidation of the Stalinist reign of necessity, Lukács continued to insist, in terms of his moral discourse, that there is bound to be a positive alternative — the realization of non-alienated humanity — despite 'the necessary historical *détour*'. And he did this even at the time when he personally had to experience 'tragedy *en route*' to the anticipated goal during his imprisonment in Moscow and the simultaneous deportation of his son, the engineer Ferenc Jánossy, to a Siberian labour camp. A few years later, in 1947, even the great positive expectations reappeared in Lukács's writings, describing postwar developments in these terms:

> The true democracy — the new democracy — produces everywhere real, dialectical transitions between private and public life. The turning point in the new democracy is that now man participates in the interactions of private and public life as an *active subject* and not as a *passive object*. ... The *ethically emerging new phase* demonstrates above all that one man's freedom is not a hindrance to another's freedom but its precondition. The individual cannot be free except in a free society. ... The now emerging self-consciousness of mankind announces as a perspective the end of human 'prehistory'. With this, man's self-creation acquires a new accent; now as a trend we see the emergence of a unity between the individual's human self-constitution and the self-creation of mankind. *Ethics is a crucial intermediary link in this whole process.*[50]

Thus, even if he wildly overstated the positive meaning of the ongoing transformations, he was still talking about social and political changes in conjunction with which he envisaged ethics to fulfil its role as the 'crucial intermediary link' of the advocated emancipatory process. The officially glorified 'year of turning' (1949), following the Cominform's break with Tito's Yugoslavia, put an end to all that, imposing the strictest Stalinist rule also in Hungary. This turn of events — a gruesome caricature of the great historical turning point projected by the Marxian socialist movement — endangered Lukács again, subjecting him to violent attacks and even to the threat of imprisonment during the 'Lukács debate' of 1949-51. Understandably, therefore, the hope attached to politics deserted him. Only once more in his life, during the October uprising of 1956, Lukács assumed a direct political role. He became Minister of Culture in Imre Nagy's government, for which he was deported to Romania; and after being released he continued to suffer attacks for eight years for his unforgivable sins. Nonetheless, Lukács's passionate advocacy of an alternative way of ordering human life — through the direct intervention of ethics — remained as strong as ever, even if it had to sound more abstract than ever in the last years of his life.

CHAPTER SEVEN

FROM THE CLOSED HORIZON OF HEGEL'S 'WORLD SPIRIT' TO PREDICATING THE IMPERATIVE OF SOCIALIST EMANCIPATION

7.1 *Individualistic conceptions of knowledge and social interaction*

7.1.1

THE relationship between consciousness and reality, and between individual and totalizing consciousness, proved to be an intractable problem to philosophers for centuries. Knowledge obtained on the basis of merely individual experience has always been considered rather problematical by philosophy, just as in the field of art and literature the artist's aim was never confined to registering the immediate impressions of particular individuals. Paradoxically, though, the true object of knowledge — that which is concealed behind deceptive appearance — had to remain elusive, from Plato's 'forms' to the Kantian 'thing in itself', so long as the problem could not be formulated in terms of 'social consciousness': an inherently historical concept. The great difficulty consisted in perceiving 'universal validity' in the actual, spatio-temporally limited experience of particular human beings. This necessarily appeared an unsolvable dilemma so long as 'the universal' was thought of as an ideal opposed to the actuality of lived experience.

The introduction of the idea of a historically developing social consciousness, no matter under what name, cut effectively through the Gordian knot of this paradox. For now 'universality' was conceived as *inherent* in, and not as *opposed* to, dynamically evolving particularity. Thus, the specific historical identity of, for instance, a particular work of art, could be recognized to be not the *negation* of 'universality' but, on the contrary, its *realization:* a far cry from Plato's conception of art as the ontologically and epistemologically inferior 'copy of the copy'. For the work of art could achieve universality only and precisely in so far as it succeeded in grasping — by the means at the disposal of the artist in his unique medium of activity — the spatio-temporally specific characteristics of actual experience as significant moments of social/historical development. The dialectical unity of the particular and the universal was, thus, conceived as 'continuity in discontinuity' and 'discontinuity in continuity': an approach diametrically opposed to 'noumenal forms' and statically permanent metaphysical 'essences'. Thus, history and permanence, as well as individual and social consciousness, appeared as inseparably interrelated in a dialectical conception.

Significantly, this awareness of both the historical and the collective dimension of consciousness came to the fore with an age of immense social turmoil: the French Revolution and the Napoleonic wars, which co-involved the whole of Europe — and not only Europe — in a series of violent confrontations and realignments. More crumbled then within the space of a mere few years than in centuries beforehand. With such elemental upheavals, the floodgates to an incomparably more dynamic social development had swung wide open, and thinkers like Hegel took notice of this, even if in an abstract, speculative form.

However, even the Hegelian philosophy — which represented the peak in the development of bourgeois historical consciousness — could not overcome the limitations of its horizon, namely the 'standpoint of political economy' (Marx). In fact, Hegel's concept of the *'List der Vernunft'* (the cunning of Reason) displayed in a graphic form both the fundamental achievements and the structural limitations of this approach. On the one hand, it emphatically underlined the objectivity of historical trends, since it was said to prevail over against the limited and self-centred plans of particular individuals, overruling the subjective bias necessarily inherent in the individual wills. On the other hand, though, it hypostatized the fact of social interaction as a mythical *supra-individual* entity. Indeed, it was the latter that mysteriously assumed charge of history, superimposing its own 'design' on the world of real individuals, making them act out in an unconscious way *its* 'destiny', *its* 'Theodicaea', in the spirit of an ultimately theological teleology.

But even if we remove the mythical hypostatization from the Hegelian scheme, this structure of thought cannot account for actual historical transformations, since it lacks the concept of a genuine *collective agency*. What is hypostatized (not only by Hegel but by many other philosophers as well) in the form of the supra-individual construct — be it the cunning of 'Reason', the Odyssey of the 'World Spirit', the 'hidden hand' of the 'commercial spirit', or indeed the 'vicissitudes of consciousness' in general — is but the unconscious totalization of atomistic individual interactions within the framework of the capitalist market. And since the true agency of history — social groups and classes, as opposed to isolated individuals — cannot be grasped by such philosophy, in that the tensions and inner contradictions of the way in which 'pre-history' unfolds would have to be laid bare for that, a maze of *individual* conflicts must be substituted for the *class* antagonisms which display the hallmarks of the prevailing system of domination.

It is this substitution of mythically inflated individual conflictuality for — ideologically inadmissible — social contradictions which produces the impenetrable opacity of the historical totality, generating thus in its turn the 'World Spirit' (or its conceptual equivalent in the systems of other philosophers) so as to be able to superimpose order on the mysteries of atomistic individual interaction. For while the unfolding of history under the impact of social antagonisms is not only *intelligible* in terms of successive systems of domination, but also demonstrates the necessary disintegration, sooner or later, of *any particular* system of domination — which is precisely what is apriori inadmissible from the ideological standpoint of political economy — the hypothesis according to which atomistic individual interactions produce a coherent historical totalization, rather than utter chaos, is a completely arbitrary postulate. Indeed, a great thinker like Hegel cannot leave matters at such a level of intellectual inconsistency. He introduces the concept of 'world historical individuals' — Napoleon, for instance, as mentioned before — through whose agency the 'World Spirit' implements its design in the world of temporal changes and historical transformations. Thus an ingenious philosophical solution is found by displacing the original mystery (that of atomistic individual interactions resulting in an historical order) by two other mysteries — one supra-individual: the 'World Spirit', and the other individual in a very special, elitistic way, namely the World Spirit's mysteriously chosen agent: the 'world historical individual' — while preserving the internal consistency of the individualistic approach, in total conformity to the standpoint of political economy.

7.1.2

IT is important to stress here that the same determinations which produce the idea of a Robinson Crusoe — both in fiction and in political economy, as Marx pointed out in the *Grundrisse* — are also responsible for all such individualistic conceptualizations of knowledge and social interaction, from the Cartesian 'ego' and Hobbes' epistemology as well as social philosophy to the Kantian and Hegelian systems and their 20th century counterparts, notwithstanding the time and circumstances that separate them from one another. The fact that atomistically isolated individuality is an artificial construct; that the real individual is unceremoniously subsumed under his class from the first moment of groping for consciousness; that he is enmeshed in the network of social determinations not only because of his own class allegiances, but also on account of the prevailing reciprocity of class confrontations in virtue of which the individual is in fact subject to a *twofold* class dependency; — all this is peripheral or irrelevant (belonging to the ontologically inferior 'phenomenal/empirical world', or, in Sartre's words, to the merely '*subjective* experience of an *historic* man'[51]) if *conflict* is perceived as emanating from the *individuals'* essential constitution, and not from the historically specific and transcendable conditions of their *social existence*. Once, however, this atomistic/individualistic view of the nature of social conflict becomes the premise of philosophy, history itself is either made intelligible in the way we have seen in Kant and Hegel — that is ultimately with the help of a theological teleology — or it is assigned an intensely problematical and ontologically secondary status, as with Heidegger and the 'pre-marxisant' Sartre.

Indeed, over the last two centuries of bourgeois philosophical development we can only witness an involution in this respect. For the nearer we get to our own times, the more radical becomes the dismissal of even the possibility of a social consciousness engaged in actual totalization of experience in a socially coherent and meaningful way. Kant still tried to connect the limited individuals with the most comprehensive category to which they belonged, namely humanity. By the time we reach the 'atheistic existentialism' of *Being and Nothingness*, attempts like this are dismissed not on account of their philosophical shortcomings but *in principle*, as hopelessly misconceived in even trying to address themselves to such issues. To quote Sartre:

But if God is characterized as radical absence, the effort to realize humanity as ours is forever renewed and *forever results in failure*. Thus the humanistic 'Us' — the Us-object — is proposed to each individual consciousness as an ideal *impossible* to attain although everyone keeps the *illusion* of being able to succeed in it by progressively enlarging the circle of communities to which he does belong. This humanistic 'Us' remains an *empty concept*, a pure indication of a possible extension of the ordinary usage of the 'Us'. Each time that we use the 'Us' in this sense (to designate suffering humanity, sinful humanity, to determine an *objective historical meaning* by considering man as an object which is *developing its potentialities*) we limit ourselves to indicating a certain concrete experience to be undergone in the presence of the absolute Third; that is, of God. Thus the limiting-concept of humanity (as the totality of the Us-object) and the limiting concept of God imply one another and are correlative.[52] To be sure, the problem of totalization is insoluble — both at the level of consciousness and at that of concrete material practices — without an adequate grasp of *mediation*. Equally, it is fairly obvious that such mediation is missing not only from Kant — who *directly* connects each individual, taken in isolation, with the generic category of Humanity by means of an *abstract moral postulate* — but also from nearly all other versions of individualistic philosophy. But this is not what Sartre is concerned about. On the contrary, he curtly dismisses the very idea of mediation as an *illusion,* together with the possibility of realizing positive human potentialities through objective historical development.

And yet, 'humanity as ours' does indeed exist in an alienated form and practically asserts itself as world history through the inescapable realities of the world market and the division of labour on a world scale. Nor does the concept of mankind developing its objective potentialities imply in the least the formulation of an impossible ideal, viewed from the illusory standpoint of the 'absolute Third', God. All that is required in order to make sense of 'humanity as ours' is, instead, to grasp the disconcerting reality of the material and ideal structures of domination in the dynamic process of their objective unfolding and potential dissolution, not from the standpoint of the 'absolute Third' but from that of a self-developing collective subject.

Naturally, the author of *Being and Nothingness* cannot opt for a similar line of solution, in view of his extreme stance with regard to the nature of conflict, founded according to Sartre on the 'ontological solitude of the For-itself': an idea that carries implications diametrically opposed to assigning positive potentialities to a collective subject. Hence Hegel's half-hearted attempts at facing the dilemma of historical totalization within an individualistic social horizon — attempts which, nevertheless, resulted in his greatest achievements, intellectually belying the limitations of their ideological half-heartedness — must be philosophically undone and dismissed as naive 'epistemological and ontological optimism':

> In the first place Hegel appears to us to be guilty of an epistemological optimism. It seems to him that the truth of self-consciousness can appear; that is, that an objective agreement can be realized between consciousnesses — by authority of the Other's recognition of me and my recognition of the Other. ... But there is in Hegel another and more fundamental form of optimism. This may be called an ontological optimism. For Hegel indeed truth is the truth of the Whole. And he places himself at the vantage point of truth — i.e., of the Whole — to consider the problem of the Other. ...individual consciousnesses are moments in the whole, moments which by themselves are *unselbstaendig* (dependent), and the whole is a *mediator* between consciousnesses. Hence is derived an ontological optimism parallel to the epistemological optimism: plurality can and must be surpassed toward the totality.
>
> [By contrast]...the sole point of departure is the interiority of the cogito. ...No logical or epistemological optimism can cover the *scandal* of the plurality of consciousnesses. If Hegel believed that it could, this is because he never grasped the nature of that particular dimension of being which is self-consciousness. [For] even if we could succeed in making the Other's existence share in the apodictic certainty of the cogito — i.e., of my own existence — we should not thereby 'surpass' the

other toward an *inter-monad totality*. So long as consciousnesses exist, the *separation and conflict* of consciousnesses will remain;...[53] Conflict is the original meaning of being-for-others.[54]

It goes without saying, if the only totalization we can envisage is one that aims at establishing an 'inter-monad totality', there can be no hope for success. Characteristically, however, Sartre blocks the road even to the possibility of success by dismissing *mediation* — and the key importance of the concept of the *whole* as its necessary frame of reference — as nothing more than an optimistic ontological illusion, and as such totally devoid of a real (Heidegger/Sartrean) ontological foundation. The only conceivable 'authentic' agency compatible with this 'non-optimistic' ontology is and remains the atomistically isolated individual. The idea of a collective subject as the potential totalizer is turned down not on account of practical considerations but, again, as a matter of *ontological* impossibility:

> The oppressed class can, in fact, affirm itself as a We-subject only in relation to the oppressing class. ...But the experience of the 'We' remains on the ground of *individual psychology* and remains a simple symbol of the longed-for unity of transcendences. ... the subjectivities remain out of reach and *radically separated*. ...We should hope in vain for a human 'we' in which the intersubjective totality would obtain consciousness of itself as a unified subjectivity. Such an ideal could be only a *dream* produced by a passage to the limit and to the absolute on the basis of *fragmentary, strictly psychological experiences*. ...It is therefore useless for humanity to seek to get out of this dilemma: one must either transcend the Other or allow oneself to be transcended by him. The essence of the relation between consciousnesses is not the *Mitsein* (being-with); it is *conflict*.[55]

Thus, in view of the alleged ontological necessity of conflict arising out of the essential constitution of atomistic individuality — the existentialist version of Hobbes' *bellum omnium contra omnes* — there can be no way out of the vicious circle of domination and subordination. It is this self-imposed ontological straitjacket that keeps Sartre from realizing his aim when he tries fifteen years later to come to terms with the tangible issues of real history in his *Critique of Dialectical Reason*. One cannot underline enough the total honesty of his commitment to look in the *Critique* for a solution radically different in its social perspective from that of *Being and Nothingness,* nor indeed the great importance of the problems he struggles with. It is all the more significant, therefore, that his inability to abandon the atomistic ontological preconceptions of his earlier work makes him go more and more around in circles the nearer he gets to the threshold of the task he sets himself: that of understanding *real* history. Instead, Sartre fails to complete more than the 'preliminary' volume, in which he ends up reiterating on nearly all major issues his former ontological position, against the original intentions, in the context of what he himself can only describe as the *'formal* structures of history'.

7.1.3

AS to the whole tradition of 'possessive individualism',[56] the concept of *class interest* is conspicuous in it by its absence. This is well in keeping with its model of conflict as emanating from abstract individuals who fight for interests strictly of their own as self-oriented/self-seeking — and thereby necessarily isolated — individuals. Once, however, interest and conflict are defined in such atomistic terms, the admissible kinds of action and social change implicitly follow. Since the problem of totalization is conceptualized from the point of view of a system of social metabolism already more or less firmly established: that of a commodity society,[57] rational action can only be what fits well within the horizons of such a society. By contrast, what is totally inadmissible — indeed: a conceptual taboo — is to envisage an effective *alternative* to the prevailing system of 'rational' social metabolism.

This is what makes intelligible the ideology of building the conflict theory of 'possessive individualism' on the shoulders of the abstract individual, conceptually obliterating the harsh reality of class interests. For no separate individual, nor some more or less haphazard aggregate of 'sovereign' individuals, could conceivably represent a viable alternative to an established social order. At the same time, conversely, any particular set of *class interests* of necessity can only be articulated as an *alternative* to the one which it tries to oppose. Thus, picturing the abstract *individual subject* as the originator and bearer of conflict corresponds to the — however unconscious — need to idealise the prevailing system of social/economic intercourse and to rule out any alternative to it. For the individuals in conflict, pursuing their drives and appetites, reciprocally affect one another, limiting at the same time the successful realization of any particular self-seeking strategy.[58] Their interchanges and clashes result in an ultimate '*equilibrium*' within the framework of this model of atomistic/parallellogrammatic individual interaction. No wonder, therefore, that the equilibrium-seeking bourgeois conceptualizations of the social process — which take the 'dynamic equilibrium' of self-propelling commodity production for granted as the necessary horizon of social life in general — cling to their atomistic/individualistic model of explanation. Equally, no wonder that within the framework of such a model no coherent theory of totalization can be formulated even by the greatest figures of this tradition.

7.2 *The problem of 'totalization' in* HISTORY AND CLASS CONSCIOUSNESS

7.2.1
BETWEEN March 1919 and Christmas 1922, as a critical reflection over his own philosophical past and over the various intellectual and political forces which contributed to the defeat of the Hungarian Council Republic, Lukács produced a powerful critique of the development of bourgeois thought in *History and Class Consciousness:* a work which in this respect remains unsurpassed even today. Insisting that the method of philosophy cannot be 'authentically totalizing' if it remains contemplative,[59] this is how he summed up his position on some of the key issues:

> The individual can never become the measure of all things. For when the individual confronts objective reality he is faced by a complex of ready-made and unalterable objects which allow him only the subjective responses of recognition or rejection. Only the class can relate to the whole of reality in a practical revolutionary way. ... And the class, too, can only manage it when it can see through the reified objectivity of the given world to the process that is also its own fate. For the individual, reification and hence determinism (determinism being the idea that things are necessarily

connected) are irremovable. Every attempt to achieve 'freedom' from such premisses must fail, for 'inner freedom' presupposes that the world cannot be changed. Hence, too, the cleavage of the ego into 'is' and 'ought', into the intelligible and the empirical ego, is unable to serve as the foundation for a dialectical process of becoming, even for the individual subject. The problem of the external world and with it the structure of the external world (of things) is referred to the category of the empirical ego. Psychologically and physiologically the latter is subject to the same deterministic laws as apply to the external world in a narrow sense. The intelligible ego becomes a transcendental idea (regardless of whether it is viewed as a metaphysical existent or as an ideal to be realised). It is of the essence of this idea that it should preclude a dialectical interaction with the empirical components of the ego and *a fortiori* the possibility that the intelligible ego should recognise itself in the empirical ego. The impact of such an idea upon the empirical reality corresponding to it produces the same riddle that we described earlier in the relationship between 'is' and 'ought'. ... Of course, 'indeterminism' does not lead to a way out of the difficulty for the individual. The indeterminism of the modern pragmatists was in origin nothing but the acquisition of that margin of 'freedom' that the conflicting claims and irrationality of the reified laws can offer the individual in capitalist society. It ultimately turns into a mystique of intuition which leaves the fatalism of the external reified world even more intact than before. (pp.193-5.)

In contrast to such approaches, Lukács indicated the adoption of 'the standpoint of totality' as the only feasible line of solution, arguing that since 'the intelligibility of objects develops in proportion as we grasp their function in the totality to which they belong..., only the dialectical conception of totality can enable us to understand reality as a social process'. (p.13.) And as the material agency capable of operating in accordance with the standpoint of totality, Lukács pointed to the proletariat and its 'non-psychological' class consciousness, attempting to account for the advances and failures of the revolutionary movement with reference to the development of 'ascribed' or 'imputed' class consciousness[60] on the one hand, and the 'ideological crisis of the proletariat' on the other.

We shall return in a moment to some of the very problematical features of Lukács's solution. But first it is necessary to stress not only the validity of his magisterial critique of the 'antinomies of bourgeois thought', but also of his intellectual demolition of social democratic 'economism', 'fatalism', etc., demonstrating in numerous contexts the renewed historical urgency of an active, radical intervention of social consciousness in the ongoing struggles. Equally, his analysis of 'hegemony'—which not only anticipated but also directly inspired Gramsci's reflections on the subject — is of the greatest importance.[61] Not to forget, of course, the theoretical/methodological as well as practical significance of pushing into the foreground of socialist debates the long lost perspective of an 'authentic totalization'.

7.2.2

IT is necessary to underline that Lukács's advocacy of 'the standpoint of totality' was directed against two major practical targets.

On the one hand, he counterposed it to the narrow tactical orientation of the Second International, with its illusory 'evolutionism' and the undialectical separation of 'means' and 'ends'. For the leading figures of the Second International adopted this position in order to be able to glorify the means at the expense of the original socialist aims which they abandoned in favour of a totally opportunistic 'realism' and 'pragmatism'.

But the second target was equally important to Lukács, even if later on — as a result of the successful Stalinization of the Third International — it became more and more difficult to voice the criticisms implicit in his position, defined in an oblique way[62] already in *History and Class Consciousness*. It was in fact the newly emerging tendency of bureaucratization in the Communist movement itself which Lukács tried to castigate with his own, rather idealised, image of the party. He often emphasised the importance of self-criticism, both in relation to Marxist theoretical work and as a fundamental principle of party organization. His oblique way of criticizing bureaucratization consisted in opposing to the 'parties of the old type' — namely the very real contemporary objects of his own concern — his ideal picture of the party which was said to be *'assigned* the sublime role of bearer of the class consciousness of the proletariat and the conscience of its historical vocation'. (p.41.) This is how he characterized the 'old type' of party organization:

> The party is divided into an active and a passive group in which the latter is only
> occasionally brought into play and then only at the behest of the former. The
> 'freedom' possessed by the members of such parties is therefore nothing more than
> the freedom of more or less peripheral and never fully engaged observers to pass
> judgement on the fatalistically accepted course of events or the errors of individuals.
> Such organizations never succeed in encompassing the total personality of their
> members, they cannot even attempt to do so. Like all the social forms of civilisation
> these organisations are based on the exact mechanized division of labour, on bureau-
> cratisation, on the precise delineation and separation of rights and duties. The mem-
> bers are only connected with the organisation by virtue of abstractly grasped aspects
> of their existence and these abstract bonds are objectivised as rights and duties.
> (pp.318-9.)

To rub salt into the wounds, a few paragraphs later the point of this indirect way of talking about the present by castigating the 'parties of the old type' emerged quite clearly when Lukács insisted that without a conscious adhesion and involvement of its members, party discipline 'must degenerate into a reified and abstract system of rights and duties and the party will relapse into a state typical of a party on the bourgeois pattern'. (p.320.)

Nor did Lukács stop at simply presenting a critique of the institutional framework of postrevolutionary transformations in terms confined to the re-quirements of party democratization. He raised the crucial issue of democrati-zation also as regards the necessary self-activity of the popular masses and the institutional organs of such self-activity which they have brought into being in the course of the great revolutionary upheavals of the past, from 1871 in Paris to 1917 in Russia and elsewhere. Thus, in one of the most striking essays of *History and Class Consciousness* Lukács appealed to the far-reaching institutional potentiality of the Workers' Councils. To quote an important passage:

> Every proletarian revolution has created workers' councils in an increasingly radical
> and conscious manner. When this weapon increases in power to the point where it
> becomes the organ of the state, this is a sign that the class consciousness of the
> proletariat is on the verge of overcoming the bourgeois outlook of its leaders. The
> revolutionary workers' council (not to be confused with its opportunist caricatures)
> is one of the forms which the consciousness of the proletariat has striven to create

ever since its inception. The fact that it exists and is constantly developing shows that the proletariat already stands on the threshold of victory. The workers' council spells the political and economic defeat of reification. In the period following the dictatorship it will eliminate the bourgeois separation of the legislature, administration and judiciary. During the struggle for control its mission is twofold. On the one hand, it must overcome the fragmentation of the proletariat in time and space, and on the other, it has to bring economics and politics together into the true synthesis of proletarian praxis. In this way it will help to reconcile the dialectical conflict between immediate interests and ultimate goal. (p.80.)

Ironically, however, by the time *History and Class Consciousness* was published, in 1923, not only the Hungarian Council Republic was militarily defeated, but everywhere else, including Russia, where workers' councils still existed, they had effectively lost all their power. Indeed, they had become a tragic reminder of the contradiction between the original aspirations of the revolution and the sociohistorical constraints which by then actually prevailed also in postrevolutionary Russia.

It was therefore by no means accidental that *History and Class Consciousness* was condemned by the Comintern itself, through the personal intervention of high ranking authorities like Bukharin and Zinoviev, not to mention scores of attacks to which its author had been subjected by less well known writers and functionaries for the views expressed in this influential book. Only in one of his last works — *Demokratisierung heute und morgen*[63] — could Lukács reformulate in the most explicit terms his condemnation of the fateful negative impact of party bureaucratization under the conditions of postrevolutionary developments, reiterating at the same time in a qualified form his belief in the world-historical significance of the Workers' Councils that spontaneously emerged on several occasions in the past from the struggles of the socialist movement.[64]

7.3 'Ideological crisis' and its voluntaristic resolution

7.3.1

IT is necessary to undertake here a critical examination of some major tenets of *History and Class Consciousness* with regard to the author's claims concerning the conditions of a conscious collective intervention in the social process for the purpose of instituting a radical structural change.

To anticipate in one sentence: Lukács's own solutions to the important issues he raises are problematical in that, for a variety of internal/theoretical and practical/political reasons, he is unable to define in tangible material terms the conditions under which the advocated and envisaged conscious collective totalization of knowledge and experience could actually take place. Consequently, he is forced to look for answers at a purely ideological — indeed at an abstract methodological — level.

We can see this quite clearly in Lukács's unrealistic evaluation of bourgeois planning as 'the *capitulation* of the class consciousness of the bourgeoisie before that of the proletariat'. (p.67.) The social crisis itself is repeatedly defined by Lukács as an '*ideological crisis*' and, correspondingly, the revolutionary task is identified with the '*struggle for consciousness*'. (p.68.)

The reason for Lukács's insistence on the claimed bourgeois *capitulation* to proletarian class consciousness is to be able to emphasise the absurdity of 'a strange counterpart to this', namely that 'at just this point in time certain sectors of the proletariat *capitulate* before the bourgeoisie' (p.67.) through their acceptance of the perspective of socialdemocratic reformism. If only the proletarians could overcome their *ideological crisis!* For in Lukács's view it is absolutely vital that they should realize clearly that 'as the bourgeoisie has the intellectual, organisational and every other advantage, the superiority of the proletariat *must* lie exclusively in its ability to see society from the centre, as a coherent whole'. (p.69.)

We would look in vain for a concrete analysis of the objective trends of development of contemporary capitalism in *History and Class Consciousness*. Everything is projected to the level of ideology and the struggle of competing class consciousnesses. In the absence of objective pointers of development we are presented, not surprisingly, with a succession of moral imperatives as our guide to the future:

> Class consciousness is the 'ethics' of the proletariat, the unity of its theory and its practice, the point at which the economic necessity of its struggle for liberation changes dialectically into freedom. By *realising* that the *party* is the historical embodiment and the *active incarnation* of class consciousness, we see that it is also the *incarnation of the ethics of the fighting proletariat*. This *must* determine its politics. Its politics may not always accord with the empirical reality of the moment; at such times its slogans may be ignored. But the ineluctable course of history will give it its due. *Even more,* the *moral strength* conferred by the correct class consciousness will bear fruit in terms of practical politics.
>
> The true strength of the party is *moral*; it is fed by the trust of the spontaneously revolutionary masses whom economic conditions have forced into revolt. It is nourished by the *feeling* that the party is the objectification of their own will (*obscure* though this may be to themselves), that it is the visible and *organised incarnation of their class consciousness*. Only when the party has fought for this *trust* and *earned it* can it become the leader of the revolution. For only then will the masses spontaneously and instinctively press forward with all their energies towards the party and towards their own class consciousness. (p.42.)

Thus we are offered a curious double postulate, representing an abstract opposition to the actuality of the situation.

- First, the 'real' ('non-psychological') class consciousness of the proletariat is turned into a moral imperative to which the workers ought to conform in the course of fulfilling their historic mission.

- And second, the party is postulated as the 'active and organized incarnation of class consciousness', provided that it is able and willing to conform to the moral determination of its essential character — its moral strength derived from being the 'incarnation of the ethics of the fighting proletariat' — and thereby 'earn the trust' required for realizing its stipulated historic mandate.

Once the reality of both the class and the party is viewed through the refracting prism of this double *Sollen* ('ought-to-be'), everything else, too, appears in the same light. Engaging with particular issues is seen 'as a *means of education* for the *final battle* whose outcome depends on closing the gap between the psychological consciousness and the imputed one'. (p.74.) Truly positive developments can only be expected after 'the school of history completes the education of the proletariat and confers upon it the leadership of mankind'. (p.76.) The condition of success is defined as the work of consciousness upon consciousness — both in the working class at large and within the party — aimed at overcoming the 'ideological crisis'. For, according to Lukács, 'it is an *ideological crisis* which must be solved *before* a practical solution to the world's economic crisis can be found'. (p.79.)

Significantly, the author's great sensitivity for dialectical solutions deserts him here, in that he defines the issues at stake in terms of 'before' and 'after': something he would never do at the level of analysing the general philosophical principles involved. Also, he avoids the question of *how* to solve the ideological crisis as such (and by the force of ideology alone) if the bourgeoisie so emphatically has the 'intellectual, organisational and every other advantage', as he himself earlier asserted. The educational work of consciousness upon consciousness, coupled with the positional advantage and qualitative superiority of the postulated totalizing proletarian class consciousness, is supposed to overcome all such practical difficulties.

In the same vein, in Lukács's attempts to explain the non-realization of revolutionary potentialities, the absence of favourable objective social/economic conditions is minimized, so as to be able to ascribe responsibility for the difficulties and failures to ideological and organizational factors. Talking about the claimed tendency of mass strikes to become a direct struggle for power Lukács characteristically insists that

> the fact that this tendency has not yet become reality even though the economic and social preconditions were *often fulfilled,* that precisely is the ideological crisis of the proletariat. This ideological crisis manifests itself on the one hand in the fact that the objectively extremely precarious position of bourgeois society is endowed, *in the minds of the workers* with all its erstwhile stability; in many respects the proletariat is still caught up in the old capitalist *forms of thought and feeling.* On the other hand, the bourgeoisification of the proletariat becomes institutionalised in the Menshevik workers' parties and in the trade unions they control. These organisations ... strive to prevent [the workers] from turning their *attention to the totality,* whether this be territorial, professional, etc., or whether it involves synthesising the economic movement with the political one. In this the unions tend to take on the task of atomising and de-politicising the movement and *concealing its relations to the totality,* whereas the Menshevik parties perform the task of establishing the *reification in the consciousness* of the proletariat both *ideologically* and on the level of *organisation.* They thus ensure that the consciousness of the proletariat will remain at a certain stage of relative bourgeoisification. They are able to achieve this only because the proletariat is in a state of *ideological crisis,* because even in theory the natural — ideological — development into a dictatorship and into socialism is out of the question for the proletariat, and because the crisis involves not only the economic undermining of capitalism but, equally, the ideological transformation of the proletariat that has been reared in capitalist society under the influence of the life-forms of the bourgeoisie. This ideological transformation does indeed owe its existence to the economic crisis which created the objective opportunity to seize power. The course it actually takes does not, however, run parallel in any *automatic* and *'necessary'* way with that taken by the objective crisis itself. *This crisis can be resolved only by the free action of the proletariat'.* (pp.310-11. Lukács's italics in the last sentence.)

We can see in the last passage also a revealing way of discrediting *'necessary'* by identifying it — thanks to a peculiar use of inverted commas — with *automatic*. Naturally, the dialectician Lukács is well aware of the difference between the necessity of complex social determinations and the crude reductionism of mechanical and automatic shortcuts as explanatory hypotheses. And yet, he identifies the two in the context of his discourse on the work of consciousness upon consciousness, in order to establish the '*free action* of the proletariat' as a result of the successful solution of its ideological crisis.

Similarly, a few pages earlier — talking about the possible economic outlets to future capitalist developments — Lukács counterposes in a somewhat rhetorical fashion 'the pure theoretical world of economics' to the 'reality of the class struggle'. (p.306.) He describes the feasible economic outlets as mere 'expedients', adding that 'for capitalism expedients can certainly be thought of in and for themselves. Whether they can be put into practice *depends, however, on the proletariat*. The proletariat, the actions of the proletariat, block capitalism's way out of the crisis'. (*Ibid.* Lukács's italics.) Abstractly this is, of course, true. But this abstract truth rests on the false assumption of the *free agency* of the proletariat: a condition to the realization of which Lukács is unable to see the obstacles in other than purely ideological terms. And, again, the vital objective conditions are discredited by the strange inverted commas and by the tendentious setting up of a straw-man target with the help of the terms 'fatalistic' and 'automatic':

> The new-found strength of the proletariat is the product of objective economic 'laws'. The problem, however, of converting this potential power into a real one and of enabling the proletariat (which today really is the mere object of the economic process and only potentially and latently its co-determining subject) to emerge as its subject in reality, is *no longer* determined by these 'laws' in any *fatalistic and automatic* way. (*Ibid.*)

The straw-man character of this target is displayed also in the total redundancy of its 'no longer'. For social forces and their consciousness have *never* been — nor could they *ever* be — determined in a 'fatalistic and automatic way', as Lukács knows only too well. Yet he needs such easy targets in the context of his discourse on the 'struggle for consciousness'. For his exclusivistic appeal in favour of an urgent and concentrated effort to overcome the diagnosed 'ideological crisis' as the paramount obstacle to revolutionary advance would reveal itself as rather problematical if he had to concede that, in the blockage we actually experience, massive objective forces are at work and their effectiveness is greatly strengthened, rather than weakened, precisely by the fact that they do not impose their paralysing determinations in a 'fatalistic and automatic' fashion.

To be sure, every social agency must articulate at the level of its social consciousness the objective determinations by which it is moved: a condition by no means invalidated by the category of 'false consciousness'. Equally, it is easy to grant that social consciousness (or 'false consciousness') cannot be *reduced* to direct material determinations, let alone to 'automatic' and 'fatalistic' outside forces. From this, however, it does not follow that one may proceed the other way round, reducing objective material/social factors, laws and forces to acts of consciousness, even though they undoubtedly appear *in* consciousness, be that in a correct or in an upside-down fashion. For turning the upside-down images the 'right way up again' will not eliminate their objective ground of determination, no matter how successful the work of consciousness upon consciousness temporarily might be in its effort to produce an 'ideological clarification'.Indeed, leaving such grounds of determination intact is likely to end up reproducing sooner or later the same upside-down images which the enlightening consciousness so laboriously tried to weed out from its target-consciousness.

In Lukács's voluntaristic subordination of some of the most powerful objective forces — characteristically described as 'mere economic expedients' — to the 'reality of the class struggle' we find precisely this tendency to inverted reductionism. (And he is by no means the only philosopher guilty of that.) The unrealistic overemphasis placed on political and ideological factors goes hand in hand with fatefully underestimating capital's power of recovery and continuing rule. Lukács's suggestion that capitalist stability exists only 'in the minds of the workers' — who thus perceive in a totally irrational form 'the objectively extremely precarious position of bourgeois society' — is a graphic example in this respect.

The voluntaristic inverted reductionism implicit in such assertions has always been one of the principal reasons for the legendary influence of *History and Class Consciousness* not only on Left-oriented Marxism in the 1920s and 1930s but also on 'Critical Theory' — both at the time of its inception and in the postwar years — and, later still, on the student movement in the 1960s, especially in Germany.[65] Published at a time when capital was well on the way to secure its stability on a new foundation, as the end-of-war revolutionary wave had died down, *History and Class Consciousness* passionately refused to accept the emerging state of affairs and directly appealed to the ideal of totalizing consciousness[66] as its sole ally against the heavy odds of the new stability. No wonder, therefore, that it continued to find favourable echoes in socially rather isolated but defiant intellectual movements which tried to articulate, in similar circumstances of social immobility — against the background of the apparent integration[67] of the working class and its traditional organizations — the idea of a conscious rebellion against the power of reification.

7.3.2

THE adoption of this kind of solution by Lukács at the time of writing *History and Class Consciousness* must be situated in the context of the conflicts and rival strategies of the deeply divided international socialist movement. As is well known, this division came about at the turn of the century, although its roots go back to the final years of the First International in Marx's lifetime. It became manifest already in the bitter controversies surrounding his *Critique of the Gotha Programme*. Such developments coincided with the new imperial drive of the major capitalist countries in the last third of the nineteenth century, giving a new lease of life to capital which also provided the scope for working class accommodation within the suitably adjusted Western parliamentary framework.

Thus, under the new conditions the earlier, rather small, socialist groups and organizations of the leading capitalist countries could become *mass* parties, in their *national* setting, as Lenin had pointed out. But the price they had to pay for such growth was the loss of their global perspective and radical stance. For the two were (and will remain also in the future) inextricably tied together.

Socialist radicalism was then (and remains even more today) feasible only on condition that the antagonist of capital strategically assessed the potentialities as well as the inescapable structural limitations of its adversary from a *global* standpoint.

Under the historical conditions of the new imperial drive, however, nationalistic reformism constituted the general trend in the working class movement to which there were only very few exceptions. As to the exceptions themselves, they could arise mainly as a result of the complicating circumstance of *dependent development,* as in the case of Russia, for instance. Russia's dependent capitalist development — in conjunction with the repressive political anachronism of the Czarist regime that, unlike its Western counterparts, offered no peace and parliamentary accommodation to the working classes — provided a more favourable ground for a radical socialist movement. But precisely on account of these rather special circumstances the roads followed by the organized working class had to part for a long time to come.

Understandably, the Russian socialist movement, as the revolutionary movement of a mass-oriented but tightly organized political *vanguard,* had to adapt itself to the specificities of its sociohistorical setting; just as the legalized and mass-vote-oriented parliamentary parties of Western Social Democracy articulated their strategic tenets in accordance with the political demands arising from the complicated, indeed contradictory material interests of their economically much more advanced and imperialistically poised national predicament.

Ideology alone could not bridge the cleavage that objectively separated these movements in terms of the different *degrees* of development of their countries; of their relatively privileged or dependent *type* of development; of the more or less favoured *position* which the particular countries concerned occupied in the global system of imperialist hierarchies; of the character of the respective *states* as developed over a long historical period; and of the feasible *organizational* structures of the socioeconomic and political/cultural transformation that could be envisaged within the framework of the established (or inherited) material base and its complex superstructure in each particular country. This is why Lenin's remarks in the aftermath of the Russian revolution, depicting the latter as the model and as the 'inevitable and near future'[68] of the capitalistically advanced Western countries, had to turn out to be so hopelessly optimistic, whereas Rosa Luxemburg's words that 'In Russia the problem could only be posed; it could not be solved in Russia'[69] stood the test of time.

The difficulties became particularly acute a few years after the first world war, following the defeat of the uprisings outside Russia. For once the 'revolutionary wave' receded and the capitalist regimes on the losing side of the war became relatively stable again, the cleavage in the sociohistorical predicament of the mutually opposed working class movements mentioned above — which in the immediate after-war situation not only *seemed to be,* but for the brief historical moment of the end-of-the-war collapse of the defeated regimes (though decidedly not of the victors who could count on the spoils of the war) *actually was* much narrower — widened enormously, resulting in a breach much greater than ever before.

The temptation to bridge it through *ideology* in the newly formed Communist Parties of the Third International became irresistible. All the more since the material structures of *development* and *underdevelopment* asserted themselves in the world with increasing severity, rather than diminishing in importance. Western capitalist countries had some objective possibilities open to them through which they were able — for a relatively long historical period — to *displace* (though by no means to *resolve*) their contradictions. This in its turn made the revolutionary discourse of the leading intellectuals of the Third International in the West very problematical, as Lukács later self-critically admitted, characterizing his own position, together with that of his comrades associated with the periodical *Communism,* as 'messianic utopianism'. (p.xviii.) For they tended to ignore the objective possibilities at the disposal of their historical antagonist, greatly underrating capital's 'staying power' in their insistence that 'the actual strength of capitalism has been so greatly weakened that ... *only ideology stands in the way'.* (p.262.)

Lenin's own discourse was quite distinct even when in the fight against reformist opportunism he laid the stress on ideology, in that he addressed himself to people who had to cope with the problems and contradictions of a very different setting. The two basic factors of his socioeconomic and political predicament — the burden of dependent capitalist development in Russia and the extreme repressive measures of the Czarist police state — made his strategy viable under the circumstances. Yet, even in his case the advocacy of the *clandestine* form of party organization as the universally valid guarantor of the correct ideology and strategy, to be applied also in Germany and elsewhere in the West, and later his direct ideological appeal to the *model* character of the Russian revolution, had their insuperable dilemmas. Once the strategic orientation of *'socialism in one country'* prevailed in Russia after Lenin's death with dogmatic finality, the general line of the Third International — which continued to insist on the model character of Soviet developments — was in fact a contradiction in terms as far as the prospects of development for a genuine international socialist movement were concerned. It was therefore not in the least surprising that the Third International should come to the sorry end which it eventually reached.

7.3.3
THE failure to engage in a thorough analysis of the ongoing Western capitalist transformations, adopting instead the proposition according to which the Russian model represented the 'near and inevitable future' of capitalism in general, brought with it some truly peculiar conclusions even in the case of such outstanding and profoundly committed revolutionary intellectuals as Lukács. With regard to the question of legal or illegal forms of action he asserted in *History and Class Consciousness* that

> The question of legality or illegality reduces itself for the Communist Party to *a mere question of tactics,* even to a question to be resolved on the *spur of the moment,* one for which it is scarcely possible to lay down general rules as decisions have to be taken on the basis of *immediate expediencies.* (p.264. Lukács's italics.)

At the same time, Lukács revised his earlier enthusiasm for Rosa Luxemburg's position and reinterpreted some of her views in such a way that they bore no resemblance to her actual statements. Thus, concerning the possible change of capitalistic structures into socialist ones, he attributed to her the view that capitalism is 'amenable to such change "through legal devices" within the framework of capitalist society'. (p.283.) In fact she had only scorn for such an idea, putting into relief in the most graphic way the absurdity of *Bernstein* looking for legislatively effective 'collars' where none could be found.[70] Worse still, Lukács also asserted — and to give it greater weight he even italicized — the most surprising proposition of all, according to which Rosa Luxemburg *'imagines the proletarian revolution as having the structural forms of bourgeois revolutions'*. (p.51.) Yet, as a matter of fact, she repeated again and again that 'history is not going to make our revolution an easy matter like the bourgeois revolutions. In those revolutions it sufficed to overthrow that official power at the centre and to replace a dozen or so of persons in authority. But we have to work from beneath. Therein is displayed the mass character of our revolution, one which aims at transforming the *whole structure of society'*.[71]

This was not an accidental misreading on Lukács's part; nor indeed the result of 'opportunistic capitulation to party orthodoxy', as often claimed. It was, rather, the consequence of not giving sufficient weight to the fact that the *material ground of solidarity* of the international working class movement had been shattered at the turn of the century. No *ideological* counter-moves could put things right in this respect while leaving the material ground itself intact.

Nor was it really feasible to remedy the situation by *political organizational* efforts alone. Not even by the best possible ones. For the great difficulty which the socialist movement had to face concerned the fundamental socioeconomic metabolism of the global capital system. No direct ideological appeal to the consciousness of the proletariat could, so to speak, 'jump the gun' of such objective developments, nullifying or overruling thereby the organic character of the developments in question, when capital could still find vast outlets for displacing its contradictions on the basis of its *global ascendancy,* notwithstanding the setbacks it suffered through the victory of the Russian revolution.

Characteristically, therefore, even the *organizational* questions tended to be reduced to *ideological* concerns. The party was defined as the carrier of the purely 'ascribed' or 'imputed class consciousness of the proletariat', and imputed class consciousness was described as follows:

> By relating consciousness to the whole of society it becomes possible to *infer* the thoughts and feelings which men *would have* in a particular situation if they were *able* to assess both it and the interests arising from it in their impact on immediate action and on the whole structure of society. That is to say, it would be possible to *infer* the thoughts and feelings *appropriate* to their objective situation. ... Class consciousness consists in fact of the *appropriate and rational* reactions *'imputed'* [zugerechnet] to a particular *typical position* in the process of production. (p.51.)

In the same way, Lukács's attempt to ascribe to ideology the crucial role everywhere, dominated his diagnosis of the unfolding socioeconomic processes as well:

> With the crises of the War and the post-war period ... the idea of a 'planned' economy has gained ground at least among the more progressive elements of the bourgeoisie. ... When capitalism was *still expanding* it rejected every sort of social organization ... If we compare that with current attempts to harmonize a 'planned' economy with the class interests of the bourgeoisie, we are forced to admit that what we are witnessing is the *capitulation of the class consciousness of the bourgeoisie before that of the proletariat.* Of course, the section of the bourgeoisie that accepts the notion of a

'planned' economy does not mean by it the same as does the proletariat; it regards it as a *last attempt to save capitalism* by driving its internal contradictions to breaking-point. Nevertheless this means *jettisoning the last theoretical line of defence*. (As a strange counterpart to this we may note that at just this point in time certain sectors of the proletariat *capitulate before the bourgeoisie* and adopt this, the most problematical form of bourgeois [party] organization.) With this the whole existence of the bourgeoisie and its culture is plunged into *the most terrible crisis*. ... This *ideological crisis* is an unfailing sign of decay. The bourgeoisie has already been thrown on the defensive; however aggressive its weapons may be, it is fighting for self-preservation. *Its power to dominate has vanished beyond recall*. (p.67.)

The historical fact that the 'strange counterpart' (of socialdemocratic reformism) to the 'capitulation of the class consciousness of the bourgeoisie before that of the proletariat' had arisen not 'at just this point in time' but at least three decades before the 'post-war period' (i.e. even before Bernstein) did not seem to matter to Lukács's diagnosis. Nor did he attempt to explain what had caused it.

Similarly, he did not feel the need to undertake a serious analysis of the global capitalist economy and its recent trends of development within their own terms of reference. His ideology-oriented discourse provided both the diagnosis and the solution in strictly ideological/theoretical terms: as the 'jettisoning of the last line of *theoretical defence*' and the '*ideological crisis*' resulting from it.

However, since the paradoxical 'strange counterpart' to the ideological crisis of the bourgeoisie was conceptualized in the same way, the solution to this paradox was theorized in an identical spirit, within ideology. Accordingly, it was asserted that

the stratifications within the proletariat that lead to the formation of the various labour parties and of the Communist Party are no objective, economic stratifications in the proletariat but simply stages in the development of its class consciousness. (p.326.)

Consequently, the possible solution to the identified problems could only be defined by Lukács in ideological/organizational terms, as 'the *conscious, free action* of the *conscious vanguard* itself. ... the overcoming of the *ideological crisis,* the struggle to acquire the correct proletarian class consciousness'. (p.330.)

As to the paradox of the 'strange counterpart' itself, Lukács's answer conformed to the same pattern. It was given in the form of assigning to political organization the *ideological mission* of rescuing 'the great mass of the proletariat which is instinctively revolutionary but has not reached the stage of clear consciousness' (p.289.) from the hands of its opportunistic leadership.

The importance of the objective factors was consistently minimized by Lukács in order to enhance the plausibility of his direct ideological appeal to an idealized proletarian class consciousness and to its 'active, visible and organized incarnation', the equally idealized party. The crisis of the capitalist system was exaggerated out of all proportions so as to suggest that, had it not been for the 'minds of the workers', the established order could not sustain itself any longer. In this way, the neglect of the material factors gave the illusion to Lukács that the economic and social preconditions of revolutionary transformation were '*often fulfilled*' and only the 'minds of the workers' had to be modified by the 'active and visible incarnation of their class consciousness' in order to gain victory over the '*objectively extremely precarious* condition of bourgeois society'.

Thus the historically produced and objectively sustained stability (i.e. the successful pre-war imperial drive and the post-1919 re-stabilization and expansion) of Western capitalist society was brushed aside by Lukács as devoid of real existence, in that allegedly it existed only 'in the minds of the workers'. Likewise, the manifold objective stratifications within the actually existing working class were denied an objective status and were described, instead (somewhat mysteriously, on the model of Weberian 'typology' positively embraced in *History and Class Consciousness* in several contexts), as 'stages' in the self-development of proletarian class consciousness. As a result of this approach, the historical task of 'what is to be done' had to be defined as the work of consciousness upon consciousness. This is how Lukács — one of the most original and truly dialectical thinkers of the century — ended up proclaiming with undialectical one-sidedness the earlier quoted proposition according to which the 'ideological crisis' of the proletariat 'must be solved *before* a practical solution to the world's economic crisis can be found'.

7.4 The function of Lukács's methodological postulate

7.4.1

WHEN Lukács insists that 'the party is assigned the sublime role of bearer of the class consciousness of the proletariat and the conscience of its historical vocation', he does this in open defiance of 'the superficially more active and "more realistic" view [which] allocates to the party tasks concerned predominantly or even exclusively with organisation'. (p.41.) In this defiant evaluation of the prevailing historical conditions, the working class — notwithstanding its internally divisive stratification and accommodating submission to the power of capital acknowledged by Lukács — is *ascribed* its totalizing class consciousness, and the party is *assigned* the role of being the actual bearer of that consciousness, despite the clearly identifiable and highly disturbing tendencies of narrow 'realism' and bureaucratization in the international communist movement. Thus, in the absence of the required objective conditions, the idea of a conscious totalization of the manifold conflicting social processes in the direction of a radical socialist transformation becomes extremely problematical. It has to be turned into a postulate, to be kept alive for the future, and a theory must be devised which is capable of asserting and reasserting its validity in the face of whatever defeats and disappointments the emerging actual future may still have in store for the beleaguered socialist movement.

These determinations carry far-reaching consequences for Lukács's approach. Against the prevailing negative conditions he cannot simply offer *likely* improvements, under determinate — and materially/politically/organizationally specified — circumstances. He must offer nothing less than *certainty*, in order to be able to counterbalance all given and possible evidence pointing in the undesired direction. Thus, absolutely nothing can be allowed to put under the shadow of a doubt 'the certainty that capitalism is doomed and that — ultimately — the proletariat will be victorious'. (p.43.) If the class shows no convincing signs of 'bridging the gap between its *ascribed* and *psychological* class consciousness', and if, worse still, the 'visible and organised incarnation' of class consciousness, the party — because of its growing 'realism' and bureaucratization — seems to be unable to fulfil the functions *assigned* to it, all that must be pushed aside by the imperative of the postulated final outcome.

The reason why Lukács's discourse must be transferred to an abstract methodological plane here becomes visible. For the defiant validity of the distant positive perspective which he must predicate can only be established — against all the visible and, as he argues, *conceivable* evidence to the contrary — in terms of a purely methodological discourse. The way Lukács himself puts it, in immediate continuation of our last quote:

> There can be no 'material'[72] guarantee of this certitude. It can be *guaranteed methodologically* — by the dialectical method. (p.43.)

The trouble is, though, that the 'methodological guarantee' offered by Lukács is at times in danger of becoming a new form of *apriorism* which tends to discard *substantive* issues as irrelevant while, in fact, they should be kept at all times under close scrutiny.

7.4.2

WE can find the sources of Lukács's idea concerning the dialectical certitude of victory against the facticity of material domination in Rosa Luxemburg's polemics against Bernstein's denunciation of Marxian dialectics as a mere 'scaffolding'. She writes in response to such a view:

> When Bernstein directs his keenest arrows against our dialectic system, he is really attacking the specific *mode of thought* employed by the conscious proletariat in its struggle for liberation. It is an attempt to break the sword that has helped the proletariat to pierce the darkness of its future. It is an attempt to shatter the intellectual arm with the aid of which the proletariat, though *materially* under the yoke of the bourgeoisie, is yet enabled to triumph against the bourgeoisie. For it is our *dialectical system* that shows to the working class the *transitory* character of this yoke, proving to the workers the *inevitability of their victory,* and is already realizing a *revolution in the domain of thought*.[73]

In contrast to Lukács's position, however, the method of the *dialectical system* on the basis of which Rosa Luxemburg predicates, just like Lukács, the *'inevitability of proletarian victory'*, is not separated by her from the substantive propositions of the Marxian theoretical framework. Content in Luxemburg is not opposed to method. On the contrary, she insists on the theoretical coherence of the Marxian propositions as a comprehensive system whose particular theses must be understood in the context of the whole. She rejects Bernsteinian reformist opportunism both in substantive terms — in that it is incapable of elaborating a *positive theory* — and on methodological grounds, stressing its failure to go beyond the parasitic theoretical practice of nothing but attacks on some *isolated theses* of the Marxian doctrine. This is how she puts it in the same work:

> Opportunism is not in a position to elaborate a *positive theory* capable of withstanding criticism. All it can do is to attack various *isolated theses* of Marxist theory and, just because Marxist doctrine constitutes one *solidly constructed edifice,* hope by this means to shake the *entire system,* from the top to its foundation.[74]

Indeed, Luxemburg puts into relief that the reformist attempt to go beyond Marx represents in fact a return to pre-Marxist positions, but one that under the new circumstances is totally devoid of the relative historical justification of the original theoretical tenets as linked to an earlier phase in the development of the socialist movement. And in her effort to grasp also in her negative critique the strategically vital substantive issues of the fully up-to-date socialist struggle, she focuses attention, in terms of well specified theoretical contents, on the regressive and hopelessly unrealistic Bernsteinian reorientation of the socialist movement from the sphere of *production* to that of *distribution*.[75] Thus, methodology and doctrine constitute an inseparable *unity* in Rosa Luxemburg's conception of the Marxian dialectical system.

7.4.3

LUKACS passionately shares with Luxemburg the radical rejection of the reformist position and her stress on the importance of the dialectical method in the face of the historically given material adversity. However, under the prevailing — most unfavourable — historical circumstances, he tends to ascribe to what Rosa Luxemburg calls a 'revolution in the domain of thought' a self-sustaining potentiality, thanks to the stipulated irrepressible power of dialectical methodology over all adversity.

In this sense, for instance, an important point raised by Franz Mehring is bypassed by Lukács in the name of method, turning a serious shortcoming into a virtue: 'Mehring's question', he writes, 'about the extent to which Marx overestimated the consciousness of the Weavers' Uprising does not concern us here. *Methodologically* [Lukács's italics] he has provided a *perfect* description of the development of revolutionary class consciousness in the proletariat'. (p.219.)

Such opposition of method and content is intended to remove the contingent factors from the theory, establishing thus its perspectives on foundations free from empirical and temporal fluctuations. However, in his attempt to provide a secure defence — in terms of the long-term temporality of dialectical methodology — against the ideologically often exploited immediacy of daily political and economic confrontations, Lukács ends up with an extreme paradox:

> Let us assume for the sake of argument that recent research had disproved once and for all every one of Marx's individual theses. Even if this were to be proved, every serious 'orthodox' Marxist would still be able to accept all such modern findings without reservation and hence dismiss all of Marx's theses *in toto* — without having to renounce his orthodoxy for a single moment. Orthodox Marxism, therefore, does not imply the uncritical acceptance of the results of Marx's investigations. It is not the 'belief' in this or that thesis, nor the exegesis of a 'sacred' book. On the contrary, orthodoxy refers exclusively to *method*. (p.1. Lukács's italics.)

It goes without saying that if a theory is being attacked, like Marx's had been, in terms of its substantive propositions, to 'confine discussion to their methodological premises and implications' (p.xliii.) is not likely to provide a truly effective defence. However, well beyond the question of defence, Lukács's methodological paradox is very problematical primarily because it disrupts the inherent dialectical relationship between method and the substantive ground on which it arises, thus rendering rather suspect *both* the general methodological principles themselves — which can function in such a self-sustaining universe of disembodied abstractions — and the particular theses and propositions articulated within their totalizing framework. Indeed, inasmuch as some of Marx's own conclusions are questionable, in that they exhibit the substantive limitations of his age, the adopted method of rigorous deductive anticipations, used in order to articulate both the monumental outlines and the minute specific details of the theory on the basis of the — historically very limited — available evidence, is by no means devoid of its internal problems.[76]

It must be emphasised, again, that the dialectician Lukács who deals with these problems at the most abstract level of philosophical analysis, in his powerful critique of the antinomies and contradictions of bourgeois thought, is fully aware of the necessary interrelationship between form and content, method and substance, categories and social being, general dialectical principles and particular theses, propositions, and conclusions. It is all the more significant, therefore, that under the pressure of the determinations mentioned above he is forced to go against his own better judgement and propound the self-sufficient validity of method as such.

The need to provide firm guarantees with regard to the 'certainty of the final victory', coupled with the difficulties of finding from his perspective other than purely 'methodological guarantees' for positive developments under the prevailing historical circumstances, produce an approach which remains with Lukács for the rest of his life.[77] Having defined the problems at stake — partly as a critique of the Second International, and more importantly: in response to the recent defeats of several European revolutionary uprisings as well as to the growing 'realism' and bureaucratization of the parties of the Third International — in terms of the *certainty of the final victory,* rather than in that of the necessarily contradictory *transitional* stages that might lead to that 'final victory', the question of a guarantee had to be purely methodological. And the other way round: a purely methodological guarantee, concerned with the most general outlines of the theory, could provide no great service for assessing the bewildering fluctuations of the specific events and changing relation of forces, other than reasserting its own validity with regard to the *general* trend of development.

Thus, in Lukács's case there could be no question of looking for *material* guarantees, even if only of a much more limited kind. Material guarantees, that is, which would be concerned with the contradictorily unfolding transitional trends and transformations — on both sides of the great social confrontation — together with their unevenness, relapses, and more or less extensive structural blockages. To pursue such an alternative approach was radically incompatible with Lukács's philosophical and political horizon. Understandably, therefore, conscious comprehensive transformatory strategy could not be defined in tangible material terms within his horizon. It had to be, instead, defiantly asserted *against* the disheartening setbacks of the given sociohistorical reality as a fundamental philosophical *postulate,* in conformity to the Lukácsian *methodological guarantee* as its supporting ground.

7.5 The hypostatization of 'imputed class consciousness'

7.5.1
THE most problematical characteristics of Lukács's approach arise from an essentially uncritical attitude towards the concept of the class itself. The hypostatization of class consciousness and collective will in the form of an idealized party is a necessary consequence of this uncritical attitude. While he is absolutely right to stress that only *collective subjects* can be considered the true agents of

history, he obscures the all-important Marxian line of demarcation between history and *'pre-history'*. He does this first by ascribing to the class some functions which it cannot possibly fulfil; and second, in order to extricate himself from this contradiction, by hypostatizing the fulfilment of the stipulated functions through the agency of the party as the 'organized incarnation of proletarian class consciousness'.

According to Marx, the class — including the 'class for-itself' — is necessarily tied to *pre-history*. Consequently, the idea of a conscious collective totalization on a class basis, notwithstanding the qualitative differences between the contending classes, is and remains a problematical concept. To postulate, therefore, an organization (the idealized party) and a social/material force (the proletariat as the similarly idealized *'identical subject-object* of history') is an attempt to do away with this problem by simply asserting that the 'historical embodiment' of proletarian class consciousness *is itself* the already existing bridge between 'prehistory' and 'real history', adding that the task will be *fully* accomplished in consciousness, by bridging the gap between the proletariat's 'psychological' and its 'imputed' class consciousness. Various constituents of the actual state of affairs are used by Lukács merely as a *springboard* towards the postulated solution, as we shall see in a moment. And since the existing situation is described in terms of the most extreme contrasts, so as to be able to present the class with the stark alternatives of its 'destiny' (to 'ignominiously perish or accomplish its task in full consciousness', etc.), Lukács makes it impossible for himself to escape the dilemmas arising from the postulated solutions.

We can take as an example of how Lukács uses reality as a springboard towards the ideal the way in which *History and Class Consciousness* deals with the problem of *stratification* within the working class. He acknowledges that 'the stratification of the problems and economic interests within the proletariat is, unfortunately, almost wholly unexplored'. However, the problem is immediately left behind in the spirit of his discourse on the 'ideological crisis' by saying that the real question concerns the

> degrees of distance between the psychological class consciousness and the adequate understanding of the total situation. These gradations, however, can no longer be referred back to socio-economic causes. The objective theory of class consciousness is the theory of its objective possibility. (p.79.)

Thus, the question of stratification is merely used as an aside to dramatically underline the 'ideological crisis'. Two paragraphs later, in the concluding lines of the essay, Lukács raises the question of proletarian 'self-criticism'. Significantly, however, in sharp contrast to Marx[78] — who defines it as unceasing radical reexamination and *practical* restructuring of the objective social forms and institutions created by the socialist revolution — he narrowly confines it to the level of consciousness, by equating 'the struggle of the proletariat against itself' with the struggle 'against the devastating and degrading *effects of the capitalist system upon its class consciousness'*. (p.80.) Here we have another example of that 'inverted reductionism' which we have seen above, calling for a merely ideological remedy and for an organization — the party — capable of administering such a remedy.

An even more important example is the treatment of 'reified consciousness' itself. Lukács insists that there is only an 'objective possibility' to overcome 'the purely *post festum* structure of the merely "contemplative", reified consciousness of the bourgeoisie' (p.317.) which is shared under capitalism by the workers too. This diagnosis produces a grave dilemma, since

> for each individual worker, because his own consciousness is reified, the road to achieving the *objectively possible* class consciousness and to acquiring that *inner attitude* in which he can *assimilate* that class consciousness must pass through the process of comprehending his own immediate experience only after he has experienced it; that is to say, *in each individual the post festum character of consciousness is preserved*. (pp.317-8.)

We can see, again, that reality is used as a springboard from which to take off in the direction of the idealized solution. In support of that solution, the actual situation is described in such a way that in view of the all-pervasive character of reification — dominating the consciousness of *each individual worker* — only a fully conscious collective agency (the party), which by the very definition of its nature escapes these determinations, can offer a glimmer of hope. No mediation can arise from the actually given situation, since the individuals concerned are fatefully trapped by the reification of their consciousness. Thus, the vital requirement of transition through the necessary mediation between the existing state of affairs and the future socialist society must be hypostatized and located in the party which thereby itself becomes '*the concrete mediation between man and history*'. (p.318. Lukács's italics).

Naturally, 'mediation' conceived in this way — i.e., as a *separate* organ, contrasted with a mass of workers who as individuals are each and every one cursed with a 'reified consciousness' — can only be an abstract postulate. It fails to meet the Marxian criteria of a successful mediation between 'pre-history' and 'real history' (not '*between man and history*'), defined by Marx as the materially grounded *self-activity* and *self-mediation* of the totality of associated producers in the necessary phase of *transition* to the qualitatively higher stage of sociohistorical development.

Paradoxically, by the idealization of the working class as the actual possessor of 'the standpoint of totality', Lukács creates for himself a situation from which there can be no way out except by leaping from imperative to imperative. For as soon as he asserts that the proletariat (as the radically new collective subject of history) acts in accordance with the 'standpoint of totality', his attempt to explain the dominant features of the actually existing conditions of development forces him to admit the sharp discrepancy between the stipulated ideal and the actual state of affairs. Thus, in order to be able to bridge the gap between the ideal construct and the rather disconcerting real situation, Lukács is led to an imperatival *substitution* — the party — as the actual embodiment and practical realization of the proletarian 'standpoint of totality' and of the proletariat's 'conscious collective will'. (p.315.) As a result, the originally critical intent of the theory is undermined and Lukács is left trapped by an apologetic idealization of his own making, against his own intentions. For once the new idealization becomes the central point of reference, the reality of the class appears that much darker and its actual class consciousness that much more reified, while its counter-image, by the same token, all the brighter and *practically* (or practicably) beyond reproach.

7.5.2

IT is not the case that Lukács *sets out* to produce an uncritical assessment of the party and its relationship to the working class. As we have seen, he voices serious critical reservations for which he is in fact promptly taken to task by the Comintern in no uncertain fashion. Nevertheless, he *ends up* with an essentially uncritical posture through the *inner logic* of his own reasoning, and not as a result of Stalinist institutional pressure. This logic has three main constituents:

- (1) the adoption of the Hegelian concept of 'the identical subject-object' and its identification with the proletariat as the radically new collective subject of history;
- (2) the concomitant postulate of the 'standpoint of totality' and its ascription to the class consciousness of the proletariat;
- (3) the imperatival consummation of the first two in the idealized party as the actual incarnation of both ethics and knowledge and, thereby, the practical 'mediation between man and history'.

As far as the internal theoretical determinations are concerned, the apologetic dimension of Lukács's assessment of the party in his conception as a whole arises, with a perverse logical consistency, from the idealistic/Messianic characteristics of the first two. For, once the historical stakes and the correspondingly stipulated social processes are defined in such absolute terms, only the imperatival counter-image of the actually existent can categorically overrule the harsh evidence of the prevailing 'bad immediacy'. Hence the 'ought' of the party must be super-imposed upon the empirical reality of the class and its 'psychological' class consciousness. It must be depicted as the absolutely necessary corrective with regard to all possible deviation from the *already given* right direction, and as the measure of advance towards the 'final aim' — defined in terms of 'bridging the gap between the psychological and the imputed class consciousness' — of which, by definition, only the idealized party can be the judge.

To be sure, according to Lukács the party in question *ought to* conform to the requirements which make it *worthy* of the historical functions ascribed to it, as we have seen above. Thus, as far as the openly stated intentions are concerned, the relationship is envisaged in potentially critical terms. Nevertheless, the uncritical dimension creeps into Lukács's theory as a result of the purely abstract character of the second imperative. For the party, the imperatival corrective to the class and to its immediately given class consciousness, is not only a moral 'ought', but also an actually existing practical/institutional reality (and an important *power structure* after the revolution), with an objective dynamic of its own. By contrast the second 'ought' — the set of ideal requirements and moral determinations to which the party is expected to conform — has no guarantee or objective force whatsoever behind it and must rely for its implementation exclusively on this abstract and practically powerless appeal to the postulated moral 'ought' itself.

Thus, it is by no means surprising that *History and Class Consciousness* is full of inner tensions. On the one hand, it firmly champions the cause of popular involvement and self-determination through the Workers' Councils, and on the other it advocates the 'renunciation of individual freedom' in the name of the 'realm of freedom':

The bourgeoisie no longer has the power to help society, after a few false starts, to break the 'deadlock' brought about by its economic laws. And the proletariat has the opportunity to turn events in another direction by the conscious exploitation of existing trends. This other direction is the conscious regulation of the productive forces of society. To desire this consciously, is to desire the 'realm of freedom' ... The conscious desire for the realm of freedom can only mean consciously taking the steps that will really lead to it. And in the awareness that in contemporary bourgeois society individual freedom can only be corrupt and corrupting because it is a case of *unilateral privilege* based on the unfreedom of others, this desire must entail the *renunciation of individual freedom*. It implies the *conscious subordination* of the self to that collective will that is *destined* to bring real freedom into being.(pp.313-5.)

Similarly, we find on the one hand the advocacy of a truly egalitarian society and a passionate denunciation of 'unilateral privilege' (as we have just seen), and on the other the defence of *party hierarchy*, with the summarily unilluminating justification that 'while the struggle is raging it is *inevitable* that there should be a hierarchy'. (p.336.)

Naturally, Lukács is by no means blind to what he calls 'the danger of ossification' (*Ibid.*) within the party. Since, however, the party constitutes the apex of his imperatival pyramid, in the absence of objective institutional guarantees and corresponding social/material forces which could assert their strategies of self-emancipation on a truly mass scale, in accordance with the institutionally and organizationally safeguarded possibilities of self-activity both within and outside the party, all that he can rely on is a long list of 'oughts' (even if they are repeatedly called 'must' by Lukács himself[79]). Such imperatives are sustained in *History and Class Consciousness* with regard to the danger of bureaucratic 'ossification' by nothing more firmly anchored than yet another 'ought' — wishfully represented as a factual 'is' — namely that 'The decisively novel aspect of [party] organization is that it struggles with a *steadily growing awareness* against this inner threat'. (*Ibid.*)

It is difficult to see how could one attempt to reconcile Lukács's acute critical perception of the growing tendencies of 'realism' and 'bureaucratization' in the international communist movement with his uncritical idealization of the party's 'steadily growing awareness' of the dangers which it had to face, with all their far-reaching implications for the prospects of a socialist advance. The truth of the matter is, of course, that they simply cannot be reconciled. On the contrary, Lukács's often far-sighted critical sensitivity and his self-disarmingly uncritical hypostatization of the party as the only conceivable agency of the required positive solution constitute a contradictory synthesis. They belong to the insurmountable inner tensions of a theory which desperately tries to do away with the objective contradictions of a historically unfavourable social reality by means of methodological/theoretical and moral postulates as well as by its direct exhortatory appeals to an 'imputed' class consciousness.

CHAPTER EIGHT
THE LIMITS OF 'OUT-HEGELING HEGEL'

8.1 A critique of Weberian rationality

8.1.1

MAX Weber's influence on *History and Class Consciousness* turns out to be most problematical. The Weberian theory of 'ideal types', at this stage of Lukács's development, is in no way subjected to critical scrutiny, as several of his positive references to 'typology' testify.

As a result, Marx's concept of class consciousness suffers an idealist twist in Lukács's theoretical framework, rendering the idea of 'imputed' or 'ascribed' class consciousness so malleable that it can substitute an idealized imperatival matrix for the actual historical manifestations of class consciousness, minimizing the relevance of the latter on account of its alleged 'psychological' and 'empirical' contaminations.

Similarly, as already mentioned,[80] the mystifying Weberian conflation of the functional and structural/hierarchical aspects of the social division of labour — under the ahistorical legitimatory use to which Weber himself puts the category of 'specialization' in his scheme of things — has a negative impact on the conceptual framework of *History and Class Consciousness*. And the most damaging of the Weberian influences proves to be the evaluation of capitalist 'rationality' and 'calculation'.

In Lukács's later work[81] we are offered an incomparably more realistic treatment of these problems than in the famous transitional volume of 1923. Yet, there is a tendency to ignore the seminal contribution of the older Lukács to philosophy, dismissing his own criticism of *History and Class Consciousness* as nothing more than capitulation to Stalinist pressure. George Lichtheim, for instance, once went as far as to publish an article on Lukács's philosophical development with the sonorous title: 'An Intellectual Disaster'. And, strangely enough, he could not see the dubious character of mounting such a haughtily moralizing attack on Lukács in the columns of *Encounter,* the C.I.A. sponsored English periodical.[82]

Thus, while Lukács's later achievements were rejected with a far from justifiable apriorism, denying even the author's elementary right to assume a critical position towards his own work in the light of his subsequent intellectual development, precisely the most problematical aspects of *History and Class Consciousness* have been and continue to be hailed as the chief inspiration of 'Western Marxism', as one can find this in Merleau-Ponty's preconceived characterization and summary dismissal — in his *Adventures of the Dialectic* — of almost the whole of Lukács's work written after the early nineteen twenties, under the label of 'Pravda Marxism', not to mention Adorno's notorious denunciatory tirades against the Hungarian philosopher.

Up to a limited extent the bias in favour of the young Lukács is understandable, even if far from justifiable. For *History and Class Consciousness* is a work of *transition* in which the author is engaged in his first systematic attempt to go beyond the methodological constraints once shared with his famous philosophical contemporaries, including Simmel, Lask, Dilthey, Husserl, Scheler and Weber. Lukács's early philosophical works — from *Aesthetic Culture* and *Soul and Forms* to the *Heidelberg Philosophy of Art*, the *Theory of the Novel* and the *Heidelberg Aesthetic* — abundantly testify to his complete identification with the general approach of the philosophical tradition from which he tries to extricate himself after 1918.

It is, therefore, by no means hard to explain that the methodological principles of this tradition, embraced by Lukács not as a matter of academic exercise but as a deeply felt existential commitment very early in his youth, continue to haunt him not only in *History and Class Consciousness* but for a number of years well after the publication of his famous work of transition. This is one of the main reasons why Lukács dedicates so much space to the discussion of methodological issues both in *History and Class Consciousness* and in his subsequent writings all the way down to the mid 1930s, in an authentic effort of critical self-examination and disengagement from his own philosophical past.

By the same token, it is equally understandable that some important left-wing intellectuals (like Walter Benjamin and Marcuse, for instance) who were facing the same problems as Lukács in the aftermath of the October revolution and the great upheavals of the 1920s, should respond with real enthusiasm, in the course of their own search for a viable radical approach, to a work engaged in a far-reaching critical re-examination of their shared philosophical heritage. They could do this even if (or perhaps precisely because) the links with the past retained by the author of *History and Class Consciousness* (e.g. the later self-critically rejected re-formulation of the Hegelian principle of Subject/Object identity which we shall see in a moment, or the likewise Hegelian conflation of the categories of objectification and alienation/reification, etc.) were in some contexts most problematical with regard to the advocated objectives.

7.1.2

THE burden of the Weberian influence is particularly telling in this respect. For, set against Lukács's consciously professed aim to explain the problems and contradictions of the contemporary world in the spirit of the Marxian conceptual system in *History and Class Consciousness*, it is truly astonishing to find in this work that he quotes with wholehearted approval the following passage from Weber, concerning the structural affinity between the capitalist state and the business enterprises of commodity society:

> Both are, rather, quite similar in their fundamental nature. *Viewed sociologically*, a 'business-concern' *is* the modern state; the same holds good for the factory: and this, precisely, is what is *specific* to it historically. And, likewise, the power relations in a business are also of the same kind. The *relative independence* of the *artisan* (or cottage craftsman), of the landowning *peasant*, the owner of a *benefice*, the *knight and vassal* was based on the fact that he himself owned the tools, supplies, financial resources or weapons with the aid of which he fulfilled his economic, political or military function and from which he lived while this duty was being discharged. Similarly,

the *hierarchic dependence* of the worker, the clerk, the technical assistant, the assistant in an academic institute and the civil servant and soldier has a comparable basis: namely that the tools, supplies and financial resources essential both for the busi- ness-concern and for economic survival are in the hands, in the one case, of the *entrepreneur* and, in the other case, of the *political master*. (p.95.)

And Lukács continues his full endorsement of the Weberian approach by adding that 'He [Weber] rounds off this account — very pertinently — with an analysis of the *cause* and the social implications of this phenomenon':

> The modern capitalist concern is based *inwardly* above all on *calculation*. It requires for its survival a system of justice and an administration whose workings can be *rationally* calculated, *at least in principle*, according to fixed general laws, just as the probable performance of a *machine* can be calculated. It is as little able to tolerate the dispensing of justice according to the judge's sense of fair play in individual cases or any other irrational means or principles of administering the law ... as it is able to endure a patriarchal administration that obeys the dictates of its own caprice, or sense of mercy and, for the rest, proceeds in accordance with an inviolable and sacrosanct, but irrational tradition. ... What is *specific to modern capitalism* as distinct from the *age-old capitalist forms* is that the *strictly rational organization of work*, on the basis of *rational technology* did not come into being anywhere within such irrationally consti- tuted political systems nor could it have done so. For these modern businesses with their *fixed capital* and their *exact calculations* are much too sensitive to legal and administrative *irrationalities*. They could only come into being in the *bureaucratic state* with its *rational laws* where ... the judge is more or less an *automatic statute-dispensing machine* in which you insert the files together with the necessary costs and dues at the top, whereupon he will eject the judgment together with the more or less cogent reasons for it at the bottom: that is to say, where the judge's behaviour is on the whole *predictable*. (p.96.)

Yet, if we have a closer look at the first quotation (p.95), it transpires that, far from identifying the real historical specificities of 'modern capitalism', as Weber claims, his main concern is their radical obliteration under a heap of superficial functional characteristics. For in terms of his characterization 'the artisan or cottage craftsman, the landowning peasant, the owner of a benefice, and the knight and vassal' are, amazingly, all brought to a common denominator if *'viewed sociologically'*, namely if one simply accepts the stipulated Weberian categorization at face value, without submitting it to the necessary critical scrutiny. As a frequently recurring methodological proviso of Weber's copious writings, the same sort of escape-clause is offered in the second quotation (p.96.), where Weber asserts that even if sociohistorical evidence goes against his circular categorization, it must be nonetheless considered valid, since the claimed characteristics of the 'modern capitalist' system are said to hold *'at least in principle'*.

As a result of defining his terms of reference in this way — i.e. by stipulating a *mechanical* identity between the 'business-concern' and the state ('a business- concern *is* the modern state; the same holds good for the factory'), thereby reducing one to the other, in much the same way as 'vulgar-Marxists' produce their undialectical reductions while grinding a very different axe — Weber is able to assert:

(1) that the close economy/politics correlation is specific to *'modern capitalism'* only, 'as distinct from the *age-old capitalist forms* of acquisition', hence the general

Marxian orienting principle which asserts the dialectical primacy of economic determinations — 'in the last analysis' — is *demoted* to a very limited status, on account of its alleged 'historical specificity'; and

(2) that the fundamental consideration in the capitalist system is the *'hierarchic dependence* of the worker, the clerk, the technical assistant, the assistant in an academic institute and the civil servant and soldier', hence it all boils down to a question of direct power relations in which the primacy goes to the *political* and not to the *economic*. Besides, the nature of the interconnection between the political and the economic is not indicated at all. Everything is supposed to be settled miraculously by the persuasive power of the mere *analogy* between the 'modern state' and the 'business-concern'.

Thus, at the end of the first quote we are offered an incredible 'explanation', derived from the 'ideal type' of the Weberian analogy. It asserts, without the slightest attempt to examine the relevant sociohistorical evidence, that the essential 'tools, supplies and financial resources' are *'in the hands,* in the one case, of the *entrepreneur* and, in the other case, of the *political master'*.

To suggest, though, that the medley category of 'artisan/cottage craftsman, landowning peasant, the owner of a benefice, and the knight and vassal' stands for a genuine *independence* (even if a 'relative' one, so as to provide Weber with yet another convenient escape-clause, in case he is pressed on this point), as opposed to the *'hierarchic dependence'* of the various social groups compressed into the other confused medley category of 'the worker, the clerk, the technical assistant, the assistant in an academic institute and the civil servant and soldier', is blatantly absurd. For it tendentiously disregards a multiplicity of heavy-handed dependencies — from absolutistic sociopolitical dependency and hierarchy at an earlier historical stage of development to the legally buttressed economic system of exploitative mortgage commitments and various kinds of rent and lease-related and/or bank-controlled indebtedness in more recent times — to which the allegedly 'independent' social groups in question are subjected.

As to the Weberian counter-image to such idealized 'independence', — namely the assertion according to which the levers of hierarchic dependency under modern capitalism are 'in the hands' of the mythical 'entrepreneur' and the equally mythical 'political master' — such a view deserves comment only in so far as it betrays the author's social partisanship and ideological eagerness, notwithstanding the adopted guise of detached objectivity. Just as his cynical characterization of the 'rationally calculable and predictable' behaviour of the judges as 'automatic statute-dispensing machines' shows his ideological allegiance at the end of the second passage quoted by Lukács.

8.1.3

WEBER'S aim is the tendentious depiction of the capitalistic relations as the insurmountable horizon of social life itself. This is why his eternalizing conception of historical 'alternatives' is tied to capitalism in one form or another, ranging from the claimed 'age-old capitalist forms of acquisition' (in other words, in his sense acquisition equals capitalism, ancient as well as modern) to the 'rational specificity' of 'modern capitalism'.

Moreover, by arbitrarily transubstantiating the historically indeed very specific and *limited* form of capitalism (the *entrepreneur*-dominated system) into the *general model* of 'modern capitalism' as such — at a time when the tendency is clearly visible (not only to Lenin and Rosa Luxemburg but to far less radical thinkers as well) that the entrepreneurial phase of capitalism is destined to become very soon a *historical anachronism,* since it is already in the process of being effectively displaced by the system of *monopoly capital* well beyond the power of control of even the biggest *entrepreneur* — the real sociohistorical dynamics of the ongoing process of transformation can be conveniently obfuscated. After all, Weber happens to be a contemporary of, and an enthusiastic German officer in, the ill-fated imperialist enterprise and carnage of the first world war which had a great deal to do with the irreconcilable interests and rival aspirations of the dominant monopolistic forces.

Thus, while on the one hand the Weberian concept of 'capitalism' is ahistorically extended so as to embrace, in a most generic sense, thousands of years of socioeconomic and cultural development, at the same time, on the other hand, the materially grounded specificity of capitalism as a historically circumscribed *antagonistic socioeconomic system,* with its *contending classes,* and with the incurable *irrationality* of its crisis-prone structure, is transformed into a fictitious entity: a social order characterized by the 'strictly rational organisation of work', coupled with a 'rational technology' as well as with a correspondingly 'rational system of laws' and a befitting 'rational administration'. And of course all this coalesces without any major problem into a strictly rational and calculable overall system of *unchangeable bureaucratic control,* both in the various 'business-concerns' themselves and in the 'bureaucratic state' which politically comprehends them, under the rule of the 'entrepreneur', on the one hand, and the 'political master', on the other. For in Weber's view any attempt at questioning and challenging this bureaucratic system of capitalist 'rationality' must be considered 'more and more utopian', since 'the ruled cannot dispense with or replace the bureaucratic apparatus of authority once it exists'.[83]

Thus, the eternalization of the ruling capitalistic relations as the unalterable horizon of social life is successfully accomplished by Weber, thanks to a series of definitional assumptions and categorical assertions.

Lumping together in the Weberian conceptual framework a multiplicity of heterogeneous social groups — both in the category of the 'independents' and in the case of those condemned forever to 'hierarchical dependency,' — serves the purpose of doing away precisely with the truly relevant category of *contending classes.* Yet, it is a mystification to claim that the 'entrepreneur' and the 'political master' are in control of the system of 'hierarchical dependency' to which everybody else seems to be subjected, no matter to which social group they may belong. Such mystification, however, is an ideologically *necessary* one. For it leaves no room in the Weberian discourse for the agencies of antagonistic social classes, let alone for the feasibility of any rationally viable strategy for turning the *subordinate class* into one in control of the social order.

As a matter of fact the worker does not stand in dependency to the 'entrepreneur' and the 'political master': a suggestion that both trivializes and mystifyingly personalizes the real nature of the power relationships at issue. He is subjected to a materially as well as politically enforced *structural dependency* to *capital* whose objective dictates and structural imperatives must be carried out by the ruling personnel too, both in the 'business-concerns' and in the 'bureaucratic state', at no matter which particular historical phase of development we might be thinking of in the long trajectory of the capitalist system of production and ever-enlarged reproduction. Besides, the mystifying personalization of the claimed 'entrepreneurial' and 'political masterly' control of the given system obliterates the fact that — far from having the objective conditions of the social metabolism 'in their hands', as Weber claims — also those in a position of command are in reality inserted into a network of objective determinations and interdeterminations that confers a strict mandate on their activity, even if their 'freedom' is exercised in the interest of capital's rule over society, rather than in opposition to that rule.

8.1.4

IN truth both the Weberian idealization of 'rational calculability' under modern capitalism, and the bewildering personalization of the question of dependency, can only sidetrack us from identifying the real forces and tendencies of the ongoing development. For what really matters is that

> the consolidation of what we ourselves produce into a *material power above us,* growing *out of our control,* thwarting our expectations, *bringing to naught our calculations,* is one of the chief factors in historical development up till now.[84]

Dependency of *all* individuals from such uncontrollable and *rationalcalculation-negating* power has never been stronger than under 'modern capitalism'. Individuals may have all kinds of illusions with regard to their greater freedom under the capitalist system of production and social interchange. In reality, however, 'they are less free, because they are to a greater extent governed by material forces',[85] i.e., in the words of the rather more sharply formulated German original, they are dominated by — or 'subsumed under' — the power of things.[86]

To suggest, therefore, as Weber does, that the entrepreneurially expected and predicted results of the capitalist economic enterprise can be rationally calculated 'just as the probable performance of a *machine* can be calculated' is a grotesque — and utterly wishful — overstatement. It is a typical feature of Weberian analogies that even their scanty plausibility would seem to apply in one direction only: the direction of the eagerly anticipated and socially apologetic conclusions of the author.

The moment we try to test them by asking the question whether the correlations predicated between the members of the asserted relationships hold true in both directions — i.e., in the present case, by asking whether one could say it aloud in public, without blushing, that the performance of machines is as predictable as the 'rational predictability' of the capitalist business enterprise — they deflate themselves instantly and reveal the ideological interests beneath the allegedly objective Weberian reasoning and its peculiar constructs. For if the probable performance of machines could be no more reliably calculated than the performance of the capitalist business enterprise, in that case the probability of Cape Canaveral moon-shots landing on the lawn of the White-House would be much greater than the likelihood that they might ever reach their predicted destination.

As regards the 'predictability' of the judges in administering the 'rational laws' of the capitalist state, to claim that their decisions are 'rationally calculable'

— because they behave like 'statute-dispensing machines' — offers us precious little in addition to the cynical joke itself. For it avoids or begs the question of *how and why* the statutes themselves are produced in the first place in the way in which they happen to be.

Also, and again characteristically for Weber, such description says absolutely nothing about the *class* character of the laws themselves which are written into the statute books before they can be 'dispensed'. Weber prefers, instead, the myth of pure 'rationality', dulling even the young Lukács's critical sense in *History and Class Consciousness* when he talks of the *'rational systematisation* of all statutes regulating life' as arrived at 'in a *purely logical* manner, as an exercise in *pure legal dogma'* etc. (p.96.) Indeed Weber goes as far as suggesting, in a totally idealist fashion, that the 'modern Occidental state' is the 'creation of the Jurists'.[87]

The reality is, of course, much more prosaic than that. For one thing, it is by no means true that judges behave simply like 'statute-dispensing machines', except in purely routine matters, which do not explain anything, least of all the claimed 'rational' constitution of the statutes themselves. Indeed, the 'learned judges' are perfectly willing and capable of producing in strictly legal terms totally unexpected judgements, as well as twisted explanations to suit the occasion — brushing aside without the slightest hesitation the relevant statutes, thus violating the 'rational law' itself which they are supposed to dispense, dutifully — whenever the social confrontation requires that they should do so in a situation of some major conflict. Not to mention the fact that even with regard to the secondary question of who are the people who actually possess the wealth so as to be able to 'insert the necessary costs and dues at the top' in order to receive 'ejected' by the presiding judges the desired judgement 'at the bottom', the blatantly obvious *class* character of such 'paradigmatically rational' exercise cannot be disregarded.

The far from 'rationally reassuring' truth of the matter is, of course, that the currently enforced system of statutes had been constituted (and continues to be modified in its fundamental outlines and socially vital dimensions) above all for the purpose of securing and safeguarding capital's control over the social body, thereby simultaneously also perpetuating the *structural subordination* of labour to capital. This is also the main reason why we are presented at times with the most baffling — apparently quite 'irrational' — *non-enforcement* of certain key statutes in some major social confrontation against one Trade Union, while the same statute happens to be strictly enforced against another Union which is considered by the representatives of the ruling class to be the principal 'enemy within'.

We had some graphic examples of such apparent 'irrationalities' and 'formal inconsistencies' in recent years; in the British miners' strike, for instance, when a — for the Tory Government's strategy potentially most damaging — conflict with the most powerful Union, the Transport and General Workers Union, was deliberately avoided by the 'fearlessly independent and objective' judiciary dispensers of our system of 'rational law', in flagrant violation of its statutes, in order to be able to concentrate the Government's fire with that much greater severity and effectiveness on the National Union of Mineworkers. Similar tactics could be observed on the occasion of two major disputes of the printworkers' unions, including the peculiarly unequal punishment meted out to the N.G.A. as against the less radical SOGAT. In any case, let anyone try to explain the various anti-union legislative measures in terms of 'strict rationality', 'pure logic', 'pure legal dogma', 'rational administration', and the like.

No doubt, we can witness an awesome 'predictability of the judges' in all situations of fundamental social conflict; whenever, that is, the stakes are defined in *structurally* significant terms. However, such predictability is not in the least intelligible in terms of 'pure logic' and 'pure rationality'. On the contrary; the logic and rationality with which we are confronted in the administration of the law belong to the category of 'applied rationality', arising from — and with a powerful *rationalizing* effect championing the cause of — more or less consciously pursued, and in any event clearly identifiable, *class interest*.

8.1.5

ANOTHER context in which we can see the problematical character of the Weberian concepts concerns the relationship between *exchange* and *use* and the categories closely connected with this relationship.

As we know, under the conditions of modern historical development capitalist exchange succeeds in one-sidedly dominating use in direct proportion to the degree to which generalized commodity production stabilizes itself. Thus we are presented with the complete *overturning* of the former dialectical primacy of *use* over *exchange*. Accordingly, capital asserts also in this respect its rigid material determinations and interests with total disregard for the consequences. As a result, use-value corresponding to need can acquire the right to existence only if it conforms to the aprioristic imperatives of self-expanding exchange-value.

To appreciate the full import of this structural subordination of *use* to *exchange* in capitalist society, we have to situate it in the context of a number of other important practical dualisms which have a direct bearing upon it — notably the interrelationship between *abstract* and *concrete, quantity* and *quality,* and *time* and *space*.

In all three instances we should be able to speak, in principle, of a *dialectical* interconnection. However, on closer inspection we find that in their historically specific manifestations under the conditions of commodity production and exchange the objective dialectic is *subverted* by capital's reified determinations and *one* side of each relationship rigidly dominates the other. Thus the *concrete* is subordinated to the abstract, the *qualitative* to the quantitative, and the living *space* of productive human interactions — whether we think of it as 'nature to hand' in its immediacy, or under its aspect of 'worked-up nature', or take it as the work-environment in the strictest sense of the term, or, by contrast, with reference to its most comprehensive meaning as the vital framework of human existence itself under the name of the *environment* in general — is dominated by the tyranny of capital's *time-management* and *time-accountancy,* with potentially catastrophic consequences.

Moreover, the way in which all four complexes are brought into a common interplay with one another under the determinations of capital greatly aggravates the situation. For, contrary to Lukács's Weberian interpretation of some of Marx's seminal ideas in *History and Class Consciousness,* the problem is not that the 'contemplative stance' of labour '*reduces* space and time to a common denominator and *degrades time to the dimension of space'* (p.89.) but, on the contrary, that *'Time is everything, man is nothing'*.[88]

In fact the *reduction* which we find here concerns *labour* in its *qualitative specificity*, and not time and space as such. A reduction indeed through which qualitatively specific and rich 'compound labour' is turned into thoroughly impoverished 'simple labour', simultaneously also asserting the domination of the *abstract* over the *concrete* as well as the corresponding domination of *exchange-value* over *use-value*.

Three quotations from Marx help to clarify these connections. The first comes from *Capital* and contrasts the position of Political Economy with the writings of classical antiquity:

> Political Economy, which as an independent science first sprang into being during the period of manufacture, views the *social division of labour* only from the standpoint of manufacture, and sees in it only the means of producing more commodities with a given quantity of labour, and, consequently, of cheapening commodities and hurrying on the *accumulation of capital*. In most striking contrast with this accentuation of *quantity* and *exchange-value*, is the attitude of the writers of classical antiquity, who hold exclusively by *quality* and *use-value*. ... If the growth of the quantity is occasionally mentioned, this is only done with reference to the greater abundance of *use-values*. There is not a word alluding to *exchange-value* or to the cheapening of commodities.[89]

The second quotation highlights the way in which the *reduction* exercised by the political economists obliterates the *social determinateness* of individuals — depriving them thereby of their *individuality,* since there cannot be true individuality and particularity in abstraction from the rich multiplicity of social determinations — in the service of the dominant ideological interests. It reads as follows:

> Society, as it appears to the political economist, is *civil society,* in which *every individual* is a totality of needs and only exists for the other person, as the other exists for him, in so far as each becomes a *means* for the other. The political economist *reduces* everything (just as does politics in its *Rights of Man*) to *man,* i.e., to the *individual* whom he *strips of all determinateness* so as to class him as *capitalist or worker*.[90]

The concern expressed in the third quotation is in close affinity with the previous one whose implications point to the dialectic of true individuality arising from the manifold mediations of social determinateness, as opposed to the reductive abstraction of the political economists that directly links *abstract individuality* and *abstract universality*. The passage in question brings into focus the relationship between simple and compound labour and the subordination of men to the rule of quantity and time. This is how Marx puts it:

> Competition, according to an American economist, determines how many days of simple labour are contained in one day's compound labour. Does not this *reduction* of days of compound labour to days of simple labour suppose that simple labour is itself taken as a measure of value? If the mere *quantity* of labour functions as a *measure* of value regardless of *quality*, it presupposes that simple labour has become the pivot of industry. It presupposes that labour has been equalized by the *subordination of man* to the *machine* or by the extreme *division of labour*; that *men are effaced by their labour*; that the pendulum of the clock has become as accurate a measure of the relative activity of *two workers* as it is of the speed of *two locomotives*. Therefore we should not say that one man's hour is worth another man's hour, but rather that *one man* during an hour is *worth just as much as another man* during an hour. *Time is everything, man is*

nothing; he is at the most *time's carcase*. *Quality* no longer matters. *Quantity* alone
decides everything; hour for hour; day for day;[91]

Thus, within the framework of the existing socioeconomic system a multiplicity
of formerly dialectical interconnections are reproduced in the form of perverse
practical dualisms, dichotomies, and antinomies, reducing human beings to a
reified condition (whereby *they* are brought to a common denominator with,
and become replaceable by, 'locomotives' and other machines) and to the ignominious status of *'time's carcase'*. And since the possibility of practically manifesting and realizing the *inherent worth* and human specificity of all individuals
through their essential productive activity is blocked off as a result of this process
of alienating reduction (which makes 'one man during an hour worth just as
much as another man'), *value* as such becomes an extremely *problematical concept*.
For, in the interest of capitalist profitability, not only can there be no room left
for the actualization of the individuals' specific worth but, worse still, *counter-
value* must unceremoniously prevail over value and assert its absolute domination as the only admissible practical value-relation, in direct subordination to
the material imperatives of the capital system.

8.1.6

IN his 1967 Preface to *History and Class Consciousness* (p.xxxvi.), describing the
impact of Marx's *Economic and Philosophic Manuscripts of 1844* on his intellectual
development, Lukács mentions that he knew some related Marxian texts that
should have led to a radical change in his interpretation of the issues at stake
already at the time of writing *History and Class Consciousness*. However, the
literature in question could not exercise a real influence on him, because he read
Marx through Hegelian spectacles.

The same is true as regards the negative, obfuscating effect of the thick
Weberian spectacles which the Hungarian philosopher still wears in *History and
Class Consciousness*. For, as the available evidence shows, by the early 1920s he is
familiar with Marx's analyses of the perverse and inhuman dominance of capitalist time-accountancy in the established socioeconomic order. He even quotes
in *History and Class Consciousness* a highly relevant passage on the subject from
Marx's *Poverty of Philosophy*. Nevertheless, he remains utterly blind to its meaning, due to the opacity of the Weberian spectacles of 'rationality' and 'rational
calculation' which he unquestioningly accepts as positive insights into the nature
of the capital system.

It is quite significant in this respect that, as a critical reckoning also with his
own past, many of Lukács's later works directly engage in a radical reassessment
of capitalistic 'rationality', emphasising the structurally insurmountable *irrationality* of this system of production and social reproduction.

References to Weber are not very frequent, although the theoretical connections are clearly visible. And in *The Destruction of Reason* — Lukács's systematic
analysis of the philosophical tradition of irrationalism in the last century and a
half, assessed within the framework of its socioeconomic and historical setting
— he subjects also the work of his former teacher and friend, Max Weber, to a
most searching criticism.

Accordingly, in the chapter entitled 'German Sociology in the Wilhelmine
Age' (pp.601-19, dedicated to the discussion of Weber's work), Lukács points

out that the Weberian conception of rationality and 'rational calculability' is based on the arbitrary identification of *technology* and *economics,* in accordance with a 'vulgarizing simplification that acknowledged only mechanized capitalism as the authentic variety' (*ibid.,* p.607).

Moreover, Lukács underlines a few lines further on in *The Destruction of Reason* that the Weberian conception

> necessarily entailed standing the capitalist economy on its head, in that the popularized surface phenomena took priority over the problems of the productive forces' development. This abstracting distortion also enabled the German sociologists to ascribe to ideological forms, particularly law and religion, a causal role equivalent and indeed superior to economics. That, in turn, now entailed an ever-increasing *methodological substitution of analogies for causal connections.*
>
> For instance, Max Weber saw a strong resemblance between the *modern state* and a *capitalist industrial enterprise.* But since he dismissed on agnostic-relativist grounds the problem of primary causation, he stuck to mere description with the aid of analogies. ... This thinking always culminated in proof of the economic and social impossibility of socialism. The seeming historicity of sociological studies was aimed — even if not explicitly — at arguing the case for capitalism as a necessary, no longer essentially changeable system and at exposing the purported internal economic and social contradictions which, it was claimed, made the realization of socialism impossible in theory as in practice.

Thus the correlation asserted by Weber between the modern state and the capitalist business-concern — a mechanistic and utterly superficial equation which, as we saw in Section 8.1.2 above, was still hailed in *History and Class Consciousness* as a major theoretical insight — is dismissed in *The Destruction of Reason* as the paradigm example of an extremely problematical methodology, in the service of a combative ideology whose more or less veiled object is to undermine any belief in the possibility of socialist development.

This critique is extended by Lukács to the whole arsenal of the highly influential Weberian methodology. For, as Lukács argues in *The Destruction of Reason:*

> Weber's sociology was full of formalistic analogies. Thus he formally equated, for instance, ancient Egyptian bureaucracy with socialism, councillors (Räte) and estates (Stände); thus in speaking of the irrational vocation of leader (charisma), he drew an analogy between the Siberian shaman and the social democrat leader Kurt Eisner, etc. As a result of its *formalism, subjectivism and agnosticism,* sociology, like contemporary philosophy, did no more than to construct specified types, set up typologies and arrange historical phenomena in this typology. ... With Max Weber this problem of types became the central methodological question. The setting up of purely constructed 'ideal types' Weber regarded as a question central to the task of sociology. According to him a sociological analysis was only possible if it proceeded from these types. But this analysis did not produce a line of development, but only a *juxtaposition of ideal types selected and arranged casuistically.* The course of society itself, comprehended in its uniqueness on Rickertian lines and not following a regular pattern, had an *irremediably irrationalistic character* ...
>
> It is evident from this that Weber's sociological categories — he defined as 'chance' the most diverse social formations such as might, justice, the State and so on — will yield simply the abstractly formulated psychology of the calculating individual agent of capitalism. ... Weber's conception of 'chance' was, on the one hand, modelled on the Machist interpretation of natural phenomena. And on the other, it was condi-

tioned by the psychological subjectivism of the 'marginal utility theory'; it converted the objective forms, transmutations, happenings, etc., of social life into a tangled web of — fulfilled or unfulfilled — 'expectations', and its regular principles into more or less probable 'chances' of the fulfilment of such expectations. It is likewise evident that a sociology operating in this direction could go no further than *abstract analogies* in its generalizations. (*Ibid.*, pp.611-3.)

In this way, in *The Destruction of Reason* the once greatly admired methodological pillars of the Weberian conceptual edifice are subjected to a radical critique by Lukács. He draws a sharp line of demarcation between what he considers to be the necessary criteria of genuine rationality — i.e., a rationality fully in consonance with the objective dialectic of the historical process — and the often even explicitly anti-socialist and thoroughly subjectivist ideological system of the German sociologist. And he insists that the Weberian system, notwithstanding all claims to objectivity, 'value-neutrality' (Wertfreiheit) and 'strict rationality' put forward by its originator, remains trapped within the *'irremediably irrational'* confines of formalistic analogies.

8.1.7

THE same critical attitude characterizes Lukács's subsequent writings on Weber. Thus, in his last work, *The Ontology of Social Being,* the Weberian theory of rationality and its application to the sphere of morality — which must result in a completely *'relativistic conception of values'*[92] — is firmly rejected by Lukács.

It is dismissed by him as the embodiment of an approach to the problems of moral judgement which can only lead into a blind alley. For in Lukács's view it represents a combination of the two typical false extremes that — notwithstanding their claims to the contrary — remain stuck to the fetishism of appearance and bring with them nothing but the capitulation of moral reason to the established order. According to Lukács what we are offered in such conceptualizations of the role of moral reason and in the thereby postulated meaning of the pluralism of values is

> on the one hand a clinging to the *immediacy* in which the phenomena present themselves in the world of appearance, and on the other hand an *over-rationalized,* logicized and hierarchical system of values. These equally false extremes, when they alone are brought into play, produce either a *purely relativistic empiricism* or else a *rational construction* that cannot be adequately applied to reality; when brought alongside they produce the appearance of an *impotence of moral reason* in the face of reality.[93]

Thus, within the framework of *The Ontology of Social Being* there can be no room for even one of the most influential aspects of Weberian theory towards which Lukács once felt a great sympathy. It is rejected on the ground that such an approach is capable of producing only fetishistic mystification and moral impotence. For the demobilizing impact of a 'purely relativistic empiricism' cannot possibly be counterbalanced by even the most ingenious schemes of over-rationalizing typology, in that in substantive terms and with regard to their corresponding ideological orientation the whole enterprise remains trapped in the prosaic but by Weber romanticized 'iron cage' of capitalist immediacy.

Admittedly, the problematical Weberian influence is never completely overcome by Lukács, as we shall see later. But, nonetheless, there is another important issue as well in relation to which we can see Lukács's conscious critical reckoning with the 'over-rationalizing' approach of his erstwhile philosophical companion. This issue concerns the category of *manipulation* which not only in his last work but in general during the last twenty years of his life occupies an increasing importance in the thought of Lukács. So much so, in fact, that he censures even Engels for what in his view amounts to a significant failure to perceive a potentially most destructive tendency in the orientation of science and technology; one that begins to manifest itself already under late nineteenth century capitalistic developments.

As a result of the tendency in question, Lukács insists, the once unambiguously liberating and therefore rightly celebrated potential of 'genuine, world-embracing science' is practically counteracted and ultimately nullified by the articulation of science as *'mere technological manipulation'*,[94] in the service of extremely dubious objectives.

It is unimportant in the present context whether the category of 'manipulation' is adequate to deal with the problems put into relief by Lukács in his many references to the dangers inseparable from the denounced economic and cultural/ideological practices. (I do not believe for a moment that it is.) What matters here is that a great deal of what is accepted by the author of *History and Class Consciousness* at face value from the Weberian mythology of the capitalist socioeconomic and cultural/legal/political order as 'rationality' and 'rationalization' is unhesitatingly consigned by the older Lukács to the category of *manipulation*.

8.2 Paradise lost of 'Western Marxism'

8.2.1

THE principal reason why Merleau-Ponty idealizes Lukács's *History and Class Consciousness* in his *Adventures of the Dialectic* as the classic embodiment of 'Western Marxism' (in contraposition to 'Pravda Marxism') is the Hungarian philosopher's treatment of the Hegelian problematic of the identical subject-object.

To his credit, Merleau-Ponty is perfectly willing to admit that his reconstruction of Lukács's meaning is done 'very freely ... in order to measure today's communism, to realize what it has renounced and to what it has resigned itself'.[95] In tune with this aspiration, the general tendency of Merleau-Ponty's *Adventures of the Dialectic* is the theoretical legitimation of extreme relativism. This is why he wants to go even beyond his own intellectual idol, Max Weber, saying that 'this great mind'[96] 'does not pursue the *relativization of relativism to its limits*'.[97] Accordingly, Merleau-Ponty looks for a suitable corrective to Weber and announces to have found it in the young Lukács. For in Merleau-Ponty's view the exemplary merits of the position assumed by the Hungarian philosopher in *History and Class Consciousness* must be recognized on account of the claimed fact that

> He does not reproach Weber for having been too relativistic but rather for not having been relativistic enough and for not having gone so far as to 'relativize the notions of subject and object'. For, by so doing, one regains a sort of totality.[98]

Merleau-Ponty needs the 'relativization of relativism to its limits' for two, closely interconnected, reasons.

First, in order to be able to relativize in such a way the meaning of what should or should not be considered progressive in the field of sociopolitical action that his earlier rejection of 'compromises with colonial and social oppression'[99] should be completely reversed. Thus, the new-found relativism gives Merleau-Ponty the excuse to condemn what he now labels as the absolutistic 'moralizing failure'[100] of the anti-colonial militants who argue and fight for the right to self-determination in the still remaining French colonial territories. In his newly adopted stance Merleau-Ponty castigates them on the ground that 'they do not envisage any compromise in colonial policy'.[101] Sadly, in this first sense, the 'relativization of relativism to its limits' is used by Merleau-Ponty to glorify French colonial policy — and to do so at the time of the Algerian war and General de Gaulle's recall to power — as 'an African Marshall Plan'.[102] And he concludes his apologetic self-identification with the exploiters and oppressors by proclaiming that 'we can no longer say that the system is made for exploitation; there is no longer, as it used to be called, any "colony of exploitation".'[103]

The second reason for which the virtues of extreme relativism are praised by the French philosopher concerns the nature of the theoretical framework itself in which the complete overturning of the earlier genuinely advocated practical political stance of the radical intellectual Merleau-Ponty can be accomplished. For only a few years before writing Adventures of the Dialectic, the 'marxisant' phenomenologist sharply condemns those American former Marxists who, in his view, joined the 'league of abandoned hope'. He censures them for having 'jettisoned every kind of Marxist criticism, every kind of radical temper. The facts of exploitation throughout the world present them with only scattered problems which must be examined and solved one by one. They no longer have any political ideas'.[104] And the radical Merleau-Ponty — at the time of writing the quoted article still Sartre's comrade in arms — sums up his position against the members of the 'league of abandoned hope' like this:

> all things considered the recognition of man by man and the classless society are less vague as principles of a world politics than American prosperity, and the historical mission of the proletariat is in the last analysis a more precise idea than the historical mission of the United States.[105]

Two and a half years after the publication of Adventures of the Dialectic the 'Marxist philosophy of history' is summarily dismissed by Merleau-Ponty who now states that 'the very idea of a proletarian power has become problematical'.[106]

This shift is theoretically prepared in the 'very free' interpretation of History and Class Consciousness which relativizes not only the subject and object — in the most general terms, for the professed purpose of 'regaining a sort of totality' — but specifically the relationship of philosophy to the material basis of social life. Thus Merleau-Ponty empties the Marxian theoretical framework of its content by establishing — not by analysis built on textual and historical evidence but by a thoroughly arbitrary decree — a later most fashionable opposition between the 'philosophical' young Marx and the originator of scientific socialism. As a result of this line of approach the so-called 'Western Marxism' — the 'relativization of relativism to its limits' in philosophy — is invented by Merleau-Ponty, in order to radically undermine with its help not only the Marxism of Marx's followers but of Marx's conceptual framework as well. Characterized as a sort of Marxism 'before the fall', the idealized 'Western Marxism' is said to represent a — somewhat mythical — antidote not only to the 'dogmatic Pravda-Marxists' but, much more significantly, to the historically known Marx himself.

It is for the establishment of this dubious theoretical objective that the 'very free' reconstruction of Lukács's line of argument in *History and Class Consciousness* is needed. In the end we are told that the — totally relativized — Marxism approved by Merleau-Ponty is none other than

the *pre-1850* one. After this comes 'scientific' socialism, and what is given to science is taken from philosophy. ... In his later period, therefore, when Marx reaffirms his faithfulness to Hegel, this should not be misunderstood, because what he looks for in Hegel is no longer philosophical inspiration; rather, it is rationalism, to be used for the benefit of 'matter' and 'ratios of production', which are considered as an order in themselves, an external and completely positive power. It is no longer a question of saving Hegel from abstraction, of recreating the dialectic by entrusting it to the very movement of its content, without any idealistic postulate; it is rather a question of annexing Hegel's logic to the economy. ... *The conflict between 'Western Marxism' and Leninism is already found in Marx* as a conflict between dialectical thought and naturalism, and the Leninist othodoxy eliminated Lukács's attempt as Marx himself had eliminated his own first 'philosophical' period.[107]

Naturally, Merleau-Ponty's arbitrary periodization runs into difficulties right from the moment of its first formulation. For the French philosopher, after declaring that the commended 'philosophical' Marx is the 'pre-1850 one', is immediately forced to put the clock back by no less than five years, all the way down to the 'young philosophical' Marx. Accordingly Merleau-Ponty asserts in the next line of his *Adventures of the Dialectic,* without bothering to sort out the contradiction in his periodization, that *'The German Ideology* already spoke of destroying philosophy rather than realizing it'.[108] Thus not even the pre-1850 Marx is allowed to join the exalted rank of 'Western Marxism'. Such a status is assigned only to a Marx who never existed.

As we can see, then, the relativistic reconstruction of *History and Class Consciousness* in the *Adventures of the Dialectic* serves a very precise and extremely problematical ideological purpose. In personal terms, sadly, it marks an important stage in the course of Merleau-Ponty's intellectual and political development from his sarcastic condemnation of the 'league of abandoned hope' to his unreserved self-identification with its conservative ideological tenets.[109]

8.2.2

TO be sure, Lukács's celebrated work has absolutely nothing to do with Merleau-Ponty's anti-Marxist ideological intentions. Nor could one identify in the author of *History and Class Consciousness* the intellectual ancestor of those who counterpose the young 'philosophical' Marx to the later 'scientific economist' thinker.[110] On the contrary, Lukács is fully justified in underlining in his Preface to the 1967 edition of *History and Class Consciousness* that

I included the early works of Marx in the overall picture of his world-view. I did this at a time when most Marxists were unwilling to see in them more than historical documents that were important only for his personal development. Moreover, *History and Class Consciousness* cannot be blamed if, decades later, the relationship was reversed so that the early works were seen as the products of the true Marxist philosophy, while the later works were neglected. Rightly or wrongly, I had always treated Marx's works as having an *essential unity*. (p.xxvi.)

The real difficulties lie elsewhere in *History and Class Consciousness*. As Lukács himself puts it in 1967, he tries to '*out-Hegel Hegel*' in his 'purely metaphysical construct' which depicts the proletariat as the 'identical subject-object of the real history of mankind'. (p.xxiii.)

As a result of approaching the problems of sociohistorical development in this spirit, Lukács ends up with 'an edifice boldly erected above every possible reality' (p.xxiii.), reproducing at the same time also the mystifying Hegelian conflation of the concepts of 'alienation' and 'objectification': a procedure which must be considered doubly bewildering in a materialist historical conception that explicitly aims at identifying the objective, materially effective leverage of social emancipation. For, once *objectification* is discarded as 'reification' and 'alienation', there remains no conceivable ground on which even the theoretically most sophisticated emancipatory strategy could be successfully implemented in the real world.

However, if Lukács tries to 'out-Hegel Hegel' in *History and Class Consciousness*, Merleau-Ponty goes a great deal further than that in his *Adventures of the Dialectic*. For he attempts to 'out-Weber Weber' with Lukács's help, in order to 'relativize relativism to its limits'. Furthermore, the French philosopher quite simply refuses to appreciate anything else that one can find in *History and Class Consciousness* beyond the Hegelian problematic of the identical subject-object. And even the latter is taken on board in Merleau-Ponty's *Adventures of the Dialectic* only in an 'out-Webered', extremely relativized and subjectivized form. In a form, that is, from which all references to the actual conditions of existence of the proletariat and to the strategic requirements of their transformation — present, at least to some extent, in *History and Class Consciousness*, even if in a very problematical form — completely disappear. Thus by far the most questionable aspect of *History and Class Consciousness* is turned into a neo-Weberian mythology, whereas all the real theoretical accomplishments of this important work of transition are wilfully ignored.

Moreover, even the question of relativism is characteristically misrepresented in Merleau-Ponty's ideologically motivated reinterpretation of *History and Class Consciousness*. For he applauds Lukács for allegedly going beyond Weber by 'pursuing the relativization of relativism to its limits'. Yet, the only place in *History and Class Consciousness* where we can find something vaguely resembling Merleau-Ponty's claim is where Lukács insists that

> Only the *dialectic of history* can create a radically new situation. This is not only because *it relativizes all limits*, or *better*, because it puts them in a *state of flux*. Nor is it just because all those forms of existence that constitute the counterpart of the absolute are dissolved into processes and viewed as concrete manifestations of history so that the absolute is not so much denied as endowed with its *concrete historical shape* and treated as an aspect of the process itself. (p.188.)

Thus, while Merleau-Ponty's ideal of 'pursuing the relativization of relativism to its limits' (whatever that curious notion might mean) has for its subject the French philosopher's out-Webered Weber: i.e., the relativistic philosopher himself, Lukács is in fact talking about something completely different. He raises the issue of relativization (or, better, as he adds, the question of putting the limits of things 'in a state of flux', underlining thereby their inherently *processual* character) with reference to the dialectic of history as such. It is the latter that *'relativizes all limits'* in the course of *its* objective unfolding within the framework of which everything must assume a *'concrete historical shape'*. Indeed, only a few lines after the passage quoted from page 188 Lukács — anticipating and rejecting Merleau-Ponty's left-handed compliment — states quite categorically that *'it is highly misleading to describe dialectical materialism as "relativism".'* (p.189.)

8.2.3

BUT really to do justice to the author of *History and Class Consciousness,* we must quote another passage as well from this work in order to show how far Lukács goes in his insistence on the far from relativistic character of the determinations which in his view emanate from the *objective dialectic* of history. In the final section of the most important essay of *History and Class Consciousness,* 'Reification and the Consciousness of the Proletariat' — concerned with the difficulties of finding a way 'to disrupt the reified structure of existence' (p.197) under the concrete historical shape of capitalist society — Lukács forcefully argues that

> the structure can be disrupted only if the *immanent contradictions* of the process [as a developing historical totality] are made conscious. Only when the consciousness of the proletariat is able to point out the road along which the dialectics of history is *objectively impelled,* but which it cannot travel unaided, will the consciousness of the proletariat awaken to a consciousness of the process, and only then will the proletariat become the *identical subject-object of history* whose praxis will change reality. If the proletariat fails to take this step, the contradiction will remain unresolved and will be *reproduced* by the *dialectical mechanics of development* at a higher level, in an altered form and with *increased intensity*. It is in *this* that the *objective necessity of history* consists. The deed of the proletariat can never be more than to take the *next step* in the process.[111] (pp.197-8.)

As we can see, in his effort to underline the inescapably objective nature of the ongoing historical process Lukács does not hesitate to resort to such an odd — at first sight even self-contradictory — concept as the 'dialectical mechanics of development' (die dialektische Mechanik der Entwicklung).[112]What he means by it is that the dialectic of history (that is, the dialectic of the overall historical development, 'Gesamtentwicklung') is itself *objectively impelled* — as a dialectically productive mechanism — to bring out into the open, at an ever-increasing intensity, the underlying contradictions of capitalist society as the *objective necessity of the process of development* ('die objektive Notwendigkeit des Entwicklungsprozesses'), even if the consciousness of the proletariat *fails* to live up to its 'historic mission'.

From this vision two conclusions follow.

- First, that there can be no such thing as the *permanent* integration of the proletariat, only a strictly *temporary* one. The 'dialectical mechanics' and the 'objective necessity of development' make it impossible for the proletariat to become permanently integrated into the exploitative and dehumanizing capitalistic framework. For the 'Gesamtprozess' continues to reproduce the antagonistic immanent contradictions of capitalist society, both at a higher level and with an increasing intensity, precisely because the dialectic of history is 'not aided' in its objectively impelled drive towards the resolution of the contradictions in question by the actualization of the proletariat's *potential* (or 'ascribed') class consciousness. Accordingly, the contradictions must be faced by the workers again and again, no matter how much effort is invested in the various schemes of accommodation through which the ruling order — with the active collaboration of socialdemocratic reformism — tries to sweep them under the carpet.

- The second conclusion concerns the dramatic alternatives implicit in the objective tendencies of actual historical development in the age of global capitalism and imperialism. On this point the author of *History and Class Consciousness* is in full agreement with Rosa Luxemburg's dictum: *'socialism or barbarism'*.[113] For according to Lukács the objective dialectic of historical necessity cannot secure by itself a *positive* outcome to the ultimately quite unavoidable confrontations whereby the two hegemonic classes of the given productive order — capital and labour — must fight out their conflicts to a historically viable conclusion, under the pressure of the 'dialectical mechanics of development'. The proletariat is said to be 'the identical subject-object of the historical process, i.e. the first subject in history that is (objectively) capable of an adequate social consciousness'. (p.199.) But *'capable'* remains the key operative term. It all hinges therefore on the successful actualization of the 'objective capability' constantly reiterated by Lukács.

The categories we have seen in the passage quoted from pages 197-8 of *History and Class Consciousness* are brought into focus by Lukács in order to set the theoretical framework in which these two conclusions can be drawn. They are in fact spelled out with utmost clarity, and without even the slightest hint of the 'relativization of relativism to its limits', in the final words of Lukács's essay on 'Reification and the Consciousness of the Proletariat'. They read as follows:

> As the antagonism becomes acute *two possibilities* open up for the proletariat. It is given the opportunity to substitute its own positive contents for the emptied and bursting husk. But also it is exposed to the danger that *for a time at least* it might adapt itself *ideologically* to conform to these, the emptiest and most decadent forms of bourgeois culture. ... The *objective economic evolution* could do no more than create the position of the proletariat in the production process. It was this position that determined its point of view. But the objective evolution could only give the proletariat the *opportunity* and the *necessity* to change society. Any transformation can only come about as the product of the — *free* — action of the proletariat itself. (pp.208-9.)

True to his general line of approach, Lukács again defines the impediment to a positive resolution of the identified contradictions in terms of *ideology*. An impediment which in his view could be overcome by the work of consciousness upon consciousness, made instrumentally/organizationally feasible in the form of the party's enlightening ideological activity, provided that the party itself becomes worthy of its historic task, as we have seen it argued by Lukács in another context. This circumstance, however, does not deprive Lukács's diagnosis of the situation, and his discussion of the way in which the 'reified structure of existence' (*'die verdinglichte Struktur des Daseins'*) could be disrupted, of their objective terms of reference.

Thankfully, in *History and Class Consciousness* not everything is left to the magic device of the 'identical subject-object of history' which the author took over from Hegel and from the idealist philosophical tradition brought by the great German dialectician to its highest level. There are also the categories of 'objective historical necessity'; the 'dialectical mechanics of development'; the 'objective necessity of the process of development'; the 'concrete historical shape'[114] of objects, tendencies and structures; the 'struggle between collective capital and collective labour', etc., with which Merleau-Ponty's quasi-mystical discourse on the 'relativization of relativism to its limits' is totally incompatible.

As far as Lukács is concerned, there can be no question of 'regaining a sort of totality'. For him 'totality' is not something romantically lost and even more romantically found again through its subsumption under the idealist category of 'subject-object identity'. No matter how inadequate Lukács's treatment of the adopted Hegelian postulate, in his conception, even at the time of writing 'Reification and the Consciousness of the Proletariat', the historically concretized subject-object identity is only *part* of the whole story.

Totality in *History and Class Consciousness* is the unfolding overall historical process (Gesamtprozess) which asserts itself — for better or worse — in its objective, and inseparably dialectical, historical necessity whether we become conscious of it or fail to do so. Although Lukács considers with unrealistically high hopes and expectations the power of consciousness directly to transform in the desired direction the 'reified world', nevertheless he does not try to equate the *objective process* of historical development with the *'consciousness* of the process'. (p.197.)

This is why the conceptual framework of *History and Class Consciousness,* notwithstanding all its problematical features, cannot be brought to a common denominator with its 'very free' reconstruction by Merleau-Ponty in his *Adventures of the Dialectic.* In fact Lukács explicitly rejects not only *'every "humanism" or anthropological point of view'* (pp.186-7.) — which were supposed to be the hallmarks of 'young philosophical Marx' and of the early Lukács himself — but the French philosopher's much admired relativism as well. He forcefully and clearly argues that 'relativism moves within an essentially *static* world' (p.187.), representing a *dogmatic* philosophical position due to its failure to treat both human beings and their concrete historical reality dialectically. *(Ibid.)*

8.3 Lukács's 'identical subject-object'

8.3.1

AS mentioned already, *History and Class Consciousness* is a most important work of transition. Indeed, it marks a watershed in Lukács's intellectual development in the sense that it remains a crucial point of reference for its author throughout his life, both negatively and as a positive foundation of his vision. For, on the one hand, in the course of his subsequent reflections on the fundamental problems of philosophy, all the way to his last work of synthesis, *The Ontology of Social Being,* Lukács is consciously engaged in a severe but deeply believed and justified critical reckoning with the line pursued in *History and Class Consciousness.* At the same time, on the other hand, he remains faithfully attached — even more than he himself seems to realize — not only to the problems raised in this volume of essays, but also to the solutions envisaged to them as far back as

1918-1923, no matter how debatable some of them might be, as we have seen in his Preface to the 1967 edition of *History and Class Consciousness* with regard to the question of methodology.

As far as the issue of subject-object identity is concerned, it represents not only one of the most problematical aspects of *History and Class Consciousness* but also of bourgeois philosophical developments in general.

Paradoxically, the ground from which the problem itself arises could not be more tangible. For the relationship between subject and object, in its original constitution, is inseparable from the conditions of production and reproduction of the human agency and from the assessment of the object (the means and material of production) without which no social metabolic reproduction — through the historically specific mode of human interchange of the individuals among themselves and with nature — is conceivable. Yet, through the refracting prism of philosophical mystification (ideologically linked to insurmountable class interests), the tangible substance of the underlying concrete material and social relationships is metamorphosed into a metaphysical riddle whose solution can only take the form of some unrealizable ideal postulate, decreeing the identity of subject and object. And precisely because the issue, in its fundamental structural determination, concerns the relationship between the *working subject* and the object of its productive activity — which under the rule of capital cannot help being an intrinsically exploitative relationship — the possibility of disclosing the real nature of the problems and conflicts at stake, with a view of transcending them in other than a purely fictitious form, must be practically non-existent. For inasmuch as the thinkers — be they bourgeois political economists or philosophers — identify themselves with the standpoint (and corresponding material interests) of capital, they must envisage a 'solution' in a way that leaves the *practically overturned* relationship between the working subject and its object in reality itself absolutely intact.

The problem here concerns the perverse overturning effect of the historically unfolding social division of labour which culminates in the capital system. An important passage from Marx's *Grundrisse* helps to throw light on the nature of the material processes which in the end are transfigured — and utterly misrepresented — in the well known idealistic postulates of subject-object identity. Marx sets out from a critique of Proudhon and makes the points that

just as the *working subject* is a natural individual, a natural being, so the first *objective condition* of his labour appears as nature, earth, as an inorganic body. He himself is not only the organic body, but also inorganic nature as a *subject*. This condition is not something he has produced, but something he finds to hand; something existing in nature and which he presupposes. ... the fact that the worker finds the objective conditions of his labour as something *separate* from him, as *capital*, and the fact that the capitalist finds the workers *propertyless*, as *abstract labourers* — the exchange as it takes place between value and *living labour* — assumes a historic process, however much capital and wage-labour themselves reproduce this relationship and elaborate it in objective scope, as well as in depth. And this historical process, as we have seen, is the evolutionary history of both capital and wage-labour. In other words, the extra-economic origin of property merely means the historic origin of the bourgeois economy, of the forms of production to which the categories of political economy give theoretical or ideal expression. ...

The original conditions of production cannot initially be themselves produced —

they are not the results of production. ... for if this reproduction appears on one hand as the appropriation of the *objects* by the *subjects,* it equally appears on the other as the moulding, the subjection, of the objects by and to a subjective purpose; the transformation of the objects into results and repositories of *subjective activity.* What requires explanation is not the *unity* of living and active human beings with the natural, inorganic conditions of their metabolism with nature, and therefore their appropriation of nature; nor is this the result of a historic process. What we must explain is the *separation* of these inorganic conditions of human existence from this active existence, a separation which is only fully completed in the relationship between wage-labour and capital. In the relationship of slavery and serfdom there is no such separation; what happens is that one part of society is treated by another as the mere inorganic and natural condition of its own reproduction. The slave stands in no sort of relation to the objective conditions of his labour. It is rather labour itself, both in the form of the slave as of the serf, which is placed among the other living things (*Naturwesen*) as inorganic conditions of production, alongside the cattle or as an appendage of the soil. In other words: the original conditions of production appear as *natural prerequisites,* natural conditions of existence of the producer, just as his living body, however reproduced and developed by him, is not originally established by himself, but appears as his prerequisite.[115]

As we can see, the possibility of disclosing the actual character of the relationship between the working subject and his object, together with the emancipatory potentiality inherent in such a disclosure, arises only under the conditions of capitalism, as a result of a long process of historical and productive development. For in complete contrast to the slave who 'stands in no sort of relation to the objective conditions of his labour', the working subject of 'wage-slavery' does indeed enter the objective framework of capitalist enterprise as a working *subject.* This is so despite the fact that his subject-character is immediately obliterated at the point of entry into the 'despotic workshop', which must be run under the absolute authority of the usurping pseudo-subject, *capital,* transforming the real subject, the worker, into a mere cog in the capital system's productive machinery. All the same, at the time of the formal constitution of their economic relationsip the worker is supposed to be not the obedient servant but the sovereign *equal* of the personification of capital, so as to be able to enter, as a *'free subject',* into the required contractual agreement.

However, since the working subject under the capital system is condemned to the existence of an *'abstract labourer',* because he is *propertyless* — quite unlike the slave and the serf who are by no means 'propertyless' but an *integral part* of property, and therefore very far from being 'abstract' —, the 'wage slave' is completely at the mercy of capital's ability and willingness to employ him upon which his very survival depends. This, again, could not be more contrasting with the original (primitive) relationship between the working subject and the objective (necessary) conditions of his productive activity. For that relationship is characterized by 'the *unity* of living and active human beings with the natural, inorganic conditions of their metabolism with nature'.

Thus, the real issue of the subject-object relationship is how to *reconstitute, at a level fully consonant with the historically achieved productive development of society, the necessary unity of the working subjects with the attainable objective conditions of their meaningful life-activity.* The *identity* of the subject and object never existed; nor could it ever exist. Moreover, the *unity* of subject and object which we find at earlier phases of history could only be a primitive one. It has been disrupted and destroyed by subsequent phases of historical development. Only a romantic day-dreamer could envisage its resurrection. Nonetheless, the *qualitatively different* reconstitution of the unity between living labour as the active subject, and the objective conditions required for the exercise of creative human energies, in accordance with the historically achieved level of productive advancement, is both feasible and necessary. The socialist project already well before Marx tried to orient itself precisely towards the realization of this objective.

The opposition — and indeed under the rule of capital the antagonistic contradiction — between living labour and the necessary conditions of its exercise is an obvious absurdity: the dirtiest trick of Hegel's *'List der Vernunft'* ('cunning of Reason'). The philosophical mystification manifest in the postulate of the subject-object identity is the necessary corollary of this objective, but nonetheless absurd, relationship as perceived from the standpoint of capital. For the contradiction in question can only be acknowledged in terms that remain fully compatible with the structural imperatives of capital as the eternalized mode of control of the social metabolism. This is why the actually feasible social remedy of reconstituting at a qualitatively higher level the *unity* of the working subject with the objective conditions of its activity must be metamorphosed into the totally mystical postulate of the *'identical* subject-object'.

THE Hegelian conflation of *objectification* and *alienation* is only another aspect of the same problematic. Lukács therefore at best only begs the question when he suggests in his 1967 Preface to *History and Class Consciousness* that

Hegel's reluctance to commit himself on this point [concerning the relationship between the hegemonic classes of capitalist society] is the product of the wrong-headedness of his basic concept. (p.xxiii.)

In fact Hegel's alleged 'wrong-headedness' explains no more than the answer received by the Indian critic who is satirized by the author of *History and Class Consciousness*. For the critic who questioned the idea that the world rests on the back of an elephant, yet 'On receiving the answer that the elephant stands on a tortoise [his] "criticism" declared itself satisfied'. (p.110.) The question which is left unanswered by the suggestion of Hegel's 'wrong-headedness' is: what are the objective determinations at its root? For, as Lukács knows better than most, Hegel is far too great a thinker to be accused of plain 'philosophical confusion'.

The trouble is not that Hegel is 'reluctant to commit himself' with regard to the fundamental social issues at stake, as Lukács claims. On the contrary, the great German philosopher is fully committed to the standpoint of capital, as evidenced also by the peculiar, and in the last resort utterly apologetic, solution which he gives to the immanent contradictions of the 'master/slave dialectic' in *The Phenomenology of Mind,* notwithstanding his acknowledgement of the potentially emancipatory dynamic implicit in that dialectic.[116] It is of course true, as Lukács says in his 1967 Preface, that

in the term alienation Hegel includes every type of objectification. Thus 'alienation' when taken to its logical conclusion is identical with objectification. Therefore, when the identical subject-object transcends alienation it must also transcend objectification at the same time. But as, according to Hegel, the object, the thing exists only as an alienation from self-consciousness, to take it back into the subject would mean the end of objective reality and thus of any reality at all. (pp.xxiii-xxiv.)

However, this particular categorial conflation is by no means an isolated occurrence in the Hegelian conceptual universe. Rather, his work as a *whole* is characterized by the systematic — and utterly bewildering — conflation of the categories of *logic* with the objective determinations of *being*. This characteristic emanates from the Hegelian attempt to conjure up the impossible within the grandiose edifice of his philosophical system: namely, the final 'reconciliation' of the antagonistic contradictions of the perceived sociohistorical reality through the conceptual devices of the *'Science of Logic'*.

The mystical postulate of the identical subject-object, which is supposed to transcend objectivity/estrangement/alienation, is a paradigm categorial embodiment of this state of affairs. For while the underlying contradiction as perceived and acknowledged by Hegel is a very real one, the envisaged 'transcending reconciliation' leaves everything in the real world completely untouched. The Hegelian 'opposition of *in-itself* and *for-itself,* of consciousness and self-consciousness, of *object* and *subject* ... is the opposition, *within* thought itself, between abstract thinking and sensuous reality or real sensuousness'.[117] Thanks to such conceptualization of the dichotomies of bourgeois philosophy, the contradictions of real life — inherent in capital's unyielding power of alienation and reification — can be both acknowledged (for a fleeting moment) and made permanently to disappear through their 'appropriating' reduction into abstract *'thought entities'*. A reduction that carries with it the ideologically motivated elimination of their *social determinateness* in every single domain of the monumental Hegelian philosophical enterprise. To quote Marx:

> the appropriation of what is estranged and objective, or the annulling of objectivity in the form of *estrangement* (which has to advance from indifferent foreignness to real, antagonistic estrangement) means equally or even primarily for Hegel that it is *objectivity* which is to be annulled, because it is not the *determinate* character of the object, but rather its *objective* character that is offensive and constitutes estrangement for self-consciousness. ... A peculiar role, therefore, is played by the act of *superseding* in which denial and preservation — denial and affirmation — are bound together. Thus, for example, in Hegel's *Philosophy of Right, Private Right* superseded equals *Morality,* Morality superseded equals the *Family,* the Family superseded equals *Civil Society,* Civil Society superseded equals the *State,* the State superseded equals *World History*. In the *actual world* private right, morality, the family, civil society, the state, etc., remain in existence, only they have become ... moments of motion.[118]

It is, thus, Hegel's ambivalent attitude to the antagonisms of society — his perception of their significance from the standpoint of capital, coupled with an idealist refusal to acknowledge their untranscendable negative implications for the given order in the framework of the unfolding historical development — which is responsible for producing this curious 'philosophic dissolution and restoration of the existing empirical world'[119] of which the mysteriously alienation-transcending postulate of the identical subject-object is a most revealing example.

The reason why it is necessary to envisage this fictitious solution to the dehumanizing domination of living labour (the working subject) by its simultaneously objectified and alienated counterpart, i.e. 'stored up labour' or capital, is because the only really feasible solution — the historically adequate reconstitution of the necessary *unity* of living labour with the objective conditions of its productive activity — is an *absolute taboo* from the standpoint of capital. For the formulation of such a programme necessarily implies the end of the absurd *separation* of the inorganic conditions of human existence from the working subject. A 'separation which is only fully completed in the relationship between wage-labour and capital'. Indeed, this alienated and — in relation to the working subject — ruthlessly dominating/'adversarial' separateness constitutes the very essence of capital as a mode of social control. Thus, no political economists or philosophers who identify themselves with the standpoint of capital can conceivably envisage the reconstitution of the unity in question, in that the latter would ipso facto imply not only the end of capital's rule over society but simultaneously also the liquidation of the vantage point from which they construct their theoretical systems.

This is why the ideologically convenient dualisms and dichotomies of bourgeois political economy and philosophy, coupled with their miraculous 'transcendences', cannot be explained simply in terms of the internal conceptual determinations of the various theories concerned. For they become intelligible only if we relate them to the manifold *actual* dualisms and antinomies of the prevailing socioeconomic order from which they necessarily arise.

AS regards the latter, at the core of commodity society's dichotomously articulated structure of domination and subordination we are confronted by the most absurd of all conceivable dualisms: the opposition between the *means* of labour and *living* labour itself. If we have a closer look at it, we find not only that the means of labour (capital) dominates labour, but also that through such domination the only truly meaningful subject/object relationship is completely *overturned* in actuality. As a result, the real subject of essential productive activity is degraded to the condition of a readily manipulable object, while the original object and formerly subordinate moment of society's productive activity is elevated to a position from which it can usurp the role of human subjectivity in charge of decision-making. This new 'subject' of institutionalized usurpation (i.e. capital) is in fact a pseudo-subject, since it is forced by its fetishistic inner determinations to operate within extremely limited parameters, substituting its own blind material dictates and imperatives for the possibility of consciously adopted design in the service of human need.

Characteristically, parallel to the developments which produce the oppressive/exploitative *practical* relationship between the working subject and its object in the course of modern history, we find that philosophy either simply codifies (and legitimates) the stark opposition between subject and object in its naked immediacy, or makes an attempt to 'overcome' it through the ideal postulate of an 'identical subject-object'.

As mentioned before, the latter is a thoroughly mystical proposition which takes us absolutely nowhere, since it leaves the existing dualism and inversion of the relationship concerned in the actual world exactly as it was before the appearance of such 'transcending criticism'. And precisely because the practical dualism and overturning of the real subject/object relationship is constantly *reproduced* in actuality, we are repeatedly presented in philosophy, in one form or another, with the problematic of subject/object duality, as seen from the standpoint of bourgeois political economy. For a social standpoint of that kind cannot possibly question the actuality of this *inversion,* let alone capital's exploitative domination of labour corresponding to it. Consequently the solution of the problem at issue remains permanently beyond its reach as set by the blind material imperatives of its own pseudo-subjectness.

In this sense there is indeed here before us a curious 'subject/object identity', even if its unvarnished reality could not be more different from its abstract philosophical conceptualization and idealization. It consists in the arbitrary identification of the *object* (means of labour, capital) with the position of the *subject* (by way of deriving the 'self-consciousness' or 'subject-identity' of philosophical discourse from the thinker's self-identification with the objectives that emanate from the material determinations of capital as *self-positing subject/object),* coupled with the simultaneous elimination of the *real subject* (living labour) from the philosophical picture. No wonder, therefore, that the elusive quest for the 'identical subject/object' persists to our own days as a haunting philosophical chimera.

8.3.2

LUKACS'S critical reassessment of the problematic of subject-object duality in *History and Class Consciousness* arises directly from the solution adopted towards it by classical German philosophy in the form of the idealist postulate of the 'identical subject-object', primarily in the work of Schiller and Hegel. Also, the Weberian preoccupation with 'formal rationality' and 'calculation' leaves a heavy imprint on Lukács's diagnosis of the issues involved and on the way in which he tries to articulate a viable alternative to the line of approach followed in these matters by bourgeois political economy and philosophy.

The central essay of *History and Class Consciousness,* 'Reification and the Consciousness of the Proletariat', attributes the failure of bourgeois philosophy to tackle the existentially unavoidable problem of reification to its uncritical incorporation of the formalizing tendency of modern science into philosophy. This is how Lukács sums up his position on the subject:

> Philosophy stands in the same relation to the special sciences as they do with respect to empirical reality. The formalistic conceptualisation of the special sciences becomes for philosophy an immutably given substratum and this signals the final and despairing renunciation of every attempt to cast light on the reification that lies at the root of this formalism. ... By confining itself to the study of the 'possible conditions' of the validity of the forms in which its underlying existence is manifested, modern bourgeois thought bars its own way to a clear view of the problems bearing on the birth and death of these forms, and on their real essence and substratum. (p.110.)

The critique of the apparently irresistible tendency to reification-enhancing formalism and 'rational objectification' (p.92.) under capitalist conditions is pursued by Lukács with great rigour in *History and Class Consciousness.* He subjects Kantian philosophy — considered by him as representative of the bourgeois philosophical tradition in its entirety — to a radical criticism, on the ground that its attempt to go beyond formalism by merely stipulating the necessity of content 'can do no more than offer it [namely the unrealized principle of the necessity of content] as a methodological programme, i.e. for each of the discrete areas it can indicate the point where the real synthesis *should* begin, and where it would begin if its *formal rationality* could allow it to do more than predict *formal possibilities* in terms of *formal calculations'*. (pp.133-4.)

At the same time Lukács is equally anxious to stress the practical/axiological implications of the line adopted by modern bourgeois philosophy. For in his view such philosophy

consciously refrains from interfering with the work of the special sciences. It even regards this renunciation as a critical advance. In consequence its role is confined to the investigation of the *formal presuppositions* of the special sciences which it neither corrects nor interferes with. And the problem which they by-pass philosophy cannot solve either, nor even pose, for that matter. Where philosophy has recourse to the structural assumptions lying behind the form-content relationship it either exalts the *'mathematicizing' method* of the special sciences, elevating it into the method proper of philosophy (as in the Marburg school), or else it establishes the *irrationality of matter*, as logically, the 'ultimate' fact (as do Windelband, Rickert and Lask). But in both cases, as soon as the attempt at systematisation is made, the unsolved problem of the irrational reappears in the problem of *totality*. The horizon that delimits the totality that has been and can be created here is, at best, culture (i.e. the culture of bourgeois society). This culture cannot be derived from anything else and has simply to be accepted on its own terms as *'facticity'* in the sense given to it by classical philosophers. ... [Thus] there appears in the thought of bourgeois society the double tendency characteristic of its evolution. On the one hand, it acquires increasing control over the *details* of its social existence, subjecting them to its needs. On the other hand it loses — likewise progressively — the possibility of gaining intellectual control of society as a *whole* and with that it loses its own *qualifications for leadership*. (pp.120-1.)

The last point made by Lukács is particularly important for understanding the theoretical strategy followed by the Hungarian philosopher not only in *History and Class Consciousness* but also in his later years. For the question of knowledge — including the concern with the methodologically vital principle defined by Lukács as 'the standpoint of totality' — is inseparable in his conception from the question of *legitimacy and value*, which in the final analysis must be disentangled in the sphere of *ethics:* a never quite realized lifelong project for the author of *History and Class Consciousness*. (Even his last work, *The Ontology of Social Being,* is full of references to a forthcoming systematic study of *Ethics* which he could never take beyond the point of preparatory notes, with too big gaps in them to be turned even in decades of hard work into a sustainable theoretical enterprise. Only fragments of this project could materialize in some related writings, above all in the final summation of his aesthetic ideas, the monumental *Specificity of the Aesthetical*.[120])

In *History and Class Consciousness* some of Lukács's weightiest objections to the philosophy of the class that had 'lost its qualifications for leadership' directly concern the great practical issues of ethics. He dismisses 'modern rationalism' as a form of *irrationality* on account of its failure to face up to those practical issues, arguing that in the various rationalistic systems 'the "ultimate" problems of human existence persist in an irrationality incommensurable with human understanding'. (p.113.) Thus, in the spirit of his concern with the 'ultimate problems of human existence', Lukács's critique of formalism acquires its full significance only in the context where he puts into relief that in modern bour-

geois philosophy
ethic becomes purely formal and lacking in content. As every content which is given to us belongs to the world of nature and is thus unconditionally subject to the objective laws of the phenomenal world, practical norms can only have bearing on the inward forms of action. The moment this ethic attempts to make itself concrete, i.e. to test its strength on concrete problems, it is forced to borrow the elements of content of these particular actions from the world of phenomena and from the conceptual systems that assimilate them and absorb their 'contingency'. The *principle of creation collapses* as soon as the first concrete *content* is to be created. (pp.124-5.)

IN opposition to Kantian and neo-Kantian ethical formalism, in *History and Class Consciousness* Lukács is looking for a solution — and finds it in his version of the identical subject-object — in terms of which 'the principle of creation' does not collapse when it comes into contact with concrete (historically specific) content. In this pursuit the direct inspiration comes as much from Schiller as from Hegel. For in the work of Schiller he finds a conception of nature

in which we can clearly discern the ideal and the tendency to overcome the problems of a *reified existence*. 'Nature' here refers to authentic humanity, the true essence of man liberated from the false, mechanizing forms of society: man as a perfected *whole* who has inwardly overcome, or is in the process of overcoming, the dichotomies of theory and practice, reason and the senses, form and content; man whose tendency to create his own forms does not imply an *abstract rationalism* which ignores concrete content; man for whom *freedom and necessity are identical*. (pp.136-7.)

Using art (seen in the light cast upon it by Schiller's attempt to go beyond Kant) as his model, Lukács addresses himself to the problem whose solution remained elusive to post-Cartesian philosophy: 'to create the subject of the "creator".' (p.140.) He immediately adds to the characterization of the philosophical task expressed in the last sentence (a task visualized already by Vico in terms of the 'creative subject of history') an idea that becomes a constantly recurring theme of his subsequent writings, including *The Ontology of Social Being;* namely, that the envisaged quest facing philosophy of necessity 'goes beyond *pure epistemology*'. (*Ibid.*)

This conclusion is well understandable. For, as we have seen, in Lukács's view what is at stake directly concerns 'the ultimate problems of human existence' which are not amenable either to formalistic (and ultimately 'mathematicizing', pseudo-scientific) or to purely epistemological solutions. As such, the existential problems are profoundly 'content-bound' (i.e. in their innermost nature *onto-logical*) and simultaneously also practical/'value-bound' (i.e. they cannot be tackled at all without putting into relief their intrinsic relationship to the fundamental issues of *ethics*).

With this view the Weberian idea of 'value-neutrality' is rejected by Lukács without hesitation, despite the fact that in his diagnosis of the situation several Weberian 'Leitmotifs' concerning formalism and rationalization survive. Equally, Weber's suggestion that the existential problems of ethics must be treated as the private preoccupations of strictly individual subjects (who have their arbitrarily chosen, and in relation to the contrasting choices of other individual subjects totally irreconcilable, 'private demons' to obey) is considered by Lukács to be a non-starter. For it can only aggravate the dualism of classical German (and not only German) philosophy which counterposes the 'ethical act' of the 'ethically acting individual subject' to empirical reality in the form of a meta-physical construct, so that

> the *duality* is itself introduced into the *subject*. Even the subject is split into phenome-non and noumenon and the unresolved, insoluble and henceforth permanent conflict between freedom and necessity now invades its innermost structure. (p.124.)

Weber can offer no help in this respect. Quite the contrary. For the Weberian solution retains the dualism criticized by Lukács and makes it worse by trans-forming the individual choices into total arbitrariness, to suit the needs of extreme *subjectivism*. Thus on this point Weber's approach represents a sharp contrast to the Kantian attempt to underpin *objectively* the ethical acts of individual subjects by imposing on them the severe requirement for the 'uni-versalization' of their moral maxims, in accordance with the 'categorical impe-rative' revealed to them by their own 'practical reason', on the ground of the particular individuals' freedom that emanates from the 'intelligible' or noumenal world to which they are said to belong as moral agents.

For Lukács the challenging task which bourgeois philosophy had to fail to come to terms with remains as before: 'to overcome the *reified disintegration of the subject* and the — likewise reified — rigidity and impenetrability of its *objects*'. (p.141.) He sees the realization of the identified task as the irreversibly unfolding tendency of the contemporary historical development itself, which in his view had been already conceptualized, even if in a most inadequate form, by the best representatives of bourgeois philosophy. In other words, the author of *History and Class Consciousness* embraces the problematics inherited from classical Ger-man philosophy, but tries to find a non-formalist and collectively oriented solution to its haunting dilemmas. A solution which in Lukács's judgement is radically incompatible with the social and theoretical standpoint of the class that had irretrievably lost its once well deserved 'qualifications for leadership'.

Thus the identical subject-object of *History and Class Consciousness* enters the stage as the carrier of its author's moral and intellectual condemnation of the class into which he was born, as seen from the historical vantage point of the class with which he unreservedly identifies himself in the course of the revolu-tionary upheavals that follow the first world war. The role which the identical subject-object in *History and Class Consciousness* is supposed to fulfil is not abstractly theoretical but primarily practical/moral. Accordingly, all the central categories of *History and Class Consciousness* are articulated in such a way that their author's ethical message should transpire through them with unmistakable clarity.

Indeed, none of the key categories of this work make any sense at all if abstracted from their historically concrete practical/moral context. Lukács's concerns for the 'bourgeois loss of totality' and for its obverse, the historical appearance of the 'standpoint of totality' on a proletarian class basis; for the 'transcendence of reified consciousness'; for the overcoming of the 'reified disintegration of the subject' through the historical intervention of the 'ethically acting collective subject'; for the abolition of 'impenetrable objectivity' thanks to the 'act of consciousness overthrowing the objective form of its object'; and for the realization of philosophy by the agency of the 'identical subject-object of history', are all brought together by the Hungarian philosopher in a synthesis which enables him to announce the successful overcoming of the 'duality of *thought and existence'* (p.203.), thanks to the irrepressible objective dynamics of the historical dialectic and its collective agent, the potentially self-conscious proletariat.

8.3.3

ALL this is perfectly in tune with Lukács's definition of class consciousness in another essay of *History and Class Consciousness*, 'The Marxism of Rosa Luxemburg', written a few months earlier than 'Reification and the Consciousness of the Proletariat'.[121] In fact the essay on reification is intended by Lukács as the philosophical proof — the detailed demonstration of the much needed 'methodological guarantee' (p.43.) — through which the correctness of the strategically and organizationally vital conclusions asserted in the earlier essay can be sustained. For in 'The Marxism of Rosa Luxemburg' the nature and role of class consciousness is defined in solemn *ethical* terms, as the 'ethics of the proletariat', as we have seen in Section 7.3.1 in a key passage quoted from page 42 of *History and Class Consciousness*. At the same time the necessary strategic instrument of the anticipated historical transformation, the party is legitimated in identical terms, on the ground of its stipulated moral mandate, in accordance with its being defined as 'the incarnation of the ethics of the fighting proletariat' and as 'the organized incarnation of proletarian class consciousness'.

In his later reflections on the failure of classical German philosophy 'to exhibit concretely the "we" which is the subject of history' (p.145.) and to discover the concrete subject of historical genesis, the *'methodologically indispensable subject-object'* (p.146.) — namely the ethically active collective subject: the proletariat — Lukács puts the emphasis on the importance of emancipatory praxis as opposed to mere contemplation. He rightly insists that in transformatory praxis it is impossible to maintain 'that *indifference* of form to content' (p.126.) which characterizes the formalistic and rationalistic philosophical conceptions. For the non-contemplative attitude of praxis in relation to its object operates on the basis of selecting content *relevant* to its pursuit. Significantly, further on in the same essay on 'Reification and the Consciousness of the Proletariat', the criterion of *truth* is also defined by Lukács as *'relevance to reality'* (p.203), underlining again the praxis-oriented ethical dimension of the author's 'non-epistemological' conception of knowledge. And he makes it clear that the reality he is talking about 'is by no means identical with empirical existence. This reality *is not*, it *becomes'*. *(Ibid.)* Thus, focusing on the question of *becoming* — which happens to be inseparable from the more or less conscious and inescapably value-bound collective agency of historical transformation — is what he considers crucial for understanding reality as historical process.

Given his intense ethical preoccupations, Lukács sees the task of philosophy, which he shares with the great ancestors, like this: 'to discover the principles by means of which it becomes possible in the first place for an "ought" to modify existence'. (p.161.) In his view even the outstanding figures of bourgeois philosophy could not discover the principles in question because of their incorrigibly[122] contemplative and socially apologetic attitude to the problem of knowledge. As a solution, he puts into relief the totalizing class consciousness of the proletariat — which is simultaneously also its ethics — so as to make intelligible the activity of the 'methodologically indispensable subject-object of history' as a *meaningful* enterprise.

Inevitably, however, the framework within which Lukács's critique is articulated imposes its limitations on his own solutions. The forceful rebuttal of the unfulfilled aspirations of classical German philosophy — to discover the principles by means of which 'ought' can modify existence — induces Lukács to spell out his own solution of the problem in terms of an *'ought-to-be'*, although his explicit aspiration is to demonstrate the transcendence of the dichotomy between 'is' and 'ought' from the vantage point of the 'identical subject-object of real history'. And the difficulties are even greater than that. For, in the spirit of a thoroughly imperatival discourse, the Lukácsian 'ethics of the proletariat' presents us with a *double 'ought'*.

- First, in the sharpest possible opposition which he sets up between the stipulative 'ascribed consciousness' of the proletariat and its empirical reality.

- And second, in the superimposition of the idealized party — as the mysterious 'incarnation of the ethics of the proletariat' — on the recognizable forms of actual historical existence, notwithstanding the contradictions manifest in the relationship between party and class which Lukács perceives but idealistically brushes aside by saying that the party *'must* determine its politics' on the basis of the insight that 'its strength is *moral'*.

Equally problematical is that, although Lukács criticizes Kant for the circumstance that the 'necessity of content' which he prescribes has only the status of a generic *methodological programme* in his philosophy, without ever being substantively implemented, yet, so much of what he himself has to say remains on the plane of the rightly deplored *methodological postulates*. The number of Lukács's purely methodological exhortations is legion. Even the most important category of *History and Class Consciousness,* the collective historical agent, is philosophically established and legitimated by him as the *'methodologically indispensable subject-object'*.

8.3.4

THESE characteristics are the consequence of a twofold determination. On the one hand, entering the Kantian/Hegelian framework of discourse for the purposes of an 'immanent critique' carries with it that Lukács's diagnosis of the problems and tasks of philosophy is adjusted to the intellectual parameters of that discourse. This is so even when the relationship to classical philosophy is spelled out by Lukács negatively, by pursuing the ideal of 'an inwardly synthesising philosophical method' (p.109) — and other tasks formulated by bourgeois philosophy, as we have seen above — which the objects of his critical sublation could not realize. For in his 'inwardly synthesising' negation he remains in dependency on the the object of his immanent critique. It is therefore by no means accidental that Lukács is totally uncritical towards the Hegelian conflation of the categories of *alienation* and *objectification,* despite the fact that Marx's theoretical achievements in this regard are present also in the works well known to the author of *History and Class Consciousness* (e.g. *Capital* and the seminal Introduction to the *Grundrisse),* and not only in the *Economic and Philosophical Manuscripts of 1844,* which were still unpublished in the early 1920s.

The second aspect of the closely intertwined twofold determination shaping *History and Class Consciousness* is even more important.

• It concerns the social and political circumstances under which the former Deputy Commissar for Culture and Education in the militarily defeated Hungarian Council Republic has to come to terms with political and theoretical work in emigration, within the horizon of the revolution 'at the weakest link of the chain' as the only available sociopolitical frame of reference. This is what constitutes the 'übergreifendes Moment' of the complex dialectical determinations at work in this period of Lukács's intellectual and political development.

• As already mentioned in the context of the 'methodological guarantee of proletarian victory' postulated by Lukács in *History and Class Consciousness,* he had to witness not only the foreign intervention and the crushing of the revolution in Hungary, but also the ebbing away of the European revolutionary wave that filled him with Messianic hope at the time of his conversion to communism. Now, under the circumstances of 'enforced leisure', as he puts it in the December 1922 Preface to *History and Class Consciousness* (p.xli.), 'Reification and the Consciousness of the Proletariat' sets itself the task of demonstrating the 'certainty of victory' in strictly theoretical terms, in the absence of more tangible proofs. It is therefore quite wrong to see the problematical aspects of Lukács's discourse in *History and Class Consciousness* simply as the 'survival of Hegelian influences'. They 'survive' because they are *needed* under the circumstances — when the sociohistorical constraints of the 'weakest link' assert themselves in reality with a vengeance — as the vehicle of the whole enterprise aimed at securing theoretical victory over the bourgeoisie and its culture. And this victory is supposed to be achieved by demonstrating the contradictions and the necessary failure of bourgeois culture, providing at the same time — through an 'immanent critique' formulated from the 'standpoint of totality' as aimed at by Hegel himself but in Lukács's view attainable only from the vantage point of the proletariat: the one and only historically concrete 'identical subject-object' — also the solutions pursued in vain by classical German philosophy.

The vital existential confrontation of the two hegemonic classes over the control of society's metabolic processes and over the 'ultimate questions of human life' is thereby transferred to the plane of a contest over true — non-contemplative, value-bound —*understanding* and its 'conditions of possibility'. Victory is already foreshadowed in the way in which Lukács formulates the problem itself, insisting that

> the *concrete totality* of the historical world, the *concrete and total historical process* is the only point of view from which *understanding becomes possible.* (p.145.)

Despite the major advances made by bourgeois thought towards understanding the nature of knowledge, in the end the task must defeat the philosophers concerned, according to Lukács. For

> Here in our newly won knowledge where, as Hegel puts it in the *Phenomenology,* 'the true becomes a Bacchantic orgy in which no one escapes being drunk', reason seems to have lifted the veil concealing the sacred mystery at Sais and discovers, as in the parable of Novalis, that it is itself the solution to the riddle. But here, we find once again, quite concretely this time, the decisive problem of this line of thought: the problem of the *subject of the action,* the subject of the *genesis.* For the unity of the *subject and object,* of *thought and existence* which the 'action' undertook to prove and to exhibit finds both its fulfilment and its substratum in the unity of the genesis of the

determinants of thought and of the history of the evolution of reality. But to *comprehend* this unity it is necessary both to discover the *site* from which to resolve all these problems and also to exhibit *concretely* the '*we*' which is the *subject of history*, that 'we' whose action is in fact history. (*Ibid.*)

As we can see, Lukács accepts, again, the problematic formulated by classical philosophy. And he does so not because he is a prisoner of Kantian/Hegelian influences, but because the problematic in question provides him with the weapons required for the successful pursuit of the postulated *theoretical victory*. For he can immediately add to the lines just quoted that 'at this point classical philosophy turned back and lost itself in the endless labyrinth of conceptual mythology. ... it was unable to discover this *concrete subject of genesis, the methodologically indispensable subject-object*'. (pp.145-6.) The fact that the 'methodologically indispensable subject-object' itself is part of the criticized conceptual mythology does not seem to worry him. For he needs the category of the 'identical subject-object' as the 'subject of creation' responsible for the results of concrete historical action (in the sense of historical/intellectual genesis) and — on account of its 'standpoint of totality' and corresponding praxis — as the guarantor of attaining true knowledge and also of achieving the unity of *thought and existence*.

The obstacles which defeated classical philosophy are defined by Lukács in strictly theoretical terms; likewise the way of overcoming them, by adopting the standpoint of the 'methodologically indispensable subject-object' of historical/intellectual genesis. As Lukács puts it:

only by overcoming the — *theoretical* — duality of philosophy and special discipline, of methodology and factual knowledge can the way be found by which to annul the *duality of thought and existence*. (p.203.)

Thus the burden of reality itself in creating and reproducing the *practical dualisms and inversions* at the roots of the theoretical ones is minimized or pushed into the background, because the solutions exhibiting the 'certainty of victory' must be themselves envisaged within the parameters of the theoretical discourse undertaken by Lukács in his '*immanent critique*' of the results and failures of his philosophical predecessors.

We are told that capitalistic 'isolation and fragmentation is only *apparent*' (p.92) and that 'atomisation is only an *illusion*' (p.93), even if a necessary one. The conflation of *alienation and objectivity* is thus not simply the result of a failure to see the 'wrong-headedness of Hegel's basic concept', as Lukács puts it in 1967, but something positively welcome in his scheme of things at the time of writing *History and Class Consciousness*. For by concentrating his attack on the 'necessary illusions' of 'reified consciousness' the author can seriously entertain the illusion that theoretical illumination — the work of consciousness upon consciousness — can produce the required *structural changes* in the social reality itself, provided that reality as such is seen as historical process. This is why he must also attack the reflection theory of knowledge, characteristically misinterpreting a passage he quotes from Engels because it does not fit into his scheme of things.[123]

Also, in the spirit of the self-same conflation of alienation and objectification, he complains that 'the *object* of thought (as something *outside*) becomes *alien* to the *subject*' (p.200.), and he identifies '*reified facts*' with the '*empirical world*' as such (p.203.), counterposing to empirical reality the 'higher reality' of the 'complex of processes'. *(Ibid.)* In the same way, Marxian dialectic is described as a procedure in which 'the *objective forms* of the objects are themselves transformed into a process, a *flux'* and everything is 'intensified to the point where *facts are wholly dissolved into processes'.* (p.180.) This is done in order to make 'possible for the proletariat to discover that it is itself the *subject* of this process [i.e., of the capitalist process of production and reproduction] even though it is in chains and is for the time being *unconscious* of the fact'. (p.181.)

The uncomfortable *fact* that in the real world the proletariat — as a result of the *practically accomplished* and consolidated alienation and inversion of the relationship between the working subject and its object — is emphatically *not* the subject of the reproduction process, but happens to be *objectively* reduced to the status of a mere condition (and cost) of production, totally at the mercy of capital's imperatives and 'rationalizing/economizing' decisions, cannot matter in this conception, because facts have been by now 'wholly dissolved into processes' in order to suit the convenience of the identical subject-object and its 'labyrinth of conceptual mythology'. All that is needed is to turn the *'unconscious'* proletariat — at present captive of its 'psychological consciousness' — into a proletariat fully conscious of its *subject* status; a task to be achieved by means of ideological clarification and theoretical illumination. The idea is modelled on the Hegel/Novalis parable of 'lifting the veil', so that the proletariat can discover — like Reason in the passage quoted a moment ago from page 141 of *History and Class Consciousness* — that it is itself 'the solution to the riddle'.

The sobering fact that the position of the subject must be reconquered by labour and radically *reconstituted* in the — by Lukács dismissively treated — 'empirical world' itself, through objectively feasible *material mediations* which restructure the antagonistic division of labour historically constituted under the rule of capital, does not seem to carry any weight at all in *History and Class Consciousness*. Instead, in tune with the need to transform the objective constraints of the 'weakest link' into plausible and materially effective assets, *'structural change'* is postulated as a direct result of — or even as synonymous with — change *in consciousness*.

This is how we end up with miraculously reification-transcending equations and transformations, like 'understood *hence restructured'* (p.189) and 'this *knowledge* brings about an *objective structural change* in the object of knowledge'. (p.169) And all this is supposed to come about thanks to the insight that the 'rigid *epistemological doubling* of subject and object' (p.169) ought to be theoretically abandoned and replaced by the 'identical subject-object', whereafter 'the rigidly reified existence of the objects of the social process will dissolve into *mere illusion'* (p.179) and — to crown it all with the ultimate piece of magic — *'the act of consciousness overthrows the objective form of its object'.* (p.178)[124] Naturally, if the existing objective structural relationships can be transformed in the way postulated by Lukács, in that case it is only a question of time before all identifiable difficulties can be consigned to the past.

Thus, retaining the Hegelian frame of reference of 'objectivity/alienation' — a conceptual framework which makes it possible for Lukács to pose and solve the problems the way he does in *History and Class Consciousness* — proletarian victory over bourgeois philosophy and culture can be accomplished *within theory,* through the postulated de-objectifying 'act of consciousness', without having to change in the real world anything at all. This is how it becomes also possible to confer a spurious plausibility on the earlier quoted assertion according to which the *ideological crisis* of the proletariat must be solved *before* a practical solution to the world's economic crisis can be found', completely overturning thereby the Marxian *relative primacy* of the material factors that represent the 'übergreifendes Moment' in the *dialectical* (and not idealistically or mechanical/materialistically one-sided) relationship between social being and social consciousness.

8.3.5

NATURALLY, Hegel looms very large in these transcending/superseding equations. For inasmuch as he represents the climax of classical philosophy, nothing could be in Lukács's view better evidence for the theoretical validity and magnitude of the announced proletarian victory than going beyond him by solving the problems which had to elude even Hegel. According to the author of *History and Class Consciousness*

> Hegel represents the *absolute consummation of rationalism,* but this means that he can be superseded only by an interrelation of thought and existence that has ceased to be contemplative, by the *concrete demonstration* of the *identical subject-object.* (p.215.)

And Lukács justifies the line of approach which he follows in *History and Class Consciousness* by intimately associating the central problematic of 'Reification and the Consciousness of the Proletariat' with the Hegelian categorial framework in general which he considers to be valid — after being rendered concrete through the 'concrete demonstration of the identical subject-object' — also for the Marxian philosophical enterprise. Indeed Lukács insists that 'Hegel's postulate that the concept is "reconstituted being"'[125] is only possible on the assumption of the *real creation of the identical subject-object'.* (p.217.)

This is where the contrast with the Marxian conception of the categories as *Daseinsformen* (forms of existence) — which is taken by Lukács to be equivalent to the Hegelian postulate of the concept as 'reconstituted being', hence the need to demonstrate the concrete 'possibility' of the Hegelian notion — becomes clear. For Marx is not in the least interested in projecting the 'certainty of proletarian victory' by embracing and 'inwardly' overcoming or concretizing the 'consummated rationalist' problematics and the categorial framework of classical bourgeois philosophy through an 'immanent critique'. Rather, he is concerned with elaborating the required — practically viable — strategies by means of which such victory can actually materialize in the real world. Marx's Introduction to the *Grundrisse,* in which he briefly sums up his interpretation of the categories as 'Daseinsformen', is already known to Lukács at the time of writing *History and Class Consciousness.* Significantly, however, he cannot make use of the substance of the Marxian approach as regards the idealistically mystified categories of classical philosophy,[126] because of the incompatibilities between Marx's scathingly demystifying views on the subject and his own continued adhesion to the mythology of the identical subject-object.

Marx's ideas on the nature and origin of even the most abstract but genuine categories of philosophy and political economy (as opposed to the artificial products of conceptual mythology) are on the whole perfectly straightforward.

In fact he is quite amused by the philosophical mystification with which the subject is surrounded. He writes in a letter to Engels:

> what would old Hegel say in the next world if he heard that the general [*Allgemeine*] in German and Norse means nothing but common land [*Gemeinland*], and the particular, *Sundre, Besondere,* nothing but the separate property divided off from the common land? Here are the *logical categories* coming damn well out of *'our intercourse'* after all.[127]

The idea that one must first subscribe to the idealist notion of the identical subject-object before one can make sense of the categories as forms of existence is, thus, at an astronomical distance from the Marxian conception. For the latter seeks to demonstrate its truth through the tangible evidence supplied by 'our intercourse' and not through aprioristic philosophical deductions. This is so whether we think of the categories of 'Allgemeine' and 'Besondere' in their relationship to the common (and later divided) land, or of the general category of 'labour' — as contrasted with the historically known, specific forms and varieties of labour, confined to the limited means and material of labour as their ground of exercise — in its practically demonstrable links to the post-physiocratic conditions of development under which 'abstract labour' becomes materially dominant by means of the victoriously advancing capitalistic industrial enterprise.

It goes without saying that it would be quite impossible to squeeze the category of the 'methodologically indispensable subject-object of history' out of the material and cultural intercourse of real life. For its rightful domain is that 'endless labyrinth of conceptual mythology' from which not even the most ingenious philosophical effort can extricate it.

CHAPTER NINE
THEORY AND ITS INSTITUTIONAL SETTING

9.1 The promise of historical concretization

9.1.1

THERE is a point in *History and Class Consciousness* where Lukács is willing to concede that his account of the postulated identical subject-object is not 'truly concrete'. However, we are presented with this admission only towards the very end of the long essay on 'Reification and the Consciousness of the Proletariat', and even then only with the disappointing proviso that 'the individual stages of this process cannot be sketched here'. (p.205.)

Thus, even if in the form of this qualified afterthought, Lukács unequivocally states that the task undertaken by him in *History and Class Consciousness* cannot be considered really accomplished without the necessary 'historical concretization' which he frequently pleads for and celebrates in his work as the theoretically all-important guiding principle that secures the superiority of the Marxian approach over classical bourgeois philosophy, including Hegel. As Lukács puts it, after asserting that what needs to be done in order to provide the required proof for the validity of the conclusions reached by him in *History and Class Consciousness* cannot be carried out 'here':

> Only then [i.e. only after the successful realization of the advocated programme of concrete historical demonstration] would it be possible to throw light on the intimate dialectical process of interaction between the socio-historical situation and the class consciousness of the proletariat. Only then would the statement that the proletariat is the identical subject-object of the history of society become truly concrete. (pp.205-206.)

The fact is, though, that the promised concretization of the role of the proletariat as the identical subject-object of history is missing not only from *History and Class Consciousness* but also from Lukács's subsequent writings. Indeed, as a result of his encounter with Marx's *Economic and Philosophical Manuscripts of 1844*, nearly a decade after the publication of *History and Class Consciousness*, Lukács abandons the notion of the identical subject-object altogether.

However, one's misgivings about the missing sociohistorical concretization are not confined to the obvious negative impact of the mythical subject-object identity on Lukács's assessment of the concrete potentialities and characteristics of development of the socio-historical agency in *History and Class Consciousness*. The larger issue concerns the appraisal of the objective conditions under which the idea of a conscious collective totalization of knowledge and experience — and with it the effective control of the manifold contradictory tendencies of actual historical development — can become real. For only through the successful articulation of the necessary modalities and instruments of *material mediation* can the emancipatory possibilities of the socialist project become real in the course of the envisaged transition from the capitalist 'realm of necessity' to the 'realm of freedom', i.e., in terms of the Marxian vision embraced by Lukács, from the more or less blindly determined 'pre-history' of humanity to the consciously and co-operatively lived 'true history' of mankind.

For a variety of reasons, Lukács's answer on this issue in *History and Class Consciousness* is not very helpful. The distance that separates the two social orders — 'the "leap from the realm of necessity into the realm of freedom", the conclusion of the "prehistory of mankind"', (p.247) — is bridged by him purely verbally, through the announcement of some general 'regulative principles'. Thus he declares, on the one hand, that 'the category of the radically new, the standing of the economic structure on its head, the change in the direction of the process, i.e. the category of the leap *must* be taken seriously in practice'. (p.249.) And, on the other hand, he asserts that

> The *leap* is a lengthy, arduous *process*. Its essence is expressed in the fact that on every occasion it denotes a turning in the direction of something qualitatively new; conscious action directed towards the comprehended totality of society comes to the surface; and therefore — in *intention* and basis — its home is the realm of freedom. (p.250.)

However, no indication is given as to the almost forbidding difficulties involved in 'standing the economic structure on its head', nor indeed of the tangible practical measures that must be adopted in order to be able 'to take the category of the leap/process seriously in practice'. Even more problematical is Lukács's attempt to skate over the immense theoretical and practical complexities implicit in the envisaged transition not simply from one social-economic and cultural/political order to another, but to one which is simultaneously expected to signal the end of all class domination, together with the radical supersession of the division of labour and of the separate political state. All such complexities are supposed to be done away with by the stipulative/definitional characterization of the circumstances according to which 'in intention and basis' the home of all conscious action within the regulatory framework of the 'leap/process/qualitatively new' can only be the realm of freedom.

Thus, conscious proletarian action *by definition* unfolds in the realm of freedom — considered as a leap/process — no matter how far removed it happens to be from the *actual state* of a socialist society. Moreover, in another passage even the requirement of self-consciousness is removed retrospectively from the definition of historically significant (hegemonic) action — which is said to move inexorably, in its 'unconscious aspiration', towards the envisaged radical human emancipation — when Lukács asserts that

> If the 'realm of freedom' is considered in the context of the process that leads up to it, then it cannot be doubted that even the earliest appearance of the proletariat on the stage of history indicated an *aspiration towards that end* — admittedly in a *wholly unconscious* way. (p.313.)

Underrating the significance of the given state of affairs as 'merely empirical facts and conditions' (to be '*wholly dissolved*' in the process'), coupled with a voluntaristic overemphasis on the abstract notion of 'process as such' at the expense of the really existent, are characteristic of the whole of *History and Class Consciousness*. They find their rationale precisely in this determination on Lukács's part to assert (in contraposition to the empirically given) the already existing *actuality* of 'the realm of freedom' and the *inevitability* of its full realization (p.250), preventable only by humanity's catastrophic regression into 'a new barbarism' (p.306), no matter how great the burden of 'facticity' pointing in the opposite direction under the historically prevailing circumstances. Thus, the 'process' becomes the mythical *subject* of historical action, whereas the actually existing class is considered to be the mere *'repository'* of the process. (p.321.)

The postulated 'identical subject-object of history' is needed by Lukács in order to enable him to produce this substitutionist personification of the 'process', with a dual function. On the one hand, the identical subject-object — which becomes synonymous with the process of consciously pursued historical transformation — can be equated with 'imputed class consciousness', and the latter transferred into the vanguard party as the 'active incarnation of class consciousness'. At the same time, on the other hand, the actually given proletariat can be characterized as the *'repository'* of the historical process (in its necessary unfolding), thereby eliminating the difficulties inherent in the non-revolutionary behaviour of the revolutionary class. In this way we are reassuringly presented with a historical agency which is revolutionary even when it is in actuality non-revolutionary, and conscious even when it is 'wholly unconscious'.

Understandably, therefore, within the framework of this aprioristic discourse the significance of concrete material mediations — through which the eventual attainment of the 'realm of freedom' would become plausible in concrete historical terms — is practically non-existent. The theoretical elaboration of the necessary modalities and instruments of material mediation leading to the envisaged future could not be considered an *asset* in terms of such a discourse but only a *hindrance*. For it would remove the aprioristic *certainty* of proletarian victory repeatedly announced by Lukács not only in the context — and on the evidence — of dialectical methodology (as we have seen above), but in numerous other passages as well, defining the role of totalizing consciousness as 'the conscious acceleration of the process in the *inevitable direction'*. (p.250.) This is why he must also maintain that 'However little the final goal of the proletariat is able, even in theory, to influence the initial stages of the early part of the process directly, it is *in principle* a synthesising factor and so can never be completely absent from any aspect of that process'. (p.313.)

9.1.2

ONE of the principal theoretical reasons why Lukács is led to pursue this line of argument emanates from his unrealistic diagnosis of the obstacles to be overcome in the interest of socialist transformation by means of the dictatorship of the proletariat.

Contrary to Marx's characterization of the problems, Lukács theorizes in a very restricted sense the reifying contradictions that affect labour's relations to capital. He treats them in his reflections on the required practical strategies as confined to the dimension directly linked to — and also effectively removable by the expropriation of — the capitalists. He quotes a passage from Marx's *Capital* according to which

> the domination of the products of past labour over living surplus-labour lasts only as long as the *relations of capital;* these rest on the particular social relations in which *past labour* independently and overwhelmingly *dominates over living labour'*. (p.248.)[128]

Disregarding the crucial fact that the hierarchically articulated relations of capital (the long established capitalistic division of labour that rules over every single factory, etc.) are *material relations* of domination which assert themselves primarily through the given instrumentality of production itself, Lukács comments on the quoted passage in a way which transforms the contradictory *material relationship* of past (i.e. accumulated, objectified/alienated) and present or living labour into the *abstract temporal opposition between 'past and present'*. He does this in order to be able to metamorphose the historical task itself, together with all its persistent — and under the circumstances even overwhelming — *material constraints,* into a matter of *consciousness* (i.e. into the advocated enlightening work of consciousness upon consciousness).

This is how Lukács's argument runs in the essay entitled 'The Changing Function of Historical Materialism':

> The social significance of the dictatorship of the proletariat, socialization, means in the first instance no more than that this domination will be taken out of the hands of the *capitalist*. But as far as the proletariat — regarded as a class — is concerned, its own labour now ceases objectively to confront it in an autonomous, objectified manner. Through the fact that the proletariat takes over simultaneously both all labour which has become objectified and also labour in the process of becoming so, this opposition is *objectively abolished* in practice. With it disappears also the corresponding opposition in capitalist society of *past and present* whose relations must now be changed structurally. However lengthy the objective process of socialization may be, however long it takes the proletariat to *become conscious* of the changed inner relationship of labour to its objectified forms *(the relation of present to past),* with the dictatorship of the proletariat the decisive turning has been taken. (p.248.)

Thus the irreconcilable contradiction between capital and labour, emanating from a substantive material relationship, is transfigured into the abstract temporal opposition between 'past and present', facilitating thereby the — purely imaginary — 'resolution' of the fundamental structural antagonism of the capital system thanks to the revolution. The fact that the 'weakest link' has immense objective limitations, both internally and in its inescapable relations to the global capital system, cannot carry any weight in this line of argument. In Lukács's view the radical transformation of society is *objectively accomplished* by the political act of 'taking the domination of labour out of the hands of the capitalist'. At one point he even talks about the *'inner willingness'* of the former ruling class 'to *accept the rule of the proletariat'* (p.266.), provided that the dictatorship of the proletariat refuses to make concessions towards the former capitalists. After that, what still remains to be achieved through the process of 'socialization' is to make the workers *become conscious* of the nature of the changes that have already taken place, so that they can recognize and fully acknowledge the *unproblematical identity of present and past* under the dictatorship of the proletariat. The thorny issues — which arise from materially anchored and in many ways still antagonistic conflicts — concerning postrevolutionary labour's inherited relations to capital thus simply cease to exist as a result of Lukács's idealist hypostatization of the identity of past and present. In this way, thanks to an abstract theoretical postulate, even the generic opposition between past and present 'disappears', although the material structures corresponding to it to a very large extent actually survive in postrevolutionary society.

This line of reasoning is the same as the one we have seen in the case of the identical subject-object. For the latter was assigned its key position in Lukács's theory because it was expected to fulfil the role of making 'disappear the distinction between theory and practice',[129] even though in the given historical reality one had to witness the manifestations of the glaring contradiction between theory and practice of which the persistent bureaucratization in postrevolutionary Russia provided a most acute example.

9.1.3

IN reality the emancipation of labour from the rule of capital is inseparable from the necessity to supersede/overcome the hierarchical and antagonistic *social division of labour*. This cannot be achieved by the *political* act of *abolishing* the juridical domination of the capitalist over labour. For the objective structures of the inherited social division of labour — the existing material articulation of production — remain basically unchanged in the aftermath of any socialist revolution, even under the most favourable historical conditions and relations of power. By politically negating the specific capitalist form of private ownership, through the 'expropriation of the expropriators' and the concomitant institution of state ownership, many of the substantive conditions of the socioeconomic metabolism — at the level of the all-important labour process of society — persist, even if the 'personification of capital' (Marx) on a *hereditary* basis is outlawed under the circumstances, although it is by no means guaranteed to remain so.

What is of overriding importance in this respect concerns directly the practical levers available for effectively controlling the operating conditions of production. Commodity fetishism, and the doubly mystifying juridical form in which the material determinations of capital's rule over the social metabolism are articulated in the legal and political sphere, obfuscate these matters beyond belief. For in reality capital is itself essentially a *mode of control*, and not merely a — legally codified — *entitlement* to control. This is true irrespective of the fact that under the specific historical conditions of capitalist society the entitlement to exercise control over production and distribution is 'constitutionally' assigned, in the form of hereditary property rights — well protected by the state — to a limited number of individuals.

From the point of view of capital as a mode of control the important matter is the necessity of an *accumulation-securing* expropriation of surplus-value, and not its contingent form. The latter is bound to be modified anyway — even within strictly capitalist parameters — in the course of capital's inexorable self-expansion, in accordance with the changing intensity and scope of practically feasible capital-accumulation under the given historical circumstances. Accordingly, the question of capital's domination over labour, together with the concrete modalities of its overcoming, must be made intelligible in terms of the *material structural determinations* upon which the varying possibilities of personal intervention in the societal reproduction process arise. For, paradoxical as it may sound, the objective power of decision making, and the corresponding unwritten (or non-formalized) authority of capital as a mode of actual control, *precedes* the strictly mandated (i.e. by the objective imperatives of capital itself strictly mandated and only contingently codified) authority of the capitalists themselves.

In this sense, addressing the issue of the capitalists' *entitlement* to dominate labour — a right that can be instantly 'taken away' or 'abolished' by the dictatorship of the proletariat, or indeed later restored through some kind of counter-revolutionary intervention — can only bring very limited changes in the structural framework of the transitional society. The real target of emancipatory transformation is the *complete eradication of capital as a totalizing mode of control* from the social reproductive metabolism itself, and not simply the *displacement* of the capitalists as the historically specific 'personifications of capital'. For the failure, for whatever reason, to bring about the objective structural eradication of capital itself from the ongoing reproductive processes, must sooner or later create an intolerable vacuum at the level of the vital metabolic control of society. And that would necessitate the establishment of new forms of '*personification*', inasmuch as the prevailing structural articulation of socioeconomic control continues to be marked by the objective characteristics of the inherited hierarchical social division of labour whose innermost nature calls for some kind of iniquitous personification.

It goes without saying, to look for viable answers with regard to these weighty material constraints is only possible within the framework of a realistic theory of transition which sets out from the premiss that the 'radically new' of the anticipated 'new historic form' is not conceivable without the painful enterprise of an all-embracing *material restructuring* of society's productive and distributive intercourse. And the latter in its turn involves the *practical* establishment of the necessary forms of *material mediation* through which capital's eradication from the social metabolic process becomes feasible in due course.

In the absence of even an attempt to formulate such a theory, Lukács's discourse on the 'radically new' in *History and Class Consciousness* tends to exhaust itself in the proclamation of some generic regulative principles, and in the solemn announcement of a whole series of purely verbal solutions which he gives to his own sharply defined paradoxes concerning the essential identity of the '*leap*' and the '*process*'. The concrete sociohistorical problems of transition are taken on board only to the extent to which they can be reduced to the abstractly and rather unrealistically formulated relationship between *economics and violence*, so that the efficacy of *political intervention* — in the form of the dictatorship of the proletariat — should appear fully adequate to mastering the encountered problems. Thus Lukács offers his readers the following diagnosis and solution:

> If the principles of human existence are about to break free and take control of mankind for the first time in history, then economics and violence, the objects and the instruments of struggle, stand in the foreground of interest. Just because those contents which were before called 'ideology' now begin — changed, it is true, in every way — to become the real goals of mankind, it becomes superfluous to use them to adorn the economic struggles of violence which are fought for their sake. Moreover, their reality and actuality appear in the very fact that all interest centres on the real struggles surrounding their realization, i.e. on economics and violence. Hence it can no longer appear paradoxical that this *transition* is an era almost exclusively preoccupied with economic interests and characterized by the *frank use of naked force*. Economics and violence have started to act out the *last stage* of their historical existence, and if they seem to dominate the arena of history, this cannot disguise the fact that this is their *last appearance*. (p.252.)

The problem with this kind of discourse is that it fails to take any notice of all those tendencies of development — visible already at the time of the publication of Bernstein's *Evolutionary Socialism* — on the basis of which reformist social democracy becomes the dominant form of articulation of the working class movement in the dominant Western capitalist countries. Such tendencies bring with them the most mystifying varieties of the 'mixed economy'; of the social-democratically administered and idealized 'welfare state'; of the disarming parliamentary practices of 'consensus politics'; of the willing participation of privileged and socialdemocratically led Western labour in the imperialistic ventures of its ruling class, etc., instead of conforming to the Lukácsian expectation of the 'frank use of naked force' which is supposed to mark the 'last stage' of social development before mankind accomplishes its full liberation.

More importantly still, as far as Lukács's assessment of the situation is concerned, the absence of any vision of what might constitute a real transition towards the desired new historic form of collective self-emancipation proves to be self-defeating even within its own terms of reference, under the given historical circumstances. For more or less at the same time when Lukács writes the exalted words quoted above on the last historical relationship between economics and violence (June 1919), he is also forced to confront in Hungary the greatly deteriorating economic conditions, the slackening of labour discipline, the dramatic fall in productivity, etc., which threaten *from within* its own social basis the very survival of the few months old proletarian dictatorship.

Having postulated the identity of *theory and practice* and the disappearance of the opposition between *past and present* — both with reference to the self-knowledge of the identical subject-object of history, as modelled by Lukács on the individual's *moral* knowledge of himself and on his corresponding sense of responsibility[130] — it must appear bewildering to the Hungarian philosopher that such a situation should arise. At the same time, the confines of the young Lukács's theory with regard to the possibilities of a solution are both limited and problematical. For as a result of the reduction of the problems of transition to the relationship between economics and violence, there can be only two alternatives compatible with Lukács's line of reasoning. Either, he must preach the 'power of morality over institutions and economics', in the form of an idealist direct appeal to the moral conscience and heightened sense of responsibility of the individual proletarians, for the purpose of radically improving their labour practices. Or, he must project, in the same discourse, the fateful consequences of the necessity imposed by the unfavourable material circumstances upon the proletariat as a class 'to turn its dictatorship against itself', in case the individual proletarians fail to live up to the moral imperative of the advocated socialist labour discipline, as we have seen it argued by Lukács in his essay on 'The Role of Morality in Communist Production',[131] written in the same period.

The uncomfortable truth is, though, that the political measures of the proletarian dictatorship, including the 'frank use of naked force', are by themselves structurally incapable of establishing the 'identity of theory and practice' and of positively superseding 'the opposition between past and present'. And by the same token, they are far from suitable to offer a positive solution to what Lukács calls 'the falling production of the transitional period'. (p.252.) Unfortunately, however, the historically concrete and feasible remedies cannot be reconciled with Lukács's terms of reference in *History and Class Consciousness*.

9.2 Changing evaluation of the workers' councils

9.2.1

DURING the time that elapses between writing the first and the last essay of *History and Class Consciousness*, we can witness a significant change in Lukács's position in relation to one of the most important potential organs of material and political mediation in the age of transition from capital's rule over society to a socialist order. This change concerns the evaluation of the *Workers' Councils* as the practically feasible bridge between the inherited socioeconomic and political structures and those that must be articulated in a *positive* way in order to be able 'to take seriously the category of leap into the realm of freedom'. For in Marx's view the social form which defines itself through the (admittedly necessary but by no means sufficient) 'expropriation of the expropriators' — thereby remaining tied to the 'negation of the negation' — could not be considered a truly self-sustaining form, because of the contradictions arising from its continued dependency on the negated object.

The positive ethos of the new society could only be found in the emancipated self-activity of its members and in the corresponding institutional/instrumental complexes which flexibly respond to the needs of the social individuals, instead of opposing them through their own — predetermined — material inertia. Only in such an institutional/instrumental framework can one take seriously the category of *conscious* collective totalization — that is: fully co-operative harmonization — of the social individuals' freely chosen aims and objectives, in sharp contrast to the system ruled by the 'invisible hand' of the market. For the latter is characterized by a wholly *unconscious totalization* that makes capital's own objectives prevail behind the backs of the particular individuals, even when they are idealized in bourgeois philosophy as 'world-historical individuals'.

It is in this context that the mediatory and emancipatory potential of the Workers' Councils becomes visible. The passage quoted in Section 7.2.2 above from Lukács's famous essay on 'Class Consciousness' — written in March 1920, before he had received and taken to heart Lenin's critique of his own share of 'Left-wing communism, an infantile disorder' — makes these connections very clear, putting the emphasis on the elimination of the bourgeois separation of the legislature, administration and the judiciary, on the overcoming of the proletariat's fragmentation, and on bringing economics and politics together in the new synthesis of a historically concrete and effective proletarian praxis. (p.80.) By contrast, the discussion of the same institutional complex in one of the last essays of *History and Class Consciousness* — 'Towards a Methodology of the Problem of Organization', written in September 1922 — is highly critical (and even if not explicitly but by implication self-critical, on account of the views held one year earlier by the author), as we can see in the following quotation:

> only after years of acute revolutionary conflict had elapsed was it possible for the Workers' Council to shed its *utopian, mythological character* and cease to be viewed as the *panacea for all the problems of the revolution;* it was years before it could be seen by the non-Russian proletariat for what it really was. (I do not mean to suggest that this process of clarification has been completed. In fact I doubt it very much. But as

it is being *invoked only by way of illustration,* I shall not enter into discussion of it *here.)* (pp.296-7.)

Unhappily, though, as a result of the sociopolitical involution in postrevolutionary Russia which culminates a few years later in the triumph of Stalinism, the postponing clause designated by the word 'here' becomes a very long time for Lukács. It is worth mentioning at this point that in his correspondence with Anna Seghers, Lukács is called upon to reply to the criticism levelled against him that he often bypasses important issues by saying something like 'this is not the place to discuss them'. He defends himself by insisting that the *complexity* of the problems does not allow one to do them justice, but at the same time the subject matter under discussion requires at least a brief reference to the missing dimensions.

This is, of course, true in some instances, but by no means the whole truth. For in numerous theoretically and politically important contexts where Lukács invokes the same exempting qualifications we have to look for other reasons, which in fact demonstrate again the intimate connection between methodology and its substantive socio-political ground of determination.

The adoption of the 'not here' proviso — which often turns out to mean 'never' — cannot be explained in terms of 'complexity'. Rather — as in the case quoted above — it is Lukács's feeling of unease about maintaining a position which he cannot adequately justify in theoretical and political terms. For the significant change that takes place — as a result of regressive sociopolitical developments in Russia — in his own evaluation of the Workers' Councils in the last essays of *History and Class Consciousness* would call for a much more adequate explanation than a summary negative reference to those who see in them a 'panacea for all the problems of the revolution'. What makes forbiddingly 'complex' to deal with this problem of far-reaching practical significance is not some insurmountable theoretical complexity but the party-disciplinary taboo surrounding it, which must be 'internalized' by the devoted party member.

Likewise, one of the strategically most important issues of the socialist movement — the relationship between the broad popular masses and the political party — is treated by Lukács with unease after his evaluation of Rosa Luxemburg's work changes in accordance with the party line. What is at stake in this issue is formulated by Luxemburg with striking clarity in her debate with Bernstein. She writes:

> The union of the broad popular masses with an aim reaching beyond the existing social order, the union of the daily struggle with the great world transformation, this is the task of the social democratic movement, which must logically grope on its road of development between the following two rocks: abandoning the mass character of the party or abandoning its final aim, falling into bourgeois reformism or into sectarianism, anarchism or opportunism.[132]

As a matter of fact, Lukács's position is very close to that of Rosa Luxemburg in the first essays of *History and Class Consciousness*. It is all the more revealing, therefore, that in the last essays (by which time the party announces the need to struggle against the 'Luxemburgists') he has to pursue a curious, contorted reasoning, in a rationalizing effort to turn the monumental historical dilemma so clearly expressed in Luxemburg's words — which must be faced even today, or perhaps today more than ever before — into a question of Weberian 'typology of the sects'. This is how he argues:

It makes no difference whether, by a process of mythologising, a correct flair for revolutionary action is unreservedly attributed to the masses or whether it is argued that the 'conscious' minority has to take action on behalf of the 'unconscious' masses. Both these extremes are offered here only as illustrations, as even the most cursory attempt to give a typology of the sects would be well beyond the scope of this study. (pp.321-2.)

The trouble is, though, that the 'illustration' transforms a vital concern — one that directly affects the *core* of all feasible socialist strategies — into a matter of small sects whose 'typology' one day might perhaps be sketched out by the philosopher. In this way the illusion is created that the problem can be theoretically resolved by 'equidistancing' oneself from the 'two extremes offered here only as illustrations'.

Yet, social reality itself stubbornly refuses to put up with such idealistic 'typological' solutions which would wishfully relegate the dramatic conflicts of the social core to its *periphery*. For one of the two 'small-sect extremes' — that which attributes 'flair for revolutionary action to the masses' (even if not 'unreservedly', as one of Lukács's reductive and disqualifying qualifications would want to have it) — in fact corresponds to the position of Rosa Luxemburg and many others who want to build their strategies of the socialist movement on the 'spontaneity of the masses', without neglecting thereby the role of consciousness. At the same time, the other 'marginal sectarian extreme' becomes more and more the *dominant*—and eventually under Stalin's rule the *exclusive*—strategic line of postrevolutionary developments.

Undoubtedly, Lukács wants to assume a practically effective critical position also in relation to the second 'sectarian' approach. For he applies also to the latter his damning characterization of the sect, insisting that 'the structure of its consciousness is closely related to that of the bourgeoisie'. (p.321.) However, his criticism is condemned to missing its target. First, because—by disregarding the massive practical/institutional power behind the criticized strategic position — we remain, again, within the realm of consciousness, expecting the solution of the problem put into relief by Lukács from the insight, thanks to the work of consciousness upon consciousness, that sectarianism is quite untenable, in view of the affinity between its structure of consciousness and bourgeois consciousness. And second, because a *mainstream* development in the international socialist movement, with immense theoretical and practical consequences for the future, is treated as a *marginal* phenomenon (of sects), so as to be containable within the parameters of a purely methodological-ideological critique.

This is how Lukács's 'aesopic language' of criticism originates, well before Stalin succeeds in eliminating his rivals from the political stage in Russia. The effectiveness of such a language is greatly limited by its very nature, since references to the material/institutional structures and trends of the unfolding development are transposed in it to an abstract methodological plane where as a rule it is very difficult to pinpoint their substantive target. At the same time, the fact that the author makes only *methodological* claims with regard to the objects of his criticism, without indicating their direct material/organizational implications, this fact can provide him with a significant margin of *protection* against the retaliatory measures of those who have at their disposal much more than purely methodological weapons. As Lukács himself puts it in *History and Class Consciousness*, in his September 1922 essay: 'Towards a Methodology of the Problem of Organization':

> On the level of *pure theory* the most disparate views and tendencies are able to co-exist peacefully, antagonisms are only expressed in the form of discussions which can be *contained* within the framework of one and the same organization *without disrupting* it. But no sooner are these same questions given organizational form than they turn out to be sharply opposed and even *incompatible*. (p.299.)

Keeping his own critical discourse primarily on the methodological plane and presenting its substantive objects in an 'aesopic language' happens to be Lukács's more or less conscious way of securing 'peaceful co-existence' for himself, without abandoning what he considers the intellectual's right and duty to join in the struggle for emancipation the way he can. And he wants to secure such 'peaceful co-existence' — to which his methodological discourse seems to be the most conducive in difficult times, when *substantive dissent* is automatically condemned as 'organizational *factionalism*', with disastrous consequences for all those who indulge in it — not simply for his own benefit, but as a disciplined party member whose absolute duty is to avod 'disrupting the organization': a sin which he would judge unforgivable to everybody, including himself.

Thus, it is right to stress again and again that the problematical position assumed by Lukács in relation to the dominant 'sectarian' direction is not the result of 'opportunistic accommodation' and 'capitulation', in response to the criticism which he receives from party functionaries *after* the publication of *History and Class Consciousness*. As we can see, it is unmistakably identifiable in *History and Class Consciousness* itself. The hypothesis (or accusation) of opportunism and capitulation — which, moreover, refuses to take any notice of even the simple facts of chronology — cannot explain anything in the case of someone who, like Lukács, personally had to give up so much when he made his irrevocable choice to identify himself unreservedly with the destiny of the party.

9.2.2

NEVERTHELESS, stressing all this can only underline the significance of the fact that Lukács's retreat from his original evaluation of the Workers' Councils is inseparable from the way in which the issue itself is *practically* treated by the party under the conditions of postrevolutionary development. Only in one of his last writings — *Demokratisierung heute und morgen,* whose publication was forbidden in Hungary for twenty years after its completion and for seventeen years after the author's death — could Lukács return to the discussion of the historical past of the Workers' Councils with approval,[133] and even then only in the most general terms, denying their relevance for the present.

To be sure, the Workers' Councils should not be considered a 'panacea for all the problems of the revolution'. Nevertheless, without some form of genuine *self-management* the difficulties and contradictions which all postrevolutionary societies have to face become chronic, and they may even carry the danger of a relapse into the reproductive practices of the old order, even if under a different type of controlling personnel. At the time of their spontaneous constitution, in the midst of some major structural crisis of the countries concerned, the

Workers' Councils attempted to assume, on more than one occasion in history, precisely the role of viable self-management, together with the *self-imposed* responsibility — which happens to be implicit in, and practically inseparable from, the assumed role — for carrying the enormous and long-lasting burden of restructuring the inherited social reproductive framework.

In the absence of historically specific and institutionally articulated forms of genuine self-management from the theoretician's horizon — and here it is quite unimportant whether they call themselves Workers' Councils or by another, self-chosen, name, so long as they are capable of fulfilling the role of effective material mediation between the old and the envisaged socialist order — all talk about 'abolishing the *split between rights and duties*' (p.319) is bound to remain merely stipulative, confined to the advocacy of some 'ought-to-be', instead of confronting the difficulties inherent in the production of workable practical strategies. This is why Lukács, after dismissing the idea of self-management through the collective agency of the Workers' Councils as 'utopian mythology' and 'panacea for all the problems of the revolution', without attempting to put anything historically concrete and institutionally safeguarded in the place of the criticized material complexes, must end up with the idealization of a self-confirmatory 'dialectical methodology', using the latter as an idealist substitute for the necessary and feasible organs of participatory social control.

Thus, paradoxically, after complaining about the utopian and mythological character of the ideas associated with the socioeconomic and political practices manifest through the *historical reality* of the Workers' Councils, Lukács offers the *mythology* of theory itself realizing the task of practical transformation on condition that it becomes 'purely dialectical'. And he does not seem to be disturbed by the fact that he creates only the semblance of resolving the surveyed problems by offering no more than a series of *abstract imperatives* ('ifs' coupled with 'musts'), instead of the necessary *affirmatives* supported by tangible sociohistorical evidence. This is how Lukács argues his case:

> The fact that proletarian class consciousness becomes autonomous and assumes objective form [through the party] is only meaningful for the proletariat *if* at every moment it really embodies for the proletariat the revolutionary meaning of that moment. In an objectively revolutionary situation, then, the correctness of revolutionary Marxism is much more than the 'general' correctness of its theory. Precisely because it has become wholly practical and geared to the latest developments the theory *must* become the guide to every day-to-day step. And this is only possible *if* the theory divests itself entirely of its purely theoretical characteristics and becomes *purely dialectical*. That is to say, it *must* transcend in practice every tension between the *general* and the *particular,* between the *rule* and the *individual* case 'subsumed' under it, between the *rule* and its *application* and hence too every tension between *theory* and *practice*. (p.333.)

However, we would look in vain in the last essays of *History and Class Consciousness* for institutionally concrete forms of social practice through which the 'tension' (in reality the sharp contradiction) between the general and the particular, the rule and its application, the rule and the 'individual case' (i.e. in reality the historically existing individuals themselves) subsumed under it, as well as (in the most comprehensive terms) the opposition between theory and practice could be transcended. Yet, only through the actual material mediation of such

— institutionally articulated and safeguarded — forms of social practice could the tension/contradiction between the broad masses of the people and the party (i.e. in the postrevolutionary society between the people and the emerging party-state) be progressively superseded within the framework of a likewise progressively self-determined productive activity which the members of Lukács's 'conscious vanguard' fully share — with all its rewards and burdens — with all the other members of the working community.

Witnessing the tragic historical developments under the impact of external 'encirclement' and internal 'bureaucratization' in post-revolutionary Russia, which inevitably paralyze and in the end outlaw *practically* (even if not formally) the spontaneously constituted Workers' Councils, the author of *History and Class Consciousness* is unable to argue in favour of strengthening the autonomous power of decision making of the popular masses. Instead, he offers — again — purely verbal remedies to the conflicts and contradictions which he perceives.

The way in which he describes the acknowledged 'tensions' within the working class and its organizations tends to deprive them of their objective weight. He explains the tensions and contradictions (at times with the help of utterly bewildering conceptual equations and transformations) by aprioristically decreeing that

> the *sharp split* in the organization between the conscious vanguard and the broad masses is only an aspect of the *homogeneous but dialectical* process of development of the whole class and of its consciousness. (p.338.)

Thus, even the greatest challenges which postrevolutionary societies have to struggle with in their protracted attempts to overcome the inherited structural division of the social body into the rulers and the ruled, the leaders and the led, the educators and the educated, can be wishfully hypostatized by Lukács as by definition transcended through the 'homogeneous but dialectical' development of imputed class consciousness. No amount of historical evidence to the contrary (the contrary being declared by Lukács to have the status of merely 'empirical/psychological consciousness') could break through the walls of an ideological fortress constructed from such an impregnable line of reasoning.

9.2.3

ADMITTEDLY, Lukács's reflections on the subject are not without a significant critical intent. For after rejecting what he calls 'utopian hopes or illusions', (p.335) with direct and indirect references to the Workers' Councils, he is willing to grant that 'we must discover *organisational devices and guarantees' (Ibid.)* in order to be able to realize the envisaged socialist aims. However, he ascribes entirely to capitalist reification the continuing (in his view primarily ideological) problems, on the ground that the 'inward transformation' of the individuals cannot be achieved 'as long as capitalism still exists'. *(Ibid.)* Thus, Lukács diagnoses the situation in such a way that the encountered problems themselves should appear to press for their — one and only feasible — solution through the organisational intermediary of the idealized party.

Inevitably, therefore, also the critical dimension of the Lukácsian strategy — i.e. the yet to be discovered 'organisational devices and guarantees' — must be conceived in terms that can be accommodated *within* the party, without imposing the slightest objective constraint on the sovereign power of decision making of the party itself through the links which it must have to other bodies and institutional/organizational forms. In other words, in Lukács's theoretical framework the dialectic of history in relation to the party could never be thought of as a dynamic totality of which the party itself is only a *part*. For the party is said to represent the active — processual — element of history as well as the 'visibly incarnated standpoint of totality', and through these two fundamental constituents the principle of collective totalization as such must be vested in it. Thus, the party's innermost nature is defined as the visible and — for the first time ever in history — conscious incarnation of the identical subject-object of the totalizing process, whereas the revolutionary class is considered only the 'repository' of the process, with no conceivable (consciously justifiable) claim over the institutionally/organizationally concrete and active incarnation of proletarian consciousness. And since the party is viewed as the organizational embodiment of the only valid vantage point — the 'standpoint of totality' — in relation to the social reality, it would be a contradiction in terms to consider it as only a *part* of the historically unfolding totality, which would make it subject to the constraints and changing requirements of the overall strategic framework of socialist transformation.

It is thus amply clear that Lukács's idealization of the party is not the consequence of his alleged 'capitulation to Stalinist orthodoxy'. As all attentive readers of *History and Class Consciousness* can confirm it for themselves, the sins which he is supposed to have committed ten years after the publication of his most famous work, under the direct pressure of Comintern (and associated party bureaucratic) strictures, in order to save his own privileged position in the international communist hierarchy, are in fact present in *History and Class Consciousness* itself which Lukács's ideological adversaries like to misrepresent as the quintessential product of a mythical Western Marxism 'before the fall'. In fact the earlier quoted essay on 'Class Consciousness' in which Lukács characterizes the party as 'the historical embodiment and the active incarnation of class consciousness' as well as the 'incarnation of the ethics of the fighting proletariat' is written by him in March 1920. This predates by three months even Lenin's qualified critique of Lukács's 'left-wing communism', not to mention the (at the time most powerful) Comintern leader's — Zinoviev's — summary condemnation of *History and Class Consciousness* in the aftermath of its publication.

In his self-critical response to renewed attacks in the early 1930s Lukács adopts the same position on the party which we can find in *History and Class Consciousness*. He distances himself mainly on theoretical grounds from the famous work repeatedly condemned by high-ranking party functionaries. His own critique of *History and Class Consciousness* is primarily concerned with the problems of 'reflection' theory, the identical subject-object, the conflation of alienation and objectivity, and similar issues.

As we have seen in Chapter 6, Lukács's undeniable idealization of the party can be made intelligible in terms of the author's intellectual formation, centred from a very early stage in his development on the notion of the historically required *moral* agency: one capable of meeting the challenge of a much needed radical renewal 'in an age of total sinfulness'.[134] This is what he is deeply convinced to have found in the party — with its 'moral mission', corresponding to its claimed objective determination as 'the ethics of the fighting proletariat', etc. — from the very moment of joining the Hungarian Communist Party as one of its first recruits.

However, putting the record straight on this score does not make the problems themselves any easier. It only helps to explain why Lukács must define the — yet to be achieved — practical aspect of mediation in party-organizational terms. He can only look for the necessary guarantees against the perceived dangers of bureaucratization and ossification on the plane of enlightened, and as a matter of principle periodically changing, party leadership (the plane of an 'ought-to-be'), coupled with '*iron discipline*' and the consciously adopted as well as by the criticized individuals willingly accepted policy of renewed *purges*.[135]

All this we can find in *History and Class Consciousness* itself, a long time before Stalin succeeds in securing a totally unchallengeable position in the Russian party as well as in the international communist movement. In tune with his passionate moral orientation, Lukács refuses to accept as the proper criterion of party membership anything less than the individuals' involvement with their '*total personality*' in the activity of the party, accepting the demands of the party unhesitatingly and unquestioningly in accordance with the same criterion. He insists that understanding the inherent 'link between the total personality and *party discipline*' represents 'one of the most exalted and important intellectual problems in the history of revolution'. (p.320.) Accordingly, submission to '*iron discipline*' is approved and commended by Lukács not under accommodation-imposing external pressure but, on the contrary, on the fully interiorized ground that the 'demand for *total commitment*' in the name of the necessary iron discipline
> tears away the *reified veils* that cloud the consciousness of the individual in capitalist society. (p.339.)

Following this line of thought to its logical conclusion as far as the role of the individual is concerned, Lukács also insists, with total sincerity, that
> The conscious desire for the realm of freedom ... must entail the *renunciation of individual freedom*. It implies the conscious subordination of the self to that *collective will* that is destined to bring real freedom into being ... This conscious collective will is the *Communist Party*. (p.315.)

Viewing everything from this perspective, it is understandable why Lukács must confine the task of historical mediation to the question of *political organization*, in that for him the party is itself 'the *concrete mediation between man and history*'. (p.318.) From the adoption of this position it follows for him that '*Organisation* is the form of mediation between theory and practice'. (p.299.) As to the concrete issues of transformatory practice that must be faced in the course of the struggle, their condition of satisfaction according to Lukács boils down to the imperative 'to form active political units (parties) that *could mediate* between the action of every member and that of the whole class'. (p.318.)

Thus, we are confined again to the domain of the general regulative principles, looking for answers on the plane of yet another 'ought-to-be', even though the recommended principle of 'mediating between the action of every member of the party and that of the whole class' is put forward by Lukács with the intent to respond to the historically specific needs — the concrete 'what is to be done?' — of the revolutionary struggle. However, the all-important question of '*how to mediate?*', in tangible and institutionally/organizationally safeguarded terms, is considered not only superfluous but totally inadmissible. For the party as the historically specific incarnation of imputed class consciousness is itself supposed to be by its very nature the 'concrete mediation' not just between the individuals and the class but altogether *between man and history*.

The actual and potential conflicts within the advocated 'political units' are brushed aside by Lukács with the help of the general assertion that 'the *unifying factor* here is *discipline*'. (p.316.) As to the 'organizational devices and guarantees' that must be discovered in the interest of avoiding ossification, they are never spelled out beyond a brief reference to the general desideratum that party hierarchy ought to be based 'on the suitability of certain talents for the objective requirements of the particular phase of the struggle'. (p.336.) A principle which, according to Lukács, ought to be implemented in the form of consciously accepted and welcome 'reshuffles in the party hierarchy'. *(Ibid.)*

The viability of Lukács's critical recommendations is questionable, therefore, on two grounds. First and primarily, because the question of mediation is restricted to the issue of party political organization. And second, because even in its own terms of reference the effectiveness or impotence of Lukács's critical intent remains entirely dependent on the far from demonstrated willingness of those in the party hierarchy who hold the power of decision making to 'reshuffle' themselves, on the basis of their conscious self-critical admission that as 'talents' they are no longer 'suitable for the objective requirements of the struggle' under the changed circumstances.

9.3 Lukács's category of mediation

9.3.1

ONCE the question of mediation is defined in the way we have seen in the last Section — i.e. by assigning (or ascribing) to the party the ontological status of being 'the concrete mediation between man and history' — there is no room left for other than the aprioristic assertion and reiteration that the problem has been solved 'in principle', even though it is painfully obvious that the practical task of emancipatory transformation, with all its potential setbacks and even massive reversals, has hardly been initiated.

In order to be able to sustain its optimistic/aprioristic message, Lukács's discussion of mediation is primarily concerned with demonstrating that bourgeois thought remains at the level of *immediacy*, whereas the proletarian 'standpoint of totality' is in principle capable of making proper use of the 'category of mediation' in theory, thanks to the objective situation of the class itself in relation to the social totality. For

> while the bourgeoisie *remains enmeshed in its immediacy* by virtue of its class role, the proletariat is driven by the specific dialectics of its class situation to abandon it. ... The unique element in its situation is that its *surpassing of immediacy* represents an *aspiration* towards society in its *totality* regardless of whether this aspiration is *conscious* or whether it remains *unconscious* for the moment. This is the reason why its *logic* does not permit it to remain stationary at a relatively higher stage of immediacy but forces it to persevere in an uninterrupted movement towards this totality, i.e. to persist in the dialectical process by which immediacies are constantly annulled and transcended. (pp.171-4.)

The accent in Lukács's discourse concerning the category of mediation is on constantly reasserting that the world of immediacy yields only a false image of reality whose structure is itself mediated, and only bourgeois thought can — and *must* — be satisfied with that false appearance. As Lukács puts it in a characteristic passage of *History and Class Consciousness*:

> The category of mediation is a lever with which to overcome the mere immediacy of the empirical world and as such it is not something (subjective) foisted on to the objects from outside, it is no value-judgement or 'ought' opposed to their 'is'. It is rather the manifestation of their *objective structure*. This can only become apparent in the visible objects of consciousness when the *false attitude* of bourgeois thought to objective reality has been *abandoned*. Mediation would not be possible were it not for the fact that the empirical existence of objects is *itself mediated* and only *appears* to be unmediated in so far as the *awareness of mediation* is lacking so that the objects are torn from the complex of their true determinants and placed in artificial isolation. (p.163.)

Thus the *category* of mediation is put into relief as the proof of the qualitative superiority of the theoretical conception corresponding to the class position and class interest of the proletariat over that of its class adversary. Coupled with the statement according to which the party itself is the 'concrete mediation between man and history', the question of mediation seems to be solved not only 'in principle' but also for good. For if reality itself is already mediated, and the party is identifiable as the agency fully and consciously engaged in the realization of the concrete tasks of the historical process, in that case addressing the issue of material (including institutional/organizational) mediations — which would inevitably have to focus on the *temporal* dimension of the party, with all its sociohistorical specificities and limitations, rather than situating it *above* such constraints in virtue of its claimed mediatory position 'between man and history' — must be considered not only redundant but even counter-productive.

9.3.2

UNDERSTANDABLY, it is very important to present the issues in this light from the point of view of a thinker who is in the course of abandoning, with profound conviction, the standpoint of the class into which he was born, and of adopting a radically different theoretical vantage point which he would never cease to commend to his fellow intellectuals. However, considered in relation to the objective needs and specific emancipatory tasks of mediatory *practice,* the same discourse turns out to be much more problematical. For it is very far from being the case that the postrevolutionary reality is itself already mediated with regard to its fundamental transformatory objectives. To this end the much needed subjective and objective conditions can only be created in the course of the actual process of radical restructuring itself, and, precisely, through the successful articulation of the historically feasible forms of material mediation.

Knowing that the new development for the proletariat means, as Lukács insists, 'that workers *can* become conscious of the social character of labour, it means that the abstract, universal form of the societal principle as it is manifested *can* be increasingly concretized and overcome' (p.171.) may be reassuring for the theoretician who is looking for reassurance. But by theoretically proclaiming that these *possibilities* have appeared on the historical horizon, they are not ipso facto turned into tangible material *realities;* nor is thereby the task of 'increasing concretization' even begun, let alone completed.

Likewise, to assert that 'the forms of mediation in and through which it becomes *possible* to go beyond the immediate existence of objects as they are given, *can* be shown to be the *structural principles* and the real tendencies of the objects themselves' (p.155) is far from solving the problem. For what is at stake is the *creation* of the indispensable forms of *concrete material and institutional mediation* which both flexibly respond to the immediate demands of the given sociohistorical situation and at the same time assume the function of restructuring the inherited metabolic framework of deeply iniquitous, hierarchical social division of labour.

- The 'category of mediation' on its own is quite impotent to produce the required material changes. Transformatory mediations call for the sustained practical intervention of a real-life social agency, and not for the self-referential unreality of an idealistically hypostatized philosophical standpoint in the role of an apriori successful substitute-agency.

- In any case, the proposition according to which the difficulties are solved by simply abandoning the 'false attitude of bourgeois thought' from which 'the awareness of mediation is lacking' (i.e. the recognition that 'the empirical existence of objects is *itself mediated*') offers a rather one-sided characterization of the actual state of affairs. For one thing, by becoming aware — as a result of having abandoned the false attitude of bourgeois thought — that in reality everything is mediated, the self-same reality does not become any more mediated than before in its general constitution, and it remains quite unmediated with regard to the specific historical tasks of socialist-oriented transformatory mediations. More importantly, still, even if we can assert that in reality everything is always mediated, this — generic — truth indicates very little about the specific character of the dynamic relations involved. For the mediations in question always assume the concrete form of tendencies and *counter-tendencies*. It is the conflictual interaction of such tendencies and counter-tendencies that produces in any particular historical moment the dominant (but by no means permanent) forms of mediation.

As we have seen, Lukács forcefully stresses that the historically given forms of mediation are the 'structural principles and the real tendencies of the objects themselves'. (p.155.) At the same time, however, he neglects the complicating and potentially derailing role of the counter-tendencies necessarily generated on the terrain of social practice. This is by no means accidental. For in his discourse the matter has been irrevocably settled in virtue of the structural inability of bourgeois class consciousness even to become aware of mediation, let alone to deal with its complications and objective constraints in social practice. In Lukács's view the irreversible tendency of the historical dialectic is the abolition of the bourgeois order. He never tires of reasserting that the objective conditions of this abolition have been 'often satisfied'. If only the proletariat could overcome its 'ideological crisis', he says, the victory would be complete and irreversible.

9.3.3

THE systematic under-estimation of bourgeois class consciousness constitutes one of the main pillars of Lukács's thought in *History and Class Consciousness*. He underrates not only the theoretical ability of the bourgeoisie to grasp the 'category of mediation', in that doing so would affect in a negative way — directly or indirectly — its fundamental class interests. More importantly, he denies the bourgeoisie the ability to *counter* on the practical terrain of sociohistorical mediations, with structurally significant and lasting (rather than purely manipulatory[136] and hence ephemeral) effect, the moves of its class adversary.

Lukács's theoretical neglect of the vitally important counter-tendencies in the unfolding of the historical dialectic is a necessary consequence of this unrealistic attitude to the limitations of bourgeois class consciousness and to the corresponding ability of the class adversary to intervene in the process of socioeconomic, political, and cultural/ideological mediations.

Yet, whenever we refer to the 'structural principles and objective tendencies' of the social world, we must bear in mind that the tendencies we are talking about cannot be divorced from their counter-tendencies which — at least temporarily — can displace or even reverse the current trends. For every tendency is in fact necessarily counteracted—to a greater or lesser degree—by its contrary in the course of capitalist development. This objective condition of complicated tendential interactions is further enhanced (and in its implications for socialist strategies in the short run much aggravated) by the intrinsically contradictory nature of capital itself. Whatever might be the immediately feasible conscious corrective changes in this respect, the negative impact of the tendential/counter-tendential interactions inherited from the past is bound to remain a major problem for the postcapitalist phase too, at least for a considerable period of time.

In the social metabolism of the capital system characterized by Marx in terms of its dominant tendencies,[137] the by no means naturalistic tendential laws of development enumerated by him are opposed by their powerful counterparts. Thus, capital's irrepressible tendency to *monopoly* is (to be sure, in different ways in different phases of capitalistic developments, which goes also for the others) effectively counteracted by *competition;* likewise, *centralization* by *fragmentation; internationalization* by national and regional *particularism; economizing* by extreme *wastefulness; unification* by *stratification; socialization* by *privatization;* the tendency to *equilibrium* by the counter-tendency towards the *breakdown of equilibrium,* etc.

The outcome of the conflictual interchanges of the various tendencies and counter-tendencies is determined by their overall configuration, on the basis of the objective characteristics of each. Theoretical relativism in this respect can be avoided only with reference to the *ultimate limits* (i.e. the immanent nature) of capital itself which determine the *global* (or 'totalizing') tendency of capital's most varied manifestations. But this global tendency can only prevail — with its objective characteristics and determining force — through the manifold partial and conflictual interactions themselves.

- Naturally, all these conflictual interactions, in their historical specificity, can only be made intelligible if full allowance is made for a significant — and to a large extent consciously pursued — *reciprocally corrective feedback* on the part of the rival social agencies, within the material parameters of their *ultimately* (but, it cannot be stressed enough, only ultimately) insurmountable overall limits. This is why the question of mediation cannot be settled in an apriori fashion, with the help of the 'category of mediation' assigned to the theoretical vantage point of one class only.

Capital's ability to displace its contradictions works through the agency and mediatory practice of the class which positively identifies its interests with the objective limits of this system of social metabolic control. Accordingly, this class is more than willing (and to a large extent able) to adjust its strategies — both nationally and internationally, whether we think in the first respect of the 'mixed economy', the 'welfare state' and 'consensus politics', etc., or internationally of the acceptance of the so-called 'non-ideological' inter-state relations, in place of the earlier openly pursued interventionist wars or of the 'cold war' — when the changing relation of forces so demands, in order to put the emerging trends to its own use.

9.3.4

THE major strategic adjustments adopted by the 'personifications of capital' under the force of historical circumstance represent *objective structural changes,* even though they are of necessity articulated within the ultimate structural limits of capital. It would be, therefore, quite wrong to consign them to the self-reassuring category of 'manipulation' (or 'ideological manipulation'), which could be more or less easily countered by the work of consciousness upon consciousness, provided that it is armed with the insight that 'the awareness of mediation is lacking' in bourgeois class consciousness. As Marx argued,

> No social order is ever destroyed before all the productive forces for which it is sufficient have been developed, and new superior relations of production never replace older ones before the material conditions for their existence have matured within the framework of the old society.[138]

This is what sets the ultimate structural limits to capital as a social metabolic control, embracing the whole *epoch* for which its productive forces can be developed and extended. Thus, the mediatory transformations open to capital as a mode of control are co-extensive to whatever may be compatible with these *epochally* set limits. Moreover, capital and labour are so closely intertwined in the ongoing social metabolic process that the feasible mediatory adjustments are necessarily conditioned — for better or worse — by the strategic moves of capital's social adversary, and of course *vice versa.*

Lukács's discourse on the limits of bourgeois class consciousness is derived from the consideration of the *ultimate* epochal limits, but it pays no attention to the intervening historical periods of capital's potential development and mediatory transformation. This is why he greets the practice of capitalist 'planning' as the 'capitulation of bourgeois class consciousness before the consciousness of the proletariat' when it is nothing of the kind. Assessing in this way an important aspect of capital's (for the time being successfully) unfolding tendency towards *monopolistic control* is all the more problematical since even the socialist modality of *planning* — as opposed to its caricature in the form of the so-called *command economy* — can only be *made* (i.e. actually constituted, rather than again assumed as a self-evident and self-reassuring category) in the course of articulating the institutionally/organizationally concrete and workable forms of *material mediation.* For only through the latter can socialist strategies of planning practically demonstrate the new social order's claims to representing a superior mode of production, on the basis of the genuine *self-management* of the most diverse reproductive units and their coherent integration into a viable social whole.

We can see, then, that Lukács's analysis of mediation falls short of its promise in two major respects.

First, because by underrating the ability of the bourgeoisie to deal with the problems that emerge from its conflictual relationship to labour by means of the required mediatory adjustments, he ignores labour's ever-growing need (as the stakes are getting higher) to meet the newly defined challenge by elaborating its own mediatory responses to the — often bewildering — changes adopted by the social adversary.

And second, by offering a framework of theoretical postulates and categories as the solution of the encountered problems — from the identity of subject and object, past and present, theory and practice, qualitative leap and gradual process (to name but a few), on the one hand, and the proletarian exclusivity claimed in relation to the categories of mediation, planning, etc., on the other — Lukács offers a rosy picture of the tasks that lie ahead. For as far as the envisaged socialist society is concerned, not only the *'awareness* of mediation is lacking' but the much needed and for emancipatory purposes usable *actual structures* meditation are themselves still objectively missing. Besides, whenever and wherever they are likely to come into being, they are bound to remain for the entire period of transition subject to all kinds of constraints, contradictions and potential relapses.

CHAPTER TEN

POLITICS AND MORALITY:
FROM *HISTORY AND CLASS CONSCIOUSNESS* TO
THE PRESENT AND FUTURE OF DEMOCRATIZATION,
AND BACK TO THE UNWRITTEN *ETHICS*

10.1 *Appeal to the direct intervention of emancipatory consciousness*

10.1.1

ONE of Lukács's greatest dilemmas concerns the relationship between the material base of society and the various forms of social consciousness. He pursues the problems related to it throughout his life with great passion and intellectual rigour, looking for emancipatory solutions to the identified contradictions through the direct intervention of social consciousness. This is why he dedicates so many works to the ethically inspired study of aesthetic issues, convinced that the development of art and literature — in the form of their successfully unfolding 'Struggle for Liberation', as the two hundred pages long closing chapter of his monumental *Aesthetics* makes it explicit even in its title — is inextricably enmeshed with the cause of human emancipation.

However, the great difficulty with regard to such a vision is that those forms of social consciousness in which the emancipatory interest is particularly strong, as undoubtedly it happens to be in the domain of aesthetic discourse, in reality cannot directly respond to the needs and demands of the social base in order to shape through their intervention the material structural framework of the established social order. For the more fully articulated the legal and political superstructure becomes in the course of historical development, the more comprehensively it embraces and dominates not only the material reproductive practices of society but also the most varied 'ideal forms' of social consciousness.

As a result, theoretical, philosophical, artistic, etc. practices can intervene in the process of social transformation only indirectly, via the necessarily *biased mediation* of the legal and political superstructure. Paradoxically, therefore, the effective exercise of these potentially emancipatory forms of social consciousness (including art and literature) needs as its vehicle the instrumental complexes of the legal and political superstructure, although the latter — in its vitiating all-pervasiveness under the conditions of the capitalist socioeconomic and political formation — constitutes the most obvious and immediate target of its critique. Many things can change in this respect after the revolution. Nevertheless, in view of the continued division of labour and the concomitant strengthening of the role of the postrevolutionary state — in sharp contrast to the idea of its 'withering away' — the need to subject to a radical critique the legal and political superstructure in the interest of emancipation loses none of its former importance and urgency in the historical epoch of transition, as the experience of all postcapitalist societies testifies.

Lukács is, of course, perfectly aware of the problematical character of politics as such, and not only of its capitalist variety. He knows very well that the necessarily averaging and levelling legal determinations through which the state can deal with the encountered problems are most inadequate to their irrepressible variety and mode of emergence from the social soil, out of the everyday life-activity of the individuals who are motivated by their 'non-reducible' personal aspirations. This is why even at the time of his most active involvement in direct political activity, as one of the leaders of the Hungarian Communist Party during the shortlived Council Republic and a few years thereafter, he defines the historical role of the party itself in essentially *moral* terms. As we have seen above, he insists that the historical legitimacy of the party arises on the one hand from its actual fulfilment of its moral mandate, and on the other from the fact that it offers the required scope for the realization of the *'full personality'* of the individuals who join its ranks in order to dedicate themselves to the cause of socialist transformation. Another way in which Lukács attempts to bypass the constraining network of political instrumentality in *History and Class Consciousness* is the formulation of *direct appeals* to ideology and to the imputed consciousness of the proletariat, coupled with repeated claims that the objective conditions for a radical structural change are already given and only the 'ideological crisis' stands in the way of accomplishing the great leap forward to the 'new historic form'.

But what happens to the philosopher's discourse if the party, for whatever reason, is unable to live up to the kind of moral determination of its essence which Lukács offers in *History and Class Consciousness?* Clearly, in the light of postrevolutionary historical experience it is impossible to continue to idealize the party as 'the mediation between man and history', etc. Under the circumstances of forced collectivization and Stalinist show trials it is no longer possible to substitute for the contradictory reality of the actually existing party — the exclusive decision making body of a centralized party-state — a set of moral imperatives which could sound perfectly plausible in the immediate aftermath of the 1917 October revolution which became victorious against overwhelming odds under the leadership of the Leninist party. Understandably, therefore, given Lukács's expulsion from the field of direct political activity as a result of the defeat of his 'Blum Theses', not to mention his imprisonment for a while in Stalin's Russia, the ethically inspired definition of the party, in the key of *History and Class Consciousness*, becomes untenable in the eyes of the Hungarian philosopher himself.

Although in view of his irrevocable commitment to the international communist movement Lukács must somehow come to terms with the ongoing developments after his own defeat as a political leader — hence his uneasy *rationalization* of the Stalinist strategy of 'socialism in one country' to the very end of his life, including the works in which he is openly critical of Stalin[139] — this is done in a way which is qualitatively different from the exalted *idealization* of the 'identical subject-object' and of the morally mandated 'active incarnation of proletarian class consciousness' in *History and Class Consciousness*.

There is some resignation in this change of perspective from the end of the 1920s. A touch of resignation becomes visible in Lukács's writings after the defeat of his 'Blum Theses' not in the sense that the author would allow anyone to cast a pessimistic shadow of doubt on the feasibility of the promised radical socialist transformation. It is the *time-scale* of Lukács's expectations that changes fundamentally once the formerly idealized instrumentality of the revolution as 'the ethics of the proletariat' is recognized to be problematical.

This resignatory shift in the envisaged time-scale is inevitable since in Lukács's vision, even after his forced exit from active politics, there can be no alternative to take the place of the emancipatory instrumentality of the party itself. Not even in the form of advocating the establishment of some limited but genuinely autonomous institutional counterweight to the latter's bureaucratizing tendencies readily acknowledged by Lukács himself. Thus, on the one hand (in contrast to the perspective put forward by the Hungarian philosopher in *History and Class Consciousness*) after 1930 we are no longer told that the material conditions of a radical supersession of capitalism have been effectively realized and only the ideological crisis stands in the way of the final victory. At the same time though, on the other hand, it is repeatedly stated by Lukács, with undiminished conviction and passion, that

> Only under the conditions of realized socialism will the subordination of men to society be superseded, opening up for them a normally balanced and healthy subject-object relationship both to their inner and to their external world.[140]

As to the time required for such a truly radical transformation, after deploring the 'paradoxical situation' that the mainstream of socialist literature simply fails to take any notice of the central problem of the 'Struggle for Liberation', as manifest in the historical development of art and literature, Lukács writes:

> The difficulty is to demonstrate that the forces capable of victoriously accomplishing this struggle for liberation reside in socialism, in the socialist culture. However, we believe that this difficulty belongs only to the given historical moment, and therefore, viewed from a world-historical standpoint, it is only transient. The question in which our considerations culminated belongs to a world-historical perspective. It is the duty of philosophy to clarify the theoretical grounds of such problems, but by no means to anticipate prophetically or utopistically their concrete forms and phases of realization. ... in terms of historical transformations of this kind not only years but even decades count very little. ... For us the important thing is the perspective of overall development. Judged from such a perspective, the objective and subjective blockages of the decades under Stalin are not, in the last analysis, decisive. For, despite everything, the mainstream of development was the strengthening and consolidation of socialism.[141]

Thus, since the socioeconomic and political framework of postcapitalist societies cannot be subjected to a radical critique by Lukács, he must opt for the time-scale of a long-drawn-out 'world-historical perspective' as a substitute for such a critique. And he can sustain the viability of the adopted perspective only as a matter of faith, rather than as a theoretically demonstrable position. This is why he chooses as one of his favourite mottoes

> a somewhat modified saying of Zola: *'La vérité est lentement en marche et à la fin des fins rien ne l'arrêtera'*.[142]

In this way Lukács can envisage a positive solution 'in the fullness of time' to the problems and contradictions of 'actually existing socialism' which he — either because of external political constraints or on account of internal theoretical reasons — cannot spell out in concrete terms. Inevitably, therefore, the historically specific tasks of practical, materially effective, mediation through which advances could be made under the established conditions towards the anticipated 'world-historical solution' of society's burning problems, must occupy a secondary position, if appear at all, in this perspective. The problematic of mediation is kept alive as the concern of aesthetics and ethics. The 'Struggle for Liberation' becomes synonymous with the realization of 'this-worldliness' in consciousness, and the corresponding emancipation of individuals from the power of religion; a struggle for which in Lukács's view the paradigm example is provided by the long historical progression of art and literature towards fully overcoming the tutelage and domination of religion.

Obviously, then, this way of characterizing the struggle for liberation bears the heavy imprint of the 'force of postrevolutionary circumstance' under which the author of *History and Class Consciousness* and the former Minister of Culture and Education in the Hungarian Council Republic is compelled to recast his original perspective. At the same time this change also shows how problematical it is to assess the needs and potentialities of the present (and of the foreseeable future as well) within Lukács's classical-culture-oriented perspective in which the names of Aristotle, Goethe, Hegel and Thomas Mann loom ever larger.[143] For although the far-away world-historical development of a fully unified humanity may indeed overcome the need to find in religion 'the heart of a heartless world' (as Marx puts it in *The German Ideology*), nevertheless, as a matter of unavoidable practical mediation between the present and the future in many parts of our contemporary world — from Nicaragua to Brazil and from El Salvador to much of Africa — one can hardly conceive of dispensing with the emancipatory potential and combative action of religious movements deeply committed to the cause of liberating the oppressed from the tutelage and domination of very real economic and political forces.

10.1.2
IN an important sense, after the 1920s the problem remains exactly as before as far as Lukács is concerned. Namely: how to make an emancipatory impact on the (by now postrevolutionary) social base by means of the direct intervention of social consciousness. Indeed, after the consolidation of Stalinism the possibility of a positive change must be defined by Lukács more strongly than ever in precisely such terms (talking also of 'ideological freedom struggle'), in view of his enforced retirement from the field of political decision making and action.

As a result of the complete Stalinization of the Comintern and of the ensuing defeat of the Hungarian party faction led by Lukács after the death of the outstanding former syndicalist leader Eugene Landler, the author of *History and Class Consciousness* (and of the 'Blum Theses') is no longer in any position of authority to intervene in the debates concerning political strategy and party organization, not even in purely methodological terms. Thus, his advocacy of solving the problems of the socialist movement through the work of consciousness upon consciousness—an idea prominent already in *History and Class Consciousness*, even if still linked to the question of the party's moral mandate and ability to provide the necessary scope for the realization of the 'full personality' of its active members, as we have seen above — becomes from the perspective forced upon Lukács by the changed political circumstances the only feasible avenue to follow. As a dedicated party member, he accepts the role assigned to him under the new circumstances, taking a most active part in the heated discussions over cultural and literary policy. But — with the exception of a few days in October 1956, as Minister of Culture in Imre Nagy's government — he never plays a direct political role. Nor indeed does he even claim the right to such a role in his definition of the moral mission and responsibility of the intellectuals. He unquestioningly assigns to the party as such the function of formulating both strategy and day-to-day policy. The intellectuals are expected to provide a purely advisory service to the party leadership, as in 'Kennedy's Brains Trust',[144] and to fulfil an educational role in society at large.

The relationship between the party and its intellectuals under Stalin's rule is very different from the way in which the international communist movement functions on the whole up to the end of the 1920s. For intellectuals (understandably as a rule of bourgeois origin) can play a very important role in shaping the strategic orientation of the socialist forces right from the *Manifesto of the Communist Party* all the way down to the consolidation of Stalinism. Lenin's famous statement (often quoted by Lukács himself) that an adequate political consciousness can only be brought into the socialist workers' movement 'from outside', by the party's dedicated intellectuals, is based on this historical fact. Even in the 1920s, some leading intellectuals can still make a significant impact on party policy through their direct interventions in the ongoing debates, in their capacity as political figures. This is so not only in Russia but also in the Communist parties of Western countries. It is enough to mention in this respect the names of Gramsci, Karl Korsch and Lukács himself.

The process of Stalinization puts a drastic end to all critical intervention by communist intellectuals in the political process. As a matter of bitter irony, it is one of the Russian intellectual politicians who (just like Bukharin and many others) later himself falls victim to the Stalinist purges of intellectuals and politicians — Grigorii Zinoviev — who introduces into the party debates the reference to 'professors' as a term of abuse and automatic political disqualifier. At the Fifth Congress of the Communist International he dogmatically condemns Lukács, threatening him with punishment, on account of the views expressed in *History and Class Consciousness*, declaring that

> If a few more of these professors come and dish out their Marxist theories, then the cause will be in a bad way. We cannot, in our Communist International, allow theoretical revisionism of this kind to go unpunished.[145]

The truth, that at the time of Zinoviev's Comintern strictures Lukács (a few years earlier a very rich man) lives with his family in exile under conditions of extreme hardship, dedicating himself fully to party work — indeed, as a matter of fact, the first time ever he becomes a professor is after his return to Hungary, in 1946 — counts obviously for naught when the interest of Stalinist 'Gleichschaltung' (uniformization) finds it intolerable to allow the continuation of open political and theoretical debates in the international communist movement. The real tragedy of all this is that in the course of the Stalinist liquidation, expulsion, and silencing of intellectual politicians and political intellectuals, the critical assessment of the adopted strategies becomes quite impossible, with the most devastating consequences for many decades to come not only in Russia, but indirectly — through the deterring effect of Stalinist developments — also in the capitalistically advanced countries of the West. The author of *History and Class Consciousness* is only one of the important communist intellectuals whose much needed political contribution to the cause of socialist transformation is utterly marginalized as a result of these changes.

10.2 The 'guerilla struggle of art and science' and the idea of intellectual leadership 'from above'

10.2.1

TO be sure, Lukács conducts for the rest of his life a kind of 'guerilla struggle' against party bureaucracy, as circumstances permit. Although he cannot address himself even indirectly to the issues of socioeconomic and political strategy, he criticizes — in 'Aesopic language', as he puts it later — some main tenets of the publicly decreed cultural and literary policy of the party (for instance the Zhdanovist conception of 'socialist realism' and 'revolutionary romanticism'), stubbornly pursuing his own 'heretic' line also on some major philosophical matters (e.g. in defence of Hegel — and of dialectics in general — against the officially proclaimed interpretations). Indeed, after returning to Hungary in 1946, he formulates the theory — attacked by Rudas, Révai and others in the acrimonious 'Lukács debate' between 1949-52 — according to which the writer should be allowed to be a *guerilla fighter,* instead of being required to behave as an army *foot-soldier* in carrying out the strategy of the party. In the same spirit, as an important general principle of his aesthetic theory, he writes much later — as an openly defiant rejection of the party's condemnation of his views on the artist's right to be a guerilla fighter — in *Die Eigenart des Aesthetischen* that

> the artistic, i.e. this-worldly, interpretation of biblical myths is the result of a quiet but tenacious *guerilla struggle* between art and church, even if at first this is not stated openly, and even if perhaps neither the artistic producer nor the consumer becomes conscious of this state of affairs.[146]

According to Lukács 'every real work of art is an *anti-Theodicaea* in the strictest sense of the term',[147] and, consequently, art and science have a great deal in common in this respect. And when he states that 'art and science stand in an irreconcilable antagonism to religion',[148] he reiterates his principle about the simultaneous 'guerilla struggle' and 'co-existence' of both the artists and the scientific intellectuals with the ruling institution of the age (which could be quite easily applied to the present as well), underlining that

> This theoretical assertion is not in the least weakened by the fact that for a long time their relationship is characterized by *silencing compromises* coupled with *irrepressible guerilla struggles.*[149]

All the same, Lukács has to recognize that the margin of action of the cultural/ intellectual guerilla fighter is rather limited in relation to the decision-making processes of the present. This is why he has to refer constantly to the 'world-historical perspective' and 'world-historical sense' of the surveyed developments. Categories which in the key of hope (Lukács's *Prinzip Hoffnung*) put the negative trends in perspective and compensate for the disappointments of the present.

Inevitably, thus, in Lukács's assessment of the all-important questions of 'what is to be done?' and 'how to do it?', the answers are formulated, more and more as time goes by, within the framework of a constantly anticipated — but never fully worked out — *ethical* discourse, with its emphasis on the *individuals'* direct role in mastering adversity and emancipating themselves from the *social* reality of alienation through their victory over their own 'particularism'. We shall see the main ingredients of this discourse further on in this chapter. But before we can have a closer look at the characteristic features of Lukács's conception of the role which ethics is called upon to play in the socialist transformation of society, it is necessary to indicate some objective constraining factors in his situation, as well as their internalization by the Hungarian philosopher, which lead to the passionate advocacy of the ethical imperatival solution on his part.

It is highly significant in this respect that even in the late sixties, well after Khrushchev's secret speech against Stalin, Lukács's critical evaluation of what went wrong after the revolution and how to put things right is confined — with the exception of the, for twenty years unpublishable, essay on *Democratization* — strictly to the domain of culture. And even the 1968 exception, concerning the need for democratization, offers only a general *methodological* critique of Stalinism, without entering into the *substantive* issues of the Stalinist strategy of 'socialism in one country'. The latter is accepted by him to the end without reservation, as we have seen also in note 139. The fact that in his 1967 Preface to *History and Class Consciousness* Lukács reiterates the earlier opposition between method and substantive theoretical propositions, insisting on the validity of the Marxian conception on purely methodological grounds, acquires its political significance in this context.

Although his own political role is abruptly terminated towards the end of the 1920s as a result of the authoritarian intervention of Comintern bureaucracy, Lukács refuses to question the socioeconomic and political changes of that decade. His criticism of postrevolutionary developments is spelled out only in relation to the negative *cultural* consequences of the Stalinist methods, stressing in his answer to '8 domande sul xxii congresso del PCUS' that

> Today [in 1962] the situation is in reality less favourable than in the nineteen twenties, when the Stalinian methods were not yet perfected, nor systematically applied to all fields of cultural production. ... The great task of socialist culture is to show to the intellectuals, and through them to the masses, their spiritual homeland. In the twenties, notwithstanding the great political and economic difficulties, this was successfully accomplished, to a large extent. The fact that later on such tendencies have been greatly weakened in the international arena of culture is the consequence of the Stalinian period.[150]

Thus the acceptance of the political and socioeconomic changes of the postrevolutionary decades greatly reduces Lukács's margin of action as a critic. All he can do is to claim *exceptional* status for the domain of literary and artistic creation, and to oppose — openly or by implication only, as the political conjuncture of the day allows it — those measures which tend to interfere with the advocated organic development of culture. Lenin's authority is invoked by Lukács within this perspective, in accordance with a line of approach that tries to enlarge the margin of relatively autonomous cultural activity in the spirit of the 'guerilla fighter'. He quotes Lenin's writings, published well before the October revolution, without raising the issue that the postrevolutionary situation would call for a radical reexamination of the quoted passages in the light of the fundamentally altered circumstances.

Two examples should suffice here to illustrate both Lukács's great political difficulties and the problematical solutions which he puts forward in order to overcome the difficulties in question. The first concerns the relationship between literary creation and the party (i.e. the question of party discipline to which creative intellectuals should or should not be required to conform); and the second, the role of the intellectuals in general in the development of socialist consciousness and in the decision-making processes of the transitional society.

In his attempt to enlarge the margin of the writer's autonomous action Lukács frequently asserts that Lenin's famous article on party literature 'does not at all refer to imaginative literature'.[151] The evidence for this thesis is in fact very shaky: a letter by Krupskaya in which, from the distance of many years, she reports that in her recollection Lenin did not intend to include creative literature in the category of party literature. Lenin's text, however, speaks otherwise. For he refers, unmistakably, to the issue of 'the freedom of *literary creation*',[152] emphasising at the same time that

> there is no question that literature is least of all subject to mechanical adjustment and levelling ... in this field greater scope must undoubtedly be allowed for personal initiative, individual inclination, thought and fantasy, form and content.[153]

And Lenin's conclusion is that while *mechanical* control is not admissible, the principle of 'party literature' must indeed apply also to the field of creative literature.

This issue graphically illustrates Lukács's dilemma and the necessary limits of his opposition to Stalinist theories and practices. Not simply because he must use Lenin's authority in support of his own principle — which pleads for granting a privileged position to creative literature — but because his defence of literature against bureaucratic interference must assume the form of an extremely problematical principle. If Krupskaya and Lukács were right on this point, Lenin would be clearly in the wrong. For there is nothing objectionable about stipulating — in the Czarist Russia of 1905, when Lenin publishes his disputed article — that creative writers who want to join the party (when they are perfectly free not to join it) should accept their share of the common task, in a form which is appropriate to their medium of activity, i.e., which acknowledges the special relationship between literary form and content, as well as the importance of personal initiative, individual inclination and fantasy.

The situation is, however, radically different after 1917, when the party is no longer a persecuted minority but the unchallenged ruling power of the country. Thus the real issue is not the relationship between literature and the party but that between the party and the total institutional framework of *postrevolutionary* society. And no amount of creative freedom in literature could conceivably remedy the contradictions of the latter. Lukács's noble defence of Solzhenitsyn, for instance, against opponents who 'read into his works far-fetched political ideas and credit them with great political impact'[154] — a defence based on the aesthetic argument that literature is political 'only in our sense of a mediation which is frequently very remote, since between the artistic level of this portrayal and its indirect effect actual social connections do exist, but are distantly mediated'[155] — makes out, again, a special case for literature, desperately minimizing, in support of this plea, the fact that the works in question are bound to have a great political impact in a society which at the time of the publication of Lukács's essay on Solzhenitsyn's novels (1969) is very far from having realized its declared programme of de-Stalinization. We can clearly see in the light of this example that — far from being a calculated accommodation as his bourgeois critics suggested — the internalization of the political constraints of the Stalinist period becomes a genuine 'second nature' to Lukács. For even as late as 1969, when the danger of brutal consequences being suffered by dissenting intellectuals is no longer real, he cannot reassess these problems in terms different from those into which the decades of Stalin's rule trapped the critical socialist aspirations of people like him.

The second example is concerned with a matter of quite fundamental importance. As mentioned already, in support of his own definition of the role and responisbility of the intellectuals we can find in Lukács's works many references to Lenin's statement according to which socialist consciousness must be brought into the workers' movement 'from outside'. Even in his essay on *Democratization* — written almost seventy years after Lenin formulated the idea in question — it occupies a central place in Lukács's line of reasoning. Thus he argues that

> Everybody who is willing to think these questions through can see that today — as we have stated already — the idea of a socialist-oriented democratizing movement can only be brought into the consciousness of the people if directed, to say it with Lenin, 'from outside'; it cannot arise there spontaneously.[156]

Lukács realizes, of course, that it is somewhat problematical to cling to a principle seven decades after its original formulation, disregarding the specific historical circumstances under which Lenin had to write his work — *What Is to Be Done?* — in which the celebrated remark appeared. Curiously, however, Lukács is convinced that he can successfully extricate himself from this difficulty by turning Lenin's historically defined proposition into a *general methodological principle*. He adopts this position after conceding that Lenin's proposition was formulated as a strategic guide-line of the Russian revolutionary movement in response to the demands and constraints of a specific historico-political and ideological conjuncture.[157]

Lukács's aim in invoking the principle of 'from outside' is to secure for the intellectuals a role and a margin of action commensurate to the historical significance of the task they are called upon to fulfil and which, according to the recommended principle, no other social force than the intellectuals can fulfil. This orientation is advocated by Lukács in the same spirit in which he suggests in his reply to '8 domande sul xxii congresso del PCUS' that if the intellectuals are enabled to find their 'spiritual homeland', in that case 'through them the masses' will find it too. At the same time it is accepted by him — as an unhappy internalization of the Stalinist constraints — that no autonomous initiative of a genuine mass character can arise under the prevailing sociohistorical circumstances. Emancipatory initiative thus becomes synonymous in Lukács's thought with the autonomous theoretical intervention of intellectuals committed to the cause of socialist transformation. Intellectuals who are capable of offering the right kind of advice to those in the party who are actually — and in Lukács's view also rightfully — in charge of decision-making.

In this way, the time-bound qualifiers of Lenin's historically defined strategic guide-line become quite irrelevant, indeed a drawback, as far as Lukács is concerned. For with the excuse of the changed circumstances the bureaucrats can deny the intellectuals the margin of action Lukács is looking for. Paradoxically, this is why he lines up Lenin's authority on his side and transforms the Russian revolutionary leader's sociohistorically specific guide-line into a general methodological principle. He does this in order to confer upon the principle in question a validity that transcends the given — unfavourable — historical conditions and political circumstances.

No matter how positively intended by Lukács, this reasoning is fatally flawed. For, unwittingly, it accepts a perspective that blocks the road to the solution of the grave structural problems and contradictions of postcapitalist societies by perpetuating a relationship — between the 'socially conscious intellectuals' and the 'unconscious' or 'false-conscious' masses — which is in need of being radically challenged.

10.2.2

CRITICS of Lenin's organizational principle like to point out that he formulated it at a time when he was 'under Kautsky's influence'. This is quite unjustified. It is true that Lenin approvingly quotes a passage in *What Is to Be Done?* from an article written by Kautsky in which it is stated that 'socialist consciousness is something introduced into the proletarian class struggle from without {von Aussen Hineingetragenes} and not something that arose within it spontaneously'.[158] However, Lenin deliberately and completely ignores the more problematical — positivistically overstretched — elements of the same Kautsky article concerning the relationship between 'science and technology' and the proletariat.

Lenin's interest in stressing the disputed point is in fact directly related to the controversy raging in the Russian party at the time of writing *What Is to Be Done?* on the kind of political organization required to bring about the socialist revolution under the circumstances of the brutally repressive Czarist regime. The crucial question in this respect is, according to Lenin, whether the creation of a *mass* political organization should be the aim of Russian Social Democracy, or a rather restricted one, capable of operating successfully despite the pressures, constraints and dangers inseparable from the clandestine conditions imposed upon it. Given the circumstances of the Czarist police state, Lenin opts for an organization of *professional revolutionaries* who can operate under the conditions of *strict secrecy*.

At the same time Lenin could not be clearer in stressing that 'To concentrate all secret functions in the hands of as small a number of professional revolutionaries as possible does not mean that the latter will *"do the thinking for all"* and that the rank and file will not take an active part in the movement'.[159] The last thing that he is willing to contemplate even under the prevailing historical circumstances (not to mention the more distant future) is the perpetuation of the divide between intellectuals and workers. On the contrary, he insists in the same work that

> all distinction as between workers and intellectuals, not to speak of distinctions of trade and profession, in both categories, must be effaced.[160]

Thus, arguing the necessity to retain as the orienting framework of the *present,* in 1968, the principle of 'from outside' is hopelessly inadequate, on several counts.

First, because it does not reflect correctly the spirit of Lenin's work, only its letter, taken out of its historical context. For, as we have seen in the last quotation, in Lenin's *What Is to Be Done?* the historically given relationship between intellectuals and workers is in fact explicitly questioned, with an aim to efface the existing differences in the course of the revolutionary advance of the movement.

Second, because the absence of the specific conditions (i.e. of the repressive Czarist police state) in terms of which Lenin justifies the recommended organizational principle of the vanguard party — the organization of a limited number of professional revolutionaries who can work in strict secrecy — calls for a radical reassessment of the principle itself in postrevolutionary societies, in accordance with the changed historical conditions, instead of conferring upon it the indeterminate validity of Lukács's 'general methodological principle'.

And third, because the difficulties and contradictions of postrevolutionary societies cannot be overcome by perpetuating, and in an important sense — as far as the relationship between party intellectuals and workers is concerned — even aggravating, the structural divisions of the inherited social order.

- THE third consideration, just mentioned, happens to be for us by far the most important. For after the revolution, when the party holds the reins of power and social control, there can be no such thing any longer as plain 'from outside'. The so-called *from outside* — vis-à-vis the masses of workers — becomes simultaneously also the hierarchically self-perpetuating *from above*. Intellectual leadership, thus, cannot be exercised in postrevolutionary societies simply 'from outside', as under the conditions of capitalist rule, when workers and progressive intellectuals alike are at the receiving end of that rule. Under the changed circumstances, by contrast, 'intellectual leadership' becomes institutionalized *political control of the masses,* exercised *from above* and enforced with all means at the disposal of the postcapitalist state. And, of course, this negative circumstance is not made any better just because it happens to be unavoidable in the *immediate aftermath* of the conquest of power, in view of the objective constitution and determining force of the inherited material power structures.

- Accordingly, the new historic task is the radical restructuring of the given hierarchical power structures, on a genuinely *mass* basis, in contrast to the painfully visible perpetuation of the division of society into the rulers (or, with a more palatable name, the leaders) and the ruled, in the name of the allegedly unavoidable necessity to introduce socialist consciousness into the workers' movement 'from outside'. The once appropriate justification of the adopted strategic measures can no longer be considered historically legitimate. For, after the conquest of power, socialist consciousness cannot be developed from the — no longer existent — 'outside', and even less from the actually existing and counter-productive *above*. It can only be generated *from within* the mass basis of postrevolutionary society, by the *masses themselves,* in response to the tasks and challenges which they have to confront in their attempts to solve — through the hard learning and reciprocally adjusting processes of co-operatively planned productive activity — the material, political and cultural problems of their everyday life.

• Clearly, then, arguing in favour of the recognition and frank public acknowledgement of this incontestable shift from 'outside' to 'above', as a result of the conquest of power, does not mean in the least an uncritical 'plea for the spontaneity of the masses'. Characteristically, all those who have a vested interest in hiding the fact that their own way of exercising control 'from outside' has become equivalent to *imposing it from above,* like to disqualify, automatically, all serious concern with these matters by saying that to raise the issue itself amounts to a 'capitulation to spontaneity'. Yet, in reality the question is not 'spontaneity versus consciousness' at all. It is, on the contrary, the autonomous development of a consciousness adequate to the demands and challenges of the new conditions. And that means not only that such consciousness can only be developed *from within,* by those who have to struggle with their severe existential problems. It also means that the consciousness in question, if it is to be successful at all in addressing itself both to the daily concerns of the people and to the task of restructuring the given socioeconomic order, must be articulated not in relation to generic strategic objectives but in terms of historically *specific tasks,* in accordance with the dynamically changing parameters of the adopted *material mediatory forms* that link the present to the future.

• The latter condition takes us back again to the necessity of *'from within'* under the conditions of postrevolutionary societies. For the strategy of 'from outside' is at best capable of enabling the working people to acquire the — undoubtedly very important — consciousness that it is necessary to conquer power in order to change significantly their conditions of life. But it cannot show the popular masses how to build and manage — autonomously, since the success of the whole enterprise depends precisely on that — the new social order. To envisage the *autonomy* of the associated producers by 'developing' their consciousness *from outside,* not to mention *from above,* is an obvious (and in its practical implications totally absurd) contradiction in terms.

As we all know, there is plenty of evidence in the annals of history for the overthrow of antiquated and oppressive social and political orders. Intellectuals of bourgeois origin, like Lukács, who turned against the class into which they were born, could render a great service to the cause of socialist transformation by evaluating such historical experience in the service of proletarian revolutions. However, there is no historical precedent at all for embarking on the task which the agency of postcapitalist restructuring is called upon to face. Consequently, under the changed circumstances intellectuals (and especially the former bourgeois intellectuals whose conditions of everyday life are quite different from those of the popular masses) know *far less* about 'what is to be done' in relation to the specific problems of postrevolutionary societies and their corresponding material mediatory forms of potential solution than the working classes whose daily bread is directly affected by the success or failure of the measures that need to be adopted. Thus, unlike before the conquest of political power, intellectuals are in no way in a privileged position on the plane of knowledge with regard to the qualitatively new historic task of overcoming the power of capital through the radical restructuring of the inherited socioeconomic and political order.

10.3 In praise of subterranean public opinion

10.3.1

WE can see from what follows below, how helpless even a great intellectual like Lukács becomes in the face of these difficulties. In a section of his book on *Democratization* he appeals to the party to pay attention to the 'subterranean public opinion' of the popular masses. As an example in support of his plea, Lukács mentions that according to his experience in the field of culture, extending over several decades:

> the success or failure, the deeper or rather superficial impact of books and films, etc., depends much more from this 'public opinion' than from criticism, and least of all from official criticism.[161]

At the same time he has to concede that 'It is much more difficult to demonstrate the same effect in economic matters'.[162] The only example he can offer, and even that only by switching to *capitalist* countries, is the effectiveness of 'working to rule' in a railway dispute.[163] Although Lukács advocates that the party should pay attention to this public opinion, he does not see the need for making significant institutional changes in order to render effective the critical views emanating from below. He wants to retain the sovereign decision-making power of the party also in this regard, without envisaging some sort of institutional guarantee for translating into practical measures the 'subterranean public opinion' which he praises.

Unfortunately, however, on closer inspection even Lukács's hopeful but institutionally far from secured plea to the party turns out to be totally beside the point. This is because the issues at stake are themselves quite different from Lukács's illustrative example. In the field of culture the 'subterranean public opinion' of the popular masses can assert itself (although even there only to a very limited extent) by means of the individuals voting with their feet and with the money in their pockets as to which particular book or film to favour or reject, as particular individuals. They have, by contrast, nothing analogous at their disposal in 'economic matters'.

- On this terrain Lukács's model, according to which the separate individuals as self-conscious individuals can — with the anticipated, radically reforming consequences — 'choose between alternatives', quite simply does not work. For in the case of what he calls 'economic matters' the issue is not really 'economic' at all — i.e. it is not selective economic consumption, set alongside and comparable to selective and with regard to the officially favoured products dismissive cultural consumption — but a matter of politically articulated *structural power relations*. It concerns first of all the *allocation of the socially produced surplus,* together with the thorny issue of *who allocates it?* The question of asserting 'subterranean public opinion in economic matters' analogously to welcoming or rejecting the cultural products on offer can only arise subsequently, on the basis of the existing power relations. In other words, it presupposes the radical redefinition of the vitally important matter of *control* over the total social product in the existing socioeconomic and political order.

In this sense, to expect the solution of the grave material problems of post-capitalist societies from the party's sympathetic response to the selective impact of 'subterranean public opinion in economic matters' — a public opinion which in reality is quite devoid of selectively applicable and fully effective material resources — is far from realistic. We might just as realistically expect the radical reform of the capitalist system — its metamorphosis into 'people's capitalism', as conservative politicians go on promising it — from the economic impact of housewives 'shopping around' (as the self-same politicians constantly invite them to do) in more or less identical supermarkets, controlled with self-serving complicity (cynically projected as 'healthy competition') by a handful of giant firms.

We must have a closer look at these problems in their proper context, in Chapters 17, 19, and 20. Now it is necessary only to underline that in the real world of postcapitalist societies the not too promising way in which the frustrated 'subterranean public opinion' of the workers could express its view of the prevailing socioeconomic power relations of 'equality' was encapsulated in the deadly serious popular joke — and corresponding productive practices — according to which 'Everything is fine: *we* pretend to work, *they* pretend to pay'. In other words, the target of popular irony was not a *particular* economic measure or product whose negative aspects could be satisfactorily dealt with by the party's sympathetic listening to *vox populi*. Rather, it had to be the established system of adversarial relationship between the workers and those who effectively controlled both the hierarchical social division of labour and the allocation of the material rewards of the labour process.

10.3.2

THIS brings to the fore a quite fundamental difficulty. For, as a matter of fact, the meaning of the development of socialist consciousness in postcapitalist societies is perfectly straightforward and the measure of its success or failure is quite tangible. Namely the degree to which the emerging social relations bring with them the supersession of the opposition (and continued antagonism) between the *'We'* and the *'They'* by the communality of *'Us'*. But, of course, this cannot be simply the question of Lukács's 'work of consciousness upon consciousness' (no matter how well-intentioned) by means of which enlightened and enlightening consciousness directly affects its target-consciousness — the consciousness of the popular masses — 'from outside'.

The barriers between the 'We' and the 'They' can only be dismantled through the sustained practical enterprise that directly addresses itself to the burning existential problems of the people. As to the latter task, its realization is feasible only on the basis of the *autonomous* material/institutional articulation of the control-dimension of the labour process as a whole by those who actively engage in it. This alone can provide both the objectives and the necessary means for the self-development of socialist mass consciousness. As Rosa Luxemburg had put this point a very long time ago:

> Socialism will not be and cannot be inaugurated by decree: it cannot be established by any government, however admirably socialistic. Socialism must be created by the masses, must be made by *every* proletarian. Where the chains of capitalism are forged, there must the chains be broken. That only is socialism, and thus only can socialism

be brought into being.[164] *The masses must learn how to use power by using power. There is no other way.*[165]

Bearing these relations in mind, it becomes clear that it is extremely problematical that in 1968, after nearly *seventy years* of Lenin's *What Is to Be Done?* (which also means five decades of Soviet power), Lukács still has to idealize the strategy of successfully introducing, one fine day, socialist consciousness 'from outside' into the working class.

If the key issue in this respect is the practical articulation of the material/institutional forms of communitarian production and consumption through which the development of socialist consciousness in the popular masses — in relation to the specific tasks and material challenges of their situation — first becomes possible, in that case the historic function of the decision making structures of 'from above' inherited from the old order (including the Leninist party which is catapulted in the course of the conquest of power into the structural position of 'above') can only be to act as a *midwife* to the birth of autonomous self-management. Everything else — whatever its relative historical justification — can only prolong the long decades (now approaching a whole century from the time of *What Is to Be Done?*) in which the roots of socialist mass consciousness might indeed one day be established and strengthened to the point of becoming ineradicable. In the meantime, however, the necessary failure of attempting to solve these problems 'from outside' (which means: from the vantage point of some self-perpetuating hierarchy ruling society from above) will remain a stark reminder of the continuing power of capital in a new form, as well as of the danger of capitalist restoration safeguarded on a hereditary basis for as long as capital — in whatever form — retains the levers of social metabolic control.

10.4 Capital's second order mediations and the advocacy of ethics as mediation

10.4.1

THE cleavage between the political framework of Lukács's quest for emancipation and the emancipatory objectives themselves envisaged by the Hungarian philosopher could not be greater. This is why in the systematic works written in the last fifteen years of his life the role of mediation can only be assigned to the imperatives of ethics in general, considered together with the closely related 'liberation struggle' of art and literature.

The question of 'autonomous action', contrasted with its denial by existing forms of domination, is defined by the author of *Eigenart des Aesthetischen* and of the *Ontology of Social Being* in its most general terms of reference: he centres the issue on the 'human species' as such becoming 'master of its own destiny'. Thus the subject of truly autonomous action is no longer a historically identifiable social class — as we have seen it theorized in *History and Class Consciousness,* with reference to the proletariat and its 'standpoint of totality' — but humanity in general. Nor is there much room left in this discourse for the 'moral mission of the party' as the conscious embodiment and the active carrier of the proletariat's all-emancipating standpoint of totality. The great obstacle to be overcome is 'absolute transcendence' (religious or secular), and the proper sphere of autono-

mous action is celebrated as the realization of 'this-worldliness'. We are told by
Lukács that

> since the *for-itself* of artistic creativity ... rejects all *absolute transcendence*, in the
> category of *this-worldliness* we find expressed the most profound affirmation of the
> world by humanity, its self-consciousness that — as human species — it is *master of
> its own destiny*.[166]

In this way Lukács remains always faithful to the Marxian perspective of radical
socialist transformation but in terms of ever more distant temporal references.
Since he had fully committed himself to seeking solutions on the margin of
action created by the 'weakest link of the chain', and subsequently of 'socialism
in one country', he cannot question in substantive terms the fateful determinations and consequences of this margin of action for the historically given socialist
movement. His reservations continue to be expressed in strictly *methodological*
terms, coupled with a noble moral appeal to the ultimate perspective of a 'humanity master of its own destiny'. The burning issue of how to make the *workers*
in postcapitalist societies become 'masters of their own destiny' is hardly raised
at all, and when it is raised it is immediately subsumed under abstract methodological considerations about Stalin's subordination of 'theory to tactics', or of
his 'crude manipulation' of society, as contrasted with the 'subtle manipulation'
by which Lukács characterises contemporary capitalism. It is therefore by no
means surprising that the frightful cleavage between 'actually existing socialism'
and the fully emancipated humanity of his vision can only be filled by the postulate of ethics as mediation. Thus, in the same spirit which we have seen in the
last quotation, the author of *Eigenschaft des Aesthetischen* insists that

> *Ethics* is the crucial field of the fundamental, all-deciding struggle between *this-
> worldliness* and *other-worldliness*, of the real superseding/preserving transformation of
> human particularity. Thus the problems arising in this respect can only be properly
> answered in an Ethic.[167]

The promise of elaborating such an Ethic is the constantly recurring theme of
Lukács's writings in the last fifteen years of his life. This project originated in
fact a long way in the past, as we have seen above, and it was never even remotely
fulfilled nor altogether abandoned, as the posthumously published pages of his
Versuche zu einer Ethik testify. We shall see in Section 10.5 how problematical the
whole enterprise was from the very beginning, when the Kantian philosophical
framework was still heavily conditioning Lukács's view of ethics in his 'Kierkegaardized Hegelian' phase of development; and paradoxically even more so
when in 1956 he seriously embarked again on the road of finally realizing his
long cherished project. Now we must briefly look at the way in which Lukács
tries to confront the problem of alienation in his *Ontology of Social Being* by
postulating the mediatory and emancipatory intervention of ethics.

Distancing himself from the subject-object identity championed in *History
and Class Consciousness*, Lukács recalls that in the Hegelian attempt to elucidate
the relationship between freedom and necessity — defining their reciprocity by
saying that 'the truth of necessity is freedom'[168] — 'substance is transformed
into subject on the path towards the identical subject-object'.[169] We find something similar in Lukács's *Ontology*, even if he makes no explicit claim for a new
subject-object identity. Nonetheless, although it is no longer suggested that the
proletariat is the identical subject-object of history, Lukács reiterates the idea in

an altered form in relation to 'labour as the positing subject'. He discusses reality
in terms of a *dual causality:* (1) the series of *'teleological positings'* performed by
labour, and (2) the chain of *causes and effects* set in motion by the positing of goals
by labour. Labour in its most general sense is the identical subject-object of the
world of teleological positing through which 'history as the ontological reality
of social being'[170] is created. In this sense not only the human species (inseparably, of course, from the individuals) is created but also *reality* itself which in
nature only existed as *possibility.*

> Without transforming this existent possibility of the *natural* into *reality,* however, all
> labour would be condemned to failure, would in fact be impossible. But *no kind of*
> *necessity* is recognized here, simply a *latent possibility.* It is not a blind necessity here
> that becomes a conscious one, but rather a latent possibility, which without the labour
> process will always remain latent, which is consciously raised by labour to the sphere
> of reality. But this is only one aspect of possibility in the labour process. The moment
> of transformation of the *labouring subject* that is stressed by all those who really
> understand labour is, when considered ontologically, essentially a systematic *awak-*
> *ening of possibilities* that were previously dormant in man as mere possibilities.[171]

From this characterization of the relationship between 'mere possibility' and the
reality-creating power of 'teleological positing' Lukács derives a conception of
freedom which he can directly put to his ethical use. He insists that the most
important aspects of this process concern 'those effects that labour brings about
in the working man himself: the necessity for his self-control, his constant battle
against his own instincts, emotions, etc. ... this self-control of the subject is a
permanent feature of the labour process'.[172] Naturally, the only way to maintain
the 'self-control of the subject' as a 'permanent feature of the labour process' is
if we abstract, as Lukács does, from the *actuality* of the labour process under the
rule of capital (including the Soviet type capital system), when talking about
labour's 'self-control' bears no relation to the tyrannically enforced conditions
of alienated control over the working subjects.

This abstraction is necessary for Lukács for his own purposes, inseparable
from the role he wants to assign to ethics. He accomplishes his theoretical aim
in this context (1) by describing 'the working subject' as labour in general (or
the human race as such, unproblematically equated with its individual members), and (2) by presenting a form of consciousness — just like in *History and*
Class Consciousness where, as we have seen, the proletariat could be treated as
conscious even when 'fully unconscious' — which can be readily reconciled, in
Lukács's pursuit of a noble ethical purpose, with the actual absence of consciousness. This is how he argues his case:

> What is involved already in labour itself, is something much more [than a formal
> similarity between labour and ethics]. Irrespective of how far the performer of this
> labour is aware of it, in this process he produces himself as a member of the human
> race, and hence produces the human race itself. We may even say that the path of
> struggle for self-mastery, from natural determination by instinct to conscious self-
> control, is the real path to true human freedom. ... the struggle for control over
> oneself, over one's own originally purely organic nature, is quite certainly an act of
> freedom, a foundation of freedom for human life. Here we encounter the species
> character in human being and freedom: the overcoming of the mere organic mute-
> ness of the species, its forward development into the articulated and self-developing
> species of man who forms himself into a social being, is from the ontological and

genetic standpoint the same act as that of the rise of freedom. ... the most spiritual and highest freedom must be fought for with the same methods as in the original labour, its outcome, even if at a much higher stage of consciousness, has ultimately the same content: the *mastery of the individual acting in the nature of his species over his merely natural and particular individuality*.[173]

Thus, in this discourse on labour in general the vicious circle of capital's second order mediations — interposed between the actually existing working subjects and the objects of their productive enterprise — is left out of sight. Its place is taken by the idea that *'labour* constantly interposes whole series of mediations between man and the immediate goal which he is ultimately concerned to achieve'.[174] In abstraction from the relation of forces and its ruthless enforcement in the historically created and really existing labour process this is, of course, true. But this abstract truth is totally invalidated by capital's mode of controlling and ultimately destructive mediating force which requires a qualitatively different assessment. All the more because a vicious circle of controlling mediations interposes itself between the working subjects and their productive activity also in the postcapitalist capital system. About the latter, however, partly for political and partly for internal theoretical reasons, Lukács cannot speak.

Just as Lukács's 'methodological guarantee of victory' in *History and Class Consciousness* could not be invalidated by the non-realization of the postulated proletarian 'ascribed consciousness', since the way in which it was defined provided also the postulate of its unchallengeable validity, in the same way in the *Ontology of Social Being* the category of 'objective intention' or 'ontologically immanent intention' sustains the claimed validity of the projected perspective. As Lukács puts it:

> Even the most primitive form of labour which posits utility as the value of its product, and is directly related to the satisfaction of needs, sets a process in motion in the man who performs it, the *objective intention* of which — irrespective of the extent to which this is adequately conceived — leads to the real unfolding of man's higher development. ... there can be no economic acts — from rudimentary labour right through to purely social production — which do not have underlying them an *ontologically immanent intention towards the humanization of man* in the broadest sense.[175]

The point of this approach is to provide the ontological foundation for Lukács's discourse on the ethical obligation of the individuals who can choose between real alternatives through which they can emancipate themselves as particular individuals from the power of alienation. This is why he must also insist that 'Even the most complicated economy is a resultant of *individual teleological positings* and their realizations, both in the form of *alternatives*.'[176] The fact that the alternatives are nullified — not by 'crude' or 'subtle manipulation' but by the *necessary mode of operation* of the capital system in all of its forms — has to be considered secondary or irrelevant in a discourse which is anxious to secure the success of the advocated struggle against the power of alienation thanks to the choice of the right alternatives by the particular individuals in their fight against their alienated particularism, within the given domain of their everyday life.

10.4.2

VICTORY over alienation is envisaged by putting into relief the categories of 'possibility' and 'duty', addressed by Lukács with uncompromising ethical rigour to the particular individuals. This is clearly expressed in *The Ontology of Social Being* when Lukács argues that despite the gravely constraining social parameters of alienation

> it is a real *possibility* for every single individual and — from the standpoint of the development of their real personality — their *inner duty* to achieve victory, autonomously, over their own alienation, irrespective of how that alienation has been constituted. ... the role of ideology in the individuals' becoming victorious over their alienated mode of living perhaps never has been greater than in the present age of de-ideologized subtle manipulation.[177]

This way of approaching the problem is unavoidable for Lukács, in view of his evaluation of postcapitalist developments. For he both wants to fight alienation under the existing circumstances and is prevented from doing so by his theorization of the actually prevailing conditions of development. He is never willing to abandon the illusion that as a result of the historical breakthrough 'at the weakest link of the chain'

> an *essentially socialist society* is in the process of construction, no matter how problematical it has become in some respects. With regard to this fundamental question bourgeois wisdom has ended up with a disgraceful fiasco, since it expected from the very beginning a quick collapse and again and again from the time of the NEP a return to capitalism. ... The important fact is that notwithstanding all problematic features a *new society* is being made, with *new human types*. ... the transformation of the people of the old class society into human beings who feel and act as socialists, depite the distortions, weaknesses, the slowing down of the process, and the obstacles created by Stalin's crude manipulation, continued in an *objectively irresistible* way.[178]

Even the repressive political expropriation of surplus-labour under the conditions of the 'essentially socialist' postrevolutionary society is transfigured and idealized in this vision, despite the hierarchical/authoritarian mode of controlling production and distribution under the postcapitalist capital system, with all its painfully obvious iniquities and differentiations. Thus we are told by the author of *The Ontology of Social Being* that 'Socialism differs from the other social formations "only" in this that in it society as such, society in its totality is the one and only *subject* of appropriation; consequently, this form of appropriation is no longer a principle of differentiation of the relationship between particular individuals and social groups.'[179] Inevitably, then, within the confines of this conception the margin of critical intervention in the actually unfolding social process must be extremely narrow, even if Lukács remains firmly convinced that the particular individuals are still very far from realizing the possibilities inherent in — and the duties emanating from — their 'species-belonging'.

Correctives to the acknowledged negative trends are offered by Lukács partly in *methodological* terms and partly on the plane of what he considers to be possible *individual* self-emancipatory action. The 'historical necessity' of postrevolutionary developments under Stalin is reasserted — with reference to Hitler's aggressive war plans. This is qualified with the methodological critique that 'daily/topical contents were rigidly turned into dogmas'.[180] As before, also in *The Ontology of Social Being* Lukács repeatedly stresses that he is only concerned 'with the method ... the dominance of tactics over theory'.[181] Also in relation to the present he can only offer as a way out from the encountered difficulties the advisability of a 'theoretical/methodological return to Marx', in contrast to 'hastily adopted theoretical conclusions'.[182]

As to the postulated self-emancipation of the individuals, Lukács's diagnosis of the existing state of affairs and of the available margin of action is theoretically based on the assertion that

> objective economic development has made it ontologically feasible for the human species the possibility of establishing its being for-itself.[183]

In truth, though, the 'ontological feasibility' of the here asserted 'possibility of humanity for-itself' constitutes an extremely tenuous ground. All the more since the accomplishments of 'objective economic development' — much like at the time of writing History and Class Consciousness, when we were told that the material conditions of human emancipation were 'often satisfied' and only the 'ideological crisis stood in the way' — are exaggerated by Lukács beyond belief, in order to be able to establish the viability of his ethical discourse about the individuals' choice between alternatives. For the actually accomplished 'objective economic development' under the rule of capital had brought with it not only material advancement (and even that in an extremely discriminatory and iniquitous way for the overwhelming majority of humankind) but also the tragic condition that the 'possibilities' of emancipation — a category absolutely central to Lukács's discourse[184] — have been turned into destructive realities. As a result, the dominant aspect of fully developed capital is not that of a 'potential emancipator' but the actual grave-digger for humanity. Thus the objectively existing situation — and not the idealized 'reality' projected by Lukács as emerging from the abstract possibilities of his hopeful perspective — is much graver than what could be counter-acted by any amount of individual opposition to 'manipulated prestige-consumption' through which the people in his view are 'nailed to their particularism'.[185]

Nevertheless, on the tenuous ground of the 'ontological feasibility of a possible humanity for itself' postulated by Lukács he proclaims that

> the road to a real, ideologically well conceived victory over alienation is today better paved — as a perspective — than ever before. ... it depends from the individual himself, whether he lives in a reified and alienated way or wishes to turn into reality with his own deeds his real personality'.[186]

The concept of 'process', in sharp opposition to the 'reified immediacy of mere appearance', played a very important role in History and Class Consciousness. The same is true of Lukács's Ontology of Social Being. For he repeatedly insists that 'alienation, in terms of being, is never a state of affairs but always a process':[187] 'the given immediacy of alienation is a mere appearance'.[188] Thus, according to him, the struggle against the process of alienation 'imposes on the individuals the duty to reach constantly new decisions and to translate them into practice'.[189] Indeed, this duty of 'emancipating oneself from one's own alienation'[190] in his view can be lived up to consciously by the individuals concerned even when it is not pursued in full consciousness. For 'The strongest weapon against alienation at the individuals' disposal is their life-content-shaping conviction — which can be no more than a vague feeling or presentiment — that species-character-for-itself [in which they can participate] is a real existent'.[191]

Recalling Goethe and Schiller (not as aesthetic ideals to be somehow imitated by contemporary literature but as originators of some ethically valid ontological messages), the author of The Ontology of Social Being describes the exemplary individual worthy of the great ethical challenge as a man who has 'sufficient insight, strength of decision making, and courage, to reject from himself all tendencies to alienation',[192] reminding us thereby of the Kantian dictum that 'ought implies can'. For in Lukács's view there can be no way of avoiding the responsibility inseparable from the challenge that 'in everyday life ... every single individual, who is in direct contact with other individuals, ought to decide *in favour or against their own alienation*'.[193] The social perspective adopted by the individuals in their effort to confront their own alienation may well be a *tragic* one.[194] As we know, Lukács's conviction — adopted from Hegel — concerning the unavoidability of 'tragedy in the realm of the ethical' goes back a very long way. What decides the issue in his eyes is that with the help of the commended positive perspective (repeatedly contrasted by Lukács with hope) the individual can '*internally* raise himself above his own particularity intertwined with and bogged down in alienation'.[195]

Thus the paralyzing material mediations of the actually existing capital system are not allowed to cast their shadow on the author's belief in the proper way of gaining victory over alienation. His attention is focussed, instead, on the possible role which ethics can play by inspiring the individuals to 'internally raise themselves above their alienated particularism' in their everyday life. This way of bypassing the vicious circle of capital's material mediations through the postulated intervention of 'ethics as mediation' is coupled with another postulate in the role of a possible social agency of sorts, emerging from the many individual protests against 'manipulation'. This is said to take the form of the 'aversion of many individuals (or small groups) condensed into a mass movement'.[196] As a proof of the emergence of this new way of confronting alienation in the spirit of his positive perspective, the author of *The Ontology of Social Being* can only offer, reminiscent of Marcuse's *One-Dimensional Man* and other writings, a fantastic overestimation of the student movement, projecting that 'the social integration of many individual revolts produces *mass movements* which are sufficiently strong to take up the struggle against the existing ground of human alienations'.[197] In *History and Class Consciousness* labour in the form of the historically existing working class, with its totalizing 'ascribed consciousness', was represented as the social agency of emancipation. In *The Ontology of Social Being* labour appears as the foundation of 'teleological positing' in general and the 'model for all freedom'.[198] This is the theoretical ground on which the individuals' 'choice between alternatives' — in favour or against their own alienation — is expected to fulfil the mediating emancipatory role of ethics in a world locked into the vicious circle of capital's second order mediations.

10.5 The political boundary of ethical conceptions

10.5.1

AS we can see, there is a great deal of resignation in this vision, despite Lukács's appeal to the pathos of his ultimately positive perspective. At times his nostalgia for the combative past of the working class movement — which had resulted at the time also in his own conversion to Marxism and inspired the volume of essays on *History and Class Consciousness* — clearly transpires in *The Ontology of Social Being* when Lukács compares the present conditions of existence to those of the period of revolutionary turmoil. This is how he sums up the difference:

The spontaneous objective linkage of the daily class struggle for immediate economic objectives with the great questions of how it would be possible to make human life meaningful for everybody, undoubtedly this was one of the principal reasons why in those days the working class movement exercised an irresistible power of attraction well beyond the ranks of the proletariat. Naturally, there are confrontations over socioeconomic issues also in contemporary society. However, in most cases precisely the pathos of the early working class movement is missing from them. This is because under the present circumstances the objects of dispute in the advanced capitalist countries do not possess any longer such direct significance for the elemental life process and destiny of the great majority of workers.[199]

It goes without saying that this diagnosis is problematical even in relation to the working classes of the capitalistically most advanced countries, not to mention the fact that even if it were correct, that would still leave at least four fifth of the socially oppressed and in economical terms monstrously disadvantaged people in the world out of consideration. However, what is important in the present context is that the nostalgic tone of the last quotation indicates a retreat from politics stronger than ever in Lukács's writings.

This is in sharp contrast not only with the views held by Lukács in the 1920s but also with his high expectations — in the immediate postwar years — concerning the sociopolitical transformations under the 'people's democracy', as we have seen in Section 6.4.2. In the passage quoted on page 303, from a lecture delivered at the end of 1947, he was claiming that 'now man participates in the interactions of private and public life as an *active subject* and not as a *passive object*'. By contrast in his essay on *Democratization* he had to admit that under the post-revolutionary regimes 'the working masses lost their character as the *subjects* of social decision making: they have become again *mere objects* of the ever-more-powerful, ubiquitous bureaucratic system of regulation which dominated all aspects of their life'.[200] And even if the profound objective reasons of how it became possible to end up with the complete reversal of the original socialist expectations were never investigated by Lukács, who left the matter at con-demning 'bureaucratization' and the method of Stalinist 'crude manipulation' (neither of which can be considered a serious causal explanation), this cannot alter the fact itself that the acknowledged perversion of the socialist ideals was a terrible blow to the Lukácsian positive perspective. For in the past it was an integral part of the positive expectations of all those who remained in the orbit of the 'revolution at the weakest link' — an expectation forcefully reasserted after Khrushchev's secret speech against Stalin — that socialist developments in the East would exercise a great 'power of attraction' over the working classes in the capitalistically advanced Western countries, instead of constituting a terrible deterrent, as 'actually existing socialism' (claimed to be socialist even in Lukács's last completed work, *The Ontology of Social Being,* as we have seen above) had in fact turned out to be.

The retreat from politics in the last fifteen years of Lukács's life is a compli-cated matter. It is not simply the consequence of the deportation and attacks he suffers after 1956. Paradoxically, he adopts the position of his last major works in this respect precisely in order to be able to remain faithful to the perspective opened up by the revolution at the weakest link, no matter how unfavourable the political circumstances and organizational forms linked to it in the present. Thus *The Ontology of Social Being* is an attempt to demonstrate as regards the ongoing objective development the 'irresistible advance towards the realization of humanity for-itself', and subjectively the indisputable validity of fully 'dedicating oneself to the cause of socialism'[201] even when the 'great cause' appears to have deserted those who believe in it, as a result of stunted development and 'crude manipulation' in the sphere of political decision making. This is Lukács's last line of defence for the perspective he derived from October 1917 and maintained to the end in the face of all adversity.

Here I recall a conversation we had in the Summer of 1956, when Lukács was telling me about his plan to finally write his *Ethics*. I argued that he would never be able to write it, because the precondition for tackling the acute problems of ethics would be to undertake a radical critique of postrevolutionary politics; and that was quite impossible under the circumstances. I repeated this conviction in an essay on Lukács — 'Le philosophe du "tertium datur" et du dialogue co-existentiel'[202] —, written in 1958 and subsequently also reprinted in German in the *Festschrift*[203] dedicated to him on his eightieth birthday, in 1965. With reference to this long-standing plan so dear to Lukács I wrote in my essay that 'He still nourishes the intention [to write his ethics] the realization of which could not become possible without a *fundamental change* in the present conditions, or else *the problems of this ethics would have to be confined to the most abstract spheres*'.[204] The general sketch of the Ethics — with the title: *Die Stelle der Ethik im System menschlichen Aktivitäten,* 'The Place of Ethics in the System of Human Activities' — was readily worked out by Lukács after the completion of his *Aesthetic,* as described by him in a letter from Budapest dated 10 May 1962. Twenty months later, however, when I asked in a letter, how he was getting on with the *Ethics,* he complained that it was proceeding 'very slowly. It has proved necessary for me to write first a long introductory part on the ontology of social being, and the latter, too, proceeds very slowly'.[205] As it happened, the 'introductory part' turned out to be *The Ontology of Social Being* and the *Prolegomena* attached to it, and the *Ethics* could never be written.[206] It could not be written by Lukács even when the danger of political imprisonment had receded from the horizon in the last five years of his life.

What is at issue here is the *internalization* of the fundamental constraints of postrevolutionary developments, combined with a reassertion of the socialist alternative in the broadest possible terms, expressed in relation to the far-away perspective of the 'realization of humanity for-itself'. This is how not only the projected Lukácsian *Ethics* is turned into *The Ontology of Social Being* but philosophy in general, with regard to its crucial themes, is defined as an ontology. As Lukács puts it:

> The central content of philosophy is the human species, that is *the ontological picture of the universe and society* from the point of view of what they were in themselves, what they have become, and what they are, so that philosophy should be able to produce the always actually existing type of possible and necessary species-character; thus it synthetically unifies in its picture of species-belonging the two poles: the world and man.[207]

This view is closely connected with the explicit rejection of the demand to make philosophy practical in the sense of linking it to the category of Lenin's 'next link of the chain', which Lukács finds appropriate in *political practice* only, thereby establishing — in contrast to *History and Class Consciousness* — a sharp opposition between praxis-oriented politics and philosophy proper. He insists that 'the typical picture of true philosophy does not contain any category at all which would stand even in a distant relationship with that of the "next link of the chain".'[208] This is obviously in part the philosopher's self-defence against the danger of 'bureaucratic manipulation' and 'the dogmatic imposition of tactics over theory'. But it is at the same time much more than that. For by adopting the ontological standpoint of philosophy advocated by Lukács, the reader is expected to agree that the disheartening contradictions, major setbacks, and tragedies which people are bound to encounter — both in the East and among the working classes of the capitalistically advanced Western countries — are 'purely episodic' in the inexorable process of fully realizing 'humanity for-itself'. And to that process every single individual not only *can* but also has the *inner duty* to actively contribute.

10.5.2

IN Lukács's essay on 'Tactics and Ethics' (early 1919) we find the astonishing assertion that 'Hegel's system is devoid of ethics'.[209] It is preceded by an even more astonishing claim according to which he had 'discovered the answer to the ethical problem: that adherence to the correct tactics is in itself ethical'.[210]

These two statements were typical of a phase in Lukács's development when he was convinced to have found the solution to the relationship between politics and ethics by stipulating their *unproblematical unity*. Even the question of individual responsibility seemed to be easily resolved by asserting that 'The sense of *world history* determines the *tactical* criteria, and it is *before history* that he who does not deviate for reasons of expediency from the narrow, steep path of correct action prescribed by the philosophy of history which alone leads to the goal, undertakes responsibility for all his deeds.'[211]

History and Class Consciousness was born from this spirit, envisaging a totalizing consciousness capable of understanding the 'correct action prescribed by the philosophy of history'. At the same time this spirit of revolutionary enthusiasm (or 'Messianic utopianism' in Lukács's characterization of 1967) also called for a strategic embodiment and organized carrier of the hypostatized consciousness: the party. And, reassuringly, the party itself was said to be capable of providing the necessary guidance on 'the narrow, steep path of correct action', thanks to the direct ethical determination of its nature, arising in Lukács's view from the moral mandate conferred upon it by history. In this way the party could *de jure* assume the 'leadership of society' (lost by the bourgeoisie according to the author of *History and Class Cosnciousness*) and 'activate the total personality'[212] of all those who were willing to 'undertake responsibility for all their deeds'. As far as the politically dedicated individuals were concerned, they had nothing to lose and everything to gain from their acceptance of the 'correct tactics' and from 'the renunciation of individual freedom'.[213] For in this way — and only in this way — they could find ethically adequate fulfilment in the realization of their 'total personality'. Thus, in the period when the essays of *History and Class Consciousness* were written *ethics* itself could be conceived by Lukács as unproblematically and *directly political* because *politics* was seen as *directly ethical*.

The situation is radically different when Lukács embarks on writing his *Ethics* which turns out to be an *Ontology*. At first, in the Summer of 1956, it seems that post-Stalin society is beginning to move in the right direction, even if very slowly, promising the possibility of a serious reexamination of the relationship between ethics and politics. The brutal repression of the October uprising in Hungary puts an abrupt end to such hopes. Thus, inasmuch as the project can be carried on at all, the burning issues of ethics, in their unavoidable relationship to politics, must be transferred to the most abstract sphere of ontology. To be sure, this is not only because of the political dangers to which the Hungarian philosopher is exposed for a number of years after 1956, but also on account of his way of internalizing and rationalizing the 'force of circumstance' (including what he calls the 'necessary historical détour' under Stalin) going back a very long way in the past. For his postulate — in 1919 — that political action is *directly ethical* under the authority of the morally mandated party, is not less problematical than the way in which the political dimension of ethics is treated in the *Ontology* and in the fragmentary notes of his *Versuche zu einer Ethics*. (In the latter, tellingly, the entry on Politics occupies the space of one slender page; and even if we add to that the entry on Freedom — most of which is concerned in the most general terms with the question of 'mastery over nature and over ourselves'[214] and not with politics — the total amount is less than five pages out of nearly one hundred.)

Politics and morality are so closely intertwined in the real world that it is hardly imaginable to confront and resolve the conflicts of any age without bringing into play the crucial dimensions of both. Thus, whenever it is difficult to face the problems and contradictions of politics in the prevailing social order, theories of morality are also bound to suffer the consequences. Naturally, this relationship tends to prevail also in the positive direction. As the entire history of philosophy testifies, the authors of all major ethical works are also the originators of the seminal theoretical works on politics; and vice versa, all serious conceptualizations of politics have their necessary corollaries on the plane of moral discourse. This goes for Aristotle as much as for Hobbes and Spinoza, and for Rousseau and Kant as much as for Hegel. Indeed, in the case of Hegel we find his ethics fully integrated into his *Philosophy of Right,* i.e. his theory of the state. This is why it is so astonishing to read in Lukács's 'Tactics and Ethics' that 'Hegel's system is devoid of ethics': a view which he later mellows to saying that the Hegelian treatment of ethics suffers the consequences of his system and the conservative bias of his theory of the state. It would be much more correct to say that — despite the conservative bias of his political conception — Hegel is the author of the last great systematic treatment of ethics. Compared to that, the twentieth century in the field of ethics (as well as in that of political philosophy) is very problematical.

No doubt this has a great deal to do with the ever narrowing margin of alternatives allowed by the necessary mode of functioning of the global capital system which produces the wisdom of 'there is no alternative'. For, evidently, there can be no meaningful moral discourse on the premiss that 'there is no alternative'. Ethics is concerned with the evaluation and implementation of alternative goals which individuals and social groups can actually set themselves in their confrontations with the problems of their age. And this is where the inescapability of politics makes its impact. For even the most intensely committed investigation of ethics cannot be a substitute for a radical critique of politics in its frustrating and alienating contemporary reality. The slogan of 'there is no alternative' did not originate in ethics; nor is it enough to reassert in ethical/ontological terms the need for alternatives, no matter how passionately this is felt and predicated. The pursuit of viable alternatives to the destructive reality of capital's social order in all its forms — without which the socialist project is utterly pointless — is a practical matter. The role of morality and ethics is crucial to the success of this enterprise. But there can be no hope of success without the joint re-articulation of socialist moral discourse and political strategy, taking fully on board the painful lessons of the recent past.

Lukács's discourse on ethics operates at a level of abstraction where the actually existing — alienated and alienating — material mediations are of a secondary importance, since ethics as such is supposed to fulfil the crucial role of mediation between the individuals' particularism and humanity for-itself. The postcapitalist capital system and its state formation is never subjected to a substantive partial critique (beyond the already mentioned references to 'voluntaristic tactics' and 'crude manipulation'), let alone to the comprehensive radical critique which it would require. Likewise, the labour process is discussed in the most general terms, without identifying the grave contradictions (and inhumanities) of subjecting the actually existing labour force to the ruthless dictates of the politically regulated extraction of surplus-labour in the name of socialism. Inasmuch as the division of labour is discussed at all, it is treated in such a way that we remain hopelessly trapped within the existing parameters of the Soviet type capital system, as we shall see it in Chapter 19.

Given the historical conditions of existence under the rule of capital and of its state formations, with their authoritarian denial of meaningful practical alternatives (even when claiming democratic credentials), it would be obviously a self-delusion to postulate today the harmonious relationship and unity of politics and ethics. Since the dominant forms of politics are very far from being ethical, ethics itself cannot be unproblematically political in the sense of attaching itself to the mainstream of politics. On the contrary, in an age when the structural crisis of capital is inescapably manifest also in the field of politics, the potential emancipatory role of ethics is unthinkable without its self-definition as the radical socialist critique of politics locked into the institutional framework of the capital system, including most of the original defensive organs of the working class movement. This is the only sense in which ethics can be political today, envisaging the *constitution* of a potential unity of politics and ethics in the practical enterprise of superseding the power of political decision making alienated from the social individuals, in the spirit of the Marxian project. But precisely in this sense, the framework of operation of this ethics for the foreseeable future can only be the existing circle of capital's second order mediations, and not the postulate of an abstract and generic mediation between 'individual particularism' and 'humanity for-itself'. Indeed, its measure of success can only be its ability to constantly maintain awareness of and reanimate practical criticism towards the real target of socialist transformation: to go beyond capital in all of its actually existing and feasible forms through the redefinition and practially viable rearticulation of the labour process.

Lukács's ontological discourse on ethics has at its centre of reference the dualism of individual and society and the way in which ethics could in principle intervene in order to overcome it. He insists that

> Only in ethics can the socially necessary dualism be transcended: in ethics the victory over the particularism of the individuals assumes the form of a unified tendency; the ethical demand here finds the centre of personality of the acting man; the individual chooses between the demands which in society are necessarily antinomous/contradictory, and the decision which is expressed in the form of a choice is dictated by the inner command to recognise as his own duty what befits his own personality — and all this unifies the human species and the personality who is victorious over his own particularism.[215]

However, it is most problematical to think of this process as effectively breaking through the existing vicious circle of capital's second order mediations, inducing the overwhelming majority (if not the totality) of individuals — rather than some exceptional 'world historical personalities', like Goethe — to conform to the model postulated by Lukács and create the idealized unity between their personality and humanity for-itself under circumstances when capital always reconstitutes and intensifies the existing antinomies/contradictions as a matter of its necessary mode of operation. Indeed, there are some passages in Lukács's writings when he admits that in the course of human development the *task* (Aufgabe) which he ascribes to ethics — just as he ascribed to the proletariat and to its party: the 'mediation between man and history', a morally operative 'totalizing consciousness' in *History and Class Consciousness* — becomes *'socially possible only in a classless society'* ('nur in klassenloser Gesellschaft möglich').[216] But, then, the mediating/contradiction-transcending power of ethics is projected for a stage to which it cannot apply, since it is supposed to have overcome the antagonisms of society, with their 'necessarily antinomous/contradictory demands' over the individuals. This is what puts Lukács's noble ontological discourse on ethics in perspective, helping to explain why its repeatedly promised 'concretization' could never be accomplished.

10.6 The limits of Lukács's last political testament

10.6.1

AFTER re-reading his essay on *Democratization* — condemned and kept under lock by the party leadership for twenty years as 'politically dangerous'[217] — Lukács had serious misgivings about it. He wrote in a letter to his German publisher that 'as a brochure it is too scientific, and as a scientific study it is too brochure-like'.[218] In truth this essay was much more problematical than the reservations of its author indicated. For it tried to offer solutions to acute political and socioeconomic problems on the plane of abstract methodological and rather remote ontological discourse, without indicating the necessary material and institutional mediations through which the identified difficulties and contradictions of the present could be overcome by a critical strategic pursuit. Again, characteristically, Lukács promised to take up the — in his own view unsatisfactorily analyzed — issues and develop them properly, in contrast to their 'brochure-like' treatment, in his projected *Ethics*. He could not admit to himself that many of the acute political and socioeconomic issues of postrevolutionary development received the same kind of unmediated treatment in his *Ontology of Social Being* and in the fragments of the unrealizable *Ethics* as in the manuscript on *The Present and Future of Democratization*. For the constantly repeated proposition that 'only ethics can overcome the dualism between the individuals' particularism and their species-character', etc., functioned everywhere as a mere postulate in relation to the discussed problems. He never attempted to spell out concretely, how the postulated ethical remedy could be effectively applied, not to a few more or less marginal aspects but to the grave contradictions and explosive material as well as political/ideological antagonisms of 'actually existing socialism'. On the contrary, his advocacy of ethics as the only feasible mediation tended to assume the role of a — noble but illusory — *substitute* for socially specific forms of critical intervention. It concentrated on the far-away perspective of a fully realized 'humanity for-itself', missing at the same time the tangible target of absolutely necessary socialist negation: the alienated and forcibly imposed mode of *control* exercised over labour in the actually existing, astronomically far from socialist, postcapitalist societies.

The problem was Lukács's *internalization* of the fundamental constraints of postrevolutionary developments, and not an opportunistic personal accommodation to the party line. The notion of 'opportunistic accommodation' is totally contradicted by the fact that for a long time after he died Lukács's principal political writings were considered 'politically dangerous' by the Hungarian party. As a matter of fact in 1968 he courageously rejected the Russian invasion of Czechoslovakia in forceful terms, and he wrote in a letter addressed to György Aczél, Secretary to the Politbureau responsible for cultural affairs, with a request to pass on a copy to János Kádár, the party leader:

> I cannot agree with the solution of the Czechoslovak problem and with the position assumed in it by the MSzMP [the Hungarian Socialist Workers Party]. Consequently, I must withdraw from the public role I played in the last few years. I hope that developments in Hungary will not lead to such a situation in which administrative measures against true Hungarian Marxists would force me again into the intellectual internment of the last decade.[219]

Even before the military repression of the 'Prague Spring' and Lukács's protests against it there was a move in Party Headquarters to initiate a new ideological and political debate against the Hungarian philosopher. The question was raised in a Memorandum written by the Moscow trained and guided Miklós Óvári, a Secretary to the party's Central Committee, dated 21 February 1968. 'This plan — inspired from abroad — amounted to no less than to make the MSzMP initiate an ideological trial'[220] against Lukács. Although under the circumstances, due to concern about the likelihood of a major international scandal, this plan was not implemented, 'the danger of an ideological trial was hanging over the head of the accused to the end of his life'.[221] But despite all such dangers, intensified after the invasion of Czechoslovakia, Lukács not only completed his essay on *Democratization* but went on giving defiantly outspoken interviews to Western journalists and intellectuals. He did this just as he defied with great moral integrity and considerable risk to himself the Russian and Hungarian authorities at the time when he was deported to Romania after the uprising of 1956. For he not only categorically refused to say one critical word against the former Prime Minister Imre Nagy, despite their well known political differences (for instance over the advisability of leaving the Warsaw Pact in the fateful days of October 1956, when Lukács voted against it only with his close friend and political ally Zoltán Szántó when János Kádár voted with Nagy for the abandonment of the Pact), insisting that 'when Imre Nagy and I are free to walk the streets of Budapest, I am willing to express with full openness my political disagreements with him; but I make no confessions against my *fellow-prisoner*'.[222] And when in the same setting Zoltán Szántó yielded to inquisitorial pressure and spoke out against Nagy, Lukács broke off at once and demonstratively his lifelong friendship with the man who made confessions against a fellow-prisoner.[223]

Thus the limitations of Lukács's solutions did not arise from political appeasement or fear for his own personal safety, let alone from looking for favours which he might have thought to be able to obtain through accommodation. They were integral to the main tenets of his world view with which he fully identified himself. The reason why he could not envisage a more radical critique of the established order than he actually voiced was because the vital parameters of his conception as a whole — articulated at the time when he embraced the perspective of 'the weakest link' and worked out in detail his ideas as a Marxist in the period of the great confrontations over the issue of 'socialism in one country', remaining in the orbit of the Russian revolution to the end — were incompatible with adopting such a critique. This is why he kept repeating the false paradox that 'even the worst form of socialism is qualitatively better than the best capitalism'.[224] And this is why even in his politically most radical essay on *Democratization,* which incorporated his heart-felt critical reflections over what had happened in Czechoslovakia, he did not hesitate to dismiss the manifestations of doubt over the socialist character of so-called actually existing socialism as 'bourgeois stupidity and slander'.[225]

In contrast to the time when as a politically most active intellectual Lukács insisted that 'adherence to the correct tactics is in itself ethical', in the last three and a half decades of his life (and especially in the last fifteen years of it) the prevalence of tactics — *vis-à-vis* theory and strategy — acquired an extremely negative connotation in his thought. But parallel to this change we also witnessed his totally unjustifiable acceptance of the *duality* and rightful separation of politics and intellectual activity, the practical decisions of politicians and the theoretical concerns of people in the field of ideology. This is how he could assert in the series of interviews conducted at the request of the party leadership a few months before he died, in January 1971, but released for publication — under the title of 'György Lukács's political testament'[226] — only in April 1990, that 'I do not wish to meddle in daily political matters. I do not consider myself a *politician.* ... I only raise the issue from the standpoint of the *ideological* success of democracy'.[227] He expressed much the same position a few years earlier in his praise for President Kennedy's 'Brains-Trust',[228] naively expecting significant improvement to 'actually exsisting socialism' from the recommended division of labour between politicians and intellectuals.

The internalization of the constraints of the 'weakest link' had brought with it for Lukács that the postrevolutionary state under the control of the party could not be subjected to any substantive critique. This is why in his search for alternatives he ended up not only with the self-defeating advocacy of separating political and intellectual activity, expecting thereby in vain the creation of a margin of autonomous activity with which the established postcapitalist system was *structurally incompatible,* but also with the totally false alternative to the existent: 'a well thought out, *realistic division of labour between the party and the state'.*[229] For nothing could be more *unrealistic* than that, as the suppression of his essay on *Democratization* and of his 1971 interviews — given at the request of the party deeply worried at the time about the wave of mass strikes in Poland — had also clearly demonstrated. In fact the whole system had to implode before Lukács's limited criticism and marginal proposals for the improvement of the established conditions could even see the light of day, not to mention the question of being acted upon.

The margin of feasible political critique within the parameters of Lukács's conceptual framework, as worked out in the orbit of the 'revolution at the weakest link of the chain', was always — and remained to the end of his life — extremely narrow. Thus in his 'political testament' he could only recommend the authorization of *'ad hoc* organizations', for strictly limited periods and for the realization of pathetically narrow objectives, as a way of instituting socialist democracy. He argued that the party should

> allow the average man to organize for the realization of some concrete, in their life important matters. To illustrate this with an example, let us suppose that there is an important street in Budapest without its own pharmacy. I cannot see the reason why the people living in this street should not be allowed to create an *ad hoc* organization whose task is to obtain permission from the local council for the establishment of the street pharmacy. ... I am absolutely unable to see what danger might possibly follow for our council republic from the opening of this pharmacy. ... What I consider essential is that in the everyday issues of everyday life such a freedom of movement and democracy should arise, for only through its help will it be possible to trim the bad effects of bureaucratism.[230]

Lukács's extreme naivety consisted not only in not seeing that the leadership of the established party-state was incapable of making even such localized concessions but, much more so, in imagining that even if the party bosses (recognized by Lukács as the only rightful political decision makers) could positively respond to his limited proposals, that could significantly improve the future prospects of the historically doomed system. He could not admit to himself that the incurable basic contradiction of the established postcapitalist capital system was the *necessarily* authoritarian mode of control of the socioeconomic metabolism, operating a politically enforced — highly antagonistic — extraction of surplus-labour, with its own form of 'personification of capital'. In this system the criticized 'bureaucratism' was not a marginal matter whose 'bad effects' could be suitably 'trimmed' with the help of duly self-abolishing 'ad hoc organizations' and street pharmacies generously conceded by the authorities. Socialist democracy, to be meaningful at all, requires the *substantive equality* of the associated producers determining both the objectives of their life-activity and the mode of realizing the chosen objectives, in sharp contrast to being ruled by the imperatives of a *hierarchical structural division of labour* and its political enforcers, no matter how well advised the latter might be by the politically self-effacing intellectuals, in accordance with the Lukácsian scheme of the 'necessary duality of politics and intellectual activity'. Unhappily, Lukács could not envisage a mode of social metabolic reproduction without the perpetuation of the division of labour, as we shall see in some detail in Chapter 19, with all of the worse than problematical implications of such a division of labour for the permanently subordinate position of labour. This is why in his political testament he had to look for a way of successfully squaring the circle, which he designated by the wishful term of 'socialist hierarchy'.[231]

10.6.2

IN his attempt to find an 'ontological foundation' for his peculiar notion of 'socialist hierarchy' Lukács started out by saying that 'in Stalin's time, when exclusively the quantity of production was pushed into the foreground, the concept of good work had disappeared, the honour of good work became less important in the factory than it used to be there before'.[232] That *quality-control* can be just as ruthlessly imposed on the labour force by the personifications of capital as the dictates of *quantity,* obviously this simple fact — on which the success of many Western capitalist enterprises depended — could find no place in Lukács's arguments. For he had to pursue the romantic notion of 'good work', for which he could only offer an artisanal example: a 'good blacksmith' contrasted with a 'bad blacksmith', for two reasons. The first was to find a 'spontaneous hierarchy' among workers, which could be used to regulate them without antagonisms and the danger of the 'wild-cat strikes' witnessed in Poland and feared by the party[233] (an incredibly utopian wishful thinking), and the second, to use the concept of 'good work' as the justification of hierarchy in society at large.

Thus Lukács generalized what he took to be the meaning of a conversation he had in 1919, during the Hungarian Council Republic, with a 'good blacksmith' (untroubled by the fact that there are not many artisanal blacksmiths, good or bad, in the productively advanced enterprises of the world today), and asserted that 'This hierarchy among the workers absolutely existed still in 1919; the Stalinist period to a large extent destroyed it, putting a purely quantitative production in its place'.[234] And he went on arguing that the proper solution to the debated issues was to make

> the position of the worker in the factory depend on how good a worker he is. For only from good work can develop the kind of human self-esteem, which we find in countless scientists and writers and which was just as much present in the workers in the past... Thus the question of improving quality is extremely important for the reorientation of work itself: from being work producing simply quantitative results to making it prevail as good work, and to turn good work into the fundamental category of the workers' life.[235]

This is how Lukács wanted to produce 'socialist hierarchy' based on the ontology of labour. He went as far as to suggest that already in humanity's prehistory, hundreds of thousands of years ago

> the first cultured worker was the man who, probably, when producing a stone-axe, made the least frequent errors, and therefore he made it the least frequently necessary to throw away the stone which he started to sharpen on the ground that he sharpened it badly.[236]

Lukács's need to look for such dubious ontological foundations was understandable in the absence of any substantive critique of the existing socioeconomic foundations and their state formations. On his totally untenable — but categorically asserted — assumption that 'In the economic life of the socialist states ... the socialization of the means of production had forcibly created such objective relations which will *always qualitatively differ* from the relations of class societies',[237] potential correctives to the falsely described *actual* social relations of postcapitalist (and not in the slightest socialist) states had to be confined to the question of developing in everyday life the individual workers' prestige-consumption-rejecting *'proper subjectivity,* so that one day it should be possible for them to become the free human beings of the communist social formation',[238] and doing this on the plane of general social ontology, inspired and mediated by ethics.

The trouble with this vision was always that nothing in actuality corresponded to the assumed 'socialization of the means of production' (which happened to be only *statalized* but not *socialized)* nor indeed to the *'socialist* state'. For the latter in reality defined itself through the authoritarian superimposition of its all-embracing political command structure over the labour force, in diametrical opposition to the socialist idea of it being — strictly for a transitional period, with a view of moving towards the 'withering away of the state'[239] — under the control of the associated producers. Thus Lukács's abstract ontological discourse about 'good work' as the 'fundamental category of the workers' life', from the quality-conscious stone-axe sharpening primitive ancestors all the way to the 'properly subjective free human beings of communist society', simply bypassed the question of material mediations, instead of undertaking the vitally necessary radical critique of the established forms of socioeconomic and political mediation. Fifty two years earlier, in 'Tactics and Ethics', Lukács appealed to the moral consciousness of the workers, urging them to adopt a high labour discipline, and warning them that if they fail to do so it will be necessary 'to create a legal system through which the proletariat *compels* its own individual members, the proletarians, to act in a way which corresponds to their class-interests: *the proletariat turns its dictatorship against itself*.[240] In 1971, after more than five decades of 'proletarian dictatorship' whose proletarian credentials he was compelled to doubt in the light of actual historical experience, he also had to concede that the 'legal system' created after the revolution had failed to achieve what he once expected of it. Since, however, the critique of the postrevolutionary state formation remained for him an internalized taboo, together with the 'economic life of the socialist states', the only mediation which he could conceive was, again, a morally inspired — in its intention noble but in reality totally ineffective — direct appeal to the idea of 'good work'.

This time Lukács's appeal was not addressed to the workers themselves, who were utterly powerless in instituting the quality-oriented changes advocated by Lukács in his critique of the Stalinist cult of quantity, but to the leading party and state functionaries — the 'personifications of capital' in the postcapitalist capital system — who, naturally, took no notice whatsoever of his noble ontological discourse, burying the tapes of his interviews for twenty years in the party archives and releasing them only after losing control of the Hungarian state apparatus. At the same time, when the dying Lukács was recommending that, in tune with the ontological foundation of his vision, the 'economic life of the socialist states' should be conducted in accordance with the principle of 'good work', the crucial isssue of the *control* of society's *decision making* processes under the actually given conditions was left totally untouched. The notion of the individual workers conquering in their everyday life — through their ethical struggle against their own alienation and 'prestige-consumption' — their *'proper subjectivity*, so that one day it should be possible for them to become the *free human beings* of the *communist* social formation', could offer no help at all as to how the members of the actually exisiting labour force might become under the given conditions even minimally more free from their subjection to the socio-economic and political imperatives of the postcapitalist capital system. The control of social metabolic reproduction was left by Lukács to the party and the state, envisaging improvements only through the 'realistic division of labour between the party and the state'. In his critical reflection on the existing state of affairs he assigned to the 'masses', as a major positive improvement, the role of 'feed-back' (whether 'subterranean' or open), insisting that 'to lead the workers *truly* is possible only if we really *lead* them, meaning that we take note of the needs which arise in them; and if these needs are correct, in that case we satisfy them, and if they are not correct, we dispute them with the workers and we try to win them over to the correct standpoint'.[241] The possibility that the workers should judge it for themselves whether or not their needs are 'correct', and make their own decisions over the question of how to control the social metabolic order in order to satisfy their needs on the basis of their own judgement, instead of accepting 'the correct standpoint' from people standing in the 'socialist hierarchy' above them — no matter how well meaning and ethically inspired those people might be — simply could not enter into the framework of a discourse which postulated the permanence of the division of labour.

Thus, Lukács's abstract ontological discourse and his hopeless attempt to directly connect the disputed issues of the antagonistic postrevolutionary order with the most general perspective of a far-away 'humanity for-itself', postulating the viability of 'ethics as the only possible mediation' between the present and the remote future, were organically linked to his inability to *critically confront* the existing forms and institutions of social metabolic control with a view of identifying the materially effective forms of feasible mediation between the existing conditions — through their necessary radical negation — and the desired future. In other words, by remaining unreservedly in the orbit of the 'revolution at the weakest link of the chain' — often repeating the dual maxims of 'right or wrong, it is my party' (without even once hearing: 'right or wrong, he is our Lukács') and 'even the worst socialism is better than the best capitalism' — he could only see remedies to the perceived problems and explosive contradictions of postcapitalist societies in terms of broad ontological/ethical regulative principles, hypostatizing substantively different results on the plane of a very distant future even when believing to provide remedies for the present.

As a result, Lukács 's margin of consciously pursued critical intervention had to be not only extremely narrow but at times even directly contradicting his own intentions. We have seen how naive and limited his views were on the way of instituting 'socialist democracy' through the authorization of self-abolishing 'ad hoc organizations', with objectives like the establishment of street pharmacies: forms of 'democratic organization' which contradicted the idea of even minimally democratic action in that they remained completely at the mercy of uncontrolled authorities of decision making. Similarly, Lukács tried to distance himself from the enthusiasts of market reform, but quickly ran into self-contradiction — because of his painfully narrow margin of criticism — the moment he tried to spell out his criticism. For the premiss of his reflection on the subject was his acceptance of the official Hungarian 'new economic mechanism', which made his margin of dissent hopelessly restricted. Thus, on the one hand, he could only offer vague general propositions, that the market measures should be 'multi-dimensional' and complemented by a 'manifold complex democratization',[242] without asking the question whether the acceptance of the *tyranny of the market* is compatible with the desideratum of a 'manifold complex democratization'. And on the other hand, when in the 1971 interviews he was advocating economic changes, he could only do this by directly connecting his ontological/ethical ideal of 'good work' with the prospect of market competition. He was arguing that

> it is a shame and a disgrace that in Budapest, the capital of an agrarian country, bread is so bad. The state bread factories are unable to change this. I am convinced that if three neighbouring agricultural co-operatives decide to set up together a bread factory in Budapest, and they produce good bread, that would solve the problem of bread-supplies in Budapest. We spoke a moment ago about the question of good work. Well, if these agricultural co-operatives try to win in the competition against the state bread factories, they can only succeed in this endeavour with the help of *good work*. Only if in the co-operative bread factories they bake *good* bread. We can see here to what a large extent there is a spontaneous socialism in the new agrarian developments.[243]

As we all know, it is possible to bake good bread also under the conditions of cut-throat capitalist competition and ruthless exploitation, without any appeal to Lukács's ontological/ethical ideal of 'human self-esteem-producing good work', much nearer on the trajectory of human self-realization to the Hungarian philosopher's stone-axe sharpening ancestor than to his postulated 'humanity for-itself'. Thus, Lukács's way of looking for, and discovering, 'spontaneous socialism' in the anticipated successful competition of the would-be co-operative bread factories against their state-run rivals, within the framework of the wishfully projected 'multi-dimensional' and 'democratized' market of the Hungarian 'new economic mechanism', revealed the unsurpassable limitations of his approach: the direct connection of a general ontological vision with the 'bad immediacy' of the present which it wanted to correct. It demonstrated the tragic unreality of the solutions which could be seen from the fatefully narrowed down perspective of even someone of Lukács's moral and intellectual stature: a veritable 'tunnel vision' produced in the orbit of the revolution which was not only *unfinished* but *unfinishable* even in the biggest country, contrary to the doctrine of 'socialism in a single country' accepted also by Lukács. A vision reiterated in a 'political testament' at a time when the postcapitalist capital system that emerged after the 'revolution at the weakest link of the chain' continued to be buffeted not by the missing insight of its political decision makers into the wisdom of authorizing 'ad hoc organizations' and co-operative bread factories but by a profound historical crisis, due to the irreconcilability of its inner structural antagonisms.

*
*   *

IN *History and Class Consciousness* Lukács quoted Hegel's poetic way of summing up the relationship between truth and Reason in the *Phenomenology:* ' "the true becomes a Bacchantic orgy in which no one escapes being drunk", *Reason* seems to have *lifted the veil* concealing the sacred mystery at Sais and discovers, as in the parable of Novalis, that *it is itself the solution of the riddle.*' (p.145.) And he continued:

> But here, we find once again, quite concretely this time, the decisive problem of this line of thought: the problem of the subject of the action, the subject of the [historical] genesis. For the unity of subject and object, of thought and existence which the 'action' undertook to prove and to exhibit finds both its fulfilment and its substratum in the unity of the genesis of the determinants of thought and of the history of the evolution of reality. But to comprehend this unity it is necessary both to discover the site from which to resolve all these problems and also to exhibit concretely the 'we' which is the subject of history, that 'we' whose action is in fact history. *(Ibid.)*

In *History and Class Consciousness,* and for a very long time thereafter, Lukács had maintained that by *lifting the veil* of ideological mystification the party — as the practical embodiment of class consciousness and the ethics of the proletariat — can conclusively demonstrate that the proletariat is the solution to the riddle of consciously shaped history. In this spirit he asserted that

> The party as a whole transcends the *reified divisions* according to nation, profession, etc., and according to modes of life (economics and politics) by virtue of its action. For this is oriented towards revolutionary unity and collaboration and aims to establish the true unity of the proletarian class. And what it does as a whole it performs likewise for its individual members. Its closely-knit organization with its resulting iron discipline and its demand for total commitment *tears away the reified veils* that cloud the consciousness of the individuals in capitalist society. (p.339.)

Moreover, in his idealization of the Russian proletariat and its party Lukács asserted in *History and Class Consciousness,* his representative theorization of the encircled Russian revolution, that

> The ideological maturity of the Russian proletariat becomes clearly visible when we consider those very factors which have been taken as evidence of its backwardness by the opportunists of the West and their Central European admirers. To wit, the clear and definitive crushing of the internal counter-revolution and the uninhibited illegal and 'diplomatic' battle for world revolution. The Russian proletariat did not emerge victoriously from its revolution because a fortunate constellation of circumstances played into its hands. (This constellation existed equally for the German proletariat in November 1918 and for the Hungarian proletariat at the same time and also in March 1919.) It was victorious because it had been steeled by the long illegal struggle and hence had gained a clear understanding of the nature of the capitalist state. (p.270.)

Here we are not concerned with the idealizing omission of the vastness of resources which in their time defeated even Napoleon without any contribution by the ideological clarity and self-consciousness of the Russian proletariat, or of the fact that the Hungarian Council Republic could be overthrown with relative ease by a massive military intervention, with the full involvement of the Western 'democratic' powers. What matters in the present context is the loss of perspective which could postulate the viability of the 'revolution at the weakest link of the chain'. For, tragically, the author of *History and Class Consciousness* had to discover that 'lifting the veil' was not enough to solve the riddle, neither for Hegel's 'Reason' nor for the proletariat as the 'identical subject-object of history', nor indeed for those intellectuals who believed themselves to be able to remove the 'cloud from their consciousness in capitalist society' by dedicating their 'total personality' to the party, like Lukács himself.

The hopeful message that the key to resolving the 'ideological crisis' — and thereby the historical crisis — was to view and reshape society from the 'stand-point of totality', in accordance with the proletariat's 'imputed' or 'ascribed' class consciousness, had to remain a voice in the wilderness under the conditions of development of the actually existing postcapitalist capital system. For the party of the postrevolutionary party-state did not just 'tear away the reified veils' of pre-revolutionary capitalist society. It replaced them by a thick canvas of its own, preaching 'socialism in a single country' in whose name it went on ruth-lessly repressing every single aspiration brought into this world by the original socialist project. Thus, instead of building 'socialism in a single country', it had succeeded in turning the working class — the historical agency of socialist emancipation—against the very idea of socialism. As a result, the earlier spon-taneous revolt of the workers against capitalist exploitation had been effectively disarmed by the frightful exploitative and repressive practices of a system which claimed to be socialist. Even the international expectations confidently ex-pressed in Lukács's last quote, concerning 'the uninhibited illegal and "diplo-matic" battle for world revolution', had been turned into their diametrical opposite, in that the Stalinist state turned itself into a mountain-size obstacle to world revolution, instead of pursuing a policy in its favour.

Through all these retrogressions the 'riddle' that must be resolved by those who refuse to abandon the socialist perspective had become more impenetrable, yet at the same time more painfully pressing, than ever before. For in the course of postrevolutionary transformations it became undeniable that the task of clearly identifying the obstacles towering before the forces of emancipation could not be confined to gaining 'a clear understanding of the nature of the *capitalist* state'. The difficulties even on the plane of the political struggle had been compounded by the devastating historical experience of the state preaching and enforcing the imperatives of 'socialism in a single country'. The disheartening years of this experience had brought with them the unavoidable necessity to confront the inner antagonisms of the postrevolutionary capital system as a whole and the tyrannical anti-labour practices of the *postcapitalist* state. For the latter, in the original expectations, was supposed to fulfil its limited historical functions and move in the direction of the 'withering away' of the state as such in the strictly transitional form of the 'proletarian dictatorship' of the associated producers, instead of transforming itself into an all-powerful and self-perpetu-ating organ exercising its absolute domination over all facets of material and cultural production.

It goes without saying, Lukács was by no means the only one to be deeply affected by the contradictions of the unfolding postrevolutionary developments. There were many intellectuals and members of numerous political organizations on the left who defined their own position in response to the 'revolution at the weakest link of the chain' and remained in its orbit for decades, either with positive disposition towards it, or by assuming a qualified negative stance as the main defining characteristic of their political perspective. Even the principal intellectuals of the 'Frankfurt School', from Walter Benjamin to Marcuse, once oriented themselves in this sense. However, most of them assumed in the end a deeply pessimistic stance not simply in relation to Soviet developments but in every way. Marcuse, too, who at the peak of the student movement in the West addressed his audience in the key of optimistic excitement, turned subsequently inwards and predicated with infinite gloom that *'In reality evil triumphs;* there are only *islands* of good to which one can *escape* for short periods of time'.[244] Not to forget those members of the Frankfurt Institute for Social Research who, like the most prominent of them, Adorno, were rightly castigated by Lukács in his 1962 Preface to *The Theory of the Novel* for having made their peace with capitalist oppression while assuming a pose of self-indulgent elitistic disdain in relation to its 'vulgar mass-cultural' manifestations. For, in Lukács's words:

> they have taken up residence in the 'Grand Hotel Abyss', a beautiful hotel, equipped with every comfort, on the edge of an abyss, of nothingness, of absurdity. And the daily contemplation of the abyss between excellent meals or artistic entertainments, can only heighten the enjoyment of the subtle comforts offered.

Although Lukács himself — for a variety of political and internal theoretical reasons which we have seen above — could not subject the postrevolutionary social order to the necessary radical critique, it remained a legitimate and valid part of his discourse to reject with intellectual consistency and passion the perspective of self-disarming pessimism. By the time when the irrevocable collapse of the Soviet system would have threatened even his 'Prinzip Hoffnung' he was no longer alive.

The implosion of the Soviet type capital system had brought a seven decades long historical experience to its conclusion, making all theorizations and political strategies conceived in the orbit of the Russian revolution — whether positively disposed towards it or representing various forms of negation — historically superseded. The collapse of this system was inseparable from the structural crisis of capital which began to assert itself in the 1970s. It was this crisis which clearly demonstrated the vacuity of the earlier strategies, from Stalin's projection of establishing the highest stage of socialism on the foundation of 'overtaking U.S. capitalism' in per capita pig iron production to the equally absurd post-Stalinist slogan of building a fully emancipated communist society by 'defeating capitalism through peaceful competition'. For under the capital system there can be no such thing as 'peaceful competition'; not even when one of the competing parties continues to delude itself of being free from the crippling structural constraints of capital in its historically specific form.

The disintegration of the Communist parties in the East took place parallel to the implosion of the Soviet system. In the Western capitalist countries, however, we were witnessing a much more complicated process. For the crisis of the Western Communist parties preceded the collapse in Russia and elsewhere in the East by well over a decade, as the fate of the once most powerful French and Italian Communist parties demonstrated. This circumstance, again, underlined the fact that the crucial underlying cause was the deepening structural crisis of the capital system in general, and not the difficulties of political response to the baffling vicissitudes in Russia and in Eastern Europe. To be sure, after the implosion of the Soviet system all of the Western Communist parties tried to use the events in the East as the belated rationalization and justification for their abandonment of all socialist aspirations. Most of them even changed their name, as if that could alter anything for the better. Indeed, the same kind of rationalization and reversal of actual historical chronology, in the interest of justifying an obvious turn to the right, characterized also the Italian Socialists and the British Labour Party. The real problem was that under the new circumstances of capital's structural crisis the former working class parties, Communist and non-Communist alike, had no strategy to offer as to how their traditional constituency — labour — should confront capital which was bound to impose on the working people growing hardship under the worsening conditions. Instead, they resigned themselves to the meek — called 'realistic' — acceptance of what could be obtained from the shrinking margins of capital's troubled profitability. Understandably, in terms of political ideology this turn of events presented a much greater problem to the Communist than to the non-Communist parties. The stillborn strategies of 'Eurocommunism' and 'great historic compromise' were attempts to come to terms with this difficulty, in the hope of finding a new constituency in the 'middle ground' while retaining some of the old rhetorics. But it all came to nothing and ended in tears for many devoted militants who once genuinely believed that their party was moving in the direction of a future socialist transformation. The disintegration of the left in Italy, among others, in the last few years bears witness to the gravity of these developments, underlying the enormity of the challenge for the future.

The historical perspective of globally extending and under favourable conditions immeasurably improving the achievements of the 'encircled revolution at the weakest link of the chain' — a perspective once shared by the Communist parties, as well as by many other political movements on the left — now belongs irretrievably to the past. However, the challenge to 'gain a clear understanding of the nature of capital' in all its forms, including the necessity to grasp the contradictory nature of its state formations, happens to be that much greater today. This is largely due to the historical exhaustion of the perspective — and of its more or less direct negations — which for so many years retained its orienting power, but now lost it completely. For seven decades of development could but painfully underline that, as Marx had put it:

> The specific economic form, in which *unpaid surplus-labour* is pumped out of direct producers, determines the relationship of *rulers and ruled,* as it grows directly out of production itself and, in turn, reacts upon it as a *determining element.*[245]

In this sense, the reasons for the tragic historical failure of more than seven decades of Soviet power must be sought, in order to be avoided in the future, both in the experienced modality of 'pumping unpaid surplus-labour out of direct producers', and in the stark reality of the historically known postrevolutionary state, as 'determining element', which — instead of releasing the forces of autonomous decision making through which the state as such could in due course 'wither away' — ruthlessly imposed on society the postcapitalist capital system's political extraction of surplus-labour, perpetuating, with disastrous consequences, a 'relationship of rulers and ruled'. For, obviously, there can be no socialism even in the totality of countries, let alone in a single country, within such a framework of socioeconomic and political determinations.

HISTORICAL LEGACY OF THE SOCIALIST CRITIQUE 2:

RADICAL BREAK AND TRANSITION IN THE MARXIAN HERITAGE

'Men must change from top to bottom the conditions of their industrial and political existence, and consequently their whole manner of being.'

Marx

'In Frankfurt, as in most old towns, it had been the practice to gain space in wooden buildings by making not only the first but also the higher storeys project over the street, which incidentally made narrow streets, in particular, sombre and depressing. Finally a law was passed permitting only the first storey of a new house to project over the ground floor, while the upper storeys had to keep within the ground floor limits. In order to avoid losing the projecting space in the second storey, my father *circumvented this law,* as others had done before him, by shoring up the upper parts of the house, taking away one storey after another from the bottom upwards and as it were *slipping in the new structure,* so that although *finally none of the old house was left,* the whole new building could be considered as mere renovation.'

Goethe

CHAPTER ELEVEN

MARX'S UNFINISHED PROJECT

HOW did it come about that Marxism succeeded in identifying the ultimate targets of a radical socialist transformation but not the forms and modalities of transition through which that target could be reached? Is the Marxist conception compatible with a fully elaborated theory of transition that specifies the conditions of a socialist transformation, including some viable strategies for cutting through the maze of bewildering contradictions and reversals which have appeared in the course of postrevolutionary developments? In other words, can Marxism offer in this respect something more concrete and practically applicable than the reassertion of its belief in the abstract, even if in its frame of reference correct, dialectical principle concerning 'continuity in discontinuity and discontinuity in continuity'?

The general principles of a theory must be clearly differentiated from their application to specific conditions and circumstances, even though in their turn the latter necessarily reenter into the dynamic reconstitution of the fundamental principles themselves. It is the task of a theory of transition to articulate the specific concerns of the ongoing social process, identifying with precision their temporal limitations, in the broad framework of the most comprehensive principles that guide the evaluation of all detail. If this is not done, any change in the historical circumstances which invalidates some *limited* tenets can be presented as the refutation of the theory as a whole: a favourite ploy of the adversaries of Marxism. But there is a much more important dimension to this problem from the point of view of the socialist movement. For claiming *general* validity where only a limited one is due produces the pressure for the apologetics of 'explaining away' any departure from the claimed norm, when in fact the very idea of such a norm runs counter to the spirit of a movement advocating fundamental change. Furthermore, once the institutionally enforced apologetics can no longer maintain its hold, the exposure of the formerly hidden contradictions to public gaze in the absence of a theory that clearly identifies their relative weight and specific place in the overall development generates disorientation, disillusionment and even cynicism. Thus the constraints of Marxist theory with regard to the problems of transition assert themselves today as a matter of great practical concern.

11.1 From the world of commodities to the new historic form

AS a point of departure, let us quote an important passage from Marx's *Grundrisse*. It goes as follows:

> All these statements correct only in this *abstraction* for the relation from the *present standpoint*. Additional relations will enter which *modify them significantly*.[246]

This quotation clearly exemplifies a cardinal rule of Marx's method: the constant deepening and revision ('significant modification') of all major points, in the light of the unfolding sets of complex relations to which they belong. In another methodologically very important passage virtually the whole of the Marxian programme is sketched out in a few lines:

> The exact development of the concept of capital is necessary, since it is the *fundamental concept* of modern economics, just as capital itself, whose abstract, *reflected image* is its concept, is the *foundation* of bourgeois society. The sharp formulation of the *basic presuppositions* of the relation must bring out *all the contradictions* of bourgeois production, as well as the *boundary* where it drives *beyond itself*.[247]

Thus everything must be grasped within the inner logic of its manifold contexts, in accordance with the objectively unfolding determinations and contradictions through which capital 'drives itself beyond itself'. This is why Marx asserts that:

> Nothing can *emerge* at the end of the process which did not appear as a *presupposition* and precondition at the *beginning*. But, on the other hand, everything also has to come out.[248]

The theoretical task, according to these methodological principles, consists in the identification and elucidation of all those objective presuppositions and preconditions which have an important bearing on any particular point at issue. The critical enterprise sets out from the immediacy of the investigated *phenomena* and, through the comprehension and explanation of the relevant *conditions and presuppositions* of their structural setting, acts as a midwife to the objectively emerging *conclusions*. The latter, in their turn, constitute the necessary presuppositions and preconditions of other sets of relations in this dialectical and inherently objective system of reciprocal determinations.

This may sound a little complicated and therefore a further illustration is called for. It is provided by Marx's brief outline of the general plan of his writing:

> In this first section, where exchange values, money, prices are looked at, commodities always appear as *already present*. The determination of forms is simple. ... This still presents itself even on the surface of developed society as the directly available world of commodities. But by itself, it points *beyond itself* towards the economic relations which are posited as relations of production. The *internal structure of production* therefore forms the second section; the concentration of the whole in the *state* the third; the *international* relation the fourth; the *world market* the *conclusion* in which production is posited as a *totality* together with all its moments, but within which, at the same time, *all contradictions come into play*. The world market then, again, forms the *presupposition of the whole* as well as its substratum [Träger]. *Crises* are then the general intimation which points *beyond the presupposition*, and the *urge* [Drängen] which drives towards the adoption of a *new historic form*.[249]

As we can see, we are led from the identification of the preconditions and presuppositions of the 'simple forms' to the '*conclusion*' of the world market which in its turn constitutes the '*presupposition* of the whole'. Only such 'conclusion' of the overall process can bring into play the conjoined totality of contradictions without which there can be no question of a structural crisis. The activation of the global contradictions and the ensuing crises, on the other hand, 'intimate' — mark well: only *intimate*, but by no means *automatically produce* — the new historic form 'beyond the presupposition'. Without the intimation of this new historic form we would remain locked inside the vicious circle of *capital's reciprocal presuppositions*. At the same time, the realisation of that which is only intimated by the crises is the most complex of all the envisaged social processes. It presents almost prohibiting difficulties of conceptualisation because it escapes the rules of any deterministic matrix. In other words, the 'new historic form' cannot be defined in terms of the prevailing system of presuppositions, preconditions and predeterminations precisely because it derives its historical novelty from bringing to the fore the 'realm of freedom' through the conscious choices of the associated producers, beyond the collapse of capital's economic determinism, at a juncture in history when 'all contradictions come into play' and cry out for a radically new type of solution.

The same problem is expressed in a passage in which Marx identifies the ultimate target to aim at as a society without reification: 'where labour in which a *human being* does what a *thing* could do has ceased'. And, again, the realisation of this society is only 'intimated' with reference to the *barrier* of capital itself:

> Capital's ceaseless striving towards the general form of wealth drives labour beyond the limits of its natural paltriness [Naturbedürftigkeit], and thus creates the *material* elements for the development of the *rich individuality*, which is as allsided in its production as in its consumption, and whose labour also therefore appears no longer as labour, but as the full development of activity itself in which *natural necessity* in its direct form has *disappeared*; because a *historically* created need has taken the place of the *natural* one. This is why capital is productive; i.e., an essential relation for the development of the social productive forces. It ceases to exist as such only where the development of these productive forces themselves encounters its barrier in capital itself.[250]

Thus the *eruption* of even the totality of capital's contradictions, in the global setting of social development, can only result in a devastating structural crisis at the barrier in question. It cannot produce by itself the *qualitative leap* to the social universe of the new historic form, since such leap presupposes the *resolution* of the fundamental contradictions, not merely their condensation and explosion.

This is the uncomforting conclusion implicit in Marx's reasoning, even if we envisage a relatively straightforward development, without the appearance of complicating and confounding historical factors which produce perplexing intermediary stages and 'halfway houses'. And how much more difficult will everything be if we allow, as indeed we must, for the constitution of 'adulterated' and 'hybrid' forms and varieties of capital in the course of actual social development towards its saturated global articulation that alone can bring fully into play all those contradictions which Marx was talking about? Clearly, an adequate theory of transition is an essential requirement of advance under such circumstances.

What is at issue here is capital's disturbing success in *extending* the limits of its own historical usefulness. And this is not simply a question of the 'premature' historical conditions under which the socialist revolution erupted in Russia, in the aftermath of a total military collapse, at a time when the social production forces were very far indeed from reaching their 'barrier in capital itself'. More important is in this respect capital's inherent ability to respond with flexibility to crises, adapting itself to circumstances which, *prima facie*, appear to be hostile to its continued functioning. We must have a closer look at these problems in their proper setting.[251] What needs to be stressed at this point is that without realistically confronting and constantly reassessing the *dynamic* limits of capital, every successful extension of those limits will continue to be hailed as a nail in the coffin of Marxism by its adversaries.

11.2 Historical setting of Marx's theory

IN any creative appropriation of Marx's original conception several important considerations must be kept in mind. The *first* concerns the requirement of orienting ourselves in the *spirit* of his work. For after a long period of static reverence, it has now become fashionable to be 'critical' of Marx, without properly understanding or even wishing to understand the vital dialectical contexts and qualifications of his assertions. If, for example, in the past his alleged thesis on 'proletarian immiseration' had to be defended at all costs, today it is quoted *ad nauseam* as a self-evident refutation of Marx's system as a whole, notwithstanding the fact that he was clearly envisaging the possibility of the worker's 'affluence' ('may his pay be high or low', as he put it in *Capital* and in the *Critique of the Gotha Programme*) which his disingenuous critics today just as conveniently ignore as his wishfully oversimplifying 'defenders' did in the past.

As we have seen before, it was Marx's explicit methodological principle to constantly revise and 'significantly modify' his propositions, in conformity with the requirements of the changing sets of relations in terms of which the various concepts were defined, with increasingly richer connotations. Without such revision they would have remained onesided 'abstractions', as he himself called them as regards their first formulation. When later, under the pressure of political determinations, the defence of socialist principles against 'Revisionism' became a major concern in the working class movement, this carried with it the understandable enunciation of political and theoretical *orthodoxy*[252] and the neglect of Marx's dialectical method, culminating in the end in a complete subordination of theory to (Stalinist) political orthodoxy. Appealing to the spirit of Marx's work, therefore, means first of all this: to undertake the necessary *internal critique* in Marx's own words: that is the 'significant modification' of some specific propositions, in the light of the theory as a whole, and thus the removal of all removable 'abstractions' and onesidedness.

The *second* consideration is closely linked to the first and arises from the unfinished character of Marx's project. We have seen that the *'presuppositions of the whole'* which have an obvious qualifying significance for everything else, including the earliest discussion of the 'simple forms', could not be spelled out before the *'fifth section'*. The latter was supposed to analyse the *world market* as the framework in which the 'totality of *moments*' becomes visible, together with the 'totality of *contradictions*', as they come into play in the form of *crises* on a *global* scale. Now from the point of view of a theory of transition the vital question concerns the possible *displacement* of capital's contradictions which cannot even be touched upon, let alone systematically examined, without an adequate investigation of the overall framework in which such contradictions can be displaced: namely the global confrontation of capital as a complex totality with the totality of labour.

As we all know, out of the five massive 'sections' envisaged by Marx in the outline of his project quoted above, he was only able to write the first two. And even the second he could only sketch out in an incomplete form, in that the third volume of *Capital* broke off at the point where he just started the discussion of *classes*, as an integral part of the analysis of the relations of production. One and three quarter sections completed out of a projected five (or six, if we add the anticipations concerning the 'new historic form')!

We can only conjecture as to how Marx might have revised the parts he had already completed if he had succeeded in writing the missing 'sections', reaching thereby the vantage point of the overall 'conclusion' and ultimate 'presuppositions of the whole', together with an adequate determination of capital's barriers on a global scale. What is more important though, as well as thoroughly feasible, is to render explicit, in the context of our own problems, various aspects of Marx's theory which appear only implicitly in the original formulations, since their proper development belongs to the unwritten sections. Thinking about such problems is very far from being an academic exercise. On the contrary, it is a practical challenge, arising from the unavoidable reassessment of some important partial tenets of Marx's theory from the point of view of his conception as a whole.

It is a weighty proof of the coherence and vitality of the Marxian system that the century that elapsed since his death did not make superfluous the task of elaborating the missing 'sections' in the spirit in which he had originally sketched them out. But nothing could be more alien to his spirit than to go on pretending that we are in possession of a fully completed and watertight system, awaiting only its practical implementation by good old 'cunning of history'.

THIS takes us to the *third*, and by far the most important consideration: the impact of postMarxian social developments on the orientation of theory.

The horizons of a historical epoch inevitably set the limits of all theory, even the greatest. The 'presuppositions of the whole', conceived within the horizons of a historical epoch, circumscribe the articulation of all details and partial presuppositions. This is why in theory, too, 'nothing can emerge at the end of the process which did not appear as a presupposition and precondition at the *beginning*'.

Major historical upheavals, however, create *new beginnings* and drastically redraw the boundaries of the earlier presuppositions and preconditions. We shall have a look at some relevant examples later on.[253] What belongs here is the need to stress that while *in principle* Marx could have completed the missing parts of his monumental enterprise in the spirit in which he outlined them, the radically different implications of a *new* historical epoch even in principle are not readily accessible to a theory constituted within the earlier horizons. This does not mean that the new requirements, emanating from the changed determinations of the 'new beginnings', are *incompatible* with the theory in question. But it does mean that a significant modification of the theoretical 'presuppositions of the whole' is called for in order to make the original theory fit the changed historical horizons.

In this sense, as far as Marxist theory is concerned, the *displacement* of capital's contradictions and the emergence of *new types of contradictions* in the postcapitalist societies represent the most challenging new 'presuppositions of the whole'. These are paradigm questions for a theory of transition, and Marxism, in conformity with the horizons of its original historical setting, was certainly not conceived as such. Indeed, Marx himself curtly refused to speculate about the problems that might arise on the soil of the 'new historic form'. Nor did matters improve in this respect for a long time. For later on 'revisionism' gave a very bad name indeed to any concern with the problems of transition. Understandably, therefore, given the disastrous practical performance of revisionist parties and their strategy of a 'gradual transition to socialism' nothing less than the idea of a 'radical break' could satisfy those who remained faithful to their revolutionary aspirations. However, this response itself tended to reinforce a problematical feature of the original conception, instead of helping to modify the theory in accordance with the changed historical circumstances.

All this clearly underlines the difficulties facing a Marxist theory of transition which must respond to not easily reconcilable demands and determinations. For such a theory must be both flexible in its constituents, giving their full weight to the tortuously shifting actual circumstances, and at the same time uncompromisingly firm in its strategic orientation towards the new historic form. Today, given the collapse of the societies of 'actual socialism' in the general setting of capital's structural crisis, the critical examination of these matters is no longer an abstract speculation about some remote future, as used to be in Marx's lifetime. And while Marx could still condemn such speculations as a *diversion* from the real tasks, today the position is completely reversed. For now it is the avoidance of these problems which constitutes an intolerable 'diversion' from the call of producing some viable socialist strategies for the future in the making.

11.3 The Marxian critique of liberal theory

IN his discussion of the origins of Marxism, Lenin named three 'sources':
   (1) Classical Political Economy;
   (2) German Philosophy; and
   (3) Utopian Socialism.
Indeed, a 'critical settling of accounts' was essential for the formation of Marx's thought, and the accent had to be put on a radical *negation* of the social standpoint of these conceptions.

In Marx's 'Critique of Political Economy' — the recurrent title or subtitle of all his major works — the limitations of the liberal/bourgeois horizon were shown to be responsible for the necessary failure of even this peak of liberal theory to solve its problems. As to Hegel, the assertion that the German philosopher shared 'the standpoint of political economy', clearly indicated that Marx judged the ultimate limitations of the Hegelian philosophy in the same terms. And, finally, Utopian Socialism had to be rejected as the bad conscience of liberalism. For despite their professed sympathies, utopian socialists could not go beyond the point of delivering moralistic sermons which failed to alter the established social order.

The radicalism of this critique was necessary not only for theoretical but also for practical/political reasons. Theoretically, the radical negation of the liberal approach was a prerequisite to elaborating a scientific world-view which aimed at transcending the 'fetishism of commodity' from the standpoint of the 'new historic form'. And politically, it was necessary to undermine the dominant intellectual edifice of liberalism whose influence constituted a major obstacle to the development of the still very young working class movement. This negative influence was manifest in the form of: (1) the disorienting confusions of a pseudo-socialist 'vulgar economy'; (2) varieties of philosophical mystification; and (3) the impotence of utopian wishful thinking. Naturally, at times the three appeared combined in a heady mixture, in currents like Proudhonism. Thus Marx's devastating critique of the liberal position originated on the soil of a political movement groping for its own voice and independent strategic orientation. Liberalism had to be attacked because it represented the principal obstacle to the emancipation of the working class movement from 'enlightened bourgeois' political/intellectual tutelage.

THE radical rejection of the liberal problematic carried with it that Marx's centre of interest shifted to the investigation of the antagonistic contradictions which tend to *explode* the established social order, together with the anticipation of the new historic form as the only feasible *solution* to such contradictions. The fact that the only feasible solution is by no means *ipso facto* also a *necessity*, had no urgent topicality for Marx — though, of course, he was theoretically aware of the problem, as we have seen in his references to the only *intimated* new historic form.

Socialism for him was a *reality*, in the positive and negative forms in which it *existed* then; and that was enough. *Negatively*, as the ever-intensifying contradictions of capital, foreshadowing its ultimate breakdown (hence the 'intimation'). And *positively*, as the growing political movement of the working class oriented towards the establishment of a socialist order. Liberal theory's interest in *continuity* (and in *transition* for the sake of continuity) had to be pushed into the background in order to unearth in every stable relation of capital the underlying instability tending towards the *break* as the *'übergreifendes Moment'* (the 'moment of overriding importance').

Naturally, Marx was too great a dialectician to disregard continuity altogether. It was a matter of *stress* or relative proportions. The 'übergreifendes Moment' had to be a *break* in the objective development and ultimate shipwreck of capital. Just how long the process in question might take; what tortuous forms it might assume; how many disappointments, reversals and possible failures will it have to struggle with; or, for that matter: what kind of new contradictions could arise from the tangential determinations of social stability as such — all these questions had to be rather peripheral to Marx's conception under the circumstances.

Liberal theory, in an important sense, is nothing but a theory of transition: and a most peculiar one at that. It operates within the framework of a set of *ideological assumptions* as its *permanent* points of reference, producing the *semblance* of a movement towards an end which is always unquestionably taken for granted. Thus 'acquisitive human nature'; the inescapable conflict of self-seeking individuals; the miraculously beneficial 'invisible hand' and the equally miraculous 'maximization of individual utilities'; the hierarchically ordered set of social relations in 'civil society' and the corresponding political state, are the absolute parameters whose *continuity* constitutes the central objective of the *structurally apologetic* liberal theory of transition.

In liberalism we are presented with a programme of transition from the *absolutes* of the advocated society to their most effective *preservation*. In other words, we are offered a 'transition' from the *given* sets of social relations to their *reproduction* — through varieties of 'social engineering', the 'art of compromise', the politics of 'consensus', etc., — in a partially altered but *structurally identical* form. Thus nothing could be a more fitting description of the liberal theory of transition than the dictum according to which *plus ça change, plus c'est la même chose* ('the more it changes the more it is the same thing'). This is why liberal theory as such is ahistorical and anti-historical,[254] which made it imperative for Marx to radically reject the liberal problematic as a whole in the course of his elaboration of the materialist conception of history.

11.4 Dependency on the negated object

THE Marxian theory of transition could take absolutely nothing from the liberal approach, since it had to be *structurally subversive* — no matter how flexible — and not apologetic. It had to be genuinely historical and *open-ended*, instead of being locked within the confines of the liberal 'absolutes' — (from 'human nature' to the modern state, and from the 'invisible hand' to the self-seeking pursuit of private utility within the horizons of the capitalist market). It had to orient itself towards the constitution of the real *social-individual* subject, instead of the largely fictitious model of *isolated individuality* (which served to misrepresent the enforced power relations, emanating from capital's reified imperatives, as ideal manifestations of the individual freely pursuing its sovereign choice of 'pleasure' and 'utility'). And it had to be critical even in relation to its own ideal: uncompromisingly *self-critical*, as Marx insisted in *The Eighteenth Brumaire*[255] and elsewhere.[256] Since, however, in all these respects Marx could not simply be critical of the liberal approach, but had to counterpose to the latter a *diametrically opposite* view, understandably, the problematic of transition tended to be pushed to the periphery in the course of pursuing the inner logic of polemical confrontations.

An important example is provided in this respect by the issue of *'production in general'*. For obvious reasons, Marx had to reject the constant attempt of liberal political economists to represent the conditions of *capitalist* production as synonymous with the conditions of *production in general*. They did this by arbitrarily asserting the identity of *capital* with the instrument of production as such, and by avoiding or crudely begging the question as to the origin of capital itself. In rejecting such 'eternalization of historical relations of production',[257] the accent had to be firmly on the *specific* qualities of the social/economic processes, insisting that 'there is no production in general', in order to sharply put into relief the ideological interests of the liberal position:

> The aim is to present production — see e.g. Mill — ... as encased in *eternal natural laws* independent of history, at which opportunity *bourgeois* relations are then quietly smuggled in as the inviolable natural laws on which *society in the abstract* is founded. This is the *more or less conscious purpose* of the whole proceeding.[258]

Our complete agreement with Marx's biting conclusions, however, cannot remove the feeling of unease over his summary dismissal of some valid lines of enquiry as 'flat tautologies'. For even if John Stuart Mill's analysis of the *'Stationary State'*[259] of society is full of mystification, it also happens to be concerned with a fundamental issue: the ultimate limits of *production as such,* and not merely of capitalist production.

THIS issue *haunted* liberal/bourgeois theory ever since Adam Smith[260] for a very good reason: the fear that capital might encounter one day its *absolute limit.* Under the circumstances when that fear becomes an unavoidable reality — which is fast happening today — the investigation of the conditions of production as such ceases to be a matter of 'flat tautologies'. Rather, it acquires a dramatic topicality because the *limits of capital* collide with the elementary conditions of the *social metabolism* itself, and thus acutely and chronically threaten the very survival of humanity.

It is in this context that critical considerations of the ecology become a vitally necessary part of Marxist theory. Naturally, ours must be a *structurally* different approach as compared to the liberal/bourgeois preoccupation with these issues. For the latter can only aim at manipulatively 'managing' production *within* and in subjection to the *limits of capital,*[261] whereas the object of Marxism is their historical *transcendence.* In this respect a concept that requires fundamental reassessment is that of capital's 'productive advance'. For at a time when the staggering productivity of capital enables it to swallow up the total material and human resources of our planet, and vomit them out again in the form of chronically under-utilised machinery and 'mass consumer goods' — and much worse: immense accumulations of weaponry bent on destroying civilization potentially a hundredfold — in a situation like this *productivity* itself becomes an intensely *problematical* concept in that it appears to be inseparable from fatal *destructiveness.*

Confronted by the emergence of such destructiveness, the conclusion is inescapable: capital's tremendous power of productivity which 'drives labour beyond the limits of its natural paltriness' cannot be simply *inherited* by the 'new historic form'. For the disconcerting truth is that while in relation to the qualitatively higher requirements of the new historic form (namely the development of Marx's 'rich individuality') the liberating and need-fulfilling power of this productivity is a *mere potential,* in terms of the successfully prevailing and self-perpetuating needs of capital-production it is a *devastating actuality.* This is why, paradoxically, the capitalist instruments and modalities of production must be *radically restructured* and reoriented before they can be 'inherited'.

11.5 The social embeddedness of technology and the dialectic of the historical/transhistorical

HOW is it feasible to open this vicious circle and provide an answer without begging the question? Again, we are facing a paradigm problem of transition, with far-reaching consequences at stake. For the social embeddedness of capitalist technology carries with it that it is structured for the sole purpose of the expanded reproduction of capital at *whatever social cost*. Thus, the frightening exponential growth of capital's destructiveness is not the result of political determinations — varieties of the 'cold war' are no more than lame *a posteriori* ideological justifications of an already prevailing state of affairs — but represents the innermost necessity of the present-day 'productivity' of capital. For the way things stand today, capital would be threatened with a total collapse if its destructive-productive outlets were suddenly to be blocked off.

The discussion of the place of the 'military-industrial complex' as a structural necessity in the contemporary development of capital belongs elsewhere in this study.[262] At the same time, it cannot be stressed enough: the productivity of present-day capital in its *necessary* orientation towards the destructiveness of the military-industrial complex is not merely *incapable* of providing the anticipated liberating power for the new historic form. Much worse than that: it represents, in fact, a Himalayan obstacle towering in front of any effort concerned with the aims of emancipation.

In this sense, unless some viable strategies of transition succeed in breaking the vicious circle of the by now catastrophic social embeddedness of capitalist technology, the 'productivity' of capital will continue to cast its dark shadow as a constant and acute threat to survival, rather than being that accomplishment of 'the material conditions of emancipation' which Marx so often greeted with praise. For while it is true that 'machinery is no more an economic category than the *bullock* that drags the plough',[263] it is far from being the case that 'the way in which machinery is utilised is *totally* distinct from the machinery itself'.[264] And in any event, the military-industrial complex, with its infernal machinery, is certainly no bullock. Nor can the power of productivity articulated within its confines be 'inherited' as anything other than the heaviest of all conceivable millstones around one's neck.

The difficulty here consists in drawing the extremely fine line of demarcation between the *historically specific* and the *transhistorical* constituents of social development. While this distinction is never absolute but concerns the *differential* rates of change, it is nevertheless a matter of great importance. As we have seen, the context of polemical confrontations made it necessary for Marx to heavily stress the historical specificities and underscore the weight of the transhistorical factors. He rightly insisted that 'every succeeding generation finds itself in possession of the productive forces won by the previous generation, which *serve it* as the *raw material* for new production'.[265] What needs to be added to this statement in the present connection is that such forces not only serve the new generation but simultaneously also *chain it* to the rock of past determinations, thus making things far more problematical than the expression 'raw material' would suggest.

This constitutes a condition of particular gravity when the issue at stake is not just how to make the transition from one generation to another, but how to accomplish the qualitative jump from the world of capital to the 'realm of the new historic form'. For, paradoxically, technology — (which might be considered 'in principle neutral' in some respects, until, that is, such view is 'significantly modified' by the force of other, overriding considerations) — in reality acquires, through its necessary social embeddedness, the weight of over-powering *inertia* of a *transhistorical* factor. This is why we have to confront the paralysing force which *serves* the military-industrial complex[266] and *chains down* (or at least holds back) all efforts that aim at its restructuring in the event of a *political* conquest of power. It goes without saying, this is a negative factor of massive dimensions which multiplies the difficulties of envisaging a successful conquest and consolidation of power under present-day circumstances.

THE social metabolism works through a multiplicity of interlocking factors and processes which exhibit vastly different rates of change among themselves. At one pole, we find those which are subject to the speediest fluctuations — e.g., daily political events and the correspondingly zig-zagging adjustments in the associated institutional forms — while at the other: the stubborn persistence of deeply rooted structures, values and aspirations which reproduce themselves with relatively little change. The latter are subject to comparatively slow change not only *within* a given historical period, or in the course of transition from one phase of development of a particular social system to another of its phases, but even across the distant boundaries of significantly different social formations (the 'nuclear family', for instance). Naturally, it is such relatively constant or transhistorical structures which represent the greatest challenge from the point of view of transition to the new historic form, implying a radical transformation of all social structures.

In this context we can see again the significant negative dependency of Marxist theory on the object of its radical negation: the liberal problematic. In opposition to the 'eternalizing' tendencies of liberalism, it was essential to insist on the historically specific dimensions of the family and on the apologetically fictitious character of the liberal conception of 'human nature'. Nevertheless, after we redressed the tendentiously distorted balance and succeeded in rescuing history from the circular orbit of a narrow ideological interest, we are still left with a no less acute problem. That is: how to produce the required *faster* rate of change in structures which show very *low differential rates of change* across historical boundaries, as a result of a variety of greatly intertwined determinations.

Thus, the family in its actual form of existence is not only the historically specific 'bourgeois family' but simultaneously also the not so specific 'nuclear family' — and the former inextricably interlocked with the latter — which regulates the social metabolism *as such* in a most significant sense. Similarly, while 'acquisitive human nature' is an anti-historical liberal fiction, the incontestable reproduction of acquisitive aspirations well beyond the boundaries of fundamental social changes, extending over several historical epochs and social formations, underlines also in this respect the need for a thorough reassessment of these issues — in terms of the complex dialectic of historical specificity in its relation to the transhistorical — in response to some practical challenges which assert themselves with growing intensity today.

11.6 Socialist theory and party-political practice

MARX'S *Critique of the Gotha Programme* ended with the cryptic phrase: *dixi et salvavi animam meam* (I have spoken and saved my soul). It indicated the strange difficulties under which Marx had to write his remarks in the first place. What made things worse was that sixteen long years had to elapse before Marx's critical notes could be published, and even then only after some bitter fight against powerful opposition. Nor did it all end there. For following the publication itself, the *'socialist bosses'* [267] continued their attacks to which Engels had to respond defensively in a letter to Kautsky: 'If we dare not say this [the criticism] openly today, then when?'[268] Engels put his finger on a most delicate matter when he wrote in another letter to Kautsky: 'it is also necessary that people finally stop treating Party functionaries — their own servants — with the eternal kid gloves and standing most obediently instead of *critically* before them, as if they were *infallible bureaucrats'*.[269]

All this revealed that a new type of constraint had appeared in the development of the socialist movement: the *internalisation* (and concomitant rationalisation) of the immediate requirements and contradictions of the movement itself. Only a few years before the controversies surrounding the Gotha Programme Marx could still proudly write:

> The Commune did not pretend to *infallibility*, the invariable attribute of all governments of the old stamp. It published its doings and sayings, it initiated the *public* into all its *shortcomings*.[270]

Now, in complete contrast, he had to address his remarks in strictest confidence to a mere handful of friends: 'only to absolve his conscience and *without any hope of success'*,[271] as Engels later admitted. For even one of the mere handful on his side in 1875, August Bebel,[272] had to a large extent accommodated himself to the internal pressures by the time Marx's *Critique of the Gotha Programme* appeared, accepting the suppression of criticism with the 'justification' — sadly familiar to members of the socialist movement ever since — that criticism of party leaders *helps our enemies*.[273] Engels' conscious efforts to 'tone down' Marx's remarks and 'dispense some tranquillizing morphine and potassium bromide in the introduction', as he put it, could not produce a 'sufficiently soothing effect'[274] in the minds of the 'infallible socialist bosses' who preferred to hide behind the spectre of the mythically inflated 'enemy'.

Thus, one could witness the complete reversal of the original intentions in more than one vitally important respect. The passionate advocacy of conducting matters under *public* scrutiny, without any attempt at hiding *shortcomings*, collided with the self-serving interests of *secrecy* and 'confidentiality'. The principle of *self-criticism*, under the pressure of such interests, assumed the stultifying form of *censorship* willingly implemented as *self-censorship* in the name of party unity. Engels commented with bitter irony:

> It is indeed a brilliant idea to put German socialist science, after its liberation from Bismarck's Anti-Socialist Law, under a new Anti-Socialist Law to be manufactured and carried out by the Social-Democratic Party authorities themselves. For the rest, it is ordained that trees shall not grow into the sky.'[275]

To all this we must add the issue with perhaps the most far-reaching implications: the realisation of Marx's fundamental concern with the *'unity of theory and practice'* in the form of the complete subordination of theory to narrow party-political practice, with its *'propensity to coercive measures'* (Engels) in the name of *'party discipline'*.[276]

Obviously, then, this was a reversal of quite fundamental importance. To say, as Engels did, that 'all the people who count *theoretically* are on my side',[277] was a very poor consolation indeed. For how could it come about that those who did not count theoretically 'counted' *practically/politically?* The very possibility of raising the matter in this way could only underline the threatening character of such developments for the future of the socialist movement. Engels addressed himself to Bebel, in an effort to enlist his help for checking the dangerous trend of bureaucratization and suppression of criticism:

> You — the Party — *need* socialist science, which cannot exist without freedom of movement. For that one has to put up with inconveniences, and it is best to do so with grace, without flinching. Even a slight tension, not to speak of a *rift between the German Party and German socialist science* would be a misfortune and an unparalleled disgrace.[278]

Engels put his warning in the conditional, hoping to strengthen the persuasive force of his appeal by not pointing too obviously his finger at those directly responsible. As history tells us, he was talking about an already existing state of affairs which became much worse, as time went by, instead of redressing the 'rift between socialist science and the party'. His diagnosis of the situation, formulated in the same letter to Bebel, sounds truly prophetic in the light of the subsequent development of the organized socialist movement:

> It is self-evident that the executive and you personally maintain, and must maintain, an important *moral* influence [Engels' italics] on the *Neue Zeit* as well as on everything else being published. But that must suffice for you and it can, too. The *Vorwärts* is always boasting about the *inviolable freedom of discussion*, but one does not see much of it. You just don't know how strange such *propensity to coercive measures* appears here abroad, where one is accustomed to seeing the oldest *party chiefs duly called to account* in their own party (for instance, the Tory government by Lord Randolph Churchill). And then you must also not forget that *in a big party discipline can by no means be so tight as in a small sect*, and that the *Anti-Socialist Law* which hammered the Lassalleans and the Eisenachers together...and made such close cohesion necessary *no longer exists*.

As we can see, Engels soberly identified at the time of their emergence the dangers of:

- (1) the transformation of a *moral* authority into the dictatorial powers of a 'bureaucratic' *ex officio* authority;
- (2) the suppression of the *freedom of discussion*;
- (3) the introduction of a system of *coercive measures*;
- (4) the assertion of the *infallibility of party chiefs* (which put the socialist party below the level of the bourgeois parties, though it was supposed to exercise a 'ruthless self-criticism' as a demonstration of its 'inner power');
- (5) the imposition of the *artificial* discipline of a *small sect* on a *mass party* (in other words: the triumph of *enforced sectarianism*, functioning through the multiplication of coercive measures and the religious cult — the 'personality cult'? — of 'infallibility'); and
- (6) the artificial cultivation of the crisis mentality of a *state of emergency* as the self-evident and unquestionable justification of the most blatant, systematic violation of all principles, organisational forms and practices of any conceivable socialist democracy.

11.7 New developments of capital and its state formations

SERIOUS as these internal problems of the socialist movement appeared even by themselves, they were very far from representing the sum total of the new complications. Nor did they represent simply a 'conflict of principles', or a contradiction between 'ideals and reality'. As Marx insisted already in his early writings[279] and went on reiterating on several occasions,[280] those who adopted the perspectives of scientific socialism and historical materialism 'have no *ideals* to realize, but to set free the elements of the new society with which old collapsing bourgeois society is pregnant'.[281] The difficulties concerned the objective constituents of social change on both sides of the equation: the strategies aimed at setting free 'the elements of the new society' on the one hand, and the prospects of development of 'old collapsing bourgeois society' on the other. People tended to read Marx's metaphor with optimistic one-sidedness which ignored its implicit warning: namely, that pregnancies of old wombs often result in miscarriages or badly handicapped offspring.

If new difficulties appeared on the horizon of the socialist movement, that was mainly due to the strange ways in which the contradictions of capital tended to surface and find their solution so as to reappear with ever-increasing complexity. The 'old society' was being shaken at all levels, from the economic foundations to the political machinery of government. And yet, it managed not only to survive but to emerge perplexingly more powerful from every major crisis.

Marx described the corrupt state power of the Second Empire as 'the *last possible form* of class rule',[282] adding elsewhere that 'on the European continent at least' this kind of governmental rule has become '*the only possible state form*'[283] in which the appropriating class can maintain its mastery over the producing class. And he announced in the same context the *death of parliamentarism* as the logical next step, following the collapse of this 'ultimate' state form. Speaking of the crisis of the Second Empire he wrote: 'This was the state power in its *ultimate* and most prostitute shape, in its supreme and basest reality, which the Paris working class had to overcome, and of which this class alone could rid society. As to *parliamentarism*, it had been *killed by its own charges* and by the Empire. All the working class had to do was *not to revive it.*'[284]

We have to recall here Engels who — in his Introduction to *The Civil War in France* — spoke of 'the irony of history'[285] in producing the very opposite of conscious intentions. It is indeed the irony of history in a rather bewildering form: in the twists and turns of these developments. For could there be a bigger irony of history than seeing socialist representatives — including some of the more radical ones, like Bebel — engaged in suppressing or censoring Marx's writings and boycotting Engels[286] under the pressure of their own involvement with the vicissitudes of parliamentarism? Instead of vanishing from the historical stage, together with the 'last possible form' of state rule, parliamentarism reappeared with a newly acquired power: to divide against itself the selfsame movement which cannot succeed in its aims without the radical supersession of such political forms.

Since Marx's political analyses were always an integral part of a much greater complex, his assertions on the 'ultimate' state form — as the 'last possible form of class rule' — anticipated a likewise irrevocable process of dissolution of capital itself. Naturally, he was talking about a *historical* process whose units of time are not days — not even years — but whole *epochs*, embracing the life-span of possibly many generations. Speaking of the age of Social Revolutions he wrote:

> The working class know that they have to pass through *different phases* of class-struggle. They know that the superseding of the *economic* conditions of the slavery of labour by the conditions of free and associated labour can only be a *progressive work of time*, ... that they require not only a change of *distribution*, but a *new organization of production*, or rather the delivery (setting free) of the social forms of production in present organised labour, (engendered by present industry), of the trammels of slavery, of their present class character, and their *harmonious national and international coordination*. They know that this work of regeneration will be again and again relented and impeded by the resistance of vested interests and class egotism. They know that the present 'spontaneous action of the natural laws of capital and landed property' — can only be superseded by 'the spontaneous action of the *laws of the social economy* of free and associated labour' by a *long process* of development of new conditions... But they know at the same time that great strides may be made at once through the Communal form of *political* organization and that the time has come to *begin* that movement for themselves and mankind.[287]

Clearly, no illusions here about the feasibility of speedy solutions through the success of *political* revolutions. For even that which appeared in many socialist dreams as the most promising of quick remedies: a radical change in the mode of *distribution*, was soberly linked to the requirement of a new organization of *production* as its necessary foundation, reasserting the dialectical links of the two, in complete harmony with Marx's earlier writings.

In this sense, as constituents of the *general* perspectives of a socialist transformation *without a time scale*, Marx's guiding principles contained in our last quote have maintained their fundamental validity to our own days. The dilemmas appeared in the context of *temporal* changes. They have arisen with respect to the evaluation of specific social/economic as well as political events and trends of development. In other words, the undeniable deviation of the objective historical trends from the 'classical model' raised with a certain urgency the complications of any transition to socialism, carrying with it the necessity of elaborating specific theories of transition, in accordance with the new modalities of crisis and the changing configuration of socio-economic conditions and historical circumstances.

It was in response to such trends of development that Marx's most radical follower, Lenin, defined *Imperialism* as the '*Highest Stage* of Capitalism'. This put the Second Empire in perspective: as a very 'underdeveloped' form indeed of capital's true potentialities, both at the economic and at the political level. To be sure, Lenin, too, saw the new, higher stage as the 'last phase' — and in that sense his conception is equally subject to major historical qualifications. Nevertheless, he pushed into the centre of analysis the problematic of capital's ruthless global expansion and its manifold contradictions as graphically exemplified by the inherent structural weaknesses — to the extent of a potential rupture — at determinate linkages of its global chain.

Within the logic of such perspective (concerned with utilising to the full the objective potentialities of *particularly* weak links in order to break the chain), there could be no question of *one* revolution and transition to socialism: there had to be *many*. From this shift in perspective two major implications followed: one very hopeful, the other dense with the dangers of a new mine-field. The first opened up the possibilities of an assault on capital's forbidding global power, with the promise of partial successes and the consolidation of some specific postcapitalist positions by exploiting the inner contradictions of capitalism, instead of engaging it in its entirety in the form of uneven direct confrontations. (Indeed, to our own days, all spectacular successes against the capitalist forma-tion grew out of this type of 'guerilla' strategy and combat.) The second impli-cation, however, pointed in the opposite direction. For it foreshadowed the *adjustment* of capital's global structure to the challenge of the partial ruptures. And there was absolutely nothing to indicate, let alone to apriori guarantee, that such adjustments would turn out to be necessarily detrimental to capital's continued survival in the foreseeable future.

11.8 A crisis in perspective?

MARX identified the real target of socialist attacks as *superseding* (not sud-denly/politically abolishing) 'the *social* enslavement of the producers ... the *economic* rule of capital over labour'[288] of which the bourgeois state was only the 'forcible perpetuation' but not the *cause*. Understandably, though regretfully, he was not interested in exploring in any detail the ways in which capital could succeed in displacing — thus temporarily resolving — its contradictions, thereby postponing for a much longer period than one would wish the eruption of its structural crisis. He greeted the Commune (in his moving celebration of its heroic days) as irrefutable evidence for the effective activation of such crisis: hence his references to the age of the *social revolution*. The imagery of disinte-grating Rome, in his frequent recall of events from ancient history meant as warnings to the present, helped to intensify the expectation of a dramatic collapse. The task of a detached reconsideration of the possibilities and forms of a new lease in capital's life-cycle — carrying with it a corresponding continu-ation and intensification of the 'social enslavement of the producers' — could not suit him even temperamentally.

The middle 1870s, precisely in this respect, brought upon him a veritable crisis: one very far from being due simply to the need to 'struggle against depressing ill health'.[289] Those who wasted their time (and ours) by pursuing an imaginary break between 'young Marx' and 'mature Marx', thus noisily barking up the wrong tree, failed to notice the obvious — though, of course, from neo-Stalinist perspectives invisible — problem: Marx's inability to bring *Capital* to a (to him) satisfactory conclusion, despite all those years of heroically sustained effort. True, he suffered a great deal from ill health. But, as a matter of fact, in the 1870s his health improved to a heartening degree, as Engels himself noted.[290] Marx's greatest difficulties were *inner* ones, and he himself implicitly revealed them by voicing a feeling of unease about the abandoned manuscript of *Capital*. For 'Part III. [of Volume II.], dealing with the reproduc-tion and circulation of social capital, seemed to him *very much in need of revision*'.[291]

Marx's feeling of unease concerned the chapters dealing with *capital's extended self-reproduction*, and within it, with the question of consumption — which constituted his last involvement with the manuscript of *Capital*, four years before his death. He took up the most recent formulations of the problem concerning the way in which capital needs consumption for its self-renewal, but he treated it rather polemically, without exploring its implications to their logical conclusion as far as their positive potentialities for capital were concerned. He quoted from an article (published in *The Nation* in October 1879) some passages in which the Secretary of the British Embassy in Washington, a certain Mr. Drummond suggested that:

> There is no reason why the working man should not desire as many comforts as the minister, lawyer, and doctor, who is earning the same amount as himself. He does not do so, however. The problem remains, how to raise him as a *consumer* by rational and healthful processes, not an easy one, as his ambition does not go beyond a diminution of his hours of labour, the demagogues rather inciting him to this than to raising his conditions by the improvement of his mental and moral powers.

The same Mr. Drummond also quoted an American company secretary who promised 'beating England' not only with regard to the *quality* of production (which, he claimed, had already been accomplished) but also through *lower prices*, to be achieved in his company's case (a cutlery factory) by lowering the unit costs of both *steel* and *labour*.

Marx's comments were passionately negative. First, he retorted with irony that 'These particular ministers, lawyers and doctors will certainly have to be satisfied *merely with desiring* many comforts.' And then he went on to spell out with utter sarcasm his opposition to the very idea of such developments:

> *Long hours of labour* seem to be the secret of these 'rational and healthful processes', which are to raise the condition of the worker by improving his 'mental and moral powers' and making a rational consumer out of him. In order to become a rational consumer of the capitalists' commodities, he must before all else — but the demagogues prevent him — begin by letting his own labour-power be consumed irrationally and in a way contrary to his own health, by the capitalist who employs him. ... Reduction in wages and long working hours: this is the kernel of the 'rational and healthful process' that is to raise the workers to the dignity of rational consumers, so that they 'make a market' for the 'things showered on them' by civilization and the progress of invention.[292]

To be sure, the unctuous hypocrisy of the Embassy Secretary's article deserved every word of Marx's strictures. At the same time, however, in the heat of polemics tending to focus on the most obnoxious aspects, some important implications of the consumerist perspective displayed in Mr. Drummond's comments were allowed to pass completely unnoticed. For even if in the eyes of capital's apologists the socialist militants could appear as nothing more than mere 'demagogues', this circumstance did not prevent them from perceiving — from the standpoint and in the interest of capital — that there is at least a potential *conflict* between the *effectiveness* of militancy and the level of development of the system of consumption as tied to the far from inflexible limitations of the capitalist market. They realised (though, of course, in a contradictory fashion, one-sidedly following to their extreme conclusion the imperatives of capital, often — but by no means always — in the form of mere wishful thinking) that the appearance of the *worker as a mass consumer* would *radically* extend the market, producing an apparently, and to them hopefully, limitless outlet for capitalist expansion.

While such people were 'naive' (to put it mildly) to imagine that *long hours* could be maintained as a norm on account of 'culturally' stimulated appetites for inessential consumption — as, of course, there could be no question of rejecting even the most unhealthy long hours so long as the workers' *bare livelihood* was at stake — they also perceived that a working day well beyond the dictates of the absolutely essential means of subsistence can be successfully imposed on the working class, so long as the relatively long hours are linked to a major expansion in consumption. Hence the references to 'invention' were far more than mere demagoguery in this line of reasoning. The objective was the successful expansion of the market: its radical, i.e., qualitative transformation into a *mass consumer market*. This was to be achieved through the integration of the workers' demands — and in their explicit hope also the workers themselves, after freeing them from their 'demagogues' — in this new market. Consequently, the reduction of the *cost* of labour (and by no means necessarily its *price* which could actually increase) was just as welcome as whatever other step pointing in the same direction.

In this *'quantification of quality'* (a process aiming from the point of view of capital at the establishment of a qualitatively more *favourable* market, defined as a *mass* consumer market), *quality* itself was treated as a necessary but *insufficient* consideration. Hence the great stress on the quantitative demand for significantly improving price levels both in terms of raw materials and as cost of labour. Furthermore, the proposed changes simultaneously affected the interests of both a given unit of a *national capital* (in this case, a particular portion of American capital in its competition with British capital) and the interests of *capital as such;* and both of them very much for the better. (This is why the *British* Secretary of Embassy could rightfully enthuse so much about *U.S.A.* developments.) Thus the issue at stake was not only the limited competition of particular capitals, in relation to which Marx's sarcasm would have been very much to the point since, indeed, 'Every capitalist naturally wants the worker to buy his particular commodities.'[293] It affected simultaneously also the 'fundamental or absolute competition' (Marx) between capital and labour, in that by making itself structurally more advanced and flexible capital *as such* improved its competitive position vis-à-vis labour for as long a historical period as the new market relations could maintain their progress. In relation to all these problems the ability of the working classes to 'make a market for the things showered upon them', clearly, presented a much weightier challenge than its curt dismissal by Marx seemed to suggest.

Significantly, on the pages that immediately follow the discussion of Mr. Drummond's article, Marx put great emphasis on the importance of the continued expansion of 'Department II' (means of consumption) in the reproduction of capital. For 'there would be relative *over-production* in Department I [means of production] corresponding to this simultaneous *non-expansion* of reproduction on the part of Department II.'[294] Naturally, this conclusion by itself did not predicate that there *would be* over-production, with its ensuing crisis; nor indeed that there would not be one. For the issue at this point was merely to establish the necessary implications of the constituent parts for one another and for the development of the capital system as a whole.

The likely direction of *actual* developments was, of course, closely tied to the success or failure of the strategies advocated by the British Secretary and his masters, requiring a precise definition of the historical specificities and changing conditions of the various factors involved. While the dream of an unhampered expansion of capital through 'productive consumption' is as old as bourgeois political economy itself, the last quarter of the nineteenth century actually initiated a phase in the development of the world commodity market which promised to make that dream come true, deeply affecting for a long period of time the orientation of the socialist movement itself. Marx witnessed the *beginnings* of this new phase as well as the *first signs* of its negative impact on the prospects of a socialist victory. Hence his inner difficulties: from *dixi et salvavi animam meam* to that of failing to assign their full weight to the greatly improved potentialities of global capital in his own theoretical framework. It was precisely with respect to these developments that Marx's feeling that 'his treatment of the reproduction and circulation of social capital was very much in need of revision' was fully justified.

CAPITAL needed new ways for its continued survival and rule, and it found two major outlets for coping with the threat of reaching its own structural limits. The first consisted in the relentless *intensification* of its domination *internally*; the second in the expansion and multiplication of its power on a *global* scale. In the second respect, this meant moving from its rather underdeveloped form under the Second Empire — and its parallel formations elsewhere — to a *system of Imperialisms* (which by no means represented the *ultimate* limits of its international articulation). And with regard to its internal development, the new phase carried with it what might be called an *'internal colonization'* of its own 'metropolitan' world, through the extension and intensification of the 'double exploitation' of the workers: both as producers and as consumers. In contrast to its mode of functioning in the colonies and 'independent' neo-colonial territories, in the 'metropolitan' areas the growth of consumption — in the service of capital's expanded self-reproduction — acquired an ever-increasing significance. Accordingly, on the internal plane the new phase was marked by a radical transition from *limited consumption* to massively extended and *'managed consumption'*, with far-reaching implications and painfully real consequences for the development of the working class movement.

CHAPTER TWELVE

THE 'CUNNING OF HISTORY' IN REVERSE GEAR[295]

12.1 'List der Vernunft' and the 'cunning of history'

THE Marxist notion of the 'cunning of history' was formulated as a 'materialist standing on its feet' of Hegel's *List der Vernunft* ('cunning of Reason'). According to Hegel, the latter is: 'an artful device which, while seeming to refrain from activity, looks on and watches how specific determinateness with its concrete life, just where it believes it is working out its own self-preservation and its own private interest, is, in point of fact, doing the very *opposite*, is doing what brings about *its own dissolution* and makes itself a *moment in the whole*.'[296]

In the Hegelian conception a positive outcome to this clash of particular interests — through their fitting subsumption in the divinely unfolding whole — is *apriori* assured, since:

> The rational, the divine, possesses the *absolute power* to actualize itself and has, *right from the beginning*, fulfilled itself; ... The world is this actualization of divine Reason; it is only on its *surface* that the play of *contingency* prevails.[297]

The apologetic character of Hegel's conception of 'being active on Reason's behalf' is brought out with particular clarity in his *Philosophy of Mind*, in his discussion of the ages of man. Hegel's treatment of this problem graphically displays the conservative nature of the liberal theory of 'transition'. For, the moment we reach 'civil society' — the structurally unalterable domain of bourgeois interests — the 'dialectical movement' becomes a pseudo-progression whose meaning resides in preserving all the 'essential' (i.e., structurally unalterable) conditions:

> He [the adult man] has plunged into the Reason of the actual world and shown himself to be active on its behalf. ... If, therefore, the man does not want to perish, he must recognize the world as a *self-dependent* world which in its *essential* nature is *already complete*, must *accept the conditions* set for him by the world and wrest from it what he wants for himself. As a rule, the man believes that this *submission* is only forced on him by necessity. But, in truth, this *unity* with the world must be recognized, not as a relation imposed by *necessity*, but as *the rational*. ... therefore the man behaves quite rationally in *abandoning* his plan for completely transforming the world and in striving to realize his personal aims, passions, and interests only within the framework of the world of which he is a part. ... although the world *must be recognized as already complete in its essential nature*, yet it is not a dead, absolutely inert world but, like the *life-process*, a world which perpetually creates itself anew, which while *merely preserving itself*, at the same time *progresses*.[298]

In accord with the standpoint of classical bourgeois political economy, Hegel uses the *organic* model of the 'life-process' (which operates with a time-scale radically different from that of the social world) so as to be able to project the *semblance* of an advancement while constantly reiterating the necessary *conserva-*

443

tion of the conditions which are said to be 'already complete in their essential nature'. As we can see, in the framework of such an 'organic' conception which takes 'civil society' for granted, the real *must* of 'necessary submission' is transubstantiated into the fictitious 'must' — in truth an impotent 'ought': a mere *Sollen* — of 'advancement', culminating in the apotheosis of the philosophies of right, ethics and religion:

> It is in this conservation and advancement of the world that the man's work consists. Therefore on the one hand we can say that the man *only creates what is already there;* yet on the other hand, his activity *must* also bring about an advance. But the world's progress occurs only on the *large scale* and only comes to view in a *large aggregate* of what has been produced. ... This knowledge, as also the *insight into the rationality of the world*, liberates him from mourning over the *destruction of his ideals.* ... the substantial element in all human activities is the same, namely, the *interests of right, ethics, and religion.*[299]

Thus, the organic character of the 'life-process' fits doubly well into Hegel's scheme of things. First, because it is *cyclic-repetitive*; and second, in that it exhibits the almost timeless temporality of natural history if measured on the dramatic time-scale of social/political events and transformations. On both counts the model of the 'life-process' can only serve the 'eternalization' of the established conditions.

Accordingly, for Hegel it would have been quite absurd to suggest that the 'cunning of Reason' might bring about a clash of antagonistic interests of such severity whereby it outwits not just the conflicting parties, but simultaneously *itself* as well, by bringing about the *destruction* of the 'whole', rather than the 'actualization of divine Reason' through the rational integration of all contradictions as happily interlocking 'moments of the self-sustaining whole' (Hegel). True to the liberal/apologetic 'standpoint of political economy' (Marx), the conflict of interests was indeed both acknowledged and *eternalized* in this Hegelian conception. For it assigned to the mere *surface* what it called 'the play of contingency', thus categorically excluding the possibility of structural changes in the divinely prefigured and permanent whole.

AS to the materialist transformation of the 'cunning of Reason', we must be aware of another inherent difficulty: namely, the application of an *individualistic model* to fundamentally *non-individualistic* processes and transformations. For Hegel this problem did not exist, for two main reasons:

- (1) The time-scale of his organic model was perfectly in tune with the individualistic framework of his conception of interactions, in that he did not have to produce real historical progression out of the chaotic-anarchic interplay of individual wills. Far from it, since the *necessary* 'outcome' was anticipated from the very beginning as 'already given' and 'already complete', while the interplay of the infinity of individual wills on an infinite time-scale was destined merely to act out what was 'notionally' required by the predeterminations of 'Divine Reason';
- (2) The difficulty involved in making the transition from the disparate individuals to the all-embracing *universality* of the historic process was easily resolved by:
  (a) *apriori* postulating the individuals' *'unity* with the world'; and

(b) by stipulating a similar unity between the human individual and *humanity as such*. (In Hegel's words: 'The sequence of ages in man's life is thus rounded into a *notionally determined totality* of alterations which are produced by the process of the *genus* with the *individual*.'[300] As we can see, the mystifying concept of 'genus-individual' mentioned in Marx's *Theses on Feuerbach* is not confined to materialism. It characterizes the entire philosophical tradition that shares the 'standpoint of political economy'.)

Thus, the historically relevant individuals were the *genus-individuals* who necessarily/rationally acted out the divinely prefigured destiny of the species on the corresponding time-scale of the 'perpetually self-renewing life-process', in relation to which the aberrations of the 'play of contingency' could only produce a mere ripple on the surface.

THERE are no such avenues open to a materialist conception of history. It is therefore rather perplexing to see how Engels uses the 'cunning of history' — the 'resultant' of the many conflicting individual wills — to explain historical movement:

> That which is willed happens but rarely; in the majority of instances the numerous desired ends *cross and conflict* with one another... Thus the conflicts of *innumerable individual wills* and individual actions in the domain of history produce a state of affairs *entirely analogous* to that prevailing in the realm of *unconscious nature*. The ends of the actions are *intended*, but the results which actually follow from these actions are *not intended*; ... Men make their own history, whatever its outcome may be, in that *each person* follows his own consciously desired end, and it is precisely the *resultant* of these *many wills* operating in *different directions* and of their manifold effects upon the outer world that constitutes history.[301]

If this is an accurate account, it is somewhat mysterious why some kind of an order (history) rather than *total chaos* should result from the many wills relentlessly pushing in 'innumerable different directions'.

The 'cunning of history' as the lawful *resultant* of millions of self-oriented centrifugal forces is not a very plausible explanation of history. For if there is no cohesion or direction of some sort already in the individual wills themselves (though, of course, not in their every momentary or capricious fluctuation), then one would either need some magic power to account for the ultimate cohesion and movement, or one would be forced into a position that tends to underestimate the importance of conscious individual determinations in favour of some 'inner general laws' and separate 'historical causes'.

As a matter of fact, there are times when Engels' formulations fall into the second category. Thus, for instance, when he insists that:

> the course of history is governed by *inner general laws*. ...the many individual wills active in history for the most part produce results quite other than those intended — often quite the *opposite*; their motives, therefore, in relation to the total result are likewise *of only secondary importance*. ... What are the *historical causes* which transform themselves into these motives in the brains of the actors?[302]

The *genus-individual* and the 'cunning of Reason' represent Hegel's way of avoiding the conclusion of anarchy and chaos while conveniently retaining the individualistic framework of eternalized 'civil society' in which fundamental *social antagonisms* are mystifyingly transsubstantiated into *individual* conflicts. Accordingly, neither the genus-individual nor the 'cunning of Reason' are suitable to be assimilated into a materialist conception of history. For they represent two sides of the same coin. Together with Hobbes' bellum *omnium contra omnes* (war of *all against all*), they belong to a certain type of theory with which Marx's conception of the *social individual* — oriented and motivated within the framework of a specific *social consciousness* — has really nothing in common.

THE fundamental difference between a speculative and a materialist conception of history is not established by renaming the 'cunning of Reason' as the 'cunning of history', but by identifying the dynamic constituents of actual historical development in their *radical openness*: i.e., without any preconceived guarantee of a positive outcome to the clash of antagonistic forces. This is why in the Marxian conception the 'new historic form' can only be *intimated* (as Marx puts it in the *Grundrisse*), since its *actual* constitution involves the necessity (the one and only 'inevitability' in these matters) of traversing the nuclear minefield of capital, with its far from happy implications for history itself. Marx firmly stated that:

> A social order *never perishes* before *all* the productive forces for which it is broadly sufficient have been developed, and new superior relations of production *never replace* older ones before the material conditions for their existence have *matured* within the womb of the old society. Mankind thus always sets itself only such tasks as it can solve, since closer examination will always show that the task itself arises only when the material conditions for its solution are already present or at least *in the process of formation*.[303]

The actual historical development is, thus, by no means closed here, notwithstanding the vulgar-fatalist view attributed to Marx by some followers and adversaries alike. For he only talks about the process of *formation* of the *material conditions* of a *possible* solution (which is 'necessary' in the non-fatalist sense of being *required*, as well as in the equally non-fatalist sense of predicating the ultimate *maturation* of the contradictions themselves, but in no way the *happy solution* of these contradictions). And though the sentence that follows the last quote — 'The prehistory of human society therefore closes with this social formation.'[304] — might create the impression of a closure, even there the issue is simply to stress that *inasmuch as* the process is successfully accomplished, it marks a qualitatively new phase in the development of mankind.

To claim that Marx guarantees the 'inevitability' of socialism, on the sole ground of the ongoing (and far from finished) *formation* of the *material* conditions of a *possible* solution — while, in fact, he dedicated his whole life to the task of realizing some other vital conditions, such as the elaboration of an adequate socioeconomic theory and political strategy — is nothing short of preposterous. His statement is concerned with the general *tendencies* of a certain *type* of social development: one marked by the rather blind determinations of 'prehistory' in which the 'cunning of history' is allowed to run riot. That is to say, it is not concerned with the tortuous ways, and disconcerting transitional specificities, through which the formation of the material and non-material conditions of a possible solution may be retarded, endangered, and even reversed for a shorter or longer period of time, under the ever-increasing pressure of capital's *global* articulation through which *'alle Widersprüche zum Prozess kommen'* ('all contradictions come into play').[305]

12.2 The reconstitution of socialist perspectives

HOW did it come about that the 'cunning of history' — which was supposed to help, so to speak *ex officio*, the rising historical forces against the old ones, so as to secure the actualization of the new order — instead of doing its job, went into reverse gear and started to move in the opposite direction, extending beyond recognition the vitality of that 'social anachronism' which seemed to be on its last leg (as the 'last possible form of class rule', etc.) in the middle of the nineteenth century? And, in view of the fact that these developments did not take place in the Hegelian speculative universe but on the real ground of human history, what are the chances and conditions of bringing to a halt this reckless driving at full rearward speed towards the precipice, with visibility confined to the miserable little rear-view mirror: a far cry indeed from the claimed totalizing vision of the 'cunning of Reason'?

The answer to the first question presents itself in two parts, in that:

(1) since the middle of the nineteenth century the socialist forces developed some internal contradictions whose negative impact well exceeded the depressing prospects that already induced Marx to draw the earlier mentioned sad conclusion in his *Critique of the Gotha Programme: dixi et salvavi animam meam* (I said it and saved my soul), in his own words 'without any hope of success' of influencing the momentous decisions that had to be taken at the time by the opposing wings of the German movement; and

(2) in the same period of time capital itself succeeded in significantly changing its character and mode of operation: not with respect to its *ultimate limits*, but as regards the *conditions* of maturation of its contradictions as known to and theorized by Marx.

As to the second question, concerned with changing the present situation for the better, the answer obviously depends on the full maturation of the contradictions themselves. For only this objective process can block both 'the line of least resistance' and the existing outlets for the *displacement* of the contradictions, on both sides of the social antagonism.

IF it is true that a social order never perishes before *all* the productive forces for which it is broadly sufficient have been developed within its framework, this truth has far-reaching implications for the ways in which a particular social formation may be replaced by another. For it is not a matter of indifference in this respect, whether a crisis leads to a total breakdown and collapse of the social order in question — in which case the productive forces obviously cannot be further developed in its confines — or, under the impact of a *major* crisis, new modalities of functioning are introduced in order to prevent that breakdown. Once, however, such changes are introduced, they become more or less consciously adopted — at any rate *integral* — parts of the new set of 'hybrid' relations, thus radically redefining the terms in which a subsequent *fundamental* (i.e., not just 'periodic') crisis may be envisaged. This is because the 'hybrid' adjustments have significantly extended the potentialities for a continued development of the productive forces within the established framework, thereby imposing the need for a profound readjustment also in the strategies of the adversary.

In this sense, the old order's viability is now positively affected to a degree simply unimaginable before. Nor should one assume that this is a 'once only' option. On the contrary, such changes generate the conditions of their own self-renewal, by injecting a number of new 'variables' — each with objective characteristics and potentialities of its own — whose interplay becomes yet again the objective ground for generating new potentialities and their combinations, carrying with it the further extension of the *earlier* limits and productive powers (though, of course, not the *ultimate* limits) of the established social order. And since the forces involved in such interchanges are themselves inherently *dynamic* social forces, with *consciousness* (and 'false consciousness') of their shifting interests, on *both* sides of the fundamental social antagonism, these readjustments must be conceptualized as an *ongoing process* whose *ultimate* or 'absolute' limits cannot be readily prefigured, although they exist nonetheless. The more or less explicit denial of such limits produces the futile submissiveness of 'revisionist' or 'social democratic' perspectives (from Bernstein to Anthony Crosland and his even smaller present-day followers), while their voluntaristic direct translation into crisis-consciousness assumes equally damaging political forms, from varieties of Stalinism to manifestations of small-group sectarianism which imaginarily act out the 'permanent revolution' by adopting the psychology of a permanent state of emergency.

The ultimate limits mentioned above concern the broadest *historical* conditions of the process, and not its transient fluctuations. For so long as these transformations unfold on an antagonistically contested terrain, no emancipatory step is safe from the dangers of retrogression, no matter how favourable the *ultimate* historical relation of forces for the 'new historic form' might be *once* the old order fails to develop the productive forces. While the social confrontations effectively persist, the outcome remains fundamentally *open*. This is because the stakes in the actual confrontations are not summarily *'everything or nothing'* — except in very rare situations of quasi-apocalyptic crisis (and even then not for long) — but the solution of *this* or *that* particular set of problems or contradictions, with the possibility of regrouping after a partial defeat, or, indeed, of losing out as a result of the unsuspecting consumption of some indigestible fruits of victory.

IT is in the innermost nature of the confrontation between capital and labour that *neither* of the two principal antagonists can be simply left slaughtered on the battlefield. The 'abolition of capital' as an *act* (in contradistinction to a long-drawn-out *process* of *restructuring*) is just as completely unrealistic as the 'abolition of the state' or the sudden 'abolition of labour'. The three stand and 'fall' together. (In fact Marx speaks of *'Aufhebung'*, which is a complex historical process of 'supersession-preservation-raising to a higher level'.) This makes the transition to socialism not only complex but, at the same time, opens up a vast terrain for the manifestations of the supposedly benevolent 'cunning of history' at its worst.

When Malenkov was First Secretary of the Soviet Party, he summed up his view of history by assuring his audience that since the first world war resulted in the victory of the Soviet Revolution, and the second was instrumental in the emergence of the Peoples' Democracies and China, the third world war would produce with historical inevitability the victory of socialism all over the world. The whole thing now sounds like a macabre joke, although Malenkov was speaking quite seriously, on a solemn occasion. The point is, though, that no reassurance can be derived from the broadest general perspectives of historical development. For the issues are always decided in their actual context, on the ground of their shifting social/historical specificities, transitional determinations, as well as retrogressions.

Thus, the historical perspectives of a socialist transformation cannot be simply *reaffirmed*. They must be constantly *reconstituted* on the basis of fully acknowledging the actual transformations (by no means always for the better) of the social forces involved in the changing confrontations. If we cannot account for the negative aspects of social development since Marx's death as they affect the prospects of a transition to socialism, any amount of faithful self-assurance is bound to sound like singing in the dark.

AS we know, Marx unequivocally stated that each nation is 'dependent on the revolutions of the others' and, therefore, 'communism is only possible as the act of the dominant peoples "all at once" and simultaneously, which presupposes the universal development of productive forces and the world intercourse bound up with them.'[306] Many years later — in fact as late as 1892 — Engels reiterated essentially the same position by saying that 'the triumph of the European working class ... can only be secured by the cooperation of at least England, France and Germany'.[307]

In the same work of 1845 in which Marx spoke of the simultaneous revolutions of the 'dominant peoples', he also considered, as an exception to the rule, the possibility of a socialist revolution erupting in an *underdeveloped* country, as a result of *uneven development*. In his view, thanks to the objective potentialities of the latter, 'to lead to a collision in a country, this contradiction need not necessarily have reached its extreme limit in that particular country. The competition with industrially more advanced countries, brought about by the expansion of international intercourse, is sufficient to produce a *similar* contradiction in countries with a *less advanced* industry (e.g., the *latent proletariat* in Germany brought into more prominence by the competition of English industry).'[308]

Another important passage of this work explored the problem of uneven development both internally and in its broadest international context:

> It is evident that large-scale industry does not reach the same level of development in all districts of a country. This does not, however, retard the class movement of the proletariat, because the proletarians created by large-scale industry assume leadership of this movement and carry the whole mass along with them, and because the workers excluded from large-scale industry are placed by it in a still worse situation than the workers in large-scale industry itself. The countries in which large-scale industry is developed act in a similar manner upon the more or less non-industrial countries, insofar as the latter are swept by world intercourse into the universal competitive struggle.[309]

Thus, alternative types of development for the eruption of socialist revolutions were also considered by Marx and Engels, even if they were not put into the foreground of their overall strategy.

AS it happened, actual historical developments disregarded the rule and produced a complicated variant of the exception. Naturally, Marx's adversaries never ceased to repeat ever since, with self-congratulatory delight, that history refuted Marxism. Let them have their fun while they can, since they refuse to see the obvious: namely, that what really matters is the undeniable fact of the eruption of such revolutions, and not their particular variations under determinate historical circumstances. And in any case, Marx did not leave this problem in the form in which it appeared in *The German Ideology*, indicating even there, as he did, the possibility of socialist revolutions in less advanced countries. He developed that idea further, in his correspondence with Vera Zasulich, with regard to the specific conditions — and potentialities — of Russia where the anticipated revolution later in fact unfolded.

While recalling this, it is nevertheless important to recognize the weighty implications of the fact that once the *exception* succeeds in asserting itself on the scale at which it actually did, from then on it becomes the *rule* in relation to which everything else has to adjust itself.

To be sure, ideally 'it would have been better', had the original hopes and expectations prevailed. For such a bewildering act of the real 'cunning of history', whereby the exception is turned into the rule, is bound to prolong the 'birth-pangs of the new historic form'. However, actual history does not deal in counter-factual conditionals. The emergence of 'brute facts', produced by the complex interplay of multi-faceted social/historical forces, always significantly reconsitutes the ground on which further action may and must be carried on.

In this sense, social history is really *made of exceptions*. For its 'laws' are *tendencies* actualized by particular social agencies — which follow conscious aims and, *within limits*, constantly readjust their actions in relation to the more or less successful realization of those aims—and not *physical laws* of the natural universe that carry radically different determinations, on an incomparably longer time scale. On the model of the natural sciences, the unexpected occurrence of the exception could be treated as an aberration, reasserting thus the validity of the original rule. In the social universe, however, there are no such solutions (or consolations). Despite everything. there is no way of going back on the world historical impact of events like the October revolution, since they create radically *new equations* for all social forces, as well as for the original terms of the theory. Once such monumental 'exceptions' consolidate themselves, any continued insistence on an eventual return to the 'classical rule' would be like 'waiting for Godot'.

12.3 *The emergence of capital's new rationality*

TODAY it remains as true as ever that 'communism is only possible' as the sustained action of the 'dominant peoples', but its conditions of realization have fundamentally altered. It would be an oversimplification to say that this change occurred suddenly, in 1917, although the Soviet revolution, obviously, brought an immense further change in the complex determinants involved.

The point is, that the emergence and consolidation of several important factors many years earlier pointed in the same direction. To sum it up in one sentence: the transition to socialism has become incomparably more complicated in view of the fact that capital, in response to the challenge presented by the development of the socialist movement, acquired a 'new rationality' as a form of self-defence and a way of counter-acting or neutralizing the gains of its adversary. While this new rationality did not and could not mean the *elimination* of its 'irrationality' and 'anarchic character' noted by Marx, it nevertheless significantly *extended* the earlier limits. It must be stressed though that these characteristics were never treated by Marx himself — unlike by some of his followers — as *absolute* determinations, but as relative and *tendential* factors, affecting the relationship of the *parts* with the *whole*, as well as the contradiction between the *immediate* measures and their *long-term* consequences. In this sense, partial and short-term rationality was never denied to capital; only the possibility of a successful and lasting integration of the partial determinations in a comprehensive whole, which is evidently a question of *limits*.

LET us have a brief look at some of the most important aspects of this set of problems.

(1) The Marxist theory of class consciousness — including its treatment by Lukács, as we have seen above — is in need of 'significant modification' (Lenin). While the concepts of 'class *of* civil society', 'class *in* civil society', and 'class *for* itself' remain valid as far as they go, they obviously do not go far enough and cannot come to grips with a number of serious difficulties. The problem is not merely that Marx's discussion of classes in Volume III of *Capital* is broken off at its very beginning, but that later developments modified in reality itself some important characteristics of the class consciousness of *both* capital and labour. (One might legitimately ask here: is it purely coincidental that Marx's analysis of classes in *Capital* was interrupted — six years before he died — precisely at the time when the new complications, arising out of these developments, just started to become visible? Or, could it be, perhaps, that such new problems added to Marx's internal difficulties which are identifiable also in other contexts?)

The 'latent proletariat' (Marx), for instance, has been 'actualized' in every major country; and by no means always in the sense in which it had been anticipated. To mention only one important aspect of this problem: the proletariat, through its — however 'partial' and 'short term' — interests in the prevailing capitalist order in the countries of some 'dominant peoples', has *also* become a 'class *of* civil society', against the original expectations. And unless the time-scale of such developments, as well as the conditions of their reversal, are defined with some precision, the various theories of 'working class integration' will continue to exercise their disorienting influence.

Similarly, the limitations of bourgeois class consciousness need a more realistic assessment than what we have become accustomed to. This concerns above all the ruling class's ability to unify to a very large extent its fragmented constituents in line with its overall class interests, both *internally*, vis-à-vis its indigenous working class, and *externally*, in its confrontation with the *international* dimension of labour's self-emancipation. All these problems directly or indirectly involve the need for a thorough reexamination of the relationship betweeen the ruling class and the state, in its comprehensive international as well as local setting. In other words, it requires a sober reassessment of the ruling class's ability to reproduce, relatively undisturbed, the totality of state and inter-state relations, despite their inner contradictions: safeguarding, thus, a vital precondition to the continued survival of capital in the global framework of the world market.

(2) Politically, the ruling class responded to the challenge of its adversary by more or less consciously 'suspending' some of its sectional interests and divisions. This trend came to the fore with dramatic force already at the time of the Paris Commune: brutally suppressed within a short time, thanks to Bismarck's complete turnabout, releasing the French prisoners of war against the Communards and providing thus a most devastating material, political and military proof of bourgeois class solidarity. Nor did it all stop just there. For Bismarck was busying himself in 1871-1872 for the establishment of an international framework of action against the revolutionary movement. In October 1873 his plan was in fact implemented, through the formation of the Three Emperors' League of Germany, Russia and Austria-Hungary, with the unifying conscious aim of taking common action in the event of a 'European disturbance' — caused by the working class — in any particular country.

At the same time, this shrewd representative of the ruling classes, internally did not confine his strategy to repressive measures, like his Anti-Socialist Law: a fitting equivalent at home to his international scheming. He simultaneously pursued the — complementary — plan of trying to accommodate the German working class, and by no means entirely without success. Indeed, one of the main reasons why Marx truly detested Lassalle was his conviction that Lassalle was 'intriguing with Bismarck'.[310] Furthermore, certain practical measures, introduced into the economy by the 'Iron Chancellor', created such confusion among socialists that Engels had to take them to task in no uncertain fashion:

> Since Bismarck went in for *State-ownership* of industrial establishments, a kind of *spurious socialism* has arisen, degenerating, now and again, into something of flunkey-ism, that without more ado declares *all* State-ownership, even of the Bismarckian sort, to be socialistic.[311]

In the long decades that followed the defeat of the Commune, the bourgeoisie on the whole successfully maintained its claim to being the 'national class', as the fate of Social Democracy during the First World War clamorously demonstrated. Even with respect to colonialism, the class as a *whole* emerged stronger than ever after the end of its direct political-military rule, despite the fact that sections of the British and French ruling classes suffered a temporary set-back through the dissolution of their Empires. It did so by instituting in the form of *neo-capitalism* and *neo-colonialism* an incomparably more 'rational', 'cost-effective' and dynamic system of exploitation than the earlier version of direct colonial/military domination.

Parallel to these developments, the ruling class as a *whole* successfully adapted itself in international terms to the loss of vast areas of the planet — the Soviet

Union, China, Eastern Europe, parts of South East Asia, Cuba, etc. — and internally strengthened its position through the invention and successful management of the 'mixed economy', the 'welfare state', and the politics of 'consensus'. And last but definitely not least, the institution (again, by the ruling class as a whole) of a 'new international order' which succeeded in eliminating — in what was supposed to be the 'Age of Imperialism and inevitable world wars' —violent collisions among the major capitalist powers now for over fifty years, and, given the existing constraints with regard to the possible consequences of reciprocal self-destruction, it looks like doing so indefinitely.

We must remember in this respect that Stalin repeated as late as 1952 — in a work hailed as his 'political testament' — his fantasies about the benevolence of the 'cunning of history', by proclaiming his belief in the inevitability of another imperialist world war and through it the self-destruction of capitalism, insisting that the fundamental contradiction was *among* capitalist powers and not between 'capitalism and socialism'. Thus he assumed a totally anti-Marxist position, since Marx always maintained that the basic social antagonism was between capital and labour, while the contradictions between particular capitals were secondary and subordinate to the former. This is how Stalin 'argued' his case, in a chapter entitled 'Inevitability of Wars between Capitalist Countries':

Take, first of all, Britain and France.Undoubtedly, they are imperialist countries. Undoubtedly, cheap raw materials and secure markets are of paramount importance to them. Can it be assured that they will endlessly tolerate the present situation, in which, under the guise of 'Marshall Plan aid,' Americans are penetrating into the economies of Britain and France and trying to convert them into adjuncts of the United States economy, and American capital is seizing raw materials and markets in the British and French colonies and thereby plotting disaster for the high profits of the British and French capitalists? Would it not be truer to say that capitalist Britain, and, after her, capitalist France, will be compelled in the end to break from the embrace of the U.S.A. and enter into conflict with it in order to secure an independent position and, of course, profits?

Let us pass to the major vanquished countries, Germany (Western) and Japan. These countries are now *languishing in misery* under the jackboot of American imperialism. Their industry and agriculture, their trade, their foreign and home policies, and their whole life are fettered by the American occupation 'regime'. Yet only yesterday these countries were great imperialist powers and were shaking the foundations of the domination of Britain, the U.S.A. and France in Europe and Asia. To think that these countries will not try to get on their feet again, will not try to smash the U.S. 'regime,' and force their way to independent development, is to believe in miracles. ...

What guarantee is there, then, that Germany and Japan will not rise to their feet again, will not attempt to break out of American bondage and live their own independent lives? *I think* there is no such guarantee. *But it follows from this that the inevitability of wars between capitalist countries remains in force.*[312]

Written at a time when the German and Japanese 'economic miracles' were already in full swing, not to mention the first major steps for establishing the E.E.C., the logic of these lines — 'I think ... therefore ... it follows' — was truly remarkable, on account of its subjectivism and voluntarism.

The relevance of the change in inter-capitalist rivalry must be assessed in its broader context. For as a logical extension of competition at its most extreme, violent collisions among capitalist states used to constitute an integral part of capital's development and normal functioning. Thus the change we have witnessed in this respect provides a major proof of capital's ability to rectify some of the most perverted aspects of its irrational rationality, even if such change came about primarily through the nuclear constraint, and not as a result of a positive deliberation. At the same time it must be stressed that the question of limits is all-important also in this respect. For this forced expansion of capital's rationality simultaneously deprives it of its ultimate competitive weapon: the destruction of its antagonist. This, in its turn, blocks a formerly vital avenue for the displacement of contradictions, and thus reactivates some explosive tendencies of the internal social dynamics, with potentially extreme severity.

(3) In the last hundred years the capitalist order has gone through some major economic developments whose impact greatly extended its rationality and ability to cope with its problems. While the first 'mainstream' reaction to the new tendencies was always rather narrow, the more imaginative representatives of the ruling class tended to prevail in the longer run. This was because they received powerful support from the beneficial economic developments themselves, which objectively changed the conditions in favour of the adoption of — from the point of view of the class as a *whole* — more rational policies and measures.

To mention but a few:

— the successful development of the mass consumer economy;[313]

— the adoption of Keynesian strategies, conceived in the aftermath of a disastrous economic crisis;

— the postwar acceptance of nationalization on a substantial scale;

— the flexible adaptation of capital to the demands and strains of the 'mixed economy';

— the establishment of the International Monetary System and the creation of a large number of multinational institutions (from the E.E.C. to E.F.T.A., G.A.T.T., I.M.F., etc.), in conformity with the overall interests of capital;

— the so far highly successful adaptation of the bourgeois national state to the needs of the 'multinationals' (in truth: giant national 'transnational' corporations) and to the expanding system of the 'military-industrial complex';

— the successful operation of a global system of domination which maintains the 'third world' in paralyzing dependency, supplying the bourgeoisie not only with vast resources and outlets for capital-expansion, but also with a revenue large enough to offset to a significant extent the tendential fall of the rate of profit, in addition to the compensation provided by the monopolistic concentration and centralization of capital.

Moreover, as I have argued in April 1982, when 'The Cunning of History in Reverse Gear' was published in Italy:

while the aggressive fantasies of a *military 'roll-back'* of 'actual socialism' proved to be an utter failure, the success of *neo-capitalist penetration* through its growing economic tentacles represents a *much more serious danger* also in this respect.

To understand the relative importance of the latter trend, we have to bear in mind that the indebtedness of several East European countries — especially Poland and Hungary — to Western capitalism is quite phenomenal. Hungary, for instance, is in debt to the tune of more than 2,000 dollars per head of population. (Given the considerably lower level of income in these countries in comparison to their Western counterparts, the per capita debt is thus much higher than it appears at first sight. In Hungary, for instance, the per capita Gross National Product amounts to less than $2,000 per annum, in contrast to the U.S. where it is ten times higher, well in excess of $20,000.)

Naturally, such debts must be serviced, and the sheer magnitude of interest payments alone may impose enormous strains — as the Polish economy testifies — on the countries concerned. Not to mention the ironical consequences of *importing inflation* into the 'planned economy' with the blessing of Western capital. And this is only one of the many ways in which the growing network of economic relations functions in favour of the capitalist countries. Others include:

— disproportionately one-sided trade relations;

— exporting, for the sake of Western currency, goods in which there is a shortage at home (including food, disregarding even the danger of food riots, as we have seen in the case of Poland);

— developing certain sectors of the economy primarily for the sake of Western markets;

— producing finished products on behalf of capitalist concerns, for sale abroad;

— subcontracting to Western firms for the supply of components;

— production under capitalist licence and disbursing the concomitant royalty payments;

— purchasing entire capitalist plants which involves, again, substantial royalty payments, often for antiquated products and processes;

— highly inflated 'unofficial' conversion rates for Western currency, in the context of the tourist trade and elsewhere;

— constructing luxury hotels and even gambling casinos (economic 'no-go areas' for the local population) and leasing them to Western capitalist enterprises on terms highly advantageous to the latter.[314]

Also, it was possible to identify very clearly some baffling developments which displayed the direct negative impact of East European societies on the livelihood and struggles of the Western working class itself. Thus, three years after this Chapter first appeared, the Hungarian periodical *Magyar Hirek*[315] proudly reported that:

> This year 280,000 blue jeans will be produced under the licence of the English Lee Cooper firm by the Karcag factory of the Budapest Clothing Cooperative. This quantity is more than double the number of farmer trousers [the Hungarian name for blue jeans] they made last year.

By coincidence, the same week it was announced in Britain that the Levi-Strauss firm — a major competitor to Lee Cooper's — was closing down two of its Scottish factories, adding 500 more workers to the already very high number of unemployed in Scotland. While the date is, of course, a mere coincidence, the real connection is very far from being accidental. It represents, in fact, one of the many ways in which Western capitalism can turn its ability to exploit even the relatively underpaid East European workforce to its own advantage and use the mobility of capital — while preaching the 'need for labour mobility' as the magic remedy to unemployment — against its own labour force.

Another significant, as well as extremely painful, example has been provided by the doubling of Polish coal exports to Margaret Thatcher's Britain during the miners' strike. Indeed, to make things worse, this happened under circumstances when Lech Walesa's Solidarnošc organisation (in contrast to some local groups of Polish workers) failed to make as much as a verbal gesture of solidarity towards the British miners.

But perhaps the most ironical case was the one that raised some eyebrows even in conservative newspapers. As *The Times* reported:

> Mr Eddy Shah, the owner of Messenger Group Newspapers, will print his new national newspaper on presses leased through the London Subsidiary of the Hungarian National Bank, it was disclosed yesterday. The financial alliance has taken unions by surprise, as the Hungarian International Bank is wholly controlled by Hungary's Communist Government. Mr Shah is widely seen as an anti-union employer, since he defeated the National Graphical Association in late 1983 in a dispute at his Warrington works over the closed shops. Mr Shah said he had approached several British banks and financers, but they were all 'scared of the political implications'. ... Mr Tim Newling, managing director of Hungarian International, said his Hungarian directors had been consulted and had agreed that Mr Shah's plan 'stacked up very well'.[316]

What was particularly disturbing about such 'purely financial' deals was not merely that a 'socialist country' should get involved at all in the business of someone who is 'widely seen as an anti-union employer', but that it should acquire — of necessity, on account of the 'risk capital' which it had put at the disposal of its curious business partner — a stake in the success of an enterprise that could not help being intensely political (and no one could have any doubt on which side of the political divide) even if Mr Shah wanted his national newspaper to stand above politics.

This is why I have argued at the time that the already visible trends and measures were more than sufficient to illustrate that the unfolding developments were quite serious as regards their weight and impact on the 'societies of actual socialism' even as things stood then, not to mention their *implications for the future.*

IN view of all these transformations, we may well find Engels' optimistic assertion — according to which 'The capitalist has no further social function than that of pocketing dividends, tearing off coupons, and gambling on the Stock Exchange, where the different capitalists despoil one another of their capital' — somewhat premature and utopian.[317] The problem here is not simply that certain expectations did not materialize. Much more important is the positive aspect of this issue: namely that the intervening developments created some objective conditions and functions which must be realistically tackled, by devising a suitable alternative to the existing — significantly rationalized — mode of functioning of present-day capital. For a one-sided negation carries with it the danger of merely losing the instruments of capital's undoubtedly limited, but within its limits most effective rationality, leaving us badly entangled in chronic economic difficulties of which the history of the 'societies of actual socialism' provides many an unhappy example.

12.4 Contradictions of an age of transition

THE negative consequences of the same period of development for socialist forces may be summarized much more briefly, since the obverse side of capital's success — given in the form of fairly obvious negative implications on each point mentioned above — need not be spelled out here. Nevertheless, it is necessary to underline some particularly important problems.

In the first place, the split of the socialist movement into radical and reformist branches, as well as its fragmentation into national particularisms, against the original expectations of a growing international cohesion, remain a major challenge for the future. Similarly, the institutionally entrenched opposition between (largely ineffective) theory and self-sustaining (authoritarian-bureaucratic) political practice shows very few signs of changing, and thus remains an equally serious problem for socialists today.

On another plane, the immediate pressures on the Western working class movement — for securing and safeguarding employment; for improving or even just maintaining the attained standard of living; etc. — make it objectively interested and involved in the continued success of 'organized capitalism', with the concomitant temptations of complicity in sustaining even the 'military-industrial complex', with the frightening 'justification' that the latter is a major provider of jobs. An equally striking complicity is manifest in the 'metropolitan' working class' participation, as a beneficiary, in the continued exploitation of the so-called 'third world': an integral, but structurally dependent and exploited part of the one and only real world.

As to the 'societies of actual socialism', the process of so-called *'socialist accumulation'* initiated in 1917 had turned sour. Which means that for a long time to come we must continue to suffer the consequences of the 'brute historical fact' that not the 'dominant peoples all at once and simultaneously' initiated the socialist revolution, but a tragically underdeveloped country, under the strain of massive internal and external pressures, sacrificing too much — a great deal of its own socialist forces — in the course of defending itself while trying to accomplish a professed aim (the production of the 'material presuppositions and preconditions') which Marx simply — and from the epochal frame of reference of the overall theory justifiably — took for granted. Furthermore, under the impact of the arms race, with its astronomical costs, every partial socialist achievement was constantly endangered and potentially nullified. The issue was not only the staggering, and ill affordable, size of the material resources themselves which were locked up in arms production, instead of developing and satisfying the needs of Marx's 'rich social individual'. It was equally a question of the overall orientation of the economy, directly or indirectly linked to the requirements of 'high technology' arms production, in competition with Western capital; not to mention the type of social control suitable to keep in tune with such economy, oriented towards the maximal politically enforced extraction of surplus-labour.

It transpires, thus, that the 'cunning of Reason' today is, at best, a simpleton, and the 'cunning of history' is bent on terminating history itself.

BUT even so, it would be quite wrong to take them too seriously and draw unduly pessimistic conclusions. For while time is not necessarily on our side, the objective limitations of capital *as such* should not be understated.

This takes us back to the all-important question of the *ultimate* limits which *remain in operation* at all times. This cannot be stressed enough, precisely because they often slip out of sight. Yet, they remain operative even when a successful readjustment and extension of the earlier limits creates an economically and politically stable and for the 'old order' favourable situation for a relatively long period of time. They operate underneath all adjustments by circumscribing the range of feasible options, thus emphatically preventing the successful reversal of the *fundamental* trends themselves. In this sense, but in this sense only, there is a real *irreversibility of historical time*, even if its particular moments must be treated with utmost care and sober evaluation.

On a historically relevant scale, an *age of transition* is initiated the moment the dominant forces of the old order are *forced* by an *acute crisis* to adopt remedies which would be totally unacceptable to them without that crisis, introducing, thus, an *alien body* into the original structure, with *ultimately* destructive consequences, no matter how beneficial the immediate results.

To be sure, any self-respecting oyster would strongly object to the injection of sand — a nasty irritant — into its flesh. Yet, once the grain of sand is there, the oyster succeeds not only to survive for a considerable time, but even to produce a shiny pearl, which may appear to have solved the problems by multiplying perhaps a millionfold the oyster's value. As we know, however, none of the real problems of our world are solved by pearl-production. Nor is it the case, as reformists think, that the introduction of sand into capital's flesh, and the ensuing multiplication of its value, turns capital-oyster into a transitional formation happily on its way to the Social-Democratic paradise and its strange idealization by the propounders of 'market socialism'. For an oyster is an oyster — and eventually a dead oyster — no matter how inflated its exchange value.

The *age of transition* to socialism — our inescapable *historical* predicament — does not mean in the slightest that the various countries involved in such transformation all actually exhibit a determinate degree of approximation to the socialist goal on a linear scale. It does not even mean that we are bound for sure to get there, since the frightening and ever-increasing accumulation of the powers of destruction — thanks to the suicidal inclinations of the 'cunning of history' — may precipitate us into Rosa Luxemburg's 'barbarism', rather than guaranteeing the socialist outcome.

NEVERTHELESS, we may speak of the age of transition to socialism meaningfully in that:

Capital is presented with a dangerously *narrowing* range of feasible alternatives to the full activation of its structural crisis. Thus:

— the *shrinking* size of the world *directly* controlled by private capital in the twentieth century;

— the sheer magnitude of the *resources* required for displacing its contradictions, within the constraints of an ominously *diminishing return;*[318]

— the slowly emerging *saturation* of the global framework of profitable capital production;[319]

— the chronic difficulties encountered in and generated by raising the necessary revenue for keeping in existence the *parasitic* sections of capital, at the expense of its *productive* parts;

— the noticeable weakening of the *ideological power* of manipulative institutions (which were originally established under the circumstances of postwar economic expansion and its twin brother: the 'welfare state') at times of recession and growing 'structural unemployment'.

Characteristically, this is the only context in which the apologists of capital have, at long last, taken notice of the existence of *structural* conditions and determinations. But, of course, the admission that unemployment is now 'structural' is stated — with a logic worthy of capital's 'analytical' wisdom — not so as to call for a change in the *structure* (the social order) in which such consequences are unavoidable. On the contrary, in order to *justify* and maintain the selfsame structure intact, at whatever human cost, accepting 'structural unemployment' as the *permanent* feature of the one and only conceivable structure.

We can see here, again, the 'eternalization of bourgeois conditions', even in the face of a dramatically obvious and highly disturbing historical development. Yesterday the oracle said: *'Full Employment in a Free Society'* (see the Lib-Labouring Lord Beveridge's book of the same title); today it talks about 'structural unemployment'. But, of course, nothing has really changed, and especially: nothing ought to change. For unemployment is 'structural', and therefore it is here to stay to the end of time.

All these trends indicate a very real movement *towards* the ultimate limits of capital as such, and hence they show the *historical* actuality of a painful but inescapable process of transition.

CHAPTER THIRTEEN

HOW COULD THE STATE WITHER AWAY?

THE history of postcapitalist states, in sharp contrast to original expectations, confronts us with some weighty problems that may be summed up as follows:

(1) To acknowledge that there has been no sign of the state's 'withering away', would amount to no more than an evasive understatement. For actual developments not merely did not live up to expectations; they moved in the opposite direction, massively strengthening the power of the political over against the social body. The anticipated short historical phase of proletarian dictatorship, to be followed by a sustained process of 'withering away' — to the point of the retention of purely administrative functions — did not materialise. Instead, the state assumed control over all facets of social life, and the dictatorship of the proletariat was promoted to the status of being the permanent political form of the *entire* historical period of transition.

(2) To add insult to injury, the capitalist state itself — again, contrary to expectations — did not become an extreme authoritarian state: fascist type state formations remained episodic in the history of capitalism up to the present time. While no one should underestimate the danger of right-wing dictatorial solutions at times of acute crises, such solutions, nevertheless, seem to be very much at odds with the objective requirements of the capitalist process of production and circulation at its relatively undisturbed phases of development. The long established 'civil society', articulated around the structurally entrenched economic power of competing private capitals, both secures and safeguards the capitalist domination of the political state and, through it, of society as a whole. Any reversal of such power relations in favour of the authoritarian political state at times of acute crises is a double-edged sword indeed, threatening the established order as much as defending it: by disrupting the *normal* mechanism of structural domination and by bringing into play the frontal collision of antagonistic forces, in place of the overpowering inertia of the formerly accepted state of affairs. The customarily prevailing relationship between 'civil society' and the political state greatly enhances the ideological power of mystification of the bourgeois political state — by advertising itself as the insuperable model of non-interference and individual freedom — and, through its very inertia, it constitutes a paralysing material obstacle to any strategy of transition. For it imposes on its socialist adversary the imperative of promising 'freedom from state domination' in the near future, while, in fact, the sustained socialist power of the postcapitalist state (the modalities of which are very far from being even touched upon, let alone fully exhausted, by summary references to the 'proletarian dictatorship') over against the inherited, capitalistically structured 'civil society', is a condition *sine qua non* of the necessary structural change.

(3) To state that 'acting within political forms belongs to the old society' (in

view of the continued existence of a separate political sphere) is as true in its ultimate perspectives as it is inadequate as far as the problems of transition are concerned. Since the *act* of liberation cannot be separated from the *process* of liberation, and since the political state, while being conditioned, is simultaneously also a vital conditioning factor, the socialist emancipation of society from the oppressive rule of the political sphere necessarily presupposes the radical transformation of politics as such. This means that the advocated transcendence of the state can only be accomplished through the heavily conditioning instrumentality of the state itself. If this is the case, as undoubtedly it happens to be, how can we escape from the vicious circle? For even if we all agree that the political state in its essential characteristics belongs to the old society, the question remains: how to turn the inherited state into a genuinely *transitional* formation from the all-embracing and necessarily *self-perpetuating* structure which it has become in the course of capitalist development. Without a realistic identification of the necessary theoretical mediations and the corresponding social/material forces involved in such transitional change, the programme of abolishing politics through a socialist reorientation of politics is bound to sound problematical.

(4) To question the validity of Marxism on account of its conception of the state is a matter of far-reaching implications. Indeed, it is in no way comparable to the tendentiously belaboured but peripheral disputes over the fact that socialist revolutions erupted in underdeveloped rather than in advanced capitalist countries. As I have argued in the last chapter,[320] Marx's idea of 'uneven development' could in fact account for discrepancies in that respect. And in any case his theory was primarily concerned with the plain necessity of socialist revolutions, and not with the inevitably changing circumstances and modalities of their practical unfolding. By contrast, should the Marxian theory of the state be invalidated, that would render Marxism as a whole thoroughly untenable, in view of the centrality of its belief in the dialectical reciprocity between base and superstructure, the material foundations of society and its political sphere. (To be sure, it is precisely in this sense that the so-called 'crisis of Marxism' has been repeatedly interpreted in the recent past, jumping in panicky haste to aprioristic conclusions from the mere assertion of that crisis, instead of tackling its constituents from a positive perspective.) What makes the matter particularly acute is that it has *direct* political implications for the strategies of all existing socialist movements, in the East and West alike, at this critical time in history. In this sense, it is not simply the heuristic value of a social theory that is called into question but something incomparably more tangible and immediate. This is why a searching examination of the Marxian theory of the state, in the light of postrevolutionary developments, is unavoidable today.

13.1 *The limits of political action*

MARX'S earliest conception of politics was articulated in the form of a threefold negation, aimed at putting in perspective the potentialities and limitations of the political mode of action. Understandably, given the circumstances of what he called the 'German misery', the accent had to be put on the severity of these limitations. Whatever changes appeared in this respect in Marx's later writings, the prevalently negative definition of politics remained a central theme of his work to the very end of his life.

Marx's negation was directed at three clearly identifiable objects, and the conclusions derived from their assessment fused into an imperative[321] to identify the constituents of a radically different mode of social action.

- The first object of his criticism was German underdevelopment itself, and the hopelessness of political action under the constraints of a semi-feudal capitalism: a world situated in terms of the French political calendar well before 1789, as he put it.
- His second object of negation was Hegel's political philosophy, which elevated to the level of a claimed 'science' the illusions of producing the much needed change, while remaining in fact within the confines of the anachronistic political mould.
- And, finally, the third prong of Marx's attack was directed at the limitations of even the most advanced French politics. For while the latter was 'contemporary' to the present in strictly political terms, it was, nevertheless, hopelessly inadequate as far as the imperative of a radical social transformation was concerned, under the conditions of the growing social antagonism.

Thus, the inner logic of Marx's critical assessment of *German* political limitations pushed him from the first critical stance of simply rejecting the local political constraints towards a radical questioning of the nature and inherent limits of *political action as such*. This is why there had to be a break with his first political comrades at a very early stage in his development. For the latter the critique of Hegel could only mean rendering German politics a little more 'contemporary to the present'. By contrast, for Marx it was just a preamble to advocating a very different mode of social action: one that started from the premiss of consciously rejecting the crippling determination of social action by the necessary one-dimensionality of *all politics* 'properly so called'. The task of understanding the 'anatomy of bourgeois society' — through a critical evaluation of political economy — was the next logical step, in that the positive counterpart to his threefold negation had to be situated on a material plane, if it was to avoid the illusions of not only Hegel and his epigones but also of the contemporary French socialists who tried to impose their politically constrained view on the orientation of the emerging working class movement.

Talking about the political bias in the outlook of his socialist comrades, Marx complained that 'Even radical and revolutionary politicians seek the root of the evil not in the *essential nature* of the state, but in a definite *state form,* which they wish to replace by a different state form. From the political point of view the *state* and the *system of society* are not two different things. *The state is the system of society*.'[322] For Marx it was imperative to get *outside* the 'political point of view' in order to be truly critical of the state. He insisted that

> The mightier the state, and the more *political* therefore a country is, the less is it
> inclined to grasp the *general* principle of *social* maladies and to seek their basis in the
> principle of the state, hence in the *present structure* of society, the active, conscious and
> official expression of which is the state. The political mind is a political mind precisely
> because it thinks *within* the framework of politics. The keener and more lively it is,
> the more *incapable* is it of understanding *social* ills. The classic period of political

intellect is the French Revolution. Far from seeing the source of social shortcomings in the principle of the state, the heroes of the French Revolution instead saw in social defects the source of political evils. Thus Robespierre saw in great poverty and great wealth only obstacles to pure democracy. Therefore he wished to establish a universal Spartan frugality. The principle of politics is the *will*. The more one-sided and, therefore, the more perfected the political mind is, the more does it believe in the omnipotence of the *will*, the more is it blind to the natural and spiritual limits of the will, and the more incapable is it therefore of discovering the source of social ills.[323]

Politics and *voluntarism* are, thus, wedded together and the unreality of wishful political remedies emanates from the inherent 'substitutionism' of politics as such: its necessary *modus operandi* which consists in substituting itself for the *social* and thus denying to the latter any remedial action that cannot be contained within its own — self-oriented and self-perpetuating — framework. To oppose within the confines of politics Stalin's 'substitutionism', advocating the replacement of the 'bureaucrat' by the 'enlightened political leader', is, therefore, another form of political voluntarism, however well-intentioned. For the question is, according to Marx, which one is the truly comprehensive category: the political or the social. Politics, the way it is constituted, cannot help substituting its own partiality for the authentic universality of society, superimposing its own interests on those of the social individuals, and appropriating to itself the power to arbitrate over conflicting partial interests in the name of its own usurped universality.

Non-substitutionist politics, therefore, would imply a whole range of social mediations — and, of course, the existence of the corresponding social/material forces — which represent an acute problem for us but were absent from the historical horizon within which Marx was situated all his life. Hence the retention of the prevalently negative definition of politics even in his latest writings, notwithstanding his sober appreciation of a necessary involvement in politics (as opposed to 'abstentionism'[324] and 'indifference to politics'[325]), be that for the purposes of negation or for acting, even after the conquest of power, 'within the old forms'.

The way Marx perceived it, the contradiction between the social and the political was irreconcilable. Given the antagonistic character of the social base itself, perpetuated as such by the political framework, the state was irredeemable and therefore had to go. For

> confronted by the consequences which arise from the unsocial nature of this civil life, this private ownership, this trade, this industry, this mutual plundering of the various circles of citizens, confronted by all these consequences, impotence is the law of nature of the administration. For this fragmentation, this baseness, this slavery of civil society is the natural foundation on which the modern state rests, just as the civil society of slavery was the natural foundation on which the ancient state rested. The *existence of the state* and the existence of *slavery* are inseparable. ... If the modern state wanted to abolish private life, it would have to *abolish itself*, for it exists only in the contradiction to private life.[326]

Thus, stressing the need to abolish the state in order to resolve the contradictions of civil society was coupled with the realisation that the state — and politics in general, as we know it — are by their very nature incapable of abolishing themselves.

The imperative to abolish the state was emphatically put into relief, but not in voluntaristic terms. On the contrary, Marx never missed an opportunity for reiterating the utter futility of voluntaristic efforts. It was clear to him from the very beginning, that no material factor can be 'abolished' by *decree*, let alone the state itself: one of the most overpowering of all material factors. Talking about the French Revolution's attempt to abolish pauperism by decree, he focussed on the inescapable limitations of politics as such:

> What was the result of the Convention's decree? That one more decree came into the world, and one year later starving women besieged the Convention. Yet the Convention represented the maximum of political energy, political power and political understanding.[327]

If the state was as powerless as this in the face of tangible social problems the claimed mastery of which constituted its tenuous legitimation, how could it conceivably confront the full burden of its own contradictions, for the sake of abolishing itself in the interest of general social advancement? And if the state itself was incapable of undertaking such task, what force of society could do so? These were the questions that had to be answered in that they were put on the historical agenda by the growing socialist movement itself. The widely differing answers which we can find in the annals of the epoch speak of qualitatively different strategies of men engaged in the struggle.

13.2 *Main tenets of Marx's political theory*

AS far as Marx himself was concerned, the answer was forcefully and clearly formulated in the early 1840s, with repeated warnings against voluntarism and adventurism as 'Leitmotifs' of his political vision. The main points of Marx's answer may be summed up as follows:

- (1) The state (and politics in general, as a separate domain) must be *transcended* through a radical transformation of the whole of society, but it cannot be *abolished* by decree or, for that matter, even by a whole series of political/administrative measures;
- (2) The coming revolution cannot be simply a political one; it must be a *social* revolution if it is not to be trapped within the confines of the self-perpetuating system of social/economic exploitation;
- (3) Social revolutions aim at removing the contradiction between partiality and universality which political revolutions of the past always reproduced, subjecting society as a whole to the rule of political partiality,[328] in the interest of the dominant sections of 'civil society';
- (4) The social agency of emancipation is the proletariat because it is forced by the maturation of the capital system's antagonistic contradictions to overthrow the prevailing social order, while it is incapable of superimposing itself as a new dominant partiality — a ruling class kept by the work of others — on the whole of society;
- (5) Political and social/economic struggles constitute a dialectical unity and consequently the neglect of the social/economic dimension deprives the political of its reality;
- (6) The absence of objective conditions for implementing socialist measures,

ironically, can only result in carrying out the adversary's policies in the event of a premature conquest of power;[329]

- (7) The successful social revolution cannot be local or national — only political revolutions can confine themselves to a limited setting, in keeping with their own partiality — it must be *global/universal*; which implies the necessary transcendence of the state on a *global* scale.

CLEARLY, the elements of this theory constitute an organic whole from which they cannot be separated one by one. For each of them refers to all the others, and they acquire their full meaning through their reciprocal interconnections. This is fairly obvious in considering 1, 2, 5, 6 and 7 together, since they are all concerned with the inescapable objective conditions of social transformation, conceived as a complex social totality with an inner dynamism of its own. Numbers 3 and 4 seem to be the 'odd ones out', in that advocating the resolution of the contradiction between partiality and universality appears to be an unwarranted intrusion of Hegelian Logic into Marx's system, and number 4 looks like an imperatival translation of this abstract logical category into a pseudo-empirical entity.

To be sure, Marx's adversaries interpreted his theory precisely in such terms, denying objective reality to the concept of the proletariat and 'invalidating' his theory as a whole on account of its 'unverifiability', etc. In truth, however, Marx's procedure is perfectly legitimate, even if the connection with Hegel cannot — nor should it — be denied. For the similarity between Hegel's 'universal class' (the idealised bureaucracy) and Marx's proletariat is superficial, since their discourses belong to quite different universes. Hegel wants to preserve (indeed glorify) the state and invents the bureaucratic 'universal' class as a quintessential *Sollen* (an 'ought to be'). The latter fulfils its function of reconciling the contradictions of warring interests by preserving them, thus safeguarding and securing the permanence of the established structure of society in its antagonistic form. Marx, in complete contrast, is concerned with the *transcendence* of the state and politics as such, and he identifies the proletariat's paradoxical universality (a not-yet-given, still-to-be-realised universality) as a necessarily *self-abolishing partiality*.

Thus, while Hegel's fictitious 'universal class' is a *classless* entity (and as such a contradiction in terms), Marx's proletariat is thoroughly class-like (and in that sense inevitably partial) and real. In its 'historic task' it has an objectively grounded universalizing *function* to fulfil. At the same time, its partiality is also unique, since it cannot be turned into an *exclusive ruling* condition of society. Consequently, in order to 'rule', the proletariat must generalise its own condition of existence: namely the inability to rule as a partiality, at the expense of other social groups and classes. (Obviously, this is in total contrast to the bourgeoisie and other ruling classes of past history which ruled precisely by excluding and subjugating other classes.) It is in this sense that 'classlessness' (the establishment of a classless society) is linked to the peculiar class rule of 'self-abolishing partiality' whose measure of success is the generalisation of a mode of existence totally incompatible with (exclusively self-favouring) class rule.

The rule of partiality over society as a whole is always sustained by politics as the necessary complementary to the iniquitousness of the established material power relations. This is why the emancipation of society from the rule of partiality is impossible without radically transcending politics and the state. In other words, so long as the proletariat acts *politically*, it remains in the orbit of partiality (with serious implications as to how the proletariat itself is necessarily affected by the rule of its own partiality), whereas the realisation of the *social* revolution advocated by Marx involves many other factors too, well beyond the political level, together with the maturation of the relevant objective conditions.

Naturally, the proletariat, so long as it exists, is situated at a greater or lesser distance from the realisation of its 'historic task' at any particular point in history, and the assessment of the class's changing sociological composition and relationship to other forces, together with its relative achievements and failures, etc., requires detailed investigations in accordance with the specific circumstances. In the present context the point is simply to stress the unbreakable links between points 3 and 4 above and the rest of Marx's political theory. For, on the one hand, it is precisely his category of objectively grounded *universality* which puts politics in perspective: by getting 'outside' politics (which means beyond the constraints imposed by 'thinking within the framework of politics', as he puts it). This must be done in order to be able to *negate* the chronic partiality of politics; and to do this not from an abstract metaphysico-logical level, but from the basis of the one and only non-fictitious (not *Sollen*-like) universality, i.e., the fundamental *metabolism* of society, the *social*. (Such grasp of universality is both historical and transhistorical, in that it highlights the necessarily changing conditions of the social metabolism while also indicating the ultimate limits beyond which even the most powerful means and mode of this metabolism — capital, for instance — lose their vitality and historical justification.) On the other hand, the *proletariat* as an actual social/economic reality was a leading actor on the historical stage well before Marx. It demonstrated its ability to gravitate towards a 'revolution within the revolution' already in the immediate aftermath of 1789, attempting to acquire an independent role, in its own interest, in contrast to its subordinate position up until then within the Third Estate. In this way, negating the newly-won political framework the moment it came into being, as Pierre Barnave shrewdly observed from the standpoint of the emerging bourgeois order as far back as 1792. Thus, to deny the actuality of the proletariat is a curious twentieth century pastime.

• The fact that Marx theoretically linked the proletariat to the necessity of the *social* revolution and to the condition of universality, was not a dubious functional requirement of a system still dependent on Hegel, but a profound insight into the world-historically novel character of the social antagonism between capital and labour. The progression from local tribal interchanges to world history, from action confined to an extremely limited sphere to one reverberating across the world, is not a matter of conceptual transformations but concerns the actual development and reciprocal integration of increasingly more comprehensive and complex structures. This is why solutions of a partial kind — which are perfectly feasible, indeed unavoidable, at an earlier stage — must be displaced by more and more all-embracing ones in the course of world-historical development, with an ultimate tendency towards 'hegemonic' solutions and towards universality. Marx's characterisation of the proletariat, thus, reflects and articulates the highest intensity of hegemonic confrontations and the historical impossibility of partial solutions at a determinate stage of global/capitalistic developments.

- Significantly, in its own way Hegel's theory incorporated this problematic, even if in a mystified form. He fully acknowledged the imperative of a 'universal' solution which should supersede the collisions of warring partialities. However, thanks to the 'standpoint of political economy' (i.e. the standpoint of capital) which Hegel shared with his great English and Scottish ancestors, he was forced to transubstantiate the perceived elements of an inherently contradictory reality into the pseudo-empirical, 'universalistically' reconciliatory fantasy-figure of the selfless state-bureaucrat. But even such mystifications cannot obliterate Hegel's achievements on account of which he stands at a qualitatively higher level of political theorising than anyone else before Marx, including Rousseau. Those who tried to censure (and heavily censor) Marx for his alleged 'Hegelianism' while glorifying Rousseau, forgot that in comparison to the paradigm *categorical imperative* of the latter's 'General Will', Hegel's attempt to embody his category of political universality in an actual social force, despite its class biassed subjectivism, is objectivity itself. However half-hearted and contradictory this Hegelian attempt at sociologically circumscribing the political will was, it was a sign of the times and as such it reflected an objective historical challenge, representing a giant step in the right direction.

- Thus — returing to the main points of Marx's political theory taken as a whole — it becomes clear that none of the other points make sense if the social agency of revolutionary transformation is abandoned. For what could it mean to say that the state can only be 'transcended' but not 'abolished' (whether in a limited national setting or on a global scale) if there is no social force willing and able to undertake the task? Similarly with all the other points. The distinction between social and political revolution has a content only if some existing social agency or agencies can *actually* make sense of it, through the precise aims and strategies of their action and through the new social order arising from that action. In the same way, it is impossible to predicate an all-embracing close reciprocity between politics and economics before a fairly advanced stage of social/economic development; which in its turn presupposes that the major forces of society be actually engaged in an inextricably political as much as economic confrontation with one another. Likewise, revolutions are 'premature' or 'belated' only in terms of the specific dynamics of the agencies in question, defined with reference to both the relevant range of objective circumstances and the greatly varying requirements of conscious action. Peasant revolutions of the past, for instance, were defined as 'premature' not so much on account of some voluntaristic engagement in violent confrontations but, rather, in view of a hauntingly *chronic* insufficiency of this agency with respect to its own aims: some sort of a 'historical conspiracy of circumstances' that imposed on the peasant masses the burden of fighting for someone else's causes — and even winning them on occasions — while suffering heavy defeats for themselves. On the other hand, several colonial revolutions of the postwar years seem to be 'belated' even when they are 'premature', and defeated even when they appear to be successful. For under the historically constituted and still prevailing relation of forces the 'underdeveloped' revolutionary agency is defined by its massive dependency on the inherited structures of 'neocolonialism' and 'neocapital-ism'.

• Naturally, the interconnections we have just seen are no less in evidence the other way round. This is because the 'proletariat' as a vital concept of Marx's theory derives its meaning precisely from those objective conditions and determinations that are articulated, on the basis of the dynamic social reality which they reflect, in the points briefly surveyed a few pages earlier. Without the latter, references to the proletariat amount to no more than empty 'catchwords' so scornfully condemned by Marx in his polemics against Schapper and others, as we have seen in note 329 above.

Thus, the transcendence of the state and its initiator, the proletariat (or, to use a theoretically more precise term, labour: the structural antagonist of capital), inseparably belong together and constitute the pivotal point of Marx's political theory. There is no romanticism involved in stressing their importance in this way: just a note of caution. For all those who want to expurgate them from Marx's conceptual framework should realise how much more — in fact nearly everything else — would have to be thrown with them overboard.

13.3 Social revolution and political voluntarism

THERE can be no question about the fundamental validity of Marx's approach to politics insofar as he is concerned with the *absolute parameters* — the *ultimate* criteria — which define and strictly circumscribe its role among the totality of human activities. The difficulties lie elsewhere, as we shall see later on. The core of Marx's political conception — the assertion that politics (with particular gravity in its version as tied to the modern state) *usurps* the powers of overall social decision-making for which it *substitutes* itself — is and remains completely unassailable. For abandoning the idea that socialist politics must concern itself in all its steps, even the minor ones, with the task of *restituting* to the social body the usurped powers, inevitably deprives the politics of transition of its strategic orientation and legitimation, thus necessarily *reproducing* in another form the inherited 'bureaucratic substitutionism', rather than creating it anew on the basis of some mythical 'personality cult'. Consequently, socialist politics either follows the path set to it by Marx — *from substitutionism to restitution* — or ceases to be socialist politics and, instead of 'abolishing itself' in due course, turns into authoritarian self-perpetuation.

To be sure, there are many unanswered questions and dilemmas that must be examined in their proper context. What will be particularly important to assess is this: to what extent and in which way the changing historical conditions and acute pressures of the unfolding social antagonism may significantly modify the Marxist political strategy without destroying its core. But before we can turn to these questions it is necessary to have a closer look at Marx's relationship to his political adversaries inasmuch as it affected the formulation of his theory of the state.

In sharp contrast to Hegel's 'false positivism', Marx never ceased to stress the essentially *negative* character of politics. As such, politics was suitable to fulfil the *destructive* functions of social transformation — like the 'abolition of wage slavery', the expropriation of the capitalists, the dissolution of bourgeois parliaments, etc.: all achievable by decree — but not the *positive* ones which must arise from the restructuring of the social metabolism itself. Because of its inherent *partiality* (another way of saying 'negative'), politics could only be a most inadequate *means* to serve the desired end. At the same time, the measure of approaching the latter was to be precisely the degree to which such constraining means could be discarded altogether, so that ultimately the social individuals should be able to function in a direct relationship with one another, without the mystifying and restrictive intermediary of the 'cloak of politics'.

Since the negating subjectivity of the will that runs riot in politics can say 'yes' only by saying 'no', the usefulness of politics as such was considered extremely limited even after the conquest of power. It is not surprising, therefore, that the *Critique of the Gotha Programme* expected of it in the society of transition no more than a negative intervention, asking it to act 'unequally' on the side of the weak, so that the worst inequalities inherited from the past should be faster removed. For while socialism required the greatest *positive* transformation in history, the negative modality of politics ('class *against* class', etc.,) made it, on its own, completely inadequate to the task.

Marx conceptualised the way of overcoming the problematical relationship between politics and society by consciously superimposing on the political revolution its hidden social dimension. He insisted that

> whereas a social revolution with a political soul is a paraphrase or nonsense, a political revolution with a *social* soul has a rational meaning. Revolution in general — the *overthrow* of the existing power and *dissolution* of the old relationship — is a *political act*. But socialism cannot be realised without revolution. It needs this political act insofar as it needs *destruction and dissolution*. But where its *organising* activity begins, where its *proper object*, its soul comes to the fore, there socialism throws off the *political cloak*.[330]

From such vantage point — in his critical assessments of Proudhon and Stirner, Schapper and Willich, Lassalle and Liebknecht, Bakunin and his associates, as well as the authors of the Gotha Programme — Marx succeeded in laying down the broad outlines of a strategy free from voluntaristic constituents.

For Marx the necessity of the revolution was neither an economic determinism (of which he is frequently accused), nor a sovereign act of the arbitrary political will (of which he is, curiously, also accused). Those who judge him in these terms only prove that they themselves are unable to think without the prefabricated schematism of such false alternatives. For Marx the social revolution stood for a number of determinate functions. It had to arise on the ground of some objective conditions (which constituted its necessary prerequisites) so as to go far beyond them in the course of its development, radically transforming both the circumstances and the people involved in the action. It was precisely this dialectical objectivity and complexity of the social revolution that disappeared through its Procustean reduction into the one-dimensional political act — whether we think of the pre-revolutionary theories of anarchist voluntarism or of the equally arbitrary, and far more damaging, reductionist and substitutionist political practices of postrevolutionary 'bureaucratism'.

The first question, therefore, concerned the grasp of the nature of both the social revolution and its agency. Bakunin conceived the latter as a 'revolutionary

General Staff composed of devoted, energetic and intelligent individuals... The number of these individuals should not be too large. For the international organisation throughout Europe *one hundred* serious and firmly united revolutionaries would be sufficient.'[331] To this self-myth of the 'revolutionary General Staff' corresponded, naturally enough, a mythical conception of the revolution itself as well as of its masses. The revolution was said to be 'slowly maturing in the *instinctive conscience* of the popular masses' (not in the objective conditions of the social reality), and the role of the 'instinctive masses' was confined to that of being the 'army of the revolution' (the 'cannon fodder', as Marx rightly exclaimed).[332]

Marx's condemnation of such views could not have been more scathing. Speaking of Bakunin he wrote:

He understands absolutely nothing of social revolution, only its political rhetoric; its *economic* conditions simply do not exist for him. ... Willpower, not economic conditions, is the basis of his social revolution.[333]

Marx called Bakunin's views 'schoolboyish rot' and reiterated that 'a radical social revolution is bound up with definite historical conditions of economic development; these are its premisses. It is only possible, therefore, where alongside capitalist production the industrial proletariat accounts for at least a significant portion of the mass of the people. And for it to have any chance of victory, it must be able *mutatis mutandis* at the very least to do as much directly for the peasants as the French bourgeoisie did in its revolution for the French peasantry at that time. A fine idea to imagine that the rule of the workers implies the oppression of rural labour!'[334]

THE multidimensional, objective determinations of the social revolution which foreshadowed an extended time-scale ('15, 20, 50 years', as Marx put it against Schapper's romantic fantasies) also implied the necessity of renewed upheavals and the unworkability of accommodations. For

- (1) Given the historically attained stage of social antagonism between capital and labour, there was no possibility of 'partial emancipation' and 'gradual liberation';[335]
- (2) The ruling class had too much to lose; it would not yield on its own accord; it must be overthrown in a revolution;[336]
- (3) The revolution cannot succeed on a narrow basis; it requires 'the production on a *mass scale*' of a revolutionary consciousness, so that the revolutionary class as a whole can 'succeed in ridding itself of all the muck of ages and become fitted to found society anew' — which is possible only through the *practice* of actual revolutionary transformations;[337]
- (4) Learning how to master the difficulties, burden, pressures and contradictions of the exercise of power requires active involvement in the revolutionary process itself, on a painfully long time-scale.[338]

As we can see, social necessity in the Marxian conception is not some mechanical determinism. Quite the contrary: it is a dialectical grasp of what needs and can be accomplished on the ground of the objectively unfolding tendencies of reality. As such, it is inseparable from a consciousness that adjusts itself to the changing conditions and sobering lessons of the world which it tries to transform. The varieties of anarchistic voluntarism, from Proudhon to Bakunin,[339] stand diametrically opposed to such view, since they fail to understand the weighty economic dimension of the task. They substitute their subjective images of agitational fervour for the objective conditions even when they talk about 'the force of circumstances'. Marx, on the other hand, articulates his conception in terms of a completely different time-scale, envisaging for a long time to come the role of *opposition* for the working class movement before the question of *government* would ultimately arise.[340]

The inherent limits of the political forms (even the most advanced ones), in contrast to the fundamental metabolic dimension of the social revolution, are summed up in a key passage of Marx's analysis of the Paris Commune. It reads as follows:

> As the state machinery and parliamentarism are not the *real life* of the ruling classes, but only the organised general organs of their dominion, the political guarantees and forms of expression of the old order of things, so the Commune is not the *social movement* of the working class and therefore of a general regeneration of mankind, but the organised *means* of action. The Commune does not do away with the class struggles, through which the working classes strive to the abolition of all classes and, therefore, of class rule (because it does not represent a peculiar interest. It represents the liberation of 'labour', that is the *fundamental and natural* condition of individual and social life which only by *usurpation*, fraud and artificial contrivances can be shifted from the few upon the many), but it affords the rational medium in which that class struggle can run through its different phases in the most rational and humane way.... The working class know that they have to pass through different phases of class struggle. They know that the *superseding* of the *economic* conditions of the slavery of labour by the conditions of free and associated labour can only be the *progressive work of time*, ...that they require not only a change of *distribution*, but a new organisation of *production*, or rather the delivery (setting free) of the social forms of production in present organised labour, (engendered by present industry), of the trammels of slavery, of their present class character, and their harmonious national and *international* coordination. They know that this work of *regeneration* will be again and again relented and impeded by the resistance of vested interests and class egotism. They know that the present 'spontaneous action of the natural laws of capital and landed property' can only be *superseded* by 'the *spontaneous* action of the laws of the social economy of free and associated labour' by a *long process* of development of new conditions.[341]

Thus the real task, with all its immense complications, only *begins* where political subjectivism imagines to have solved it for good.

The issue at stake is the creation of the 'new conditions': the transcendence/ supersession of the 'spontaneous action of capital's natural law' — i.e., not its simple political 'abolition', which is inconceivable — and the long-drawn-out development of a *new spontaneity*, 'the spontaneous action of the laws of the social economy' as the radically restructured mode of the new social metabolism. The expressions 'general regeneration of mankind' and 'work of regeneration', linked to a repeated emphasis on the necessity of 'different phases' of development through a 'progressive work of time', clearly indicate that the power of politics must be very limited in this respect. Hence, to expect the generation of the new spontaneity (i.e., a form of social intercourse and mode of life-activity that becomes 'second nature' to the associated producers) by some political decree, be it the most enlightened one, would be a contradiction in terms. For while *distribution* is immediately amenable to change by decree (and even that only to an extent strictly limited by the socially attained level of productivity), the material conditions of *production* as well as its hierarchical organisation remain exactly the same the day after the political revolution as before. This is what makes it practically impossible for the workers to become the anticipated 'free associated producers' for a long time to come even under the politically most favourable circumstances.

Furthermore, the qualification that the socialist 'regeneration of mankind' necessarily calls for a 'harmonious national and international coordination' as well, puts politics in perspective again. For it is in the nature of political voluntarism to misrepresent also this dimension of the problem. It treats the failure of realising the Marxian requirement as a simple political deficiency for which its own policies cannot be held responsible — the famous 'encirclement', with its automatic self-justification — while, in truth, the 'harmonious national and international coordination' concerns the vital conditions of labour itself: the profound interrelatedness of objective economic structures on a global scale.

Such is, then, the true nature of the 'work of regeneration', the true magnitude of its multidimensional objectivity. The rule of capital over labour is fundamentally *economic*, not political in character. All that politics can do is to provide the 'political guarantees' for the continuation of a materially already established and structurally entrenched rule. Consequently, the rule of capital cannot be broken at the political level, only the guarantee of its *formal* organisation. This is why Marx, even in his most positive references to the political framework of the Paris Commune, defines it *negatively* as a 'lever for *uprooting* the economic foundations of class rule', indicating the positive task in 'the economic emancipation of labour'.[342] And further on in the same work, Marx compares the 'organised public force, the state power' of bourgeois society to a 'political *engine*' that 'forcibly perpetuates the *social* enslavement of the producers of wealth by its appropriators, of the *economic rule of capital* over labour',[343] again making it amply clear what had to be the fundamental objective of the socialist transformation.

It must be underlined here that Marx's adversaries completely failed to understand the necessary interconnection between *the state, capital and labour*, and the existence of quite different levels and dimensions of possible change. Due to their reciprocally self-sustaining interrelationship, the state, capital and labour could only be done away with simultaneously, as a result of the radical structural transformation of the entire social metabolism. In this sense all three could not be 'overthrown/abolished' but only 'transcended/superseded'. This constraint, in its turn, necessarily carried with it both the extreme complexity and the long-term temporality of such transformations.

At the same time, all three had a dimension immediately accessible to change, without which the very idea of a socialist transformation would have been a romantic pipe-dream. It consisted in the social specificity of their historically prevalent form of existence. That is to say, in the attained level of concentration and centralisation of capital ('monopoly/imperialist', 'semi-feudal', 'colonially dependent','underdeveloped','military-industrial-complex orientated', or whatever else); in the corresponding variety of specific capitalist state-formations (from the Bonapartist state to Tsarist Russia just before the revolution, and from the 'liberal' states running the British and French Empires to Fascism and to the present-day varieties of military dictatorship engaged in neo-capitalist 'development', under the tutelage of our great democracies); and finally, in all those specific forms and configurations through which 'wage labour', in close conjunction with the dominant form of capital, reshaped the productive practices of each country, making it possible for capital to function as a truly interconnected global system.

It was at this level of sociohistorical specificity that direct intervention in the form of 'overthrow/abolition' could and had to be envisaged as a first step. But success depended on understanding the dialectic of the historically specific and the transhistorical, linking the necessary first step of what could be immediately overthrown to the *strategic* task of a long sustained 'transcendence/supersession' of capital itself (and not just capitalism), of the state in all its forms (and not merely the capitalist state), and of the *division of labour* (and not simply the abolition of wage labour). And while the *political* revolution could score successes at the level of the immediate tasks, only the *social* revolution as conceived by Marx—with its positive 'work of regeneration' — could promise lasting achievements and truly irreversible structural transformations.

13.4 Critique of Hegel's political philosophy

Bakunin's ultimate argument in favour of the immediate abolition of the state was a reference to *human nature* which, he claimed, is tempted by the very existence of the state into perpetuating the rule of a privileged minority over the majority. In this curious way, 'libertarian anarchism' displayed its liberal-bourgeois ancestry, with all its contradictions. For the liberal theory of the state was founded on the self-proclaimed contradiction between the assumed total *harmony of ends* (the ends necessarily desired by all individuals, in virtue of their 'human nature'), and the total *anarchy of means* (the necessary *scarcity* of goods and resources, which makes them fight and ultimately destroy one another by *bellum omnium contra omnes*, unless they somehow succeed in establishing over above themselves a *permanent* restraining force, the bourgeois state). Thus, *deus ex machina*, the state was invented in order to turn 'anarchy into harmony' (to harmonise the anarchy of means with the wishfully postulated harmony of ends), by reconciling the violent antagonism of two powerful *natural* factors — 'human nature' and material scarcity — thanks to the absolute permanence of its own 'artificial contrivance', to use Marx's expression. The fact that the stipulated 'human nature' was merely a self-serving assumption and that 'scarcity' was an inherently *historical* category, had to remain concealed in liberal theory beneath its multiple layers of *circularity*. It was the latter that enabled the representatives of liberalism to freely move backwards and forwards from arbitrary premises to the desired conclusions, establishing on the apriori foundations of such ideological circularity the 'eternal legitimacy' of the liberal state.

Bakunin, in his own version of the stipulated relationship between the state and an arbitrarily assumed 'human nature', simply reversed the equation, claiming that the *natural* tendency for *class* domination (what an absurd notion!) will, somewhat mysteriously, disappear with the revolutionary state's immediate self-abolition by decree. And since the sovereign frame of reference of Bakunin's wishful act of self-abolition remained the elitistically conceived politics of the 'General Staff', references to 'human nature', again, could only serve the purpose of legitimating the circularity of self-perpetuating politics.

Marx, by contrast, insisted that the political act of decreed self-abolition is nothing but self-contradiction, since only the radical restructuring of the *totality* of social practice can assign to politics an ever-diminishing role. At the same time he stressed that critically challenging the predominant, arbitrary conceptions of 'human nature' — for 'human nature' in reality was nothing but the 'community of men',[344] the 'ensemble of social relations'[345] — was an elementary condition for escaping from the strait-jacket of inherited political circularity.

NATURALLY, the circularity in question was not simply a philosophical construct but, as we shall see in a moment, a theoretical reflection of the practical perversity of class society's political self-reproduction across the ages. This is why Marx kept it at the forefront of his attention also in his *Critique of Hegel's Philosophy of Law.*

Commenting on Hegel's definition of the monarchy ('Taken without its monarch and the articulation of the whole which is the indispensable and direct concomitant of monarchy, the people is a formless mass and no longer a state.')[346] Marx wrote:

> This whole thing is a *tautology.* If a people has a monarch and an articulation which is its indispensable and direct concomitant, i.e., if it is articulated as a monarchy, then extracted from this articulation it is certainly a formless mass and a quite general notion.[347]

If a great philosopher, like Hegel, indulges in such violations of logic, there must be more to it than mere 'conceptual confusion', this pseudo-explanatory trouvaille of 'analytical philosophy' which 'explains' what it terms 'conceptual confusion' by circularly asserting the presence of conceptual confusion.

Indeed, the Hegelian leapfrogging from tautology to tautology — from the just seen definition of the monarchy to the circular determination of the political sphere, and from the tautological characterisation of the 'universal class' to proving the 'rationality of the state' by its mere assertion — is a striking feature of this political philosophy, but by no means unique to it. Underneath it all we find the ideological determinations which induced liberal theory as a whole to argue from unsustained premises to the desired conclusions (and *vice versa*), so as to be able to 'eternalise' the bourgeois relations of production, together with their corresponding state formations.

What was specific to Hegel was that, living at a juncture of history which displayed in an acute form the explosion of social antagonisms — from the French Revolution to the Napoleonic wars and to the appearance of the working class movement as a hegemonic force, envisaging its own mode of social metabolic control as a radical alternative to the existent — he had to face openly many a contradiction that remained hidden from his predecessors. If he was more contrived in his philosophy than such predecessors, that was largely because he had to be far less 'innocent' than them, attempting to embrace and integrate within his system a far greater range of objective problems and contradictions than they could even dream about. If in the end he could only achieve this in an abstract/logical, often definitional/circular, and cerebralised fashion, that was primarily due to the insuperable taboos of his bourgeois 'political-economist standpoint'. The penalty he had to pay for sharing that standpoint was the mystifying conflation of the categories of *logic* with the objective characteristics of *being* while he was attempting to conjure up the impossible, namely, the final 'reconciliation' of the antagonistic contradictions of the perceived sociohistorical reality.

THE Hegelian characterisation of the 'universal class' is a graphic example of such ideological circularity and conflation. We are told that

> The universal class, or, more precisely, the class of civil servants, *must* purely in virtue of its character as *universal*, have the *universal* as the end of its *essential* activity.[348]

By the same token, the 'unofficial class' displays its suitability to fit into the Hegelian scheme of things by 'renouncing itself' so as to acquire a true political significance. But, as Marx rightly comments, the claimed political act of the 'unofficial class' is a 'complete transubstantiation'. For 'in this political act civil society *must* completely renounce itself as such, as unofficial class, and assert a part of its essence which not only has nothing in common with the *actual* civil existence of its essence, but *directly opposes* it.'[349] Thus the fictitious universality (by stipulated essence) of the 'universal class' carries with it the equally dubious redefinition of the actual forces of 'civil society', so that the contradictions of the social world should be reconciled, in accordance with the 'Idea', in the idealised domain of the Hegelian state.

As Marx exclaims, 'the bureaucracy is a *circle* from which no one can escape.'[350] This is because it constitutes the operative centre of a circular construct which reproduces, even if in a bewildering fashion, the actual perversity of the bourgeois world. For the political state as an abstraction from 'civil society' is not Hegel's invention but the result of capitalistic developments. Nor are 'fragmentation', 'atomism', 'partiality', 'alienation', etc., figments of Hegel's imagination, no matter how idealistically he treats them, but objective characteristics of the dominant social universe, as is the challenge of 'universality' mentioned above. Indeed, Marx does not simply turn his back to this problematic. He reorients it towards its objective ground, by insisting that

> The abolition/supersession [Aufhebung] of the bureaucracy can only consist in the *universal* interest becoming *really* — and not, as with Hegel, becoming purely in thought, in abstraction — a *particular* interest; and this is possible only through the particular interest *really* becoming *universal*.[351]

In other words, the circle of bureaucracy (and of modern politics in general) is a very real circle from which one must organise a correspondingly real escape.

Marx also acknowledges that 'Hegel's keenest insight lies in his sensing the *separation* of civil and political society to be a *contradiction*. But his error is that he contents himself with the appearance of its dissolution, and passes it off as the real thing.'[352] The fact that Hegel cannot find a way out of the perceived contradiction is, again, not his personal limitation. For the practice of simply assuming a necessary relationship between a 'civil society' (torn apart by its contradictions) and the political state (which resolves or at least keeps in balance these contradictions) was, as we have seen, a characteristic feature of liberal theory in general, fulfilling, thanks to its ahistorical circularity, a much needed social/apologetic function. When Hegel 'presupposed the separation of civil society and the political state (which is a modern situation), and developed it as a necessary moment of the Idea, as an absolute truth of Reason,'[353] he merely adapted the general practice of liberal theory to the specific requirements of his own philosophical discourse.

The greatest deficiency of Hegel's approach is the way in which he deals with the need for 'mediation' (though, it cannot be stressed enough, the difficulty of mediation exists for him as a constantly recurring problem, while in liberal theory in general it tends to be narrowly reduced to a question of more or less ready-made 'balancing' instrumentality, if it is not ignored altogether). Hegel realises that, if the state is to fulfil the vital functions of totalisation and reconciliation assigned to it in his system, it must be constituted as an *organic* entity; one adequately fused with society, and not mechanically superimposed upon the latter. In this spirit he goes on to say that

> It is a prime concern of the state that a *middle class* should be developed, but this can be done only if the state is an organic unity like the one described here, i.e., it can be done only by *giving authority to spheres of particular interests*, which are relatively independent, and by appointing an army of officials whose personal arbitrariness is broken against such authorised bodies.

The problem is, though, that the picture we are here presented with is nothing but a stipulated/idealised version of the political state-formation of divided 'civil society'; one that preserves all the existing divisions and contradictions while conveniently conjuring away their ultimate destructiveness. As Marx put it in his comments appended to these lines: 'To be sure the people can appear as one class, the middle class, only in such an organic unity; but is something that keeps itself going by means of the *counterbalancing of privileges* an organic unity?'[354]

Thus, the envisaged solution is even self-contradictory (defining 'organicity' in terms of a perilously unstable 'counterbalancing' of hostile centrifugal forces), not to mention its fictitious character which predicates a *permanent* remedy on the basis of an ever-intensifying real conflictuality. In this wishful 'Aufhebung' of the growing social contradictions through the magic circle of an omniscient bureaucracy and the heaven-sent expansion of the 'middle class', we are provided with a veritable model of all twentieth century theories of social accommodation, from Max Weber to the 'managerial revolution', from Max Scheler and Mannheim to the 'end of ideology', and from Talcott Parsons to the 'knowledge-oriented post-industrial society' of 'modernity' and 'post-modernity' as the ultimate solution. (But mark again, Hegel only says that this middle class *should be* developed', while twentieth century apologists claim that it has *actually* arrived already, bringing with it the end of all major social contradictions.[355])

The modern political state in reality was not constituted as an 'organic unity' but, on the contrary, was imposed upon the *subordinate* classes of the *materially* already prevailing power relations of 'civil society', in the preponderant (and not carefully 'counterbalanced') interest of capital. Thus the Hegelian idea of 'mediation' could only be a false mediation, motivated by the ideological needs of 'reconciliation', 'legitimation', and 'rationalisation'. (The latter in the sense of accepting and idealising the prevailing social relations.)

Hegel's 'logical inconsistencies' arise from the soil of such motivations. The established facticity and separateness of 'civil society' and its political state are simply assumed as given, and as such they are kept apart; hence the crude circularity of Hegelian 'tautologies' and self-referential definitions. At the same time, the need for producing an 'organic unity' generates the more subtle 'dialectical circularity' of mediations (which, in the end, turns out to be anything but dialectical). The criss-crossing of reciprocal references arranged around a middle term creates the semblance of a movement and genuine progression, while in fact it reflects and reproduces the brutally self-sustaining dual facticity of the given social order ('civil society' and its political state-formation), only now in a deductively 'transubstantiated' abstract philosophical form.

As Marx observes, 'If civil classes as such are political classes, then the mediation is not needed; and if this mediation is needed, then the civil class is not political, and thus also not this mediation. ... Here, then, we find one of Hegel's inconsistencies within his own way of reviewing things: and such *inconsistency* is an *accommodation*.'[356] Thus, ultimately, what gives the game away is the apologetic character of its 'mediation'. It reveals itself as a sophisticated reconstruction of the ahistorically assumed dualistic reality — and eternalised as such — within the Hegelian discourse, and no real mediation at all. As Marx puts it: 'In general, Hegel conceives of the syllogism as middle term, a *mixtum compositum*. We can say that in his development of the rational syllogism all of the transcendence and mystical dualism of his system becomes apparent. The middle term is the wooden sword, the concealed opposition between universality and singularity.'[357]

The logical deficiency here referred to is, thus, not a matter of conceptually not knowing the difference between 'universality' and 'singularity', but that of a perverse necessity to *conceal* the irreconcilable opposition between them as they actually confront one another in social reality. Worse still, the need for preserving the given in its dominant facticity, produces an overturning of the actual sets of relations inasmuch as it disregards the new hegemonic/universal potential of labour and misrepresents a *subservient partiality* — the idealised state bureaucracy — as 'true universality'. This is why the lofty enterprise of the Hegelian 'rational syllogism' culminates in the prosaic modality of apologetic rationalisation. Understandably, therefore, the 'wooden sword' of false mediation only manages to carve out of the sand dunes of this conceptual universe a spitting image of the dualistic bourgeois world. (This is all the more telling in view of Hegel's explicit rejection — could it be through the voice of 'bad conscience'? — of all forms of philosophical dualism.)

All this is by no means surprising. For once the reciprocal circularity of 'civil society' and its political state is assumed as the absolute premise of political theory, the 'rules of the game' enforce themselves with iron determination. It is painful to witness the way in which a thinker of Hegel's stature is reduced in size, almost to the point of writing 'schoolboy nonsense', under the impact of such determinations. This is how Marx characterizes Hegel's self-imposed straitjacket:

> The sovereign, then, had to be the middle term in the legislature between the executive and the Estates, and the Estates between him and civil society. How is he to mediate between what he himself needs as a mean lest his own existence becomes a one-sided extreme? Now the complete absurdity of these extremes, which inter-

changeably play now the part of the extreme and now the part of the mean, becomes apparent. ...This is a kind of *mutual reconciliation society*. ... It is like the lion in *A Midsummer Night's Dream* who exclaims: 'I am the lion, and I am not the lion, but Snug.' So here each extreme is sometimes the lion of opposition and sometimes the Snug of mediation. ... Hegel, who reduces this absurdity of mediation to its abstract logical, and hence pure and irreducible, expression, calls it at the same time the speculative mystery of logic, the rational relationship, the rational syllogism. *Actual extremes cannot be mediated* with each other precisely because they are actual extremes. But neither are they in need of mediation, because they are opposed in essence. They have nothing in common with one another; they neither need nor complement one another.[358]

Seeing, thus, Hegel shipwrecked on the rocks of his false mediation, Marx realised that it was the very premises of politics itself that needed drastic revision in order to break its vicious circle. For so long as 'mediation' remained tied to the political state and its supporting anchorage, the established 'civil society', the critical aspirations of political theory had to be systematically frustrated, allowing for only an institutionally constrained margin of easily integrated protest. Envisaging *structural* change in terms of the accepted premises was apriori out of the question. For the prevailing order helped to reproduce itself also by riveting philosophy to the dead weight of dualistic immobility, and by restricting 'mediation' to the self-serving circularity of traditional political discourse.

THERE are times in history — as a rule its periods of transition — when the inner contradictions of particular social formations come to the fore with much greater clarity than under normal circumstances. This is because at such times the principal forces of the ongoing social confrontation put forward their rival claims more openly as hegemonic alternatives to one another. This gives not only a greater fluidity but also a greater transparency to the social processes. By the time the contesting forces settle down to a more firmly regulated (indeed, to a large extent institutionalised/routinised) mode of interaction, under the predominance of one of them — and for what appears to the participants an indeterminate period of time — the lines of social demarcation become increasingly more blurred. The formerly acute conflict loses its cutting edge and its animators appear to be assimilated or 'integrated', at least for the time being.

Hegel's philosophy is the product of such a historical period of dramatic fluidity and relative transparency. Fittingly, he completed the monumental synthesis of *The Phenomenology of Mind* in Jena at the time when Napoleon — the subject of his greatest hope for a radical transformation of the anachronistic social structures of the 'Ancien Régime' all over Europe — was marshalling his forces for a decisive battle on the surrounding hills. And even though by the time of writing his *Philosophy of Right* Hegel had settled into a more conservative mould, his philosophy as a whole confronted and embodied — notwithstanding its mystifications — the dynamic contradictions of the not-yet-consolidated world of capital, together with the sombre recognition of the menacing world-historical potential of its antagonist.

Given the vastness of the Hegelian vision, and the way in which it articulated the incommensurable complexities of this restless age, with its apparently unending cycles of revolutions and counter-revolutionary upheavals, Marx could not have had a more fertile point of departure in his 'critical settling of accounts' with the standpoint of capital. For the Hegelian system clearly demonstrated — consciously, through its genuine insights, and unconsciously, through its class-imposed contradictions and mystifications — what an immense role politics plays in the extended self-reproduction of the world dominated by capital; and *vice versa:* in what an elemental way the 'civil society' of the capital system shapes and reproduces the political formation in its own image. The ultimate secret of the astonishing, naked circularity of Hegel's sophisticated political philosophy was this: the real circle of capital's self-expanding reproduction from which there seemed to be no escape, thanks to the interlocking *dual circles* of 'civil society/political state' and 'political state/civil society', with their reciprocal *assumption* of and *derivation* from each other, and with capital at the core of both.

The abstract dualism of Hegelian political philosophy, thus, revealed itself as the sublimated expression of the suffocatingly real world of a 'dual-concentric' circularity through which capital politically reproduces itself: by apriori defining the very terms and framework of 'reform' that promises to 'supersede' (by means of some fictitious 'mediation') its deep-seated structural deficiencies, without questioning in the slightest the fatal immobilising power of the political circle itself. This is why the task of emancipation had to be radically redefined in terms of breaking the vicious circle of politics as such. This had to be done, according to Marx, so as to be able to pursue the struggle against the power of capital at the level where it really hurts: well beyond the false mediations of politics itself, on capital's own material ground.

13.5 The displacement of capital's contradictions

MARX worked out his conception of the socialist alternative at the closing stage of this dramatic period of transition, just before capital succeeded in firmly consolidating its newly won position on a global scale: first by resolving its national rivalries for the next historical phase through the Napoleonic wars; and later by ruthlessly extending its sphere of domination to the farthest corners of the planet through its various empires. His formative years coincided with the defiant appearance of the working class as an independent political force all over Europe, culminating in the achievements of the Chartist movement in England and in revolutionary uprisings of growing intensity in France and Germany in the 1840s.

Under these circumstances, the relative transparency of the social relations and their antagonistic contradictions greatly favoured the formulation of Marx's comprehensive synthesis which consciously traced the dynamics of the fundamental tendencies of development. He was always looking for the 'classical'[359] configuration of forces and events, highlighting their ultimate structural significance even when starting out from the raw everydayness of their phenomenal manifestations.[360] It was, undoubtedly, this ability to situate the minutest detail within the broadest perspectives which made Engels write in 1886: 'Marx stood higher, saw further and took a wider and quicker view than all the rest of us.'[361]

But, of course, such ability, in order to realise itself, had to find its objective complement in the given sociohistorical reality itself. For it would have been futile to see farther and wider, from the vantage point of an individual talent no matter how great, if all that one could perceive amounted only to vague outlines and confounding complexities, on the soil of inconsistent social movements, bent on blurring the real lines of demarcation and — preoccupied with the narrow practicalities of accommodation and compromise — avoiding like plague the open articulation of their latent antagonisms. The intellectual desert of the age of reformist Social Democracy bears eloquent witness to this depressing truth.

It was the historical coincidence of the type and intensity of Marx's personal qualities with the dynamic transparency of the age of his formative years which enabled him to work out the fundamental outlines — the veritable 'Grundrisse' — of the socialist alternative. By defining the meaning of socialist politics as the total restitution of the usurped powers of decision making to the community of associated producers, Marx laid down the synthesizing core of all radical strategies that may arise under the changing conditions of development. The validity of these outlines extends over the whole historic period that goes from capital's world-wide domination to its structural crisis and ultimate dissolution, and to the positive establishment of a truly socialist society on a global scale.

However, to stress the epochal validity of Marx's overall vision, emphasizing its organic links to the relative transparency of the age that made it possible, is not meant to suggest that such ages are nothing but pure blessing for theory, in the sense that they do not impose any limitation on the world-views which originate on their soil. For, precisely because they put sharply into relief the basic polarities and alternatives, they tend to push into the background tendencies and modalities of action which point towards the continued reproduction of the prevailing social order; just as extended periods of compromise and accommodation create a general climate of opinion that strongly discourages the articulation of radical criticism, dismissively labelling it as 'Messianic' and 'Apocalyptic'.

Marx was in his element at times when the manifestations of crisis were at their most intense. By the same token, he experienced great difficulties from the 1870s (which represented a period of major success in capital's global expansion). Such difficulties presented themselves not only politically, in relation to some important organisations of the working class, but also theoretically, in assessing the new turn of developments. Reflecting this, the intellectual production of his last fifteen years bears no comparison to the previous decade and a half, nor with the fifteen years just before that.

Not that he changed his approach as 'old Marx'. On the contrary, his work retained its most remarkable unity even under the *internally* most difficult circumstances. Throughout his life he was looking for tendencies and signs of development which would provide cumulative evidence for the validity of the 'fundamental outlines'. They were streaming forward, in great abundance, during the historic phase of the more open and transparent, sharp alternatives; so much so, in fact, that they could hardly be contained even within the massive works of creative explosion of the first twenty five years. Given the then prevailing relation of forces and the great fluidity of the overall socio-historical situation, the possibility of capital's structural collapse was an *objective* one. It was the latter that found its forceful articulation in Marx's correspondingly dramatic writings. For these were times when even the London *Economist* had to admit — as Marx enthusiastically quoted it in a letter to Engels — that capital all over Europe 'escaped only by a hair's-breadth from the impending crash'.[362]

The difficulties started to multiply for him at the time when those immediate possibilities receded, opening new outlets for stabilisation and expansion which capital did not fail to exploit in its subsequent global development. It was under such conditions, with contradictory objective alternatives *within* the major classes on both sides of the great divide — and not only *between* them — that also the internal divisions in the practical strategies of the working class movement strongly surfaced, inducing Marx to write at the end of his comments on the Gotha Programme, with a tone of militant resignation: *dixi et salvavi animam meam*, as we have seen above.

Two points must be firmly made in this context. First, that the passing away of some objective, historically specific possibilities of change does not eliminate the fundamental contradictions of capital itself as a mode of social metabolic control, and hence it does not invalidate Marx's overall theory, concerned with the latter. And second, that an attempt to identify the difficulties and dilemmas inherent in some of Marx's conclusions is not the projection of 'hindsight' upon his work (which would be totally ahistorical, thus inadmissible), but rests on explicit or implicit elements of his own discourse.

To be sure, the apologists of the established order greet every escape from the crisis as their final victory as well as the ultimate refutation of Marxism. Since they cannot and will not think in historical terms, they fail to grasp that the *boundaries of the capital system* may indeed historically expand — through opening up new territories, protected by colonial empires, or by the more up-to-date ways of 'neocapitalism' and 'neocolonialism'. Equally, they may expand through 'internal colonisation', i.e., the ruthless establishment of new productive outlets at home, safeguarding the conditions of their sustained expansion by a more intensive exploitation of both the producer and the consumer, etc.—without thereby doing away with the *structural limits* and contradictions of capital as such.

Marx's theoretical framework can easily weather all these wishful refutations. For it is oriented towards the central contradictions of capital, pursuing their unfolding from the early developments to the global domination and to the ultimate disintegration of this controlling force of social production. Specific historical evidence is relevant in this framework of analysis to the extent to which it affects the basic structural relations, on the broadest historical time-scale, — which happens to be the appropriate temporality of the basic categories scrutinised by Marx. To judge such a theoretical system — which is primarily concerned with the *ultimate* limits of capital and with the conditions/necessities of reaching them — on the short-term temporality of alleged 'predictions' as to what exactly the day after tomorrow might or might not bring, is utter futility, if not blatant hostility dressed up as a 'scientific' quest for 'verification' or 'falsification'.

Marx would indeed be refuted if it was proved that the limits of capital are *indefinitely* expandable: namely, that the power of capital is itself limitless. Since, however, to prove such thing is quite impossible, his adversaries prefer to *assume* it as the circular axiom of their own world of 'piecemeal social engineering'. The latter, thus, becomes the self-evident measure of all criticism and, as such, by definition, cannot possibly be itself the subject of scrutiny and criticism. At the same time, Marxism may be freely denounced and dismissed as 'unverifiable ideology', 'holism', 'metaphysical deductionism', and who knows what else.

But even beyond such hostile views, there persists a serious misconception of the nature of Marx's project. On the one side, there is the expectation/accusation of immediate predictive implications, together with disputes over their realisation or non-realisation, as the case might be. On the other, in complete contrast, we find the characterization of Marx's conception as a self-articulating, quasi-deductive system, without empirical connections, following its own rules of 'theoretical production', thanks to the somewhat mysterious 'discoveries' of its 'scientific discourse' concerning the 'continent of history'.

Against the first misconception it cannot be stressed enough that, inasmuch as Marx's aim is the identification of capital's fundamental contradictions and ultimate limits, the characterization of the given sociohistorical setting (from which predictions may follow about the near future) is always subject to manifold qualifications, in view of the virtually endless number of variables at work, and therefore must be treated with extreme care. This is by no means a conveniently prefabricated escape clause, nor an attempt to take refuge from the difficulties of facing reality in the clouds of a self-referential discourse. The point is that contradictions may be *displaced* as a result of the specific interplay of determinate forces and circumstances, and there can be no *apriori* way of prefiguring the concrete forms and particular historical boundaries of displacement when, in fact, the dynamic configurations of the interplay itself are impossible to freeze into an arbitrary, schematic mould.

Saying this in no way implies a defensive denial of the predictive aspirations and value of Marxist theory. For the question of displacement refers to the *specificity* of these contradictions, and not to the determination of the *ultimate limits* of the capital system. In other words, the contradictions of capital are displaced only *within* such limits, and the process of displacement may continue only to the point of the ultimate *saturation* of the system itself and the blocking of the expansionary outlets (the conditions of which can be defined with precision), but not endlessly or indefinitely. Margins of displacement are created by a multiplicity of contradictions given in a specific configuration and by the unevenness of development, and decidedly not by the *disappearance* of the contradictions themselves. Thus the concepts of 'displacement', 'saturation', and 'structural crisis' acquire their meaning in terms of the ultimate limits of capital as a global system, and not in terms of any one of its transient forms. Displacement means *postponing* (not liquidating) the saturation of the available outlets and the maturation of the fundamental contradictions. It also means *extending* capital's given historical boundaries but not eliminating its ultimately explosive objective structural constraints. In both cases we are talking about inherently temporal processes which foreshadow a necessary closure of the cycles involved, though, of course, on their own time-scale. And while all this certainly puts the predictive anticipations of Marxist theory in perspective, it also reasserts their legitimacy and validity with the greatest emphasis in terms of the appropriate time-scale.

As to the claimed deductive character of Marx's discourse — some say: its most unhappy mixture of Hegelian deductivism and scientism/positivism/empiricism — this question concerns the relationship between reality and the theoretical framework. No doubt, Marx's method of presentation (and his positive references to Hegel) may at times create the impression of a strictly deductive procedure. Besides, things are further complicated by the fact that Marx apodeictically concentrates on the fundamental conditions and determinations; on the necessities at work in all social relations; on the objective dynamism of the unfolding contradictions; and on the explanation of men and ideas — as situated within the parameters of a strictly defined material foundation — in terms of a subtle but no less objective necessity of dialectical reciprocity.

However, this forceful articulation of the necessary connections, centred on a few vital categories — e.g., capital, labour, surplus-value, modern state, world market, etc. — does not mean the replacement of social reality by the deductive matrix of a self-referential discourse. Nor, indeed, the superimposition of a set of abstract categories of the 'Science of Logic' on actual relations, as happens to be the case with Hegel; categories whose connections and reciprocal derivations are formally/deductively/circularly established on the mystifying ground of complex ideological determinations, as we have seen a few pages ago.

The apodeictic rigour of Marxian analysis as arising from the necessary connections of his system of categories is not the *formal* characteristic of a 'theoretical practice', but his way of conveying the *objectively* structured architecture of the social totality. For categories, according to Marx, are not timeless philosophical constructs but DASEINSFORMEN: forms of being, condensed reflections of the essential relations and determinations of their society. What defines with precision the theorizable character of any given society is the *specific configuration* of its dominant objective categories. In this sense, while several categories of modern bourgeois society originated on a very different soil, and some of them are indeed bound to extend over postcapitalist formations as well, it is the unique combination of CAPITAL, WAGE-LABOUR, WORLD MARKET and the MODERN STATE which *together* identify the *capitalist formation* in its historical specificity.

The way in which some categories cross the frontiers of different social formations, shows the objective dialectic of the *historical* and the *transhistorical* at work. This must be grasped in theory both in terms of the objectively different levels and scales of *temporality* and as a vital characteristic of the given social *structures*. (The latter exhibit the correlation between the historical and the transhistorical in the form of *continuity* in discontinuity, and *discontinuity* in even the apparently most stable continuity.) In Marx's view, stressing these links and determinations serves to articulate in theory the historical dynamism of the social processes and the objective structural characteristics of all the relevant factors which together constitute the real ground of all categorial condensations and reflections. Thus, the contrast with deductivism and with all past conceptions of the nature and importance of categories could not be greater.

MARX'S real dilemmas (which affected his theory in significant ways) concerned the question of capitalist crisis and the possibilities of its displacement inasmuch as they were visible in his age. As already mentioned, raising this issue is not the projection of hindsight on a work articulated from a very different vantage point, but an attempt to understand the theoretical consequences of his conscious decision to assign a subordinate position to certain — already in his life-time discernible — tendencies which to us appear to possess in their own historical context a much greater relative weight. This is a problem of great complexity, since a number of very different factors come together in it to produce the result in question, and none of them could yield an acceptable answer if taken separately.[363] The main factors here referred to are:

- (1) the dramatic polarities and alternatives of Marx's formative years (making the collapse of capitalism, in view of its far more limited developmental/expansionary outlets at the time, historically quite feasible);
- (2) Marx's method of analysis, as arising from the soil of such dramatic alternatives and greatly favoured by them in their call for sharply drawn outlines and for the articulation of the central antagonisms (and by the same token not favouring, of course, a method of manifold qualifications which would not dare to go beyond the amassed details of 'overwhelming evidence');
- (3) the principal political confrontations in which Marx happened to be involved (especially his struggle against anarchist political voluntarism); and
- (4) the main intellectual targets of his critique (above all Hegel and the 'standpoint of political economy').

All these determinations and motivations combined, produced that negative definition of politics which we have seen above, carrying with it not only the radical rejection of the liberal problematic, but also an extreme scepticism with regard to the possibilities of displacing the structural crisis of capital for much longer. It must be stressed, this applies to Marx's work as a whole, including the last few years when he crossed out some excessively optimistic remarks from his letters.[364] At the same time it cannot be repeated enough, since it is generally ignored, that this problem existed for Marx as a serious *dilemma*. And even though he resolved it the way he did, he was, nevertheless, fully aware of the fact that the advocated solution was not without its great difficulties.

TO appreciate how involved and delicate a matter this is, we have to set side by side two of his letters: one well known, the other strangely forgotten. Various critics and 'refuters' of Marx are fond of quoting the first in which he tells Engels that he is 'working frantically, well into the night' to complete his economic studies, so as to have 'clearly worked out at least the fundamental outlines [the *Grundrisse*] before the deluge'.[365] In the light of the apparently chronic crisis of the middle 1850s — which could not be ignored or readily dismissed even by the *Economist*, as we have seen above — Marx's expectation of 'deluge' and the excited tone of his letter are well understandable.

However, his reflections do not stop there. For he sizes up with great realism the full burden of the socialist undertaking, as it transpires through the other, much neglected, letter:

> One cannot deny, bourgeois society lives its second 16th century which, *I hope*, will take it into the grave, just as the first one brought it into life. The historic task of bourgeois society is the establishment of the WORLD MARKET, at least in its basic outlines, and a mode of production that rests on its basis. Since the world is round,

it seems that this has been accomplished with the colonisation of California and Australia and with the annexation of China and Japan. For us the difficult question is this: the revolution on the Continent is imminent and its character will be at once socialist; will it not be necessarily crushed in this little corner of the world, since on a much larger terrain the development of bourgeois society is still in the *ascendant*.[366]

One could not sum up more clearly even today the problems at stake, though from our own historical vantage point the various trends of development surveyed by Marx assume a rather different significance. For, indeed, the viability of capital is inseparable from its full expansion into an all-embracing world system. Only when that process is accomplished can the *structural* limits of capital come into play with their devastating intensity. Until that stage, however, capital maintains the dynamism inherent in its historical ascendancy. And together with this dynamism capital retains, of course, also its power to bend, subdue, and crush the forces that oppose it in many 'little corners' of the world, inasmuch as its socialist opponents do not produce adequate strategies to counter the growing power of capital on its own terrain.

Thus, the crucial question is this: under what conditions can the process of capital-expansion come to a close on a truly global scale, bringing with it necessarily the end of crushed and perverted revolutions, opening thereby the new historic phase of an irrepressible socialist offensive. Or, to put it in another way: what are the feasible — though by no means inexhaustible — modalities of capital's revitalisation, both with respect to its direct outlets and as regards its power to acquire new forms that significantly extend its boundaries within the framework of its ultimate structural determinations and overall historical limits.

The real magnitude of the problem becomes clearer when we remind ourselves that even today — well over 150 years after Marx first articulated his vision — the world of capital still cannot be considered a fully extended and integrated global system, even if by now it is not far from being that. This is where we can also see that we are not imposing this problematic on Marx in hindsight, since the objective trends of capital's actual and potential development were unhesitatingly acknowledged by him with reference to its historical 'ascendancy' all over the world, in contrast to what was likely to happen in the 'little corner' of Europe. The differences concern the *relative weight* of the trends identified and the temporalities involved. For while the world is certainly round, it is equally true that capital has the power of discovering new continents for exploitation which were formerly hidden beneath the crust of its own relative inefficiency and underdevelopment. Only when there are no more 'hidden continents' to be discovered, only then may one consider the process of capital's global expansion fully accomplished and its latent structural antagonisms — the central object of Marx's analysis — dramatically activated.

The difficulty is that capital can restructure its outlets according to the requirements of an *intensive totality* when the limits of its *extensive totality* are reached. Until that point, capital too pursues 'the line of least resistance', whether we are thinking of the historical changes in the mode of exploiting the 'metropolitan' working classes or of its different ways of ruling the colonised and 'underdeveloped' world. For only when the flow of *'absolute surplus-value'* is no longer adequate to its need for self-expansion, only then is the incomparably vaster territory of *'relative surplus-value'* fully explored, removing the obstacles from the road of capital's unhindered development due to the original ineffi- ciency of its natural greed. In this sense, the size of the 'round world' may well be doubled, or even multiplied tenfold, depending on a number of other — including political — conditions and circumstances. Similarly, under the pres- sure of its own inner dynamic as well as of various other factors beyond its control, capital can assume a multiplicity of 'mixed' or 'hybrid' forms — which all help to extend its life-span.

In this perspective it matters very little that the expected 'deluge' of the 1850s and 1860s did not materialise. First, because capital's collapse does not have to take the form of a deluge at all (though, of course, at some stage even the latter cannot be excluded). And second, because what really does matter — the struc- tural disintegration of capital in *all* its historically viable forms — is a question of the time-scale that adequately matches the inherent nature of the social determinants and processes involved. If a particular thinker's 'revolutionary impatience' — his subjective temporality — conflicts with the objective histori- cal time-scale of his own vision, that by itself does not invalidate his theory in the slightest. For the validity of his views hinges on whether or not his overall historical perspective objectively grasps the fundamental trends of development as they unfold on no matter how long a time-scale. Subjective temporality should not be confused with *subjectivism*. The former — like Gramsci's optimistic *will,* contrasted by him to the 'pessimism of the *intellect'* — is an essential mo- tivating force that sustains the individual under difficult circumstances, within the horizons of a world-view which must be judged on its own merits. Subjec- tivism, by contrast, is an arbitrary image that substitutes itself for the required comprehensive view of the world and runs diametrically counter to the actual trends of development.

While undoubtedly in Marx's work, too, one can detect a conflict of varying intensity between the subjective and the objective scales of temporality (a much sharper one in the 1850s and 1860s than after the defeat of the Paris Commune), he never allowed even his most optimistic hope to undermine the monumental architecture of his 'fundamental outlines'. He warned with great realism that

> The doctrinaire and necessarily fantastic anticipations of the programme of action for a revolution of the future diverts us from the struggle of the present'.[367]

Marx was able to put the present in this way in its proper perspective because he assessed it from the temporally not hurried, global point of view of capital's social formation in its entirety—from its 'ascendancy' to its pregnancy with the 'new historic form'—which alone can assign their true significance to all partial events and developments. And since we continue to live in the orbit of the same broad historical determinations, Marx's overall conception is — and remains for a long time to come — the inescapable horizon of our own predicament.

13.6 *Temporal ambiguities and missing mediations*

WITHIN such horizons, however, the relative weight of the forces and tenden- cies which confront us requires a significant redefinition. To put the key issue in one sentence: the *mediations* so stubbornly resisted by Marx are no longer anticipations of a more or less imaginary future but ubiquitous realities of the present. We have seen that the way in which the Marxian system was constituted brought with it both the radically negative definition of politics and the abhorrence of mediations as the miserable practice of reconciliation and complicity with the established order. The break had to be envisaged as the most radical possible, allowing even socialist politics an extremely limited, strictly transient role. This is clearly expressed in the following passage:

> since the proletariat, during the period of struggle to overthrow the old society, still acts on the basis of the old society and consequently within political forms which more or less belong to that society, it has, during this period of struggle, not yet attained its *ultimate structure*, and to achieve its *liberation* it employs means which will be *discarded after the liberation*.[368]

In this uncompromising negativity towards politics a number of determinations came together and reinforced one another. They were: the contempt for the political constraints of 'the German misery'; the critique of Hegel's conception of politics, on account of the 'false positivity' of its reconciliations and mediations; the rejection of Proudhon and the anarchists; extreme doubts about the way the German working class's political movement was developing; etc. Understandably, therefore, Marx's negative attitude could only harden, if anything, as time went by, instead of positivistically 'maturing', as the legend would have it.

The most important factor in Marx's radical rejection of mediations was the global historical character of the theory itself and the relatively premature conditions of its articulation. Far from the time of any actual 'deluge', his conception was spelled out well before one could see what alternative ways capital could pursue to displace its internal contradictions when they erupted on a massive scale. Thus Marx was looking — to the very end of his life — for strategies that could prevent capital from penetrating into those territories which it had not fully conquered yet, so as to secure its earliest possible demise. For, with regard to the maturation of capital's structural contradictions, it was not a matter of indifference how far the sphere of domination of this mode of production would extend. So long as new countries could be added to capital's existing domain, the corresponding increase in material and human resources would help the development of new productive potentialities and, therefore, postpone the crisis. In this sense, the eruption and consummation of a structural crisis within the constraints of capitalistic developments in the 1850s and 1860s — i.e., without an effective economic integration of the rest of the world within the dynamics of global capital expansion — would have meant something radically different from facing the same problem in the context of the incomparably more flexible resources of a successfully completed world system. If, therefore, important territories could have been prevented from being engulfed by capital, in principle that should have accelerated the maturation of its structural crisis.

It is highly significant precisely for this reason that Marx's last important project concerned the nature of developments in Russia, as evidenced by the immense care with which he tried to define his position in relation to 'archaic modes of production' in the draft letters to Vera Zasulich. In his spirited defence of the future potentialities of the archaic modes — containing also the tempting polemical remark that capitalism itself 'has reached its withering stage and soon will become nothing but an "archaic" formation', which he later rightly cut out from his letter[369] — he was eager to explore the viability of a direct move from the existing form of 'archaic collectivism' to its historically superior, namely socialist form, bypassing altogether the capitalist phase. At the same time, he was also trying to find political inspiration and ammunition for the *social* revolution in the postulated need to defend the existing archaic-collectivist form, with all its positive potentialities, from being destroyed by the capitalistic processes. By contrast, as a result of the developments that had actually taken place in the intervening decades, Lenin's approach could not have been more different. He started out from the firm premise that the capitalist penetration into Russia had been irretrievably accomplished, and therefore the task was to break the 'weakest link' of the global chain so as to precipitate a chain reaction for the *political* revolution of the world capitalist system.

MARX'S frame of reference was the *whole historical phase* of capital's social formation, from its original accumulation to its ultimate dissolution. One of his principal concerns was to demonstrate the inherently *transitional character (Übergangscharakter)* of the capitalist system *as such*, in constant polemics against the 'eternalization' of this mode of production by bourgeois theoreticians. Inevitably, such concentration on the broad historical framework brought with it a shift in perspective which sharply emphasised the fundamental outlines and basic determinants and treated the partial transformations and mediations as of secondary importance; indeed as often directly responsible for the detested mystifications and mediatory reconciliations.

In any case, when one's frame of reference is a whole historical phase, it is very difficult to keep constantly in view — while addressing oneself to the immediate present — that the conclusions are valid on a long-term scale of temporality; and it is particularly difficult to do so at the level of political discourse, which aims at direct mobilisation. If, however, this ambiguity of temporalities is left unresolved, its necessary consequences are ambiguities at the core of the theory itself. To illustrate this, let us concentrate on a few directly relevant examples.

The first of them can be found in the penultimate quotation above in which Marx assigns politics to the old society. He speaks of an *'ultimate* structure' which must be reached, insisting at the same time that politics 'will be *discarded* after the *liberation'*. Just how is it possible to 'discard' politics after the liberation, is very far from being clear. But beyond this, the real ambiguity concerns *'liberation'* itself. What is its precise temporality? It cannot be the conquest of power only (though in the primary sense of the term it could be), since Marx links it to the *'ultimate* structure' (schliessliche Konstitution) of the proletariat. This means, in fact, that the act of liberation (the political revolution) falls well short of liberation as such. And the difficulties do not stop even there. For the 'ultimate structure' of the proletariat is, according to Marx, its necessary self-abolition. Consequently, we are asked to accept simultaneously that politics can be unproblematical — in the sense that the proletariat can simply *use* it as a *means* to its own sovereign end, whereafter it is discarded — and that it is extremely problematical, in view of its belonging to the 'old society' (and therefore inescapably conditions and fetters all emancipatory efforts), for which reason it must be radically transcended.

All this sounds somewhat bewildering. And yet, there is absolutely nothing wrong with this conception if it is assigned to its appropriate, *long-term*, scale of temporal reference. The difficulties start to multiply when one tries to make it operational in the context of immediate temporality. In that case it becomes suddenly clear that the translation of the long-term perspectives into the modality of immediately practicable strategies cannot be done without first elaborating the necessary *political mediations*. It is the structural gap of such missing mediations which is being filled by the theoretical ambiguities, matching the unresolved ambiguity of the two — fundamentally different — time-scales involved.

An equally serious theoretical ambiguity surfaces in *Wages, Price and Profit:* a work in which — in contrast to narrow Trade Unionist strategies — Marx recommends to the working class that

> Instead of the conservative motto, 'A fair day's wage for a fair day's work!' they ought to inscribe on their banner the *revolutionary* watchword, 'Abolition of the Wages System!'[370]

Undoubtedly, Marx's advocacy of attacking the *causes* of social evils, instead of fighting necessarily lost battles against the mere *effects* of capital's ongoing self-expansion, is the only correct strategy to adopt. However, the moment we try to understand the practical/operational meaning of 'abolition of the wages system', we are struck by a major ambiguity. For the scale of immediate temporality — the necessary frame of reference of all tangible political action — defines it as the abolition of private property and thus as the 'expropriation of the expropriators', which can be achieved by decree in the aftermath of the socialist revolution. Not surprisingly, this is how Marx's 'revolutionary watchword' concerning the abolition of the wages system has been interpreted as a rule.

The trouble is, though, that there is a great deal in the 'wages system' that cannot be abolished by any revolutionary decree and, consequently, must be transcended on the long-term time-scale of the new historic form. For immediately after the 'expropriation of the expropriators' not only the inherited means, materials and technology of production remain the same, together with their links to the given system of exchange, distribution and consumption, but the very organisation of the labour process itself stays deeply embedded in that *hierarchical social division of labour* which happens to be the heaviest burden of the inherited past. Thus, on the necessary scale of long-term temporality — the only one fit to achieve *irreversible* socialist transformations — the Marxian call for the 'abolition of the wages system' not only does not mean abolition of the *wages system:* it does not mean *abolition* at all.

The real target of the strategy advocated by Marx is the hierarchical social division of labour, which simply cannot be *abolished*. Just like the state, it can only be *transcended* through the *radical restructuring* of all those social structures and processes through which it necessarily articulates itself. Again, as we can see, there is nothing wrong with Marx's overall conception and its long-term historical temporality. The problem arises from its direct translation into what he calls a 'revolutionary watchword' to be inscribed on the banner of the given movement. For it is simply *impossible* to translate the *ultimate* perspectives *directly* into practicable political strategies.

As a result also in this respect the gap of *missing mediations* is filled by the profound ambiguity of Marx's terms of reference as linked to their temporal dimensions. And while he is absolutely right in insisting that 'the working class ought not to exaggerate to themselves the *ultimate* working of these *everyday* struggles',[371] the passionate reassertion of the validity of the broad historical perspectives does not solve the problem.

The conflict in temporality reveals an inherent difficulty in the realisation of the strategy itself; one that cannot be eliminated by metaphors and ambiguities but only by the historically feasible material and institutional mediations. For the dilemma, in its stark reality, is this: the revolutionary act of liberation is not quite liberation (or emancipation) itself, and the 'abolition of the wages system' is very far from being its real transcendence.

It is the historical unavailability of the necessary practical mediations which makes Marx settle for a solution that simply reiterates the ultimate aim as the general rule to guide the immediate action, bridging the gap between the far-distant horizon and what is practically feasible in the proximate future by saying that the working class *ought to* use 'their organised forces as a *lever* for the *final* emancipation of the working class, that is to say, the *ultimate* abolition of the wages system.'[372]

Thus, the crucial issue for socialist politics is: how to gain a firm hold on the *necessary mediations* while avoiding the trap of *false mediations* constantly produced by the established order so as to integrate the forces of opposition. For the actuality of a given set of 'bad mediations' — with all their 'false positivity' rightly condemned by Marx — can only be countered by another set of specific mediations, in accordance with the changing circumstances. In other words, the accommodating pressures of *immediate* temporality cannot be effectively transcended by simply reasserting the validity of the overall historical horizons. And while the social formation of capital is, as Marx says, undoubtedly *transitory* in character (if considered on its proper historical scale, embracing the whole epoch), from the point of view of the forces *immediately* engaged in fighting its deadening domination, it could not be farther from being transitory. Thus, to turn the socialist project into an *irreversible reality*, we have to accomplish many *'transitions within the transition'*, just as under another aspect socialism defines itself as constantly self-renewing *'revolutions within the revolution.'*

IN this sense, the radical transcendence of the state is one side of the coin, representing the *ultimate* horizons of all socialist strategy. As such it must be complemented by the other side, namely the project of concrete *mediations* through which the ultimate strategy can be progressively translated into reality. The question is, therefore, how to acknowledge, on the one hand, the demands of *immediate temporality* without being trapped by it; and on the other: how to remain firmly oriented towards the ultimate *historical* perspectives of the Marxian project without becoming remote from the burning determinations of the immediate present.

Since for the foreseeable future the horizons of politics as such cannot be transcended, this means simultaneously 'negating' the state and operating on its terrain. As the general organ of the established social order, the state is inevitably biassed in favour of the immediate present and resists the actualisation of the broad historical perspectives of a socialist transformation which postulates the state's 'withering away'. Thus the task defines itself as a dual challenge for:

- (1) instituting non-state-organs of social control and growing self-management which can increasingly take over the most important areas of social activity in the course of our 'transition within the transition'; and, as conditions permit, for

- (2) producing a conscious shift in the state-organs themselves — (in conjunction with (1) and by means of the necessary internal and global mediations) — so as to make feasible the realisation of the ultimate historical perspectives of the socialist project.

TO be sure, all such developments are tied to the maturation of some objective conditions. Confronting the problematic of the state in its entirety involves a multiplicity of internal and external determinations in their close interconnectedness, in that the state is both the general organ of a given society and represents the links of the latter with the social totality of its historical epoch. Consequently, the state is, in a sense, *mediation par excellence*, since it combines around a common political focus the totality of internal relations — from the economic interchanges to the strictly cultural ties — and integrates them to varying degrees also into the global framework of the dominant social formation.

Since capital, in Marx's life-time, was very far from its present-day articulation as a truly global system, equally, its overall political command structure as a system of globally interconnected states was far less visible in its precise mediatedness. It is, therefore, by no means surprising that Marx never succeeded in sketching even the bare outlines of his theory of the state, although the latter was assigned a very precise and important place in his projected system as a whole. Today the situation is quite different, in that the global system of capital, under a variety of very different (indeed contradictory) forms, finds its political equivalent in the totality of interdependent state- and inter-state-relations. This is why the elaboration of a Marxist theory of the state is both possible and necessary today. Indeed, it is vitally important for the future of viable socialist strategies.

THE Marxian proposition that *'Men must change from top to bottom the conditions of their industrial and political existence, and consequently their whole manner of being'* remains more than ever valid as the necessary strategic direction of the socialist project. For the defeats suffered in the twentieth century were to a large extent due to the abandonment of the real target of socialist transformation. That is: the necessity to win the epochal war by going irreversibly beyond capital (this is what is meant by reaching the 'new historic form'), instead of being satisfied with ephemeral victories in a few battles against the weaker divisions of capitalism (e.g. the economically backward and militarily defeated Czarist system in Russia), remaining at the same time hopelessly trapped by the alienating self-expansionary imperatives of the capital system itself. Indeed, what makes matters worse in this respect is that a socialist revolution even in the most 'advanced capitalist' country would in no way alter the need for, and the diffi-culties involved in, going beyond capital.

Economic backwardness is only one of the many obstacles that must be overcome on the road to the 'new historic form', and by no means the greatest of them. The temptation to relapse into the formerly settled ways of running the social metabolism in a formerly dominant 'advanced capitalist' country, once the worst conditions of the crisis which precipitated the revolutionary explosion had been left behind — so as to be able to follow again 'the line of least resistance' at the expense of others who find themselves in dependency to the 'metropolitan developed country' in question — cannot be underrated. The successful reali-zation of the task of radically restructuring the global capital system — with its multi-faceted and unavoidably conflicting internal and international dimen-sions — is feasible only as an immense historic enterprise, sustained over many decades. It would be reassuring to think, as some people had actually suggested, that once the capitalistically advanced countries embark on the road of socialist transformation, the journey will be an easy one. However, it is usually forgotten in such sanguine projections that what is at stake is a monumental leap from the rule of capital to a *qualitatively* different mode of social metabolic control. And in that respect the fact of being tied by a more perfected network of structural determinations to the reproductive and distributive practices of 'advanced capitalism' represents a rather dubious asset.

The imperative to go beyond capital as a social metabolic control, with its almost forbidding difficulties, is the shared predicament of humanity as a whole. For the capital system by its very nature is a global/universalistic mode of control which cannot be historically superseded except by a likewise all-embracing social metabolic alternative. Thus every attempt to overcome the constraints of a historically determinate stage of capitalism — within the structural parameters of the necessarily expansion-oriented and crisis-prone capital system — is bound to fail sooner or later, irrespective of how 'advanced' or 'underdeveloped' the countries which attempt to do so might be. The idea that once the relation of forces between capitalist and postcapitalist countries changes in favour of the latter, humanity's journey to socialism will be 'plain sailing', is naive at best. It was conceived in the orbit of the 'encircled revolution', attributing the failures of the Soviet type system to external factors (also when talking about the 'in-ternal sabotage of the enemy'), ignoring or wilfully disregarding the material and political antagonisms necessarily generated by the forcibly surplus-labour extracting postcapitalist order both under and after Stalin. It is the *internal* dynamics of development which ultimately decides the issue, potentially decid-ing it for the worse even under the best external relation of forces.

Thus, the concept of *irreversibility* of socialist transformation is meaningful only if it refers to the point of no return in the internal dynamics of development, beyond the structural determinations of capital as a mode of social metabolic control, fully embracing all three dimensions of the inherited system: CAPITAL, LABOUR, and the STATE. The *qualitative leap* in Marxian discourse — the well known aphorism in *The Eighteenth Brumaire of Louis Bonaparte* about 'Hic Rhodus, hic salta!' — anticipates the time when the long sustained struggle to move beyond capital becomes *globally irreversible* because it is fully in tune with the *internal* development of the countries concerned. And in Marx's view that becomes possible only as a result of the cumulative corrective impact of radical self-criticism exercised by the social agency of emancipation, labour, which must be not nominally (as seen so far, under the authority of the postcapitalist 'personifications of capital') but genuinely and effectively in charge of the social metabolic process.

Clearly, however, the process of socialist transformation — precisely because it must embrace all aspects of the interrelationship between *capital, labour,* and the *state* — is conceivable only as a form of transitional restructuring based on the inherited and progressively alterable leverage of material mediations. As in the case of Goethe's father (even if for very different reasons), it is not possible to pull down the existing building and erect a wholly new edifice in its place on totally new foundations.Life must go on in the shored up house during the entire course of rebuilding, 'taking away one storey after another from the bottom upwards, slipping in the new structure, so that in the end none of the old house should be left'. Indeed, the task is even more difficult than that. For the decaying timber frame of the building must be also replaced in the course of extricating humankind from the perilous structural framework of the capital system.

Disconcertingly, the 'expropriation of the expropriators' leaves the edifice of the capital system standing. All it can achieve on its own is to change the *type* of personification of capital, but not the need for such personification. Often even the personnel can remain the same (as not only the significant continuity in the commanding economic and state personnel in postrevolutionary societies demonstrated but even more so the post-Soviet restoratory moves all over Eastern Europe), changing, so to speak, the party membership card only. This is because the three fundamental dimensions of the system — CAPITAL, LABOUR, and the STATE — are *materially* constituted and linked to one another, and not simply on a legal/political basis.

Accordingly, neither capital, nor labour, nor indeed the state can be simply *abolished* by even the most radical juridical intervention. It is, therefore, by no means accidental that historical experience had produced plentiful examples of the *strengthening* of the postrevolutionary state, but not even the smallest step in the direction of its 'withering away'. For postrevolutionary labour in its immediately feasible mode of existence, whether in formerly advanced capitalist or in underdeveloped countries, remains directly tied to the substance of capital, i.e. the latter's material existence as the ongoing structural determination of the labour process, and not to its historically contingent form of juridical personification. The substance of capital as the materially embedded, incorrigibly hierarchical, expansion-oriented and accumulation-driven determining power of the social metabolic process, remains the same for as long as this system — whether in its capitalist or in its postcapitalist forms — can successfully exercise the historically alienated controlling functions of labour. By contrast the political/juridical forms of personification through which the objective reproductive imperatives of the capital system ('the rule of wealth over society' in Marx's words) continue to be imposed on labour *can and must* vary in tune with the changing historical circumstances, in that such variations arise as necessary attempts to remedy some major disturbance or crisis of the system within its own structural parameters. This is true not only in the historically rather rare cases of dramatic shift from a capitalist to a postcapitalist form of social metabolic reproduction but also in the much more frequent and in its character on the whole temporary changes from liberal-democratic to military-dictatorial varieties of capitalism, and back again to the economically more viable liberal-capitalist form. The only thing that must remain constant as regards the personifications of capital in all such metamorphoses of the controlling personnel, across centuries, is that their functional identity must be always defined in *contra-position* to labour.

Given the inseparability of the three dimensions of the fully articulated capital system — capital, labour, and the state —, it is inconceivable to emancipate labour without simultaneously also superseding capital and the state as well. For, paradoxically, the fundamental material supporting pillar of capital is not the state but labour in its continued structural dependency from capital. Lenin and others spoke of the unavoidable necessity 'to smash the bourgeois state' as the immediate task of the proletarian dictatorship in the aftermath of the conquest of political power. At the same time, as a warning, Lukács projected the picture of the proletariat 'turning its dictatorship against itself', as we have seen above. The difficulty is, though, that the conquest of state power is very far from equalling the control of social metabolic reproduction. It is indeed possible to smash the bourgaois state through the conquest of political power, at least to a significant extent. However, it is quite impossible to 'smash' labour's inherited structural dependency from capital. For that dependency is materially secured by the established hierarchical structural division of labour. It can be altered for the better only through the radical restructuring of the totality of social reproductive processes, i.e. through the progressive rebuilding of the inherited edifice in its entirety. Preaching the necessity — and the ethical rightfulness — of high labour discipline, as Lukács tried to do, avoids (at best) the question of who is actually in charge of the productive and distributive determinations of the postrevolutionary labour process. So long as the vital controlling functions of the social metabolism are not effectively taken over and autonomously exercised by the associated producers, but left under the authority of a separate controlling personnel (i.e. the new type of personification of capital), labour itself self-defeatingly continues to reproduce the power of capital over against itself, materially maintaining and extending thereby the rule of alienated wealth over society.

This is what makes all talk about the 'withering away of the state' totally unrealistic under such circumstances. For in the aftermath of the 'expropriation of the expropriators' and the institution of a new, but equally separate and superimposed, controlling personnel, the authority of the latter must be politically established and enforced in the absence of the old juridical entitlement to control the productive and distributive practices on the basis of private property ownership. Thus the *strengthening* of the postrevolutionary state not simply in relation to the *outside* world — which, after the defeat of the interventionist forces in Russia was in fact unable to exercise a major impact on the course of *internal* developments — but over against the *labour force,* for the sake of the politically regulated maximal extraction of surplus-labour, becomes a perverse structural necessity, and not a more or less easily corrigible 'bureaucratic degeneration', to be rectified on the political plane, thanks to a new 'political revolution'. As the implosion of the Soviet capital system demonstrated, given the enormously strengthened state power in the country it was much easier to engineer a *political counter-revolution from above* than to realistically envisage a *political revolution from below* as the corrective to the contradictions of the established order. For even if a new political revolution of the masses could prevail for a while, the real task of fundamental restructuring of the postcapitalist capital system would still remain. By contrast Gorbachev's pretended 'perestroika' did not have to restructure anything at all in the domain of the given hierarchical/structural social metabolic control. For its proclamation of the 'equality of all types of property' — i.e. the *juridical restoration of the rights of capitalist private property* for the benefit of the few — operated in the sphere of the personifications of capital, making only 'justifiably' hereditary (in the name of the promised 'economic rationality' and 'market efficiency') what they already controlled *de facto*. Instituting legal/political changes on the plane of entitlement to property is a child's play compared to the burdensome and prolonged task of superseding capital's mode of controlling the social reproductive order.

The 'withering away of the state' — without which the idea of realizing socialism cannot be seriously entertained for a moment — is inconceivable without the 'withering away of capital' as the regulator of the social metabolic process. The vicious circle of labour being locked into its structural dependency from capital, on the one hand, and into a subordinate position at the level of political decision making by an alien state power on the other, can only be broken if the producers progressively cease to reproduce the material supremacy of capital. This they can only do by radically challenging the hierarchical structural division of labour. It is therefore most important to bear in mind that the perverse strengthening of the postcapitalist state is not a self-sustaining cause but inseparable from the structural dependency of labour from capital. This contradictory determination of labour under the continued rule of capital (even if in a new form) asserts itself despite the fact that capital always was — and can only be—reproduced as the embodiment of labour in an alienated and self-perpetuating form. Since, however, the antagonistic determination in question is inherent in the *material command structure of capital*, which is only *complemented by* but not *grounded in* the state as the system's comprehensive political command structure, the problem of labour's self-emancipation cannot be addressed at the level of politics only (or even primarily). The countless 'revolutions betrayed' across modern history provide painfully abundant evidence in this respect.

The necessary critique of state power, with the aim of radically curtailing and ultimately superseding it, acquires its sense only if it is practically implemented in its social-metabolic/material-reproductive setting. For the 'withering away' of the state implies not only the 'withering away' of capital (as the objectified and reified controller of the social reproductive order) but also the self-transcendence of labour as subordinate to capital's material imperatives enforced by the prevailing system of structural/hierarchical division of labour and state power. This is possible only if all controlling functions of the social metabolism — which must be under all forms of the rule of capital vested in the material and political command structure of an alienated decision making power — are progressively appropriated and positively exercised by the associated producers. In this sense the objective structural (in contrast to by itself unsustainable political/juridical) displacement of the personifications of capital through a system of genuine *self-management* is the key to a successful rebuilding of the inherited structures.

NOTES to Part Two

[1] The Petöfi Circle — named after the great revolutionary poet and the most radical leader of the 1848-49 uprising and war of independence against the Habsburg domination of Hungary — was in 1956 the most effective public forum for articulating the demand for the eradication of Stalinism in the country; a process that culminated a few months later in the October uprising.

[2] László Sziklai, 'Megkésett prófécia? Lukács György testamentuma', *Népszabadság*, 31 December 1988, p.7.

[3] Rezsö Nyers, 'The Present and Future of Restructuring', *The New Hungarian Quarterly*, Spring 1989 (No. 113), pp.24-5.

[4] I have discussed these problems in 'The Meaning of Rosa Luxemburg's Tragedy', *The Power of Ideology*, pp.313-37.

[5] 'Lukács György politikai végrendelete: kiadatlan interjú 1971-böl', ('G. Lukács's Political Testament: Unpublished Interview from 1971'), *Társadalmi Szemle*, vol. XLV, April 1990, pp.63-89.

[6] Lukács, 'The Metaphysics of Tragedy' (1910), in *Soul and Form*, Merlin Press, London, 1974, p.160.

[7] *Ibid.*, p.162.

[8] *Ibid.*, pp.167-8.

[9] *Ibid.*, p.171.

[10] *Soul and Form* (Die Seele und die Formen) was Lukács's first internationally acclaimed book. It contained a group of beautifully written essays, articulated around a few recurrent 'Leitmotifs'. 'The Metaphysics of Tragedy' was the concluding piece and the final summation of the ideas developed in this volume.

[11] *Ibid.*, p.160.

[12] *Ibid.*, pp.173-4.

[13] Lukács, *The Theory of the Novel*, Merlin Press, London, 1971, p.12.

[14] *Ibid.*, p.20.

[15] *Ibid.*, p.21.

[16] *Ibid.*, p.18.

[17] *Soul and Form*, p.172.

[18] Lukács, *History and Class Consciousness*, Merlin Press, London, 1971, p.192.

[19] *Ibid.*, p.193.

[20] As Lukács wrote in his 1962 Preface to *The Theory of the Novel*:

> The fact that Ernst Bloch continued undeterred to cling to his synthesis of 'left' ethics and 'right' epistemology (cf. e.g. *Philosophische Grundfragen I, Zur Ontologie des Noch-Nicht-Seins*, — 'Fundamental Questions of Philosophy: The Ontology of Not-Yet-Being' — Frankfurt 1961) does honour to his strength of character but cannot modify the outmoded nature of his theoretical position.

(*Op. cit.*, p.22.)

[21] See Ernst Bloch, 'Discussing Expressionism' and Georg Lukács, 'Realism in the Balance' in the volume: E. Bloch, G. Lukács, B. Brecht, W. Benjamin, Th. W. Adorno, *Aesthetics and Politics*, NLB, London, 1977, pp.16-59. Both Bloch's and Lukács's articles originally appeared in 1937.

[22] *Soul and Form*, p.18.

[23] *Ibid.*, p.174.

[24] Georg Lukács, *Political Writings, 1919-1929: The Question of Parliamentarism and Other*

Essays, NLB, London 1972, p.14.

[25] As Lukács put it:

The first such thesis is: that the development of society is determined exclusively by forces present within that society (in the Marxist view, by the *class struggle* and the transformation of the relations of production). The second: that the direction of this development can be clearly determined, even if it is *not yet fully understood*. The third: that this direction has to be related in a certain, albeit *still not fully understood* fashion, to human objectives; such a relationship can be perceived and *made conscious*, and the process of making it conscious exerts a positive influence on the development itself. And finally, the fourth thesis: that the relationship in question is possible because, although the motive forces of society are independent of every *individual* human consciousness, or its will and its objectives, their existence is inconceivable except in the form of *human consciousness, human will and human objectives*. Obviously the laws which have to become effective in this relationship are reflected for the most part in an obscure or distorted manner in the *consciousness of individual* human beings.

Ibid., pp.14-15.

[26] *Ibid.*, p.15.

[27] The last two quotations *Ibid.* p.15

[28] *Soul and Form*, p.17.

[29] *Ibid.*, p.93.

[30] *Ibid.*, p.31.

[31] *Ibid.*, p.18.

[32] *Ibid.*

[33] See Lukács's posthumously published volumes, *Heidelberger Philosophie der Kunst (1912-1914)*, and *Heidelberger Aesthetik (1916-1918)*, edited by György Márkus and Frank Benseler, Luchterhand Verlag, Darmstadt & Neuwied, 1974.

[34] *Ibid.*, p.32.

[35] 'What Is Orthodox Marxism?' (first version, 1919), in Georg Lukács, *Political Writings, 1919-1929*, p.26

[36] 'Tactics and Ethics', in *Political Writings, 1919-1929*, p.8.

[37] *History and Class Consciousness*, p.312.

[38] *Political Writings, 1919-1929*, p.27.

[39] *Ibid.*, p.26.

[40] *Ibid.*, p.27.

[41] *Ibid.*, p.8.

[42] *Ibid.*, p.9.

[43] *Ibid.*

[44] *Ibid.*, pp.26-27.

[45] *Ibid.*, p.10.

[46] Ernst Bloch, *Das Prinzip Hoffnung*, Aufbau-Verlag, Berlin, 1959.

[47] 'I am personally rather opposed to Bloch's "Principle of Hope". This view does not concern only Bloch. For a very long time I shared the Epicurean conception of Spinoza and Goethe rejecting fear and hope which they considered dangerous for the freedom of true humanity.' From a Letter to his German Publisher, Frank Benseler, 21 January 1961, quoted on pp.21-22 of Lukács's *Versuche zu einer Ethik*, edited by György Iván Mezei, Akadémiai Kiadó, Budapest, 1994.

[48] Lenin, *Letter to the Hungarian workers*, 27 March 1919.

[49] Lukács, 'Party and Class', in *Political Writings, 1919-1929*, p.36.

[50] Lukács, 'A marxista filozófia feladatai az új demokráciában'. (The Tasks of Marxist Philosophy in the New Democracy. Text of a lecture given at the Congress of Marxist Philosophers in Milan, on 20 December 1947.) Published as a separate volume in Budapest, 1948. Quotation taken from pp.11-12.

[51] Sartre, *Being and Nothingness,* Methuen, London, 1969, p.429.

[52] *Ibid.,* p.423. While one can understand why the author of *Being and Nothingness* takes his stand in this way, it is astonishing to see Althusser assume the same position (in his attacks on 'theoretical humanism' as well as in his curious theory of ideology), castigating dissenting Marxists from the standpoint of a twentieth century bourgeois idea *par excellence.*

[53] Sartre, *Op. cit.,* p.240

[54] *Ibid.,* p.364.

[55] *Ibid.,* pp.422-9. For the connections of these problems with Sartre's philosophy as a whole, see Chapter 5 of my book, *The Work of Sartre: Search for Freedom,* Harvester Press, Brighton, 1979, pp.158-243.

[56] To use a term put into relief by C.B. Macpherson which fittingly characterizes a trend that goes well beyond his own concerns, all the way down to our own days. See Macpherson's influential book, *The Political Theory of Possessive Individualism: Hobbes to Locke,* Oxford University Press, London, 1962.

[57] This happens to be the case even prior to the bourgeois revolution which is essentially *political* in character. Its ideologists argue in favour of bringing the ruling institutions 'rationally' in line with the requirements of a productive system capable of satisfying individual appetites and the spontaneous inclinations of 'human nature', not to mention later stages when the dictates of a fully developed commodity society are taken for granted as the self-evident presuppositions of social theory.

[58] Of course, this needs serious qualifications. For we know only too well that *some* self-seeking strategies actually succeed at the expense of others. However, it is impossible to make their success intelligible without focusing on the prevailing social relations of domination and subordination. By contrast, bourgeois theories of atomistic individual interaction have to operate, on the one hand, with the fictions of the 'benevolent state' and the equally benevolent 'hidden hand' as the guardians of the social interest (which implies acting against intolerable individual excesses), and on the other hand they are forced to appeal to mythically inflated psychological characteristics ('entrepreneurial spirit', 'personal initiative', etc.) and resort to self-contradictory assumptions — the notion of 'individual material incentive' to make intelligible the strangely discriminatory manifestations of an alleged 'human nature' in powerfully driving forward some individuals while failing to motivate others — in order to produce anything like a plausible explanation of the dynamics of actual social processes.

[59] Lukács, *History and Class Consciousness,* Merlin Press, London, 1971, p.221. Page numbers in brackets refer to this edition.

[60] A concise and clearly written book which took its inspiration from Lukács in the 1930s is Franz Jakubowski's *Ideology and Superstructure in Historical Materialism* (Allison & Busby, London, 1976, 132pp.), first published in 1936 under the title: *Der ideologische Überbau in der materialistischen Geschichtsauffassung.* In the postwar years Lucien Goldmann applied with great success some of Lukács's key concepts — especially that of 'ascribed consciousness' — to the study of philosophy and literature. See his *Immanuel Kant* (NLB, London, 1971, French: 1948); *The Human Sciences and Philosophy* (Jonathan Cape, London, 1966, French: 1952 and 1966); *The Hidden God* (Routledge & Kegan Paul, London, 1967, French: 1956); *Recherches Dialectiques* (Gallimard, Paris, 1958); *Pour une sociologie du roman* (Gallimard, Paris, 1964); *Lukács and Heidegger* (Routledge & Kegan Paul, London, 1977, French: 1973). For a recent study of reification in the Lukácsian spirit, see José Paulo Netto, *Capitalismo e reificaçâo,* Livraria Editora Ciéncias Humanas, Sâo Paulo, 1981.

[61] See, for instance, pp.52-3, 65-6, 68-9, and 79-80.

[62] It is oblique in that Lukács does not explicitly name his adversaries — like Béla Kun: one of Stalin's favourites at the time — and the policies they advocate. His criticism is

formulated in general, rather abstract terms. Nevertheless, the objects of his criticism, however oblique, are at this point in time still clearly identifiable political/organizational complexes. By contrast from the nineteen thirties, following the defeat of his 'Blum Theses' and therewith the end of his direct political role, Lukács is confined to philo-sophical/literary subjects, and his critical references to political strategies are couched in greatly mediated 'Aesopic language', as he himself puts it after 1956.

[63] *Demokratisierung heute und morgen* ('Democratization today and tomorrow'), a search-ing examination of the contradictions of both Western democracy and the Stalinist type of development, written in German in 1968, mainly in response to the Soviet interven-tion in Czechoslovakia; published in Hungarian twenty years later under the title: *A demokratizálódás jelene és jövöje* ('The present and future of democratization', Magvetö Kiadó, Budapest, 1988), briefly discussed in Section 6.1.1 and in Chapter 10.

[64] In this latter work, Lukács more than once reminds his readers of the spontaneous establishment of Workers Councils in the course of revolutionary upheavals, pointing to the events of 1871, 1905 and 1917. This is how he sums up his views on the subject in one of the key passages of his book on *Democratization*:

> The task of socialist democracy as the transitional social form leading to the 'realm of freedom' is precisely the supersession of the dualism between private man and citizen. The great mass movements mentioned already, which always prepared and accompanied the socialist revolutions, prove that this is not an ideal construct. Naturally, what we have in mind here is the way in which the councils were constituted in 1871, 1905 and 1917. We have shown already that this movement — which had for its aim the rational solution of the workers' vital existential problems, from the everyday concerns of work and housing to the great issues of social life, in accordance with their elementary class needs — was squeezed out by a bureaucratic machine after the victorious ending of the civil war; we have shown that Stalin later on unchallengeably consolidated the bureaucratic regulators and practi-cally liquidated the whole council system. ... Thus, the working masses lost their character as the *subjects* of social decision making: they have become again *mere objects* of the ever-more-powerful, ubiquitous bureaucratic system of regulation which dominated all aspects of their life. With this, the road of socialist development that could have led towards the 'realm of freedom' had been practically blocked. (Quoted from the Hungarian edition, pp.159-61.)

However, as we shall see in Chapter 10, even in 1968, when Stalin can be openly criticized without fear of imprisonment or worse, the Workers Councils are celebrated by Lukács as belonging to past history, without any realistic prospect for their reconsti-tution under present-day circumstances. This is in line with the partial reversal of Lukács's original enthusiasm for the Workers Councils; a reversal which takes place already in the last essays of *History and Class Consciousness*. (On this issue see Chapter 9.)

It is also important to point out in the present context that, unlike in *History and Class Consciousness*, in *The Present and Future of Democratization* there is no more mention of the necessary 'elimination of the bourgeois separation of the legislature, administra-tion and the judiciary.' Since Lukács is now resigned to the idea that one cannot aim at more than the establishment of a 'realistic division of labour between the Party and the State', the task of eliminating the bourgeois separation of powers is replaced in his study written in 1968 by the much more abstract and institutionally unspecified demand for 'the supersession of the dualism between private man and citizen', as we have seen in the last quote.

[65] See the representative volume *Geschichte und Klassenbewusstsein Heute: Diskussion und Dokumentation* by F. Cerutti, D. Claussen, H-J. Krahl, O. Negt and A. Schmidt, prepared in 1969 but published only in 1971 by Verlag de Munter, Amsterdam. See also Hans-Jürgen Krahl's important collection of essays, *Konstitution und Klassenkampf: zur*

historischen Dialektik von bürgerlicher Emanzipation und proletarischer Revolution, Verlag Neue Kritik, Frankfurt, 1971. For a critical reexamination of this experience and its relation to the early Lukács, see Furio Cerutti, *Totalitá, bisogni, organizzazione: ridiscutendo 'Storia e coscienza di classe',* La Nuova Italia, Firenze, 1980.

66 The following sentence is a typical example of the passionately heightened character of this direct appeal: 'Unless the proletariat wishes to share the fate of the bourgeoisie and perish wretchedly and ignominiously in the death-throes of capitalism, it must accomplish this task *in full consciousness.*' (p.314. Lukács's italics.)

67 It was by no means accidental that another seminal influence in shaping the ideology of the student movement was Marcuse's *One-Dimensional Man* (Routledge & Kegan Paul, London, 1964). For Marcuse insisted that the formerly oppressed people, 'previously the ferment of social change, have "moved up" to become the ferment of social cohesion', leaving only the outcasts in opposition and thereby a 'hope without hope' that 'in this period, the historical extremes may meet again: *the most advanced consciousness of humanity,* and its most exploited force'. (pp.256-7).

68 Lenin, '"Left-Wing" Communism — An Infantile Disorder', Collected Works, Vol. 31, p.22.

It is true that Lenin asserts in the previous sentence that 'soon after the victory of the proletarian revolution in at least one of the advanced countries, a sharp change will probably come about; Russia will cease to be the model and will once again become a backward country (in the "Soviet" and the socialist sense).' *(Ibid.,* p.21.) This is the sentence which Lukács likes to quote in his critique of Stalininst developments. However, to do so is a completely one-sided presentation of Lenin's line of argument. For he continues his article immediately after the sentence just quoted like this:

> At the present moment in history, however, it is the *Russian model* that reveals to *all* countries something — and something highly significant — of their *near and immediate future.* Advanced workers in all lands have realized this; more often than not, they have grasped it with their revolutionary class instinct rather than realized it. *(Ibid.,* p.22. The word 'all' is italicized by Lenin.)

Thus, the adoption by the Third International of the perspective according to which the Russian revolution and its aftermath represented the 'near and immediate future' of even the capitalistically most advanced countries cannot be dissociated from Lenin. This is not altered by the fact that he had to formulate this strategic evaluation of the given historical conditions in opposition to the 'leaders of the Second International, such as Kautsky in Germany and Otto Bauer and Friedrich Adler in Austria, who have failed to understand this, which is why they have proved to be reactionaries and advocates of the worst kind of opportunism and social treachery'. *(Ibid.,* p.22.) For Rosa Luxemburg was no less opposed to them than Lenin, condemning their blindness as regards the world historical significance of the Russian revolution in the sharpest possible terms.

69 Luxemburg, *The Russian Revolution,* The University of Michigan Press, 1961, p.80.

70 Luxemburg, *Reform or Revolution,* Pathfinder Press, New York, 1970, p.50.

71 Luxemburg, *Spartacus,* Young Socialist Publications, Colombo, 1971, p.27.

72 Notice again the characteristic use of inverted commas, in line with our earlier examples.

73 Luxemburg, *Reform or Revolution,* p.58.

74 *Ibid.,* p.59.

75 This is how Rosa Luxemburg argues the points at issue in immediate continuation of our last quote:

> This shows that opportunist practice is essentially irreconcilable with Marxism. But it also proves that opportunism is incompatible with socialism (the socialist movement) in general, that its internal tendency is to push the labour movement into bourgeois paths, that opportunism tends to paralyze completely the proletarian class

struggle. The latter, considered historically, has evidently nothing to do with Marxist doctrine. For, before Marx, and independently from him, there have been labour movements and various socialist doctrines, each of which, in its own way, was the theoretic expression, corresponding to the conditions of the time, of the struggle of the working class for emancipation. The theory that consists in basing socialism on the moral notion of justice, on a struggle against the mode of *distribution,* instead of basing it on the struggle against the mode of *production,* the conception of class antagonisms as an antagonism between the poor and the rich, the effort to graft the 'cooperative principle' on capitalist economy — all the nice notions found in Bernstein's doctrine — already existed before Marx. All these theories were *in their time* [Luxemburg's italics], in spite of their insufficiency, effective theories of the proletarian class struggle. They were the children's seven-league boots in which the proletariat learned to walk upon the scene of history.

But after the development of the class struggle and its reflex in its social conditions had led to the abandonment of these theories and to the elaboration of the principles of scientific socialism, there could be no socialism — at least in Germany — outside of Marxist socialism, and there could be no socialist class struggle outside of the social democracy. From then on, socialism and Marxism, the proletarian struggle for emancipation, and the social democracy were identical. That is why the *return to pre-Marxist socialist theories* no longer signifies today a return to the seven-league boots of the childhood of the proletariat, but a return to the puny worn-out slippers of the bourgeoisie. *(Ibid.,* pp.59-60.)

Significantly enough, in a general discussion of methodology, concerned with the development of European philosophy in the last three centuries, Sartre reiterates the point made by Rosa Luxemburg about anti-Marxist attempts to go 'beyond Marx'. He writes:

The periods of philosophical creation are rare. Between the seventeenth century and the twentieth, I see three such periods, which I would designate by the names of the men who dominated them: there is the 'moment' of Descartes and Locke, that of Kant and Hegel, finally that of Marx. These three philosophies become, each in its turn, the humus of every particular thought and the horizon of all culture; there is no going beyond them so long as man has not gone beyond the historical moment which they express. I have often remarked on the fact that an 'anti-Marxist' argument is only the apparent rejuvenation of a pre-Marxist idea. A so-called 'going beyond' Marxism will be at worst only a return to pre-Marxism; at best, only the rediscovery of a thought already contained in the philosophy which one believes he has gone beyond.

Sartre, *The Problem of Method,* Methuen, London, 1963, p.7.

[76] Some of these problems are discussed in the present volume Chapters 11-13 of Part Two and in 'The Division of Labour and the Postcapitalist State' of Part Four.

[77] In his essay on 'Class Structure and Social Consciousness', Tom Bottomore understandably voiced his surprise 'that Lukács should repeat, with great approval, in his new preface of 1967, the passage which opposed method to content in the opening essay of *History and Class Consciousness'.* (See *Aspects of History and Class Consciousness,* ed. by I. Mészáros, Routledge & Kegan Paul, London, 1971, p.55.) However, if we remember the function which the idea of a 'methodological guarantee' for the certainty of victory plays in Lukács's thought, then the reassertion of its validity in 1967 is far from surprising. In fact Lukács's constant polemics in defence of the dialectical method against 'mechanical materialism' and 'vulgar Marxism', in his eyes also fulfil an important political function, in the struggle against sectarianism and its undialectical cult of immediacy. The long line of works in this respect goes from his critique of Bukharin's *Historical Materialism* through his essay on 'Moses Hess and the Problems of Idealist

Dialectic' to *The Young Hegel, The Desctruction of Reason,* and, ultimately, to *The Ontology of Social Being.* Indeed, as the conditions of open ideological and political debate disappear with the consolidation of Stalinism, the discourse on how to overcome the proletariat's 'ideological crisis' is more and more confined to arguing in abstract theoretical terms in favour of the dialectical method, expressing, thus, in the 'Aesopic language' of philosophical methodology Lukács's greatly mediated political aspirations. *(The Young Hegel* is the most important document of this 'Aesopic phase' in Lukács's development.)

Another important aspect of this problem is Lukács's insistence throughout his life that there can be only one 'true Marxism' (i.e., 'orthodoxy' in inverted commas, in order to contrast it with institutionally imposed orthodoxy). At the same time, in accordance with the innermost character of his discourse — centred on the notions of the 'ideological crisis' and the 'responsibility of intellectuals' to pave the way out of that crisis — he is deeply concerned about enlarging the intellectual influence of Marxism.

Thus the two determinations come together in the methodological definition of 'true Marxism'. On the one hand, it must be able to exercise a critical/excluding function against 'Stalinist dogmatism', 'mechanical materialism', 'vulgar Marxism', etc., without frontally attacking the powerful institutional objects of this critique on political/economic issues. And on the other hand, the definition of Marxism must be flexible enough to embrace in a 'non-sectarian' way, from a fairly broad political spectrum, all serious scholars and intellectuals who are willing to make the positive step towards Marxism.

Both these aspects are clearly visible in a lecture given in Rome, Milan and Turin in June 1956 — (*La lotta fra progresso e reazione nella cultura d'oggi,* Feltrinelli, Milano, 1957) — when Lukács can for the first time, after the XX Congress of the Soviet Party, openly challenge his adversaries. He insists that in the interest of the 'clarifying propaganda of true Marxism' (p.18), aimed at exercising 'ideological influence ... to lead in a new direction the non-Marxist intellectuals' (p.34) and thus 'to influence the ideological ferment and development of the world' (p.46), it is necessary 'to break definitively with sectarianism and dogmatism' (p.44) The rejected 'Stalinist dogmatism' (p.34) is defined, again, primarily in methodological terms: as the 'absence of *mediation*' (p.5), the reifying 'confusion of *tendency* with accomplished *fact*' (p.7), the *'mechanical* subordination of the *part* to the *whole*' (p.9), the assertion of an 'immediate relationship between the *fundamental* tenets of the theory and the problems of the *day*' (p.10), the 'dogmatic restriction of dialectical materialism' (p.36) and, most importantly, as the misconceived belief that *'Marxism is a collection of dogmas'* (p.45). He also states categorically that the only way to exercise ideological influence is through *'immanent* critique' (p.25) which puts the methodological issues into the foreground.

It is in the same spirit that he praises in the 1967 Preface to *History and Class Consciousness* his old methodological 'definition of orthodoxy in Marxism which I now think not only objectively correct but also capable of exerting a considerable influence even today when we are on the eve of a Marxist renaissance'. (p.xxv.)

[78] 'Bourgeois revolutions, like those of the eighteenth century, storm swiftly from success to success; their dramatic effects outdo each other; men and things seem set in sparkling brilliants; ecstasy is the everyday spirit; but they are short-lived; soon they have attained their zenith, and a long crapulent depression lays hold of society before it learns soberly to assimilate the results of its storm-and-stress period. On the other hand, proletarian revolutions, like those of the nineteenth century, criticize themselves constantly, interrupt themselves continually in their own course, come back to the apparently accomplished in order to begin it afresh, deride with unmerciful thoroughness the inadequacies, weaknesses and paltriness of their first attempts, seem to throw down their adversary only in order that he may draw new strength from the earth and rise again, more gigantic, before them, recoil ever and anon from the indefinite prodigiousness of their own aims, until a situation has been created which makes all turning back impossible,

and the conditions themselves cry out:

Hic Rhodus, hic salta!

Here is the rose, here dance!'

Marx, 'The Eighteenth Brumaire of Louis Bonaparte', in Marx and Engels, *Selected Works*, Lawrence & Wishart, London, 1958, vol. 1, pp.250-51.

[79] '...the activity of every member must extend to every possible kind of party work. Moreover this activity must be varied in accordance with what work is available so that party members enter with their whole personalities into a living relationship with the whole of the life of the party and of the revolution so that they cease to be mere *specialists* necessarily exposed to the *danger of ossification*. ... Every hierarchy in the party must be based on the suitability of certain talents for the objective requirements of the particular phase of the struggle. If the revolution leaves a particular phase behind ... what is needed in addition [to a change in tactics and methods] is a reshuffle in the party hierarchy: the selection of personnel must be exactly suited to the new phase of the struggle.' (pp.335-6.)

We can also notice here the influence of Weberian mystification — which systematically confuses the *technical/specialist* and the *social/hierarchical* division of labour, so as to be able to justify the second under the cover of the first — in the way in which the question of 'ossification' is raised. For in reality the latter is not a matter of 'over-specialized' individual functionaries, nor can it be prevented by some utopian cult of the 'Renaissance personality'. It concerns primarily the social institutions themselves, calling for adequate *institutional/organizational* remedies and guarantees.

What is fundamentally wrong with the social division of labour is not that different individuals fulfil different functions in society but that their 'specializations' (often devoid of any content, representing in fact a 'speciality' only in name) arbitrarily locate them at some determinate point on the scale of the given social hierarchies and subordinations. Hence, what needs to be radically questioned is not 'specialization' as such but the pernicious character of assigning people in a *hierarchical* order to their place in society under the pretext of functional specialization.

[80] See the last two paragraphs of note 79.

[81] This is true already of his essay on 'Moses Hess and the Problems of Idealist Dialectics' (1926). See in this respect also *The Young Hegel* (first German edition 1948, completed during the war), *The Destruction of Reason* (1954), and his last major work, *The Ontology of Social Being*. (With regard to the latter, see in particular Volume 2, Chapter II, which deals with the complex issues of *Reproduction*.)

[82] In this respect Lichtheim only followed Adorno's equally self-righteous assault a few years earlier, in the same kind of periodical, shortly after Lukács had been released from deportation — thanks to a sustained international protest — and published one of his books in West Germany, as an act of openly declared defiance against the government which condemned him, having become an unpublishable *persona non grata* not only in East Germany but everywhere in the East, including Hungary. Adorno considered West Germany his own crown territory for granting or refusing to grant admission to Marxist social theories. So long as Lukács was confined to the East, Adorno used to pay great compliments to him, but could not tolerate the trespasser. (For Lichtheim's article, see the May 1963 issue of *Encounter*. As to Adorno's attack on Lukács — entitled 'Erpresste Versöhnung': 'Forced Reconciliation' — see the German equivalent of *Encounter: Der Monat*, November 1958.)

[83] *From Max Weber: Essays in Sociology*, ed. by H.H. Gerth and C. Wright Mills, Routledge & Kegan Paul, London, 1948, p.229.

[84] MECW, Vol. 5, pp.47-8.

[85] *Ibid.*, p.79.

[86] 'In der Wirklichkeit sind sie natürlich unfreier, weil mehr unter sachliche Gewalt

subsumiert.' MEW, Vol. 3, p.76.

[87] *From Max Weber: Essays in Sociology,* p.299.

[88] Marx, *The Poverty of Philosophy,* MECW, Vol. 6, p.127.

[89] Marx, *Capital,* Vol. 1, pp.364-5.

[90] Marx, *Economic and Philosophic Manuscripts of 1844,* p.129.

[91] Marx, *The Poverty of Philosophy,* pp.126-7.

[92] Lukács, *The Ontology of Social Being: Labour,* Merlin Press, London, 1980, p.93.

[93] *Ibid.*

[94] *Ibid.,* p.126.

[95] Maurice Merleau-Ponty, *Adventures of the Dialectic,* Heinemann, London, 1974, pp.57-58.

[96] *Ibid.,* p.25.

[97] *Ibid.,* p.31.

[98] *Ibid.* Characteristically for Merleau-Ponty's 'very free' interpretation of *History and Class Consciousness,* no textual evidence is offered by him in support of this sweeping assertion.

[99] Merleau-Ponty, 'The USSR and the camps', *Signs,* Northwestern University Press, 1964, p.272.

[100] 'On Madagascar', *Signs,* p.331.

[101] *Ibid.,* p.329.

[102] *Ibid.,* p.332.

[103] *Ibid.,* p.333.

[104] 'The USSR and the camps', *Signs,* p.269.

[105] *Ibid.,* p.270.

[106] 'On Madagascar', *Signs,* p.329.

[107] Merleau-Ponty, *Adventures of the Dialectic,* pp.62-4.

[108] *Ibid.,* p.62.

[109] I have discussed at some length Merleau-Ponty's political and intellectual development in *The Power of Ideology.* See in particular pp.153-6 and 161-7.

[110] We can find the same contradiction which we have seen in Merleau-Ponty's *Adventures of the Dialectic* also in Louis Althusser's periodization of Marx's intellectual development, even though the ideological intent of the communist philosopher is diametrically opposed to that of his model. Regrettably, however, Althusser accepts Merleau-Ponty's self-contradictory classification, reversing only the 'sign' of his false equation. In contrast to Merleau-Ponty, in his first two volumes of essays — *For Marx* and *Reading Capital* — Althusser praises the 'scientific Marx' against the 'philosophical young Marx', who in his view is supposed to be guilty of Hegelianism, on account of his concern with the 'ideological concept' of alienation. Later, however, he discovers that 'mature Marx', too, including the author of *Capital,* heavily indulges in the same sins. Trapped by the logic of the adopted schematism, Althusser reaches the peculiar conclusion that only the few pages of the *Critique of the Gotha Programme* (1875) and the *Marginal Notes on Wagner* (1882) should be considered proper Marxist works, free from the denounced ideological aberrations. (See in this respect Althusser's Introduction to the Garnier-Flammarion edition of volume 1 of Marx's *Capital,* published in Paris in 1969.) This shows that it is not enough to reverse the ideological intent of the intellectual and political adversary without submitting to a critical scrutiny its theoretical substance. For a failure to do the latter carries with it the unhappy consequence that one remains captive to his legends.

[111] The words 'this' and 'next step' are italicized by Lukács. And renewing his rejection of the view that strategic flexibility of dialectical materialism could be considered a form of relativism he adds in a footnote:

> Lenin's achievement is that he rediscovered this side of Marxism that points the way to an understanding of its *practical* core. His constantly reiterated warning to seize

the 'next link' in the chain with all one's might, that link on which the fate of the totality depends in that one moment, his dismissal of all utopian demands, i.e. his 'relativism' and his 'Realpolitik': all these things are nothing less than the practical realisation of the young Marx's *Theses on Feuerbach*. (p.221.)
The word 'practical' is italicized by Lukács.

[112] Lukács, *Geschichte und Klassenbewusstsein. Studien über marxistische Dialektik*, Malik Verlag, Berlin, 1923, p.216. The English translation which I have here corrected renders 'die dialektische Mechanik der Entwicklung' as the 'dialectical mechanics of history'.

[113] As Lukács puts it in another essay, 'Critical Observations on Rosa Luxemburg's *Critique of the Russian Revolution*':

socialism would never happen 'by itself', and as the result of an inevitable natural economic development. The natural laws of capitalism do indeed lead inevitably to its ultimate crisis but at the end of *its* road would be the destruction of all civilization and a new barbarism.

History and Class Consciousness, p.282. Italics by Lukács.

[114] 'Reification and the Consciousness of the Proletariat', *History and Class Consciousness*, p.188. And in another passage of the same work Lukács argues that 'the concrete totality of the historical world, the concrete and total historical process is the only point of view from which understanding becomes possible'. (p.145.)

[115] Marx, *Pre-Capitalist Economic Formations*, Lawrence and Wishart, London, 1964, pp.85-7. For an alternative translation see the Penguin edition of Marx's *Grundrisse*, pp.488-90.

[116] See in this respect the essay, 'Kant, Hegel, Marx: Historical Necessity and the Standpoint of Political Economy' in my book: *Philosophy, Ideology and Social Science*, pp.143-95.

[117] Marx, *Economic and Philosophic Manuscripts of 1844*, p.149. Marx's emphases.

[118] *Ibid.*, pp.159-62. Marx's emphases.

[119] *Ibid.*, p.150.

[120] *Die Eigenart des Aesthetischen*, published by Luchterhand Verlag, Neuwied am Rhein, 1963, in two massive 'half-volumes', 850pp. and 887pp. respectively. Several hundred pages of this work deal, directly or indirectly, with ethical questions.

[121] 'The Marxism of Rosa Luxemburg' was written in January 1921, and the much longer 'Reification and the Consciousness of the Proletariat' after March 1921, completed in the course of 1922.

[122] According to Lukács incorrigibly because class interests tie the vision of this philosophy to the immediacy of the established mode of everyday life. For although 'intellectual genesis must be identical in principle with historical genesis', the development of bourgeois thought 'has tended to wrench these two principles apart.' So much so, in fact, that

as a result of this duality of method, reality disintegrates into a multitude of irrational facts and over these a network of purely formal 'laws' emptied of content is then cast. And by devising an *'epistemology'* that can go beyond the abstract form of the immediately given world (and its conceivability) the *structure is made permanent* and acquires a *justification* — not inconsistently — as being the necessary 'precondition of the possibility' of this world view. But unable to turn this 'critical' movement in the direction of a true creation of the object — in this case of the thinking subject — and indeed by taking the very opposite direction, this 'critical' attempt to bring the analysis of reality to its logical conclusion ends by returning to the same immediacy that faces the ordinary man of bourgeois society in his everyday life. It has been conceptualized, but only immediately. (p.155.)

[123] Engels is — rightly — dismissive of the idea of *'ready-made* things'. He contrasts the latter with the category of 'a complex of processes'. Lukács, however, after quoting with approval Engels' rejection of 'ready-made things', asks with revealing eagerness the

rhetorical question: 'But if there are *no things*, what is "reflected" in thought?' (p.200.) As if the 'complex of processes' counterposed by Engels to the *mechanical* notion of ready-made things also had to exclude the idea of the *dialectical configuration* of — decidedly not 'ready-made' — things. Lukács has to make the conceptual shift that fallaciously equates *things* with *ready-made things* because he wants to maintain that 'In the theory of "reflection" we find the theoretical embodiment of the *duality of thought and existence*, consciousness and reality, that is so intractable to the reified consciousness.' *(Ibid.)* To extricate 'reified consciousness' from its predicament, Lukács offers the good offices of the 'identical subject-object' which is supposed to overcome the duality of thought and existence by way of its innermost constitution (i.e. by definition). Unhappily, though, this solution traps all those who adopt it in the 'endless labyrinth of conceptual mythology' which Lukács condemns in the practice of classical philosophy.

124 The last sentence is italicized by Lukács in its entirety.

125 Hegel, *Werke*, vol. 5, p.30.

126 In the three chapters of *The Ontology of Social Being* available in English the interested reader can find a radically different approach to these issues, including a profound critical account of the Hegelian categorial framework.

127 Marx, *Letter to Engels*, 25 March 1868.

128 The quotation is from page 391 of *Capital*, vol.3. The passage as a whole, in which Marx discusses the fetishism of interest-bearing capital, reads as follows:

> The concept of capital as a fetish reaches its height in interest-bearing capital, being a conception which attributes to the accumulated product of labour, and at that in the fixed form of money, the inherent secret power, as an automaton, of creating surplus-value in geometrical progression, so that the accumulated product of labour, as the *Economist* thinks, has long discounted all the wealth of the world for all time as belonging to it and rightfully coming to it. The product of past labour, the past labour itself, is here pregnant in itself with a portion of present or future living surplus-labour. We know, however, that in reality the preservation, and to that extent also the reproduction of the value of products of past labour is *only* [Marx's italics] the result of their contact with living labour; and secondly, that the domination of the products of past labour over living surplus-labour lasts only as long as the *relations of capital*, which rest on those particular social relations in which past labour independently and overwhelmingly dominates over living labour.
> *(Ibid.,* pp.390-91.)

129 Lukács writes in a footnote in an early essay — *Tactics and Ethics* — first published in Hungarian in 1919:

> The concept of consciousness was first noted and elucidated in classical German philosophy. 'Consciousness' refers to that particular stage of knowledge where the subject and the object of knowledge are substantively *homogeneous*, i.e. where knowledge takes place from within and not from without. (The simplest example is man's moral knowledge of himself, e.g. his sense of responsibility, his conscience as contrasted with the knowledge of the natural sciences, where the known object remains eternally alien to the knowing subject for all his knowledge of it.) The chief significance of this type of knowledge is that the *mere fact of knowledge* produces an *essential modification in the object known*; thanks to the *act of consciousness*, of knowledge, the tendency inherent in it hitherto now becomes more assured and vigorous than it was or could have been before. A further implication of this mode of knowledge, however, is that the *distinction between the subject and object disappears*, and with it, therefore, the *distinction between theory and practice*. Without sacrificing any of its purity, impartiality or truth, *theory becomes action, practice*.

In the passage to which this footnote is appended Lukács — characteristically, in the same spirit in which he deals with these problems in *History and Class Consciousness*, as we have seen in the previous section — minimises the power of material determinations (the 'blind forces of nature' which Marx refers to in his characterization of the capitalistic socioeconomic metabolism) as *'mere appearance'*, in order to be able to offer as the required remedy the act of enlightening consciousness. Thus he insists, again and again, that such material determinations 'are a mere appearance which can survive only until those blind forces have been *awakened to consciousness'* by the knowledge supplied through the agency of the identical subject-object. (Both quotations are from page 15 of Lukács, *Political Writings, 1919-1929,* New Left Books, London, 1972.)

Naturally, the difficulties are much greater than that. For the knowledge of the preponderant material determinations, no matter how accurate, does not by itself remove their force of inertia, even if it can indicate the way in which the latter task can be accomplished through the sustained transformatory intervention of *social practice*. It is worth reminding ourselves here of Marx's sober evaluation of his own theoretical achievements, which he put in perspective by saying that with the discovery of the component parts of the air the atmosphere itself remained unchanged. By contrast, according to the Lukácsian postulates of the identical subject-object and of the identity — *by definition* — of theory and practice, the atmosphere is supposed to be 'structurally changed' by the self-illuminating act of consciousness itself, thanks to the claimed discovery that from the standpoint of the identical subject-object the power of material determinations is 'a mere appearance'.

[130] See the first quotation in note 79.

[131] See the Section entitled 'Lukács's Solution' of the essay: *Political Power and Dissent in Postrevolutionary Societies* in Part Four of the present volume.

[132] Rosa Luxemburg, *Reform or Revolution,* New York, 1970, pp.60-61.

[133] See the passage quoted from Lukács's book on *Democratization* in note 14.

[134] See his pre-Marxist work, *The Theory of the Novel,* and the Preface written in 1962 for its unaltered German edition, published by Luchterhand Verlag in 1963 and in English by the Merlin Press in 1971.

[135] Lukács writes in *History and Class Consciousness,* in his essay entitled 'Towards a Methodology of the Problem of Organization':

> The much vilified and slandered question of *party 'purges'* is only the negative side of the same issue [of true democracy]. Here, as with every problem, it was necessary to progress from utopia to reality. For example, the demand contained in the 21 Conditions of the Second Congress that every legal party must initiate such purges from time to time proved to be a utopian requirement incompatible with the stage of development reached by the newly-born mass parties in the West. (The Third Congress formulated its views on this issue with much greater caution.) However, the fact that this clause was inserted was nevertheless no 'error'. For it clearly and unmistakably points in the direction that the Communist Party must take in its internal development even though the manner in which the principle is carried out will be determined by historical circumstances. ... the more clearly and energetically the process mediates the necessities of the moment by putting them in their historical perspective, the more clearly and energetically will it be able to absorb the individual in his isolated activity; the more it will be able to make use of him, bring him to a peak of maturity and judge him. (pp.338-9.)

Naturally, Lukács's acceptance of the purges in no way condones the physical liquidation of those censured, which becomes the hallmark of Stalinist politics in the 1930s.

[136] The exaggerated importance assigned by Lukács to 'manipulation' has a great deal to do with the conceptual space created for this category in *History and Class Consciousness.*

[137] It must be stressed that Marx is well aware of the significance of objective counter-tendencies in the socioeconomic process, and often qualifies his analyses of the dominant tendencies in this sense.

[138] Marx, *A Contribution to the Critique of Political Economy*, Lawrence & Wishart, London, 1971, p.21.

[139] The following passage — from Lukács's reply to an international round table questionnaire of the periodical *Nuovi Argomenti*, on the XXII Congress of the Soviet Communist Party, with the participation of Paul Baran, Lelio Basso, Isaac Deutscher, Maurice Dobb, Pietro Ingrao, Rudolf Schlesinger, Paul Sweezy and Alexander Werth — is representative of his views in this respect:

> Since the revolutionary wave which had been unleashed in 1917 had faded away without instituting a stable dictatorship in any other country, it was necessary to confront with resolution the problem of building socialism in one (backward) country. It is in this period that Stalin revealed himself a remarkable and far-sighted statesman. His forceful defence of the new Leninist theory of the possibility of a socialist society in one country against attacks mainly by Trotsky represented, as one cannot help recognizing today, the salvation of Soviet development. ... What today we consider despotic and anti-democratic in the Stalinian period, has a very close strategic relationship with Trotsky's fundamental ideas. A socialist society led by Trotsky would have been at least as little democratic as Stalin's, with the difference that strategically it would have oriented itself through the dilemma: a catastrophic politics or capitulation, instead of the — substantially accurate — thesis of Stalin, asserting the possibility of socialism in one country. (The personal impressions which I formed on the basis of my meetings with Trotsky in 1921 convinced me that, as an individual, he was drawn towards the 'personality cult' even more than Stalin.)... With all its errors, Stalin's industrialization was able to create the conditions and technological requirements for winning the war against Hitler's Germany. However, the new world situation confronts the Soviet Union, in the economic field, with tasks altogether new: she must create an economy able to overtake, in all areas of life, the most advanced capitalism, that of the United States, and to raise the standard of living of the Soviet people above the American level. An economy able to lend all sorts of help, both systematic and permanent, to other socialist states as well as to economically backward peoples on their way to emancipation. To this end new methods are required, more democratic, less bureaucratically centralized than those that were allowed to develop up to now. The XXII Congress has opened the way to a grandiose and varied system of reforms. Here I limit myself to recalling only the extremely important decision that in future elections to Party positions 25 percent of the old leaders cannot be reelected.

'8 domande sul XXII Congresso del PCUS', *Nuovi Argomenti*, No. 57-58, July-October 1962, pp.117-32.

As we all know, the advocacy of surpassing the United States in per capita production was already one of Stalin's favourite ideas. As to the suggestion that the periodic replacement of 25 percent of party officials might be considered a 'grandiose reform' — an idea well in line with Lukács's proposal in *History and Class Consciousness* to ask the party functionaries to 'reshuffle' themselves from time to time — is very naive, to put it mildly. For such reforms — even if they are implemented, which is by no means guaranteed, as the subsequent decades of development testify — leave the fundamentally undemocratic structural division of society into the leaders and the governed quite unchanged.

[140] Lukács, *Aesthetik Teil I: Die Eigenart des Aesthetischen*, Luchterhand Verlag, Neuwied and Berlin, 1963, vol. 2, p.856.

[141] *Ibid.*, pp.870-71.

[142] 'Truth is slowly pursuing its forward march, and in the end of ends nothing can hold it back.' Lukács, 'Postscriptum 1957 zu: Mein Weg zu Marx.' In *Georg Lukács: Schriften zur Ideologie und Politik*, ed. by Peter Ludz, Luchterhand Verlag, Neuwied and Berlin,

1967, p.657.

[143] Significantly, Goethe gets the last word in Lukács's *Aesthetics:*
> Wer Wissenschaft und Kunst besitzt,
> Hat auch Religion;
> Wer jene beiden nicht besitzt,
> Der habe Religion.
> (If you have Science and Art,
> You have Religion, too;
> If you do not possess both,
> You should have Religion.)

Eigenart des Aesthetischen, vol. 2, p.872.

Something for which Lukács has been criticized a great deal — his categorical rejection of 'avant-gardism' — can only be understood in terms of the same perspective. For, as he insists again and again:

> in a world-historical sense, the capitulation of avant-gardism before the amorphous contemporary religious need — which tends to destroy all artistic objectivity — represents a mere episode in the course of artistic development. *(Ibid.,* p.830.)

[144] I quoted in *Lukács's Concept of Dialectic* a passage from pp.78-9 of *Gespraeche mit Georg Lukács* (Rowohlt Verlag, Hamburg, 1967) in which the author rather naively idealized President Kennedy's Brains-Trust, as a model to be adopted also in the socialist countries, so as to play the role of corrective to bureaucracy. In Lukács's view, with the Brains-Trust

> a new organizational principle has appeared, namely a *duality* and a co-activity of theory and political practice, which is no longer unified in one person — and which happened to be unified only once, if at all — but which, on account of the extraordinary widening of the tasks, can be brought about today only in such a *dual form.*

The reality was, of course, quite different. I could not help feeling at the time that 'Almost every single element of Lukács's assessment is hopelessly out of touch with reality. George Kennan, perhaps the best brain of Kennedy's Brains-Trust, has a much lower opinion of this "organizational form". He knows that its actual working principle is: "Leave your brains and ideals behind when you enter this Brains-Trust", that is if your ideals happen to differ from those of the "top-level bureaucrats" ("hohen Bürokraten"). He wrote after his resignation from Kennedy's team that the only occasion when those bureaucrats could not prevail over him was when he donated his blood after the Skopje earthquake: they could not prevent *that* from happening. Also, the issue is not whether we abound in men of the stature of a Marx or a Lenin. The rarity of intellectually creative political talent is not an "original cause", but rather the *effect* of a certain type of social development, which not only prevents the emergence of new talent, but destroys the talent available through political trials (cf. the numerous Russian intellectuals and politicians liquidated in the 1930s), through the expulsion of men of talent from the field of politics (Lukács, for instance), or through bending them to the acceptance of the narrow political perspectives of the given situation (e.g. the great talent, by the highest standards, of a Joseph Révai). ... The advocated "organizational form" as the synthesis between theory and practice is a mere utopian postulate. It is no more than a pious hope to expect the frustrated Kennan's bureaucrats to give way to his insights and proposals, just as much as it is a mere wishful thinking to expect the solution of the great structural problems of international socialism to come from the self-conscious and willing recognition by Party First Secretaries that they are neither Marxes nor Lenins. If it is true, as it may well be, that we are today confronted with an "extraordinary widening of tasks" ("ausserordentliche Verbreitung der Aufgaben"), this makes it all the more urgent and vital to insist on the reciprocal interpenetration of theory and politics, theory and practice, rather than to offer a justification of their alienation and "necessary duality" by idealizing an organizational form, a non-existent and unworkable Brains-Trust. Nothing could be more illusory than to expect the solution of our problems from the "Brains-Trust" of abstract intellectuals and narrowly pragmatic politicians. The alleged "Verbreitung der Aufgaben" needs for its solution the reciprocal interpenetration of theory and prctice in all spheres of human activity and at all levels, from the lowest to the highest, and not the sterile stalemate of academics and politicians at the top. In other words the task is the *radical democratization and restructuring* of all social structures and not the utopian reassembly of *existing hierarchies.*'

Mészáros, *Lukács's Concept of Dialectic,* Merlin Press, London, 1972, pp.89-91; first published in a volume edited by G.H.R. Parkinson, *Georg Lukács, The Man, His Work and His Ideas,* Weidenfeld & Nicholson, London, 1970.

[145] G. Zinoview, 'Gegen die Ultralinken' (1924), *Protokoll des V. Kongresses der Kommunistischen Internationale,* Moscow, 1925. Reprinted in *Georg Lukács: Schriften zur Ideologie und Politik,* ed. by Peter Ludz, pp.719-26.

[146] *Die Eigenart des Aesthetischen,* vol. 2, p.742.

[147] *Ibid.,* p.837.

[148] *Ibid.,* p.847.

[149] *Ibid.*

[150] *Nuovi Argomenti,* No. 57-58, pp.130-31.

[151] Lukács, 'Solzhenitsyn's Novels' (1969), p.77 of Lukács, *Solzhenitsyn,* Merlin Press, London, 1970. The discussion that follows below is taken from my review article on Lukács's *Solzhenitsyn, New Statesman,* 26 February 1971; reprinted on pp.105-14 of the Merlin Press edition of *Lukács's Concept of Dialectic.*

[152] Lenin, 'Party Organization and Party Literature' (1905), *Collected Works,* vol. 10, p.46.

[153] *Ibid.*

[154] Lukács, 'Solzhenitsyn's Novels', p.80.

[155] *Ibid.,* p.81.

[156] Lukács, *A demokratizálódás jelene és jövője,* p.192.

[157] *Ibid.,* p.187.

[158] Lenin, *What Is to Be Done?* (1902), in *Collected Works,* vol. 5, p.384.

[159] *Ibid.,* p.465.

[160] *Ibid.,* p.452.

[161] Lukács, *A demokratizálódás jelene és jövője,* p.171.

[162] *Ibid.*

[163] *Ibid.,* pp.171-2.

[164] Rosa Luxemburg, *Spartacus,* Merlin Press, London, 1971, p.19.

[165] *Ibid.,* p.27.

[166] Lukács, *Eigenart des Aesthetischen,* vol. 2, p.831.

[167] *Ibid.,* pp.836-7.

[168] As Hegel puts it: 'This truth of necessity, therefore, is Freedom: and the truth of substance is the Notion — an independence which, though self-repulsive into distinct independent elements, yet in that repulsion is self-identical, and in the movement of reciprocity still at home and conversant only with itself.' Hegel, *Logic,* translated by William Wallace, The Clarendon Press, Oxford, 1975, p.220.

[169] Lukács, *The Ontology of Social Being: Labour,* Merlin Press, London, 1980, p.121.

[170] *Ibid.,* p.134.

[171] *Ibid.,* pp.123-4.

[172] *Ibid.,* p.134.

[173] *Ibid.,* pp.135-6.

[174] *Ibid.,* p.101-102.

¹⁷⁵ *Ibid.*, pp.86-7.
¹⁷⁶ *Ibid.*, p.83.
¹⁷⁷ Lukács, *A társadalmi lét ontológiájáról, Szisztematikus fejezetek* (The Ontology of Social Being, Systematic Chapters), Magvető Kiadó, Budapest, 1976, vol. 2, pp.786-7.
¹⁷⁸ *Ibid.*, p.777.
¹⁷⁹ *Ibid.*, p.248.
¹⁸⁰ *Ibid.*, p.319.
¹⁸¹ *Ibid.*, p.561. Lukács also adds on the same page that 'we do not contest, whether or not the tactical decisions were correct or false. The important thing is that Stalin's point of departure was always tactical'.
¹⁸² *Ibid.*, p.320.
¹⁸³ *Ibid.*, p.332.
¹⁸⁴ The use of the category of possibility in the *Ontology of Social Being* is countless. Thus Lukács argues, to quote a typical sentence in this respect, that the individuals' struggle against their own alienation '*can* influence overall social development *potentially,* and under certain conditions it is *possible* for it to obtain significant objective weight'. *Ibid.*, p.768.
¹⁸⁵ *Ibid.*, p.739.
¹⁸⁶ *Ibid.*
¹⁸⁷ *Ibid.*, p.624.
¹⁸⁸ *Ibid.*, p.625.
¹⁸⁹ *Ibid.*
¹⁹⁰ *Ibid.*
¹⁹¹ *Ibid.*
¹⁹² *Ibid.*, p.734.
¹⁹³ *Ibid.*, p.735.
¹⁹⁴ *Ibid.*, p.758.
¹⁹⁵ *Ibid.*
¹⁹⁶ *Ibid.*, p.809.
¹⁹⁷ *Ibid.*, p.741. And on page 809 of the same book Lukács asserts that 'the student revolts are growing into an international mass movement'.
¹⁹⁸ Lukács, *The Ontology of Social Being: Labour,* p.136.
¹⁹⁹ Lukács, *A társadalmi lét ontológiájáról,* vol. 2, pp.791-2.
²⁰⁰ Lukács, *A demokratizálás jelene és jövője,* p.160.
²⁰¹ Lukács, *A társadalmi lét ontológiájáról,* vol. 2, p.772. This problem is discussed at length on pages 773-8 of volume 2.

We find the intellectual ancestor of this idea of unreservedly dedicating oneself to the great cause in *History and Class Consciousness,* when Lukács talks about the 'active engagement of the total personality'. (p.319.) However, the big difference is that in *History and Class Consciousness* the idea is directly linked to the party, insisting that its condition of realization is 'the discipline of the Communist Party, the unconditional absorption of the total personality in the praxis of the movement'. (p.320.) In *The Ontology of Social Being,* by contrast, Lukács grants not only that dedication to a progressive cause can assume alienated forms but also that 'even if exceptionally, nonetheless it is possible that some people should identify themselves with socially regressive causes in a subjectively/humanly authentic way'. (p.773.)
²⁰² Mészáros, 'Le philosophe du "tertium datur" et du dialogue co-existentiel', in *Les grands courants de la pensée mondiale contemporaine,* vol. vi, Marzorati Editore, Milano, 1961, pp.937-964,
²⁰³ See 'Die Philosophie des "tertium datur" und des Koexistenzdialogs', in Frank Benseler (ed.), *Festschrift zum achtzigsten Geburtstag von Georg Lukács,* Luchterhand Verlag, Neuwied & Berlin, 1965, pp.188-207.

[204] 'Il nourrit encore cette intention dont la réalisation ne serait possible qu'après un *changement fondamental* des circonstances actuelles, ou bien *les problèmes de cette éthique devront se limiter aux sphères les plus abstraites*'. (Marzorati ed. p.952, *Festschrift* p.205.)

[205] Lukács's letter from Budapest is dated 13 January 1964.

[206] The notes and sketchy remarks recently published under the title of *Versuche zu einer Ethik*, although most valuable for the researcher specializing in Lukács's work, add very little to what we can find already in the *Eigenart des Aesthetischen* and in *The Ontology of Social Being*.

[207] Lukács, *A társadalmi lét ontológiájáról*, vol. 2, p.529.

[208] *Ibid.*, p.727.

[209] Lukács, *Political Writings 1919-1929*, pp.6-7.

[210] *Ibid.*, p.6.

[211] *Ibid.*

[212] Lukács, *History and Class Consciousness*, p.319.

[213] *Ibid.*, p.315.

[214] Lukács, *Versuche zu einer Ethik*, p.75.

[215] Lukács, *A társadalmi lét ontológiájáról*, vol. 2, p.330.

[216] Lukács, *Versuche zu einer Ethik*, p.124.

[217] László Sziklai, 'Megkésett prófécia? Lukács György testamentuma' ('Belated prophecy? György Lukács's testament'), *Népszabadság*, 31 December 1988.

[218] Lukács, Letter to Frank Benseler, 18 December 1968; quoted in Sziklai's review article of Lukács's book on *Democratization* cited in the last note.

[219] Lukács, Letter to György Aczél, 24 August 1968, published in *Társadalmi Szemle*, April 1990, p.89.

[220] Károly Urbán, 'Megbékélés? Lukács és az MSzMP 1967/68-ban' ('Reconciliation? Lukács and the MSzMP in 1967/68'), *Magyar Nemzet*, 2 April 1990.

[221] *Ibid.*

[222] 'Lukács György politikai végrendelete' ('György Lukács's political testament'), *Társadalmi Szemle*, April 1990, p.84.

[223] This took the form of not only the sharpest possible moral condemnation of an old friend but also of an open defiance as to how the imprisoning authorities might respond to the manifestation of open contempt towards their man who had 'returned to the fold'. The way in which this happened was unquestionably authenticated by Miklós Vásárhelyi: one of Imre Nagy's best friends and closest political advisers who had to spend several years in prison after Prime Minister Nagy's execution. He told me in December 1990 that the people deported to Romania shared a dining room and used to sit in small groups of friends and family members around the available tables. Lukács and his wife Gertrúd shared a table with Zoltán Szántó and his wife. The morning after Szántó made his incriminating confession, at breakfast time Lukács and Gertrúd walked to the table they shared up until then with him, picked up their plates and cutlery, and sat down next to Szilárd Ujhelyi, who had no family members with him and was always eating alone at his table. That was the fully justified end to a very long friendship.

[224] Quoted in György Aczél and István Sziklai, 'Feljegyzés a Politikai Bizottságnak' ('Memorandum for the Politbureau', written 24 June 1966), *Társadalmi Szemle*, April 1990, p.88.

[225] Lukács, *A demokratizálás jelene és jövője*, p.178.

[226] 'Lukács György politikai végrendelete', *Társadalmi Szemle*, April 1990, pp.63-85.

[227] *Ibid.* pp.66-7.

[228] See Hans Heinz Holz, Leo Kofler, Wolfgang Abendroth, *Gespräche mit Georg Lukács*, ed. by Theo Pinkus, Rowohlt Verlag, Hamburg, 1967, pp.78-9.

[229] Lukács, *A demokratizálás jelene és jövője*, p.194.

[230] 'Lukács György politikai végrendelete', p.76.

231 *Ibid.*, p.69.
232 *Ibid.*, p.68.
233 See pp.65-7 of this interview.
234 *Ibid.*, p.69.
235 *Ibid.*, pp.69-70.
236 *Ibid.*, p.67.
237 Lukács, *A demokratizálás jelene és jövője*, p.178.
238 *Ibid.*
239 More about these problems in Chapters 13 and 20.
240 See 'Lukács's solution' in 'Political Power and Dissent in Postrevolutionary Societies', pp.816-8 of the present volume.
241 'Lukács György politikai végrendelete', p.65, Lukács's italics.
242 Lukács, *A demokratizálás jelene és jövője*, p.200.
243 'Lukács György politikai végrendelete', p.77, Lukács's italics.
244 Herbert Marcuse, *Die Permanenz der Kunst*, Carl Hanser Verlag, Munich, 1977, p.53.
245 Marx, *Capital*, vol. 3, p.772.
246 Marx, *Grundrisse*, Penguin Books, Harmondsworth, 1973, p.341.
247 *Ibid.*, p.331.
248 *Ibid.*, p.304.
249 *Ibid.*, pp.227-8. See also p.264, where Marx writes:
   After capital, landed property would be dealt with. After that, wage labour. All three presupposed, the movement of prices, as circulation now defined in its inner totality. On the other side, the three classes, as production posited in its three basic forms and presuppositions of circulation. Then the state. (State and bourgeois society. Taxes, or the existence of the unproductive classes. The state debt. Population. The state externally: colonies. External trade. Rate of exchange. Money as international coin. Finally the world market. Encroachment of bourgeois society over the state. Crises. Dissolution of the mode of production and form of society based on exchange value. Real positing of individual labour as social and vice versa.)
As we can see, we are presented with the same progression, depicting the inner logic of capital's need for trade on an ever-increasing scale. The vital condition of satisfying that need is the state, both internally and in its external relations. All this is riddled with contradictions of growing intensity and scale, leading to a structural crisis and ultimately envisaging the dissolution of this social formation. The new historic form is, again, only *'posited'* (or 'necessarily intimated'), as the real *unity of individual and social labour*: i.e., as a social formation free from the contradiction of opposing one to the other.
250 *Ibid.*, p.325.
251 See in particular Chapters 14 , 15 18, and 20 of the present study.
252 See for instance Lukács's spirited defence of Rosa Luxemburg in *History and Class Consciousness* (in the essay on 'The Marxism of Rosa Luxemburg'). He also attempted in the same work particularly in the essays on 'What is Orthodox Marxism?' and 'Reification and the Consciousness of the Proletariat' to put into relief the dialectical nature of Marx's method and tried to reconcile it with the requirements of radical theoretical/political 'orthodoxy'. Very soon, however, the narrowest possible conception of orthodoxy prevailed in the Third International, which amounted in fact to no more than the unquestioning acceptance of the latest party-political (Stalinist) decrees. Of such view of 'orthodoxy', naturally, Marx's dialectical method itself had to fall a victim for a long historical period.
253 See Chapter 12.
254 As we have seen in Chapter 1, Hegel presents an extremely complicated case in that he goes well beyond the usual liberal solution according to which 'history existed up to now but no longer'. But even his conception founders in the end on the rocks of the

structurally apologetic requirements of 'the standpoint of political economy'.
[255] See the passage quoted from Marx's *Eighteenth Brumaire of Louis Bonaparte* in note 78.
[256] See, for instance, Marx's *Civil War in France*.
[257] Marx, *Grundrisse*, p.85.
[258] *Ibid.*, pp.86-7.
[259] See Book IV., Chapter VI. of John Stuart Mill's *Principles of Political Economy*.
[260] See Adam Smith's considerations on the 'progressive state of society' in *An Inquiry Into the Nature and Causes of the Wealth of Nations*. As J. S. Mill rightly observed: 'The doctrine that, to however distant a time incessant struggling may put off our doom, the progress of society must "end in shallows and in miseries", far from being, as many people still believe, a wicked invention of Mr. Malthus, was either expressly or tacitly affirmed by his most distinguished predecessors...' *Principles of Political Economy*, Longmans, Green & Co., London, 1923, p.747.
[261] See the apologetic character of much of *'The Limits to Growth'* debate.
[262] See Part Three, in particular Chapter 16.
[263] Marx, *The Poverty of Philosophy*, Lawrence & Wishart, London, 1936, pp.112-3.
[264] Marx, *Letter to P.V. Annenkov*, 28 December, 1846.
[265] *Ibid.*
[266] Under a different aspect, the same problem confronts us in the form of the trans-national division, organisation and development of technology — cynically adapted even to the immediate requirements of beating strikes — in conformity to the present-day needs of capital.
[267] Engels, *Letter to F.A. Sorge*, 11 February, 1891.
[268] Engels, *Letter to K. Kautsky*, 3 February, 1891.
[269] Engels, *Letter to K. Kautsky*, 11 February, 1891.
[270] Marx, *The Civil War in France*, Foreign Languages Press, Peking, 1966, p.80.
[271] Engels, *Letter to A. Bebel*, 1-2 May, 1891.
[272] Bebel was the recipient of Engels' uneasy letter, quoted in the last sentence.
[273] 'this fright [of publication] was essentially based on the consideration: what will the enemy make of it? Since the thing was printed in the official organ, the exploitation by the enemy will be blunted and we put ourselves in a position where we can say: See how we criticize ourselves — we are the only party that can allow itself to do this; try and imitate us! And this is also the correct standpoint which should have been taken in the first place.' (Engels, *Letter to K. Kautsky*, 3 February, 1891.)

Bebel's main objection was directed at publishing Marx's letter to W. Bracke (dated 5 May, 1875, with comments on the Gotha Programme), saying that it concerned the party leadership the criticism of which placed weapons in the hands of the enemy. (See Bebel's *Letter to Engels*, 30 March, 1891.)

In another letter to Kautsky (dated 23 February, 1891) Engels returned again to the subject: 'The fear that it would put a weapon in the hands of our opponents was unfounded. Malicious insinuations, of course, are being attached to anything and everything, but on the whole the impression made on our opponent was one of *complete bewilderment at this ruthless self-criticism* and the feeling: what an inner power must be possessed by a party that can afford such a thing! That can be seen from the hostile newspapers you sent me (for which many thanks) and from those to which I have otherwise had access. And, frankly speaking, that really was my intention when I published the document.'
[274] Engels, *Letter to K. Kautsky*, 15 January, 1891.
[275] Engels, *Letter to K. Kautsky*, 23 February, 1891.
[276] Engels, *Letter to A. Bebel*, 1-2 May, 1891.
[277] Engels, *Letter to F.A. Sorge*, 4 March, 1891.
[278] Engels, *Letter to A. Bebel*, 1-2 May, 1891.

[279] See his *Introduction to the Critique of the Hegelian Philosophy of Right* as well as Part I of *The German Ideology*.

[280] Most emphatically in the *Manifesto of the Communist Party*.

[281] Marx, *The Civil War in France*, p.73.

[282] *Ibid.*, p.167.

[283] *Ibid.*, p.228.

[284] *Ibid.*, p.232.

[285] *Ibid.*, p.13.

[286] 'The Berliners' boycott of me has not been lifted, I hear and see nothing by letter...' (Engels, *Letter to Kautsky*, 11 February, 1891.) And again: 'there is a plan to release a fraction edict to the effect that the publication [of Marx's *Critique*...] took place without their prior knowledge and that they disapproved of it. They can willingly have the fun. ... In the meantime, I am boycotted by these gentlemen, which is quite all right with me, since it saves me wasting a lot of time.' (Engels, *Letter to F. A. Sorge*, 11 February, 1891.)

[287] Marx, *The Civil War in France*, op. cit., p.172.

[288] *Ibid.*, p.229.

[289] Engels, *Preface* to Marx's *Capital*, Vol. II.

[290] 'Marx has come back from Carlsbad quite changed, vigorous, fresh, cheerful and healthy, and can soon get down seriously to work again.' (Engels, *Letter to W. Bracke*, 11 October, 1875.)

[291] Engels, *Preface* to Marx's *Capital*, Vol. II.

[292] Marx, *Capital*, Vol. II, Penguin Books, Harmondsworth, 1978, pp.591-2.

[293] *Ibid.*, p.591.

[294] *Ibid.*, p.593.

[295] First published in Italian as part of a longer study: 'Il rinnovamento del marxismo e l'attualità storica dell'offensiva socialista', *Problemi del Socialismo*, January-April 1982, pp.5-141, and in English in *Radical Philosophy*, No. 42. (Winter/Spring 1986), pp.2-10. This study is now published with minor changes in Chapters 11-13 and 18. Notes 316-19 of Part Two and Section 18.4 has been added to this volume.

[296] Hegel, *The Phenomenology of Mind*, Allen & Unwin, London, 1966, p.114.

[297] Hegel, *Philosophy of Mind*, Clarendon Press, Oxford, 1971, p.62.

[298] *Ibid.*, pp.62-3.

[299] *Ibid.*, p.63.

[300] *Ibid.*, p.64.

[301] Engels, *Ludwig Feuerbach and the End of Classical German Philosophy*, in Marx and Engels, *Selected Works*, Vol. II., p.354.

[302] *Ibid.*, pp.354-5.

[303] Marx, 'Preface to the Critique of Political Economy', in *A Contribution to the Critique of Political Economy*, Lawrence & Wishart, London, 1971, p.21. Unfortunately, in this translation the word 'always' ('immer') is rendered as *'inevitably'*, thus encouraging a fatalist/determinist reading.

[304] *Ibid.*

[305] Marx, *Grundrisse*, p.228.

[306] Marx and Engels, *Collected Works*, (Henceforth quoted as MECW), Vol. 5., p.49. *(The German Ideology)*

[307] Engels, Introduction to the English Edition of *Socialism: Utopian and Scientific*, Marx and Engels, *Selected Works*, Vol. II., p.105.

[308] MECW, Vol. 5., pp.74-5.

[309] *Ibid.*, p.74.

[310] See Engels, *Letter to Kautsky*, 23 February, 1891.

[311] Engels, *Socialism: Utopian and Scientific*, *Selected Works*, Vol. II., p.135.

312 Stalin, *Economic Problems of Socialism in the U.S.S.R.*, Foreign Languages Press, Peking 1972, pp.34-6.

313 Though it is politically understandable, events and developments which represent just as much capital's success as labour's victory, are often one-sidedly hailed by socialists, overrating their importance for the advancement of the movement itself (from the repeal of Bismarck's Anti-Socialist Law and other versions of anti-labour legislation to the 'welfare state' and the consumer economy).

To be sure, the working class has a vital share in all such achievements. However, it is more than a mere coincidence that these conquests become possible at times when capital is in a position not only to digest them, but also to turn the extracted concessions into major gains for itself. In other words, these improvements come into being at times when, as a result of capital's inner dynamic — of which its relation to labour is, of course, a key factor — the repressive posture proves to be not only outdated and redundant, but indeed a fetter to the further expansion of its power and wealth.

Naturally, for exactly the same reasons — which assert *capital's* prevalent interests in these matters — things may move in the opposite direction for a shorter or longer period of time, under specific historical conditions and circumstances: as not only the emergence of Fascism demonstrated, against the background of a massive economic crisis, but also the recent emergence of the 'Radical Right', with its ruthless legislative measures directed against labour.

314 Mészáros, 'L'astuzia della storia a marcia indietro', pp.46-7 of the Italian study referred to in note 295.

315 *Magyar Hirek*, 2 February, 1985.

316 See *The Times*, 11 April 1985.

317 Ironically — yet another 'irony of history'? — this judgment is made in a work entitled: *The Development of Socialism from Utopia to Science.* (The quotation is from Marx and Engels, *Selected Works*, Vol. II., p.136.)

318 The destructiveness that goes with these developments had by now assumed such proportions that it directly threatens human survival. See Chapter 5 in this respect.

319 Due to the major deficiencies asserting themselves in the domain of profitable capital production and accumulation, indebtedness has become an ultimately uncontrollable problem in some of the leading capitalist countries, Britain included. Nowhere are the dangers more evident than in the United States: the preponderant hegemonic power of the global capital system. I have been arguing since 1983 that the real debt problem is not that of the 'Third World' but the spiralling indebtedness — both internal and external — of the United States, foreshadowing the danger of a massive international economic earthquake when the U.S. will default on its debt in one form or another. Those who continue to assert that the U.S. economy — the world's greatest debtor by far — will 'grow out' of its precarious financial predicament close their eyes to all factual evidence, so as to be able to turn the actually prevailing causal relationship between growth and ever-escalating indebtedness upside down. For, as Paul Sweezy and Harry Magdoff stressed it in an important study:

> The trouble with this line of reasoning is that policies of this kind have been pursued during Reagan's two terms in office more vigorously than ever before at the very time when overall economic expansion has been most obviously dominated by the ever more rapid expansion of debt. There have been periods in the history of capitalism when growing out of debt actually happened and on a large scale, too, but to talk about it here and now is a good example of putting the cart before the horse: in this country today, debt is the *motor* of growth, not the *by-product* of growth.

(Paul M. Sweezy and Harry Magdoff, *The Irreversible Crisis*, Monthly Review Press, New York 1988, p.70.)

The severity of the situation in which growing indebtedness has to fulfil the contradictory role of the 'motor of growth', designed to rescue the economy (for as long as such practices can be sustained) out of its tendency to stagnation, can hardly be overstated:

The stimulatory medicine that Keynesian theory prescribes for depressions — massive doses of deficit spending — has already been used up. There is nothing left in the entire bag of tricks. The reality of stagnation on a scale not experienced for half a century now stares us in the face. ...

Among the forces counteracting the tendency to stagnation, none has been more important or less understood by economic analysts than the growth, beginning in the 1960s and rapidly gaining momentum after the severe recession of the mid-1970s, of the country's debt structure (*government, corporate, and individual*) at a pace far exceeding the sluggish expansion of the 'real' economy. The result has been the emergence of an unprecedentedly huge and fragile financial superstructure subject to stresses and strains that increasingly threaten the stability of the economy as a whole.

Between 1970 and 1980, the ratio of debt to GNP advanced from 1.57 to 1.7. That, it turned out, was only a prelude to the debt explosion in the 1980s. By 1987, the total outstanding debt was *2.25* times as large as that year's GNP...

What is particularly noteworthy is that debt dependency in the last fifteen years has been steadily increasing to compensate for a weakening private economy. Total government expenditures have been a major economic influence throughout the post-Second World War years, rising from 13.5 percent of GNP in 1950 to *20.4 percent* in 1987. But while in the earlier years, surpluses in good years more or less balanced the deficits of recession periods, later on the pattern changed. *Deficits* began gradually to outweigh surpluses during the 1960s, and thereafter reliance on deficits rapidly increased. During the 1970s as a whole, deficits were needed to pay for *8 percent* of federal government expenditures, whereas during the first seven years of the present decade this proportion more than doubled to *17 percent*....

[In the consumer economy, lending by banks and finance companies] has propped up sales of homes and consumer durable goods, it has also piled up a mountain of consumer debt that is fast approaching an unsustainable limit: in 1970 the outstanding consumer debt amounted to about 67 percent of after-tax consumer income; in 1987 it was close to *90 percent*....

Nonfinancial business has been no stranger to the feverish accumulation of debt. ... Unable to find profitable productive investment opportunities in the face of excess capacity and flagging demand, they have been eager participants in the merger, takeover, and leveraged buyout frenzy that has swept the country in recent years, becoming in the process both lenders and borrowers on an enormous scale. For all these reasons, nonfinancial corporations as a whole now carry a debt load of about *$1.5 trillion,* which, according to Felix Rohatyn, of the Lazard Frères investment banking firm, *exceeds their total net worth by 12 percent.* Moreover, Rohatyn points out, since 1982 the cost of servicing this debt has been absorbing *50 percent* of the entire corporate cash flow. By comparison, during the 1976-79 recovery this cost averaged only 27 percent. ...

Aware as the monetary authorities may be of the dangers that lie ahead, their hands are nonetheless tied. And the reason is precisely the fragility of the system. Interference by the government or the monetary authorities, other than efforts to put out fires when they flare up, carries with it the potential of setting off a chain reaction. This explains why at every critical juncture existing restraints on further financial expansion have been relaxed in order to avoid a major breakdown. The removal of controls has in turn opened the door to still more innovations that add to the fragility. *(Ibid.,* pp.11, 13-4, 16-7, and 20.)

Undoubtedly, recent developments in Eastern Europe can open up some new possibilities for profitable capital accumulation in the dominant Western capitalist countries, above all in the Federal Republic of Germany. However, given the relatively limited scale of such economic openings, as well as the political complications inseparable from them, it would be very naive to expect the solution of the structural defects of the Western capital system as a whole from the new market-opportunities emerging in the East.

320 See Section 12.2 of the present volume.

321 He even spoke about a 'categorical imperative', in the context of discussing the social agency — the proletariat — which he considered both necessary and adequate to the task of structural change. See his 'Critique of Hegel's Philosophy of Law. Introduction.'

322 Marx, 'Critical Marginal Notes on an Article by a Prussian', MECW, Vol. 3, p.197.

323 Ibid., p.199. We can see here very clearly how strongly Marx is opposed to any mechanical and reductionist position.

324 See Marx and Engels, 'Fictitious Splits in the International; Circular from the International Working Men's Association'. (Written in January-March, 1872.)

325 See Marx, 'Indifference to Politics'. (Written in January, 1873.)

326 Marx, 'Critical Marginal Notes on the Article by a Prussian', p.198.

327 Ibid., p.197.

328 'Germany, as the deficiency of the political present constituted as a particular world, will not be able to throw down the specific German limitations without throwing down the *general* limitations of the *political* present. It is not the radical revolution, not the *general* human emancipation which is a utopian dream for Germany, but rather the *partial*, the merely political revolution, the revolution which leaves the pillars of the house standing.' Marx, 'Contribution to Critique of Hegel's Philosophy of Law. Introduction', MECW, Vol. 3., p.184.

329 This point is well illustrated by the confrontation between Marx and Schapper: 'I have always defied the momentary opinions of the proletariat. We are devoted to a party which, most *fortunately* for it, cannot yet come to power. If the proletariat were to come to power the measures it would introduce would be petty-bourgeois and not directly proletarian. Our party can come to *power* only when the conditions allow it to put *its own* view into practice. Louis Blanc is the best instance of what happens when you come to power prematurely. In France, moreover, it isn't the proletariat alone that gains power but the peasants and the petty-bourgeois as well, and it will have to carry out not its, but *their* measures.' (Marx, at the 'Meeting of the Central Authority, September 15, 1850', MECW, Vol. 10, pp.628-9.)

This sober realism could not contrast more with Schapper's bombastic voluntarism at the same meeting: 'The question at issue is whether we ourselves chop off a few heads right at the start or whether it is our own heads that will fall. In France the workers will come to power and thereby we in Germany too. Were this not the case I would indeed take to my bed; in that event I would be able to enjoy a different material position. If we come to power we can take such measures as are necessary to ensure the rule of the proletariat. I am a fanatical supporter of this view... I shall certainly be guillotined in the next revolution, nevertheless I shall go to Germany... I do not share the view that the bourgeoisie in Germany will come to power and on this point I am a fanatical enthusiast — if I weren't I wouldn't give a brass farthing for the whole affair.' (*Ibid.*, p.628.) As we can see, Schapper (who died in ripe old age in his bed) supports the soundness of his voluntaristic conception of politics by nothing else than twice repeating that he 'fanatically believes' in it.

Marx is right in stressing in opposition to Schapper and others like him that 'The revolution is seen not as the product of *realities* of the situation but as the result of an effort of *will*. Whereas we say to the workers: you have 15, 20, 50 years of civil war to go through in order to alter the situation and to *train* yourselves for the *exercise of power* it is said: we must take power *at once*, or else we may as well take to our beds. Just as the democrats abused the word "people" so now the word "proletariat" has been used as a mere phrase. To make this phrase effective it would be necessary to describe all the petty bourgeois as proletarians and consequently in practice represent the petty bourgeois and not the proletarians. The *actual* revolutionary process would have to be replaced by revolutionary *catchwords*. This debate has finally laid bare the differences in principle which lay behind the clash of personalities...' *(Ibid.,* pp.626-7.)

[330] Marx, 'Critical Marginal Notes on the Article by a Prussian', MECW, Vol. 3, p.206.

[331] Quoted in Marx and Engels, 'The Alliance of Socialist Democracy and the International Working Men's Association'. (Written in April-July, 1873.)

[332] *Ibid.*

[333] Marx, 'Notes on Bakunin's *Statehood and Anarchy*', (written in December 1874-January 1875), MECW, vol.24, p.518.

[334] *Ibid.*

[335] See Marx's 'Contribution to Critique of Hegel's Philosophy of Law. Introduction.'

[336] See *The German Ideology*, MECW, Vol. 5, p.53.

[237] *Ibid.,* pp.52-3.

[338] See in this respect not only Marx's polemics against Schapper, but also his analyses of the Paris Commune of 1871.

[339] 'Mr Bakunin has only translated Proudhon's and Stirner's anarchy into the barbaric idiom of the Tartars.' Marx, 'Notes on Bakunin's *Statehood and Anarchy*', MECW, vol. 24, p.521.

[340] 'It is self-evident that a secret society of this kind which aims at forming not the *government* party of the future but the *opposition party of the future* could have but few attractions for individuals who on the one hand concealed their personal insignificance by strutting round in the theatrical cloak of the conspirator and on the other wished to satisfy their narrow-minded ambition on the *day* of the next revolution, and who wished above all to seem important at the moment, to snatch their share of the proceeds of demagogy and to find a welcome among the quacks and charlatans of democracy.' Marx, 'Revelations Concerning the Communist Trial in Cologne'. (Written in December 1852.) MECW, Vol. 11, p.449.

[341] Marx, *The Civil War in France*, pp.171-2.

[342] *Ibid.,* p.72.

[343] *Ibid.,* p.229.

[344] 'But the *community* from which the worker is isolated is a community the real character and scope of which is quite different from that of the *political* community. The community from which the worker is isolated by his own labour is life itself, physical and mental life, human morality, human activity, human enjoyment, human nature. Human nature is the true community of men. The disastrous isolation from this essential nature is incomparably more universal, more intolerable, more dreadful, and more contradictory, than isolation from the political community.' Marx, 'Critical Marginal Notes on the Article by a Prussian', MECW, Vol. 3, pp.204-5.

[345] From one of Marx's 'Theses on Feuerbach'.

[346] Quoted by Marx in his *Critique of Hegel's Philosophy of Right*, Cambridge University Press, 1970, p.29.

[347] *Ibid.*

[348] *Ibid.,* p.76.

[349] *Ibid.,* p.77.

[350] *Ibid.,* p.77.

[351] *Ibid.,* p.48.

[352] *Ibid.,* p.76.

353 *Ibid.*, p.73.

354 *Ibid.*, p.54.

355 Mannheim, for instance, who enthusiastically approves Scheler's grotesque idea that ours is 'the epoch of equalisation' [Zeitalter des Ausgleichs], claims at the same time that formerly antagonistic classes 'are now, in one form or another, *merging into one another.'* (See *Ideology and Utopia*, Routledge & Kegan Paul, London, 1936, p.251.) He adds to this fiction another bit of fantasy about the 'free-floating intelligentsia' [freischwebende Intelligenz] — a first cousin of Hegel's 'universal' bureaucrat — which is supposed to 'subsume in itself *all* those interests with which social life is permeated.' *(Ibid.*, p.140.) I discussed these problems in 'Ideology and Social Science' *(The Socialist Register,* 1972; reprinted in my book, *Philosophy, Ideology and Social Science*, Harvester/ Wheatsheaf, Brighton, and St. Martins Press, New York, 1986, pp.1-56.)

356 Marx, *Critique of Hegel's Philosophy of Right*, p.96.

357 *Ibid.*, p.85.

358 *Ibid.*, pp.88-9.

359 A long time before analysing the 'classical' conditions of capitalist development in England and in the writings of 'English political economy, i.e., the scientific reflection of English economic conditions' ('Critical Marginal Notes on the Article by a Prussian', p.192.), Marx discussed the social turmoil of Germany in the same terms, insisting that 'Germany is just as much *classically* destined for a *social* revolution as it is incapable of a *political* one.' *(Ibid.,* p.202, Marx's emphases.)

360 *The Eighteenth Brumaire of Louis Bonaparte*, and *Civil War in France* are masterful examples of this Marxian achievement. In both works he sets out from the 'red-hot immediateness' of current events — which frightens away traditional historians — and, by integrating them within the sharply defined outlines of the prevalent historical tendencies, derives from them some major theoretical insights. The latter illuminate not only the scrutinised events themselves, but simultaneously also the epoch as a whole, becoming thus new building blocks and further supporting evidence of Marx's constantly developing vision. The ability to treat facts and events as classically significant manifestations of major social trends and forces is inseparable from the stark apodeicticity of the overall vision that guides it (determining, by the way, also the methodology of its 'classical' orientation in the conception and presentation of the fundamental theoretical propositions). The conditions of possibility of this vision were precisely the fluidity and transparency of an age of transition — with the relative openness and clarity of purpose of the contesting alternatives — which characterised the social confrontations of Marx's formative years.

361 Engels, 'Ludwig Feuerbach and the End of Classical German Philosophy', in Marx and Engels, *Selected Works*, Moscow, 1951, Vol. 2, p.349.

362 Letter dated 8 December, 1857. MEW, Vol. 29, p.225.

363 See in this respect also the first two pages of Section 13.6 on 'Temporal Ambiguities and Missing Mediations'.

364 Compare his draft letters to Vera Zasulich with the final version. (Written end of February/beginning of March, 1881.)

365 Marx, Letter to Engels, 8 December 1857. (MEW, Vol. 29, pp.222-5.)

366 Marx, Letter to Engels, 8 October 1858. (MEW, Vol. 29, p.360.)

367 Marx, Letter to Domela Nieuwenhuis, 22 February 1881.

368 From Marx's 'Conspectus of Bakunin's Book *State and Anarchy*'.

369 MEW, Vol. 19, p.398.

370 Marx, *Lohn, Preis und Profit*, ('Wages, Price and Profit', published in English under the title: 'Value, Price and Profit'), MEW, Vol. 16, p.153, and MECW, Vol. 20, p.149.

371 MECW, Vol. 20, p.148.

372 *Ibid.*, p.149.

PART THREE

STRUCTURAL CRISIS OF THE CAPITAL SYSTEM

'If capital increases from 100 to 1,000, then 1,000 is now the point of departure, from which the increase has to begin; the tenfold multiplication, by 1,000 percent, counts for nothing; profit and interest themselves become capital in turn. What appeared as surplus-value now appears as simple presupposition etc., as included in its simple composition.'

Marx

'In the form of government contracts for army supplies the scattered purchasing power of the consumers is concentrated in large quantities and, free of the vagaries and subjective fluctuations of personal consumption, it achieves an almost automatic regularity and rhythmic growth. Capital itself ultimately controls this automatic and rhythmic movement of militarist production through the legislature and a press whose function is to mould so-called "public opinion". That is why this particular province of capitalist accumulation at first seems capable of infinite expansion.'

Rosa Luxemburg

'Competition separates individuals from one another, not only the bourgeois but still more the workers, in spite of the fact that it brings them together. ... Hence every organized power standing over against these isolated individuals, who live in conditions daily reproducing this isolation, can only be overcome after long struggles. To demand the opposite would be tantamount to demanding that competition should not exist in this definite epoch of history, or that the individuals should banish from their minds conditions over which in their isolation they have no control.'

Marx

CHAPTER FOURTEEN

THE PRODUCTION OF WEALTH AND THE
WEALTH OF PRODUCTION

THE first issue which we have to consider concerns the possibility of a radically different approach to the development of human productive potentialities, in response to genuine need; as opposed to the established practice of social reproduction, subordinated to the alienated imperatives of ever-expanding capital-production, irrespective of its implications for human need.

The reason why this issue must be in the forefront of our attention is twofold. First, because it is no longer credible that the *disjunction* of need and wealth-production — which happens to be a necessary characteristic of generating wealth under the rule of capital — can indefinitely sustain itself even in the capitalistically most advanced and privileged countries; let alone that it can satisfy 'in due course' (through its glorified 'dynamism') the elementary needs of the vast majority of humankind which it now so callously disregards. And second, because the belief that there can be *no alternative* to the dominant productive practices is based on the false theorization of the relationship between production, science and technology, conceived and characteristically distorted from the standpoint of capital which it eternalizes. Such a view is quite untenable. For the dominance of capital's mode of production goes back only a few centuries in human history, and to establish its absolute permanence would require much more than the wishful assertions of its defenders.

Naturally, from the standpoint of capital's eternalizing self-perception the relationship of the present both to the past and to the future must be wantonly misrepresented. With regard to the past, it must count for nothing that for thousands of years, prior to the triumph of the capital system, the characteristics of productive activity were qualitatively different from our present modality of social reproduction. They were oriented towards aims that could not be more contrasting with the pursuits of ruthless capital-accumulation. As to the future, what must be apriori rejected from the standpoint of capital is that it is possible to identify today, in a tangible way, both the practical requirements and the appropriate operating principles on the basis of which an alternative — humanly rewarding and fulfilling — system of production could be instituted and maintained in existence.

14.1 The disjunction of need and wealth-production

14.1.1
THE complete subordination of human needs to the reproduction of exchange-value — in the interest of capital's expanded self-realization — has been the salient feature of the capital system from the outset.

This contrasted in the sharpest possible way with the productive practices of the ancient world. Indeed, the shift brought about by the consolidation of the rule of capital as an all-comprehensive system of control constituted the radical reversal of the orienting principles which characterized production in classical antiquity. To quote Marx:

> In antiquity ... *wealth does not appear as the aim of production*... The question is always which mode of property creates the best citizens. Wealth appears as an end in itself only among the few commercial peoples — monopolists of the carrying trade — who live in the pores of the ancient world, like the Jews in medieval society. ... Thus the old view, in which *the human being* appears as *the aim of production,* regardless of his limited national, religious, political character, seems to be very lofty contrasted to the modern world, where *production appears as the aim of mankind and wealth as the aim of production.*[1]

In order to make the production of wealth the aim of mankind, it was necessary to separate use-value from exchange-value, under the supremacy of the latter. This characteristic, in fact, was one of the main secrets of capital's dynamic success in that the given limitations of need did not constrain its development. For capital was oriented towards the production and enlarged reproduction of exchange-value, and thus could run ahead of existing demand to a significant extent and act as a powerful stimulus for the latter.

Naturally, the organization and division of labour had to be fundamentally different in societies where use-value and need played the key regulatory function. Two examples suffice here to illustrate the sharp contrast between the capitalist mode of production — oriented towards the multiplication of material wealth through the self-expansion of exchange-value — and the societies which organized their life on the basis of very different principles, even though the role of exchange was already quite significant in their metabolic intercourse with nature. The first is described by Marx as follows:

> Those small and extremely ancient *Indian communities,* some of which have continued down to this day, are based on possession in common of the land, on the blending of agriculture and handicrafts, and on an unalterable division of labour, which serves, whenever a new community is started, as a plan and scheme ready cut and dried. Occupying areas of from 100 up to several thousand acres, each forms a compact whole *producing all it requires*. The chief part of the product is destined for *direct use* by the community itself, and does not take the form of a commodity. Hence, production here is independent of that division of labour brought about, in Indian society as a whole, by means of the exchange of commodities. It is the *surplus alone* that becomes a *commodity,* and a portion of even that, not until it has reached the hands of the *State,* into whose hands from time immemorial a certain quantity of these products has found its way in the shape of rent in kind. The constitution of these communities varies in different parts of India. In those of the simplest form, the land is tilled in common, and the produce divided among the members. At the same time, spinning and weaving are carried on in each family as subsidiary industries. Side by side with the masses thus occupied with one and the same work, we find the 'chief inhabitant', who is judge, police, and tax gatherer in one; the book-keeper, who keeps the accounts of the tillage and registers everything relating thereto; another official, who prosecutes criminals, protects strangers travelling through and escorts them to the next village; the boundary man, who guards the boundaries against neighbouring communities; the water-overseer, who distributes

the water from the common tanks for irrigation; the Brahmin, who conducts the religious services; the schoolmaster, who on the sand teaches the children reading and writing; the calendar-Brahmin, or astrologer, who makes known the lucky or unlucky days for seed-time and harvest, and for every other kind of agricultural work; a smith and a carpenter, who make and repair all the agricultural implements; the potter, who makes all the pottery of the village; the barber, the washerman, who washes clothes, the silversmith, here and there the poet, who in some communities replaces the silver smith, in others the schoolmaster. This dozen individuals is *maintained at the expense of the whole community.* If the population increases, a new community is founded, on the pattern of the old one, on unoccupied land. The whole mechanism discloses a systematic division of labour; but *a division like that in manufactures is impossible,* since the smith and the carpenter, &c., find an *unchanging market,* and at the most there occur, according to the sizes of the villages, two or three of each, instead of one.[2]

The second example is equally revealing. It is concerned with the inner determinations of production and distribution within the framework of the guild system and in relation to the demands and interests of merchant capital which objectively conflicted with the constitutive principles and productive practices of the guilds. Under the prevailing historical circumstances, the guilds had to defend themselves against the subversive tendency of expanding merchant capital, and the reason why they could be successful for a very long time in their defensive action was their orientation towards the production of use-values.

This is how Marx characterises the functioning of the guild system in its complex historical setting:

> The rules of the guilds, by limiting most strictly the number of apprentices and journeymen that a single master could employ, prevented him from becoming a capitalist. Moreover, he could not employ his journeymen in any other handicraft than the one in which he was a master. The guilds zealously repelled every *encroachment by the capital of the merchants,* the only form of free capital with which they came in contact. A merchant could buy every kind of commodity, but *labour as a commodity he could not buy.* He existed only on sufferance, as a dealer in the products of the handicrafts. If circumstances called for a further division of labour, the existing guilds split themselves up into varieties, or founded new guilds by the side of the old ones; all this, however, without concentrating various handicrafts in a single workshop. Hence, the guild organisation, however much it may have contributed by separating, isolating, and perfecting the handicrafts, to create the material conditions for the existence of manufacture, *excluded division of labour in the workshop.*[3]

Thus, both examples underline the historically exceptional character of the capitalist system of production and distribution which first had to subdue, in the course of its historical unfolding, a number of spontaneous natural determinations, before it could successfully impose on humanity the material imperatives of its own functioning. It is important to remember in this respect that

> It is not the *unity* of living and active humanity with the natural, inorganic conditions of their *metabolic exchange with nature,* and hence their appropriation of nature, which requires explanation or is the result of a historic process, but rather the *separation* between these inorganic conditions of human existence and this active existence, a separation which is completely posited only in the relation of *wage labour and capital.*[4]

This is a fairly obvious truth which is, nevertheless, totally (and conveniently) ignored by the apologists of the capital system. For this system cannot successfully control the social metabolism unless it makes *permanent* all those artificial separations which constitute the *necessary presuppositions* of its own *modus operandi*, postulating them as determinations emanating from unalterable *'human nature'* itself.

14.1.2

TO be sure, the original natural correlations cannot be reestablished at a much more advanced stage of social development. For the whole system of human needs, together with their conditions of gratification, is radically altered in the course of historical transformations. And while the question of the *'unity* of active humanity with the *natural, inorganic conditions* of their metabolic exchange with nature' remains an open challenge, its realization is only conceivable at the most advanced level of productive interchange with *both* dimensions of nature. It has to embrace nature *'outside'*, confronting (with its manifold properties and adaptable forces, as well as with its indomitable resistances) the human natural being, and nature *'inside'*, i.e. historically developing 'humanity's own nature' (which includes the natural, inorganic conditions of human interchange with nature).

This means a qualitatively different and productively most advanced reconstitution of the long lost *unity* of the organic and inorganic conditions of human existence. This is not a *technological* but a *social* challenge of the highest order, since it implies the conscious mastery and all-sidedly beneficial regulation of the conditions of creative human interaction. A process unfolding under circumstances when social reproduction is no longer dominated by the burden of — at first natural but later paradoxically and bewilderingly more and more *man-made — 'scarcity'*. Under circumstances, that is, when the up to the present fragile and in many ways illusory 'mastery of man over nature' will no longer be bought, strictly for the benefit of the ruling minority, at the price of subjugating the vast majority of humankind to the alienating demands of commodity production.

Accordingly, it must be kept in mind that the problematical achievements of the capital system arose from a self-contradictory strategy that naively or wantonly ignored the requirement of a proper 'mastery of men over their organic and inorganic conditions of existence' as the necessary precondition of a socially viable human mastery over the forces of nature. At the same time it must be also remembered that the socialist critique of capital's contradictions cannot be formulated from the perspective and in terms of the constraining metabolic practices of past socioeconomic formations. For, compared to the dynamism of capital, tending from the outset towards its global articulation and domination, the structural limitations of the earlier forms of production — which rule them out on account of their inability to meet the socialist requirement of providing 'to each according to their needs' — are clear enough.

The self-enclosed and self-sufficing Indian communities had to pay a very high price indeed for the way in which the conditions of existence of their people continued to be reproduced with repetitively self-imposing stability. The price that had to be paid was that the potentially positive impact of a universal productive interchange with other communities (a fundamental characteristic of the capitalist formation) was necessarily denied to them. For exchange as such played a strictly marginal role in their social metabolism. But even the productive and distributive processes described in the second example — a socioeconomic framework in which the penetration of exchange-value was much more in evidence than in the small Indian communities — could not escape the limitations of the type and range of consumption compatible with the intrinsic determinations of that system. For, as Marx had put it into relief:

> With the urban crafts, although they rest essentially on exchange and on the creation of exchange-values, the *direct and chief aim* of this production is subsistence as craftsmen, as master-journeymen, hence *use-value*; not *wealth,* not exchange-value as *exchange-value*. Production is therefore always subordinated to a *given consumption,* supply to *demand,* and *expands only slowly*.[5]

As we can see, then, to oppose use-value to the capitalist dominance of inexorably expanding exchange-value is very far from being able to offer the sufficient conditions of a successful socialist transformation. For various historically known systems of societal reproduction oriented towards the production of use-value tended to impose severe limitations on the admissible productive and consumptive practices of the systems in question. Indeed, their ultimate historical demise could not be made intelligible without reference to such limitations which tended to undermine their viability in their — sooner or later unavoidable — confrontations with the incomparably more dynamic capitalist mode of production and societal reproduction.

It is therefore necessary to couple the socialist critique of capitalist value-relations, and the affirmation of the vital positive role of use-value, with an indication of a practically feasible way out of the contradictions of the precapitalist forms of socioeconomic interchange insofar as they arise from their approach to use value. Contradictions which systematically prevent the development of the potential wealth of production through the negative determinations of limited consumption and one-sided demand. For a failure to identify the objective and subjective conditions of positively overcoming such constraints would carry with it uncomfortable implications for the anticipated socialist mode of production and reproduction as inevitably 'the generalization of misery'. Indeed, it would make the Marxian discourse — on not merely restoring use-value to its past importance but promoting it to its proper, potentially dynamic and creative role in regulating the social metabolism — devoid of all practical relevance. Thus it is by no means accidental that in Marx's theory the great emphasis laid on the orienting determination of use-value in a future socialist society is inseparable from the question of the *all-sided* development of the social individual's *needs and productive capacities.* For such a development is feasible only within the unrestricted — i.e. no longer class-interest- and class-conflict-determined — framework of 'universal intercourse' and *'universal exchange' of human capacities and accomplishments* (discussed in Chapter 19), as opposed to *universally dominant exchange-value*.

14.2 Fetishistic and true meaning of property

14.2.1

IN the course of capital's historical unfolding — which imposed on humankind the production of wealth as the all-absorbing aim — the real character of wealth properly so called completely disappeared from sight. It was obliterated by a reified conception, wedded to equally fetishistic material structures and relations which determined the overall social metabolism in all its dimensions.

In this respect, one of the most important categories whose meaning was perversely altered under the impact of capital's reifying determinations was that of *property*. Parallel to — and in conjunction with — the developments which separated (and alienated) from the active subject of social reproduction the 'inorganic conditions of human existence', the meaning of 'property' changed beyond recognition. Characteristically, it became identified with the *'thing'* of commodity production and exchange, and above all with the institutionalized guarantee of capitalist reproduction (i.e. 'objectified, alienated and stored up labour' assuming the form of legally protected capital assets and ever-expanding exchange-value).

The *raison d'être* of such changes is not too difficult to identify. For through its radically perverted meaning, the capitalist concept of 'property' can play a vital part in legitimating the established — apriori prejudged and materially fixed, as well as legally/politically safeguarded — relations of production and the dominant mode of appropriation (and expropriation) corresponding to it, in sharp contrast to its original meaning. For:

> *Property* originally means no more than a human being's relation to his *natural conditions* of production as *belonging to him,* as his, as presupposed along with *his own being*; relations to them as natural presuppositions of his self, which only form, so to speak, *his extended body.* He actually does not relate to his conditions of production, but rather has a *double existence,* both *subjectively* as he himself, and *objectively* in these *natural non-organic conditions of his existence.* ... Property originally means — in its Asiatic, Slavonic, ancient classical, Germanic form — the relation of the working (producing or self-reproducing) *subject* to the *conditions* of his production or reproduction *as his own.* It will therefore have different forms depending on the conditions of this reproduction. Production itself aims at the reproduction of the producer within and together with these, his objective conditions of existence.[6]

The capitalist mode of social reproduction could not be more distant from this original determination of production and property. Under the rule of capital, the working subject can no longer consider the conditions of his production and reproduction as *his own property.* They are no longer the self-evident and socially safeguarded presuppositions of his *being,* nor the natural presuppositions of his *self* as constitutive of 'his extended body'. On the contrary, they now belong to a reified 'alien being' who confronts the producers with its own demands and subjugates them to the material imperatives of its own constitution. Thus the original relationship between the subject and object of productive activity is completely overturned, reducing the human being to the dehumanized status of a mere 'material condition of production'. 'Having' dominates 'being' in all spheres of life. At the same time, the real self of the *productive agents* is destroyed through the fragmentation and degradation of work while they are subjugated to the brutalizing requirements of the capitalist labour process. They are acknowledged as legitimately existing 'subjects' only as the *manipulated consumers* of commodities. Indeed, they become the more cynically manipulated — as the fictitious 'sovereign consumers' — the greater the pressure of the decreasing rate of utilization.

Naturally, under such circumstances and determinations the productively active human beings cannot occupy their rightful place as a human beings in capital's equations, let alone can they be considered within the parameters of the capital system as the true aim of production. The commodified and reified social relationship between the productive subjects and their now independent controller — who, as a matter of materially constituted and legally enforced rights, acts as the sole proprietor of the conditions of the worker's production and self-reproduction — appear mystifying and impenetrable. Equally, the task of social reproduction and metabolic interchange with nature is fetishistically defined as the reproduction of the objectified/alienated conditions of production of which the sentient human being is no more than a strictly subordinated part, as a 'material factor of production'. And since the established productive system, under the rule of capital, cannot reproduce itself unless it can do so on an ever-enlarged scale, production not only must be deemed the aim of mankind but — as a mode of production to which there cannot be any alternative — it must be premissed by the never-ending multiplication of material wealth as the aim of production.

14.2.2

THE productive dynamism of the capital system, whatever its inhumanities, is in evidence throughout the history of its national and global expansion whose impact the earlier forms of social reproduction are far too powerless to withstand. Naturally, the formerly unimaginable growth of wealth that goes with such dynamism — so long as it can last — constitutes the historical legitimacy of this system. However, given the inherent contradictions of the capital system, and the concomitant wastefulness of its mode of operation, its productive development cannot be sustained indefinitely.

Thus, at a time when the capitalistic self-expansion of exchange-value is in crisis, if we want to address ourselves seriously to the problems of development and 'underdevelopment', in order to investigate the conditions of a viable socialist alternative, it is unavoidable to challenge the very *horizons* of capital's self-reproducing 'wealth' within which there can be no solution to such problems. In other words, the issue at stake is an absolutely fundamental one in relation to which everything else could only qualify, at best, as a *temporary* palliative.

In practical terms the issue we are concerned with is: how to make the human being again the aim of production, in accordance with the immense *positive potentialities* of the — to some extent already existing but destructively embedded — production forces. To do this, instead of devising various pseudo-scientific rationalizations of capital's productive practices which prevent the actualization of the positive potentialities, preserving the existing relations of production and the iniquitous, hierarchical division of labour. Inevitably, this involves a radical redefinition of *'wealth'*, in the same spirit in which the capitalistically distorted meaning of *'property'* needs a radical redefinition. For

> when the limited bourgeois form is stripped away, what is *wealth* other than the *universality of individual needs, capacities, pleasures, productive forces etc.*, created through *universal exchange*? The full development of human mastery over the forces of nature, those of *so-called nature* as well as of *humanity's own nature*? The absolute working out of his *creative potentialities*, with no presupposition other than the previous historic development, which makes this totality of development, i.e. the *development of all human powers as such the end in itself*, not as measured on a *predetermined* yardstick?

Where he does not reproduce himself in one *specificity*, but produces his *totality*? Strives not to remain something he has *become*, but is in the absolute movement of *becoming?* In bourgeois economics — and in the epoch of production to which it corresponds — this complete working out of the human content appears as a complete emptying-out, this universal *objectification* as total *alienation*, and the tearing-down of all limited, one-sided aims as sacrifice of *the human end-in-itself* to an entirely *external end.*[7]

Given these considerations, we can well understand why some people who argue from the reified *presuppositions* of capital's self-oriented 'productive wealth' — whether they favour 'growth' or are against it — must remain trapped within the contradictions of alienated objectification and its uncontrollable, ultimately self-destructive 'external ends', even when they claim to look for and offer a way out of those contradictions. And that is precisely the position of all those who end up with the advocacy of false dichotomies — like, for instance, 'growth and catastrophic collapse or global equilibrium through zero growth' — as a result of their failure to question the vicious circle of the reified wealth-orientated capital system, treated by them as the unalterable alpha and omega of social life itself.

In complete contrast, the removal of capital's 'predetermined yardstick' as the measure of all human endeavour means that the life-activity of the associated individuals must be radically reoriented in its entirety. For capital's yardstick can measure only the higher or lower degree of success to conform to the imperative of managing production as the aim of mankind, in subservience to the expansion of utilitarian/commodified material wealth as the aim of production. This is why in Marx's view human endeavour must be reoriented towards the *wealth of production* (i.e., 'the universality of *individual* needs, capacities, pleasures, productive forces, etc.') and towards an increasingly richer — but of course not in a narrowly material sense 'richer' — *self-reproduction* of the *social* individuals as the consciously adopted end-in-itself. For capital is by far the most powerful spontaneous regulator of production known to mankind up to the present and cannot be replaced by a socioeconomic vacuum. The rule of capital over society can be overcome only by a materially sound and humanly rewarding reproductive order which takes over all of the vital metabolic functions of this mode of control without its contradictions.

Production is either consciously controlled by the associated producers in the service of their ends, or it controls them by imposing its own structural imperatives as the inescapable presuppositions of social practice. Thus, only *self-realization* through the *wealth of production* (and not the alienating and reified *production of wealth*) as the aim of the social individuals' life-activity can offer a viable alternative to capital's blind self-reproductive spontaneity and its destructive consequences. This means the production and actualization of all creative human potentialities no less than the continued reproduction of the material and intellectual conditions of social interchange.

In this sense, what is 'utopian' is decidedly not the socialist reorientation of production as an alternative to the now prevailing practices, whatever its practical difficulties. On the contrary, an utterly bleak form of pessimistic utopianism happens to characterize precisely the advocacy of 'well tried' and 'realistic' — though, as a matter of fact, in the longer run totally unreal — solutions. For

the 'realistic' prescriptions advocated by those who dismiss the Marxian perspective as nothing but 'utopianism' remain trapped within the horizons of
self-propelling wealth-production even when they talk of some wishful regulatory mechanisms while preserving unchanged the overall framework of structural inequality.

14.3 Productivity and use

14.3.1

THE prospects of human emancipation are inseparable from the required
advancement in — historically feasible — productivity. This is not simply a
matter of a *quantitative* increase in the amount of goods at the disposal of a
particular society, measured on a *per capita* basis. A number of *qualitative* considerations are much more important in conceptualizing the role of productive
achievements in the course of historical development than the quantitative
expansion of productive outlets.

Indeed, once the social metabolism leaves behind the stage characterized by
the satisfaction of needs only in terms of the bare necessities of survival, a strictly
quantitative assessment of the ongoing productive improvements becomes extremely problematical, if not altogether meaningless. Nevertheless, at a highly
advanced stage of historical development, under the conditions of generalized
commodity production—after countless centuries of reciprocal interaction between newly arising needs and corresponding productive practices, which inevitably go with a great variety of qualitative differentiation already well before
the global triumph of capital — the fetishism of quantification completely
dominates the qualitative dimension of the reproduction process. Such perversity becomes intelligible only with reference to the intrinsically contradictory
way in which capital's productive system itself is, of necessity, articulated. For
this particular mode of societal reproduction is overburdened with an ultimately
explosive contradiction that turns its *positive* potentialities into *destructive* realities. This turn of development becomes the more pronounced the more closely
the structural limits of the capital system — the limits of ever-more-wasteful
quantification and expansion in a world of finite resources — are approached.

The quantitative dimension of the material emancipatory requirements is
underlined by Marx when he states that the advocated new society presupposes
'a great increase in productive power, a high degree of its development. ...
without it privation, want is merely made general, and with want the struggle
for necessities would begin again, and all the old filthy business would necessarily be restored.'[8] Since, however, increased productivity from the earliest phase
of historical development is inseparably linked to the dialectic of expanding
needs (together with the expanded reproduction of their conditions of gratification),[9] the qualitative aspect of productive expansion is implicit in the creation
and satisfaction of the new needs already at the most primitive stages of human
history. This is so even if the emergent qualitative differentiation in the structure
of historically developing needs can be materially identified only later on. It can
be perceived when the constraints of 'bare necessity' are no longer overpowering
in the social metabolism, thanks to the appearance and progressive expansion

of the socially produced *surplus,* no matter how iniquitously appropriated under the circumstances.

In this sense, the historical advancement represented by the capitalist stage of productive developments (embracing, after all, only a few centuries of the total history of humankind) is an actual *relapse* if considered with regard to its impact on the dialectic of need and productivity. For it radically disrupts the previous relationship which prevailed, as already mentioned, over thousands of years. It removes — as it must — not only the *limiting* determinations of need-orientated production, but simultaneously also the possibility of *controlling* the destructive tendencies which arise from the total domination of *quality* by the imperatives of unrestrained quantitative capital-expansion. This is why the pro-blematics of *need, quality* and *use* must occupy a central place in the socialist reorientation of production and distribution. Indeed, the orienting criteria of need, quality and use apply to all aspects of socialist production and distribution, from the satisfaction of the elementary material requirements of the social me-tabolism to the various efforts aimed at enhancing the most mediated dimen-sions of cultural reproduction.

14.3.2

THE reductive and reifying quantification in evidence everywhere under the rule of capital carries far-reaching consequences for the alienated, dehumanized and impoverished exercise of the functions of living labour. To quote Marx:

> If the mere *quantity* of labour functions as a measure of value regardless of *quality,* it presupposes that simple labour has become the pivot of industry. It presupposes that labour has been equalized by the *subordination of man to the machine* or by the extreme division of labour; that *men are effaced by their labour*; that the pendulum of the clock has become as accurate a measure of the relative activity of *two workers* as it is of the speed of *two locomotives.* Therefore, we should not say that one man's hour is worth another man's hour, but rather that one man during an hour is worth just as much as another man during an hour. Time is everything, *man is nothing*; he is, at the most, *time's carcase. Quality* no longer matters. *Quantity* alone decides everything; hour for hour, day for day;[10]

Thus, since human beings can only be fitted into the productive machinery of the capital system as cogs of the overall mechanism, their human qualities must be considered only a hindrance to the optimal efficacy of a system which has its own logic and measure of legitimation. Accordingly, the same criteria must be applied to the assessment of human performance as to that of locomotives, thereby not even just equating with but *subordinating* sentient and troublesome[11] humankind to the undemanding efficacy of much more easily managed profit-able mechanical devices.

Furthermore, to make matters worse, whereas the efficacy (or value) of the *productive* worker can be objectively assessed within the capitalistic framework of accountancy with suitable accuracy, in the same way as the locomotive can be — and that is precisely how the machine can become a direct competitor to the productive worker — the 'worth' ascribed to the *unproductive* and *parasitic* constituents of the capitalistic process of production and distribution (from fraudulent stock-market manipulators to anti-trade-union labour relations 'ex-perts' and commercial or political advertising agents) is open to the most arbitrary determinations. Indeed, the nearer we get to the most advanced stage of 'advanced capitalism', the more pronounced is the shift in the direction of the non-productive and parasitic constituents.

AS an illustration of the nature of such a shift we may take Baran's example of a hypothetical bakery in which 80 workers are productively and 20 non-productively employed. The non-productive workers are engaged as follows:

> five men are commissioned to change continually the shapes of the loaves; one man is given the task of admixing with the dough a chemical substance that accelerates the perishability of bread; four men are hired to make up new wrappers for the bread; five men are employed in composing advertising copy for bread and broadcasting same over the available mass media; one man is appointed to watch carefully the activities of other baking companies; two men are to keep abreast of legal developments in the antitrust field; and finally two men are placed in charge of the baking corporation's public relations.[12]

If we bear in mind that the inherent purpose of production is supposed to be the satisfaction of human need, it transpires that under the prevailing conditions, on the contrary, *'utility'* can be successfully equated with *anti-need,* and in that sense with the need-negating practical assertion of *anti-value.* At the same time, the unproductive and parasitic constituents of the system can run riot, in the absence of any objective measure whatsoever for assessing the contribution or non-contribution of such constituents to the production of social wealth. Instead, they themselves can arbitrarily determine the course of wealth-distribution in virtue of their privileged position in the *command structure of capital,* whether as 'captains of industry' or as political guardians of the bourgeois state. Thus, to add insult to injury, they can absurdly elevate themselves to the exalted status of 'the creators of wealth' so as to appropriate, in accordance with that lofty status, a major portion of the social product to which they contribute absolutely nothing of substance.

Admittedly, these contradictions, with all their grotesque manifestations, become particularly acute only under 'advanced capitalism'. Nevertheless, the conflict between productive and non-productive labour appears already at a very early stage of capitalistic developments, even if it cannot assume at the time of its emergence the *extravagant* forms with which we are familiar today. For the necessary precondition of the latter is the prodigious expansion of society's productive power which enables — and, as we shall see later, under the conditions of 'advanced capitalism' indeed necessitates — the allocation of an increasingly greater portion of social wealth for the production of *institutionalized waste.*

14.4 Contradiction between productive and non-productive labour

14.4.1

THE contradiction between productive and non-productive labour is inherent in the fundamental antagonism between the interests of capital and those of labour and, as such, it is insurmountable. It arises in the first place from the exploitative character of the capitalist labour process itself and from the necessity of finding a form of control suitable to its perpetuation. As Marx puts it:

The *directing motive,* the end and *aim* of capitalist production, is to extract the greatest possible amount of *surplus-value,* and consequently to *exploit* labour-power to the greatest possible extent. As the number of the co-operating labourers increases [in the capitalist factory], so too does their resistance to the domination of capital, and with it, the necessity for capital to overcome this resistance by counter-pressure. The *control* exercised by the capitalist is not only a special function, due to the nature of the social labour-process, and peculiar to that process, but it is, at the same time, a function of the exploitation of a social labour-process, and is consequently rooted in the unavoidable antagonism between the exploiter and the living and labouring raw material he exploits. ... If, then, the control of the capitalist is in substance *twofold* by reason of the twofold nature of the production process itself — which, on the one hand, is a social process for producing *use-values,* on the other, a process for creating *surplus-value* — in form that control is *despotic.* As co-operation extends its scale, this despotism takes forms peculiar to itself. Just as at first the capitalist is relieved from actual labour so soon as his capital has reached that minimum amount with which capitalist production, as such, begins, so now, he hands over the work of direct and constant *supervision* of the individual workmen, and groups of workmen, to a *special kind of wage-labourer.* An industrial army of workmen, under the command of a capitalist, requires, like a real army, *officers (managers),* and *sergeants (foremen, overlookers),* who, while the work is being done, *command* in the name of the capitalist. The work of supervision becomes their established and exclusive function. When comparing the mode of production of isolated peasants and artisans with production by slave- labour, the political economist counts this labour of superintendence among the *faux frais* [false costs or useless expenses] of production. But when considering the capitalist mode of production, he, on the contrary, treats the work of control made necessary by the co-operative character of the labour process as identical with the different work of control, necessitated by the capitalist character of that process and the *antagonism of interests* between capitalist and labourer. It is not because he is a *leader* of industry that a man is a capitalist; on the contrary, he is a leader of industry because he is a *capitalist.* The leadership of industry is an *attribute of capital,* just as in feudal times the functions of general and judge were attributes of landed property. Auguste Comte and his school might therefore have shown that feudal lords are an *eternal necessity* in the same way that they have done in the case of the lords of capital.[13]

Later extensions of the non-productive, anti-value generating constituents of the capitalist labour process share the same premisses and are built on the self-same material foundations. They belong to those 'false costs and useless expenses of production' which are, nevertheless, absolutely vital to the survival of the system: a contradictory determination from which they cannot be extricated.

Moreover, beyond a certain point of capitalistic developments, as we shall see below, the quantitative changes in the extension of the non-productive dimension turn into a *qualitative* redimensioning of the whole structure. As a result, the undisturbed functioning of the genuinely productive constituents becomes ever-more-dependent on the maintenance and further growth of the *parasitic* sectors — on which increasing numbers of people depend for their livelihood, while others depend on the latter as consumers of their products — thereby paradoxically adding to the contradictions of the overall complex also when offering remedies to its more or less openly acknowledged dysfunctions.

This is where the intrinsic limitations of the capitalist orienting principles of production come to the fore. The deepening crisis of the established system cannot be resolved in terms of simply expanding the 'production of wealth', since within its framework 'wealth' is equated with *surplus-value,* and not with the production of *use-value* by means of the creative application of *disposable time.* At the same time the liberating potential of *increased productivity* is dissipated and nullified through the cancerously growing 'false costs' of control in the service of the exploitative dimension. The Marxian proposition concerned with reorienting production from its subordination to surplus-value (i.e. from the capitalist 'production of wealth' which sets up the multiplication of reified wealth as the aim of production) towards a need- and use-orientated, as well as creativity-enhancing, socialist 'wealth of production', is attempting to address itself precisely to such — within capital's framework insurmountable — difficulties.

14.4.2

What is at issue here, as far as the advocated socialist productive practices are concerned, is nothing less than the *complete reversal* of the prevailing — and in its one-sidedly quantitative terms most effective, no matter how wasteful — approach to the question of utility. The contrast is highlighted in Marx's words when he asserts that:

> In a future society in which *class antagonism* will have ceased, in which there will no longer be any classes, *use* will no longer be determined by the *minimum* time of production; but the *time* of production devoted to an article will be determined by the degree of its *utility*.[14]

Naturally, this conception presupposes the ability of the associated producers to overcome the constraints of *scarcity* and organize their life on the basis of a truly rational allocation of not only the available and dynamically utilized (i.e. in such essentially *qualitative* sense genuinely expandable) material resources but, above all, in accordance with the liberating potentialities of *disposable time.*

THE concept of disposable time, taken in its positive and liberating sense, appeared well before Marx, in an anonymous pamphlet entitled *The Source and Remedy of the National Difficulties,* published in London in 1821. In some passages quoted by Marx this pamphlet offered a remarkable dialectical grasp of both the nature of the capitalistic production process and — by focusing attention on the vitally important categories of 'disposable time', 'surplus labour', and 'shortened working day' — the possibility of escaping from its contradictions:

> *Wealth is disposable time* and nothing more. ... If the whole labour of a country were sufficient only to raise the support of the whole population, there would be no *surplus labour,* consequently nothing that can be allowed to *accumulate as capital.* ... Truly *wealthy a nation,* if there is no interest or if the *working day* is 6 hours rather than 12.[15]

Reorienting social production in accordance with the spirit and categorial framework of this anonymous pamphlet is, of course, thoroughly incompatible with the logic of capital. For, due to the inherently contradictory nature of capital as the overall regulator of the social metabolism, advancements in *productivity* — and the potential increase in positively allocated *disposable time* — cannot be harmoniously contained within its framework.

Improved productivity, to be sure, is a necessary aim of the *individual* capitalist, inasmuch as it can secure *competitive advantage* to him. However, nothing positive is implied by this circumstance with regard to genuine *use* corresponding to *human need,* since the connection is purely *accidental* from the point of view of the individual capitalist. The latter is not in the slightest interested in 'need' or 'use' but merely in the *realization* of his capital on an extended scale. Nor could indeed the individual capitalist be interested in need and use over which he has no control. For he has no guarantee whatsoever of finding in the mysterious domain ruled by the 'invisible hand' the *capitalistically legitimate* 'effective demand' and consumption-capacity equivalent to his own commodities. Even less has he any way of determining the use to which the social product in its entirety might be put.

Worse still, while the productive system of capital *de facto* creates *'superfluous time'* in society as a whole, on an increasing scale, it cannot conceivably acknowledge the *de jure* existence of such socially produced surplus-time as potentially creative *disposable time*. On the contrary, it must assume a *negative/destructive/dehumanizing* attitude towards it. Indeed, capital must callously disregard the fact that the concept of 'superfluous labour', with its 'superfluous time', in reality refers to *living human beings* and possessors of *socially* useful — even if *capitalistically* redundant or inapplicable — productive capacities.

14.4.3

Productivity, in all forms of society, is inextricably linked to the kind of *utility* and *utilization* which happens to be compatible with the dominant productive practices of that society. Naturally, the same goes for the capitalist social order. Given the structural limitations and contradictions of this universally commodifying, profit-orientated socioeconomic order, the scope of its productivity is hopelessly constrained — and its direction beyond a certain point of the unfolding historical development radically perverted — by the way in which the demands of capital-expansion practically define the criteria of *'usefulness'* to which everything must conform. As Marx observes in the *Grundrisse* on the perverse determination of 'usefulness' and 'uselessness' arising from the untranscendable limits of capital-utilization:

> It is a law of capital to create *surplus labour, disposable time*; it can do this only by setting *necessary labour* in motion — i.e. entering into exchange with the worker. It is its tendency, therefore, to create as much labour as possible; just as it is equally its tendency to *reduce* necessary labour to a minimum. It is therefore equally a tendency of capital to *increase* the labouring population, as well as constantly to posit a part of it as *surplus population* — population which is *useless* until such time as *capital can utilize it*. (Hence the correctness of the theory of surplus population and surplus capital.) It is equally a tendency of capital to make human labour (relatively) *superfluous*, so as to drive it, as human labour, towards infinity. Value is nothing but objectified labour, and surplus value (realization of capital) is only the excess above that part of objectified labour which is necessary for the reproduction of labouring capacity. But labour as such is and remains the presupposition [of capitalist production], and surplus labour exists only in relation with the necessary, hence only in so far as the latter exists. Capital must therefore constantly posit *necessary* labour in order to posit *surplus labour*; it has to multiply it (namely the simultaneous working days) in order to multiply the surplus; but at the same time it must *suspend* them as *necessary*, in order to posit them as *surplus labour*. ... the newly created surplus capital can be realized as such only by being again exchanged for living labour. Hence the tendency of capital simultaneously to *increase* the labouring population as well as to *reduce* constantly the necessary part (constantly to posit a part of it as *reserve*). And the increase of popu-

lation itself the chief means for reducing the necessary part. At bottom this is only an application of the relation of the *single working day*. Here already lie, then, all the *contradictions* which modern population theory expresses as such, but does not grasp. Capital, as the positing of surplus labour, is equally and in the same moment the positing and the not-positing of necessary labour; it exists only in so far as necessary labour both exists and does not exist.[16]

Thus, the contradictory system of capital practically asserts its own — historically *specific* — limits as the limits of *production in general*. It acknowledges and legitimizes human need (and corresponding utilization of the available material and human resources) only to the extent to which doing so is in agreement with the imperatives of capital's expanded self-realization. Whatever falls outside such parameters, must be deemed 'useless', 'unutilizable' and intolerably 'superfluous', irrespective of the consequences. Indeed, capital's restless drive forward — in the process of its ever-enlarging self-reproduction — prevents it from paying attention to the destructive developments arising from the contradiction between superfluous and necessary labour. For capital itself can only exist 'in so far as necessary labour both exists and does not exist', i.e. in so far as it succeeds in reproducing the underlying contradiction (however precarious the situation) and thereby itself as well.

Furthermore, the contradictions of capital's unique *'microcosm'*, identifiable in the inner determinations and tensions of the *single working day*, are inevitably reproduced throughout the *'macrocosm'* of the capitalist mode of production. Reification becomes ubiquitous because under the rule of capital the specific characteristics of all productive activity, from the smallest local units to the factories of the gigantic transnational corporations, are necessarily constituted in conformity to the material and organizational imperatives of the *commodity structure* which apply no less to *living labour* than to the means and material of production.

14.5 The command structure of capital: vertical determination of the labour process

14.5.1

IN this way, thanks to the dehumanizing fact that living labour itself is turned into a *commodity* which can function (as a productive force) and biologically sustain itself (as an organism) only by entering the framework — and submitting itself to the material and organizational demands — of the dominant *exchange relations*, the major obstacles that heavily constrained the scope and dynamism of earlier productive systems are successfully removed. As commodified living labour becomes *'time's carcase'*, it becomes possible to structure the resulting (reifiable) working days — both horizontally and vertically — in accordance with the requirements of capital's enlarged self-reproduction.

It is this very process of quantifying reduction and reification of living labour that brings with it the *universal* diffusion and domination of the commodity structure; once, that is, the conditions of its universalisability are historically satisfied. As to the latter question, the capitalist commodity structure becomes *universalisable* — in the sense that absolutely everything can be subsumed under it — precisely because under the new circumstances commodified living labour can be organized and controlled with great flexibility and dynamism. This control is exercised both horizontally and vertically, as the emergent structural imperatives of the capitalist division of labour (under their manifold functional and social/hierarchical aspects) prescribe it.

The *horizontal* flexibility of the new organizational determinations carries with it, on the one hand, that the uniquely structured (i.e. in a yet to be discussed sense thoroughly *homogenized*) working day of the capitalist labour process, in sharp contrast to the limited potentialities of previous modes of production, can be both *multiplied and divided indefinitely,* as the conditions of successful capital-accumulation permit and the advancement of the functional division of labour requires it. At the same time, on the other hand, the selfsame horizontal flexibility also means that the multiplicity of co-existent and co-operating working days can be arranged and supervised *side by side* — so to speak 'under the same roof' even when spread over many countries — in a functionally suitable and dynamically modifiable pattern. This type of development stretches from the relatively primitive workshop of the early manufacturing period all the way to the highly complex and diffused simultaneity of massive transnational factories in our own times.

14.5.2

THE *vertical* structuring, however, is even more important for securing the dynamic development of the capital system. For it is precisely the ability of capital to order the multiplicity of working days also in a *vertical/hierarchical* pattern that constitutes the *guarantee* of the safe applicability and full diffusion of the horizontal organizational principle itself, together with the productive potentialities inherent in it. (E.g. economies of scale, of spatio-temporal, material and intellectual resource-utilization, etc.)

It is this vertical dimension that directly corresponds to the historically unparalleled *command structure of capital* whose function is to safeguard the vital interests of the ruling system. That is to say: the interests of securing the continued expansion of surplus-value on the basis of the maximum practicable *exploitation* of the totality of labour (though, of course, in conjunction with *differential rates* of exploitation in different countries and industries across the ages, as this is made possible by the prevailing relation of forces in the global framework of capital). Such interests must be secured through the proper functioning of capital's command structure, whatever the scope and complexity of the horizontal organization (functional fragmentation/division and simultaneous reunification) of the total capitalistically *utilizable* working days. (The latter are, of course, very far from equalling the total socially *available* working days which could be put, under a very different mode of social metabolic control, to humanly rewarding use.)

Accordingly, the horizontal structuring factor is allowed to advance at any given time only to the extent to which it is duly controllable within capital's reproductive horizon by the vertical dimension. In other words, it can proceed to the extent to which the ensuing productive developments remain *containable* within the parameters of capital's imperatives (and corresponding limitations), as opposed to becoming 'dysfunctional' to the system. (We may recall in this context that the European Chief Executive of the Ford Corporation, Mr Bob Lutz, was threatening the *liquidation* of some major plants of the company if 'uneducated governments' and 'intransigent trade unions' — acting so as to reduce the total number of exploitable working days — dared to challenge the *status quo*. He objected to any attempt to interfere with the capitalistic verti-cal/hierarchical determination of what could be considered tolerable and what must be ruled out as absolutely inadmissible, in order to prevent the appearance of dysfunctional elements in the *overall* framework of the American transnational corporation in question. See in this respect p. 868 of the present volume.)

Here we can also see that ultimately not the horizontal factor but the ines-capable determinations of the vertical/hierarchical dimension decide the histo-rical unfolding and advancement — as well as the distorted development or underdevelopment — of the capital system, in its parts no less than in its entirety.

The control demands of vertical ordering constitute always the *overriding* moment in the relationship of the two dimensions, even during the long his-torical period of capital's ascendancy, when a dialectical reciprocity between the horizontal and vertical structuring principles is much in evidence. This dialec-tical reciprocity, with the vertical dimension as its *'übergreifendes Moment'*, brings with it in the course of capitalistic developments some highly adaptable struc-tures of control, on a monumental scale. (We witness, for instance, the switch from the limited paternalistic entrepreneurial system to the readily expandable joint stock managerial framework.) Changes of this kind take place in response to the needs of the unfolding functional/horizontal division of labour, with its vast international ramifications, while successfully containing the latter entirely within the class parameters of capital's vertically enforced vital interests.

However, once the historical phase of capital's relatively unproblematical ascendancy is left behind, the *overriding moment* is turned into a *one-sided* and ultimately disruptive *direct determination* of the interchange between the two dimensions. It thereby *prevents* the actualization of those positive productive potentialities which appear, as necessarily frustrated and repressed potentialities, on the horizon. In a most important sense this correlation marks out very clearly the insuperable *structural limits* of the capital system as a mode of production and social metabolic reproduction.

14.6 The homogenization of all productive and distributive relations

14.6.1

THE historically unique *homogenization* of all productive and distributive rela-tions completes capital's vicious circle. This homogenization is an *absolute* con-dition of the social metabolic order controlled by capital. For without it the capital system could not reproduce itself, in view of the cleavages and contra-dictions which it necessarily brings into being in the course of its historical articulation.

For one thing, the *unity* of need and production — characteristic of earlier modes of metabolic interchange with nature inasmuch as 'their aim is man' in that they orient themselves towards the production of use-values — is totally disrupted in the capital system. Indeed, to be more precise, the latter is characterized by a *double disruption*.

First, the producers are radically *separated* from the material and instruments of their productive activity, thereby making it impossible for them to produce for their own use, since they are no longer even partially in control of the production process itself.

And second, the commodities produced on the basis of such separation and alienation cannot emerge directly from the production process as *need-related use-values*. They require the intervention of an *extraneous* moment for their metamorphosis into use-values in order to make possible the continuity of production and the overall reproduction of the capital system. In other words, since the great mass of the produced commodities cannot conceivably constitute use-values for their *owners* (the comparatively insignificant number of capitalists), they must enter capital's *exchange relation* — whereby they can function as use-values for their *non-owners* (i.e. overwhelmingly the workers) — in order to be realized for the benefit of capital's expanded reproduction as *values*.

Moreover, it is a vital structuring determination of the system that capital cannot renew itself without appropriating the *surplus-labour* of society (i.e. under capitalism the *surplus-value* produced by commodified *living labour* with which capital must exchange the mass of available commodities, so as to realize them as values and begin again, on an extended scale, the capitalist cycle of production and reproduction). Consequently a new kind of *unity* must be generated which is capable of *displacing* the contradictions of this double disruption (even if it can never fully *overcome* them) while maintaining the structural cleavages in existence.

Bewilderingly, it is the double disruption itself which serves as the material basis of the unity without which capital could not function. Its first moment — the radical separation of the workers from the means and material of their productive activity and self-reproduction — deprives them of any influence on the way in which the specific productive functions which they must perform in their place of work are assigned to them, not to mention the way in which the overall reproduction process is determined and organized. At the same time, the second moment — the necessity to enter capital's exchange relation for the sake of mere survival — locks the workers firmly into the ruling system, totally at the mercy of capital. For the fragments of the commodities which the individual workers produce are both beyond their control (as a result of the alienation of the means and material of production) and at the same time useless to them, because of their fragmentariness, compared even to the elementary needs of the individual workers. Furthermore, even the one and only real possession of the workers — their labour power — cannot constitute use-value for them, but only for capital which sets it into motion. This is how the double disruption between need and production is turned into an immensely powerful labour-enslaving operational unity, asserting itself through the interlocking determinations and dictates of the labour process, on the one hand, and the exchange relation, on the other. In this way the capital system is enabled to operate — with great dynamism and efficacy throughout the historical phase of its ascendancy — thanks to the separation of living labour from its objective conditions of exercise, complemented by the subjugation of need and use-value to the reifying determinations of exchange-value.

The overall purpose and motivating force of the capital system cannot conceivably be the need-orientated production of use-values but only the successful *valorization/realization* and constant *expansion* of the given mass of accumulated material wealth. Within the framework of such all-embracing motivational determinations the structural location of use-values is in fact extremely precarious. Not only must all use-values corresponding to human need constitute a strictly *subordinate* moment in the capitalist strategy of valorization. Also, they can be grossly interfered with and indeed relegated to a position of secondary importance in the overall reproduction process — inasmuch as they are replaced by varieties of institutionalized waste — when the deepening structural crisis of capital demands such solutions, as we shall see later on.

Here the point that must be underlined is that the inherently constraining and distorting determinations and contradictions of the commodity structure do not arise at some far advanced stage; they are operative from the very outset. For the capital system, paradoxically, can only function if it both forcefully asserts the absolute validity of such determinations and contradictions, whatever their practical implications, and simultaneously brings them into an operationally manageable balance.

Thus, on the one hand, this system must assume a *positive/affirmative* attitude towards the reproduction of the existing contradictions and adversarial relations. For the capitalist mode of production itself, as a historically limited metabolic process, cannot help being other than the material embodiment and temporary equilibration of the irreconcilable structural antagonism between capital and labour. At the same time capital must also find the necessary objective *guarantees* for the practical/operative cohesion of all the multifarious conflicting constituents of its own system. In order to be able to function, capital must *suspend* the inner antagonisms and disintegrative tendencies of its mode of control as much as feasible under the changing historical circumstances.

The constant advances in productive performance required for the expanded reproduction of capital would be quite inconceivable without such guarantees. Indeed, they are so important that the determination of their nature and impact cannot be left to the fallibility of subjective management decisions and forms of control. Rather, the required guarantees must become integral parts of the objective articulation of the capitalist system of production as a closely interlocking whole.

This means that all classes of people who are active within capital's framework of interlocking determinations are confronted by a set of inescapable structural imperatives. Accordingly, the latter—precisely because they are objective *structural imperatives*—must be reflected in the conceptualizations, as well as properly implemented through the actions, of both management and labour. Hence the vital role of the universally diffused commodity structure and of the 'fetishism of commodity' arising from it. For on the plane of the traditional adversarial confrontations and 'labour disputes' the commodity structure diverts attention from the feasible *strategic* alternative to the ruling system and makes the disputes centre on *partial* economic issues. As a result labour, even when successful with its demands formulated in such terms — in an expansionary phase of development — remains firmly locked into the vicious circle of the capital system.

14.6.2

THE process through which the necessary guarantees are produced — and also *renewed* — in the course of capitalistic developments consists in the *homogenization* of the most minute constituents of the system with the whole. Historically such a homogenization takes place in accordance with capital's fundamental material determinations which correspond to its specific — i.e. inherently economic — exploitative parameters. In other words, since the exploitative parameters of this particular system of production and distribution are circumscribed in such a way that surplus-value must be extracted from living labour (and appropriated by expansion-oriented capital) through a set of complex *economic* mechanisms, the homogenization in question must also assume in the course of its historical unfolding an essentially economic character.

The alienation of the means and material of labour from living labour could not constitute by itself the sufficient condition for the undisturbed functioning of the capitalist metabolic process. It must be complemented by the radical and permanent separation of *all* the vital controlling functions of both the labour process and distribution of the social product from labour itself.

To accomplish the task of bringing the labour process fully in line with the already achieved separation and alienation of the means and material of labour from the worker, capital must set in motion a process of dehumanizing homogenization — dividing labour into its smallest capitalistically utilizable and universally commensurable elements — through which living labour can be allocated to productive tasks and successfully controlled as the needs of commodity production and exchange dictate it.

This homogenization in fact amounts to both the extreme *fragmentation* and complete *degradation*[17] of work and its carrier, the worker. The *master-journeyman* of the guild system was not only the owner of the means and material of his productive activity but also the possessor (and of course the controller) of a multiplicity of skills which he himself *unified* in his work and *objectified* in his product. In the sharpest possible contrast, the minute fragment which the particular wage labourer is condemned to monotonously contribute to the total labour of society is completely subsumed under, and dominated by, the ubiquitous commodity structure. As mentioned before, the constraining way in which capitalistically alienated and homogenized labour-power (and productive activity) is circumscribed, it cannot conceivably constitute use-value for its owners (the workers) but only for its non-owners (i.e. its potential buyers: the capitalists). Consequently, productive activity, and the workers totally dependent on it for their livelihood, lose even the semblance of autonomy. Only by radically challenging the system in its entirety as a mode of control can one envisage a way out of this predicament of structural dependency.

Also, as a commodity, the fragmentary contribution of the wage labourer is *commensurable* and *equalizable,* in an accurately determinable ratio, with the commodities offered by the capitalist on the market. As a result, commodified and homogenized labour satisfies the all-important condition of integrating (in a way and to the extent to which such an integration is feasible within the confines of the capital system) the *extraneous* moment of *exchange* with the vital reproductive requirements of the *production* process.

Thus, to present us with the most extreme paradox of all, it is commodified labour itself which helps to suspend the contradiction between production and exchange. For it helps to secure — by participating in and submitting itself to the *peculiar unity* of the two, objectively contradictory, moments — the necessary *continuity of production*. This mode of societal reproduction can go on undisturbed until the crises of *failed accumulation* and *overproduction* periodically disrupt the whole set of relationships and necessitate their reconstitution, in tune with the new circumstances.

In this way the earlier mentioned broken *unity of need and production* is 'mended', even if in a characteristically perverse form, so as to suit the limits of capital's metabolic process. For what counts now as 'need' is not the human need of the producers but the structural imperatives of capital's valorization and reproduction. *Use-values* become legitimate in relation (and in strict subordination) to the latter. Accordingly, the worker can gain access to a determinate range and quantity of use-values — whether or not they correspond to his real needs — so long as capital *legitimates* them as viable and profitable, on the basis of the reconstituted unity of need (exchange) and production (reproduction), within the framework of the ongoing homogenization. The worker thus *internalizes* the needs and imperatives of capital as his own, as inseparable from the exchange relation, and thereby he accepts the imposition of *capitalistically viable* use-values as if they emanated from his own needs.[18] And worse than that. For simultaneously the worker also chains himself, through the *internalization* of what he accepts to be his own 'legitimate' needs, to the fortunes of the ruling productive system. So that in due course, under the conditions of internalized 'consumer capitalism', the worker has in fact far more to lose than his '*external chains*' if he dares to contest the established order.

But the most important aspect of this process of homogenization is that the de-skilling division and fragmentation of labour that goes with it in the framework of commodity production totally deprives living labour of the power of *overviewing* and *controlling* the labour process of society, together with its distributive dimension.

In this respect, the transformation of objectified labour into capital, and therewith the permanent institutionalization of the alienated means and material of labour as the property of capital, must be considered the *secondary aspect* of capital's authoritarian rule over labour. This is so irrespective of its importance both historically, in the violent process of capitalist 'original accumulation' (and expropriation), and with regard to the future. For precisely because the fundamental issue at stake is the *overall control* of the labour process by the associated producers, and not simply the question of how to overturn the established *property rights,* it must be constantly kept in mind that the 'expropriation of the expropriators' is only the necessary prerequisite and *first step* towards the required changes. This is true also in relation to the past. For the institutionally reinforced alienation of the means and material of labour from the worker constituted only the material precondition of the perversely fragmenting and homogenizing capitalistic articulation of the labour process and of the labourer's complete subjugation to the rule of capital as a 'detail worker', confined to the control of *infinitesimal* productive functions, and no control whatsoever over the distribution of the total social product.

Nothing is really accomplished by — more or less easily reversible — changes in property rights alone, as the postwar history of 'nationalizations', 'de-nationalizations', 're-nationalizations' and 'privatizations' amply testifies. Legally induced changes in property relations have no guarantee of success even if they embrace the overwhelming majority of private capital, let alone if they are confined to its bankrupt minority. For what needs to be radically altered is the way in which the reified 'microcosm' of the single working day is utilized and reproduced, despite its inner contradictions, throughout the homogenized and equilibrated 'macrocosm' of the system as a whole.

The capitalist property relations represent no more than the material prerequisites and legally sanctioned guarantees to the *substantive* articulation of this overall complex of social metabolic reproduction. It is the latter which is in need of radical restructuring, so that a qualitatively different and consciously controlled 'macrocosm' should be built up from the autonomous self-determinations of qualitatively different 'microcosms'. The exchange relation to which labour is subjected is no less enslaving than the separation and alienation of the material conditions of production from the workers. By reproducing the established exchange relations on an extended scale labour can only multiply the power of alien wealth over against itself. The sad history of the co-operative movement in capitalist countries, despite their once genuine socialist aspirations, speaks eloquently in this respect. But even the strategy of overturning the property relations of private capitalism through the 'expropriation of the expropriators' can only scratch the surface without the radical restructuring of the inherited exchange relations, leaving capital in postcapitalist societies — even if in an altered form — fully in control of the reproduction process. Thus nothing could be more absurd than the attempt to institute socialist democracy and the emancipation of labour through the enslaving fetishism of 'market socialism'.

14.7 *The curse of interdependence: vicious circle of the 'macrocosm' and constitutive cells of the capital system*

14.7.1
Accordingly, the challenge that must be faced with regard to all aspects of the relationship between productivity and use is this: how to undermine the constantly renewed capitalistic reproductive process of quantity- and exchange-value oriented homogenization and replace it by need- and use-value oriented qualitative processes.

Obviously, the difficulties involved even in just identifying the main characteristics of the rival capitalist and socialist strategies, together with their practical implications for future developments, are daunting. For the same process that must be considered from the standpoint of capital as the *blessing of homogenization* presents itself from the standpoint of labour as the *curse of interdependence* (and *dependence*). A curse because the homogeneity of capitalist value-relations practically asserts itself as a jungle-like network of closely interwoven determinations. The parts of this network (including commodified labour) reinforce one another and safeguard the viability of the whole. Thus they seem to deny even the remote possibility of escape from this vicious circle.

The gap between the quantifying homogenization of the established system and Marx's earlier quoted anticipation — according to which under socialism use will no longer be determined by the minimum time of production but, on the contrary, the time of production devoted to an article will be determined by the degree of its substantive utility — is obviously unbridgeable. For, given the intrinsic characteristics of the rival systems of metabolic control, the question of alternatives defines itself as the choice between mutually exclusive 'macrocosms' whose constituent parts, down to the smallest elements of the single working day as well as to the most intimate moments of everyday life, are likewise mutually exclusive.

This is why there is no possibility of *reform* leading to *structural transformations* within the parameters of the capitalist mode of production; which also explains why all such attempts, in their by now almost one hundred years long history — from Bernstein's *Evolutionary Socialism* to its postwar imitations — failed to make the slightest dent in the edifice of the established order. They failed to do so despite all promises concerning the *gradual* but nonetheless *complete* rebuilding of the established order in the spirit of socialism. For the possibility of a sustainable modification of even the smallest parts of the capital system implies the necessity of, constantly renewed, *two-pronged* assaults on its constitutive 'cells' or 'microcosms' (i.e. on the way in which the single working days are organized inside the particular productive enterprises) as well as on capital's self-regulating and within its structural limits self-renewing 'macrocosm' in its entirety.

Naturally, the recognition that the strategy of *gradualist/evolutionary* socialism within the restrictive parameters of capital cannot amount to more than a contradiction in terms, does not mean that the *revolutionary* strategy of socialist transformation is not in need of the appropriate material and institutional *mediations*. 'Mediation' as such should not be confused with 'gradualism' and 'reformism', even if it involves measures which can only be implemented step by step. What decides the issue is the way in which the partial steps are integrated in a coherent overall strategy whose target is not simply the improvement of the workers' living standard (which happens to be strictly conjunctural and reversible in any case) but the radical restructuring of the established *division of labour*.

This applies to the horizontal as much as to the vertical dimension of the division of labour. For under the capital system the horizontal dimension — which is supposed to be neutral according to the postulated 'strict functionality' and 'instrumental rationality' of its organizing principles — is in fact necessarily vitiated by the vertical imperatives of perpetuating the structural subordination of labour. For even the claimed purely functional determinations, which are said to arise from self-justifying scientific and technological considerations, are in fact adopted only if they conform to the real test of operational legitimation: their role with regard to the incorrigibly expansion-orientated nature of the capital system, disregarding even their potentially most damaging impact on the labour force. This is why the capitalist factory cannot be simply transplanted to the social soil of the 'new historic form', contrary to the belief of even some socialist thinkers, including Lukács, that 'a factory built for capitalist purposes can carry on producing quite untroubled in a socialist society without introducing any substantive changes, and *vice versa*', as we have seen above. Accordingly, the necessary socialist mediations become viable only if they undertake the radical reconstitution of the relationship between productivity and use under all its aspects, activating the creative expansion of human needs and potentialities against their present-day subordination to the reifying imperatives of the established reproductive system.

14.7.2

THE problems of mediation, as they arise in the context of socialist transformations, will be discussed later on. Here, to conclude the present chapter, it must be stressed that the dominant tendencies of capitalistic developments today make the incompatibilities of the two, alternative systems of social control, even more pronounced. For the inherently problematical, yet in its own way in the past highly effective, capitalist unity of need, use, and production is itself under a heavy cloud today. What is at issue here is not only the destructive dissipation of capital's productive potentialities, in tune with the most absurd manifestations of the decreasing rate of utilization, but also the aggravating fact that such wasteful practices do not seem to fulfil any longer their earlier function in the societal reproduction process. For the 'productive destruction' once celebrated by reputable economists has lost its productive power, transforming itself into an ultimately crippling drain on the basic social metabolic requirements of the planetary household.

The importance of these developments cannot be over-stated. For in the not too distant past the destructive dissipation of almost unimaginably vast quantities of productive powers and resources could be turned to capital's advantage with relative ease, positively contributing thereby to the successful response of the system to the structural imperative of its expanded self-reproduction. Today, by contrast, formerly unexperienced conflicts and contradictions break out into the open, since the once almost universally applauded practice of institutionalized waste-generation (and corresponding destruction of material and human resources on a prohibitive scale) no longer seems to be able to produce the results that could continue to legitimate it. Indeed, the way in which waste-production functions today carries with it grave implications for the metabolic viability of the capital system itself. For it seems to interfere with, and seriously disrupt, the uneasy equilibration of capital and labour which the precariously reconstituted unity of need and production discussed above safeguarded in the past. In a past, that is, when — notwithstanding all waste — capital could successfully 'deliver the goods' as directly consumable use-values to the individual workers, with two qualifications. First, it could do so only in the privileged 'advanced capitalist' countries, callously denying at the same time the satisfaction of even the most elementary needs of the working people in all the others; and second, even in the handful of privileged countries the goods delivered could not be other than grossly distorted (often quite artificial) use-values, practically imposed on society in the interest of capital's self-legitimation, as required by various conjunctural shifts in the dominant exchange relations.

In the last few decades we could witness significant changes in this respect which redefined in important ways the productive and distributive parameters of postwar capitalism in its entirety. The end of undisturbed expansion, lasting two and a half decades after the Second World War, had brought with it the necessity to intensify the rate of exploitation even in the most privileged capitalist countries, as we have seen above in various contexts. At the same time the plight of two and a half billion people in the 'Third World'—a staggering number of which more than one billion have to survive, in 1995, on less than $1 per day, as now acknowledged even by the Secretariat of the United Nations—failed to improve in response to the loudly trumpeted but pathetically inadequate strategies of 'modernization' and 'development aid'. Today, under the impact of their growing problems and socioeconomic failures, even the richest 'core' countries of the global capital system refuse to allocate for the purpose of alleviating world poverty the miserable 0.7 percent of GNP to which they had once committed themselves. Indeed, ever greater masses of people are now being condemned to experience the conditions of abject poverty also in the 'advanced capitalist' countries, even if — for the time being — not yet to the same extent and intensity as what must be endured in the 'Third World'.

The conclusion is therefore inescapable: *'production as the aim of mankind'* in its confinement to *'wealth as the aim of production'* — the strategy of social metabolic reproduction successfully pursued by capital in the course of its historical ascendancy — has tragically failed humanity even in the system's own terms of reference. Whatever 'improvements' may be offered within the framework of capital's mode of control must be subject to the constraints and contradictions of *'production as the aim of mankind'* restricted to alienated material wealth as the aim of production. For the improvements defined in such terms can promise under the historically attained level of development of globally over-stretched capital only more of the same thing of which even the presently available less is far too much, on account of its unavoidably destructive consequences.

In the euphoria prevailing for quite some time after the Second World War, following the establishment of the United Nations and a number of major international economic agencies inspired by the Bretton Woods agreements, the personifications of capital promised the enlightened social and economic relations of a radically different world, absurdly reiterating their promise of a 'New World Order' also in the aftermath of the dramatic implosion of the Soviet system. However, absolutely nothing of the solemn promises of a 'fair and just society to the benefit of all' came to fruition. On the contrary, given the necessary premisses and operational imperatives of capital as a mode of control, all that this system could achieve was to turn its once more or less temporary conjunctural and periodic crises into a chronic structural crisis, directly affecting for the first time in history the whole of humankind. This is why, as things stand today, only a qualitative reorientation of social metabolic reproduction can show a way out of humanity's truly global crisis. A reorientation from the inescapably constraining and wasteful *production of wealth* toward a humanly enriching *wealth of production*, with its *optimal* as opposed to a perilously *decreasing* rate of utilization. Naturally, such a reorientation implies quite fundamental changes in all domains and at all levels of socioeconomic and cultural production, within the framework of a radically altered/non-hierarchical organization of labour in both the 'macrocosm' and the constitutive cells of an alternative social order. Only in this way can the 'curse of interdependence' and the perverse homogenization that go with the horizontal and vertical division of labour under the rule of capital be broken: a difficult subject to which we have to return in the remaining chapters.

CHAPTER FIFTEEN

THE DECREASING RATE OF UTILIZATION UNDER CAPITALISM

15.1 From maximizing the 'useful course of commodities' to the triumph of generalized waste-production

15.1.1

ONE and a half century ago Charles Babbage — a most remarkable but relatively little known early 19th century thinker[19] who had a profound interest in political economy — wrote in praise of the sound economic principles applied to the conversion of 'materials of little value' into useful and valuable products:

> The worn-out saucepans and tin ware of our kitchens, when beyond the reach of the tinker's art, are not utterly worthless. We sometimes meet carts loaded with old tin kettles and worn-out iron coal-skuttles traversing our streets. These have not yet completed their useful course; the less corroded parts are cut into strips, punched with small holes, and varnished with a coarse black varnish for the use of the trunk-maker, who protects the edges and angles of his boxes with them; the remainder are conveyed to the manufacturing chemists in the outskirts of the town, who employ them in combination with pyroligneous acid, in making a black die for the use of calico printers.[20]

Reading such accounts today is like being catapulted back to a prehistoric age in order to witness, with some amusement, the pathetic productive practices of capitalist cave-man, although the time that separates us from them is quite insignificant on the scale of human history. For in the sixteen decades that elapsed since the days of Babbage the measure of advancement of 'advanced capitalism' had become the efficacy with which *waste* can be generated and dissipated on a monumental scale.

That the tendency towards waste generation is not a 'deviation' from the 'spirit of capitalism' and from the idealized 'sound economic principles' — which were supposed to establish the permanent superiority of this productive system — transpires clearly even from certain passages of Babbage's own book, although the underlying determinations remain hidden to its author.

For one thing, while Babbage enumerates what he considers to be the threefold advantages of capitalist machinery and manufacture as:

(1) the addition which they make to human power;

(2) the economy they produce of human time; and

(3) the conversion of substances apparently common and worthless into valuable products,[21]

he must soon admit that the importance of the second overrides everything else, including the criteria by which materials and productive instruments are meant to serve useful purposes, rather than being discarded as worthless. This is how

547

Babbage stresses the crucial role of time: 'So extensive and important is this effect [i.e. the economy of human time], that we might, if we were inclined to generalize, embrace almost all the advantages under this single head'.[22] Since, however, Babbage — just like all the other major bourgeois political economists — can only see the *positive* side of these developments, he cannot pay attention to the destructive implications of the capitalist *tyranny of (minimal) time* required for production, to which all other considerations must be subordinated. For the same tendency of universal quantification that reveals itself from the standpoint of labour as a force which degrades the human being into *'time's carcase'*, appears from the point of view of capital as an indisputably objective measure and the ideal solution to all possible legitimate disputes between capital and labour:

> It would, indeed, be of great mutual advantage to the industrious workman, and to the master-manufacturer in every trade, if the machines employed in it could register the quantity of work which they perform, in the same manner as a steam-engine does the number of strokes it makes. The introduction of such contrivances gives a greater stimulus to honest industry than can readily be imagined, and removes one of the sources of disagreement between parties, whose real interests must always suffer by any *estrangement* between them.[23]

It is because of this identification with the 'standpoint of political economy' that Babbage's critical observations can only amount to isolated insights, and their far-reaching implications for the future development of the capitalist system must remain hidden to him.

Significantly enough, after recommending that machinery should be constructed to the highest possible standard, Babbage observes that:

> Machinery for producing any commodity in great demand, *seldom actually wears out*; new improvements, by which the same operations can be executed either more quickly or better, generally superseding it *long before* that period arrives: indeed, to make such an improved machine *profitable*, it is usually reckoned that in *five years* it ought to have paid itself, and *in ten* to be superseded by a better.[24]

Moreover, he also notices that: 'During the great speculations in the patent-net trade, the improvements succeeded each other so rapidly, that machines which had never been finished were abandoned in the hands of their makers, because new improvements had superseded their utility.'[25] Thus, it seems to Babbage, the negative implications of such phenomena can be safely ignored as — however regrettable — *aberrations*, since they only appear under the non-typical (i.e. from the standpoint of capital as a whole theoretically not necessary) conditions of *'speculation'*.

Similarly, a *general tendency* of capitalist production is seen only as pertaining to *special circumstances*, and thereby finding its full justification in the differential price of labour:

> The effect of competition in cheapening articles of manufacture *sometimes* operates in rendering them *less durable*. When such articles are conveyed to a distance for consumption, if they are broken, it often happens, from the price of labour being higher where they are used than where they were made, that it is *more expensive to mend* the old article, than to *purchase a new*.[26]

Thus, the fact that in its general tendency the capitalist mode of production is an enemy of *durability*, and therefore in the course of its historical unfolding it must undermine the durability-oriented productive practices in every possible way, including the deliberate subversion of quality, must be thoroughly ignored.

Instead, the manifestations of this tendency must be justified in terms of the necessity of competition, the rational utilization of labour resources — both of them treated as entirely beneficial (ideal) necessities — and the like. The possibility that serious negative consequences might arise from the *saturation* of the market, due to the permanence of certain products, appears in Babbage's work for a moment, in a limited context:

> If it [a product like plate glass] were indestructible, the price would continually diminish; and unless an increased demand arose from new uses, or from a greater number of customers, a single manufactory, unchecked by competition, would ultimately be compelled to shut up, driven out of the market by the permanence of its own productions.[27]

However, the author's unreservedly positive reading of capital's productive and distributive tendencies prevails again, and suggests the optimistic solution of all such problems:

> Articles become old from actual decay, or the wearing out of their parts; from improved modes of constructing them; or from changes in their form and fashion, required by the varying taste of the age. In the two latter cases, their utility is but little diminished; and, being less sought after by those who have hitherto employed them, they are sold at a reduced price to a class of society rather below that of their former possessors. Many articles of furniture, such as well-made tables and chairs, are thus found in the rooms of those who would have been quite unable to have purchased them when new; ... Thus a *taste for luxuries is propagated downwards in society*; and after a short period, the numbers who have acquired *new wants* become sufficient to excite the ingenuity of the manufacturer to reduce the cost of supplying them, whilst he is himself benefited by the extended scale of demand.[28]

Naturally, within such perspective, the question cannot arise what might happen when the limits of the capitalist system are reached and its contradictions cannot be removed by 'propagating the taste for luxuries downwards in society'. In fact the existence of real antagonisms and irreconcilable contradictions cannot be admitted at all. The system is supposed to work for the benefit of everyone, as demonstrated also by the downwards propagation of the taste for luxuries. Inasmuch as conflicts are acknowledged at all, they must be conceptualized as temporary difficulties that can be overcome by the application of the proper scientific/technological and managerial/organisational methods.[29] Advancements in productivity are considered apriori good and desirable. The conditions under which such advancements are obtained cannot be questioned, nor indeed their potentially harmful implications, since they constitute the — capitalist — framework and measure of all possible evaluation. Not surprisingly, therefore, the negative dimension of all the dominant tendencies of the ongoing socioeconomic development must remain hidden from even the best and most honest thinkers who contemplate them from the standpoint of political economy and visualize the difficulties of the system as readily amenable to the kind of solutions which happen to be compatible with capital's productive and distributive parameters.

15.1.2

IN the course of history, advancements in productivity inevitably change the pattern of consumption as well as the way in which both the goods to be consumed and the instruments with which they are produced will be utilized.

Furthermore, such advancements profoundly affect the nature of productive activity itself, determining at the same time also the ratio with which a given society's total available time is going to be distributed between the activity required for its basic metabolic interchange with nature and all the other functions and activities in which the individuals of the society in question engage.

The decreasing rate of utilization is, in a sense, directly implicit in the advancements accomplished with regard to productivity itself. In the first place it manifests itself in the *changing ratio* with which a society has to allocate determinate quantities from its total available time for the production of the quickly *used-up* goods (e.g. food) as against those that remain *usable* (i.e. *re-usable*) for a longer time: a ratio which obviously tends to shift in favour of the *latter*. Without this shift a sustainable and potentially emancipatory productive development would be inconceivable.

It is therefore extremely problematical that beyond a certain point in the history of 'advanced capitalism' this process — which is intrinsic to productive advancement in general — is completely *reversed*, in a most bewildering form: in that the *'throw-away society'* establishes the equilibrium between production and consumption necessary for its continued reproduction only if it can artificially *'use-up'* at a great speed (i.e. prematurely discard) vast quantities of commodities which formerly belonged to the category of relatively *durable* products. Thus, it maintains itself as a productive system by manipulating even the purchase of so-called *'durable consumer goods'* in such a way that they must be thrown onto the rubbish heap (or sent, for scrap, to gigantic 'car cemeteries', etc.) well before their useful life is over. Indeed, as we shall see later on, 'advanced capitalism' also invents a type of production — centred around the military/industrial complex — in relation to which the traditional challenge of consumption (utility) can only marginally apply, if at all. So that the resulting products can join the mountains of 'used-up' commodities the moment they leave the factory gates, while destructively consuming in the course of their production immense material and human resources.

Since the changing ratio of productive activity to be divided between the immediately 'used-up' and the 're-usable' goods in favour of the latter is an intrinsic characteristic of productive advancement, a society's wealth and level of economic development can be up to a point adequately measured by it. Consequently, it is in principle desirable that more and more of a society's resources should be allocated towards the production of *re-usable* (and, of course, genuinely *used* and *re-used*) goods — from durable and aesthetically enjoyable housing to time-saving and comfortable means of transport, or for that matter from sculptures and paintings to literary and musical works of art, etc. — so long as the basic needs of *all* members of society are adequately satisfied.

The decreasing rate of utilization of the socially produced goods and services, as well as of the productive forces and instruments that must be employed for their production, is a corollary of this shifting primary ratio in favour of more durable products. Here, however, the issue becomes much more complicated. For while the shift towards expending an increasingly greater amount of the socially available productive resources on re-usable goods (rather than on the quite elementary necessaries required for the physical/biological reproduction of the individuals) happens to be an unambiguously positive attainment, the same could not be said about the decreasing rate of utilization in its capitalistic variety. The latter is by no means intrinsic to productive advancement as such, since a number of very special conditions must be first satisfied — above all the separation of the producers from the means and material of their productive activity, and thereby their forcible alienation from the objective conditions of their self-reproduction — before it can be set fully in motion under the expansionary dynamic of capitalism. Nor are indeed the complex manifestations of the decreasing rate of utilization on the plane of production and consumption unproblematical in their 'advanced capitalist' form.

An example concerning the development of the instruments of production well illustrates the differences. In this respect, the constant use of the available instruments of production is confined to extremely primitive stages of historical development, when the given tools are almost literally the primitive producer's 'extended inorganic body'. As human productive capacities — and their tangible objectifications in the form of productive utensils — improve and cumulatively become also more varied, significant changes take place with regard to their utilization in the labour process. Accordingly, considered from the vantage point of a much more advanced stage, the specialization manifest in the multiplicity of different tools employed by the craftsman, who unites a variety of skills in one person (e.g. the master-journeyman), inevitably carries with it that some of the instruments of production (indeed: even their majority) remain idle while others are being used by him.

This kind of *'under-utilization'*, however, is radically different from the one we experience under the conditions of capitalism. For the master-journeyman himself is not in the least idle when he uses the saw instead of the chisel or hammer. By contrast, the capitalist instrument of production — an increasingly more intertwined productive machinery, articulated through the minute division and re-unification of labour, in accordance with the earlier discussed vertical and horizontal determinations of the capitalist labour process — is by its very nature a *social* instrument that can be productively employed only in common.

The inherently social articulation of the capitalist productive machinery implies, as the precondition of its *healthy* state, the *necessity* of its *continuous* utilization. This is a requirement that must be satisfied; if, that is, the 'chain-reaction' of so-called 'temporary dysfunctions' resulting in more or less extensive destructive consequences is to be avoided. Consequently the under-utilization (or non-utilization) of the capitalist productive machinery under determinate socioeconomic conditions (e.g. periodic crises; but, as we shall see in a moment, less and less only under the circumstances of such crises) is the manifestation of a serious *social disease*. It contrasts sharply with the craft system's unavoidable normality of switching from one segment of an individually co-ordinated process of multifarious skill-exercise to another. For the latter is in full conformity and adequacy to the inherent characteristics of the given mode of production and the historically attained level of development of the socially accumulated productive skills and instruments.

Thus, an analysis of the historical development of production in relation to the decreasing rate of utilization presents us with a paradoxical, indeed contradictory, pattern. For, on the one hand, for a long historical period it goes hand in hand with the positively shifting ratio between used-up and re-usable goods; and while it does so, it remains *unproblematical* as regards its further extension, but also very limited in its extent, confining most of the benefits to an extremely small part of the social whole (and thus proving to be *problematical* on account of its necessarily *limited* character). By contrast, on the other hand, the tendency for the decreasing rate of utilization acquires its full scope only with the unfolding of capital's productive potentialities which promise the supersession of the contradictions associated with the up until then limited character of the tendency. However, the dynamic of capitalist developments cannot simply remove the earlier limitations from the path of the decreasing rate of utilization. It simultaneously must also render some of the new manifestations of the decreasing rate very *problematical* from the very beginning, and *increasingly* so as time goes by. For, as a result of the absurd reversal of productive advancements in favour of quickly 'used-up' products and destructively dissipated resources, 'advanced capitalism' tends to impose on humanity a most perverse kind of *'from hand to mouth'* existence: one totally devoid of any justification with reference to the limitations of the productive forces and potentialities of mankind accumulated in the course of history.

15.2 *The relativization of luxury and necessity*

15.2.1
NEVERTHELESS, no one can dispute that a qualitative, and at first 'civilizing', change takes place in relation to the various productive manifestations of the decreasing rate of utilization through the development of capitalism. All kinds of constraints are swept away as the formerly unimaginable dynamic of capital asserts itself with irresistible efficacy, notwithstanding its manifold contradictions.

One of the most important fronts on which the battle is fought (and won) concerns the legitimation of *'luxury'*. The issue — whose theorizations go back to the times of classical antiquity — is contested with great vigour from the end of the 17th century, in the face of both ideological and practical opposition.

To be sure, it takes some time before the *full implications* of the role of 'luxury' in the expansion of capitalist production can come to the fore. Yet, the positive assessment of 'luxury' is present from a very early stage of capitalistic developments. It is welcomed both as a vital motivating factor (promising individual rewards to all, and in particular to the members of the dominant classes), and as the clearly advantageous sphere of productive expansion for the system as a whole. Indeed we can see in this context that the Weberian 'spirit of capitalism' is not only irrelevant for understanding the way in which the capitalist system of production and distribution functions in the 20th century; it is also profoundly misleading with regard to its fundamental tendencies of development from the very outset.

Weber's way of theorizing such matters acquires its plausibility by systematically conflating *motivation* with *causality* and obliterating the latter by the former. Such method puts irremovable obstacles in the path of historical understanding. For while the *subjective rationalizations* of some individual capitalists may fall into the Weberian pattern — and even then only for a relatively short period of time — the *objective determinations* of the capitalist system as a *causal network* cannot be made intelligible without bringing into focus the *necessary* adoption of *'luxury'* (i.e. its *practical 'rehabilitation'*, whatever the rhetorics) as the orienting framework of productive expansion.

The radically new attitude to 'luxury' is inherent in the way in which capitalism defines its relationship to *use-value* and *exchange-value*, attacking the constraints associated with production orientated towards use-value, together with the direct or indirect rationalization of the severely constricted mode of production and consumption inseparable from it. Thus the *practical rehabilitation* of 'luxury' represents an *objective structural imperative* of the capital system as the new regulator of the social metabolism. The spontaneously changed productive practices themselves have the *historical priority* also in this respect, and they find their suitable theoretical expressions — which insist on the productive dynamics and all-round beneficial character of the once morally condemned 'consumption of superfluities' — parallel to the consolidation of the new system.

This is how Adam Ferguson — one of the greatest figures of the Scottish Enlightenment (who is by no means uncritical towards the inhumanities and contradictions of the capitalist system of production and exchange) — sums up many centuries of controversy on the subject, with particular concern for the debates of the early 18th century. He comes out emphatically in favour of 'luxury', as far back as 1767 — by which time the grooves of further socioeconomic development, in this respect as well as in many others, are firmly set:

> We may propose to stop the advancement of arts at any stage of their progress, and still incur the censure of luxury from those who have not advanced so far. The house-builder and the carpenter of Sparta were limited to the use of the axe and the saw; but a Spartan cottage might have passed for a palace in Thrace: and if the dispute were to turn on the knowledge of what is *physically necessary* to the preservation of human life, as the standard of what is *morally lawful*, the faculties of physic, as well as of morality, would probably divide on the subject, and leave every individual as at present, to find some rule for himself. The casuist, for the most part, considers the practice of his own age and condition, as a standard for mankind. If in one age or condition, he condemn the use of a coach, in another he would have no less censured the wearing of shoes; and the very person who exclaims against the first, would probably not have spared the second, if it had not been already familiar in ages before his own. A censor born in a cottage, and accustomed to sleep upon straw, does not propose that men should return to the woods and the caves for shelter; he admits the reasonableness and the utility of what is already familiar; and apprehends an excess and corruption, only in the newest refinement of the rising generation.[30]

Thus, the question of 'luxury' must be *relativized*, against the claims of *moralizing absolutism*, so as to make possible the legitimation of the productive practices orientated towards the increase of the 'wealth of the nation' by means of the vast expansion in the quantity and variety of individually consumable commodities. This is how the new-found dynamic of production becomes the aim of mankind and the multiplication of wealth the aim of production.

15.2.2
THE relativization and legitimation of luxury, and the adoption of — individualistically orientated — material wealth-production as the aim of mankind,

inevitably also means the *relativization of values*. For the productive system within whose framework such objectives are accomplished is based on *competition* and on the concomitant assertion and justification of the *rival interests* — as well as associated *values* — of the contending parties who put forward their exclusivistic claims for the division of the social product.

This relativization of luxury and necessity, destruction and production, vice and virtue — together with the underlying interests and contradictions — is spelled out, with a clear and unashamed admission of the exploitative character of the system, in Bernard Mandeville's *Fable of the Bees*, published more than sixty years before Ferguson's seminal *Essay on the History of Civil Society* quoted above:

> Vast Numbers thronged the fruitful Hive;
> Yet those vast Numbers made 'em thrive;
> *Millions endeavoured to supply*
> Each other's Lust and Vanity;
> Whilst other Millions were employ'd
> To see their Handy-works destroy'd;
> They furnished half the Universe;
> Yet had more Work than Labourers.
> Some with vast Stocks, and little Pains
> Jump'd into Business of great Gains;
> And some were damn'd to Sythes and Spades,
> And *all those hard laborious Trades;*
> Where willing Wretches daily sweat,
> And wear out Strength and Limbs to eat;
>
> And all those, that, in Enmity
> With down-right Working, *cunningly*
> Convert to their own Use the Labour
> of their good-natur'd heedless Neighbour.
> These were called Knaves; but bar the Name,
> The grave Industrious were the Same.
> All Trades and Places knew some Cheat,
> No Calling was without Deceit.[31]

Indeed, not even what is traditionally considered the paradigm of virtue: *Justice*, can escape Mandeville's sardonic characterization as a form of vice, practised in favour of the Rich:

> Justice her self, famed for fair Dealing,
> By Blindness had not lost her Feeling;
>
> Yet, it was thought, the Sword she bore
> Check'd but the Desp'rate and the Poor;
> That, urged by mere Necessity,
> Were tied up to the wretched Tree
> For Crimes, which not deserv'd that Fate,
> But *to secure the Rich and Great.*[32]

Other conceptions of society and human nature — like Lord Shaftesbury's moral theory categorically rejected by Mandeville — postulated the natural sociability of man and the pursuit of the public good chosen by the individuals who follow the rules of Reason and Good Sense. They also assumed that Virtue and Vice

— the first on the side of the public good while the second lined up against it — are permanent realities: the same in all countries and all ages. By complete contrast, Mandeville asserts in all his writings that

> things are *Good and Evil* in reference to *something else*, and according to the Light and Position they are placed in. What pleases us is good in that regard, and by this Rule every Man wishes well for himself to the best of his Capacity, with little Respect to his Neighbour. ... When the Corn stands thick in the Spring, and the generality of the Country rejoyce at the pleasing Object, the Rich Farmer who kept his last Year's Crop for a better Market, pines at the sight and inwardly grieves at the prospect of a plentiful Harvest.[33]

And yet, this is very far from being an arbitrary conception, concerned with glorifying the irreconcilability of tastes and subjective motives. On the contrary, Mandeville is eager to underline that the identified relativities rest on a *firm material ground*. Indeed, he repeatedly states that such relativities are deeply rooted in the mutually reinforced objectivity of twofold determinations: the changing *social conditions* and circumstances on the one hand, and *nature* (or 'human nature') on the other. Accordingly, in his view the insurmountable relativity of Vice and Virtue, and the paradoxical but inescapable dependence of human life on both—though primarily on 'private Vices'—is explained in terms of 'the condition of the Social Body and the Temperament of the Natural'.[34]

The various, often aphoristically and satirically formulated aspects of Mandeville's conception constitute a coherent whole. His views on society, 'sociability', the state and the legal system, the 'Body Politick' and the forms of rule and subjection appropriate to it, productive activity, and 'Civil Society', are complemented by a notion of nature and 'human nature' that closely fits the overall framework of social reproduction he describes with undisguised approval.

Mandeville can perceive all kinds of contradictions with the sharpest eye, but only to the extent to which they are compatible with the dynamically expanding socioeconomic order that he champions, whatever its contradictions. In truth, he ascribes a highly positive role to contradictions in the 'natural unfolding' of human affairs. The difficulty he has to solve in constructing an alternative model of society and human nature to the scornfully rejected ideas of Lord Shaftesbury and others is twofold:

First, as a 'natural' grounding to the society riddled with contradictions — with which he nonetheless fully identifies himself — he must assume that human nature itself is inherently contradictory. As he puts it: 'This Contradiction in the Frame of Man is the Reason that the Theory of Virtue is so well understood, and the practice of it so rarely to be met with.'[35]

Secondly, however, he must also maintain that a social order beneficial to all can emerge on a natural basis that brings with it the necessary disjunction of theory and practice as far as the individuals and their perception of their own motivations are concerned. He disposes of the second difficulty by stressing the total insufficiency of the particular human individuals in the order of nature. In this spirit, addressing himself to man, Mandeville says: 'fickle timerous Animal, the Gods have made you for Society, and design'd that Millions of you, when well joyned together, should compose the strong *Leviathan*. A single Lyon bears some sway in the Creation, but what is a *single Man*? A small and inconsiderable part, a *trifling Atom* of one great Beast.'[36]

Thus, we are offered a conception of the social order in which the ubiquitous contradictions not only do not *destroy* but actually *reinforce* the cohesion of the overall system. For whatever might be considered defective, is defective strictly as regards the *parts* which nevertheless, paradoxical as he admits this to be, add up to a well integrated and felicitously functioning *whole*; just as later, in Adam Smith's view, the 'invisible hand' fully remedies the faulty calculations of the individuals. According to Mandeville: 'the frailties of Men often work by *contraries* ... But the vicissitudes of Fortune are necessary, and the most lamentable are no more detrimental to Society than the Death of the Individual Members of it. ... The various *Ups and Downs* compose a Wheel that always turning round gives motion to the *whole Machine*.'[37] This is why Mandeville can sing the praises of the way in which the contradictions of the parts produce the harmony of the whole:

> *Thus every Part was full of Vice,*
> Yet the whole Mass a Paradice;
>
> The Worst of all the Multitude
> Did something for the common Good.
> *This was the State's Craft, that maintain'd*
> The Whole, of which each Part complain'd:
> This, as in Musick Harmony,
> Made Jarrings in the Main agree;
>
> The Root of evil Avarice,
> That damn'd ill-natur'd baneful Vice,
> Was Slave to *Prodigality*,
> That Noble Sin; whilst *Luxury*
> Employ'd a Million of the Poor.
> And odious Pride a Million more.
> Envy it self, and Vanity
> Were Ministers of Industry;
> Their darling Folly, Fickleness
> In Diet, Furniture, and Dress,
> That strange ridic'lous Vice, was made
> The very Wheel, that turn'd the Trade.
> Their Laws and Cloaths were equally
> Objects of *Mutability*;
> For, what was well done for a Time,
> In half a Year became a Crime;
> Yet whilst they alter'd thus their Laws,
> Still finding and correcting Flaws,
> *They mended by Inconstancy*
> Faults, which no Prudence could foresee.
> Thus Vice nursed Ingenuity,
> Which join'd with Time, and Industry
> Had carry'd Life's Conveniencies,
> It's real Pleasures, Comforts, Ease,
> To such a Height, *the very Poor*
> Lived better than the Rich before;
> And nothing could be added more.[38]

Thus the characteristics of the capitalist system of production and distribution (from Prodigality to Fickleness and from Inconstancy to Mutability etc.) are located as ineradicable Vices/Virtues in human nature itself, providing through the assertion of their 'Contraries' the necessary fuel for the perpetual motion of the Wheel that drives forward the 'Whole Machine' of Civil Society and the Body Politick. This is how Luxury becomes unreservedly rehabilitated and positively exalted. It is assigned a place of paramount importance in the Whole, in that the conditions of producing and expanding Luxury bear witness to the truth of the author's proposition, namely that 'Private Vices' result in 'Publick Benefits'.

The beneficial 'contraries' and contradictions in Mandeville's conception are those which readily fit in with the diverse interests of competing capitals, both in the sphere of manufacture (ruled by the principles of mutability, prodigality and luxury), and in agriculture; the latter as exemplified by the rich farmer who speculates with last year's corn he deliberately withheld from the market, cursing the good weather and the prospects of a plentiful harvest welcomed by others. By contrast, the most basic competition of capitalist society, that between capital and labour — which has the character of an irreconcilable antagonism — cannot be acknowledged within the categorial framework of this 'enlightened egotism'. Just like all the other classics of political economy, Mandeville too remains totally blind to the developing explosive potential of this antagonism. In the same spirit as his ideological comrades in arms, he too assumes that the subordinate position of the Poor in the established productive system is a *permanent condition* of the social order, unaffected in its substance by all feasible (and admissible) change in circumstance.

In this respect the pursuit of knowledge gives way to the interest of rationalizing capital's exploitative relationship to the worker. In fact Mandeville is at great pains to show that the necessary waste and destruction inseparable from the established system of production are primarily to the benefit of the Poor. For even if only the losses suffered through shipping disasters were eliminated:

> it would be detrimental to all other Branches of Trade besides, and *destructive of the Poor* of every Country, that Exports any thing of their own Growth or Manufacture. The Goods and Merchandizes that every Year go to the Deep, that are spoyl'd at Sea by Salt Water, by Heat, by Vermin, destroy'd by Fire, or lost to the Merchant by other Accidents, all owing to Storms or Tedious Voyages, or else the neglect or rapacity of Saylors; such Goods I say and Merchandizes are a considerable part of what every Year is sent abroad throughout the World, and must have employ'd great Multitudes of Poor before they could come on Board. A Hundred Bales of Cloth that are Burnt or Sunk in the Mediterranean, are as *Beneficial to the Poor in England*, as if they had safely arriv'd at Smyrna or Aleppo, and every Yard of them had been Retail'd in the Grand Signior's Dominions. The Merchant may break, and by him the Clothier, the Dyer, the Packer and other Tradesmen, the Midling People may suffer, but *the Poor that were set to Work about them can never lose.*[39]

The blatant contradiction that the workers are supposed to find gratification and fulfilment in working *for others* is resolved by postulating the *voluntary* character of wage slavery. This is how Mandeville puts it:

> What a Bustle is there to be made in several Parts of the World, before a Fine Scarlet or Crimson Cloth can be produced, what multiplicity of Trades and Artificers must be employ'd! ...When we are thoroughly acquainted with all the Variety of Toil and

Labour, the Hardships and Calamities that must be undergone to compass the End I speak of ... When we are acquainted with, I say, and duly consider the things I named, it is scarce possible to conceive a Tyrant so inhuman and void of Shame, that beholding things in the same View, he should exact such terrible Services from his Innocent Slaves; ... But if we turn the Prospect, and look on all those Labours as so many *voluntary Actions*, belonging to different Callings and Occupations, that Men are brought up to for a Livelyhood, and in which *everyone works for himself*, how much soever he may *seem* to Labour for others: If we consider, that even the Saylors who undergo the greatest Hardships, as soon as one Voyage is ended, even after Ship-wreck, are looking out and solliciting for employment in another: If we consider, I say, and look on these things in another View, we shall find that the *Labour of the Poor*, is so far from being a Burthen and an Imposition upon them; that *to have Employment is a Blessing*, which in their Addresses to Heaven they Pray for, and to procure it for the generality of them is the *greatest Care of every Legislature*.[40]

In Mandeville's view, the State of a 'large stirring Nation'[41] — like that of capitalistically as well as colonially expanding England — has the responsibility of promoting with its policies the true virtues of productive development.[42] At the same time, the class character of the state and of its laws is also clearly disclosed by Mandeville with reference to the task of safeguarding private property in order to make sure that the material reproduction process functions as it should:

Trade is the Principal, but not the only Requisite to aggrandize a Nation; there are other Things to be taken Care of besides. The *Meum* and *Tuum* must be *secur'd*.[43]

As it befits all conceptions formulated from the standpoint of the capitalist system, the social and political order recommended by Mandeville is one of strict hierarchy and subjection, ruled by disciplined 'Labouring for others' through which those who labour 'find their own Ends', thanks to a 'cunning Manage-ment':

by Society I understand a Body Politick, in which Man either subdued by Superiour Force or by Persuasion drawn from his Savage State, is become a *Disciplin'd Creature*, that can find *his own Ends* in *Labouring for others*, and where under one Head or other Form of Government each Member is render'd Subservient to the Whole, and all of them by cunning Management are made to Act as one.[44]

Characteristically, considerations of how to deal with the 'working Poor' (who are repeatedly said to find their own ends in labouring for others) are always subordinated to postulating the *absolute permanence* of their present condition, as the otherwise relativist Mandeville insists, with undisguised paternalism and cynicism:

I have laid down as Maxims *never to be departed from*, that the Poor should be kept *strictly to Work*, and that it was Prudence to relieve their Wants, but *Folly to cure them*; ... I have named *Ignorance* as a necessary Ingredient in the Mixture of Society: From all which it is manifest that I could never have imagined, that *Luxury* was to be made *general* through every part of a Kingdom. I have likewise required that *Property should be well secured*, ... no Foreign Luxury can undo a Country: The height of it is never seen but in Nations that are vastly populous, and there only in the *upper part* of it, and the greater that is the larger still in proportion must be the *lowest*, the Basis that supports all, the multitude of *Working Poor*.[45]

What is, according to Mandeville, of the greatest importance is that the Poor (those who 'bear the Brunt of every thing, the meanest indigent Part of the

Nation, the working slaving People'[46]) should be always *'well managed'*[47] — i.e. firmly controlled both at work and in society at large, within a framework in which 'Property was well secured'[48] — so that they should fulfil the task assigned to them, namely the production and expansion of the wealth of the nation. 'For how excessive soever the Plenty and Luxury of a Nation may be, *some Body must do the work.'*[49] By the same token, if the poor are well managed, they provide a double benefit to society: *working* as well as *consuming*; both necessary for the expansion of the nation's wealth. For: 'it is in the Interest of Rich Nations, that the greatest part of the Poor should almost *never be Idle*, and yet *continually spend what they get'*.[50]

15.2.3

These are major insights into the real motivating spirit and objective structural imperatives of the capitalist system from its origins to the present, arrived at notwithstanding the limitations of Mandeville's social standpoint. The conclusions he draws about the nature of 'luxury' are particularly important. Being a truly radical thinker within the boundaries of his class horizon, he seizes the issue at its roots by bringing into focus its vital practical implications:

> If every thing is to be *Luxury* (as in strictness it ought) that is not *immediately necessary* to make Man subsist as he is a living Creature, there is nothing else to be found in the World, no not even among the naked Savages; ... This definition every body will say is too rigorous; I am of the same Opinion, but if we are to abate one Inch of this Severity, I am afraid we shan't know where to stop. ... if once we depart from calling every thing Luxury that is not absolutely necessary to keep a Man alive, then there is *no Luxury at all*; for if the *wants of Men* are innumerable, then what ought to *supply* them has *no bounds*;[51]

> So that many things, which were once look'd upon as the invention of Luxury, are now allow'd even to those that are so miserably poor as to become the Objects of publick Charity, nay counted so *necessary*, that we think no Human Creature ought to want them.[52]

And Mandeville focuses on something highly significant when he points out, with supreme irony, that the rationalizations of the past — which condemned Luxury and Riches and exalted Poverty — showed a revealing disjunction between 'Theory and Practice' in general, as well as, in particular, between 'the Words and the Lives' of the people who used to deliver their noble sermons on abstinence while themselves indulging in the benefits of wealth. His sharp satirical judgement sounds irresistible when he takes to task Seneca himself, one of the most revered moralists of the past:

> I could swagger about *Fortitude* and the *Contempt of Riches* as much as *Seneca* himself, and would undertake to write twice as much in behalf of *Poverty* as ever he did, for the *tenth part of his Estate*.[53]

Leaving personalities apart, the ideology of abstract moralism — while promising the poor their proper reward in the 'world of beyond' for their suffering in the real world, in which they were forced by political and/or economic necessity to earn their livelihood and 'find their own ends' in labouring for others — rationalized a state of society in which procuring the 'luxurious *superfluities'* of the few (who, as a just retribution, are said to be prevented from getting through 'the eye of the needle') simultaneously meant the denial of basic *necessities* to the overwhelming majority.

Undoubtedly, the unfolding productive and distributive practices of the capital system bring major changes in this respect, at least for the 'large stirring Nations'. Since there can be no production without consumption of some kind, the expansion of capitalist production necessitates the broader distribution of the produced goods. This tendency is enhanced as time goes by, particularly since it is linked to a complementary tendency towards *mass production* through the advancement of the division of labour and the development of machinery the potentials of which cannot be adequately implemented and economically exploited on the basis of confining its products to the limited number of the rich. Thus, although it is a great exaggeration to say that as a result of these developments 'The very Poor lived better than the Rich before', it is nevertheless quite true that a much greater number of the 'working poor' became 'useful' — both as producers and consumers — and did not have to be disposed of as 'vagrants' and 'vagabonds' by hanging: the way in which hundreds of thousands of them were done away with in the not too distant past (72,000 under Henry VIII alone).

What must be strongly underlined here is that we are talking about an *objective tendency* of development, and not simply of its differing conceptualizations by bourgeois political economists. The interminable controversies of the latter are in fact theoretical expressions (and rationalizations) of the contradictions inherent in the tendency itself. If, therefore, Mandeville, Lauderdale and Malthus take the side of 'Luxury', whereas Say, Ricardo and others side with 'thrift' and 'saving', they only express different aspects of the same — intrinsically contradictory — tendency of development. It is therefore quite arbitrary to appoint one side to the exalted status of 'the spirit of capitalism' while totally ignoring the other. All the more since the disregarded tendency happens to be in fact the historically dominant one.

15.3 Tendencies and counter-tendencies of the capital system

15.3.1

GIVEN the immanent nature of capital characterized by Marx as the 'living contradiction', every major tendency of this productive and distributive system can only be made intelligible if we take fully into account the specific *counter-tendency* to which the tendency in question is objectively linked, even if in their relationship one side of the contradictory interdeterminations, of necessity, takes the upper hand, in accordance with the prevailing sociohistorical circumstances. Thus, capital's tendency to *monopoly* is counteracted by *competition;* likewise *centralization* by *fragmentation, internationalization* by national and *regional particularisms, equilibrium* by the *breakdown* of equilibrium, etc.

The same is true of the tendential law of the *decreasing rate of utilization*. As we have seen above, at first this tendency asserts itself as the rehabilitation of 'LUXURY' and 'PRODIGALITY' — together with the expansion of the circle of consumption which thereby embraces also an increasing number of the 'working Poor', providing them with a growing range of commodities, as the developing productive forces make that both possible and necessary — without however abandoning 'AVARICE', 'THRIFT' and 'SAVING', treated as subordinate moments of capitalism in its ascendancy. The same tendency, under the conditions of fully developed capitalism, assumes the form of extreme WASTEFULNESS and DESTRUCTION, but again it is counteracted — to varying degrees — by the imperative of saving as well as by the unavoidable necessity to reconstitute capital in the aftermath of the periodic destruction of its 'over-produced' magnitude, in the interest of the survival of the capital sytem.

However, two important qualifications are needed here for a proper assessment of the way in which the dominant tendencies (and counter-tendencies) of capitalist development historically unfold and structurally assert themselves. First, that since the functioning of this system throughout its history is characterized by the prevalence of the law of *uneven development*, the tendencies mentioned in the last paragraph can manifest in very different ways in different parts of the world, depending on the more or less advanced level of development of the given *national* capitals, as well as on the more or less dominant position of the latter within the framework of *global* capital.

Thus, it is possible that *one side* of the objectively interlinked tendency/counter-tendency *predominates* in *one* country, whereas the *other* prevails in a *different country*. It is enough to think in this respect of the extreme hardship, 'thrift', and 'tightening of the belt' to which the Brazilian and Mexican working classes, among others, must be subjected since the evaporation of their respective 'miracles' of expansionary development, while the United States in particular, and the capitalistically advanced countries of the West in general, have to continue to waste vast amounts of resources under the pressure of the decreasing rate of utilization. Nevertheless, it must be stressed at the same time that one can only talk of the *pre*-dominance of one of the interlinked sides of this tendential law, in that — however absurd this is — even in the 'underdeveloped world' the capitalistically advanced sectors cannot escape the imperatives of waste-production at the present juncture of history, given the globally intertwined character of the capital system.

15.3.2

THE second qualification is equally important. It concerns the inner determinations of the various tendencies themselves as well as their relative weight in the totality of capitalist developments. For whatever their transformations, changes in emphasis, and shifts with regard to each other, or in relation to their specific counter-tendencies, in different places and at widely differing times in history — i.e. what we may consider their strictly transient characteristics, identifiable in terms of the *conjunctural interrelationship* of the diverse forces and determinations of which they themselves constitute a specific part in the given sociohistorical setting — they also possess an immanent logic of their own in accordance with which they unfold *across history*, and thereby objectively circumscribe the *limits* of global capitalist development.

In this sense, while the dialectical reciprocity of the manifold tendential interactions defines the characteristics of any particular tendency or counter-tendency as *relative* to the *overall* configuration of the *given* social forces and determinations, there can be no question of historical *relativism* and 'equidistance from God' in the spirit of post-Ranke-type historiography. For in each case *one* side (or one of the principal aspects) of the various tendencies mentioned above asserts itself as *dominant* — i.e. in Marx's terminology it constitutes the 'über-greifendes Moment' of the relevant dialectical complex — across the *global trajectory* of capitalist development. This is so notwithstanding the fact that (considered in terms of their own particular histories) they can show great variations, and even complete reversals, from one phase of global capitalist history to the other.

Thus, MONOPOLY tends to prevail over COMPETITION in the long run, as the capital system historically progresses towards its ultimate structural limits as a productive system. Moreover, the early *monopolistic* manifestations that charac-terize the 'empire-building' practices of the 'large stirring Nations', in due course give way — as a clear example of the possible reversals referred to a moment ago — to the predominance of forceful *competition* (and to the concomitant anti-monopolistic measures of the capitalist state) in the middle period of capitalistic expansion. But this happens only to be reversed again with an awesome finality in the twentieth century, and particularly in the last few decades, in favour of giant monopolies,[54] while maintaining with complete hypocrisy the resounding rhetorics of competition as the ultimate legitimation of the private enterprise system.

Significantly, even the practice of 'de-nationalization' (or 'privatization') has undergone a major change in this respect in the postwar period. For at first the ruling class was satisfied with the restoration of the British steel industry, for instance, to competing private capitals, once its earlier bankruptcy had been remedied through the public funding of 'nationalization'. Soon enough, how-ever, the troubles started all over again, necessitating not only a second round of bankruptcy-absorbing state-intervention and 'nationalization', but simulta-neously also the ideologically most embarrassing admission of yet another major capitalist failure. Understandably, therefore, in recent years the *dominant form* of 'de-nationalization' became the establishment of *nation-wide private monopolies* — from British Telecom to British Gas and Electricity, as well as the water supplies — which quite cynically eliminated even the possibility of competition (and the economic risks inherent in it) within the confines legislatively controlled by the capitalist state in question.

In the same way as in the case of monopoly and competition, with regard to the historically unfolding tendency and counter-tendency of *centralization* versus *fragmentation* the 'übergreifendes Moment' is the first. Likewise, the *internation-alizing* tendency of capital quite obviously predominates in our times over against the identifiable national and regional *particularisms*, in the form of the irresistibly growing power of *transnational* corporations, in all major capitalist countries, even if the antagonisms inherent in these relationships cannot be resolved. And what is no less important, the upsetting and *breakdown of equilib-rium* happens to be the ultimately dominant tendency of the capital system, and not its complementary tendency to *equilibrium*. This is so notwithstanding the countless theories and practical policies dedicated to the task of safeguarding equilibrium in the course of 20th century capitalist developments. The ulti-mately overriding character of the tendency to the breakdown of equilibrium (i.e. its self-assertion as the 'übergreifendes Moment') is evidenced in our epoch by the 'ever-diminishing return' the system receives from the ever-increasing efforts invested in reconstituting—with the help of unashamedly direct state-intervention — the periodically (but more and more frequently) lost equilibrium, whereas in the more distant past the need for the reconstitution of equilibrium seemed to be able to take care of itself.

The predominance of one side over against the other is equally true in relation to our specific concern. For the *decreasing rate of utilization* by now assumed an overpowering position within the capitalist framework of socioeconomic metabolism, notwithstanding the fact that by now astronomical magnitudes of waste must be incurred in order to be able to impose on society some of its most bewildering manifestations. At the same time, as we shall see below, the imperative for providing the prohibitively large funds required for the ever-expanding production of waste asserts itself today in formerly unimaginable form even in the capitalistically most advanced countries: by imposing 'cuts' and 'savings' on every important area of social reproduction, from education to health care, not to mention the elementary demands of the social security system. As if the governments of the various capitalist states wanted to demonstrate every day the truth of the Marxian proposition that capital is the 'living contradiction'.

15.4 *The limits of economically regulated surplus-extraction*

15.4.1

MANDEVILLE offers a 'rigorous' definition of 'Luxury', expressed in terms of the basic physical/biological necessities that must be satisfied in order to secure the survival of living human beings. At the same time he rightly adds that if we abandon this definition of 'Luxury' (i.e., whatever is above bare necessities) — as in his view we should, because it is 'too rigorous' — 'we shan't know where to stop'.

Such a conclusion points to a fundamental *practical dilemma* which happens to be *absolutely insoluble* within the framework of the capital system. For the latter — not as a matter of defective (and in principle corrigible) knowledge, but as a result of immanent determinations and contradictions — truly 'does not know where to stop'.

Mandeville himself indicates two of the principal difficulties at issue. First, that the paradoxical way in which the capitalist productive system advances means that it brings with it an increase in 'the *Necessaries* of Life without any *Necessity*'.[55]

In other words, the problem is that within the framework of this system there can be no objective criteria as to what kind of productive targets should be adopted and pursued, and what others might in the longer run turn out to be rather problematical. Moreover, the absence of such criteria is by no means accidental. For so long as the limits of the capital system are not reached, the question of devising some alternative to increasing 'the Necessaries of Life without any Necessity' seems to be totally devoid of practical significance. And since those who identify themselves with the standpoint of capital cannot acknowledge the existence of objective structural limits to the capital system as such (perceivable only from the critical standpoint of a radical alternative), preferring to assume that as far as the viability of this mode of production is concerned 'only the sky is the limit', they must remain blind to the negative implications of the question. This happens to be true even of the relatively few thinkers who raise the issue — as Mandeville does — in a limited context, characterizing thereby only the behaviour of particular individuals whose 'inconsiderateness' cannot reflect negatively on the emerging 'felicitous whole'.

The second difficulty raised by Mandeville is treated by him in the same spirit, so that its implications remain hidden even from this sharp-witted and profoundly original thinker. Significantly, though, the *equivocation* in his terms of reference speaks loud enough for itself. For when Mandeville states with approval that the necessary implication of having abandoned the one and only rigorous definition of Luxury is that *'there is no Luxury at all'*, he immediately runs away from facing up to the question of objective limits by the equivocating shift from *'is'* to *'ought'* in his reflections; when, that is, he curiously concludes his line of argument by asserting that 'if the wants of Men *are* innumerable, then what *ought to* supply them *has no bounds'*.

Naturally, from stating that something *'ought not* to have bounds', it does not follow in the sligthest that it *does not actually* have them. But, of course, acknowledging the objective limitations of actuality would ipso facto render the notion of 'unlimited wants' extremely problematical. And this is where the objective social/structural determinations at the roots of a certain type of thought become visible. For inasmuch as the standpoint of capital is incompatible with the acceptance of limits, Mandeville's insensitivity towards the highly problematical character of the stipulated 'innumerable wants of Men' reveals itself as being far from accidental. Accordingly, his enthusiastic depiction and positive legitimation of the new relationship between allegedly boundless or unlimitable wants and their satisfaction must be made plausible (and acceptable) by way of postulating the matching boundlessness of gratification as 'grounded' in *ought*. (The real state of affairs is, of course, quite different, in that the 'wants' themselves are neither biologically fixed nor boundless but socially redimensioned and conditioned at all times — i.e. restricted or stimulated,[56] as the case might be — in accordance with the productive potentialities and determinations of the established metabolic interchange with nature.)

Furthermore, the fact that in response to his critics Mandeville is willing to introduce a *limiting* condition by excluding the 'working Poor' from the generous diffusion of 'Luxuries', does not remove at all the identified difficulties. First, because *some* 'Luxuries' — though, characteristically, this is proclaimed, again, without defining *which* ones and *how many* of them — are said to be legitimately given over to the working poor, both in order to motivate them for harder work and to stimulate the welcome expansion of production and trade. And second, since it is admitted that 'Luxury' is an incorrigibly *historical* category — so that things considered 'Luxuries' in the past today are 'counted so *necessary*, that we think no Human Creature ought to want them' — the limitations with regard to the poor proposed by Mandeville ('give them some but not too much') are utterly useless as a workable guiding principle. For as a result of capital's irrepressible expansionary dynamic (positively embraced by Mandeville himself), whatever appears to be 'too much' one day becomes 'too little' at some other time; not because of growing enlightenment, but because capital's productive system itself is constricted by the limitations of consumption, and therefore must sweep the constraints of 'too little' out of the way.

15.4.2

THE inability to set some meaningful and practically observable limits is one of the most important defining characteristics of capitalistic developments, with far-reaching implications for the viability of the system. It is in this respect highly symptomatic that, despite the innumerable attempts, bourgeois political economy cannot provide an adequate definition of 'productive and unproductive consumption' (nor for that matter of 'productive and unproductive labour'), since the intolerability of limits in general undermines the possibility of formulating objective limiting criteria in the particular.

To be sure, from the very beginning 'usury' and 'avarice' must be denounced as unproductive and parasitic, since the objective interests and structural imperatives of capital's productive expansion require that all forms of capital must be *'put to work'*, just as the 'poor' (the formerly useless 'vagrants' and 'vagabonds') must be *'put to work'*. Once, however, all this is stated and practically achieved, it cannot be specified what kind of work — work to which both capital and labour are now effectively 'put' through the dominance of industrial capital — and what kind of commodities emerging from the labour process may be considered more rather than less acceptable. For from the standpoint of capital, so long as they are expansionary, they all come to the same thing.

This is also the reason why at a much later historical stage in the course of capitalist developments *growth as such* must become a value in itself (nay: *the* paradigm of value), without examining the nature of the advocated growth in the given setting, let alone its longer term human implications. Instead, conveniently self-sustaining tautology rules the day, defining *productivity as growth*, and *growth as productivity*. Nor is this simply a matter of elementary logical requirements, and even less of theoretical niceties. The practical dimension of the problem is that since the capital system cannot set limits to itself, also, it cannot differentiate between the *growth of a child* and the *growth of a cancer*. For in terms of capital's reductive practical equations — as well as in their convoluted theoretical rationalizations — both must be brought to the same common denominator: the 'productivity of cells'.

Such practical inadmissibility of limits in the capital system arises from the way in which the formerly prevailing productive relationship to *use* is fundamentally altered in the course of historical development. As a result, *'useful'* becomes synonymous with *'saleable'*, whereby the umbilical cord of the capitalist mode of production with direct human need can be completely severed while retaining its semblance. At the same time, the earlier practised forms of *exchange* — which were directly related to human need, whatever their limitations in other respects — are superseded by the domination of *exchange-value*, so that subsequently one cannot conceptualize exchange as such unless it is defined in terms of formally equalized commodity-transactions that take place within the strictly quantifying framework of reified exchange-relations.

'Universal exchange' in this conceptual framework cannot mean other than the universal adoption of exchange-value as the exclusive practical orienting principle of material and intellectual production. A notion diametrically opposed to its Marxian meaning, defined as bringing into full co-operative interchange — beyond the restrictive rule of commodified and exploitative exchange-relations

to which labour is subjected — the full range of creative human potentialities, from material productive skills to science and to the enriching enjoyment of works of art. Thus, the capitalist equation of 'exchange' with 'exchange-value' is fallacious not only in relation to the — limited, constraining, and therefore rather problematical — forms of exchange which we can identify in the past. It appears even more fallacious and arbitrary in the light of its potentially unrestricted — socially creative as well as individually fulfilling — realization as truly *universal exchange* in the future.

15.5 The decreasing rate of utilization and the meaning of 'disposable time'

15.5.1

AS we have seen in the last chapter, even in the productive system of the urban crafts (where exchange-value already plays an important role) 'the direct and chief aim of this production is subsistence as craftsmen, as master-journeymen, hence use-value; not wealth, not exchange-value as exchange-value. Production is therefore always subordinate to a given consumption, supply to demand, and expands only slowly.'[57] Thus, since production is heavily constrained by the limitations of demand so that it can expand only slowly, the rate of utilization of any particular product must be high, and the number of people drawn into the circle of expanding consumption comparatively low. Any significant advance in this respect necessarily presupposes the removal of the primary obstacle to accumulation: the *unpurchasable* (or non-commodifiable) character of labour power. For the merchant against whose interference the guilds jealously guard their domain 'could buy every kind of commodity, but labour as a commodity he could not buy.'[58]

Under these circumstances 'On the whole, the labourer and his means of production remained closely united, like the snail with its shell, and thus there was wanting the principal basis of manufacture, *the separation of the labourer from his means of production*, and the *conversion* of these means into *capital*.'[59] Once, however, the forcible separation of the labourer from his means of production (and self-reproduction) is accomplished, the road is wide open to an incomparably more dynamic development. For the targets of production are no longer directly tied (and subordinated) to the limitations of the given consumption but can to a significant extent run ahead of it, thereby stimulating in the form of their new reciprocity both production and 'supply-led demand'.

Nevertheless, this weapon (which is unique to capital) is a double-edged sword. For the removal of the earlier constraints to consumption, and the adoption of an *active/stimulative* (and, as time goes by, increasingly more *manipulative*) role in relation to demand, simultaneously also means the loss of capital's ability to set limits to its own productive procedures (which in the case of earlier systems of production were circumscribed by the given demand in its equivalence to direct use) without slumping thereby into inactivity and crisis.

Capital treats *use-value* (which directly corresponds to need) and *exchange-value* not merely as separate, but in a way that radically subordinates the former to the latter. As mentioned already, in its own time and place this represents a radical innovation that opens up formerly unimaginable horizons for economic development. An innovation based on the practical realization that any particular commodity may be constantly in use, at one end of the scale, or indeed never be used at all, at the other extreme of the possible rates of utilization, without losing thereby its usefulness as regards the expansionary requirements of the capitalist mode of production.

As a result, new productive potentialities open up to capital in that it is of no consequence whatsoever for its system whether the maximum or the minimum rate of utilization characterizes someone's relationship to a given product. For it does not affect in the slightest the only thing that really matters from capital's point of view. Namely: that a certain quantity of exchange-value has been realized in the commodity in question through the act of sale itself, irrespective of whether it is subsequently subjected to constant use, or indeed to very little, if any (e.g. the photographic camera which I may use only once a year, on holiday, if at all), as the case might be. For capital defines 'useful' and 'utility' in terms of *saleability*: an imperative that can be realized under the hegemony and within the domain of *exchange-value* itself.

As Marx points out, 'the exchange-value of a commodity is not raised by its use-value being consumed more thoroughly and to greater advantage.'[60] The same applies, however, exactly the other way round too. Accordingly, if we lower the use-value of a commodity, or create conditions whereby it can only be consumed 'less thoroughly and to smaller advantage', that practice, no matter how reprehensible from some other point of view, is not going to affect its exchange-value either. Once the commercial transaction has taken place, self-evidently demonstrating the 'usefulness' of the commodity in question through its actual sale, there is nothing more to be worried about from capital's point of view. Indeed, the less a given commodity is really used and re-used (rather than quickly used-up: which is perfectly all right for the system), while the effective demand for the same type of use is successfully reproduced, the better this is from capital's standpoint: in that such *under-utilization* produces the saleability of another piece of commodity.

In this sense, what is truly advantageous to capital-expansion is not the increase in the rate at which (or in the degree to which) a commodity — for instance a shirt — is utilized but, on the contrary, the decrease in the hours of its daily use. For so long as such decrease is accompanied by a suitable expansion in society's purchasing power, it creates the demand for another shirt. To put it in more general terms, if the *rate of utilization* of a particular type of commodity could be *decreased* from say 100 percent to 1 percent, while maintaining constant the demand for its use, the potential multiplication of exchange-value should be correspondingly one hundredfold (i.e., the staggering figure of 10,000 percent). In point of fact, this tendency for reducing the actual rate of utilization has been precisely one of the principal ways in which capital succeeded in achieving its truly incommensurable growth in the course of historical development.

However, on the other side of the capitalistic socioeconomic equation we find that — as a result of capital's inner dynamic and antagonistic contradictions — an originally highly positive acquisition turns into its diametrical opposite, with no conceivable solution within the framework of commodity production.

In precapitalist economic formations, when 'the labourer and his means of production remain closely united, like the snail with its shell,' the productive system must develop — or remain constricted — in all its fundamental dimensions. This is indeed what determines the primary meaning of *'economy'* as *'economizing'*. For the available means of production, both positively and in a negative sense, circumscribe the type of productive activity that must be pursued in the given society, in direct relation to the needs of its members — subject to the practical qualification arising from the more or less strategic position of the different social classes within the structural framework of society. Accordingly, even if the *politically* imposed and enforced surplus-extraction — which is hopelessly inefficient anyway, compared to its *economically* regulated extraction in capitalist society — may be said to represent in strict economic terms a certain amount of waste, under the direct control of the privileged (as their monuments, from pyramids to feudal palaces, testify), the societal reproduction process as a *whole* is ruled by the principle of genuine economy, with regard to both labour and the material resources employed. The limitations of the labour process — embracing the various types and skills of labour, its materials and instruments, and its products: all set in direct relation to *need* and *use* and constituting a closely intertwined *unity* — turn out to be also the historically determined limitations of its capacity for waste-production.

All this radically changes with the rise of capitalism. Flexible though the capital system is in so many ways, it cannot simply reproduce itself on a 'stationary' basis, no matter how much theoretical day-dreaming is dedicated to such desideratum once the contradictions of the capitalist mode of production break out into the open. On the contrary, it must prove its 'healthy state' by being very far from 'steady' and 'stationary', reproducing all its conflicting constituents on an ever-enlarging scale. For, as Marx illustrates the point:

> If capital increases from 100 to 1,000, then 1,000 is now the point of departure, from which the increase has to begin; the tenfold multiplication, by 1,000 percent, counts for nothing; profit and interest themselves become capital in turn. What appeared as surplus-value now appears as simple presupposition etc., as included in its simple composition.[61]

Capital's practical relationship to 'economy' is necessarily subordinated to such determinations. The imperatives of profitability on an inexorably growing scale — as exemplified in the last quote — carry with them the bewildering consequence that no matter how 'calculating' and 'rationalizing' or 'economy-conscious' the particular enterprises might (indeed *must*) be, in the interest of their own survival in the market place, the system as a *whole* is utterly *wasteful;* and it must continue to be so in ever-escalating proportions.

A closer look at the economy practised in the particular enterprises removes the mystery of how and why such 'economy' of the parts should produce the wastefulness of the whole, disclosing that the contradiction between the 'micro-' and 'macro-economic' determinations of the capital system is only an apparent one in this respect. For in reality the 'economy' of the particular firm is a *pseudo-economy*. It is not only *compatible* with waste but represents the *necessary mode* of implementation — as well as the spontaneous form of legitimation — of waste in the constitutive cells (i.e. the 'microcosms') of the system.

The ubiquitous operative determination in the capital system is and remains the imperative of *profitability*. It is this that must overrule all other considerations, whatever the implications. In this sense, anything that secures the continued profitability of the particular firm, *ipso facto* also qualifies it for being considered an *economically viable* enterprise. Consequently, no matter how absurdly wasteful a particular productive procedure might be, so long as its product can be profitably imposed on the market, it must be welcomed as the right and proper manifestation of capitalist 'economy'. Thus, to take an example, even if 90 percent of the material and labour resources required for the production and distribution of a profitably marketed commodity — say a cosmetic product: a face cream — goes straight into the physical or figurative (but nonetheless with regard to the costs of production just as real) electronic/advertising rubbish bin, as packaging of one sort or another, and only 10 percent is dedicated to the chemical concoction which is supposed to deliver the real or imaginary benefits of the cream itself to the purchaser, the obviously wasteful practices here involved are fully justified, since they meet the criteria of capitalist 'efficiency', 'rationality' and 'economy' in virtue of the proven *profitability* of the commodity in question.

16.5.2

THESE dubious productive practices are inseparable from the decreasing rate of utilization which itself can only be made intelligible if related to the forcible separation of the 'snail from its shell'. For once the (no matter originally how constraining) close unity of the labourer with the means of production is destroyed through their alienation from the working subject, the constituent parts of the labour process can, and must, follow their own course of self-oriented development, resulting in the end in the kind of absurd manifestations which we are all familiar with.

We must bear in mind that the alienation of the means of production from the producers is simultaneously also the perverse *metamorphosis* of such means of production into *capital*. Accordingly, the logic to which they must from now on conform is none other than that of necessarily self-expanding (or perishing) capital as such.

In this sense, the development of the means of production is no longer directly linked to (and more or less forcefully spurred on by) the development of human *needs*. Nor can it directly respond to, and benefit by, the potentialities arising from the advancement of production-related knowledge itself. Rather, since the means of production have been *converted into capital* (i.e., they constitute the means of production of the given society only inasmuch as they can practically define and economically prove themselves as an *organic part of capital*), they must *oppose* themselves to human needs if the logic of capital demands it, superimposing on existing and potentially unfolding human needs the so-called '*needs of production*' that directly correspond to the interest of safeguarding capital-expansion. Similarly, advancements in scientific know-how can now be turned into actually employed means of production not on the ground of, and in response to, human needs, but only if doing so enhances the interests of the capital system. This is why some inherently productive lines of enquiry are not only not pursued, but even a great deal of already existing knowledge, together with countless practical inventions, are 'shelved' or altogether repressed whenever they happen to conflict with the interests of capital. Indeed, given the alienating metamorphosis of the means of production into reified capital, the productive machinery of this system can and must be articulated in such a way that it should serve destructive rather than productive purposes if the imperatives of capital's continued self-reproduction so decree.

Thus, with regard to their immanent logic, the means of production are no longer genuine *means* but a determinate portion of *self-imposing* capital. As 'means of production' they represent a specific form of capital. However, inasmuch as they constitute only a *part* of capital as such, they are subjected to the intrinsic determinations of this productive system as a whole. Their 'independent development' is independent only from the producers' aims and needs; it is, by contrast, totally dependent for its viability on its strict conformity to the law of continued capital-expansion. Since the means of production embody a determinate *magnitude of capital*, they must grow (or perish if unable to grow enough) as stipulated by that magnitude itself, whether or not there is an authentic productive justification (measurable by need) for their growth. The circular definition of *productivity as growth* and *growth as productivity* finds its explanation (and possible correction) with reference to this perverse practical relationship that banishes the producers (as potentially 'rich social individuals'), together with their needs — whose unfettered development and gratification could make them truly rich — from capital's equations, substituting for them itself as its own end.

The fact that the expansionary dynamic of the means of production itself is primarily determined by the logic of capital as such, and not by the particularity of its form of existence as material and instruments of production, has serious repercussions for the decreasing rate of utilization. They are in evidence not only in the domain of plant and machinery, but in the operation of the capitalist system of production and distribution taken in its entirety.

As mentioned before, *self-expanding capital* must show profitable return on the *totality* of its additional units, compounding thereby not only its own power but also the complications (and contradictions) that go with the necessity to turn surplus-value into the mere presupposition of the new cycle of expansion. And so this process must continue indefinitely, irrespective of how immense is already the accumulated magnitude of capital that must be considered in *all* its forms (including, of course, the means of production) nothing more than the mere point of departure of the renewed drive for expansion.

Thus, the very moment in which it is born, the death sentence is immediately pronounced on that determinate portion of capital which is allocated to the means of production. This is due to the imperative to be transcended, in the course of capital's inexorable multiplication, as the historically constituted (and likewise, in its capacity as a contingently given magnitude of capital, always hopelessly limited) means of production. In its historical genesis the capitalist system could not acquire its necessary momentum for development without forcibly alienating the means of production from the producers and *converting* them into *capital*. At the same time, in its actual mode of operation a significant portion of capital must constantly *reconvert* itself into the given means of production on an ever-enlarging scale, so as to metamorphose itself *back into capital* on a still larger scale, in order to be able to embark on its cycle of enlarged self-reproduction again and again. Paradoxically, therefore, the larger the magnitude of capital dedicated to the means of production (as it must be, given the equation of self-expanding capital under one of its forms of existence with the instruments and material of production), the greater the pressure to supersede it by an ever-greater-magnitude of capital consigned to the same sort of existence, awaiting the execution of its own sentence upon itself.

Furthermore, since the expansionary dynamic must assume, as a result of such imperatives, the form of the concentration and centralization of capital, the relatively inefficient parts of total social capital must inevitably fall by the wayside, as they become prematurely 'surplus to requirements'. They turn out to be *capitalistically useless* (on account of becoming unprofitable in their mode of operation), even if they could contribute a great deal to the production of *socially useful* products under the conditions of a less concentrated overall articulation of capital; and even more so if we transfer the accumulated assets outside the framework of capital into a non-adversarial social reproductive system rationally managed by the associated producers.

In this way, following the logic of its immanent determinations, the inexorable tendency to the concentration and centralization of capital — arising originally both from the capital/labour antagonism and from the conflictual interchanges of a great multiplicity of competing capitals — prevails no less under the conditions of arbitrary monopolistic imposition and 'short-circuiting' of some of the system's inner determinations than before, activating and intensifying thereby the tendency for the decreasing rate of utilization on the plane of capital-utilization itself. The much idealized category of the *'economy of scale'* (which in the end amounts to little more than the apologetic rationalization of cannibalistic big capital's insatiable appetite to gobble up its smaller brothers and cousins) displays quite well the growing unviability of not only small but even medium-size capital in the face of the decreasing rate of capital-utilization with which only the largest complexes seem to be able to cope at all at the present juncture of history, and even they by no means satisfactorily.

It is enough to remind ourselves in this respect of the current state of the motor car industry. Not only because so many medium to large car manufacturers have disappeared in the last three decades all over the world, from the US to Britain, France, Italy, Germany, etc., but because even such comparatively big and state-subsidized firms as the former British Leyland (rebaptised as The Rover Group, in preparation for the 'privatization' of the profitable parts of the 'Group') and Renault — which both swallowed up quite a number of fairly large companies in their own time of expansion, using the same rationalization of the 'economy of scale' — continue to experience major difficulties in terms of their apparently chronic inability to live up to the productive requirements of the ever-growing 'proper economy of scale'. Besides, a closer look reveals that in reality we are facing here a vicious circle, since the absorption of yesterday's 'surplus-capacity' (in the name of the selfsame 'economy of scale', which is supposed to be dictated by 'rationality' itself and is presented as such often in order to justify the publicly financed heavy losses) turns out to be tomorrow the newly under-utilized 'surplus-capacity'. And, of course, that will be in its turn assimilated the day after tomorrow by an even bigger corporation, with its allegedly now at last fully adequate 'economy of scale'; so as to start all over again, in due course, the whole process of surplus-capacity-generating 'capacity-rationalization'.

15.5.3

CONSIDERED in relation to *productivity* as such, the forcible separation of the 'snail from its shell' is by no means less problematical. For, since capital usurps all the controlling functions of the socioeconomic metabolism while the producers themselves are completely excluded from setting the targets of production in relation to their need, there can be no other direction given to the development of productivity itself than the maximization of profit.

The fact that the means of production are converted into capital and must be valorized as such on an ever-expanding scale brings with it the development of *technology* as a paradoxically self-oriented productive practice. It is paradoxical in the sense that it is both *autonomous* (in that it is freed by capital from the immediate constraints of human needs, and thereby it is enabled to pursue up to a point its own line of development), and *slavishly subordinated* to the profit-oriented dictates of capital's immanent logic. As a result, technology can *race ahead* in the realization of its self-posited objectives, irrespective of the negative implications of such autonomous orientation both with regard to the decreasing rate of utilization — manifest on the one hand in the *over-produced mass of commodities*, and on the other in the accumulated *surplus productive capacity* — and with regard to its impact on living labour. Checks and restraints can be brought into the picture only *post festum*, after the infliction of the damage. At the same time, the correctives feasible within the confines of capitalism are rather limited in that the negative impact of technological autonomy — which seems to contradict under the circumstances of crises the system's vital interests — is in fact fully in tune with capital's inalterably profit-oriented material dictates, even if it is preferable from the standpoint of capital to keep the underlying contradictions hidden from sight.

Thus, the contradictions are bound to erupt with painful regularity, whatever the wishful tales of *'capitalist planning'*. Remedial action within the global framework of the capital system is feasible only as a form of *post festum* corrective that preserves the overall profitability of the system, whatever *partial* anticipatory correctives and manipulatory methods might be devised in more limited contexts. Even the military/industrial complex as a 'planned' corrective can only have a limited impact in this respect, no matter how massive its size in any particular country for a given historical epoch. As far as living labour is concerned, the material imperatives of profit-seeking capital in the domain of productive technology must be imposed in one way or in another; if not by sugar-coating the bitter pill then by some more drastic means. Labour's periodically exploding *'Luddite'* responses to such impositions are extreme manifestations of this contradiction. But even if the latter assumes a far less striking form, it remains an *antagonistic* contradiction, no matter how much effort is spent on trying to talk it (or wish it) out of existence. For it is necessarily reproduced with every cycle of expanded conversion of productive machinery and technology into capital and *vice versa* in direct subordination to the material imperative of profitability.

The claims and demands of the workers, in their constantly renewed confrontations with capital, can only be met to the degree to which they can be accommodated within such a framework of orientation. The fact that even the best and most honest thinkers who conceptualize the ongoing developments from capital's standpoint cannot acknowledge the antagonistic character of such confrontations, this fact itself puts sharply into relief the problematical nature of all the practical efforts that must be, nonetheless, devised to deal with them.

Moreover, given the conditions under which the fundamental — yet, as we have seen, to both Mandeville and Babbage apparently quite invisible — structural antagonism of the capitalist social order asserts itself, it can only yield *contradictory* results to *both* sides of this irreconcilable confrontation. For labour gains concessions at the price of being forced into the position of constantly reducing the amount of *necessary labour* required for securing the continuity of the capitalist reproduction process, without acquiring though the power to make acceptable the legitimacy (and necessity) of organizing production in accordance with the principle of *disposable time*: the only viable safeguard in the long run against being subjected to the extreme hardship and indignity of *mass unemployment*. And capital, on the other hand, succeeds in transforming labour's gains into its own profit and dynamic self-expansion by relentlessly increasing the *productivity* of labour; without however finding a proper solution to the mounting complications and perilous implications of *chronic unemployment and concomitant over-production* that foreshadow its ultimate breakdown as a socially viable mode of productive reproduction.

Science itself is mobilized in the service of the demands emanating from the selfsame fundamental antagonism. Thus, under the prevailing circumstances, science is one-sidedly subordinated in its primary function to capital's vital need to turn to its advantage its own concessions and labour's periodic gains. Accordingly, scientific activity is practically orientated (and constantly reorientated, whatever the illusions of 'self-developing pure science'), in accordance with its position within the framework of the capitalist division of labour, towards the dual task of inventing more and more 'cost-effective' (that is to say: primarily *labour-saving*) productive *machinery* on the one hand, and of devising the methods and processes suitable for the *profitable mass production* of commodities, on the other. This is how it becomes possible to superimpose on the overall dynamic of the capitalist labour process (in its inseparability from the corresponding imperative and dynamic of the 'valorization' process) the necessary-labour-saving productive determinations that can match in scope the ever-increasing magnitude of capital as the new presupposition and point of departure of the profit-orientated expansionary cycle.

15.5.4
THE decreasing rate of utilization is the necessary concomitant of all these determinations. Both labour's own contribution towards the productive reduction of necessary labour time, and capital's objective imperative to turn to its own use labour's gains, carry with them the decreasing rate of utilization on several planes; from the mode of functioning of living labour itself (assuming, as time goes by, the form of growing unemployment) to the over-production/under-utilization of commodities, and to the ever-more-wasteful utilization of productive machinery. The only conceivable way out of such contradictions from the standpoint of labour — namely, the general adoption and creative utilization

of *disposable time* as the orienting principle of societal reproduction — is of course anathema to capital, since it cannot be fitted into its framework of expanding self-reproduction and valorization. Thus, the drive for the multiplication of reified wealth and for the concomitant increase in society's abstract productive powers cannot be halted, whatever its implications for the decreasing rate of utilization and for the associated wastefulness in managing society's material and human resources.

From the standpoint of living labour it is perfectly possible to envisage disposable time as the condition that fulfils some vital positive functions in the life-activity of the associated producers (functions which it alone can fulfil), provided that the lost unity between need and production is reconstituted at a qualitatively higher level than it ever existed in the historical relationship between 'the snail and its shell'. In complete contrast, however, 'disposable time' from capital's standpoint is necessarily perceived as something either to be exploited in the interest of capital-expansion (from the sale of 'Do-it-yourself' tools and materials to the extreme commercialization of every 'leisure-activity', be that sex, religious worship or art), or as idle 'wasted time', inasmuch as it cannot be profitably exploited. This is why the capitalist tyranny of *minimal time* (allowed in production), wedded to the decreasing rate of utilization (in the spheres of both production and consumption), must prevail without hindrance until the system as a whole breaks down under the weight of its own contradictions.

The alternatives open to capital in this respect are, in fact, rather limited. The capitalist system of production and consumption can continue to function so as to postpone 'the moment of truth' with regard to its own limits so long as:

(1) the given circle of consumption can successfully expand, so that a large and *growing* labour force can keep pace with the imperative of increased productivity, absorbing the available products without difficulties; or

(2) a relatively limited or *stationary* labour force — i.e., in practical terms, that of the capitalistically advanced countries — can provide a sufficiently dynamic demand to match the need generated for capital-expansion within the system, both by enlarging the range, and by speeding up the rate, of its consumption.

These are of course not aprioristic philosophical determinations but real historical possibilities. As such, they must be actualized (i.e., turned into tangible, and in the final analysis limiting/constricting, socioeconomic realities) through the multifaceted interchanges that take place within the global framework of societal reproduction in which the various tendencies and counter-tendencies of the capital system assert themselves.

Thus, considering the first possibility, it is not a matter of indifference which particular way the capital system is in fact historically articulated with regard to the relationship between the 'metropolitan' centres of capital and the rest of the world. Once, however, the objective structural relationships which we are familiar with are brought into being and become consolidated through Western capitalist penetration and imperialist (or neo-imperialist) domination, subordinating the 'Third World' to the interests of the leading capitalist countries, the possibility of enlarging the consuming circle so as to include in it the world population as a whole suffers a massive setback.

It is not surprising, therefore, that the postwar strategies devised for the 'modernization' of the 'Third World' within the framework of the capital system could hardly even scratch the surface of the structural problems of the societies concerned. At the same time, the dynamic of capitalist expansion, too, had to retreat into the confines of the dominant Western countries, relying primarily on the second possibility mentioned above, coupled with the multiplication of waste beyond belief within the boundaries of 'advanced capitalism' itself. Attempts at redefining the relationship between the 'Third World' and the West in the 'enlightened self-interest' of the latter (e.g. by the *Brandt Reports)* were therefore devoid of a real constituency to address themselves to and were thus condemned from the start to disappear without trace. The stark reality of the prevailing conditions could leave no room for effective enlightenment, but only for some 'charitable' interventions on the occasion of the gravest emergencies (like the famine in Ethiopia). Indeed, as a general rule, Western-oriented developmental theories and corresponding institutional practices of 'modernizing' intervention in the 'Third World' could only assume hopelessly inadequate charity-like and paternalistic postures. For the substantive enlargement of the historically constituted (and extremely restricted) consuming circle itself — without which only the crumbs from the table of capitalistically advanced countries could be 'redistributed' — would require a radical change in the established power relations of dependency and domination. However, the global system of capital, locked into the lopsided dynamic of its existing structural articulation in favour of the 'North', is objectively incompatible with such a change.

15.5.5

THE *decreasing rate of utilization* negatively affects all three fundamental dimensions of capitalistic production and consumption, namely those of:

1) goods and services;
2) plant and machinery; and
3) labour-power itself.

WITH regard to the first, the tendency is noticeable through the accelerating speed of circulation and turnover of capital that becomes necessary with the unfolding of 'consumer-capitalism', in order to compensate — as much as feasible under the circumstances — for some of the most damaging negative tendencies of economic development.

At first there seems to be no problem, since the expansionary needs of capitalist production can be satisfied by drawing into the framework of rather more than just basic consumption new, formerly excluded, groups of people; or by making available also to the working classes, at least in the capitalistically advanced countries, commodities formerly reserved to the privileged; as, for instance, the broad diffusion of the motor car testifies, in conjunction with the changing pattern of housing and the shift of the workers away from their place of work (in contrast to Victorian mill-towns) to suburban areas (but, of course, not in the 'Third World', as the tragedy of Bhopal, due to the operations of U.S. transnational Union Carbide, testifies).

Beyond a certain point, however, the commodities destined for 'high mass-consumption' are no longer sufficient to keep the wolves of the crisis of productive expansion (due to the absence of suitable capital-accumulation outlets) from the door. Thus, it becomes necessary to devise ways in which one can *reduce* the rate at which any particular type of commodity is used, deliberately *shortening* its useful life-span, in order to make it possible to throw a continuing supply of overproduced commodities into the whirlpool of accelerating circulation. The notorious 'planned obsolescence' of mass-produced 'durable consumer goods'; the displacement and neglect, or deliberate run-down, of goods and services that offer an inherently higher potential for utilization (e.g., *public transport*) in favour of those in which the rate of utilization tends to be much lower, even minimal (like the privately owned motor car) while they absorb a massive portion of society's purchasing power; the artificial imposition of almost completely unused productive capacity (e.g., the 'overkill' of a complex computer, used as a 'word processor' in an office where a straightforward typewriter would be quite sufficient); the increased waste resulting from the introduction of new technology, directly contradicting the promised savings in material resources (e.g., the computerized 'paperless office' that uses five times more paper than ever before); the deliberate 'extermination' of repair skills and services so as to compel the customers to buy costly new parts or products when the throw-away objects themselves could be easily mended (e.g., compelling people to purchase a complete car silencer system costing £160 in place of a £10 welding job which would be perfectly adequate for the purpose), etc., all belong to this category, ruled by the underlying imperatives and determinations for wastefully decreasing the practicable rates of utilization.

However, despite the cynical practice of 'built-in obsolescence', as well as of all the manipulative advertising efforts that aim at producing the same 'premature obsolescence' by other means, it is not very easy to guarantee — on the necessary scale and with the consistency required to make it reliable from the point of view of expansion-orientated capital — the motivation for wastefully discarding perfectly usable goods, given the economic constraints of individual households, even in the richest countries, and the conflicting demands imposed upon their resources. Thus, much more secure guarantees must be found, on a sufficiently large scale and in a directly institutionalizable form, so that capital's relentless drive forward, as coupled with its tendency to reduce the rate of utilization, should go on unhindered.

As we shall see in some detail in the next chapter, this guarantee to capital is provided by the emergence and state-sponsored consolidation of the 'military/industrial complex' that *temporarily* displaces several major contradictions. It appropriates and dissipates apparently limitless resources and over-produced capital funds, without adding in the slightest to the realization-problems and competitive pressures, as capital-expansion orientated towards real consumption, of necessity, would. At the same time, the astronomical wastefulness (which should be quite incompatible with the normally glorified criteria of economic efficiency and 'good house-keeping') finds its automatic justification and legitimation in an appeal to the ideology of 'national interest' and 'national security', under the combined legislative, juridical and administrative power of the state that acts in unison with the military/industrial complexes concerned. In this way, not only are the negative consequences of the decreasing rate of utilization not immediately felt but, on the contrary, thanks to the direct institutional underpinning provided by the state on a massive scale and in virtually every area of economic activity, for a determinate historical period they can be turned into formerly unimaginable, extremely powerful levers of capitalist expansion; as we could witness it in the postwar decades.

WE find similar difficulties and complications, affecting the requirements of capital-expansion, on the plane of plant and machinery too. The decreasing rate of utilization here manifests itself in the form of the *chronic under-utilization* of plant and machinery, coupled with an ever-increasing pressure for artificially *shortening the cycle of amortization* of the same, in order to counteract the tendency itself. Accordingly, we are very far today from Charles Babbage's diagnosis of the capitalist imperative to renew machinery once in every *ten years*. For our 'throw-away society' today often resorts to the bewildering 'productive' practice of scrapping brand new machinery after very short use, or even without inaugurating it, so as to either replace it by something 'more advanced', or to leave its place vacant under the conditions of a 'downward pressure' in the economy. Naturally, such absurd wastefulness in the field of productive-capacity-utilization cannot become the general rule. Nevertheless, also the *general rule* has been significantly changed in the 20th century, and particularly in the last four decades, compared to the 'leisurely pace' at which perfectly usable plant and machinery used to be discarded in Babbage's epoch.

That the practices adopted as a result of the objective trends and pressures of modern capitalist development are apologetically rationalized through the convenient ideology of 'technological innovation' — for who in his right mind would dare to question the necessity of motherhood for the survival of humankind? — does not alter the fact that we are facing here a fundamental structural problem of growing severity. And, again, we must notice the direct buttressing function of the state in generously providing, even to the richest multinational corporations, the much needed funds for 'plant renewal' and 'development'; funds which the idealised 'entrepreneurial spirit' of private competition can no longer profitably produce. Not to mention the modern capitalist state's permanent involvement in materially sustaining (and subsidizing) the private enterprise system through the finance and organization of both directly technology orientated and so-called 'basic research'.

AS to the third aspect of our problem, concerned with the use or non-use of socially available labour-power, it happens to constitute the potentially most explosive of capital's contradictions. For — unfortunately from the point of view of capital—labour is not only 'a factor of production', in its capacity of labour-power, but also the 'mass-consumer' so vital for the normal cycle of capitalist reproduction and the realization of surplus-value. This is why the individual capitalist likes so much the improving purchasing power of *someone else's labourer*. Indeed, under suitable conditions, in principle he is not opposed even to the improvement of the material conditions of the working class as a whole; that is to say: at times when such improvements do not conflict with the requirements of profitability, since they can be financed from growing productivity within the dynamics of enlarged reproduction. Hence the possibility, indeed the necessity, of 'high wage economies', or varieties of the 'welfare state', under the circumstances of undisturbed capital-expansion, as we have witnessed during the relatively long postwar phase of development in the capitalistically advanced countries.

However, the decreasing rate of utilization with regard to labour-power (which manifests itself in the form of growing unemployment) cannot be reversed by conjunctural factors and measures. Disconcertingly for capital, treating labour as a mere 'factor of production' cannot be maintained indefinitely, not even by ideologically exploiting the fictitious opposition between the worker and the consumer, so as to be able to subdue the worker in the name of the mythical 'Consumer' writ large. For *in the last analysis* (and notwithstanding all the apologetic ideological clichés produced by so-called 'economic science' about the claimed 'maximization of marginal utilities' on a strictly individualistic basis) the two are basically the same. Indeed the healthy or 'dysfunctional' state of the capitalist economy is ultimately determined on the ground of this (from the standpoint of capital extremely uncomfortable) structural identity between labour and 'mass-consumer' which assigns to labour, on both counts, an objectively strategic position in the overall system, even if the people concerned are as yet not conscious of the emancipatory potentialities inherent in it.

The negative practical implications of this fundamental identity come to the fore with irrepressible evidence and finality through the unfolding tendency of the decreasing rate of utilization. Moreover, in relation to labour this tendency assumes the form of a yawning contradiction. For on one side we find capital's *ever-increasing* appetite for 'mass consumers', whereas on the other its *ever-diminishing* need for living labour.

It is, in fact, the antagonistic and ultimately explosive contradiction between these two fundamental but irreconcilable needs of capital that dominates the discourse of modern bourgeois economic theory, offering the imaginary 'reconciliation' of the contradiction in question by rewriting its terms of reference and redefining the substance of its constituents for the purpose of ideological rationalization. Accordingly, 'economic science' not only invents *'the Consumer'* as a separate entity, but also conjures up the capitalist as *'the Producer'*,[62] thereby fictitiously reducing the strategic role of labour to a negligible minimum. In this way, 20th century bourgeois political economy simultaneously reflects and legitimates, in a characteristically upside-down fashion, the most anti-social and dehumanizing tendency of capital for the brutal ejection of living labour from the labour process.

To be sure, so long as the decreasing rate of utilization can produce outlets for capital-expansion through the, no matter how wasteful, multiplication of goods and services, as well as through the accelerating rate of amortization of plant and machinery mentioned above, the third and most dangerous dimension of this tendency — that which directly affects labour as the living subject of the labour-process — may remain latent. Indeed, the latency of this third dimension, coupled with the exploitation of the other two (both in strictly economic terms and through the active involvement of 'consensus-politics' in capitalistically advanced countries) may create the illusion of the permanent 'integration' of labour. As a result, the profound structural problems and contradictions of the existing socioeconomic system can be conceptualized as 'temporary dysfunctions' essentially *technological* in character, from which it would seem to follow that they are amenable to similarly *technological solutions* as a matter of course.

Only when the potentialities of the first two dimensions — as manifest in relation to (1) goods and services; and (2) plant and machinery — for displacing the contradictions inherent in the decreasing rate of utilization do not reach far enough, only then is the savage mechanism of ejecting living labour in massive numbers from the production process activated. It assumes the form of *mass unemployment*, even in the most advanced capitalist countries, irrespective of its consequences for the position of the 'mass consumer' and for the necessary implications of the consumer's worsening position in a 'downward spiral' of development of the economies concerned.

Under such circumstances, when an ever-growing proportion of living labour becomes *superfluous labour-power* from the point of view of capital, apologetic 'economic science' suddenly discovers that the displacement of labour is a structural problem and begins to talk about *'structural unemployment'*. All that it forgets to add is 'merely' that mass unemployment is *structural to capital only*, and not to the advancement of the production process as such. The blame, inasmuch as recognized at all, is put squarely at the door of 'technological progress' itself which, of course, no one can conceivably oppose, except perhaps in the name of the pessimistic utopia of disenchanted liberal thought called 'steady-state economy'.

Thus, thanks to the mystifying conflation of a major social trend with its technological setting, and thanks to the arbitrary subordination of the former to the latter, the problems inherent in the *cumulative* impact of the three dimensions put together — which reciprocally intensify the negative power of each taken separately — need not even be noticed, let alone effectively counteracted at the plane of social practice. This is why, true to form, even at a time of mass unemployment that affected the mining communities in Britain with even greater savagery than other areas of industrial production, the ruling body of the 'nationalized' coal industry (British Coal) had to impose its socially *absurd* but capitalistically *rational* (!) demand for the introduction of the *six day workweek*, in place of the traditional *five day week*, so as to be able to *lengthen the exploitable time* of its greatly reduced labour force, in tune with the decreasing rate of utilization advancing at all three planes of production and consumption discussed above.

The only viable alternative to such practices (namely: to look for solutions in the direction of reorienting social production from the tyranny of minimal time towards the maximization of *'disposable time'*) would obviously call for the adoption of a radically different *social accountancy*, in place of the relentless pursuit of profit. But, of course, the category of *disposable time*, as a positive and creatively utilizable orienting principle of social interchange, is totally incompatible with the interests of the established order.

CHAPTER SIXTEEN

THE DECREASING RATE OF UTILIZATION AND THE CAPITALIST
STATE: CRISIS-MANAGEMENT AND CAPITAL'S DESTRUCTIVE
SELF-REPRODUCTION.

16.1 Capital's line of least resistance

16.1.1

THE decreasing rate of utilization happens to be one of the most important and
far-reaching tendential laws of capitalistic developments. It must be stressed, of
course, that this tendency (which is closely linked to the imperatives of capital-
expansion) fulfilled very different functions at different phases of such developments. Thus, the move from making available two pairs of shoes to the worker,
instead of one, can only be considered a positive one, whatever the motivations
and determinations behind it on the capitalist side. In fact, such expansion in
consumption, on a scale incomparable with earlier productive systems, is one of
the most significant aspects and real achievements of 'mobile property's civilizing victory'. To quote Marx:

> In spite of all 'pious' speeches he [the capitalist] searches for means to spur them [the
> workers] on to consumption, to give his wares new charms, to inspire them with
> new needs by constant chatter etc. It is precisely this side of the relation of capital
> and labour which is an essential civilizing moment, and on which the historic justi-
> fication, but also the contemporary power of capital rests.[63]

However, the emergence of the military/industrial complex on the basis of the
same tendency is an entirely different matter. Indeed, the destructive manifestations of this tendential law — which were hardly visible in Marx's lifetime —
came to the fore with dramatic emphasis in the 20th century, and particularly
during the last four or five decades. Accordingly, the old socialist anticipation
of overcoming SCARCITY through the production of formerly unimaginable ABUN-
DANCE needs a radical reexamination in the light of the same developments.

Evidently, Marx could not even dream about the emergence of the mili-
tary/industrial complex as an all-powerful and effective agent for displacing
capital's inner contradictions. He described the dynamic of capital's enlarged
self-reproduction — which, in his view, would also generate, despite the
conscious intentions of the individual capitalists, the material conditions of a
socialist transformation — in the following terms:

> The great historic quality of capital is to create this surplus labour, superfluous labour
> from the standpoint of mere use value, mere subsistence; and its historic destiny
> [Bestimmung][64] is fulfilled as soon as, on one side, there has been such a development
> of needs that surplus labour above and beyond necessity has become a general need
> arising out of individual needs themselves — and, on the other side, when the severe
> discipline of capital, acting on succeeding generations [Geschlechter], has developed

general industriousness as the general property of the new species [Geschlecht] — and, finally, when the development of the productive powers of labour, which capital incessantly whips onward with its unlimited mania for wealth, and of the sole conditions in which this mania can be realized, have *flourished to the stage* where the possession and preservation of general wealth require a lesser labour time of society as a whole, and where the labouring society relates *scientifically* to the process of its progressive reproduction, its reproduction in a *constantly greater abundance*; hence where labour in which a human being does what a *thing could do* has ceased. ... Capital's ceaseless striving towards the general form of wealth drives labour beyond the limits of its natural paltriness [Naturbedürftigkeit], and thus creates the material elements of the *rich individuality* which is *as all-sided in its production as in its consumption,* and whose labour also therefore appears no longer as labour, but as the *full development of activity itself* in which *natural necessity* in its direct form has *disappeared*; because a *historically created need* has taken the place of the natural one. This is why capital is productive; i.e., an essential relation for the development of the social productive forces. It ceases to exist as such only where the development of these productive forces themselves encounters its barrier in capital itself.[65]

The problem is, though, that capital in its unbridled form — that is, under the conditions of generalized commodity production which define, and circumscribe the limits of, capitalism — sets into motion not only great productive potentials, but simultaneously also massive diversionary as well as destructive forces. Consequently, disturbing as this must sound to socialists, such diversionary and destructive forces provide capital in crisis with new margins of expansion and new ways of overcoming the barriers which it encounters.

Thus, the inner dynamic of productive advance as predicated by the objective potentialities of science and technology is gravely distorted, indeed fatefully derailed, with a tendency towards the *perpetuation* of capitalistically viable practices — however wasteful and destructive — and the *blocking* of alternative approaches that might interfere with the fetishistic requirements of self-expanding exchange value. In this sense, the 'historically created needs' that replace the natural ones under the constraints of generalized commodity production are extremely problematical and, therefore, must be radically questioned from the point of view of the advocated socialist emancipation which they not only do not necessarily anticipate but, on the contrary, actively oppose.

16.1.2

WE can see the dilemmas involved in these developments in the context of growing *consumption* which, in theory, should be inherently emancipatory. To quote Marx:

> the production of relative surplus value, i.e. production of surplus value based on the increase and development of the productive forces, *requires the production of new consumption*; requires that the *consuming circle* within circulation expands as did the productive circle previously. Firstly quantitative expansion of existing consumption; secondly: creation of *new needs* by propagating existing ones in a wide circle; thirdly: production of new needs and discovery and creation of *new use values*.[66]

However, the positive outcome of this dialectical interplay between production and consumption is very far from being secure, since the capitalistic drive for the expansion of production is not at all necessarily linked to *human need* as such, but only to the abstract imperative of the *'realization'* of capital.

Naturally, the latter is feasible in more ways than one. The first and histori-cally primary—as well as fundamentally positive — way of pursuing the process of capital's ever-expanding self-realization through the dynamic interplay bet-ween production and consumption is described by Marx, in part reminiscent of Babbage, like this:

> For example, if, through a doubling of productive force, a capital of 50 can now do what a capital of 100 did before, so that a capital of 50 and the necessary labour corresponding to it become free, then, for the capital and labour which have been set free, a new, qualitatively different branch of production must be created, which *satisfies and brings forth a new need*. The value of the old industry is preserved by the creation of the fund for a new one in which the relation of capital and labour posits itself in a new form. Hence exploration of all of nature in order to discover new, useful qualities in things; universal exchange of the products of all alien climates and lands; new (artificial) preparation of natural objects, by which they are given new use values. The exploration of the earth in all directions, to discover new things of use as well as new useful qualities of the old; such as new qualities of them as raw materials etc.; the development, hence, of the *natural sciences* to their *highest point*; likewise the discovery, creation and satisfaction of *new needs arising from society itself*; the *cultivation of all the qualities of the social human being,* production of the same in a form *as rich as possible in needs,* because rich in qualities and relations — *production of this being as the most total and universal possible social product,* for, in order to take *gratification in a many-sided way,* he must be capable of many pleasures [genussfaehig], hence cultured to a high degree — is likewise a *condition of production founded on capital.* This creation of new branches of production, i.e. of qualitatively new surplus time, is not merely the division of labour, but is rather the creation, separate from a given production, of labour with a new use value; the development of a constantly expanding and more comprehensive system of different kinds of labour, different kinds of production, to which a *constantly expanding and constantly enriched system of needs* corresponds. ...
>
> Thus capital creates the bourgeois society, and the universal appropriation of nature as well as of the social bond itself by the members of society. Hence the great civilizing influence of capital; its production of a stage of society in comparison to which all earlier ones appear as mere local developments of humanity and as nature-idolatry. For the first time, nature becomes purely an object for humankind, purely a matter of utility; ceases to be recognized as a power for itself; and the theoretical discovery of its autonomous laws appears merely as a ruse so as to subjugate it *under human needs,* whether as an object of consumption or as a means of production. In accord with this tendency, capital drives beyond national barriers and prejudices as much as beyond nature worship, as well as all traditional, confined, complacent, encrusted satisfactions of present needs, and reproductions of old ways of life. It is destructive towards all of this, and *constantly revolutionizes it,* tearing down all the barriers which hem in the development of the forces of production, the *expansion of needs,* the *all-sided development of production,* and the exploitation and exchange of natural and mental forces.[67]

Unfortunately, however, there can be no guarantee that the positive potentiality pointing in the direction of a socialist transformation will prevail. For, from the standpoint of self-expanding exchange-value, the obvious alternative to the line of development here described by Marx is to *abort* it well before it irretrievably undermines capital's power of overall control. This implies a need on capital's part to pursue a strategy of 'realization' which not only overcomes the immediate limitations of fluctuating market demand, but at the same time also succeeds in radically disengaging itself from the *structural constraints* of use-value as tied to human need and real consumption.

Once this is accomplished, and thereby the humanly meaningful measure of legitimate aims and objectives is repudiated as an intolerable fetter to 'development', the road is wide open to *displace* many of capital's inner contradictions. And this can go on for as long a historical period as the new outlets and modalities of realization remain free from the pressures of *saturation* on the one hand, and from serious difficulties in securing the necessary *resources* for the cancerously growing and ever-more-wasteful[68] pattern of production on the other.

This type of, by Marx unexpected, structural change in the capitalistic cycle of reproduction is accomplished through a radical shift from genuinely *consumption-orientated* production to *destruction*.

To be sure, a great variety of other forms of waste-production are also tried out for the same purpose, and they continue to be practised ever since, as we have seen with reference to 'planned obsolescence', etc. However, they prove to be far too limiting in the course of capitalistic developments in relation to the structural imperatives of the system. Thus, it becomes necessary to adopt the most radical form of waste — i.e., the direct destruction of vast quantities of accumulated wealth and worked-up resources — as the dominant way of disposing of overproduced capital.

The reason why such a change is feasible at all within the parameters of the established production system is because *consumption and destruction* happen to be *functional equivalents from the perverse standpoint of the capitalistic 'realization' process*. Thus, the question as to whether normal consumption — i.e., the human consumption of use-values corresponding to need — or 'consumption' through destruction will prevail, is decided on the ground of the comparatively better suitability of one or the other to satisfy the overall requirements of capital's self-reproduction under the changing circumstances.

In practice we find, of course, a combination of the two, even under the worst circumstances. Nevertheless, we can clearly perceive a growing tendency in favour of the second — namely *destructive pseudo-consumption* — in the course of twentieth century capitalistic developments in the dominant Western countries.

It was Rosa Luxemburg who first noticed, before the outbreak of the first world war, in 1913, the great advantages of militarist production for capitalist accumulation and expansion. This is how she characterized the underlying material determinations:

> In the form of government contracts for army supplies the scattered purchasing power of the consumers is concentrated in large quantities and, free of the *vagaries and subjective fluctuations of personal consumption,* it achieves an almost automatic *regularity and rhythmic growth.* Capital itself ultimately controls this automatic and rhythmic movement of militarist production through the legislature and a press whose function is to mould so-called 'public opinion'. That is why this particular province of capitalist accumulation at first seems capable of *infinite expansion.* All other attempts to expand markets and set up operational bases for capital largely depend on historical, social and political factors beyond the control of capital, whereas production for militarism represents a province whose *regular and progressive expansion* seems primarily determined by *capital itself.*[68]

Naturally, since the time when Rosa Luxemburg wrote in these terms about 'militarist production', we have witnessed the emergence and consolidation of the *'military/industrial complex'*, which is a qualitatively different phenomenon in its relationship to the state. However, the basic material determinations remain the same from the point of view of the capitalistic realization process, only their implementation now assumes a considerably more advanced — i.e., economically more flexible and dynamic, as well as ideologically less transparent and therefore politically less vulnerable — form.

16.1.3

In this respect, just as in many others, capital follows *the line of least resistance*. In other words, if it finds a capitalistically more viable or easier *functional equivalent* to a course of action which its own material determinations would otherwise predicate (i.e., by 'otherwise' meaning the expansion of production corresponding to the development of 'rich human need', as described by Marx), it is bound to opt for what is more obviously in keeping with its overall structural configuration, maintaining the control which it already exercises, rather than pursuing some alternative strategy that would necessitate a departure from well established practices.

Accordingly, while, *in principle,* it is true that the development of capitalist production 'requires that the *consuming circle* within circulation *expands* as did the productive circle previously',[69] a preferable functional equivalent is available to capital in the form of *accelerating* the speed of circulation within the consuming circle itself (by increasing the number of transactions in the *already given* circle), rather than embarking on the more complicated and risky venture of enlarging the circle as such.

Other things being equal, this is a much easier course from the point of view of capital. First, because the expansion of the consuming circle carries with it the difficult economic task of establishing a more elaborate commercial network that extends over some formerly untried and unsecured areas. And second, because the operation of an enlarged circle of consumption involves a far from negligible shift in the prevailing pattern of *distribution,* with all its ideological and political complications. (See in this respect in England, for instance, the sharp contrast between restricted consumption as managed by — Conservative or Liberal — Victorian paternalism, and the greatly enlarged consuming circle of the postwar era, with its *consensus politics*.[70])

Thus, only when the course corresponding to the 'line of least resistance' is unable to meet any longer the requirements of capitalistic development, only then are the alternatives pursued, so as to *displace* the underlying contradictions and thereby prevent the activation of the liberating potentials inherent in the 'socialization of production' so hopefully contemplated by Marx.

16.1.4

THE same goes for the relationhip between *absolute* and *relative surplus-value*. Undoubtedly, looking back from the vantage point of the present, it seems obvious that the ultimate dynamism of capitalistic developments cannot be explained without its more sophisticated motor of exploitation: the production of relative surplus-value. In comparison, the extortion of absolute surplus-value must appear not only crude, but also wastefully inefficient.

However, two fundamental considerations are omitted from such reasoning, and both happen to be crucial for understanding the dynamic of 'underdevelopment'.

First, that *historically* the ruthless expropriation of *absolute* surplus-value, even in its most cruel form,[71] is the necessary point of departure and material foundation for the more refined (and also ideologically more bewildering) variety of capitalist exploitation. In other words, the production and appropriation of relative surplus-value on an ever-expanding scale, in view of its being a specific mode of *re*-production, necessarily presupposes, not just analytically/conceptually but also in real historical terms, its actual material constitution — i.e., its original *production* — through the comparatively more transparent exploitative mechanism of absolute surplus-value.

Second, that even at a considerable distance from the historical phase of 'primitive accumulation', the shift to the predominance of relative surplus-value — and one can *never* speak of more than its *predominance,* since the practice of 'sweat-shop' type exploitation remains with capitalism even at its most 'advanced' stage, no matter how 'enlightened' its labour-legislation — is decidedly not the result of some 'natural progression', whatever the self-serving mystifications of capitalistically inspired developmental theories of 'modernization'. On the contrary, this shift is the outcome of hard struggles and extreme confrontations which *eventually* succeed in breaking (on this particular terrain, without necessarily affecting the others) capital's ability to follow the line of least resistance, materially *incorporating*[72] the gained concessions into the productive practices and institutional structures of capitalist society.

Naturally, when this shift is effectively accomplished, under the pressure of weighty political and economic determinations, *ipso facto* capital's line of least resistance is itself significantly redefined. Thus, the objective incorporation of the 'concessions', through a complex mechanism of 'feed-back', into a flexible set of dynamic and institutionally safeguarded[73] productive practices, significantly enlarges the boundary of capital-expansion. The powerful expansionary imperative of such developments favours in the dominant capitalist countries, for determinate periods of time, even the official adoption and successful implementation of Keynesian-type economic strategies as the temporary common denominators of structurally opposed and ultimately irreconcilable class interests.

But even so, the threat of contractionary reversals and collapses, under the name of 'monetarism' or whatever else, is always in the background even in the capitalistically most advanced societies, foreshadowing the need to intensify also the 'metropolitan' rate of exploitation in the circumstances of a major crisis. (It is at such times that labour's demands can no longer be contained within the narrow confines of contesting the relative distribution of available surplus-value: a hopeless contest from the point of view of labour against the necessary presupposition of adequate profit margins to secure investment and expansion. Accordingly, under the conditions of a structural crisis, *defensive gains* — normally accommodated well within the margins of expanding profit — are no longer feasible, and the objective of the social confrontation radically changes to contesting the hegemonic alternative between capital and labour as diametrically opposed modes of control of social reproduction.)[74]

Furthermore, the continued extortion of absolute surplus-value remains an irreplaceable constituent of the expansionary dynamism itself throughout the history of capitalistic developments, including their least problematical phases. This is clearly evidenced in the use to which 'sweat-shops', immigrant workers, 'Gastarbeitern', home-based 'piece-workers', etc., are put in the capitalistically advanced countries. Not to mention the immense material benefits which the latter continue to derive by extracting vast quantitites of surplus-value, at the highest practicable rate of exploitation, from the rest of the world.

As to the 'underdeveloped' countries themselves, their strategies of 'modernization' are nullified not only by the chronic insufficiency of 'primitive accumulation', but also by the equally grave condition that they are unable to escape from the straitjacket of absolute surplus-value as the overpowering regulator of their socioeconomic metabolism. And since they are not in a position to colonize and plunder, as well as systematically exploit ever after, the 'advanced' countries, the persistent inadequacy of capital-accumulation wedded to the preponderance of absolute surplus-value constitute a veritable vicious circle for their development.

Nor is all this as simple as some one-sided dependency theories might suggest. For while it is certainly true that the paralyzing circularity of the two fundamental deficiencies just mentioned amounts to a massive socioeconomic factor, with all its *structurally* retardatory consequences, at the same time it is also true that the postwar situation is totally unintelligible without the full complicity of the local ruling classes in producing and preserving the crippled structure of chronic underdevelopment.

To be sure, the neo-colonially safeguarded exploitation of absolute surplus-value eminently suits the interests of 'metropolitan capital' and its insatiable appetite for easily repatriable super-profits, in accordance with its line of least resistance under the circumstances. However, it should not be forgotten that the neo-colonial 'modernization' of the capitalist system of production which retains in the 'third world' the admittedly quite anachronistic preponderance of absolute surplus-value, also happens to accord well with the interests of 'underdeveloped' capital and *its* line of least resistance at the given stage of development. It is precisely on the basis of this identity of interests that the different sections of global capital can successfully operate, in full complicity with one another, the most openly exploitative and antiquated economic practices on their shared line of least resistance in the overall framework of capitalist production.

16.1.5

THE importance of these developments in our context — both as regards the successful manipulation of the 'consuming circle' and the continued extortion of absolute surplus-value — is that, as a result, capital's margin of manoeuvre is considerably *enlarged* and the maturation of its inner contradictions *postponed*. For the fact that capital can continue to accumulate by way of the most intense exploitation of absolute and relative surplus-value, and that at the same time (contrary to Marx's expectations which were well grounded in the 19th century) it is far from being inexorably driven 'to enlarge the periphery of circulation',[75] means that the limits to capital-expansion are significantly extended and the objective conditions of saturating capital's global framework of profitable operations significantly redefined. Naturally, such change in its turn also means that the tendencies which point towards the necessity of a socialist alternative are effectively *blocked* for as long as the newly created conditions prevail, enabling capital to maintain its control over the socioeconomic metabolism thanks to the suitably redrawn line of least resistance. Redrawn indeed in a way which could be hardly more contrasting with the earlier imperative to enlarge the consuming circle as such.

This is the point where we can clearly see the vital significance of the decreasing rate of utilization in twentieth century capitalist developments. For as long as the decreasing rate can profitably increase, nay multiply, the number of transactions in the already given circle, there is no reason whatsoever for taking the risk 'to enlarge the periphery of circulation'. Consequently, vast sections of the population can be safely ignored by capitalist developments even in the 'advanced' countries, not to mention the rest of the world which is kept in a state of enforced underdevelopment. Besides, the *complementarity* of the continued extortion of absolute surplus-value with no matter how great productive advances[76] secures that, inasmuch as it becomes necessary to enlarge the consuming circle in the Western capitalist countries, capital is well compensated for and needs not face the potentially most disruptive consequences of the decreasing rate of profit, since they are effectively displaced not only by monopolistic practices but also by the operation of the decreasing rate of utilization as combined with the ruthlessly exploitative mechanism of absolute surplus-value.

Moreover, since the decreasing rate of utilization opens up new possibilities for capital-expansion, it acquires a very special role in the realization process of 'advanced' capitalism. In the first place, in virtue of its ability to deal with the pressures arising from the interaction between production and consumption due to the constraining limits of the given periphery of circulation, it functions as the irreplaceable *means* to accomplish the required reproduction on an *enlarged* scale while artificially holding back the tendency to enlarge the consuming circle itself. Subsequently, however, the greater the dependency of the overall process of reproduction on the decreasing rate of utilization, the more obviously the latter becomes an *end-in-itself* in that it is perceived as the possibility of *unlimited* expansion, on the assumption that the rate itself can be lowered without ultimate hindrance. For, in ideal terms, conceptualized from capital's standpoint (in the same spirit in which under rather different historical conditions political economists postulate 'perfect competition' as the system's ideal mode of operation), the nearer the established mode of production and consuption could approximate the *zero rate* of utilization, the more scope such approximation would automatically create for continued production and unlimited expansion, having completely removed the 'dysfunctional nuisance' — or in Rosa Luxemburg's words 'the vagaries and subjective fluctuations' — of actual consumption.

No matter how *absurd* this assumption might be in its final implications, the productive practices associated with it provide a powerful operational base for capitalist developments under circumstances when the alternative course of action envisaged by Marx could only intensify capital's contradictions. The aim and orienting principle of production thus becomes: how to secure *maximum* feasible expansion (and corresponding profitability) on the basis of the *minimum* rate of utilization that maintains the *continuity* of enlarged reproduction.

As it happens, this kind of orientation in the first place spontaneously asserts itself as an objective imperative and tendency of capitalist production in *particular* firms and branches of industry well before it is conceptualized in a general form and implemented on a *comprehensive* scale through the direct involvement of various state organs. Naturally, the adoption of such an aim favours the emergence and increasing dominance of precisely those types of economic enterprise that can match up to the necessary requirements of the productive processes in question with the greatest dynamism and efficacy. As a result, under the impact of these determinations, it is not the *enlargement* of the periphery of circulation that constitutes an inexorable trend of capitalistic developments but, on the contrary, the *artificial restriction* of the consuming circle and the *exclusion* of the 'underprivileged' masses (i.e. the overwhelming majority of humankind) from it both in the 'advanced' countries and in the 'Third World', thanks to the perverse productive possibilities opened up to the capitalist system by the decreasing rate of utilization.

16.2 *The significance of the military/industrial complex*

16.2.1

THE agency willing and able to cut the Gordian knot of how to combine maximum feasible expansion with the minimum rate of utilization presented itself for capital in the shape of the military-industrial complex, following a number of failed attempts to deal with the problems of overproduction in less wasteful ways after the world economic crisis of 1929-33. Although the first steps towards finding a solution to overproduction through militarist production were taken already before the first world war, as we have seen in Rosa Luxemburg's prophetic remarks, its *general* adoption occurred only after the second world war.

Pursuing this line of orientation, the leading powers of Western capitalism took a leaf out of Hitler's book of post-1933 'economic miracles' and adapted it to the sociopolitical realities of their liberal-democratic institutions. For their earlier attempts to overcome the crisis—by the combined strategies of manipulative 'demand management' (hence the rise to prominence of Madison Avenue) on the one hand, and of 'New Deal' type state-intervention on the other — miserably failed to resolve the problem of mass unemployment and depression until well after the expansionary requirements of the war effort radically redefined the whole framework of economic activity.

Furthermore, and notwithstanding all self-serving Keynesian and neo-Keynesian mythologies to the contrary, the real material ground of expansion was the new dynamism of the military/industrial complex already in existence (even if as yet far from fully extended) at the time of the Bretton Woods agreements which the latter only helped to enhance. Thus, the various strategies of Keynesianism were *complementary* to the unhindered expansion of the military/industrial complex, rather than independently applicable to truly productive and in socialism also viable conditions. (If nothing else, this should be a warning to all those who are trying to devise—on neo-Keynesian lines—'alternative economic strategies' for the future.) After all, Keynesian theory was already fully worked out in the immediate aftermath of the 1929-33 crisis, and in its broad outlines well before that. Yet, it had to remain a cry in the wilderness — despite the author's quite exceptional establishment-connections — in the absence of a suitably wasteful, but at the same time both dynamic and ideologically respectable material vehicle of state-sponsored implementation.

Naturally, there can be no question of *uniformity* with respect to the emergence and consolidation of the military/industrial complex in the capitalistically advanced countries. Not only because the law of uneven development continues to apply to them, just as before; but also because in some instances quite special extra-economic conditions are imposed on a number of them for some time by the victors in the postwar years. Thus Japan and Germany, for instance, are restricted by their respective Peace Treaties as regards their immediate possibilities of rearmament, with unavoidable consequences for the relatively slow and selective reconstruction of their military industries.

Undoubtedly, in this respect the US military/industrial complex occupies the overwhelmingly dominant position from the very beginning, followed by Britain, France and Italy, proportionate to their relative economic possibilities. However, one should not have the illusion that the postwar economic development of Japan and Germany has nothing to do with the fortunes of the military/industrial complex. As a matter of fact, they are locked into it in more ways than one, both on the plane of their national economies and internationally. To mention the most important ways in which their own development is dependent on the postwar role of the military/industrial complex:

First, with the establishment of the new military alliances, nearly all the original Peace Treaty restrictions are quickly removed and thereby both Japan and Germany are enabled to set up and expand (practically as much as they please) their own military/industrial complexes, in virtually every field of military production, with the sole exception of nuclear armaments.

Second, since the military industry — under US hegemony — is an international enterprise, Japan and Germany participate in its postwar development from a very early stage, directly and indirectly, in a variety of forms, from optics to electronics and from chemistry to metallurgy. Such participation is of a major importance for the establishment and/or modernization of whole branches of industry on which the Japanese and German 'miracles' of postwar economic development are founded. Moreover, highly profitable direct military orders also play an important role. (As Paul Sweezy pointed it out recently in 'Economic Reminiscences: Review of the Month' — May 1995, p.5 — 'the Korean War was a turning point not only for the United States but also for Germany and Japan: the much-touted German and Japanese "miracles" both had their origins in a surge of Korean War orders'.)

Third, the close interconnection between the economies of all Western capitalist countries and the United States. This happens to be the most significant factor for assessing the true weight and importance of the military/industrial complex for the continued 'healthy' functioning of global capital. For by far the most extensive and dynamic economy of the Western world — that of the United States — is sustained in its steady expansion, throughout the postwar period, by astronomical (and notwithstanding the grave US internal and international debt maintained) defence budgets. As it happens, all advanced capitalist societies are heavily dependent for their ability to sustain the existing levels of production in their own countries on the expanding market of the United States, which in its turn is quite unthinkable without securing those astronomical defence budgets (and deficits) on which the expansionary dynamic of the US economy as a whole so heavily relies.

These considerations — which also help to explain the Western attitude to the US debt problem — apply to Japan and Germany no less than to all the other capitalistically advanced countries. Thus, even in the case of the countries in which the *direct* share of the local military/industrial complex in the national economy is relatively small (compared to the US and a few others), the continued productive expansion of the national economies concerned cannot be separated from the global importance of militarist production in the sense just described, with regard to their apparently incurable dependency on the US economy and on the preponderant military/industrial complex within the latter.

16.2.2

THE great innovation of the military/industrial complex for capitalistic developments is to obliterate in a practically effective way the literally vital distinction between *consumption* and *destruction*. This 'innovation' offers a radical solution to a contradiction inherent in self-positing value as such in all its forms, even though becoming acute only under the conditions of contemporary capitalism.

The contradiction here referred to arises from the various objective *barriers* to self-expanding wealth which must be transcended at all costs if value as an independent operational force is to realize itself in accordance with the intrinsic determinations of its nature. This is why in imperial Rome, as Marx noted, alienated and independent value as consumption-oriented wealth

> appears as *limitless waste* which logically attempts to raise consumption to an imaginary boundlessness by *gulping down salads of pearls* etc.[77]

The problem at stake is twofold. First, it concerns society's *limited resources* and hence the necessity of *legitimating* their allocation between not merely feasible but actually competing alternatives. And second, it has to do with the constitution of the *consumer* himself; that is to say, with all the natural and socioeconomic as well as cultural *limitations of his appetites*.

The military/industrial complex successfully addresses itself to both of these fundamental constraints. For, with regard to the first dimension, while contemplating the ancient Roman practice of 'conspicuous waste' which takes the form of 'gulping down salads of pearls', the conclusion as to its decadent gratuitousness is irresistible, whereas the truly limitless waste of 'gulping down' resources equivalent to billions of such salads over the years, while countless millions have to endure starvation as their inescapable 'fate', succeeds in legitimating itself as totally unquestionable patriotic duty.

Similarly, in relation to the second vital aspect, the military/industrial complex successfully removes the traditional constraints of the consuming circle as defined by the limitations of the consumers' appetites. In this respect it cuts the highly entangled Gordian knot of 'advanced' capitalism by restructuring the framework of production and consumption in such a way as to remove for all intents and purposes the need for real consumption. In other words, it allocates a massive and ever-increasing portion of society's material and human resources to a parasitic and *self-consuming* form of production which is so radically divorced from, and indeed opposed to, actual human need and corresponding consumption that it can envisage as its own *rationale* and ultimate end even the total destruction of mankind.

16.2.3

IT cannot be stressed enough, capital did not simply *stumble* upon the solutions structurally embodied in the institutional articulation and productive practices of the military/industrial complex. On the contrary, one can identify here a fateful consistency and direction in the sense that the determinations and imperatives which culminated in the 'solutions' which we have just seen, originally surfaced at a very early stage of capitalistic developments, even if in a very different form. For capitalism as such is built on the insoluble contradiction between use-value and exchange-value, stipulating the necessary, and ultimately most destructive, subordination of the former to the latter. This contradiction manifests itself from the very beginning also as an intractable problem of *legitimation* to which the apologists of capital's iniquitous system of 'possessive individualism' can offer solutions only in the form of sophistry and mystification, from the cerebralized deduction and rationalization of the exploitative use of money and 'tacit consent' by the founding father of Liberalism, John Locke,[78] to the fictitious 'consumer Sovereignty' of so-called 'marginal utility theory'.

Similarly, the constraints arising from the practical limitations of the consumer's appetites are resented and brushed aside, as much as feasible, throughout the history of capitalism. Attempts of this kind, in fact, grow in intensity parallel to the unfolding of capital's productive potentialities. As we have seen with reference to Mandeville's work, the 'protestant work ethic' and its condemnation of 'luxury' could *never* represent more than one side of the coin. By the time we reach the epoch of 'planned obsolescence', it seems hard to believe that anybody could ever have paid even the slightest attention to such rules of conduct.

To be sure, in this respect too, capital's opposition to its own limitations has to assume a contradictory form. Hence the earlier mentioned telling approval of higher wages for the workers of *other capitalists* — the welcome purchasers of what one offers for sale — coupled with the exhortation of the virtues of wage-restraint in the name of 'cost-effectiveness' and 'sound house-keeping': sanctimonious rationalizations of the dominant partial interests dressed up as universal values. And since the expansion of exchange-value is the fundamental concern of this society, every form of mystification is used to pretend that the production of an ever-increasing quantity of exchange-value, no matter how obviously wasteful, is in full agreement with the best principles of 'economic rationality', efficaciously corresponding to some 'real demand'.

Accordingly, the question of *real use* is conjured away and the mere act of *commercial transaction* becomes the only relevant criterion of 'consumption', thereby characteristically conflating the concepts of *use* and *exchange*. Thus, just as we have witnessed earlier the self-serving and totally mystifying equation of the *'producer'* with the *capitalist,* so as to eliminate from the stage the embarrassing real producer, the worker, here we are presented with the tendentious identification of the *purchaser* with the *'consumer'* so-called.

Thanks to this latter mystification, two delicate problems are conveniently solved with one stroke. First, the question whether there is some real consumption — corresponding to human need — subsequent to the necessary preliminary step of 'contractual' transaction, cannot even arise, since the very act of transferring the commodity to the new owner in exchange for money to be reinvested, completes capital's circuit of enlarged reproduction. And second, commodities can now be *heaped up* without any difficulty of justification, since the act of purchase itself can, in principle, 'consume' an *unlimited* quantity of goods (without consuming in reality *anything at all*) in view of the fact that it is not tied to the necessarily limited appetites of real human beings.

In this sense it is by no means accidental that Locke is so preoccupied with making a speedy transition from *real use* — in his view narrowly and wastefully circumscribed by the constraints of nature as evidenced both in the perishability of the objects to be consumed and in the limitations of human appetites themselves — to the *pseudo-consumption* emanating from the 'use of money by common consent'. For the latter provides, according to him, the justifiable ground for 'heaping up' and 'hoarding up' wealth, so that 'a man may rightfully, and without injury, possess more than he himself can make use of by receiving gold and silver, which may continue long in a man's possession without decaying for the overplus.'[79] Indeed, by putting the cart before the horse, Locke can even misrepresent the artificial and iniquitous practices of hoarding up social wealth and excluding others from its benefits as being in full agreement with, nay as directly arising from, nature itself. For he argues that: 'Find out something that hath the use and value of money amongst his neighbours, you shall see the same man will begin presently to enlarge his possessions.'[80]

It is in this respect truly ironical in which way the circle from Locke's age to the present is completed, and the original ground of justification of the dominant productive practices completely overturned. For Locke's principal argument (favouring the use of money and justifying the grossly iniquitous accumulation of wealth) was that together they *eliminate waste,* which obviously must be in the interest of every single member of society. However, by the time the system of accumulation championed by Locke reaches its full articulation, waste is no longer a regrettable marginal aspect of the way in which this system functions, but an integral and deliberately cultivated part of it. Indeed, waste is very far from being restricted in it to the perishable products of nature. On the contrary, it runs riot in all areas of production and consumption, thereby completely destroying all those justifications (and rationalizations) which Locke could marshall in his deductions in favour of the system. The alleged guarantor of the properly economic use of the available resources — the accumulable and successfully self-enlarging wealth, said to be activated by the 'durability' of money — turns out to be the greatest enemy of durability as such and the agency of utter wastefulness. Ironically, it succeeds in the end in 'raising consumption to an imaginary boundlessness' by inventing the instant perishability of even the most durable material substances: by 'working them up' in the form of the instruments of war and destruction, which happen to be wasteful/destructive of human resources in the extreme, even if they are never used at all.

16.2.4

THE military/industrial complex not only perfects the ways in which capital can now deal with all these structural limitations and contradictions, but also makes a 'quantum leap' in the sense that the scope and the sheer size of its profitable operations becomes incomparably larger than could be conceived at earlier stages of capitalistic developments. This quantum leap creates formerly unimaginable outlets, qualitatively modifying thereby the relation of forces in capital's favour for a period directly proportional to the size of the newly created productive outlets themselves.

If the mystifications and deceits of earlier stages resembled the rather crude means and methods of the penny-cheating shopkeeper (who could be found out anyway with relative ease), their equivalents under 'advanced capitalism' are only comparable to some multinational swindle of gigantic proportions, involved in the manipulation of astronomical sums between computer terminals and the cover up of even the most fraudulent transactions[81] thanks to an ideologically well buttressed institutional network in which the activities of the embezzler, paymaster, auditor, law-maker and judge are all rolled into one.

Accordingly, if a major portion of the available resources is openly allocated for waste-production, equating the production of the means of destruction with production full stop, all this must take place, of course, strictly for the unobjectionable purpose of 'providing much needed jobs'. Nor need one reckon any more with the difficulties due to the constraints of human appetites and personal income. For the 'consumer' is no longer simply the available aggregate of limited individuals. Indeed, thanks to the major transformation of the dominant productive structures of postwar capitalist society, coupled with the corresponding realignment of their relationship to the capitalist state (both for economic purposes and for securing the necessary ideological/political legitimation), from now on the mythically fused producer/purchaser/consumer is nothing less than 'The Nation' itself.

This happens to be another fundamental innovation of the military/industrial complex. For while the former misrepresentation of the *purchaser* as the *consumer* could only push aside the embarrassing question of human appetites and the traditional requirement of producing goods with real use corresponding to such appetites, it was not suitable to offer solutions to the financial constraints attached to individual 'consumer Sovereignty' as frustrating the alienated expansionary needs of the capitalist realization process itself. Only 'The Nation' could promise to satisfy the dual requirements of providing an inexhaustible purse on the one hand, in order to make possible capital's enlarged self-reproduction, and a bottomless pit, on the other, to swallow up all the resulting waste.

16.2.5

THE consequences of the changes and perverse innovations here surveyed could not be more disturbing as regards the positive anticipations quoted in Section 16.1.2 from the *Grundrisse*. Indeed, if we adopt an optimistic reading of Marx's conceptual exploration of capital's productive potentialities, we are likely to end up with a greatly distorted overall picture of the actual trends of development. For in the course of the last century, and in particular in the postwar period, capital's line of least resistance has been forcefully reconstituted in such a way that the expansion of the periphery of circulation and the growth of use-value corresponding to human need is no longer a necessary requirement of expanded reproduction. On the contrary, thanks to the ongoing transformations and structural adjustments, *other things being equal,*[82] it becomes possible to nullify, or at least significantly to claw back, labour's earlier acquisitions from the margins of relative surplus-value even in the capitalistically most advanced countries without suddenly endangering the realization process itself. After all, one should not forget that the military/industrial complex *versus* the Welfare State is not merely a crying *contradiction* of contemporary capitalism. It is simultaneously also an effective, even if by no means permanent, *solution* to some of capital's self-reproducing contradictions, in the customary form of their displacement. The recent 'resoluteness' and ensuing successes of the so-called 'Radical Right' — this arch-conservative ideological legitimator and political standard-bearer of the dominant class interests — indicate both the urgency of the underlying determinations and the ability of the ruling order to pursue a course that actually reverses the postwar trend 'to enlarge the periphery of circulation' without seriously disrupting, for the time being at least, the socioeconomic metabolism of Western capitalism.

Since capital as such is totally devoid of a humanly meaningful frame of reference and measure with regard to its self-expansionary production targets, the shift from *consumption-orientated* production to 'consumption' through *destruction* can come about without any major difficulty at the plane of production itself. At the same time, the obstacles to the necessary ideological/political rationalization and legitimation of such changes can be readily dismantled through the manipulation of 'public opinion' and the joint control of the mass media by the dominant private interests and the capitalist state.

Moreover, the method of solving the accumulated problems by activating the mechanisms of destruction is by no means something radically new, appearing only with the recent development of capitalism. On the contrary, that is precisely the way in which capital succeeded, throughout its history, in extricating itself from situations of crisis: i.e., by unceremoniously destroying overproduced and no longer viable units of capital, thereby conveniently both increasing the concentration and centralization of capital and reconstituting the overall profitability of total social capital. The innovation of 'advanced' capitalism and of its military/industrial complex is that now the earlier practice — catering for the exceptional and emergency requirements of crises — is *generalized* and turned into the *model of normality* for the everyday life of the whole system oriented towards production for destruction as a matter of course, in conformity with the tendential law of the decreasing rate of utilization capable of approaching, in theory, the *zero rate*.

This new-found normality of the capitalist system enables it to *displace* (but, of course, not to *eliminate*) a fundamental contradiction of developed capital: overproduction. For, thanks to the ability of the military/industrial complex to *impose* its needs on society, the age-old wishful thinking of bourgeois political economy — the claimed identity of supply and demand — is manipulatively realized, *for the time being,* within its framework.

Marx rightly took to task the political economists who tried to conjure away

the contradiction between production and consumption by suggesting that:
supply and demand are ... identical, and should therefore necessarily correspond. *Supply,* namely, is allegedly *a demand measured by its own amount.*[83]
However, what the political economists could only dream about is now successfully implemented *by decree* of the all-powerful military/industrial complex acting in unison with the capitalist state.

Thus both supply and demand are cynically relativized, so as to enable the *legitimation of actual supply by fictitious 'demand'.* As a result, the supply in question (no matter how wasteful, dangerous, unwanted and destructive) is forcibly imposed upon society by unchallengeable legal devices and becomes the supreme 'demand of the Nation'. It is, indeed, truly and effectively *'measured by its own amount',*[84] and protected by the more than obliging state against the limitations of even the most elementary (but of course rather inconvenient) capitalistic criteria of 'rational cost-accounting' by inflation-proof annual military budget increases, at the expense of all social services and real human need.

16.2.6
THANKS to all these shifts and changes, capital acquires a new mode of managing the objective determinations of socioeconomic development, including its own contradictions at the plane of the crucial interplay between production and consumption, minimizing for an entire historical period even the most severe implications of the latter for the eruption of crises. Accordingly, since setting in motion and 'scientifically' exploiting the mechanisms of destruction corresponds to capital's line of least resistance, in direct opposition to the expansion of humanly meaningful use-value, *none* of the theoretically feasible positive features of capital's productive development anticipated in the earlier quote from the *Grundrisse* need come to fruition within the productive boundaries of this social formation.

In this sense, the 'severe discipline of capital, acting on succeeding generations' can *never* bring about a state where one could characterize society as having appropriated 'general industriousness'. Nor indeed is capital likely to produce an all-comprehensive and constantly richer consuming circle, as well as a *development of needs* corresponding to the latter through which 'surplus labour above and beyond necessity' can become a 'general need arising out of individual needs themselves'. Such objectives not only cannot be achieved within the social horizons of the capitalist mode of production, but even the earlier trend towards realizing their most elementary preconditions suffers a grave setback when capital's line of least resistance begins to stipulate the ruthless ejection of a growing number of people from the labour process even in the most 'advanced' capitalist countries, instead of embracing the totality of mankind in the effective pursuit of general industriousness and genuine productivity.

The same reversal applies to the development of science and the transformation of productive practices in accordance with its inherent potentialities which were meant to favour the expansion of use-value and the dialectical interaction of progressively expanding use-value with the unfolding of human needs. For, as a result of capital's new requirements and determinations, *science* is diverted from its positive objectives and assigned the role of helping to multiply the forces and modalities of destruction, both directly, on the payroll of the ubiquitous and catastrophically wasteful military/industrial complex,[85] and indirectly, in the service of 'planned obsolescence' and other ingenious manipulative practices, devised for keeping the wolves of overproduction from the door in the consumer-industries.

In the same way, the alienated needs and perverse productive requirements of capital's self-realization not only do not allow the creation of the *material elements* of the rich individuality which is as all-sided in its production as in its consumption'; nor indeed the full development of human needs and potentialities (which is primarily a social/cultural challenge) but, on the contrary, the *artificial needs* of destructive capital-expansion tend to compete with, to undermine, and in the frequent event of incompatibilities to suppress with utmost callousness even the most elementary needs of by far the greater part of mankind. Understandably, therefore, the production of a *'constantly greater abundance'* becomes an ever more elusive dream — the ever-receding light at the end of the ever-lengthening tunnel — notwithstanding the staggering increase in society's *abstractly* 'productive' powers, which are condemned to remain abstract and sterile, nay *counter-productive,* because of their capitalistic social embeddedness and destructive dissipation.

16.3 From 'great thunderstorms' to a depressed continuum: crisis-management and capital's destructive self-reproduction

16.3.1

PERHAPS the most significant and far-reaching aspect of capital's successful redefinition of its own line of least resistance (and thereby the temporary displacement of its contradictions) concerns the radically new way of managing crises, compared to the not too distant past. Here, again, a quotation from the *Grundrisse* is most instructive. In his discussion of the contradiction between *production and consumption* (or *production and exchange*) under capitalism, and of the one-sided perception of the problems at stake by bourgeois political economists, notably Ricardo and Sismondi, Marx writes:

> Ricardo himself, of course, has a suspicion that the exchange value of a commodity is not a value apart from exchange, and that it proves itself as a value only in exchange; but he regards the barriers which production thereby encounters as accidental, as barriers which are overcome. He therefore conceives the overcoming of such barriers as being in the essence of capital, although he often becomes absurd in the exposition of that view; while Sismondi, by contrast, emphasizes not only the encounter with the barriers, but their creation by capital itself, and has a vague intuition that they must lead to its *breakdown.* He therefore wants to put up barriers to production, from the outside, through custom, law etc., which of course, as merely external and artificial barriers, would necessarily be demolished by capital. On the other side, Ricardo and his entire school never understood the really *modern crises,* in which this contradiction of capital *discharges itself in great thunderstorms* which increasingly threaten it as the *foundation of society and of production itself.*[86]

To be sure, the contradiction here described by Marx is an insurmountable contradiction of capitalist society. The dramatic change, though, in contrast to Marx's fitting characterization of the earlier phases of development, is that capitalist crises under the new conditions — *so long* as the material and ideological/political prerequisites of the latter can be objectively reproduced — need not take at all the form whereby the contradiction between production and exchange 'discharges itself in *great thunderstorms*'.

IT is this new-found ability of capital to avoid thunderstorms under the present circumstances that has been misconceived by Marcuse and others as a fundamental structural remedy. In their view the radically altered nature of the prevailing conditions is characterized by the 'integration' of the working classes and the triumph of 'organized capitalism' over the contradictions of 'crisis capitalism'.[87]

In truth, however, 'organized capitalism' is by no means less burdened with crises than so-called 'crisis capitalism'. Quite the contrary. For, as a matter of fact, the elaboration and perfection of the methods of 'crisis management' came about in direct response to the pressures of a deepening crisis.

Also, it is quite wrong to suggest (as Lucien Goldmann does, following in the footsteps of Marcuse) that 'we have arrived at a particular turning in the evolution of Western society, *a turning marked by the appearance of self-regulating economic mechanisms*',[88] since capitalism, in fact, has *always* been ruled by its historically specific self-regulating mechanisms. Indeed, the self-assertive power of such mechanisms is absolutely *inseparable* from the capitalist socioecomic formation as such and constitutes one of its most important defining characteristics as a specific form of social control.

The real innovation of postwar developments in the present context can be pinpointed in the shift from the traditional pattern of consumption to a very different type in which the interests of the military/industrial complex predominate. The new system is characterized by the institutionalized under-utilization of both productive powers and products on the one hand, and by the ongoing, constant rather than sudden, dissipation or destruction of the results of over-production through a practical redefinition of the supply/demand relationship in the suitably restructured production process itself on the other hand. It is precisely this major shift in the relationship between production and consumption that enables capital to do away, *for the time being,* with the spectacular collapses of the past, like the dramatic Wall Street crash of 1929. In this way, however, the crises of capital are by no means radically overcome but merely '*spread out*', both in a *temporal* sense and with regard to their *structural* location in the overall framework.

Admittedly, *so long* as the present relationship between the dominant interests and the capitalist state prevails and successfully imposes its demands on society, there will be no big thunderstorms, at fairly distant intervals, but precipitations of increasing frequency and intensity all over the place. Thus, the former '*abnormality*' of crises — once alternating with much longer periods of undisturbed growth and productive development — under the present conditions can become in smaller daily doses the *normality* of 'organized capitalism'. Indeed, the peaks of capital's historically well known *periodic crises* could be — *in principle* — replaced altogether by a linear pattern of movement.

It would be, however, a great mistake to read the absence of extreme fluctuations or suddenly erupting thunderstorms as the evidence of a healthy and sustainable development, rather than as the representation of a *depressed continuum*, exhibiting the characteristics of a *cumulative, endemic,* more or less *permanent* and *chronic* crisis, with the ultimate perspectives of an ever-deepening *structural crisis*.

16.3.2

IN the final analysis, the institutionally safeguarded structural integration and diffusion of the objective components of the capitalist crisis — which we have been witnessing now for quite some time — does not decrease their weight and severity, no matter how effective it may be in its function of displacement and 'equalization'.

Perfecting the machinery of 'crisis management' is an essential part of capital's successful reconstitution of its line of least resistance, enabling it to confront its inherent limits and displace its major contradictions with greater effectiveness under the present historical circumstances. Equally, there can be no doubt that to counter capital's new acquisitions and powerful innovations will require the articulation of new strategies by the socialist forces at present thoroughly baffled by their adversary's ability to keep under control the traditional determinants and manifestations of its own crises.

Nevertheless, the limits of capital remain structurally untranscendable and its contradictions *ultimately explosive,* notwithstanding the postwar record of commodity society in *temporarily* overcoming those limits, as well as in 'diffusing' and de-fusing the contradictions.

The limits of capital are not statically given but represent a dynamic challenge to both capital and labour. Indeed, its ultimate limits manifest themselves as the limits to expanded reproduction, and it is in the innermost nature of capital to confront them so as to subdue them, in a restless drive forward, irrespective of the consequences. However, as Marx forcefully stressed:

> From the fact that capital posits every such limit as a *barrier* and hence gets *ideally* beyond it, it does not follow that it has *really* overcome it, and, since every such barrier contradicts its character, its production moves in contradictions which are constantly overcome but just as constantly posited. Furthermore. The *universality* towards which it irresistibly strives encounters *barriers in its own nature,* which will at a certain stage of its development, allow it to be *recognized* as being itself the greatest barrier to this tendency, and hence *will drive towards its own suspension.*[89]

AND yet, it is necessary to voice some words of caution. Not so much with regard to the optimistic anticipations of the last sentence which do not directly concern us in the present context. In any case, Rosa Luxemburg put the records straight in this respect when she insisted on the dramatic alternative between *'socialism or barbarism'*. For capital can, at best, only drive forward to the point of presenting us with the alternative itself, but not towards its resolution by its own suspension. Rather the opposite, in that capital's perilous inner logic can drive it towards resolving the alternative only in its own favour, radically aborting the prospects of a socialist outcome through its barbarous material determinations.

The point at issue here concerns the dominant modality in which contemporary capitalism can impose its structural imperatives (and ensuing crises) on society with the help of the increasingly more interventionist state. As we have seen, 'organized capitalism' is not less but more deeply affected by crises than so-called 'crisis capitalism'. Yet, it seems to be able to cope with difficulties and emergencies of formerly unimaginable magnitude as a matter of course. The barriers which capital 'encounters in its own nature' with regard to both production and consumption do not seem to affect significantly its power of self-expansion. Also, its manifest failure to accomplish at the plane of production the 'universality towards which it irresistibly strives' does not seem to undermine its power of universal social domination, even in the productively most under-developed regions.

To understand these bewildering characteristics of contemporary capitalism, a vital distinction must be drawn between *production* and *self-reproduction*. The reason why this distinction is so important is because capital is not in the least concerned with production as such, but only with *self-reproduction*. Likewise, capital's 'irresistible drive towards universality' only concerns its tendency to global expansion in the interest of its self-reproduction, but not the interests of humanly meaningful and rewarding production.

Naturally, under determinate historical circumstances capital's expanded self-reproduction and genuine production can in a positive sense *coincide,* and while they do, the capitalist system can fulfil its 'civilizing role' of increasing the productive powers of society and spur on, up to the point not only permitted but also dictated by its own interests, the emergence of 'general industriousness'. However, the necessary conditions of genuine production, and those of capital's enlarged self-reproduction, not only need not always coincide but, on the contrary, may even diametrically oppose one another.

In sharp contrast to the predominantly productive social articulation of capital in Marx's lifetime, contemporary capitalism has reached the stage where the *radical disjunction* of genuine production and capital's self-reproduction is no longer some remote possibility but a cruel reality, with the most devastating implications for the future. For the barriers to capitalist production today are overcome by capital itself in the form of securing its own reproduction — to an already large and constantly growing extent — inescapably as *destructive self-re-production,* in antagonistic opposition to genuine *production*.

In this sense, capital's limits can no longer be conceptualized as merely the material obstacles to a greater increase in productivity and social wealth, and thus as a *brake* on development, but as the direct challenge to the very survival of mankind. And in another sense, the limits of capital can turn against it as the overpowering controller of the social metabolism not when its interests collide with the general social interest of increasing the powers of genuine production — the first impact of such collision could be felt, in fact, a long time ago — but only when capital is no longer able to secure, by whatever means, the conditions of its *destructive self-reproduction* and thereby causes the breakdown of the overall social metabolism.

As we have seen before, capital is totally devoid of a humanly meaningful measure and framework of orientation, while its inner drive for self-expansion is apriori incompatible with the concepts of checks and limits, let alone with that of a positive *self-transcendence*. This is why it corresponds to capital's line of least resistance to carry the material practices of *destructive enlarged self-reproduc-*

tion to the point where they raise the spectre of global destruction, instead of accepting the required positive restraints in the interest of production for the satisfaction of human need.

ONCE upon a time contemplating the production of *abundance* and the supersession of *scarcity* was thoroughly compatible with the capitalistic processes and aspirations. Today such objectives, within the horizons of capitalist 'development' and 'modernization', only appear in the ideological rationalizations of the established system's most cynical apologists. This fact alone, if nothing else, tells us a great deal about the real meaning of capital's structural reconstitution — in close conjunction with the corresponding adjustments in the directly and indirectly supportive operation of the capitalist state — in the last few decades.

Way back, in the age of Mandeville, the main concern with regard to the role of the state was, as we have seen, to use its power inside the country so that 'Property should be well secured' and that 'the Poor should be kept strictly to work'; and internationally, in order to sustain the forces of capital in their enterprise of colonial expansion, in the interest of the growing wealth of the 'large stirring Nations'.

Today the situation is radically different. Not in relation to 'securing Property' and 'keeping the Poor strictly to work': objectives that must remain the permanent concern of the system as long as the capitalist mode of production and its state formations survive. The radical difference is visible in this that the capitalist state must now assume a direct interventionist role at *all planes* of social life, actively promoting and managing the destructive consumption and dissipation of social wealth on a monumental scale. For without such *direct intervention* in the social metabolic process, no longer only in a situation of emergency but on a *continuous basis,* the extreme wastefulness of the contemporary capitalist system could not be maintained in existence.

CHAPTER SEVENTEEN

CHANGING FORMS OF THE RULE OF CAPITAL

17.1 *The meaning of capital in the Marxian conception*

17.1.1

TO understand and appreciate Marx's approach to the nature of capital and of the social formation dominated by the imperatives of ever-extended capital production, it is necessary to bear in mind the fundamental methodological principles which guide his analyses. They are made explicit in a key passage of the *Grundrisse* as follows:

> Bourgeois society is the most developed and the most complex historical organization of production. The categories which express its relations, the comprehension of its structure, thereby also allow insights into the structure and the relations of production of all the vanished social formations out of whose ruins and elements it built itself up, whose partly still unconquered remnants are carried along within it, whose mere nuances have developed explicit significance within it, etc. *Human anatomy contains a key to the anatomy of the ape*. The intimations of higher development among the subordinate animal species, however, can be understood *only after the higher development is already known*. The bourgeois economy thus supplies the key to the ancient, etc. But not at all in the manner of those economists who smudge over all historical differences and *see bourgeois relations in all forms of society*. One can understand tribute, tithe, etc., if one is acquainted with ground rent. But one must not identify them. Further, since bourgeois society is itself only a *contradictory* form of development, relations derived from earlier forms will often be found within it only in an entirely stunted form, or even travestied. For example, *communal* property. Although it is true, therefore, that the categories of bourgeois economics possess a truth for all other forms of society, this is to be taken only with a grain of salt. They can contain them in a developed, or stunted, or caricatured form etc., but always with an essential difference. The *so-called historical presentation of development* is founded, as a rule, on the fact that the latest form regards the previous ones as steps leading up to itself, and, since it is only rarely and only under quite specific conditions able to *criticize itself* — leaving aside, of course, the historical periods which appear to themselves as times of decadence — it always *conceives them one-sidedly*. The Christian religion was able to be of assistance in reaching an objective understanding of earlier mythologies only when its own self-criticism had been accomplished to a certain degree, so to speak *dynamei*. Likewise, bourgeois economics arrived at an understanding of feudal, ancient, oriental economics only after the *self-criticism of bourgeois society* had begun. In so far as the bourgeois economy did not mythologically identify itself altogether with the past, its critique of the previous economies, notably of feudalism, with which it was still engaged in direct struggle, resembled the critique which Christianity levelled against paganism, or also that of Protestantism against Catholicism.
>
> In the succession of the economic categories, as in any other historical, social science, it must not be forgotten that their subject — here, modern bourgeois society — is

always what is given, in the head as well as in reality, and that these *categories* therefore express the *forms of being, the characteristics of existence,* and often only individual sides of this specific society, this subject, and that therefore *this society by no means begins only at the point where one can speak of it as such;* this holds for science as well. This is to be kept in mind because it will shortly be decisive for the order and sequence of the categories. ... *Capital* is the *all-dominating* economic power of bourgeois society. It must form the *starting point* as well as the *finishing point.* ... It would therefore be unfeasible and wrong to let the economic categories follow one another in the same sequence as that in which they were *historically* decisive. Their *sequence* is determined, rather, by their relation to one another in modern *bourgeois society,* which is precisely the *opposite* of that which seems to be their natural order or which corresponds to *historical* development. ... The purity (abstract specificity) in which the trading peoples — Phoenicians, Carthaginians — appear in the old world is determined precisely by the predominance of the agricultural peoples. Capital, as *trading-capital,* or *money-capital,* appears in this abstraction precisely where *capital is not yet the predominant element* of societies. Lombards, Jews take up the same position towards the agricultural societies of the Middle Ages. ...The order obviously has to be (1) the *general abstract determinants* which obtain in more or less all forms of society, but in the above-explained sense. (2) The categories which make up the *inner structure* of bourgeois society and on which the fundamental classes rest. Capital, wage labour, landed property. Their inner relations. Town and country. The three great social classes. Exchange between them. Circulation. Credit system (private). (3) Concentration of bourgeois society in the form of the *state.* Viewed in relation to itself. The 'unproductive' classes. Taxes. State debt. Public order. The population. The colonies. Emigration. (4) The *international* relations of production. International division of labour. International exchange. Export and import. Rate of exchange. (5) The *world market and crises.*[90]

As we know, several parts of the Marxian project as summed up here could not be completed by him. Regrettably, only the problems enumerated under (2) were worked out in detail in Marx's published books and posthumous manuscripts; but even among those the fundamental question of class relations were hardly touched upon, since the manuscript of the third volume of *Capital* broke off at the very beginning of his discussion of the subject. Nevertheless, Marx's general approach to the whole complex of problems to be investigated is clear enough in the passage quoted above. It shows us the reasons behind the choice Marx made in concentrating on the categories required for understanding the inner structure of the social order from which the transition to a qualitatively different system of societal reproduction had to be made if humanity was to survive.

The important methodological principle adopted by Marx — that in investigating the essential defining characteristics of the most advanced, bourgeois, form of economy the key to the 'anatomy of the ape' must be sought in human anatomy, and not vice versa, as the purportedly historical but in reality most unhistorical approaches to the subject attempted to do — enables him to put at the centre of his analysis capital as the *all-dominating* power of the existing social metabolic order. This choice is made in order to be able to demonstrate both the *positive* aspects of this reproductive system, which made capital prevail as the *all-dominating* power of society, and the *negative* ones which are bound to lead to its disintegration. This is why capital in its *fully developed form* 'must form the *starting point* as well as the *finishing point*'.

Naturally, the adoption of this course of analysis does not mean that in Marx's view the *historical antecedents* of the capital system do not matter, or that *capital* somehow suddenly appears with the *capitalist* formation, springing out of the clouds of mystery as Pallas Athene from the head of Zeus. On the contrary, as Marx shows in various contexts, all aspects of capital's fully developed form — including the commodification of labour power, which is the most important step in reaching the most developed, capitalist, form — appear to some degree in history a long time before the capitalist phase, some of them thousands of years earlier. Concentrating on the fully developed form is necessary both for showing the tendency toward the system's dissolution and as part of the Marxian critique of political economy. For, as regards the latter, the historical *specificity* and the necessary *transience* of the capital system is apologetically denied by all those — from the 18th century to the theories of Max Weber, Hayek, and their followers — who use the *partial* and *sporadic* historical antecedents of capital as an *all-dominating system* in order to *eternalize* the *capitalist* mode of controlling humanity's social metabolic reproduction.

As usual, the apologists of capital ascribe their own sins to Marx, so as to be able to absolve themselves of such sins by implication, by perversely condemning him. Thus, economic determinists as they actually are, in that they uncritically identify themselves with the standpoint and interests of capital, they condemn Marx as an 'economic determinist' — for having dared to expose the self-expansionary economic determinism of their cherished system. In the same way, they accuse Marx of putting an 'end to history' in his references to a future socialist order — because he dared to demonstrate the inner contradictions and the disintegrating tendencies of the still all-dominating capital system. In reality when they themselves 'smudge over all historical differences and *see bourgeois relations in all forms of society*', they are the ones who put an end to the historical dynamics. For by suppressing the *specificities* of the partial historical antecedents of the existing socioeconomic system, they end up liquidating the historical dynamics altogether, in that they make the historical process culminate in the, forever frozen, capitalist present. The present, in their view, cannot be considered historically specific and *transient* precisely on that score, as the claimed culmination and final consummation of all history. In complete contrast, Marx — who is supposed to have put an end to history — insists on the irrepressibility of the historical dynamics when he emphasises the specificity of *both the antecedents and the fully developed form* of capital production, and thereby offers a view of historical time which is *open-ended* in the direction of the *future* no less than in that of the *past*.

Terminating history in the present must destroy the historical character even of the events and processes leading to it, turning them into some kind of *predestination* which is meant to justify the acceptance of the present, whether in the form of resignation (if the thinker in question is man enough to acknowledge its negative and problematical aspects) or in the form of a more or less mindless apologetic glorification of the existent. Also in this respect, everything seems to appear in history first in a tragic form and at a later stage as a farce. Thus, the Hegelian termination of history goes with a great philosopher's recognition and resigned acknowledgement of 'tragedy in the realm of the ethical', as we have seen before. By contrast, the uncritical self-identification of many 20th century thinkers with the *standpoint of all-dominating capital* produces the farcical celebration of not only the morally unjustifiable but, self-contradictorily, also of what should be considered unsustainable even in the economic terms of the established social reproductive order itself which they want to perpetuate.

The combative dimension of Marx's critique of the 'eternalizing' tendencies of bourgeois political economy and philosophy is thus inseparable from the methodological principles adopted by him at the precise junction of historical development when he conceived his work. The 'categories of being' *(Daseinsformen)* of developed capitalist society are the necessary *'starting point as well as the finishing point'* of his approach. On this conceptual basis the whole of the Marxian analysis was intended to be carried to its conclusion, in relation to the problems enumerated under points (4) and (5), by demonstrating the insoluble structural crisis of the system, which he expected to unfold through the antagonisms emanating from the international division of labour and the world market. This is one of the main reasons why the idea of 'socialism in one country' had to be a non-starter for Marx. Furthermore, in the passage quoted above Marx also indicated that some of the categories which had to be analysed in *Capital,* as the categorial forms of relations derived from earlier forms of development, are preserved in the modern bourgeois order 'in an entirely stunted, travestied, or caricatured form' — 'for example, communal property', in his words, and indeed the stunted/travestied character of productively advanced social labour as such under the rule of capital. Consequently, given the *contradictory* character of the advanced capitalist order firmly put into relief by Marx, absolutely fundamental changes were required in order to make the inherited productive powers suitable to serve the aims of the freely associated producers in the alternative social metabolic order envisaged by him. For without the radical supersession of the 'stunted/travestied' character and antagonistic structural determinations of the formerly prevailing social division of labour the power of capital would reassert itself and nullify all socialist aims.

In the analysis of the fully developed productive and distributive relations of capital the historical antecedents could be rightly treated as subordinate moments of the present, using the methodological principle expressed with reference to the 'anatomy of the ape'. For under a given social metabolic order, as it actually functions, all of the past relations and historical antecedents which were in any affinity with the now effectively ruling order are already *subsumed,* as its subordinate determinations, whether in a more developed — i.e. positively incorporated — or in a 'stunted, travestied or caricatured form'. All this, however, radically changes in the event of the overthrow of the system in question through a socialist-inspired *political revolution.*

At that point, when many formerly consolidated relations become fluid and the *possibility* of creating alternative structures through a sustained *social revolution* arises, the inherited capitalist forms refuse, with all their might, to be consigned to the position of the ape. And more than that, in the new situation also the once subservient 'apes' actively side with the temporarily displaced former all-dominating power. Indeed, in the immediate postrevolutionary situation capital and its constituents all become flying dragons, spitting fire at all those who try to change the old order in the earlier form of which also the subordinate moments were firmly integrated and possessed their subsidiary but very real functions. And most important of all, even 'stunted and travestied' social labour — as tied for its continued existence to capital in the established division of labour — is in danger of siding with them. It is in danger of doing so, against its own practically realizable interests, unless within the framework of a radical socialist strategy the associated producers can really assume the position of an agency in charge of controlling the transitional social metabolic order, aiming to go *beyond capital* not only in its directly inherited, but, more importantly, also in its feasible postrevolutionary forms.

This is the setting we know from 20th century history, with its devastating impact on the socialist project. Naturally, Marx could in no way imagine the kind of developments which produced the disintegration we have witnessed in the recent and not so recent past. All the less since in his vision a viable socialist transformation had to arise — and could only arise — from the structural crisis of the global capital system, with its antagonistic international social division of labour and deeply troubled world market.[91] However, in the light of our own historical experience the *self-critique* of the socialist revolution and its actual unfolding — which we find in Marx only as a general principle, as briefly mentioned in his *Eighteenth Brumaire of Louis Bonaparte* — must be an integral part of understanding the contradictory reality of capital also in its postcapitalist varieties. Understandably, Marx's work could not deal with this vital issue, since he could not in any way take into account the historical specificities under which the bewildering postrevolutionary developments unfolded and in the end have brought about the implosion of the Soviet type postcapitalist capital system. Nevertheless, as we shall see in Section 17.1.4, the way in which he characterized capital's fully developed order as an 'organic system' that must be superseded precisely as an *organic system,* because its constituents reciprocally sustain one another — instead of limiting change to its juridical dimension only, while maintaining intact in many respects the inherited capital-relation — helps to throw light on what went wrong and offers important warning signs for the future.

17.1.2

WE can see Marx's fundamental concern in trying to combine the main tenets of his theory with the critique of political economy. The economists he must criticise for 'eternalizing' the established order project the prehistory of capital into the present. The point of doing so is that they should be able to maintain that what is true of the earliest phase of capital's development — 'accumulation prior to labour and not sprung out of it' — is also true of the fully developed capital system:

> This act by capital which is independent of labour, not posited by labour, is then shifted from the prehistory of capital into the present, into a moment of its reality and of its present activity, of its self-formation. From this is ultimately derived the eternal right of capital to the fruits of alien labour, or rather its mode of appropriation is developed out of the simple and 'just' laws of equivalent exchange. ... [in reality in the present] the worker constantly creates a double fund for the capitalist, or in the form of capital. One part of this fund constantly fulfils the conditions of his own existence and the other part fulfils the conditions for the existence of capital. As we

have seen, in the case of the surplus capital — and surplus capital in relation to its antediluvian relation to labour — all *real, present capital* and each of its elements has equally been *appropriated* without exchange, without an equivalent, an objectified, appropriated *alien labour*.[92]

It is the necessary critique of political economy — on account of its eternalizing identification with the standpoint of capital — which induces Marx to concentrate on the stage of development where the continued appropriation of labour is the presupposition for the continued reproduction of the system. The original accumulation of capital is in this respect secondary. For by the time the disputed relations concern the fully developed form of the system, the earliest forms of accumulation have been radically altered. They must be faced in that radically altered form if one wants to raise the question of an alternative socioeconomic order. The latter must be a viable alternative to the actually existing system, and not to its distant ancestry. To be sure, the historical constitution of capital becomes highly relevant again in the aftermath of a socialist revolution, when it becomes painfully obvious that — just as it could not arise, nor assert its power suddenly — capital cannot be consigned to past history by a sudden negation of its being, no matter how radical the political intent to do so. However, when we talk about the fully developed form of the capital system, as Marx does in his critique of political economy, the accent must be put on the conditions under which labour power becomes a commodity for the worker himself, and as a result production becomes

> the production of commodities to its *complete* extent, over the *whole* of its length and breadth. Only then are *all* products converted into commodities ... the commodity as the *necessary* form of the product, and therefore the *alienation* of the product as the necessary form of its *appropriation,* imply a *fully developed division of social labour,* while on the other hand it is only on the basis of capitalist production, hence also of the capitalist division of labour within the workshop, that all products *necessarily* assume the *commodity form,* and all producers are therefore necessarily commodity producers. It is therefore only with the coming of capitalist production that *use* value is first *generally* mediated through *exchange* value.[93]

In a sense we are talking here about a paradoxical form of development. For we see commodity as the *presupposition* of capital — in its historical formation — appear also as its *product* at the fully developed stage of capital production. To quote Marx:

> The commodity, as the elementary form of bourgeois wealth, was our starting point, the presupposition for the emergence of capital. On the other hand, *commodities* now appear as the *product of capital.* This circular course taken by our presentation, on the one hand, corresponds to the *historical development* of capital, one of the *conditions for the emergence* of which is the *exchange of commodities, trade in commodities;* but this condition itself is formed on the basis provided by a number of *different stages of production,* which all have in common a situation in which capitalist production either does not as yet exist at all or exists only sporadically. On the other hand, the exchange of commodities in its full development and the *form of the commodity* as the universally necessary social form of the product first emerge as a *result of the capitalist mode of production.*[94]

The point is that without understanding the *perverse circularity* of the capital system — through which labour as *objectified* and *alienated labour* becomes capital and, as *personified capital,* confronts as well as dominates the worker — there can be no escape from the vicious circle of capital's expanded self-reproduction as the most powerful mode of social metabolic control ever known in history. For the power dominating the worker is the circularly transformed power of social labour itself, assuming a 'stunted/travestied form' and asserting itself in 'the *fetishistic* situation when the *product is the proprietor of the producer*'.[95] In other words, 'the "social character", etc., of the worker's labour confronts him, both "notionally" and "in fact", as not only alien, but hostile and antagonistic, and as *objectified* and *personified* in capital'.[96] Thus, in order to break out of the vicious circle of capital as a mode of social metabolic control, it is necessary to confront the fetishism of the system in its fully developed form. A task which requires understanding that

> Capital is no more a *thing* than money is. In capital, as in money, *definite social relations of production between persons* are expressed *as the relations of things* to persons, or definite social connections appear as *social characteristics belonging naturally* to things. ... Money cannot become capital without being exchanged for labour capacity as a commodity sold by the worker himself. Labour, on the other hand, can only appear as wage labour when its own objective conditions meet it as egoistical powers, as alien property, value existing for itself and holding fast to itself, in short as capital. ... these objective conditions must from the formal point of view confront labour as alien, *independent* powers, as value — objectified labour — to which living labour is the mere means of its own preservation and expansion.[97]

The form of domination in which capital — objectified and alienated labour — rules in its circular self-reproduction over labour is very different from the earlier forms of domination. None the less

> The capital-relation is a *relation of compulsion,* the aim of which is to extract surplus labour by prolonging labour time — it is a relation of compulsion which does not rest on any personal relations of domination and dependence, but simply arises out of the difference in economic functions. This capital-relation as a relation of compulsion is common to [several] modes of production, but the specifically capitalist mode of production also possesses other ways of extracting surplus value. [when surplus value is created only by *prolonging labour time*, we find the production of *absolute surplus value*.] Therefore, where this is the sole form of production of surplus value, we have the *formal subsumption of labour under capital*.[98]

The examples offered by Marx at this point to illustrate the precapitalist forms of formal subsumption of labour under capital are *usurers' capital* and *merchants' capital*.[99] By contrast the historical specificity of the fully developed capitalist form of domination is what he calls the *'real subsumption of labour under capital'*,[100] characterized by large scale production involving science and machinery and securing the dominance of *relative* surplus value, in contrast to the prevalence of *absolute* suplus value under the conditions of the formal subsumption of labour. Domination of the labour force in one way or another is what all forms of production share with capital production, with the exception of the primitive communist system founded on *communal* property, which Marx considers 'naturally arisen'.[101] Given the fetishism of the capital system, the illusion is created — and, of course, eagerly perpetuated with all power at the disposal of the ruling ideology — that the relationship between capital and labour under the modern capitalist order is free from domination. The reality is very different:

> This constant sale and purchase of labour capacity, and the constant confrontation between the worker and the commodity produced by the worker himself, as buyer

of his labour capacity and as constant capital, appear only as the *form mediating* his subjugation to capital, the subjugation of living labour as a mere means to the preservation and increase of the objective labour which has achieved an independent position vis-à-vis it. This perpetuation of the relation of capital as buyer and the worker as seller of labour is a form of mediation which is immanent in this mode of production; but it is a form which is only distinct in a formal sense from other, more direct, forms of the enslavement of labour and *property in labour* on the part of the owner of the conditions of production. It *glosses over* as a mere *money relation* the real transaction and the perpetual dependence, which is constantly renewed through this mediation of sale and purchase. Not only are the conditions of this *commerce* constantly reproduced; in addition to this, what one buys with, and what the other is obliged to sell, is the result of the process. The constant renewal of this relation of *sale and purchase* only mediates the permanence of the specific relation of dependence, giving it the deceptive *semblance* of a transaction, a contract between *commodity owners* who have equal rights and confront each other equally freely.[102]

Thus the historically specific form of domination and exploitation of labour characteristic of the capital system ultimately rests on foundations with very deep roots in history. This is why emancipating labour from its formal and real subsumption under capital is unthinkable without radically challenging and overcoming domination and exploitation in general, which assumed so many different forms in history while retaining their subjugating substance. No wonder, therefore, that the juridical displacement of private capitalists in Soviet type postrevolutionary societies could not even scratch the surface of the problem. If anything, this problem was further complicated by a change in form from the directly economic extraction of surplus value under capitalism to the politically controlled and enforced extraction of surplus labour under the postcapitalist capital system. For the directly economic extraction prevailing under the capitalist variety of this mode of social metabolic reproduction is exerted, according to Marx, 'in a manner more favourable to production'.[103] To a large extent this is due to the fetishistic mode of managing the relationship between capital and labour, with its mystificatory tendency to hide the ruthless compulsion prevailing as a matter of normality and under the delusory appearance of freely entered contracts. As we shall see in Section 17.4, the failed attempt of Gorbachev's 'perestroika' tried to combine the two modes of exploitative surplus labour extraction, under the fantasy projections of 'market socialism', assuming that their shared domination of labour is by itself sufficient to compensate for the missing objective requirements of the primarily economic modality of compulsion practicable under fully developed capitalism.

Given the mythology of the 'free enterprise system', there is a tendency to forget that even the fully articulated economic mode of compulsion has at its disposal the 'reserve powers' of the state in case of major disturbances. As to the historical origins of this system, it is systematically obliterated from memory that the direct exercise of even the most extreme forms of violence — the execution of many thousands of 'vagrants' and 'vagabonds' produced through forced enclosures — was essential for securing the conditions favourable to the development and operation of capital. For, as Marx recalls it:

> With free labour, wage labour is not yet completely posited. The labourers still have support in the feudal relations; their supply is still too small; capital hence still unable to reduce them to the minimum. Hence statutory determination of wages. So long

as wages are still regulated by statute, it cannot yet be said either that capital has subsumed production under itself as capital, or that wage labour has attained the mode of existence adequate to it. ... [In England] Wages again regulated in 1514, almost like the previous time. Hours of work again fixed. Whoever will not work upon application, arrested. Hence still *compulsory labour* by free workers at the given wages. They must be first *forced* to work within the conditions posited by capital. The propertyless are more inclined to become vagabonds and robbers and beggars than workers. The last becomes normal only in the developed mode of capital's production. In the prehistory of capital, state coercion to transform the propertyless into *workers* at conditions advantageous for capital, which are not yet here forced upon the workers by competition among one another.[104]

The crucial condition for the existence and functioning of capital is that it should be able to exercise *command over labour*. Naturally, the modalities through which this command can and must be exercised are subject to historical changes, capable of assuming the most bewildering forms. But the *absolute condition* of objectified and alienated command over labour — exercised indivisibly by capital and no one else, under whichever of its actually existing and feasible forms — must always remain. Without it, capital would cease to be capital and disappear from the historical stage.

The way in which capital actually attains its fully developed form is a very long and complicated historical process. As the all-dominating power of social metabolic reproduction capital arises from constituents which in their original setting, of necessity, play a subordinate role, even if a dynamically increasing one in relation to the other forces and reproductive determinations of the given society. In the course of its historical unfolding capital progressively overcomes the resistances which it encounters and acquires 'sovereign power' to rule over all facets of the societal reproduction process:

the process in which money or value-for-itself originally becomes capital presupposes a *primitive accumulation* by the owner of money or commodities, which he has achieved as a *non-capitalist*, whether by saving, or by his own labour, etc. Therefore, while the presuppositions for the transformation of money into capital appear as given, external *presuppositions* for the emergence of *capital*, as soon as capital has become capital, it creates its own presuppositions, namely the possession of the real conditions for the creation of new values without *exchange* — by means of its own production process. These *presuppositions*, which originally appeared as prerequisites of its becoming, and therefore could not arise from its *action* as *capital*, now appear as results of its own realization, reality, as brought into being by it, not as *conditions of its emergence*, but as *results of its own being*.[105]

This is how capital becomes truly *causa sui:* 'its own cause', reproducing itself as a power which must be transcended under *all* its aspects precisely because of its self-constituting (and in the absence of a viable alternative even after a major reversal successfully self-reconstituting) power of *causa sui*. Capital must be superseded in the totality of its relations, otherwise its all-dominating mode of social metabolic reproduction cannot be displaced even as regards matters of relatively minor importance. For 'capital is not a simple relation, but a *process*, in whose various moments it is always capital. ... exchange did not stand still with the formal positing of exchange values, but necessarily advanced towards the subjection of production itself to exchange value'.[106] What is really at stake, then, is capital's process of circular self-constitution and expanded self-reproduction in its most developed form. Any attempt to gain control over capital by treating it as a 'material thing' tied to a 'simple relation' with its private owner — instead of instituting a sustainable alternative to its dynamic process 'in whose various moments it is always capital' — can only result in catastrophic failure. No juridical device can by itself remove capital from the social metabolic process as the necessary *command over labour* under the historically long prevailing and after the revolution unavoidably inherited circumstances. It is not possible to restitute the alienated power of command over labour to labour itself by simply targeting the private capitalist personifications of capital, but only by replacing the established 'organic system' as the all-embracing and dominating controller of societal reproduction. And that requires the substantive self-emancipation of labour, in contrast to the juridical fiction of emancipation tragically pursued in dependency to the inherited fetishism of capital — as a 'mechanism' and material entity capable of 'socialist accumulation' — under the Soviet type postcapitalist systems. The fact that capital itself, which in Marx's view must be fully superseded, is so deeply rooted in history — reaching back in its origins at least as far as Ancient Greece and Rome[107] — can only underline the heavy material burden of this simple truth.

17.1.3

THE capital-relation could not be more contradictory. For it is characterized by a twofold split on the side of labour, and a doubling up on the side of capital parasitic on labour's split. And to make it all even more contradictory, the splits in the capital-relation are bridged — while the relationship is historically tenable — by an irreconcilable structural antagonism. What makes the capital-relation tenable for a determinate historical epoch is that, in the absence of the required social metabolic alternative, capital and labour — and not the private capitalist owner and its juridically safeguarded material possessions — are inextricably tied together in the material reproduction process, unable to survive by themselves without the continued mutual reproduction of each other as well as of their structural antagonism. Nevertheless, not *despite* its contradictoriness but precisely *through* it, the capital-relation is constituted and maintained in existence, for as long as it can be, as an *organic system,* asserting itself as *capital's expanded reproduction process* 'in whose various moments it is always capital'. This is why all past attempts to eliminate the structural antagonism of the system — from 'people's capitalism' to socialdemocratic accommodation and capitulation — proved to be not only futile but also totally misconceived, and must do so also in the future. Capital, for as long as its dynamic reproduction process is objectively sustainable, has nothing to fear from conflict. On the contrary, it thrives on conflicts and contradictions even on its own side, among the plurality of capitals, and is strengthened by successfully asserting its power and command over labour in the course of reproducing the profound structural antagonism of its organic system. In fact this is how capital progresses from the modest local beginnings of its sporadic appearance to its monstrous global power over labour today. Once capital ceases to dominate and ruthlessly exploit labour — as the fictitious notion of 'participatory labour sharing power with capital' would want it, projecting an 'enlightened' form of capital and its caring 'social market' as the framework of a happy future relationship — it loses its ability to control the social metabolic process altogether.

On the side of labour the twofold split we are here concerned with is visible in that

- (1) the real *subject* of the production process objectifies itself in the form of capital/alienated labour, and thereby loses its subject character as the ability required for the *overall control* of the social reproduction process, although in a telling contradictory form it must retain the conscious ability to perform the countless *particular* productive tasks directly assigned to it by the personifications of capital; and

- (2) social labour, absolutely necessary for capital's advanced production process, is split into its fragments, confronting capital in the domain of both production and distribution as *isolated* workers. This relationship prevails in the interest of maintaining total social capital's control over the totality of labour by the historically practicable mode of — directly economic or politically mediated — competition among the fragmented multiplicity of labour.

This is why the social labour process can only be of a *'stunted/travestied'* type under the rule of capital, no matter how advanced might be the established horizontal and vertical division of labour, remaining necessarily stunted/travestied — even if with added complications for the continued rule of capital — also under its known postcapitalist varieties. We can also see in this context that competition among the fragments of labour is secondary, in the sense of being subsidiary to the management of the fundamental structural antagonism between capital and labour. It is the customary form in which that antagonism asserts and successfully reproduces itself, serving the purpose of capital's expanded self-reproduction. (As we have seen above, the conditions economically favourable to capital in the first place did not directly arise from its economic production process. They had to be politically imposed on recalcitrant — 'vagrant' and 'vagabond' — labour by the most savage form of state legislation, instituted by 'great kings', like Henry VIII. Capital needed a great deal of helpful 'pump-priming' then, and in our age — far from reassuring for its continued rule — it badly needs political help again, and indeed to a much greater extent than 'pump priming'.) If the competition among the fragmented totality of labour were not secondary or subsidiary determination but primary to the articulation and operation of the system, that would maintain capital's command over labour on a permanent basis, thanks to labour's necessary default over its own interests as the only feasible alternative to the established reproductive order. However, the weakness of fragmented and internally torn labour, from which capital's continued strength is derived, is in the final analysis also capital's weakness. For without the internal division and fragmentation of labour — which capital can ferment, and through its state formations even legislatively intensify up to a point, but over which it cannot exercise ultimate control — the rule of capital over society cannot be indefinitely sustained. The fragmentation and competition characteristic of the 'stunted/travestied' forms of social labour under the rule of capital are not only *capable* of suspension; they are *bound* to be suspended — if humankind is to survive. Not because the pious preaching emanating from the grotesque 'Justice and Fairness Commissions' of 'New Labour' is destined to conquer the hearts of the personifications of capital sitting on its even more grotesque 'Business Commissions', but through the unfolding of the capital system's increasingly devastating structural antagonisms on a global scale.

The contradictory doubling up on capital's side — a process which is parasitic on the alienated objectification and division of labour, as mentioned above, and therefore can be historically transcended by eliminating the ground of its formation through the institution of a non-fetishistic mode of productive objectification — follows the same pattern as seen on the side of labour. It manifests, on the one hand, as the question of capital's peculiar *subjectivity,* and on the other, as the relationship between the particular constituents of capital and its aggregative totality.

- Capital as subject is a *usurped,* and for the requirements of a rational production process not only *superfluous* but also *damaging* and increasingly *destructive* subject. Even in the classical accounts of the system's most enthusiastic defenders the consciousness attributable to this subject is located *outside* the head of the particular decision makers. The correctness of their decision making is stipulated on the basis of a guiding *'invisible hand'*, but the body to which that hand is attached, together with its infinitely benevolent and superior — all-comprehending — head, remains a complete mystery. This is how the morally rightful and economically correct mode of comprehensive interaction, to the benefit of all, can be not only gratuitously *assumed* but also apriori exempted from all critical scrutiny even in the face of the greatest possible disturbances, since the latter are supposed to be of necessity happily sorted out sooner or later by the possessor of the 'invisible hand'. The projection of this scheme of things is not accidental, nor the aberration of a particular thinker. It is a necessary conception in as much as the requirement of *comprehensive rationality* is rationally incompatible with the capital system, in contrast to its feasible alternative based on the self-determined productive and social metabolic practices of the freely associated producers. For in order to achieve comprehensive rationality capital not only would have to harmoniously unify under some mythical common denominator (perhaps 'invisible hand' mark two) its own conflicting constituents — the inescapable plurality of capitals without which capital as such is inconceivable — depriving itself thereby of its own actually existing material ground and productive dynamism. At the same time capital would also have to maintain unaltered its *domination over labour* within the framework of its newfound 'stationary state': one projection more absurd than the other.

- The setting in which the rational interaction — and corrective action — of capital's particular subjects is supposed to take place is the idealized market. Thus the irrationality of the system as a whole must be simultaneously both acknowledged and denied. It must be acknowledged that the particular personifications of capital cannot possess the rational overview of the whole, only the partial rationality required to run their limited productive enterprises; for without acknowledging this circumstance there would be no need for the corrective action of the 'invisible hand' and its market. In this way the *semblance* of a rational reproductive order is created by the subsumption of the more or less blind decisions of capital's particular subjects under the market-oriented, allegedly rational, cohesiveness of the overall reproductive framework. Yet, the acknowledgement of the market's corrective rationality amounts at the same time also to the admission of the defectiveness of a system subject to the good work of such — far from adequate — corrective machinery. A deficiency which capital itself must try to overcome, primarily by its *monopolistic* tendency, directly contradicting thereby not only its own inner dynamism, but also the self-mythology of its universally beneficial 'market society'.

However, no matter how far advanced the tendency to monopoly, capital's particular subjects can never be fully aggregated in a rational whole, in view of the always necessarily specific conditions of capital's antagonistic confrontation with labour, under changing historical and local circumstances, aggravated by the law of uneven development. If the structural antagonism with labour did not exist, and the capital system's continued existence did not depend on its ability to successfully reproduce it, there would be no need whatsoever for the personifications of capital. The objective structural imperatives of the system would unproblematically prevail on the basis of their willing 'rational acceptance' by a non-recalcitrant labour force. The insurmountable problem for the capital system is that it has no *automatic* machinery at its disposal — neither in the domain of production nor in the field of circulation — to which social labour, even in its fragmented and 'stunted/travestied form' — could be subordinated as a simple appendage, willingly submitting itself to the authority of productive and distributive 'rationality' embodied in some 'neutral mechanism'. One should not confuse the mythology of the market with its — actually limited — ability to fulfil its ascribed functions, denied and negated even by capital's monopolism whenever it suits the convenience of the system. The viability of the market is in fact subject to a number of fundamental contradictions, including the fluctuations and instabilities due not only to the conflicting interests of the plurality of capitals, but even to the limiting impact of the self-assertive determinations of fragmented labour. As to the production sphere, the situation is not much better. For although in the form of advanced productive machinery — obtained by expropriating science as the historically developed collective knowledge of society — capital comes the closest to being able to define and treat labour as Aristotle's *'talking tool'*, this is a much more unstable mode of controlling the labour process than the original system of slave labour. For its success depends on enforcing — whether through direct economic compulsion or by political force — the permanent submission of labour. This is because the combination of labour under the authority of capital's most advanced productive machinery is

> just as subservient to and led by an alien will and an alien intelligence ... as its material unity appears subordinate to the *objective unity* of the *machinery,* of fixed capital, which, as *animated monster,* objectifies the scientific idea, and it is in fact the coordinator, does not in any way relate to the individual worker as his instrument; but rather he himself exists as an animated individual punctuation mark, as its living isolated accessory. ... Hence, just as the worker relates to the product of his labour as an alien thing, so does he relate to the combination of labour as an alien combination, as well as to his own labour as an expression of his life, which. although it belongs to him, is alien to him and coerced from him ... Capital therefore is the existence of social labour — the combination of labour as subject as well as object — but this existence as itself existing independently opposite its real moments — hence itself a *particular* existence apart from them. For its part, capital therefore appears as the predominant subject

and owner of *alien labour,* and its relation is itself as complete a contradiction as is that of wage labour.[108]

Thus the real problem of the *subject-object relationship* facing labour is not the philosophical assertion of a mythical Hegelian 'subject-object identity' in history in general. It is the tangible practical task of removing the paralysing contradiction through which the real subject of production is treated by capital — labour's alienated objectification turned into the controlling power and 'predominant subject' of the labour process — as the degraded object of the societal reproduction process and the 'living isolated accessory' to capital's productive machinery at the present stage of historical development. This contradiction finds its counterpart in the equally contradictory determination of capital itself from which the latter, unlike labour, cannot be extricated. Nor is it possible to remove the structural antagonism from the capital system which totally vitiates its claims to being not only rational, but indeed the only truly rational and efficient economic system. The particular controlling subjects as personifications of capital — who must respond to both the general challenge of structural antagonism and to its necessarily specific manifestations in their own situation — can never be fully aggregated to a rationally sustainable whole. They are constituted not simply as an abstract and efficiency-oriented *'economic consciousness'* but simultaneously also as a *combative will.* Without the latter they would not be able to fulfil the functions assigned to them, and therefore would make no sense whatsoever from capital's standpoint. Their rationality in the domain of capital's economic pursuit of expanded self-reproduction in general, as well as in relation to the economic success of their particular enterprises, is strictly circumscribed by the need to reproduce their *command over labour* — locally and in society at large — which must take precedence over the so-called 'instrumental rationality' of their idealized 'economic calculation' so dear to the heart of the system's past and present apologists. To believe, as we are told, that the contradictions on the side of both capital and labour either do not exist, or that they will be never recognized and acted upon by those who are suffering their devastating impact, requires also believing that people are blind idiots and mesmerized forever by the promise of capital's universally beneficial 'economic calculation', despite the system's monstrous failures directly affecting the life-chances of thousands of millions. Marx's assessment of the development of social consciousness is much more plausible, emphasizing that 'The recognition of the product as its own, and its awareness that its separation from the conditions of its realisation is an injustice — *a relationship imposed by force* — is an enormous advance in consciousness, *itself the product* of the capitalist mode of production and just as much the KNELL TO ITS DOOM as the consciousness of the slave that he *could not be the property of another* reduced slavery to an artificial, lingering existence, and made it impossible for it to continue to provide the basis of production'.[109]

17.1.4

WE must pursue these problems further in their proper setting in the remaining chapters. What we have to consider at this point are Marx's views on the mystifying fetishism and simultaneous personification at the core of the capital-relation. He quotes with approval young Engels's first characterization of the

personification of both capital and labour as inseparable from the mutual determinations of the capital-relation:

> The relation of the manufacturer to his operatives is ... purely economic. The
> manufacturer is 'Capital', the operative 'Labour'.[110]

And Marx adds here, putting into relief the peculiar nature — in a sense even
completely fraudulent character — of the labour market forced upon the worker, in which the transactions required for the operation of the capitalist variety
of capital's reproduction process can take place:

> It is not a mere buyer and a mere seller who face each other, it is a *capitalist* and a
> *worker;* it is a capitalist and a worker, who face each other in the sphere of circulation,
> on the market, as *buyer* and *seller.* The relation as *capitalist* and *worker* is the presup-
> position for their relation as buyer and seller.[111]

We shall see in Section 17.4 that the total failure to understand the difference
between a straightforward transaction of sale and purchase and the type required
for securing capital's command over labour in the specifically capitalist order
(through the operation of the labour market) underlined the absurdity of 'market socialist' fantasies and made a mockery out of Gorbachev's 'socialist' pretences. But well beyond such failures, the potentially fateful implications of
maintaining the capital-relation in any one of its feasible postcapitalist varieties
present a warning also for the future. For just as capital did not rain out of the
sky fully formed in the 17th or 18th century, it is likewise inconceivable that
the capital-relation would quietly fade away in the aftermath of a socialist
political revolution which removes the private capitalists from the countries
concerned.

The problem is not that, displacing the capitalists in some countries while
leaving their position unaffected in others, the capitalists remaining in control
of the metabolic process elsewhere can gang up against the revolution and en-
circle it. It is much worse than that. For the fundamental stake is and remains
the *internal dynamics* of the social reproduction process and capital's *command over
labour.* By removing the capitalists from a country's economic decision making
framework — whether we have in mind one isolated country or any number of
them — the *command over labour* is by no means *ipso facto* restituted to labour.
The capitalist owner of the means of production functions as the *personification
of capital.* Without capital the capitalist is nothing: a relationship which obviously does not hold the other way round. In other words, it would be quite
absurd to suggest that without the private capitalist owners of the means of
production capital itself is nothing. For the possible personifications of capital
are by no means confined to the private capitalist variety; not even within the
framework of an 'advanced capitalist' system. The mode of functioning of 'nationalized industries' in the post-Second World War period, with as complete a
subjection of labour in what were supposed to be 'publicly owned and controlled'
industries to the command of capital as anywhere else in the capitalist economy,
supplied plenty of evidence for this fact. To take only one example, the ruthlessly
aggressive role fulfilled by the 'National Coal Board' in Britain — in total
collusion with a 'Radical Right' Conservative Government — against the miners
during their one year long strike clearly demonstrated that altering the juridical
form of ownership and replacing one type of personification of capital by another
changes absolutely nothing in labour's subjection to the structural determina-

tions of the system. Not even if it is done on a large scale, rather than most selectively, in the bankrupt industries, as socialdemocratic governments have done it, deluding themselves — or just pretending — that they were 'conquering the commanding heights of the economy'. For as long as capital retains its substantive regulating power over the social metabolism, in any form, the need for finding a form of personification of capital suitable to the circumstances remains inseparable from it. Capital as such is inherent in the inherited adversarial structuring principle of the labour process. If that structuring principle is not radically superseded in the course of a viable practical articulation of the socialist project — which anticipates the control of social metabolic reproduction through the autonomous self-determinations of the associated producers — capital is bound to reassert its power and find the new forms of personification required for keeping recalcitrant labour under the control of an 'alien will'. That 'alien will', in any of its feasible varieties appropriate to the circumstances, is absolutely irreplaceable in the operation of an *adversarial system,* when command over labour is objectively alienated from labour. Without its new personifications capital could not continue to fulfil its long sustained and deeply embedded reproductive functions, endangering thereby the social metabolism as a whole, in the absence of an effective and all-embracing alternative controlled by labour itself which could match in every way capital's totalizing mode of control.

Although Marx could not imagine the historical conditions under which the problem of a new type of personification of capital became acute in the 20th century, we can find some warnings in this regard in his writings, even if not always clearly expressed or fully articulated. To take an important example, his critique of the illusion of realizing socialism by doing away with the capitalists while retaining capital as such is explicit in several places in his writings, although the problem is not pursued in a direction which could indicate the feasible alternative forms of capital's rule and corresponding modality of personification, under very different historical circumstances. Thus, in the *Grundrisse* Marx underlines that 'the idea held by some socialists that *we need capital but not the capitalists* is altogether wrong. It is posited within the concept of capital that the *objective conditions* of labour — and these are its own product — take on a *personality* towards it'.[112] The same critique of socialist wishful thinking is more fully spelled out in another context where Marx writes:

> In the first act, in the exchange between capital and labour, labour as such, existing *for itself,* necessarily appears as *the worker.* Similarly, here in the second process: capital as such is posited as a value existing for itself, as egotistic value, so to speak (something to which money could only aspire). But capital in its being-for-itself is *the capitalist.* Of course, socialists sometimes say, we need capital, but not the capitalist. (For example John Gray, *The Social System,* p.36, and J.F. Bray, *Labour's Wrongs,* pp.157-76.) Then capital appears as a pure thing, not as a relation of production which, reflected in itself, is precisely the capitalist. I may well separate capital from a given individual capitalist, and it can be transferred to another. But, in losing capital, he loses the quality of being a capitalist. Thus capital is indeed separable from an individual capitalist, but not from *the* capitalist who, as such, controls *the* worker.[113]

Capital 'in its being-for-itself' is the *necessary personification of capital* which may or may not be the private capitalist owner of the means of production, depending on the specific historical circumstances. What decides the matter is the *capital-*

relation itself in which the *controller* of the worker — who must be under the capitalist form of capital's rule *the* capitalist and not the particular or individual capitalist, the latter being subsidiary to the concept of capital as such — confronts and dominates *the* worker. The *necessary* conditions in all conceivable forms of the developed capital-relation — including the postcapitalist forms — are:

- (1) the *separation* and *alienation* of the *objective conditions* of the labour process from labour itself;
- (2) the *superimposition* of such objectified and alienated conditions over the workers as a separate power exercising *command over labour;*
- (3) the *personification of capital* as *'egotistic value'* — with its usurped subjectivity and pseudo-personality — pursuing its own *self-expansion,* with a *will* of its own (without which it could not be 'capital-for-itself' as the controller of the social metabolism); a will not in the sense of 'individual caprice', but in the form of setting as its internalized aim the fulfilment of the expansionary imperatives of capital as such (hence the grotesque notion of 'socialist accumulation', to be accomplished under the unchallengeable rule of the Soviet type bureaucrat; it is also important to stress here that it is not the bureaucrat who produces the perverse Soviet type capital system, however much he is implicated in its disastrous running, but, rather, the inherited and reconstituted postcapitalist form of capital gives rise to its own personification in the form of the bureaucrat, as the postcapitalist equivalent to the formerly economic-extraction-oriented capital system which had to give rise to the private capitalist); and
- (4) the equivalent *personification of labour* (i.e. the personification of the workers as 'Labour' destined to enter a contractual/economic or a politically regulated dependency relation with the historically prevailing type of capital), confining the subject-identity of this 'Labour' to its fragmentary productive functions — whether we think of the category of 'Labour' as wage labourer under capitalism or as the norm-fulfilling and over-fulfilling 'socialist worker' under the postcapitalist capital system, with the latter's own form of vertical and horizontal division of labour.

Capital can, thus, readily change the *form of its rule* for as long as these four basic conditions — which are constitutive of its 'organic system' and compatible with all kinds of transformation in detail without changing their substance — are not radically superseded through the formation of an alternative, genuinely socialist, *organic system.*

The question of *irreversibility* — which must concern all socialists, especially in the light of 20th century reversals — is not simply a matter of instituting political and military guaranties capable of withstanding concerted capitalist assaults. The political defence of the socialist revolution is, of course, always important. But no political and military force alone is capable of resisting the internal disintegrative and restoratory power of postcapitalist capital in the absence of profound positive transformations in the social metabolic order itself, irrespective of how strong the postcapitalist state might be in relation to its external adversaries; a truth amply confirmed by the implosion of the Soviet system. Irreversibility depends primarily on the ability of the associated producers to turn their alternative social reproductive order into a truly organic system whose parts reciprocally sustain one another. For once such a mode of social metabolic reproduction is operational, capital can oppose it only from a socially and historically retrograde, and in the end totally unsustainable, position. Such a situation is qualitatively different from what we have witnessed in the recent past, when 'advanced capitalism' — despite its massive contradictions — could successfully attack the Soviet type postcapitalist capital system on its own terms, claiming superiority towards it on the ground of accumulation-enhancing 'economic calculation' and related 'market efficiency', against which the Soviet system, based on its own type of subjection and exploitation of labour, had no defence whatsoever.

I argued on many occasions, but it cannot be stressed enough, that Marx's object of critique was not *capitalism* but *capital*. He was not concerned with demonstrating the deficiencies of *'capitalist production'* but with the great historical task of extricating humankind from the conditions under which the satisfaction of human needs must be subordinated to the *'production of capital'*. To extricate humankind, that is, from the dehumanizing conditions under which it is possible to gain legitimacy only for those use values, no matter how badly needed, which can be fitted into the straitjacket of the system's profitably produced exchange values. He treated with sarcasm all those who wanted to 'reform' the existing system of *distribution* while retaining capital's mode of *production* fetishistically intact. Thus he insisted that

> It is highly absurd when e.g. John Stuart Mill says: 'The laws and conditions of the production of wealth partake of the character of physical truths ... It is not so with the distribution of wealth. That is a matter of human institutions solely.'[114] The 'laws and conditions' of the production of wealth and the laws of the 'distribution of wealth' are the same laws under different forms, and both change, undergo the same historic process; are as such only moments of a historical process. It requires no great penetration to grasp that, where e.g. free labour or wage labour arising out of the dissolution of bondage is the point of departure, there machines can only *arise* in antithesis to living labour, as property alien to it, and as power hostile to it; i.e. that they must confront it as capital. But it is just as easy to perceive that machines will not cease to be agencies of social production when they become e.g. property of the associated workers. In the first case, however, their distribution, i.e. that they *do not belong* to the worker, is just as much a condition of the mode of production founded on wage labour. In the second case the changed distribution would start from a *changed* foundation of production, a new foundation first created by the process of history.[115]

Understandably, therefore, distribution viewed in this light cannot be brought one inch nearer to the envisaged socialist objective of giving 'to each according to their contribution to production' — let alone to the more advanced regulatory principle of 'to each according to their needs' — without an elemental transformation of the whole of the production and societal reproduction process. Moreover, it must be also remembered that in the dialectical relationship between production and distribution the former has the relative primacy. There can be no question of turning the envisaged alternative social reproductive order into an organic system without the dialectical unity of production and distribution. The pursuit of the value of a 'more equitable society' — the vacuous and therefore unrealizable promise of social democracy — makes no sense, because the underlying objective is not the conquest of *full equality*, which must be asserted as the orienting principle of both production and distribution if it is to have any chance of success. For all improvements in the domain of distribution are necessarily nullified sooner or later if they are not fully complemented by an ever deepening transformation of the production sphere. And *vice versa,* changes aimed at establishing socialist interrelations in production will get absolutely nowhere without the corresponding restructuring of the inherited, profoundly iniquitous, system of distribution.

The changes required in production and distribution amount to the total eradication of capital from the social metabolism as *command over labour* — which in its turn is inconceivable without irreversibly superseding the *alienated objectification* of labour under all its aspects, including the political state — and the simultaneous prevention of the *personification* of both capital and labour in the sense mentioned above. Subjecting to social control the material possessions of the private capitalists is a relatively easy part of this enterprise. For 'the capitalist himself only holds power as the *personification of capital*'.[116] No matter how bewildering might be the form in which the personifications of capital control the objective reproduction process, they control it *on behalf of capital* itself. Thus they should not be misconceived as the subject of the social metabolic process 'in whose various moments' capital as such is the real (however perversely reified) *commanding subject,* remaining 'always capital' even in its personified instances. As Marx puts it in his characterization of capital's self-expansionary process:

> The reproduction and *valorisation,* i.e. the *expansion,* of these *objective conditions* is simultaneously their reproduction and their new production as the wealth of an alien subject, indifferent to and independently confronting labour capacity. What is reproduced and newly produced is not only the *being* of these objective conditions of living labour but *their being as alien* to the worker, as confronting this living labour capacity. The *objective* conditions of labour gain a *subjective* existence as against living labour capacity — *capital* gives rise to the *capitalist*.[117]

To prevent capital from giving rise to the capitalist — or to its feasible equivalents under different sociohistorical conditions — it is necessary to do away with capital altogether, i.e. with the self-perpetuating capital-relation itself. In every context where Marx addresses himself to these problems he makes it clear that *the causal relationship runs from capital to the capitalist,* and not the other way round. He makes it equally clear that only the freely associated producers can overcome the underlying contradictions. For the capital-relation as such is grounded on the antagonistically alienated objectification of social labour. At the same time, the capital-relation remains unstable, no matter how massive are the forces reproduced and progressively enlarged in it, precisely in view of its insurmountable structural antagonism. This is also the reason why it can be radically altered by reconstituting the labour process in accordance with its directly social character, in place of its perverted sociality under the rule of a separate power of metabolic control.

The perverted development of social labour, which makes labour contradictorily ever more powerless the more productively advanced it becomes, is the result of an alienating historical transformation whereby

> the objective conditions of labour assume an ever more colossal independence, represented by its very extent, opposite living labour, and social wealth confronts labour in more powerful portions as an alien and dominant power. The emphasis comes to

be placed not on the state of being *objectified,* but on the state of being *alienated,* ... on the condition that the monstrous objective power which social labour itself erected opposite itself as one of its moments belongs not to the worker, but to the personified conditions of production, i.e. to capital.[118]

In the *'monstrous objective power'* of capital, representing the *'personified conditions of production'*, we find the twofold contradiction (1) between subjectivity and objectivity (i.e. alienated objectivity perversely assuming the form of the commanding subject), and (2) between the individual and the social. The second contradiction assumes a particularly bewildering form between the all-dominating general pseudo-subject (capital itself) and its particular exemplifications (i.e. the individual personifications of capital). It is particularly bewildering because at the roots of capital's historical constitution as (usurped but effectively ruling) subject we find nothing but social labour's own alienated subjectivity and potentially conscious power of control over its self-activity. It is this set of contradictions which condenses and reproduces itself in the form of the *structural antagonism* between capital and labour under determinate historical circumstances, losing its originally most potent productive justification and legitimacy with the end of capital's historical ascendancy. There can be no way of alleviating or removing the contradictions of the system 'little by little'. For the self-expansionary dynamics of the capital system makes it necessary also for its contradictions and structural antagonisms to be renewed on an ever-enlarged scale, assuming global proportions in the course of historical development. (It is far from accidental that two World Wars had to be fought in the 20th century, and a Third 'Great War' was avoided only because of the certainty of humanity's self-destruction if it was allowed to erupt.[119])

This is the ultimate meaning of capital's inexorable *'globalization'*, extending the system's 'monstrous objective power' over everything, without the slightest ability, however, of altering — let alone of fully eliminating — the adversarial inner determination of its own nature, from its smallest constitutive microcosms to the most comprehensive systemic relations on the global scale. And since the structural antagonism of the capital system is what objectively defines it, in its parts as much as a whole, no substantive change is feasible in that respect within the framework of capital's social reproductive order. The structural antagonism of the system is removable only through the radical supersession of the capital-relation itself which — as an 'organic system' — dominates the social metabolism in its entirety.

Contrary to the views of all defenders of the capital system who rely on the argument of 'complexity', and its presumed 'natural' foundation corresponding to the necessity to divide the productive functions of labour in the course of historical advancement, the issue is not at all the unavoidable horizontal social division of labour and the complexity arising from it.

It is rather the *division* of the associated *elements of the production process* themselves, and their *achievement of an independent position* vis-à-vis each other, which proceeds as far as their reciprocal personification.[120]

The alienated 'reciprocal personification' characteristic of capital's mode of controlling the social metabolism, in all of its historically known and feasible forms, is not the consequence of producing with the help of more developed productive machinery. It is the *necessary alienation of control* over all aspects of the societal reproduction process — including control over productive machinery and scientific research — from social labour within the framework of capital's 'organic system'. In the theories which shift the issue from the alienation of control from (and the ensuing command over) labour to the apparently neutral problem of 'complexity', said to be due to the allegedly 'natural division of labour' — a characteristic shift and 'sleight of hand' always serving the interest of the 'eternalization' of the established relations of social metabolic reproduction — we find a blatant ideological mystification under the cover of 'scientific objectivity'. But even so, it is not enough to demonstrate the vested interests at work in producing such mystifications. In positive terms, the solution of all these problems is dependent on the objective requirements and determinations of a viable practical alternative to capital's *organic system.*

The historical constitution of capital's organic system — with far-reaching implications for the constitution of other such systems — is characterized by Marx in these terms:

> It must be kept in mind that the new forces of production and relations of production do not develop out of *nothing,* nor drop from the sky, nor from the womb of the self-positing Idea; but from within and in antithesis to the existing development of production and the inherited, traditional relations of property. While in the completed bourgeois system every economic relation presupposes every other in its bourgeois economic form, and everything posited is thus also a presupposition, this is the case with every organic system. This organic system itself, as a totality, has its presuppositions, and its development to its totality consists precisely in subordinating all elements of society to itself, or in creating out of it the organs which it still lacks. This is historically how it becomes a totality. The process of becoming this totality forms a moment of its process, of its development.[121]

In this sense, the capital system constitutes a vicious circle, because 'everything *posited* in it is also a *presupposition*'. In order to turn into reality the historic task of a new — socialist — 'positing', it is necessary to break capital's circular 'presuppositions' in all domains, from the control of the direct production process in the particular enterprises to the correlated all-embracing state practices. As regards the first, it is absolutely necessary to bring about a real, and not merely juridical, *unification* of 'the historically *divided elements of the production process*' as an effectively functioning alternative to the inherited mode of social metabolic control. As to the second, the process of the state's 'withering away' is also a question of progressive unification. For in this domain the *separate legality and state administration* necessarily complement and help to reproduce the capital system's *iniquitous appropriation,* based on the incurable structural iniquities of a mode of production with a separate/alienated command over labour.

Thus the question of going *beyond capital* hinges on the ability or failure of the associated producers to create a new — genuinely and sustainably socialist — 'organic system': a coherent social totality which not only breaks the vicious circle of capital's self-sustaining organic totality but puts an irreversible open-ended development in its place. The tragedy of Soviet type postcapitalist societies was that they failed to orient themselves towards the realization of this difficult historic task. They followed, instead, the 'line of least resistance' — by positing socialism without radically overcoming the *material presuppositions* of the capital system — which condemned them to failure. For, given the active restoratory power of those constituents of the formerly established 'organic totality' which are not subjected to change, following the 'line of least resistance' makes one fall back sooner or later into the reproductive determinations of the objectively constituted 'organic system' one is trying to leave behind. Marginalizing the private capitalists as the old type of personification of capital is very far from being enough to secure success. For the socialist revolution — not as a, hopelessly insufficient, political act, but as the constantly renewed 'social revolution' (or 'permanent revolution') of the associated producers — must 'subordinate all elements of society to itself'. At the same time it must also create out of the inherited but progressively restructured organic system 'the organs which it still lacks', in order to be able to turn itself into its own, qualitatively different type of organic and irreversible totality. A new organic system irreversible towards the retrograde past but creatively open-ended towards the future. This is the vital meaning of the Marxian distinction — whether explicitly made or only by implication — between *capital* and *capitalism* for the present and the future.

17.2 'Socialism in one country'

17.2.1
THE question of what could constitute secure foundations for socialist development had arisen a long time before the October revolution. As we have seen earlier, Marx's answer was a resounding no to the idea of achieving socialism in a single country, since the conditions under which such a transformation could be envisaged, given the global dynamics of capital, were inseparable from the maturation of the system's productive potentialities and the unfolding of its antagonistic contradictions within the framework of the world market.

The criterion of 'universality' by which the viability of the socialist alternative had to be judged was laid down as far back as *The German Ideology,* and it could never be abandoned by Marx and Engels. This is why they insisted that the 'dominant peoples all at once and simultaneously' had to embark on the road towards socialism in order to secure a positive outcome: one 'which presupposed the universal development of the productive forces and the world intercourse bound up with them'.[122] Nor is it possible to argue — not only in the light of the catastrophic collapse of the Soviet system but on the basis of any serious scrutiny of postrevolutionary developments — that Stalin's notorious strategy of 'socialism in one country' had ever the slightest chance of being realized. Apologists of Stalinism — like Santiago Carillo, who later pioneered *'Euro-communism'* with the same blindness with which he had served and justified Stalin's most disastrous policies throughout the long decades of his tyranny — argued even as late as 1974 that 'the idea of building socialism in a single country was correct. The communists were right about that.'[123] Santiago Carillo reluctantly conceded to Marx and Engels only that they were right in saying — a pathetic tautology which they never uttered — 'that the *complete* victory of socialism can only be universal, that is to say that as long as there continue to exist in the world capitalist countries that are economically the most developed, those countries will constitute an obstacle to the development of socialism in the other countries.'[124]

The truth of the matter is that what was always at stake and remains so also today is not the question of 'underdevelopment' or socioeconomic backwardness but the viability or unreality of the adopted *socialist strategy*. Irrespective of what has happened in Soviet society, this issue is vital for all socialist movements, even in the capitalistically most developed countries. The 'Asiatic backwardness' and the hostile capitalist encirclement may explain some aspects of Soviet postrevolutionary transformations, but are very far from an adequate explanation. Equally, and for the future more importantly, the idea nourished by many new-left-oriented socialists in the past, that the 'democratic state' of the West provides the guarantees that the disasters of Soviet type postrevolutionary development can be avoided by the socialist movements of 'advanced capitalist' countries, can hardly be considered more sound than a self-reassuring illusion. The fundamental issue that cannot be avoided is the *power of capital* and the need to overcome it. Capital is not going to hand over its power to the representatives of some 'democratically elected' anti-capitalist party just because the etiquette of democratic behaviour in the postulated states with 'democratic traditions' would seem to make it the proper thing to do.

The Russian revolution erupted against the historical background of the first global crisis of *capitalism,* in the closing phase of the First World War. The war offered temporary solutions and advantages to some of the victorious participants, e.g. Britain and France, while greatly aggravating the conditions of the others, including Czarist Russia and Germany. What is important to bear in mind in this context is that in the course of historical development capital reached a stage when the earlier processes of social metabolic reproduction through which it originally triumphed — the most favourable and dynamic mode of extracting surplus value by overwhelmingly economic means — proved to be no longer sufficient to the self-expansionary requirements of the system. Marx characterized the conditions most favourable to capital's mode of social metabolic control as those under which *'capital can proceed from itself as its own presupposition',* i.e. when 'it ceases to need any *extraneous help'*.[125] The 20th century signalled a major change in this respect, with an ever greater direct role which the state had to assume in order to provide the much needed 'extraneous help' to the economic reproductive constituents of the capital system, all the way to fighting wars of formerly quite unimaginable magnitude. The all-embracing conflicts of the most powerful states which attempted to solve the underlying socioeconomic problems by redefining the inter-state relations of power,through violent confrontations, marked the irretrievable end of the phase in capital's development when the political dimension of the system was far less pronounced than the role fulfilled by the direct economic processes.

Ever since the onset of such a change, the advocates of capitalist purity regularly proclaim their belief in 'free competition' and continue to protest against 'state interference'; only to complain just as regularly, with great disappointment, that their words of wisdom are not at all, or only most insufficiently, heeded. The last thing they would be willing to admit is that there might be an objective causal foundation to the fact that this is so, no matter how faithfully the personifications of capital active in the political sphere might try to follow their advice. For the 'pure mechanisms' of their idealized system are incapable of fulfilling their reproductive functions on the required expanded scale. Consequently, capital's mode of social metabolic control cannot prevail under present-day conditions without heavily relying on the politically managed 'extraneous help' which, in the view of the various representatives of the 'Radical Right', should be considered anathema to the system.Thus even one of the most revered ideologists of monetarism, Milton Friedman, has to admit that the overall record of their camp is 'practical failure' (his words), despite the 'change in the climate of opinion' which is evident in the 'transition from the overwhelming defeat of Barry Goldwater in 1964 to the overwhelming victory of Ronald Reagan in 1980 — two men with essentially the same programme and the same message'.[126] This is how Milton Friedman describes what he considers to be a disheartening 'practical failure', namely that 'the developments since 1962 in the world of practice differ markedly from those in the world of ideas' (i.e. his own work):

> The United States, for which I know the situation best and with which *Capitalism and Freedom* dealt, is clearly further from a truly liberal society in 1986 than it was in 1962 [the year in which Friedman's celebrated book was first published].
>
> A simple measure is the ratio of government spending to national income. For all tiers of government — federal, state and local — spending was 43.8 percent of national income in 1985, compared with 34.7 percent in 1962. As a further benchmark, the corresponding fraction was 15 percent in 1930 [i.e. before Roosevelt's 'New Deal']. ... [Even if we take into account the necessary technical adjustments] the direction of change is clearly the same. In the 32 years from 1930 to 1962, the US government took over from its citizens the spending of 21 percent of the amount initially under their control; in the next 23, it took over 9 percent of the remainder. This is hardly a story of easing of government control.[127]

Nine years later, in 1995, the situation is worse than ever before from the point of view of Milton Friedman and others who preach the same sermon,[128] despite the sustained efforts of all 'Radical Right' governments in the intervening decade in several 'advanced capitalist' countries. The reasons for the acknowledged 'practical failure of governments' go much deeper than what could be theorized under the pseudo-explanatory concept of the mysterious 'change in the climate of opinion', coupled with the even more baffling impotence of this change of climate in affecting policy on a lasting basis. For the failure must be admitted by the intellectual spokesmen of the Radical Right against the background of ideologically impeccable conservative governmental efforts to harmonize policies with the 'changed climate'. As another adherent of the Radical Right puts it: 'Take but one example which, to me at least, is a *mystery*. In the 19th century, one of the standard arguments for democracy, as opposed to despotic government, was that it tended to be *fiscally responsible*. This assertion remained true up to about 1960. ... Beginning in the 1960s, most of the democracies began running *large peacetime deficits.*'[129] In reality, though, the ever-increasing direct involvement and 'fiscal irresponsibility' of the capitalist state is not mysterious at all. For we have witnessed a significant reversal of some fundamental trends of development in the 20th century, resulting in an incurable 'hybridization' of the capital system which at the peak of its historical ascendancy could reproduce itself and dynamically extend its power by primarily economic processes. The major historical events of the century testify to far-reaching structural changes in this respect, as well as to the chronic failure to bring the system's antagonisms under control.

Considered in this context, the Russian 'break of the chain at its weakest link' in 1917 was a major historical development *sui generis,* in the sense that it attempted a *postcapitalist* solution to the crisis of *capitalism* on a vast territory of the planet while remaining within the structural confines of the *capital system.* Naturally, there were also other, very different, ways of confronting the profound crisis of capitalism, from Mussolini's fascist Italy in 1922 to Roosevelt's 'New deal' in America in the 1930s and, of course, in Hitler's Germany. All of these countries remained not only well within capital's structural parameters but, in contrast to Soviet Russia, also firmly on capitalist ground. At the same time, what was characteristic of *all* of the 20th century attempts to deal with the capitalist crisis was that, in no matter how different ways, they all provided, without a single exception, massive state intervention as the *'extraneous help'* required by the system for its continued survival.

The suggestion by the Radical Right apologists of the system, according to which the 'fiscal irresponsibility' of the contemporary capitalist state is not due to changes 'in the real world',[130] but only to pernicious and more or less easily corrigible intellectual influences, exercised by misguided economists on the minds of policy-makers, is a complete misdiagnosis of the situation. For their principal culprit in this respect, Keynes, responded in fact to major, and in his view most alarming, historical developments which he wanted to counter — in order to secure the survival of the capitalist order — with the help of the recommended measures, arguing that

> In conditions of *laissez-faire* the avoidance of wide fluctuations in employment may prove impossible without a far-reaching change in the psychology of investment markets such as there is no reason to expect. I conclude that the duty of ordering the current volume of investment cannot safely be left in private hands.[131]

As to the social interests defended by the Keynesian approach, they transpired very clearly in another passage of *The General Theory:*

> Whilst, therefore, the enlargement of the functions of government, involved in the task of adjusting to one another the propensity to consume and the inducement to invest, would seem to a nineteenth-century publicist or to a contemporary American financier to be a terrific encroachment on individualism, I defend it, on the contrary, both as the only practicable means of avoiding the destruction of existing economic forms in their entirety and as the condition of the successful functioning of individual initiative. .... The authoritarian state systems of today seem to solve the problem of unemployment at the expense of efficiency and of freedom. It is certain that the world will not much longer tolerate the unemployment which, apart from brief intervals of excitement, is associated — and in my opinion inevitably associated — with present-day capitalistic individualism. But it may be possible by a right analysis of the problem to cure the disease whilst preserving efficiency and freedom.[132]

Thus, far from being anti-liberal, even if not *pro-laissez-faire,* the Keynesian solutions wanted to deal with the disturbingly obvious capitalist crisis, 'in the real world', in a way which would safeguard the system through the increasing — but strictly subsidiary or complementary — involvement of the state in the economic reproduction process, short of which the author feared the worst also for the once 'financially responsible democracies'. The trouble with the Keynesian remedies was not only that they failed to solve 'the problem of unemployment' but also that the projected solution to a number of related issues proved to be illusory. However, the failure to solve on a lasting basis the problem of unemployment was by no means only the fate of the Keynesian recommendations. It was true of all of the attempted ways of dealing with the crisis of capitalism, including in the longer run also the measures adopted by the Russian postcapitalist system. The various attempted solutions could only temporarily alleviate mass unemployment, for shorter or longer periods of time, according to their specific sociohistorical circumstances. In the end the Keynesian remedies had to be rejected in the Western 'advanced capitalist countries' when their cost started to become unmanageable. However, the monetarist alternative solutions attempted after the Keynesian phase with enormous zeal and great political enthusiasm — by Labour governments as much as by their Conservative rivals — proved to be no less of a failure than their predecessor. They also shared Keynes's inability to address *causes,* trying to remedy the situation by intervening only at the level of *effects* and *consequences,* which could work only conjuncturally, for very limited periods of time.

We may recall here that Keynes never offered a theoretical explanation of the causes of 'no longer tolerable unemployment' as linked to the historically specific determinations of the capitalist economy. Instead, given his blind acceptance of the standpoint of capital as the only rationally feasible regulator of social metabolic reproduction — the absolute *causa sui,* exactly as it appeared and appears in the books of the monetarists, — Keynes contented himself with the wishful projection that state-interventionist manipulation of the *negative symptoms* encountered would produce *permanent positive remedies.* No changes had to be envisaged to the antagonistic structural determinations of the existing order, admitted to be characterized by 'class war' in which Keynes openly and proudly declared his total allegiance to the bourgeoisie.[133] Arguing from such premises, the only admissible explanatory 'hypothesis' of the identified problem of unemployment — a hypothesis fulfilling at the same time the role of an automatic justification of the system's no longer deniable 'dysfunctions' and failures — was a crude *technological determinism.* No rational being was supposed to question the force of such an argument in 'explaining' unemployment. An argument which automatically absolved the socioeconomic order itself of all blame and responsibility for the misery of the people, in that

> For the *moment* the very rapidity of technical changes is hurting us and bringing difficult problems to solve. Those countries are suffering relatively which are not in the *vanguard of progress.* We are being afflicted with a new disease of which some readers may not yet have heard the name, but of which they will hear a great deal in the years to come — namely, *technological unemployment.* ... But this is only a *temporary phase of maladjustment.* All this means in the long run that mankind is solving its economic problem.[134]

Sixty five years later (which included the massively employment-boosting period of a World War and the after-war decades of reconstruction), in 1995, the 'temporary phase of maladjustment' is still with us, and there is no sign of the postulated happy outcome of 'mankind solving its economic problem'. Yet the same vacuous diagnosis and prognostication is offered today by labourite neo-Keynesian revivalists no less than by the anti-Keynesian monetarists, as well as by all the other ideological representatives of the Radical Right who project the miraculous future remedial action of the existing problems by *'the third wave'*. The fact that in the intervening sixty five years only the *opposite* of the Keynesian expectations was realized, in that now also the 'countries in the vanguard of progress' are being 'afflicted with the new disease' of chronic unemployment, is wilfully disregarded, as if it did not happen or did not matter. Again and again, the pseudo-causal explanation of *'technological change'* is put forward both for identifying the problem and for postulating its automatic solution. At the same time, two of Keynes's ideologically most revealing fallacies are perpetuated. First, that there is such a thing as 'mankind's *economic* problem' which is amenable to a *technological/economic* solution, if not today then certainly in the first years of the 21st century (and especially with the help of 'laptop computers'). And second, that *increased productivity of labour* is *ipso facto* the cause of unemployment, and not the determining power of the given *socioeconomic framework* in which any advancement in labour productivity is bound to be first evaluated — i.e. put to humanly fulfilling or fetishistically constrained and dehumanizing use — according to the values and practical orienting principles inherent in the prevailing mode of social metabolic control.

Manipulating the symptoms of unemployment without confronting their causes was, of course, only one of the major problems in relation to which the capitalist crisis had to be tackled, so as to provide the *'extraneous help'* which the system badly needed. Other important areas in which the state had to intervene with its 'extraneous help', in an attempt to manage the crisis of capitalism include:

- (1) direct support for securing the capitalistically vital *continuity of production* under circumstances when a deteriorating trend was observable in this respect, due to the 'vagaries of the market' and to the integration of productive enterprises on an ever-increasing scale;[135]
- (2) facilitating the inexorable trend to *monopolistic* development, providing protection to the principal monopolist interests, often under the cloak of regulating mergers in observance of 'free competition' and in accordance with the 'national interest'; the slavishly and cynically fulfilled facilitating role of 'democratic politics' in the service of big business has a great deal to do with the general contempt expressed in opinion polls towards politics and politicians today;
- (3) the reversal of the trend which characterized the system at the peak of capital's historical ascendancy, when we saw 'The separation of *public works* from the *state*, and their migration into the domain of the works undertaken by *capital itself*' which indicated 'the degree to which the real community has constituted itself in the form of capital';[136]
- (4) providing the funds absolutely vital for the normal functioning of the social metabolic process inasmuch as they directly affect the reproduction of the labour force — i.e. general education and heavily state subsidized health service of one type or another — which the capitalist enterprises are incapable of financing by themselves;
- (5) direct state involvement in the extended reproduction of fixed capital without which the system would collapse. For 'it is in the *production of fixed capital that capital posits itself as end-in-itself* and appears active as capital, to a *higher power than it does in the production of circulating capital*. Hence, in this

respect as well, the dimension already possessed by fixed capital, which its production occupies, within total production, is the measuring rod *of the development* of wealth founded on the mode of production of capital';[137]

- (6) massive direct subsidies put at the disposal of capitalist enterprises in a variety of forms, from research funds to lucrative state contracts, and from the maintenance of the 'infrastructure' to the most grotesque ways of financing pseudo-market agricultural practices within the framework of the European 'Common Agricultural Policy', for instance;

- (7) rescuing — through 'nationalization' — not only some major capitalist enterprises but even whole branches of industry when they become bankrupt, and returning them in due course to the 'competitive private sector' (with great hypocrisy and political cynicism, in the form of far from competition-oriented private monopolies and quasi-monopolies) once their economic viability has been secured through heavy state investment, financed from general taxation;

- (8) running the *social security* system — often requiring enormous funds, and now increasingly under the shadow of state bankruptcy — not only as some sort of a safeguard against social explosions, but also for maintaining, in no matter how inadequate a form, a significant amount of purchasing power which would be otherwise totally lost to capital.

The various attempts to deal with the crisis of capitalism in the 20th century all had to address these issues. They had to do what they could in providing the required 'extraneous help' which made the system look very different indeed from its form attained at the peak of capital's historical ascendancy. Naturally, the postcapitalist Soviet system provided its own way of dealing with the problems which the other responses to the capitalist crisis tried to solve in a very different form by remaining, on the whole, within the primarily economic parameters of extracting surplus labour even when political determinations played a major part in regulating their internal and external relations. The situation, however, greatly worsened in the 1970s, with the onset of the global structural crisis of the capital system as such, exposing the inadequacy of the 'extraneous help' which the state could provide under the circumstances of the deepening *systemic crisis*.

Significantly, the viability of the Soviet type system became not only most problematical but quite untenable under these conditions, as an integral part of the general structural crisis. For in the postrevolutionary situation it could define itself negatively for a long time, in its opposition to capitalism, offering its mode of overcoming the crisis of capitalism by securing a form of industrial development through the institution of its own form of — postcapitalist — extraction of surplus labour. The exhaustion of this way of securing the expanded reproduction of capital within a directly state-managed postcapitalist framework coincided with the unfolding structural crisis of the *capital system* as a whole, bringing with it in a most dramatic form the implosion of the Soviet type social metabolic order. At the time of the Soviet collapse, this development was greeted by the defenders of capital as a triumphant return all over the world to the *status quo ante*. By now, however, it should be clear enough to all those who are willing to open their eyes that the triumph was an optical illusion, magnified to cosmic proportions by capitalist wishful thinking. The wishful thinking in question eagerly announced a new era of undisturbed expansion on a global scale by integrating into the system as equal partners all of the capitalistically underdeveloped postcapitalist countries. The spokesmen of 'advanced capitalism' at once promised a massive 'modernizing' economic and financial help to the countries of the Eastern block, dangling even the carrot of a generous 'New Marshall Plan' before the noses of the credulous. It looked for a while that mountains were in labour, but as it turned out only scrawny mice were born. For just as the long promised 'modernization' to the benefit of the 'Third World' did not materialize in the past, in the same way virtually nothing came of the earlier propagandized modernizing aid. And no wonder. For the economies of the 'advanced capitalist' countries badly needed themselves the 'extraneous help' — in every shape and form in which they could get it — without which the whole system could not secure its continued viability.

Ironically, therefore, instead of representing a genuine triumph, the implosion of the Soviet type economy only underlined the unviability of solving the crisis of the global capital system on a lasting basis by massive direct state involvement in the social metabolic process. A solution which up until the collapse of 'actually existing socialism' appeared to be a — no matter how problematical, nevertheless practicable — alternative. As it happens, the need for 'extraneous help' is now greater than ever before, affecting with acute problems and challenges every single country, including the capitalistically most advanced ones. Indeed, the 'extraneous help' that would have to be provided today is of such a nature and magnitude that it cannot be accommodated within the confines of the established system of social metabolic control. This is why the twentieth century crisis of *capitalism* has been turned into the structural or systemic crisis of the *capital system* itself. Thus, instead of the projected undisturbed expansion which was supposed to provide a potential solution to the global capitalist crisis, we have entered a phase of unprecedented instability of which the predicament of the former societies of 'actually existing socialism' is a seriously aggravating constituent.

17.2.2

THE postrevolutionary Soviet development successfully managed for a long time the capitalist crisis which constituted its necessary point of departure and gave it its original impetus. To do so, it had to provide, in a very different form to what was practicable in strictly capitalist terms, the 'extraneous help' required — in relation to the problems mentioned in the last section — by the established social metabolic order in an extreme situation of emergency, aggravated by international capitalist intervention which fed and prolonged also the internal civil war. Thus the postrevolutionary regime had to confront not only the profound crisis of the inherited system, but it had to attempt also the establishment of an alternative — postcapitalist — reproductive order; one capable of securing the conditions of sustainable socioeconomic expansion in a hostile global environment.

Under the circumstances, even if the postrevolutionary leaders wanted to do so (which, of course, they did not), they could not have followed the capitalist road. Not even the 'state capitalist' one. Lenin used the term 'state capitalism' at first in a polemic context, turning it against the 'Left Communists' who raised the issue. These were his words:

> According to the 'Left Communists', under the 'Bolshevik deviation to the right the Soviet Republic is threatened with evolution towards state capitalism'. They have really frightened us this time! And with what gusto these 'Left Communists' repeat this threatening revelation in their theses and articles. It has not occurred to them that state capitalism would be a *step forward* as compared with the present state of affairs in our Soviet Republic.[138]

Later Lenin admitted that his reflections on 'state capitalism' were guided by the hope that within the framework of the New Economic Policy the government could 'lease out concessions'[139] to foreign and local capitalist enterprises, which would in his view legitimate the use of the term in that the capitalist concessions would remain strictly under the control of the Soviet state. However, as Lenin also acknowledged later, 'concessions have not developed on any considerable scale',[140] and he abandoned the term altogether, switching his interest to the prospects of co-operatives and arguing that 'co-operation under our conditions nearly always coincides fully with socialism'.[141] Moreover, as is well known, the New Economic Policy itself was later completely abandoned, and the subsequent development of the Soviet economy could be in no way characterized as capitalist or state capitalist. To do so would only confuse matters, diverting attention from the real problems and contradictions of the Soviet type postcapitalist system. Also, to characterize the Soviet system as capitalist or state capitalist before its collapse makes it totally mysterious why the regime under Gorbachev and his successors desperately tried to restore capitalism, if they already had it, as it is alleged, ever since the 1920s; and why indeed even up to the present day they could only partially succeed in this enterprise.

It was the failure of de-Stalinization and the worsening crisis of the Soviet system to lead to the pressure in the ruling circles for the restoration of capitalism. This happened under circumstances when the capital system as such had entered its historic phase of structural crisis, making the viability of the earlier known forms of 'extraneous help' for solving the problems of the system extremely problematical. A long time before Gorbachev's attempted 'perestroika' and failed, I tried — while stressing that the Soviet type system remained under the rule of capital — to characterize the main differences between capitalism and the postcapitalist form of managing the socioeconomic metabolism as follows:

> The capitalist formation extends only over that particular phase of capital production in which:
>
> (1) *production for exchange* (and thus the mediation and domination of use-value by exchange-value) is *all-pervasive*;
>
> (2) *labour-power* itself, just as much as anything else, is treated as a *commodity*;
>
> (3) the drive for *profit* is the fundamental regulatory force of production;
>
> (4) the vital mechanism of the *extraction of surplus-value,* the radical separation of the means of production from the producers, assumes an *inherently economic form*;
>
> (5) the economically extracted surplus-value is *privately appropriated* by the members of the capitalist class; and
>
> (6) following its own *economic imperative* of growth and expansion, capital production tends towards a *global integration*, through the intermediary of the world market, as a totally interdependent system of economic domination and subordination.

To speak of capitalism in post-revolutionary societies, when out of these essential defining characteristics only one — number four — remains, and even that in a *radically altered* form in that *the extraction of surplus-labour is regulated politically and not economically,* can be done only by disregarding or misrepresenting the objective conditions of development, with serious consequences for the possibility of gaining insight into the real nature of the problems at stake.

Capital maintains its — by no means unrestricted — rule in post-revolutionary societies primarily through:

(1) the material imperatives which circumscribe the possibilities of the totality of life-processes;

(2) the inherited social division of labour which, notwithstanding its significant modifications, contradicts 'the development of free individualities';

(3) the objective structure of the available production apparatus (including plant and machinery) and of the historically developed and restricted form of scientific knowledge, both originally produced in the framework of capital production and under the conditions of the social division of labour; and

(4) the links and interconnections of the post-revolutionary societies with the global system of capitalism, whether these assume the form of a 'peaceful competition' (e.g., commercial and cultural exchange) or that of a potentially deadly opposition (from the arms race to more or less limited actual confrontations in contested areas).

Thus the issue is incomparably more complex and far-reaching than its conventional characterization as merely the imperative of capital accumulation, now renamed 'socialist accumulation'.[142]

It cannot be emphasised enough, our main concern here is not historical, concerned with the specificities and limitations of postrevolutionary developments undertaken within the confines of great socioeconomic backwardness; a revolution which on top of its extremely unfavourable internal conditions had to face also the onslaught of the hostile capitalist world. The immense difficulties of moving from the rule of capital to a self-regulating socialist order must be confronted even by the economically most developed country. For in such a country, given the much higher concentration and centralization of capital, the immediate pressure for maintaining the continuity of production — and thereby the viability of the newly instituted social metabolic reproduction process—is bound to be even greater than in a relatively underdeveloped society. Moreover, the necessity to switch from the inherited—primarily economic—mode of expropriating surplus-value to a viable form of politically regulated surplus-labour-extraction in the aftermath of a socialist revolution cannot be avoided, no matter how economically advanced the country or countries concerned.

The power of capital cannot be overcome in the material domain under its control by some kind of spontaneous economic action, even if economic knowledge is sufficiently developed and diffused in society as a whole (which is out of the question, given the qualitative novelty of the tasks that must be undertaken, and the knowledge needed for them cannot be legitimated by the inherited capital system and its 'personifications'). The vital first step involves radically changing the mode of regulating the production and allocation of the economic surplus. This is feasible in the first place only through an autonomous — and in the course of the unfolding revolution socially sustainable — political process, whether we have in mind an underdeveloped or a capitalistically most developed country. A veritable 'sea-change' is required, everywhere, in order to embark on the road towards a new 'organic system'. The proper political regulation of socioeconomic intercourse is a vitally important part of this enterprise, especially in the early phases of the difficult transition towards a fully self-regulating socialist metabolic order. For the modern state formation is an essential constituent of capital's organic system, and the move towards the socialist alternative is inconceivable (1) without taking over all of the old state's protective functions vis-à-vis the capital system, as the negative aspect of the postcapitalist political enterprise, and (2) without successfully articulating the autonomous and positive regulatory functions through which the associated producers can themselves put to their chosen ends the fruits of their surplus-labour in the course of creating the socialist organic system.

If the positive aspect of the task is not pursued right from the beginning, there can be no hope of carrying to a successful conclusion the socialist revolution. Indeed, sooner or later even the negative functions undertaken by 'expropriating the expropriators' are bound to fail. For the fundamental issue in this respect is the *antagonistic* structural relationship within the labour process itself under the rule of capital. This is the case in every domain and at every level of the social metabolism, from the 'microcosms' of the local economic enterprises to the most comprehensive reproductive interrelations. If in this respect the politically regulated extraction of surplus-labour after the revolution is not actually controlled by the associated producers themselves, but by a political authority superimposed on them, that kind of relationship would inevitably reproduce the incurable antagonism of the old labour process. This must be the case even if the type of personification of capital confronting postrevolutionary labour would have to change in accordance with the altered sociohistorical circumstances.

One of the most difficult problems in this respect is what Lenin called 'the significance of the dictatorship of the proletariat in the economic sphere ... the dictatorship by the workers in economic relations'.[143] His answer inevitably carried the marks of the historical situation in which economically backward Russia found itself, and Lenin was the first to admit it by stressing that 'we, the Russian proletariat ... are behind the most backward West-European country as regards our level of culture and the degree of material and productive preparedness for the introduction of socialism'.[144] Thus he could only answer his own question about the 'significance of the dictatorship of the proletariat in the economic sphere' by insisting that

> the work of learning practically how to build up *large-scale production* is the guarantee that we are on the right road, the guarantee that the class-conscious workers in Russia are carrying on the struggle against *small proprietary disintegration* and disorganization, against petty-bourgeois indiscipline — the guarantee of the victory of communism.[145]

To be sure, the dangers of 'small proprietary disintegration and disorganization' were real enough. Thus the adoption of the overall socioeconomic objective 'to build up large-scale production' had meant embarking on the necessary and right road, in contrast to the temptations to go along with 'small proprietary' demands. However, while large-scale production is undoubtedly a necessary *material prerequisite* to a successful socialist development, it is certainly not '*the guarantee of the victory of communism'*. The objective constraints of the given historical situation forced even Lenin to look for reassurances which turned out to be most problematical. For Lenin could not envisage the possibility of an objective contradiction between the dictatorship of the proletariat and the proletariat itself. Thus on some vital issues, concerning both the exercise of state power and its relationship to the proletariat, he radically altered his position after the October revolution, with far-reaching consequences for the working class. In contrast to the pre-revolutionary intentions which predicated the fundamental identity of the *'entire armed people'*[146] with state power, there appeared in Lenin's writings a separation of state power from 'the working people', whereby *'state power* is organizing large-scale production on *state-owned* land and in *state-owned* enterprises on a national scale, is *distributing labour power* among the various branches of economy and the various enterprises, and is *distributing among the working people* large quantities of articles of consumption *belonging to the state'*.[147] The fact that the *'distribution of labour-power'* was a relationship of *structural subordination* did not seem to trouble Lenin, who bypassed the issue by simply describing the new form of separate state power as 'the proletarian state power'.[148] Thus the objective contradiction between the dictatorship of the proletariat itself disappeared from his horizon at the very moment it surfaced as centralized state power which determines on its own the distribution of labour-power.

At the most generic level of class relations — corresponding to the polar opposition between the proletariat and the bourgeoisie — the contradiction did not seem to exist. The new state had to secure its own material base and the central distribution of labour-power appeared to be the only viable principle for achieving this, *from the standpoint of the state already in existence*.[149] In reality, however, it was 'the working people' themselves who had to be reduced to and distributed as labour-power: not only over immense geographical distances — with all the upheavals and dislocations inevitably involved in such a centrally imposed system of distribution — but also 'vertically' in each and every locality, in accordance with both the material dictates of the inherited production structures and the political dictates inherent in their newly constituted principle and organs of regulation.

These problems were closely connected with the dilemmas concerning the socialist revolution 'at the weakest link of the chain'. Lenin argued that 'thanks to capitalism, the material apparatus of the big banks, syndicates, railways, and so forth, has grown' and 'the immense experience of the *advanced countries* has accumulated a stock of engineering marvels, the employment of which is being hindered by capitalism', concluding that the Bolsheviks (who were in fact confined to a *backward country)* could 'lay hold of this apparatus and set it in motion'.[150] Thus the immense difficulties of transition from one particular revolution to the irrevocable success of a global revolution (which is beyond the control of any one particular agency, however class-conscious and disciplined) were more or less implicitly brushed aside by voluntaristically postulating that the Bolsheviks were capable of taking power and 'retaining it until the triumph of the world socialist revolution'.[151] Thus, while the viability of a socialist revolution at the weakest link of the chain was advocated, the imperative of a world revolution as a condition of success of the former reasserted itself in a most uneasy form: as an insoluble tension at the very heart of the theory. But what could one say in the event the world socialist revolution did not come about and the Bolsheviks were condemned to hold on to power indefinitely? Lenin and his revolutionary comrades were unwilling to entertain that question, since it conflicted with certain elements of their outlook. They had to claim the viability of their strategy in a form which necessarily implied anticipating revolutionary developments in areas over which their forces had no control whatsoever. In other words, their strategy involved the contradiction between two imperatives: first, the need to go it alone, as the *immediate* (historical) precondition of success (of doing it at all); and second, the imperative of the triumph of the world socialist revolution as the *ultimate* (structural) precondition of success of the whole enterprise.[152]

In the aftermath of the October revolution, for as long as the hope of a global revolution could be nourished, Lenin's strategic concern was to 'hold the fort' until the situation became truly favourable, thanks to the revolution in the advanced countries, enabling the Bolsheviks 'to lay hold of the advanced productive apparatus and set it in motion'. This is why even the notion of 'state capitalism' could be entertained by Lenin as a very limited phase strictly supervised by the state. After great disappointments this perspective had to be abandoned and a more positive definition of socialism in the country had to be given. Thus Lenin wrote in 1923:

> Now we are entitled to say that for us the mere growth of co-operation ... is identical with the growth of socialism, and at the same time we have to admit that there has been a radical modification in our whole outlook on socialism. The radical modification is this; formerly we placed, and had to place, the main emphasis on the political struggle, on revolution, on winning political power, etc. Now the emphasis is changing and shifting to peaceful, organizational, "cultural" work.[153]

This change of emphasis could be used later by Stalin for his own purposes in asserting the actual development of 'socialism in one country'. This was quite illegitimate. For Lenin ended the same article with a sobering note, underlining that

> This *cultural revolution* would now suffice to make our country a completely socialist country; but it presents immense difficulties of a purely *cultural* (for we are illiterate) and *material* character (for to be cultured we must achieve a certain development of the material means of production, must have a certain *material base*).[154]

Thus, even in his most positive reflections on the margin of emancipatory action in postrevolutionary Russia, Lenin refused to 'radically modify' his earlier view that socialism will have to be 'created by the revolutionary co-operation of the proletarians of *all* countries'.[155]

Whatever might be the constraining and complicating socioeconomic circumstances, two conclusions are inescapable even for the industrially most advanced capitalist countries in the light of 20th century historical experience. The *first* concerns the political form required for attempting to break the rule of capital. Whether it is called the 'dictatorship of the proletariat' or by some other name, the need remains acute for instituting a transitional state form capable not only of matching and overcoming the power of capital, but also of progressively 'withering away' in due course, parallel to the transfer of the traditional state functions to the social body. This transitional form of political control could not be, of course, in sharper contrast to the postrevolutionary seizure of power converting itself into a more than ever centralized and strengthened separate state organ through which the new type of 'personifications of capital' can appropriate to themselves the levers of controlling the social metabolic functions and perpetuate the structural subordination of labour to the reproductive imperatives of the capital system. The *second* conclusion is implicit in Lenin's last quotation. For, as he stressed, the success or failure of socialism depends on the efficacy of the *'cultural revolution'*, as linked to the *'growth of co-operation'* mentioned in the preceding quote.

This is where we can see how inseparably the two practical conclusions are intertwined in the prospects of any country attempting a socialist transformation, no matter how economically underdeveloped or advanced they might be. For the essential defining characteristic of the postrevolutionary political form — if it is to overcome the power of capital and fulfil its role in the realization of socialism — is its orientation towards the establishment of a *non-adversarial* mode of *overall* social metabolic control. This means co-ordinating the *co-operative* 'micro-structures' or societal productive cells into a *comprehensive* reproductive framework, which is feasible only if the institutional articulation of the postrevolutionary political form and the practices in tune with it are *non-hierarchical*. The incorrigibly hierarchical overall political command structure of capital arises on the ground of the necessary adversarial inner determination of its reproductive constituents, due to the structural antagonism between capital and labour which the political system embodies and consolidates. The failure of all past attempts to establish 'co-operatives' on capital's material ground was, therefore, unavoidable, given the interlocking determinations of the material and political domain and the hierarchical adversarial character of both. But precisely for this reason, the political form of postrevolutionary society can fulfil its anticipated transitional role, and 'wither away' in due course, only if it is articulated in conjunction with a simultaneously developing non-adversarial co-operative material domain. And vice versa, the 'cultural revolution' stressed by Lenin has for its necessary objective not only the elimination of illiteracy and the development of theoretical and practical productive skills on the broadest possible basis. At the same time, the fundamental strategic objective of the advocated cultural revolution is the establishment of the new — non-adversarial and positively co-operative — material reproductive 'microcosms' which can harmoniously coalesce within the overall framework of the non-hierarchical postrevolutionary political form and progressively take over the latter's at first unavoidably separate functions.

17.2.3

THE slogan of 'socialism in one country' — officially embraced by the Communist International as part of its own programme — was immensely damaging for the socialist movement not only in Russia but all over the world. It has led not only to the hopeless distortion of every major theoretical tenet of the originally envisaged socialist transformation. Worse than that, the country in which it was implemented became the yardstick of socialism as 'actually existing'; a yardstick which could be used as a stick — indeed as a bludgeon — with which the adversaries of socialism could beat its supporters. As to the Soviet

Union itself, the matter could not even be left at deluding the people only with the 'completion of socialism in one country'. After the passing of some decades it had to be asserted that complete socialism had been already realized, and now the highest phase of social development, *communism* — whose orienting principle is: 'from each according to their ability, to each according to their needs' — was in the process of being accomplished. Naturally, the postcapitalist personifications of capital could preach such an absurdity only with the greatest *cynicism* in a country in which even the basic necessities (from food and clothing to decent housing) were lacking for countless millions, while they treated themselves with boundless generosity, 'according to their needs' (or, rather, greedy wants) by setting up an elaborate network of special shops, luxury holiday resorts, hunting lodges, dachas, etc. Thus, not only 'socialism' but even 'communism' had already arrived, for them. The precipitous speed with which at the time of the Soviet system's implosion the same 'socialist leaders' had embraced the orienting principles of capitalist 'market society', could only confirm that the quality essential for operating the profoundly iniquitous capital system in any one of its feasible varieties, while pretending that everything is done in the interest of the popular masses, is boundless cynicism.

At the time of his exile in Alma Ata, in 1928, Trotsky — still hoping to reverse the trend of Stalinist accommodation within the Communist International — tried to put the record of theoretical debates straight in a memorandum addressed to the Sixth Congress of the Comintern. Understandably, this memorandum was suppressed by Stalin because Trotsky had pointed out the complete travesty of Lenin's position in the course of the unfolding debates by Stalin, including the doctoring of his own views held in the past:

In 1924 Stalin outlined Lenin's views on the building of socialism as follows:
'The overthrow of the power of the bourgeoisie and the establishment of a proletarian government in one country does not yet guarantee the complete victory of socialism. The main task of socialism — the organization of socialist production — still remains ahead. Can this task be accomplished, can the final victory of socialism in one country be attained, without the joint efforts of the proletariat of several advanced countries? *No, this is impossible.* To overthrow the bourgeoisie, the efforts of one country are sufficient — the history of our revolution bears this out. For the final victory of socialism, for the organization of socialist production, the efforts of one country, particularly of such a peasant country as Russia are insufficient. For this the efforts of the proletarians of several advanced countries are necessary. Such, on the whole, are the characteristic features of the Leninist theory of the proletarian revolution.'
One must concede that the 'characteristic features of the Leninist theory' are outlined here quite correctly. In the later editions of Stalin's book this passage was altered to read in just the opposite way. [Accordingly] Stalin said in November 1926:
'The party always took as its starting point the idea that the victory of socialism in one country means the possibility to build socialism in that country, and this task can be accomplished with the forces of a single country.'
We already know that the party never took this as its starting point. On the contrary, 'in many of our works, in all our speeches, and in our entire press', as Lenin said, the party proceeded from the opposite position, which found its highest expression in the program of the C.P. S.U.[156]

The Stalinist juggernaut rolled on relentlessly and in April 1925 Stalin obtained official approval for the doctrine of 'socialism in one country' at the fourteenth conference of the party. According to Isaac Deutscher 'Trotsky did not challenge the dogma until 1926, when it had already gained wide acceptance'.[157] Deutscher explained Stalin's doctrinal victory in this way: 'The truly tragic feature of Russian society in the twenties was its longing for stability, a longing which was only natural after its recent experiences. The future had little stability in store for any country, but least of all for Russia. Yet the desire at least for a long, very long, respite from risky endeavours came to be the dominant motive of Russian politics. Socialism in one country, as it was practically interpreted until the late twenties, held out the promise of stability. On the other hand, the very name of Trotsky's theory, 'permanent revolution', sounded like an ominous warning to a tired generation that it should expect no Peace and Quiet in its lifetime.'[158] Although it is true that in the confrontation over the issue Stalin's 'immediate purpose was to discredit Trotsky and to prove for the *nth* time that Trotsky was no Leninist',[159] Stalin could also use his doctrine as the theoretical justification and pseudo-Leninist legitimation of his policy of forced collectivization. For he could claim that the 'extension of socialism' to the country-side through collectivization had put an end to the danger of *'small proprietary disintegration and disorganization, and petty-bourgeois indiscipline'* against which Lenin sounded the warnings quoted above. In truth, however, Stalin's policy caused immense damage to the country's agricultural development — not to mention its human costs — from which the Russian economy could not fully recover even to the present day.

The cynicism with which the doctrine of 'socialism in one country' was treated by the ruling political elite transpired in the conversations Trotsky had in 1926 in Berlin — when he had to spend some time there for medical treatment — with Eugene Varga. As Deutscher recalled it:

> While he stayed at the Berlin embassy, Trotsky spent many hours in discussions with Krestinsky, the Ambassador, and E. Varga, the Comintern's leading economist. The subject of his discussions with Varga was socialism in a single country. Varga admitted that as an economic theory Stalin's doctrine was worthless, that socialism in one country was moonshine, but that it was nevertheless politically useful as a slogan capable of inspiring the backward masses. Recording the discussion in his private papers, Trotsky remarked of Varga that he was 'the Polonius of the Comintern'.[160]

Thus, in one way or another, 'socialism in one country' became the accepted orthodoxy throughout the international communist movement. The question *whether* the Soviet system could realize socialism within the adopted socioeconomic and political framework became a taboo; the only legitimate question was *how long* it would take to achieve the irreversible and complete transition to socialism. Yet, against those who argued that the Soviet transitional régime could only move in the direction of socialism Trotsky stressed later — in 1936, the year of the first great show trials in Moscow — that 'In reality a backslide to capitalism is wholly possible'.[161] However, although Trotsky's next sentence stated that 'A more complete definition will of necessity be complicated and ponderous',[162] he did not theoretically elaborate his insight about the wholly possible backslide into capitalism under the Stalinist system. He went on describing the Soviet Union as a *'degenerate workers' state'*, expecting a solution from a political revolution through which 'the workers would overthrow the bureaucracy'.[163]

One of the old Bolsheviks in Trotsky's opposition group, Christian Rakovsky — who also fell victim to the Stalinist terror — characterized the aims and merits of their group in this way: 'The opposition will always retain as one of its merits, as against the party, a merit which nothing can remove, the fact that it has, in good time, sounded the alarm on the terrible decline of the spirit of activity of the working classes, and on their increasing indifference towards the destiny of the dictatorship of the proletariat and of the Soviet state'.[164] He also asked the important questions:

> ... what has happened to the spirit of revolutionary activity of the party and of our proletariat? Where has their revolutionary initiative gone? Where their ideological interests, their revolutionary values, their proletarian pride have gone? You are surprised that there is so much apathy, weakness, pusillanimity, opportunism and so many other things that I could add myself? How is it that those who have a worthy revolutionary past, whose present honesty cannot be held in doubt, who have given proof of their attachment to the revolution on more than one occasion, can have been transformed into pitiable bureaucrats?[165]

However, despite the author's noble intentions, the solutions proposed were very far from meeting the challenge and matching the size of the identified problems. Perhaps understandably, since the debate unfolded in the domain of political confrontations, with the participation of people who all their adult life were active as political leaders, remedies were only envisaged in the form of improving the methods of political leadership, linked to the task of re-educating the working class. Rakovsky could go as far as stressing that 'it is not only a question of a change of personnel but firstly a change in methods'.[166] And he added: 'It is necessary to re-educate the working masses and the party masses within the framework of the party and of the trade unions. This process will be long and difficult; but inevitable. It has already started'.[167]

As we all know, none of these hopes were realized in the course of subsequent developments. In the diagnoses offered by Rakovsky and his friends, too much stress was laid on the corrupting psychological impact of privileges leading to bureaucratization, which seemed to beg the question. In the end the suggestion failed to answer Rakovsky's most relevant question: 'How is it that those who have a worthy revolutionary past, whose present honesty cannot be held in doubt, who have given proof of their attachment to the revolution on more than one occasion, can have been transformed into pitiable bureaucrats?'. In his attempt to explain the bewildering and most disheartening developments Rakovsky spoke about a 'functional differentiation' which 'power has introduced into the bosom of the proletariat' and concluded from it that 'The function has modified the organism itself; that is to say that the *psychology* of those who are charged with the diverse tasks of *direction* in the administration and the economy of the state, has changed to such a point that not only objectively but subjectively, not only materially but also morally, they have ceased to be a part of this very same working class.'[168] This perspective, which addressed correctly some of the manifestations of the postrevolutionary social malady but not their deep-seated causes, wanted to undo the damage by advocating a return to genuine revolutionary political morality through the change in the methods — as well as, of course, in the personnel — of the political leadership, coupled with the education of the working class, a task conceived in the same spirit.

Tragically, the contradictions were much more fundamental than what could be amenable to such solutions. They have arisen from the reproduction of the *adversarial* and *hierarchical* character of the rule of capital in a new — postcapitalist — form. The controlling personnel superimposed on labour, and its ever more tyrannical methods, opposed by the marginalized former revolutionary leaders (in the end liquidated by Stalin), were the concomitant of the Soviet type system remaining fatefully trapped — despite the original revolutionary intentions and the corresponding initial political steps taken for 'expropriating the expropriators' — within the structural confines of the capital system as an order of social metabolic reproduction with its own, ruthlessly self-expansionary, logic. If the politically enforced extraction of surplus labour retains its adversarial and hierarchical character — which it must if control over the labour process is not exercised by the associated producers themselves, — then the objective conditions of labour (which under capitalism are personified in the private expropriators of surplus-value) will have to find their new type of personification of capital. 'Psychological corruption' is the consequence, rather than the original cause, of such primarily objective determinations.

To do away with the privilege-seeking psychology — characterized as the 'motor harem' in one of Rakovsky's references[169] — it is necessary to overcome the structural subordination of labour to capital through the fully co-operative principle advocated by Lenin in 1923, alas in vain. For labour subjected to the material imperatives of capital-expansion, as controlled by a power superimposed on the labour process also under the known forms of political surplus-labour-extraction, remains dominated by alienation both in the sense of being ruled by an alien decision-making power, and in that the fruits of surplus-labour are alienated from it. Thus, in Marx's words, when labour's objective conditions of exercise are unaccountable to living labour, asserting themselves, instead, as 'value existing for itself and holding fast to itself, in short as capital ... these objective conditions must from the formal point of view confront labour as alien, independent powers, as value — objectified labour — to which living labour is the mere means of its own preservation and expansion'.[170] The privilege-seeking psychology and its ideological legitimation rightly deplored by Rakovsky and his comrades is grounded in these objective determinations and power relations. Accordingly, the acceptance of the postrevolutionary capital system's alienating and dehumanizing imperatives by Stalin and his supporters, and their imposition with brutal efficacy on the social body, were the secrets of Stalin's — at first to the old Bolsheviks quite astonishing — success.

17.3 The failure of de-Stalinization and the collapse of 'really existing socialism'

17.3.1

FOR all too obvious reasons, Stalin did his best to confine the validity of the Marxian conception of capital strictly to capitalism, grossly distorting thereby the meaning of his work. For in the interest of postcapitalist capital-apologetics it had to be emphatically denied that the Marxian categories had any relevance to the critical understanding of the alienating antagonisms and socioeconomic deficiencies of the established order. In his last lengthy writing, intended as the theoretical elaboration of the problems of political economy — and in particular of 'socialist' political economy — Stalin proclaimed that:

> I think that we must also discard certain other concepts taken from Marx's *Capital* — where Marx was concerned with an analysis of *capitalism* — and artificially pasted on to our socialist relations.I am referring to such concepts, among others, as 'necessary' and 'surplus' labour, 'necessary' and 'surplus' product, 'necessary' and 'surplus' time. Marx analyzed capitalism in order to elucidate the source of exploitation of the working class — surplus value — and to arm the working class, which was bereft of means of production, with an intellectual weapon for the overthrow of capitalism. It is natural that Marx used concepts (categories) which fully corresponded to *capitalist relations*. But it is strange, to say the least, to use these concepts now, when the working class is not only not bereft of power and means of production, but, on the contrary, is *in possession of the power and controls the means of production*.[171]

Pursuing the fiction of total harmony, the apologetic intent became clear when Stalin insisted that it is 'strange to speak now of "necessary" and "surplus" labour: as though, under our conditions, the labour contributed by the workers to society for the extension of production, the promotion of education and public health, the organization of defence, etc., is not just as necessary to the working class, now in power, as the labour expended to supply the personal needs of the worker and his family.'[172] Thus, the crucial question of *who controlled* the allocation of labour power as regards both the adopted production targets and the distribution of the total social product — i.e. whether it was allocated by the associated producers themselves, exercising their control within the framework of a fully co-operative mode of production and distribution, or under the new personifications of capital who ruthlessly enforced their system's imperatives through an authoritarian state machinery — could be conveniently brushed aside with the help of Stalin's primitive demagoguery, greeted with total sycophancy as the ultimate revelation of socialist wisdom. If for maintaining the existing system in power countless millions of workers had to be sent to forced labour camps, that was also 'just as necessary to the working class' as the means of consumption to its individual members (of which they had very little, especially in the labour camps where millions of them had to perish). For the working class was supposed to be 'in possession of power and in control of the means of production'.

That the dismissed category of *surplus labour* not only existed in Soviet society but also continued to be allocated with great political arbitrariness — as well as with immense wastefulness, due to the ultimate uncontrollability of recalcitrant labour — was obviously quite inadmissible. All kinds of fantasies had to be pursued and reassuringly decreed to be already realized, or to be well on the way to full realization. After the claimed successful completion of 'socialism in one country', nothing less than the potential achievements of the highest state of communism had to be declared as being within fairly easy reach. Thus not only the abolition of the opposition between town and country but even that between mental and physical labour had to be postulated, removing them with the same magic wand — reference to the juridical overthrow of capitalism — which disposed of the antagonism arising from the alienated structural subordination of labour to the established hierarchical system. This is how Stalin 'argued' his case:

> The economic basis of the antithesis between mental and physical labour is the exploitation of the physical workers by the mental workers. Everyone is familiar with the gulf which under capitalism divided the physical workers of enterprises from the managerial personnel. We know that this gulf gave rise to a hostile attitude on the part of the workers towards managers, foremen, engineers and other members of the technical staff, whom the workers regarded as their enemies. Naturally, with the abolition of capitalism and the exploiting system, the antagonism of interests between physical and mental labour was also bound to disappear. And it really has disappeared in our present socialist system. Today the physical workers and the managerial personnel are not enemies, but comrades and friends, members of a single body of producers who are vitally interested in the progress and improvement of production.[173]

In this way nothing further needed to be changed in the organization of the labour process. Great advances could be claimed without changing anything at all. It could be pretended that under 'our present socialist system' the control of labour was non-hierarchical and purely technical, and the people involved in it were 'comrades and friends', constituting a 'single body of producers'. The political tyranny through which a forced rate of extraction of surplus-labour was secured under the given system of postcapitalist capital production was nowhere mentioned. There could be no room for such considerations in the proclaimed 'scientific political economy'. For in Stalinist fiction-land the workers were 'in possession of state power and in control of the means of production'. No task or height of achievement could be considered too great for the claimed 'single body of producers'. The Stakhanovite scheme cynically used by the state to force upon the workers exploitative 'norms' and work methods was described as 'socialist emulation', projecting great things for the future. The contrast between the pre-Stakhanovite past and the present was characterized in this way:

> Before the socialist emulation movement assumed mass proportions, the growth of our industry proceeded very haltingly, and many comrades even suggested that the rate of industrial development should be retarded. This was due chiefly to the fact that the cultural and technical level of the workers was too low and lagged far behind that of the technical personnel. But the situation changed radically when the socialist emulation movement assumed a mass character. ... among the workers whole groups of comrades came to the fore who had not only mastered the minimum requirements of technical knowledge, but had gone further and risen to the level of the technical personnel; they began to correct technicians and engineers, to break down the existing norms as antiquated, to introduce new and more up-to-date norms, and so on. What should we have had if not only isolated groups, [!? not a 'mass emulation movement'?!] but the majority of the workers had raised their cultural and technical level to that of the engineering and technical personnel? Our industry would have risen to a height unattainable in other countries.[174]

A prospect of development like this surely must have put the fear of god into the Americans, as well as into the Japanese and the Germans! Modelling itself on this Stalinist discourse, in which the wishfully projected future was inextricably fused with the most peculiar description of the present, the later strategies of 'winning the peaceful competition over advanced capitalism', thanks to the claimed apriori superiority of the established system, maintained the same voluntaristic attitude to the economic facts and social relations of 'actually existing socialism', with disastrous consequences for the future.

There was another way as well in which Stalin's last lengthy writing anticipated later developments. By the Spring of 1952, when 'Economic Problems of Socialism in the U.S.S.R.' was published, the Soviet economy was experiencing major difficulties, after the relatively unproblematical years of postwar reconstruction, with its high rate of growth. Running the economy on the basis of a permanent state of emergency, which characterized many years of Soviet economic development, could no longer meet the requirements of both a much more sophisticated — increasingly high technology-oriented — military production and an expanding demand for consumer goods of at least tolerable quality. During the long years when the Soviet economy was managed on the basis of an artificially cultivated state of emergency — apart from the war years when the emergency was real enough — the productivity of labour was very low, to a significant degree due to the fact that a sizeable portion of the labour force was locked up in labour camps. However, the recalcitrance of labour was much more widespread than the numbers in forced labour camps. It embraced the overwhelming majority of the working class; partly because of the antagonistic mode of controlling the labour process, and partly because of the very meagre remuneration received by the workers. Attempts to 'liberalize' the direct political control of the labour process could only be made after Stalin's death, ascribing all the failures and contradictions of the past, in Khrushchev's secret speech, to Stalin's 'personality cult'. By contrast, Stalin's celebrated writing on the 'Economic Problems of Socialism in the U.S.S.R.' tried to address the chronically neglected issues of the consumer industry, even if in a half-hearted and rather confused way.

Given the Stalinist régime's ideological rationalization and legitimation, the author's confusion was due to the congenital inability to see the postrevolutionary developments in their objective historical perspective. The constraints under which the Soviet postcapitalist capital system operated had to be theorized as non-existent or, worse still, transubstantiated into permanent and model socialist achievements. The fact that after 'breaking the weakest link of the chain' the postrevolutionary society had to find its own solutions to several dimensions of the capitalist crisis out of which it had emerged, remaining thereby in dependency to the objective conditions which it had to negate, was left totally out of sight when viewed through the distorting prism of 'socialism in one country'. As mentioned in note 135, within the framework of the postcapitalist socioeconomic order's expansionary requirements and potentialities, neither the pressure for achieving the 'maximum realization of capital, and the maximum continuity of the production process through circulation time posited as zero', nor the fundamental difficulties of maintaining an economically sustainable proportionality between departments A (the production of the means of production) and B (production for direct consumption by the labour force) seemed to exist at all for a long time after the revolution.Under the significantly changed post-Second World War circumstances, however, these problems had reemerged with a vengeance, and could not be treated with the vacuous slogans of Stalinist mythology, like the earlier mentioned Stakhanovite 'socialist mass emulation'. Thus Stalin proclaimed 'the law of balanced (proportionate) development of the national economy, which has superseded the law of competition and anarchy of production', arguing that

> In this same direction, too, operate our yearly and five-yearly plans and our economic policy generally, which are based on the *requirements* of the *law* of balanced development of the national economy.[175]

The meaning given here to 'law' was quite bewildering. For whereas *competition* and *anarchy* were *objective laws* of development, the proclaimed 'law' of proportionate or 'balanced development of the national economy' was no more than a *requirement*, and under the Soviet type postcapitalist capital system an extremely problematical and wishful one. The disintegration of 'actually existing socialism' had a great deal to do with this kind of economic reasoning, which tried to run the economy, with great arbitrariness, on the basis of utterly fictitious laws. On top of it, Stalin wanted to maintain, under all circumstances, the 'primacy of the production of means of production', asking the rhetorical question: 'what would be the effect of ceasing to give primacy to the production of the means of production?' and answering it with a circular declaration that

> The effect would be to destroy the possibility of the continuous expansion of our national economy, because the national economy cannot be continuously expanded without giving primacy to the production of means of production.[176]

Whether the 'continuous expansion of the national economy' can be actually sustained by sticking to the adopted strategies and methods of giving primacy to the production of means of production was never asked. It was simply assumed that once that course is pursued, the declared objective of 'continuous expansion' — whose absolute and permanent desirability was also simply assumed, and progress towards it was measured in the most primitive terms, like the quantity of pig-iron production in comparison to the U.S. — would be automatically secured; another utterly wishful proposition. For the antagonistic nature of the existing control of the labour process turns 'proportionality' into an empty *desideratum* and the linked idea of 'continuous productive expansion of the national economy' into an all-promising but unworkable propaganda device. The projected results of economic development are realizable in the longer run only in a genuinely socialist socioeconomic framework whose productive targets are set not by an alien body, but by all those who have to call upon their own resources so as to translate them into reality, measuring the attainment of their chosen objectives on an inherently *qualitative* basis, as we shall see in Chapters 19 and 20. Without that the possibility of sustainable productive development is bound to be nullified as time goes by, as indeed in the Soviet type postcapitalist system it emphatically has been, whatever successes might be achieved at first under the circumstances of postrevolutionary emergency.

By the time Stalin wrote his piece on the 'Economic Problems of Socialism in the U.S.S.R.', there were serious difficulties about making the desideratum of 'proportionality' live up to expectations. Securing 'continuous expansion' within the framework of a system run on the basis of an artificially extended state of emergency, giving primacy to the production of means of production with extreme wastefulness, was becoming less and less tenable. Other ways had to be attempted to give a boost to the economy. This is how Stalin came to give his blessing to the pursuit of profit in Soviet economic enterprises, although —

given the other regulatory requirements which he wanted simultaneously to remain in operation — also in this respect to a large extent one could only speak of desiderata. He declared that

> the operation of the law of value is not confined to the sphere of *commodity circulation*. It also extends to production. ... As a matter of fact, *consumer goods*, which are needed to compensate the *labour power* expended in the process of production, are produced and realized in our country as *commodities* coming under the operation of the *law of value*. It is precisely here that the law of value exercises its influence on production. In this connection, such things as *cost accounting and profitableness*, production costs, prices, etc., are of actual importance in our enterprises. Consequently, our enterprises cannot, and must not, function without taking the law of value into account. Is this a good thing? It is not a bad thing. Under present conditions, it really is not a bad thing, since it trains *our business executives* to conduct production on rational lines and *disciplines* them. It is not a bad thing because it teaches our executives to count production magnitudes, to count them accurately, and also to calculate the real things in production precisely ... It is not a bad thing because it teaches our executives systematically to improve methods of production, to lower production costs, to practise cost accounting, and to make their enterprises pay. It is a good practical school which accelerates the development of *our executive personnel* and their growth into genuine *leaders of socialist production* at the present stage of development.[177]

Much of what has been decreed here was theoretically quite unfounded and had to remain in the realm of fantasy. For the Soviet system could not operate on the basis of commodity production and circulation, under the law of value, above all for the simple reason that it did not have a proper market, and least of all a labour market. And many things can be regulated in an economy with tolerable reliability with the help of a pseudo-market, but certainly not the allocation and firm control of labour power.

Nevertheless, even if in the form of desiderata only, something new appeared on the horizon through Stalin's intervention at a time when the Soviet economy was experiencing serious decline in production at the close of the post-war phase of reconstruction. It was the officially sanctioned notion that in the future much greater attention must be paid to the chronically neglected consumer goods industry, 'producing commodities for circulation', in order to 'compensate labour power' on the basis of proper 'cost accounting', adequate 'profitableness', 'discipline', etc. Naturally, the original socialist idea that the workers themselves should decide for themselves both their productive targets and the mode of operating production and distribution could not fit into this conception. The workers existed in it only as 'labour power' to be compensated by profitably produced commodities. Decisions over immediate productive tasks had to be left to *'our business executives'* and to the *'executive personnel'* in general, apart from the party leaders, of course, who remained in charge of the overall decision making process in a system operating the politically enforced extraction of surplus labour, notwithstanding Stalin's distaste for the Marxian category of surplus labour, among many others. The antagonistic mode of social metabolic reproduction prevailing under the postcapitalist capital system had to be consecrated in this way also for the future, with whatever variations and innovations in the conduct of the technical and business executive personnel might have been envisaged on the way. As to the system's self-legitimatory claims of being 'completed socialism', that question could be handled with the same cynical declaratory ease as many other questions in the past. All that was needed was to proclaim that the underlying purpose of the newly advocated changes in the economy was to 'accelerate the development of *our executive personnel* and their growth into genuine *leaders of socialist production*'. If you believed that, you could believe anything. But if you still wondered how the division of society into 'labour power' and 'socialist business executives' (as well as their other privileged brethren) could be reconciled with the idea of a classless society, and 'communism around the corner' in which the distinction between mental and physical labour disappears, that question could be also disposed of in the same way, by definition. Thus Stalin decreed, sprinkling even a pinch of 'self-critical' salt over the matter, that

> The essential distinction between them, the difference in their cultural and technical levels, will certainly disappear. But some distinction, even if inessential, will remain, if only because the conditions of labour of the *managerial staffs* and those of the *workers* are not identical. The comrades who assert the contrary do so presumably on the basis of the formulation given in some of my statements, which speaks of the abolition of the distinction between industry and agriculture, and between mental and physical labour, without any reservation to the effect that what is meant is the abolition of the *essential* distinction, not of all distinction. That is exactly how the comrades understood my formulation, *assuming* that it implied the abolition of all distinction. But this indicates that the formulation was unprecise, unsatisfactory. It must be discarded and replaced by another formulation, one that speaks of the abolition of essential distinctions and the persistence of inessential distinctions between industry and agriculture, and between mental and physical labour.[178]

Thanks to this 'new formulation', which could shove in or out of the categories of 'essential' and 'inessential' whatever suited the conjuncturally changing requirements of social apologetics, the workers could forever remain 'labour power' (respectful of the orders received, and grateful for their 'compensation' with consumer commodities), and the political and business managers could likewise forever qualify for the position of 'leaders of society' and 'leaders of socialist production'. There was no need to change the structural subordination of labour to the ruthlessly enforced mode of hierarchical social reproductive control, because the subordination of labour — the 'condition of labour for workers' as compared to that of 'managers' — was an 'inessential' determination, and therefore could be rightfully considered absolutely permanent. The 'only' question that remained unanswered in all this was: what was going to be the impact, if any, of such verbal magic on the objective social antagonism itself which deeply affected the labour process under the Soviet type postcapitalist capital system, with devastating consequences for all of the desiderata listed by Stalin in his 'political-economic testament'?!

17.3.2

IT was left to Stalin's heirs to try and answer the last question. Not surprisingly, they could not come up with viable solutions to the challenges they had to face, despite their political condemnation of Stalin's authoritarian 'personality cult'. Their 'good intentions' announcing the programme of 'de-Stalinization' had to fail because their diagnosis of the situation, and the proposed remedies in tune with it, were formulated essentially from the same standpoint which had prevailed in the past. For, as personifications of capital, the last thing they could even consider, let alone radically question, was the *structural subordination of labour to capital* in their system, and the unavoidable negative consequences of operating within such a socioeconomic framework.

The nearly four decades of Soviet reform attempts after Stalin's death, from Khrushchev's assumption of power all the way to the final implosion of the system under Gorbachev, were full of inconsistencies and contradictions, not only with regard to the economy but also in political terms. Thus, on the plane of politics, not long after denouncing Stalin in his secret speech as a monstrous tyrant, Khrushchev did not hesitate to order the bloody suppression of the Hungarian uprising in October 1956, only to be emulated in the same spirit by the new party boss — Brezhnev — who deposed him and put a brutal end to Dubcek's 'socialism with a human face' in Czechoslovakia in August 1968, after twelve more years of openly declared 'democratization' and 'de-Stalinization'. As to the economy, the political leaders of the Soviet Union in the post-Stalin era always tried to achieve, in one way or another, the impossible. For they tried to inject *capitalist* methods of cost-accounting and 'profitableness' into a *post-capitalist* system incompatible with such practices, while retaining unaltered the *political* mode of enforcing the centralized authoritarian extraction of surplus labour instituted by Stalin. In the end, when they realized that their preferred solution was unworkable, they opted, characteristically, for the restoration of capitalism.

Throughout the long decades of the attempted reforms the contradiction that remained insoluble had arisen from the leadership's futile desire to resolve the deep-seated *social antagonism* of the Soviet postcapitalist system by inventing some neutral *mechanism*. The suggestions entertained by the political leadership ranged from the improvement of the technical devices of central planning — thanks to the application of mathematical tools advocated by leading economists — all the way to the idea of full 'marketization'. Even the latter had to be characterized as for the purposes of socialist economic development unproblematically suitable — indeed, in the view of many advocates the *ideal* — 'rational mechanism'. Debates on the desirability and feasibility of introducing technical improvements in planning and better mechanisms of overall social accountancy were initiated already in the late 1950s,[179] and they acquired ever greater prominence in the 1960s.[180] The stubborn recalcitrance of labour as the root cause of the main troubles could not be faced ideologically, since its removal required the unthinkable institution of a radically different mode of controlling the social metabolic process of reproduction as a whole.

Practical experiments were set up in well controlled regions on the line of exploring the possible adoption of a more flexible instrument for regulating the relationship between the central planning authorities and the local productive enterprises. The publication of Liberman's *Pravda* article in the Autumn of 1962 was preceded not only by a meeting — in April 1962 — of the Scientific Council of the Soviet Academy of Sciences officially in charge of 'scientific planning', which had to approve, as in fact it did, Liberman's proposals.[181] More importantly, even the debate behind closed doors of the Academy was preceded by the experiments carried out in various enterprises in the region of Kharkov[182] on the basis of which Liberman's proposal's were made. The political brief for the whole enterprise was also indicated in Nemchinov's article about the resolution of the XXII Party Congress 'to realize the grandiose programme of building the *material-technical basis of communism* and of the world's most advanced industry', with the help of *'new instruments of economic regulation'*.[183] The hope vested in the 'new instruments' bordered on the miraculous: the permanent solution of humanity's yearning for motherhood and apple-pie, thanks to the anticipated *'maximum results through minimal investment'*.[184] The working class, as a collective social subject, was never allowed to appear even for a fleeting moment in this discourse, which must have added a great deal to its attractiveness in the eyes of the party leaders. The potentially troubling idea of *antagonism* was removed from it with the help of a magic wand, postulating that the proposed reforms *'eliminate the antagonism of interest between the particular enterprises and society'*.[185] Thus, between the two legitimated 'subjects' the interests of the working class — the class which, after all, had to bear the burden of everything, whether in the unreformed state of the economy or as 'improved' by repeatedly projected 'new rational mechanism' — could rightfully disappear from the horizon even in the context of the 'grandiose programme of building the material-technical basis of communism'.

After Khrushchev's fall the attempts to solve the growing socioeconomic problems of the Soviet system by technical means continued unabated. After all, no party leader, from Stalin to Gorbachev — nor indeed their 'democratic' counterparts in the West — could object to the promise of an untroubled supply of motherhood and apple-pie. In 1965 some economic reforms were in fact introduced in the Soviet Union which also stimulated a more open discussion of the difficulties persisting under Khrushchev, even if the painfully obvious but unpalatable conclusions about the underlying social antagonism could not be openly spelled out. Nevertheless, a famous airplane designer, O.I. Antonov, reported in a book published in 1965 the manifestation of indifference — bordering on hostility — of some groups of workers. According to an example highlighted by Antonov:

> two workers who were employed to unload bricks quickly from trucks did so by throwing them on the ground, usually breaking some 30 percent of them. They knew that their actions were both against the interests of the country and against simple common sense, but their work was assessed and paid on the basis of a time indicator. Therefore, they would be penalized — indeed would not be able to make their living — if they were to arrange the bricks carefully on the ground. Their way of doing the job was bad for the country, but, on the face of it, good for the plan! So they acted against their consciences and intelligence, but with a deep feeling of bitterness against the planners: 'You don't want it done in a way good husbandry would have it, you keep pressing only for quicker and quicker! Well then, get your bricks! Bang! Bang!' Thus, all over the country, decent and responsible citizens, perfectly rational beings, acted in wasteful, almost criminal ways.[186]

However, even here the fundamental question of social antagonism remained an unmentionable taboo. Legitimate questioning had to be confined strictly to the *inflexibility* of the plan, leaving the matter of the *radical exclusion of the workers* from the planning process completely out of account. Within the confines of such a discourse, the rational solution appeared to be: allocate a certain amount of time to the function of 'arranging the bricks carefully on the ground', and then the workers will happily reconcile their 'consciences and intelligence' with the requirements of the plan. Consequently, the economy will flourish, in that the deplored 30 percent wastage — in whichever work practice it might otherwise arise — would be eliminated. To be sure, the pursuit of inflexible quantitative targets was in this way indicted. However, the only thing the would-be reformers could offer as the appropriate corrective remedy — not simply in the case of Antonov, but in general, in the theories of the more or less explicitly mathematically oriented economists — was the incorporation of a suitable range of 'feed-back loops' into the central plan.

Thus the question of *quality* was hopelessly misconceived. For by maintaining the determination of the plan by a separate body — one superimposed on the workers — had inevitably meant also retaining the arbitrary quantification of its centrally ordained targets, no matter how many 'flexible feed-back loops' might have been incorporated into the control devices. For in the framework of a socialist economy *quality* concerns the recognition of the genuine human *needs* of the self-determining labour force, together with the selection of the most appropriate means and forms of action for the realization of the chosen ends. This applies to the productive tasks both in terms of the expenditure of the required human skills/energies and the materials used up in the relevant practical processes, assuming thereby responsibility not only for the local decisions but also for their broader social context and viability, established on the basis of co-operative reciprocity with other social metabolic units. The required *feed-back* is therefore an integral part of this kind of social reproductive organization, qualitatively determining its own orientation on the basis of which also quantitative wastefulness can be eliminated or reduced to an absolute minimum. By contrast, the idea of achieving an *optimal* rate of production, in accordance with the centrally envisaged efficiency-requirements of a predetermined 'flexible plan', projecting also the corrective impact of a multiplicity of 'feed-back loops' predetermined from above, is at best the pure wishful thinking of 'enlightened absolutists', if not a complete absurdity. For in 'realistic' terms, only an *infinity* of such feed-back loops could account for all possible local variations and eventualites — not to mention the *impossibility* of anticipating as well as properly redressing by technical corrective measures the immense complications which are bound to arise from the adversarial character of the existing relationship of postcapitalist capital and labour maintained in force as before. Such a system of centrally regulated 'feed-back loops' could therefore result only in a chaotic paralysis in place of a successful plan, making a complete mockery of the claims to flexibility and realism of the whole reform enterprise.

However, planners and reform-minded economists refused to give up the idea of squaring the circle — by eliminating the system's social antagonisms through technical devices — not in the world of pure mathematics but in the societies of 'actually existing socialism'. They were carried away by their belief in the irresistible power of the advocated 'new instruments and mechanisms', conferring particularly high expectations upon the methods of computerized mathematical economics and anticipating optimal results from the adopted methods. As a book published in 1967 — the fiftieth anniversary of the Russian revolution — raved about it:

The Institute for Economic Research of Gosplan and the Economics Institute of the

Academy of Sciences of the USSR have elaborated the first inter-sectoral balance of the production and distribution of the social product for 1970, which determines the optimal rhythms and proportions of the sectors and the national economy in its entirety. Scientists are backed up in this enterprise by electronic machines. Academician Fedorenko declares that, at the time of deciding the 5 year plan of Armenia's national economy, the computers had to find the most rational variant of employment, increase in the productivity of labour, and the most complete utilization of investment. They accomplished this task brilliantly in only 16 hours, while an economist, equipped with an automatic arithmometer, would have taken 720 years! Mathematical methods and electronic calculators have made it possible to compose several variants of the dynamism and *structural modifications* in the development of the national economy over a long time-scale. They have made possible the achievement of the best variant of economic development. ... Thus we shall soon have a *complex model* of the *optimal variant* of the economic plan.[187]

If only the actually existing Soviet economy could show the same ratio of advancement, from 720 years to 16 hours, as the production of its 'complex but optimal' electronic model, that would certainly make U.S. pig-iron production disappear altogether from the face of the earth, compared to the achievements of the 'new mechanisms'. There remained, though, one niggling little difficulty which turned all such elevated prognostication into dust. It was the intractable and even unmentionable fact that whereas the high-speed electronic computers could offer all kinds of dynamic variations and *'structural modifications'* as regards the data they have been fed with, in accordance with the self-serving predeterminations of the established order faithfully reflected in the modelling programs themselves, the one 'structural modification' that had to remain absolutely out of the question was the *structural subordination of labour* to the material and political imperatives of the Soviet type postcapitalist capital system.

In this scheme of things workers, with identifiable interests, were recognized only as *fragmented individual consumers* who might be conceded some limited *individual material incentives*. That was the basis on which the reform-economists could postulate the realization of the principle according to which 'that which is advantageous to society ought to be advantageous to the particular enterprise. And vice versa, that which is not advantageous to society, ought not to be advantageous to any productive enterprise at all'.[188] For 'labour is valued above all by the manner in which the consumers purchase the products and by the one and only qualitative index of profitability.'[189] Nemchinov, too, in another of his most influential articles, praised 'the individual material interests of the workers',[190] insisting at the same time that the 'feed-back loops' championed by him 'ought to be regulated in advance',[191] by the central planning authorities. Naturally, Nemchinov dutifully repeated the 'principle' that — in an economy run on the basis of decision making processes from which the workers were structurally excluded — 'all that is useful and advantageous to the national economy as a whole ought to be advantageous to the enterprise as well'.[192] Curiously, however, on the same page he also asserted that the mechanism of centrally predetermined feed-back loops (advocated by him and accepted by the party leadership) — which he also called 'the planning system based on economic calculation' — would put an end to the undesirable practices of 'economic voluntarism'.

Tragically, however, in the period of the debates on the 'liberalization' and

'democratization' of the economy, the repression of recalcitrant workers continued as before. Nor could one rationally expect to see a major change in the
situation by the postulated idea of *eliminating the antagonism of interest between the
particular enterprises and society'* through the improved mechanisms of planning,
even if they could be made to work with greater economic efficiency. For the
particular enterprises were run on the same authoritarian basis as society was.
The antagonism that needed to be eliminated, but could not be, was the
continued structural antagonism between postcapitalist capital — enforced
with ruthless political and military means by its personifications — and labour.
Thus, the year of the celebrated and much romanticized *Pravda* debates on
economic reform also witnessed the massacre of more than one hundred workers
who demonstrated against aggravated work conditions and savage cuts in their
wages in the southern Russian town of Novocherkassk. And that was the time
of the officially proclaimed 'improvement in the individual material incentives'
of the workers as consumers. Such events have become public knowledge only
in the late 1980s, but of course they were not unknown to party leaders, planning officials and prominent economists. As one of the worker participants, Petr
Siuda — who was jailed, and in 1991 murdered — commented in 1988 on the
brutal repression of the protesting workers:

> The mask was torn from the regime that claimed it was a popular government and
> that the enterprises belonged to the people. The events showed that our society is,
> in fact, *antagonistic,* that the state stands above the people. It's not the people's state.
> It exists to protect a class of exploiters — the party-state bureaucrats, whose platform
> is Stalinism. The class of the exploited stands facing them, left with nothing but the
> ideals of the revolution as a sort of pacifier.[193]

Conflicts and explosions like the events in Novocherkassk clearly demonstrated
that much more was needed than the adjustment of the Soviet planning processes to the technical devices of the belatedly discovered computer age. For insurmountable structural reasons, however, the meaning of such events could not
be taken on board by the ruling personnel. Everything had to be pressed into
the only acceptable mould of 'improved mechanisms', no matter how remote
might have been their connections with the ever more pressing problems of
'actually existing socialism'.

Re-reading the reform debates of the 1960s one is struck by their affinity —
both in principal themes and in their characteristic unreality — with Gorbachev's 'perestroika' program. Some of the old 'good intentions' are renewed in
the writings of the last Soviet Party Secretary and his 'catastroiking' collaborators with even greater emphasis than in the past, leading them as surely towards
Dante's hell as their predecessors twenty odd years earlier. The gravity of the
situation, in a country which was called upon to face its contradictions but could
not move one inch in the direction of resolving them, transpires when we recall
that in three and a half decades of programmatic 'de-Stalinization' nothing could
be significantly changed in the established economic order.

Just like before, great expectations were attached by Gorbachev and followers
to 'economic mechanisms' and to the idea of conceding — quite undeliverable
— 'individual material incentives' to the workers as consumers. Indeed, also the
idea of 'democratization' became prominent as 'glasnost' was wedded to 'perestroika'. It is salutary to compare the 'Regulations of the Socialist State Enter-

prises' approved by the Council of Ministers of the U.S.S.R. on the 4th of October 1965, announcing measures for democratizing the internal organization and decision making processes of industrial enterprises,[194] with Gorbachev's similar reform projects: both producing absolutely nothing. Yet Gorbachev could boast, with the customary rhetorics and unreality of the Soviet Party's General Secretary, that

> No one will go so far in the development of democracy as we will because this is the essence of the socialist system. We are extending socialist democratism into all spheres, including the economy. Nowhere in the West do they *elect directors* and foremen, nowhere in the West do work collectives *endorse* plans. And this is what constitutes our socialist democracy.[195]

The fact that the 'election' of directors — from a predetermined list — had to be *approved* (or rejected) by the *central authorities,* and that the workers could only *endorse* the plan but in no way really shape it, seemed to make no difference whatsoever to the Soviet State President and Party Secretary, even though his claimed 'socialist democratism' as the 'essence of the socialist system' generated sardonic laughter among the workers. He paid a compliment to the working class, saying 'how *realistic* it has been in advancing demands stemming from the new situation',[196] i.e. that it had put up with getting nothing more tangible than the rhetorics of 'socialist democratism'. And he confidently anticipated that the 'levelling of pay'[197] would disappear for good, opening up great possibilities for the 'individual material incentives' of the workers as consumers in the future, even if the working class had to maintain its 'realism' in the present.

However, the moment of truth had to come when the structural problems had to be confronted. For in that situation it was no longer sufficient to postulate solutions with reference to the working class's 'realism' in accepting both its continued structural subordination and the restoration of capitalist private property ideologically rationalized as 'well justified income differentials' in contrast to the evil 'levelling of pay'. Thus the pressure for the 'new realism' had to discard its rhetorical garb and appear in its naked ugliness. Some issues concerning the move from the pre-perestroika mode of controlling the extraction of surplus labour to the intended new one will be discussed in the next section. What is necessary to recall in the present context is the kind of unashamed cynicism with which the working people were completely excluded again from the possibility of controlling the social reproductive process when the moment of truth arrived, with changes advocated by the 'democrats' in the name of following the only viable road. A few quotations from an article by the mayor of Moscow at the time, Gavril Popov, illustrates this issue graphically. This is how he characterized the situation in 1990 and the necessity to deal in an authoritarian way with the recalcitrant popular masses in an article published in the *New York Review of Books* well before Gorbachev's final demise:

> Clearly, we could not have overthrown the powerful totalitarian system without the active participation of millions of ordinary people. But now we must create a society with a variety of different forms of ownership, including private property; and this will be a society of inequality. There will be contradiction between the policies leading to denationalization, privatization, and inequality on the one hand and, on the other, the populist character of the forces that were set in motion in order to achieve those aims. The masses long for fairness and economic equality. And the further the process

of transformation goes, the more acute and the more glaring will be the gap between those aspirations and economic realities. We must create an effective economy. But the masses of workers participating in the economy are not thinking about how to organize work more effectively; they are thinking about being consumers and of having more goods to consume. ... the model of complete democracy we have been trying to follow is bound, in my view, to encounter serious difficulties: first through strikes and then through the consequences of yielding to the demands of left-wing populism, starting at the lower levels of the soviets, and then going higher and higher. Therefore it seems to me that we must make an intense effort to find new and different political mechanisms to bring about the transformations that must take place if we are to move into a new society. It is absolutely obvious to me that the purely democratic model now being pursued is leading to contradictions that can only grow more severe in the future. The participants in the political struggle in our countries today lack the element that is most needed for them to shape a workable society: new forms of property. And in order for new forms of property and new political forces that would reflect them to appear, we need time. But that is precisely what we do not have. If we cannot soon denationalize and privatize property, we will be attacked by waves of workers fighting for their own interests. This will break up the forces of perestroika and put its future in question. The first conclusion from the analysis I have been making is that we must speed up changes in the forms of ownership. The second is that we must seek new mechanisms and institutions of political power that will depend less on populism. The euphoria of the previous period, when we prevailed swiftly and easily, has no place in dealing with the future.[198]

Thus the ambiguity had to be removed, in pursuit of solutions which eluded the 'reformers' not only five years after Gorbachev's election to the highest post in the Soviet Party but even today, yet another five years later; not to mention the four decades that elapsed since Stalin's last years and his attempts to reha- bilitate commodity production in the consumer industries, as we have seen above. No more nonsense about letting the workers pursue their interests as consumers through 'socialist democratism'. The stress had to be laid where it belonged: on the 'effective organization of work', fully in tune with Stalin's demand for 'discipline'. God forbid that there should be any room for 'waves of workers fighting for their own interests'. As a commentator had put it:

Around the same time as the Independent Miners' Union was founded [in 1990], the self-management movement [of the workers] finally seemed to be taking off after years of false starts. Ironically, it arose at a time when Gorbachev was turning away from the original official conception of market reforms as a renewal of socialism (in practice, it had always been far short of this), toward promoting the market reform as the restoration of capitalism. This meant privatization of the state enterprises and the abandonment of the self-management idea. This shift was reflected in a govern- ment directive to end election of management by workers and in the new 1990 Law of enterprises, which essentially abolished the STKs [the work-collective councils].[199]

This is how the long-drawn-out agony of the Stalinist system was in the end consummated, after four decades of totally failed reform attempts. The 'Polonius of the Comintern' (in Trotsky's words) and Stalin's house-economist, Eugene Varga, summed up with great cynicism the underlying problem, trying to turn its authoritarian solution into a self-sustaining *absolute law* of all economic activity, as externally ordained activity. In this sense he wrote that *'Production must be directed'*, quoting a truncated sentence from Marx's *Capital* according to which 'All combined labour on a large scale requires, more or less, a directing authority, in order to secure the harmonious working of the individual activities'.[200] But this is the continuation of Marx's sentence:

and to perform the general functions that have their origin in the action of the combined organism, as distinguished from the actions of its separate organs. A single violin player is his own conductor; an orchestra requires a separate one. The work of directing, superintending, and adjusting, becomes one of the functions of capital, from the moment that the labour under the control of capital, becomes co-operative. Once a function of capital, it acquires special characteristics. The directing motive, the end and aim of capital production, is to extract the greatest possible amount of surplus-value, and consequently to exploit labour-power to the greatest possible extent. As the number of the co-operating labourers increases, so too does their resistance to the domination of capital, and with it, the necessity for capital to overcome this resistance by counter-pressure. The control exercised by the capitalist [the personification of capital] is not only a special function, due to the nature of the social labour-process, and peculiar to that process, but it is, at the same time, a function of the exploitation of a social labour-process, and is consequently rooted in the unavoidable antagonism between the exploiter and the living and labouring raw material he exploits.[201]

The real issue was, therefore, the *incurably antagonistic* command of capital over labour which prevailed not as an ideal harmonization of individual activities but, on the contrary, *despite* the — ultimately untenable — fact that the *general functions* of the labour process, expropriated by capital, 'have their origin in the combined organism' of, from now on to the end of time irrepressible and irreversible, *co-operative labour*. Although for centuries the alienation of control from, and its ruthless superimposition on, recalcitrant labour, could be maintained, indeed, during the long historical ascendancy of the capital system it could even represent a necessary advancement, despite its inhumanities, all this came to a close with the eruption of the chronic crisis of capitalism out of which also the various postcapitalist attempts of resolving that crisis emerged. Thus the historical challenge for the labour movement presented itself as a necessity to resolve the antagonism the only way it was feasible: by putting an end to the alienating and dehumanizing command of capital over labour through really harmonizing the general functions of the labour process with its absolutely vital co-operative requirements. This was and remains the unavoidable historical challenge on which the Soviet type postcapitalist system necessarily foundered, by following the line of least resistance and perpetuating — although in altered but hopelessly unsustainable forms, from Stalin's open repression and concomitant labour camps to the failed socioeconomic reforms of 'de-Stalinization', including Gorbachev's 'perestroika' — the separate command system and alienated rule of capital over labour.

As we all know, or at least should know, Marx was not concerned with asserting the apologetic platitude that 'production must be directed'. On the contrary, his life-project was dedicated to finding an *alternative* to the expropriation of the function and power of direction by capital, advocating as the only viable alternative the autonomous exercise of social metabolic control by the associated producers themselves. This had to mean *either going radically beyond capital, or getting absolutely nowhere*— as it actually happened — either in the socialdemocratized 'welfare state' countries of Western capitalism, or through all conceivable reforms undertaken within the margin of action allowed by the authoritarian directive determinations of the postcapitalist capital system. As the tragic history of the Stalin era — which 'had for many years taught workers that you risked a two-year prison sentence for arriving twenty minutes late'[202] — and its four decades long aftermath conclusively demonstrated, the personifications of capital could shed their skins and grow new ones, but they could not eliminate the antagonisms of the capital system and remove the dilemma facing labour. Nor could indeed the disintegration of the socialdemocratic and communist parties in the West resolve the structural crisis of 'advanced capitalism'. Despite false appearances to the contrary, Marx's stark alternative mentioned above confronts labour as the structural antagonist of capital today more than ever before, calling for the radical rearticulation of the socialist movement which, in its known forms of defensive articulation, could not match up to the magnitude of the historical challenge.

17.4 The attempted switch from political to economic extraction of surplus-labour: 'glasnost' and 'perestroika' without the people

14.4.1

IN November 1989, *Soviet Weekly* published an article with the title: 'A farewell to the primitive view of socialism'. It was written by one of President Gorbachev's advisers, Oleg Bogomolov: a member of Parliament and the head of what was called at the time in Moscow (perhaps in jest) the 'Institute of Socialist Economics'. The expression 'primitive view of socialism' summed up with great accuracy the author's position, even if not in the intended sense. For this was his conclusion regarding the state of the world and the historical realization of the socialist project:

> The convergence theory — under which capitalism and socialism get closer as they progress, and will eventually meet as a single system — in no way looks as primitive as it did. The West is moving towards a better society, which it refers to as 'post-industrial' and 'information-based'. We usually refer to that kind of society as the *first stage of communism*.[203]

In this way President Gorbachev's trusted adviser embraced not only the values implicit in Daniel Bell's 'post-industrial' reveries but also their crude corollary made explicit in Robert Tucker's assertion according to which 'Marx's concept of communism is more nearly applicable to present-day America, for example, than his concept of capitalism.'[204]

Thus, through its capitulation to some very old thinking in the capitalist West, the so-called 'New Thinking' of the Soviet Union under Gorbachev tried to define its peculiar new value-orientation. The former rulers and propagandists of the Stalinist system, with constant references to the 'irreversibility' of their 'new course', were eager to demonstrate to Reagan, Thatcher, Bush, and others like them, the rock-solid finality of their conversion to an enthusiastic belief in the virtues of the (socially as yet unqualified) 'market economy'. As a proof of their good faith, they appealed to the idea of a universal consensus and to their from now on unshakable belief in the effective predominance of 'universal human values' in the contemporary world.

Naturally, in reality all this amounted to no more than 'singing in the dark', since nothing could be presented as evidence in order to sustain the proclaimed Gorbachevian position other than its repeated proclamation. Consequently, in order to find self-assurance in their negotiations with the White House, as well as some kind of justification when presenting their case at home, the ideologists of the new Soviet wishful thinking postulated the fiction of a materially well grounded consensual East/West value-system. In this spirit Gorbachev's last 'Ideology Chief' (as he was officially called), Vadim Medvedev, declared — disregarding all historical evidence to the contrary — that the capitalist commodity-money relations and the market were the instrumental embodiments of universal human values and 'a major achievement of human civilization',[205] insisting that for this reason in the policies pursued by the decision-makers of perestroika the 'class approach' had to be replaced by *the universal human approach*.[206]

This approach to values — characterized by the grotesque belief that they can be plucked out of thin air, without any reference to their *social foundation* — was adopted by leading Soviet bureaucrats in all walks of life, from international diplomacy to ethnic relations. Thus the eventually ill-fated Foreign Minister, Alexander A. Bessmertnykh, announced the triumph of the 'pragmatic approach' over the 'ideological approach'[207] by declaring that

> the essence of the new thinking [in international diplomacy] is to bring to the foreground not egotistic, but *increasingly altruistic interests*. Altruism ceases to be an attribute of the romantic school of diplomacy. It has suddenly become an element of the modern thinking.[208]

In this way the sociohistorical antagonism of capital and labour was reconciled in the wishful postulate of universal 'increasingly altruistic interests'. And this is what Bessmertnykh called 'a realistic vision of reality'![209]

In the same spirit, the wholesomely titled 'Chairman of the Inter-Departmental Scientific Council on the Studies of Ethnic Processes of the Presidium of the USSR Academy of Sciences', Julian Bromlei, summed up his own 'realistic view of the reality of nations' in general, and of the Soviet Union in particular, by insisting that the term 'the Soviet people'

> reflects a reality, a state and territorial entity that has common cultural features, traditions, values and *unified self-awareness*. The millennia-long history of humankind has seen many of such entities; take the present *Indian and Indonesian peoples* in the developing world, the people of Switzerland in the West and *Yugoslav people* in the Socialist countries. Thus the Soviet people is a *natural phenomenon* which differs from similar societies mainly in its Socialist parameters and corresponding spiritual values. Clearly, we should bear in mind that the *Soviet nation* consists of a variety of *ethnic groups*.[210]

This is how the Stalinist fiction of 'the Soviet nation' — which was in fact proclaimed by Stalin on the basis of degrading the various national communities of the Soviet Union, including the Ukraine and exempting only the Russian, to the status of mere 'ethnic groups' (an utterly arbitrary procedure for which none other than Lenin called the Georgian Stalin a 'Great-Russian gendarme') — could be perpetuated in theory (but not for long in practice) in the name of the allegedly enlightened and humanistic/liberating principles of 'the new thinking'. The common denominator seemed to be the voluntaristic superimposition of materially unfounded but nonetheless wishfully declared values — whether called 'spiritual values' or by some other name — on the given sociohistorical reality. The painfully evident contradictions of the latter were supposed to be resolved by the projected values, thanks to the persuasive power of their self-evident rightness, as decreed by 'the new thinking'.

The recent fountain-head of all these ideas was, of course, Party General Secretary and State President Mikhail Gorbachev. He claimed that Clausewitz and power politics 'now belong to the libraries' because

> For the first time in history, basing international politics on moral and ethical norms that are common to all humankind, as well as humanizing interstate relations, has become a vital requirement.[211]

Since he refused to acknowledge the fairly obvious difference (and in this case also the striking contradiction) between 'requirements' (or 'imperatives') and the actually existing social interests, Gorbachev kept on repeating his moral sermon about 'the priority of universal human values',[212] while his adversaries asserted — in the Gulf and elsewhere — with the most brutal and open aggressiveness, their continued happy adhesion to Clausewitz's well tried 'library' principles.

In truth, 'universal human values' could not be simply assumed in the existing societies of destructive class antagonisms. They had to be first created by overcoming such antagonisms, as envisaged by the socialist project. Sadly, however, since Mikhail Gorbachev and his collaborators had learned their trade as politicians under Stalinism, they had no contact with the original meaning of the socialist project. This is why in their wishful advocacy of universally acceptable solutions they could only proceed by postulating 'universal human values' as if they were already given, dismissing at the same time, as we have seen above, the 'class approach' from the imaginary height of the 'supremacy of a general human approach'. Consequently, they could only ground the non-existent, all-conflicts-reconciling universal values on the fiction of 'increasingly more altruistic interests', brought into this troubled world of ours from the womb of 'the new thinking'.

Gorbachev went on proclaiming that 'it is essential to rise above ideological differences'[213] but refused to inquire into the conditions of realization (if any) of such wish. His book on *Perestroika* consisted of a long list-wish, wrapped up in the customary party rhetorics of the General Secretary. At the same time, the book made no attempt at showing how to translate into reality the desired political objectives. Ironically, while pursuing his marathon course of wishful thinking, the author of *Perestroika* also proclaimed that 'In real politics there can be no wishful thinking.'[214] He did this as an intended indisputable authentication of his own credentials as a realistic politician, in place of demonstrating the soundness of the chosen course of action. He thought that by saying that 'we proposed the policy of perestroika to which there was *no alternative*'[215] the weighty questions concerning the *viability* of perestroika had been automatically resolved, on the self-evident authority of the postulated necessity itself.

Unfortunately, however, as historical experience reveals, voluntaristic wishful thinking — often wedded to a direct appeal to the authority of claimed moral imperatives — tends to predominate in politics precisely at times when the advocated political objectives are poorly grounded, due to the inherent weakness of those who promote them. Direct appeal to morality in such political discourse is used as an imaginary *substitute* for identifiable material and political forces which would secure the realization of the desired objectives. This makes such political discourse extremely problematical, no matter how high-sounding its 'universalistic' moral claims. Thus, when Gorbachev's 'Ideology Chief', echoing his General Secretary, insisted that 'We have made our choice ... our society has embarked on the right road, and the *one-way traffic* along this road is becoming *irreversible*',[216] he failed to ask some vital questions about the *destination* and *acceptability* (or otherwise) of the 'irreversible one-way traffic'. Thus, substituting the vacuity of moral slogans about 'the universal human approach' for a serious analysis of what went terribly wrong under Stalinism in postrevolutionary societies brought with it the Ideology Chief's absurd conclusion which embraced the capitalistic market as the *'guarantee of the renewal of socialism.'*[217]

17.4.2

AS we have seen in Section 17.3.1, the idea of imposing on the labour force the burdensome consequences of the 'discipline' that went with 'cost-accounting and profitableness' through 'commodity production and circulation of consumer goods' — which on the face of it, in contrast to its actuality which oppressed only labour, was supposed to apply to the 'business executives' and the 'leaders of socialist production' — goes back to Stalin's last years. The three decades of reform-attempts after Stalin's death were also trying to achieve their objectives by some form of 'cost-accounting' and 'marketization', by declaring not only the legitimacy of profit but even by promoting it to the exalted status of the 'one and only indicator of quality', according to the distinguished economist Liberman.

The fact that a vast area of Soviet industrial production had nothing whatsoever to do with *consumer goods,* vitiated these attempts all the time. For even if the advocated reforms could produce the desired improvements of 'rational cost-accounting and profitableness' — which they could not, for a variety of reasons — that would still leave the greater part of the economy in a precarious state under the changing circumstances. It was quite fallacious to wish to generalize Liberman's Kharkov experiments — based on the eminently consumer-related *clothing* industry — to the whole of the economy. The fact that a very substantial part of the economy, the armaments industry and its linkages, cannot be run on the basis of the proclaimed 'cost-accounting' and 'market discipline' even in the capitalistically most developed countries of the West, made the fantasies of solving the problems of the economy in the USSR on such lines too fantastic to be taken seriously by any standard. Since, however, the fundamental contradiction of the Soviet economy — the insuperable *antagonism* between postcapitalist capital and recalcitrant postrevolutionary labour — could not even be mentioned, let alone addressed in the form of viable practical measures, all that remained was the margin of wishful manipulative solutions and their ideological equivalents, like declaring that the 'disciplined pursuit of profit' was a high — indeed in the sphere of production and 'commodity circulation' the highest possible — socialist virtue.

There was, however, a fundamental difference between the path followed by

Mikhail Gorbachev and his team and the earlier reform attempts. It was the willingness of the West's favourite Soviet politician to go 'all the way', i.e. to *fully restore capitalism* if need be, in the name of 'cost-accounting' and 'market discipline'. This is what explains why the so-called 'Gorby-mania' had to be so highly promoted in the West. In sharp contrast, the earlier reform attempts always wanted to reconcile their dream about revitalizing the Soviet economy through capitalist cost-accounting and profit-oriented commodity production and circulation with the central state-management of the established social reproductive system, under the unchallengeable authority of the party: a system they called socialist. Thus, before Gorbachev's election to the position of General Secretary there could be no question of celebrating the United States as the society which had achieved the 'first stage of communism'; nor indeed of commending the capitalist market as 'the guarantee of the renewal of socialism'.

Not by accident, right from the beginning the refrain of Gorbachev's speeches became the sentence he shared with the most conservative Western politicians, like Margaret Thatcher: 'there is no alternative'. Thus he kept on repeating in one way or another that 'We are unanimous in our belief that perestroika is indispensable and indeed *inevitable,* and that we have *no other option'*.[218] The particular policy formulations of Gorbachev and his team fluctuated and frequently also contradicted one another, but the general line consisted in the institution of 'market mechanisms' copied from the West and the submission of the workers to the corresponding 'market discipline'. Hillel Ticktin rightly argued at a very early stage of the perestroika reforms that 'the hidden agenda is almost certainly to introduce the market', adding that Gorbachev's 'call for both more and less centralization, reiterated at the [Party] Congress, in fact means something else than appears at first sight. He wants the market, but has to retain maximum control at the centre to avoid the system disintegrating before the alternative is in place'.[219]

To what extent the 'architects of perestroika' — from Yakovlev to Gorbachev and to their eager underlings — have imagined or envisaged from the outset that the objective logic of their course of action was the restoration of capitalism, is difficult to judge. No doubt some of them may have had illusions that they could carry on by retaining a very large degree of central political control while switching in the main to an economic mode of managing the extraction of surplus labour. They saw in the latter the most viable material ground as well as the 'rational guarantee' and justification of instituting for themselves not just perks and insecure party privileges (exposed to the threat of political changes even in the case of a Khrushchev), but the possibility of acquiring substantive amounts of inheritable capitalist private property. They certainly anticipated the introduction of changes in that sense in the name of the 'perestroika' ideology of the *'full equality of all types of property'* (including, of course, capitalist private property), which would be constitutionally secured by the so-called 'law-governed state'. Gorbachev pontificated against the evil of the *'levelling of pay'* and some of his economists 'theorized' that the proper — economically rational and efficacious — differential in income would be (and of course should be) 1 to 10, and even 1 to 15. At the same time, the working class could only expect more severe work discipline from the 'law-governed state of society', under the threat — and simultaneous ideological justification — of 'objective market imperatives'. In the foreseeable future the only certainty the working class could look forward to was the necessity of 'economically rational' mass unemployment.

By October 1990 the assertion of 'there can be no alternative' was clearly spelled out in terms of the acceptance of the Soviet system's capitulation to the 'world civilization' of global capitalism. The rationalization of the openly adopted policy read like this in Gorbachev's reform document:

> 'There are *no alternatives* to the market. Only the market can ensure the satisfaction of *people's needs,* the *fair distribution of wealth,* social rights, and the strengthening of *freedom and democracy.* The market would permit the Soviet economy to be *organically linked* with the world's, and give our citizens *access to all the achievements of world civilization.'* Agreements on financial and economic support for the market reform will be sought through talks with the International Monetary Fund, the European Community and foreign governments. All accounts with Comecon countries will be settled at world prices in hard currency from January 1991. Aid to foreign countries will be reduced and put on commercial basis.[220]

Understandably, within the framework of such a reform policy, notwithstanding all of the continued cynical talk about the 'people's needs' and the 'fair distribution of wealth' (the worst joke of all), provisions had to be made for the redefinition of ruling class legitimacy, even if at first with a cautious phraseology. Thus one of the leading ideologists of 'perestroika', Tatyana Zaslavskaya argued that

> The creation of a *business class* is plainly part and parcel of a *market economy* — but which of the existing classes is this new class to be created out of? That is the question.[221]

Zaslavskaya's rhetorical question was in reality a very easy one to answer. For the Soviet type personifications of capital were in an eminently advantageous position to turn themselves into the new 'business class' not only in Russia but everywhere in Eastern Europe, as indeed they did in no time at all. Talking about Poland, the London *Economist* acknowledged in fact that 'Several "private" companies, employing Ursus [state tractor factory] workers and materials — and *owned, invariably, by Ursus directors* — have been formed.'[222] The really difficult question was whether the adopted course of capitalist restoration would work out the way it was intended and anticipated. As to the idealized 'market economy', that was, of course, simply a code-word for the commended capitalist economy, both in the East and in the Western press. The moment the required moves in the direction of capitalist restoration had been made, the code-word became redundant. Thus *The Economist,* which for a long time was also addicted to the code-word of 'market economy' when talking about capitalism in the East, spoke quite openly after the big changes. Significantly, in its uncamouflaged discourse following the accomplished fact of the Soviet capitulation to the prospect of capitalist restoration — the actualization of what Gorbachev called 'making perestroika irreversible' — doubts started to creep into the earlier ludicrously triumphalistic perspective:

> The task that confronts the economies of Eastern Europe is only now becoming clear. The region's political transformation, extraordinary though it has been, was just the start. A much bigger challenge lies ahead. It is not merely *to build capitalism,* but to build it from the wreckage of an existing, and *still sort of functioning,* economic system; to maintain support for policies that are *sure to make many, if not most, people worse off,*

at least for a while; and hardest of all, to disappoint hopes of a quick recovery without destroying the ambition to succeed in the years to come. ... *Building capitalism is bound to be painful,* if only because communism was so good at assigning workers and capital to jobs that made no sense. Rapid *privatization cannot even ensure that the transition will succeed.* The most that can be said is this: it is the only approach not guaranteed to fail.[223]

With regard to the Soviet Union itself, *The Economist* advocated the 'Chilean model' of military dictatorship. Naturally — true to its customary cynicism and hypocrisy — it did so in the name of introducing into the Soviet Union what it called 'liberal economics', arguing that

> It may be that a push from the president, backed where necessary by the *army* to ensure vital supplies or to *break politically motivated strikes,* is the only way to get things going. ... It might, just might be the Soviet Union's turn for what could be called *'the Pinochet approach to liberal economics'.*[224]

The absurdity of such a perspective should have been visible to any sane person on two counts. First, because Chile was fully integrated into the Western capitalist system well before General Pinochet appeared on the stage, with U.S. blessing and active support, as a great 'liberal economist', which was obviously not the case as far as the Soviet Union was concerned. And the second fundamental difference was the size of the two countries. For even if a Russian Pinochet could be somehow invented, not only Milton Friedman's 'Chicago boys' but all of the Chicago gangsters put together could not shrink the Soviet Union down to the size suitable for being readily subsumed under prosperous American tutelage, not to mention the annoying 'dysfunctions' of Western capitalist prosperity itself.

Evidently, however, such 'trifling' differences could not count in the eyes of either the Leader writers of *The Economist* or of perestroika 'democrats' and economists; the latter no doubt all avid readers of *The Economist.* Thus Sergei Stankevich joined in the chorus of newborn 'liberal economics' and declared that *'Democrats* must finally realize that *authoritarian rule* is bad, but absence of power is *even worse.* Hence they have to *support stronger executive power,* though with certain conditions.'[225] Naturally, the fact that no self-respecting authoritarian ruler gives a broken farthing for the 'certain conditions' which the 'democrats' might think to be able to impose on his exercise of 'stronger executive power' as their fig-leaf and alibi, could carry no weight whatsoever in the eyes of the 'democrats' opting for authoritarian rule. The same perspective was expressed, even more unashamedly, in an interview given by perestroika-democrat economist Sergei Kugushev. The question 'Isn't it wrong to introduce a market at gunpoint?' was answered by him like this:

> The many cases of countries that went from totalitarianism to a market show that every time reform was successful because of very harsh rule, if not the use of military force. There are two ways to introduce a market: German and Japanese way, and the Latin American and South-East Asian way. In the first, the reform was effectively carried out by an occupation administration. That is not open to us. We can only go for market reforms through strong rule — a typical example is Chile. Basically it is a strong government supported by the army, with the aim of ensuring normal economic development. We should take a closer look at this model, because I consider it the most likely in our situation.[226]

In all these projections the truly relevant questions — will it work? can it work?

why not if it cannot? and what is to be done if it cannot? — were not only never answered, they were not even seriously asked by those who championed pere-stroika. Not even after five long years of failed reforms, when clouds gathering on the horizon were becoming ever darker, by which time even the *ex officio* optimistic propaganda-sermons of *The Economist* could only offer the dubious negative assurance that the 'painful building of capitalism' in the East is 'not guaranteed to fail'. The gap between this perspective and Gorbachev's October 1990 reform document — according to which 'Only the market can ensure the satisfaction of *people's needs,* the *fair distribution of wealth,* social rights, and the strengthening of *freedom and democracy*' — could hardly have been greater, which was a very sad reflection indeed on the 'realistic view of reality' adopted by the Soviet State President and Party General Secretary; the man who was not only happy to 'do business with Margaret Thatcher' but also demonstrated the grasp and soundness of his judgement by lending his name to the venture of interna-tional capitalist crook, Robert Maxwell, for setting up the '*Gorbachev-Maxwell Institute of Minnesota*'.

The final outcome of the policies pursued by Gorbachev and his team was the break up of the U.S.S.R., the implosion of the Soviet postcapitalist capital system, and the utter failure of perestroika itself. In the heady days of peres-troika, the marketization pursued by its champions was celebrated and ration-alized as 'the guarantee for the renewal of socialism'. However, as the logic of the 'restructuring' developments unfolded, the attempted shift from the politi-cal extraction of surplus labour to its primarily economic mode of extraction ran into the most glaring contradictions. These contradictions were not confined to the unpalatable fact that the truth of the claimed 'renewal of socialism' turned out to be the 'painful building of capitalism'. They also manifested in the way in which the legitimation of the process undertaken by Gorbachev had to be turned completely upside down.

At the time of first announcing the intended 'restructuring' reforms, the great 'democratic' argument in favour of 'market socialism' was that it would inevi-tably curtail the power of political arbitrariness, authoritarianism, bureaucracy, etc. However, as time went by and no positive results could be shown, while the negative consequences of Gorbachev's 'perestroika' policy were plentiful, deeply affecting the overwhelming majority of the Soviet population, the tune of ideological rationalization and legitimation of the strategy pursued had to be radically changed. This is how — instead of putting and end to authoritarianism and bureaucratic arbitrariness, and instituting in their place, on the secure material foundations of 'market socialism', the promised 'freedom and demo-cracy' — the advocacy of the most authoritarian forms of state control was gaining momentum. Whether it was promoted under the 'Pinochet model of liberal economics' or under some other name (like Gavril Popov's 'new mecha-nisms and institutions of political power' as a way of defeating working class demands and providing a guarantee against 'left-wing populism'), the objective was always the same: acquiring the means and institutional forms through which the restoration of capitalistic market relations could be secured and maintained in operation. This is how the circle was fully closed. The 'market mechanism', which at first was presented as the necessary *means* to the noble end of the promised 'revival of socialism' and 'freedom and democracy' for the broad masses of the people, had become the ultimate self-justifying *end-in-itself* to which everything else had to be subjected. Naturally, in the eyes of the realigned personifications of postcapitalist capital no price could be considered too high for reaching the end of which they were the real beneficiaries. If the realization of the desired end called for the appearance of the Russian Pinochet — to be backed not only by the army but even more so by the ruling elite in the process of redefining itself as the 'new business class' — so much the better. This is what turned out to be the far from edifying meaning of 'perestroika' and 'market socialism' as attempted in the Soviet Union not simply without but emphatically against the people.

17.4.3
YET, despite turning the originally idealized reform project upside down, the enterprise did not work out. The failure of perestroika had a great deal to do with the arbitrary way in which the Soviet personifications of capital under Gorbachev's leadership tried to transplant some relations of social metabolic control from capitalistically advanced Western societies into a politico-economic setting which objectively resisted them. As mentioned in Chapter 2, the implosion of the Soviet capital system was due above all to the contradiction between the Soviet state's role in forcefully enhancing the socialization of production by political means during almost seven decades after the revolution, and the post-Brezhnev regime's need to bring recalcitrant — but by the party itself collectively organized and managed — labour under the firmest possible control of a quasi-automatic 'market mechanism' within the framework of perestroika.

Nourished also by the mythologies prevailing in Western capitalist countries, the market was for a long time misconceived in the East as a neutral and easily transplantable 'mechanism', in wishful ignorance that it was lacking its essential supporting pillars in Soviet society. But even when finally it started to sink in that the perestroika strategy was encountering major resistance, the nature of the resistance was again misdiagnosed as something that could be quite readily brought under control through the proper — if need be openly authoritarian — 'political mechanisms'. The postcapitalist personifications of capital never wanted to admit to themselves that their fundamental role in society was to impose the material imperatives of an objectively determined *capital system* on labour. They made a myth out of their own 'leadership' as a disembodied determination, divorced from its unsavoury — labour-oppressing — social metabolic functions. Thus when they embarked on perestroika they failed to realize that the proper restructuring of the established postcapitalist system would require much more than the 'leaders' themselves turning inside out their own political coats — as indeed invariably and unhesitatingly they did — and make labour devotedly follow them as a result of the promised benefits of 'market socialism' in its inseparability from 'freedom and democracy'. Even when they started the debate about the need for a 'business class', they refused to admit to themselves that it would require a major earthquake to switch from the long established and still functioning political extraction of surplus labour to a fully marketized system which they would continue to control dressed in their new coat as 'the business class'.

The reform document which spelled out Mikhail Gorbachev's final capitulation to capitalist marketization in the Autumn of 1990 had for its speech-writer Stanislav Shatalin, the leading economist of Brezhnev's 'administrative command system' once rhetorically denounced by Gorbachev. In fact commentators could not help recalling at the time that 'It is ironic that Shatalin should hold such a position. While Leonid Brezhnev was in power, Shatalin made an important academic contribution to the strengthening of the planned economy, winning the Soviet Union's State Prize in 1968. Now he believes the ministerial monolith that sends production orders to every factory from Volgograd to Vladivostok should be destroyed if the economy is to move towards the free-market principles.'[227] Characteristically, the leading light of the 'stagnation era' assumed a key role in elaborating Gorbachev's strategy of 'free market' restoration. As a journalist reported from Moscow:

> Shatalin belongs to the coterie of Soviet intellectuals on whom Gorbachev relies heavily for advice. For two men now partners in consigning communism to the dustbin of history, Shatalin and Gorbachev have had a surprisingly short relationship. They first met at an economics conference in Moscow last October where Shatalin, who describes himself as a convinced social democrat, claims he converted Gorbachev from communism to social democracy. Since then, Gorbachev's position has become markedly more radical.[228]

The idea of transplanting the ways and means of — by the 1990s not even mildly reformist but openly liberal-bourgeois — Western social democracy to the Soviet Union in the midst of its most acute structural crisis had to be stillborn. For neither turning the leaders' political coat, nor aping the policies adopted by Western socialdemocratic parties in a fundamentally different economic and political/institutional setting could be considered sufficient even for scratching the surface of the crisis experienced by the Soviet postcapitalist system. The conditions for making a reformist socialdemocratic strategy succeed in the Soviet Union were totally absent, and even five years later, in 1995, there was no sign whatsoever of their materialization.

The socialdemocratic parties of the West have themselves gone through quite fundamental changes from the time of their foundation in the 19th century to the point when they meekly integrated themselves into the Western parliamentary framework, accepting its anti-labour constraints and progressively abandoning their original emancipatory strategies. Rosa Luxemburg prophetically summed up, way back in 1904, the meaning of the reformist — and in the end disastrously self-abolishing — trend of socialdemocratic political development by stressing that its parliamentary leadership *'must dissolve the active, class-conscious sector of the proletariat in the amorphous mass of an "electorate".'*[229] In another work she also underlined that

> only by an insight into all the fearful seriousness, all the complexity of the tasks involved, only as a result of a capacity for critical judgement on the part of the masses, which capacity was systematically killed by the Social Democracy for decades under various pretexts, only thus can the genuine capacity for historical action be born in the German proletariat. ... As bred-in-the-bone disciples of parliamentary cretinism, these German Social Democrats have sought to apply to revolution the home-made wisdom of the parliamentary nursery: in order to carry anything, you must first have a majority. The same, they say, applies to revolution: first let's become a "majority". The true dialectic of revolutions, however, stands this wisdom of parliamentary moles on its head: not through a majority to revolutionary tactics, but through revolution-

ary tactics to a majority — that is the way the road runs.[230]

The original Marxian strategy — which suffered a historic defeat already at the time of the rejection of Marx's 'Critique of the Gotha Programme' by German social democracy — was conceived as a way of fighting the *atomization* of the working class and its inevitable domination, as a fragmented multiplicity of individuals, by the self-perpetuating capital system. Talking about the need for collective unity in his early reflections on the subject, Marx emphasized that competition separated the workers from one another even more than the bourgeois, and he argued that the organized power — i.e. capital and its state formation — standing over against the isolated workers

> who live in conditions daily reproducing this isolation, can only be overcome after long struggles. To demand the opposite would be tantamount to demanding that competition should not exist in this definite epoch of history, or that the individuals should banish from their minds conditions over which in their isolation they have no control.[231]

The socialist movement was expected to provide the necessary counter-weight to capital, enabling the individual workers to break out of their isolation which their objective situation in their workplace, and their contractual subordination to capital in the labour market, continued to perpetuate. We should recall that 'in the production process of capital labour is a totality whose individual component parts are alien to one another ... they are forcibly combined ... subordinate to the objective unity of machinery, of fixed capital ... [and the worker only exists] as an animated individual punctuation mark, as *capital's living isolated accessory*'.[232] The situation is made worse for the workers by the functioning of the capitalist labour market. For they have to enter a contractual relationship with the personifications of capital as isolated individual workers, compelled — on the pain of losing their livelihood — to accept the pre-existent conditions of work in the enterprise to which they are assigned and the predetermined rules of labour discipline through which the authoritarianism of the workshop can be 'rightfully' exercised. This is how the dual pillars of the capitalistic variety of the capital system: the *authoritarianism of the workshop* and the *tyranny of the market* not only complement one another but also create the illusion of individual freedom. For *in theory* the workers could refuse to consent — but of course not *in actuality* — to the terms of the contract determined by the inescapable dictates of the labour market. In truth:

> The capital-relation is a *relation of compulsion,* the aim of which is to extract surplus labour by prolonging labour time — it is a relation of compulsion which does not rest on any personal relations of domination and dependence, but simply arises out of the difference in economic functions.[233] ... To be sure, the *relation of production* itself creates a new *relation of domination and subordination* (and this also produces *political,* etc., expressions of itself).[234] ... The constant sale and purchase of labour capacity, and the constant confrontation between the worker and the commodity produced by the owner himself, as buyer of his labour capacity and as constant capital, appear only as the *form mediating* his subjugation to capital ... It *glosses over* as mere *money relation* the real transaction and the perpetual dependence, which is constantly renewed through this mediation of sale and purchase. Not only are the conditions of this *commerce* constantly reproduced; in addition to this, what one buys with, and what the other is obliged to sell, is the result of the process. The constant renewal of this relation of *sale and purchase* only mediates the permanence of the specific relation

of dependence, giving it the deceptive *semblance* of a transaction, a contract between *commodity owners* who have equal rights and confront each other equally freely.[235]

Against this socioeconomic background, given the actually isolating and mystificatory power of the material reproduction process itself, only socialist consciousness — provided that it 'gripped the labouring masses' — could produce a viable alternative mode of controlling social metabolic reproduction. Thus in the original socialist project the organization of fragmented and atomized labour and its transformation into an effective class-conscious collective force was — and remains for us to the end of the capital system — a vital historic task which the reformist social democracy of the West obviously failed to realize. Quite the contrary, as time went by the parties of the Second International more and more actively contributed to preserving the fragmentation and atomization of labour by expropriating to themselves the role of all *legitimate opposition and reform*. All protest had to be strictly confined to what could be accommodated within the limits of the 'parliamentary nursery', without disturbing the existing relation of forces between capital and labour, disarming and outlawing thereby all *spontaneous working class protest* and delivering *practically disenfranchised* labour to the unhindered rule of capital in the name of the 'democratic electorate'.

However, it is necessary to underline here that in this fateful involution of Western social democracy — from its original articulation as a force committed to the emancipation of labour, via its intermediary form as an organization still professing the institution of socialism in due course through gradual reform, to finally becoming a bourgeois liberal party and the champion of the eternal rule of capital and of its untranscendable 'market economy' — the material reproductive structures of the existing social order strongly helped to sustain such transformation. The market was not only the effective regulator of the capital-relation in the globally dominant Western countries, where social democracy flourished (and, tellingly enough, it could flourish only there). Also, thanks to their dominance in the global pecking order of capital, the capitalistically advanced Western countries could secure for themselves massive privileges, out of which relative defensive gains could be conceded to their respective working classes (or at least to some sections of them) through the parliamentary agency of reformist social democracy and the associated trade unions. The axiomatic orienting principle of reformist social democracy was never to challenge the undisturbed functioning of the capital-relation, accepting thereby labour's permanent structural subordination to capital in exchange for marginal improvements in the standard of living of the 'electors' in very limited areas of the planet, without ever asking the question: for how long was it possible to safeguard even such marginal improvements. Nevertheless, the material vehicle sustaining the transformation of social democracy from its original emancipatory commitments to an agency of minimal socioeconomic reform, to be instituted and managed by the Western 'welfare state', was a most powerful one. It was propelled by the global expansion of the capital system from the 'European little corner of the world' to cover the whole of the planet, under the hegemony of a handful of 'advanced capitalist' countries. Significantly enough in this respect, the historical moment of reformist social democracy was terminated with the end of capital's global expansionary phase, as the system's structural crisis erupted in the early 1970s. As a result we had to experience the beginning of anti-labour legislation by labourite governments and the metamorphosis of socialdemocratic parties — which up until then still claimed at least some allegiance to the working class — into liberal-bourgeois political organizations all over Western Europe.

Thus the original Marxian strategy of countering the fragmentation and atomization of labour by internationally oriented socialist parties, fulfilling their historic mission in the development of the class consciousness of the workers as *'mass consciousness'*, had to founder on the success of capital's global expansion and the mystificatory power of the capital-relation daily reproducing itself on an extended scale through the market. This is why the 'dissolution of the active, class-conscious sector of the proletariat in the amorphous mass of an electorate' through the agency of reformist social democracy could succeed in the capitalistically advanced countries. The notable counter-example in this respect was, of course, Lenin's very different 'social democratic' party, which ended up with the conquest of state power in Russia. But the Bolshevik Party was not an exception to the general rule of socialdemocratic accommodation which prevailed in the West under the impact of unhindered capital expansion. For the country in which Lenin succeeded in following a very different strategy to socialdemocratic reformism was capitalistically most underdeveloped, occupying a subordinate position in capital's international order, constituting 'the weakest link of the chain'. A country which, to top it all, happened to be also humiliatingly defeated in the internally destabilizing first 'Great War', in a century aptly described by Gabriel Kolko as a *'Century of War'.*[236]

Naturally, the fact that the original radical orientation of socialdemocratic parties gave way to ever more diluted (and in the end totally abandoned) labour reformism in all capitalistically advanced countries represents a great challenge for the future of socialism. To make it worse, the parties of the Third International — which were formed in order to keep alive the original socialist project of revolutionary transformation — also fully caved in under the impact of the same determinations, embracing the positions of the mildest of mild reformism which they had bitterly opposed for decades. We have to address these problems in some detail in the next chapter. In the present context our concern is why the attempt by perestroika ideologists to breathe life into their reform project when they proclaimed their adhesion to social democracy had to fail, despite their repeated public insistence that 'only the market can ensure the satisfaction of *people's needs,* the *fair distribution of wealth, social rights,* and the strengthening of *freedom and democracy'.*

In the article quoted above in which Shatalin confessed his unreserved conversion to social democracy it was also reported from Moscow that, in keeping with the vacuous rhetoric of perestroika for five years, he announced that 'We aim to take everything from the state and *give it to the people'.*[237] As if reformist social democracy ever achieved anything even remotely resembling the desideratum of 'giving everything to the people' anywhere in the world!

Two things were hopelessly wrong with the socialdemocratic market fantasy of the Autumn 1990 perestroika reform proposals. First, that the Soviet type postcapitalist capital system was devoid of a proper market, and therefore could not regulate the allocation of labour power to productive tasks on the basis of contractual market relations. And the second, that even if after a number of years — through the joint effort of foreign capital and the successful self-conversion of the Soviet postrevolutionary personifications of capital into fully fledged private capitalists — a tolerably functioning market system could be established in the Soviet Union, even that would not secure to the thus 'restructured' postcapitalist order the advantages which a handful of privileged Western capitalist countries possessed at the time of the global expansionary phase of capital, on the basis of which they could acquire the wealth necessary for the (by now everywhere greatly threatened) social security funds of the 'welfare state'.

Apart from its commercial relations with the capitalist West throughout the postrevolutionary decades, some sort of internal 'quasi-market' did exist in the Soviet Union, in the form of the 'commodity circulation' through which 'labour power' had to be 'compensated for the effort expended in the process of production', according to Stalin's last writing on political economy.[238] But that was very far indeed from constituting a labour market. The defining characteristic of the labour market is that the parties involved in the exchange relation are not simply 'buyers and sellers' who could in principle alternate their position and role, at times being buyers and at other times sellers. On the contrary, they are *particular personifications* of the *structurally entrenched* but necessarily particularized capital-relation — i.e. *particular* personifications of both capital and labour — who enter into a contractual relationship of commercial transaction with one another. There was nothing comparable to this in the Soviet type capital system. Moreover, due to the immense labour requirements of the industrial developments followed both before and under Stalin and his successors, there was no unemployment problem in the Soviet Union, and the *right to labour* became even constitutionally guaranteed in the 1930s. The adoption of such an approach to labour would be inconceivable — and of course quite intolerable — in the capitalist order. For the constitutional right to labour would rule out the possibility of an 'industrial reserve army', with all its advantages to capital, nullifying at the same time the inherently economic mode of allocating labour power within the framework of the capitalist labour market. In other words, if entitlement to work could be made constitutionally guaranteed and enforced in the capitalist system, that would undermine and ultimately destroy its labour market, rendering thereby the specifically capitalist — primarily economic — mode of controlling the extraction of surplus value altogether unsustainable.

The *political* mode of extracting surplus labour became necessary in the Soviet type capital system precisely because it was structurally incompatibile with the objective requirements of setting up and maintaining in operation a postrevolutionary labour market. This is what made it genuinely postcapitalist, in that the socioeconomic reproduction process could not be regulated in it by a clearly identifiable and effectively functioning *plurality of private capitals*. State power was conquered in 1917 by the Bolshevik Party which remained after the revolution not only the controller of the direct state functions but also in charge of supervising — in its totality as well as in its minute details — the material and cultural reproductive process.

This created a unique capital-labour relation in postrevolutionary society. On the one hand, the new — Soviet — type of personifications of capital, subject to the absolute authority of the central plan enshrined in law, could not exercise even a limited autonomy as individual decision makers in control of the reproduction process, in contrast to their capitalist counterparts. This was all the more paradoxical since the same individuals were simultaneously also participating in the maximum of authoritarian arbitrariness and voluntarism characteristic of the decisions and actions of the party leadership as a collective entity. On the other hand, in the postrevolutionary capital-relation labour could not be fragmented and atomized on the model of the capitalist labour process, despite the fact that the Stalinist party tried to impose in a most authoritarian form — including imprisonment and mass labour camps — the most severe labour discipline, holding workers criminally responsible as individuals for their failure to conform to the norm laid down for them. However, the fragmentation and atomization of labour characteristic of capitalism could not prevail under the postrevolutionary capital system. There were three main reasons for this. First, the immense enterprise of industrialization — as well as forced collectivization and forced industrialization — was inconceivable without the highest degree of the socialization of production, inevitably and directly affecting the consciousness of the labour force. Second, the ground of legitimation of 'building socialism' was the working class, and all talk about the 'proletarian dictatorship' and the 'leading role of the party' in it had to exclude quite explicitly the possibility of capitalist restoration and the subjection of labour to the alienating fetishism of commodity. In this sense the party itself had to justify its credentials and legitimate itself on the ground of its claimed representation of the class of labour. And the third reason why the authoritarian discipline to which individual workers were subjected, no matter how severe, could not produce the result desired by the party leadership was that it could never be admitted that the recalcitrance of labour was a matter of *class antagonism*. It had to be treated in the ideology of the system as the work of the mythical 'enemy', maintaining at the same time the complementary mythology of a unified working class fully devoted to building socialism — and later the highest state of communism — in one country. The workers, however, knew all too well that when they were violating the prescribed norms on a mass scale, in front of one another, and performing their role at a much lower level of productivity than they could, involved in all kinds of 'going slow', 'moonlighting', etc., they were not acting on behalf of a mysterious outside enemy but on their own behalf, in solidarity with one another which made their recalcitrant behaviour possible at all in an authoritarian system.

The essential defining characteristics of all feasible forms of the capital system are: the *highest practicable extraction of surplus labour by a separate controlling power, in a labour process conducted on the basis of the hierarchical structural subordination of labour to the material imperatives of production oriented towards accumulation — 'value holding fast to itself' (Marx)*[239] *— and towards the continued enlarged reproduction of accumulated wealth*. The particular forms of the personification of capital can considerably vary, so long as the forms assumed conform to the requirements emanating from the system's essential defining characteristics. Thus in the Soviet type system in which capital's controlling functions were vested in the party as such, and not in particular individuals even at the top echelons of the party (who could be eliminated without seriously disrupting the system), the leaders of the party were genuine personifications of capital in their collective capacity only. This made their personal position precarious, and the economic viability of such a mode of exercising control — so to speak 'by proxy' and without permanently safeguarded assets, unlike the managers in the capitalist system — rather problematical. This constituted one of the great weaknesses of the Soviet capital system as viewed from the standpoint of its personifications of capital. The other major weakness from the same standpoint was the insufficient fragmentation and atomization of labour which could be remedied only by the establishment of a fully effective labour market.

Gorbachev's perestroika tried to remedy both weaknesses. It attempted to change the Soviet capital system by switching from the political extraction of surplus labour to its primarily economic mode of control through the market, even if it took a few years before the true character and magnitude of the required changes could be identified and more or less openly spelled out. Even as late as 1990 the obvious direct exploitative implications of 'privatization' had to be approached in a round-about way, as the cat approaches hot porridge. Thus when finally the old rhetoric of 'serving the people and nothing but the people' had to be modified, though by no means completely abandoned, and Gorbachev's spokesman, Deputy Prime Minister Leonid Abalkin, revealed that 'The choice has already been made. We can no longer continue balancing between two stools',[240] he tried to justify the adopted course by saying that:

> People had to see there was no alternative. Without such a transition [to the 'free market'] the country has no future as a great power. Unless we go over to a new system, we will deprive ourselves and our children of the benefits of a great power, of being a place where people will not be ashamed to live. We have to make sacrifices, but there is no option.[241]

Let people have the consolation prize that they were living under a 'great power' so that they should swallow without a grumble the bitter pill of 'no option' as the 'only choice' available and made above their heads by their leaders. At the same time Gorbachev's spokesman 'stopped short of calling for a *new employing class*. The concept of *"exploitation"* was extremely *emotional and sensitive'*, he said.[242] The indirect defence of the coming capitalist exploitation was offered by Abalkin with the most peculiar argument, by asking 'whether anyone living on the earning of others was automatically an exploiter; what about pensioners?'[243] As if pensioners never earned the pensions for which they worked throughout their adult life! And to put the crowning touch to his defence of the adopted course, Abalkin also added that 'Soviet workers must always have a right to be consulted and share in decision-making'.[244] This he said after indicating that 'the choice has already been made', admitting also that the role of the people was 'to see there was no alternative'. In other words, the people's 'share in decision-making' was to 'participate' by accepting the 'no option choice' made on their behalf by their perestroiking leaders.

Obviously, however, things could not be left in such a suspended state of animation between the rhetorically claimed allegiance to the people and the actual decision taken to establish the 'free market'. In the past the contradiction between even the most blatantly far-fetched kind of rhetorics — promising fully realized communism 'for the younger generation' — and the painful reality of never ending hardship and material shortages could be *managed*, though of course never *resolved,* under the authority of the party. The labour force was controlled not only through the administrative machinery and security forces of the state, in conjunction with the commanding personnel of the particular industrial and agricultural enterprises, but also through the so-called 'transmission belts' of central policy — the trade unions and other mass organizations, from the Komsomol to women's organizations — and the grass root organizations of the party itself in the work-places. Once Gorbachev and his team decided that there was no alternative to the establishment of the 'free market', i.e. to the restoration of capitalism, the old forms of legitimating centrally made decisions — by discussing and approving them at the local level in the work-place party organizations and at the meetings of the 'transmission belts' — became a potential threat to the imposition of 'perestroika', when the people started to vote against the 'no alternative' decisions taken by Gorbachev and company in the name of 'glasnost' and 'democracy'.

The greatest problem was presented, of course, by the party itself. Naturally, it did not concern its top leadership which, as the postrevolutionary personification of capital, was eager to turn itself into individually autonomous holders of major economic assets and decision makers in the economically regulated extraction of surplus labour. The problem was the party as the hegemonic mass organization of Soviet society, with its unique mode of legitimating — in the name of the working class and the dictatorship of the proletariat — the political extraction of surplus labour. It was this kind of legitimation which happened to be totally incompatible with capitalistic marketization in which the masses of people cannot have any regular voting power, even in the sense of calling for mere approval. There could be no chance of instituting the labour market and thereby subjecting the labour force to the 'iron determinations' of its 'economic rationality' for as long as the unpredictable party organizations of the workplace — which became totally unpredictable, under the impact of the reforms introduced, in the immediate aftermath of Gorbachev's publicly declared 'glasnost' and 'perestroika' — remained in existence. In fact the critique of 'democracy' became louder and louder as the 'democrats' argued for its suspension or elimination. As one of them put it: *'Democracy can never come before the market; it is the result of a market'.*[245]

Significantly, in order to cut this 'Gordian knot', Boris Yeltsin started to ban party work in the factories in the Spring of 1991 by Russian presidential decree. But, of course, the problem was much bigger than what could be handled in such a 'piecemeal' fashion. Something even more drastic was required in order to resolve the dilemma concerning the relationship between 'democracy' and 'market' to the liking of perestroika democrats. Debates were raging already in 1990 and they intensified in 1991. In a sharp polemical article Gorbachev's military adviser, the later mysteriously suicided Marshal Sergei Akhromeyev, attacked one of the most agile political chameleons, at the time one of Yeltsin's closest counsellors in these terms:

> My congratulations to Dr Arbatov: having faithfully served Nikita Khrushchev, Leonid Brezhnev and Yuri Andropov, he then worked with Mikhail Gorbachev; he was a member of the communist party's central committee for 20 years, and worked to promote the socialist cause; and now, as Yeltsin's assistant, he seems finally to have found a leader whose views he shares. I would be interested to know whether Dr

Arbatov is going to remain in the communist party.[246]

Akhromeyev did not live long enough to get the answer to his question, in the most unexpected form. It turned out that Dr Arbatov did not have to leave the party. Not because for some incomprehensible reason he might have wanted to remain faithful to one of his commitments of the past, but because there was nothing left for him to leave. For the General Secretary of the party, Mikhail Gorbachev dissolved the party by decree. As former dissident historian Roy Medvedev commented: 'It's political suicide. Gorbachev was elected as head of the Soviet Communist Party. By dissolving the party he has removed the ground from under his own feet, taken away the basis of his own legitimacy as leader. Can you imagine Giulio Andreotti outlawing the Italian Christian Democrats? He would be forced to resign from the government the next day. This is what will happen to Gorbachev.'[247] To be sure, Gorbachev, by appointing himself President of the Soviet Union, made what he thought to be a sufficient provision for securing for himself the top political decision making power irrespective of what might happen to the party. Where he totally miscalculated was in never imagining the possibility of the break-up of the U.S.S.R. itself.

What had brought matters to a head was the disastrous failure of Gorbachev's perestroika policies and the likely success of the widespread call for his replacement as General Secretary. Paradoxically, he was only saved in that post by Yeltsin's decrees against the workplace organizations of the party. This is how Medvedev described the unfolding of events:

> They would have dismissed him at the July Congress. I have information to prove it. The party secretariat had received dozens of resolutions from regional committees. Sixty percent of them wanted Gorbachev out. Many were even demanding his expulsion from the party. It was as clear as daylight that everybody had lost faith in him. But then Yeltsin issued his proclamation of independence and everyone was afraid of what would happen. He started to ban party work in the factories. Many of the party chiefs thought that Gorbachev, once again, was the only one who would be able to save their bacon. This is the reason that they didn't get rid of him immediately. But tension was extremely high.[248]

The order for the dissolution of the party was made in the immediate aftermath of the coup in which Gorbachev played a most peculiar role. When the Moscow Party Secretary was arrested and was asked in front of the television cameras about his involvement in the 'coup' he answered: 'what coup? It was a charade'. Be that as it may, in relation to the people arrested:

> Rumour has been circulating in Moscow for some time that the trial of the coup leaders will be held behind closed doors. ... If the court does not disclose the truth, the whole truth, and nothing but the truth about the 'Soviet leadership's conspiracy', this infant democracy and the credibility of two presidents — Gorbachev and Yeltsin — may be damaged beyond repair. ... According to one version, the circle of top officials who knew the coup was coming goes far beyond the few now held in Remand Centre 4 — and includes Mikhail Gorbachev himself. ... There are probably more puzzles in the events of August than we shall ever get answers to, even in an open trial. And there is speculation that three of the main coup plotters may not live that long: people say one may die of a heart attack or a stroke, another of cirrhosis of the liver, another will have poison smuggled into his cell. Not as unlikely as it sounds, given the series of mysterious suicides[249] immediately after the coup.[250]

Naturally, 'the truth, the whole truth, and nothing but the truth about the

Soviet leadership's conspiracy' has not been disclosed by the trial that never was. Predictably, there could be no trial because the accused were threatening great revelations about the real culprits who were not indicted. It may take a very long time before it can be credibly explained, if ever, what has really happened in Moscow in August 1991. All we can ask now is this: what has been actually achieved by the unfolding events?

The change of guard from Gorbachev and his team to Yeltsin's 'democrats' underlined the absurdity of Gorbachev's endlessly repeated declarations of 'no alternative', as the fountain-head of this wisdom has been first sidelined and then altogether pensioned off, just like his 'no alternative' soul-mate in Britain, Margaret Thatcher. Much more important than that was, of course, the dissolution of the Soviet Party by the decree of its General Secretary. For it removed the principal obstacle from the chosen course of restoring capitalism through the establishment of a proper commodity and labour market.

However, the removal of ambiguities through the dissolution of the old form of legitimating the postrevolutionary capital system, and the opening up of the road for the conversion of the Soviet type personifications of capital into fully fledged private capitalists does not mean that the restoration of capitalism in the former Soviet Union is now guaranteed to succeed. The perestroika reforms, to be sure, failed, as did the Stalinist system before them. But two failures, no matter how clamorous, do not add up to a success. For, so far at least, even though no less than twelve years have passed since Gorbachev received in Britain Margaret Thatcher's blessing as the Soviet politician 'we can do business with', *none* of the grave problems affecting the Soviet postcapitalist system has been resolved. Today the crisis is as great as ever before, although the catastrophic unemployment that would necessarily follow from the full marketization of commodity production and the operation of the corresponding labour market is nowhere yet on the horizon, despite the 'sound economic advice' constantly received from the West, and not least from the Editors and Leader writers of the London *Economist*. The only restructuring that had a chance of relatively trouble-free success was one that would have had to alter the structural determinations and the adversarial/antagonistic labour process of the postrevolutionary reproductive system. Given the fact, however, that the parameters of 'perestroika' reform were premissed on the continued rule of postrevolutionary capital, following that road was obviously out of the question. Perestroika without the people and against the people had to fail. Now even *The Economist* can promise only the 'painful building of capitalism'. But 'the truth, the whole truth, and nothing but the truth' in this respect includes the far from reassuring conclusion that the pain of the anticipated painful building of capitalism will reverberate well beyond the boundaries of the former Soviet Union.

CHAPTER EIGHTEEN

HISTORICAL ACTUALITY OF THE SOCIALIST OFFENSIVE

THE present 'crisis of Marxism' is largely due to the fact that many of its representatives continue to adopt a *defensive* posture, at a time when we have historically turned an important corner and should engage in a socialist offensive, in keeping with the objective conditions available to us. Indeed, paradoxically, the last twenty five years that increasingly manifested capital's structural crisis — and hence the beginning of the necessary socialist offensive in a *historical* sense — also witnessed a greater than ever willingness of many Marxists to get involved in all kinds of wholesale revision and compromise, in search of new defensive alliances, and nothing really to show as a result of such fundamentally disoriented strategies.

The disorientation in question is, thus, by no means simply ideological. On the contrary, it involves all those institutions of socialist struggle that were constituted under defensive historical circumstances and therefore pursue, under the weight of their own inertia, modes of action which directly correspond to their defensive character. And since the new historical phase inevitably brings with it the sharpening of the social confrontation, the increased defensive reaction of the given institutions (and strategies) of working class struggle is to be expected — but not to be idealized — under the circumstances. Sadly, however, the existing defensive structures and strategies take their own presuppositions for granted and look for solutions which remain anchored to the conditions of the old, and by now surpassed, historical phase.

All this must be stressed as firmly as possible in order to avoid the illusion of easy solutions. For it is not enough to argue in favour of a new ideological/political orientation if the relevant institutional/organizational forms are retained as they exist today. If the current disorientation is the combined manifestation of practical/institutional and ideological factors in their rather inert response to the changed historical circumstances, it would be naive to expect a remedy from what people like to describe as 'ideological clarification'. Indeed, while obviously the two must develop together, the 'übergreifendes Moment' in this dialectical reciprocity at the present juncture is the practical/institutional framework of socialist strategy which badly needs restructuring in accordance with the new conditions. These are the problems we have to address in the present chapter.

18.1 *The necessary offensive of defensive institutions*

18.1.1

TO say that we are contemporaries to the new historical phase of socialist offensive does not mean in the slightest that from now on the road is smooth and victory near. The phrase 'historical actuality' does not imply more than it explicitly states: namely that the socialist offensive confronts us as a matter of *historical* actuality, in contrast to our objective predicament not so long ago, dominated by inescapably defensive determinations. Consciousness does not automatically register social changes, no matter how important, even if *eventually* ('in the last analysis') they are bound to filter through the prevailing channels and modes of political and ideological mediation. But before we reach the stage of the 'last analysis', the inertia of the previous mode of response — as articulated in determinate strategies and organizational structures — continues to dominate the way in which people define their own alternatives and margins of action. In this sense, the discourse on 'class consciousness' that reproaches the proletariat for 'lack of combativity', so long as the instruments and strategies of socialist action remain defensively structured, demonstrates only its own vacuity.

The historical actuality of the socialist offensive in the first instance amounts to no more than the uncomforting negative fact that — due to the changed relation of forces and circumstances — some earlier forms of action ('the politics of consensus', 'the strategy of full employment', 'the expansion of the Welfare-State', etc.) are objectively blocked, calling for major readjustments in society as a whole. From this initial 'brute negativity' it does not follow, however, that the readjustments in question will be positive ones, mobilising the socialist forces in a conscious effort to present themselves as carriers of the alternative social order fit to replace the society in crisis. Far from it. Since the changes required are so drastic, the probability is that people will follow the 'line of least resistance' for a considerable time, even if it means suffering significant defeats and imposing major sacrifices upon themselves, rather than readily accept the 'leap into the unknown'. Only when the options of the prevailing order are exhausted, only then may one expect a *spontaneous* turn towards a radically different solution. (The complete breakdown of the social order in the course of a lost war and the ensuing revolutionary upheavals known from past history well illustrate this point.)

Nevertheless, the difficulties of an adequate socialist response to the changed historical situation do not alter the character of the situation itself, even if they put again into relief the potential conflict between scales of temporality — the immediate and the broad historical framework of events and developments. It is the objective character of the new historic conditions that *ultimately* decides the issue, whatever delays and diversions may follow under the given circumstances. For the truth is that there is a *limit* beyond which forced accommodation and newly imposed sacrifices become intolerable not only *subjectively* for the individuals concerned, but *objectively* as well for the continued functioning of the still dominant social/economic framework. In this sense, and none other, the historical actuality of the socialist offensive — as synonymous with the end of the system of relative improvements through consensual accommodation — is bound to assert itself in the longer run. To assert itself both in the required form of social consciousness and its strategic/instrumental mediation. Even if there can be no guarantees against further disappointments and defeats in the shorter run. For even if it is true that human beings have a boundless capacity to endure absolutely anything imposed upon them, including the worst possible conditions (which is rather doubtful), the resilience of the global system of capital amounts to far less than that today.

18.1.2

The objective potentialities of the socialist offensive are inherent in the structural crisis of capital itself, as we shall see in a moment. Now the point is to stress a major contradiction: the absence of adequate political instruments that could turn this potentiality into *reality*. Furthermore, what makes things worse in this respect is that the self-awareness of the organizations concerned is still dominated by past mythologies, depicting the Leninist party, for instance, as the institution of strategic offensive *par excellence*.

To be sure, all instruments and organizations of the working class movement were brought into being in order to overcome some major obstacles on the road to emancipation. In the first instance they were the outcome of spontaneous explosions, and as such they represented a *moment* of attack. Later, as a result of conscious efforts, coordinated structures emerged both in particular countries and on an international scale. But none of them could actually go beyond the horizon of fighting for specific, limited objectives, even if their *ultimate* strategic aim was a radical socialist transformation of the whole of society. One should not forget that Lenin brilliantly — and realistically — defined the Bolsheviks' objectives between February and October 1917 as securing 'Peace, Land and Bread' so as to create a viable social base for the revolution. But even in basic organizational terms the 'Vanguard Party' was constituted in such a way that it should be able to *defend* itself against the ruthless attacks of a police state, under the worst possible conditions of clandestinity, from which inevitably followed the imposition of absolute secrecy, a strict command structure, centralization, etc. If we compare the self-defensively closed structure of this Vanguard party with Marx's original idea of producing 'communist consciousness on a mass scale' — with its necessary implication of an inherently open organizational structure — we have some measure of the fundamental difference between a defensive and an offensive posture. When the objective conditions implicit in such aim are in the process of unfolding on a global scale, only then may one realistically envisage the practical articulation of the required organs of socialist offensive.

In truth, Lenin had no illusions in this regard, even if some interpretations tend to rewrite his objectives in the light of retrospective wishful thinking. He based his strategy for breaking the 'weakest link of the chain' on his interpretation of the law of uneven development, insisting at the same time that

> *political* revolutions can under no circumstances whatsoever either obscure or weaken the slogan of a *socialist* revolution ... which should not be regarded as a *single act*, but as a *period* of turbulent political and economic upheavals, the most intense class struggle, civil war, revolutions and counter-revolutions.[251]

In this spirit, he expected the political revolution of October to open up the 'period of turbulent political and economic upheavals', manifest in a whole series of revolutions all over the world, until the conditions of a socialist victory were firmly secured. When the wave of revolutionary upheavals had died down without significant positive results elsewhere, he soberly remarked that one could not hand back power to the Czars, and went on with the job of defending what could be defended under the circumstances. He was originally hoping to combine the political potential of the 'weakest link' with the economically mature conditions of the 'advanced' capitalist countries. It was the failure of the world revolution that forcibly truncated his strategy, imposing on him the crippling constraints of a desperate defence.

Whereas Lenin always retained his awareness of the fundamental difference between the political and the social (he called it socialist) revolution, even when he was irrevocably forced into defending the bare survival of the political revolution as such, Stalin obliterated this vital distinction, pretending that the *first step* in the direction of a socialist victory represented socialism itself, to be simply followed by stepping onto the 'highest stage of Communism' in an encircled country. Naturally, with such an apologetic shift in strategy, the real difference between defensive and offensive structures and developments also disappeared, since everything had to be crudely subordinated to the defence of Stalinism and hailed simultaneously as the greatest possible victory for the socialist revolution in general. And while Lenin, in the absence of the world revolution, saw the task on the whole as a *holding operation* (to be relieved by favourable world developments in due course), Stalin made a virtue out of misery. He transubstantiated the prevailing political response to the given constraints into a general (and thereafter compulsory) *social ideal*, arbitrarily superimposing on all social and economic processes the voluntaristic practice of trying to solve problems by authoritarian *political dictates*.

Thus, we could witness a big diversion from the original intentions not only in terms of the fundamental objectives but also with respect to the corresponding institutional and organizational forms. Marx's overall conception had for its strategic objective the comprehensive social revolution, in terms of which men must change 'from top to bottom the conditions of their industrial and political existence, and consequently their whole manner of being'.[252] Accordingly, the forms and instruments of the struggle had to match the essentially *positive* character of the undertaking as a whole, instead of being blocked at the *negative* phase of a *defensive* action. This is why Marx, addressing himself to a group of workers, reminded them that they should not content themselves with the negativity of 'retarding the downward movement' when the task consisted in 'changing its direction'; that they should not apply 'palliatives' when the problem was how to 'cure the malady'. And he went on to make the general point that it was not enough to negatively/defensively engage in the

> unavoidable *guerilla fights* incessantly springing up from the never ceasing encroachments of capital or changes of the market.[253]

However, when it came to spelling out the *positive* side of the equation, under the prevailing conditions of capital's relative underdevelopment — still far from its real barriers and structural crisis — he could only point to the fact of an ongoing process of objective development, but to no tangible institutional and strategic mediations for turning that process to a lasting advantage. As he put it, the workers 'ought to understand that, with all the miseries it imposes upon them, the present system simultaneously engenders the *material conditions* and the social forms necessary for an economical reconstruction of society'.[254] Thus he was able to indicate a positive ally in the maturing material conditions of society, but he could go no further than that. Insisting as he did more than once in the same lecture that 'guerilla war' defensively fights only the effects of the system, he could only offer the metaphor of a 'lever' to be used for a fundamental change, in no way identifying where and how that lever might be inserted into the strategic centre of the negated system so as to be able to produce the advocated radical transformation.

It would have been a miracle, had it been otherwise. For the socialist movement, after the first — more or less spontaneous — explosions and attacks born out of despair, found itself in a situation of setting itself very limited targets, in response to the challenges it had to face in the context of particular national confrontations, against the background of capital's global expansion and dynamic development. Accordingly, the First International soon experienced great difficulties which eventually led to its disintegration. And no amount of retrospective mythology can turn even the Paris Commune into a major socialist offensive: not simply because it was brutally defeated, but primarily in view of the fact strongly stressed by Marx himself that it was not socialist at all.[255] Naturally, the debates concerning the Gotha Programme and the strategic orientation of the German working class movement were very much under the shadow of the same defensive determinations. The objective conditions for envisaging even the bare possibility of a hegemonic offensive were nowhere in sight, and in their absence the severe limitations of the feasible organizational forms and strategies were also pushed into relief. This is why Marx, after defining the necessary conditions of a successful socialist revolution in terms of 'the positive development of the means of production', unhesitatingly declared as late as 1881:

> It is my conviction that the critical juncture for a new International Workingmen's Association has not yet arrived and for this reason I regard all workers' congresses, particularly socialist congresses, insofar as they are not related to the *immediate* given conditions in this or that *particular nation*, as not merely useless but harmful. They will always fade away in innumerable stale generalized banalities.[256]

Needless to say, the Second International did not bring any improvement in this respect. On the contrary, through its 'economism' it miserably capitulated to the dominant social/economic determinations of the overall defensive predicament. It substituted the pedestrian practice of 'gradual change' to the requirements of a comprehensive strategy, directly translating at the same time its vision of defensive capitulation into the ossified organizational structure of a 'Social Democracy' corruptly wedded to capitalist parliamentary manipulation. Well in keeping with that, the postwar period of capitalist expansion — hailed by many as the permanent solution of capital's contradictions, as well as the structural integration of the working class — found its most enthusiastic spokesmen and administrators in this pseudo-socialist movement of socialdemocratic capitulation.

Contrary to the Second International — which, in a sense, is still with us today — the historical moment of the Third International was a relatively brief one. The revolutionary wave in the closing stages of the first world war gave it a big original impetus, but hardly twenty months after its founding Congress Lenin had to admit that

> It was evident that the revolutionary movement would inevitably slow down when the nations secured peace.[257]

Significantly, the same speech that acknowledged the passing of the revolutionary wave in the West, heavily concentrated on the question of economic concessions to capitalist countries, approvingly quoting Keynes about the importance of Russian raw materials for the reconstitution and stabilization of the global economy of capital and consciously adopting it as the strategy of the foreseeable future. By the time the strategists of the German 'March Action' embarked on their voluntaristic 'offensive', the dice of objective determinations were heavily loaded against any such offensive, putting a tragic seal on the fate of revolutionary socialist movements for a long time to come.

The world of capital weathered also the storm of its 'Great Economic Crisis' of 1929-33 with relative ease, without having to face a major hegemonic confrontation from socialist forces despite the mass suffering caused by this crisis. For the fact is that 'Great' as this crisis was, it was very far from being a *structural* crisis, leaving an ample number of options open for capital's continued survival, recovery and stronger than ever reconstitution on an economically sounder and broader basis. Retrospective political reconstructions tend to blame personalities and organizational forces for such recovery, particularly with respect to the success of Fascism. Yet, whatever the relative weight of such political factors, one should not forget that they must be assessed against the background of an essentially defensive historical phase. It is pointless to rewrite history with the help of counter-factual conditionals, whether they concern the rise of Fascism or anything else. For the fact that really matters is that at the time of the crisis of 1929-33 capital actually did have the *option of Fascism* (and similar solutions) which it no longer possesses today. And objectively that makes a world of difference as far as the possibilities of defensive and offensive action are concerned.

18.1.3

Given the way in which they had been constituted — as integral parts of a complex institutional framework — the organs of socialist struggle could win individual battles, but not the war against capital itself. For the latter a fundamental restructuring would be required, so that they complement and intensify each other's effectiveness, instead of weakening it through the 'division of labour' forced upon them by capital's 'circular' institutionality within which they originated. The two pillars of working class action in the West — parties and trade unions — are in fact inseparably linked to a third member of the overall institutional setting: Parliament, through which the circle of civil society/political state is closed and becomes that paralyzing 'magic circle' from which there seems to be no escape. To treat trade unions, together with other (far less important) sectoral organizations, as somehow belonging to 'civil society' alone, in virtue of which they can be used against the political state for a profound socialist transformation, is no more than romantic wishful thinking. For the institutional circle of capital in reality is made of the *reciprocal totalizations* of civil society/political state which deeply interpenetrate and powerfully support one another. Thus, it would take much more than knocking down one of the three pillars — Parliament, for instance — to produce the necessary change.

The problematic side of the prevailing institutional framework is tellingly captured by expressions like 'trade union consciousness', 'party bureaucracy', 'parliamentary cretinism', to name but one in each category. Parliament, in particular, has been the target of many a justified criticism, and up to the present time there is no satisfactory socialist theory as to what to do with it beyond the conquest of power: a fact that loudly speaks for itself. While the classics of Marxism fought against 'Indifference to Politics' and the equally sectarian advocacy of 'boycotting Parliament', they did not envisage an 'intermediary stage' (which might in fact be a very long historical phase). A stage that in a meaningful sense retains at least some important features of the inherited parliamentary framework while the long-drawn-out process of radical restructuring is accomplished on the required comprehensive scale. Marx, for instance, raised this possibility by implication, in an aside arising in the context of revolutionary change tied to the use of force as a rule. This is how he tackled the problem in an important but little known speech:

> The worker will some day have to win political supremacy in order to organize labour along *new lines*: he will have to defeat the *old policy* supporting *old institutions*...
> But we have by no means affirmed that this goal would be achieved by identical means. We know of the *allowances* we must make for the *institutions, customs and traditions* of the various countries; and we do not deny that there are countries such as America, England, and I would add Holland if I knew your institutions better, where the working people may achieve their goal by *peaceful means*. If that is true, we must also recognize that in most of the continental countries it is *force* that will have to be the lever of revolutions; it is *force* that we shall some day have to resort to in order to establish a reign of labour.[258]

It is arguable whether the issue at stake is simply a question of 'allowances' that must be made for some inherited constraints: the importance of Parliament is far too great to be dealt with in passing and in the company of 'customs and traditions'. Understandably, in Marx's conception of politics as *radical negation*, Parliament usually appears in its almost grotesque negativity, summed up with the dictum: 'To delude others and by deluding them to delude yourself — this is *parliamentary wisdom* in a nutshell! Tant mieux!'[259] Is it really 'so much the better' or is it 'so much the worse'?

Since Parliament profoundly affects all institutions of socialist struggle which happen to be closely linked to it, surely it must be so much the worse. And if you add to this fact the consideration — raised by Marx as a serious historical possibility, and not as an empty gesture of fractionalist party propaganda — that revolutionary change may use *peaceful means* as its vehicle, in that case the imperative of radically reorienting 'parliamentary wisdom' for the realization of socialist aims becomes so much more pressing.

The experience of the societies of 'actual socialism' clearly shows that it is impossible to demolish just one of the three pillars of the inherited institutional framework, since one way or another also the remaining two go with it. This is fairly obvious when we think of the purely nominal existence of the trade unions in these societies, just as the experience of Poland and the resurfacing of bitterly independent trade unionism from limbo in the form of 'Solidarity' made it amply clear that balancing society on top of the one remaining pillar is totally untenable in the longer run. Less obvious, though, is what happens to the party itself in the aftermath of the conquest of power. While it may retain some organizational features of Lenin's 'vanguard party' as constituted under the conditions of illegality and struggle for mere survival against the Czarist police state, by becoming the unchallengeable ruler of the new state it ceases to be a Leninist party

and becomes in fact the *Party-State*, imposing and also suffering all the consequences which this change necessarily carries with it. Thus, transfer of power
from one set of individuals to another (a laughably commonplace occurrence in
the parliamentary framework), or even a partial shift in policy under changed
circumstances, becomes extremely difficult, if not impossible.

THE nature of the overall institutional framework determines also the character
of its constituent parts, and vice-versa, the particular 'microcosms' of a system
always exhibit the essential characteristics of the 'macrocosm' to which they
belong. In this sense no change can become other than purely ephemeral in any
particular constituent, unless it can fully reverberate through all channels of the
total institutional complex, thus initiating the required changes in the whole
system of reciprocal totalizations and interdeterminations. To win 'guerilla
fights', as Marx insisted, was not enough, since they could ultimately be
neutralized or even nullified by the assimilative and integrative power of the
ruling system. The same was true of winning *individual battles* when the issue
was ultimately decided in terms of the conditions of winning the *war* itself.
    This is why the historical actuality of the socialist offensive is of an immense
significance. For under the new conditions of capital's structural crisis it becomes
possible to win much more than some great (but in the end badly isolated) *battles*
like the Russian, Chinese and Cuban revolutions. At the same time, there can
be no question of minimizing the painful character of the process involved, requiring major strategic adjustments and correspondingly radical institutional/
organizational changes in all areas and across the whole spectrum of the socialist
movement.

18.2 From cyclic to structural crisis

18.2.1

AS mentioned before, the crisis of capital we are experiencing today is an all-
embracing structural crisis. There is nothing special, of course, in linking capital
to crisis. On the contrary, crises of varying intensity and duration happen to be
capital's *natural* mode of existence: ways of progressing beyond its immediate
barriers and thus extending with ruthless dynamism its sphere of operation and
domination. In this sense, the last thing that capital could envisage is a *permanent*
supersession of all crises, even if its ideologists and propagandists frequently
dream about (or indeed claim the achievement of) nothing less than that.
    The *historical* novelty of today's crisis is manifest under four main aspects:
- (1) its *character* is *universal*, rather than restricted to one particular sphere (e.g,
    financial, or commercial, or affecting this or that particular branch of
    production, or applying to this rather than that type of labour, with its
    specific range of skills and degrees of productivity, etc.);
- (2) its *scope* is truly *global* (in the most threateningly literal sense of the term),
    rather than confined to a particular set of countries (as all major crises have
    been in the past);
- (3) its *time scale* is extended, continuous — if you like: *permanent* — rather
    than limited and *cyclic*, as all former crises of capital happened to be.

- (4) its *mode* of unfolding might be called *creeping* — in contrast to the more spectacular and dramatic eruptions and collapses of the past — while adding the proviso that even the most vehement or violent convulsions cannot be excluded as far as the future is concerned: i.e, when the complex machinery now actively engaged in 'crisis-management' and in the more or less temporary 'dispalacement' of the growing contradictions runs out of steam.

To deny that such machinery exists and that it is powerful, would be extremely foolish. Nor should one exclude or minimize capital's ability to add new instruments to the already vast arsenal of its continued self-defence. Nevertheless, the fact that the existing machinery is being brought into play with increasing frequency and that it proves less and less effective as things stand today, is a fair measure of the severity of this deepening structural crisis.

HERE we must concentrate on a few constituents of the unfolding crisis. If in the postwar period it has become embarrassingly unfashionable to talk about capitalist crisis — yet another sign of the defensive posture of the labour movement mentioned above — it was not only due to the successful practical operation of the machinery that displaces (through diffusing as well as de-fusing) the contradictions themselves. It was also due to the ideological mystification (from 'the end of ideology' to the 'triumph of organized capitalism' and 'working class integration', etc.) which misrepresented the *mechanism of displacement* as a structural remedy and *permanent solution*.

Naturally, when the manifestations of the crisis cannot be hidden any longer, the same ideological mystification that yesterday announced the final solution of all social problems today attributes their reemergence to purely *technological* factors, belching out its apologetic platitudes about 'the second industrial revolution', 'the collapse of work', 'the information revolution', and the 'cultural discontents of post-industrial society'.

To appreciate the historical novelty of capital's structural crisis, we have to locate it in the historical context of twentieth century social, economic and political developments. But first, it is necessary to make some general points about the criteria of a structural crisis, as well as about the forms in which its solution may be envisaged.

To put it in the simplest and most general terms, a structural crisis affects the *totality* of a social complex, in all its relations with its constituent parts or sub-complexes, as well as with other complexes to which it is linked. By contrast, a non-structural crisis affects only some parts of the complex in question, and thus no matter how severe it might be with regard to the affected parts, it cannot endanger the continued survival of the overall structure.

Accordingly, the displacement of contradictions is feasible only while the crisis is partial, relative and internally manageable by the system, requiring no more than shifts — even if major ones — *within* the relatively autonomous system itself. By the same token, a structural crisis calls into question the very existence of the overall complex concerned, postulating its transcendence and replacement by some alternative complex.

The same contrast may be expressed in terms of the limits any particular social complex happens to have in its immediacy, at any given time, as compared to those beyond which it cannot conceivably go. Thus, a structural crisis is not concerned with the *immediate* limits but with the *ultimate* limits of a global structure. The immediate limits may be extended in three different ways:

- (a) by modifying some parts of a complex in question;
- (b) by changing, as a whole, the system to which the particular sub-complexes belong; and
- (c) by significantly altering the relationship of the overall complex to other complexes outside it.

Consequently, the greater the complexity of a fundamental structure and of its relationships with others to which it is linked, the more varied and flexible are its objective possibilities of adjustment and its chances of survival even under extremely severe conditions of crisis. In other words, partial contradictions and 'dysfunctions', even if severe in themselves, can be displaced and diffused — within the *ultimate* or *structural limits* of the system — and the countervailing forces or tendencies neutralized, assimilated, nullified, or even turned into an actively sustaining force of the system in question. Hence the problem of reformist accommodation. However, all this should be kept in perspective, in contrast to the grotesquely overstated theories of 'working class integration' which were fashionable not so long ago. For the undeniable integration of the leadership of most working class parties and trade unions should not be confused with the hypostatized — but structurally impossible — integration of labour as such into the capital system.

At the same time it must be stressed that when the manifold options of internal adjustment begin to be exhausted, not even the 'curse of interdepend-ence' (which tends to paralyse the forces of opposition) can prevent the ultimate structural disintegration. Naturally, given the inherent character of the struc-tures involved, it is inconceivable to think of such disintegration as a sudden act, to be followed by an equally speedy transformation. The 'creeping' but relentlessly advancing structural crisis can only be grasped as a contradictory process of *reciprocal adjustments* (a 'war of attrition' of sorts), to be brought to a conclusion only by a long and painful process of *radical restructuring* inevitably tied to its own contradictions.

18.2.2
AS far as the world of capital is concerned, the manifestations of the structural crisis can be identified in its various internal dimensions as well as at the level of the political institutions. As Marx had repeatedly stressed, it is in the nature of capital to drive beyond the barriers it encounters:

> The tendency to create the world market is directly given in the concept of capital itself. Every limit appears as a barrier to be overcome. Initially, to subjugate every moment of production itself to exchange and to suspend the production of direct use values not entering into exchange... But from the fact that capital posits every such limit as a barrier and hence gets ideally beyond it, it does not by any means follow that it has really overcome it, and, since every such barrier contradicts its character, its production moves in contradictions which are constantly overcome but just as constantly posited. Furthermore, the universality towards which it irresistibly strives encounters barriers in its own nature, which will, at a certain stage of its development, allow it to be recognized as being itself the greatest barrier to this tendency, and hence will drive towards its own suspension.[260]

In the course of actual historical development capital's three fundamental dimensions — production, consumption and circulation/distribution/realization — tend to strengthen and expand one another for a long time, providing also the necessary internal motivation for each other's dynamic reproduction on an ever-extended scale. Thus in the first place the *immediate* limitations of each are successfully overcome, thanks to the reciprocal interaction of the others. (E.g., the immediate barrier to production is positively superseded by the expansion of consumption, and vice-versa.) In this way, the limits truly appear to be no more than mere barriers to be transcended, and the immediate contradictions are not only displaced but directly utilized as levers for the exponential increase in capital's seemingly boundless power of self-propulsion.

Indeed, there can be no question of a *structural* crisis so long as this vital mechanism of self-expansion (which is simultaneously also the mechanism of internally transcending or displacing contradictions) continues to function. There may be all kinds of crises of varying duration, frequency, and severity directly affecting one of the three dimensions and *indirectly,* until the blockage is removed, the system as a whole, without, however, calling into question the *ultimate limits* of the overall structure. (For instance, the crisis of 1929-33 was essentially a 'realization crisis', at an absurdly low level of production and consumption as compared to the postwar period.)

To be sure, the structural crisis does not originate in some mysterious region of its own: it resides in and emanates from the three internal dimensions mentioned above. Nevertheless, the dysfunctions of each taken separately must be distinguished from the fundamental crisis of the whole which consists in the *systematic blockage* of the vital constituent parts.

It is important to make this distinction because — given the objective interconnections and reciprocal determinations — under specific circumstances even a temporary blockage of *one* of the internal channels may with relative ease drive the whole system to a halt, thus creating the *semblance* of a structural crisis, together with some voluntaristic strategies arising from the misperception of a temporary blockage as a structural crisis. It is worth remembering in this context Stalin's fatefully optimistic evaluation of the crisis of the late 1920s, and its devastating consequences for his policies both internally and on the international plane.

18.2.3

ANOTHER misconception that must be cleared out of the way is that structural crisis refers to some *absolute* conditions. This is not so. To be sure, all three fundamental dimensions of capital's continued functioning have their absolute limits which can be clearly identified. (For instance, the absolute limits of production may be expressed in terms of the means and material of production, which in their turn may be further specified as the total collapse of the supply of certain key raw materials, or as the equally total collapse — not just 'underutilization' — of the available productive machinery, for whatever reason, as, for instance, the irresponsible and reckless misuse of energy resources.) But while such considerations are certainly not irrelevant, they suffer from the avoidance of social specificities (as many environmentalist arguments testify), thereby unnecessarily weakening their own weapons of critique by linking them to doomsday expectations which need *never* materialize.

- Capital's structural crisis which we started to experience in the 1970s relates, in fact, to something far more modest than such absolute conditions. It means simply that the threefold internal dimensions of capital's self-expansion exhibit increasingly greater disturbances. Thus they not only tend to disrupt the normal process of growth but also foreshadow a failure in their vital function of displacing the system's accumulated contradictions.

- The inner dimensions and inherent conditions of capital's self-expansion constituted from the very beginning a *contradictory* unity, and not an un-problematical one, in that one had to 'subjugate' the other (as Marx had put it: to 'subjugate every moment of production itself to exchange') so as to make the overall complex work. At the same time, so long as the expanded reproduction of each could continue undisturbed — i.e., so long as it was possible to dig increasingly bigger holes in order to fill the earlier smaller ones with their contents — not only each of the contradictory internal dimensions could be strengthened separately but they could also function together in a 'contrapuntal' harmony.

- The situation radically changes, however, when the interests of each on its own cease to coincide with those of the other even in the last analysis. From that moment on, the disturbances and antagonistic 'dysfunctions', rather than being absorbed/dissipated/diffused and de-fused, tend to become *cumulative* and thus *structural*, carrying with them a dangerous blockage in the complex mechanism of *displacing contradictions*. Thus what we are confronted with is no longer simply 'dysfunctional' but potentially very explosive. For capital never-ever *solved* even the smallest of its contradictions.

- Nor could it do so, since by its very nature and inherent constitution capital *thrives* on them (and can safely do so up to a point). Its normal way of dealing with contradictions is to intensify them, to transfer them to a higher level, to displace them to a different plane, to suppress them as long as it is possible to do so, and when they cannot be suppressed any longer, to export them to a different sphere or to a different country. This is why the increasing blockage in displacing and exporting capital's inner contradictions is so dangerous and potentially explosive.

It goes without saying, this structural crisis is not confined to the social/economic sphere. Given the inescapable determinations of capital's 'magic circle' earlier referred to, the profound crisis of 'civil society' loudly reverberates on the whole spectrum of political institutions. For under the increasingly more unstable socioeconomic conditions, new and much stronger 'political guarantees' are needed which cannot be provided by the capitalist state as it stands today. Thus the ignominious demise of the 'Welfare State' only puts the seal of open admission on what is no less than the *structural crisis of all political institutions* which has been fermenting under the crust of 'consensus politics' for well over two decades. What needs to be stressed here is that the underlying contradictions by no means fizzle out in the crisis of *political* institutions but affect the whole of society in a way never experienced before. Indeed, the structural crisis of capital reveals itself as a veritable *crisis of domination* in general.

Anyone who might feel that this sounds too dramatic should just look around, in whatever direction. Is it possible to find any sphere of activity or any set of human relations not affected by the crisis? A hundred and forty years ago Marx could still speak about 'the great civilising influence of capital', emphasising that through it

> for the first time, nature becomes purely an object for humankind, purely a matter of utility; ceases to be recognized as a power for itself; and the theoretical discovery of its autonomous laws appears merely as a ruse so as to subjugate it under human needs, whether as an object of consumption or as a means of production. In accord with this tendency, capital drives beyond national barriers and prejudices as much as beyond nature worship, as well as all traditional, confined, complacent, encrusted satisfactions of present needs, and reproductions of old ways of life.[261]

And where does it all lead to? For capital can have no other objective than its own self-reproduction to which everything else must be absolutely subordinated, from nature to all human needs and aspirations.

Thus the civilising influence comes to a devastating end the moment the ruthless inner logic of capital's expanded self-reproduction encounters its obstacle in human needs. One year's military budget in the U.S.A. alone amounts (in 1981) to the figure of 300 billion dollars, (and who knows how much more in addition to that, under various other budgetary covers), which defies human comprehension. At the same time the most elementary social services are subjected to callous cuts: a true measure of capital's 'civilising work' today. Yet, even such sums and cuts are very far from being sufficient to enable capital to follow its undisturbed course: one of the striking proofs of the crisis of domination.

The systematic devastation of nature and the continued accumulation of the powers of ultimate destruction — globally to the tune of well over one trillion dollars per annum — indicate the frightening material side of capital's absurd logic of development, together with the complete denial of the elementary needs of countless starving millions: the forgotten side and receiving end of the wasted trillions. The paralysing human side of this development is visible not only in the obscenity of enforced 'underdevelopment' but everywhere even in the capitalistically most advanced countries.

The prevailing system of domination is in crisis because its historical *raison d'être* and justification has disappeared, and no amount of manipulation or naked repression can reinvent it. Thus, keeping thousands of million in destitution and starvation when the wasted trillions could feed them *fifty times* over puts the enormity of this system of domination in perspective.

The same is true of those other great human issues which started to mobilize people a relatively short time ago. Sociological literature had produced so many nice fairy tales, for decades, about 'generation conflict' (in the true spirit of 'the end of ideology', attempting to turn the nasty signs of class contradictions into the noble vicissitudes of timeless generations); now they really have something to write about. However, the prefabricated schemes of psycho/sociological mystification do not fit the real picture. For the so-called 'generation conflict' was automatically resolved the moment it was apologetically predicated, in that all 'youthful rebellion' was supposed to grow in due course into the sound maturity of mortgage payments and savings for an old-age pension, so as to secure commodity-existence all the way to the grave and beyond, through the eternal reproduction of capital's new 'generations'. The self-reassuring idea was that whatever difficulties 'nature' may present us with — and the notion of 'generations' was supposed to be simply a category of nature — capital will, thankfully, resolve them as a matter of course.

The truth, however, turned out to be the exact opposite, since capital does not resolve but *generates* the real conflict of generations, on an ever-extending scale. Millions of young people are denied the chance of a job in every major capitalist country, unceremoniously obliterating the not so old memory of courtship about 'youth culture', while continuing to squeeze every possible drop of profit out of the remnants of such culture. At the same time, millions of older people are also forced to join the dole queues, and millions more are under an immense pressure for 'early retirement' from which the most mobile section of contemporary capital — finance capital — can suck some more profit for a while at least. Thus the age-group of the 'useful generation' is shrinking to somewhere between 25 and 50, and it is *objectively* opposed to the 'unwanted generations' condemned by capital to enforced idleness and the loss of their humanness. And since now the middle generation is squeezed between the 'useless young' *and* the 'useless old' — until, that is, it becomes itself superfluous, when capital deems so — even the temporal planes of these contradictions become all-confounding.

Typically, the solutions proposed do not even scratch the surface of the problem, underlining that, again, we are confronted with an insoluble inner contradiction of capital itself. For what is really at stake is the role of labour as such in capital's universe once a very high level of productivity is reached. To cope with the contradictions generated thereby, a major upheaval would be needed, affecting not only the immediate conditions of work itself but all facets of social life as well, even the most intimate ones. Capital, by contrast, can only produce the material conditions for the development of the autonomous social individual so as to negate them immediately. It negates them materially at times of economic crises, as well as at the political and cultural levels in the interest of its own continued survival as the ultimate framework of domination.

Since capital can only function by way of contradictions, it both creates the family and destroys it; both produces the economically independent young generation with its 'youth culture' and undermines it; both generates the conditions of potentially comfortable old age, with adequate social provisions, and sacrifices them to the interests of its infernal war-machinery. Human beings are both absolutely needed by capital and totally superfluous to it. If it was not for the fact that capital needs living labour for its extended self-reproduction, the nightmare of the neutron-bomb holocaust would certainly come true. But since such 'final solution' is denied to capital, we are confronted with the dehumanizing consequences of its contradictions and with the growing crisis of the system of domination.

Perhaps the latter is nowhere more obvious than in the intensifying struggle for women's liberation. The economic grounds of the past historical justification of women's oppression have irretrievably been destroyed, and capital's productive advance itself played a central role in this. But again we can see the inherent contradictions. In one sense — for its own purposes — capital helps to liberate women so as to be able to better exploit them as members of a much more varied and conveniently 'flexible' labour force. At the same time it needs to retain their social subordination on another plane — for the uncomplicated reproduction of the labour force and for the perpetuation of the prevalent family structure — so as to safeguard its own domination as the absolute master of the social metabolism itself.

Thus, it clearly emerges that the partial successes can evaporate from one moment to the next — women are among the first to be forced back into unemployment or into miserably remunerated part-time labour — since capital's *overall* interests predominate over the more limited ones. Given the fact that the real stake is the prevailing system of domination and that significant successes in women's liberation are bound to make deep inroads into it, ultimately undermining its viability, anything that cannot be kept strictly within the bounds set by the pursuit of profit must be resisted. At the same time, capital's major involvement in the destruction of all economic justification of women's oppression make it impossible to resolve this problem by way of an *economic* mechanism. (In fact, purely in economic terms, the balance often points in the opposite direction, thus contributing to the sharpening of this contradiction.)

Since the family is the true microcosm of society — fulfilling beyond its immediate functions also the requirements of securing the continuity of property, to which we must also add its role as the basic unit of distribution and its unique ability to act as the 'transmission belt' of the prevailing value-structure of society — the cause of women's liberation directly or indirectly affects the totality of social relations, in all their untenability.

The apparent stalemate in this respect at the present time, under the immediate pressures of the economic crisis, is rather deceptive. For looking at it from the perspective of a longer time-scale we can see a dramatic change, in that the *three* generation family we had before the last war has now effectively turned into a *one generation* family: with all its highly beneficial consequences for the expansion of the consumer-economy.

But even that is no longer enough. Hence the contradictory pressures for further changes — although, in fact, we have run out of the possibility of such changes *while* retaining the exisiting family structure — and the equally great pressures, if not even greater ones, to move in the opposite direction, restoring the old, patriarchal 'family values', in the interest of capital's continued survival. It is the simultaneous presence and intensity of forces irrepressibly pulling in ways like this in opposite directions which makes the present, structural crisis of capital a veritable crisis of domination.

18.2.4

IN comparison to all this, the crisis of 1929-33 was evidently of a very different kind. For no matter how severe and prolonged that crisis was, it affected only a limited number of capital's complex dimensions and mechanisms of self-defence, corresponding to its relatively underdeveloped state at the time with respect to its overall potentialities. But before those potentialities could be fully developed, some major political anachronisms had to be swept away, as it transpired with rather brutal clarity and far-reaching implications during the crisis.

By the time the crisis erupted in 1929, capital reached the final stages of its transition from 'extensive totality' to the relentless exploration and exploitation of the hidden continents of 'intensive totality', as a result of the great productive boost it received during the first world war and through the postwar period of reconstruction. While different countries were affected in different ways (depending on capital's relative degree of development and on their status as victors or losers), the new contradictions erupted essentially because the qualitative productive advances of the period could no longer be contained within the historically antiquated power relations of the prevailing 'extensive totality'.

Marx noticed already in the late 1870s that U.S. capital represented by far the most dynamic force of the global system: a truth which sounded half a century louder in the 1920s. And yet, despite the vital role American capital played in winning the war, the still prevailing political status quo of global domination (established a long time earlier) condemned it to being very much the second fiddle to British imperialism: an anachronism that, obviously, could not be tolerated indefinitely.

Not surprisingly, therefore, the imperative of a new departure had crystallized during the 'Great World Crisis'. For the devastating pressures of this apparently never ending crisis made it abundantly clear that U.S. capital had to remake the entire world of capital in its own more dynamic image, and that it had no alternative to doing so if it wanted to overcome not merely the immediate critical conditions but also the prospect of chronic depression. Accordingly, beneath the intense rhetorics of Roosevelt's Inaugural Address in 1933 the really significant message was the radically new perspective of *neocapitalist* colonialism under American hegemony. For it foreshadowed not only Churchill's frustrations during the war as well as the Yalta agreements but — above all — the takeover of the British and French Empires for all intents and purposes, together with the relegation of the historically antiquated varieties of imperialism and colonialism to the Second Division, where they effectively already belonged, in the higher stakes for the domination of capital's 'intensive totality'.

Liberal mythology likes to remember Roosevelt as the 'man of the people' and as the tireless champion of a 'New Deal' for them. In truth, however, his claim to lasting historical fame, even if somewhat dubious, rests on being a far-sighted representative of capital's new-found dynamism, in virtue of his pioneering role both in elaborating the overall strategy and in skilfully laying the practical foundations for neocolonialism.

This meant a two-pronged attack in the framework of a truly *global* orientation. On the one hand, since the imperative of a new departure had arisen on the basis of the great productive advance and the crisis created by its driving to a halt, with respect to its homeward terms of reference the new strategy involved the full exploration of all the hidden continents of 'internal colonialism': hence the 'New Deal' and the development of an expanding consumer-economy on more secure foundations. At the same time, the need for securing and safeguarding the continued expansion of the home economic base necessarily implied on the other hand the ruthless removal of all the 'artificial barriers' of past colonialism (and corresponding protectionist/underdeveloped capitalism).

This neocapitalist strategy of conquering 'intensive totality' was a truly *global* conception also in the sense that it attempted to come to terms with the existence of the Soviet Union, not only for its own sake but also in order to be in a better position to control the emerging anti-colonial movements.

Naturally, all this was supposed to succeed under the unquestionable hegemony of U.S. capital which later went on advertising, with typical vulgarity, its arrogant self-confidence by insisting that the twentieth century was 'the American Century'. And, of course, in view of the inherent dynamism of the historically most advanced form of capital, the 'new world order' (and its 'new economic order') was supposed to come into being and remain with us forever through the agency of purely *economic* forces and determinations: so said the rhetorics, from Roosevelt's First Inaugural Address to 'the end of ideology'.

However, the facts could not speak more differently. For they bitterly put into relief one of the greatest ironies of history, namely: that although an incomparable economic dynamism and a potentially great new productive advance was at the roots of the original Rooseveltian strategy, its actual implementation — far from being satisfied with *economic* mechanisms, in tune with the even today still persisting myth of 'modernization' — required the most devastating war known to man, the second world war, for its 'take-off', not to mention the emergence and domination of the 'military-industrial complex' in its real 'drive to maturity'.

While American capital had much more than simply the initiative in all these developments — indeed it completely dominated them throughout, securing for itself a position of overwhelming advantage through which it can chalk up astronomical budget deficits and make the rest of the world pay for them — they affected and benefited 'total social capital' (constituted as a global entity) in its drive for self-expansion and domination.

To be sure, several national constituent parts of the totality of capital had to suffer humiliating immediate defeats, but only so as to rise stronger than ever from the ashes of temporary disintegration. The German and Japanese 'miracles' speak for themselves in this respect. In other cases, notably that of British capital, the impact was much more complicated, for a variety of reasons, concerned mainly with the rearguard struggle over the dissolution of the British Empire. But even in such instances, there can be no denying that in the end a not negligible degree of dynamic restructuring came about under the American challenge.

The overall result of these transformations was a significant *rationalization of global capital* and the establishment of a framework of financial/economic and state relations which, all in all, was much more suitable for the displacement of many contradictions than the system previously in existence.

18.2.5

THUS, the 1929-33 crisis was by no means a structural crisis from the point of view of capital as a global formation. On the contrary, it provided the necessary stimulus and pressure for the realignment of its various constituent forces, in accordance with the objectively changed power relations, greatly contributing thereby to the unfolding of capital's tremendous potentialities as inherent in its 'intensive totality'.

Externally this meant:
- (1) a dramatic move from poly-centred, outdated, wastefully interventionist political/military imperialism to a dynamic, economically much more viable and integrated system of global domination under U.S. hegemony;
- (2) the establishment of the International Monetary System and a number

of other important organs for the incomparably more rational regulation of inter-capital relations than the poly-centred framework had at its disposal;

- (3) the export of capital on a large scale (and through it the most effective perpetuation of dependency and enforced 'underdevelopment'), and the secure repatriation, on an astronomical scale, of rates of profit totally unimaginable at home; and

- (4) the relative incorporation, to varying degrees, of the economies of all postcapitalist societies into the framework of capitalist interchanges.

On the other hand, *internally* capital's great success story could be described in terms of:

- (1) using various modalities of state intervention for the expansion of private capital;

- (2) the transfer of bankrupt but essential private industries to the public sector, and their utilization for supporting through state funds in yet another way the operations of private capital, to be followed in due course by the transformation of such industries into private monopolies or quasi-monopolies, once they have become highly profitable again through the injection of massive funds financed from general taxation;

- (3) the successful development and operation of an economy of 'full employment' during the war and for a considerable period of time also after the war;

- (4) the opening up of new markets and new branches of production on the plane of the highly stretched 'consumer-economy', together with capital's success in generating and sustaining extremely wasteful patterns of consumption as a vital motivating force of such an economy; and

- (5) to crown it all, both in its sheer economic weight and political significance, the establishment of an immense 'military/industrial complex' as the controller and direct beneficiary of by far the most important portion of state intervention, and with it simultaneously also the removal of well over one third of the economy from the unwelcome fluctuations and uncertainties of the market.

Although the intrinsic value of all these achievements is extremely problematical (to put it mildly), there can be no doubt whatsoever as to their significance from the point of view of capital's dynamic self-expansion and continued survival. Precisely because of their central importance in 20th century capitalist developments, the severity of today's structural crisis is heavily underlined by the fact that several of the characteristics mentioned above are no longer true, and that the underlying tendency points in the direction of their reversal altogether: from a trend towards a new poly-centrism (think of Japan and Germany, for instance), with potentially incalculable consequences, to persistent mass unemployment (and its obvious implications for the consumer-economy) as well as to the threatening disintegration of the international monetary system and its corollaries. It would be foolish to take for granted as permanent even the powerfully entrenched positions of the military-industrial complex and its ability to extract and allocate to itself, undisturbed, the surplus required for its continued functioning on the current, still astronomical scale.

SOME people argue that since capital managed to solve its problems in the past, it will indefinitely do so also in the future. They might even add that if the crisis of 1929-33 spurred capital to the dramatic changes we have witnessed ever since, the present structural crisis is bound to produce lasting remedies and permanent solutions. The trouble with such reasoning is that it has absolutely nothing to back up the wishful thinking which desperately tries to pursue the 'line of least resistance' when it is no longer feasible to do so.

While it is always rather vacuous and dangerous to argue from nothing more than mere analogies of the past, it is self-contradictory to do so when the issue at stake is precisely the structural crisis and breakdown of some, up to now vital, mechanisms and determinations, manifesting itself as the crisis of established control and domination as such. The conditions for a solution of the present crisis can be specified, as we shall see in a moment. Thus, unless it can be demonstrated that capital's contemporary trends of development can actually satisfy these conditions, any talk about its inherent ability to always solve its problems is nothing but 'whistling in the dark'.

Another line of reasoning insists that capital has at its disposal an immense repressive force which it can freely use, as much as it pleases, for the solution of its mounting problems. Though it is by no means true that there are no constraints — even major ones — on the actual and potential use of naked force by capital, it is unquestionably the case that the already accumulated forces of destruction and repression are frightening, and still multiplying. But even so, the truth remains that nothing is ever solved by force alone, nor has been. Legends to the contrary — concerning Nazism and Stalinism, for instance — are often used merely to explain away a great deal of more or less active complicity of allegedly powerless sections of the population.

In addition, there is a far weightier consideration which concerns the inherent characteristics of capital itself. To put it simply, capital is a most efficient force for mobilising the complex productive resources of a society fragmented in many parts. It does not matter to capital how many: the ability to cope with fragmentation is precisely its great asset. However, capital is definitely not a system of unifying *emergency*, nor could it become one on a long-term basis, for reasons of its own internal constitution. It is by no means accidental in this respect that Fascist type state formations are viable today only at the periphery of the global capital system, in dependency and subordination to some liberal-democratic 'metropolitan' centre.

Thus, whatever the temporary successes of 'iron-fisted' authoritarian attempts might be in delaying or postponing the 'moment of truth' — and the chances of even such short-term successes should not be underrated — they can only aggravate the crisis in the longer run. For the structural problems described above amount to a major blockage in the global system of production and distribution. As such, they call for adequate structural remedies, not for their multiplication by forced postponement and repression. In other words, they require a positive intervention in the troubled productive process itself for checking its dangerously growing contradictions, with a view to ultimately removing them as the pace of actual restructuring permits. As against this, to present the possibility of capital resorting, while it can, to rule by way of a completely unstable, hence necessarily *transient,* state of *emergency*, as the *permanent* condition of its future *normality*, is a truly absurd notion.

18.2.6

THE conditions of managing the structural crisis of capital are directly linked to some major contradictions which affect both the internal problems of the various systems involved and their relationships with one another. They may be summed up as follows:

- (1) The internal social/economic contradictions of 'advanced' capital manifesting in increasingly more lopsided development under the direct or indirect control of the 'military-industrial complex' and the system of transnational corporations;
- (2) The social, economic and political contradictions of postcapitalist societies, both internally and in relation to one another, leading to their disintegration and thereby to the intensification of the structural crisis of the global capital system;
- (3) The increasing rivalries, tensions and contradictions among the leading capitalist countries, both *within* the various regional systems and *among* them, putting enormous strain on the established institutional framework (from the European Community to the International Monetary System) and foreshadowing the spectre of a devastating trade war;
- (4) The growing difficulties of maintaining the established neocolonial system of domination (from Iran to Africa and from South East Asia to Central and Southern America), coupled with the contradictions generated within the 'metropolitan' countries through the production units established and managed by 'expatriate' capital.

As we can see, in all four categories — each of which stands for a multiplicity of contradictions — the tendency is the intensification, and not the decrease of the existing antagonisms. Furthermore, the severity of the crisis is underlined by effectively confining intervention to the sphere of *effects,* making it prohibitively difficult to tackle their *causes*, thanks to the earlier mentioned 'circularity' of capital's civil society/political state through which the established power relations tend to reproduce themselves in all their surface transformations.

Two important examples illustrate this with savage conclusiveness. The first concerns the military-industrial complex, the second the chronic insolubility of the problems of 'underdevelopment'.

Much hope is expressed about finding the resources for a positive and viable economic expansion through reallocating a major portion of the military expenditure for socially long overdue measures and purposes. However, the permanent frustration of such hopes arises not only from the immense economic weight and naked state power of the military-industrial complex but also from the fact that the latter is more the manifestation and effect of the deep-seated structural contradictions of 'advanced' capital than their cause. Naturally, once it exists, it continues to function *also* as a contributory cause — and the greater its economic and political power the more so — but it does not *produce* them in the first place. From the point of view of contemporary capital, if the military-industrial complex did not exist, it ought to have been invented. (As mentioned earlier, in a sense capital simply 'stumbled upon' this solution during the war, after Roosevelt's somewhat naive attempt to *reculer pour mieux sauter* from the launching pad of the New Deal, resulting in very little advance indeed in a continued depression rather than in a real jump.)

The military-industrial complex fulfils with great effectiveness two vital functions, displacing temporarily two massive contradictions of 'overdeveloped' capital.

The first, mentioned a short while ago, is the transfer of a significant portion of the economy from the treacherous sea of uncontrollable market forces to the sheltered waters of highly profitable state finance. At the same time it also maintains intact also the mythology of economically superior and *cost-effective private enterprise*, thanks to the apriori absolution of *total* wastefulness and *structural bankruptcy* by the ideology of patriotic fervour.

The second function is no less important: to displace the contradictions due to the *decreasing rate of utilization*[262] which dramatically asserted itself during the last few decades of developments in the capitalistically advanced countries.

This is why, so long as a structural alternative is not found for dealing with the causal foundations of the successfully displaced contradictions here referred to, the hope of simply reallocating the prodigious resources now vested in the military-industrial complex are bound to remain nullified by the prevailing causal determinations.

The same is true of the intractable problems of enforced 'underdevelopment'. Naturally, it would suit 'enlightened capital'—a true contradiction in terms, if ever there was one—to extend its sphere of operation into every pore of 'underdeveloped' society, fully activating its material and human resources in the interest of its renewed self-expansion. Hence the efforts of *Brandt Commissions* and similar enterprises which manage to voice a great many partial truths while failing to notice the global one: that the 'underdeveloped' world is *already* fully integrated into the world of capital, and fulfils in it a number of vital functions. Thus, again, we can see an attempt to alleviate the *effects* of the dominant mode of integration while leaving their *causal determinations* untouched.

What is systematically ignored in such wishful proposals is that it is quite simply impossible to have it both ways: to maintain 'advanced' capital's highly stretched and absurdly 'overdeveloped' system of production in existence (which necessarily postulates the continued domination of a vast 'hinterland' of enforced underdevelopment) and at the same time to propel the 'Third World' to a high level of capitalistic development (which could only reproduce the contradictions of western 'advanced' capital, multiplied by the immense size of the population involved).

Capital's managers currently in charge know much better what the real score is — and so did Edward Heath and Willie Brandt themselves, when they were heading their respective governments — and cast aside these reports with the cynical 'realism' that directly corresponds to the aggressive reassertion of the dominant U.S. interests:

United States' Secretary of State said today that it was unrealistic to speak of a big transfer of resources from developed to developing countries. Mr Haig's emphasis was on using conventional market forces [sic!] to alleviate the plight of the poorest countries. There had to be 'a more open trading system with improved rules'. Foreign assistance had to be coupled with 'sound domestic policy and self-help'. In the view of the United States that meant relying on economic incentives and individual freedom. 'Suppression of economic incentives ultimately suppresses enthusiasm and invention...Those governments that have been more solicitous of the liberties of their people have also been more successful in securing both freedom and prosperity.'[263] To hear a paradigm representative of the repressive military-industrial complex sing the timeless virtues of 'conventional market forces' and 'individual freedom' is indeed a supreme irony. Sadly, however, it also happens to be a true measure of the utter hopelessness of expecting solutions from improvements in the realm of effects while leaving the causal determinants of capital's real world follow their established course which *structurally* reproduces those effects, with deepening gravity, on an ever-enlarging scale.

If the condition of resolving the structural crisis is tied to the solution of the four sets of contradictions mentioned above, the prospects of a positive outcome are far from promising from the point of view of capital's continued global expansion and domination. For one can see very little chance of success even in regard to relatively limited objectives, let alone in the lasting solution of the contradictions of all four categories combined. The probability is, on the contrary, that we shall continue to sink deeper into the structural crisis, even if there are bound to be some conjunctural successes as well as those resulting from a relative 'upturn', in due course, in the merely *cyclic* determinants of capital's present-day crisis.

18.3 The plurality of capitals and the meaning of socialist pluralism

18.3.1

REFLECTING over the debates of the Gotha Programme, Engels sarcastically commented on what he considered the deplorable influence of Wilhelm Liebknecht, the main author of the Programme: 'From bourgeois democracy he has brought over and maintained a real *mania for unification*.'[264] Sixteen years earlier, at the time of the planned Unity Congress, Marx made a similar point about the question of unification, though without the personal references. He acknowledged that 'the mere fact of unification is satisfying to the workers', but in the same sentence he stressed that 'it is a mistake to believe that this momentary success is not bought at too high a price.'[265]

It is important to remember this sceptical attitude towards 'unity' and 'unification' in order to put in perspective the recent advocacy of pluralism. For it would be quite wrong to treat this problem as something arising either from purely tactical considerations or from the practical constraints of an unfavourable relation of forces which no longer allows the pursuit of consistent socialist policies but calls, instead, for the strategy of elaborate compromises.

Another dimension of this problematic is that for many years the working class movement was subjected to Stalinist-inspired pressures which tried to enforce 'unity' so as to automatically suppress criticism in the interest of the 'Leading Party'. The self-appointed spokesmen of such 'unity' never bothered to define the tangible socialist objectives of the advocated organizational *Gleichschaltung* (i.e., forcing into a set mould), nor indeed to size up the objective conditions of formulating coordinated socialist strategies, together with the immense difficulties of their realization.

There are some very powerful reasons why Marx and Engels considered 'unity' and 'unification' as rather problematical concepts: the existing objective divisions and contradictions in the various constituents of the socialist movement. Such divisions and contradictions, in view of their complex internal and international ramifications, could not be simply wished or legislated out of existence; even less so than the eighteenth century French Convention could dream about abolishing pauperism by decree. It was not necessary to wait for the eruption of the Sino-Soviet conflict and the war between China and Vietnam to realize that merely postulating or enunciating the 'unity of socialist forces' contributes absolutely nothing to removing their problems, inequalities and antagonisms. The task of developing a force strong enough to successfully challenge capital on its own ground implied from the very beginning the necessity of building on the given foundations which show a great diversity and conflict of interests, as determined by the inherited social division of labour and the long prevailing differential rates of exploitation.

Since the problem was how to constitute a socialist *mass* consciousness on the available foundations while simultaneously engaging in unavoidable confrontations for the realization of *limited* aims and objectives, it was essential to find ways of preserving the integrity of the *ultimate* perspectives without losing contact with the *immediate* demands, determinations and potentialities of the historically given conditions. For Bakunin and the anarchists this problem did not exist (just as it was of no concern to all subsequent breeds of voluntarism), since they were not interested in the production of a socialist mass consciousness. They simply assumed the spontaneous convergence of the 'instinctive conscience of the popular masses' with their own views and strategies.

Marx, by contrast, saw the organizational question as:

(1) remaining faithful to socialist *principles*, and

(2) devising viable and flexible *programmes of action* for the various forces which share the broad common objectives of the struggle. This is how he summed up his views about the Unity Congress in the last quoted letter:

> The Lassallean leaders came because circumstances forced them to come. If they had been told in advance that there would be *no bargaining about principles*, they would have had to be content with a *programme of action* or a plan of organization for common action. Instead of this, one permits them to arrive armed with mandates, recognizes these mandates on one's part as valid, and thus *surrenders* unconditionally to those who are themselves in need of help.

Irrespective of the specific circumstances of the Gotha Congress, the 'high price' referred to by Marx concerned the compromise of *principles*, in pursuit of an illusory 'unity' in place of the feasible and necessary *common action*.

Just as in those days, this happens to be again an issue of paramount importance. For today — perhaps more than ever, in view of the bitter experiences of the recent and not so recent past — the much needed forms of *common action* cannot be conceived without a conscious strategic articulation of a *socialist pluralism* which recognises not only the existing differences but also the need for an adequate 'division of labour' in the general framework of a socialist offensive. In opposition to the false identification of 'unity' as the only way of championing socialist *principles* (while, in fact, the unrealistic pursuit and imposition of unity carried with it the necessary *compromise of principles*), Marx's rule remains valid: there can be *no bargaining about principles*.

But the obverse side of this rule is equally valid: namely, that the elementary condition of realising the principles of a socialist transformation (which, after all, involves the totality of 'associated producers' in the common enterprise of changing 'from top to bottom the conditions of their industrial and political existence, and consequently their whole manner of being') is the production of a socialist *mass consciousness* in the only feasible form of self-developing *common action*. And the latter, of course, can only arise out of the truly *autonomous* and *coordinated* (not hierarchically ruled and manipulated) constituents of an *inherently pluralist* movement.

In the socialist movement for a long time it was customary to *underestimate* the ability of the bourgeoisie to achieve unity. At the same time, there was a corresponding tendency to greatly *overestimate* both the possibilities and the immediate importance of working class unity. Furthermore, the same conceptions which assessed unity so much out of focus with reality also had a tendency to see the conquest of power as the *solution* of the problems confronting the socialist revolution, rather than their *real beginning*.

Naturally, if the socialist revolution is seen as primarily *political* in character, rather than as a multidimensional, and therefore necessarily 'permanent' *social* revolution, as Marx defined it, in that case the production and preservation of unity overrides everything in importance. If, however, it is recognized that the acquisition of power is only the *starting point* for unearthing the real difficulties and contradictions of that transformation 'from top to bottom, of the whole manner of being' of the associated producers, — difficulties and contradictions many of which cannot be even imagined before actually encountering them in the course of the ongoing transformation itself — then the need for genuinely pluralist strategies asserts itself as a matter of both immediate urgency and continued importance.

In this respect, while it is abstractly true that the ruling class's unity 'can only reveal itself vis-à-vis the proletariat,'[266] it is also highly misleading. For insofar as everything is subordinated to the fundamental contradiction between capital and labour under capitalism, bourgeois unity inevitably fulfils the function of strengthening one side of this antagonism. The trouble is, though, that the same is true of the other side; and even more so, as we shall see in a moment. Consequently, the abstract truth conceals a misrepresentation of major importance, born from wishful thinking. In other words, it denies or ignores that there is a devastatingly *real* foundation to the ruling class's unity: its *actual* rule and the tangible *power* (both material/economic and political/military) that goes with it.

By contrast, proletarian unity is a problem, a task, a challenge, even an imperative in determinate situations of emergency, but not a spontaneously given actual state of affairs. It may be brought into being for a more or less limited period and for a determinate purpose, but it may never be assumed as an unproblematically persistent condition even after its successful accomplishment in a specific socio-historical situation. On the contrary; it has to be constantly *recreated* under the changing circumstances for as long as the objective grounds of inequality (due to the inherited hierarchical social division of labour and differential rates of exploitation mentioned earlier) remain with us in any form whatsoever, as they are bound to for a much longer historical period of transition than one would wish.

18.3.2

THE 'bourgeois mania for unity' referred to by Engels has its solid foundation in the dominant economic order of society and its institutional guarantor, the capitalist state. The political manipulations of formal unity (at times successfully masquerading even as 'general consensus') amount to no more than putting the seal of approval on a *de facto* already prevailing state of affairs, thus providing its *a posteriori* 'legitimation'.

Being effectively in power as a class — and not only politically, thanks to the repressive instrumentality of the state, but in the *positive* sense of regulating the fundamental social metabolism itself — provides a powerful objective ground for a unifying self-identity well before the question of an acute political confrontation with the opposing class may arise. And even as far as the internal divisions of bourgeois 'civil society' are concerned, in view of the irrepressible objective tendency of concentration and centralization of capital the winning side is always the 'unitarian' one (i.e. big capital). The power of the latter multiplies just as certainly as the drive towards monopoly quickens its pace and creates the grotesquely unequal parties to the once idealized but now ever more blatantly predetermined and automatically resolved internal 'competition'. Hence the ever-increasing *sham pluralism* of the social order of capital in all its contemporary permutations.

One of the most powerful political/ideological mystifications of capital is, in fact, its pretence to 'pluralism' through which it succeeds in ruthlessly prescribing the framework of all admissible opposition to its own rule. While at the liberal/democratic phase of capitalist developments the claim to pluralism still meant something (even if not much more than the possibilities inherent in John Stuart Mill's 'negative freedom'), ever since the onset of the *monopolistic* phase the margin of real alternatives has been getting narrower and narrower, to the point of its almost complete disappearance in recent times. If the monetarist nightmare today finds its crude, inarticulate articulation in T.I.N.A. ('there is no alternative', as Ministers carry on repeating, like a broken gramophone record, the cynical message of capital's real freedom), that can only underline the gravity of the structural crisis. Besides, it also underlines the difficulties of a continued misrepresentation of the *absolute tyranny* of capital's economic determinism as 'the greatest good of the greatest number' and the apotheosis of 'traditional market forces and individual freedom'.

In truth, right from the beginning 'pluralism' was an extremely problematical concept for capital. Not only — and not even primarily — because of its *tendency* towards monopoly, but because of the *absolute presupposition* of monopoly as its *starting point*: i.e., the monopoly of private property by the few and the apriori exclusion of the vast majority as the necessary prerequisite of capital's social control. (It is worth mentioning here that state-monopoly of the means of production retains this vital presupposition of the capital system and thereby perpetuates the rule of capital under a different form.) All subsequent rules of capital's 'pluralist' game were decreed on this absolute monopolistic foundation: in its own interest, and to be broken in the interest of its continued rule, whenever the circumstances so required.

It was assumed as self-evident right from the beginning that 'there can be no alternative' to the monopoly of the means of production, nor to the free reign of capital's steamrolling economic determinism. If someone — followers of Marx, for instance — dared to question the destructive manifestations and implications of such economic determinism, they had to be condemned as dangerous 'economic determinists' from the standpoint of capital's one-dimensional and uni-directional freedom. The meaning of capital's 'pluralism' never amounted to more than simply acknowledging the *plurality of capitals* while simultaneously also insisting on total capital's absolute right to *monopoly*, both *tendentially* and *de facto*.

Thus, not only there can be no affinity between socialist pluralism and capitalist pseudo-pluralism (which does not and cannot offer a bigger margin of alternative action than is required by the narrow self-interest of a plurality of competing capitals, and even that only so long as their limited competition remains viable); they are, in fact, diametrically opposed to one another.

The meaning of capital's pluralism is visible at the political level in the farcical ritual of 'competing' for power between Democrats and Republicans in the U.S., just as much as in the successful manipulation of political power on behalf of capital by one wretched party in Italy, the Christian Democrats, for well over four decades and a half without interruption. (That the rule of Japanese capital is effectively linked to a curious one-party system, cleverly exploiting the traditional allegiances of a paternalistic society, is obvious even to its capitalist critics.) And in the somewhat more complicated cases of England and Germany (where Social Democracy openly boasted about its ability to better administer a 'modern' capitalist 'mixed economy' than the conservative alternative, self-delusorily trying to legitimate its claim to being 'the natural party of government' on such a noble foundation), only the form of 'pluralist' mystification is different, not its substance. This is why the conservative Edward Heath and the socialdemocratic Willy Brandt end up on the same side in a tame critique of the system when *both* their parties happen to be in government. And this is why Willy Brandt's successor, Helmut Schmidt, can only conceptualize (and denounce) the possibility of a socialist challenge to capital's rule as 'political destabilization'.

In all these cases 'pluralism' means a *systematic political disenfranchizing* of labour in its confrontation with capital, in the form most appropriate to the local circumstances. The 'pluralism' of changing governments (how many of them in postwar Italy, without the slightest change at all?) provides the *permanent alibi* for categorically rejecting any real change and for cynically enforcing the imperative according to which 'there can be no alternative' to capital's devastating economic determinism. Furthermore, the institutions of capital's pseudo-pluralism not only provide the immediate political guarantees of its continued rule. They also act as a mystifying shield that automatically diverts all criticism from its real target (namely the vicious circle of capital's destructive self-expansion to which everything must be unquestioningly subordinated) to the personalized irrelevance of its willing administrators who fall over backwards in outbidding one another as to who can keep the mechanism of the system better oiled.

Thus, the possibility of 'consensual' change is conveniently relegated to a margin of action apriori set by the premiss that 'there is no alternative' to the requirements of capital's self-expansion (no matter how destructive), success-fully enforcing thereby the dictates of the narrowest kind of economic determi-nism as the ultimate fulfilment of freedom. For the diversionary target of consensual political opposition makes it sure that whenever governments are booted out of office by bitterly disillusioned 'sovereign' electorates for 'breaking their promises', the awesome responsibility and dubious viability of the so-cial/economic order which they serve and on whose behalf they make and break those promises is never even mentioned. Accordingly, while 'pluralist' govern-ments may come and go with mystifying frequency, the rule of capital remains absolutely intact.

18.3.3
IN complete contrast, the elementary condition of success of the socialist project is its inherent pluralism. It sets out from the acknowledgement of the existing differences and inequalities; not to preserve them (which is a necessary concomi-tant of all fictitious and arbitrarily enforced 'unity') but to supersede them in the only viable form: by securing the active involvement of all those concerned.

The latter, it goes without saying, is impossible without the elaboration of specific strategies and 'mediations', arising from the particular determinations of changing needs and circumstances, which represent the greatest challenge to contemporary Marxist theory. For the one and only broadly held view that can serve as a common framework of reference for the great variety of politically more or less organized and conscious socialist forces is the *rejection* of the ubiquitous slogan that 'there is no alternative'. And even that cannot be assumed as unproblematically given. Not only because it is a *negativity* which needs its positive articulation in order to become viable as a mobilising strategy, but also because in the first instance it amounts to no more than merely asserting that 'there *ought to be* an alternative'. However, it remains the necessary starting point. For those who accept the wisdom of 'there is no alternative' — in the name of the 'triumph of organized capitalism', or the 'integration of the working class', or whatever else — could hardly claim *also* to offer the perspective of a socialist transformation, even if sometimes, curiously, they continue to do so.

Just as capital is structurally incapable of pluralism (other than one of a very limited kind, and even that becoming more and more restricted with the advance of capital's necessary concentration and centralization), so the socialist enterprise is *structurally unrealizable* without its full articulation in the manifold autonomous ('self-managing'), and thus irrepressibly pluralist projects of the ongoing *social revolution*.

The broad general principle rejecting capital's economic determinism pro-vides no more than a necessary point of departure in relation to which all particular groups (inevitably reflecting a multiplicity of given interests and divisions) must define their position in the form of interconnected, and if conditions permit also coordinated, but definitely not identical specific objec-tives and strategies. What is at stake is to devise a viable alternative to an immensely complex global system which has on its side the 'curse of interde-pendence' in resisting change.

This is expressed with brutal clarity in the words of Sir Roy Denman, E.E.C.'s chief negotiator for many years on international trade relations:

There is no alternative. People are not *insane* enough to want a *massive unravelling of the whole system.* Yet the dangers are very great, the situation is more serious now than at any time since the last war.[267]

Thus, the spokesmen of capital, even when they are forced to acknowledge the severity of the crisis, can find reassurance in the prevailing 'sanity' that protects and imposes the system as the one to which 'there is no alternative'. And even though it cannot be all that reassuring to be left with nothing more solid than the ultimate *fiat* of 'sanity' in defence of capitalist insanity, it remains true that *a massive unravelling of the whole system* is the only real alternative to capital's deepening structural crisis.

No one can seriously suggest that Sir Roy Denman's 'insanity' — the 'massive unravelling of the whole system' and its replacement by a viable one — could be accomplished by small groups of fragmented, isolated people. In reality, there can be no escape from Marx's programme of constituting a socialist mass consciousness through the practical enterprise of engaging in actually feasible and inherently pluralist common action.

While it becomes painfully obvious that capital's alternatives today are more and more confined to manipulative fluctuations between varieties of *Keynesianism* and *monetarism,*[268] with perilously less and less effective oscillatory movements tending toward the 'absolute rest' of a depressed continuum, the socialist rejection of the tyranny of 'no alternative' must be positively articulated in the form of intermediary objectives whose realization can make strategic inroads, even if in the first instance only partial ones, into the system to be replaced.

WHAT decides the fate of the various socialist forces in their confrontation with capital is the extent to which they can make tangible changes in everyday life now dominated by the ubiquitous manifestations of the underlying contradictions. Thus, it is not enough to focus on the structural determinants — even if it is done with insight, from an adequate vantage point — if at the same time their directly felt manifestations are left out of sight, because their socialist strategic implications are not visible to those concerned. For the meaning of socialist pluralism — the active engagement in common action, without compromising but constantly renewing the socialist principles which inspire the overall concerns — arises precisely from the ability of the participating forces to *combine* into a coherent whole, with *ultimately* inescapable socialist implications, a great variety of demands and partial strategies which in and by themselves need not have anything *specifically socialist* about them at all.

In this sense, the most urgent demands of our times, directly corresponding to the vital needs of a great variety of social groups — for jobs and education as well as for a decent health care and social services, together with the demands inherent in the struggle for women's liberation and against racial discrimination — are, without one single exception, such that, in principle, every genuine liberal could wholeheartedly embrace them. It is rather different, though, when we consider them not as single issues, in isolation, but jointly, as parts of the overall complex that constantly reproduces them as unrealized and systematically unrealizable demands.

Thus, it is the *condition* of their realization that ultimately decides the issue, (defining them in their plurality as *conjointly* socialist demands) and not their character considered separately. Consequently, what is at stake is not the elusive 'politicization' of these separate concerns through which they might in the end fulfil a direct political function in a socialist strategy, but the *effectiveness* of asserting and sustaining such largely self-motivating 'non-socialist' demands on the broadest possible front.

The immediate concerns of everyday life, from health care to grain production, are not directly translatable into the general values and principles of a social system. (Even comparisons become relevant and effective only when there is a shortfall in one area as a result of the more or less unjustifiable demands of another; like today's cuts in vital social services in the interest of the war-industry.) Any attempt at imposing a direct political control on such movements, following the rather unhappy tradition of the not so distant past, is in danger of being counterproductive (even if for the best intentions of 'politicization'), instead of helping to strengthen their autonomy and effectiveness.

It is an important sign of the historically changed conditions that these demands and the forces behind them can no longer be 'incorporated' or 'integrated' into capital's objective dynamics of self-expansion. In view of their chronic insolubility, as well as their immediate motivating power, they are likely to set the framework of social confrontation for the foreseeable future. Naturally, no matter how important even on their own, the issues referred to above were mentioned here only as *examples* belonging to a much larger number of specific concerns through which socialist aspirations and strategies must mediate themselves today.

Another type of demand involves a more obvious and direct social/political commitment, although even this set cannot be characterized as specifically socialist. For instance, the intensifying struggle for preserving peace against the vested interests of the military-industrial complex, or the need for curbing the power of the transnationals, or indeed for establishing a basis of cooperation and interchange in order to secure the conditions of real development in the 'Third World'. While it is fairly obvious that capital cannot meet any of these demands, and thus its control over the forces behind them is diminishing, it is also true that the liberating potential of its slipping control cannot be realized without the articulation of adequate socialist strategies and corresponding organizational forms.

The demands that directly manifest the necessity of a socialist alternative concern the inherent wastefulness of capital's mode of functioning. For, paradoxically, capital manages to impose on society the 'iron law' of its *economic determinism* without knowing the meaning of *economy* at all. There are four main directions in which the necessary wastefulness of capital asserts itself with increasingly more harmful consequences, as the ultimate limits of its productive potential are approached:

- (1) the uncontrollable demand for *resources* — i.e., capital's irrepressibly rising 'resource-intensity', of which 'energy-intensity' is only one aspect — irrespective of the consequences for the future, or for the environment, or indeed for repressing the needs of the people afflicted by its so-called 'developmental strategies';
- (2) the growing *capital-intensity* of its production processes, inherent in the necessary concentration and centralization of capital, and greatly contribut-

ing to the production of 'underdevelopment' not only on the 'periphery' but even in the heartland of its 'metropolitan' domain, generating massive unemployment and devastating a once flourishing and in many respects perfectly viable industrial base;

- (3) the accelerating drive for the *multiplication of exchange-value*, at first simply *divorced* from but now more and more openly *opposed* to 'use-value' in the service of *human need*, for the sake of maintaining capital's rule over society intact; and

- (4) the worst kind of waste: the waste of people, through the mass production of *'superfluous people'* who, both as a result of capital's 'productive' advances and its increasing difficulties in the 'realization process', cannot fit any longer into the narrow schemes of the production of profit and the wasteful multiplication of exchange-value. (The fact that the mass-produced 'superfluous time' of the growing number of 'superfluous people' is the once only given life-time of real people, cannot be, of course, of any concern to capital's devoted personifications.)

18.3.4

IN relation to all these tendencies and contradictions of capital, demands for a change can only be formulated in terms of a global socialist alternative. It is in this respect that the renewal of Marxism is so vital. For despite the criticisms concerning the 'crisis of Marxism', there is no serious alternative theory anywhere in sight which might be able to address itself to these problems in their complexity and comprehensiveness.

Apart from the recent hostile critics of Marx (like the 'new French philosophers' and their 'post-modernist' stable-mates) who may be safely ignored on account of their all too obvious ideological interests and corresponding intellectual standard, the various critical reflections tend to focus on limited aspects of the current social crisis. They offer answers and solutions which are applicable only partially, and avoid precisely those comprehensive issues which define the strategic horizons of any viable alternative.

While it is necessary to resist the inclination of some Marxists to dismiss this type of criticism as 'populist' — for, surely, there must be an important place for socialist inspired 'populism' in a genuinely pluralist framework of common action — the concern with local issues and 'grass root' forms of organization, as well as with the task of understanding their historical traditions and 'peculiarities', is far from sufficient on its own. It must be complemented by tackling their much broader ramifications and links with the social totality, so that their cumulative impact strengthens the chances of socialist strategy, instead of pulling in the direction of fragmentation and dispersal.

If in the past Marxist theory had a tendency to neglect such concerns, preferring to concentrate on the general principles of the socialist alternative, that was to a significant extent due to the historically *defensive* conditions. So long as such conditions prevailed, the repeated reassertion of the *ultimate* validity of the overall perspectives — in a defiant dismissal of capital's untroubled self-expansion as ultimately irrelevant — was understandable, indeed necessary, even if problematical. Under the changed conditions of the necessary *offensive*, however, the self-reassuring restatement of the general perspectives in the abstract — as a declaration of faith — is completely out of place. For Marx's dictum about '*hic Rhodus, hic salta*' calls for integrating the totality of social demands, from the most immediate 'non-socialist' everyday concerns to those openly questioning capital's social order as such, into a theoretically coherent as well as instrumentally/organizationally viable strategic alternative.

Thus, the real issue is how to set firmly an overall direction to follow while fully acknowledging the constraining circumstances and the power of immediacy opposed to ideal shortcuts. The Marxian social revolution defines the period of transition in terms of identifiable objectives, together with the theoretical, material and instrumental mediations necessary for their realization. In this sense, to name a few vital issues, the question that must be pursued is: how is it possible

- (1) to produce a *radical change* while safeguarding the necessary *continuity* of the social metabolism (which calls for the sustained practical application of the Marxian methodological principle concerning the dialectical reciprocity between continuity and discontinuity);

- (2) to restructure 'from top to bottom' the *whole* edifice of society which simply cannot be pulled down for the purposes of a total reconstruction, as we have seen in Part Two;

- (3) to move from the prevailing *fragmentation* of the social forces to their *cohesion* in the creative enterprise of the *associated producers* (which implies the successful development of socialist *mass consciousness* through assuming *responsibility* for the consequences of self-managed productive and distributive practices);

- (4) to accomplish a genuine *autonomy* and *decentralization* of the powers of decision making, in opposition to their existing concentration and centralization which cannot possibly function without 'bureaucracy';

- (5) to transcend the division and 'circular inertia' of *civil society/political state* through the unification of the functions of *work* and *decision making*;

- (6) to abolish the everywhere prevailing *secrecy* of government by instituting a new form of *open self-government* by the people concerned.

Many important themes of twentieth century Marxist theory are integral parts of tackling these issues of transition, just as the question of reassessing the role of trade unions and parties in the framework of socialist pluralism has been brought to the forefront again. Some may wish to deny that such issues are important today. But those who do not take that view should not find it difficult to agree that actively engaging with them may well be the most fruitful way of tackling the 'crisis of Marxism'.

18.4 The need to counter capital's extra-parliamentary force

18.4.1

WE live in an age when — due to the internal dynamics of 'hybridization' of the established mode of social metabolic control — the *political* dimension is much more prominent than in the classical phase of capital's historical ascendancy, despite all protestations of the 'radical right' to the contrary. Naturally, the proper assessment of this problem should not be restricted to the direct political institutions, like parliament. It is much broader and more deep-seated than that. In fact the changes which we have witnessed in the functioning of parliament itself — changes tending to deprive it even of its limited autonomous functions of the past — cannot be circularly explained in terms of the changing electoral machinery and the corresponding parliamentary practices. Spokesmen and women of the hypostatized 'absolute sovereignty of parliament' and their rhetorical clashes with their parliamentary colleagues over the mirage of 'losing sovereignty to Brussels' (for instance), are wide off the mark. They seek remedies to the deplored changes where they cannot be found: within the confines of the parliamentary political domain itself. The problem is, though, that the ongoing, and from a self-referential political perspective utterly bewildering, developments can only be understood in the comprehensive framework of the material and cultural reproduction process. For it is the latter that requires the fulfilment of determinate but changing functions from the political sphere in the course of the historical transformations and self-assertive adjustments of the dominant social metabolic order as a whole.

As we have seen above in various contexts, 20th century developments were characterized by the growing weight of 'extra-economic' factors. In other words, the 20th century has witnessed the rise to prominence of 'extra-economic' forces and procedures which used to be considered with great scepticism, and rejected as alien to the nature of the capital system at the time of its triumphal historical ascendancy. When with the onset of the structural crisis of the system, in the 1970s, the representatives of the 'radical right' broke with the Keynesian form of consensual capitalist state intervention (dominant for a quarter of a century after the Second World War), many of the politicians involved instantly forgot not only that they themselves were deeply implicated in the sinful practices which they now sonorously denounced. They blinded themselves also to the fact — and it is unimportant here whether with the help of hypocrisy and cynical pretence or out of genuine ignorance—that the altered course required at least as great a state intervention in the socioeconomic processes (now more than ever on behalf of big business) as the Keynesian variety beforehand. The only difference was that, in addition to the generous help given to big business — from massive tax incentives to corrupt 'privatization' practices,[269] and from abundant research funds (especially for the benefit of the military/industrial complex) to the more or less open facilitation of the tendency to monopolism—the 'radical right' had to impose also a whole range of repressive laws on the labour movement. Ironically, the repressive laws against labour had to be introduced 'softly softly' through the good offices of 'democratic parliaments', in order to deny to the working classes even the defensive gains of the past, in accordance with the narrowing margins of profitable capital-accumulation under the circumstances of the unfolding structural crisis.

Thus the importance of political struggle and the radical critique of the state — including its 'democratic institutions', with parliament at their apex — has never been greater for the prospects of labour's emancipation than in the present historical phase of the pretended 'rolling back the boundaries of the state'. As it has become painfully obvious through the worsening plight of billions of people, the capital system — even in its most advanced form — has miserably failed humankind. The same can be said of its political dimension of social metabolic control. For even the most advanced state form of the capital system — the liberal-democratic state, with its parliamentary representation and institutionalized formal democratic guarantees for 'justice and fairness', together with its alleged safeguards against the abuse of power — has failed to deliver any of its claimed self-legitimating promises.

The crisis of politics all over the world, including the parliamentary democracies in the capitalistically advanced countries — often assuming the form of understandable bitterness and a resigned withdrawal from political activity by the popular masses — is an integral part of the deepening structural crisis of the capital system. The claims of 'empowering the people' — be that under the ideology of 'people's capitalism' (armed with a handful of non-voting shares) or under the slogans of 'equal opportunity' and 'fairness' in a system of incorrigible structural inequality — are too absurd to be taken seriously even by its prominent propagandists. The future is, on the contrary, likely to bring ever greater imposition of regressive political determinations over the everyday life of the popular masses, rather than the repeatedly promised 'rolling back the boundaries of the state'. There can be no way of opting out of politics, no matter how disheartening its dominant institutional forms and their self-perpetuating practices. But precisely for that reason, politics is too important to be left to politicians; and, indeed, democracy worthy of its name is far too important to be left to capital's actually existing and feasible parliamentary democracies and to the corresponding narrow margin of action of parliamentarians; even of 'great parliamentarians'.

When the title of 'great parliamentarian' is conferred upon representatives of the Left , it is used by the conservative system (with a small 'c', including the Labour Party's right wing leadership) as a way of congratulating and patting itself on the back.Such political figures are supposed to be 'great parliamentarians' because, as the legend goes, they have 'learned to master the rules of parliamentary procedure' and with their help 'continue to raise uncomfortable issues'. However, the truly uncomfortable truth is that the issues thus raised are invariably ignored, or ruled 'out of order' in parliament itself. In this way the apologists of the substantively anti-socialist parliamentary system can demonstrate to 'democratic public opinion' that there can be no other way of dealing with the problems of society than submission to the rules of the parliamentary game and the strict observance of its procedures which produce 'great parliamentarians' also on the political Left. *Futility* and *political marginalization* are the criteria for being promoted to the exalted rank of 'great parliamentarians' on the Left. Thus a few of them are allowed into the hall of fame in the interest of putting the system of parliamentary democracy beyond and above all conceivable 'legitimate criticism'.

In truth, given the political marginalization inseparable from the acceptance of parliamentary constraints as the only legitimate framework of political action, conformity to the internalized rules of the parliamentary game — even if it is practised with radical intent — can only produce the *parliamentary self-imprisonment* of the Left. Ironically, the way the parliamentary system actually functions, now even people with impeccable right-wing credentials — but great illusions about their own role in determining the outcome of political debates — like Roy Hattersley, are unhappy about the blind conformism with which they have to accept the latest rules of the parliamentary game. They have to complain, of course totally in vain, that the party leadership should pay more attention to its once professed principles. In fact we witness today the liquidation of even the mildest socialdemocractic principles in the name of securing a 'broad electoral alliance'. Revealingly, thus, Hattersly is arguing — in an article published in the *Independent* on 12 August 1995 under the title: 'Roy Hattersley tells Tony Blair where he has gone wrong' — that

> I am a passionate believer in New Labour, a long time opponent of old Clause IV [the clause promising the common ownership of the means of production] and a heretic who wants completely to sever Labour's formal links with the trade unions. But I nevertheless understand why party members worry that we have become so preoccupied with the problems of the middle classes that we have begun to overlook the needs of the disadvantaged and the dispossessed. ... Ideology is what keeps parties consistent and credible as well as honest. In the long term, the party's public esteem would be protected by a robust statement of fundamental intention. Socialism — which is proclaimed in New Clause IV — requires the bedrock of principle to be the redistribution of power and wealth. If that objective were reasserted, many of the problems would disappear.

The fact that the Labour Party— of which not so long ago Hattersley was the Deputy Leader — failed to 'redistribute power and wealth' throughout its long history, does not seem to worry the author of this article. The *Times* leader is much more realistic when it sings the praises of Tony Blair, saying that 'The "new Labour" ideology championed by the Opposition leader bears little relation to the socialism of the past. It is *pragmatic, friendly to business'*.[270]

18.4.2

THE narrowing margin of profitable capital-accumulation greatly affected the prospects of the labour movement even in the capitalistically most advanced countries. For it not only worsened the standard of living of the labour force in full employment (not to mention the conditions of countless millions of unemployed and underemployed people), but, as mentioned in the last section, also curtailed the possibilities of their self-defensive action as a result of authoritarian legislation imposed on the working classes by their allegedly democratic parliaments.

As of today, this process is by no means completed. There is no year in which the working classes are not confronted by new legislative measures devised against their traditional defensive organs and forms of action. At the same time the parliamentary form of representation itself has become extremely problematical even in its own terms of reference.

Once upon a time the justification for the relative autonomy of parliamentary representatives — an argument still used for rationalizing the non-accountability of parliamentary representatives to their electors — was summed up in these terms by Hegel:

> their relation to their electors is not that of agents with a commission or specific instructions. A further bar to their being so is the fact that their assembly is *meant to be a living body in which all members deliberate in common and reciprocally instruct and convince each other.*[271]

In the actual functioning of parliaments nothing corresponds today to the Hegelian characterization even to the limited extent to which they could be once described in such terms. Whatever might be the views held by the particular members of parliament on which they would like to 'deliberate in common and reciprocally instruct and convince each other', the arguments they might be able to master in favour of their views, even if strongly held, carry no weight. For as a matter of fact the so-called 'three line whip' compels them to vote according to the dictates of their party leadership, on pain of 'losing their whip' as a result of which they are subsequently 'deselected' as parliamentary candidates. This practice is followed not only in dealing with major political issues but even on debates about the desirability of introducing dog licences. There is no difference in this respect between the major political parties. 'Left of centre' Labour Prime Minister Harold Wilson once threatened, with brutal authoritarianism, his dissenting colleagues on the left of the party by saying to them that unless they behaved he would not *'renew their dog licences'.*

This is a most challenging problem for the future. For in the course of this century we have witnessed the degradation of parliamentary politics — once rooted in the plurality of capitals and in the margin of relative gains that could be derived from the corresponding divergence of interests also to sections of the working class — to some sort of a *conspiracy* against labour as the antagonist of capital. This kind of conspiracy takes place not so much *between* parties but *within* each of them. Between them only in the sense that the unholy 'consensus politics' of these decades — despite the institutionalized fog-generation of parliamentary 'adversarial politics' — also belongs to this issue. However, the most important aspect is the internal constitution and functioning of the parties themselves, including the parliamentary parties of labour. For the way they are constituted and run excludes any possibility of even raising the question of how to alter the established mode of social metabolic control. On the contrary, all parliamentary political activity is confined — both in government and in opposition — to the stabilization or re-stabilization of the capital system. This is why now for a long time the guiding thread of parliamentary politics has been how to *disenfranchise* labour (not openly and formally but in substantive terms), so as to nullify its gains obtained through the instrumentality of the early working class parties and trade unions. The policy somersaults of the British Labour Party (now respectfully calling itself 'New Labour'), and the similar 'disengagement' of the Italian Communist Party from all of its former principles and beliefs, are good illustrations of the way in which the antagonist of capital has been effectively disenfranchised in the course of these developments.

The principal role of Socialdemocratic parties (under a variety of names, including those of the rebaptized former Communist parties) is nowadays confined to *delivering labour to capital,* and using the people as *electoral fodder* for the purposes of the spurious legitimation of the perpetuated status quo under the pretext of the 'open' and 'fully democratic' electoral process. This uncritical parliamentary accommodation of working class parties was by no means always the case, even though the 'strict observance of parliamentary procedures' to which they were expected to submit when they entered the electoral arena was always extremely problematical. For the labour movement, at the time of its inception, had much broader and incomparably more radical objectives than what could be realized within the framework of the principal political organ created by the bourgeoisie in the ascendant: Parliament. Indeed, even the German socialdemocratic movement — which started to yield to accommodatory pressures already in Marx's lifetime — continued to promise a radical social transformation through the implementation of strategic reforms until it openly capitulated to the demands of bourgeois national expansionism at the outbreak of the First World War. Now, however, with the end of capital's historical ascendancy, the margin of even the most limited reform in favour of labour is practically non-existent. Thus the mainstream of 'reform' and parliamentary legislation has for its objective the castration of the labour movement in general, and not just the total isolation of the handful of its committed socialist parliamentarians.

Every single institution of the system is fully involved in this enterprise, notwithstanding the mythology of 'democratic guarantees' which are supposed to be provided by the 'division of powers': a mythology that infected even some well known intellectuals on the left. What is supposed to be one of the principal democratic guarantees — the 'fearlessly independent judiciary' — continues to demonstrate on every possible occasion its 'independent' ability to extend the repressive laws of 'democratic parliament' against labour fully in tune with the interests and imperatives of the established order. Its behaviour during the one year long miners' strike provided striking examples of 'judiciary militancy'. But, of course, the judiciary does not need a major social confrontation, like the miners' strike, to fulfil its class conscious anti-democratic role. It does so as a matter of normality on every key issue. Thus a recent — and in domestic law final — judgement by the British law lords attacks the trade unions even in their basic wage-negotiating function, undermining thereby their very existence. As reported in the *Financial Times:*

> The law lords unanimously ruled yesterday that employers were legally entitled to withhold pay rises from employees who refused to sign personal contracts that removed their union-based negotiating rights.[272]

This transparently class-conscious judgement was in fact a retrospective extension of a 1993 anti-union law by the Conservative government in Britain, although procedures of this kind are usually misrepresented, with characteristic hypocrisy, as 'politically independent legal clarification'. What beats, however, even the hypocrisy of such anti-democratic acts is the 'reasoning' in which they are wrapped up in order to make them appeal to the credulity of those who are credulous enough to take them seriously. Thus

> Lord Slynn argued there was no evidence that withholding a salary increase from those who remained in the union was meant to prevent or deter union membership, even if *derecognition* in itself might make the union less attractive to members or potential members.[273]

There can be no doubt about the mental gymnastics and acrobatics at work in producing rationalizations like this, which call for the unique ability to stand on one's head for the duration of writing lengthy supreme court judgements without even blushing. At the same time, such acts of the highest independent democratic judiciary also confirm with eloquence that the *'separation of powers'* under the rule of capital can only mean one thing: the *institutionalized and legally enforced separation of power from labour and its exercise against the interests of labour.* This is why there can be no hope for instituting meaningful structural changes even in a million years within the confines of the established and well entrenched sociopolitical framework. The permanent frustrations and invariable defeats of genuine socialists who hoped to achieve their objectives now for well over a century through parliamentary reforms were and remain unavoidable precisely for this reason. Their far from simply personal failures underline the wisdom of the great Hungarian poet, Attila József, who wrote:

> *even the best tricks of cat won't catch the mouse*
> *at the same time outside and inside the house.*[274]

18.4.3

THE critique of the parliamentary system from a radical perspective did not begin with Marx. We find it powerfully expressed already in the 18th century in Rousseau's writings. Starting from the position that sovereignty belongs to the people and therefore it cannot be rightfully alienated, Rousseau also argued that for the same reasons it cannot be legitimately turned into any form of representational abdication:

> The deputies of the people, therefore, are not and cannot be its representatives; they are merely its stewards, and can carry through no definitive acts. Every law the people has not ratified in person is null and void — is, in fact, not a law. The people of England regards itself as free; but it is grossly mistaken; it is free only during the election of members of parliament. As soon as they are elected, slavery overtakes it, and it is nothing. The use it makes of the short moments of liberty it enjoys shows indeed that it deserves to lose them.[275]

At the same time Rousseau also made the important point that although the power of legislation cannot be divorced from the people even through parliamentary representation, the administrative or 'executive' functions must be considered in a very different light. As he had put it:

> in the exercise of the legislative power, the people cannot be represented; but in that of the executive power, which is only the force that is applied to give the law effect, it both can and should be represented.[276]

In this way Rousseau, who has been systematically misrepresented and abused by 'democratic' ideologues even of the 'socialist jet-set' because he insisted that *'liberty cannot exist without equality'* [277] — which therefore ruled out even the best feasible form of representation as necessarily discriminatory/iniquitous hierarchy — had put forward a much more practicable exercise of political and administrative power than what he is usually credited with or indeed is accused of doing. Significantly, in this process of tendentious misrepresentation, both of the vitally important principles of Rousseau's theory, usable in a suitably adapted form also by socialists, have been disqualified and thrown overboard. Yet the truth of the matter is that, on the one hand, the power of fundamental decision making should never be divorced from the popular masses, as the veritable horror story of the Soviet state system, run against the people by the Stalinist bureaucracy in the name of socialism in the most authoritarian fashion, conclusively demonstrated it. At the same time, on the other hand, the fulfilment of specific administrative and executive functions in all domains of the social reproductive process can indeed be *delegated* to members of the given community, provided that it is done under rules autonomously set by and properly controlled at all stages of the substantive decision making process by the associated producers.

Thus the difficulties do not reside in the two basic principles themselves as formulated by Rousseau but in the way in which they must be related to capital's

material and political control of the social metabolic process. For the establishment of a socialist form of decision making, in accordance with the principles
of both inalienable rule-determining power (i.e. the 'sovereignty' of labour not
as a particular class but as the universal condition of society) and delegating
specific roles and functions under well defined, flexibly distributed and appropriately supervised, rules would require entering and radically restructuring
capital's antagonistic material domains. A process which would have to go well
beyond what could be successfully regulated by considerations derived from
Rousseau's principle of inalienable popular sovereignty and its delegatory corollary. In other words, in a socialist order the 'legislative' process would have to
be fused with the production process itself in such a way that the necessary
horizontal division of labour — discussed in Chapter 14 — should be complemented by a system of self-determined *co-ordination* of labour, from the local to
the global levels. This relationship is in sharp contrast to capital's pernicious
vertical division of labour which is complemented by the 'separation of powers' in
an alienated and on the labouring masses unalterably superimposed 'democratic
political system'. For the vertical division of labour under the rule of capital
necessarily affects and incurably infects every facet also of the horizontal division
of labour, from the simplest productive functions to the most complicated balancing processes of the legislative jungle. The latter is an ever denser legislative
jungle not only because its endlessly multiplying rules and institutional constituents must play their vital part in keeping firmly under control the actually
or potentially challenging behaviour of labour, watchful over limited labour
disputes as well as safeguarding capital's overall rule in society at large. Also,
they must somehow reconcile at any particular temporal slice of the unfolding
historical process — to the extent to which such reconciliation is feasible at all
— the separate interests of the plurality of capitals with the uncontrollable
dynamics of the totality of social capital tending towards its ultimate self-assertion as a global entity.

In a recent rejoinder with Rousseau's critique of parliamentary representation, Hugo Chávez Frias, the leader of a radical movement in Venezuela — the
Movimiento Bolivariano Revolucionário (MBR-200) — writes in response to
the chronic crisis of the country's sociopolitical system:

> With the appearance of the populist parties the suffrage was converted into a tool
> for putting to sleep in order to enslave the Venezuelan people in the name of demo-
> cracy. For decades the populist parties based their discourse on innumerable pater-
> nalistic promises devised to melt away popular consciousness. The alienating political
> lies painted the 'promised land' to be reached via a rose garden. The only thing the
> Venezuelans had to do was to go to the electoral urns, and hope that everything will
> be solved without the minimal popular effort. ... Thus the act of vote was transformed
> into the beginning and the end of democracy.[278]

The author of these lines stands the second highest in popular esteem in Venezuela (second only to Rafael Caldera) among all public figures, embracing all walks
of life, way above all aspiring party politicians. Thus he could easily win high
public office if he so wanted, which refutes the usual argument that people who
criticize the existing political system only do so because they are unable to meet
the arduous requirements of democratic elections. As a matter of fact Hugo
Chávez at the time of writing (in 1993) rejects the 'siren song' of political opinion

formers — who try to pacify people by saying that there is no need to worry about the crisis because there is 'only a little time' to go to the new elections — for very different reasons. He points out that while the usual political advice calls for 'a little more patience' until the election scheduled a few months ahead, 'every minute hundreds of children are born in Venezuela whose health is endangered for lack of food and medicine, while billions are stolen from the national wealth, and in the end what remains of the country is bled dry. There is no reason why one should give any credence to a political class which demonstrated towards society that it has no will at all to institute change.'[279] For this reason Chávez counterposes to the existing system of parliamentary representation the idea that 'The sovereign people must transform itself into the object *and the subject* of power. This option is not negotiable for revolutionaries.'[280] As to the institutional framework in which this principle should be realized, he projects that in the course of radical change

> Federal state electoral power will become the political-juridical component through which the citizens will be depositories of popular sovereignty whose exercise will thereafter really remain in the hands of the people. Electoral power will be extended over the entire sociopolitical system of the nation, establishing the channels for a veritable polycentric distribution of power, displacing power from the centre towards the periphery, increasing the effective power of decision making and the autonomy of the particular communities and municipalities. The Electoral Assemblies of each municipality and state will elect Electoral Councils which will possess a permanent character and will function in absolute independence from the political parties. They will be able to establish and direct the most diverse mechanisms of Direct Democracy: popular assemblies, referenda, plebiscites, popular initiatives, vetoes, revocation, etc. ... Thus the concept of *participatory* democracy will be changed into a form in which democracy based on popular sovereignty constitutes itself as the *protagonist* of power. It is precisely at such borders that we must draw the limits of advance of Bolivarian democracy. Then we shall be very near to the territory of *utopia*.[281]

Whether such ideas can be turned into reality or remain utopian ideals cannot be decided within the confines of the political sphere. For the latter is itself in need of the type of radical transformation which foreshadows from the outset the perspective of the 'withering away of the state'. In Venezuela, where in many parts of the country as much as 90 *percent of the population* demonstrates its 'rebellion against the absurdity of the vote through its electoral abstention',[282] the traditional political practices and the apologetic legitimatory use to which the 'democratic electoral system' is put, falsely claiming for the system the unchallengeable justification of a 'mandate conferred by the majority', no condemnation of vacuous parliamentary paternalism can be considered too sharp. Nor can it be seriously argued that high electoral participation is itself the proof of actually existing democratic popular consensus. After all, in some Western democracies the act of voting is compulsory and may in fact add up in its legitimatory value to no more than the most extreme forms of openly critical or pessimistically resigned abstentionism. Nevertheless, the measure of validity for subjecting to the necessary radical critique the parliamentary representational system is the strategic undertaking to exercise the 'sovereignty of labour' not only in political assemblies, no matter how *direct* they might be with regard to their organization and mode of political decision making, but in the self-determined productive and distributive life-activity of the social individuals in every single domain and at all levels of the social metabolic process. This is what draws the line of demarcation between the socialist revolution which is socialist in its *intent* — like the October Revolution of 1917 — and the *'permanent revolution'* of effective socialist transformation. For without the progressive and ultimately complete transfer of material reproductive and distributive decision making to the associated producers there can be no hope for the members of the postrevolutionary community of transforming themselves into the *subject* of power.

18.4.4

IN the second half of the 20th century no one has argued more forcefully in favour of finding legislative guarantees against the abuse of political power and the violation of human rights than Norberto Bobbio. Conscious of the inhumanities committed in the name of socialism under the Soviet-type system, he tried to combine the best features of liberalism with the aspirations of democratic socialism. Firmly rejecting the idea of 'direct democracy', he advocated the institution of guarantees and improvements in human rights through the parliamentary legislative system.[283] Significantly, however, the improvement of existing conditions by means of formally guaranteed rights advocated by Bobbio has become progressively more dependent on changing the *material* determinations and imperatives of the capital system. Accordingly, a radical critique of this system as a social metabolic order would seem to be the necessary precondition for assessing the legislative measures compatible with it.

In a 1992 interview Bobbio stressed that in our age the right to liberty and work, coupled with the individual's entitlement to social security provisions, must be complemented by the rights of the present and future generations to live in an unpolluted environment, with the right to self-regulated human procreation and guarantees of privacy against all encroachments on it by the ubiquitous all-controlling state, as well as with legally secured guarantees against the grave dangers increasingly affecting the genetic patrimony.[284] Much as one can agree with all these demands, it is disturbingly clear that even the parliamentary enactment of the advocated rights and guarantees — with the possible exception of the formally proclaimed 'right to liberty' which is, however, materially emptied of all content in practice for the overwhelming majority of humankind by the established mode of social metabolic control — would become possible only by successfully confronting the massive material and political vested interests militating against them. Besides, formal enactment would by itself provide no guarantees for their implementation, as countless solemnly proclaimed democratic constitutional principles and just as countless unenforced laws decorating the existing statute books amply testify. For they remain unenforced precisely because they would, or even just might, curtail the power of capital. In a world of chronic unemployment, with constant attacks even on the meagre remnants of the 'Welfare state' and the social security system, under the pressure to maximally exploit everything, from unrenewable resources to the ethically most questionable advances made in bio- and information-technology in direct subordination to the dictates of profitable capital-accumulation, one could only dream about enforcing the diametrical opposite of such developments by the good offices of an enlightened legislature. Equally, it would be nothing short of a miracle if a system of reproductive control which is structurally incapable of planning and restraining the harmful impact of its own mode of operation even for the day after tomorrow could codify and respect the rights of *future generations* clearly in conflict with its material imperatives. Naturally, this circumstance does not invalidate the Italian philosopher's point that the left should fight in every way it can to make people conscious of the merits of such demands, as part of its critique of the established social order. But it puts sharply into relief the hopeless limitations of the available legislative institutions for solving the deep-seated material reproductive problems identified by Bobbio himself.

Social democracy in its long history at first followed the path of trying to introduce major changes in the prevailing class relations through parliamentary reform and — after a few decades of failure to advance the objectives of socialist transformation — ended up totally reneging on them. This was by no means accidental or simply due to 'personal betrayal' of their erstwhile principles by the socialdemocratic parliamentary representatives. Their enterprise of instituting socialism by parliamentary means was doomed from the outset. For they envisaged the realization of the *impossible*. They promised to gradually transform into something radically different — that is, into a socialist order — a system of social reproductive control over which they *did not and could not have any meaningful control* in and through parliament.

As we have seen above, capital — by its very nature and innermost determinations — is *uncontrollable*. Therefore, to invest the energies of a social movement into trying to *reform* a substantively *uncontrollable* system, is a much more futile venture than the labour of Sisyphus, since the viability of even the most limited reform is inconceivable without the ability to exercise control over those aspects or dimensions of a social complex which one is attempting to reform. And that is what made the socialdemocratic parliamentary enterprise self-contradictory and doomed from the outset. For the socialdemocratic parties continued to delude themselves and their electors, for decades, that they would be able to institute 'in due course', through parliamentary legislation, a *structural reform of the uncontrollable capital system*.

The blind alley of social democracy was by no means the original path of the socialist movement. Following the road of parliamentary reform and accommodation became the dominant orientation in the political parties of the working class only with the emergence and consolidation of the Second International. Naturally, the blind apologists for the abandonment of all socialist objectives by the present-day leadership of socialdemocratic and labour parties try to retrospectively rewrite history, grotesquely suggesting that

> The original — and, for its day, audacious — *aim of socialism* was *democratic capitalism*. It was not until the 1840s, when *Marx and Engels hijacked the term*, that 'socialism' became a project whose ambition was to destroy capitalism. Clause 4 [of the British Labour Party's seventy year old constitution] remains a fundamentally Marxist text, for all its slippery language and the wishes of its authors to distance Labour from the worst excesses of Lenin's dictatorship of the proletariat. Hence the importance of [present leader] Blair's announcement. He is challenging his party, at last, to *bury Marxist socialism*.[285]

The historical facts, wilfully brushed aside by all apologists, speak otherwise. For the radical negation of the capitalist order goes back a long way before Marx and Engels had set their eyes on England. The persecuted secret societies engaged in working-class-oriented negation of the established order's incorrigible — and thus unreformable/'undemocratizable' — structural iniquities go back at least as far as the French Revolution and its turbulent aftermath. As a matter of fact Marx's first acquaintance with the uncompromising demands of radical anti-capitalist socialism took place precisely in such secret working class societies during his stay in France as a young man, well before he started to write his seminal *Economic and Philosophic Manuscript of 1844.* Anybody who can seriously commit to paper the proposition that a world-historical revolutionary movement can be invented by two exiled young German intellectuals who 'hijack the term socialism' is as completely out of contact with reality and all sense as someone who can pontificate, just because he fancies it, that by replacing the long held commitment to public ownership in Clause 4 of the Labour Party's constitution with the unprincipled verbal concoction of 'New Labour', Tony Blair can actually 'bury Marxist socialism' — 'if he finds the right words', as the wishful projection puts it.

The derailment of the working class movement occurred in the last third of the 19th century, and its negative consequences became pronounced with the parliamentary success — and accommodation — of the socialdemocratic and labour parties. The success itself could only be considered a Pyrrhic victory in its long-term impact on the cause of labour's emancipation. For the price which had to be paid for it was the fateful structural weakening of labour's fighting potential, caused by the acceptance of the parliamentary constraints as the only legitimate framework of contesting the rule of capital. In practical terms this had meant catastrophically dividing the movement into the so-called *'political arm'* and the *'industrial arm'* of labour, with the illusion that the 'political arm' would serve or represent, by legislatively codifying, the interests of the class of labour organized in the capitalist industrial enterprises by the particular trade unions of the 'industrial arm'. As time went by, however, everything turned out to be exactly the other way round. The 'political arm', instead of asserting its political mandate in close collaboration with the 'industrial arm', used the rules of the parliamentary game in order to subordinate the trade unions to itself and to capital's ultimate political determinations enforced through parliament. Thus, instead of politically strengthening the fighting force of the 'industrial arm' in its confrontations with capitalist enterprises, thereby enhancing the emancipatory potential of labour, the 'political arm' confined the trade unions — in the name of its own political exclusiveness — to *'strictly economic labour disputes'*. In this way what was supposed to be the 'political arm of labour' ended up with playing a crucial part in actively imposing on labour — by the force of 'representational parliamentary legislation' — capital's vital interest: to ban *'politically motivated industrial action'* as categorically inadmissible 'in a democratic society'.

Both reformism and its necessarily precarious achievements were corollaries of this split articulation of the labour movement as 'political arm' and 'industrial arm'. Operating in that split mode — within the comprehensive political command structure of capital as the rational framework of legitimacy and democratic authority — had brought with it the necessary acceptance and internalization of the *objective material constraints of capital.* At the same time reformist labour retained for a while the contradictory idea that socialist objectives were fully compatible with capital's material constraints. In this spirit it was postulated — by Harold Wilson and other labour leaders — that by 'conquering the commanding heights of the economy' it will be possible to realise socialism 'one day'. In reality 'conquering the commanding heights' amounted to nothing more than the nationalization of bankrupt sectors of capitalist industry, generously compensating their former owners for their worthless assets: a process which could be in any case very easily reversed through parliamentary acts of 'privatization' once their profitability to capital has been secured through generous state investment, financed from tax revenue squeezed out of the common people. Ironically, this road, with its self-contradictory twists and turns, has led from the reformist entrapment of the labour movement to the complete disintegration of socialdemocratic reformism itself, whereby not only the once professed socialist 'ultimate aims' had to be openly renounced but even references to the term 'socialism' had to be avoided like plague.

Another irony which underlines the perverse logic of parliamentary accommodation within the anti-labour confines of capital's comprehensive political command structure is the fate of the 'revolutionary' parties of the Third International. It puts sharply into relief that fundamental *structural* determinations were at work in the clamorous defeats suffered by the institutionalized left in the course of the century. Indeed, to make matters worse, the defeats were suffered despite the deepening crises of the ruling socioeconomic and political order. In this sense, the 'Italian road to socialism' and the subsequent 'great historic compromise' of the Italian Communist Party within the same constraints of parliamentary representation and accommodation, with an identical split between the 'political arm' and the 'industrial arm' of Italian labour as seen in countries with socialdemocratic and labour parties, proved to be as disastrous for the socialist movement as the disintegration of socialdemocratic varieties of reformism.

Thus, in the light of the bitter historical experience to which labour has been subjected by the failure of the parliamentary parties of both the Second and the Third International, it is not too difficult to see that there can be no hope for an effective rearticulation of socialist radicalism without overcoming the contradictions which necessarily arise from the self-defeating division between the 'political arm' and the 'industrial arm' of labour. For, paradoxically, the reformist separation and compartmentalization of labour's 'two arms' can only amount to the paralyzing *'headlessness'* of the movement: i.e. to the more or less conscious internalization of capital's logic both in terms of its material constraints and its legislatively safeguarded 'democratic' political regulatory principles. For conformity to the rules of the system aprioristically determines in capital's favour what may and what may not be 'rationally disputed and contested' not only in the political domain, but even more so as regards the feasibility of questioning and challenging the established framework of social metabolic reproduction. Thus, as a result of the compartmentalized split in tune with those rules, the 'political arm' loses the material power through which the labour movement could effectively counter capital's logic and self-assertive power, and struggle not just for minimal — by the existing structural framework containable and, if need be, reversible — concessions, but for the institution of an alternative social reproductive order. At the same time, while the 'political arm' is rendered impotent by depriving itself of the combative material power of productive labour — which is vitally important for capital's continued reproduction — the 'industrial arm' is compelled to abandon even the *thought* of legitimately concerning itself not only with major structural change but with any political objective whatsoever. It is forced to settle, instead, for marginal improvements; and even its pursuit of such marginal and partial improvements must be strictly subordinated to the *conjunctural* shifts and limitations of the *particular* units of capital with which the local units of the 'industrial arm' are by the law allowed to enter into 'economic dispute'.

18.4.5

THE insurmountable problem here is — and remains without a fundamental reorientation of the strategic target of socialist transformation — the nature of power under the rule of capital. Reformist politicians, whether of the socialdemocratic kind or those who fantasized about the 'Italian road to socialism' within the crippling confines of actually existing capitalism, never faced up to this problem. Indeed they could not face up to it because doing so would have exposed the unrealizable character of their self-contradictory strategies. For just as they were trying to *reform the uncontrollable,* they also assumed as the leverage through which they would bring about the promised transformation of the established social order *a power that did not and could not exist.* Their postulated leverage could not exist for the simple reason that *the power of total social capital as the controller of social metabolic reproduction is indivisible,* notwithstanding the mystifications perpetuated by bourgeois ideology about 'the division of powers' in the political sphere.

Understandably, therefore, the strategies built on the two pillars of (1) *reforming the uncontrollable,* and (2) *'conquering the commanding heights'* of the established system through the leverage of a *non-existent power,* had to end with the self-imposed defeat of the historical left. As we have seen above this had to apply, *mutatis mutandis,* also to the postrevolutionary societies of Soviet type 'actually existing socialism'. For although the postrevolutionary 'personifications of capital' in Soviet type societies did not operate in and through a parliamentary setting, they failed to confront the *uncontrollability of capital* where it massively asserted itself: i.e. as the regulator of social metabolic reproduction. Thus, given their failure to identify the real target of strategic intervention and restructuring, at the social metabolic level, they tried to exercise power in an extreme voluntaristic way, as an attempt to remedy their actual *powerlessness* with regard to the objective material imperatives and the blindly followed — but increasingly more defectively fulfilled — expansionary requirements of the postcapitalist capital system.

The fact that capital as a mode of social metabolic reproduction is uncontrollable — the veritable *causa sui* compatible with 'improvements and correctives' only at the level of *effects and consequences,* but not at that of the system's causal foundations, as we have seen already in various contexts — means not only that capital is *unreformable* but also that it *cannot share power* even in the short run with forces aiming to transcend it in the no matter how long a run, as their 'ultimate aim'. This is why socialdemocratic strategies of 'gradual reform' had to come to absolutely nothing in terms of socialist transformatory potential. For as long as capital remains the effective regulator of the social metabolism, the idea of 'equal contest' between capital and labour — an idea perpetuated and enhanced by the rituals of parliamentary confrontation of 'labour's representatives' with their legislative adversaries: a confrontation of 'no contest' whose self-contradictorily accepted premiss is the permanence of capital's material ground — is bound to remain a mystification. The limited political disputes in parliament, in the strictly regulated and by the instruments and institutions of 'legitimate violence' underpinned framework of capital's comprehensive political command structure, cannot be a *contest with capital* but only *among* its more or less diverse constituents. Those parliamentary constituents which, whether they profess their allegiance to various business interests or to sections of reformist labour, willingly accept their submission to the necessary constraints of defining their legislative objectives in accordance with the self-serving rules of total social capital's 'constitutional state'. At the same time the representatives of labour who try to maintain a radical critical stance are either kept out of parliament or become totally marginalized in it. In contrast to the parliamentary system the 'personifications of capital' in postcapitalist societies operated under a very different but equally harmful mystification. They vainly tried to treat capital either as a *material entity* — the neutral depository of 'socialist accumulation' — or as an equally *neutral mechanism: the 'social market'*, ignoring that capital is in reality always a *social relation*. Thus the *fetishism of capital* dominated postcapitalist societies as much as it ruled them under capitalism, even if the new rule of capital had to assume a different form.

The relationship between capital and labour cannot be considered *symmetrical*, with the possibility of *balancing the contested power* between the two, let alone of changing it *in labour's favour*. The concept of 'balance of power' as the regulator of internal sociopolitical power belongs to the world of capital only, affecting with 'legitimate concern' the changing interrelations of the smaller and larger constituents of total social capital as articulated at any particular point in history. The ever-growing 'legislative jungle' mentioned in Section 18.4.3 is the necessary concomitant of this type of structural articulation of social capital as a whole. From this type of articulation — subject to the practical qualifications arising from the monopolistic trend of the system — necessarily follows also the balance-oriented contest *among* particular constituents of capital in the legislative arena. And that includes also the limited possibilities of legislative action accorded to sections of reformist labour on the margins of the constantly renewed and just as constantly overthrown internal balancing contest of capital's changing units. (A good example of this type of balance-oriented marginal improvement is Sir Winston Churchill's 'enlightened' legislation in 1906 over *minimum wage* levels 'in favour of labour', as well as the recent controversies in the European Union concerning the demand for equal remuneration to be given to groups of labour moving from one member country to another. Naturally, the complete overthrow of the good old 'minimum wage legislation' by the 'Radical Right' under Margaret Thatcher and her successors, overthrown despite its impeccable Churchillian legislative ancestry, demonstrates the extreme precariousness of such 'labour's conquests' under significantly altered historical circumstances, just as the present controversy hides the underlying self-protective capital interests and the necessary fragility of labour measures associated with them.)

While the interests of capital's particular constituents can be successfully — even if strictly temporarily — balanced, there can be no question of balancing the interests and the corresponding power of capital and labour with one another. Labour is either the *structural antagonist and systemic alternative to capital* — in which case 'sharing power' with capital is an absurd self-contradiction — or remains the structurally subordinate part (the constantly endangered 'cost of production') of capital's expanded self-reproduction process, and as such totally *devoid of power*. The effective power of labour in the existing socioeconomic order is *partial* and *negative,* like the *strike weapon.* Thus it cannot be sustained in its negativity indefinitely, since the necessary practical premiss of its operation — even if we are thinking of the quite extraordinary one year long British miners' strike—is the continued functioning of the social metabolic order whose working parts must be able to take over also the burden of temporarily withdrawn labour. The idea of a political general strike is a radically different proposition. If it is to be successful it must have for its objective a fundamental change in the social reproductive order itself, otherwise its impact is bound to be subsequently nullified, as with general strikes in the past. Thus the paradox of power facing the socialist movement is that the exercise of labour's actually existing but *negative* power is unsustainable in the long run even in its *partiality,* and only its *potentially* positive power is truly sustainable, as by its very nature it cannot be confined to the pursuit of *partial* objectives. For the condition of its actualization is that the positive power of labour as the systemic alternative to capital's mode of control should envisage itself as the radical structuring principle of the social metabolic order as a whole. Thus, whichever way we look at it — whether in its partially contesting negativity or as the positive potentiality of comprehensive socialist transformation — it becomes clear that under no circumstances can one think of the power of labour as shared with capital (or the other way round), notwithstanding the well known illusions and the ensuing necessary defeats of parliamentary reformism.

From the non-symmetrical relationship between capital and labour also follows that — in complete contrast to the practices of representation affecting the internal relations of the plurality of capitals — *labour cannot be represented.* In a sense it is also true that *capital cannot be represented.* But it is true with a radical difference compared to the position of labour. The idea of capital itself being represented in the parliamentary domain can only project the mirage of *shared and balanced power* between *capital and labour,* as we find it in the countless fairy tales of bourgeois and reformist ideology. However, the postulate of 'equality' and 'fairness', on the ground that neither labour nor capital as such are directly represented in the legislative domain, which is supposed to be regulated by a somewhat mysterious 'process of the law itself', in tune with Max Weber's idea that the 'jurists' were the autonomous creators of the 'Occidental state', is also nothing but a self-serving camouflage of the existing power relations. For the big difference is that capital as a whole is not represented because it *needs no representation* since it is already *fully in control of the social metabolic process,* including the effective — extra-parliamentary — control of its own comprehensive political command structure, the state. Labour, on the other hand, cannot be represented *in principle,* because its possible forms of 'representation' — even if they could be organized in the political sphere on the basis of 'fairness' and 'justice', which they cannot conceivably be in view of the existing material and ideological power relations — would of necessity remain utterly sterile. For they could not alter the extra-parliamentary structural determinations of capital's profoundly entrenched mode of social metabolic reproduction.

Naturally this does not mean that the historically evolved system of parliamentary representation is irrelevant to the assertion of capital's rule over society. Nor can one indeed see its value to capital only because of its undoubted power of ideological mystification. Far from it. For parliamentary representation is able to fulfil some vitally important functions in the existing social metabolic order. In part the essential regulatory role of parliament consists in legitimating (and thereby also 'internalizing') the imposition of the strictest rules of 'constitutional legality' on potentially recalcitrant labour. But the role of parliament is by no means limited to that. Indeed, in the historical development of parliament making labour submit to self-legitimating 'constitutional legality' came second to its original and primary function. That crucial function consisted and consists in enabling the *plurality of capitals* to find the necessary (even if always temporary) *modus vivendi* and *balance of power among themselves* at any given temporal slice of the system's unfolding dynamics. This is how capital as total social capital can assert its rule in the political sphere under the conditions of 'parliamentary democracy'.

As we have seen above, the capital system is made up from incorrigibly *centrifugal* constituents, on the basis of an equally incorrigible *adversarial* structural relationship common to all of its parts, from the smallest reproductive 'microcosms' to the biggest transnational corporations. It is capital as a social totality which brings under control (and *must* do so in a suitable way) the centrifugal force. It can do this through those universally prevailing rules and structural determinations which objectively define capital itself as a mode of social metabolic control. The determinations in question are *internal* not only to the system as a whole but also to all of its parts. In other words, they must be *shared* by all of capital's manifold particular constituents, notwithstanding their conflicting interests vis-à-vis one another. Without sharing them — which simultaneously also means sharing the vital *common interest* to be parts of the controlling system of social metabolic reproduction, from which the self-interested class consciousness of the 'personifications of capital' arises — they could not operate among themselves as a plurality of capitals asserting their particular interests within the overall structural constraints and self-preserving dynamism of their system in any given historical situation. This is how capital as such, articulated as the actually existing mode of social metabolic reproduction, can bring under control the untranscendable centrifugal force of its constituent parts. Not by simply *overruling* that force — whereby the capital system would cease to be a viable system *sui generis* — but by *complementing* it through the imperative of overall systemic reproduction, thereby restraining only the *disintegrative* impact of the insurmountable *conflictual* interactions.

This is how the state of the capital system acquires its great importance not simply as the overall regulatory framework of contingent *political* relations but as an essential material constituent of the system in its entirety, without which capital could not assert itself as the controlling power of the established mode of social metabolic reproduction. Accordingly, under the circumstances of 'constitutional democracy' the parliamentary system is an essential part of bringing the centrifugal force of the plurality of capitals under suitable control. In this process the interests of the multiplicity of capitals can be adequately represented. For the representation of even the most diverse capital interests in parliament, under the comprehensive political command structure of capital, is fully in tune with the overall determinations of social metabolic control. Apart from the structural antagonism between capital and labour which affects, of course, also capital's particular constituents, the conflicts of the plurality of capitals are played out — subject to the restraining overall determinations mentioned above — among themselves. They can *never* be directed against the capital *system* without which the plurality of conflicting capitals cannot be even imagined, let alone exist. Thus the regulatory force of parliamentary representation, as far as the plurality of capitals is concerned, is fully adequate both as genuine *representation* and as the *preservation* (or 'eternalization') of a power — the power of social metabolic control — *already in existence*. But precisely for that reason, labour cannot be represented in principle. For the vital interest of labour is the *radical transformation* of the established social reproductive order, and not its *preservation:* the only thing compatible with parliamentary representation as such under the comprehensive political command structure of capital. This is how the non-symmetrical relation between capital and labour nullifies the emancipatory interests of labour in the political sphere under all historically known forms of the parliamentary system.

There is another way in which parliamentary politics serves the interests of capital as a metabolic system as well as the interests of its manifold constituents. For according to the changing dynamics of development of total social capital, parliament can provide the framework of quite far-reaching shifts in the system's strategic operation vis-à-vis labour, such as the move from the postwar decades of 'Butskellism' (or paternalistic 'one-nation Toryism') to the savagery of Thatcherite 'Radical Right' strategies. Highly revealing in this respect is the sharp contrast between two parliamentary solutions to capital's unfolding structural crisis as perceived and commended by different sections of British capital in 1979. For the same year which had initiated the fifteen year long domination of British parliament by Margaret Thatcher's government had also witnessed the eclipse of the earlier political line of the Conservative Party, as encapsulated in a nostalgic interview broadcast on BBC Television by former Prime Minister Harold Macmillan in February 1979. This is how 'Super-Mac' — who later sarcastically denounced the Thatcher government on account of its corrupt privatization policies as a short-sighted and vulgar practice of 'selling off the family silver' — summed up his proposed solution to the no longer deniable crisis, trying to remain in tune with the spirit of Keynesian Welfare-state-oriented 'consensus politics' followed by the dominant sections of British capital after the Second World War for two and a half decades:

> So perhaps the way would be somehow to get everybody together and say, *'Boys, it's all in our hands;* let's get down and do it, add to the total production of *marketable wealth'*. That's what we want. ... On the home side, I am sure people would welcome a real lead — *'Boys and girls, let's get together* and make this marvellous world we could

make for ourselves'. ... I am quite certain that there are forces now which, if we could only get them to *unite, whether in government or unity of the great organizations of employers and trade unions*, or the churches — all the people who influence opinion — who would say 'It's enough; we must make a *new start'*. It's a *moral issue;* we must have the determination and we must rebuild our courage.[286]

A few months after this interview, the Conservative Party under Margaret Thatcher's leadership was elected to government. Within a short period of time *all* of the 'one-nation' Tory Members of Parliament were condemned as 'wets' and consigned to the political wilderness as brutally as the left-wing members of the Labour Party were later, under the leadership of former left-wingers Michael Foot and Neil Kinnock. Far from addressing themselves to the 'boys and girls' in order to urge them to unite with government and with the 'great organizations of employers and trade unions', for the sake of the 'moral issue' of making together 'a new start' in the improved 'production of marketable wealth', the *change of guard* in the Conservative Party (and not only in that party) had put as the principal item on the political agenda the 'constitutional' oppression of the defensive organs of the working class. The 'boys and girls' in parliament — Macmillan's former colleagues — were busy introducing punitive anti-labour laws, coupled with appropriate industrial and financial measures conceived and instituted in the same spirit in favour of capital. And the shift from the political dominance of some sections of capital to more aggressive ones was by no means a British development only. On the contrary, the unfolding structural crisis of the capital system had brought with it very similar political, industrial and financial measures, as well as their ideological rationalizations, everywhere in the 'advanced capitalist' countries.

Hard as it may be to believe our eyes when we read the passage quoted below, we have to pay attention to it as a typical example coming from the 'Radical Right' in the U.S. It encapsulates the 'objective economic theory' of a leading American financial expert/speculator and influential lobbyist, James Dale Davidson.[287] He argues the 'scientific' merits of the anti-labour line in this way:

> As an investor, you should be always wary of commonly held presumptions about economic relationships. This is especially true for a topic like [surprise, surprise!] wages, when special pleading and political considerations stand in the way of the truth. The truth is that whatever their intentions, employers in market societies have a devil of a time 'exploiting' the workers. Indeed, this is almost impossible where workers are free to develop their talents and move from one opportunity to another. [i.e. in the never-nowhere-land of 'people's capitalist' utopia.] Surprisingly [this time a real surprise], it is far more common for workers to exploit capitalists. In general, this is the function that labour unions perform. They raise wage rates above the market-clearing level. The result is that investors receive a smaller portion of the revenue of the firm than they would otherwise. ... the existence of democratic institutions during periods when technology increases scale economies more or less guarantees that the workers will exploit the capitalists.[288]

Characteristically, the ruthless intervention of 'democratic parliaments' in undermining even the limited defensive power of trade unions is not even mentioned in the description of the unfolding changes instituted in capital's favour, from the large-scale casualization of the labour force to the concomitant criminalization of those who fight against it. Everything is ascribed with customary scientific objectivity to strictly *technological* factors. As if the political forces which the author as lobbyist is eager to influence with all means at his disposal did not exist at all. Thus the anti-union laws of the recent past are supposed to be totally irrelevant to understanding these developments. We are told that rationally un-objectionable technology alone 'explains why *unions are now faltering* in Western societies, as technology is reducing scale economies. It explains why *income differentials are widening* once more, as essentially unskilled workers are obliged to find employment at market-clearing wages'.[289] That is, in reality, 'obliged to find employment' *if they can,* not at 'market-clearing wages' but often at well below subsistence-level wages, given the devastating impact of *chronic unemployment* in the idealized 'properly scaled economies' of the contemporary capital system. Evidently, all this has nothing to do either with the savagery of anti-union laws or with the dehumanizing brutality of 'structural unemployment'. Indeed, unemployment itself must be the most cunning device ever devised by labour to 'exploit the capitalists and investors', poor helpless dears, by obliging them to 'receive a smaller portion of the revenue than they would otherwise'; otherwise, being, if the unemployed allowed them to operate the economy under the more generously revenue-producing conditions of full employment.

However, coming back to reality from the carefully crafted fantasy-world of cynical capital-apologetics, there are two further aggravating conditions to be considered here. The first is that labour accommodating itself to the paralysing constraints of the parliamentary framework at the time of capital's deepening structural crisis cannot help being gravely affected by the negative impact of the shifts within total social capital's power structure and by the narrowing margin of action which they can provide to labour even for the most limited defensive gains. Reformist labour's present-day submission to forces diametrically opposed to the interests of the working classes demonstrates that the historical phase of defensive strategies has run its course. The socialdemocratization of the Western Communist parties, coupled with the transformation of the traditional socialdemocratic and labour parties into the mildest possible advocates of lib-labouring — and even in its own terms of reference ineffective — puny socioeconomic and political reform, offer painfully obvious illustrations of the defeat suffered by the historical left through these shifts and changes within the constraints of parliamentary accommodation. The fact that some prominent right-wing politicians of the British Labour Party now find themselves marginalized for their 'unacceptably outspoken left-wing views', said to damage the prospects of 'New Labour' in government — indeed unacceptable to the extent that they themselves feel obliged to announce their retirement from active politics at the next general election, avoiding thereby the humiliation of 'deselection' — is an ironical twist in this unhappy but most eloquent cautionary tale. It underlines in its own way, through the party leadership's adopted 'preparation for government' which cannot tolerate even the unfulfilled promises of the old Clause 4, that whenever reformist Labour may be in government, capital always remains in charge.

The second aggravating condition is even more serious, in that it calls into question the very survival of humanity. For despite the worsening socioeconomic conditions and the elimination of the margin of even minor adjustments in favour of labour — with the active involvement of authoritarian legislative measures and the complicity of its own party — capital is unable to solve its structural crisis and successfully reconstitute the conditions of expansionary dynamics. On the contrary. In order to remain in control of the social metabolism at all, it is compelled to encroach over territories which it cannot control and utilize for the purposes of sustainable capital-accumulation. Moreover, for the sake of remaining in charge of societal reproduction, at whatever cost to humankind, capital must undermine even its own political institutions which in the past could function as a partial corrective and as some sort of safety valve. In a past, that is, when the road of expansionary displacement of capital's accumulating contradictions was still more or less wide open. Today, by contrast, the options of the capital system are being narrowed down everywhere, including the domain of politics and parliamentary adjustive action. This narrowing down of the options of expansionary recovery brings with it the imperative to directly dominate also politics by a most unholy 'consensus politics' between age-old capital and 'New Labour', in fitting complement to the authoritarian tendencies of the 'New World Order' by no means only in the British Labour Party. The consummation of this unholy consensus — far from being capital's ultimate triumph, as the absurd fantasies about the 'end of conflictual history' predicated it — would foreshadow the danger of a major collapse, affecting not only a limited number of capital's centrifugal constituents, and not even just a key strategic sector like international finance, but the global capital system in its entirety. The need for countering the destructive extra-parliamentary force of capital by the appropriate extra-parliamentary action of a radically rearticulated socialist movement acquires its relevance and urgency precisely in view of this danger.

18.4.6

WHEN the historical phase of defensive gains is exhausted, labour as the structural antagonist of capital can only advance its cause — even minimally — if it goes on the offensive, envisaging as its strategic target the radical negation and the positive transformation of the mode of social metabolic reproduction also when fighting for the realization of more limited objectives. For only through the adoption of a viable overall strategy can the partial steps become cumulative, in sharp contrast to all known forms of labour reformism which disappeared without a trace like a few drops of water in the desert sand.

Defensive gains in the past were always closely tied to expansionary phases of the capital system. They were carved out from the margin of concessions which the system could not only afford but also positively turn to its advantage. Even under the most favourable circumstances they could not bring the promised 'gradual' realization of socialism one inch nearer. For by their very nature they could be only *conjunctural concessions,* affordable under conditions favourable to capital itself and only by 'reflected glory' helpful also to labour. Once, however, the historical phase of capital's expansionary concessions is left behind, the total capitulation of reformist labour we witnessed in the last few decades accompanies it. This is because under such conditions not only further defensive gains by labour are out of the question, but even many of the past concessions must be clawed back, subject only to the potential destabilizing impact on capital's continued self-reproduction if too much is taken back within a short space of time. This is what moderates the tendency for the equalization of the differential rate of exploitation in the capitalistically advanced countries for as long as the total social capital of the countries concerned can compensate for it through its neo-colonial domination of areas of the planet which provide for 'metropolitan capital', thanks to a higher rate of practicable exploitation, a much higher rate of profit. Nevertheless, even such currently alleviating factors are bound to be temporary and displaced with the unfolding of capital's structural crisis.

There are some people — who fancy themselves as 'realists' — who insist (with slogans like 'the party is over') that the experienced constraints affecting the system must be accepted as permanent, asking us to accept also the permanence of labour's structural subordination to capital. They think that the radical phase of labour militancy is gone forever, adding that even in the past it was nothing but a big mistake and a romantic illusion at best; not to mention the 'theorists' and 'spin-doctors' of 'New Labour' who ascribe the past revolutionary aspirations of the socialist movement to the 'word-highjacking' skills of young Marx and Engels.

The trouble with the ideas of those who postulate the permanent submission of labour to the rule of capital is that they must also hypostatize the absolute permanence of the capital system. And that can be done only by totally blinding oneself even to the most destructive aspects of capital's mode of social metabolic control, which are visible not only to socialists but to all those who are willing to make the most elementary environmental calculations. The strategic perspective of reformist labourism was in the past untroubled by such concerns, and therefore the distinction between 'the rule of society over wealth' as opposed to the alienating 'rule of wealth over society' could have no meaning whatsoever for it. However, today these problems cannot be ignored any longer. Nor is it possible to equate necessarily self-deflating and disintegrating labour reformism with labour itself. As should be obvious enough by now, the history of labour reformism is characterized by its progressive accommodatory integration into the political command structure of capital, and thus also by its *complete disintegration through its capitulatory integration even as reformism.*

In this way the 'realists' who project the unproblematical harmony between capital and socialdemocractic labour simply beg the question. For only accommodatory reformist labour can be imagined in unproblematical harmony with capital, tying itself to the destiny of the latter not only during the system's historical ascendancy but even in its destructive and disintegrative phase of development. This conception also shows a singular inability to see that the class of labour itself cannot avoid being the *structural antagonist of capital,* even if under conditions favouring the reformist perspective — i.e., when labour's defensive gains can be readily conceded by capital and used for the purposes of its dynamic accumulatory expansion — the demands of socialdemocratic labour can be reconciled with and contained well within the limits of the system. All this is, however, radically altered when the road of dynamic expansion is blocked (for whatever reason), and labour is expected to subject forever its aspirations — even when they directly arise from its elementary needs — to the imperatives of capital's 'reason', preached by its own reformist leaders as 'necessary realism'. Under such altered conditions, if prolonged (as they must be on account of the system's structural crisis), the antagonist of capital is compelled to contemplate the feasibility of a strategic offensive aimed at the radical transformation of the established social metabolic order. It is compelled to do this sooner or later, even if the process of reassessing the strategic orientation of the socialist movement is bound to be a difficult one. For it will have to assume the form of learning from frustrated attempts and disappointed expectations, though hopefully also from a progressively improved approximation to the proper organizational framework and tactical measures through which the adopted strategic targets can be reached.

Another argument which is often used in favour of permanent accommodation is the threat of extreme authoritarian measures that must be faced by a socialist revolutionary movement. This argument is backed up by emphasizing both the immense destructive power at capital's disposal and the undeniable historical fact that no ruling order ever cedes willingly its position of command over society, using if need be even the most violent form of repression to retain its rule. The weakness of this argument is twofold, despite the factual circumstances which would seem to support it.

First, it disregards that the antagonistic confrontation between capital and labour is not a political/military one in which one of the antagonists could be slaughtered on the battlefield or riveted to chains. Inasmuch as there can be chains in this confrontation, labour is wearing them already, in that the only type of chains compatible with the system must be 'flexible' enough to enable the class of labour to produce and be exploited. Nor can one imagine that the authoritarian might of capital is likely to be used only against a revolutionary socialist movement. The repressive anti-labour measures of the last two decades — not to mention many instances of past historical emergency characterized by the use of violence under the capital system — give a foretaste of worse things to come in the event of extreme confrontations. But this is not a matter of either/or, with some sort of apriori guarantee of a 'fair' and benevolent treatment in the event of labour's willing accommodation and submission. The matter hinges on the gravity of the crisis and on the circumstances under which the antagonistic confrontations unfold. Uncomfortable as this truth may sound to socialists, one of the heaviest chains which labour has to wear today is that it is *tied to capital* for its continued survival, for as long as it does not succeed in making a strategic break in the direction of a transition to a radically different social metabolic order. But that is even more true of capital, with the qualitative difference that capital cannot make any break towards the establishment of a different social order. For capital, truly, 'there is no alternative' — and there can never be — to its exploitative structural dependency on labour. If nothing else, this fact sets well marked limits to capital's ability to permanently subdue labour by violence, compelling it to use, instead, the earlier mentioned 'flexible chains' against the class of labour. It can use violence with success selectively, against limited groups of labour, but not against the socialist movement organized as a revolutionary *mass movement*. This is why the development of 'communist mass consciousness' (to use Marx's expression), in contrast to the vulnerability of narrow sectarian orientation, is so important.

The second point that must be made in this context is equally important. It concerns the innermost determinations of the capital system as a necessarily expansion-oriented and accumulation-driven social metabolic order. The point is that the exercise of power through the repressive machinery of violence is extremely wasteful in the system's own terms of reference; even if undoubtedly it can serve the purpose of redressing the power relations in capital's favour in a situation of *emergency*. What must weigh heavily in the balance is that it is impossible to secure the required expansion and capital-accumulation on a permanent basis through the perpetuation of economically wasteful emergency, apart from its anything but negligible political dangers. The idea of 'Big Brother' successfully ruling over labour as a permanent condition is too fantastic even for a work of Orwellian fiction, let alone for the actuality of capital's mode of social metabolic reproduction. For the latter must perish if it is unable to secure its own reproduction through the appropriation of the fruits of ever more productive labour and the concomitant expanded realization of value, which in its turn is inconceivable without a dynamic process of 'productive consumption'. And neither ever-improving labour productivity, with the necessarily increasing socialization of the labour process as its precondition, nor the required — ever-expanding — scale of 'productive consumption' is compatible with the idea of a permanent state of emergency. Moreover, as Chomsky rightly argued many years ago, the surveillance system that must go with a successful enforcement of permanent authoritatian rule involves the absurdity (and, of course, the corresponding cost) of *infinite regress* in monitoring not only the population at large but also the monitoring personnel itself, as well as the monitors of the monitors,[290] etc. We must add here that the idea of capital's permanent rule through the use of violence must also postulate the total *unity of global capital* against the *national* labour forces which happen to be effectively under the control of capital's particular units in the existing (but by no means unified) global order. This vacuous postulate of capital's global unity and uniformity arbitrarily brushes aside not only the *law of uneven development*. It also ignores the abundant historical evidence which shows that the exercise of force on a mass scale — through war — always needed masses of people to be able to impose violence on their counterparts, motivated as a rule for many centuries by national rivalries. Indeed, the national articulation of the global capital system, far from being a historical accident, had a great deal to do with capital's need to maintain control over the labour force with at least some degree of consensus. Otherwise the inter-capitalist rivalries, all the way to the most comprehensive international conflagrations, would be unmanageably risky from the point of view of total social capital, nullifying the inner logic of the system to fight out to the full the conflict of interests and make the strongest prevail in the Hobbesian *bellum omnium contra omnes*. For in every situation of major inter-capitalist confrontation the capital system itself would be in danger of being overthrown by its labour antagonist, in the absence of a sufficiently high degree of consensus — present as a rule to a very high degree in national conflicts — between capital and labour belonging to the same side. (In fact some radical socialists tried to counter this consensus, unsuccessfully, with the programme inviting the workers at the outbreak of the First World War 'to turn their weapons against their national bourgeoisie'.) Thus, to sum up, all of the arguments in favour of capital's permanent rule through the imposition of violence on a mass scale suffer from having to define their conditions of realization in a self-contradictory way. Accordingly, as mentioned in Section 18.2.5, to project the rule of capital, in its direct antagonistic confrontation with labour, by way of a completely *unstable*, hence *necessarily transient*, state of *emergency*, as the *permanent* condition of its future *normality*, is a mind-boggling notion. To be sure, no one should doubt that the use of violence may *postpone* for a shorter or longer period of time the success of labour's positive emancipatory efforts; but it cannot *prevent* the exhaustion of capital's productive potentialities. On the contrary, if anything, it can only *accelerate* their exhaustion if violence is used on a mass scale, thereby radically undermining the objective conditions of capital's rule.

THE great difficulty for labour as the antagonist of capital is that while the only viable target of its transformatory struggle must be the social metabolic power of capital — with its not simply personal but objective structural/hierarchical control over the material productive sphere, from which other forms of 'personifi- cation' may (and as time goes by under misconceived strategies also *must*) arise — this all-important target cannot be reached without gaining control over the political sphere. Moreover, the difficulty is compounded by the temptation to believe that once the political institutions of the inherited capitalist system are neutralized, the power of capital is itself firmly under control: a fateful belief which could only lead to the well known historical defeats of the past.

As we have seen in Chapter 2, the capital system is made up from incorrigibly *centrifugal* constituents, complemented as their *cohesive* dimension not only by the unceremoniously overruling power of the 'invisible hand' but also by legal and political functions of the modern state. The failure of postcapitalist societies was that they tried to counter the centrifugal structuring determination of the inherited system by *superimposing* on its particular adversarial constituents the *extreme centralized command structure* of an authoritarian political state. This they did in place of addressing the crucial problem of how to *remedy* — through internal restructuring and the institution of *substantive democratic control* — the adversarial character and the concomitant centrifugal mode of functioning of the particular reproductive and distributive units. The removal of the private capitalist personifications of capital therefore could not fulfil its role even as the *first step* on the road of the promised socialist transformation. For the adversarial and centrifugal nature of the inherited system was in fact retained through the superimposition of centralized political control at the expense of labour. Indeed, the social metabolic system was rendered more uncontrollable than ever before as a result of the inability to productively replace the 'invisible hand' of the old reproductive order by the voluntaristic authoritarianism of the 'visible' new personifications of postcapitalist capital. Inevitably, this brought with it the growing hostility of the mistreated subjects of politically extracted surplus-la- bour towards the postrevolutionary order. The fact that the labour force was subjected to ruthless political control, and at times even to the most inhuman discipline of mass labour camps, does not mean that the Soviet type personifi- cations of capital were in control of their system. The uncontrollability of the postcapitalist reproductive system manifested itself through its chronic failure to reach its economic targets, making a mockery of its claims regarding the 'planned economy'. This is what sealed its fate, depriving it of its professed legitimation and making its collapse only a matter of time. That in the final stages of existence of the Soviet type system the postrevolutionary personifica- tions of capital desperately tried to smuggle into their societies the 'invisible hand' by the back door, rebaptizing it — in order to make it palatable — as *'market socialism'*, could only underline how hopelessly uncontrollable the post-capitalist system had remained even after seven decades of 'socialist control', in the total absence of a substantive democratic control of its productive and distributive units.

It stands to reason that the reconstitution and substantive democratization of the political sphere is a necessary condition for making an inroad into capital's mode of social metabolic control. For the power of capital is not, and cannot be, confined to the direct productive functions. In order to successfully control the latter, capital must be complemented by its own mode of political control. The material command structure of capital cannot assert itself without the system's comprehensive political command structure. Thus, the alternative to capital's mode of social metabolic control must likewise embrace all complementary aspects of the societal reproduction process, from the direct productive and distributive functions to the most comprehensive dimensions of political decision making. Since capital is *actually* in control of all vital aspects of the social metabolism, it can afford to define the sphere of political legitimation as a strictly *formal* matter, thereby apriori excluding the possibility of being legitimately challenged in its *substantive* sphere of operation. Conforming to such determinations, labour as the antagonist of actually existing capital can only condemn itself to permanent impotence. For the institution of a viable alternative social metabolic order is feasible only through the articulation of *substantive democracy,* defined as the self-determined activity of the associated producers in politics no less than in material and cultural production.

It is a unique feature of the capital system that, as a matter of normality, the material reproductive functions are carried on in a separate compartment, under a command structure substantially different from capital's comprehensive political command structure embodied in the modern state. This separation and 'diremption', as constituted in the course capital's historical ascendancy in its orientation for self-expanding exchange-value, is in no way disadvantageous to the system itself. Quite the contrary. For the economic/managerial personifications of capital can exercise their authority over the particular reproductive units, in anticipation of a feed-back from the market, to be translated in due course into corrective action, and the state fulfils its complementary functions partly in the international sphere of the world market (including the safeguard of capital-interests in wars if need be), and partly vis-à-vis the potentially or actually recalcitrant labour force. Thus on both counts the structural antagonist of capital is firmly kept under control by the established compartmentalization and the radical alienation of the power of decision making — in all spheres — from the producers in a system well suited to the requirements of capital's expanded reproduction and accumulation.

In complete contrast, the alternative — socialist — mode of reproductive control is unimaginable without successfully overcoming the existing diremption and alienation. For the necessary condition of carrying out the direct material reproductive functions of a socialist system is the restitution of the power of decision making — in all spheres of activity and at all levels of co-ordination, from the local productive enterprises to the most comprehensive international interchanges — to the associated producers. Thus the 'withering away of the state' refers to nothing mysterious or remote but to a perfectly tangible process which must be initiated right in the present. It means the progressive reacquisition of the alienated powers of political decision making by the individuals in their transition towards a genuine socialist society. Without the reacquisition of these powers neither the new mode of political control of society as a whole by its individuals is conceivable, nor indeed the *non-adversarial* and thereby *cohesive/plannable* everyday operation of the particular productive and distributive units by their self-managing associated producers.

The reconstitution of the unity of the material reproductive and the political sphere is the essential defining characteristic of the socialist mode of social metabolic control. Creating the necessary mediations towards it cannot be left to some far-away future time, like the apologetically theorized 'highest stage of communism'. For if the mediatory steps are not pursued right from the outset, as an organic part of the transformatory strategy, they will be never taken. Keeping the political dimension under a separate authority, divorced from the material reproductive functions of the labour force means retaining the structural dependency and subordination of labour, making thereby also impossible to take the subsequent steps in the direction of a sustainable socialist transformation of the established social order. It was in this sense both revealing and fateful that the Soviet system *reinforced* the separate state functions against the labour force under its control, superimposing the *dictates* of its political apparatus on the direct productive processes under the pretext of 'planning', instead of helping to activate the autonomous power of decision making of the producers. Even the time scale of eternity could not turn a social metabolic order trapped by such hopelessly alienating structural determinations into a self-managed socialist system.

18.4.7

UNDER the circumstances of actually existing 'advanced capitalism' the worsening condition of the labour force cannot be countered — let alone the painful structural dependency of labour challenged — without a fundamental rearticulation of the socialist movement from its defensive posture to one capable of offensive action. For not only the traditional parliamentary mode of political control but also the reformist accommodation of labour within it have run their historical course.

What is important to bear in mind here is that the renewal of the parliamentary form of political legislation itself is unavoidable if the labour movement is to achieve anything at all under the present circumstances. Such a renewal can only come about through the development of an *extra-parliamentary* movement as the *vital conditioning force* of Parliament itself and of the legislative framework of transitional society in general. As things stand today, labour as the antagonist of capital is forced to defend its interests not with one but both hands tied behind its back. One tied by forces openly hostile to labour and the other by its own reformist party and trade union leadership. The latter fulfil their special functions as personifications of capital within the labour movement itself in the service of total accommodation, and indeed capitulation, to the 'realistic' material imperatives of the system. What is left, then, under the present crippling articulation of the mass labour movement as the only weapon to carry on the fight with — head-butting against steel spikes — is not what one might consider to be suitable even as a strictly defensive weapon; despite the fact that the spokespersons of 'New Labour' enlist the services of 'the great and the good' of capitalist society in their 'Justice Commissions' in order to proclaim that the ongoing contest fully conforms to the requirements of 'fairness' and 'justice'. Under these conditions the alternative facing the labour movement is either to resign itself to the acceptance of such constraints, or to take the necessary steps to untie its own hands, no matter how hard that course of action might be. For nowadays the former reformist leaders of labour openly admit, as Tony Blair did it in a speech delivered in Derby appropriately on April Fool's day, that 'The Labour Party is *the party of modern business* and industry in Britain'.[291] This represents the final phase of the total betrayal of everything belonging to the old socialdemocratic tradition that could be betrayed. As we can read in *The Times* of London:

> Labour, in its famous 'prawn cocktail' strategy of City lunches [under former leader John Smith], has approached business before. But the new commission [on 'Public Policy and British Business', set up by Labour on the model of its 'Justice Commission'], especially in its arm's-length relationship with the party, is different. 'The idea of the "prawn cocktail" offensive was to show that we didn't mean harm', says one Blair colleague. 'This goes beyond that: we want to show that *we can do business with business'.*[292]

The only question is, how long will the class of labour allow itself to be treated as April's Fool, and how long can the strategy of capitulating to big business be pursued beyond the coming Pyrrhic electoral victory. After all, we know not only that Margaret Thatcher could 'do business with Gorbachev', and *vice versa,* in the same spirit of 'there is no alternative' which is now being championed by 'New Labour' as 'the party of modern business'. We also know what happened to both Gorbachev and Baroness Thatcher in the end, as well as to their once glorified strategies.

The contest between capital and labour within the framework of the parliamentary system was never 'fair and equal', nor could it ever be. For capital as such is not a *parliamentary force,* despite the fact that its interests can be properly represented in parliament, as mentioned before. What necessarily prejudges against labour the political confrontation with capital confined to parliament is the incorrigible circumstance that total social capital cannot help being the *extra-parliamentary force par excellence.* This remains so even when the representatives of the plurality of capitals assert the interests of their system as a whole against labour, and also sort out the legal/political regulatory aspects of their particular differences of interest among themselves, with the help of the 'parliamentary rules of the game'.

Naturally, when it comes to imposing the dictates of capital on the parliamentary governments of labour, no nonsense can be tolerated from Labour Prime Ministers. Nearly ten years ago Sir Campbell Adamson — a former Director General of the Confederation of British Industry — made a telling confession in a television interview. He revealed that he had actually threatened Harold Wilson (at the time Labour Prime Minister of the British Government) with a *general investment strike* if Wilson failed to respond positively to the ultimatum of his Confederation. Adamson candidly admitted that the threatened action would have been *unconstitutional* (in his own words), adding that 'fortunately' in the end there was no need to proceed with the planned investment strike because 'the Prime Minister agreed to our demands'.

Thus *constitutionality* itself is a plaything for the representatives of capital, to be ruthlessly and cynically used as a self-legitimating device against labour. The personifications of capital, when they abuse 'democratic constitutionality', are, of course, not sent to the Tower of London, as they undoubtedly would have been for an equivalent outrage against their king in the late Middle Ages. On the contrary, they are knighted or elevated to the House of Lords, even by Labour Governments. As to the people who might think that this is the 'peculiarity of the English', they should remember what happened to the President — the *ex officio* guardian of the American Constitution — in the much talked about 'Irangate Contra Affair'. The U.S. Congressional Committee investigating that affair had concluded that the Reagan Administration was guilty of '*subverting the Law and undermining the Constitution*'. But, of course, this judgement — despite its grave implications for the professed 'rule of law' (never noticed by the Hayeks of this world), did not affect in the slightest the guilty 'Teflon President'; nor did it result in the introduction of the required constitutional safeguards in order to prevent similar violations of the U.S. Constitution in the future.

As far as the political representatives of labour are concerned, the issue is not simply that of personal failure or yielding to the temptations and rewards of their privileged position when they are in office. It is much more serious than that. The trouble is that when as heads or Ministers of goverments they are supposed to be able to politically control the system they do nothing of the kind. For they operate within the political domain apriori prejudged in capital's favour by the existing power structures of its mode of social metabolic reproduction. Without radically challenging and materially dislodging capital's deeply entrenched structures and mode of social metabolic control, *capitulation* to the power of capital is only a question of time; as a rule almost managing to outpace the speed of light. Whether we think of Ramsay MacDonald and Bettino Craxi, or Felipe Gonzáles and François Mitterrand — and even long imprisoned Nelson Mandela, the new-found champion of the South African arms industry[293] — the story is always depressingly the same. Often even the wishful anticipation of the 'realistic and responsible role' which is supposed to be appropriate to an expected future high ministerial position is enough to produce the most astonishing somersaults. Thus Aneurin Bevan, once the idol of the Labour left and the most fiery opponent of the nuclear arms race in Britain, did not hesitate to denude himself of his socialist principles and shout down his former left-wing comrades at the Party's annual policy-making conference, saying that as the designated Foreign Secretary of a future Labour Government he could not be expected 'to walk into the international negotiating chamber naked, and sit around the conference table like that while defending the interests of the country', i.e. the privileged position of British imperialism as a member of the exclusive 'nuclear club'.

The working class was an 'afterthought' to the bourgeois parliamentary system, and was always treated by it in that way after entering its corridors. For it could never even remotely match capital's power as the effective material foundation of the parliamentary political system. Even if the formal rules and the material costs of entering parliament could be made equitable — which, of course, they cannot be, in view of the monstrous inequality of wealth between the classes, as well as the educational and ideological advantages enjoyed by the ruling class as the material and cultural controller of the 'ruling ideology' — even that would not significantly alter the situation. For the fundamental question concerns the *structural* relationship between the parliamentary political framework and the existing mode of social metabolic reproduction totally dominated by capital.

The diremption of economics and politics which eminently suited the historical development of the capital system presented, by contrast, an enormous challenge to the labour movement, which it could not meet. The failure of the historical left was inextricably tied to this circumstance. For the defensive articulation of the socialist movement both directly *reflected* and *accommodated itself* to this diremption. The fact that the fateful acceptance of such structural determinations was not a gladly, voluntarily undertaken act but a *forced accommodation* does not alter the fact of labour's entrapment by the available, hopelessly narrow, margins of self-emancipatory action within the given framework. It was a forced accommodation in the sense that it was imposed upon labour as the *necessary precondition* for being allowed to enter the parliamentary domain of 'political emancipation' and corresponding limited reformist material improvements, once that road was embarked upon by the originally extra-parliamentary radical oppositional forces. The space for this type of reformist articulation of the mass labour movement was opened up in the 'European little corner of the world', with its imperialistically dominated global 'hinterland', by the dynamic expansionary — and thus affordably 'permissive' — phase of capital's development in the second half of the 19th century, and it took almost a century to run its historical course. The hopelessly paralysing separation of the 'political arm' and the 'industrial arm' of labour mentioned earlier was an appropriate complement to and support of this type of development, offering in a most discriminatory way some limited material advantages to the working classes of a handful of privileged countries at the expense of the super-exploited masses in the rest of the world. The projection that a *radical structural change* — socialism achieved by gradual reform — would one day arise from the unquestionable *acceptance of the incorrigible structural constraints of the system* was a delusion right from the beginning, even if at first some reformist politicians and trade union leaders genuinely believed in it. It was, of course, a contingent historical fact that the socialist movement, after very different beginnings, accepted the separation of its 'political arm' from its industrial body, in order to be able to operate within the parliamentary framework created by the personifications of capital for defending and managing the interests of the capital system. However, the triumph of the reformist strategy in the socialist movement was by no means accidental or the consequence of contingent personal aberrations and bureaucratic betrayals. It was the inevitable concomitant of fitting the movement into the preestablished parliamentary political framework and accommodating it to the peculiar structural diremption between politics and economics characteristic of the capital system. The success of the socialist offensive is inconceivable without radically challenging these structural determinations of the established order and without reconstituting the labour movement in its integrality; not only with its 'arms' but also with the full consciousness of its transformatory objective as the necessary and feasible strategic alternative to the capital system.

18.4.8

THE insoluble problem within the existing framework of political institutions is the fundamental inequality between capital and labour in the material power relations of society as a whole, asserting itself for as long as the established mode of metabolic reproduction is not radically altered. It is important to quote in this respect a passage from Marx's *Economic Manuscripts of 1861-63*. It reads as follows:

> Productive labour — as value producing — always confronts capital as the labour of *isolated* workers, whatever social combinations those workers may enter into in the production process. Thus whereas capital represents the social productive power of labour towards the workers, productive labour always represents towards capital only the labour of the *isolated* worker.[294]

If by some miracle parliaments passed a law tomorrow, even unanimously, that from the day after tomorrow all this should be different — i.e. that the social power of productive labour should be recognized by capital and that productive labour should not be represented vis-à-vis capital as the labour of isolated workers — all that would not make the slightest difference. Nor could it. For capital, as materially constituted — through alienated and stored up labour — *actually* and *objectively* represents the social productive power of labour. This objective relationship of structural domination is what finds its adequate embodiment also in the political institutions of the capital system. This is why the plurality of capitals can be properly represented within the framework of parliamentary politics whereas labour cannot be. For the existing — incorrigibly iniquitous — material power relations make labour's 'representation' either *vacuous* (as the *strictly political* parliamentary representation of the *materially subordinate* class of labour) or *self-contradictory* (whether we talk about the electoral representation of the *isolated* worker, or of the 'democratic participation' of the radical *structural antagonist* of capital which is nonetheless happily predisposed to accepting the crumbs of marginal reform-oriented accommodation). No political reform can conceivably alter these material power relations within the parameters of the existing system.

What makes it worse for all those who are looking for significant change on the margins of the established political system is that the latter can claim for itself genuine constitutional legitimacy in its present mode of functioning, based on the historically constituted *inversion* of the actual state of affairs. For inasmuch as the capitalist is not only the 'personification of capital' but functions also 'as the personification of the *social* character of labour, of the *total workshop* as such',[295] the system can claim to represent the vitally necessary productive power of society vis-à-vis the individuals as the basis of their continued existence, incorporating the interest of all. In this way capital asserts itself not only as the *de facto* but also as the *de jure* power of society, in its capacity as the objectively given necessary condition of societal reproduction, and thereby as the constitutional foundation to its own political order. The fact that the constitutional legitimacy of capital is historically founded on the ruthless expropriation of the conditions of social metabolic reproduction — the means and material of labour — from the producers, and therefore capital's claimed 'constitutionality' (like the origin of all constitutions) is unconstitutional, this unpalatable truth fades away in the mist of a remote past. The *'social productive powers* of labour, or *productive powers of social labour,* first develop historically with the specifically capitalist mode of production, hence appear as something immanent in the capital-relation and inseparable from it.'[296] This is how capital's mode of social metabolic reproduction becomes *eternalized and legitimated* as a lawfully unchallengeable system. Legitimate contest is admissible only in relation to some minor aspects of the unalterable overall structure. The real state of affairs on the plane of socioeconomic reproduction — i.e. the actually exercised productive power of labour and its absolute necessity for securing capital's own reproduction — disappears from sight. Partly because of the ignorance of the very far from legitimable historical origin of capital's 'primitive accumulation' and the concomitant, frequently violent, expropriation of property as the precondition of the system's present mode of functioning; and partly because of the mystifying nature of the established productive and distributive relations. For

> the *objective conditions of labour* do not appear as subsumed under the worker; rather, he appears as subsumed under them. CAPITAL *EMPLOYS* LABOUR. Even this relation in its simplicity is a personification of things and a reification of persons.[297]

Nothing of this can be challenged and remedied within the framework of parliamentary political reform. Nor even under the most favourable circumstances, like the 1945 political landslide in favour of the Labour Party, which followed in Britain the revival of the critique of the system on account of the sacrifices that had to be endured by the popular masses during the long years of inter-war depression and the subsequent war. It would be absurd to expect the abolition of the *'personification of things and the reification of persons'* by political decree, and just as absurd to expect the proclamation of such an intended reform within the framework of capital's political institutions. For the capital system cannot function without the perverse overturning of the relationship between persons and things: capital's alienated and reified powers which dominate the masses of people. Similarly, it would be a miracle if the workers who confront capital in the labour process as 'isolated workers' could reacquire mastery over the social productive powers of their labour by some political decree, or even by a whole series of parliamentary reforms enacted under capital's order of social metabolic control. For in these matters there is no way of avoiding the irreconcilable conflict over the material stakes of *'either/or'*.

Capital can neither abdicate its — usurped — social productive powers in favour of labour, nor can it *share* them with labour. For they constitute the overall controlling power of societal reproduction in the form of *'the rule of wealth over society'.* Thus it is impossible to escape in the domain of the fundamental social metabolism the severe logic of *either/or.* For either wealth, in the shape of capital, continues to rule over human society, taking it to the brink of self-destruction, or the society of associated producers learns to rule over alienated and reified wealth, with productive powers arising from the self-determined social labour of its individual members. Capital is the *extra-parliamentary force par excellence* which cannot be politically constrained in its power of social metabolic control. This is why the only mode of political representation compatible with capital's mode of functioning is one which *effectively denies* the possibility of contesting its *material power*. And precisely because capital is the extra-parliamentary force par excellence, it has nothing to fear from the reforms that can be enacted within its parliamentary political framework. Since the vital issue on which everything else hinges is that 'the *objective conditions of labour* do not appear as subsumed under the worker' but, on the contrary, 'he appears as subsumed under them', no meaningful change is feasible without addressing this issue both in a form of politics capable of matching capital's extra-parliamentary powers and modes of action, and in the domain of material reproduction. Thus the only challenge that could sustainably affect the power of capital is one which would simulta- neously aim at assuming the system's key productive functions, and at acquiring control over the corresponding political decision making processes in all spheres, instead of being hopelessly constrained by the circular confinement of legitimate political action to parliamentary legislation.

To be sure, the castration of socialist politics is perfectly consistent with the power relations of capital and with its only feasible mode of operation, *in all its forms*. Since 'the objective conditions of labour do not appear as subsumed under the worker', rather the opposite, therefore the worker treated as isolated worker in the labour process can be legitimately considered in the same way in the other important spheres of the societal reproduction and distribution process. In poli- tics he or she can legitimately act as the (isolated) 'electors' who make their decisions strictly alone in the privacy of the polling booth. And in the materially most important sphere of 'productive consumption' which completes the cycle of capital's expanded reproduction, they can appear again as — strictly indivi- dual/isolated — 'sovereign consumers' who bear no relationship to their class. Instead, they act by consulting — this time not their *'political and moral conscience'* in the secrecy of the electoral booth, as they did it in their capacity as 'sovereign electors' — but their *'rational consciousness'* (or 'rational faculty') in calculating and maximizing their 'private marginal utilities'. The Soviet type postcapitalist system retained the same relationship, despite the abolition of the private capi- talist form of personification of capital. The worker remained subsumed under the objective conditions of labour, under the authoritarian control of the state as managed by the postcapitalist personifications of capital. Treated as isolated workers, who could under no circumstances organize themselves vis-à-vis the controlling authority of the labour process, they could be rewarded as 'Stak- hanovite' exemplary individuals (to be emulated by others), or punished and sent in their millions to the labour camps as 'criminal saboteurs' and 'enemy agents'; but labour as such could not acquire legitimacy as the active collective agent of the labour process, let alone assume control over social metabolic reproduction as a whole. Although under the prevailing circumstances of authoritarian 'planning' the idea of 'consumer sovereignty' could not be main- tained, none the less the matter of consumption was also regulated on an individual — and at that as a rule most discriminatory — basis, both in relation to 'Stakhanovites' and 'exemplary party workers'. Even the fiction of 'secret ballots' was maintained, whereby the 'socialist individuals' were supposed to consult their 'moral and political conscience' in the privacy of the polling booth, and come up with the expected uniform state-legitimating answers. All this was by no means surprising. For substantive differences in the field of politics and in that of 'productive consumption' would be feasible only by radically altering the structuring principle of the capital system which must keep the workers — one way or another — subsumed under the objective conditions of their own labour.

The extra-parliamentary power of capital can only be matched by labour's extra-parliamentary force and mode of action. This is all the more important in view of the complete disintegration of the once proclaimed and pursued parliamentary reformism of the labour movement, in the interest of delivering labour to capital as fragmented electoral fodder. Rosa Luxemburg wrote, prophetically, a very long time ago that

> parliamentarism is the breeding place of all the opportunist tendencies now existing in the Western Social Democracy. ... [it] provides the soil for such illusions of current opportunism as overvaluation of social reforms, class and party collaboration, the hope of pacific development toward socialism, etc. ... With the growth of the labour movement, parliamentarism becomes a springboard for political careerists. That is why so many ambitious failures from the bourgeoisie flock to the banners of the socialist parties. ... [The aim is to] *dissolve* the active, class conscious sector of the proletariat in the *amorphous mass of an 'electorate'*.[298]

The dissolution of which Rosa Luxemburg spoke as a threat has been fully completed to date, using the notion of an 'amorophous electorate' as its ideological legitimatory ground. Through this process not only openly reformist Western Social Democracy but also the once programmatically revolutionary affiliates of the Third International turned themselves into bourgeois liberal parties, consummating thereby the capitulation of the 'political arm' of labour before the 'rational' and 'realistic' imperatives of capital. All this came about much more easily than could be at first imagined. For the process of dissolution and disintegration of labour's defensive strategies was objectively helped along and sustained by the material power relations of the capital system which in the process of production and consumption can recognize only the isolated worker and consumer, and in the political domain the isolated elector equivalent to the powerless worker. This is why in the end 'representational' politics had to be degraded to the level of a public relations exercise everywhere, appropriately vomiting out of its belly and catapulting to the top of parliamentary politics — instead of realizing the promised 'Italian road to socialism' — 'representative' creatures like media tycoon Silvio Berlusconi, — of all places in the country of, once upon a time, Gramsci's Communist Party.

Naturally, in the countries of 'advanced capitalism', against the background of the clamorous historical failure of reformism and representational politics in general, the much needed change is unthinkable without the radical reconstitution of the labour movement — in its integrality and on an international scale — as an extra-parliamentary force. The self-defeating division between the 'political arm' and the 'industrial arm' of labour proves every day that such a division is a hopeless historical anachronism. Not only in view of its obvious failure in the political arena in the course of a whole century, but also because of its inability to embrace within its framework the countless millions of the *unemployed* 'superfluous people', ejected from the labour process at an alarming rate by the dehumanizing imperatives of 'productive capital'. The labour force still employed, defining its strategies as an organized political movement, cannot afford to disregard any longer the profound grievances — as well as the great potential force — of these countless millions. All the less because tomorrow the same fate is bound to afflict growing sections of today still employed labour. Given the slavishly facilitating role of politics in the service of capital's mode of social metabolic control — ideologically rationalized and justified under the labels of 'increased productivity', 'competitive advantage', 'market discipline', 'globalization', 'cost-efficiency', meeting the challenge of the 'five little tigers', or whatever else — very little can be expected from the parliamentary institutions as they are articulated today. Only a radical intervention at the level of the established order's wastefully 'economizing' material reproductive processes can successfully redress the powerlessness of labour, provided that it can assert itself against the now prevailing most unfavourable odds through the concerted action of a mass extra-parliamentary movement. This is what puts the historical actuality of the socialist offensive into relief.

It must be emphasised again that, as mentioned in Section 18.1.1, the historical actuality of the socialist offensive — due to the exhaustion of the self-serving concessions which capital could make in the past to a defensively articulated labour movement — does not mean that the success is assured and its realization is in our immediate vicinity. Being *'historical'* here indicates, on the one hand, that the necessity of instituting some fundamental changes in the orientation and organization of the socialist movement has appeared on the historical agenda; and, on the other, that the process in question unfolds under the pressure of powerful historical determinations, pushing the social agency of labour in the direction of a sustained strategic offensive if it wants to realize not only its potentially all-embracing transformatory objectives but even its limited ones. The road ahead is likely to be very hard, and certainly not one that can be side-stepped or altogether avoided.

The historical *mediations* required as viable steps towards the realization of labour's alternative social metabolic order are inherent both in the pursued objective — a radical intervention not confined to the political sphere but directly challenging the material structures of the capital-relation itself which subsume labour under the alienated and reified objective conditions of its exercise, condemning the social subject of the production process to the utter powerlessness of isolated workers — and in the inescapably extra-parliamentary mode of action through which it can be progressively translated into reality. For by the very nature of this enterprise, to have any chance of success at all, already the *first steps* must confront and overcome — even if at first only in relatively limited contexts — the pernicious diremption of politics and economics which suits only capital's mode of social metabolic control, as the self-defeating separation of labour's 'political arm' from its 'industrial arm' proved it with painful conclusiveness in the last hundred years.

It must be also stressed that the materially effective practical negation of the dominant reproductive structures through extra-parliamentary organization and action does not imply lawlessness or even an aprioristic rejection of parliament itself. Nonetheless, it involves an organizationally sustained challenge to the crippling constraints which the parliamentary 'rules of the game' *one-sidedly* impose on labour as the antagonist of capital. Naturally, the question of legislation cannot be ignored or wished out of existence even in a genuinely socialist society of the future. What decides the issue is the relationship between the associated producers and the rules which they set themselves through appropriate forms of decision making. To be sure, Marx is right that in a developed socialist society many of the unavoidable regulatory requirements can find their solution through *customs* and *traditions* established by the autonomous decisions and spontaneous interrelations of the individuals living and working in a non-adversarial framework of society. Without that the supersession of politics as an alienated domain is inconceivable, making therefore also the 'withering away of the state' unthinkable. But it is also clear that for the foreseeable future many of the overall regulatory requirements of society are bound to remain tied to formal legislative procedures. This is why the 'parliamentary wisdom of deluding others as well as oneself', quoted in Section 18.1.3, must be considered 'so much the worse' and not 'so much the better'.

Thus the role of labour's extra-parliamentary movement is twofold. On the one hand, it has to assert its strategic interests as a social metabolic alternative by confronting and forcefully negating in practical terms the structural determinations of the established order as manifest in the capital-relation and in the concomitant subordination of labour in the socioeconomic reproduction process, instead of helping to restabilize capital in crisis as it happened at important junctures of the reformist past. At the same time, on the other hand, the political power of capital which prevails in parliament needs to be and can be challenged through the pressure which extra-parliamentary forms of action can exercise on the legislative and executive, as witnessed by the impact of even the 'single issue' anti-poll-tax movement which played a major role in the fall of Margaret Thatcher from the top of the political pyramid. Without a strategically oriented and sustained extra-parliamentary challenge the parties alternating in government can continue to function as convenient reciprocal *alibis* for the structural failure of the system towards labour, thus effectively confining the role of the labour movement to its position as an inconvenient but *marginalizable afterthought* in capital's parliamentary system. Thus in relation to both the material reproductive and the political domain, the constitution of a strategically viable socialist extra-parliamentaty *mass* movement — in conjunction with the traditional forms of labour's, at present hopelessly derailed, political organization, which badly needs the *radicalizing pressure and support* of such extra-parliamentary forces — is a vital precondition for countering the massive extra-parliamentary power of capital.

CHAPTER NINETEEN

THE COMMUNAL SYSTEM AND THE LAW OF VALUE

19.1 The claimed permanence of the division of labour

19.1.1

SINCE the target of socialist emancipation is the radical transcendence of the inherited hierarchical social division of labour, it matters a great deal how effectively the transitional forms of material mediation can undertake the task of restructuring the metabolic framework of postrevolutionary society. For a failure to bring progressively under control the forces which continue to reproduce the iniquitous structural parameters of hierarchical decision making bequeathed by the past, condemns the socialist project at best to stagnation, if not to relapse and involution. Indeed, while it goes without saying that the social division of labour cannot be simply abolished by any act of government, no matter how well-intentioned, it remains equally true that in a most profound sense the yardstick of socialist achievements is the extent to which the adopted measures and policies actively contribute to the constitution and deep-rooted consolidation of a *substantively* democratic (i.e. in its mode of operation in all spheres truly non-hierarchical) mode of overall social control and self-management. Thus, the strategic importance of a socialist thinker's views on the division of labour cannot be overstated.

On this issue we find in Lukács's *History and Class Consciousness* an unhappy blend of disparate elements. On the one hand, the Weberian influence survives in that the Hungarian philosopher attributes the negative impact of the social division of labour to capitalistic 'rationalization', 'abstraction' and 'specialization'. He writes with regard to the last named tendency that 'The specialization of skills leads to the destruction of every image of the whole'. (p.103.)

In truth, however, a very high degree of specialization is perfectly compatible with an adequate image of the whole, so long as the practitioner of the skills in question is not forcibly separated from the power of decision making without which the meaningful participation of the social individuals in the constitution of the whole is inconceivable. What turns living labour into 'abstract labour' under capitalism is not *specialization* as such, but the rigid and dehumanizing confinement of the specialists' functions to the task of unquestioning execution, due to the fact that *labour* as such is radically excluded from *property* on the ground of which — and in accordance with the objective structural imperatives of which — the key decisions are made and the manifold partial functions of the social body are combined into a whole.

At another level, Lukács is scathing in *History and Class Consciousness* in his denunciation of the alienating division of labour, using even the dubious argument of 'human nature' in support of his position. He writes that

The division of labour, alien to the nature of man, makes men ossify in their activity,
it makes automata of them in their jobs and turns them into the slaves of a routine.
(p.335.)

In the same spirit — though again with a touch of Weberian mystification,
invoking as the ground of justification for the criticized phenomena the notion
of 'purposeful action' as such — he argues that

the requirements of purposeful action also compel the Party to introduce the division
of labour to a considerable degree and this inevitably invokes the dangers of ossification, bureaucratization and corruption. *(Ibid.)*

Thus, there is an insuperable inner tension in Lukács's characterization of the
problem. For although he makes it clear that he is aware of the negative and
potentially dangerous effects of the hierarchical social division of labour on the
actual mode of functioning of the party itself, nevertheless he reinforces his
justification for the retention of hierarchy by adding to the general clause of
'purposeful action' the highly problematical and in no way substantiated
judgement according to which 'while the struggle is raging it is *inevitable* that
there should be a hierarchy'. (p.336.)

Lukács's utopian recommendation, mentioned in Chapter 7, that the periodically 'reshuffled' hierarchy in the party 'must be based on the suitability of
certain talents for the objective requirements of the particular phase of the
struggle' *(Ibid.)* cannot eliminate the tension between condemning the division
of labour as 'alien to the nature of man' and wanting to retain it until the struggle
is completely over. It only exposes the author of *History and Class Consciousness*
to bureaucratic attacks on account of raising the issue at all.

19.1.2

THE impact of subsequent historical developments on Lukács is even more
problematical in this respect. For after the practical elimination of the structures
and institutional forms (e.g. the Workers' Councils) in which the originally
envisaged overcoming of the division of labour could be realistically attempted
in postrevolutionary societies, the very idea of its advocacy becomes more and
more abstract, to the point of entirely 'withering away', instead of being theoretically reassessed in the light of historical experience, in the interest of helping
to supersede the burdensome inheritance of the past.

Thus, the old Lukács's book on *The Present and Future of Democratization*
reproduces in the form of a sharp contradiction the tension we could see manifest
already in the last essays of *History and Class Consciousness*. For, on the one hand,
in this work of 1968 the author reasserts his positive belief in the validity of the
historical past of the Workers' Councils (though coupled with the repeated
pessimistic assertion that in the historical period ahead of us there is no
possibility for the reappearance of a 'spontaneous mass movement' corresponding to this form of self-management, dismissing those who advocate it as
'enthusiastic dreamers'[299]), and at the same time, on the other hand, he abandons
altogether the idea of overcoming the division of labour. (In this sense, therefore,
even if the Workers' Councils somehow appeared again, they could not make
in Lukács's view much difference.)

To justify his change of position on this important issue Lukács even claims,
without supplying the slightest evidence in support of his claim, that the older

Marx — 'in contrast to his youthful views in which the division of labour itself appears as a principle which must be transcended under communism'[300] — is only interested in pruning the 'oppressive effects' of the division of labour. The truth of the matter is, though, that Marx remains convinced to the end of his life that the division of labour is oppressive through and through, and not only in some of its prunable 'effects'. Ironically, therefore, Lukács — who, in opposition to fashionable legends, so often rightly emphasised the fundamental continuity between 'young Marx' and 'mature Marx' — ends up, for reasons of his own, with the same sort of legend.

At the time of writing on *Democratization* — the summer of 1968 which saw the forced obliteration of the hopes and measures of the 'Prague Spring' by Brezhnev's military intervention — the popular movement behind the ferment in Czechoslovakia cannot be praised by Lukács as a 'spontaneous mass movement'. Even less can he uphold the Workers' Councils, which spontaneously re-emerged in October 1956 in Hungary, as a recent historical example of a promising — or at least as a symptomatic and forewarning — mass movement. For what is today called by the Hungarian party a 'popular uprising' was at that time officially condemned as an imperialist-inspired 'counter-revolution'. (For the sake of the record, the spontaneous mass movement of 'Solidarnosc' in Poland was not yet on the historical horizon. Thus Lukács could not be accused of overlooking its potential impact.) Understandably, therefore, the pessimistic evaluation of the institutionally feasible practical mediations through which the contradictions of the present could be progressively overcome, coupled with the abandonment of the Marxian idea of transcending the division of labour as the consciously adopted and constantly reaffirmed strategic direction of socialists in the age of transition, Lukács confines his own theoretical perspective to a very narrow margin. On the premiss of the indefinitely retained hierarchical structures, he sees the way out of the encountered difficulties through a *'realistic division of labour between the party and the state'*,[301] arguing at the same time and in the same spirit that

> a factory built for capitalist purposes can produce smoothly without significant changes under socialism, and vice versa.[302]

In this perspective the role of the masses is confined to giving 'feed-back signals' from below to which those in charge of the state and the party ought to listen. As to the question of transition towards the higher stage of socialist society in which 'to each according to their need' is expected to be the ruling principle, Lukács — embracing one of the most problematical categories of positivistic sociology — sees the obstacles that prevent its realization in *'prestige-consumption'*. He argues that

> So long as the satisfaction of needs ... takes the form largely of *prestige-consumption*, i.e. it is in the first place not concerned with true existential needs but constitutes a means in the competitive struggle for higher social prestige and rank, so long the communist principle cannot be realized.[303]

Quite apart from the fact that the direct causal connections, inasmuch as they exist at all, between 'prestige-consumption' and industrial development, are represented upside-down when Lukács claims that 'The economic basis of the unprecedented development of the consumer industry and of the so-called services is precisely the *prestige-competition of the consumers'*,[304] one fails to see the relevance of this discourse on 'prestige-consumption' to the problems of the actually existing postcapitalist societies. For the latter in reality were struggling at the time of Lukács's reflections, after so many years of existence, with the quite elementary difficulties of how to supply their people with the basic necessities of life and how to shorten the intolerable queues for almost everything, from food to housing, and not with the pseudo-problem of 'how to keep up with the Joneses'.

The only thing that makes intelligible (though by no means justifiable) the use of such peculiar arguments is that with their help, in the absence of a historically concrete analysis of the prevailing *objective conditions* and contradictions in the socioeconomic base as well as in the political framework of postcapitalist societies, Lukács can again concentrate the fire of his critique on the 'defective *subjective factor*'. And, characteristically enough, the rectification of the defects diagnosed in this way is envisaged by the author of *The Present and Future of Democratization* — not in the form of a conscious and sustained attack on the iniquitous, hierarchical social division of labour by means of the successful articulation of the appropriate material mediations and institutional guarantees. He expects success from a direct appeal to the individuals' consciousness of their 'species-belonging' (while calling others, with much more modest and objectively much more feasible aims in mind, 'enthusiastic dreamers') and to the vague notion of the 'reformed everyday life' of the selfsame individuals.

19.1.3

LUKACS'S theoretical postulate which asserts the free interchangeability of the factories built for capitalist and socialist purposes, and thereby the smooth functioning of production on such a materially 'neutral' basis, treats fetishistically the concepts of technology and 'pure instrumentality'. (And he tends to do the same in relation to the so-called 'purely economic determinations', used in his discourse on the mission to be assigned to the freedom-producing 'subjective factor' vis-à-vis its mechanistic counter-image.) This postulate of material/instrumental neutrality is as sound as the idea that one can run the *hardware* of a computer without *software*. For even when one might have the *illusion* that this could be done, since the 'operating system' etc. need not be loaded separately from a floppy or hard disk, the relevant software is in fact already built into the hardware. And, of course, no software could be considered 'neutral' (or indifferent) to the purposes for which it has been devised.

The same goes for the factories built for capitalist purposes which bear the indelible marks of the 'operating system' — the hierarchical social division of labour — in conjunction with which they were constituted. To stay with the computer analogy, a system structured around a CPU (Central Processing Unit) is quite unsuitable for an operating system intended for 'decentralized' Parallel Processors, and vice versa. Thus, a productive system that wants to activate the full participation of the associated producers requires a multiplicity of adequately co-ordinated 'Parallel Processors', as well as a corresponding operating system which is radically different from the centrally operated alternative, be that capitalist or the well-known varieties of postcapitalist *command economy* misrepresented as *'planning'*.

One might argue with greater justification the *relative* neutrality of the strictly *isolated* work-instrument: a hammer, a hand-saw, or a particular memory chip. But even in this respect the limits of neutrality very quickly show up. For although the not very efficient hand-saw has not been — nor could it ever be — completely eliminated from the high-productivity-demanding capitalist system, its use has been of necessity 'marginalized' under the conditions of capitalist mass production. Equally, it is not a matter of indifference whether the memory chip in question is capable of 8-bit or 64-bit operation, which makes it totally useless outside the frame of reference defined by such operational characteristics.

In this sense, the limits of instrumental neutrality with regard to the particular work-instruments are decided by their suitability (or otherwise) to become constitutive parts of a coherent overall system. How much more one must be aware of such determinations and constraints in the case of the capitalist factory?! For the latter is not an isolated instrument but a powerful *system* (a veritable 'microcosm'), successfully operated on the basis of the 'despotism of the workshop' (its hierarchic internal command structure), in its organic connection with the 'tyranny of the market' which links and integrates the particular productive units within the totalizing 'macrocosm' of the capitalist regulatory framework.

Thus, it is far from accidental that the retention of the division of labour — with its authoritarian command structure — in postcapitalist societies should in the end lead to the advocacy of 'market socialism' (not by Lukács, who pursues his quest for solutions — in the spirit of *History and Class Consciousness* — on the plane of the 'subjective factor', but by many others), in order to remedy the inconsistency and contradiction between the particular productive units and the overall synthesising framework of the established socioeconomic systems. For under the continued hierarchic division of labour the removal of the capitalist *internal disciplining constraint* — which defines its own *justifying rationale* in terms of successful *market-performance* — cannot be redressed by authoritarian political control either in society at large or in the particular productive units themselves. The unhappy combination of hierarchic managerial decision making in the work-place, and the well grounded resentment of the people who suffer the consequences of this 'socialist' form of alienation of their own power of decision making, can only produce the *'anarchy of the workshop'* (in the form of 'moon-lighting', material and time-wasting, poor motivation for learning new and higher skills and negligent productive skill-exercise even at the lower level, etc.) on the one hand, and on the other hand, as its corollary and wishful remedy, the ultimately counter-productive intensification of centralized bureaucratic control of which the Stalinist system represents only a particularly acute and tragic historical example.

Accordingly, the troubles and failures of the postcapitalist socioeconomic systems are not the result of unavoidable *'complexity'* as such: the favourite argument of all those who like to use the arsenal of Weberian clichés as the 'proof' for the apriori impossibility of instituting truly socialist productive relations. They are the necessary consequence of the *adversarial* structural relationship between production and control, the 'undisciplined' producers and the 'socialist' management. 'Complexity', therefore, far from being apriori 'unavoidable', is directly produced by the inner contradictions of the postrevolutionary organization and control of the productive (and reproductive) functions of society under the prevailing historical circumstances. Coupled with the burden of the past, this new form of antagonistic structural relationship between production and control *creates* — at the core of the fundamental social metabolism of postcapitalist societies — not an 'unavoidable complexity', but indeed an *uncontrollable complexity*.

It is understandable why Max Weber — an openly professed and sworn enemy of socialism — should promote 'insurmountable complexity' to the status of an *'original cause'*, since on such a premiss (which puts the cart before the horse and 'concludes' that the cart cannot possibly move) the chances of the socialist project overcoming the power of capital are rendered nil. But those who look for remedies on a socialist basis have to address themselves to the real *causal foundations* of the visibly uncontrollable complexity in order to bring them under the control of the associated producers.

However, neither Lukács's moralistic direct appeal to the individuals' sense of responsibility — expressed in 'The Role of Morality in Communist Production' in the form of the sharp alternative: either freely accepted work-discipline for the sake of high productivity or the proletariat must turn its dictatorship against itself — nor the various authoritarian attempts to superimpose discipline from above on the producers can offer a solution to these problems. For in different ways and on the ground of very different motivations, they all operate on the plane of consequences, instead of facing up to their causes.

19.2 The law of value under different social systems

19.2.1

THE division of labour is by no means the only question on which Lukács offers a very problematical interpretation of Marx. The most important corollary of his departure from the Marxian conception of the division of labour concerns the 'law of value' and its manifestations under different social-economic systems. He quotes in this regard a passage from Marx's *Capital*, omitting a most important qualification. For where Marx writes:

> We will assume, *but merely for the sake of a parallel with the production of commodities*, that the share of each individual producer in the means of subsistence is determined by his labour-time.[305]

Lukács turns the *limited parallel* in question into a universally valid and permanent law, characteristic of 'all modes of production',[306] including the highest stage of communist society. This is quite unjustifiable. For the 'mere parallel' is offered by Marx as the illustration of only *one aspect* of the problem, namely the one directly related to the 'fetishism of commodities'. His reflections on this point are meant to demonstrate the *'transparency'* and straightforward *'intelligibility'* of the social character of production and distribution under socialism, in diametrical opposition to the capitalist system which 'conceals' and fetishistically misrepresents 'the social character of private labour and the social relations between the individual producers'.[307] At the same time, Marx offers this qualified parallel with commodity production in capitalist society with reference to *quantities* of labour-time partly because that is the only language understood by bourgeois political economy, and partly because the quantitative way of measuring the individuals' entitlement to their share in the social product remains relevant also in the transitional society, although in Marx's view decidedly not at the higher stage of socialism, as we know from his references to the principle 'to each according to their need' in *The Critique of the Gotha Programme.*

All this, however, does not amount to the ahistorical permanence of the law of value, as Lukács claims. On the contrary, Marx could not be clearer in his insistence that

The exchange of living labour for objectified labour — i.e. the positing of social labour in the form of the contradiction of capital and wage labour — is the *ultimate* development of the *value-relation* and of production resting on value. Its presupposition is — and remains — the mass of direct labour-time, the quantity of labour employed, as the determinant factor in the production of wealth. But to the degree that large industry develops, the creation of real wealth comes to depend less on labour-time and on the amount of labour employed than on the power of the agencies set in motion during labour time, whose 'powerful effectiveness' is itself in turn out of all proportion to the direct labour time spent on their production, but depends rather on the general state of science and on the progress of technology, or the application of this science to production. ... As soon as labour in the direct form has ceased to be the great well-spring of wealth, *labour-time ceases and must cease to be its measure,* and hence exchange-value must cease to be the measure of use-value.[308]

This is where we can see the far-reaching consequences of building a socialist theory and strategy — nay, a theory consciously put forward by its author as the necessary foundation of all other dimensions of knowledge and social practice: the ontology of social being — on the uncritical acceptance of the idea of *'socialism in one country'.* For arguing from such a problematical premiss — as Lukács does, not only in Stalin's life-time, when the dissenters often had to pay with their lives for their temerity to dissent, but to the very end, insisting even in his openly anti-Stalinist book on *Democratization* that 'One can doubt the *objectively socialist* character of actually existing socialism only from the standpoint of *bourgeois stupidity and slander'*[309] — brings with it the need to obliterate some vital lines of demarcation.

Internalizing and rationalizing this problematical premiss — which should be at least subjected to a critical scrutiny, even if in the end the thinker comes to the conclusion that it can be maintained, despite everything — bars one from exploring certain avenues both in the search for the causal determinations that lead to the present and with regard to the question of 'what is to be done?' in order to bring about a very different future.

In this perspective, conceived from the premiss of 'socialism in one country', the failure to overcome the problems and deficiencies of a greatly underdeveloped postrevolutionary system — with its crying need for 'original accumulation' (or 'socialist accumulation'); for the development of technology and science and for their successful application to the process of production — may indeed create the illusion that the *value-relation,* with its measure of quantifiable *labour-time,* can and must remain the permanent regulatory framework of societal reproduction under all forms of production, including the highest stages of socialist society. Consequently, the margin of feasible action is confined to extremely narrow limits. Objective structural changes are declared to be no longer necessary, hopelessly exaggerating the role of the 'subjective factor', which is now undialectically separated from, and even sharply opposed to, its material ground. In the same spirit as in *History and Class Consciousness,* the subjective/ideal/ideological factor is set against the 'purely economic' one. The necessary material mediations disappear from sight, or assume the form of an abstract methodological postulate, as we shall see in a moment. Understandably, therefore, in the end no other avenue remains open to the author except that of a direct moral appeal to the individuals' consciousness. He invites the individuals to recognize — or postulates that they are bound to recognize, as a result of a mysteriously developing 'ever-purer sociality' (whose material conditions are not only not indicated, but through the assertion of the permanence of the division of labour and of its value-relation are rendered impossible to realize) — their 'conscious species-belonging'.

Marx, however, sees these matters in a radically different light. Far from accepting the permanency of the measure of labour-time, he underlines the role of *disposable time* as the measure of wealth under the conditions of an advanced socialist society. For, as he puts it,

> real wealth is the developed productive power of all individuals. The measure of wealth is then not any longer, *in any way,* labour time, but rather *disposable time.* Labour time as the measure of value posits wealth itself as founded on poverty, and disposable time as existing in and because of the antithesis to surplus labour time; or, the positing of an individual's entire time as labour time, and his *degradation* therefore to mere worker, *subsumption under labour.*[310]

Indeed, Marx forcefully argues that under the conditions of advanced socialism we witness the transformation of 'necessary labour-time' from tyrannical and degrading *measure* into being itself *measured,* in subordination to *qualitative* human criteria, 'by the *needs* of the social individual'.[311] He argues this in full conformity to an idea spelled out in a most striking way ten years earlier, according to which

> In a future society, in which class antagonism will have ceased, in which there will no longer be any classes, *use* will no longer be determined by the *minimum time* of production; but the *time* of production devoted to an article will be *determined* by the degree of its *social utility.*[312]

The question is, therefore, whether considerations of time play the role of the all-important *determinant* in the historically specific form of social metabolism, or, on the contrary, the labour time of society — both its production and allocation — is regulated and *determined* by the objectives which the members of an advanced socialist society set themselves, within the framework of a genuine *plan* devised by them. In other words, the question is whether the social individuals are able to plan in this genuine sense, allocating their time — the time of meaningful life — among a whole range of activities that correspond to their needs. A procedure which stands in stark contrast to the caricature of planning: the bureaucratic imposition of a set of productive and distributive dictates from above, ruled in its turn by the necessity to extract — in an iniquitous way — the surplus labour (and the equivalent surplus time) of the workers.

Understandably, thus, it is inconceivable to bring about this vital change in the social function of labour time — from determinant (which reduces living labour, in Marx's word, to 'time's carcass') to being determined — without a corresponding advance towards the supersession of the division of labour. For so long as time dominates society in the form of the imperative to extract the surplus labour time of its overwhelming majority, the personnel in charge of this process must lead a substantially different form of existence, in conformity to its function as the *personification and enforcer of the time-imperative*. At the same time the overwhelming majority of the individuals are '*degraded to mere worker, subsumed under labour*'.

Only the full and equal participation of all its members in the process of decision making at all levels can progressively extricate the transitional society from this contradictory and antagonism-reproducing predicament, on its road to superseding the division of labour and emancipating itself from the tyranny of time. Lukács is, therefore, perfectly consistent when he wants to retain not only the division of labour but also the value relation that goes with it. Paradoxically, however, this consistency makes the very idea of socialism extremely problematical, and the possibility of reaching its advanced stage utterly unreal.

19.2.2

WE must look at a representative passage from Lukács's *Ontology of Social Being* in order to see the difference between his approach and Marx's ideas on the subject. The tendency in Lukács's line of argument is to eliminate the qualitative distinction made by Marx between *social* and *communal* (the latter being 'gemeinschaftliche' or 'not *post festum* social') production and to subsume the latter under the former. In other words, Lukács's approach is characterized by a tendency to subsume the communal system under a form of social production which remains always subjected to and dominated by the constraints of the value-relation.

This is not simply a conceptual imprecision or an accidental slip in Lukács's theory. He *must* proceed in this way in order to be able to ground the role ascribed in the *Ontology of Social Being* (and in his writings more or less closely related to the *Ontology*, e.g. the study on *Democratization*) to value-oriented 'individual teleological positings' under all historical conditions and circumstances.

In this spirit we are told by Lukács that 'Even the most complicated economy is the *resultant* of *individual teleological positings* and their realizations, both in the form of *alternatives* ... [even though] men can scarcely follow correctly the consequences of their own decisions'. In the next sentence, anticipating an obvious objection to this proposition, Lukács asks the question: 'How therefore could their positings of value constitute economic value?' And he answers it with a categorical reassurance: 'But value itself is still *objectively* present, and its very objectivity also determines — even if without complete *certainty* on the *objective* side, or adequate *awareness* on the *subjective* — the individual teleological positings that are oriented by value'.[313]

Since the validity of these assertions is by no means self-evident, and the exempting qualifications made with regard to both the objective and the subjective side raise more questions than they really answer, this is how Lukács tries to prove his point on the authority of Marx:

the social division of labour that becomes ever more complex gives rise to values ... the division of labour mediated and brought about by *exchange-value* produces the principle of control of time by a better subjective use of it. As Marx puts it: 'Economy of time, to this all economy ultimately reduces itself. Society likewise has to distribute its time in a purposeful way, in order to achieve a production adequate to its overall needs; just as the individual has to distribute his time correctly, in order to achieve knowledge in proper proportions or in order to satisfy the various demands on his activity. Thus, economy of time, along with the planned distribution of labour time among the various branches of production, remains the first economic law on the basis of *communal* production'. [i.e. a specifically/co-operatively social *'gemeinschaft-liche'*, and not a generically *'gesellschaftliche* Produktion', I.M.] Marx speaks of this here as the law of *social* production. And rightly so, for the causal effects of the different phenomena involved combine together to give such a law, reacting thus on the *individual acts* as a decisive factor, so that individuals must adapt themselves to this law or perish. Economy of time, however, immediately involves a relation of value. ... The objective orientation of economic law to the saving of time immediately gives rise to whatever is the *optimal social division of labour* at the time, thus bringing about the rise of a social being at a higher level of sociality that becomes ever more pure.[314]

As we can see, the passage from the *Grundrisse* quoted here by Lukács directly contradicts his claim that the principle of 'economy of time' is the product of *exchange-value*. For in Marx's view the principle in question both precedes and survives the dominance of exchange-value, asserting its own validity, even if in *qualitatively* different ways, under *all* forms of production, including the *commu-nal* system. And the latter deserves its name because it is characterized not only by communal *production* but also by communal — i.e. neither abstract collec-tivist nor individualistically value-oriented — *consumption* ('gemeinschaftliche Konsumption').

However, the divergence of Lukács's position from the Marxian conception is much greater than this particular point could indicate. In order to understand the nature and theoretical function of Lukács's astonishing misreading of Marx, we must have a closer look at the passage to which he refers. But first it is necessary to underline the characteristic line of reasoning through which Lukács —much the same way as in *History and Class Consciousness*—introduces exempt-ing qualifications in order to remove the doubts and difficulties he has to face with regard to some of his key categories. In *History and Class Consciousness* he could maintain with the help of such qualifications that 'conscious proletarian action' *by definition* unfolds in the realm of freedom, thereby reassuring himself and his readers on the ground of postulating a historical agency which is revo-lutionary even when it is in actuality not revolutionary, and conscious even when it is 'wholly unconscious'. This is how the 'certainty of proletarian victory' could be asserted and reiterated in *History and Class Consciousness* with moving com-mitment despite the major defeats and setbacks, in defiance of the prevailing unfavourable sociohistorical circumstances.

In the same way, in the *Ontology of Social Being* we are invited to adopt a perspective which stipulates the certain 'rise of a social being at a higher level of sociality that becomes ever more pure', emerging out of the 'parallelogram-mic' interactive processes of individuals who, in tune with the Hegelian 'cunning of Reason',[315] 'can scarcely follow correctly the consequences of their own decisions', since they are enmeshed in the historically 'optimal' and ever more complex social division of labour. Nevertheless, the positive outcome of the higher social order is expected to arise in the form of the necessary *'resultant* of the individual teleological positings', even though we cannot find any certainty of its realization on the objective side, nor indeed an 'adequate awareness' of the 'objective intent' inherent in the individual teleological positings on the subjective side.

What is highly problematical in this vision is the absence of mediation in two fundamental respects. First, because it does not show the links which lead (or might lead) from the individuals who find themselves at the lower level of sociality (in antagonistically divided class societies) to the higher one, where the individuals' full consciousness of their 'species-belonging' is said to be the operative principle. And second, because it fails to indicate the historically specific form of mediatory interchanges through which the individuals can actually live their 'species-belonging', at no matter how high a level of sociality, in accordance with the given degree of development of their society.

This is why, most significantly, in Lukács's reading of the passage quoted from the *Grundrisse* the Marxian idea of *communal* production and consumption — and the corresponding use of time in a *qualitative/liberating* sense, in contrast to its tyrannical *quantitative imposition* on the producers, which happens to be inseparable from the value-relation — radically changes the meaning of the original. For in Marx's vision the qualitative use of time under the communal form of reproductive interchange represents the historically attainable level and mode of quite *unique mediation* of the associated producers, at the highest stages of socialism.

As a result of omitting Marx's references to the radical reorientation of time towards *quality,* in Lukács's discourse on individual teleological positings the Marxian idea, concerned with the new meaning of the 'economy of time', is completely lost. In contrast to Marx who speaks of allocating society's total disposable time on the basis of *conscious communal decisions,* Lukács interprets it as a *generic social law* that directly confronts and subdues the individuals who 'must adapt themselves to this law or perish'. Yet, given the premiss of advanced socialism posited by Marx in the context of these reflections, the peril of perishing can no longer orient, through its overpowering negativity, the life-activity of the 'rich social individuals'. Thus, in Lukács's discourse, the dualistic opposition between 'social law' (which timelessly asserts itself for him even under communal production and consumption) and 'individual teleological positings' cannot be bridged. In the absence of historically specific forms of material mediation, bridging can only be attempted by proposing emancipatory intervention on the 'subjective side', through some form of direct appeal to consciousness. All recommendations with regard to the possibility of intervention on the 'objective side' assume the form of *methodological postulates,* and thus remain essentially within the domain of the 'subjective factor'.

19.2.3

MARX'S discussion of these problems in the passage quoted by Lukács in a truncated form sets out from underlining the contrast between the quantitative and the qualitative differentiation of time, and from firmly asserting that the productive activity of living labour — the labour of particular working subjects — cannot be simply equated with 'general, self-equivalent labour time'. For under the conditions of commodity production 'labour time as subject corresponds as little to the general labour time which determines exchange values as the particular commodities and products corresponding to it as object'.[316]

The radical difference between the communal and the capitalist form of social reproduction is put into relief by Marx in response to Adam Smith's reflections on the role of money — as 'general commodity' — in the historically established and transcendable, but by bourgeois political economy eternalized, system of commodity production and exchange. He criticizes Smith's self-contradictory idea of 'general exchangeability': a totally elusive notion under the conditions of commodity society and its value relation. And yet, its postulate arises, by no means accidentally, in the service of the eternalization of the given system. Moreover, this postulate must be self-contradictory. For while the problematical concept of capitalist 'general exchangeability' has to be postulated by Smith in conformity to the requirements of an eternalized socioeconomic system, it can only be defined by the great Scottish thinker in terms of conditions under which the issue itself can no longer be raised at all.

This is how Marx argues the fundamental difference between the two systems of production and distribution, bringing into focus a number of vitally important determinations at the roots of each, with a direct bearing also on the sharply contrasting forms in which the reproductive interchange of the particular individuals is of necessity mediated under the *'post festum' sociality* of capitalism on the one hand, and the truly planned communal system on the other:

> The labour of the individual looked at in the act of production itself, is the money with which he directly buys the product, the object of his *particular* activity; but it is a particular money, which buys precisely only this specific product. In order to be general money directly, it would have to be not a particular, but general labour from the outset; i.e. it would have to be posited as a *link in general production.* But on this presupposition it would not be *exchange* which gave labour its general character; but rather its presupposed *communal* character would determine the distribution of products. The communal character of production would make the product into a *communal, general product from the outset.* The exchange which originally takes place in production — which would not be an exchange of exchange values but of *activities,* determined by *communal needs and communal purposes* — would from the outset include the participation of the individual in the communal world of products. On the basis of exchange values, labour is posited as general only through exchange. But on this [communal] foundation it would be posited as such *before* exchange; i.e. the exchange of products would in no way be the medium by which the participation of the individual in general production is mediated. Mediation must, of course, take place. In the first case, which proceeds from the independent production of individuals — no matter how much these independent productions determine and modify each other *post festum* through their interrelations — mediation takes place through the exchange of commodities, through exchange value and through money; all these are expressions of one and the same relation. In the second case, the presupposition is itself mediated; i.e. a communal production, *communality* is presupposed as the basis of production. The labour of the individual is posited from the outset as social labour. Thus, whatever the particular material form of the product he creates or helps to create, what he has bought with his labour is not a specific and particular product,

but rather a *special share of the communal production*. He therefore has no particular product to exchange. His product is not an exchange value. The product does not first have to be transposed into a particular form in order to attain a general character for the individual. *Instead of a division of labour*, such as is necessarily created with the exchange of exchange values, there would take place an *organization of labour* whose consequence would be the participation of the individual in *communal consumption*. In the first case the social character of production is posited only *post festum* with the elevation of products to exchange values and the exchange of these exchange values. In the second case the social character of production is *presupposed*, and participation in the world of products, in consumption, is not mediated by the exchange of mutually independent labours or products of labour. It is mediated, rather, by the *social conditions of production* within which the individual is active. Those who want to make the labour of the individuals directly into money (i.e. his product as well), into realized exchange value, want therefore to determine that labour directly as general labour, i.e. to negate precisely the conditions under which it must be made into money and exchange values, and under which it depends on private exchange. This demand can be satisfied only under conditions where it can no longer be raised. Labour on the basis of exchange values presupposes, precisely, that neither the labour of the individual nor his product are *directly general;* that the product attains this form only by passing through an objective [gegenständliche] mediation, by means of a form of money distinct from itself.[317]

Obviously, thus, the lines of demarcation between the communal system on the one hand, and systems dominated by the division of labour and the corresponding value-relation on the other, could not be drawn more emphatically than they are here. It is therefore all the more problematical that Lukács should use Marx's conclusions in support of his own ahistorical projection of the 'always optimal' division of labour and its law of value into the future, obliterating thereby the diametrical opposition between the *directly general* organization of the communal labour process and those in which the social character of labour can only be posited *post festum,* through the intermediary of exchange value. Indeed, it is almost incomprehensible that Lukács, who is as a rule highly appreciative of the encountered historical specificities, should pursue his ahistorical line of reasoning on this set of issues, despite the fact that the *qualitative* differences separating the societal reproductive systems are made quite explicit in the quoted passage of the *Grundrisse.*

Naturally, all this is not a matter of abstract theoretical interest only. On the contrary, what is at stake here constitutes the practically vital orienting principle of the strategies that aim at a radical restructuring of the established labour process and its exchange relation. The central issue in dispute concerns the necessary forms of *mediation* through which the hierarchical structural division of labour could give way to the *directly social* mode of production of the 'new historic form'. In other words, it is concerned with setting the *parameters* of and the *direction* in which — in Marx's words — 'instead of a division of labour' (whose material imperatives are unceremoniously imposed on the particular working subjects) the consciously self-controlled life-activity of the social individuals could be integrated into a both productively viable and humanly fulfilling whole.

Lukács's symptomatic misreading of Marx, by contrast, *conflates* the *generic* social (which includes the extremely problematical *post festum* sociality of capitalist commodity production) with the *specific,* from the *outset* socially determined and consciously organized (i.e. genuinely planned) character of the anticipated socialist system of production and consumption. (As we shall see, he must adopt this conflated category of generic sociality because his discourse on the individuals' 'triumph over their own particularism' needs it.) By doings so, however, he bars the road to understanding the significance of the necessary material mediations that could lead from the rule of capital perpetrated within the framework of the inherited structural division of labour to the communal system of production and consumption in Marx's sense. For his own line of argument simultaneously removes the need for such mediations — assigning them, instead, to the sphere of *ethics* — and rules out the possibility of their practical articulation by postulating the permanence of the division of labour (and the corresponding value relation) even at the most advanced stage of the socialist order.

19.3 Antagonistic and communal mediation of the individuals

19.3.1

THE defining characteristics of the communal system put into relief by Marx must be kept in mind if we are to take seriously the idea that the socialist project can offer a solution to the contradictions of our contemporary reproductive systems. The obstacles to the realization of the communal mode of production and consumption cannot be removed by hypostatizing the 'identity of the past and the present' under the dictatorship of the proletariat, as Lukács tried to do in *History and Class Consciousness;* nor indeed by subscribing to the idea of 'socialism in one country', coupled with the eternalization of the division of labour and its value relation, and rationalized in a way which simply takes for granted its own terms of reference: namely, the claim that the task ahead of us is the creation of a 'realistic division of labour between the party and the state'.

That a thinker of Lukács's stature should produce such a baffling interpretation of the Marxian passage quoted from the *Grundrisse,* can only be understood in relation to the constraining practical premisses mentioned in the last sentence, which objectively preclude the possibility of a reading in the sense intended by Marx. It is for the same reasons that the author of the monumental *Ontology of Social Being* must also substitute for the investigation of the tangible and feasible material mediations of the actually existing transitional societies, in their difficult and contradictory movement towards the future, the noble but unreal projection of the individuals' consciousness of their 'species-belonging'. He conceives the latter *dualistically* and can envisage the necessary mediation only through *Ethics,* as we have seen above, promising for many years the elaboration of the related problems in a work which, significantly, he can never write.

The relevance of the Marxian signposts and orienting principles which we can clearly identify in the passage quoted above is today greater than ever before, in view of the profound crisis of all three socioeconomic systems of our contemporary world. The failure of 'modernization' in the 'Third World'; the reappearance of the spectre of explosive antagonisms in the 'First World', together with the high probability of some major disaster paralysing the financial arteries of 'advanced capitalism' before long; and the implosion of nearly all post-capitalist societies, — all these circumstances highlight the sobering truth that there can be no *separate* solutions to the problems of the three systems. For the so-called 'Three Worlds' constitute *one* world only in any meaningful sense of the term, due to the profound and inextricable interconnections of the socioeconomic and political systems in question, notwithstanding all the existing divisions, structural dependencies and antagonisms. Consequently, the broad general perspective of finding a way out of the existing impasse of each can only be *one* capable of addressing itself to the problems and contradictions of all three systems, in the spirit of the original socialist project.

To be sure, the Marxian signposts and orienting principles in question can only be that, and no more. In other words, as signposts and orienting principles they need to be translated at any particular juncture of socioeconomic and cultural/political development into historically specific — hence necessarily changing —*mediatory strategies*. But precisely because by their very nature they can circumscribe only the broad general perspective of the ongoing transformation, their validity is not tied to a limited sociohistorical conjuncture. It is therefore in principle quite irrelevant whether it might take a very long time to achieve the necessary breakthrough towards socialism — not in one country alone, and not even in a dozen or more, but *irreversibly* for the *whole* of humanity — or only a few decades.

The relevance of the Marxian orienting principles asserts itself through the inescapable fact that without them the journey itself becomes extremely problematical, because it loses — with the most bewildering and disheartening consequences — its *direction*. We could witness this not only in the East but also in the total reversal of the strategic orientation of some former communist and socialist parties in Western Europe. The socialdemocratization of the communist parties in the West belongs to the same process through which the leaders of some labour and socialdemocratic parties abandoned the once professed socialist aims by self-contradictorily declaring that the task of socialists is the 'better management of capitalism'. They do not seem to realize that even if capitalism could be fully restored in all postrevolutionary societies, that would not solve one single structural contradiction of capital as a mode of social control to which the working classes are subjected. It would only remove the self-complacent justification and *alibi* of 'advanced capitalism'.

19.3.2

UNDERLINING the broad historical validity of the Marxian orienting principles, together with the need for their institutionally concrete articulation in accordance with the margin of action available to the emancipatory agencies under the prevailing circumstances, cannot be used, of course, as a convenient escape-clause. The acknowledgement that the full historical maturation of the conditions anticipated in the broad orienting framework itself might take a very long time to come about does not mean that it is enough to define the principles themselves in terms of abstract imperatives. What is needed is a precise indication of at least the *type* of action — spelled out both at the level of the relevant material productive practices and with regard to the institutional/organizational forms of human interchange — through which the communal mode of social reproduction can actually prove its viability as a practical alternative to the existent.

To put it in another way, the orienting principles cannot simply proclaim (in the form of a categorical negation) the envisaged future conditions of communal production and consumption as the *ideal counter-image* of the present, however acute the contradictions and crisis symptoms of the latter. For the other side of this equation — i.e. the *positive substance* of the socialist negation of 'post festum' sociality — can become credible only if it is made tangible in terms of the actually feasible *material mediations* between the constraints of the present and the potentialities of the future. Material mediations, that is, which are concrete and adaptable enough to be used by the social emancipatory agencies as the principled yet flexible strategic framework for the elaboration of their historically specific programmes of action.

This is where we can see the striking contrast between Lukács's general postulates and projections, spelled out in the form of moral imperatives — both in *History and Class Consciousness* and in *The Ontology of Social Being* — and the Marxian characterization of the communal form of existence in the *Grundrisse*. Paradoxically, the passing of time signals for Lukács an involution in this respect. The moral imperatival character of his discourse becomes more abstract in his last works than in *History and Class Consciousness*. As we have seen above, whereas in his youthful work of synthesis both the question of the proletariat's historic mission and that concerning the realization of the individual's 'total personality' is institutionally concretized by Lukács to the extent that he envisages the solution of such practical challenges within the framework and through the accomplishment of the 'moral mission' of the party, the same imperatival moral postulates appear in his last works without any concrete historical embodiment.

In a sense this is perfectly understandable. For in the light of post-revolutionary historical experience and Lukács's bitter disappointments as a dedicated militant, the party cannot be idealized any longer the way we find it idealized in *History and Class Consciousness*. However, Lukács's reluctant reassessment of his earlier conception from the distance of half a century does not lead to the abandonment of idealization itself. On the contrary, the appeal to moral imperatives in his last works is in evidence stronger than ever before.

Twenty five years ago, when Lukács was still working on the final summation of his vision in the *Ontology of Social Being*, intended by the author as the necessary groundwork to his long-projected *Ethics*, I chose as the epigraph of a study which tried to sketch the outlines of his philosophical development — *Lukács's Concept of Dialectic* — a sentence from one of his most important early writings, *The Theory of the Novel:*

> der Zwiespalt von Sein und Sollen ist nicht aufgehoben; the rupture between 'Being' and 'Ought' is not superseded.

I argued at the time that within the framework of Lukács's conception this all-embracing dualism can never be superseded, despite his lifelong concern for producing a solution that had to remain elusive to the antinomous structure of thought of classical German philosophy. Thus, seeing the role assigned to 'ought' in Lukács's last works could come as no surprise; only the intensity with which the moral imperative is pushed into the foreground of his reflections.

Characteristically, we are presented in the last two works of the Hungarian philosopher — *The Present and Future of Democratization* and *The Ontology of Social Being* — with the materially unmediated opposition between the poles of particularistic individuality and humanity in general. As we have seen, Lukács offers a way out of this dualism by saying that only the ideality of ethical moral consciousness (contrasted by him, in the tradition of classical German philosophy, with purely subjective morality) can provide the necessary mediation between the two poles. Also, the once firmly asserted organic connection between the individual's 'total personality' and his dedication to the cause of socialism through disciplined action (within the framework of the party) is reasserted in Lukács's last works with the strongest possible emphasis, even though without any reference to a historically concrete collective agency and its institutional/organizational articulation. What is considered by Lukács in this matter the ethically relevant organic connection is reformulated by him in the *Ontology of Social Being* in terms of the necessary correlation between the *personality-to-be-made* of the particularistic individuals and the *'great cause'* through which it becomes possible for them to triumph over their own limited particularism (provided that they fully dedicate themselves to some great cause), participating thereby in the unfolding process of humanity realizing 'humanity-for-itself'.

Thus, in the absence of any attempt to conceptualize in concrete social and historical terms the material conditions of mediation in the age of transition, in Lukács's last works of synthesis ethics as such must be assigned the role which in *History and Class Consciousness* he ascribes to proletarian class consciousness and its 'active incarnation', the party. In this way Lukács reformulates in the books written in the last decade of his life (including the fragmentary but nonetheless magisterial work on *Aesthetics*) the old dualism between 'Being' and 'Ought' in a spirit substantively echoing the volume published in the aftermath of the October revolution and of the shortlived Hungarian Council Republic, even if in a different form.

If in *History and Class Consciousness* the idealized party must be characterized as the 'concrete mediation between man and history', in Lukács's last works only *ethics* can be expected to assume an equivalent function, ideally mediating between the individuals' limited particularism and 'humanity-for-itself'. The task of identifying the historically feasible and socially specific material mediations between the present and the future is bypassed in favour of substituting for it — as the hypostatized solution of the dilemmas that must be faced by the individuals under the complicated vicissitudes of everyday life — the imperative of an ideal mediation of the practically insurmountable dualism of the two poles in the individuals' consciousness, through the self-emancipatory intervention of their moral consciousness. In this perspective it is postulated by Lukács that the individuals will become fully aware of and positively embrace the moral responsibilities that go with their 'species-belonging' — without indicating at all how such a radical change in the motivational framework of 'actually existing socialism' might come about — in response to the particular challenges which they are called upon to confront as individuals in their everyday life.

Thus, 'Der Zwiespalt von Sein und Sollen ist nicht aufgehoben'. Within such horizons it cannot be. But the most unreal aspect of Lukács's resolution of the dichotomy between 'Being' and 'Ought' is to hypostatize the realization of 'humanity-for-itself' in and through a mode of existence which reconciles the individuals to the permanence of the division of labour. Curiously, they are expected to find fulfilment in Goethe's Olympian elitism according to which 'even the *most insignificant man* can be a complete man',[318] in open contradiction to the meaning of the Marxian struggle against the hierarchical social division of labour. A struggle whose aim is precisely to find a way for overcoming the *structurally enforced* 'insignificance' of the individuals 'degraded to mere workers, subsumed under labour'.

19.3.3

IT is very important to understand the contrast between Lukács's way of dealing with the issue of mediation through the ideality of ethics (which induces him to read the *Grundrisse* the way he does) and the Marxian approach to the fundamental difference between the communal mode of social metabolic exchange and the earlier forms of sociality. For this difference has a direct bearing on the unavoidable forms of emancipatory mediation towards the future.

As mentioned already, what is most tellingly overlooked by Lukács in the passage quoted in Section 19.1.2 is the sharp opposition between *post festum* sociality — in which the individuals participate only through the division of labour and the corresponding value-relation — and the communal mode of reproductive interchange, characterized by Marx as *directly social* in its innermost determination, i.e. social *'from the outset'*. The author of *The Ontology of Social Being* cannot help committing this oversight, because his philosophical discourse — which assigns the key role to the individuals' 'decisions between alternatives', so as to give an ontological foundation to his direct appeal to their moral consciousness — must orient itself, in counter-position to spontaneously emerging sociality, towards a model of ethically defined sociality.

The unique character of the latter is established by Lukács on the ground that it is produced *in* the individuals' *consciousness,* through the direct intervention of *self-emancipatory ethical consciousness.* It is his orientation towards this — morally conceived — model of sociality which makes it necessary for Lukács also to postulate the permanence of the division of labour and its 'law of value'. For according to him the latter directly confronts the individuals, as separate individuals, with the imperative to choose between alternatives, and only their rising ethical consciousness enables them to make the right and proper decisions at the level of true sociality, in the spirit of their consciously acknowledged species-belonging.

In Marx's view, by contrast, true sociality — i.e. one that is not worn by the individuals as a strait-jacket (like the social role assigned to them through the division of labour) but corresponds to their objectively, and under fully developed communal conditions also freely, constituted being — is not produced *in consciousness* (let alone in particularistic individual consciousness, under the pressure of the imperative: 'recognise as an individual the moral implications of your species-belonging or perish'). It can only be produced *in reality* itself; or, to be more precise, in the material and cultural intercourse of the individuals' *communal* social existence which cannot be conceptualized in individualistic terms, nor can it indeed be grasped in abstraction from the historically changing and expanding needs of the social individuals.

Naturally, the productive relationship between the particular working subjects must be *mediated* in every conceivable form of society. Without it the 'aggregative totality' of the individuals who are active at any particular time in history could never coalesce into a sustainable social whole. Indeed, the historical specificity of the given form of mediation through which the individuals are linked together, by means of the historically given intermediary groupings and their institutional equivalents, into a more or less closely intertwined societal whole, happens to be of seminal importance. For it is precisely this — practically inescapable — mediatory specificity of the individuals' reproductive interrelations that ultimately defines, through the more or less direct determination of the prevailing operating conditions of production and consumption, the fundamental character of the various, historically contrasting modes of societal intercourse.

In this sense, according to Marx, under the division of labour that prevails in commodity society, the individuals are mediated among themselves and combined into an *antagonistically structured* social whole only through the capitalistic system of commodity production and exchange. And the latter is ruled by the imperative of ever-expanding exchange-value to which everything else — from the most basic as well as the most intimate needs of the individuals, to the various material and cultural productive activities in which they engage in capitalist society — must be strictly subordinated.

The communal system envisaged by Marx stands in complete contrast to this form of antagonistically structured societal mediation which cannot help ruthlessly superimposing itself on the individuals through the value relation.

The main characteristics of the communal mode of interchange enumerated in the passage quoted in Section 19.2.3 from Marx's *Grundrisse* are as follows:
- the determination of the working subjects' life-activity as a necessary and individually meaningful link in directly general production, and their correspondingly direct participation in the available world of products;
- the determination of the social product itself as inherently communal, general product from the outset, in relation to communal needs and purposes, on the basis of the special share which the particular individuals acquire in the ongoing communal production;
- the full participation of the members of society also in communal consumption proper: a circumstance that happens to be extremely important, in view of the dialectical interrelationship between production and consumption, on the basis of which the latter is rightfully characterized under the communal system as positively '*productive* consumption';
- the planned *organization* of labour (instead of its alienating *division*, determined by the self-assertive imperatives of exchange value in commodity society) in such a way that the productive activity of the particular working subjects is mediated not in a reified-objectified form, through the exchange of commodities, but through the intrinsically social conditions of the given mode of production itself within which the individuals are active.

These characteristics make it quite clear that the key issue is the establishment of a historically *new mode of mediating* the metabolic exchange of humanity with nature and of the progressively more self-determined productive activities of the social individuals among themselves.

At the same time, it is equally clear that this is not a matter of projecting upon the given reality a set of moral imperatives, however noble in aspiration, as the counter-image of the existent. Rather, what is directly at stake here is the articulation of quite tangible material practices and corresponding institutional forms. In other words, the historical viability of the communal system advocated by Marx — defined by him as the *positively* self-sustaining alternative to the antagonistically structured division of labour and its value relation — can be established only if the conditions of its anticipated actualization are spelled out in terms of concrete tasks and instruments that can match up to them. This is why Marx was always critical of the utopian counter-position of the socialist future to the existing social order as an abstract ideal to which reality had to conform.

19.4 The nature of exchange under communal social relations

19.4.1

THE most important aspect of this issue concerns the nature of *exchange* in the communal system of production and consumption. In fact it is no exaggeration to say that this aspect represents the 'Archimedean point' of the whole complex of practically necessary and feasible mediatory strategies and modes of action on which the articulation of an irreversible socialist order hinges. For the necessity of instituting a radically new type of exchange relation arises in the socialist project not as an abstract and rather remote regulative principle, but as a matter of great practical urgency.

Thus, the relevance of the advocated new form of — communal type — exchange is not a matter of a far-away social order. It is not an order in which the fully realized 'humanity-for-itself' finds itself in complete harmony with the totality of individuals who make their decisions between alternatives in accordance with the inner demands of their moral consciousness, with reference to the ideal implications of their species-belonging. On the contrary, whatever its implications for the distant future, the significance of communal type exchange consists today precisely in its more or less direct application to the problems and contradictions — and indeed to the almost prohibitive practical difficulties — with which the *transitional* society, in its painful present-day reality, is forced to struggle in order to extricate itself from the power of capital and from the concomitant hierarchical division of labour.

However, the communal exchange relation discussed by Marx is *qualitatively* different from the forms of exchange we are all familiar with. As a matter of fact, due to the ideological vested interests which try to eternalize the structural framework of the established social order, in the theoretical discourse dominant in our century — from Max Weber to Talcott Parsons and to their more or less distant followers — the concept of exchange has become synonymous with *capitalistic commodity exchange*. In all such discourse 'exchange' is also ahistorically projected a long way back into the past, so that the defenders of commodity society should be able to argue (as Max Weber does, tendentiously contrasting 'modern capitalism' with the so-called 'age-old capitalist forms',[319] setting up thereby an ideologically convenient and closed circle) that there can be no alternative whatsoever to the mode of production and consumption embodied in the capitalist social-economic order, let alone a socialist one.

In truth, though, the question of exchange cannot be confined to the capitalist system of commodity exchange (be that 'modern' or 'age-old') without violating logic, notwithstanding the contingent fact that the commodity exchange relation experienced by us had acquired its dominant position in the course of modern history. It is quite fallacious to restrict the category of exchange even to the much more generalizable concept: the exchange of *products,* which embraces also the forms that cannot fit into the profit-oriented capitalist variety. It is therefore all the more problematical to indulge in the tendentious restriction of this fundamental category of societal reproduction to the exchange of *commodities,* just because the latter happens to be all-pervasive under the conditions of generalized commodity production, in capitalist society.

The core meaning of the term 'exchange' refers to humanity's metabolic interchange with nature, on the one hand, and to the exchange relations of the particular individuals among themselves, on the other — whatever might be the historically specific forms required to realize the envisaged objectives. In this sense, the category of exchange is inseparable from that of *mediation,* clearly indicating the *processual* character of what is really at issue. By contrast, the role assigned to *products* — not to mention the special case of capitalistically legitimated *commodities,* produced under the imperative of securing profit within the framework of ever-expanding exchange-value — can constitute only a subordinate moment in this complex of problems.

It is only because under the capitalist modality of metabolic exchange with nature the *objectification* of human powers necessarily assumes the form of *alienation* — subsuming productive activity itself under the power of a *reified objectivity,* capital — that 'exchange' can and must be reduced to its fetishistic material dimension and decreed to be identical to the eternalized commodity form. Yet, the primacy in this matter surely belongs to the active/productive side, irrespective of how deeply this circumstance may be hidden by the fetishism of commodity. For even the capitalist commodity must be first produced, through the interchange and exchange of a great multiplicity of activities, before it can enter the market, in direct pursuit of profit.

The radical categorial shift introduced by Marx in his discussion of the communal system does not concern exchange as such, in its inseparability from the *absolute* condition of mediation between humanity and nature on the one hand, and among the individuals themselves, on the other. Rather, it refers to the *historically unique* form in which mediatory exchange can fulfil its functions under the communal conditions of societal intercourse, when production is organized as directly social from the outset.

Accordingly, in striking contrast to commodity production and its fetishistic exchange relation, the historically novel character of the communal system defines itself through its practical orientation towards the *exchange of activities,* and not simply of *products.* The allocation of products, to be sure, arises from the communally organized productive activity itself, and it is expected to match the directly social character of the latter. However, the point in the present context is that in the communal type exchange relation the primacy goes to the self-determination and corresponding organization of the *activities* themselves in which the individuals engage, in accordance with their need as active human beings. The products constitute the subordinate moment in this type of exchange relation, making it therefore possible also to allocate in a radically different way the total disposable time of society, rather than being predetermined and utterly constrained in this respect by the primacy of the material productive targets, be they commodities or non-commodified products.

Understandably, it is not very easy to conceptualize the exchange relation in these terms. For the fetishism of commodity prevails under the rule of capital in such a way that *commodities* superimpose themselves on *need,* measuring and legitimating (or denying the legitimacy) of the latter. This is what we are accustomed to as the normative horizon of our everyday-life. The alternative would be, of course, to have the products themselves subjected to some meaningful criteria of assessment on the basis of which they would be produced in response to need, and above all in accord with the individuals' basic need for humanly fulfilling life-activity. Since, however, the last consideration cannot possibly enter the framework of capitalist cost-accounting, because the organization and exercise of humanly fulfilling life-activity is an inherently *qualitative* concern (the judges of which can only be the *individuals* themselves, rather than the idealized 'invisible hand'), we are not expected even to think about activities as rightfully belonging to the category of need. Naturally, even less are we expected to envisage the possibility of adopting the necessary practical measures through which we could reshape productive social intercourse on a qualitative basis, in harmony with the objectives which we, as associated producers, would set ourselves in order to gratify and further develop our needs and realize our aspirations.

The Marxian characterization of the communal exchange relation — according to which what is involved in it is not 'an exchange of exchange-values but of *activities,* determined by communal needs and communal purposes' — points to a fundamental reorientation of our long established societal reproduction process. At the same time it signals the social individuals' progressive emancipation from the structurally enforced constraints of the division of labour and of its quantitatively self-imposing law of value.

19.4.2

IN the historical epoch of transition the direct relevance of this radical reorientation of the exchange relation for the socialist project presents itself under two major aspects.

- First, in that the categorial shift from the exchange of products (and, of course, under capitalism: of commodified products) to the mediatory exchange of productive activities based on a viable measure — need — offers a way out of the destructive contradictions of reified objectification, when the inexorable self-expansion of exchange-value runs out of control, in the absence of effective limiting criteria or constraints (other than the structural crisis itself).

- And the second major aspect — beyond the contradictions of the capitalist order — directly concerns the prospects of the emancipatory enterprise itself. In this regard the urgency of the communal restructuring of the established productive practices arises from the sobering circumstance that the socialist undertaking cannot even begin to realize its fundamental objectives without successfully accomplishing at the same time the shift from the exchange of products — i.e. from a form of societal reproduction oriented towards, and strictly subordinated to, the achievement of preestablished material targets, as practised for centuries and deeply embedded in the productive structures and instrumental complexes which the postcapitalist society inherits from the past — to the exchange of genuinely *planned* and *self-managed* (as opposed to bureaucratically *commanded, from above*) productive activities.

The severe problems which transitional societies have to face in the course of changing the old mode of societal reproduction, in their effort to restructure the inherited institutional and instrumental complexes, become more intelligible in the light of the Marxian distinction between the communal type exchange and the dominant exchange relations of the last centuries. The greatest problem in this respect is that production oriented towards and determined by the exchange of products — be that under capitalism or in postcapitalist societies — is radically incompatible with real *planning*.

This condition is in fact aggravated in postrevolutionary — command type — economies. For the capitalist mode of production is at least able to operate a (no matter how problematical) *substitute* for economizing with the available material and labour resources, within its own terms of reference. It can do this in the form of a *post festum feed-back* through the *market,* on the basis of which capitalistically viable adjustments can be made in the operation of the affected productive enterprises, until the next round of problems arises, so as to activate again the same type of corrective mechanism.

By contrast, the command type economy instituted by Stalin represents a paradigm case of 'falling between two stools'. For by extending its authoritarian control over the exchange of products, it deprives the given reproductive system even of a limited feed-back mechanism, without creating at the same time the conditions of genuine *planning* through the necessary shift from the product-oriented *division of labour* and its exchange relation to the communal *organization of labour* aimed at the *exchange of activities.* This is how, as a bitter irony of history, after seventy years of command economy the limited feed-back mechanism of the capitalist market can reemerge as the ideal of 'market socialism', envisaging as the solution of the encountered problems and contradictions of postrevolutionary society the 'cost-efficient' ejection of millions of workers from the labour process.

The real difficulty is that, in order to make viable the postcapitalist alternative to its historical predecessor, it is not enough to switch from the market-allocated commodity system to the centrally controlled production and bureaucratic/iniquitous allocation of goods and services. The adoption of such practices in the immediate aftermath of the revolution is understandable to the extent that it corresponds to the line of least resistance, leaving the inherited division of labour in its structural parameters intact, despite the change of personnel. At the same time, however, a veritable vicious circle is created by following the line of least resistance. For, while on the one hand the retention of the structural division of labour and its product-oriented (even if not commodified) exchange relation in postcapitalist society can only yield a bureaucratically controlled command economy, the latter type of control, on the other hand, can only reinforce the hierarchical structural division of labour and its matching form of distribution.

Not surprisingly, therefore, the 'planning' system of the command economy — aimed at the centrally controlled production and allocation of resources — is in reality a, rather defective, *post festum* 'planning', and only in fiction a genuine social planning process. For the more or less arbitrarily (or 'voluntaristically') preestablished planning targets cannot be simply imposed on a recalcitrant social body. Indeed, in actuality the arbitrarily proclaimed plans of the command economy are as a rule forcibly revised (without publicly admitting it) as a result of the encountered failures. And the fact that such revisions must take place without the crutch of the capitalist feed-back mechanism of the market does not obliterate the structural similarity with regard to the fundamental characteristics of the two, on the surface diametrically opposed, 'planning' systems. For although they obviously differ in that one of them is centrally supervised and the other is not, nevertheless the substantive common traits of the two systems are:

- 1. the *post festum* character of their correctives, and
- 2. the imposition of the feasible correctives *from above* (in one case by the 'invisible hand' of the totalizing market,[320] and in the other case by the bureaucratic state authorities).

We can see here that Lukács's characterization of the Stalinist planning system as 'manipulative' is not very helpful. For it substitutes the vague generality of 'manipulation' (which can be applied to almost anything) to the tangible characteristics of an authoritarian mode of reproductive control which, in line with its historical predecessor, perpetuates the division of labour. And precisely because Lukács himself is quite uncritical with regard to the latter, he has to look for answers like 'manipulation' which he considers to be correctable by the application of the right methodological insight.

In truth, however, the retention of the hierarchical social division of labour in the — command type — postcapitalist economy brings with it the twofold determination of its planning process mentioned above. At the same time, the clearly identifiable *structural affinity* between the two dubious planning systems, both with regard to their *post festum* temporality and authoritarian mode of operation *from above*, helps to explain why the adoption of the line of least resistance should so fatefully lead from the inherited capitalist reproductive practices (in which living labour is of necessity subordinated to the projected commodity targets) to the authoritarian submission of labour to the preestablished material imperatives of the (Stalinist) command economy.

19.4.3

THE switch from the commodity- or product-oriented mediatory exchange relation to the communal system based on the exchange of activities requires a radical democratization of society in every respect.

The intermediary stages that could lead from the authoritarian reproductive practices (and corresponding structures) of the inherited commodity exchange system to a genuinely planned organization of labour *from below* (planned, that is, on the basis of the envisaged *exchange of activities*), are not at all feasible without a profound democratization of the postcapitalist mode of decision making. For although the bureaucratic command-type system can maintain its control over society when the reproduction process is managed on a product-oriented basis (to which living labour is necessarily subordinated), even though *commodity* production as such is left behind, the same system is totally powerless when it comes to planning the production and proper co-ordination of productive activities, together with their feasible level of attainment. The ultimate sanction of the command-type system — the threat or actual institution of labour camps — can only be *counter-productive* with regard to the productivity of labour, as the great historical tragedy of Stalin's 'socialism in one country' testifies.

The communal type production and exchange of activities envisaged by Marx — in which 'instead of a division of labour' (which must be tyrannically predetermined by the projected material targets) a 'planned *organization of labour*' (planned in accord with the needs and aspirations of the working subjects concerned) is the operative principle — can only be brought into existence by the individuals concerned. For they are the ones who are called upon to produce and exercise their own work-skills, to the full of their abilities, within the setting of a properly mediated and coordinated societal *self-management*.

This is why Lukács's advocacy of instituting 'a realistic division of labour between the party and the state' is very far indeed from the Marxian theoretical framework which he sincerely believes to champion in *The Present and Future of Democratization*. For, according to Marx, the task is not the reconciliation of postcapitalist society to the structural imperatives of the division of labour. On the contrary, it is the progressive overcoming of the latter through a conscious organization of labour, planned by the active working individuals themselves who reappropriate all those controlling functions which continue to be exercised by the party and the state under the (post-revolutionary) division of labour. Only in this way can they hope to emancipate themselves from the tyranny of time and from the all-quantifying and levelling law of value.

19.5 New meaning of the economy of time: quality-oriented regulation of the communal labour process

19.5.1

THE last point that must be discussed in the present context directly arises from the Marxian contraposition of the consciously planned communal organization of labour to the inherited division of labour, on the ground that the latter is inevitably predetermined by the 'rational' imperatives of ever-expanding exchange value. This issue is concerned with the *qualitative* dimension of the 'economy of time' and, as such, it can only be raised under the new historical circumstances when the formerly prevailing law of 'minimal time' is no longer required for the successful regulation of the social metabolic process.

The reorientation of labour practices in this spirit represents, again, a veritable categorial shift, like the earlier seen opposition between the commodity- or product-determined exchange relation and the communal exchange of activities. We shall have a closer look at this problem presently. But before we can do so, it is first necessary to quote the relevant passage from Marx's *Grundrisse* — which is somewhat selectively used by Lukács in *The Ontology of Social Being* — in its integrality. It reads as follows:

On the basis of *communal* production, the determination of *time* remains, of course, essential. The less time the society requires to produce wheat, cattle etc., the more time it wins for other production, material or mental. Just as in the case of an individual, the multiplicity of its development, its enjoyment and its activity depends on an *economization of time*. Economy of time, to this all economy ultimately reduces itself. Society likewise has to distribute its time in a purposeful way, in order to achieve a production adequate to its overall needs; just as the individual has to distribute his time correctly, in order to achieve knowledge in proper proportions or in order to satisfy the various demands on his activity. Thus, economy of time, along with the *planned distribution of labour time* among the various branches of production, remains the first economic law on the basis of *communal production*. It becomes law, there, to an even *higher degree*. However, this is *essentially different* from a measurement of exchange values (labour or products) by *labour time*. The labour of individuals in the same branch of work, and the various kinds of work, are different from one another not only quantitatively but also *qualitatively*. What does a solely *quantitative* differ- ence between things presuppose? The identity of their *qualities*. Hence the quanti- tative measure of labours presupposes the equivalence, the identity of their quality.[321]

As we can see, in Marx's view 'the planned distribution of labour time' is the salient feature of regulating the communal labour process. Moreover, such a genuinely planned distribution of society's total disposable time happens to be quite unique to the communal mode of production and exchange. For under the conditions when the capitalist division of labour prevails, the antagonistic structure of production and distribution imposes on society the law of value as a blind determination. Given the division of labour and the irreconcilable adversarial relationship between control and execution (capital and labour), the products emerging from the particular units of production must be first 'elevated to exchange values and exchanged as exchange values', before one can even imagine the chaotic multiplicity of socioeconomic interrelations as an integrated societal complex. In other words, under the conditions when the capitalistic division of labour prevails, only the law of value can regulate, in this blind fashion — 'behind the back' of the human agency involved, so to speak — the metabolic exchange of society with nature, on the one hand, and the unstable coalescence of the individuals into an antagonistically structured societal whole, on the other. This is why the *post festum* sociality of the commodity system, ruled by the law of value, cannot be even mentioned in the same breath with communal sociality, let alone identified with the latter.

As Marx rightly argues, no society can function without giving a proper consideration to the 'economy of time'. However, it makes a world of difference whether such consideration is *imposed* upon the society in question by a mecha- nism that asserts itself behind the backs of the producers (like the objective imperatives of the capitalist exchange relation), or whether the social individuals active in the communal system of production and distribution determine for themselves how they allocate the total *disposable time* of their society in fulfilment of their own needs and aspirations.

The term 'law' is used in very different ways in these two cases. When it is imposed by a blindly self-assertive mechanism, it is used by Marx as analogous to the natural law through which he likes to characterize the capitalist system. But there is another sense as well of 'law'. It stands for a regulatory framework or procedure devised by a human agency in furtherance of its chosen objectives.

It is this latter meaning — 'the law we give ourselves' — which is relevant in the context of the economic use of time under the conditions of the communal system. Accordingly, Marx insists that this kind of regulation of society's disposable time is *essentially different* from a measurement of exchange values (labour or products) by labour time'.

This train of thought is in full agreement with Marx's earlier quoted condemnation of the dehumanizing rule of quantity over labour under the conditions of capitalist industry. For

> If the mere *quantity* of labour functions as a measure of value regardless of *quality*, it presupposes that ... labour has been equalized by the *subordination of man to the machine* or by the extreme *division of labour;* that *men are effaced by their labour;* ... *Time is everything, man is nothing;* he is at most *time's carcass. Quality* no longer matters. *Quantity* alone decides everything; hour for hour; day for day.[322]

Thus, according to Marx, there can be no question of emancipating society from the rule of capital without addressing ourselves to the difficult task of superseding the division of labour. A task which in its turn cannot be even conceived, let alone accomplished, without consciously restructuring the labour process in its entirety on a *qualitative* basis, so that human beings should cease to play the role necessarily assigned to them by capital — for as long as the capital system itself survives, in post-capitalist societies too — as 'time's carcass'. This is why the 'old Marx' of the *Grundrisse* and *Capital* cannot possibly abandon the position he assumed on these matters in his earlier writings.

19.5.2

IN the ideological discourse dominant in our own epoch there is a mystifying tendency to identify exchange as such with *commodity-exchange*. At the same time, we are often presented with similarly bewildering attempts to establish a necessary correlation between the economy of time and the *market*. This is totally unjustifiable for a variety of reasons.

- First, because the proclamation of this linkage arbitrarily precludes the possibility of operating a rational system of allocation of the available human and material resources outside the chaotic, and even in its own terms of reference in many ways wasteful, distributive and corrective mechanism of the market.
- Second, because the market-determined allocation of time can only operate on the basis of enforcing the requirement of *minimum time,* deciding in this crude way not only the success or failure of competing commodities, but altogether the modality of society's metabolic exchange with nature, and the legitimation or callous denial of the needs of its members. Market-oriented management of labour time is quite incapable of addressing the much more difficult question, concerned with the total available time of the social body, including that portion of it which cannot be successfully exploited within its reifying framework for the purposes of profitable commodity production.
- Third, because the development of society's productive powers in the form of science and technology — i.e. the cumulative objectification of living labour and of the collective mind, across centuries, in the form of (beneficially or destructively) usable knowledge and its instruments — makes it not only obsolete to remain locked within the confines of directly exploitable mini-

mum time; it also creates the danger of a total breakdown of the social metabolism by activating, through the profit-oriented irrational 'corrective' of the capitalist market mechanism, the stark prospects of an ultimately incorrigible *'structural unemployment'*.

- Fourth, because the very notion of 'economy of time' — even in its narrowest terms of reference — becomes utterly problematical with the development of capitalism. Inevitably, under the rule of capital this shift must assume the form of an extreme contradiction. For the capitalist system of cost-accounting can *never* completely renounce the imposition of minimum time on the production process. It must continue the maximum feasible exploitation of the labour force that remains in active employment, notwithstanding all the dangers implicit in the rising structural unemployment. At the same time, however, in conformity to the imperative to decrease the rate of utilization, the drive for economizing (characteristic of the ascending phase of capitalist development) is progressively displaced by the tendency to ever-increasing *wastefulness* which asserts itself not only in relation to goods, services and productive machinery, but also with regard to the total labour force of society. Thus, the ruthless imposition of the economy of time on the active labour force goes hand in hand with the capital system's total disregard for all those — no matter how large their number — who have to suffer the indignity of *enforced idleness* as their 'fate', because it suits the absurd wastefulness of the prevailing profit-accountancy.

- And fifth, because the increasing trend of capital's transnational articulation and monopolistic centralization turns the market itself (as we know it today) into an utterly problematical and ultimately threatened structure. This trend carries with it very serious implications for the position of labour and of its traditional defensive organizations, originally constituted within the framework of nationally centered capitalistic market society. The attacks on the earlier legally safeguarded institutional position of labour which we could witness during the last two decades in all capitalistically advanced countries, mounted at times — significantly — by Labour Governments (like Harold Wilson's administration in Britain, responsible for an ill-fated attempt to castrate the British Labour Unions by means of its notorious legislative project called 'In Place of Strife': fully implemented later by Conservative Governments), were manifestations of the underlying tensions and of the need for major structural readjustments. As we have seen above, the authoritarianism implicit in these developments represents not only a blatant attempt to 'roll back' labour's gains obtained during the last century and a half (to rôll back, that is, in the form in which such a strategic objective can be reconciled with the expansionary needs of capitalist consumer society), but also a design to impose on the 'metropolitan' labour force the labour discipline which transnational capital can operate in the 'Third World' under its control. Thus, far from amounting to a real advancement, the 'economy of time' that can be squeezed out in this way from the various sections of the global labour force is tantamount to an all-round intensification of the rate of exploitation under the conditions of 'advanced capitalism'.

IN all these respects the economy of time, in its crudely *quantifying* modality, imposes itself as a blind economic law on commodity society, even if it can only do so in a contradictory and antagonistic form. *Qualitative* considerations are radically incompatible with such an operation of the economic law of value intrinsic to the capitalist division of labour. For the law of value that regulates the exchange relation in commodity society must assert itself in the form of an *averaging and levelling mechanism* which categorically overrules, through the intervention of its 'invisible hand', all 'erratic' potential departures from the underlying material imperatives of the capital system.

By contrast, the 'economic law' discussed by Marx in the context of the communal system of production and distribution is characterized as an inherently *qualitative* regulator.

It could not be otherwise with reference to the key concept on the basis of which the social metabolism of this new reproductive sytem is made intelligible, namely, the *total disposable time* of society. For if the wealth of the communal type social order is to be measured in terms of its total disposable time, rather than in that of the fetishistically quantified *products* obtained through imposing the requirement of minimum time on the working individuals, in that case the concept of 'economic law' itself mentioned by Marx acquires a meaning qualitatively different from the law of value that prevails through the exchange relation of commodity society. 'The law we give ourselves', in order to regulate the reproductive interchanges of a truly cooperative system, is in no way comparable to the self-imposing mechanism of the natural law which can take no notice of the needs, desires and aspirations of the human individuals. In contrast, the adoption of a genuinely economizing (as opposed to profit-oriented and quite wastefully 'economical') regulator of the social metabolism by the associated producers is meant to indicate that

- (1) new areas of activity (and 'free activity') are opened up, thanks to the multiplication of society's 'total disposable time' for productive purposes in a system oriented towards the *exchange of activities,* once the viability of the activities themselves in which the individuals engage is no longer judged on the basis of narrow 'economic' (i.e. profit-oriented) criteria; only in this way would it be possible to achieve the satisfaction of needs whose existence cannot be acknowledged from the perspective, and under the pressure, of the quasi-mechanical constraint of *minimum time* (which must always remain the regulating principle of commodity-oriented production);
- (2) in close conjunction with the previous point, thanks to the greatly expanded and redefined total *disposable time* of society, time can be allocated for the production of goods and services on a *qualitative* basis, determined by consciously adopted *priorities,* irrespective of the 'man-hours' required for the realization of the chosen objectives, instead of the objectives and priorities themselves being determined on the ground of whatever can be obtained through the utilization of the readily exploitable time of the producers. This qualitative shift cannot be simply the result of an increase in productivity. The capital system is perfectly capable of that within its own terms of reference. The possibility of regulating production without undue time-constraints, in tune with consciously chosen priorities, positively arises from formerly inaccessible 'time-zones', i.e. from the domain of capitalistically non-profitable and therefore necessarily untapped human resources. This is how the total disposable time of the associated producers can be qualitatively

redefined. In its new modality, under the communal system of production and consumption, total disposable time becomes expendable on a multiplicity of activities which could not possibly enter into the earlier enforced economic equations, no matter how acute the need. Only within such parameters is it possible to envisage also a radical redefinition of *utility* — under the capital system not only materially constraining but also alienating and reifying — in the sense expressed by Marx in *The Poverty of Philosophy* quoted above. A sense — according to which the time of production devoted to an article is determined by the degree of its social utility, instead of the tyranny of minimum time being allowed to pronounce the final judgement in matters of social utility — which would make eminently good sense to all working individuals if it was not for the internalized dictates of capitalist cost-accountancy.

To be sure, the reorientation of the labour process in the spirit of these qualitative considerations is quite unthinkable without progressively overcoming the division of labour and its law of value through the material mediations of the transitional society. And by the same token, if in the proposed emancipatory strategies the division of labour and the law of value are not radically challenged, very serious consequences follow from such a departure from the original socialist project. For in that case there can be no room left for a vision of the communal labour process, as characterized by Marx, in which *quality* — and corresponding human *needs* — play the deciding role, and the quantitative allocation of time loses its formerly overpowering role as the uncontrollable *determinant* of the social metabolic process. It is, therefore, by no means surprising that Lukács cuts out Marx's crucial references to quality and to the assessment of time as 'essentially different from the measurement of exchange values' from the passage he quotes from the *Grundrisse,* attempting to use the truncated lines in support of his own ideas concerning the permanence of the division of labour and of its law of value.

19.5.3

AS far as Lukács is concerned, the Marxian considerations of quality (without which exemplary works of art, or morally exemplary actions, both advocated by him, would be inconceivable) are right and proper beyond the 'sphere of necessity', in relation to the 'realm of freedom'. For Marx, by contrast, they must be an integral part of the adopted material mediatory measures which society needs for restructuring the postcapitalist labour process itself under all its aspects, if there is to be any hope of emancipating the social individuals from the rule of capital and its concomitant hierarchical division of labour.

Marx envisages as the material basis of the emancipated society a world of *'abundance'*, i.e. conditions under which the struggle for the necessarily iniquitous appropriation of scarce resources no longer determines the life-activity of individuals. As Marx argues with reference to the universal development of the productive forces and the possibility of new human relations on that basis:

> this development of productive forces (which at the same time implies the actual empirical existence of men in their world-historical, instead of local, being) is an absolutely necessary practical premiss, because without it privation, *want* is merely made general, and with want the *struggle for necessities* would begin again, and all the

old filthy business would necessarily be restored; and furthermore, because only with this universal development of productive forces is a universal intercourse between men established, ... making *each nation dependent on the revolutions of the others,* and finally puts world-historical, empirically universal individuals in place of local ones. Without this, (1) communism could only exist as a local phenomenon; (2) the forces of intercourse themselves could not have developed as universal, hence unendurable powers: they would have remained home-bred 'conditions' surrounded by superstition; and (3) each extension of intercourse would abolish local communism. Empirically *communism is only possible as the act of the dominant peoples 'all at once' and simultaneously* which presupposes the *universal development of the productive forces* and the *world intercourse* bound up with them.[323]

Thus, according to Marx, there can be no 'socialism in one country'; nor is it possible to establish a socialist order without overcoming privation, want, and scarcity by a highly productive socioeconomic system, capable of satisfying the needs of *all* its members.

Clearly, however, it is quite inconceivable to overcome *scarcity* as such — and all that 'old filthy business' that goes with it — within the confines of the law of value and the corresponding rule of quantity. For without the conscious adoption of quality, in Marx's sense, as the measure capable of setting meaningful limits to what would otherwise amount to no more than a potentially most wasteful pursuit of wealth, irreversible progress towards the 'new historic form' can only be projected as a dream.

The actual realization of the society of abundance requires the reorientation of the social reproductive process in such a way that the communally produced goods and services can be fully shared, and not individualistically wasted, by all those who participate in directly social production and consumption. Short of this kind of conscious self-regulation, the resources and products of even the richest possible society must remain trapped within the vicious circle of *self-renewing and self-imposing scarcity* even in terms of the unrestrained appetites of relatively limited groups of people, let alone in relation to the totality of individuals.

Naturally, the full realization of this Marxian vision calls for the historically feasible articulation of the necessary material mediations in their global context, leading from the division of labour under the rule of capital (in whatever form) to a new type of communal existence that can only emerge from the process of progressive restructuring undertaken by the historically arising transitional societies. Nevertheless, even if the *full* realization of this vision — predicating the necessity of a *global* transformation — might take a very long time to come about, the practical steps required for advancement in the envisaged direction can be pursued in any postrevolutionary society, even in a relatively limited setting, without waiting for the radical reversal of the existing power relations between capital and labour on a global scale.

The retention of the global perspective, as spelled out by Marx in the last quotation, is of course necessary as the orienting framework of the practical steps and strategies through which the particular transitional societies can attempt to realize their feasible mediatory objectives. At the same time, though, progressively instituting the necessary shift towards a qualitative determination of the transitional societies' productive targets and distributive procedures —

through a radical reassessment of the prevailing rates of utilization which were adopted in the past under the constraints of the law of value — is practicable 'here and now'. The specific terms of reference of this shift can be spelled out as tangible material and cultural objectives, promising not only a, however modest, advancement in the direction of the rather distant aim of a global communal society, but also a much more realistic improvement in the individuals' standard of living, 'here and now', than what might be obtained by patching up the inherited structures of the division of labour.

The premises adopted by Lukács as a result of the great historical disappointments of the postrevolutionary decades — i.e. the earlier mentioned premisses of 'socialism in one country' and the permanence of the division of labour on the basis of which he advocates the institution of a 'realistic division of labour between the party and the state' — offer a very different perspective for solving the encountered, apparently chronic, problems. However, once we accept the structural constraints that inevitably go with such premisses, only the moral imperatives of an abstract ethical discourse postulated by Lukács remain as our slender, materially quite unsubstantiated, hope to overcome the contradictions of the present.

CHAPTER TWENTY

THE LINE OF LEAST RESISTANCE AND THE
SOCIALIST ALTERNATIVE

FOR a long time — and especially for a decade after the Second World War — it used to be taken for granted on the communist left that after the 'victory of socialism' in the greater part of the world we shall all live in an irreversible socialist order. This view represented a terrible impoverishment of the Marxian project. For by the postulated 'victory of socialism' was only meant the *political overthrow of capitalism,* on the model of the Russian revolution. The most grotesque and macabre version of this voluntaristic reductionism was expressed in the earlier mentioned insane projection by Stalin's favoured successor, Malenkov, according to which 'after the Third World War', in line with what happened after the First and the Second, the people of the whole world would belong to the 'socialist camp'. 'Historical inevitability' unfolding in this way was supposed to signal the beginning of a superior stage of historical development, applauded as such by the postcapitalist personifications of capital in total blindness to the fact that in actuality, under the projected circumstances, nothing would be left even to light a prehistoric camp fire.

It has been often asserted that the capitalist order, and of course the class conscious private capitalist guardians of it, will not leave the historical stage without a fight. This prognosis is undoubtedly correct, even if it greatly understates the difficulties and contradictions that must be confronted after a successful political revolution. For the most intractable obstacles are not erected by the personifications of capital, but by the imperatives of the capital system itself which produce and reproduce the different types of capital's necessary personifications in accordance with the changing historical conditions. Accommodation by the representatives of labour to the *line of least resistance,* which we have historically experienced at great cost to the socialist movement, is inseparable from this perverse *systemic* determination of the margin of transformatory action. This is what must be challenged if there is to be any hope of success on the originally envisaged road to socialist emancipation. For — in the light of 20th century historical disappointments — following the line of least resistance can only lead to the revitalization of capital in crisis and to the self-paralysis of its historical alternative.

In different though complementary ways both the socialdemocratic/reformist and the Stalinist — including the so-called 'de-Stalinized' — parties of the labour movement followed the line of least resistance, ending up with an equally disastrous collapse in their sphere of operation even within their own terms of reference. The roots of this historical failure were common, in that the strategic orientation of both wings of the labour movement failed to challenge the systemic determinations of capital's mode of social metabolic control. Socialdemocratic reformism had to fail because it wanted to reform capitalism while uncritically accepting its structural constraints. Thus in a self-contradictory way it wanted to institute a reformist transformation of capitalism — at first even to the extent of turning it as time went by into socialism — without changing its capitalist substance. Likewise, the postrevolutionary socioeconomic system, as we have seen above, remained trapped by the alienating structural shackles of capital as such, even though it had instituted a postcapitalist mode of extracting surplus-labour by direct political means at an enforced rate, bringing into existence a new type of enforcer of the time-imperative, as befitting the capital system in all of its historically feasible forms. This is also why all of the post-Stalin reform attempts had to fail, including Gorbachev's so-called 'perestroika'. The self-contradiction of such postrevolutionary reform attempts was no less acute than what characterized their socialdemocratic counterparts in the West. For they tried to 'restructure' the existing order without changing its hierarchical and exploitative command structure at all. It was therefore only appropriate that the way in which the parties of both the reformist and the once communist wing of the labour movement 'returned to the fold' had obliterated all of their original differences. Significantly, they have found their common denominator by becoming bourgeois liberal parties — in the East and in the West alike, including the former Italian and French Communist Parties — on the common ground of embracing capitalism and its 'market society' as the unchallengeable horizon of social life.

However, this turn of events cannot be considered the end of the road. For the capitulation of the traditional parties of the left — which followed the blind alley of the line of least resistance during the greater part of their existence — has not solved a single contradiction of the capital system. On the contrary, the ever more compromising accommodation and the final capitulation not only of labour's reformist but also its once radical political parties is the manifestation of the system's deepening contradictions. These contradictions progressively narrowed down and ultimately eliminated — in the interest of preserving capital's mode of control under the conditions of the system's structural crisis — the margin of opposition and the conquest of even limited gains for labour. Nevertheless, it would be foolish to assume that the working class will simply resign itself to being robbed of its past gains by the capitulation of its own parties to the vested interests of the established order. As Daniel Singer rightly remarked on the conflicts arising from the fact that the former parties of the left in Britain, France and Italy 'have gone far on the road of surrender',[324] following that course in the future is likely to encounter increasing resistance. Thus 'the passionate, powerful reaction to the first frontal attack on the welfare state — the attack against pensions in Italy — suggests that the task [of those who follow the course of surrender] will not be easy'.[325] In Italy, as a response to the attack on the pension rights of labout, with the telling complicity of the 'left' parties, we have already witnessed 'a series of strikes and the biggest demo in Rome's history'.[326]

At the same time, when the traditional political parties of labour turn their back on their own past and embark on a transparent defence of the ruling order, the activation of capital's absolute limits threatens the very survival of humankind. Obviously, this makes the project of socialist emancipation that much more difficult today. For the class conscious resistance of capital's personifications against all attempts at introducing meaningful change, strengthened by the frightening inertia of the established social reproductive order itself, is greatly aggravated by the urgency of time and the catastrophic prospects for the future unless the destructive forces are successfully confronted. For the only thing that can be taken for granted about the not too distant future is that the need for the inauguration of the socialist alternative on a global scale is likely to arise under the most grievous historical circumstances, when capital's mode of social metabolic control can no longer fulfil even the primary reproductive functions required of it.

Accordingly, the challenge facing socialists will present itself as the necessity to put the pieces together and make a workable social metabolic order out of the ruins of the old. The idea advocated by some former socialists — that the road to radical change will be opened up by a big labourite electoral victory, willingly conceded by the repressive material and political forces of capital as a clear mandate for socialist transformation on account of the size of such an electoral victory — belongs to the realm of pure fantasy.

In the end what decides these issues is the *internal dynamics of development* embracing the capital system as a whole. This is what gave a new lease of life to capital in the last third of the 19th century, extending its reproductive viability for nearly a century thereafter, until the onset of the system's structural crisis. Those conditions, however, have fundamentally changed for the worse as regards capital's global order. For precisely the once highly favourable internal dynamics of development has become unsustainable on the necessary objective premises of this wastefully expansion-oriented and accumulation-driven mode of social metabolic control. And that defect of *internal dynamics* cannot be compensated for in the longer run by the *external remedial devices* of theoretical baboonery and corresponding practices.

As things stand today, despite the shallow triumphalism of not so long ago, there can be no doubt about the gravity of the structural crisis affecting capital's mode of control at its roots; nor indeed about the dangers emanating from such a historically unprecedented structural crisis for the survival of humanity. The time-scale of capital's irreversible destructiveness resulting in a catastrophe can no longer be complacently measured in centuries, for the end of which the apologists of the system would postulate—as they invariably and gratuitously did in the past and still do today — the happy resolution of the existing problems. Thus the rearticulation of the socialist movement as the hegemonic alternative to capital's long entrenched exploitative and mystifying reproductive order — a positive alternative inconceivable on the line of least resistance — is both timely and literally vital in importance.

20.1 Myth and reality of the market

20.1.1

ONE of the most effective mystifications of the capital system on which the claims to its unchallengeable validity are erected by its defenders is the greatly misrepresented market.

That the various trends of bourgeois political economy should glorify such a market is well understandable. For by the claimed 'naturalness' of capitalistic exchange relations arbitrarily projected into the past, in the service of the system which they want to eternalize, they can construct a vicious circle from which there can be no escape. Since no developed social reproductive order can function without some form of exchange, the sleight of hand by which exchange relation *as such* is tendentiously — and circularly — defined so as to foreshadow, from time immemorial, its capitalistic variety, it can be readily concluded that there can be no alternative to the rule of capital as the mode of controlling social metabolic reproduction in general. What is, however, very far from understandable is why should anyone who claims to be even just vaguely sympathetic, let alone truly committed to, socialism, accept the horizons of the vicious circle in which capital necessarily maintains its stranglehold over labour and drives humanity towards self-destruction. Yet, as the disastrous vicissitudes of so-called 'market socialism' testify, the implosion of the Soviet type postcapitalist system had a great deal to do with the total blindness of the advocates of 'market socialism' towards the nature of the exchange relations which they wanted to impose on the labour force. Indeed, as another twist in this baffling tale, they put forward their — quickly deflated — claims for instituting a 'social market' in the name of providing the real *'guarantee for socialism and democracy'*, as opposed to the 'command economy'. In doing so they ignored — or as they themselves badly tainted former 'command economists' deliberately disregarded — that their intellectual ancestor in wanting to impose 'discipline' for greater 'economic efficiency' by means of commodity exchange and controlled market relations was none other than their once much adored *'great Stalin'* himself, as we have seen above.

Naturally, embracing 'the market' as the regulator of socioeconomic interchange carried far-reaching implications for the postcapitalist societies involved, leading to the — at first timid but soon enough quite open — advocacy of capitalist restoration. Thus, interviewed only a few months after the so-called 'velvet revolution':

'A market economy without any adjectives'. That is what Mr Vaclav Klaus insists is needed in Czechoslovakia, where he has been finance minister since early December. Not for him the 'social market economy', a phrase being bandied about elsewhere in Eastern Europe. This soft-spoken but smilingly confident 48-year-old economist believes that half measures will be worse than useless. To bring the market in quickly, Mr Klaus and his ministry are preparing a slew of new laws to permit western-style financial markets. ... Mr Klaus and his fellow Czechoslovak delegates in Davos were anxious to distance themselves from the 1968 reforms. But they were happy to cosy up to western business. Equity capital and not aid is what they are after, and they appear unfussed about whether it arrives through joint ventures, greenfield investments or direct purchases of Czech firms. As a good Friedmanite, Mr Klaus shows no interest in dictating the outcome of market forces: his role is to keep prices stable while business does its work.[327]

The Czech finance minister's cynical sense of realism, for which he was quickly rewarded with the Prime Ministership of his country, contrasted favourably with *The Economist's* zealous propagandistic myth-mongering about the market. For the Leader writers of the London weekly were mixing naked class interest, to be asserted against the Western labour force, with unctuous preaching over what the market should do in order to help the 'poor East European workers'. This is how they have presented their curious mixture of hypocritical 'bleeding heart' rhetorics and anti-labour ferocity:

> the [European] Community should give the Czechoslovaks, Hungarians and Poles complete freedom, not just to come and visit (they already have visa-free travel to most EC countries), but to come and work. Allowing East Europeans to work in the West would help *keep down EC wage costs,* and it would also be a fine way of educating ex-communists in the ways of capitalism and of helping them *amass the savings* needed to *rebuild their economies.*[328]

If 'O' level maths students made their calculations in this way, they would be no doubt failed in their exams, and quite rightly so. The Editors and Leader writers of *The Economist,* however, who make their mighty profits from pontificating about the world economy on the basis of such a level of arithmetical and economic skills, can get away with the most absurd fantasies and projections, just because their propaganda exercises are conceived from the standpoint of agressive bourgeois class consciousness. Thus we are expected to believe that the miserably low wages which East European workers would have to earn in the West, in order to make sense of the *Economist's* desire to 'keep down EC wage costs', would be more than sufficient not only to sustain them in Western hostels, as well as their families at home, but on top of all that also for 'amassing the savings needed to rebuild their economies'. Not to mention the fact that unemployment in OECD countries is well in excess of 40 million: a figure to which also the many millions of people who can get only part-time and casual work must be added in order to have a true picture, completed with the necessary correction of cynically falsified government statistics. One can only wonder, in amazement, where would the countless millions of East European workers (who in the view of *The Economist* should become unemployed for the sake of 'rebuilding their economies') find work in the West if the local labour force is unable to find it? In any case, there is no need at all for the advocated 'fine way of educating ex-communists in the ways of capitalism'. As it happens, East European workers are receiving that 'fine education' in great abundance already in their home countries.

The reality of the market is, of course, very different from its mythical images. All those in postcapitalist societies who once believed in the fairy-tale of benevolent marketization had to be very quickly disappointed. A good illustration of what the capitalist market really amounted to in relation to the East was provided by the violent protest against the attempted Russian access to EC fish markets. For when Russian trawlers unloaded their catch at the fish market of Grimsby, in Northern England, diesel oil was poured on it by their would-be 'trading partners', so as to render it unsaleable. Similar measures greeted the attempted import of meat and agricultural products to EC countries from Eastern Europe, including even minute quantities of raspberries from Poland. Nor do such conflicts exhaust themselves in confrontations between the EC and the former postcapitalist countries of the East. They erupt at increasing frequency among the members of the 'European Union', despite its fancy new name. In this respect it is enough to think of the 'lamb war' between France and England, the 'fish war' between England, Spain, France, and Portugal, as well as the 'wine and tomato war' between France and Italy. Indeed, much more seriously, antagonisms surface on an incomparably larger scale between the US and Japan and between the US and the European Union. The conflict between the US and Japan assumes many different forms, and refuses to go away despite all attempts at reaching some sort of compromise. As to the contradictions between the US and the European Union, the Airbus and the GATT negotiations offered some graphic examples in the recent past, at times encapsulated in the words of official spokespersons with brutal openness. Thus on the 9th of June 1991, on the 'Money Programme' of BBC 2, concerned with the conflicts surrounding the European Airbus project, the top official in charge of the commercial airlines division of the American Department of Commerce declared: 'In our experience a short, well-fought trade war can generate a long and prosperous trade peace', meaning, of course, 'on American terms'. Even more menacingly, at the time of the GATT negotiations, the US Chief negotiator, Mrs Carla Hills — President Bush's Mickey Kantor — stated: 'We are determined to open the door in defence of our business interests. We shall do it through negotiations, if we can, but if we cannot, we are going to do it *with crowbars*'. Nothing could be clearer than that.

In contrast to its mythology, the reality of the market means more or less naked power relations and ultimately irreconcilable conflicts. This can become only aggravated with the ongoing concentration and centralization of capital and the inexorable trend towards monopolistic and quasi-monopolistic development. The stakes are becoming constantly higher and the position of the 'smaller players' constantly worse. British Telecom — a giant company — has an annual turnover in excess of £13 billion and a profit of over £3 billion, thanks to its monopolistic position in Britain. And yet, it did not succeed in winning the huge contract serving the Anglo/Dutch giant company, UNILEVER. The US 'big player' AT&T — an even bigger company than British Telecom — had won it, well illustrating how immense must be the resources at the disposal of the competing forces in order to stand a chance of success in the unfolding confrontations. A far cry indeed from the piddling economic funds which were supposed to be derived from the cost-cutting yet generously repatriated wages of *Gastarbeitern* from former postcapitalist countries, as postulated by the London *Economist's* fairy-tale about 'rebuilding the economies of Eastern Europe' to the point of becoming 'healthy competitors' in the global capital system.

20.1.2

Few people denounced the 'self-regulating market' with greater passion in the 20th century than Karl Polányi. In an eloquent passage of his book, *The Great Transformation*, he argued that

> To allow the market mechanism to be sole director of the fate of human beings and their natural environment, indeed, even of the amount and use of purchasing power, would result in the demolition of society. For the alleged commodity 'labour power' cannot be shoved about, used indiscriminately, or even left unused, without affecting also the human individual who happens to be the bearer of this peculiar commodity. In disposing of a man's labour power the system would, incidentally, dispose of the physical, psychological, and moral entity 'man' attached to that tag. Robbed of the protective covering of cultural institutions, human beings would perish from the

effects of social exposure; they would die as the victims of acute social dislocation through vice, perversion, crime, and starvation. Nature would be reduced to its elements, neighbourhoods and landscapes defiled, rivers polluted, military safety jeopardized, the power to produce food and raw materials destroyed. Finally, the market administration of purchasing power would periodically liquidate business enterprise, for shortages and surfeits of money would prove as disastrous to business as floods and droughts in primitive society. Undoubtedly, labour, land, and money markets are essential to a market economy. But no society could stand the effects of such a system of crude fictions even for the shortest stretch of time unless its human and natural substance as well as its business organization was protected against the ravages of this satanic mill.[329]

The Great Transformation was first published in 1944, by which time the defeat of Fascism looked a certainty. This made the author nourish great hope for the unfolding changes, adding to a later edition of his book in an optimistic mood that

> The removal of control of money from the market is being accomplished in all countries in our day. ... From the viewpoint of human reality that which is restored by the disestablishment of the commodity fiction lies in all directions of the social compass. In effect, the disintegration of a uniform market economy is already giving rise to a variety of new societies. Also, the end of market society means in no way the absence of markets. These continue, in various fashions, to ensure the freedom of the consumer, to indicate the shifting of demand, to influence producers' income, and to serve as an instrument of accountancy, while ceasing altogether to be an organ of economic self-regulation. ... Out of the ruins of the Old World, cornerstones of the New can be seen to emerge: economic collaboration of governments and the liberty to organize national life at will. Under the constrictive system of free trade neither of these possibilities could have been conceived of, thus excluding a variety of methods of co-operation between nations. While under market economy and the gold standard the idea of federation was justly deemed a nightmare of centralization and uniformity, the end of market economy may well mean effective co-operation with domestic freedom.[330]

Most noble in intent, this prognostication proved to be extremely premature.[331] For the monstrous 'satanic mill' which the author of *The Great Transformation* wanted to see humanity rescued from was in reality the *capital system* itself, of which the 'self-regulating market' was only a transient and subordinate — if necessary to a major extent alterable — moment. It was this expansion-oriented and accumulation driven reproductive system, finding itself in ever deepening crisis, which not only enslaved humankind in its 'satanic mill' but also directly threatened it with destruction. The earlier discussed correctives introduced by the different types of personification of capital, in order to overcome that crisis, failed to achieve their objective, thereby making the danger of humanity's destruction which Polányi feared and passionately castigated that much more acute. He repeatedly insisted that 'an industrial society can afford to be free' and that 'such a society can afford to be both just and free'.[332] The trouble is, though, that the industrial society of the capital system, in any one of its historically feasible varieties, cannot afford to be either just or free. The more or less self-regulating market is an essential constituent only of that variety of the capital system in which surplus-labour is extracted with overwhelmingly economic means, but not in those in which surplus-labour extraction is controlled through primarily political forms of enforcement. However, as the troubled history of the twentieth century testifies, the politically regulated system cannot offer a greater reassurance for the survival of humankind than any of the capitalist varieties. In the meantime, the implosion of postcapitalist societies has underlined that a veritable epochal shift is needed in order to be able to leave behind the long-drawn-out historical phase of the capital system, whether the latter imposes itself through the exchange relations of the capitalist market or in any other form.

20.1.3

THE favourite device used by the apologists of the capitalist market is to link it to the postulated *'profit motive'*, said to be implanted in human beings by nature. In this way they claim to establish two axiomatic truths and the unalterable conditions corresponding to them. First, that the economic institutions resting on the 'profit motive' are *natural,* constituting thereby the vital objective ground and framework of reproductive activity which could be altered only by violating nature itself, and would be therefore necessarily condemned to fail. And second, that the required conformity to their postulated 'nature' defines and circumscribes the horizon of *'economic rationality'* to which the question of what may or may not be considered legitimate human aspirations must be subordinated. For no one in possession of the human 'faculty of reason' — rhetorically expressed also as 'no one in their right mind' — should quarrel with the authority of nature itself.

The fact that historical evidence refutes this fictitious account of *nature,* as well as the bastardized notion of *rationality* derived from it, carries no weight whatsoever in the view of those whose vested interests dictate the apology of the capital system at any cost. Also, the argument that the fateful subordination of human behaviour to the pursuit of the claimed 'economic rationality' — directly equated with the prevalence of the 'profit motive' — is bound to destroy the elementary conditions of social metabolic reproduction, fares no better. For even if it is admitted that there might be some problems lying ahead in the future — which is hardly ever done, in view of the extremely short-term temporality compatible with the standpoint of capital, coupled with the often repeated false deduction according to which 'the encountered difficulties always worked out in the past, and therefore they are going to be resolved also in the future'— all critical scrutiny of the ruling order is in the end blindly dismissed. The apologetic argument used for brushing aside our vital concerns is that the 'purely hypothetical threat' of the destructive consequences arising from the ongoing interference with nature on a vast scale must be overruled by the absolute imperative of regulating socioeconomic interchange as befits the determinations of 'human nature' and the now successfully pursued 'economic rationality' corresponding to it.

Yet, a closer examination of the hypostatized 'profit motive' reveals that not only is its historical dimension obliterated, depriving the arguments built upon it even of their rather limited historical validity, but the actual relationship between profit and productive activity is turned completely upside down by its champions. For even in the capitalist variety of the capital system, where profit plays an important role, the *primary determination* is not profit — let alone the individual capitalist's 'profit motive' — but the *expansionary imperative* of the system which cannot successfully reproduce itself unless it can do so on a constantly extended scale. Thus the appearance of the 'profit motive' is rather a consequence of the system's inner determinations than their determining cause, even if a dialectical reciprocity prevails for a determinate period of time once the individual pursuit of profit is in operation. In other words, it is because the capital system as such must be always *expansion-oriented and accumulation-driven* that — under *specific historical circumstances,* when for the socioeconomic reproductive system of capital in all of its known and feasible varieties absolutely necessary *personification of capital* assumes the private capitalist form — the imperative of *accumulation and expansion* (the real driving force of the system) can be pictured, from the standpoint of the individual capitalists, as their motivation for 'personal profit', i.e. as the 'profit motive'. But it is ludicrous to deduce from this, as Max Weber has done in his transparent attempt to refute Marx by turning his theory upside down and fictionalizing the formation of 'modern capitalism' — set by Weber with eternalizing ideological eagerness against the arbitrarily assumed background of the 'age-old capitalist forms', as mentioned above — that the established order of social metabolic control had arisen from the mysterious 'spirit of protestantism' which conveniently metamorphosed into the profit-oriented 'entrepreneurial spirit'.

The function of this kind of capital apologetic is to eliminate the historical dimension — as Weber and his followers are determined to do — even where it stares them in the face. For the immense historical transformations which have taken place under the impact of capitalistic developments cannot be simply denied; nor indeed need to be denied, as far as the standpoint of victorious capital is concerned, inasmuch as they lead to the present. What must be, however, categorically denied, from the same standpoint, is that all this could be otherwise in the future. It must be denied, no matter how inhuman, enslaving (in Weber's words permanently 'iron-cage-imposing'), and potentially catastrophic the conditions of capital's continued rule. Thus the *human agency* involved in all historical transformations must be eliminated from the stage with the help of sheer mystification, attributing the change witnessed in the past to the gratuitously and circularly hypostatized 'spirit of capitalism'. In this way, dealing with the historical origin of capitalism resembles the famous card trick: 'now you see it, now your don't'. You see it for a brief moment, as protestantism — an obviously historical phenomenon — is equated with 'the spirit of capitalism'. But, here comes the card trick. For, the moment one looks at protestantism from the other side of the stipulated equation, accepting its identity with the spirit of capitalism, the assessment of the whole issue is already beginning to lose its historical connotations. And significantly, at the next step — when the truly relevant question of capital's possible transcendence might be raised — the historical character of the relationship in question totally vanishes. For who 'in their right mind' would presume to tamper with the divine and eternal 'spirit of protestantism' as transfigured into the 'spirit of capitalism', dragging it down to a 'mere historical' level? Besides, while the credulous spectators focus their eyes on the cards ably manipulated by the illusionist in front of them on the table, distracted by the dexterity of his well designed moves, they also fail to notice that the self-justifyingly proclaimed and idealized capitalist 'economic rationality' — which is supposed to establish the apriori superiority of this system over all conceivable alternatives — has been founded on nothing more solid than pure mysticism, devised to hide and justify the fatefully uncontrollable and destructive irrationality of capital's social metabolic order, even though this means the acceptance of Weber's eternal 'iron cage'.

In truth the imperative of accumulation-driven expansion can be satisfied under changed socioeconomic circumstances not only without the subjective *'profit motive'* but even without the objective requirement of *profit,* which happens to be an absolute necessity only in the *capitalist* variety of the capital system. The requirement of *accumulation* should not be confused with the necessity of *profit.* As we have witnessed in the 20th century, during several decades of Soviet type economic development, high levels of capital accumulation can be secured by means of the politically controlled extraction of surplus labour, without even remotely resembling the capitalist system in its necessary orientation towards profit, let alone the 'entrepreneurial' and 'buccaneering spirit' of the people in command who are supposed to be driven by the subjective motivational force of the 'profit motive'. Only when Stalin wishfully initiated the switch to what later became known as 'market socialism' and stipulated the adoption of commodity relations in the consumer industry, only then was the question of profit raised — and even then, as well as later on, all the way to Gorbachev's failed reforms, quite unsuccessfully — with reference to the grotesque idea that it might better motivate 'our business executives' without transferring to them state property. As to the future, it is quite feasible to envisage a turn of events whereby the capital system in profound crisis — necessitating ever greater state intervention in order to manage the crisis — is forced to adopt a mode (or even several different modes) of reproduction in which the room for the controlling function of the personal 'profit motive' is extremely curtailed. Not only future postcapitalist systems but even a consistent state capitalist socioeconomic order, brought into being under the conditions of an extremely high degree of monopolism and sharpening antagonisms between capital and labour, can — and under the pressure of greatly worsened profit generation must — dispense with the often arbitrary and utterly wasteful control function of personal profit.

To put these matters in their proper perspective, within the framework of the fundamental objective determinations of the established mode of social metabolic reproduction, it is necessary to recall the relationship betwen capital and its personifications. For the self-serving idea that social wealth is produced in the competitive market place through the entrepreneurial virtues of the 'protestant ethic' and the 'thrifty' accumulation and reallocation of personal profit for the purposes of expanded reproduction, in the interest of all, is at best only a bad joke.

Ricardo still knew very well and was honest enough to admit that no matter how efficient and competitive the particular capitalists were against one another in the market place, their higher or lower profits as entrepreneurial units were regulated by the general framework of profitability of total capital (asserting itself through the average or 'general rate of profit'), depending on objective determinations — which make the system exhibit the falling overall rate of profit — and not on subjective motives. As he had put it: 'A fall in the general rate of profits is by no means incompatible with a partial rise of profits in particular employments. It is through the inequality of profits, that capital is moved from one employment to another. ... An extraordinary stimulus may be also given for a certain time, to a particular branch of foreign and colonial trade; but the admission of this fact by no means invalidates the theory, that profits depend on high or low wages'.[333] This is why — given his much more subtle account of the limitations of market competition among individual capitalists in affecting more than marginally, in one direction or the other, the falling rate of profits — Ricardo forcefully objected to Adam Smith who in his view 'uniformly ascribes the fall of profits to accumulation of capital, and to the competition which will result from it'.[334] Thus Ricardo had precious little use for the individual capitalists' profit motive as the guarantor of the continued dynamism and permanent health of the capital system.

The mythologies of profit-oriented 'free competition' within the framework of the universally beneficial market are cultivated also as the proof of the one and only feasible 'free society'. The reality is much more prosaic. For

> Free competition is the relation of capital to itself as another capital, i.e. the real conduct of capital as capital. ... It is *not individuals* who are set free by free competition; it is, rather, *capital* which is set free. ... Free competition is the real development of capital. By its means, what corresponds to the nature of capital is posited as external necessity for the individual capital; what corresponds to the concept of capital is posited as external necessity for the mode of production founded on capital. ... The predominance of capital is the presupposition of free competition, just as the despotism of the Roman Caesars was the presupposition of the free Roman 'private law'. As long as capital is weak, it still itself relies on the crutches of past modes of production, or of those which will pass with its rise. As soon as it feels strong, it throws away the crutches, and moves in accordance with its own laws. As soon as it begins to sense itself and become conscious of itself as a *barrier to development,* it seeks refuge in forms which, by *restricting free competition,* seem to make the *rule of capital more perfect,* but are at the same time the *heralds of its dissolution* and of the dissolution of the mode of production resting on it. Competition merely expresses as real, posits as an external necessity, that which lies within the *nature of capital;* competition is nothing more than the way in which the many capitals force the inherent determinants of capital upon one another and upon themselves. ... [Free competition] is nothing more than free development on a *limited basis — the basis of the rule of capital.* This kind of individual freedom is therefore at the same time the most complete suspension of all individual freedom, and the most complete *subjugation of individuality* under social conditions which assume the form of objective powers, even of *overpowering objects —* of things independent of the relations among individuals themselves.[335]

The objective logic of these developments is relentless, no matter how strong the illusions and how mystifying the material and ideological vested interests attached to the unfolding trends. For the capital system moves from its ascending phase, when it can afford to throw away the crutches, to a course of development when new crutches are ever more badly needed, directly contradicting both the objective dynamism and the ideological justification of the rule of capital. Thus, in accordance with the nature of capital as 'living contradiction',

> The influence of *individual capitals* on one another has the effect precisely that they must conduct themselves *as capital;* the *seemingly independent* influence of the individuals, and their *chaotic collisions*, are precisely the positing of their *general law.* Market here obtains yet another significance. The influence of capitals as individuals on each

other thus becomes precisely their positing as *general beings,* and the suspension of the seeming independence and independent survival of the individuals. This suspension takes place even more in credit. And the most extreme form to which the suspension proceeds, which is however at the same time the *ultimate positing of capital* in the form adequate to it — is *joint stock capital.*[336]

This is how the grotesquely idealized 'spirit of capitalism' consummates itself, making an absolute mockery of 'free competition' and 'free individuality', by bringing about a stage of development where finance capital and monopolism run riot. And even that cannot be all. For the nature and logic of capital can only offer the prospect of a ruthlessly corporatist order of which Hitler's Germany provided already its tangible antecedent. Given the nature of capital and the way in which it suspended and turned its once emancipatory tendencies into their opposite, the disastrous logic of this system is bound to prevail, unless a radically rearticulated socialist movement can put an end to the rule of capital and assert itself as the hegemonic alternative to the established mode of social metabolic reproduction.

20.1.4

THE 'chaotic collisions' of freely competing individual capitals, of which Marx spoke, are by now severely restricted by the necessary crutches of the capital system in structural crisis. For on the basis of what characterized its classical phase of development the system could not survive from one day to the next, let alone assert its domination on a continuing basis. Yet, the apologists of capital carry on fictionalizing and idealizing the non-existent conditions of spontaneous individual interchanges within the framework of the market, as if nothing had happened in the last century and a half to the way in which the rule of capital prevails in society. Thus Hayek, for instance, uses the pretended objectivity of the 'price mechanism' and 'market mechanism' for the purpose of cynical rationalization and pseudo-moral justification of capital's deeply iniquitous reproductive order. He writes that

> You must allow prices to be determined so as to tell people where they can make the best contribution to the rest of society — and unfortunately the capacity of making good contributions to one's fellows is not distributed according to any principles of justice. People are in a very unequal position to make contributions to the requirements of their fellows and have to choose between very different opportunities. In order therefore to enable them to *adapt themselves* to *a structure which they do not know* (and the determinants of which they do not know), we have to allow the *spontaneous mechanisms of the market* to tell them what they *ought to do.* ... Our modern insight is that prices are signals which inform people of what they *ought to do* in order to *adjust themselves* to the rest of *the system.*[337]

In Hayek's discourse the only thing that matters is the constant assertion and reassertion that people *must submit* — unquestioningly — to the imperatives of the existing structural order, even though he must admit that the principles advocated by him 'have never been rationally justified'.[338] The apologetic aim of the whole exercise transpires when he keeps repeating that people must be 'willing to *submit to the discipline* constituted by commercial morals',[339] without letting us into the secret of what makes the 'commercial morals' of capital's ruthless domination of the overwhelming majority of humankind to which Hayek himself subscribes — even acknowledging that it is opposed to all principle of justice — deserve the name 'morals'. The idea of the — idealized but non-existent 'spontaneous market mechanism' is used by Hayek only as an *ideological device* in the name of which he crudely tries to dismiss the socialist project of controlling the social metabolism through the conscious self-regulation of productive and distributive interchanges by the associated producers. Thus he writes in 'The Moral Imperative of the Market' that

> We are now in the extraordinary situation that, while we live in a world with a large and growing population which can be kept alive thanks only to the prevalence of the market system, the vast majority of people (I do not exaggerate) no longer believes in the market. It is a crucial question for the future preservation of civilization and one which must be faced before the arguments of socialism return us to a primitive morality. We must again *suppress* those innate feelings which have welled up in us once we ceased to learn the *taut discipline of the market,* before they destroy our capacity to feed the popluation through the *co-ordinating system of the market.* Otherwise, the collapse of capitalism will ensure that a very large part of the world's population will die because we cannot feed it.[340]

As we have seen also in Sections 4.3.1 and 4.3.2, Hayek's allegedly 'irrefutable proof' for the irreplaceability of the capitalist market — with reference to the size of the world population — is trotted out at every opportunity. Yet, the whole argument rests on a double-absurdity: (1) that the blindly self-expansionary and wasteful capital system can actually provide the guarantee for indefinitely sustaining the growing population of the world (when in fact it is a fateful certainty that it cannot do so even today, let alone tomorrow); and (2) that conscious human design is by definition incapable of regulating the 'spontaneous mechanism' of the social metabolic process, including the size of the population — just because Hayek's capital-apologetics and hatred of the Marxian socialist project say so.

As usual in the writings of capital's uncritical defenders, we are allowed to think of history for a brief moment, in the context of the consolidation of capitalism, when we are told that 'commercial or mercantile morals by the middle of the last century had come to govern the world economy'.[341] But, of course, there can be no question of historical change in the future. For we either 'submit' to the 'existing structures' which we do not and cannot understand, 'adjusting' ourselves to 'the rest of the system' by conforming to the 'moral imperative of the market', as we 'ought do do', or human 'civilization will be destroyed' by the 'conceit of socialists' who try to meddle with the absolutely unalterable. At the same time the reality of the market is totally misrepresented. The pretended 'moral imperative of the market' is invoked in order to remove any idea of historical alterability from this institution, so that the people at the receiving end of the established relations of domination should accept the *tyranny of the market* — its 'taut discipline' to which labour must unquestioningly *submit* — as their *moral duty.* And to sweeten somewhat the bitter pill, it must be also pretended that the capitalist market is a *neutral 'co-ordinating system'* to which no sane person should seek an alternative.

Underneath the façade of this apologetic rationalization we find a striking contradiction. For if it is true that the capitalist market is a neutral, universally beneficial co-ordinating system and a set of 'spontaneous mechanisms' working so well as Hayek claims, in that case 'what is the boot doing on the table', as a

Hungarian adage puts it. That is to say, if the nature of the market is as depicted by Hayek and other apologists like him, what is the point of projecting and enforcing strict conformity to the spontaneous determinations of the market as a *'moral imperative'* which *'ought to be' obeyed* also by dissenting socialists? What could be the role of this 'argument' other than camouflaging the author's eagerness to disqualify 'primitive' socialists — who are 'primitive' by Hayekian definition — as capable of 'modern morality'; and doing this without adding anything whatsoever to the claimed incontestable merits of the market, established for reasons of social apologetics on neutral *instrumental* ground by stipulating its unexceptionable 'co-ordinating' function and defining its nature as a 'spontaneous *mechanism*'.

In actuality, however, nothing could be further from the truth than describing the market as a neutral 'co-ordinating system' and a 'spontaneous mechanism'. The market which the apologists of capital try to idealize is in no way capable of self-reliance and neutral disposition towards its social surrounding. Far from it. For it is an integral part of the exploitative relations of a social reproductive system in which surplus labour is extracted by primarily economic means. The spontaneous development of the market to the point of embracing the reproductive processes of the various national economies is a complete myth. As Polányi rightly stressed: 'Economic history reveals that the emergence of national markets was in no way the result of gradual and spontaneous emancipation of the economic sphere from governmental control. On the contrary, the market has been the outcome of a conscious and often violent intervention on the part of government which imposed the market organization on society for noneconomic ends.'[342] As to the 'spontaneous functioning' of the market even at the peak of *'laissez faire'* capitalism, its operation is in fact subject to the weighty qualifications which we have seen in Chapter 2, with regard to the remedial action of the state made necessary by the structural defects of control in the capital system both in productive and in distributive relations. This explains not only why the emergence and consolidation of the national markets is unthinkable without major state involvement, but also the fact that the structural domination of international market relations is confined to a mere handful of economic powers. It is confined to precisely those economies whose state power can both actively sustain the dynamics of internal capital-expansion and assert the interests of the repective economic systems — in the first place often by violent noneconomic means, until, that is, their economic dominance itself can be used in the form of punitive 'economic sanctions' for the same purpose — in the international power struggle of national capitals.

Naturally, when we consider the necessarily antagonistic interchanges within the framework of the global capital system, only a lunatic — or a crude apologist like Hayek — could suggest that they can be safely left to the 'spontaneous co-ordinating system' of the 'market mechanism'. For the market in question is not a 'spontaneous co-ordinating mechanism' but an actively managed and by all means at the disposal of the dominant powers in their own favour distorted constituent of the globally prevailing/enforced system of ruthless *power relations*. In the course of historical development early colonialism gave way to imperialist domination of the planet by a few countries, and that in its turn metamorphosed after two — far from 'spontaneous' — World Wars into the now existing order of 'neo-colonialism' and 'neo-capitalist imperialism': always retaining the imperative of antagonistic structural domination as the defining characteristic of the capital system both on the internal and on the international plane. Under the ideological façade of objective and mutually beneficial market relations we find the activating power of naked material and cultural imperialism, as recently demonstrated by the GATT negotiations. To quote Daniel Singer:

> During the 1993 polemics, Regis Debray quoted the words of a Time Warner executive speaking on a French television channel: 'You French are best at making cheese and wine, or in fashion. Filming is our speciality. So let us get on with film-making and you keep on with the cheeses'. Debray summed it up, tongue in cheek: 'let us shape the minds and you stick to stomachs'. Not so fast. Our collective stomachs are financially too precious to be left to the French, as was shown in the bitter GATT battles over agriculture. But the control of the mind, the monopoly of the image, is ever more important.[343]

If the French — one of the select few prominent powers of post-colonial imperialism — can be treated in this way, it is not too difficult to imagine what position must be assigned to the countries which find themselves at the lower (not to mention the lowest) rung of the ladder corresponding to capital's global pecking order. Only the gullible political leaders of the former Soviet Union and Eastern Europe, guided by their equally gullible economic advisers, could take seriously Hayek's capital-apologetic fantasies about the market and its 'objective price signals'. They projected the miraculously beneficial impact of the 'market mechanism' for the economies of their countries, making the people pay dearly for their disastrous attempt to embrace first the mirage of 'market socialism' and then the stark reality of dependent capitalism.

To understand the reality of the market today, it is necessary to constantly bear in mind its great reliance on the state. For massive domains of economic activity are quite unviable in the contemporary capital system without the direct supporting role of the state on a phenomenal scale. This is quite obvious in the case of the military/industrial complex which constitutes a most important sector in the economies of the dominant capitalist countries. But it does not stop there, however vital militarist production itself might be for the health of 'advanced capitalism'. The so-called 'common agricultural policy' in the European Union — with its just as generously state-subsidizing counterparts in the agriculture of the United States — is an equally telling illustration of the high economic stakes involved in consciously 'cooking' the 'spontaneous co-ordinating system' of the market, as opposed to Hayek's grotesque and utterly cynical propaganda-projection of 'allowing prices to be determined so as to tell people where they can make the best contribution to the rest of society'. In Britain, for instance, the contribution of agriculture is a paltry 1.5 percent to the Gross National Product, but the state subsidies transferred to the farmers are astronomical by comparison; sheep farmers alone — a minor portion of the overall state contribution — receive an annual subsidy in excess of £370 million. Projects like the common European Airbus are likewise most generously treated at the taxpayers' expense, even if US protests against it are disingenuous, since the giant airoplane producing corporations, like Boeing and Lockheed, receive also in America immense subsidies in the form of military contracts and state financed research.

Naturally, the role of the state in directly sustaining the far from 'spontaneous mechanisms' of the capitalist market is by no means exhausted in performing the function of the milking cow, at the expense of the working people. Its role is equally important as the facilitator and protector of the monopolistic concentration and centralization of capital, as well as in general the enforcer of the laws enacted for absolutely preventing the articulation of labour's hegemonic alternative to the capital system. For given the insurmountable adversarial structural relationship of the labour process, affecting both production and the sphere of distribution, the allegedly 'spontaneous market mechanisms' could not function at all without the legally safeguarded protection of the exploitative framework of the capital system of which the market always was and remains a subordinate part. The facilitating role of the state for the establishment of monopolies and quasi-monopolies, as well as for ignoring or even openly justifying the transparent monopolistic practices of preponderant cartels, assumed scandalous proportions, cynically maintaining at the same time for public consumption the mythology of 'free competition'. To take only one example, we learned in Britain the scandalous fact that between them Tate & Lyle and Silver Spoon control more than 95 percent of sugar production and distribution, but nothing is done to redress the situation. Often the connection with corrupt political practices is also in evidence, and still makes no difference. Thus there was a major scandal about the phenomenally overpriced supply of concrete to government financed building projects — like motorways, public roads, bridges, etc. — by Lord Hanson's companies. As it happens (no doubt, they would say, by 'pure coincidence'), Lord Hanson — the head of a giant conglomerate — has been for a long time one of the biggest contributors to the British Conservative Party's finances. And now that the party of 'New Labour' looks like the certain winner of the next general election, one of the handful of prominent businessmen appointed to that party's recently established 'Commission on Public Policy and British Business' is none other than Sir Christopher Harding, 'for 20 years a director of Hanson, one of the Conservative Party's biggest donors and most active business supporters'.[344] But perhaps this is yet another 'pure coincidence'.

The *'privatizations'* promoted with hypocritical ideological zeal in the name of 'free competition' — but implemented in practice with a cynical sense of capitalistic reality — by Hayek's 'Companions of Honour' in Britain produced giant private monopolies and quasi-monopolies, with the ability to amass to themselves astronomical profits. Perhaps the only area of market relations today where direct state subsidizing practices and the various degrees of monopolism do not make a complete mockery of the propagandistic claims attached to the idealized market as the one and only viable 'spontaneous co-ordinating system', is the 'consumer-economy' of boutiques, car-boot sales, and street-corner taco stands. But who could seriously maintain that the enthusiastically praised 'ever more globalized world economy' of the contemporary capital system could be run on such a material basis?

20.1.5
IF only it could be really true that the market is a 'spontaneous mechanism', capable of regulating the capital system by its neutral and automatic 'co-ordinating action', that would be wonderful for the eternalization of the established

mode of social metabolic control. For in that case there would be no need for an alien command over labour in the form of the *personifications of capital,* since the spontaneous and automatic mechanism itself would fulfil the necessary control functions both over the labour process and over the distribution of its products. Naturally, from such a conveniently conflict-free design it would also follow that labour could have no case whatsoever for contesting the established order of things, since the operation of the system would be self-evidently natural and unalterable.

However, what exposes the real nature of the ideological schemes devised in favour of capital-apologetics is the fact that the various types of personification of capital self-evidently do exist, whereas all claimed evidence for the spontaneous functioning and natural character of the ruling order — which happens to be, on the contrary, forcibly imposed on society through the combined power of economic compulsion and the state—is missing altogether. The labour process in all known and feasible forms of the capital system — which are inconceivable as forms of social metabolic control without the enforcement of the system's time-imperative being constituted as a separate and alien subjectivity directly confronting labour — cannot help being *adversarial* and ultimately unsustainable. This is why the removal of the consciousness of conflictuality must be (and happens to be) the prime ideological objective of the rationalization and justification of the continued rule of capital. This is so whether it takes the form of the constantly projected fiction that capital's mode of control and its 'spontaneous co-ordinating system' represent the natural order and the perfect mechanism of all conceivable forms of socioeconomic reproduction, or indeed the form of the equivalent Stalinist fiction according to which there is a total identity of interest between the postcapitalist personifications of capital (the party bureaucrats and 'our business executives') and the labour force.

Understandably, the ideologists of 'advanced capitalism' find themselves at a loss when they have to explain the stubborn persistence of social conflict. The projection of the market as a socially neutral and ideally rational 'spontaneous mechanism' is both the manifestation of the wishful thinking of capital's beneficiaries, envisaging an unchallengeable order (at once contradicted by the vague intuition of their own superfluity if their projected scheme corresponded to reality), and the ideological embodiment of a transparent class interest — which makes it necessary to formulate their 'unchallengeable' projection, despite its self-contradiction — to categorically rule out the rationality of conflict and contestation. Accordingly, if they have to concede the periodic eruption of more or less severe antagonisms, they can only do so by resorting to the most absurd hypotheses of *irrationality,* imputed to their adversaries, in order to reconcile the claimed self-evident naturalness of their system and of its 'spontaneous co-ordinating mechanism' with the possibility of such an ideal world being contested at all. In this spirit Hayek insists that 'socialists have been led by a very peculiar development to *revive certain primitive instincts and feelings* which in the course of hundreds of years had been practically suppressed by commercial and mercantile morals'.[345]

Thus, what is indeed evident is not the naturalness of the idealized but inevitably contested — for in its innermost determinations adversarial — capital system, but the naked ideological interest at the root of the uncritical and fallacious arguments marshalled in its favour. The characterization of the market by Hayek and his followers has not even an infinitesimal objective descriptive constituent. All it consists in is the aprioristic rejection of the *rationality and legitimacy of contesting the system,* which is said to be totally free from even the shadow of controversy in virtue of being the ideal 'spontaneous co-ordinating system'.

The conclusion of 'rational incontestability' is *circularly assumed* in the utterly arbitrary characterization of a system of irreconcilable *structural antagonisms* — sustainable only for as long as the hierarchical domination and exploitation of labour can be enforced — as *rational co-ordination itself,* and not as a most questionable and ultimately explosive *historical* variety of productive and distributive co-ordination and control. This arbitrary and logically circular procedure exempts Hayek and his 'radical right' soul-mates from the difficult task of even attempting to objectively justify the specific, historically produced and therefore in principle historically alterable, mode of social metabolic control commended by them. At the same time it also suppresses — by idealizing definition alone — the consciousness of the structural antagonisms at the heart of their cherished system. In the end the only part of the whole discourse to which one can attach some meaning, but in no way a factually sustainable meaning, is the peremptory declaration that the people should resist the temptations of the 'primitive instincts and feelings' ascribed to the socialists, and submit, instead, to the *'taut discipline of the market'* as their *'moral duty'*. It goes without saying, this is not a rational argument but the worst kind of social demagogy.

Significantly, this is where Hayek and Stalin — and in Stalin's footsteps the postcapitalist personifications of 'market socialist' capital — had found their common denominator. For the benefits of 'taut discipline' were expected also by Stalin to emerge from the advocated extension of the 'market mechanism' and the continued operation of the law of value, as he had put it, 'not only in circulation but also in the sphere of production'. This substantive affinity between the different types of personification of capital also explains why former Stalinists in charge of the postcapitalist economy and its 'planning system' in the Soviet Union as well as in other parts of Eastern Europe so readily and enthusiastically embraced, at the time of Gorbachev's ill-fated reform attempt, Hayek's and Milton Friedman's creed. To the astonishment only of the naive who took seriously the idea of 'actually existing socialism', the postcapitalist personifications of capital very quickly started to preach — indistinguishably from their private capitalist cousins — the virtues of 'taut discipline' in the name of 'guaranteed democratization', commending as their ideally restructured new 'democratic order' the continued rule of capital with the 'innovation' that the long established and throughout the postrevolutionary decades retained authoritarianism of the workshop should be complemented by the tyranny of the market.

In the capitalist world today the arguments in favour of the market are depicting the real situation completely upside-down, betraying their apologetic ideological function. It is pretended that *'the market demands'* — in the health service, in the educational system, etc. — 'discipline', 'efficiency', 'increased economy', and the like, and therefore 'it demands *cuts'* in all domains of the welfare services. In reality the relations are exactly the other way round. For it is the profound *structural crisis* of the global capital system which demands and imposes cuts on an ever-increasing scale, pointing now in the direction of the necessity to destroy even the *pension* system; and, of course, to do so not only in Italy, but in every 'advanced capitalist' welfare state. As a result, in this upside-down world of capital's no longer readily manageable constraints and contra-dictions, the rationalizing escape route is sought by misrepresenting the unde-sirable *effects* as if they constituted the underlying original *cause* of the growing problems, and the *real causes* of the undeniable difficulties as the *avoidable effects* of the 'scrounging', 'undisciplined', 'inefficient' etc. actions of reprehensible individuals who must be induced to accept the 'taut discipline' of the market as their 'moral duty'.

Politicians often mindlessly repeat the cliché, whenever they try to justify their callous disregard for human suffering: 'don't throw money at it'. But where is the money they could 'throw at it'? It is gobbled up by the insatiable appetite of monopolies and quasi-monopolies, as well as by the other powerful capitalistic interests. The capital system in structural crisis is unable to produce any more the funds required for maintaining in existence, let alone for expanding in line with the growing need, the welfare state which not so long ago constituted its ultimate justification. This is why all kinds of phoney pseudo-market devices must be invented, wherever possible, from the educational system (for instance, the intellectually most damaging transformation of departments in universities into 'budgetary units') to the health service (e.g. the cynical slave-driving device of the so-called 'internal market'), so as to be able to impose on the labour force everywhere the conditions of increased exploitation and 'discipline', in the name of the prefabricated self-justification that all this is rightly prescribed by the one and only rational productive and distributive order to which 'there can be no alternative'.

20.2 Beyond capital: the real target of socialist transformation

20.2.1

THE temptations of envisaging transition to the socialist reproductive order by following the line of least resistance have been always great. We have seen in Section 13.6 that Marx had warned the workers against the illusion that the pursuit of 'a fair day's wage for a fair day's work' can lead in the direction of the desired transformation, advising them, instead, that 'they ought to inscribe on their banner the revolutionary watchword, "Abolition of the wages system".'[346]

However, although it is absolutely true that what needs to be attacked is the causal framework of capital's surplus-labour extraction and not simply some of its iniquitous and temporarily removable effects, the wages system itself, strictly speaking, cannot be 'abolished' even by the most consistently revolutionary decree, just as capital and the state cannot be so 'abolished'. They all have to be laboriously superseded/transcended in the course of the radical restructuring of the established social metabolic order as an 'organic whole', i.e. as a circularly self-sustaining 'organic system' the constituents of which tend to reciprocally reinforce one another. Thus the requirement of radical transcendence has far-reaching implications not only for all of the material and cultural productive and distributive dimensions of the long established hierarchical social division of labour, but also for the inherited totalizing political command structure of capital embodied after the revolution in the postcapitalist state. In this sense, going *beyond capital* means superseding capital's mode of control as an *organic system:* a task feasible only as a global enterprise.

The inextricably intertwined constituents of capital's organic system — in its capitalist and postcapitalist varieties — are:

- (1) CAPITAL, representing not only the alienated material conditions of production but also — as the *personification* of capital's material imperatives, including the earlier discussed time-imperative — the subjectivity confronting and commanding labour;
- (2) LABOUR, structurally deprived of control over the necessary conditions of production, reproducing capital on an extended scale, and at the same time — as the real subject of production and the *personification* of labour — *defensively confronting* capital; and
- (3) the STATE, as the overall political command structure of the *antagonistic* capital system, providing the ultimate guarantee for the *containment* of the irreconcilable antagonisms and for the submission of labour, since labour retains the power of potentially explosive recalcitrance despite the system's unique economic compulsion.

The principal impediment for embarking on the realization of the socialist project, and the strategic lever that must be firmly held in order to break the vicious circle of capital's organic system, is not the repressive power of the state — which can be overthrown under favourable circumstances — but the *defensive or offensive posture* of labour towards capital. Indeed, as 20th century historical evidence demonstrated, the postcapitalist systems came into being by overthrowing their respective capitalist states; but they remained, none the less, under the rule of capital, because postcapitalist labour retained its defensive/reactive posture in the control process of the postrevolutionary socioeconomic and political order.

The fatefully defensive articulation of the historical left discussed in Chapter 18, which had to result in the catastrophic disintegration not only of its reformist socialdemocratic wing but also of its once programmatically revolutionary organizations, was the necessary concomitant of the structurally defensive confrontation of labour with its adversary within the established organic system. For despite the irreconcilable structural antagonism between capital and labour — which happens to be successfully *contained,* except in rare circumstances of acute crises — the constituents of the system tend to reinforce one another as a matter of course, in the interest of the normal functioning of the established reproductive order on which also labour depends for its livelihood. The necessary practical premises of expanded reproduction circumscribe the limits of what can be contested and obtained — and also for how long a historical period — within the structural parameters of the capital system. This goes not only for the ultimately illusory character of the watchword: 'A fair day's wage for a fair day's work', but for all material and political gains that can be conceded to the working class. The margin of 'democratic' political action and the 'rules of the parliamentary game' are also determined by the same practical premises of the system, regulating social interchange in strict subordination to its expansionary imperative and to the need for containing the antagonism between capital and labour. The moment the relative gains of labour begin to conflict with the necessary practical imperatives of the capital system, they must be taken back in order to secure — at whatever political cost, including authoritarian anti-labour legislation in 'advanced capitalist democracies' — the continued viability of the established mode of social metabolic reproduction. The fact that under the pressure of the erupting structural crisis of capital the traditional — socialdemocratic and communist — parties of the socialist movement all caved in and turned themselves into bourgeois liberal parties, openly accepting the insurmountable constraints of the system as the absolute horizon of all feasible social advancement, could come as a surprise only to those who failed to consider altogether the question of limits, nourishing, instead, great illusions about the margin of feasible gains for labour.

The question of *strategic offensive* is not reducible to the need for *political action*, even if the latter is a *necessary* — but very far from *sufficient* — part of the envisaged socialist transformation. Interpretations of Marx's idea of the proletariat becoming a *'class for itself'* oversimplified the issue by suggesting that what it meant was the pursuit of radical political action. This was a strategically disorienting misconception. For even the sharpest political confrontation between capital and labour can be still the struggle of 'class against class', i.e. the political action of the proletariat as a *'class in itself'* defensively confronting capital — another *'class in itself'* — and remaining within the parameters of the socioeconomic order structurally dominated by the latter. The history of political confrontations between capital and labour during the last century and a half speaks eloquently enough on this subject, demonstrating the painful inadequacy of the *defensive articulation* of the socialist movement — from the time of its inception to the present day — to the emancipatory enterprise undertaken by it.

What decides the issue is the relationship between the objectives pursued by labour and the structural parameters of the established socioeconomic order. In this sense, whatever concessions, obtained by labour, are compatible with, and containable by, the expansion-oriented and accumulation-driven capital system, are by the same token unfit to alter the defensive posture and structurally subordinate position of capital's antagonist towards its adversary. This remains the case irrespective of how sharp might be the periodic clashes and confrontations — including even a most dramatic general strike — through which labour's gains are in the end conceded by capital. The concessions granted to labour under the 'welfare state' did not weaken capital in the slightest. Quite the contrary, they significantly contributed to the expansionary dynamic of the system over a sustained period of two and a half decades after the Second World War. Nor did such concessions alter the relation of forces in favour of labour. If anything, they weakened the combativity of labour by reinforcing the mystifications of reformism. Naturally, all this does not mean that the defensive gains of the past are not worth defending, especially when capital is bound to try and claw them back, under the pressure of a deepening structural crisis. But it does mean that the illusions attached to them throughout the history of reformist social democracy have to be exposed for what they are, instead of fantasising about the viability of labour's neo-Keynesian 'alternative economic strategy', which happens to be not only totally unreal under the circumstances of capital's structural crisis, but even if by some miracle it could be implemented, it would not constitute an alternative at all.

The hegemonic alternative of labour to the rule of capital is inconceivable without the *complete eradication of capital from the social metabolic process*. This is why the overthrow of capitalism can hardly even scratch the surface of the problem. Indeed, a good indicator of what is woefully inadequate to the realization of the socialist project is whatever can be *overthrown,* including the state and—through the 'expropriation of the expropriators'—the capitalist personifications of capital. The radical negation of the capitalist state and the likewise negative 'expropriation of the expropriators' was always considered by Marx only the necessary first step in the direction of the required socialist transformation. He insisted that even the most radical negation remains in dependency on the object of its negation. The implications of this judgement are crucial for the self-management of the associated producers envisaged as the hegemonic alternative to capital's social order. For the realization of such an order can only be an *inherently positive* enterprise. This is why the socialist revolution could not be conceived as a single act, no matter how radical in intent. It had to be described, as we have seen in Marx's *Eighteenth Brumaire,* as an ongoing, consistently *self-critical social revolution,* i.e. as a *permanent revolution* capable of providing and constantly improving the *positively self-determined* mode of control of the socialist order. No wonder, therefore, that the apologists of the established order and the disingenuous idealizers of the market have to resort to the most grotesque travesty of the Marxian project, characterizing it as the advocacy of the *'golden age of communist steady-state equilibrium'.*[347]

Thus the real objective of socialist transformation — beyond the negation of the state and of capital's personifications — can only be the establishment of a self-sustaining alternative social metabolic order. An order from which capital with all of its corollaries — including the so-called 'market mechanism', which in actuality could not be further removed from being a 'mechanism' only — has been irreversibly removed. And that means: removed not only in the form of the unavoidable critical transcendence but, much more importantly, through the *positive appropriation* and *ongoing improvement* of the vital functions of metabolic interchange with nature and among the members of society by the self-determining individuals themselves. Understandably, the defensive articulation of the socialist movement makes it impossible to pursue the objective of labour's hegemonic alternative to the established order. For the terms of reference of every particular confrontation with capital, for the purpose of even just maintaining the status quo, and even more so if the issue at stake is to obtain the thinnest slice of improvement for labour from the given margin of social wealth, are strictly circumscribed by the limits of viability of the ruling order and by the ultimately destructive logic of its expansionary material imperatives. This is why the sand-castles of reformist social democracy have turned to dust with no less dramatic finality than the false promises of the imploded Soviet type postcapitalist capital system. For both wings of the historical left failed to challenge the rule of capital, looking at the time of their inception — self-contradictorily — for sustainable improvements and gains in favour of labour, while remaining captive of their different, but equally self-defeating, defensive posture in relation to capital's social metabolic order.

Today, in the light of 20th century historical experience and the failure of all past attempts to overcome the dehumanizing constraints and contradictions of capitalism, the meaning of radical negation can only be defined as a subordinate moment of the positive project of labour's hegemonic alternative to capital itself in the sense discussed above. The rearticulation of the socialist movement as a strategic offensive to go beyond capital is in this way the necessary precondition also of partial successes which in due course, within the framework of the right strategy, can become cumulative. By contrast, without the proper target of the strategic offensive — oriented towards the socialist order as a hegemonic alternative to the existent — the journey itself is without a compass. And we certainly cannot afford the luxury of wandering for another century and a half in the blind alley of trying to produce structural changes within the paralyzing structural confines of the capital system.

Those who might think that the socialist hegemonic alternative is 'unreal' — and have no vested interest in defending at all costs the established order — should ask themselves the question: is it actually feasible and logically tenable to project the permanence of a metabolic system of societal reproduction based on the fetishistic material imperatives of capital's destructive logic? Can those who are resigned to endure the inertia of capital's self-perpetuating 'realism' seriously maintain that the *destructive uncontrollability of capital* is not casting ever darkening shadows on the horizon of human survival? For by now even the most uncritical defenders of the ruling order are forced to concede that very big problems lie ahead. The 'only' difference is that they wishfully project that the repressive power of capital will forever be able to cope with all such problems. In truth, however, what is most *unreal* is not the socialist hegemonic alternative to the rule of capital in all of its historically known and still feasible forms, but the gratuitous projection that humankind can survive much longer within the necessarily destructive structural limits of the established mode of social metabolic reproduction.

20.2.2

ONE of the prefabricated objections to the possibility of building a socialist order is the notion of *'complexity'*. It is wheeled out with monotonous repetitiveness at every opportunity. The number of *complexity merchants* is legion, but their efforts uniformly boil down to the announcement that they have found the new 'philosophers' stone', proclaimed to be much more precious than the old alchemists' would-be miracle method of producing gold, because it promises to do away, 'irrefutably', with socialism.

This new philosophers' stone is carved out from the rock of the truism that 'modern market society' is made up of many more members than the small groups of our distant ancestors. However, the transparent ideological conclusion directly derived from this profundity — by Hayek and others — is that the idea of *solidarity* is totally illusory in our times.

The enemy which must be defeated with the help of such 'arguments' is, of course, socialism. The alleged absurdity of the socialist position must be discredited and dismissed, according to Hayek, because 'an atavistic longing after the life of the noble savage is the main source of the collectivist tradition'.[348]

Those who might be tempted by the 'atavistic instincts of collectivism' are called back to their senses by Hayek — 'with reference to the idea which still prevails about solidarity'[349] — like this:

Agreement about a common purpose between a group of known people is clearly an idea that cannot be applied to a large society which includes people who do not know one another. The modern society and the modern economy have grown up through the recognition that this idea, which was fundamental to life in a small group — a face-to-face society, is simply inapplicable to large groups. The essential basis of the development of modern civilization is to allow people to pursue their own ends on the basis of their own knowledge and not to be bound by the aims of other people.[350]

Naturally, this is only the prelude. Now comes the principle which should put the fear of god into any socialist who might wish to change the existing order. It decrees that the 'limitation of our powers necessarily grows with the complexity of the structure that we wish to bring into being'.[351] As to why human beings should curtail their powers by complexity, we get the answer in the lyric eulogy of the capitalist 'market order':

Some persons are so troubled by some effects of the market order that they overlook how unlikely and even *wonderful* it is to find such an order prevailing in the greater part of the modern world, a world in which we find thousands of millions of people working in a *constantly changing* environment, providing means of subsistence for others who are mostly unknown to them, and at the same time finding satisfied their own expectations that they themselves will receive goods and services produced by equally unknown people. Even in the *worst of times* something like *nine out of ten* of them will find their *expectations confirmed*.[352]

Understandably, since he writes about a 'market order' which in his view we 'do not know and cannot know', and because of its complexity we 'cannot control' and should not try to control, Hayek here commits a few slips of the pen. By the 'constantly changing environment' he means a structural order of domination and subordination which is *never changing,* and therefore those at the receiving end — 'only' the overwhelming majority of humankind — might find it not so wonderful, after all. As to the last sentence, what it really means, once we rectify Hayek's 'subconscious' slip of the pen, is that even at the *best of times* — as a matter of the capital system's incorrigible structural determinations — more than *nine out of ten* people *cannot find their expectations confirmed* in the 'unalterably complex' and 'wonderful market order'. But who in their right mind could quarrel with 'the superior self-ordering power of the market system'?[353] Only Marx and the socialists who fail to understand the 'self-steering market processes'.[354]

Naturally, as usual in all such 'refutations' of the Marxian project of conscious intervention in the established social metabolic order — elaborated by Marx for the purpose of bringing under control its destructive and exploitative reproductive practices, on the basis of a proper understanding of how capital's structural domination of society works and through what strategic levers it could be altered — Hayek, too, offers a caricaturistic misrepresentation of the socialist position. He proclaims that 'Marxian economics is still today attempting to explain *highly complex* orders of interaction in terms of single causal effects like mechanical phenomena rather than as prototypes of those self-ordering processes which give us access to the explanation of highly complex phenomena'.[355] Needless to say, we *never* get from Hayek and his followers *any* explanation of how the 'complex

phenomena' of the 'complex market order' work. Indeed, their rational inex-
plainability is repeatedly asserted, whether by 'single causal effects' — falsely
attributed to Marx — or by any number of them, dogmatically proclaiming,
instead, that 'the creation of wealth ... cannot be explained by a chain of cause
and effect'.[356] In line with this decree, all attempts to offer some explanation are
exorcised with the swearword 'rationalism', said to be characteristic of 'socialist
intellectuals'. Accordingly, all that we need to know is that the 'market order'
is *complex,* and that it is *wonderful.* Only trouble-making socialist intellectuals
can refuse to be happy with that.

Thus, as the climax of Hayek's profundity, we are offered a matching 'deep
psychological explanation' as to why intellectuals stubbornly refuse to accept
the revolutionary explanatory value of his own refusal to consider the possibility
of a rational account of the 'market order' (the term 'capitalism' is rejected by
Hayek, because it is said to emotively and misleadingly suggest 'a clash of
interests which does not really exist';[357] one 'explanation' more objective and
convincing than the other):

> such persons [i.e. the intellectuals] are tempted to interpret more complex structures
> animistically as the result of design, and to suspect some secret and dishonest mani-
> pulation — some conspiracy, as of a 'dominant class' — behind 'designs' whose
> designers are nowhere to be found. This in turn helps to reinforce their initial
> reluctance to relinquish control of their own products in a market order. For
> intellectuals generally, the feeling of being mere tools of concealed, even if imper-
> sonal, market forces appears almost as a personal humiliation.[358]

This priceless psychology is complemented by a logic according to which the
established property relations — 'I generally prefer the less usual but more
precise term "several property" to the more common expression "private property" '[359] — are contested by labour only because 'Intellectuals, thinking in
terms of limited causal processes they had learned to interpret in areas such as
physics, found it easy to persuade manual workers that selfish decisions of
individual owners of capital — rather than the *market process itself* — made use
of widely dispersed opportunities and constantly changing relevant facts'.[360] The
proper attitude to which intellectuals should conform, in the light of this convoluted logical non-sequitur, is to accept that the objective facts in the name of
which they mislead and incite the manual workers against (capitalist) 'several
property' — instead of instructing them that what might look reprehensible
and contestable is nothing of the kind, because everything is due to the complexity of the strictly impersonal and to the workers generous 'market process
itself', for which they ought to be grateful since they owe to it their very
existence, as we have seen it argued by Hayek above — 'such objective facts
simply do not exist and are unavailable to anyone'.[361]

In this way the question of justifying capital's structural domination and
exploitation of labour cannot possibly arise, since the unalterable complexity of
the market process itself is responsible for everything, and the market order is
in any case not only irreplaceable but also 'wonderful'.[362] The purpose of the
whole exercise is to use the notion of complexity not only to forbid to practically
'tamper' with the established system of socioeconomic reproduction, but even
to attempt to *think* about the possibility of altering in any way the 'complex
market order'. While Hayek falsely accuses Marx and his followers of 'mono-

causal reductionism', in fact he is guilty of it. For he is the one who tries to hide the crudest form of material reductionism — the picture of a world in which there can be no room for conscious human design and action, due to its constitution as 'a self-maintaining structure',[363] which is arbitrarily hypostatized in the name of vague analogies with and summary references to the complexity of biology and chemistry — under the irrationalistic glorification of impenetrable 'complexity'.

Hayek's reductionism is pursued in the interest of blindly defending, under the façade of his pseudo-scientific humbug, the irreconcilable antagonisms of the (capitalist) system of 'several property'. Yet, even the most cursory glance at the relationship between his 'wonderful market order' and its political setting reveals that the established 'extended economic order' (Hayek's preferred term for the rule of capital), with its obfuscatingly baptized 'several property' — far from constituting a *self-maintaining structure* — could not be sustained for a single year without the most active involvement of the state in defence of capital's rule, let alone to the end of time as he suggests. Nor is it possible to make any sense at all of the successful operation of the capital system even for one day in crudely material terms, no matter how complex the 'market order' is supposed to be on account of the thrown-in false analogy of its 'self-maintaining structure' to the structures of biological organisms.

Plausible — and not apologetically prefabricated 'no alternative' — explanation of the capital system's successful operation, together with its limits, is possible only if we try to understand the way in which it is actually constituted. This means understanding the (far from 'mono-causal') *dialectical relationship* between the objective material imperatives and determinations of capital as a mode of social metabolic control — including its insurmountable structural antagonisms — and its necessary *personifications,* as they consciously pursue their objectives, in accordance with their position and role in the material and political command structure of the established order. For the historically characteristic personifications of capital — the necessary *system-specific regulatory subjectivity* in all of its known and feasible variations — are brought into existence largely because of the vital need to manage and contain the insurmountable antagonisms of the established order, in the interest of asserting capital's command over labour in the societal reproduction process; a function which no 'self-ordering market mechanism' could conceivably fulfil on its own.

By contrast to Marx's dialectical account, Hayek's eager capital-apologetics and aprioristic rejection of the socialist idea of rational planning turn him into a crude material reductionist and into the eager idealizer of the — non-existent — 'self-maintaining structure' of the 'infinitely complex market order'; an apologist who is forced to eliminate even the most remote possibility of conscious human intervention from the picture. Amazingly, in his belief that he can expose the 'errors' and the 'fatal conceit' of socialists, and thereby defeat them forever (as in his footsteps his Companion of Honour, Margaret Thatcher, claimed to have 'seen off socialism for good'), Hayek does not hesitate to defend the proposition that — just because *everything* cannot be known at once by either an individual or by a given collective — *any* rational assessment of the conditions of successful strategic design and action in the sphere of social metabolic reproduction is inconceivable. The only thing even more amazing than this blatantly fallacious reasoning is the blind *self-complacency* with which it is assumed by the complexity merchants, like Hayek, that the 'infinitely complex', 'self-ordering', 'self-steering', 'self-regulating', and 'self-maintaining structure' of their 'irreplaceable economic order'[364] — which, on the mysterious authority of inter-galactic buccaneering, is declared to be (no doubt at least as soundly as the evidence provided by the author in support of the rest of his theory) 'the most complex structure in the universe'[365] — is bound to remain forever free from major problems and contradictions. The trouble is that even if we foolishly assume that 'we are constrained to preserve capitalism because of its superior capacity to utilize dispersed knowledge',[366] it does not follow at all that we shall be *able* to permanently preserve it. Can anyone seriously suggest that 'the most complex structure in the universe' — which, on planet earth, is indeed constrained both by its inner social antagonisms and by the impossibility to timelessly assert its uncontrollable, more and more destructive self-expansionary drive in a soberingly *finite* 'universe' — will always remain trouble-free for humanity (including the owners of 'several property'), so as to suit the convenience of the established order? Yet, without this blindly self-complacent, but characteristically unmentioned, second assumption, the proclaimed eternalizing 'constraint to preserve capitalism' would make no sense whatsoever even in terms of Hayek's capital-apologetic logic.

ANOTHER way of playing the Joker of 'complexity' in the pack is to frighten people that if they try to replace the market through socialist planning, they will end up — by definition, thanks to the decree of those who do not want to see any alternative to the market — with an authoritarian system of mind-boggling bureaucratic complexity, generously forgiving at the same time the combined chaos and bureaucratic complexity of the established order. Thus we are told that

> The 'New Left' [meaning in the author's vocabulary the radical socialist critics of both the capitalist market and the Soviet system], by attacking the market, logically put themselves in the position of advocating the substitution, in micro-economic affairs, of the visible for the hidden hand. They have as yet given no answer to the rather obvious counter-attack; the visible hand can only operate in the form of a *highly complex administrative machine*, which must surely generate most of the *bureaucratic-centralist* distortions of Soviet experience. Who but the centre, in a *modern industrial society*, would be able to decide between ends, means and alternative uses if no *market-and-price mechanism* exists? The usual answer is to denounce the USSR as not socialist, and assert the virtues of democracy and workers' control. Workers' self-management *à la Yugoslavia* is, however, only conceivable in a market environment. Without a market the elected committee would have to take instructions from the central planners, who alone will have the necessary information about ends and means.[367]

As usual, we are presented with arbitrary assumptions, made for the purpose of circularly deriving from them the desired conclusions. First, that the 'visible hand' can only operate 'in the form of a highly complex administrative machine', and therefore its operation is bound to be inescapably 'bureaucratic-centralist'. Second, that workers' control and workers' self-management can only be conceived 'à la Yugoslavia', ignoring the decapitated nature and the well known authoritarian restriction from above of the Yugoslav forms of 'self-management', although these defects have been repeatedly pointed out by the system's radical critics. And third, that workers' self-management is 'only conceivable in a market environment', because the information required for its operation is either provided by the market-and-price mechanism or must be dictated by the central planners. Naturally, from such arbitrary but highly tendentious assumptions one can derive the conclusion, with triumphant circularity, that there can be no alternative to the market 'in a modern industrial society'. But should the apologetically and fallaciously projected threat of 'absolutely unavoidable bureaucratic complexity' distract attention from the actually existing fateful uncontrollability of the capital system, with all of its frightening implications even for tomorrow, not to mention the more distant future? Who can be persuaded by the prefabricated 'conclusions' of the author quoted above? Only those who took for granted with him the irreplaceability of the capitalist market in the first place.

What is important to bear in mind is that the real issue is not complexity as such, be the argument concerned with complexity self-servingly inflated or real, but whether or not the socioeconomic trends of development described as complex are *controllable*. There is no such thing as a plain 'modern industrial society'; nor could there ever be. The type and degree of complexity of the productive and distributive practices in any society is determined by the historically and socially specific mode of controlling its metabolic interchange with nature and among the individuals themselves, depending, of course, also on the nature of the larger units under which the particular individuals are unceremoniously subsumed or grouped potentially freely. As we know from serious studies of social anthropology, the notion that communal type early societies — which regulate their social metabolic interchanges on the basis of a very high degree of solidarity among their members — are 'simple', is nothing but a patronizing and totally ahistorical misrepresentation. It arises from the need to project the characteristics of capital's reproductive order as ideal, and as the only measure by which everything else must be pronounced 'primitively simple' if it fails to conform to the ahistorically proclaimed measure. Moreover, as we have seen in Hayek's theorizations — but the same point generally applies to all those who construct their theories in tune with the vested interests of the established order — the self-serving opposition between simple and complex is invented on the crudest mechanical ground of making a fetish out of numbers, as if the same numbers could not mean something qualitatively different in different sets or structural relations. This mechanical number-fetish is pursued in order to dogmatically rule out the possibility — even the 'logical conceivability' — of solidarity arising and having a significant impact in any 'large industrial society'. We must ask, though, how small should be the numbers in question in order to be allowed to qualify in this respect? Should they amount to 50, or 100, or maybe at the extreme limit even to 1,000? But we know well from historical experience as recent as the Second World War that under determinate circumstances not only *millions* but even *hundreds of millions* of individuals are capable of acting in solidarity with one another. If the rational pursuit of a common objective, requiring solidarity and personal sacrifice for the realization of the shared purpose, is possible under the threat of an enemy, like Hitler's Nazi Germany, why should solidarity be 'inconceivable' when the stakes are even greater, foreshadowing the total destruction of humankind if the capital system is not brought under lasting control by rational human design and matching solidarity? Only because the blindly self-complacent interest of capital-apologetics so decrees. And to take an even more recent example, the solidarity of the British miners — positively demonstrated in their one year long strike in 1984-85 — was, in the end, not defeated by the 'complexity of a large industrial society'. On the contrary, it could only be subdued by the fully mobilized economic power and repressive force of the capitalist state, ruthlessly applied by the class-conscious defenders of the ruling order against the 'enemy within', in Margaret Thatcher's give-away words.

The opposition between 'complexity' and 'simplicity' is a tendentiously conceived false opposition, in the same way as that between 'growth versus no-growth' is. They are devised for the dual purpose of automatically defending, wholesale, the existent, and for aprioristically discrediting at the same time any attempt to alter the prevailing socioeconomic relations. If we agree to enter the framework of such a discourse — operating with arbitrary blanket-justifications of the ruling reproductive order, like 'complexity', 'growth', 'large-scale modern industry', 'technology', etc. — we are bound to be trapped by its false alternatives. For we are then bombastically challenged to choose either *'sancta simplicitas'* or 'unalterable complexity', the *'golden age of communist steady-state equilibrium'* or capitalist growth, *'small-group idolatry'* or 'large-scale industrial society', the illusions of *'Rousseau's noble savage'* or 'modern technology', etc.; naturally, the second always representing the 'sensible no alternative option', whereas the first the romantic illusion that must be ridiculed. In this way we are manoeuvred into a position where we either accept to be ridiculed, or must 'realistically' conclude that there can be no structural alternative to the established order. And while we waste our time over the false alternative of 'unalterable complexity' or 'sancta simplicitas',[368] the grave issue of capital's ever more threatening uncontrollability is not even mentioned.

Naturally, it is inconceivable to remove all complexity from an all-embracing mode of social metabolic control. However, there is no reason at all why that should be done if the social agency that must carry on the vital functions of societal reproduction can positively control the productive and distributive processes on which the development of the society in question, and the self-realization of its individuals, depend.

As far as the socialist project is concerned, subjecting the 'unalterable complexity' of capital's metabolic order to a radical critique is relevant to the extent to which it helps to remove the system's uncontrollability, with its all too obvious destructive implications. The fundamental — historically created and system-specific — determinations which can be pursued in this respect promise far-reaching changes under a socialist mode of social metabolic control. They require:

- superseding the *antagonistic/adversarial* relationship in which the labour process is carried on under the hierarchical structural domination of labour by capital in all of its known and feasible forms. Only in this way is it possible to remove those — wastefully complex and extreme bureaucratic — controlling institutions and functions (including in the final analysis the state as the totalizing command structure of capital), without which this mode of social metabolic control could not survive. The far from 'unalterable complexity' here referred to does not arise from the essential *primary* reproductive functions of society as such. On the contrary, it is generated by the perverse *second order mediations* of the established order, i.e. by capital's own need of self-preservation and structurally enforced command over labour. Since control over production and distribution is alienated from labour, the separate exercise of control must be protected by the *expropriation of the knowledge* required for the societal reproductive functions. At the same time, also institutional guarantees must be created through which the alienated control over the labour process as a whole — including its dimension involving privileged knowledge — can be enforced, if necessary by the force of arms. Inevitably, both the expropriation and separate development and application of knowledge, and the successful exercise of alienated control over the productive and distributive functions of society necessitate the superimposition of *multiple layers of complexity* which can be removed not only without detriment to society but *positively enhancing* its potential for development. This is thoroughly feasible, provided that the antagonistic/adversarial determination of the labour process and the unavoidable recalcitrance of labour is overcome, removing the nightmarish layers of complexity inseparable from a system which cannot function without enforcing its separate command over labour, even if it means vitiating all aspects of the social metabolism, from the productive and distributive microcosms all the way to the most comprehensive societal reproductive structures.

- The transcendence of the *fetishism of commodity* — necessarily inherited by all postcapitalist societies from the past — is inconceivable without progressively overcoming the adversarial determination of the labour process. In capitalist society the antagonist/adversarial control of the social metabolism is inseparable from the fetishism of commodity — the alienated and mystifying 'power of things' — which imposes the material imperatives of capital's expansion-oriented order on *all* members of society, including the personifications of capital. Thus, what is really at stake in this respect is not just 'complexity' — which could be amenable, in principle, to rational control, even when it happens to be of a very high degree — but the *type* of complexity which *excludes the possibility of control,* if control means interfering even minimally with the structural parameters and blind expansionary material imperatives of the capital system. The apologetic idealization of 'changing little by little' (advocated by Popper, Hayek, and others sharing the same vested interests), indicates the untouchability of the fetishistic structural framework as a whole, and the legitimation of only such measures of 'improvement' which conform to the perverse logic of the uncontrollable material dictates. However, the postcapitalist order's attack on the fetishism of commodity — in order to render the societal productive and distributive functions *transparent* and rationally modifiable — is bound to fail, unless it is complemented by measures consciously adopted in order to prevent the appearance of a new type of personification of capital, in charge of the politically regulated extraction of surplus-labour. For the continuation of a separate command over labour, even if it assumes a form very different from its capitalist variety, reproduces the antagonistic/adversarial determination of the way in which the social metabolic functions are carried on. And once the antagonistic command over labour prevails — whether for the economically or for the politically regulated extraction of surplus-labour — the necessity of multiple layers of wasteful complexity goes with it. Given the politically enforced extraction of surplus-labour in the Soviet type postcapitalist order, even the potentiality of progressively removing the inherited fetishism of commodity is greatly curtailed. Indeed, in the light of the Stalinist experience it has become abundantly clear that, as the direct political control of the labour process by the new personifications of capital encounters major difficulties, even the need for restoring the old fetishism of commodity — from Stalin's anticipation of the wishful remedy of 'market socialism' all the way to its final consummation as the peculiar restoration of capitalism by Gorbachev and his successors — reappears with a vengeance.

Thus the key to significant changes in the complexity of social metabolic reproduction is the radical supersession of the antagonistic/adversarial determination of the labour process, whether we have in mind the capitalist, primarily economic, or the postcapitalist, direct political, extraction of surplus-labour. No socialist could or would wish to advocate the establishment of a social metabolic order which fails to meet the needs of the individuals as a result of its simplistic approach to the encountered tasks and difficulties. The test to be applied here is whether or not the complexity in question is in the service of genuine human need or militates against it. What makes the complexity of capital's mode of reproduction deeply objectionable is its self-serving perniciousness. For the fundamental operational premiss of the capital system is *its own* reproduction on an ever-expanding scale, at whatever cost. This is what makes necessary the imposition of totally *unjustifiable complexity,* arising from the parasitic need of the capital system to retain control over the individuals — the alienating 'rule of wealth over society' — often not only neglecting but ruthlessly overruling even the most elementary human need. And there is nothing that can be done about this self-serving 'complexity' without going beyond capital. For once the need for the system's expanded reproduction is taken for granted as the necessary operational premiss of all productive and distributive practices, and thereby as the unalterable precondition by which the legitimacy and viability of human need must be judged, the pernicious complexity through which capital's hierarchical structural domination over labour is enforced must also be accepted.

By progressively overcoming the antagonistic/adversarial determination of the labour process, qualitative changes can be made in greatly reducing, and in the longer run completely eliminating the enslaving complexity required by capital's uncontrollable second order mediations, as opposed to human need. It is impossible to envisage a viable socialist reproductive order while retaining the capital system's existing forms and layers of mystifying complexity. The idea that *'micro-economics'* could be and should be safely left — *'à la Yugoslavia'* — to the fetishistic and dehumanizing tyranny of the market, suitably 'regulating' at the same time *'macro-economics',* under the slogan of a fictitious *'market socialism',* is totally incoherent as a conception and utterly disastrous as a practical policy, *'à la Yugoslavia'* or *à la Gorbachev,* or indeed in any other form. The acceptance of such absurd ideas and their more or less distant corollaries, in the name of *'unalterable complexity',* can in fact only mean the total renunciation of the possibility that human beings may one day gain control over the suicidal *uncontrol-*

lability of the capital system.

20.2.3

IN the course of historical development the move from *'nulle terre sans Seigneur'* to *'l'argent n'a past de maître'* represented a veritable *sea-change*. However, to talk about sea-change in moving from the established mode of reproductive control to a social metabolic order which had succeeded in eradicating capital from the labour process is not enough. It would be much more fitting to describe it as a real *epochal shift*. For the socialist project calls for the radical supersession of the structural domination of labour. As history shows, the structural domination of labour, in one form or another, is characteristic of all class societies. This is why the metaphor of sea-change is not enough for describing the unprecedented qualitative shift involved in positively appropriating — beyond the rule of capital — the alienated control functions of humanity's metabolic exchange with nature and the vital productive and distributive interchanges of the social individuals among themselves. For even the Black Sea intercommunicates with the distant Pacific Ocean.

The epochal shift in question means not only overcoming the rule of capital in the existing order, but also ensuring that such a change remains *irreversible*. In other words, it means rendering impossible the reappearance of capital's command over labour — and, of course, the necessary personifications of capital to enforce it — in the regulation of the productive and distributive relations of society by instituting and consolidating the self-determined activity of the associated producers. This can only be achieved by

- (1) returning the objective conditions (i.e. the material and means) of production as genuine or substantive property to the producers themselves, in contrast to the historically experienced vacuous juridical definition of 'collective property' which remained in actuality under the control of a separate state authority;

- (2) by exercising strict control in the period of transition over the personifications of capital inherited from the past. This means not simply gaining control over capital's personifications as particular individuals. For, as we know, it is possible to change the personnel without significantly altering the system itself. The issue is the institution of effective social supervision over a determinate set of controlling functions which in the inherited system are assigned to a number of strategically located individuals. As the disheartening historical experience of postcapitalist societies clearly demonstrated, transition to a socialist mode of reproduction is inconceivable without the strict exercise of this type of supervision over the personifications of capital by appropriate forms of self-management. The purpose of such supervision is twofold: (a) the prevention of the abuse of power for ends incompatible with the overall socialist objectives, and (b) the progressive transfer of the control functions themselves to the social body, those functions, that is, which —in view of the nature of the inherited system—cannot be directly exercised by the various work collectives for a more or less limited period of transition;

- (3) the conscious prevention of the possibility that new types of personification — for the strategic requirements of direction — should reemerge as time goes by, in conjunction with a separate and alienable form of control over the strategic levers of social metabolic reproduction. Here it is important to recall the repeated apologetic — and totally fallacious — identification of the need for 'directing will' with the historically experienced *alienated* forms of control and *command over labour;* as if it were inconceivable that the productive and distributive relations of the individuals could be regulated in a *substantively democratic* way by the individuals themselves. On this issue, tellingly, we find a total identity between Stalin's favourite economists, like Varga quoted above, and the Western 'liberal' apologists of capital's authoritarianism in the workshop and tyranny in the market, duly complemented by an eager rejoinder by the advocates of 'market socialism'. For once the authoritarian definition of an alien 'directing will' is taken for granted as some kind of a natural law, the permanent structural subordination of labour 'follows' from it.

One of the most intractable problems which even the greatest thinkers of the bourgeoisie in the ascendant could not master concerned the 'directing will' in its broadest sense. The reason why in their explanations they had to mix rationality with complete mystery was because they could not resolve the contradiction inseparable from the standpoint of capital which they had adopted. For capital simultaneously asserts itself both as a *multiplicity of capitals,* which remain in conflict not only with their labour force but also among themselves (hence the ideals and ideology of possessive and competitive individualism), and as the *totalizer* whose laws must prevail, at all costs, over against both labour in general and over its own pluralistic constituents. Adam Smith's 'invisible hand', Kant's 'commercial spirit' and Hegel's 'world spirit' were heroic attempts to come to terms with this contradiction, while remaining enclosed within the constraining conceptual parameters of their adopted standpoint. These visions, despite the characteristic distortions of the 'standpoint of political economy', represented real insights at least into the nature of the dilemma which the great Scottish and German thinkers attempted to resolve. For they offered the idea of some kind of a 'collective' mover, even if they could only do that in the form of a benevolent *supra-individual* subjectivity, situated within an *individualistic* framework of explanation, as we have seen it in Chapter 3. Later 'improvements' on these solutions—by the first versions of 'marginal utility' theory and its descendants—amounted to a complete mystification, and as a rule were coupled with the crudest mechanistic postulates of some controlling automata. The system-specific regulatory subjectivity of capital's mode of reproduction — with all of its embarrassing implications — was thereby conveniently obliterated.

At the roots of the apologetic theories of the 'marginal revolution' we find the problem that the *objective laws* of the capital system — with a logic of its own and a tendency towards an ultimately insoluble structural crisis — cannot be admitted to exist. Thus the mysteries of the 'infinite subjective choices' of the consumers must be gratuitously assumed as the only conceivable effective regulator. This explanation has a dual function. First, it wishfully eliminates the possibility of any *rational alternative* to the established reproductive order by the decree that no 'rational design' for controlling the social metabolic process as a whole should be contemplated, since it would run counter to the idea of infinite individual utility-maximizing choices. And second, by postulating this kind of absolutely uncontrollable individualistic regulatory mechanism as an explanatory hypothesis, the idea of raising the question of *responsibility* (and potential blame) vis-à-vis the actually existing *system-specific subjectivity,* i.e. the personifications of capital, is ruled out.

It is impossible to gain control over the established mode of societal reproduction without understanding the relationship between the objective and subjective factors through which capital asserts its rule. Postulates of infinite subjective choices — within the framework of the 'market mechanism' — as the regulators of the system are not theoretical explanations but fog-generators. They dissolve the line of demarcation between the objective and the subjective and render impossible the understanding of both. The truth is that no social metabolic control can function by objective laws alone, through the exclusion of human subjectivity, or *vice versa,* no system of sustainable metabolic reproduction is intelligible on the basis of self-oriented, 'utility-maximizing' subjective choices alone.

It is necessary to understand the objective material/structural imperatives and totalizing laws of the capital system in order to be able to grasp the dialectical relationship between the historically specific *commanding/controlling subjectivity* — the personifications of capital — and the systemic need for rationally coherent anticipations and corrective actions in terms of which the particular personifications of capital have to fulfil their role in the system. In this sense Hayek's demagogic dismissal of all talk about the 'selfish decisions of individual owners of capital' is indeed a red herring. No serious socialist analysis of the antagonisms of the capital system is concerned with the 'selfish decisions of individual capitalists' on their own. That aspect is quite irrelevant to the objective assessment of what is really at stake and how the antagonisms of the system could be overcome in the future. The particular capitalists may or may not be individually selfish. If they are, the likelihood is that they will not remain for long successful capitalists. This is so not because of the intervention of some mysterious moral punishment for greedily acquiring and selfishly dissipating their profits, but because by doing so they would fail to carry out their function as personifications of capital, in conformity to the *expansionary imperative* of their system. What matters here is not the selfishness of particular capitalists, who mistreat the workers because of their blind greed and selfishness, but the structural subordination and exploitation of labour — even by the most enlightened 'caring capitalists' — as determined by the incorrigible material dictates of the system.

The rule of capital and its personifications — as system-specific subjectivity in command over labour — stand or fall together. The epochal shift required for moving beyond capital is concerned with the question of control and with the radical supersession of the alienated system of command over labour by the associated individual producers themselves. Only the shallowest liberals and social democrats could restrict the question of emancipation to the pious critique of 'selfishness'. A critique which never produced — nor could it ever produce — anything but vacuous sermons. For capital always was and necessarily remains an unrestrainable and uncontrollable mode of social metabolic control which must subdue everything that stands in its path of self-expansion. This logic could not be effectively challenged for as long as the dynamism of capital-expansion could 'deliver the goods', making perversely palatable much inhumanity and destructiveness that went with that delivery. The big difference today is that the *unrestrainability* of capital has run its historic course, making the system's *uncontrollability* too great a threat to be ignored by turning the other way. This is what confers on the Marxian socialist project greater relevance today than ever before. For only by pursuing the real target of socialist transformation — to go beyond capital — is it possible to address with any chance of lasting success even the most immediate dangers.

20.3 Beyond the command economy: the meaning of socialist accountancy

20.3.1

TO say that capital's unrestrainability has run its historic course means that the system itself has lost its viability as the controller of sustainable social metabolic reproduction. This is not a question of looking far ahead into the future. The limits are visible in our immediate vicinity, as are the dangers that go with the inability or refusal — and in capital's case the two coincide — to exercise restraint. For today even the most eager defenders of the established order, with enormous vested interests to defend, are willing to concede that some restraints must be adopted (at least in some areas of economic activity, such as the husbandry of prime material and energy resources, as well as with regard to 'population control'), even if they are unable to offer practical solutions, other than the general prescription that everything must remain well within the structural parameters of their system. They used to argue in a confidently circular fashion that the expansionary dynamics itself always successfully redefines and extends the limits. Today that argument is obviously untenable. However, despite the concession of the need for restraint, no indication is ever given how the capital system could function on that basis — i.e. *what* could be restrained in it and *who* should be in control of the restraining process meant to overrule the material imperative of expansion — while retaining its viability as a totalizing mode of social metabolic reproduction. In fact the possibility of capital's restrained operation appears in the writings of its ideologists either as the nightmare of the 'stationary state' of economic reproduction, or as something to be exorcised with a gratuitous insult against Marx, attributing to him, as we have seen above, the mindless advocacy of 'a communist steady-state equilibrium'.

Naturally, the question of restraint cannot be separated from the objective characteristics and structural determinations of the system in relation to which the need for restraint arises. In this sense, to expect from capital to restrain itself is nothing short of expecting a miracle to happen. For capital could adopt self-restraint as a significant feature of its mode of operation only by ceasing to be capital. As Marx had pointed out:

> If capital increases from 100 to 1,000, then 1,000 is now the point of departure, from which the increase has to begin; the tenfold multiplication, by 1,000 percent, counts for nothing; profit and interest themselves become capital in turn. What appeared as surplus-value now appears as simple presupposition etc., as included in its simple composition.[369]

Thus the need for restraint — even if what is at stake is nothing less than human survival — is diametrically contradicted by the innermost determinations of the capital system. For capital's mode of reproduction would collapse very quickly if it was compelled to operate within firmly circumscribed, as opposed to constantly expandable, limits. No partial remedies are conceivable in this regard, and certainly none that could be implemented by the personifications of capital in any one of their actually feasible embodiments. This is why it is necessary to envisage the institution of qualitative systemic changes at a time when the dangers arising from the uncontrollability of capital intensify, due to the system's structural unrestrainability.

Capital is the most comprehensively alienated mode of control in history, with its self-enclosed command structure. For it must operate by strictly subordinating the producers — in every respect — to a system of decision making radically divorced from them. This is an irremediable condition, due to the totalizing — and in its objective implications from the outset globally expansionary — character of the system which cannot share power, even to a minimal degree, with labour. Thus the alienated control process must be objectively defined as the inexorable *logic of capital*, which in its turn calls for the definition of the controlling personnel as the *personification of capital in command over labour*. The *separate group-identity* of the personifications of capital is the necessary corollary of capital's objective logic, corresponding to the system's key defining characteristic as a separate, alienated command structure. For this reason there can be no question of reforming the capital system even through the science-fictional cloning of the 'enlightened caring capitalists', nor indeed of radically changing it through the postcapitalist metamorphosis of the inherited system's personifications into hierarchically operating political controllers of surplus-labour extraction. For capital cannot help being a hierarchical *command system,* and its economy — through whatever historically different forms of personification it might be operated — a *command economy.*

When Gorbachev and followers denounced the Soviet 'command economy', many people responded to it with positive expectations. For before these high-ranking personifications of Soviet postcapitalist capital so dramatically changed their tune, they were indeed operating and enforcing for decades the rules of a repressive command system. What was profoundly misleading about their characterization of the issues at stake and the way of resolving them was that the projected solutions were in fact based on the most absurd illusions about the democratic potential of 'market society'. The top party and state officials in charge of the Soviet system wilfully ignored that the Western capitalist economy from which they borrowed the models of 'perestroika' was also a command economy. This is how it could be proposed in all seriousness that the restoration of capitalist private property, coupled with a modified 'economic mechanism' and 'management techniques', will *ensure the country's social democratic progress'.*[370] As the chief Soviet ideologist and a member of the Party Politburo, Vadim Medvedev, had put it:

> it was impossible to break the iron vice of the administer-and-command system, which impedes economic progress, without political reform. Subsequent critical thinking led us further, to the understanding of the need for the *reorganization of property relations.* ... Without drastic changes in production relations, *new economic management techniques* are rejected as something alien. ... The vicious circle can be

broken only by a *reform of property relations,* by admitting a variety of forms of property. The Party has opted for this approach, banking not on one or two 'advanced' or 'most Socialist' forms but on the entire set of equal forms of property. ... Perestroika has opened wide opportunities for cooperatives, lease contracts, various other contracts, household production, and individual labour activity. *Joint-stock companies* are in no way contrary to Socialist economic principles. ... We regard a far-reaching reorgani- zation of property relations and the diversity and equality of all of its forms as a *guarantee of the renewal of Socialism.*[371]

Naturally, for the personifications of capital, in whatever form, the profoundly anti-democratic nature of the command structure in which they are in control over labour, with the mandate for enforcing the material imperatives of their system, cannot present any problem. That is why they can slide with such ease from one to the other. This is true not only of those who can discover in the restoration of capitalist private property not only the 'equality' of giant monop- olistic joint stock companies with 'household production' and the local cobbler's 'individual labour activity', but also the 'guarantee of the renewal of Socialism'. In the same way, the personifications of capital operating in the Western 'de- mocratic market economy' find no difficulty with the periodic transformation of their societies into brutal dictatorships at times of major economic crises and labour unrest, despite their loudly proclaimed 'liberal' beliefs. Besides, even when they talk about democracy, they restrict its sphere of operation to the 'free political choice' of abdicating the power of decision making to party represen- tatives firmly locked into capital's political command structure, coupled with the absolutely unchallengeable premiss of the consumers' so-called 'free econo- mic choice' in the capitalist market — to be carved out of the workers' meagre resources, not to mention the fact that they are totally denied to have any say in decisions over the sphere of production and over the conditions of their working life.

But even in such vacuous definition of democracy and freedom, in contrast to the substantive authoritarianism of capital's command structure both in the domain of economics and in politics, the system needs the semblance of choice and the observance of the 'rules of the game' suitable to create the illusion of democracy. Thus, after the euphoria of 'seeing off socialism' and thereby trium- phantly reaching the 'end of history', qualifications had to creep in as to where the 'free political choice' might be if there is no 'left' that can be safely allowed to be chosen for the purpose of labour's political abdication and for the pacifi- cation of the potentially unruly masses of the people. Understandably, therefore, the leading ideological organs of the established order, like the London *Economist,* had to change their tune and sing their old song in this peculiar way:

> the death of communism leaves a void that needs to be filled quickly. ... the poor are still with us: in growing numbers in much of the southern world, in pockets of desperation in North America and Western Europe. Doing something for the un- fortunate is the chief business of the political left. ... Your great-grandchildren will be better off in 2092 if you act in the name of compassion in 1992. Here is the starting-point for something new on the left. A new left is badly needed. The end of communism has left the world standing, as it were, on one leg. The forward march cannot be resumed until the other leg is back in healthy operation.[372]

Mercifully, then, historical time is not completely dead yet. Thanks to the mag- nanimity of *The Economist,* we are allowed to postpone 'the end of history'. At least until the world grows back its missing leg, at which point we can happily resume our forward march in the, for the time being somewhat problematical, 'New World Order'.

Still, the thought of the world hopping along on one leg towards the gates of the liberal-capitalist Millennium, while its other leg slowly grows back, out of the remnants of its socialdemocratic stump, is quite hilarious. We could even laugh about it if conditions were not so desperately serious for the overwhelming majority of humankind. Here, again, we can see the abyss that separates the ascending phase of capitalist development from its present-day reality. For in the age of Enlightenment the spokesmen of the bourgeois order genuinely believed that 'enlightened self-interest' would bring its abundant benefits to the whole of humanity, wiping out poverty altogether from the face of the earth. They could do this because the inner contradictions of the capital system did not reveal as yet their necessary unfolding in the form of the *destructive dissipation of wealth*. That was in store for the human race in a future when capital's continued self-expansion could not be secured in any other way, making a mockery of the once honestly championed ideals of 'Liberty, Fraternity, Equality'. Now all talk about 'enlightened self-interest' amounts only to a cynical camouflage of the fact that the overwhelming majority of people are categorically excluded, through capital's structural hierarchy and authoritarian command system, from its exercise. They have to be contented with *The Economist's* decree that it is in the nature of *'the human predicament'* that 'the poor will be always with us',[373] coupled with the meaningless line in the same sermon, that 'It makes sense to rescue the poor [who 'will be always with us'], because the world is then likely to be a safer place'.[374] And the spokesmen of capital hasten to decree another of their laws of 'the human predicament', saying that *'The world will never be wholly dictator-free'.*[375] This is what the 'enlightened self-interest' and 'compassion' of *The Economist* boils down to, in its appeal for the creation of a new 'designer left' — like 'New Labour' in Britain — all in perfect conformity to the material dictates of capital's 'democratic'command economy, at a time when the system has fully consummated its historical ascendancy.

20.3.2

IT is obscene to call 'free and democratic' an economic system which has for its absolute material precondition the alienation of the conditions of production from the producers, and for its mode of operation the permanent imposition of an authoritarian command structure — both in the workshop and in society at large — through which the continued extraction of surplus-labour can be secured for the purposes of capital's expanded reproduction. As to the proposition according to which the restoration of capitalist property relations constitutes the 'guarantee for the renewal of Socialism', it can only prove something which the Greeks have discovered thousands of years ago; namely, that those whom the gods want to destroy, they first render insane.

The capitalist command economy represents the most sophisticated — and also the most mystifying — all-invading variety of social metabolic reproduction. Capital's exploitative domination over labour 'is only distinct in a formal sense from other, more direct, forms of *enslavement* of labour and property in labour on the part of the owner of the conditions of production. It glosses over as a mere money relation the real transaction and the *perpetual dependence,* which is constantly renewed through the relation of sale and purchase. Not only are the conditions of this commerce constantly reproduced, in addition to this, what one buys with, and what the other is *obliged* to sell, is the result of the process. The constant renewal of this relation of sale and purchase only mediates the *permanence of the specific relation of dependence,* giving the *deceptive semblance* of a transaction, a *contract* between commodity owners who have *equal rights* and confront each other *equally freely'.*[376]

None the less, it can be argued that the capitalist type of command economy represents in a sense the unsurpassable peak of all those forms of economic development in history which are based on antagonistic structural determinations. For although the ruthless imposition of the compulsion to perform surplus-labour is shared by the capitalist mode of production with earlier modes of exploitative societal reproduction, capital exerts such compulsion 'in a form more favourable to production'.[377] It is superior to the others in virtue of its incomparable inner dynamism and global expandability, thanks to its perfection of the modality — and the maximization of the quantity — of surplus-labour extraction, with *relatively* small amounts of resources wasted on extra-economic means of enforcement. For the mystifying and 'deceptive semblance of a freely entered contract between parties with equal rights' can fulfil many of the necessary functions of enforcement, creating the illusion of 'consensual' and 'democratic' relations, under actually existing conditions when labour is 'obliged' — i.e. economically compelled — to submit to the imperatives of capital's command economy and accept its 'human predicament' in the 'iron cage' (Weber) of so-called 'modern industrial society'.

This mode of social metabolic reproduction in which objectified and alienated labour — assuming the form of capital, with its own logic and material inertia — rules over labour, 'makes sense', so long as the system's incomparable dynamics of expansion itself makes sense. The question, nevertheless, remains, what kind of consciousness is judging, or is capable of judging, whether or not, for whom, and at what price, the inexorable self-expansion of capital 'makes sense'. It cannot be the collective pseudo-subject, capital. For in its substance capital is nothing more than *'the objectification of alien labour, value independently confronting labour capacity'.*[378] Inasmuch as capital can, and does, acquire consciousness and will, through the personifications of capital, it can only prejudge the issues, with ultimately fatal distortion, in its own favour. Distorted prejudgement of the road to follow must take place both in the interest of capital in general, as the totalizer of social metabolic interchange, and in relation to the partial interests of the plurality of capitals and the particular personifications of capital. The required judgement cannot be based on the interests of all members of a historically given society (including the particular workers), let alone on the interests of labour as a class whose hegemonic alternative to the existent diametrically contradicts the given order. Nor can, of course, the basis of judgement be the consideration of humanity's interests; not even when the very survival of humankind is at stake. Thus the determination of what 'makes sense' can only be done on the basis of the prevailing power relations, in accordance with the material dictates of capital's continued self-expansion. Bourgeois class interests and the material inertia of the given reproductive structures all act in the same direction. Their negations — by the earliest forms of labour protest and their intellectual conceptualizations — remain problematical and 'utopian', until a stage of socioeconomic development is reached when the viability of labour's hegemonic alternative to the established mode of control can be posited. Under such conditions it becomes possible for labour to posit the negation of the established order not as an ideal counter-image to capital's antagonistic, and therefore of necessity forcibly imposed, authoritarian command system, but as a *materially sustainable,* as well as in a *substantive* sense democratic, mode of decision making in all productive and distributive relations.

It would stand to reason that when the destructive dissipation of natural resources and social wealth becomes the objective condition of capital's expanded reproduction, the continued 'rule of wealth over society' can no longer make sense from the standpoint of sustainable societal reproduction. Indeed, the greater the inner dynamics of capital's drive for expanded reproduction — representing a vital positive asset at earlier phases of development — the more irrational it becomes to engage in it when the destructiveness on a formerly quite unimaginable scale is an integral part of the whole process. However, the trouble is that despite its threatening irrationality, the pursuit of the established mode of expanded reproduction continues to 'make sense' as much as ever before from capital's own standpoint. For capital, as *causa sui,* cannot conceivably envisage — and even less allow — any alternative to its own mode of operation, which is incorrigibly expansion-oriented. Thus, even when 'value independently confronting labour capacity' becomes simultaneously *anti-value confronting the whole of humanity,* foreshadowing the *destruction of the social metabolism* as such, even that cannot alter capital's equations. It can only render the authoritarianism of its command system more authoritarian than ever before. For the *self-oriented rationality* of capital's expanded reproduction, on the premiss of its *causa sui,* must overrule — whenever needed, even by the application of the most tyrannical forms of political repression — all alternative forms of rationality. The historical evidence of 'democratic' capital's metamorphoses into extreme forms of authoritarianism at times of major crises can offer no reassurance in this respect for the future.

To be sure, under such circumstances the continued rule of capital's mode of wealth-production over society contains a major *regressive* moment even from the standpoint of capital itself, not to mention the threat to human survival. For the introduction of ever more powerful political factors even into the normal mode of operation of the capital system (of which there is plenty of evidence in the 20th century), coupled with the direct imposition of repressive political and military measures under the conditions of emergency, significantly alter the earlier mentioned historical advantage of capitalism. Namely, that its compulsion is exercised over labour 'in a form more favourable to production'. For the regressive employment of direct political control tends to undermine the deceptive consensual stability of the system, letting loose a number of complications and contradictions, including the 'crisis of democratic politics'. Nevertheless, this kind of regression presents in no way a prohibitive problem to capital when the system's continued survival is at stake. For the bottom line remains what capital shares with earlier antagonistic forms of social metabolic reproduction: the *necessary domination of labour* and the *exploitative compulsion* that must be exercised in order to *extract surplus-labour*. The capital system historically originated on such a material basis, and its mode of operation could never be imagined, without ceasing to be capital's mode of control — let alone implemented as the fiction of 'people's capitalism' — on any other basis. This is what connects the Pacific Ocean with the Black Sea.

Describing the potential inherent in the productive achievements of capital's historical ascendancy, Marx argues that 'it creates the real conditions for a new mode of production, superseding the antagonistic form of the capitalist mode of production, and thus lays the *material basis* for a newly shaped social life process and therewith a *new social formation*. ... [For] the material conditions for its dissolution are produced within it, thereby *removing its historical justification* as a necessary form of economic development, of the production of social wealth.'[379] And he makes it clear elsewhere that the process through which this potentiality can be turned into reality is not an easy one. For it involves both the recognition that capital's insurmountable barriers are not the absolute limits of all productive development, and the ability to act in full awareness of the objectively available positive potentialities beyond the capital system's antagonisms. To quote Marx:

> The barrier to *capital* is that this entire development proceeds in a contradictory way, and that the working-out of the productive forces, of general wealth, etc., knowledge etc., appears in such a way that the working individual *alienates* himself *{sich ent-äussert};* relates to the conditions brought out of him by his labour as those not of his *own* but of an *alien wealth* and of his own poverty. But this antithetical form is itself fleeting and produces the real conditions of its own suspension. The result is: the *tendentially* and *potentially* general development of the forces of production — of wealth as such — as a basis; likewise, the universality of intercourse, hence the world market as a basis. The basis as the *possibility* of the universal development of the individual, and the real development of the individuals from this basis as a constant suspension of its barrier, which is *recognized as a barrier*, not taken for a *sacred limit*. Not an ideal or imagined universality of the individual, but the universality of his real and ideal relations. Hence also the *grasping* of his own history as a *process*, and the *recognition* of nature (equally present as practical power over nature) as his real body. The process of development itself posited and known as the presupposition of the same. For this, however, necessary above all that the *full development* of the forces of production has become the *condition of production;* and not that *specific conditions of production* are posited as a *limit* to the development of the productive forces.[380]

Thus the positive outcome depends not on the recognition by intellectuals that the historical justification of the capital system is over, but on the material force of a conscious social agency capable of eradicating capital from the social metabolic process, superseding thereby the rule of 'alien wealth' over society. If that agency proves to be unequal to the task, there can be no hope for the socialist project. But, then, there can be no hope for the survival of humanity either.

As we know, in Marx's life-time the capital system was far from subsuming under its own reproductive framework every country on the planet. Thus it was still very far from its stage of development when the destructive dissipation of natural resources and social wealth had to become an objective condition of capital's expanded reproduction. Likewise, the development of the instruments of destruction was still very far from the point where it could directly threaten human life everywhere, in sharp contrast to our own perilous conditions of existence. Accordingly, the dangers arising from both these developments could not enter Marx's horizon in their overpowering material reality. The possibility that capital's infernal war machinery could physically destroy the human race in a matter of hours, if not minutes, was in Marx's lifetime inconceivable. The grave dangers to human existence could be visible to him only in the form of some conceptual/theoretical implications of capital's uncontrollable logic, in the sense indicated by the quotation from *The German Ideology* on page 6. The same goes for the world market and the potentially lethal antagonisms arising from it. As Marx stressed, 'the tendency to create the *world market* is directly given in the *concept of capital* itself'.[381] However, we had to wait for the occupation and reproductive domination of every little corner of the world by the major capitalist powers, leading to the conflagration of two World Wars, before the destructive implications of capital's uncontrollability could be fully sized up in their massive materiality. And we have by no means reached the end of this process. For the much talked about 'globalization' — assuming the form of an apparently irresistible integration of the productive and exchange processes of the capital system in the entire world — foreshadows new antagonisms and potential destruction.

In relation to all these developments it is painfully obvious that the necessarily authoritarian articulation of capital's command economy, with all of its political corollaries, can only become more pronounced in the foreseeable future. Sadly, the recognition of the dangers is not enough. Capital's established mode of social metabolic control has two major assets, despite its contradictions. The first is the massive *inertia* of the prevailing structures, pushing everything to follow the *'line of least resistance'*. And the second, that the only social agency capable of taking up the challenge, labour, in its 'immediacy' (i.e. in its established mode of reproduction) is also locked into the vicious circle of the 'line of least resistance', subsumed under and dominated by the capital system's productive and distributive relations. We should not forget that labour in its immediacy, including its direct confrontation with capital, of necessity assumes the form of consciousness as the 'personification of labour'. In this way it is engaged in conflict with the 'personification of capital', thereby confining itself to aims containable by the structural parameters of the capital system. We have seen the tragic consequences of that posture in the clamorous defeat of the historical left. This is why we badly need the radical rearticulation of the socialist movement. Without it, there can be truly 'no alternative' to capital's destructive command economy and to whatever authoritarian devices might be required in order to impose it at all costs on society, until the whole system collapses under the weight of its own deadly inertia.

20.3.3

THE socialist movement has no chance of success against capital by raising only a set of partial demands. For such demands must always prove their viability within the preestablished limits and regulatory determinations of the capital system. To talk about parts makes sense only if they can be related to the whole to which they objectively belong. In this sense, only within the overall terms of reference of the socialist hegemonic alternative to the rule of capital can the validity of strategically chosen partial objectives be properly judged. And the criterion of assessment must be their suitability (or not) to become *lasting and cumulative* achievements in the hegemonic enterprise of radical transformation. Not surprisingly, therefore, the Bernsteinian reformist slogan which proclaimed that 'the aim is nothing, the movement is everything' — by making a fetish out of the most limited partial objectives of 'the movement' and rejecting at the same time the overall socialist aim—could only lead the socialdemocratic movement into the blind alley of capitulation.

One of the most important questions of any socialist strategy concerns the *accountancy* used for orienting and evaluating the particular steps and measures that must be adopted in the course of transition from the established order to a radically different one. For even if capital's historical phase of ascendancy can create some favourable material conditions which point in the direction of 'a newly shaped social life', as Marx had argued, the potential material assets in question become totally endangered when the system's historical ascendancy is over and capital can continue to superimpose itself on society only at the cost of undermining its own former achievements. The structural incorporation of waste-production into the expansionary dynamics of present-day capital production is a very good example of how Marx's once justifiable optimistic expectations have turned sour under the pressure of the capital system's deepening contradictions. It is therefore vital to adopt a framework of accountancy very different from the one to which we are accustomed. That is, a new framework of accountancy through which both the general direction of the socialist emancipatory strategy and its particular mediatory objectives can be reliably evaluated.

In principle, *'accountancy'* — often reduced to its most obvious aspect of *'book-keeping'* — and *'administration'*, could be considered essential (some might say absolute) moments of all present and future modes of social metabolic reproduction. This is true in the sense that no societal reproductve system can function in a sustainable way without activating its material and human resources and controlling their allocation and deployment in accordance with some principle of 'economy'.

However, despite the self-mythology of capital's 'rational principles of allocation' and 'instrumental values', there can be no question of 'neutrality'. The ideas of 'value-free' or 'value-neutral' assessment of the issues at stake, and action on the basis of the conclusions obtained in that way, belong to the apologetic fantasies of the established order. We have seen on many occasions that the claimed 'rational conclusions' are as a rule uncritically and circularly assumed from the outset by those who identify themselves with the standpoint of capital, so as to enable them to reach the ideologically desired 'conclusive proof of the superiority of their system.

In truth, as soon as we examine a little more closely capital's allegedly neutral 'book-keeping', said to be based on 'pure instrumental rationality', it becomes clear that all such book-keeping is heavily *value-laden social accountancy*. As Marx rightly observed, 'The capitalist himself only holds power as the personification of capital. This is why in double-entry book-keeping he constantly figures twice, e.g. as DEBTOR to his own CAPITAL.'[382] Characteristically, Max Weber assigned a key role to the 'discovery of double-book keeping' in his biassed representation of the capitalist order as the paradigm of rationality. In this way he was able to brush aside the primacy of *material power relations,* disregarding altogether the real nature of capital's system-specific subjectivity — the personification of capital — and its system-determined, far from purely rational, double-entry book-keeping.

The same considerations apply to *administration,* which is inconceivable without the social framework — and under the rule of capital of necessity a profoundly iniquitous and structurally predetermined and secured hierarchical social framework — through which the overall principles of societal regulation can be first of all *enacted,* and then implemented or *enforced.* Even Hayek's 'purely formal principles' of traffic regulation discussed above, which he fallaciously wanted to generalize and use, with typical ideological eagerness, for his uncritical defence of capital and its state formation, must rely on a hierarchical social network of enactment and enforcement. Not to mention the 'rational administrative decisions' taken for building (or not building) the roads themselves on which traffic can then be 'rationally regulated'. The way in which the arguments about the 'insurmountable complexity of modern industrial society' are wedded together with the claims of the capital system's insuperably 'rational administration' — and, of course, also with the claims concerning capital's universally beneficial and 'rationally efficacious book-keeping' — speaks volumes about the apologetic intent of the complexity merchants and myth-makers of capitalist 'value-neutral' rationality.

Naturally, the question of rational administration is important in socialist theory, since its practical realization is vital to the socialist project. And since the way in which the question arises is inseparable from the need to overcome the structural hierarchy of the inherited capital system — and to do so without imposing on the social individuals a new type of hierarchy, under the rule of the postcapitalist personifications of capital — the fundamental challenge in this respect concerns the necessity to do away with the *separate command over labour:* an alienated command system deeply embedded in the sphere of production which must go with a separate command structure also in the area of administration. There can be no socialist administration — deserving to be characterized as a truly rational system of administration — for as long as the practical premises of rule-enactment and rule-enforcement are set by the vitiating demands of separate command over labour, linked to any particular form whatsoever of the forcible extraction of surplus-labour. Besides, many of the perversely/adversarially devised, enacted, and with much waste enforced rules fall by the wayside if the need for regulation directly arises from the individuals concerned. This could not contrast more sharply with 20th century historical experience whereby the rules of the postcapitalist command systems were imposed upon a recalcitrant social body — the overwhelming majority of the working people — by the enforcers of capital's continued time-imperative. For postcapitalist capital's alienated control of surplus-labour-extraction could only be exercised by the postcapitalist personifications of capital, fully in tune with the alienating imperatives of the system.

The practical realization of the principles of *socialist accountancy* is a necessary and integral constituent of the originally envisaged socialist order. For only through the practical realization of such principles can the material base be secured without which the ongoing rational regulation of the social individuals' productive and distributive interchanges is not possible. Notwithstanding the myths of capital's rational efficacy and ideal economy, the capital system *never* was — nor could it ever be — truly economical in its use of material and human resources. What created the deceptive semblance of insurpassable rational economizing was the system's ability to maximize the extraction of surplus-labour. For capital, in its drive for expansion and accumulation, functioned as the most powerful *pump* ever made in history for the purpose of ruthlessly extracting surplus-labour and surplus-value from living labour.

But this characteristic, notwithstanding its importance in the course of historical development, should not be confused with real economy. For *real economy depends on the use to which the social wealth created by the producers is put*. The capital system's pump-economy resembles the British water industry which struggles with major water shortages — on the face of it quite unbelievably — every warm summer, in a country benefiting from most abundant rainfall. The mystery is resolved by focusing on the simple fact that up to one third of the water extracted by the British pump system is irresponsibly wasted through the leakages of the pipe network itself. And on top of it, the obscenely well paid managers of the privatized British water extraction and distribution system argue, in true capitalist fashion, that it is 'much more economical' to let the pipes leak and waste away all that water, rather than mend or renew the defective distribution network itself; a policy pursued, they say, 'strictly in the interest of the consumers'. In a similar way, capital's powerful pump system as a whole could hide throughout history its waste of immense resources under the spectacular results of *unhindered capital-expansion*. The 'moment of truth' only arrives when the necessity of expansion encounters major obstacles, as we experience it in our own times. The fact that under such circumstances the difficulties of profitable capital-expansion assume the form of speculative capital shortages and adventurist capital movements, against the background of the most cruel denial to satisfy the elementary needs of countless millions, can only underline that capital is, in Marx's words, the 'living contradiction'.

20.3.4

IN contrast to capital's — expansion-dictated and not need-oriented — false economy, the socialist system of accountancy must be economical in a substantive sense. For its consciously appreciated principal determining force is constituted by labour, recognized not as abstract 'labour capacity' but as living human individuals. Capital, on the other hand, can relate to the overwhelming majority of human beings only by reducing them to exploitable 'labour capacity', to be put to use in its reified form — as a 'material factor of production' — for the purpose of surplus-labour-extraction.

This is why the ruling principle of capital's expansion-oriented social accountancy must be *quantification* in every sphere of activity and in every relation, even when the term *'quality'* is employed. Hegel talked about the dialectical transformation of *quantity into quality*. In capitalist value relations transformation takes place exactly the other way round. All qualities must be turned into quantity, so as to become grist to capital's 'Satanic mills'.

To be sure, quality control plays an important role in successful capitalist production. But 'quality' here stands for the quantified performance-statistics of the product, whether we think of a motor car or of the MTBF figures[383] of computer components and HiFi equipment, etc. The most varied qualities of use value must be first subsumed under determinate quantities of exchange value, before they can acquire the legitimacy to be produced at all; and they must constantly prove their viability — not in relation to qualitatively different human needs, but under the strictly quantitative criteria of commodity exchange. Moreover, quantification rules also under the postcapitalist capital system, as we have known it so far. For even if profitability recedes into the background, reappearing again only in the wishful images of Stalinist and 'de-Stalinized' *'market socialism'*, the expansionary imperative itself remains as powerful as ever before, imposed on society in an authoritarian way through the quantity-fetish of compulsory plan-fulfilment and through the idealization of 'socialist' quantification as the plan's (fictitious) 'over-fulfilment'.

The false alternatives of 'unalterable complexity or romantic simplicity', and 'growth or no-growth', etc., arise from the inability of the capital system's ideologists to see the *qualitative* dimension of the issues at stake. Quantity-fetish must prevail in the theoretical conceptions articulated from capital's standpoint because quantity rules over all relations in the actually existing capital system. But that is not all. For recognizing the validity of genuine concern with quality, on a line radically different from what we find in the quantified 'quality control' processes of capitalist production, would open up a dangerous 'theoretical space'. It would be dangerous, because by admitting the legitimacy of concern with quality in a substantive sense, the possibility of an alternative to the existing system itself — which is incompatible with quality considerations based on human needs and oriented towards the production of use values — would have to be conceded at least by implication. This is why it is so much preferable to misrepresent the arguments of the socialist adversary, even if misrepresentation has to assume the most absurd form, as we have seen it in the grotesque caricature of Marx depicted as the simplistic advocate of 'the golden age of communist steady-state equilibrium'.

Quality as the fundamental principle of socialist accountancy is relevant also because only through the criterion of quality is it possible to confer non-fetishistic meaning on *quantity*. The well known definition of the principle regulating the share of the individuals in the total wealth produced in an advanced socialist society — 'to each according to their need' — is based on inherently qualitative considerations. The pursuit of quantity in production, no matter how spectacular might be its results for a few centuries, is quite unsustainable as the regulating principle of social metabolic reproduction which must be counted on an incommensurably longer time-scale, hopefully in hundreds of millions of years. Only a substantively quality-oriented accountancy can be viable on that scale, which goes for the socialist project no less. Accordingly, unless both *production* and *distribution* are regulated on the basis of *directly need-related substantive quality,* and on the basis of the rational acknowledgement and non-adversarial implementation of its implications for the necessity of *genuine economy* (which also means firmly ruling out the acceptance of market-imposed criteria and the rule of any 'self-regulating mechanism' whatsoever), as encapsulated in the socialist principle, the 'newly shaped social life process' and the corresponding 'new social formation' anticipated in the Marxian project cannot be considered historically viable.

Thus the socialist principle concerning the relationship between the individuals and *their* society, which aims to make it possible for the associated producers to fulfil their aspirations as self-determined social individuals, is meant not only for transcending the iniquitous hierarchical and exploitative relations of the past. It is also a vital 'insurance policy' for a sustainable future, on account of its firm quality-orientation. This is how the necessary requirement of accountancy can be brought into harmony with the aspirations of the social individuals. On the basis of the pursuit of quantity neither a sustainable accountancy nor the harmonization of the relationship between the individuals and society are conceivable. For the point of departure is then always the *available quantity*, coupled with the necessary *confrontations* over its distribution — always grossly prejudged in favour of the privileged in the social hierarchy and wasted on the parasitic requirements of maintaining in existence such a system in production and in distribution — no matter how large the given quantity might be. This must always remain so in a system which thrives not on diminishing 'scarcity' but on reproducing it, partly as a justification of its own mode of alienated control over production and distribution, claiming to be the only viable 'rational allocator of scarce resources'.

It is important to remember here the other half of the socialist regulating principle. For the two halves *together* constitute also the orienting principle of socialist accountancy. The first half is usually, and tellingly, forgotten. However, without the neglected part, the second half has no chance of being taken seriously. This is, in fact, the reason why the adversaries of socialism are so fond of quoting the second half, so as to dismiss it immediately. The full sentence goes like this: *'from each, according to their ability, to each according to their need'*. This is where we can see, again, the dialectical interrelation between production and distribution. For unless the individuals can contribute to the production of social wealth according to their *ability* — and that means: on the basis of the *full development of the creative potentialities of the social individuals* — there can be no question of meeting the requirements of the second half, i.e. the satisfaction of the individuals' needs. The connection between the needs of the individuals and quality is obvious, or at least should be obvious. It was due to the inseparability of need from quality that in the end all utilitarian attempts to devise a formula for the 'quantification of pleasure' had to be defeated. Only the mystics of 'marginal utility theory' could carry on none the less with their apologetic efforts to square that circle.

The challenge presented by the socialist principle of distribution — which refuses to subject the needs of the individuals to the tyranny of the market or to the authoritarianism of someone else's judgement over what their 'legitimate needs' might be — is that the condition of its realization is the regulation of production, by the associated individuals themselves, on the same qualitative basis, in consciously recognized direct relation to need. Subsuming 'labour capacity' under the quantitative determinations (since there cannot be any other) of a separate command structure — whether it operates through the intermediary of the market or through a direct state control system — must miserably fail both in activating human resources and in satisfying the individuals' needs. It is most significant in this respect that under the conditions of capital's accountancy, no matter how skilful the 'double-entry book-keeping' accountants might be in controlling the industrial and commercial enterprises, the greater part of the human resources already in existence and the incomparably greater potentiality of undeveloped — because under the quantifying accountancy of capital's expansion-oriented and accumulation-driven system absolutely undevelopable — creativity must all remain *untapped,* despite the *maximal exploitation of 'labour capacity'.* They cannot be put to individually rewarding and socially sustainable use because they do not fit into the quantitative determinations of *surplus-labour extraction,* under the alienating and dehumanizing imperative of *minimal time.* The measure of real wealth — the total *disposable time* (not to be confused with idle 'leisure') available to a given society in its *qualitative* potentiality and richness — cannot fit into capital's accountancy, whether the senselessly wasteful 'economic rationality' used in its control processes is double-entry book-keeping or the computerized mathematical sophistication of linear programming and simultaneous equations.

It cannot be stressed enough, the regulation of societal interchanges in accord with both halves of the socialist principle quoted above is not simply the proclamation of morally commendable equity. It originated like that during the French revolution, in the Society of Equals of Babeuf who had to pay with his life for his temerity to challenge thousands of years of hierarchy and subordination. At the time of its first formulation the material conditions of translating into social practice Babeuf's principle were missing, and that is why it had to sound for a long time as an abstract moral principle. Today the situation is radically different, although, of course, it remains true that the principle in its Marxian formulation meets the requirements of truly equitable — and by no means downward-levelling and averaging — human relations. For the need for its realization now arises from the *necessity* to make sustainable the way of activating and managing the material and human resources of social metabolic reproduction, under conditions when they become increasingly imperilled. Thus the moral commendability of the socialist regulating principle, and the ability to sustain *indefinitely* the individuals' productive and distributive relations under the qualitative criteria of socialist accountancy, coincide, even if it will take quite some time before the *practical viability* — and *necessity* — of adopting this mode of control will sink in.

20.3.5

TO take a topical example, we can see the direct relevance of socialist accountancy in a particularly important area, concerned with the false alternative of *'growth or no-growth'.* It is relevant not simply as a theoretically feasible alternative to capital's wasteful 'economic accountancy', but also as the already practicable way to break the stranglehold of the false alternative dictated by the system's expansionary imperative. Within the incurably quantitative confines of capital-accountancy, the issue can only be conceived as the pseudo-alternative of 'no growth', to be set against the existing — dangerously wasteful — growth pattern of the system. If adopted, it would freeze the existing power relations of terrible inequality, condemning the overwhelming majority of humankind to permanent misery. Nor is there any chance whatsoever that this course of action might be followed by the 'underdeveloped' economies of the former colonial territories. If we consider only three countries in Latin America — Argentina, Brazil and Mexico — and two in Asia, China and India, we find that the dynamics of their industrial development is bound to affect the lives of more than *two and a half billion* people, and through that indirectly also the rest of the world population. If the requirements of capital-accountancy are allowed to set the rules of expansionary development even in only the five countries mentioned above — to which obviously the rest of the 'underdeveloped' world would have to be added in any realistic assessment of the issues at stake — in that case the future prospects of even bare survival on this planet, let alone those of an ongoing development, become disastrous.

Thus, the only real alternative in this respect is the radical redefinition of the problem on a *qualitative* basis. We have seen in previous chapters that the decreasing rate of utilization is an objective tendency of the capital system, with extremely problematical and ultimately unsustainable consequences for the social metabolism. This is what needs fundamental remedial action which is inconceivable on the basis of quantity-fetish and capital-accountancy. By contrast, in terms of the qualitative criteria of socialist accountancy, there can be no difficulty in envisaging the *growth of utilization* — and use or utilization is, after all, what really matters in the satisfaction of human need, not the exclusive legal entitlement to little used or unused possessions — without intolerable consequences for the conditions of social metabolic reproduction. Indeed, the strategic concern with *increasing the rate of utilization* to an *optimal* level is bound to become a fundamental orienting principle of sustainable social metabolic reproduction in the not too distant future. Naturally, this way of orienting societal reproduction has far-reaching implications for human interchanges, as discussed in relation to communal production and consumption in Chapter 19. What is important to stress here is that the radical reorientation of production towards use value, in conjunction with the socially viable exchange of activities (and not commodities or non-commodified products), rationally planned by the associated individuals themselves, is feasible only in terms of the *qualitative* determinations of socialist accountancy. In other words, it works only if the production of use values can directly arise from the self-determined life-activity of the social individuals, setting thereby also to the aims of production a rational limit in a non-adversarial way. For under such circumstances the general orienting principle of quality — in choosing the activities pursued by the individuals on the basis of their creative potentialities and needs, and in the regulation of individual and communal interchanges both in production and in distribution— can be consistently applied. It can be applied as a result of overcoming the contradictions between production and control, production and consumption, and production and circulation,[384] thus superseding the *quantitative regimentation* that necessarily arises from the need of the antagonistic capital system for containing its contradictions through the power of an alienated command structure.

Another dimension of the same problem is the necessity to overcome *scarcity* in a rationally sustainable sense. Here, too, the quantity-fetish of capital-accountancy proves to be self-defeating. The necessary conversion of all qualities of use value into determinate quantities of exchange value, and the subordination of the former to the latter, bring with them the eternal reproduction of scarcity, despite the immense expansion of society's productive (and destructive) powers. For whereas natural appetites have their limits, capital's appetite for expansion, and the drive of its personifications for the accumulation of wealth under the imperative of capital-expansion, are limitless. This is why scarcity must be not simply reproduced, but reproduced with a vengeance, on an ever-increasing scale. From this historically contingent fact — which, however, also happens to be capital's insuperable necessity — the system's apologists 'conclude', by fallaciously assuming again from the outset the conclusion which should be sustained without the crutches of their arbitrary assumptions that 'human predicament means scarcity'; just because it must indeed mean sinking always deeper into scarcity on the practical premisses and operational imperatives of their system. Naturally, from this assumed 'conclusion', which makes their ahistorically defined 'human predicament' itself inseparable from absolute scarcity, it must also follow that the socialist concern with overcoming scarcity is worthy only of derision.

Accusations that the Marxian socialist project envisaged a simplistic utopian idea of abundance could not be further from the truth. For Marx knew very well that 'scarcity' and 'abundance' — like all other issues arising in the social world — must be related to their historical context and to the productive powers at the disposal of the individuals through which the difficulties facing them can be resolved. Passing judgement over 'scarcity' and 'abundance' in their abstract generality is totally meaningless, irrespective of the positive or negative attitude of the judges to the supersession of scarcity. The same goes for *utility* and *need;* hence the failure of *utilitarianism* in attempting to find abstract-generic solutions to inherently social and historical problems; a necessary failure due to the utilitarian philosophers' uncritical relationship to the 'eternalized' liberal capitalist order. For 'utility' means something radically different in relation to the historically specific social formation of capital from what it means in relation to the historically changing range and quality of human needs. The latter cannot be meaningfully discussed without putting into the centre of attention the question of *quality.* In complete contrast, capital's interest in utility categorically excludes all consideration of quality as human need, with devastating consequences also for the question of scarcity. For

> The *only utility* whatsoever which an object can have for *capital* can be to *preserve or increase it.* ... value, having become independent as such — or the general form of wealth [money] — is capable of no other motion than a *quantitative* one. It is according to its concept the *quintessence of all use values;* ... value which insists on itself as value *preserves itself through increase;* and it *preserves* itself precisely only by *constantly driving beyond its quantitative barrier* ... Thus, growing wealthy is an end in itself. The goal-determining activity of capital can only be that of growing wealthier, i.e. of *magnification,* of increasing itself. ... Fixed as wealth, as the general form of wealth, as value which counts as value, it is therefore the *constant drive to go beyond its quantitative limit: an endless process.* Its own animation consists exclusively in that; it preserves itself as a self-validated exchange value distinct from a use value only by *constantly multiplying itself.*[385]

Thus, even if capital's mode of social metabolic reproduction could be materially sustained on a permanent basis — which is for a number of reasons inconceivable — even in that case *scarcity* could *never* be overcome within the framework of capital's endless process of 'constantly driving beyond its quantitative barrier', orien-ted towards its own multiplication, ignoring the qualitative dimension of the relationship between use value and human need. The actual situation, however, is much worse than that; and not only because a world of infinite material resources does not exist. For in the total absence of regulatory criteria, derivable only from positively developing human need, capital's infernal logic and endless drive for quantitative self-expansion inevitably lead to destructive consequences. The destructiveness of capital's internal dynamics affects not only the natural environment but every facet of social metabolic reproduction. 'The growing incompatibility between the productive development of society and its hitherto existing relations of production expresses itself in *bitter contradictions, crises, spasms*. The violent destruction of capital not by relations *external* to it, but rather as a condition of its *self-preservation*'.[386] This is how we reach the historical stage where the self-contradictory logic of capital's destructive self-preservation im-poses a formerly quite unimaginable level and range of destructive production. There can be no exemption from this rule. Even major parts of capital's own productive constituents must be periodically destroyed, so that in its reconsti-tuted form capital should be led 'back to the point where it is enabled to go on fully employing its productive powers *without committing suicide*'.[387] For in terms of capital's logic the extermination of humanity is much preferable to allowing anyone to question the *causa sui* of this mode of reproduction. And since the speedy and destructive dissipation of material and human resources, as well as of the products of labour, acquire a perversely *positive* connotation in the capital system in structural crisis, because they represent 'conditions of its *self-preserva-tion*', the socialist alternative which aims at overcoming scarcity must be ana-thema to the ideologists of the ruling order.

Only within the framework of socialist accountancy is it possible to envisage overcoming scarcity. This means both the consistent assertion of *qualitative* cri-teria in evaluating society's material and human resources, and the regulation of the individuals' productive and distributive interchanges — on the basis of the exchange of activities — in accord with the principle of 'from each according to their ability, to each according to their need'. The road to follow is to some extent the same as the one required for correcting the absurdly wasteful rate of utilization now prevailing in 'advanced capitalist' countries, and for *reversing* its tendency to decrease everywhere under the destructive pressures of the capital system. However, the challenge of overcoming scarcity is broader. For optimiz-ing a given range of utilization, and reversing the decreasing tendency itself, still leave vast areas of existing consumption which are not amenable to major changes in that way. To take one example only, it is a humbling thought that the private motor car, despite its extremely low rate of utilization, causes great damage to public health and makes traffic conditions in large cities quite intolerable, not to mention its impact on road building programmes and on many historic town centres and areas of natural beauty. Obviously, therefore, only a radically different solution — in the form of free public transport of the non-polluting, and in its demand on land, etc., most economical, kind — could be rationally contemplated in this respect, eliminating altogether the private motor car from the face of the earth before long. This would also mean that the provision for the type of use to which the motor car is best suited would have to be made strictly on the basis of need, out of a public pool. It is equally obvious, however, that this kind of rationalization of the needs of the individueals for transport — although it would make sense even today — is feasible only at a more advanced stage of socialist development. For it would conflict not only with massive capitalist interests in contemporary society but also with the imperative to find productive employment for labour. And that in its turn would become possible only through a radical restructuring of the existing areas of production in their entirety, or at least in their great majority.

Overcoming scarcity is therefore a long-term project. It is feasible only in a society where the quality-oriented principles of socialist accountancy are fully operational, enabling thereby humankind to conduct its affairs on the basis of true economy. This view is in total contradiction to the concept of unqualified 'abundance' which the apologists of the existing order now attribute to the socialist idea. They do this in order to be able to proclaim the apriori impossibility of socialism, having themselves claimed in the spirit of capital-apologetics the imminent realization of abundance at the peak of postwar expansion.[388] Naturally, unqualified 'abundance' does not exclude the possibility of waste. In fact the 20th century apologists of the capital system projected the production of 'boundless abundance' — including Keynes.[389] The already clearly visible practices of frightful waste-production — which directly contradicted the possibility of achieving abundance — could not give them even a morsel of food for thought. Nothing could be further from the Marxian socialist idea than this kind of 'abundance'. For the socialist conception of overcoming scarcity has for its necessary practical premiss the realization of *true economy* within the framework of socialist accountancy, and thereby the *conscious exclusion of waste*. For waste-production does not mean only the waste of material resources but also the waste of human beings who dissipate their lives in that kind of production. Only a society in which there is no alienated command structure to impose on the individuals to waste their lives in that way, because the associated producers are themselves in full control of their productive and distributive interchanges, only that kind of society can envisage the production of abundance and the supersession of the material and intellectual deprivation of its members.

In the period of transition ahead, the importance of reversing the decreasing rate of utilization could not be overstated. In part this is because it is impossible to escape from the vicious circle of 'growth or no-growth' without concentrating on the feasible objective of growth in utilization, on the basis of enhancing the production of use values freed from the strait-jacket of exchange values. But it is important also in the sense that the principle of increasing the rate of utilization is compatible to a significant extent with the now existing exchange relations and the strictly quantitative determinations arising from the nature of money and the market. The 'rate of utilization' is a primarily qualitative concept, but it has also a quantitative dimension which can fit into the now dominant modality of exchange up to a point. But only up to a rather limited point. Beyond that point we find the radical incompatibility of socialist accountancy with capital's operative determinations, including the market and money. That is where the roads necessarily part. For further progress would require the adoption of a very different mode of living, on the basis of communal production and consumption, with important consequences for the individuals' need for housing, transport, the building of very different types of towns and cities as well as places of work and cultural development, together with the redefinition of their relationship to the countryside, and many other aspects of their daily life.

Thus, it is inconceivable to overcome scarcity without radically superseding the existing exchange relations and their intermediaries, including the market with all of its corollaries. The common sense proposition that one cannot be 'a little bit pregnant' is valid in this regard as much as in its original context. Those who imagine that socialism can be combined with the 'market mechanism' are either very naive, or (like Alec Nove) really advocate the restoration and eternal life of capitalism under the name of 'feasible socialism'. Their incoherent theoretical guiding principle is 'let us have a little bit of this and a little bit of that'. In this way they either ignore the objective incompatibilities between socialism and the capitalist exchange relations, or are perfectly happy to idealize the permanent submission of labour to the alienated command struture and dehumanizing material imperatives of the capital system.

We must recall again the inescapable dialectical relationship between production and control, production and distribution, and production and circulation which contain also the dialectic of production and consumption. The vicious circle of the capital relation is made up of many circuits, all intertwined and mutually reinforcing one another. The question of overcoming scarcity cannot be reduced to that of individual consumption. For every act of production is simultaneously also consumption, with far-reaching consequences. Whether the consumption of materials and human energy unavoidable in the production process results in inherently productive or destructive consumption, and to what extent one or the other, depends on the totality of society's reproductive relations, i.e. on the established framework of social metabolic control. This is why it is inconceivable to achieve the socialist objectives without going beyond capital, i.e. without radically restructuring the totality of existing reproductive relations. All circuits of the capital relation, without a single exception, reinforce the perverse dialectic of the incurably wasteful capital system. Consequently, overcoming scarcity is not possible without superseding all of them through the positive articulation of a new set of interrelations between production and consumption in its broadest dialectical sense. No doubt, this process will take time, perhaps a very long time. Nevertheless, the principles of socialist accountancy are valid and necessary from the beginning of the journey. For without them the dangers of ending up again and again in the blind alley of the postcapitalist past always loom large.

20.4 Beyond the illusions of marketization: the role of incentives in a genuinely planned system

20.4.1

'MARKET socialism', under a variety of names (devised to hide its capitalist nature), had two lineages. In historical sequence the first lineage was reformist social democracy, and the second Stalinism. Their common denominator was always the structural subordination of labour to capital — and to the personifications of capital in their capitalist or postcapitalist variety. Not surprisingly, therefore, in the end they fully converged, contributing in that form, to a significant extent, to the disintegration of the Soviet type postcapitalist capital system.

From Bernstein to Kautsky the radical socialist aims were dismissed, and accommodation to the capitalist market became the absolute rule. In later versions — including the 'Swedish road to socialism' which could only lead, like all the others, to the strengthening of capitalism through the state subsidy of its bankrupt sectors — the phraseology of 'mixed economy' was often used, promising for a while the achievement of socialist aims; until the structural crisis of the capital system made it wiser to abandon even the limited social welfare aims. The 'nationalizations', as a rule, consisted in bailing out some important bankrupt industries, so as to make the capitalist market as a whole more viable. Under Harold Wilson's government in Britain there was a lot of talk about the 'mixed economy' and about 'conquering the strategic heights of the economy', but all that remained hot air and empty verbiage. For the reality was well illustrated by a parliamentary debate. A Labour MP, Edward Garrett, asked the question the Labour Minister of State for Industry, Gerald Kaufman: 'A major objective of the NEB [National Enterprise Board] was to extend public ownership into profitable manufacturing industry, rather than to bail out the lame ducks. When is this likely to take place?' This is how the subject was handled:

> Mr Kaufman — Gradually. (Conservative laughter.) It has already begun. The NEB has already taken shares in Brown Boveri Kent and International Computers.
>
> Mr Michael Grylls (Conservative) — Is he claiming Brown Boveri Kent as a successful inverstment? If not, what is the most successful and profitable inverstment so far made by the NEB?
>
> Mr Kaufman — He is talking about a company in which private enterprise was totally unsuccessful and on which a rescue operation had to be conducted. The NEB has extended its holdings to make that enterprise profitable, as it will.[390]

Thus Mr Kaufman first pretended to the Labour side of Parliament that Brown Boveri Kent was not a bailing out operation. To his chagrin, the Conservative Mr Grylls knew that this was not true. Naturally, the second half of Mr Grylls' question could not be answered, concerning the NEB's 'successful and profitable investments' because there were none. This was the truth behind the slogan of 'conquering the commanding heights of the economy'. No wonder, therefore, that the British version of squeezing socialism out of the efforts to improve the capitalist market had to end in complete failure.

A socialdemocratic theorization of 'market socialism', *The Economics of Feasible Socialism* (1983), itself influenced by some earlier Stalinist reflections on the subject, was quite influential on the theorists of 'perestroika'. Characteristically, its author — Alec Nove, in his own words 'brought up in a socialdemocratic environment, son of a Menshevik'[391] — had to take the side of Stalin against Marx, dismissing wholesale the Marxian vision of socialism with this 'argument': 'What if the vision is unrealisable, contradictory? Does it make sense to "blame" Stalin and his successors for not having achieved what cannot be achieved in the real world? ... Marx's ideas on socialism are very seriously defective and misleading'.[392] The unforgivable defectiveness of Marxian ideas in Nove's view is the temerity to suggest that one should strive for the establishment of a society in which labour is not dominated and exploited. One of his 'proofs' regarding the unrealizability of the Marxian vision is more priceless than the other. Thus Nove imagines to be able to prove both the impossibility of overcoming scarcity and the impossibility of eliminating iniquities by peremptorily asserting the impossibility of unbiased information:

> No doubt any of us, 'new leftist' or no, in applying for a research grant or money for travel, would emphasise (and quite sincerely so) the value for society of whatever we are doing, and present the facts with — shall we say — appropriate cosmetics. As already stressed, in a vastly complicated society, we *simply cannot know* who is being deprived for our benefit if our application succeeds. There are, of course, degrees of dishonesty and concealment of facts, in this as in anything else. But to expect unbiased information from those interested in the results to which the information is put is to live in cloud-cuckoo-land. This would not happen if resources were unlimited; but this is where we came in.[393]

But, of course, we know very well that the real issue is not: which particular individual is disadvantaged by the grant-dispensing set-up of which the author is a beneficiary, but the whole system of iniquities of which it is a part. True to his apologetic vocation, Nove always assumes as *unalterable* — on the likewise circularly assumed arguments of 'vastly complicated society', 'necessary hierarchy', and the like — what he wants to declare in his conclusion *unchangeable*. Accordingly, we must exclude the possibility of democratic decision making and control, and therefore also give up being concerned about substantive inequality, because we cannot pinpoint the particular individual whose application for grant might not be successful as a result of his success. And since overcoming scarcity is connected with the reliability of information, we can forget from now on that problem too. The existing system of hierarchies, and the concomitant scarcities iniquitously imposed by it on those in subordinate position, can carry on functioning forever as before, thanks to the conclusive evidence supplied by the author's successful application for research and travel grants.

The same logic characterizes the defence of excluding the overwhelming majority of human beings from the exercise of their now repressed powers of decision making. We are told, on the basis of an assertion simply plucked out of thin air, that 'On balance [?!], it does seem likely that *most human beings will continue to prefer to avoid responsibility* and be glad to accept (appoint, elect) others to carry it. How many university professors wish to be vice-chancellors?'[394] If Marxian socialists do not give up their 'very seriously defective and misleading' way of thinking after reading this profundity, they never will. For, obviously, 'most human beings' are in the position in which they find themselves today in relation to the effective exercise of power because they 'prefer to avoid responsibility'. The proof that places of learning, like universities, can only be managed hierarchically is that, if we assume the existing hierarchical system as unalterable, in that case 'on balance, it does seem likely' that not many university professors — never mind lesser mortals — would wish to be vice-chancellors. A proof fully matching the previous one and worthy of another research grant. The only nagging doubt that remains is this: who is the one who 'lives in cloud-cuckoo-land'?

This doubt is reinforced when we read that 'Marx's over-emphasis on human effort, *his downgrading of use value,* should be corrected'.[395] It is well known that Marx conferred the greatest importance on the production of use value, envisaging a fundamental change in the 'new historical order' precisely through extricating use value from its subordination to, and fetishistic domination by, exchange value. If someone argued that Marx *over-emphasises use value,* that would invite a serious exchange of views. But that would be pointless in this case. For someone who can accuse him of 'downgrading use value' can only prove that his wholesale dismissal of Marx — as 'seriously defective and misleading', 'contradictory', 'utopian', suffering from a 'romantic imagination', etc. — is born out of capital-apologetic eagerness and ideological enmity, without the slightest evidence of having understood his work.

The whole purpose of Nove's advocacy of 'market socialism' is to insist on the permanent subordination of labour as a matter of unalterable necessity. We are told by him that

> it is clear that someone (some institution) has to tell the producers about what the users require. If that someone is not the impersonal market mechanism it can only be a hierarchical superior. There are horizontal links (market), there are vertical links (hierarchy). What other dimension is there?[396]

As to why one should arbitrarily equate 'horizontal links', by definition, with the market, declaring at the same time that the coordination of overall societal reproduction must be equated — again, by definition— with 'vertical links (hierarchy)', we are never told. The rhetorical question: 'What other dimension is there?' is supposed to do away with all such questions. On closer inspection, however, we find that in Nove's vision of 'feasible socialism', in contrast to the commonly held view of the *three-dimensionality* of the world, even *two dimensions* must be considered an unaffordable luxury. For the actually existing and feasible market is very far from being and ideal coordinating framework of *'horizontal links'.* It is *hierarchical* through and through, favouring in its material power relations the strong against the weak, notwithstanding all fantasy about the 'equality of all types of property', from the local cobbler and the smallest peasant household economy to the giant transnational corporation. Indeed, *vertical hierarchy* is the true defining dimension of the capital system in all of its historically known and feasible — capitalist or postcapitalist — varieties, without which it could not impose its necessary structural domination over labour. It was most appropriate, therefore, that the former Stalinist party officials and theorists of 'perestroika' should respond with such eager approval to Nove's apologetic axioms about the one and only truly essential dimension of their 'real world'.

The predictive value of Nove's *Economics of Feasible Socialism* was as sound as its theoretical tenets. For this is how he pictured his coming 'feasible socialist' society, in the spirit of socialdemocratized Stalinism:

> It is clear [?!] that the role of the state will be very great, as owner, as planner, as enforcer of social and economic priorities. The assumption of democracy makes its task more difficult, not easier, since a variety of inconsistent objectives will be reflected in political parties and the propaganda they will undertake. One hopes that an educated and mature electorate will support governments which will keep the economy in balance, avoiding inflationary excess and unemployment, allowing the market to function but not letting it get out of hand. The danger one foresees is not one of a vote to 'restore capitalism'. There was no mass movement of this sort even in countries where the Soviet-type system was intensely unpopular — for instance, Poland or Czechoslovakia.[397]

And this was the kind of analysis which was supposed to prove its realism and theoretical superiority over against Marx's 'contradictory, unrealizable, seriously defective and misleading' vision. Unfortunately for the author of *The Economics of Feasible Socialism,* none of the items of his wish-list suspended in thin air (and not only in the last quoted passage but everywhere in his book) were realized by the proponents of 'market socialism' in the East. Rather the opposite. The incompatibility between the advocated market and the proclaimed 'socialist' objectives — toned down to the point of wanting to retain only some social security services and minimize unemployment — asserted itself with brutal savagery, with a helping hand or two lent to it by the International Monetary Fund and the World Bank. Instead of benefiting from the promised greatly improved economic conditions, the working people all over Eastern Europe ended up with massive unemployment and massive inflation. The fantasy of 'market socialism' totally deflated itself the moment it was embarked upon in the USSR and everywhere else in Eastern Europe. As another former champion of 'market socialism', Wlodzimierz Brus (one of Nove's gurus), later admitted: 'The collapse of communist power in Eastern Europe in 1989 brought about renunciation of market socialism as an objective of systemic transformation; the aim became — more or less explicitly — a *return to capitalist economy*'.[398] Even that change did not come about in accord with Nove's projected scheme. There was no need whatsoever for a 'vote to restore capitalism'. The General Secretary of the Soviet Party and his colleagues did their best to achieve that objective, as we have seen in Chapter 16, and the 'democratic' President of the Russian Republic finished the job by ordering a tank regiment to shoot Parliament to pieces. Thus ended a phase of socioeconomic development in the Soviet Union which started in 1952 with Stalin's blessing.

20.4.2

THE second lineage of 'market socialism' — which used to condemn socialde-mocratic reformism before adopting much the same position — directly descended from Stalin, as we have seen above. Stalin's rejection of key Marxian categories, above all any embarrassing reference to 'surplus labour' which his system extracted with brutal authoritarianism from the labour force, his advocacy of commodity relations and profitability, together with his stress on greater discipline to be exercised by 'our business executives' with the help of marketization and the criteria of profitability, opened the road to a development whose objective logic pointed in the direction of capitalist restoration, and not towards socialism.

The close connection of 'market socialist' economic reform in postcapitalist societies with Stalin himself was usually kept under silence in the self-images of its practitioners. Indeed, as time went by the high level functionaries of the centralized planning system claimed anti-Stalinist credentials, despite the fact that they were involved up to their neck in directing and administering the 'command economy'. They continued to idealize for decades after Stalin's death the fiction of their 'socialist economy', proclaiming that 'it seems obvious [?!] that a planned socialist economy provides basic preconditions much more favourable to technological progress than those afforded by a capitalist economy'.[399] The author of these lines, the Polish economist Wlodzimierz Brus, even asserted that the 'historicist Marx' maintained the progressive nature of commodity relations 'in certain circumstances'.[400] The purpose of this curious characterization transpired a few pages further on when Brus declared that 'In given socio-economic circumstances an *increase in the scope and the importance of commodity relations* may, for a number of reasons, *greatly facilitate the development of a socialist society'*.[401] In truth, however, Marx talked about such ideas with undisguised contempt, insisting that 'There can be *nothing more erroneous and absurd* than to postulate the control by the united individuals of their total production, on the basis of *exchange value*, of *money'*.[402]

The apologetic nature of 'market socialist' reasoning in the East, in trying to combine the authoritarian planning system with profitability and commodity relations sanctioned by Stalin, was clear enough. Thus Brus asserted in the same book, before seeing the radiant capitalist light on the road to Damascus (or was it Chicago?), that 'The overall balance of the twenty-year experience of the socialist planned economy in Poland is evidently favourable'.[403] This apologetic approach was applied not only retrospectively, embracing the worst decades of Stalinist repression, but also in relation to the future, operating with the concepts of 'modernity', 'complexity', 'mechanism', and functional 'specialization'. Thus we were told that

Nowadays we more readily realize that the growth of the apparatus of economic administration (bureaucratization, in the usual meaning of the term) is not only and not even primarily the result of incompetence but is the result of the *modern organization* of productive forces, the price which *society has to pay* for the control of processes which have hitherto been spontaneous. The prophecy that economic management would be so simplified that direct management would be possible without the *permanent division of labour* has not been fulfilled. On the contrary, the *mechanism* of management has become increasingly *complicated* and the importance of *specialists* in various branches of economic life has grown.[404]

Social antagonisms in this way of depicting the ruling order did not and could not exist. The hierarchical and exploitative division of labour quite simply could not be perceived through the spectacles constructed from the conceptual matrix of 'modern organization of productive forces', 'increasingly complicated mechanism of management', and absolutely necessary 'specialists'. Bureaucratization and the division of labour had to be deemed permanent, and fully in accord with instrumental rationality, since they were represented as 'the price which society had to pay' for a modern control of reproductive processes, never mentioning which class in actuality was compelled to 'pay the price' on behalf of 'society'. The marketization advocated in the book was promising improvements through *'new techniques of management'* and *'modern information techniques',*[405] treating the market itself not as a social relation in the service of the extraction of surplus labour but as an obliging 'mechanism'.[406] This served a double apologetic purpose. For, on the one hand, it was used to hide the exploitative social role of the market, depicting it, instead, as an instrument of universal benefit; and on the other, it served to fictionalize also the existing authoritarian command system as a pure 'mechanism'. Thus we were told that 'In some circumstances a regulated *market mechanism* is (or at least may appear to be) the form better suited to a planned economy than a *command mechanism'*.[407] In case some people nourished illusions about the democratic potential of the projected marketization in the control of production, they had to be quickly disappointed. For the centralized command system had to retain its absolute primacy. The author insisted that 'transferring the control of some social resources to a lower economic level may lead to a dissipation of effort and to an underestimation of the preferences of society as a whole'.[408]

One of the most astonishing propositions of this book was that 'the possibilities for economic incentives opened up by the increased use of the market mechanism'[409] would result in the growth of *socialist consciousness*. This is how the 'argument' ran: '*if* by this means [i.e. market-driven economic incentives] the connection between individual (and collective) interests and social interests *were really to be strengthened,* this *would* not merely improve short-term economic efficiency but, most important, *would* have educational effects, providing a much more powerful impulse for the *growth of socialist consciousness* than can be derived from verbal didacticism'.[410] Granted that 'verbal didacticism' cannot produce socialist consciousness; but does that confer any sense at all on this convoluted sentence? For, as an English adage wisely puts it, 'if pigs had wings they would fly'. But they don't have wings and need troughs on the ground for feeding. This kind of 'market socialist' reasoning may have pleased some party bosses, but it had nothing to do with reality — despite the claims of the theorists of 'feasible socialism' that their solutions corresponded to a superior vantage point 'in the real world'. For the projected 'educational effects' actually worked in the *opposite* direction, enhancing the growth of discriminatory privileges and social divisiveness, not 'socialist consciousness'. Ten years before the implosion of post-capitalist societies, a journal of the market-socializing Hungarian government proudly reported — in an article entitled 'Two-car family' — the words of a top official in an agricultural cooperative: 'We must have two cars, because otherwise we could not move around on the vast land of the cooperative. I drive the 1200, my wife the 1500'.[411] This was presented as the way of the future for everyone. However, pigs refused to grow wings not only in Poland and Russia but also in Hungary. The rest of the story is well known.

But even if in the postcapitalist countries material resources, by some miracle, could have been plucked out of thin air with the same ease as the pillars of the theory projecting the 'market socialist' paradise were, what would be the good of that? In the United States the 'more than two-car family' is a reality; there are in fact 700 motor cars for every 1,000 people. Apply that figure to China and India alone — i.e. 1,500 million petrol-guzzling polluters — and the lungs of everyone on this planet are in serious danger. Apologists can, of course, always adopt a 'positive stance' towards such matters, welcoming the generalization of the US figures for the world population as a whole. For that would solve for them two intractable problems with one stroke. First, the resulting traffic jams, compelling people to crawl along sitting in their cars for hours and hours every day, would resolve Keynes's great dilemma of how to kill idle time after 2030. And second, it would also do away with the problem of chronic unemployment. For the people enjoying the blessings of the 'two-plus-car family' would choke to death well before they would have to be made redundant.

'Market socialists' in the East, before openly embracing capitalism, liked to censure in the name of '*continuity*' all those who argued in favour of a *radical transformation* of the Stalinist system. Accordingly, Brus argued that change should be sought '*not through a "second socio-economic revolution", but by working for*

the further development of the revolution which has already taken place'.[412] This was by
no means surprising. For 'market socialism' organically grew out of the crisis of
Stalinism. The collapse of the Stalinist rationalization of a permanent state of
emergency, and the total inadequacy of labour productivity under the changed
circumstances, had resulted in the half-baked attempts to rescue the postcapitalist capital system through marketizing reforms already in Stalin's lifetime.
Such reforms could be further extended after 1953, precisely because they represented the 'line of least resistance' on the substantive common ground of the
capital system in which there can be truly *'no alternative'* to the maximal extraction
of surplus-labour, controlled by some form of alienated and hierarchical command structure. The fact that the two lineages of 'market socialism' converged
and in the end fully merged into one another, as socialdemocratized Stalinism,
finding their common denominator in the open advocacy of capitalist restoration
under the control of a strong state, could come as a surprise only to those who
nourished illusions about the compatibility of market-driven exploitation with
the objectives of socialism.

20.4.3

THE abyss that separates the socialist project from the capital-apologists of
'market socialism' is clearly visible also in a much later work by Brus in which
he argues that

> Consistent pursuit of market socialism — *capital and labour markets, ownership
> restructuring,* political pluralism — must be regarded as *blurring* the habitual distinc-
> tion between capitalism and socialism, and therefore denying to socialism the
> character of a bounded successor system to capitalism (Brus and Laski 1989). This
> is not necessarily tantamount to the abandonment of *basic socialist policy objectives —
> full employment, equality of opportunity, social welfare* — or *government intervention as the
> method to achieve them.* What it does imply, however, is the abandonment of the concept
> of *socialism as a grand design* ... in other words abandonment of the philosophy of the
> revolutionary break in favour of continuity in change.[413]

Apart from the 'post-modern' phraseology of 'socialism as a grand design', we
are back to Bernstein's (and Popper's) self-contradictory strategy of 'little by
little', to be pursued within the crippling structural confines of capitalism. And,
of course, in the ideology of those who object to 'grand design' there can be no
objection to capitalism as the eternalized 'grand design' of the only appropriate
social order. Strangely, though, Brus still cannot abandon the idea of teaching
pigs how to grow wings and fly, expecting the realization of what he calls 'basic
socialist policy objectives' from the 'method'—just like earlier from the postulated 'mechanisms', 'techniques' and 'instruments', in place of the reality of social power relations — of the benevolently interventionist capitalist state.

The advocacy of *'capital and labour markets and ownership restructuring'* does not
mean only 'blurring' the distinction between capitalism and socialism but the
complete abandonment of even the most remote possibility of realizing socialist
aims. The so-called 'basic socialist policy objectives' are nothing of the kind.
'Full employment', 'equality of opportunity', and 'social welfare' are in fact the
no longer feasible aims of postwar welfare-capitalism, adopted but never realized
by 'Butskellite' governments in a handful of privileged capitalist countries.
Besides, they have been abandoned as policy objectives everywhere by the

parliamentary political organizations, including not only the reformist socialde-mocratic parties but also the former communist parties, under the pressure of capital's structural crisis. Thus, the so-called 'socialist policy objectives' are today at best vague *desiderata,* totally out of the reach of the traditional political mo-vements, demonstrating, yet again, how deeply rooted are the 'blurred' fancies of market socialism in the 'real world'.

But even if the actual material conditions did not conflict with retaining the welfare objectives of postwar capitalist expansion, their pursuit would be still at an astronomical distance from the genuine socialist emancipatory objectives. For the socialist project is not interested in the 'full employment' of the exploit-able (and of course under all feasible forms of the capital system always exploited) labour force, but in securing *meaningful work* for the members of society by the associated producers themselves; not in the vacuous promises of 'equal oppor-tunity', necessarily nullified at the very moment of their utterance by the actu-ally existing hierarchical structures of domination, but in the *substantive equality* of all individuals; not in 'social welfare' dished out to the means-tested submis-sive poor by the liberal/capitalist 'welfare state', but in the *self-determined alloca-tion of social wealth* — both material and cultural — 'to each according to their need'; and not in the eternalization of 'government intervention', but in creating the necessary material and political conditions through which the *withering away of the state* can be secured.

Naturally, for as long as the inhumanities of capitalism prevail, there will be always some liberal-minded individuals — without any connection with the utterly discredited and at the time of the implosion of the Soviet system instantly deflated 'market socialist' theories — who will condemn the perceived evils in their societies and try to find something better within the confines of the existing order. However, the problematical nature and sobering limits of such an enter-prise quickly show up. As Harry Magdoff commented on a volume published in 1994 in the US,[414] which followed that line:

> My impression of the essays in the book is that by and large, despite protestations to the contrary, the vision the authors have in mind is a nice, humane regulated capitalism. Heilbroner sums it up nicely in his foreword: "Socialisms therefore con-stitute a kind of ongoing experiment to discover what sorts of arrangements might repair the damage wrought by the existing social order". The essays by and large are concerned with issues which are germane to a capitalist society: how to get improved growth, start new enterprises, improve efficiency, encourage innovation and compe-tition. Do the people of the United States need faster growth, except for the fact that it is the only way to create jobs in a capitalist society? Are more profit-making enterprises needed? To do what — produce more cars, ferrous metals, plastics, paper; provide services of lawyers, bill collectors, real estate operators, and brokers? Why do we need improved efficiency? Efficiency for what, and by what standards? Why not less efficiency — shorter workdays, shorter work weeks, longer vacations, relaxa-tion time during dull work routines? We are a rich country with enormous potential for improving the quality of life for *all* the people, as long as the ideal standard of life is not taken as that of the upper middle class. The innovations needed are not more gadgets or information highways, but the enrichment of education, medical care, room for the creative urges to flourish — alas not grist for viable ventures in the marketplace.[415]

There was a time, towards the end of the postwar expansionary phase, when some of the leading political figures of the ruling class — like British Prime Minister Edward Heath — could still critically speak about '*the unacceptable face of capitalism*'. That phase receded to what now appears to be a very remote past, hard to believe even that it ever existed. For actually existing capitalism now cannot help showing its really existing savage face, making it *acceptable* in the name of the 'harsh conditions of competitive efficiency' (the 'five little tigers', etc.) and other labour-taming ideological rationalizations, enforced by anti-labour legislative measures. This is why the chances of a 'more humane regulated capitalism' must be today very slender indeed, not to mention the possibility of squeezing some form of 'enlightened market socialism' out of the material expansionary imperatives of capital's destructive self-preservation.

20.4.4

THE illusions of marketization are often used also as a prefabricated substitute for a genuine concern with *incentives*. For no social reproductive order can function without its own way of motivating and controlling the individuals engaged in productive activity. If the material conditions prevent the control of societal reproduction by the producing individuals themselves, some form of alienated control system is bound to take over the comprehensive coordinating functions. For the individual and collective dimensions of reproductive interchange are inextricably intertwined in every social metabolic order.

In this sense, it would be totally undialectical to counterpose overall social control — by proclaiming absurdities like 'there is no such thing as society', as Margaret Thatcher did in the footsteps of her guru and Companion of Honour, F.A. Hayek, who decreed that the term 'social' is a 'weasel word' in 'our poisoned language'[416] — to (positive and negative) individual motivation. Even in a slave-driver society the threat or infliction of more or less extreme punishment and pain act as some kind of motivation, however inhuman, for the individuals at the receiving end of the system. The same goes for the capitalist order in which the incentives of the individuals cannot be separated from the overall determinations and controlling functions of this social system, notwithstanding the mythology of 'individual consumer sovereignty'.

Thus, a dynamic socialist reproductive order, controlled by the self-determined individuals, is unthinkable without its own system of incentives befitting its fundamental aims; one which positively combines the individual motivating dimension with the systemic requirements of overall social metabolic control. This means a qualitatively different orientation to what is imposed on all individuals by the capital system. For under the latter the incentives must be directly subordinated to the material expansionary imperatives. Accordingly, the 'rule of wealth over society' must always prevail, in sharp contrast to the socialist vision of the relationship of the individuals to the production and distribution of social wealth. Under the rule of capital, in all of its historically known and feasible forms, 'material incentives' are legitimated from the standpoint and in the interest of 'economic efficiency'. This goes also for the Stalinist control of the political extraction of surplus labour, both before and after the officially blessed switch to 'commodity relations' in consumer goods production. Likewise, at the time of the open proclamation and growing practice of 'market socialism' the accent was put on '*incentives for adaptability*' to technical change of the economy as a whole',[417] in pursuit of increased production and 'improving short-term economic efficiency',[418] envisaging the operation of individual material incentives by 'tying the *bonus system* (including the participation of employees in profits through the "enterprise fund") ... to actual improvements in the rate of growth'.[419] Understandably, therefore, the idea of breaking the *rule of wealth over society* through the 'mechanism' of the socialistically 'regulated market' was always a non-starter, even if we disregard the vagueness and incoherence of the wishfully projected notion of 'regulation' which, in order to succeed, would have to put out of action the market. This is why Marx rightly insisted that nothing could be more absurd than 'to postulate the control by the united individuals of their total production, on the basis of exchange value, of money'. For doing so would sharply contradict not only the socialist orientation of the 'new social formation' as a whole; it would simultaneously also make impossible the socialist self-motivation of the individuals in that it would impose on them forever the prefabricated straitjacket of the iniquitous pursuit of exchange value and money.

A system of incentives appropriate to the 'new social life process' of a socialist society can only arise from the dialectic of production–distribution–consumption. Under the capital system we find a *truncated dialectic*. For the alienation of the means of production from the producers, and the superimposition of a separate mode of control over them, creates a *short circuit*. The operation of this short circuit — in which capital and its personifications usurp the power of control by expropriating the material conditions of production — is compatible only with the fetishistic predetermination not only of the ongoing production process itself, but also the way in which the individuals must *internalize* their feasible aims and motivating objectives, oriented towards the acquisition of products or commodified products, in subordination to the system's expansionary drive. The question of satisfying the needs of the individuals can only arise *post festum,* in tune with the *post festum* character of production itself, inasmuch as the *post festum recognized and legitimated needs* can fit into the reproductive short circuit of capital's truncated dialectic. In this way, due to the fateful distortion of distribution — through the expropriation of its absolutely necessary constituents for setting in motion the labour process: the material and means of production, thereby expropriating the power of control over the social metabolism as a whole — both production and consumption are also distorted. They suffer an incorrigible distortion in order to be able to serve both the structural imperative of expansion and the retention of control by the alienated command structure in the form of the established structural hierarchy. The illusions of 'variety' and 'diversity' in consumption are artificially cultivated in the interest of the system's self-legitimation. In reality nothing could be further from the truth. For the necessity to induce the fictionalized 'sovereign consumers' to fit their *post festum* recognized needs into the *preestablished grooves* of production under the rule of capital represents the height of *conformism*.

Thus, also in this respect the target of socialist transformation must be going beyond capital, and not merely overthrowing the private capitalist personifications of capital; let alone self-contradictorily attempting to accommodate the 'new social life process' to the crippling structural constraints of the 'capital and labour markets'. In the context of incentives the socialist hegemonic alternative to the rule of capital means radically overcoming the truncated dialectic of the system in the vital interrelationship of production–distribution–consumption. For without that, the socialist aim of turning work into 'life's prime want' is inconceivable. To quote Marx:

> In a higher phase of communist society, after the *enslaving subordination of the individual to the division of labour,* and therewith also the *antithesis between mental and physical labour,* has vanished; after labour has become not only a means of life but *life's prime want;* after the productive forces have also increased with the *all-round development of the individual,* and all the springs of *cooperative wealth* flow more abundantly — only then can the narrow horizon of bourgeois right be crossed in its entirety and society inscribe on its banners: *From each according to his ability, to each according to his needs!*[420]

Emancipating the individuals from their 'enslaving subordination to the division of labour' (in the words of 'old Marx') is tantamount to the radical reconstitution of the dialectic of production–distribution–consumption, setting out from the genuinely social control of the means of production, as opposed to their control by the capitalist or postcapitalist personifications of capital, in an alienated command structure. Only in this way is it possible to begin the creative transformation of both production and consumption, involving also the *self-determined* distribution of the individuals — as cooperatively associated and all-round developing individuals — among the different branches of productive activity, in accord with their personal inclinations and needs, as opposed to their treatment under the capital system as abstract 'labour capacity' and mere material factor of production 'efficiently allocated' from above.

Only within this framework is it possible to overcome the false opposition between *individual and social incentives,* on the one hand, and *material and non-material (cultural and moral) incentives,* on the other. The separation and alienation of control from the producers brings with it the fragmentation of the labour force whose members acquire legitimacy only as isolated individuals vis-à-vis capital, and likewise as isolated individual consumers in the market place. Thus the question of incentives, too, must be confined to the strictly individual plane. At the same time, given the necessary subordination of the needs of the individuals to the material imperatives of the system, a false opposition must be also established between material and non-material (above all moral) incentives. This is how the question of incentives is reduced in capital's 'real world' to their customary treatment as 'individual material incentives'. As we have seen above, in Hayek's theory *solidarity*—a collective moral incentive *par excellence*—is banned altogether from the 'complex modern world'. In other, less openly apologetic theories, moral incentives are either transformed into the strictly individualistic reflections of Max Weber's 'private demons',[421] or transferred to a separate religious/moral sphere, legitimated as some kind of idealistic preaching, with a most tenuous connection, if any, with the actual social metabolic process, even if not banned completely from the 'modern world'. The Stalinist mode of control of the postcapitalist capital system is not substantially different in this respect. For while it pays lip-service to moral incentives, it *arbitrarily prescribes* to the individuals the permissible content of their ideals and values, excluding the possibility of critically self-conscious *solidarity* arising from the collective labour force under its authoritarian control. Indeed, the possibility of labour solidarity contesting the political extraction of *surplus labour* — which in Stalin's view does not exist at all, as we have seen above, just like capitalist exploitation is non-existent for its apologists — must be condemned with the same dogmatic finality as Hayek rejects the contestation of economically regulated and enforced surplus labour extraction.

The socialist system of incentives is based on the *primacy of needs* over production targets, liberating itself thus from the tyranny of exchange value. This is possible only in a reproductive system in which (1) the control of production is fully vested in the producing individuals themselves, excluding thereby the superimposition of preestablished production objectives over their activity; and (2) the social character of labour is asserted directly, not *post festum*, enabling thus the individuals to *plan* their productive and distributive interchanges in a truly meaningful sense of the term. The social agency of production is constituted of particular individuals who can successfully reproduce themselves in society only as *social individuals*, even when they are at the mercy of fetishistic reproductive structures and modes of control. But precisely because under the rule of capital the social character of their production cannot be directly asserted, the individuals must be subsumed under power structures which relate to one another in antagonistic ways, narrowly determining also the nature and margin of individual material incentives compatible with them. Thus the needs of the individuals and the potentially corresponding use values must occupy a subordinate position within the reproductive framework of the capital system. Only the two important conditions mentioned at the beginning of this paragraph can secure the primacy of human needs and establish a system of incentives on qualitatively different foundations.

There could be no greater incentive for the individuals in any social order than the ability to control their own conditions of life. Naturally, for reasons which we are familiar with, this is totally denied to them under the rule of capital. Hence the false opposites which are meant to rationalize and legitimate the exclusion of non-individual and non-material incentives. Yet, since the actually existing social life process — from which the individuals cannot be extricated — is an interpersonal social process, the ability to control the conditions of life, as an incentive, is inseparably individual and collective/social by its innermost determination. At the same time, it is also a material and non-material or moral incentive. For through the real involvement of the associated producers in the control of the social reproductive process it is possible to envisage not only the removal of their formerly fully justified recalcitrance and hostility towards capital's alien command over labour, but, in a positive sense, also the activation of the individuals' repressed creative potentialities, bringing major material benefits to society as a whole as well as to the particular individuals. But, of course, the importance of this incentive — which is feasible only as the regulator of the 'new social life process' — is immeasurably greater than what could be characterized under the name of 'individual material incentives'. Since, however, the question of *control* is practically prejudged and must remain an absolute taboo under the rule of capital, it is precisely the most vital of the incentives for the life process of the individuals as self-determined autonomous individuals which cannot appear even for a fleeting moment within the horizon of the system's ideologists. On the contrary, the individual material incentives themselves must be always conceived and practically implemented in such a way that they should *divide* and actively set the individuals against one another, thereby facilitating the imposition and trouble-free management of capital's alien command structure.

Another dimension of our problem concerns the judicious apportionment of social wealth available for distribution between public funds and private consumption. This is particularly important in the period of transition. Again, the mythology of marketizing must be resisted. For the legitimation of market-driven private consumption only is blind as a policy and damaging not only to society as a whole but also to the individuals. Private consumption funds — for food and clothing, etc. — cannot meet by themselves the needs of the people, and even less so if they are market-determined, i.e. extremely discriminatory. The needs of the individuals for education, medical services, public transport, care for the aged, and the like, not to mention the crying need for social services by many groups of the socially and medically disadvantaged, can only be met from public funds. Once the basic needs of the individuals are satisfied from private consumption funds, the expansion of the public funds acquires an ever growing significance. The ratio between the two types of funds must be therefore regulated by the conscious decisions of the associated producers themselves. An improving ratio in favour of the public funds from the redistributed social wealth may become in fact a measure of the advancement of the society in question, rather than the opposite. What remains crucial in this respect, too, is the decision making process itself. For without a substantively democratic decision making by the associated producers themselves there can be no way out from the vicious circle of society's adversarially regulated — not least when within the framework of the market 'deregulated' — distributive relations.

20.5 Beyond the adversarial stalemate: from institutionalized irresponsibility to democratic decision making from below

20.5.1

IN her critique of Bernstein's strictures against the 'lack of discipline' of the workers in their cooperatives — a recurrent theme of socialdemocratic and 'market socialist' fantasies about the reformability of the capitalist order — Rosa Luxemburg argued that

> The domination of capital over the process of production expresses itself in the following ways. Labour is intensified. The work day is lengthened or shortened, according to the situation of the market. And, depending on the requirements of the market, labour is either employed or thrown back into the street. In other words, use is made of all methods that enable an enterprise to stand up against its competitors in the market. The workers forming a cooperative in the field of production are thus faced with the contradictory necessity of governing themselves with the utmost absolutism. They are obliged to take toward themselves the role of the capitalist entrepreneur — a contradiction that accounts for the *failure of production cooperatives*, which either become pure capitalist enterprises or, if the workers' interests continue to predominate, end by dissolving. Bernstein has himself taken note of these facts. But it is evident that he has not understood them. For, together with Mrs. Potter-Webb, he explains the failure of production cooperatives in England by their *lack of 'discipline'*. But what is so superficially and flatly called here 'discipline' is nothing

else than the natural *absolutist regime of capitalism,* which it is plain, the workers cannot successfully use against themselves.[422]

Under capitalism, discipline is ruthlessly imposed on labour through the *authoritarianism of the workshop* and the *tyranny of the market* (including, of course, the labour market). The drive for imposing it emanates from the expansionary imperatives of capital production, and it must prevail at all costs, no matter how inhuman and crippling the consequences. The reform attempts of Bernstein and his followers wanted to achieve their — ever diminishing and in the end totally evaporating — 'socialist' objectives without changing the structural framework of the system. Understandably, therefore, they had to welcome with wide open arms not only the need for capital's discipline but also the authoritarianism of the workshop and the tyranny of the market through which that discipline could be imposed on labour.

Capital's mode of social metabolic control by its innermost nature cannot be other than an *alienated* mode of control, whether the extraction of surplus labour is economically or politically regulated. No wonder, therefore, that Stalin — and his adherents also in the West — were allergic to the term *'alienation'*, trying to confine it to Marx's 'idealistic youthful phase' of development, despite massive evidence to the contrary. Yet, without constantly reminding ourselves of the incorrigibly alienated nature of the capital system, we cannot understand what needs to be radically superseded in the course of socialist transformation. For labour's hegemonic alternative — the object of socialist strategy — is not concerned with accommodatory reforms, devised to 'make capitalism work better', as latter-day Labour and 'New Labour' politicians advise people to do, but with establishing a radically different mode of social metabolic reproduction, consigning irreversibly to the past the coercive and exploitative determinations of capital's alienated order. To quote an important passage from the *Grundrisse:*

> In fact, in the production process of capital ... labour is a *totality* — a combination of labours — whose individual *component parts are alien to one another,* so that the overall process as a totality is not the work of the individual worker, and is furthermore the work of the different workers together only to the extent that they are {forcibly} combined, and do not [voluntarily] enter into combination with one another. The combination of this labour appears just as *subservient* to and led by an *alien will and an alien intelligence* — having its *animating unity* elsewhere — as its material unity appears subordinate to the *objective unity* of the *machinery,* of fixed capital, which, as *animated monster,* objectifies the scientific idea, and it is in fact the coordinator, does not in any way relate to the individual worker as his instrument; but rather he himself exists as an animated individual punctuation mark, as its living isolated accessory. ... Hence, just as the worker relates to the product of his labour as an *alien thing,* so does he relate to the combination of labour as an *alien combination,* as well as to his own labour as an expression of his life, which, although it belongs to him, is *alien to him and coerced from him* ... *Capital* therefore is the existence of social labour — the combination of *labour as subject as well as object* — but this existence as itself *existing independently opposite its real moments* — hence itself a particular existence apart from them. For its part, capital therefore appears as the *predominant subject* and owner of *alien labour,* and its relation is itself as complete a *contradiction* as is that of wage labour.[423]

Also in this context it is clearly visible that the contradiction of which Marx speaks cannot be overcome without going beyond capital not as a juridical entity but as a social metabolic order. This is why the Soviet type capital system had to end in failure. Its way of exercising discipline over labour could only work by making labour *'subservient* to and led by an *alien will and an alien intelligence'*. The adversarial determination of the labour process, directly controlled by the post-capitalist personifications of capital, remained fully in force, even if the ruthlessly enforced extraction of surplus labour was politically regulated, and not through the intermediary of the capitalist market. The worker could only 'relate to the product of his labour as an *alien thing,* to the combination of labour as an *alien combination,* and to his own labour as *alien to him and coerced from him'*. Capital's 'labour discipline' had to be observed everywhere even without the market, on pain of punishment. Ultimately, the forced labour camps to which masses of workers have been sent under Stalin (and not only under Stalin), enforcing the authoritarianism of the workshop in the most brutal form, made a complete mockery of the claims that alienation had been superseded in the postrevolutionary 'socialist' society.

Once the extreme political enforcement of labour discipline proved to be counter-productive, the legitimation of 'market socialism' seemed to the Stalinist personifications of capital to be the way out of the difficulties. However, the objective logic of their attempted reforms pointed towards the complete restoration of capitalism; even if it had to take three decades before it could be openly advocated that the way of the future had to be, as we have seen above, the 'consistent pursuit of market socialism — capital and labour markets and *ownership restructuring',* i.e. even the juridical restoration of the private capitalist system. The legitimation of commodity relations in consumer goods production, and the corresponding market and profit-accountancy to help enforce discipline, as Stalin imagined, was not enough. It was not possible to stop half-way in this restoratory process.

The establishment of the labour market proved to be particularly difficult. This should not have been surprising. For the labour market is a most peculiar kind of market also under capitalism. A transaction in the labour market is not a straightforward relationship of sale and purchase — unlike the acquisition and sale of consumer products — but a *structurally predetermined hierarchical power relation.* The fiction of 'contract between free and equal parties' hides the fact that the contracting individual workers are not entering the relationship as 'sovereign individuals' who could 'shop around' — in principle even between New York and New Delhi or London and Mexico City, on the model of capital markets in a 'globalized economy' — but as heavily constrained isolated individual personifications of labour confronting the personifications of preponderantly favoured capital. Labour's defensive trades unions try to remedy this state of affairs, but they can succeed only to a minimal extent even when authoritarian anti-labour legislation does not paralyse their efforts, not to mention chronic mass unemployment which delivers the knock-out blow. Thus, whereas the *mobility of capital* is undeniable and constitutes a major source of its power over labour, the 'mobility of labour' is virtually non-existent by comparision, and inasmuch as it exists under capitalism — to different degrees in different phases of the system's development — it serves primarily the domination of self-expansionary capital over labour.

The peculiar character of the labour market under capitalism was in the first place a great help to the postcapitalist capital system. For the Stalinist mode of regulation could 'mimic' some of the important defining characteristics of the inherited labour market. That could work quite well, up to a point, since the state and the postcapitalist personifications of capital could fulfil the function required of them as the structurally dominant party in the pseudo-contractual relationship. They could allocate and direct 'labour power' — in theory strictly on behalf of the workers, mimicking also in this sense the fictional 'free contract' and the autonomous self-determination of the workers who enter into it — to wherever it was needed, exercising at the same time (as capital always does) the system's separate and alienated command over the individual workers as much as over the totality of labour as a class.

An essential discipline-enhancing feature of the capitalist labour market was, however, missing; and that proved to be in the end a major reason for the un-doing of the Soviet type capital system. For under capitalism it is not simply the totality of labour which is subsumed under capital as a whole, but simultane-ously also determinate groups of workers are directly related to and dominated by a plurality of capitals. As a matter of structural determinations, capital under capitalism is articulated as a multiplicity of capitals, despite the growing — but never fully realizable — tendency to monopoly. The many capitals control the particular groups of labour under their command both through the more or less obvious authoritarianism of the workshop and their own, more or less favour-able, position in the national and international market. Also the nature and the corresponding strict limitations of *political pluralism* under the capitalist system — the 'multi-party democracy' of the parliamentary framework under the rule of capital's parliamentary and extra-parliamentary forces — are determined on such a weighty socioeconomic basis. Without acknowledging this substantive relationship, all references to an idealized 'political pluralism' — whether in the Leaders of the London *Economist* or in the theoretical writings of 'market social-ists' — belong to the category of veiled political propaganda in favour of capi-talist restoration. All four advocated policy objectives of the so-called 'consistent pursuit of market socialism' — *'capital markets, labour markets, ownership restruc-turing, and political pluralism'* — actively promoted capitalist restoration. For the only admissible 'political pluralism' which the postcapitalist personifications of capital could contemplate and tolerate in the political sphere was the kind which would secure their continued command over labour.

The principal attraction of the postcapitalist personifications of capital to marketization — from Stalin in his last years of rule to Gorbachev and company both in the USSR and in Eastern Europe — was their desire to strengthen their grip over labour by intensifying labour discipline under the changed circum-stances. Their embrace of the market was expected to achieve this end, in that the inherited authoritarianism of the workshop — which they could politically impose and even intensify without unmanageable difficulties under Stalin and after — would be complemented and greatly strengthened by the *tyranny of the market*. Given the requirements of a more intensive type of production at home and the increasingly closer links of their economies with the world market, they wanted to succeed through the new formula of combining the political extrac-tion of surplus labour with the (grotesquely misconceived) 'market mechanism', hoping to squeeze out in that way from a less recalcitrant labour force the desired higher productivity.

However, the new formula would not work. For the missing dimension of the capitalist labour market in the postrevolutionary system revealed its importance precisely at the time when the 'market socialists' tried to make fully operational a proper labour market in the USSR and in Eastern Europe. Under the capitalist system the workers are tied to their contractual position in the companies for which they work in such a way that they are induced to *internalize* the exposure of the companies in question to the vicissitudes of the national and world market. It is well known that through competition 'what corresponds to the nature of capital is posited as *external necessity* for the *individual capital* ... The *reciprocal compulsion* which the particular capitals practise upon one another, on labour etc. (the competition among workers is only *another form of the competition among the capitals),* is the free, at the same time the real development of wealth as capital'.[424] The workers cannot help participating in (by suffering the consequences of) the 'external necessity' of competition which affects the particular capitalist enterprises in the marketplace and provides them with all kinds of excuses vis-à-vis their labour force. This is how the, on the face of it baffling, situation arises that workers can accept not only *'wage restraint'* and *'wage freeze'* but even *wage cuts* and *voluntary redundancies* in order to save from bankruptcy the firms which dominate and exploit them. Naturally, this is the only kind of 'solidarity' which even Hayek would enthusiastically applaud 'in the modern world'.

This kind of market-induced discipline was what the postcapitalist personifications of capital from Stalin to Gorbachev were longing for. Stalin was anticipating improved economic discipline from the pressure for profitability of the enterprises, and Gorbachev praised the sense of realism of the workers in restraining their demands under the 'new situation' of marketizing perestroika. The last thing the postcapitalist personifications of capital could wish for was the effective solidarity between the local enterprises and their workers. The market-induced discipline, as a subordinate moment of the established mode of politically enforced extraction of surplus labour, was supposed to strengthen the grip of the central authority, not weaken it. The 'one and only qualitative index of profitability' eulogized by Liberman and Nemchinov was coupled with reassurances that the proposed mathematical 'feed-back loops' of the marketized planning process could be determined *in advance* by the *central* planning organs. By impressing on the workers in particular enterprises the need for local 'economic efficiency' and profit accountancy, the market (or pseudo-market) was expected to reinforce the unquestioning subordination of labour to postcapitalist capital — just like the kind of labour's subservient solidarity with capital in the good books of Hayek — and thereby improve the viability of the postcapitalist mode of centralized social metabolic control. Stalin in his last years, in order to strengthen the central organs of control, wanted to combine his 'socialist commodity relations' with the centrally orchestrated Stakhanovite 'socialist emulation movement', as a directly enforceable political pressure on labour for submission to higher work-norms; and Gorbachev liked to preach about the need for 'sacrifices' by the workers before they could get the promised economic benefits of the market reforms.

Yet, the objective conditions demonstrated the nonsensical character of the wishful projection of combining the political extraction of surplus labour with the market, preventing the establishment of a real labour market without the restoration of capitalism. Under the capitalist system labour's internalization of the painful consequences of the 'external necessity' of competition which affects the particular enterprises in the marketplace actually works because the threat of negative consequences is very real. Under the Soviet system, by contrast, the possibility of internalization was totally missing. For, given the way in which the postcapitalist system was constituted, the recalcitrance of labour was directed against the real controlling authority—the overall political command structure of capital as embodied in the state — and not against local managers, who could at times even collude with the workers (naturally in their own interest) in order to outwit the central authorities. To make sense of the advocacy of establishing a real labour market, it was necessary (1) to abolish the constitutional right of the workers to employment, and (2) to introduce reforms through which the 'less efficient' enterprises could (and under the advocated market competition actually would) go bankrupt. Not surprisingly, therefore, as the 'reform movement' gathered momentum, calls for *bankruptcy legislation with real teeth* figured ever more prominently on the list of 'market socialist' priorities, in close conjunction with demands for the establishment of 'capital and labour markets, ownership restructuring, and political pluralism', i.e. all four of the necessary requirements for the restoration of capitalism.

This is how the *tyranny of the market* — the directly market-related dimension of discipline to which labour must be subjected under the capitalist variety of the capital system — had to be introduced into the Soviet type capital system, ironically contributing in a most active way to its disintegration. Given the incorrigibly adversarial nature of the postcapitalist labour process and the alienated economic and political command structure required for its control, the 'improved labour discipline' anticipated in the market reforms could only be realized — contrary to the fantasies of combining 'socialist democracy' with the 'economic efficiency' of an enlightened and caring 'social market' — in the form of fusing the well entrenched authoritarianism of the workshop with the savage unemployment-producing tyranny of the market, thanks to a large extent to the capitalistically reconstituted labour market.

20.5.2

TO be sure, *discipline* is not less but much more important in the 'new social life process' of a socialist society. But with a qualitative difference. For the only discipline practicable under all feasible forms of the capital system — in view of the incorrigibly *adversarial structural determination* of its labour process — is *external* discipline, which must be superimposed in one way or another on the labour force. By contrast, the socialist alternative involves the *internally* motivated discipline of the associated individual producers. And that is feasible only if the structural antagonism between capital and labour and the adversarial stalemate resulting from it are superseded through the positive reproductive processes of the socialist hegemonic alternative to the established social metabolic order. Discipline in this positive sense means the individuals' autonomous dedication to the tasks they face, making them their own not through some external command — not even as a result of moral exhortations which in many ways resemble external commands — but because they have *actually* made the tasks their own by their self-determined deliberations and actions, defining for themselves both the objectives to be pursued and the ways and means through which they can be realized.

The question of discipline presents itself under two major aspects. The first concerns the nature of the tasks to be performed, and in that sense the appropriateness of the human *skills* which they require, together with their careful exercise for the successful completion of the given tasks. The second aspect is directly related to the *intensity* with which the individuals — who possess the required skills—are able (as a matter of disposable energy) and willing (primarily a question of attitude) to perform the work undertaken by them. Evidently, therefore, it makes a world of difference whether the individuals work under the pressure of political and economic compulsion, or dedicate themselves out of conscious deliberation both to learning and to applying the required skills, working with an intensity and care which no separate — let alone an alienated and hostile — supervisory authority can impose upon them. The only feasible solutions to these requirements within the confines of the capital system are, (1) to *fragment the tasks and work-skills* to their minutest details, effectively *de-skilling* thereby the labour force, so that the workers' power of control is minimized and even nullified, and the fragmented tasks can be assigned to some machinery to which the workers are attached as a mere appendage. At the same time, (2) the question of intensity can be managed in part by instrumental devices, such as the speedy assembly line, which — coupled with the most exploitative industrial organizational methods and techniques, like Taylorism — forces the workers to apply their energies to the point of exhaustion (hastened by the extreme monotony of the detail tasks performed); and in part by the economic and/or political compulsion which the given regulation of surplus-labour-extraction must impose on labour under the rule of capital.

Once upon a time capital's way of managing the labour process and imposing its iron discipline on labour represented a historical advance, and as such it 'made sense'. Today the situation is radically different. For, ruthlessly driving forward a stunted kind of production with the greatest practicable intensity, at a time when capital-expansion is inseparable from the system's *destructive* reproduction and self-preservation, capital's external discipline not only does not make sense any longer but represents the devastating triumph of *unreason,* just as the mindless expansion of exchange value, at the expense of vital human need, represents the crippling triumph of *anti-value.*

Right from the historical ascendancy of the capital system there were two grave reasons why the process of productive development on this socioeconomic basis could not turn out to be more positive. First, because all feasible achievements had to be accommodated within the confines of capital's expansion-oriented and accumulation-driven framework, which narrowly determined what could be and what could not be pursued as productive targets with the required 'economic efficiency', totally unmindful of the human and ecological consequences from 'day one', so to speak. And second, given the *centrifugal* determination of the capital system (discussed in Chapter 2), due to the insoluble contradiction between production and control from the smallest reproductive microcosms to the most comprehensive productive and distributive relations, it was inconceivable to remedy the *adversarial* structural framework which carried with it un-limitable wastefulness and ultimate uncontrollability. If it is true that within the capital system 'individuals are *subsumed* under social production which exists *outside* them as their *fate'*,[425] it must be an equally disconcerting truth for the defenders of capital that the 'fate' of their system is that it can never overcome the antagonisms of its structural determinations and the constantly reproduced adversarial stalemate of its social metabolic control process. For under determi-nate historical conditions labour can be dominated, exploited and for a shorter or longer duration even violently repressed by the power of capital, but never submissively integrated for good as a class into capital's incorrigibly adversarial reproductive order.

The disastrously failed 'market socialist' ventures were projecting capital and its benevolent 'social market' in a form which bore no resemblance whatsoever to the actually existing, irremediably antagonistic, capital relations. In the foot-steps of Margaret Thatcher who recited the words of Saint Francis of Assisi after her electoral victory, the political masters and propagandists of market socialism also pretended to follow Saint Francis in the role of preaching to the birds. But they did it with a big difference. For whereas one of the most radical saints in history addressed real life birds in their natural habitat, they delivered their market socialist sermons to a row of stuffed birds, shouting in excitement: 'How wonderful! It's a great miracle! The killer birds are not going to kill the song birds ever again! They all sit peacefully next to one another!' This is how — thanks to the advanced methods of imaginary bird-incantation 'in the modern world' — the enlightened, truly compassionate, and universally beneficial 'social market' came into existence in the new 'market societies', breaking all connec-tions with the actually existing market. Even Hobbes was now expected to rest in peace. For, according to the newly proclaimed world view, *bellum omnium contra omnes* has finally come to an end in the 'post-historical' Millennium.

Yet, the actually existing capital system reasserted its material imperatives and antagonisms as ever before. So much so, in fact, that it is very difficult to find even a tiny spot on our planet under the rule of capital where the contra-dictions of the system are not in evidence, whether we think of the growing disenchantment with politics or of the stubborn refusal of the *ectoplasm of 'feel-good-factor'* to materialize in the domain of economics; not to mention the serious military conflagrations in different parts of the world. The happy New World Order was supposed to have arrived with the implosion of the Soviet system and the capitulation of Gorbachev's Russia. But even in that regard the euphoria is misplaced. For sooner or later the meaning of a Hungarian adage — *'I caught a Turk, but he doesn't let me go!'* — is bound to become clear to everyone.

The social reproductive system which is incapable of taking into account the consequences of its drive forward, except on a most myopic scale and within the confines of the shortest time-span, can only be described as a system of institu-tionalized irresponsibility. The external discipline imposed on the producers in order to realize the self-expansionary objectives of this system can only aggravate the situation, even if it can secure for the time being the envisaged objectives. For such a discipline not only drives forward labour, irrespective of the conse-quences, but also eliminates the possibility of subjecting to a conscious critical examination the objectives dictated by the system and imposed from above, preventing the assessment of their viability — and therefore also their desirability — on the necessary global scale and within an appropriately long-term time horizon. The social metabolic order which regulates its reproductive processes on such a basis is, therefore, not only irresponsible but also most dangerous in the longer run.

The institutionalized irresponsibility which goes with the adversarial structural determinations of the capital system can only be overcome by changing that structure itself. This is possible only through the positive articulation of the socialist hegemonic alternative to the self-sustaining totality of capital as an organic system. The productive objectives of the socialist alternative cannot be even defined, let alone realized, without escaping from the straitjacket of self-expanding exchange value, adopting in its place as the orienting principle of societal reproduction the positive development and satisfaction of human needs, including in a prominent place the need for work 'as life's prime want'. The internal discipline of work counterposed to capital's externally imposed drill is also in need of a very different economic grounding, in terms of its relationship to labour time. For the expropriation of no matter how large a quantity of *surplus labour* and *surplus value* by capital, corresponding to ever greater quantities and intensity of surplus labour time, would be a truly miserable foundation for the requirements of a socialist labour process, which aims at the production and satisfaction of 'rich human need'. A qualitatively different relationship to the life-activity of the individuals is needed here, which is feasible only if their *disposable time* is freely made available for the ends consciously chosen by the associated producers themselves, instead of forcibly extracting from them whatever can be extracted and utilized by an alienated mode of social metabolic control, for its own self-expansionary ends, with 'economic efficiency'. But, of course, there can be no reason whatsoever why the individuals should feel internally/positively motivated to put their disposable time into the common pool of their productive and distributive practices if they are not fully in control of their life-activity.

Naturally, the existing adversarial system of institutionalized irresponsibility cannot be overcome without the establishment of a substantively democratic decision making process, which in its turn is inconceivable without a genuine planning process. In this context another false opposite must be rejected: the allegedly insurmountable opposition between 'central planning' and 'individual choice', promoted usually in the service of capital-apologetics and market-idolatry. For 'individual choice' and 'local autonomy' mean absolutely nothing if the 'autonomous' choices made by the individuals or groups of individuals at a local level are nullified by the material imperatives of the capital system and the authoritarian directives of its overall political command structure. The source of the trouble here is that the established social metabolic order is adversarial in its totality as well as in its smallest constitutive parts. Only in the realm of fiction is it possible to make prevail substantive individual choices and local autonomy while keeping the adversarial structural determinations of the capital system as a whole intact. Only by radically restructuring — i.e. substantively democratizing — the *constitutive cells* of the given order is it possible to envisage a viable alternative. For the antagonistic/adversarial comprehensive framework is both the embodiment of the adversarial microcosms and reflects itself back into them, shaping them in accordance with the overall systemic requirements. This is why the 'central planning systems' known in history had to prove a failure even in their own terms of reference — except for very limited periods, like major wars and other extreme states of emergency — in that they could not successfully prevail (not even when they used the most violent means of enforcement) over the recalcitrant elements of their adversarial microcosms. Moreover, when they were attempting to 'reform' themselves, they could envisage reform only in the form of 'decentralization' — determined from above — which preserved virtually intact the contradictions of this vicious circle, begging the question in favour of the primacy of authoritarian centralism. For, given capital's *adversarially structured* hierarchical social division of labour, the *cohesive* dimension must be superimposed *from above* on the constitutive parts of its incorrigibly *centrifugal* system. Hence the false opposition between 'central' and 'local', since everything must be ruthlessly *subsumed* — despite the rhetorics of 'individual consumer sovereignty' and 'local autonomy'—under the hierarchical structural imperatives of the capital system. Without that, capital's antagonistic/adversarial mode of reproduction could not function even for a day, let alone survive for a long historical period.

The real issue, then, is the dialectical relationship between the *whole* and its *parts*. Under the capital system the top echelons of its command structure, with their perverse centrality, usurp the place of the whole and dominate the parts, imposing on everyone their *partiality* as the *'interest of the whole'*. This is how capital's self-sustaining totality can assert itself — by undialectically short-circuiting the part/whole relationship — as an organic system. The socialist hegemonic alternative therefore involves the reconstitution of the objective dialectic of the parts and the whole in a non-adversarial way, from the smallest reproductive constitutive cells to the most comprehensive productive and distributive relations. The success of planning depends on the willing coordination of their productive and distributive activities by those who have to realize the consciously envisaged aims. Thus genuine planning is inconceivable without substantive democratic decision making from below through which both the lateral coordination and the comprehensive integration of reproductive practices become feasible. And *vice versa*. For without the consciously planned and comprehensively coordinated exercise of their creative energies and skills, all talk about the democratic decision making of the individuals is without substance. Only the two together can define the elementary requirements of the socialist hegemonic alternative to capital's social metabolic order.

NOTES TO PART THREE

[1] Marx, *Grundrisse*, pp. 487-8.
[2] Marx, *Capital*, vol. 1, pp. 357-8.
[3] *Ibid.*, pp. 358-9.
[4] Marx, *Grundrisse*, p. 489.
[5] *Ibid.*, p. 512.
[6] *Ibid.*, pp. 491-5.
[7] *Ibid.*, p. 488. The sharply criticized fact of being thus *predetermined* is italicized by the 'crude economic determinist' Marx himself.
[8] Marx and Engels, *Collected Works*, vol. 5, pp. 48-9.
[9] 'The satisfaction of the first need, the action of satisfying and the instrument of satisfaction which has been acquired, leads to *new needs*; and this creation of new needs is the *first historical act.' Ibid.*, p. 42.
[10] MECW, vol. 6, p. 127.
[11] 'Since handicraft skill is the foundation of manufacture, and since the mechanism of manufacture as a whole possesses no framework, apart from the labourers themselves, capital is constantly compelled to wrestle with the *insubordination* of the workmen. "By the infirmity of human nature," says friend Ure, "it happens that the more skilful the workman, the more *self-willed* and *intractable* he is apt to become, and of course the less fit a *component of a mechanical system* in which ... he may do great damage to the whole." Hence throughout the whole manufacturing period there runs the complaint of *want of discipline* among the workmen.' Marx, *Capital*, Foreign Languages Publishing House, Moscow, 1958, vol. 1, p. 367.
[12] Baran, *The Political Economy of Growth*, Monthly Review Press, New York, 1957, p.xx.
[13] Marx, *Capital, Ibid.*, pp. 331-2.
[14] MECW, vol. 6, p. 134.
[15] Quoted in Marx, *Grundrisse*, Penguin Books, Harmondsworth, 1973, p. 397.
[16] *Ibid.*, pp. 399-401.
[17] See in this respect Harry Braverman's classic study, *Labor and Monopoly Capital: The Degradation of Work in the Twentieth Century* (Monthly Review Press, New York, 1974), as well as a collection of essays on *Technology, the Labor Process and the Working Class* (Monthly Review Press, New York, 1976). The latter volume contains essays conceived as critical rejoinders to Braverman's book. They are: 'The Working Class Has Two Sexes' by Rosalyn Baxandall, Elizabeth Ewen, and Linda Gordon; 'Work and Consciousness' by John and Barbara Ehrenreich; 'Capitalist Efficiency and Socialist Efficiency' by David M. Gordon, 'Division of Labor in the Computer Field' by Joan Greenbaum; 'Marx as a Student of Technology' by Nathan Rosenberg; 'Social Relations of Production and Consumption in the Human Service Occupations' by Gelvin Stevenson; 'The Other Side of the Paycheck: Monopoly Capital and the Structure of Consumption' by Batya Weinbaum and Amy Bridges; and 'Marx versus Smith on the Division of Labor' by Donald D. Weiss. The volume also contains a brief reply by Harry Braverman.
See also 'Special Issue Commemorating Harry Braverman's *Labour and Monopoly Capital*', with contributions by John Bellamy Foster, Joan Greenbaum, Peter Meiksins, Bruce Nissen and Peter Seybold, *Monthly Review*, vol. 46, No. 6, November 1994.
[18] Set the apologetic myth of 'consumer sovereignty' against the reality of such transformations.
[19] Charles Babbage was a far-sighted thinker, with strong practical interests. He

advocated the productive exploitation of tidal wave energy as far back as the eighteen thirties; founded the 'science of *computation*', and even built the first (mechanical) computer, although the amazingly large scale which he adopted for that enterprise prevented its completion. In 1816 he was made Fellow of the Royal Society, but was very critical of the way in which that institution was administered at the time (through the meddling of aristocrats), and he helped to found the British Association, in 1831, as a broadly based alternative institution for the advancement of science. His book *On the Economy of Machinery and Manufactures* was a great success: 3,000 copies of the first edition were sold out within months, in 1832, and several thousands more followed later on, despite the dubious behaviour of 'The Trade' whose monopolistic practices Babbage forcefully denounced in all subsequent editions of his book.

[20] Charles Babbage, *On the Economy of Machinery and Manufacture*, 4th edition enlarged, Charles Knight, London, 1835, pp.11-2.

[21] *Ibid.*, p. 6.

[22] *Ibid.*, p. 8.

[23] *Ibid.*, p. 297.

[24] *Ibid.*, p. 285.

[25] *Ibid.*, p. 286.

[26] *Ibid.*, p. 292.

[27] *Ibid.*, p. 150.

[28] *Ibid.*, pp. 148-9.

[29] Babbage may well be considered also the founder of the 'science of management', eighty years before F. W. Taylor. The difference between their views is partly accountable for with reference to the much more advanced stage of capitalist technology in Taylor's time. More important, though, is their attitude to Trade Unions (or 'combinations'). For while Babbage wants to remove the artificial restrictions and prohibitions from their path — even if he is firmly convinced that in his 'new system of manufacture' there would be no need for separate workers' combinations — Taylor is a crude anti-unionist.

Babbage constantly insists on the importance of precise measurement and verification, trying to optimize the productive advantages of machinery by superimposing its power of control on the human agency. This is how he describes the process involved:

> One great advantage which we may derive from machinery is from the check which it affords against the inattention, the idleness or the dishonesty of human agents. ... Perhaps the most useful contrivance of this kind, is one for ascertaining the vigilance of a watchman. It is a piece of mechanism connected with a clock placed in an apartment to which the watchman has not access; but he is ordered to pull a string situated in a certain part of his round once in every hour. The instrument, aptly called a *tell-tale,* informs the owner whether the man has missed any, and what hours, during the night. (*Ibid.*, pp. 54-5.)

However, on the whole his attitude to labour is that of an 'enlightened capitalist' who strongly condemns the double exploitation of labour through the 'truck system' (which compels the workers to buy their necessaries in the factory shop, at exorbitant prices) and advocates various — though often naive — measures to alleviate the great hardship of unemployment brought upon the workers precipitously at times of 'glut'. Unintentionally demonstrating that the illusions of 'participatory popular capitalism' are almost as old as capitalism itself, he even puts forward a thoroughly utopian proposal for a 'new system of manufacturing', recommending its virtues in these terms:

> I believe that some such system of conducting manufactories would greatly increase the productive powers of any country adopting it; and that our own possesses much greater facilities for its application than other countries, in the greater intelligence and superior education of the working classes. The system would naturally commence in some large town, by the union of some of the most prudent and active

workmen; and their example, if successful, would be followed by others. The small capitalist would next join them and such factories would go on increasing until competition compelled the large capitalist to adopt the same system; and ultimately, the whole faculties of *every* man engaged in manufacture would be concentrated upon one object — the art of producing a good article at the lowest possible cost ... (*Ibid.,* p. viii.)

Convinced that the conflict between capital and labour is the cause of much waste and unnecessary complications, the main reason why he wants to introduce his new system — which would begin with a co-operative enterprise between the best workers (who invest their savings) and some small capitalists — is to remove such conflicts, arguing that:

A most erroneous and unfortunate opinion prevails amongst workmen in many manufacturing countries, that their own interest and that of their employers are at variance. The consequences are, — that valuable machinery is sometimes neglected, and even privately injured, — that new improvements, introduced by the master, do not receive a fair trial, — and that the talents and observations of the workmen are not directed to the improvement of the processes in which they are employed. (*Ibid.,* p.250.)

And this is how he sums up the principal benefits of his system:

The result of such arrangements in a factory would be,

1. That every person engaged in it would have a *direct* interest in its prosperity; since the effect of any success, or falling off, would almost immediately produce a corresponding change in his own weekly receipts.

2. Every person concerned in the factory would have an immediate interest in preventing any waste or mismanagement in all the departments.

3. The talents of all connected with it would be strongly directed to its improvement in every department.

4. None but workmen of high character and qualifications could obtain admission into such establishments; ...

5. When any circumstances produced a glut in the market, more skill would be directed to diminishing the cost of production; ...

6. Another advantage, of no small importance, would be the total removal of all real or imaginary causes for combinations. The workmen and the capitalist would so shade into each other, — would so *evidently* have a common interest, and their difficulties and distresses would be mutually so well understood, that, instead of combining to oppress one another, the only combination which could exist would be a most powerful union *between* both parties to overcome their common difficulties. (*Ibid.,* pp.257-8.)

Of course Babbage is by no means blind to the fact that:

It would be difficult to prevail on the *large capitalist* to enter upon any system, which would change the division of the profits arising from the employment of his capital in setting skill and labour in action; any alteration, therefore, must be expected rather from the *small capitalist*, or *from the higher class of workmen*, who combine the two characters; (*Ibid.,* p.254.)

Indeed, he sees that the diminution in the capitalist's share of profit, which he readily concedes to be the necessary implication of his arguments commending the new system of manufacture to the workers, might present great obstacles to the adoption of his scheme. But he attempts to overcome that difficulty by suggesting a 'presumed effect' capable of (wishfully) solving the problem:

One of the difficulties attending such a system is, that capitalists would at first fear to embark in it, imagining that the workmen would receive too large a share of the profits: and it is quite true that the workmen would have a larger share than at present: but, at the same time, it is presumed the effect of the whole system would be, that the total profits of the establishment being much increased, the smaller proportion allowed to capital under this system would yet be greater in actual amount, than that which results to it from the larger share in the system now existing. (*Ibid.*, p.258.)

F.W. Taylor copies Babbage's suggestions when he insists that as a result of adopting his own approach: 'The great revolution that takes place in the mental attitude of the two parties under scientific management is that both sides take their eyes off the division of the surplus as the all-important matter, and together turn their attention toward increasing the size of the surplus until this surplus becomes so large that it is unnecessary to quarrel over how it shall be divided.' (cf. p.88 of *Management Thinkers*, ed. by Anthony Tillett, Thomas Kempner and Gordon Wills, Penguin Books, Harmondsworth, 1970.) The big difference is that Babbage offers the workers some degree of control, through their participation in a 'co-operative' enterprise with the capitalists, while Taylor none.

However, the unreality of Babbage's utopia comes not only from his lack of understanding of the roots of the antagonism between capital and labour, and thus of their ultimate irreconcilability. Equally important is in this respect his failure to recognize the tendency for the concentration and centralization of capital and of the fact that, while remaining within the capitalistic framework, no durable obstacles can be put in the path of such tendencies. He even tries to devise a utopian technological power requirement to match his economic/organisational utopia, envisaging a potential reversion to the domestic type of manufacture — just like some people fantasise about it today in relation to a future 'cottage economy' based on computer technology — as if the ongoing concentration of wealth was due simply to technological factors:

If any mode could be discovered of transmitting power, without much loss from friction, to considerable distances, and at the same time of registering the quantity made use of at any particular point, a considerable change would probably take place in many departments of the present system of manufacturing. A few central engines to produce power, might then be erected in our great towns, and each workman, hiring a quantity of power sufficient for his purpose, might have it conveyed into his own house; and thus a transition might in some instance be effected, if it should be found more profitable, *back again from the system of great factories to that of domestic manufacture. (Ibid.*, p.290.)

As we all know, the discovery of electricity and the establishment of not only national but even globally interconnected networks of power — both electric and gas — greatly contributed to the concentration and centralization of capitalist industry, rather than to its decentralization or return to 'domestic manufacture', as Babbage expected.

[30] Adam Ferguson, *An Essay on the History of Civil Society* (1767), ed. with an introduction by Duncan Forbes, Edinburgh University Press, 1966, p.245.

[31] Bernard Mandeville, *The Fable of the Bees: or Private Vices, Publick Benefits,* Edited with an introduction by Phillip Hart, Penguin books, Harmondsworth, 1970, p. 64. First published in 1705. The Penguin edition contains various other writings added by Mandeville to his poem between 1714 and 1724. They are: 'An Enquiry into the Origin of Moral Virtue'; 'An Essay on Charity, and Charity Schools'; 'A Search into the Nature of Society'; and 'A Vindication of the Book and an Abusive Letter to Lord C'. Quotations below are taken from all these works.

[32] *Ibid.*, p.67.

[33] *Ibid.*, p.369.

Mandeville does not hesitate to push religious morality, too, aside in favour of a 'scandalously' secular view of good and evil, defined in terms of their contribution to the wealth of society:

Religion is one thing and Trade is another. He that gives most Trouble to Thousands of his Neighbours, and invents the most operose Manufactures is right or wrong the greatest Friend to the Society. (*Ibid.*, p.358.)

Similarly, for him 'sociability' is not a beneficially given characteristic implanted by nature in man, but the hard-won outcome of conflicting determinations, in that: 'the Sociableness of Man arises only from these Two things, viz. The multiplicity of his *Desires* and the *continual Opposition* he meets with in his Endeavours to gratify them.' (*Ibid.*, p.347.)

Mandeville's whole conception in this respect is summed up in the passage that follows:

I flatter my self to have demonstrated that, neither the Friendly Qualities and kind Affections that are natural to Man, nor the real Virtues, he is capable of acquiring by Reason and Self-Denial, are the foundation of Society; but that what we call Evil in this World, Moral as well as Natural, is the grand Principle that makes us Sociable Creatures, the solid Basis, the Life and Support of all Trades and Employments without exception: That there we must look for the true origin of all Arts and Sciences, and that the moment, Evil ceases, the Society must be spoil'd if not totally dissolv'd. (*Ibid.*, p.370.)

34 *Ibid.*, p.258.
35 *Ibid.*, p.187.
36 *Ibid.*, p.197.
37 *Ibid.*, pp.257-8.
38 *Ibid.*, pp.67-9.
39 *Ibid.*, p.365.
40 *Ibid.*, p.358-60.
41 'Frugality is like Honesty, a mean starving Virtue, that is only *fit for small Societies* of good peaceable Men, who are contented to be poor so they may be easy; but in a *large stirring Nation* you may have soon enough of it. 'Tis an *idle dreaming Virtue that employs no hands,* and therefore very *useless in a trading Country,* where there are vast numbers that one way or other *must be all set to Work.* Prodigality has a thousand Inventions to keep People from sitting still, that Frugality would never think of; and as this must *consume a prodigious Wealth,* so Avarice again knows innumerable Tricks to rake it together, which Frugality would scorn to make use of.' *Ibid.*, pp.134-5.

The contrast between the commended 'large and stirring Nations' which regulate their conduct on the basis of 'Private Vices', and the 'small Nations' that live in accordance with the precepts of Virtue, is a recurring theme of Mandeville's writings. His guiding criteria always remain the suitability of Virtues (or Vices) to productive expansion. In one of the passages concerning the limitations of 'small Nations' he asserts that: 'Few Vertues employ any Hands, and therefore they may render a small Nation Good, but they can never make a Great one.' (*Ibid.*, p.368.) He scornfully rejects even the adoption of 'That boasted *middle way',* on the ground that 'the calm Virtues recommended in the Characteristicks are good for nothing but to *breed Drones,* and might qualify a Man for the stupid Enjoyments of a *Monastick Life,* or at best a Country Justice of Peace, but they would never fit him for Labour and Assiduity, or stir him up to great Atchievements and perilous Undertakings.' (*Ibid.*, p.337.)

42 'The great Art then to make a Nation happy, and what we call flourishing, consists in *giving every body an Opportunity of being employ'd;* which to compass, let a *Government's* first care be to promote as great a variety of Manufactures, Arts and Handicrafts, as Human Wit can invent; and the second to encourage Agriculture and Fishery in all their Branches, that the whole Earth may be forc'd to exert itself as well as Man; for as the one is an infallible Maxim to draw vast multitudes of People into a Nation, so the other is the only Method to maintain them. It is from *this Policy,* and not the trifling Regulations of Lavishness and Frugality, (which will ever take their own Course,

according to the Circumstances of the People) that the *Greatness and Felicity of Nations* must be expected; for let the Value of Gold an Silver either rise or fall, the Enjoyment of all Societies will ever depend upon the *Fruits of the Earth, and the Labour of the People;* both which joyn'd together are a more certain, a more inexhaustible and a *more real Treasure than the Gold of Brazil, or the Silver of Potosi.'* (*Ibid.*, pp.211-2.)

43 *Ibid.*, p.142.

44 *Ibid.*, p.350.

45 *Ibid.*, pp.256-7.

46 *Ibid.*, p.145.

47 *Ibid.*, p.209.

48 *Ibid.*

49 *Ibid.*, p.145.

50 *Ibid.*, p.209.

51 *Ibid.*, p.136-7.

52 *Ibid.*, p.188.

53 *Ibid.*, p.174.

54 See the penetrating analysis of such developments in Paul A. Baran and Paul M. Sweezy, *Monopoly Capital,* Monthly Review Press, New York, 1966. See also Sweezy, 'The Resurgence of Financial Control: Fact or Fiction?', in *Monthly Review,* vol. 23, no. 6 (Nov. 1971), pp.1-33.

55 Mandeville, *Ibid.,* p.360.

56 As Marx underlines: 'Under private property ... every person speculates on creating a *new* need in another, so as to drive him to a fresh sacrifice, to place him in a new dependence and to seduce him into a new mode of *gratification* and therefore economic ruin. Each tries to establish over the other an *alien* power, so as thereby to find satisfaction of his own selfish need. The increase in the quantity of objects is accompanied by an extension of the realm of the alien powers to which man is subjected, and every new product represents a new *potency* of mutual swindling and mutual plundering. Man becomes ever poorer as man; his need for *money* becomes ever greater if he wants to overpower hostile being; and the power of his money declines exactly in inverse proportion to the increase in the volume of production: that is, his neediness grows as the *power* of money increases. The need for money is therefore the true need produced by the modern economic system, and it is the only need which the latter produces. The *quantity* of money becomes to an ever greater degree its sole *effective* attribute: just as it reduces everything to its abstract form, so it reduces itself in the course of its movement to something merely *quantitative*. *Excess* and *intemperance* come to be its true norm. Subjectively, this is even partly manifested in that the extension of products and needs falls into *contriving* and ever-*calculating* subservience to inhuman, refined, unnatural and *imaginary* appetites.' Marx, *Economic and Philosophic Manuscripts of 1844,* Lawrence and Wishart, London, 1959, pp.115-6. Marx's italics.

57 See note 26.

58 Marx, *Capital,* vol. 1, pp.358-9.

59 *Ibid.*, p.359.

60 *Ibid.*, p.324.

61 Marx, *Grundrisse,* p.335.

62 Unfortunately, Immanuel Wallerstein retains the same usage which is much more suitable to the Weberian/Parsonian framework of ideological apology than to the conceptual requirements of a critical socialist theory. For instance: 'To say that a *producer's objective* is the accumulation of capital is to say that he will seek to produce as much of a given good as possible and offer it for sale at the highest profit margin to him.' (Wallerstein, *Historical Capitalism,* Verso Editions, London 1983, p. 20.) That this is not just an isolated and inconsequential slip, is demonstrated by the recurrence of the same

baffling usage on pages 21, 22, 26, 29, and 50 of Wallerstein's book.

[63] Marx, *Grundrisse*, p.287.

[64] 'Its historical determination is accomplished' would be a more adequate rendering of Marx's expression than 'its historic destiny is fulfilled'.

[65] Marx, *Grundrisse*, p. 325.

[66] *Ibid.*, p. 408.

[67] *Ibid.*, pp. 408-10.

[68] Rosa Luxemburg, *The Accumulation of Capital*, Routledge, London, 1963, p.466.

[69] Marx, *Grundrisse*, p. 408.

[70] By the same token, a major objective pressure in the opposite direction brings with it the end of consensus politics and the need to legitimize the attacks on the material foundations of the 'Welfare State' — implying, again, a shift in the pattern of distribution, though this time one of a restrictive kind—on a more aggressively neo-conservative basis. Hence it is by no means accidental that the recent ideological rationalizations of capital's material dictates advocate with growing enthusiasm a 'return to Victorian values' as the symptoms of a structural crisis gather intensity.

[71] See in this respect Marx's powerful discussion of 'So-called Primitive Accumulation' in Part VIII. of *Capital*, Volume One.

[72] In opposition to the myths of political voluntarism, it is important to stress that these concessions, coupled with their objective material and institutional incorporation, are feasible at the time of their acquisition because they happen to coincide also with the interests of the more dynamic parts of total social capital. As a matter of historical fact, the latter tend to act under such circumstances as the 'reform wing' of the bourgeoisie and thus, temporarily, as the ally of the working classes for legislatively securing the general diffusion of more tolerable working conditions. For through the introduction of uniformly binding reforms, the 'enlightened' wing of the bourgeoisie obtains for itself considerable competitive advantages against the less dynamic and less adaptable elements of its own class. Furthermore, since under the circumstances the reform wing represents the most advanced elements of the bourgeoisie, its partial interests coincide with the overall interests of the class as a whole at a highly expansionary phase of its development. Thus, capital as a social totality concedes the 'enlightened safeguards' of labour-legislation, in accord with the shift to the predominance of relative surplus-value, not only because it can safely afford to do so, but even more so because the new productive practices greatly increase its own power and help the realization of its objective potentiality for a formerly (i.e., within the confines of absolute surplus-value) unimaginable growth and global expansion.

All this is stressed by no means in order to deny the importance of radical politics, but to better identify its strategic targets. For at the time of the shift to the predominance of relative surplus-value, as well as for a long historical period thereafter, the confrontation between capital and labour can be — mystifyingly — confined to bargaining over the distribution of the available slices of a 'growing cake', without affecting in the least the viability of capital as the overall *controlling force* of society. The situation radically changes, however, at the time of a *structural crisis*: when capital is no longer in a position of making concessions which it can simultaneously turn into its own advantage. At such times the social confrontation concerns the question of *control* as such, and not merely the relative share of the contending classes in the total social product.

[73] The consensus politics of Social Democracy and the corresponding forms of Trade-Unionism in Europe, as well as their historically very different but in their vital economic functions largely equivalent counterparts in North America and Japan, were essential constituents of the socioeconomic developments of advanced capitalist countries in the postwar era.

[74] An obvious example of the changed conditions and capital's response to them is the

enactment of anti-Trade Union laws in Great Britain, attempting to destroy defiant Trade Unions through the savage measure of the total sequestration of their funds, as witnessed in the disputes of the National Union of Mineworkers and the printing unions (SOGAT and NGA). Such measures brutally redefine the meaning of 'industrial disputes', putting traditional Trade Unions — even if they are led by defiant and class conscious officials — in an extremely precarious position.

[75] Marx, *Grundrisse,* p. 408.

[76] Indeed, as the much advertised capitalist 'transfer of technology' to the 'Third World' testifies, it is possible to combine the highest levels of productivity with the highest — and in the equivalent enterprises of the 'mother countries' totally inconceivable — rates of exploitation (with most inhuman working hours, true to the worst practices of absolute surplus-value extraction), yielding correspondingly unthinkable levels of super-profit and fast amortization of capital-investment to the 'metropolitan countries'.

[77] Marx, *Grundrisse,* p. 270.

[78] Anatole France defined (and castigated) with irony the spurious freedom and equality of liberal/democratic society as the equal prohibition applied by the law to everyone, 'without discrimination', to sleep under the bridges, irrespective of who actually needs to do so. The real irony is, of course, that the apologists of the capitalist social order are completely serious when they lay down essentially the same criteria which Anatole France satirized. Thus Locke, in an attempt to prop up his vacuous concept of *tacit consent,* so as to legitimize the total subjection of the dispossessed to the political system that serves the interests of the ruling classes, stretches the notions of *property* and *possession* to the point where it ceases to matter 'whether this possession be of land to him and his heirs for ever, or a lodging only for a week; or whether it be barely travelling freely on the highway; and, in effect, it reaches as far as the very *being* of any one within the territories of that government.' (Locke, *Two Treatises of Civil Government,* Book II, paragraph 119.)

At the roots of such blatant rationalization of the established power relations we find in Locke an equally apologetic sophistry through which he succeeds in 'deducing' the rightfulness of the unequal distribution of wealth. He badly needs all the sophistry he can master because the gap between his starting point — the acknowledgement that *'labour,* in the beginning, gave a *right of property'* (*Ibid.,* Book I, paragraph 45) — and the object of his legitimizing apology (which presupposes the total subjection and exploitation of labour) could not be greater. But just as the fiction of 'tacit consent' helped him to get out of the difficulties of political legitimation, so in the context of accounting for the established property relations the postulate of a 'common consent to the use of money' (*Ibid.*) and of a 'mutual consent' (*Ibid.,* paragraph 47) as to the general benefits of money come to the rescue. For from that postulate it can be conveniently concluded that 'it is plain that the consent of men have agreed to a disproportionate and unequal possession of the earth'. (*Ibid.,* paragraph 50.)

[79] Locke, *Op. cit.,* Book I, par. 50.

[80] *Ibid.,* par. 49. His description, in paragraph 48, of an imaginary island devoid of natural objects 'fit to supply the place of money', serves the same purpose of inventing a 'natural' justification for the established relations of man-made and institutionally safeguarded inequality.

[81] In this respect, the story of how the technological white elephant and permanent loss maker, the Anglo/French supersonic airplane *Concorde* was imposed by cynically manipulative governments on their 'Sovereign' electors, on both sides of the Channel — promising at the outset that total costs would not exceed 165 million pounds but in fact undertaking an expenditure *ten times* higher than that (and, of course, still going up, with every year of subsidized operation) — speaks for itself. Not to mention the even more lucrative and 'optimistically underestimated' defence contracts which can be

hidden from public scrutiny by legally enforced secrecy that protects the fraudulent practices of the military/industrial complex in the name of 'the national interest'.

[82] It is important to stress the need for precise historical, economic and political qualifications in this repect. For the proverbial 'other things' are never really equal. Hence the attempts at nullifying labour's earlier acquisitions must reckon with some major obstacles both at the plane of the socio-political struggle and in terms of the immanent dynamic of the economic determinations themselves. However, a more detailed assessment of these issues does not belong to the present context where the main point is to underline that, due to some important structural changes in the course of twentieth century capitalist developments, it has become possible, *in principle,* to contemplate *for the time being* even the most drastic reversal of the here discussed earlier trends in capital's favour.

[83] Marx, *Grundrisse,* p. 411.

[84] One of the most sinister aspects of the military/industrial complex's postwar ability to 'measure itself by its own amount' and to turn its lethal supply into corresponding demand, was the mushrooming of military dictatorships in the 'Third World', under the tutelage — and often direct intervention — of the 'great Western liberal democracies', above all the U.S. Far from being surprising or paradoxical, this reveals a *necessary* connection. For the military/industrial complex of developed capital badly needs the military/economic outlets which it cannot readily secure, for a variety of reasons, within the confines and legitimating modalities of its own home base. Thus, despite the rhetoric of 'Human Rights' and 'Alliance for Progress', we are presented here with a relationship of essential *complementarity* in that the pernicious supply of the 'advanced' military/industrial complex cannot generate internally the required 'effective demand' on an ever-expanding scale. By implication, however, inasmuch as the dynamic of the unfolding socioeconomic and political change — above all in Latin America, but by no means only there, as the turmoils of the Philippines and South Korea show — is likely to undermine the stability of 'Third World' military dictatorships, such development is bound to have severe repercussions for the continued viability of the military/industrial complex also in the 'advanced' capitalist countries.

[85] In Britain more than 50 percent of all scientific research is controlled by the military/industrial complex, while in the U.S. the figure is in excess of 70 percent. And in both cases the trend is on the increase.

[86] Marx, *Grundrisse,* p. 411.

[87] See, for instance, Lucien Goldman's 1966 Preface — written under Marcuse's influence — to *The Human Sciences and Philosophy,* Jonathan Cape, London, 1969.

[88] *Ibid.,* p.16. At the time of writing this Preface, Goldman was in fact so strongly convinced of the durability of the new system of 'organized capitalism' that he assigned positive significance to some of its most problematical features. He insisted that 'our criticism of *organized capitalism* (or, to use another term for the same thing, of *consumer society,* the society of *mass production*) is not intended to lead back to the past or to question the *positive achievements of modern society* (its raising of the standard of living, its *regulative mechanisms* which allow society to *avoid particularly severe crises,* etc.)' (*Ibid.,* p. 19.)

The trouble with this line of reasoning is that the vague categories of 'modern society', 'consumer society' and 'society of mass production' divert the author's attention from the most important dimension of capitalistically advanced societies, namely the overpowering position of the military/industrial complex in their socioeconomic metabolism, with its catastrophic waste of resources that foreshadows the prospect of the gravest structural crisis. Thus, one-sidedly, what is in reality built on sand can appear as solid achievements, and the power of the 'regulative mechanisms' for *avoiding* (in contrast to what could be correctly described as displacing and postponing) 'severe crises' is exaggerated beyond all proportions.

[89] Marx, *Grundrisse*, p. 410.

[90] *Ibid.*, pp.105-109.

[91] As Marx remarked on page 887 of the *Grundrisse*, in his critique of Carey's misconception of the nature of the 'disharmonies' identified and deplored by the American economist:

> What Carey has not grasped is that these *world-market disharmonies* are merely the *ultimate adequate expressions* of the disharmonies which have become fixed as abstract relations within the *economic categories* or which have a *local* existence on the *smallest* scale.

Thus in Marx's view the antagonistic inner structural determination of the capital system is pervasive at all levels, from the smallest local contexts to the most comprehensive global dimension, characterizing thereby the 'micro' structures as much as the 'macro' relations of the whole system as an international order. This is what expresses itself also in the 'Daseinsformen' of the most abstract economic categories.

[92] Marx, *Grundrisse*, p.504. Marx's italics.

[93] Marx, *Economic Works: 1861-1864*, MECW, Vol. 34, p.359. Marx's italics.

[94] *Ibid.*, p.355. Marx's italics.

[95] *Ibid.*, p.109. Marx's italics.

[96] *Ibid.*, p.429.

[97] *Ibid.*, p.413. Marx's italics.

[98] *Ibid.*, p.426. Marx's italics.

[99] See *Ibid.*, p.427 for usurers' capital and p.428 for merchants' capital.

[100] See *Ibid.*, p.429.

[101] As Marx puts it:

> Exchange begins not between the individuals within a community, but rather at the point where the communities end — at their boundary, at the point of contact between different communities. Communal property has recently been rediscovered as a special Slavonic curiosity. But, in fact, India offers us a sample chart of the most diverse forms of such economic communities, more or less dissolved, but still completely recognizable; and a more thorough research into history uncovers it as the point of departure of all cultured peoples. The system of production founded on private exchange is, to begin with, the historic dissolution of this *naturally arisen communism*. However, a whole series of economic systems lies in turn between the modern world, where exchange value dominates production to its whole depth and extent, and the social formations whose foundation is already formed by the dissolution of *communal property*.

Marx, *Grundrisse*, p.882.

[102] Marx, *Economic Works: 1861-1864*, p.465. Marx's italics.

[103] *Ibid.*, p.123.

[104] Marx, *Grundrisse*, p.736. Marx's italics.

[105] Marx, *Economic Works: 1861-1864*, p.235. Marx's italics.

This is how elsewhere Marx describes some vital aspects of capital's original formation:

> Capital comes initially from circulation, and, moreover, its point of departure is money. We have seen that money which enters into circulation and at the same time returns from it to itself is the last requirement, in which money suspends itself. It is at the same time the first concept of capital, and the first form in which it appears. ... [M-C-C-M] *this movement of buying in order to sell, which makes up the formal aspect of commerce, of capital as merchant capital*, is found in the earliest conditions of economic development; it is the first movement in which exchange value as such forms the content — is not only the form but also its own content. This motion can take place within peoples, or between peoples for whose production exchange value has by no means yet become the presupposition. The movement only seizes upon the surplus

of their directly useful production, and proceeds only on its margin. Like the Jews within old Polish society or within medieval society in general, entire trading peoples, as in antiquity (and, later on, the Lombards), can take up this position between peoples whose mode of production is not yet determined by exchange value as the fundamental presupposition. Commercial capital is only circulating capital, and circulating capital is the first form of capital; in which it has *as yet by no means become the foundation of production.* A more developed form is *money capital,* and *money interest,* usury, whose independent appearance belongs in the same way to an earlier stage. Finally, the form C-M-M-C, in which money and circulation in general appear as mere means for the *circulating commodity.*

Marx, *Grundrisse,* p.253. Marx's italics.

[106] Ibid., pp.258-9. Marx's italics.

[107] To quote Marx:

[the *Carthaginians*] had developed capital in the form of *commercial capital,* and therefore made exchange values as such into the direct [object of] production, or where, as with the *Romans,* through the concentration of wealth, particularly of landed property, in a few hands, production was necessarily directed no longer towards use by the producer himself but towards *exchange value,* hence possessed this aspect of capitalist production. (Marx, *Economic Works: 1861-1864,* p.98. Marx's italics.)

And further on in the same work he argues that

The two forms in which capital appears before it takes control of the direct relation of production — becoming in this sense productive capital — and therefore appears as the relation dominating production, are *trading capital* and *usurers' capital (interest-bearing capital).* ... For example, in India the usurer ... Here labour is not yet formally subsumed under capital. IT DOES NOT EMPLOY THE RYOT AS LABOURER; he is not a wage labourer, any more than the usurer who employs him is an industrial capitalist. ... We find the same relation between e.g. the patricians and plebeians of Rome, or the peasants owning small parcels of land and the usurers. ... *Debt slavery* in distinction to *wage slavery.* ... What we have said of usurers' capital is true of *merchants capital.* It can equally be a *form transitional to* the subsumption of labour under capital (initially its formal subsumption). This is the case wherever the *merchant* as such plays the role of MANUFACTURER. He advances the raw material. He appears originally as the *buyer* of the products of independent industries. *(Ibid.,* pp.118-120. Marx's italics and capitalization.)

As to the position in Greece, Marx emphasises that although the word 'capital' does not exist in Ancient Greek, the word *arkhais* is used by the Greeks, corresponding to the Roman *principalis summa rei creditae,* i.e. the principal of a loan. (See *Grundrisse,* p.513.)

[108] *Ibid.,* pp.470-71. Marx's italics.

[109] Marx, *Economic Works: 1861-1864,* p.246. Marx's italics and capitalization.

[110] Engels, *The Condition of the Working Class in England,* written in 1844-45. See MECW, vol.4, p.563.

On the same page Engels describes his encounter in Manchester with one of the 'enlightened' Liberal bourgeois who were in favour of repealing the Corn Law. Engels expressed his indignation about the frightful conditions of the working-people's quarters. 'The man listened quietly to the end, and said at the corner where we parted: "And yet there is a great deal of money made here; good morning, sir".' After the lines quoted by Marx, Engels continues: 'And if the operative will not be forced into this abstraction, if he insists that he is not Labour, but a man, who possesses, among other things, the attribute of labour-force, if he takes it into his head that he need not allow himself to be sold and bought in the market, as the commodity "Labour", the bourgeois reason comes to a standstill. He cannot comprehend that he holds any other relation to the operatives than that of purchase and sale; he sees in them not human beings, but hands, as he constantly calls them to their faces'. *(Ibid.)*

[111] Marx, *Economic Works: 1861-1864*, p.422. Marx's italics.

[112] Marx, *Grundrisse*, p.512.

[113] *Ibid.*, p.303. Marx's italics.

[114] John Stuart Mill, *Principles of Political Economy*, pp.199-200. The passage from which Marx's quotation is taken reads as follows:

The laws and conditions of the Production of wealth partake of the character of physical truths. There is nothing optional or arbitrary in them. Whatever mankind produce, must be produced in the modes, and under the conditions, imposed by the constitution of external things, and by the inherent properties of their own bodily and mental structure. ... It is not so with the Distribution of wealth. That is a matter of human institutions solely. The things once there, mankind, individually or collectively, can do with them as they like. They can place them at the disposal of whomsoever they please, and on whatever terms.

[115] Marx, *Grundrisse*, p.832. Marx's italics.

[116] Marx, *Economic Works: 1861-1864*, p.123. Marx's italics.

[117] *Ibid.*, p.245. Marx's italics.

[118] Marx, *Grundrisse*, p.831. Marx's italics.

[119] Someone once asked Einstein, what kind of weapons will be used in the Third World War: a question which he wisely answered by saying that he could not foresee that, but he could absolutely guarantee that the Fourth would have to be fought with stone axes.

[120] Marx, *Economic Works: 1861-1864*, p.423. Marx's italics.

[121] Marx, *Grundrisse*, p.278. Marx's italics.

[122] MECW, vol. 5, p.49.

[123] Santiago Carillo, Dialogue on Spain, with Régis Debray and Max Gallo, Lawrence & Wishart, London, 1976, p.133. First published in France in 1974.

[124] *Ibid.*, Carillo's italics.

[125] Marx, *Economic Works: 1861-1864*, p.258.

[126] Milton Friedman, 'Has Liberalism Failed?', in Martin J. Anderson (ed.), *The Unfinished Agenda: Essays on the Political Economy of Government Policy in Honour of Arthur Seldon*, The Institute of Economic Affairs, London, 1986, p.129.

[127] *Ibid.*, pp.131-2. The book mentioned by Friedman is Milton and Rose Friedman, *Capitalism and Freedom*, University of Chicago Press, Chicago, 1962.

[128] A quixotic recent rejoinder lamenting the same disheartening failure and talking abour all of us now being 'just prisoners of the state' is a book by Alan Duncan and Dominic Hobson, *From Saturn's Children*, Sinclair-Stevenson, London, 1995. Alan Duncan is a Conservative Member of Parliament.

[129] Gordon Tullock, 'Wanted: New Public-Choice Theories', in Martin J. Anderson (ed.), *The Unfinished Agenda*, p.16. This is how the author characterizes the existing 'theoretical explanations' to what he calls the 'unsolved mystery':

There are, so far as I know, three possible candidates for such a theory. One was invented by my colleague, Professor James Buchanan, one by Congressman Richard Armey of Texas [a former Professor of Economics at Texas A&M University], and the last by myself. ... All three theories are based on the impact of ideas on government. Armey explains it in terms of the baneful impact of Galbraith's book, *The Affluent Society*. Buchanan puts it down to a long-delayed response to another book, *The General Theory* of John Maynard Keynes. My theory is slightly more complicated and assumes that politicians learned from experience ... All three theories, in essence, assume that change was *not in the real world* but in behaviour, as a result of changes *within the minds of policy-makers*. Obviously, such a hypothesis is hard to test. *(Ibid.*, pp.17-8.)

The trouble is not only that such theories are 'hard to test' but that they are quite ludicrous in trying to explain monumental objective changes by the mysterious impact of a few books — let alone the 'belated' impact of one of them, from a distance of nearly three decades in the case of Keynes, so as to make the mystery denser and blame him in accordance with the monetarist tenets even more strongly — on the 'minds of policy-makers'. Underneath such 'hypotheses' we find, of course, the wishful thinking that the ideas of the 'Radical Right' will in due course similarly affect the 'minds of policy-makers', and we shall live happily ever after. What must be frustrating to those who take them seriously is to have to admit that despite the conquest of the 'minds of policy-makers' — like Ronald Reagan and Margaret Thatcher — the commended 'fiscal responsibility' remains as elusive an ideal as before.

[130] See note 129.

[131] Keynes, *The General Theory of Employment, Interest, and Money*, p.320.

[132] *Ibid.*, pp.380-81.

[133] This is how Keynes had put it:

> When it comes to the *class struggle* as such, my local and personal patriotism, like those of everyone else, except certain unpleasant zealous ones, are attached to my own surroundings. I can be influenced by what seems to *me* to be justice and good sense; but the *class war* will find me on the side of the educated *bourgeoisie*.

Keynes, 'Am I a Liberal?', in *Essays in Persuasion,* Norton & Co. Inc., New York, 1963, p.324.

[134] Keynes, 'Economic Possibilities for Our Grandchildren', in *Essays in Persuasion,* p.364. 'Technological unemployment' is italicized by Keynes.

[135] As Marx puts it in the *Grundrisse:*

> The maximum realization of capital, as also the maximum continuity of the production process, is circulation time posited as $= 0$; i.e. then, the conditions under which capital produces, its restriction by circulation time, the necessity of going through the different phases of its metamorphosis, are suspended. It is the necessary tendency of capital to strive to equate circulation time to 0; i.e. to suspend itself, since it is capital itself alone which posits circulation time as a determinant moment of production time. It is the same as to suspend the necessity of exchange, of money, and of the division of labour resting on them, hence capital itself. (p.629.)

Postcapitalist developments were at first a great asset in relation to capital's wishful objective of realizing itself in 0 circulation time. In this respect the political extraction and allocation of surplus labour was beneficial for as long as individual consumption — and the industrial production corresponding to it — had to be, and could be, kept at a very low level. At a later stage, however, the earlier asset became a major drawback for sustained socioeconomic development, underlining that the politically enforced extraction of surplus labour cannot offer by itself a lasting solution to the underlying pressures when society has to confront capital's structural crisis.

[136] Marx, *Grundrisse*, p.531.

[137] *Ibid.*, p.710. Marx's italics.

[138] Lenin, 'Left-Wing Childishness and the Petty-Bourgeois Mentality', in *Collected Works,* vol. 27, p.334.

[139] Lenin, 'On Co-operation', in *Collected Works,* vol. 33, p.472.

[140] *Ibid.*, p.473.

[141] *Ibid.*

[142] Mészáros, 'Political Power and Dissent in Postrevolutionary Societies' (1977),pp.912-913 of the present volume.

[143] Lenin, 'Left-Wing Childishness and the Petty-Bourgeois Mentality', in *Collected Works,* vol. 27, p.351.

[144] *Ibid.*, p.345.

[145] *Ibid.*, p.351.

[146] Lenin, 'Letters from Afar', in *Collected Works,* vol. 23, p.325.

[147] Lenin, 'Economics and Politics', in *Collected Works,* vol. 30, pp.108-09.

[148] *Ibid.*, p.108.

[149] Lenin himself bitterly complained in his stocktaking speech on the NEP that the newly created state organs were heavily conditioned by the old Czarist state. I quoted the relevant passages in the article referred to in note 142. See page 915 of the present volume.

[150] Lenin, 'Can the Bolsheviks Retain Power?', in *Collected Works,* vol. 26, p.130.

[151] *Ibid.*

[152] The last page is based on Section 3 ('Political Power in the Society of Transition') of the article quoted in note 142. See pp.902-05 of the present volume.

[153] Lenin, 'On Co-operation', in *Collected Works,* vol. 33, p.474.

[154] *Ibid.*, p.475.

[155] Lenin, 'Left-Wing Childishness and the Petty-Bourgeois Mentality', in *Collected Works,* vol. 27, p.346. Lenin's italics.

[156] Trotsky, *The Third International After Lenin,* Pioneer Publishers, New York, 1957, pp.35-6.

[157] Isaac Deutscher, *Stalin: A Political Biography,* Oxford University Press, London, 1967, p.293.

[158] *Ibid.*, p.291.

[159] *Ibid.*, p.282.

[160] Deutscher, *The Prophet Unarmed: Trotsky 1921-1929,* Oxford University Press, London, 1970, p.266.

[161] Trotsky, *The Revolution Betrayed,* Pioneer Publishers, New York, 1957, p.255.

[162] *Ibid.*

[163] *Ibid.*, p.256.

[164] Christian Rakovsky, 'The "Professional Dangers" of Power' (1928), in *C. Rakovsky: Selected Writings on Opposition in the USSR 1923-30,* edited by Gus Fagan, Allison and Busby, London, 1980, p.124.

[165] *Ibid.*, p.132.

[166] *Ibid.*, p.135.

[167] *Ibid.*, p.136.

[168] *Ibid.*, p.130.

[169] 'If the motor car had existed at the time of the French revolution, we would also have had the factor of the "motor harem", indicated by comrade Sosnovsky as having played a very important role in the formation of the ideology of our bureaucracy of soviets and the party.' Rakovsky, *Ibid.*, p.128.

[170] Marx, *Economic Works: 1861-1864,* p.413.

[171] Stalin, 'Economic Problems of Socialism in the U.S.S.R.' (1952), in *The Essential Stalin: Major Theoretical Writings 1905-52,* edited by Bruce Franklin, Croom Helm, London, 1973, pp.457-8.

[172] *Ibid.*, p.458.

[173] *Ibid.*, p.465.

[174] *Ibid.*, p.466.

[175] *Ibid.*, p.461.

[176] *Ibid.*, p.462.

[177] *Ibid.*, p.459.

[178] *Ibid.*, p.467. The word 'essential' is italicized by Stalin.

[179] The first major industrail reform, under Khrushchev, was enacted already at the end of 1957.

[180] E. Liberman's famous article on 'Plan, Profit, Premium' appeared in *Pravda* on the

9th of September 1962, generating a wide-spread debate lasting for years. Centred around the question of how to improve the *mechanisms* of planning and control, this debate was officially blessed by Khrushchev and the party, and it continued also after Khrushchev's fall in October 1964.

[181] As acknowledged in an article by Academician V. Nemchinov, head of the Scientific Council, in an article published in *Pravda* on 21 September 1962. The main contributions to this debate, taken a step futher in 1964, were published in Italy in a volume: Liberman, Nemchinov, Trapeznikov e altri, *Piano e Profitto nell'economia sovietica*, a cura di Lisa Foa, Editori Riuniti, Roma, 1965. Nemchinov's account of the April 1962 session of the Soviet Academy's Scientific Council is on page 31.

[182] According to Academician Nemchinov, the April 1962 meeting decided 'to support the Kharkov initiative and to extend the experiments in the same direction, mainly with reference to the introduction of new types of products and to the adoption of modern technical means of production'. V. Nemchinov, 'Obiettivo pianificato e incentivo materiale (a proposito delle proposte di Liberman)', page 31 of the volume cited in note 181.

[183] *Ibid.*, p.30.

[184] *Ibid.* For greater effect, the last words were italicized by Academician Nemchinov.

[185] *Ibid.*, p.29.

[186] Quoted in Moshe Lewin, *Stalinism and the Seeds of Soviet Reform: The Debates of the 1960s,* Pluto Press, London, 1991, p.148.

[187] V. Touradjev, *Une économie dirigée,* Editions de l'Agence Presse Novosti, Moscow, 1967, pp.142-3.

[188] E. Liberman, 'Piano, profitto, premi', in volume cited in note 181, p.24.

[189] 'Articolo di E. Liberman per la *Novosti*', in the same volume, p.166.

[190] V. Nemchinov, 'Gestione economica socialista e pianificazione della produzione', in the same volume, p.69.

[191] *Ibid.*, p.72.

[192] *Ibid.*, p.73.

[193] David Mandel, *Rabotyagi: Perestroika and After Viewed from Below, Interviews with Workers in the Former Soviet Union,* Monthly Review Press, New York, 1994, p.36. As David Mandel writes: 'In the spring of 1991 Petr was murdered in Novocherkassk, beaten and left to die in the street. In his briefcase were documents about the 1962 events. The murder remains unsolved, but the interview [published in the volume, and critical also of Gorbachev and Yeltsin] makes clear that it was in all likelihood politically motivated.' *Ibid.*, p.15.

[194] See regulation No. 731 of the Council of Ministers, especially paragraphs 95-104, as published in volume *La réforme économique en U.R.S.S., Plan, stimulants, initiative,* Editions de l'Agence Presse Novosti, Moscow, 1965, pp.178-9.

[195] Mikhail Gorbachev, *Democratization: The Essence of Perestroika, the Essence of Socialism,* A meeting at the CPSU Central Committee with the heads of the mass media, ideological institutions and artistic unions, 8th January 1988, Novosti Press Agency Publishing House, Moscow, 1988, p.14.

[196] *Ibid.*, p.7.

[197] *Ibid.*, p.11.

[198] Gavril Popov, 'Dangers of Democracy', *New York Review of Books,* 16 August 1990.

[199] David Mandel, *op. cit.*, p.12.

[200] Eugene Varga, *Politico-Economic Problems of Capitalism*, Progress Publishers, Moscow, 1968, p.25.

[201] Marx, *Capital,* vol. 1, pp.330-31.

[202] Petr Siuda in David Mandel's *Rabotyagi,* p.30.

[203] Oleg Bogomolov, 'A Farewell to the Primitive View of Socialism', *Soviet Weekly,* 4 November 1989.

204 R.C. Tucker, *Philosophy and Myth in Karl Marx*, Cambridge University Press, 1961, p.235.

205 Vadim Medvedev, 'The Ideology of Perestroika', in *Perestroika Annual* Vol 2., ed. by Abel Aganbegyan, Futura/Macdonald, London, 1989, p.31.

206 *Ibid.*, p.33.

207 Alexander A. Bessmertnykh, 'Foreign Policy — A New Course', in *Perestroika Annual* Vol. 2., p.49.

208 *Ibid.*, p.50.

209 *Ibid.*, p.49.

210 Julian V. Bromlei, 'Ethnic Relations and Perestroika', in *Perestroika Annual* Vol. 2., p.118.

211 Mikhail Gorbachev, *Perestroika: New Thinking for Our Country and the World*, Updated Edition, Fontana/Collins, London, 1988, p.141.

212 *Ibid.*, p.185.

213 *Ibid.*, p.221.

214 *Ibid.*, p.220.

215 *Ibid.*, p.264. Elsewhere in the book Gorbachev wrote: 'we are unanimous in our belief that perestroika is indispensable and indeed *inevitable*, and that we have *no other option.*' *Ibid.*, p.67. But even if this proposition could be considered true, the claimed absence of an alternative by no means establishes the viability and soundness of a chosen course of action. Politicians' claims of 'no alternative' as a rule turn out to be rationalizations of self-induced failures.

216 Vadim Medvedev, *Op. cit.*, p.40.

217 *Ibid.*, p.32.

218 Gorbachev, *Perestroika*, p.267.

219 Hillel Ticktin, 'The Political Economy of the Gorbachev Era', *Critique*, No. 17, 1986, pp.122-4. See also his comprehensive analysis of the Soviet economic system in *Origins of the Crisis in the USSR: Essays on the Political Economy of a Disintegrating System*, M.E. Sharpe, Inc., New York, 1992. Bertell Ollman's 'The Regency of the Proletariat in Crisis: A Job for Perestroika' (in his *Dialectical Investigations*, Routledge, New York, 1993, pp.109-118) offers a sobering assessment of Gorbachev's doomed reform attempt.

220 John Rettie, 'Only market can save Soviet economy', *The Guardian*, 17 October 1990.

221 Tatyana Zaslavskaya, 'Nineties nervous breakdown for democrats as things fall apart', *Soviet Weekly*, 10 January 1991.

222 'Eastern European factories: Unfinished business', *The Economist*, 10 January 1990.

223 'From Marx to the market', *The Economist*, 11 May 1991.

224 *The Economist*, 22 December 1990.

225 Sergei Stankevich quoted in *Moscow News*, 6 January 1991.

226 I. Savvateyeva, 'A Chile wind blows through the Soviet economy', *Soviet Weekly*, 21 February 1991.

227 James Blitz, 'Shatalin key to Soviet reforms', *The Sunday Times*, 16 September 1990.

228 *Ibid.*

229 Rosa Luxemburg, 'Organizational Questions of the Russian Social Democracy' (first published in *Neue Zeit*, 1904), translated under the title 'Leninism or Marxism' in R. Luxemburg, *The Russian Revolution and Leninism or Marxism*, introduction by Bertram D. Wolfe, The University of Michigan Press, Ann Arbor, 1961, p.98.

230 'The Russian Revolution' (1918), in Luxemburg, *The Russian Revolution and Leninism or Marxism*, p.30 and p.39.

231 MECW, vol. 5, p.75.

232 Marx, *Grundrisse*, pp.470-71.

233 MECW, vol. 34, p.426. Marx's italics.

234 *Ibid.*, p.431. Marx's italics.

235 *Ibid.*, p.465. Marx's italics.

236 Kolko's book offers a powerful analysis of the impact of wars on 20th century social development. To quote a passage concerned with the end of war period:

> The First World War had a far greater influence on Europe's social structure, economy, and human and demographic existence than any other event since at least the French Revolution, and it initiated those objective changes that were to alter profoundly the Continent's subjective consciousness and politics after 1917. Given the war's very uneven effects, we must consider its consequences in all their diversity, ranging from those that were catastrophic and decisive, as in the case of Russia, to those that were merely very important, as in Great Britain. Yet no European nation emerged unscathed from the experience as wartime conditions interacted with Europe's many long-standing social and economic problems and tensions to accelerate the crises confronting most of its people in ways that would have appeared inconceivable before 1914.

Gabriel Kolko, *Century of War: Politics, Conflict, and Society Since 1914,* The New Press, New York, 1994, p.87.

237 James Blitz, 'Shatalin key to Soviet reforms', *The Sunday Times,* 16 September 1990.

238 See Section 17.3.1.

239 MECW, vol.34, p.413.

240 Michael Binyon, 'Gorbachev opts for the free market: Stock exchange for Moscow', *The Times,* 10 April 1990.

241 *Ibid.*

242 *Ibid.*

243 *Ibid.*

244 *Ibid.*

245 Economist Sergei Kugushev interviewed in I. Savvateyeva, 'A Chile wind blows through the Soviet economy', *Soviet Weekly,* 21 February 1991.

246 Marshal Sergei Akhromeyev, 'They are pulling us apart', *Soviet Weekly,* 28 February 1991.

247 Roy Medvedev, 'Walking out on history', *The Guardian,* 30 August 1991.

248 *Ibid.*

249 One of the most mysterious of all those 'suicides' was the death of Marshal Sergei Akhromeyev who, in February 1991, strongly criticized the 'democrats', from Arbatov and Gavril Popov to Yeltsin, for their efforts to break up the Soviet Union.

250 Georgi Ovcharenko, 'Key trial for glasnost', *Soviet Weekly,* 17 October 1991.

251 Lenin, 'On the Slogan for a United States of Europe', *Collected Works,* Vol. 21, pp. 339-40. (Written in August, 1915.)

It is also worth mentioning in this context that according to *The Times* (22 July 1995), based on an *AP* report from Moscow,

> The [Russian] Supreme Court has awarded £9.400 damages to Valentin Varennikov, a participant in the 1991 Soviet coup, who was acquitted on treason charges last year.

What is significant about this piece of news is that Varennikov insisted at the time of the projected but, of course, never held, trial that he wanted to be publicly tried for his alleged role in Gorbachev's phoney and badly mishandled coup, so as to be able to reveal what had really happened and who gave the orders. It was, therefore, most appropriate that the 'coup that never was' should be followed by a 'trial that never was', and that the whole sordid affair be concluded with a large sum of money — in terms of Russian Rouble incomes a real fortune — being awarded to an accused by the country's Supreme Court, instead of a prison sentence.

252 Marx, *The Poverty of Philosophy*, London, Lawrence & Wishart, n.d., p.123.

253 Marx, *Lohn, Preis und Profit*, (Wages, Price and Profit), MEW, Vol. 16, p.153.

[254] *Ibid.,* (Marx's italics.)

[255] 'apart from the fact that this was merely the rising of a town under exceptional conditions, the majority of the Commune was in no sense socialist, nor could it be. With a small amount of sound common sense, however, they could have reached a compromise with Versailles useful to the whole mass of the people — the only thing that could be reached at the time.' Marx, Letter to Domela Nieuwenhuis, 22 February, 1881.

[256] *Ibid.*

[257] 'Speech Delivered at a Meeting of Activists of the Moscow Organization of the R.C.P.(B.)', December 6, 1920. Lenin, *Collected Works,* Vol. 21, pp.441-2.

[258] Reporter's Record of the Speech Made by Marx at the Meeting Held in Amsterdam on September 8, 1872. (See MEW, Vol. 18, p. 160.)

[259] Marx, Letter to N. F. Danielson, 19 February, 1881. (MEW, Vol. 35, p.157, Marx's italics.)

[260] Marx, *Grundrisse*, pp. 408 & 410. (German edition: pp.311 & 313-4.)

[261] *Ibid.,* pp. 409-10. (German edition: p.313.)

[262] These problems have been discussed in Chapters 15 and 16 above. The fact that the end of the cold war failed to deliver the 'peace dividend', leaving the military/industrial complex in a dominant position in the leading capitalist countries, underlines the importance of these deep-seated economic connections.

[263] *The Times,* 22 September, 1981.

[264] Engels, Letter to A. Bebel, 1-2 May, 1891.

[265] Marx, Letter to Wilhelm Bracke, 5 May, 1875.

[266] Lukács, 'Tactics and Ethics' (1919), *Political Writings, 1919-1929*, NLB, London, 1972, p. 31.

[267] *The Sunday Times*, 21 February, 1982. We can see, again, how the desperate imperative of a blind submission to capital's economic determinism is used by decreeing the recognition of 'no alternative' (yet another bourgeois 'law of nature') as the unquestionable criterion of 'sanity' and freedom.

[268] It is highly misleading to represent these two as polar opposites, with the suggestion that the latter introduces some major innovation in relation to the former. As a matter of fact, for a long time every variety of Keynesianism has been a Quixotic venture that carried *within itself* its Friedmanesque Sancho Panza — in the 'stop' phase of its 'stop-go' policies — and *vice versa*. But perhaps a more fitting way of grasping their true significance and impact is to recognise them as the cancer that they are in each other's bowels, reciprocally intensifying the consequences of their separate action. The fact that the cancer of monetarism had to surface recently in such a particularly obnoxious form from the Keynesian entrails — openly supporting with its claimed 'enlightened' views the most brutal military dictatorships, from Chile to El Salvador, not to mention the all-powerful U.S. military-industrial complex — only shows that the pretence of unproblematical (indeed: model) 'development' can no longer be maintained. In the meantime, the momentum of an oscillatory swing in the other direction is slowly but certainly building up: no doubt, before long we are going to be presented with another variant of Keynesian miracle-making, even if for a much shorter duration than the 'happy days' of postwar expansion. In this sense, as capital's apologists continue to remind us of the phrase, truly 'there is no alternative'. But to expect the restoration of capital's health to its former vigorous state by either of the two, or indeed by both put together, is — alongside the *fiat* of 'sanity' — another striking example of the dangerous wishful thinking that dominates our social/economic life today.

[269] 'Imagine the government, in its wisdom, set up a panel of experts whose brief was to devise a system to give privatization a bad name. Step one would be to transfer monopoly utilities into the private sector with the minimum of competition and, for the first five years, a very generous pricing regime. Step two would be to appoint

regulators who, having allowed these privatized utilities to build up a huge profits base, would lean towards the interests of shareholders rather than customers, in deciding the industry's pricing structure. Step three, a vital one this, would be to allow the directors and chairmen of these privatized utilities to confirm that monopoly industries deal in Monopoly money, by paying themselves huge salaries, with share options and golden handshakes. Never mind that many of these people do not have an entrepreneurial bone in their bodies. Never mind that most have never taken a risk in their lives. They seem to be motivated by the motto from the 1980 film *Wall Street:* "Greed is good". The government, then, has no need for such a panel. The existing system does the job very well.' If someone thinks that this quotation comes from a socialist fringe publication, they are in for a big surprise. For it is taken from an Editorial article — under the title: 'Privatization is now a dirty word' — which appeared on 14 August 1994 in by far the biggest circulation British conservative weekly paper, *The Sunday Times.* In fact the Editorial article concludes with a broken heart: 'This newspaper supports privatization. We have no truck with those who criticise the financial rewards that accrue to those who display genuine enterprise. Sadly, the government has made it all too easy for the once good name of privatization to be dragged into disrepute.'

270 'Burden of opposition', *The Times,* 11 August 1995.

271 Hegel, *The Philosophy of Right,* p.201.

272 Robert Taylor, 'Blow for unions in derecognition case', *Financial Times,* 17 March 1995.

273 *Ibid.*

274 Attila József, *Eszmélet* ('Consciousness', or more precisely, 'Prise de conscience').

275 Rousseau, *The Social Contract,* Everyman Edition, p.78.

276 *Ibid.,* p.79.

277 *Ibid.,* p.42.

278 Hugo Chávez Frias, *Pueblo, Sufragio y Democracia,* Ediciones MBR-200, Yara, 1993, pp.5-6.

279 *Ibid.,* p.9.

280 *Ibid.,* p.11.

281 *Ibid.,* pp.8-11.

282 *Ibid.,* p.9.

283 See Norberto Bobbio, *Politica e cultura,* Einaudi, Torino, 1955; *Da Hobbes a Marx,* Morano Editore, Napoli, 1965; *Saggi sulla scienza politica in Italia,* Editori Laterza, Roma & Bari, 1971; *Quale Socialismo? Discussione di un'alternativa,* Einaudi, Torino, 1976; *Dalla struttura alla funzione: Nuovi studi di teoria del diritto,* Edizioni di Comunità, Milano, 1977; *The Future of Democracy: A Defence of the Rules of the Game,* Polity Press, Oxford, 1987.

284 As Bobbio puts it:

> Hoy están en primer plano no sólo los derechos de libertad o el derecho al trabajo y la seguridad social, sino también, por poner un ejemplo, el derecho de la humanidad actual, y aun de las generaciones futuras, a vivir en un ambiente no contaminado, el derecho a la procreación autorregulada, el derecho a la privacidad frente a la posibilidad que hoy tiene el Estado de saber exactamente todo lo que hacemos. Además, quisiera señalar la gravísima amenaza a la conservación del patrimonio genético generada por el progreso técnico de la biología, amenaza a la que no podrá responderse si no es estableciendo nuevos derechos.

Norberto Bobbio, 'Nuevas fronteras de la izquierda', in *Leviatán,* No. 47, Madrid, 1992. Quoted in Gabriel Vargas Lozano, *Más allá del derrumbe: Socialismo y democracia en la crisis de civilización contemporánea,* Siglo XXI editores, México & Madrid, 1994, p.117. See especially the chapters 'Opciones después del derrumbe' and 'El socialismo liberal' for the author's thoughtful comments on Bobbio's work.

285 Peter Kellner, 'Blair can reinvent socialism — if he finds the right words', *The Sunday*

Times, 9 October 1994.

[286] 'Harold Macmillan at 85: An Interview', *The Listener,* 8 February 1979, p.209.

[287] James Dale Davidson is the founder and chairman of the right-wing National Taxpayers Union 'and the driving force behind the Constitutional Convention to Balance the Budget', according to the blurb of his book quoted below. His success in Balancing the U.S. Budget may be a good measure also of the soundness of his theories.

[288] James Dale Davidson and Sir (now Lord) William Rees-Mogg, *Blood in the Streets: Investment Profits in a World Gone Mad,* Sidgwick & Jackson, London 1988, pp.156-7. The title of the book refers to Baron Nathan Rothschild's celebrated dictum: 'The time to buy is when blood is running in the streets.'

[289] *Ibid.,* p.157.

[290] See Noam Chomsky, 'The Responsibility of Intellectuals', in *The Dissenting Academy,* edited by Theodore Roszak, Random House, New York, 1967, and Penguin Books, Harmondsworth, 1969.

[291] Philip Bassett, 'Labour shows it means to do business with business', *The Times,* 7th April 1995. Tony Blair made his confession on heading the party of British business before Labour's women's conference in Derby on the 1st of April 1995.

[292] *Ibid.* Labour's recently launched 'Commission on Public Policy and British Business', as we learn from Philip Bassett's *Times* article, 'will include among a host of luminaries David Sainsbury, head of the supermarket group, [Yeltsin adviser] Professor Richard Layard of the London School of Economics, and Sir Christopher Harding, former chairman of British Nuclear Fuels and for 20 years a director of Hanson, one of the Conservative Party's biggest donors and most active business supporters.'

[293] 'President Mandela delivered an important boost to South Africa's expanding multimillion-pound arms industry yesterday by publicly giving it his personal blessing for the first time. ... His public endorsement was welcomed by South Africa's arms manufacturers, who believe his support will help them to secure future deals. Abba Omar, speaking for Armscor, the state arms agency, said: "The President has for the first time unequivocally given his backing to the arms industry. It cannot be stressed how important his seal of approval is to us".' Inigo Gilmore, 'Mandela applauds South Africa's rising arms trade', *The Times,* 23 November 1994.

[294] MECW, vol.34, p.460. Marx's italics.

[295] *Ibid.,* p.457. Marx's italics.

[296] *Ibid.,* p.456. Marx's italics.

[297] *Ibid.,* p.457. Marx's italics and upper case emphases.

[298] Rosa Luxemburg, 'Organizational Questions of the Russian Social Democracy', published in English under the title 'Leninism or Marxism?' in the volume *The Russian Revolution and Leninism or Marxism?,* introduced by Bertram D. Wolfe, The University of Michigan Press, Ann Arbor, 1970, p.98.

[299] Lukács, *A demokratizálódás jelene és jövője,* p.172.

[300] *Ibid.,* p.155.

[301] *Ibid.,* p.194.

[302] *Ibid.,* p.181. Naturally, every self-respecting capitalist would reject the *vice-versa* part of this assertion.

[303] *Ibid.,* p.158.

[304] *Ibid.,* p.159.

[305] Marx, *Capital,* vol. 1., pp.78-9.

[306] Lukács, *A demokratizálódás jelene és jövője,* pp.111-2.

[307] Marx, *Ibid.,* p.76.

[308] Marx, *Grundrisse,* pp.704-5.

[309] Lukács, *A demokratizálódás jelene és jövője,* p.178.

[310] Marx, *Grundrisse,* p.708.

[311] *Ibid.*

[312] Marx, *The Poverty of Philosophy,* MECW, vol. 6., p.134.

[313] Lukács, *Toward the Ontology of Social Being: Labour,* Merlin Press, London, 1980, p.83.

[314] *Ibid.* pp.83-4.

[315] See the discussion of the problematic character of this model of individual and social interaction in Chapter 12, 'The Cunning of History in Reverse Gear', first published in English in *Radical Philosophy,* No. 42, Winter/Spring 1986, and in Italian in *Problemi del Socialismo,* Anno xxiii, No. 23, 1982.

[316] Marx, *Grundrisse,* p.170.

[317] *Ibid.,* pp.171-2.

[318] Quoted in Lukács's *Ontology of Social Being,* vol. 2, p.731. (Hungarian edition, Magvetö Kiadó, Budapest, 1976.)

[319] See Section 6.2

[320] No matter how much it may be idealized, the capitalist market economy is also a type of 'command economy', even if its command structure is more complicated — and also more impersonal — than that of the postcapitalist system. However, the truth about the market economy of commodity society — which is supposed to be operated on the basis of individual 'consumer sovereignty' — comes to the fore in every situation of crisis. Invariably, then, we are told that 'there is *no alternative*' to implementing the imperatives of the established system.

[321] Marx, *Grundrisse,* pp.172-3.

[322] Marx, *The Poverty of Philosophy,* pp.125-27.

[323] MECW., vol. 5, p.49.

This is how the Editors of MECW comment on Marx's idea that the realization of a communist society is feasible only in global terms:

> The conclusion that the proletarian revolution could only be carried through in all the advanced capitalist countries simultaneously, and hence that the victory of the revolution in a single country was impossible, was expressed even more definitely in the 'Principles of Communism' written by Engels in 1847. In their later works, however, Marx and Engels expressed this idea in a less definite way and emphasised that the proletarian revolution should be regarded as a comparatively long and complicated process which can develop first in individual capitalist countries. In the new historic conditions V. I. Lenin came to the conclusion, which he based on the specific circumstances of operation of the law of uneven economic and political development of capitalism in the epoch of imperialism, that the socialist revolution could be victorious at first even in a single country. This thesis was set forth for the first time in his article 'On the Slogan for a United States of Europe' (1915).

This is a complete — though by no means accidental — misunderstanding of Marx's meaning. For in the disputed passage Marx is not talking at all about the possible victory of a *proletarian revolution* in a limited area, but of the global productive prerequisites of instituting *communism* as a radically new *socioeconomic system*. Once, however, the Stalinist slogan of 'socialism in one country' becomes the compulsory wisdom to which all important theoretical considerations must be subordinated, the difference between the victorious overthrow of the bourgeoisie and the material and cultural/political conditions of a successful socialist transformation are obliterated, and the criteria laid down by Marx for the latter (criteria never revised or abandoned either by him or by Engels, nor indeed by Lenin himself whose authority is invoked by the Editors of MECW) must be thrown overboard.

As a matter of fact, Lenin's ideas on the subject, even as expressed in the 1915 article 'On the Slogan for a United States of Europe' in no way contradict Marx's views on the global prerequisites for the victory of communism as a socioeconomic system. On the contrary. For he unequivocally states that

A United States of the World (not of Europe alone) is the state form of the unification and freedom of nations which we associate with socialism — until the time when the complete victory of communism brings about the total disappearance of the state, including the democratic. ... The *political form* of a society wherein the proletariat is victorious in overthrowing the bourgeoisie will be a *democratic republic,* which will more and more concentrate the forces of the proletariat of a given nation or nations, in the struggle against states that have not yet gone over to socialism. The abolition of classes is impossible without a dictatorship of the oppressed class, of the proletariat. A *free union of nations in socialism* is impossible without a more or less prolonged and stubborn struggle of the *socialist republics* against the backward states. (Lenin, *Collected Works,* vol. 21, pp.342-3.)

Thus, Lenin forcefully reiterates the ultimately global character of the socialist enterprise. At the same time he is anxious to stress, in order to combat disarming political strategies, that a *breakthrough* towards the global socialist transformation can come about 'in several or even in a single country'. But a 'breakthrough' in the form of a successful political revolution which *aims* at the establishment of socialism is by itself very far from being the realization of a communist social reproductive order actually regulated in its everyday life by the principle: 'to each according to their needs'.

[324] Daniel Singer, 'Moment of truth for social democracy?', *Monthly Review,* June 1995, p.28.

[325] *Ibid.,* p.29.

[326] *Ibid.* See also Daniel Singer, *Is Socialism Doomed? The Meaning of Mitterrand,* Oxford University Press, 1988.

[327] 'Financial reform in Czechoslovakia: A conversation with Vaclav Klaus', *The Economist,* 10 February 1990.

[328] 'Open up', *The Economist,* 3 August 1991.

[329] Karl Polányi, *The Great Transformation,* Beacon Press, Boston, 1957, p.73.

[330] *Ibid.,* pp.252-4. These passages, quoted from the final chapter of Polányi's book, are not yet present in its English edition — published under the title *Origins of Our Time: The Great Transformation* by Victor Gollancz Ltd., London, 1945, i.e. one year after the first American edition — which itself contains 'an expansion of the last chapter', according to the author's 'Preface to revised edition'.

[331] This has been acknowledged in a recently published article by Karl Polányi's daughter, the distinguished economist Kari Polányi Levitt, who wrote that 'Polányi was premature in dismissing "market economy" and "market society" from the stage of history'. See 'Toward alternatives: re-reading *The Great Transformation*', *Monthly Review,* June 1995, p.10.

[332] Karl Polányi. *op. cit.,* p.256.

[333] David Ricardo, *Principles of Political Economy and Taxation,* (1817 and 1821), Penguin Books, 1971, pp.138-9.

[334] *Ibid.,* p.290.

[335] Marx, *Grundrisse,* pp.650-52.

[336] *Ibid.,* pp.657-8.

[337] Hayek, 'The Moral Imperative of the Market', in Martin J. Anderson (ed.), *The Unfinished Agenda,* pp.146-7.

[338] *Ibid.,* p.148.

[339] *Ibid.,* p.149.

[340] *Ibid.,* p.148.

[341] *Ibid.,* p.147.

[342] Polányi, *The Great Transformation,* p.250.

[343] Daniel Singer, 'Europe in Search of a Future', *The Socialist Register,* ed. by Leo Panitch, Merlin Press, London, 1995, p.119.

[344] See Philip Bassett's *Times* article, quoted in note 291.

[345] Hayek, *ibid.*, p.147.

[346] Marx, 'Value, Price, and Profit', in MECW, vol. 20, p.149.

[347] Alec Nove, *The Economics of Feasible Socialism*, George Allen & Unwin Ltd., London, 1985, p.15. On the same page, the author also condescendingly pontificates that 'one feels that the "ideal society" of Marx's romantic imagination is not merely unreal, it would also be dull, of little attraction to either workers or intellectuals.' The fact that Nove is filled with the feeling of dullness is supposed to conclusively settle the matter in his view. At the same time, as usual, he demonstrates his total incomprehension of Marx's position. For in his anti-Marxist ideological eagerness Nove circularly assumes the absolute permanence of the division of mental and physical labour — the opposite of which is clearly asserted by Marx with reference to the future society of the 'new historic form' — in order to be able to conclude his 'refutation of Marx' with the arbitrary assertion (proclaimed god only knows on the basis of what evidence, other than his own feeling of dullness) that 'the workers and intellectuals' would find life dull 'in the ideal society'. This kind of ideologically motivated circularity characterizes Nove's 'arguments' from the beginning to the end of his *Economics of Feasible Socialism*.

[348] Hayek, *The Fatal Conceit*, p.19.

[349] Hayek, 'The Moral Imperative of the Market', p.146.

[350] *Ibid.*

[351] Hayek, *The Fatal Conceit*, p.83.

[352] *Ibid.*, p.84.

[353] *Ibid.*, p.146.

[354] *Ibid.*, p.148.

[355] *Ibid.*, pp.149-50.

[356] *Ibid.*, p.111.

[357] *Ibid.*, p.99.

[358] *Ibid.*, p.82. In the same spirit it is also asserted by Hayek (on page 119) that 'an anti-capitalist ethic continues to develop on the basis of errors'. Responsibility for it must be attributed to the guilty socialist intellectuals, who imagine 'that their reason can tell them how to arrange human efforts to serve their innate wishes better, they themselves pose a grave threat to civilization'.

[359] *Ibid.*, p.110.

[360] *Ibid.*, p.78.

[361] *Ibid.*

[362] We have seen that in his *Fatal Conceit* Hayek declared that 'The issue of justification is a red herring'. (p.68.)

[363] *Ibid.*, p.144.

[364] *Ibid.*, p.9.

[365] 'Niente meno' — i.e. 'nothing less' — as the Italians say. *Ibid.*, p.127.

[366] *Ibid.*, p.8.

[367] Alec Nove, *Efficiency Criteria for Nationalised Industries*, George Allen & Unwin Ltd., London, 1973, p.140.

[368] See 'The Legacy of Marx, *Sancta Simplicitas*', in Alec Nove, *The Economics of Feasible Socialism*, pp.32-39.

[369] Marx, *Grundrisse*, p.335.

[370] Vadim A. Medvedev, 'The Ideology of Perestroika', in A. Aganbegyan, *op. cit.*, p.27.

[371] *Ibid.*, pp.29-32.

[372] *The Economist*, 31 December 1991, pp.11-12.

[373] *Ibid.*, p.12.

[374] *Ibid.*

[375] *Ibid.*

376 MECW, vol. 34, p.465.

377 *Ibid.*, p.457.

378 *Ibid.*, p.423.

379 *Ibid.*, p.466.

380 Marx, *Grundrisse*, pp.541-2.

381 *Ibid.*, p.408.

382 MECW, vol. 34, p.457.

383 MTBF stands for Mean Time Between Failures.

384 See on these issues Chapter 2.

385 Marx, *Grundrisse*, p.270.

386 *Ibid.* p.749.

387 *Ibid.* p.750.

388 Even some socialist thinkers were captivated at the time by this perspective. See 'Premature Theorization of the End of Scarcity' in *The Power of Ideology*, pp.63-65.

389 Keynes had even put a date to his fantasy of reaching the capitalist Millennium of boundless abundance. He projected — in 'Economic Possibilities for our Grandchildren' (1930) — that by 2030 the only remaining problem will be how to kill idle time. This was a double absurdity. For (1) without the full and continuing activation of the creative potentials of the individuals' *total disposable time* there can be no hope for overcoming scarcity even in the economically most advanced society; and (2) inasmuch as scarcity can be overcome through the creative use of total disposable time, this certainly cannot be achieved in the capital system, under the imperative of capital's chronically wasteful self-preservation.

390 'Takeover of profitable sectors has begun', *The Times*, 28 June 1976. As it transpires through the report itself, the title of this article is as misleading as the Labour Minister of State for Industry tried to be in his answer to his own colleague.

391 Alec Nove, *The Economics of Feasible Socialism*, p.ix.

392 *Ibid.*, pp.ix-x.

393 *Ibid.*, p.20. Nove's italics.

394 *Ibid.*, p.215.

395 *Ibid.*, p.211.

396 *Ibid.*, p.226.

397 *Ibid.*, p.229.

398 Wlodzimierz Brus, 'Market Socialism', in Tom Bottomore (ed.), *A Dictionary of Marxist Thought*, Blackwell, Oxford, 1991, p.339.

399 W. Brus, *The Economics and Politics of Socialism: Collected Essays*, With a Foreword by Maurice Dobb, Routledge & Kegan Paul, London, 1973, p.21.

400 *Ibid.*, p.46.

401 *Ibid.*, p.49.

402 Marx, *Grundrisse*, pp.158-9.

403 Brus, *Ibid.*, p.1.

404 *Ibid.*, p.98.

405 *Ibid.*, p.16.

406 *Ibid.*, p.28.

407 *Ibid.*, p.35.

408 *Ibid.*, p.29

409 *Ibid.*, p.49

410 *Ibid.*, p.50

411 'Két autós chalád' (Two-car family), *Magyar Hirek*, 16 June 1979, p.6.

412 Brus, *Ibid.*, p.96.

413 Brus, 'Market Socialism' (1991), *op. cit.*, p.339. The passage refers to W. Brus and Kazimierz Laski, *From Marx to the Market: Socialism in Search of an Economic System*,

Clarendon, Oxford 1989.

[414] See Frank Roosevelt and David Belkin (editors), *Why Market Socialism?*, M.E. Sharpe, Armonk, New York, 1994.

[415] Harry Magdoff, 'A Note on "Market Socialism",' *Monthly Review,* May 1995, pp.16-7. 'All' is italicised by Magdoff.

[416] See Hayek, *The Fatal Conceit,* pp.106-119.

[417] Brus, *The Economics and Politics of Socialism,* p.21.

[418] *Ibid.,* p.50.

[419] *Ibid.,* p.28.

[420] Marx, *Critique of the Gotha Programme,* in Marx and Engels, *Selected Works,* vol. 2, p.23.

[421] For Max Weber once upon a time existed the mysterious general 'spirit of protestantism' — not just 'private demons' — which created capitalism. Since, however, capitalism is eternalized in his conception, the socialist alternative must be treated in a very different way, and dismissed in the most categorical fashion.

[422] Rosa Luxemburg, *Reform or Revolution,* Pathfinder Press, New York, 1970, pp.41-42.

[423] Marx, *Grundrisse,* pp.470-71.

[424] *Ibid.,* p.651.

[425] *Ibid.,* p.158.

PART FOUR

ESSAYS ON RELATED ISSUES

I. THE NECESSITY OF SOCIAL CONTROL*

IN the deeply moving final pages of one of his last works Isaac Deutscher wrote:

> The technological basis of modern society, its structure and its conflicts are international or even universal in character; they tend towards international or universal solutions. And there are the unprecedented dangers threatening our biological existence. These, above all, press for the unification of mankind, which cannot be achieved without an integrating principle of social organization. ... The present ideological deadlock and the social status quo can hardly serve as the basis either for the solution of the problems of our epoch or even for mankind's survival. Of course, it would be the ultimate disaster if the nuclear super-Powers were to treat the social status quo as their plaything and if either of them tried to alter it by force of arms. In this sense the peaceful co-existence of East and West is a paramount historic necessity. But the social status quo cannot be perpetuated. Karl Marx speaking about stalemates in past class struggles notes that they usually ended 'in the common ruin of the contending classes'. A stalemate indefinitely prolonged and guaranteed by a perpetual balance of nuclear deterrents, is sure to lead the contending classes and nations to their common and ultimate ruin. Humanity needs unity for its sheer survival; where can it find it if not in socialism?[1]

Deutscher concluded his work by passionately stressing: 'de nostra re agitur': it all is our own concern. Thus it seems to me right to address ourselves on this occasion to some of the vital problems which stood at the centre of his interest towards the end of his life.

All the more so because the 'status quo' in question is a historically unique status quo: one which inevitably involves the *whole* of mankind. As we all know from history, no status quo has ever lasted indefinitely; not even the most partial and localized one. The permanence of a *global* status quo, with the immense and necessarily expanding dynamic forces involved in it, is a contradiction in terms: an absurdity which should be visible even to the most myopic of game-theorists. In a world made up of a multiplicity of conflicting and mutually interacting social systems — in contrast to the fantasy-world of escalating and de-escalating chess-boards — the precarious global status quo is *bound* to be broken for certain. The question is not 'whether of not', but 'by what means'. Will it be broken by devastating military means or will there be adequate social outlets for the manifestation of the rising social pressures which are in evidence today even in the most remote corners of our global social environment? The answer will depend on our success or failure in creating the necessary strategies, movements and instruments capable of securing an effective transition towards a socialist society in which 'humanity can find the unity it needs for its sheer survival'.

---

* The first Isaac Deutscher Memorial lecture, delivered at the London School of Economics and Political Science on 26 January 1971. Published as a separate volume, under the same title, by The Merlin Press, London, 1971.

1. The counter-factual conditionals of apologetic ideology

WHAT we are experiencing today is not only a growing polarization — inherent in the global structural crisis of present-day capitalism — but, to multiply the dangers of explosion, also the break-down of a whole series of safety valves which played a vital part in the perpetuation of commodity society.

The change that undermined the power of consensus politics, of the narrow institutionalization and integration of social protest, of the easy exportation of internal violence through its transference to the plane of mystifying international collisions, etc., has been quite dramatic. For not so long ago the unhindered growth and multiplication of the power of capital, the irresistible extension of its rule over all aspects of human life, used to be confidently preached and widely believed. The unproblematic and undisturbed functioning of capitalist power structures was taken for granted and was declared to be a permanent feature of human life itself, and those who dared to doubt the wisdom of such declarations of faith were promptly dismissed by the self-perpetuating guardians of the bourgeois hegemony of culture as 'hopeless ideologists', if not much worse.

But where are now the days when one of President Kennedy's principal theorists and advisers could speak about Marx and the social movements associated with his name in terms like these:

He [Marx] applied his kit-bag to what he could perceive of *one* historical case: the case of the British take-off and drive to maturity; ... like the parochial intellectual of Western Europe he was, the prospects in Asia and Africa were mainly beyond his ken, dealt with almost wholly in the context of British policy rather than in terms of their own problems of *modernization*. ... Marx created ... *a monstrous guide to public policy*. [Communism] is a kind of disease which can befall a transitional society if it fails to organize effectively those elements within it which are prepared to get on with the job of modernization. [In opposition to the Marxist approach the task is to create] in association with the non-Communist politicians and peoples of the preconditions and early take-off areas [i.e. the territories of neocolonialism] a *partnership* which will *see them through* into sustained growth on a political and social basis which keeps open the possibilities of progressive democratic development.[2]

These lines were written hardly a decade ago, but they read today like prehistoric reasoning, although — or perhaps because — the author is the professor of Economic History at the Massachusetts Institute of Technology.

In this short decade we were provided with tragically ample opportunity to see in practice, in Vietnam and in Cambodia, as well as in other countries, the real meaning of the programme of 'partnership' intended 'to see the politicians of the early take-off areas through' to the disastrous results of such partnership,[3] under the intellectual guidance of 'Brain Trusts' which included quite a few Walt Rostows: men who had the cynical insolence to call *Marx's* work 'a monstrous guide to public policy'. Inflated by the 'arrogance of military power', they 'proved', by means of tautologies interspersed with retrospective 'deductions', that the American stage of economic growth is immune to all crisis,[4] and they argued, with the help of counter-factual conditionals, that the break in the chain of imperialism was merely an unfortunate mishap which, strictly speaking, should not have happened at all. For:

if the First World War had not occurred — or had occurred a decade later — Russia would almost certainly have made a successful transition to modernization and rendered itself invulnerable to Communism.[5]

We might be tempted to rejoice at the sight of such a level of intellectual power in our adversaries, were it not terrifying to contemplate the naked power they wield in virtue of their willing submission to the alienated institutions which demand 'theories' of this kind so as to follow, undisturbed even by the possibility of an occasional doubt, their blind collision-course. The hollow constructions which meet this demand of rationalization are built on the pillars of totally false — and often self-contradictory — premises like, for instance:

1. 'socialism is a mysterious — yet easily avoidable — disease which will befall you, unless you follow the scientific prescription of American modernization';

2. 'facts to the contrary are merely the result of mysterious — yet easily avoidable — mishaps; such facts (e.g. the Russian Revolution of 1917) are devoid of an actual causal foundation and of a wider social-historical significance';

3. 'present-day manifestations of social unrest are merely the combined result of Soviet aspirations and of the absence of American partnership in the societies concerned; therefore, the task is to check-mate the former by generously supplying the latter'.

'THEORIES' resting on such foundations can, of course, amount to no more than the crudest ideological justification of aggressive American expansionism and interventionism. This is why these cynical ideologies of rationalization have to be misrepresented as 'objective social and political science' and the position of those who 'see through' the unctuous advocacy of 'seeing the politicians of the early take-off areas through' — by means of the 'Great American Partnership' of massive military interventions — must be denounced as 'nineteenth century ideologists'.

The moment of truth arrives, however, when the 'mishaps' of social explosion occur, even more mysteriously than in the 'early take-off areas', in the very land of 'supreme modernization' and higher than 'high mass-consumption': namely in America itself. Thus, not only is the model of undisturbed growth and modernization shattered but, ironically, even the slogan of 'sustained growth on a political and social basis which keeps open the possibilities of progressive, democratic development' ideologically backfires at a time when outcries against the violation of basic liberties and against the systematic disenfranchizing of the masses is on the increase. That we are not talking about some remote, hypothetical future but about our own days, goes without saying. What needs stressing, however, is that the dramatic collapse of these pseudo-scientific rationalizations of naked power marks the end of an era: not that of 'the end of ideology' but of the end of the almost complete *monopoly* of culture and politics by anti-Marxist ideology successfully self-advertised up until quite recently as the final supersession of all ideology.

2. Capitalism and ecological destruction

A decade ago the Walt Rostows of this world were still confidently preaching the *universal* adoption of the American pattern of 'high mass-consumption' within the space of one single century. They could not be bothered with making the elementary, but of course necessary, calculations which would have shown them that in the event of the universalization of that pattern — not to mention the economic, social and political absurdity of such an idea — the ecological resources of our planet would have been exhausted well before the end of that century several times over. After all, in those days top-politicians and their Brain-Trusts did not ride on the bandwagon of ecology but in the sterilized space-capsules of astronautical and military fancy. Nothing seemed in those days too big, too far, and too difficult to those who believed — or wanted us to believe — in the religion of technological omnipotence and of a Space Odyssey round the corner.

Many things have changed in this short decade. The arrogance of military power suffered some severe defeats not only in Vietnam but also in Cuba and in other parts of the 'American hemisphere'. International power-relations have undergone some significant changes, with the immense development of China and Japan in the first place, exposing to ridicule the nicely streamlined calculations of escalation-experts who now have to invent not only an entirely new type of multiple-player chess game but also the kind of creatures willing to play it, for want of real-life takers. 'The affluent society' turned out to be the society of suffocating *effluence*, and the allegedly omnipotent technology failed to cope even with the invasion of rats in the depressing slums of black ghettos. Nor did the religion of Space Odyssey fare any better, notwithstanding the astronomical sums invested in it: recently even the learned Dr. Werner von Braun himself had to link-up the latest version of his irresistible 'yearning for the stars' with the prosaic bandwagon of pollution (so far, it seems, without much success).

'The God that failed' in the image of technological omnipotence is now revarnished and shown around again under the umbrella of universal 'ecological concern'. Ten years ago ecology could be safely ignored or dismissed as totally irrelevant. Today it must be grotesquely misrepresented and one-sidedly exaggerated so that people — sufficiently impressed by the cataclysmic tone of ecological sermons — can be successfully diverted from burning social and political problems. Africans, Asians, and Latin Americans (especially Latin Americans) should not multiply at pleasure — not even at God's pleasure, if they are Roman Catholics — for lack of restraint might result in 'intolerable ecological strains'. That is, in plain words, it might even endanger the prevailing social relation of forces, the rule of capital. Similarly, people should forget all about the astronomical expenditure on armaments and accept sizeable cuts in their standard of living, in order to meet the costs of 'environmental rehabilitation': that is, in plain words, the costs of keeping the established system of expanding waste-production well-oiled. Not to mention the additional bonus of making people at large pay, under the pretext of 'human survival', for the survival of a socioeconomic system which now has to cope with deficiencies arising from growing international competition and from an increasing shift in favour of the parasitic sectors within its own structure of production.

THAT capitalism deals this way — namely its own way — with ecology, should not surprise us in the least: it would be nothing short of a miracle if it did not. Yet the exploitation of this issue for the benefit of 'the modern industrial state' — to use a nice phrase of Professor Galbraith's — does not mean that we can afford to ignore it. For the problem itself is real enough, whatever use is made of it today.

Indeed, it has been real for quite some time, though, of course, for reasons inherent in the necessity of capitalist growth, few have taken any notice of it. Marx however — and this should sound incredible only to those who have repeatedly buried him as an 'irretrievably irrelevant ideologist of nineteenth century stamp' — had tackled the issue, within the dimensions of its true social-economic significance, more than one hundred and twenty-five years ago.

Criticizing the abstract and idealist rhetoric with which Feuerbach assessed the relationship between man and nature, Marx wrote:

> Feuerbach ... always takes refuge in external nature, and moreover in nature which has not yet been subdued by men. But every new invention, every new advance made by industry, detaches another piece from this domain, so that the ground which produces examples illustrating such Feuerbachian propositions is steadily shrinking. The 'essence' of the fish is its 'existence', water — to go no further than this one proposition. The 'essence' of the freshwater fish is the water of a river. But the latter ceases to be the 'essence' of the fish and is no longer a suitable medium of existence as soon as the river is made to serve industry, as soon as it is polluted by dyes and other waste products and navigated by steamboats, or as soon as its water is diverted into canals where simple drainage can deprive the fish of its medium of existence.[6]

This is how Marx approached the matter in the early eighteen forties. Needless to say, he categorically rejected the suggestion that such developments are inevitably inherent in the 'human predicament' and that, consequently, the problem is how to *accommodate* ourselves[7] to them in everyday life. He fully realized, already then, that a radical restructuring of the prevailing *mode* of human interchange and control is the necessary prerequisite to an effective control over the forces of nature which are brought into motion in a blind and ultimately self-destructive fashion precisely by the prevailing, alienated and reified mode of human interchange and control. Small wonder, then, that to present-day apologists of the established system of control his prophetic diagnosis is nothing but 'parochial anachronism'.

TO say that 'the costs of cleaning up our environment must be met in the end by the community' is both an obvious platitude and a characteristic evasion, although the politicians who sermonize about it seem to believe to have discovered the philosophers' stone. *Of course* it is always the community of producers who meet the cost of everything. But the fact that it always *must* meet the costs does not mean in the least that it always *can* do so. Indeed, given the prevailing mode of alienated social control, we can be sure that it *will not be able to* meet them.

Furthermore, to suggest that the already prohibitive costs should be met by 'consciously putting aside a certain proportion of the resources derived from extra growth' — at a time of nil growth coupled with rising unemployment and rising inflation — is worse than Feuerbach's empty rhetoric. Not to mention the additional problems necessarily inherent in increased capitalistic growth.

And to add that 'but this time growth will be controlled growth' is completely beside the point. For the issue is not *whether* or *not* we produce under *some* control, but under what *kind* of control; since our present state of affairs has been produced under the 'iron-fisted control' of capital which is envisaged, by our politicians, to remain the fundamental regulating force of our life also in the future.

And, finally, to say that 'science and technology *can* solve all our problems in the long run' is much worse than believing in witchcraft; for it tendentiously ignores the devastating social embeddedness of present-day science and technology. In this respect, too, the issue is not *whether* or *not* we use science and technology for solving our problems — for obviously we must — but whether or not we *succeed* in radically *changing* their *direction* which is at present narrowly determined and circumscribed by the self-perpetuating needs of profit maximization.

These are the main reasons why we cannot help being rather sceptical about the present-day institutionalization of these concerns. Mountains are in labour and a mouse is born: the super-institutions of ecological oversight turn out to be rather more modest in their achievements than in their rhetoric of self-justification: namely Ministries for the Protection of Middle-Class Amenities.

3. The crisis of domination

IN the meantime, on this plane as well as on several others, the problems accumulate and the contradictions become increasingly more explosive. The objective tendency inherent in the nature of capital — its growth into a global system coupled with its concentration and increasingly greater technological and science-intensive articulation — undermines and turns into an anachronism the social/structural subordination of labour to capital.[8] Indeed, we can witness already that the traditional forms of hierarchical/structural embeddedness of the functional division of labour tend to disintegrate under the impact of the ever-increasing concentration of capital and socialization of labour. Here I can merely point to a few indicators of this striking change:

1. The escalating vulnerability of contemporary industrial organization as compared to the nineteenth century factory. (The so-called 'wild-cat strikes' are inconceivable without the underlying economic and technological processes which both induce and enable a 'handful' of workers to bring to a halt even a whole branch of industry, with immense potential repercussions.)

2. The economic link-up of the various branches of industry into a highly stretched system of closely interdependent parts, with an ever-increasing imperative for safeguarding the *continuity of production* in the system as a whole. (The more the system is stretched as regards its cycle of reproduction, the greater is the imperative of continuity, and every disturbance leads to more stretch as well as to an ever-darkening shadow of even a temporary break-down in continuity.) There are increasingly fewer 'peripheral branches', since the repercussions of industrial complications are quickly transferred, in the form of a chain-reaction, from any part of the system to all its parts. Consequently, there can be no more 'trouble-free industries'. The age of paternalistic enterprise has been irretrievably superseded by the rule of 'oligopolies' and 'super-conglomerates'.

3. The growing amount of socially 'superfluous time' (or 'disposable time'),[9] customarily called 'leisure', makes it increasingly absurd, as well as practically impossible, to keep a large section of the population living in apathetic igno-

rance, divorced from their own intellectual powers. Under the impact of a number of weighty socioeconomic factors the old mystique of intellectual elitism has already disappeared for good. Also, side by side with a growing intellectual unemployment — both potential and actual — as well as a worsening of the cleavage between what one is supposed to be educated for and what one actually gets in employment opportunities, it becomes more and more difficult to maintain the traditionally unquestioning subordination of the vast majority of intellectuals to the authority of capital.

4. The worker as a consumer occupies a position of increasing importance in maintaining the undisturbed run of capitalist production. Yet, he is as completely excluded from control over both production and distribution as ever — as if nothing had happened in the sphere of economics during the last century or two. This is a contradiction which introduces further complications into the established productive system based on a socially stratified division of labour.

5. The effective establishment of capitalism as an economically interlocking world system greatly contributes to the erosion and disintegration of the traditional, historically formed and locally varying, partial structures of social and political stratification and control, without being able to produce a unified system of control on a world-wide scale. (So long as the power of capital prevails, 'world-government' is bound to remain a futurologist pipe-dream.) The 'crisis of hegemony, or crisis of the State in all spheres' (Gramsci) has become a truly international phenomenon.

IN the last analysis all these points are about the question of *social control*.

In the course of human development, the function of social control had been alienated from the social body and transferred into capital which, thus, acquired the power of grouping people in a hierarchical structural/functional pattern, in accordance with the criterion of a greater or lesser share in the necessary control over production and distribution.

Ironically, though, the objective trend inherent in the development of capital in all spheres — from the mechanical fragmentation of the labour process to the creation of automated systems, from local accumulation of capital to its concentration in the form of an ever-expanding and self-saturating world system, from a partial and local to a comprehensive international division of labour, from limited consumption to an artificially stimulated and manipulated mass-consumption, in the service of an ever-accelerating cycle of reproduction of commodity-society, and from 'free time' confined to a privileged few to the mass production of social dynamite, in the form of 'leisure', on a universal scale — carries with it a result diametrically opposed to the interest of capital. For in this process of expansion and concentration, the power of control invested in capital is being *de facto* re-transferred to the social body as a whole, even if in a necessarily irrational way, thanks to the inherent irrationality of capital itself.

That the objectively slipping control is described from the standpoint of capital as 'holding the nation to ransom', does not alter in the least the fact itself. For nineteenth century capitalism could not be 'held to ransom' even by an army of so-called 'troublemakers', let alone by a mere 'handful' of them.

Here we are confronted with the emergence of a fundamental contradiction: that between an effective loss of control and the established form of control, capital, which, by its very nature, can be nothing *but* control, since it is constituted through an alienated objectification of the function of control as a reified body apart from and opposed to the social body itself. No wonder, therefore, that in the last few years the idea of *workers' control* has been gaining in importance in many parts of the world.

THE social status quo of not so long ago is rapidly and dramatically disintegrating in front of our very eyes — if only we are willing to open them. The distance between Uncle Tom's Cabin and the beleaguered headquarters of black militancy is *astronomical*. And so are the distances from the depressing working class apathy of the post-war period to today's, even officially admitted, growing militancy on a world-wide scale; from graciously granted presidential 'participation' to the Paris street fights; from a badly divided and narrowly wage-orientated Italian trade union movement to the unity necessary for the organization of a political general strike; or, for that matter, from the monolithic, unchallenged rule of Stalinism to the elemental eruption of massive popular dissent in Poland, in Hungary, in Czechoslovakia, and recently in Poland again. And yet, it did not take anything like light-years — not even light-minutes — to travel such astronomical distances.

Not so long ago the 'scientific' ideology of gradualist 'social engineering' — as opposed to the 'religious holism' of revolutionary change and socialism — enjoyed an almost completely monopolistic position not only in educational and cultural institutions but also in the ante-chambers of political power. But, good heavens, what are we witnessing today? The dramatic announcement of the need for a 'major *revolution*' by none other than President Nixon himself, in his recent State of the Union message; followed by the Shah of Persia's warning that he is going to spearhead the 'rebellion of the have-nots against the haves'.

And Mr. Wilson too, who mysteriously lost the word 'socialism' from his vocabulary the very minute he walked through the front door of 10 Downing Street — and it just could not be found, though his entire team of experts and advisers as well as cabinet colleagues were looking for it for almost six years through the powerful spectacles of 'pragmatic modernization', supplied completely free of prescription charges — mysteriously found the word again after leaving the Prime Ministerial residence by the back door. Indeed, in one of his public speeches he even cracked a joke about the 'Pentagon hunting for communists under the sea-bed', though at the same time by a slight fit of amnesia forgetting that he was himself fishing for communists under the Seamen's bed not that long ago.

President Nixon: a new *revolutionary*; the Shah of Persia: *leader of the world rebellion* of the have-nots; and Mr. Wilson: an indomitable *crusader against the Pentagon's anti-communist crusades*. I wonder what might come next. (I did not have to wonder for long: only a few days after this lecture was delivered, Mr. Heath — yet another 'pragmatic modernizer', of Rolls Royce fame — hastened to add, in the truest spirit of consensus-politics, his name to our illustrious list: as a vigorous *champion of nationalization*.)

However, even metamorphoses of this kind are indicative of powerful pressures whose nature simply cannot be grasped through the mystifying personalization of the issues as expressed in hollow concepts like 'bridging the credibility gap', 'acquiring a new image', etc. The hypothesis that politicians break their promises because they are 'devious' and because they 'lack integrity', only begs the question, at best. And the suggestion that they change their slogans and catchphrases, because 'they need to change their image' is the emptiest of the whole range of tautologies produced by the post-war boom of behaviourist and functionalist 'Political Science'. Concepts of this kind are nothing more than pretentiously inflated rationalizations of the practice of self-advertising through which the advertising media sell their services to credulous politicians. As Mr. Wilson himself can testify: the simple and strictly quantifiable truth is that the psephologist 'credibility gap' between this kind of 'scientific' electoral forecast and the painfully final result *exactly* equals the distance between the front door and the back door of 10 Downing Street.

IF the tone of traditional politics is changing today, it is because the objective contradictions of our present-day situation cannot be repressed any longer either by means of naked power and brute force or through the soft strangulation supplied by consensus politics. Yet, what we are confronted with is but an unprecedented crisis of social control on a world scale, and not its solution. It would be highly irresponsible to lull ourselves into a state of euphoria, contemplating a 'socialist world-revolution round the corner'.

The power of capital, in its various forms of manifestation, though far from being exhausted, does no longer reach far enough. Capital — since it operates on the basis of the myopic rationality of narrow self-interest, of *bellum omnium contra omnes*: the war of each against all — is a mode of control which is apriori incapable of providing the comprehensive rationality of an adequate social control. And it is precisely the need for the latter which demonstrates its dramatic urgency with the passing of every day.

The awareness of the limits of capital has been absent from all forms of rationalization of its reified needs, not only from the more recent versions of capitalist ideology. Paradoxically, however, capital is now forced to take notice of some of these limits, although, of course, in a necessarily alienated form. For now at least the *absolute* limits of human existence — both at the military and at the ecological plane — *must* be sized up, no matter how distorting and mystifying are the measuring devices of a capitalist social-economic accountancy. Facing the dangers of a nuclear annihilation on one side and of an irreversible destruction of the human environment on the other, it becomes imperative to devise practical alternatives and remedies whose failure is rendered inevitable by the very limits of capital which have now collided with the limits of human existence itself.

It goes without saying, the limits of capital carry with them an approach which tries to exploit even these vital human concerns in the service of profit-making. The lunatic — but, of course, capitalistically 'rational' — theories (and associated practices) of 'escalating' war-industry as the ultimate safeguard against war have dominated 'strategic thinking' now for quite some time. And recently we could observe the mushrooming of parasitic enterprises — from the smallest to the largest in size — which all try to cash in on our growing awareness of the ecological dangers. (Not to mention the ideological-political operations associated with the same issues.[10])

All the same, such manipulations do not solve the issues at stake, only contribute to their further aggravation. Capitalism and the rationality of comprehensive social planning are radically incompatible. Today, however, we witness the emergence of a fundamental contradiction, with the gravest possible implications for the future of capitalism: for the first time in human history the unhampered dominance and expansion of the inherently irrational capitalist structures and mechanisms of social control are being seriously interfered with by pressures arising from the elementary imperatives of mere survival. And since the issues themselves are as unavoidable as the contradiction between the need for an adequate social control and the narrow limits of capitalist accountancy is sharp, the necessary failure of programmes of short-sighted manipulation — in a situation which demands far-reaching and consciously coordinated efforts on a massive scale — acts as a *catalyst* for the development of socialist alternatives.

AND this is far from being the sum total of the rising complications. The mass production of disposable time mentioned earlier is now coupled not only with expanding knowledge, but also with growing consciousness of the contradictions inherent in the practically demonstrated failures, as well as with the development of new modes and means of communication potentially *capable* of bringing to light the massive evidence for the eruption of these contradictions.[11]

At the same time, some of the most fundamental institutions of society are affected by a crisis never even imagined before.

The power of religion in the West has almost completely evaporated a long time ago, but this fact has been masked by the persistence of its rituals and, above all, by the effective functioning of substitute-religions, from the abstract cult of 'thrift' in the more remote past to the religion of 'consumer-sovereignty', 'technological omnipotence', and the like, in more recent decades.

The structural crisis of education has been in evidence now for a not negligible number of years. And it is getting deeper every day, although its intensification does not necessarily take the form of spectacular confrontations.

And the most important of them all: the virtual *disintegration* of present-day family — this cell of class society — presents a challenge to which there cannot conceivably be formal-institutional answers, whether in the form of 'amending the law of trespass' or in some more ruthlessly repressive form. The crisis of this institution assumes many forms of manifestation, from the hippy cults to widespread drug-taking; from the 'Women's Liberation Movement' to the establishment of utopian enclaves of communal living; and from the much advertised 'generation-conflict' to the most disciplined and militant manifestations of that conflict in organized action. Those who have laughed at them in the past had better think again. For whatever might be their relative weight in the total picture today, they are potentially of the greatest significance without one single exception.

EQUALLY significant is the way in which the stubborn persistence of wishful thinking misidentifies the various forms of crisis. Not only are the manifestations of conflict ignored up to the last minute; they are also misrepresented the minute after the last. When they cannot be swept any longer under the carpet, they are tackled merely as *effects* divorced from their *causes*. (We should remember the absurd hypotheses of 'mysterious diseases' and of 'events devoid of any foundation' mentioned above.)

Characteristically, we find in a recent book on economics, at the foot of a page which calls for 'reducing industrial investments in favour of a large-scale replanning of our cities, and of restoring and enhancing the beauty of many of our villages, towns and resorts', the following story:

> The recent electric-power breakdown in New York, obviously to be deplored on grounds of efficiency, broke the spell of monotony for millions of New Yorkers. People enjoyed the shock of being thrown back on their innate resources and into sudden dependence upon one another. For a few hours people were freed from routine and brought together by the dark. Next-door strangers spoke, and gladdened to help each other. There was room for kindness. The fault was repaired. The genie of power was returned to each home. And as the darkness brought them stumbling into each other's arms, so *the hard light scattered them again*. Yet someone was quoted as saying, 'This should happen at least once a month'.[12]

The only thing one does not quite understand: why not 'at least once a *week*'? Surely the immense savings on all that unused electricity would more than cover the costs of a 'large-scale replanning of our cities, and of restoring and enhancing the beauty of many of our villages, towns and resorts'. Not to mention the supreme benefits inherent in practising the new-found virtue of unlit-skyscraper-corridor-brotherhood regularly on a weekly basis. For apparently it is not the mode of their social relationships that 'scatters people' apart, but the technological efficiency and monotony of 'hard light'. Thus, the obvious remedy is to give them less 'hard light' and all the unwanted problems disappear for good. That the production of 'hard light' is a social necessity, and cannot be replaced even for the duration of periodic rituals by soft candle-light, is a consideration evidently unworthy of the attention of our champions in romantic day-dreaming.

To put it in another way: this approach of wishful thinking is characterized by a curt dismissal of all those expectations which the system cannot meet. The representatives of this approach insist, with unfailing tautology, that such expectations are not the manifestation of social and economic contradictions but merely the *effects* of 'rising expectations'. Thus, not only is the challenge of facing up to the *causal foundations* of frustrated expectations systematically evaded but at the same time this evasion itself is very conveniently 'justified', i.e. rationalized.

The fact is, however, that we are concerned here with an internal contradiction of a system of production and control: one which cannot help raising expectations even to the point of a complete breakdown in satisfying them. And it is precisely at such points of breakdown that Quixotic remedies and substitutes are advocated with so much 'humanitarian' passion. Up until, or prior to, these points of crisis and breakdown, no one in his right mind is supposed to question the superior wisdom of 'cost-effectiveness', 'business-sense', 'technological efficiency', 'economic motives', and the like. But no sooner does the system fail to deliver the goods it so loudly advertised the moment before — confidently indicating, prior to the eruption of structural disturbances, its own ability to cater for expanding expectations as the self-evident proof of its superiority over all possible alternative modes of production and social control — its apologists immediately switch from preaching the religion of 'cost-effectiveness' and 'economic motives' to sermonizing about the need for 'self-denial' and 'idealism', untroubled not only by their sudden change of course but also by the rhetorical unreality of their wishful 'solutions'.

Thus, beyond the horizon of 'artificial obsolescence' we are suddenly confronted with 'theories' advocating the planning of artificial powercuts, the production of artificial scarcity — both material and as an antidote to too much 'disposable time' which involves the danger of an increasing social consciousness; of space-solidarity and artificially manipulated suspense, etc. Indeed, at a time of dangerously rising unemployment there are still with us antediluvian 'theorists' who wish to counteract the complications arising from a total lack of aim in saturated commodity-existence by seriously advocating the production of artificial unemployment and hardship, topping it all up with nostalgic speeches about lost religions and about the need for a brand-new artificial religion. The only thing they fail to reveal is how they are going to devise also an artificial being who will systematically fail to notice the grotesque artificiality of all these artificialities.

Once upon a time it suited the development of capitalism to let the genie of a ruthless conversion of everything into marketable commodities out of the bottle, even though this deed necessarily carried with it the undermining and the ultimate disintegration of religious, political and educational institutions which were vital to the control mechanism of class society. Today, however, the status quo would be much better served by a restoration of all the undermined and disintegrating institutions of control. According to our romantic critics everything would be well if only the genie could be persuaded to retire back into the bottle. The trouble is, though, that he has no intention whatsoever of doing so. Thus, nothing much remains to our romantics except lamenting upon the wickedness of the genie and upon the folly of human beings who let him loose.

4. From 'repressive tolerance' to the liberal advocacy of repression

WHEN the system fails to cope with the manifestations of dissent, while at the same time it is incapable of dealing with their causal foundations, in such periods of history not only fantasy-figures and remedies appear on the stage but also the 'realists' of a repressive rejection of all criticism.

In 1957 a gifted young German writer, Conrad Rheinhold had to flee the D.D.R. where he used to run a political cabaret in the aftermath of the Twentieth Congress. After he had some experience of life in West Germany, he was asked in an interview published in Der Spiegel,[13] to describe the main difference between his old and new situation. This was his answer: 'Im Osten soll das Kabarett die Gesellschaft ändern, darf aber nichts sagen; im Western kann es alles sagen, darf aber nichts ändern.' ('In the East political cabaret is supposed to change society, but it is not allowed to talk about anything; in the West it is allowed to talk about whatever it pleases but it is not allowed to change anything at all.')

This example illustrates quite well the dilemma of social control. For the other side of the coin of 'repressive tolerance' is the 'repression of tolerance'. The two together mark the limits of social systems which are incapable of meeting the need for social change in a determinate historical period.

When Marx died in 1883, his death was reported in *The Times* with some delay.[14] And no wonder: for it had to be reported to the London *Times* from *Paris* that Marx had died in *London*. And this, again, illustrates very well our dilemma. For it is easy to be liberal when even a Marx can be totally ignored, since his voice cannot be heard where he lives, thanks to the political and ideological vacuum that surrounds him. But what happens when the political vacuum is displaced by the rising pressure of the ever-increasing social contradictions? Will not, in that case, the frustrations generated by the necessary failure of attending only to the surface manifestations of socioeconomic troubles, instead of tackling their causes, — will not that failure take refuge behind a show of strength, even if this means the violation of the selfsame liberal values in whose name the violation is now committed? The recent case of another young refugee from the D.D.R. — this time not a political cabaret writer but someone deeply concerned about the degradation of politics to the level of cheap cabaret: Rudi Dutschke — suggests a rather disturbing answer to our question.

The issue is not that of 'personal aberration' or 'political pigheadedness', as some commentators saw it. Unfortunately it is much worse than that: namely an ominous attempt to bring the political organs of control in line with the needs of the present-day articulation of capitalist economy, even if such an adjustment requires a 'liberal' transition from 'repressive tolerance' to 'repressive intolerance'. Those who continue to nurse their illusions in these matters should read their allegedly 'impartial' daily somewhat more attentively, in order to grasp the carefully woven meaning of passages like this:

> The harder the liberal university is pressed, the less comprehensive it can *afford* to be, the more *rigorously* will it have to draw the line, and the more likely will be the *exclusion of intolerant points of view*. The paradox of the *tolerant society* is that it cannot be defended solely by *tolerant* means just as the *pacific society* cannot be defended solely by peaceful means.[15]

As we can see, the empty myths of 'the tolerant society' and 'the pacific society' are used to describe the society of a 'bellum omnium contra omnes', disregarding the painfully obvious ways in which the 'pacific society' of U.S. capitalism demonstrates its true character by saturation bombing, wholesale slaughter and massacres in Vietnam, and by shooting down even its own youth in front of the 'liberal university' — in Kent State and elsewhere — when it dares to mount a protest against the unspeakable inhumanities of this 'tolerant' and 'pacific' society.

Moreover, in such passages of editorial wisdom we can also notice, if we are willing to do so, not only the unintended acknowledgment of the fact that this 'liberal' and 'tolerant' society will 'tolerate' only to the point it can *afford* to do so — i.e. only to the point beyond which protest starts to become effective and turns into a genuine social challenge to the perpetuation of the society of repressive tolerance — but also the sophisticated hypocrisy through which the advocacy of *crude* ('rigorous') and *institutionalized intolerance* ('exclusion') succeeds in representing itself as a liberal defence of society against 'intolerant points of view'.

Similarly, the advocacy of institutionalized intolerance is extended to prescribing 'solutions' to Trade Union disputes. Another *Times* leader — significantly entitled: *A Battle Line at 10 per cent*[16] — after conceding that 'Nobody knows for sure what the mechanism which causes a runaway inflation is', and after murmuring something about the fate of 'some sort of authoritarian regime' which befalls the countries with substantial inflation, goes on to advocate *blatantly authoritarian* measures:

> What can be done to reverse the present inflationary trend? The first and immediate answer is that the country should recognize the justice of *standing firm*. Anyone in present circumstances who asks for more than 10 per cent is joining in a process of self-destruction. Anyone who strikes because he will not accept 15 per cent deserves to be *resisted* with all the influence of society and *all the power of government*.[17] ... The *first thing to do and the simplest is to start beating strikes.* [!!!] The local authorities should be given *total support* [including troops?] in refusing to make any further offer, *even if the strike lasts for months.*

We can see, then, that the *apparent* concern about the (fictitious) danger of 'some sort of authoritarian regime' — which is simply declared to be inevitably linked to major inflations — is only a cover for the *real* concern about protecting the interests of capital, no matter how grave the political implications of 'standing firm' against 'strikes lasting for months' might be. To formulate, thus, the highest priorities in terms of 'beating the strikes' is and remains *authoritarian*, even if the policy based on such measures is championed in editorial columns capable of assuming liberal positions on peripheral issues.

From the advocacy of institutionalized intolerance, in the form of 'beating the strikes with all the power of government', to the legitimation of such practices, through *anti-union laws*, is, of course, only the next logical step. And the record of consensus-politics is particularly telling in this respect.[18] For Mrs. Castle's denunciation of the *Tory* anti-union bill is not just half-hearted and belated. It also suffers from the memory of its twin brother — the ill-fated Labour bill — for which she could certainly not disclaim maternity. And when Mrs. Castle writes about *The Bad Bosses' Charter*,[19] she merely highlights the stubborn illusions of 'pragmatic' politicians who, notwithstanding their past experience, still imagine that they will be voted back into office in order to write in the statute books a 'Charter for the Good Bosses'.

From a socialist point of view, bosses are neither 'bad' nor 'good'. Just *bosses*. And *that* is bad enough: in fact it could not be worse. This is why it is vital to go beyond the paralysing limits of consensus-politics which refuses to recognize this elementary truth, and makes the people at large pay for the disastrous consequences of its mounting failures.

5. 'War if the normal methods of expansion fail'

UNDER the devastating impact of a shrinking rate of profit which must be monopolistically counteracted, the margin of traditional political action has been reduced to slavishly carrying out the dictates arising from the most urgent and immediate demands of capital expansion, even if such operations are invariably misrepresented as 'the national interest' by both sides of the 'national' consensus.[20] And just how directly policy-making is subordinated to the dictates of monopoly capital — unceremoniously excluding the vast majority of the elected representatives from the determination of all the important matters — is at times revealed in most unexpected ways by such embarrassing events as the headline-catching resignation of supposedly key decision-makers: some members of the most exclusive 'inner cabinets' (restricted to a mere handful of ministers) who protest that they had no say in deciding the crucial issues of their own Departments, let alone the national policy as a whole.

Even more revealing is the meteoric rise of the self-appointed representatives of big business and high finance to the top of political decision-making. For — given the vital role assigned to the state in sustaining, with all available means at its disposal, the capitalist system of production, at a time of an already enormous but still extending concentration of capital — so much is at stake that the traditional forms of an indirect (economic) control of policy-making must be abandoned in favour of a *direct* control of the 'commanding heights' of politics by the spokesmen of monopoly capital. In contrast to such manifestations of actual economic and political developments which we have all witnessed in the recent past and are still witnessing today, the mythology of realizing socialist ideals by 'pragmatically' acquiring control over the 'commanding heights of a mixed economy' must sound particularly hollow indeed.

Thus, politics — which is nothing unless it is a conscious application of strategic measures capable of profoundly affecting social development as a whole — is turned into a mere instrument of short-sighted manipulation, completely devoid of any comprehensive plan and design of its own. It is condemned to follow a pattern of belated and short-term reactive moves to the bewildering crisis-events as they necessarily erupt, with increasing frequency, on the socioeconomic basis of self-saturating commodity production and self-stultifying capital accumulation.

The crisis we face, then, is not simply a political crisis, but the general structural crisis of the capitalistic institutions of social control in their entirety. Here the main point is that the institutions of capitalism are inherently violent and aggressive: they are built on the fundamental premise of 'war if the "normal" methods of expansion fail'. (Besides, the periodic *destruction* — by whatever means, including the most violent ones — of over-produced capital, is an inherent necessity of the 'normal' functioning of this system: the vital condition of its *recovery* from crisis and depression.) The blind 'natural law' of the market mechanism carries with it that the grave social problems necessarily associated with capital production and concentration are never *solved*, only *postponed*, and indeed — since postponement cannot work indefinitely — transferred to the *military* plane. Thus, the 'sense' of the hierarchically structured institutions of capitalism is given in its ultimate reference to the violent 'fighting out' of the issues, in the international arena, for the socioeconomic units — following the inner logic of their development — grow bigger and bigger, and their problems and contradictions increasingly more intense and grave. Growth and expansion are immanent necessities of the capitalist system of production and when the local limits are reached there is no way out except by violently readjusting the prevailing relation of forces.

The capitalist system of our times, however, has been decapitated through the removal of its ultimate sanction: an all-out war on its real or potential adversaries. Exporting internal violence is no longer possible on the required massive scale. (Attempts at doing so on a limited scale — e.g. the Vietnam war — not only are no substitutes for the old mechanism but even accelerate the inevitable internal explosions, by aggravating the inner contradictions of the system.) Nor is it possible to get away indefinitely with the ideological mystifications which represented the *internal* challenge of socialism: the only possible solution to the present crisis of social control, as an *external* confrontation: a 'subversion' directed from abroad by a 'monolithic' enemy. For the first time in history capitalism is globally confronted with its own problems which cannot be 'postponed' much longer, nor indeed can they be transferred to the military plane in order to be 'exported' in the form of an all-out war.

BLOCKING the road of a possible solution to the grave structural crisis of society through a third world war is of an immense significance as far as the future development of capitalism is concerned. The grave implications of this blockage can be grasped by remembering that the 'Great Wars' of the past:

1) automatically 'de-materialized' the capitalist system of incentives (producing a shift from 'economic motives' to 'self-denial' and 'idealism' so dear to the heart of some recent spokesmen and apologists of the system in trouble), adjusting at the same time, accordingly, the mechanism of 'interiorization' through which the continued legitimation of the established order is successfully accomplished;

2) suddenly imposed a radically lower standard of living on the masses of people, who willingly accepted it, given the circumstances of a state of emergency;

3) with equal suddenness radically widened the formerly depressed margin of profit;

4) introduced a vital element of rationalization and co-ordination into the system as a whole (a rationalization, that is, which, thanks to the extraordinary circumstances, did not have to be confined to the narrow limits of all rationalization that directly arises from the sole needs of capital production and expansion); and, last but not least:

5) gave an immense technological boost to the economy as a whole, on a wide front.

Current military demand, however massive, simply cannot be compared to this set of both economic and ideological factors whose removal may well prove too much for the system of world capitalism. The less so since present-day military demand — which is imposed on society under 'peace-time' conditions and not under those of a 'national emergency' — cannot help intensifying the contradictions of capital production. This fact is powerfully highlighted by the spectacular failures of companies which heavily depend for their survival on mammoth defence contracts (Lockheed and Rolls Royce, for instance).

The issue is, however, far more fundamental than even the most spectacular of failures could adequately indicate. For it concerns the structure of present-day capitalist production as a whole, and not simply one of its branches. Nor could one reasonably expect the state to solve the problem, no matter how much public money is poured down the drain in the course of its revealing rescue-operations.

Indeed, it was the tendency of increasing state interventions in economic matters in the service of capital expansion which led to the present state of affairs in the first place. The result of such interventions was not only the cancerous growth of the non-productive branches of industry within the total framework of capital production but — equally important — also the grave distortion of the whole structure of *capitalist cost-accounting* under the impact of contracts carried out with the ideological justification that they were 'vital to the national interest'. And since present-day capitalism constitutes a closely *interlocking system*, the devastating results of this structural distortion come to the fore in numerous fields and branches of industry, and not only in those which are *directly* involved in the execution of defence contracts. The well known facts that original cost-estimates as a rule madly 'escalate', and that the committees set up by governments in order to 'scrutinize' them fail to produce results (that is, results other than the white-washing of past operations coupled with generous justifications of future outlays), find their explanation in the immanent necessities of this changed structure of capitalist production and accountancy, with the gravest implications for the future.

Thus, the power of state intervention in the economy — not so long ago still widely believed to be the wonder-drug of all conceivable ills and troubles of the 'modern industrial society' — is strictly confined to accelerating the maturation of these contradictions. The larger the doses administered to the convalescing patient, the greater his dependency on the wonder-drug, i.e., the graver the symptoms described above as the structural distortion of the whole system of capitalist cost-accounting: symptoms which menacingly foreshadow the ultimate paralysis and breakdown of the mechanisms of capital production and expansion. And the fact that what is supposed to be the remedy turns out to be a contributory cause of further crisis, clearly demonstrates that we are not concerned here with some 'passing dysfunction' but with a fundamental, dynamic contradiction of the whole structure of capital production at its historic phase of decline and ultimate disintegration.

6. *The emergence of chronic unemployment*

EQUALLY important is the newly emerging pattern of unemployment. For in recent decades unemployment in the highly developed capitalist countries was largely confined to 'pockets of underdevelopment'; and the millions of people affected by it used to be optimistically written off in the grand style of neo-capitalist self-complacency as the 'inevitable costs of modernization', without too much — if any — worry about the social-economic repercussions of the trend itself.

Insofar as the prevailing movement was from *unskilled* to *skilled* jobs, involving large sums of capital outlay in industrial development, the matter could be ignored with relative safety, in the midst of the euphoria of 'expansion'. Under such circumstances the human misery necessarily associated with all types of unemployment — including the one produced in the interest of 'modernization' — could be capitalistically justified in the name of a bright commodity-future for everyone. In those days the unfortunate millions of apathetic, 'underprivileged' people could be easily relegated to the periphery of society. Isolated as a social phenomenon from the rest of the 'Great Society' of affluence, they were supposed to blame only their own 'uselessness' (want of skill, lack of 'drive', etc.) for their predicament, resigned to consume the leftovers of the heavily laden neo-capitalist dinner table magnanimously dished out to them in the form of unemployment 'benefits' and unsaleable surplus-food coupons. (We should not forget that in those days some of the most prominent economists were seriously advocating programmes which would have institutionalized — in the name of 'technological progress' and 'cost-efficiency' — the permanent condemnation of a major proportion of the labour force to the brutally dehumanizing existence of enforced idleness and of a total dependence on 'social charity'.)

What was systematically ignored, however, was the fact that the trend of capitalist 'modernization' and the displacement of large amounts of unskilled labour in preference to a much smaller amount of skilled labour ultimately implied the *reversal* of the trend itself: namely the breakdown of 'modernization', coupled with massive unemployment. This fact of the utmost gravity simply *had* to be ignored, in that its recognition is radically incompatible with the continued acceptance of the capitalist perspectives of social control. For the underlying dynamic contradiction which leads to the drastic reversal of the trend is by no means inherent in the *technology* employed, but in the blind subordination of both *labour and technology* to the devastatingly narrow limits of capital as the supreme arbiter of social development and control.

To acknowledge, though, the social embeddedness of the given technology would have amounted to admitting the socioeconomic limitations of the capitalist applications of technology. This is why the apologists of the capitalist relations of production had to theorize about 'growth' and 'development' and 'modernization' *as such*, instead of assessing the sobering *limits* of *capitalist* growth and development. And this is why they had to talk about the 'affluent', 'modern industrial' — or indeed 'post-industrial'(!) — and 'consumer' society *as such*, instead of the artificial, contradictory affluence of *waste-producing commodity society* which relies for its 'modern industrial' cycle of reproduction not only on the most cynical manipulation of 'consumer-demand' but also on the most callous exploitation of the 'have-nots'.

Although there is no reason why *in principle* the trend of modernization and the displacement of unskilled by skilled labour should not go on indefinitely, as far as *technology itself* is concerned, there is a very good reason indeed why this trend must be reversed under capitalist relations of production: namely the catastrophically restricting criteria of profitability and expansion of *exchange value* to which such 'modernization' is necessarily subordinated. Thus, the newly emerging pattern of unemployment as a socioeconomic trend is, again, indicative of the deepening structural crisis of present-day capitalism.

In accordance with this trend, the problem is no longer just the plight of unskilled labourers but also that of large numbers of *highly skilled* workers who are now chasing, in addition to the earlier pool of unemployed, the depressingly few available jobs. Also, the trend of 'rationalizing' amputation is no longer confined to the 'peripheral branches of ageing industry' but embraces some of the *most developed* and modernized sectors of production — from ship-building and aviation to electronics, and from engineering to space technology.

Thus, we are no longer concerned with the 'normal', and willingly accepted, by-products of 'growth and development' but with their driving to a halt; nor indeed with the peripheral problems of 'pockets of underdevelopment' but with a fundamental contradiction of the capitalist mode of production as a whole which turns even the latest achievements of 'development', 'rationalization' and 'modernization' into paralysing burdens of chronic underdevelopment. And, most important of all, the human agency which finds itself at the receiving end is no longer the socially powerless, apathetic and fragmented multitude of 'underprivileged' people but *all* categories of skilled and unskilled labour: i.e., objectively, the *total labour force* of society.

It goes without saying, we are talking about a major *trend* of social development, and not about some mechanical determinism that announces the immediate collapse of world capitalism. But even though the storehouse of manipulative counter-measures is far from being exhausted, no such measure is capable of suppressing the trend itself in the long run. Whatever might be the rate of success of measures arising from, or compatible with, the basic requirements and limitations of the capitalist mode of production, the crucial fact is and remains that under the present-day circumstances and conditions of capital production the totality of the labour force is becoming involved in an ever-intensifying confrontation with monopoly capital — which carries far-reaching consequences for the development of social consciousness.

7. *The intensification of the rate of exploitation*
HERE we can see, again, the vital importance of blocking the road of possible solutions to the structural crisis of capitalism through the violent displacement of its problems in the form of a new world war. Under the changed circumstances some of the most powerful instruments of mystification — through which capital managed to exercise its paralysing ideological control over labour in the past — become dangerously undermined and tend to collapse altogether. For now the immense tensions generated within the system of capital production cannot be exported on an adequately massive scale at the expense of other countries, and thus the basic social antagonism between capital and labour which lies at the roots of such tensions cannot be sealed down indefinitely: *the contradictions must be fought out at the place where they are actually generated.*

Capital, when it reaches a point of saturation in its own setting and, at the same time, cannot find outlets for further expansion through the vehicle of imperialism and neo-colonialism, has no alternative but to make its own indigenous labour force suffer the grave consequences of the deteriorating rate of profit. Accordingly, the working classes of some of the most developed 'post-industrial' societies are getting a foretaste of the real viciousness of 'liberal' capital.

The interplay of a number of major factors — from the dramatic development of the forces of production to the erection of enormous obstacles to the unhampered international expansion of monopoly capital — have exposed and undermined the mechanism of the traditional 'double book-keeping' which in the past enabled capital to conform to the rules of 'liberalism' at home while practising and perpetuating the most brutal forms of authoritarianism abroad. Thus, the real nature of the capitalist production relations: the ruthless domination of labour by capital is becoming increasingly more evident as a *global* phenomenon.

Indeed, it could not be otherwise. For so long as the problems of labour are assessed merely in *partial* terms (i.e., as *local* issues of fragmented, stratified and divided groups of workers) they remain a mystery for theory, and nothing but cause for chronic frustration for politically-minded social practice.

THE understanding of the development and self-reproduction of the capitalist mode of production is quite impossible without the concept of the *total* social capital, which alone can explain many mysteries of commodity society — from the 'average rate of profit' to the laws governing capital expansion and concentration. Similarly, it is quite impossible to understand the manifold and thorny problems of nationally varying as well as socially stratified labour without constantly keeping in mind the necessary framework of a proper assessment: namely the irreconcilable antagonism between *total* social capital and the *totality* of labour.

This fundamental antagonism, it goes without saying, is inevitably modified in accordance with:

a) the local socio-economic circumstances;

b) the respective positions of particular countries in the global framework of capital production; and

c) the relative maturity of the global socio-historical development. Accordingly, at different periods of time the system as a whole reveals the workings of a complex set of objective differences of interest on *both* sides of the social antagonism. The objective reality of different *rates of exploitation* — both within a given country and in the world system of monopoly capital — is as unquestionable as are the objective differences in the *rates of profit* at any particular time, and the ignorance of such differences can only result in resounding rhetoric, instead of revolutionary strategies. All the same, the reality of the different rates of exploitation and profit does not alter in the least the fundamental law itself: i.e., the growing *equalization* of the differential rates of exploitation as the *global trend* of development of world capital.

TO be sure, this law of equalization is a long-term trend as far as the global system of capital is concerned. Nevertheless, the modifications of the system as a whole also appear, inevitably already in the short run, as 'disturbances' of a particular economy which happens to be negatively affected by the repercussions of the shifts which necessarily occur within the global framework of total social capital.

The dialectic of such shifts and modifications is extremely complex and cannot be pursued at this place much further. Let it now suffice to stress that 'total social capital' should not be confused with 'total national capital'. When the latter is being affected by a relative weakening of its position within the global system, it will inevitably try to compensate for its losses by increasing its specific rate of exploitation over against the labour force under its direct control — or else its competitive position is further weakened within the global framework of 'total social capital'. Under the system of capitalist social control there can be no way out from such 'short-term disturbances and dysfunctions' other than the intensification of the specific rates of exploitation, which can only lead, both locally and in global terms, to an explosive intensification of the fundamental social antagonism in the long run.

Those who have been talking about the 'integration' of the working class — depicting 'organized capitalism' as a system which succeeded in radically mastering its social contradictions — have hopelessly misidentified the manipulative success of the differential rates of exploitation (which prevailed in the relatively 'disturbance-free' historic phase of post-war reconstruction and expansion) as a basic *structural remedy*.

As a matter of fact, it was nothing of the kind. The ever-increasing frequency with which 'temporary disturbances and dysfunctions' appear in all spheres of our social existence, and the utter failure of manipulative measures and instruments devised to cope with them, are clear evidence that the structural crisis of the capitalist mode of social control has assumed all-embracing proportions.

8. Capital's 'correctives' and socialist control

THE manifest failure of established institutions and their guardians to cope with our problems can only intensify the explosive dangers of a deadlock. And this takes us back to our point of departure: the imperative of an adequate social control which 'humanity needs for its sheer survival'.

To recognize this need is not the same thing as issuing an invitation to indulge in the production of 'practicable' blue-prints of socioeconomic readjustment in the spirit of accomodating liberal meliorism. Those who usually lay down the criterion of 'practicability' as the 'measure of seriousness' of social criticism, hypocritically hide the fact that their real measure is the capitalist mode of production in terms of which the practicability of all programmes of action is to be evaluated.

Practicable *in relation to what*? — that is the question. For if the criteria of capital production constitute the 'neutral' basis of all evaluation, then, of course, no socialist programme can stand the test of this 'value-free', 'non-ideological' and 'objective' approach. This is why Marx himself who insists that men must change 'from top to bottom the conditions of their industrial and political existence, and consequently *their whole manner of being*',[21] must be condemned as a 'hopelessly impractical ideologist'. For how could men conceivably change from top to bottom the conditions of their existence if conformity to the conditions of capital production remains the necessary premiss of all admissible change?

And yet, when the very existence of mankind is at stake, as indeed it happens to be at this juncture of an unprecedented crisis in human history, the only programme which is really practicable — in sharp contrast to the counterproductive practicality of manipulative measures which only aggravate the crisis — is the Marxian programme of radically restructuring, 'from top to bottom', the totality of social institutions, the industrial, political and ideological conditions of present-day existence, 'the whole manner of being' of men repressed by the alienated and reified conditions of commodity society. Short of the realization of such 'unpracticability', there can be no way out from the ever-deepening crisis of human existence.

The demand for 'practicable' blue-prints is the manifestation of a desire to integrate the 'constructive' elements of social criticism; a desire coupled with the determination to devise ruthlessly effective counter-measures against those elements which resist integration, and therefore a priori defined as 'destructive'. But even if this were not so: truly adequate programmes and instruments of socio-political action can only be elaborated by critical and self-critical social practice itself, in the course of its actual development.

Thus, the socialist institutions of social control cannot define themselves *in detail* prior to their practical articulation. At this point of historic transition the relevant questions concern their general character and direction: determined, in the first place, by the prevailing mode and institutions of control to which they have to constitute a radical alternative. Accordingly, the central characteristics of the new mode of social control can be concretely identified — to a degree to which this is necessary for the elaboration and implementation of flexible socialist strategies — through the grasp of the basic functions and inherent contradictions of the disintegrating system of social control.[22]

Here we must confine ourselves to mentioning only the most important points — among them the relationship between politics and economics in the first place. As is well known, Marx's bourgeois critics never ceased to accuse him of 'economic determinism'. Nothing could be, however, further removed from the truth. For the Marxian programme is formulated precisely as the *emancipation* of human action from the power of relentless economic determinations.

When Marx demonstrated that the brute force of economic determinism, set into motion by the dehumanizing necessities of capital production, rules over all aspects of human life, demonstrating at the same time the inherently *historical* — i.e. necessarily *transient* — character of the prevailing mode of production, he touched a sore point of bourgeois ideology: the hollowness of its metaphysical belief in the 'natural law' of permanence of the given production relations. And by revealing the inherent contradictions of this mode of production, he demonstrated the necessary *breakdown* of its objective economic determinism. Such a breakdown, however, had to consummate itself by extending the power of capital to its extreme limits, submitting absolutely everything — including the supposedly autonomous power of political decision-making — to its own mechanism of strict control.

Ironically, though, when this is accomplished (as a result of an increasingly bigger appetite for 'correctives' devised to safeguard the unhampered expansion of the power of capital), monopoly capital is compelled to assume direct control also over areas which it is structurally incapable of controlling. Thus, beyond a certain point, the more it controls (directly), the less it controls (effectively), undermining and eventually destroying even the mechanisms of 'correctives'. The complete and by now overt subordination of politics to the most immediate dictates of capital-producing economic determinism is a vital aspect of this problematic. This is why the road to the establishment of the new institutions of social control must lead through a radical *emancipation of politics from the power of capital*.

ANOTHER basic contradiction of the capitalist system of control is that it cannot separate 'advance' from *destruction*, nor 'progress' from *waste* — however catastrophic the results. The more it unlocks the powers of productivity, the more it must unleash the powers of destruction; and the more it extends the volume of production, the more it must bury everything under mountains of suffocating waste. The concept of *economy* is radically incompatible with the 'economy' of capital production which, of necessity, adds insult to injury by first using up with rapacious wastefulness the *limited resources* of our planet, and then further aggravates the outcome by *polluting and poisoning* the human environment with its mass-produced waste and effluence.

Ironically, though, again, the system breaks down at the point of its supreme power; for its maximum extension inevitably generates the vital need for restraint and *conscious control* with which capital production is structurally incompatible. Thus, the establishment of the new mode of social control is inseparable from the realization of the principles of a *socialist economy* which centre on a *meaningful economy of productive activity:* the pivotal point of a rich human fulfilment in a society emancipated from the alienated and reified institutions of control.

AND the final point to stress is the necessarily global determination of the alternative system of social control, in confrontation with the global system of capital as a mode of control. In the world as it has been — and is still being — transformed by the immense power of capital, the social institutions constitute a closely interlocking system. Thus, there is no hope for *isolated partial* successes, only for *global* ones — however paradoxical this might sound. Accordingly, the crucial criterion for the assessment of partial measures is whether or not they are capable of functioning as 'Archimedean points': i.e. as *strategic levers* for a radical restructuring of the global system of social control. This is why Marx spoke of the vital necessity of changing, 'from top to bottom', the conditions of existence *as a whole,* short of which all efforts directed at a socialist emancipation of mankind are doomed to failure. Such a programme, it goes without saying, embraces the 'micro-structures' (like the family) just as much as the most comprehensive institutions (the 'macro-structures') of political and economic life. Indeed, as Marx had suggested, nothing less than a radical transformation of our 'whole manner of being' can produce an adequate system of social control.

ITS establishment will, no doubt, take time and will require the most active involvement of the whole community of producers, activating the repressed creative energies of the various social groups over matters incomparably greater in importance than deciding the colour of local lamp-posts to which their 'power of decision-making' is confined today.

The establishment of this social control will, equally, require the conscious cultivation — not in isolated individuals but in the whole community of producers, to whatever walk of life they may belong — of an uncompromising critical awareness, coupled with an intense commitment to the values of a socialist humanity, which guided the work of Isaac Deutscher to a rich fulfilment.

Thus, our memorial is not a ritual remembrance of the past but a persistent challenge to face up to the demands inherent in our own share of a shared task.

It is in this spirit that I wish to dedicate my lecture to the memory of Isaac Deutscher.

NOTES
[1] Isaac Deutscher, *The Unfinished Revolution*, Oxford University Press, 1967, pp. 110-4.
[2] W.W. Rostow, *The Stages of Economic Growth: A Non-Communist Manifesto*, Cambridge University Press, 1960, pp. 157-164.
[3] People often forget that President Kennedy was directly responsible for the escalating

U.S. involvement in Vietnam, inaugurating a whole series of disastrous policies conceived on the basis of 'theories' like the one quoted above.

⁴ Here is a graphic example of tautological apologetics based on a retrospective reconstruction of the past in the key of an idealized present of U.S. capitalism:

> The relative inter-war stagnation in Western Europe was due not to long-run diminishing return but to the *failure* of Western Europe to create a setting in which its national societies moved promptly into the age of high mass-consumption, yielding new leading sectors. And this *failure*, in turn, was due mainly to a *failure* to create initial full employment in the post-1920 setting of the terms of trade. Similarly the protracted depression of the United States in the 1930s was due not to long-run diminishing returns, but to a *failure* to create an initial renewed setting of full employment, through public policy, which *would have permitted* the new leading sectors of suburban housing, the diffusion of automobiles, durable consumers' goods and services to roll forward beyond 1929. (Rostow, *op. cit.*, p. 155.)

Thus, 'failures' (crises and recessions) are explained by the 'failure' to realize the conditions which 'would have permitted' the avoidance of those unfortunate 'failures', by producing the present-day pattern of capitalist 'high-consumption' which is, of course, the non plus ultra of everything. How those unfortunate, failure-explanatory failures came into being, we are not told. Since, however, the point of the whole exercise is the propagation of Rostow's 'objective' and 'non-parochial' *Non-Communist Manifesto* as the ultimate salvation of U.S. dominated world capitalism, by implication we can take it that the 'failures' in question must have been due to the absence of this retrospective-tautological economico-political wisdom. By what 'failures' he would explain today's rising unemployment and the associated symptoms of serious structural disturbances in the U.S. as well as in other parts of the capitalist world of 'high mass-consumption', 'suburban housing', etc., must remain, unfortunately, a mystery to us, since there are no 'new leading sectors' in sight whose creation 'would have permitted' the avoidance of present-day failures.

⁵ Rostow, *op. cit.*, p. 163.

⁶ Marx, *The German Ideology*, pp. 55-6.

⁷ *Ibid.*, p. 56.

⁸ I have discussed several related problems in 'Contingent and Necessary Class Consciousness', my contribution to *Aspects of History and Class Consciousness*, Essays by Tom Bottomore, David Daiches, Lucien Goldmann, Arnold Hauser, E.J. Hobsbawm, István Mészáros, Ralph Miliband, Rudolf Schlesinger, Anthony Thorlby, Edited by I. Mészáros, Routledge & Kegan Paul, London, 1971; reprinted in István Mészáros, *Philosophy, Ideology and Social Science'*, Harvester Press, Brighton, 1986, pp. 57-104.

⁹ See Marx, *Grundrisse der Kritik der politischen Ökonomie*, Berlin, 1953, pp. 593-4.

¹⁰ This is how the 'Voice of America' introduces its programme of interviews with intellectuals on 'Man and his Survival':

> The order of importance of great tasks has changed. Today no longer the clash of *national interests*, or the struggle for *political power* occupy the first place; nor indeed the elimination of *social injustice*. The outstanding issue by now is whether or not mankind will succeed in securing the conditions of its survival in a world it has transformed. ... No wonder that the President of the United States has dedicated two thirds of his latest 'State of the Union' message to the question of how to rehabilitate the environment from pollution. What happens, though, if man, instead of thinking about his own survival, *wastes his energies in fighting for the relative truth of various ideologies and social-political systems?* What are the first steps mankind ought to take in order *to reform itself and the world?*'

Further comment is quite unnecessary, thanks to the transparency of these lines.

[11] A capability so far very effectively paralysed by the guardians of the ruling order. For a penetrating analysis of the dynamic potentialities of the 'mass media', see Hans Magnus Enzensberger: 'Constituents of a Theory of the Media', *New Left Review*, No. 64 (Nov.-Dec. 1970), pp.13-36.

[12] E.J. Mishan, *The Cost of Economic Growth*, Penguin Books, 1969, p. 225.

[13] 6 November, 1957.

[14] On Saturday, March 17, 1883, the London *Times* published the following notice:

Our Paris correspondent informs us of the death of Dr. Karl Marx, which occurred last Wednesday, in London. He was born at Cologne, in the year 1818. At the age of 25 he had to leave his native country and take refuge in France, on account of the Radical opinions expressed in a paper of which he was editor. In France he gave himself up to the study of philosophy and politics, and made himself so obnoxious to the Prussian Government by his writings, that he was expelled from France, and lived for a time in Belgium. In 1847 he assisted at the Working Men's Congress in London, and was one of the authors of the 'Manifesto of the Communist Party'. After the Revolution of 1848 he returned to Paris, and afterwards to his native city of Cologne, from which he was again expelled for his revolutionary writings, and after escaping from imprisonment in France, he settled in London. From this time he was one of the leaders of the Socialist Party in Europe, and in 1866 he became its acknowledged chief. He wrote pamphlets on various subjects, but his chief work was 'Le Capital', an attack on the whole capitalist system. For some time he had been suffering from weak health.

What is remarkable about this piece is not only its provenance from Paris but also the way in which the class solidarity of international capital is revealed in it through reporting the concerted reactions of governments (the Prussian Government is annoyed — thus — the French Government acts) to the 'obnoxiousness' of the man who dared to write 'an attack on the whole capitalist system'.

[15] Editorial, *The Times*, 17 October, 1970.

[16] 20 October, 1970.

[17] Marx's comments on the Prussian censorship instructions throw an interesting light on this 'liberal' mode of arguing:

'Nothing will be tolerated which opposes Christian religion in general or a particular doctrine in a frivolous and hostile manner.' How cleverly put: *frivolous, hostile*. The adjective 'frivolous' appeals to the *citizen's sense of propriety* and is the exoteric term in the *public view*; but the adjective 'hostile' is whispered into the *censor's ear* and becomes the *legal interpretation* of frivolity.

In our quotation the corresponding terms are: 'the influence of society' (for the citizen's sense of propriety) and 'all the power of government' (for the authoritarian state official's ear).

[18] As the editors of the *Trade Union Register* rightly emphasize:

The similarities between the two documents [i.e. the Tory *Fair Deal at Work* and Labour's *In Place of Strife*] are considerable, and certainly more substantial than their differences. This consensus reflects the whole tendency in orthodox political circles to assume that workers (not *necessarily* trade unions) have too much freedom and power in the exercise of strike action and other forms of industrial collective pressure, and that it is legitimate for the state to legislate with a view to restraining and limiting those freedoms and powers. In view of the enormous recent increases in the authority and influence of the state itself, and of large irresponsible private industrial and commercial companies, against which the independent forces of organized labour alone stand as a guarantee of ultimate civic and political liberties, the consensus view prevailing in the political parties of the centre and right requires the

most vigorous and thorough opposition from the labour movement.
Trade Union Register 1970, Merlin Press, London 1970, p. 276.

[19] Barbara Castle, 'The Bad Bosses' Charter', *New Statesman*, 16 October 1970.

[20] When Mr. Heath nationalizes Rolls Royce (after his repeated denunciation of the measure of nationalization as a 'doctrinaire socialist nonsense'), all he carries out is, of course, nothing but the 'nationalization' of capitalist bankruptcy in a key sector of commodity production. The fact, though, that the immediate cause of this step was a contract negotiated by the outgoing Labour Government (envisaging the balancing of enormous private losses from public funds), only highlights the surrender of both parties to the dictates of the prevailing capitalist structure of production. Such dictates prescribe the transference of the non-profitable branches of industry into the 'public' (i.e. state-bureaucracy controlled) sector so that they can be turned into further subsidies at the service of monopoly capital. Thankfully, this particular act of 'nationalization' has been carried out by a Conservative Government — which makes it a less mystifying event. For had it been implemented by a Labour Government, it would have been loudly hailed as a great landmark of 'pragmatic socialism'.

[21] Marx, *The Poverty of Philosophy*, Lawrence & Wishart, London, n.d., p. 123.

[22] They are in the process of disintegration precisely because — due to their inherent contradictions — they are unable to cope with the vital functions they are supposed to carry out in the totality of social intercourse.

II. POLITICAL POWER AND DISSENT
IN POSTREVOLUTIONARY SOCIETIES*

1. 'There will be no more political power properly so called'

THE question of political power in post-revolutionary societies is and remains one of the most neglected areas of Marxist theory. Marx formulated the principle of the abolition of 'political power properly so-called' in no uncertain terms: 'The organization of revolutionary elements as a class supposes the existence of all the productive forces which could be engendered in the bosom of the old society. Does this mean that after the fall of the old society there will be a new class domination culminating in a *new political power*? No. The condition for the emancipation of the working class is the abolition of every class, just as the condition for the liberation of the Third Estate, of the bourgeois order, was the abolition of all estates and all orders. The working class, in the course of its development, will substitute for the old civil society an association which will exclude classes and their antagonisms, and *there will be no more political power properly so-called*, since political power is precisely the official expression of antagonism in civil society.'[1] And he was categorical in asserting that 'when the proletariat is victorious, it by no means becomes the absolute side of society, for it is *victorious only by abolishing itself and its opposite*. Then *the proletariat disappears* as well as the opposite which determines it, private property.'[2]

But what happens to political power in post-revolutionary societies when the proletariat does not disappear? What becomes of private property or capital when private ownership of the means of production is abolished while the proletariat continues to exist and rules the whole of society — including itself — under the new political power called 'the dictatorship of the proletariat'? For according to Marx's principle the two sides of the opposition stand or fall together, and the proletariat cannot be truly victorious without abolishing itself. Nor can it fully abolish its opposite without at the same time abolishing itself as a class which needs the new political form of the dictatorship of the proletariat in order to secure, and maintain itself in, power.

It would be mere sophistry to try and get out of these difficulties by suggesting that the new political power is not 'political power properly so-called'; in other words that it is not the manifestation of deep-seated objective antagonisms. For the existence of such antagonisms is painfully in evidence everywhere, and the severity of measures devised to prevent their eruption — by no means with guaranteed success — provides an eloquent refutation of all evasive sophistry.

Nor is it possible to take seriously for a moment the self-justifying suggestion that the political power of the post-revolutionary state is maintained — indeed

---

* Intervention at the *Convegno del Manifesto* on 'Power and Opposition in Postrevolutionary Societies', held in Venice on 11-13 November 1977. First published in English in *New Left Review*, No. 108 (March/April 1978), pp. 3-21.

intensified — in function of a purely *international* determination, in that political repression is explained as the necessary consequence of 'encirclement' and as the only feasible form of defending the achievements of the revolution against external aggression and its complementary: internal subversion. As recent history loudly testifies, 'the enemy within and without' as the explanation of the nature of political power in post-revolutionary societies is a dangerous doctrine which substitutes the part for the whole in order to transform a partial determination into a wholesale *a priori* justification of the unjustifiable: the institutionalized violation of elementary socialist rights and values.

The task is, clearly, an investigation — without apologetic preconceptions — of the specific political antagonisms which come to the fore in post-revolutionary societies, together with their material bases indirectly identified by Marx's principle concerning the simultaneous abolition of *both sides* of the old socio-economic antagonism as the necessary condition of proletarian victory. This does not mean, in the least, that we have to commit ourselves in advance to some theory of a 'new class'. For postulating a 'new class' is only another type of preconception which does not explain on its own anything at all. On the contrary, it badly needs explanation itself.

NOR does the magic umbrella term 'bureaucratism' — which covers almost everything, including the assessment of qualitatively different social systems approached from opposite standpoints, from Max Weber to some of Trotsky's followers — provide a meaningful explanation of the nature of political power in post-revolutionary societies, in that it merely points to some obvious appearances while begging the question as to their causes. In other words, it presents the *effect* of far-reaching causal determinations as itself a *causal explanation*.

Similarly, the hypothesis of 'state capitalism' will not do. Not only because it confounds the issues with some present-day tendencies of development in the most advanced capitalist societies (tendencies very briefly touched upon by Marx himself), but also because it has to omit from its analysis some highly significant objective characteristics of post-revolutionary societies in order to make the application of this problematic label look plausible. Labels, no matter how tempting, do not solve complex theoretical issues, only bypass them while giving the illusion of a solution.

BY the same token, it would be somewhat naive to imagine that we can leave these problems behind by declaring that the dictatorship of the proletariat as a political form belongs to the past, whereas the present and future are to be envisaged according to the principle of political pluralism — which, in turn, necessarily implies a conception of shared power as a 'historical compromise'. For even if we accept the pragmatic viability and relative historical validity of this conception, the question of how to constitute and exercise political power which actively contributes to a socialist transformation of society, instead of postponing indefinitely its realization, remains just as unanswered as before.

There are some worrying dilemmas here which must be answered. In the framework of the newly envisaged pluralism, is it possible to escape the well-known historical fate of Social Democracy, which resigned itself to the

illusion of 'sharing power' with the bourgeoisie while in fact helping to perpetuate the rule of capital over society? If it is not possible — if, that is, the political
form of pluralism itself is by its very nature a submission to the prevailing form
of class domination, as some would argue — in that case why should committed
socialists be interested in it in the slightest? But if, on the other hand, the idea
of pluralism is advocated in the perspective of a genuine socialist transformation,
it must be explained how it is possible to proceed from *shared power* to *socialist
power*, without relapsing into the selfsame contradictions of political power in
post-revolutionary societies whose manifestations we have witnessed on so many
occasions.

This is what gives a burning topicality to this whole discussion. The question
of political power in post-revolutionary societies is no longer an academic matter.
Nor can it be left anchored to the interests of conservative political propaganda
and dismissed by the Left as such. Quite unlike 1956 — when these contradictions erupted in such a clamorous and tragic form — it is no longer possible for
any section of the Left to turn its back to it. Facing the issues involved has
become an essential condition of advance for the entire working-class movement, under conditions when in some countries it may be called upon to assume
the responsibilities of sharing power, in the midst of the deepening structural
crisis of capital.

2. The ideal and the 'force of circumstance'

IF there has ever been a need to go back to the original sources and principles
in order to examine the conditions of their formulation, together with all the
necessary implications for present-day conditions and circumstances, it is precisely on these issues. But as soon as we admit this and try to act accordingly,
we are immediately presented with some great difficulties. For Marx's original
definition of political power as the necessary manifestation of class antagonism
contrasts the realities of class society with fully realized socialism in which there
can be no room for separate organs of political power, since 'the social life-process
... becomes production by *freely* associated men, and stands under their conscious
and planned control'.[3]

But try and replace the plan consciously arrived at by the totality of individual
producers by a plan imposed upon them from above, then the concept of *'freely*
associated men' must also be thrown out and replaced by that of a *forced*
association, inevitably envisaging the exercise of political power as separate from
and opposed to the society of producers, who must be compelled to accept and
implement aims and objectives which do not issue from their conscious deliberations but, on the contrary, negate the very idea of free association and
conscious deliberation. Or, vice versa, try and obliterate the concept of 'freely
associated *individuals*'; worse still, arbitrarily declare, in the spirit of whatever
form of Stalinism, that such concepts are purely 'ideological' remnants of a
'moralizing bourgeois individualism', even if this means that from now on,
however surreptitiously, a significant portion of Marx's own work too has to be
obliterated with the same label — and there will be no way of conceiving and
envisaging (let alone practising) the elaboration and implementation of social
planning except as a forced imposition from above.

Thus we witness the complete transformation of Marx's ideal into a reality which replaces the self-determining life-activity of freely associated social individuals by the forced association of men ruled by an alien political force. Simultaneously, Marx's concept of conscious *social* plan (which is supposed to regulate, through the full involvement of the freely associated individuals, the totality of the life-processes of society) suffers the gravest reduction, becoming a one-sided, technocratically preconceived and often unfulfilled mere *economic* plan, and thus superimposing upon society in a new form the selfsame economic determinations whose supersession constituted the framework of orientation of scientific socialism from the moment of its inception.

Furthermore, since now the two basic constituents of a dialectical unity, the association of producers and the regulatory force of the plan, are divorced from and opposed to one another, the 'force of circumstance' — which is the necessary consequence of this separation rather than its cause, whatever the historically changing social determinants at work — becomes the unqualified cause, indeed the 'inevitable cause'. And since the 'inevitable cause' is also its own justification, the transformation is carried even further, setting itself up as the only possible form of realization of Marx's ideal: as the unsurpassable *model* of all possible socialist development. From now on, since the prevailing form of political rule must be maintained and therefore everything must remain as it is, the problematical notion of the 'force of circumstance' is used in the argument in order to assert categorically that it *could not have been otherwise*, and thus it is *right* that everything should be as it is. In other words, Marx's ideal is transformed into a highly problematical reality, which in its turn is reconverted into a totally untenable model and ideal, through a most tortuous use of the 'force of circumstance' as both inevitable cause and normative justification, while in fact it should be critically examined and challenged on both counts.

TO be sure, this double perversion is not the product of one-sided theory, though it represents an apologetic capitulation of theory to the 'force of circumstance', which in its turn is brought into existence as a result of immensely complex and contradictory social determinations, including the share of theoretical failure as a significant contributory factor to the overall process. But once this process is accomplished and a uniform praise of the perverted ideals is imposed by the force of law, condemning as 'heresy' and 'subversion' all voices of dissent, critical reflection must assume the form of bitter, self-torturing irony. Such as the answer given by the mythical 'Radio Yerevan' to the question of an anonymous listener who asks: 'Is it true that we have socialism in our country?' The answer is given in an oblique form as follows: 'You are asking, Comrade, whether it is true that luxurious American motor cars will be given away Saturday afternoon on Red Square. It is perfectly true, with three qualifications: they won't be American, they will be Russian; they won't be motor cars, they will be bicycles; and they won't be given away, they will be taken away.' Cynically nihilistic though this may sound, who can fail to perceive in it the voice of impotence protesting in vain against the systematic frustration and violation of the ideals of socialism?

Admittedly, the problem of political power in post-revolutionary societies cannot be solved by simply reiterating an ideal in its original formulation. For by their very nature these problems belong to the period of *transition* which imposes its painful qualifications on all of us. All the same, there is a moral for us too in the story of 'Radio Yerevan'. It is that we should never consent to 'qualifications' which obliterate the ideal itself and turn it into its opposite. To ignore the 'force of circumstance' would be tantamount to living in the world of fantasy. But whatever the circumstances, the ideal remains valid as the vital compass that secures the chosen direction of the journey and as the necessary corrective to the power of *vis major* which tends to take over in the absence of such corrective.

3. Political power in the society of transition

IS it possible to identify the necessary socio-historical qualifications which apply the spirit of Marx's original formulations to the concrete realities of a complex historical transition from one social formation to another? How is it possible to envisage this transition in a political form that does not become its own self-perpetuation, thus contradicting and effectively nullifying the very idea of a transition which alone can justify the continued, but in principle diminishing, importance of the political form? Is it possible to have such qualifications without liquidating Marx's theoretical framework and its implications for our problem?

As we have seen, Marx's original definition concerned political power as the direct manifestation of class antagonism. This was contrasted by Marx with its opposite: the abolition of political power properly so-called in a fully realized socialist society. But what happens in between? Is it possible to break the old, entrenched political power without necessarily resorting to the exercise of a fully articulated system of political power?

If not, how is it possible to envisage a change of course 'halfway through' — namely, the radical transformation of a powerful system of *self-sustaining* political power which controls the whole of society, into a *self-transcending* organ which progressively transfers the manifold functions of political control to the social body itself, thus enabling the emergence of that free association of men and women without which the life-process of society remains under the domination of alien forces, instead of being consciously regulated by the social individuals involved in accordance with the ideals of self-determination and self-realization? And finally, if the transitional forms of political power stubbornly refuse to show signs of 'withering away', how should one assess the contradictions involved: as the failure of a 'utopian' Marxism, or as the historically determinate manifestation of objective antagonisms whose elucidation is well within the compass of Marx's original project?

MARX'S assertion about the supersession of political power in socialist society is coupled with two important considerations. First, that the free association of social individuals who consciously regulate their own life-activities in accordance with a settled plan is not feasible without the necessary '*material foundation*, or a series of material conditions of existence, which in their turn are the natural and *spontaneous* product of a *long and tormented* historical development'.[4] The emancipation of labour from the rule of capital is feasible only if the objective *conditions of its emancipation* are fulfilled whereby 'the direct material production process is stripped of the form of *penury and antithesis*', giving way to the '*free development of individualities*'.[5] By implication, so long as 'penury and antithesis' remain characteristics of the material base of society, the political form must suffer their consequences and the 'free development of individualities' is hindered and postponed.

The second consideration is closely linked to the first: Since overcoming the conditions of 'penury and antithesis' necessarily implied the highest development of the forces of production, successful revolution had to be envisaged by Marx in capitalistically advanced countries, and not on the periphery of world capitalist developments (although he touched upon the possibility of revolutions away from the socio-economically most dynamic centre, without however entering into a discussion of the necessary implications of such possibilities). Inasmuch as the object of his analysis was the power of capital as a world system, he had to contemplate a breakthrough, under the impact of a profound structural crisis, in the form of more or less simultaneous revolutions in the major capitalist countries.

As to the problems of political power in the period of transition, Marx introduced the concept of the 'dictatorship of the proletariat', and in one of his later works, *The Critique of the Gotha Programme*, he addressed himself to some additional problems of a transitional society as manifested in the politico-legal sphere. While these elements of his theory certainly do not constitute a system (the sequel to *Capital* which was supposed to develop the political implications of Marx's global theory in a systematic way was never even sketched, let alone fully worked out), they are important signposts and must be complemented by certain other elements of his theory (notably the assessment of the relationship between individual and class, and of the structural interdependence between capital and labour) which have a significant bearing on the strictly political issues, as we shall see in a moment.

IT was Lenin, as we all know, who worked out the strategy of revolution 'at the weakest link of the chain', insisting that the dictatorship of the proletariat must be considered as the only viable political form for the entire historical period of transition that precedes the highest stage of communism, in which it finally becomes possible to implement the principle of freedom. The most significant shift in his analysis was envisaging that the 'material foundation' and the supersession of 'penury' will be accomplished under the dictatorship of the proletariat in a country which sets out from an extremely low level of development. Yet Lenin saw no problem in suggesting in December 1918 that the new state will be *'democratic* for the proletariat and the propertyless in general and *dictatorial* against the bourgeoisie' only.[6]

There was a curious flaw in his usually impeccable reasoning. He argued that 'thanks to capitalism, the material apparatus of the big banks, syndicates, railways, and so forth, has grown' and 'the immense experience of the *advanced countries* has accumulated a stock of engineering marvels, the employment of which is being hindered by capitalism', concluding that the Bolsheviks (who were in fact confined to a *backward country*) could 'lay hold of this apparatus and set it in motion'.[7] Thus the immense difficulties of transition from one particular revolution to the irrevocable success of a global revolution (which is beyond the control of any one particular agency, however class-conscious and disciplined) were more or less implicitly brushed aside by voluntaristically postulating that the Bolsheviks were capable of taking power and 'retaining it until the triumph of the world socialist revolution'.[8]

Thus, while the viability of a socialist revolution at the weakest link of the chain was advocated, the imperative of a world revolution as a condition of success of the former reasserted itself in a most uneasy form: as an insoluble tension at the very heart of the theory. But what could one say in the event the world socialist revolution did not come about and the Bolsheviks were condemned to hold on to power indefinitely? Lenin and his revolutionary comrades were unwilling to entertain that question, since it conflicted with certain elements of their outlook. They had to claim the viability of their strategy in a form which necessarily implied anticipating revolutionary developments in areas over which their forces had no control whatsoever. In other words, their strategy involved the contradiction between two imperatives: first, the need to go it alone, as the *immediate* (historical) pre-condition of success (of doing it at all); secondly, the imperative of the triumph of the world socialist revolution as the *ultimate* (structural) precondition of success of the whole enterprise.

Understandably, therefore, when the actual conquest of power in October 1917 created a new situation, Lenin exclaimed with a sigh of relief: 'It is more pleasant and useful to go through the "experience of the revolution" than to write about it.'[9] And again: 'The October 25 Revolution has transferred the question raised in this pamphlet from the sphere of theory to the sphere of practice. This question must now be answered by deeds, not words.'[10] But how deeds could themselves answer the dilemma concerning the grave difficulties of accomplishing all the necessary 'material groundwork' which constitutes the prerequisite of a successful socialist transformation, without 'words' — without, that is, a coherent theory which soberly assesses the massive potential dangers involved, indicating at the same time, if feasible, the possibilities of a solution to them — Lenin did not say. He simply could not envisage the possibility of an objective contradiction between the dictatorship of the proletariat and the proletariat itself.

WHILE in March and April 1917 Lenin was still advocating 'a state *without* a standing army, *without* a police opposed to the people, *without* an officialdom placed above the people',[11] and proposed to 'organize and arm *all* the poor, exploited sections of the population in order that *they themselves* should take the organs of state power directly into their own hands, in order that *they themselves should constitute* these organs of state power',[12] a significant shift became visible in his orientation after the seizure of power. The main themes of *The State and Revolution* receded further and further in his thought. Positive references to the experience of the Paris Commune (as the *direct* involvement of *'all* the poor, exploited sections of the population' in the exercise of power) disappeared from his speeches and writings; and the accent was laid on 'the need for a *central authority*, for dictatorship and a united will to ensure that the *vanguard* of the proletariat shall close *its ranks, develop the state* and place it upon a new footing, while *firmly holding the reins of power*'.[13]

Thus, in contrast to the original intentions which predicated the fundamental identity of the *'entire armed people'*[14] with state power, there appeared a separation of the latter from 'the working people', whereby *'state power* is organizing large-scale production on *state-owned* land and in *state-owned* enterprises on a national scale, is *distributing labour-power* among the various branches of economy and the various enterprises, and is *distributing among the working people* large quantities of articles of consumption *belonging to the state*'.[15] The fact that the relationship of the working people to state power manifested as the *central distribution of labour-power* was a relationship of structural subordination did not seem to trouble Lenin, who bypassed this issue by simply describing the new form of separate state power as 'the proletarian state power'.[16] Thus the objective contradiction between the dictatorship of the proletariat and the proletariat itself disappeared from his horizon at the very moment it surfaced as centralized state power which determines on its own the distribution of labour-power.

At the most generic level of class relations — corresponding to the polar opposition between the proletariat and the bourgeoisie — the contradiction did not seem to exist. The new state had to secure its own material base and the central distribution of labour-power appeared to be the only viable principle for achieving this, *from the standpoint of the state already in existence*.[17] In reality, however, it was 'the working people' themselves who had to be reduced to and distributed as 'labour-power': not only over immense geographical distances — with all the upheavals and dislocations inevitably involved in such a centrally imposed system of distribution — but also 'vertically' in each and every locality, in accordance with both the material dictates of the inherited production structures and the political dictates inherent in their newly constituted principle and organs of regulation.

4. Lukács's solution
NO matter how problematical his conclusions, it was Lukács's great intellectual merit to have highlighted this dilemma in a most acute form, in one of his relatively unknown articles, written in the spring of 1919. The issue is important enough to warrant the long quotation needed to reproduce the train of his thought:

> It is clear that the most oppressive phenomena of proletarian power — namely, the scarcity of goods and high prices, of whose immediate consequences every proletarian has personal experience — are the direct consequences of the slackening of labour-discipline and the decline in production. The creation of remedies for these, and the consequent improvement in the individual's standard of living, can only be brought about when the causes of these phenomena have been removed.
> Help comes in two ways. Either the individuals who constitute the proletariat *realize* that they can help themselves only by bringing about a voluntary strengthening of labour-discipline, and consequently a rise in production: or, if they are incapable of this, *they create institutions which are suitable to bring about this necessary state of affairs*. In the latter case, they create a legal system through which the proletariat *compels* its own individual members, the proletarians, to act in a way which corresponds to their class-interests: *the proletariat turns its dictatorship against itself*. This measure is necessary for the self-preservation of the proletariat when correct recognition of class-interests and voluntary action in these interests do not exist. But one must not hide from oneself the fact that this method contains within itself *great dangers for the future*. When the proletariat itself is the creator of labour-discipline, when the labour-system of the proletarian state is built on a *moral* basis, then the external compulsion of the law ceases *automatically* with the abolition of class division — that is, the state

withers away — and this liquidation of class-division produces out of itself the beginning of the true history of humanity, which Marx prophesied and hoped for. If, on the other hand, the proletariat follows another path, it must create a legal system which cannot be abolished automatically by historical development. Development would therefore proceed in a direction which *endangered the appearance and realization of the ultimate aim*. For the legal system which the proletariat is compelled to create in this way *must be overthrown* — and who knows what convulsions and what injuries will be caused by a transition which leads from the kingdom of necessity to the kingdom of freedom by such a *détour*? ... It depends on the proletariat whether the real history of humanity begins — that is to say, *the power of morality over institutions and economics*.[18]

This quotation shows Lukács's great power of insight as regards the objective dialectic of a certain type of development, formulated from a rather abstract philosophical point of view. Lenin, by comparison, preferring 'deeds' to 'words', was far too busy trying to squeeze out the last drop of practical socialist possibilities from the objective instrumental set-up of his situation to indulge in theoretical anticipations of this kind in 1919. By the time he started to concentrate on the dreadful danger of an ever-increasing domination of the ideals of socialism by the 'institutions of necessity', it was too late — not only for him personally, but historically too late — to reverse the course of developments. The ideal of autonomous working-class action had been replaced by the advocacy of 'the greatest possible centralization'. For, in Lenin's words:

> Communism requires and presupposes the *greatest possible centralization* of large-scale production throughout the country. The all-Russia centre, therefore, should definitely be given the right of *direct control* over *all* the enterprises of the given branch of industry. The regional centres define their functions depending on local conditions of life, etc., in accordance with the *general* production directions and *decisions of the centre*.[19]

Accordingly, both the Soviets and the factory councils had been deprived of all effective power, and in the course of the trade-union debate all attempts at securing even a very limited degree of self-determination for the working-class base had been dismissed as 'syndicalist nonsense'[20] and as a 'deviation towards syndicalism and anarchism',[21] seen as a direct threat to the dictatorship of the proletariat.

The cruel irony of it all is that Lenin himself, totally dedicated as he was to the cause of the socialist revolution, helped to paralyse the selfsame forces of the working-class base to which he tried to turn later for help, when he perceived in Russia the fateful danger of those developments which were to culminate in Stalinism. Against this background, it is pathetic to see Lenin, a genius of realistic strategy, behaving like a desperate utopian from the beginning of 1923 to the moment of his death: insistently putting forward hopeless schemes — like the proposal to create a majority in the Central Committee from the working-class cadres, in order to neutralize the Party bureaucrats — in the hope of reversing this dangerous trend, by now far too advanced. Lenin's great tragedy was that his incomparable, instrumentally concrete, intensely practical strategy in the end defeated him. In the last year of his life, there was no longer a way out of his almost total isolation. The development he himself, far more than anybody else, had helped to set in motion made him historically redundant. The specific form in which he lived the unity of theory and practice proved to be the limit even of his greatness.

WHAT was extremely problematical in Lukács's discourse was the suggestion that the acceptance of the need for higher productivity and greater labour discipline — as a result of the philosopher's direct moral appeal to the consciousness of individual proletarians — might avert the danger so graphically described and render the creation of the institutions of necessity superfluous. What degree of labour discipline is high enough under the conditions of extreme urgency of the necessary 'material groundwork'? Is 'correct recognition of class-interest' *ipso facto* the end of all possible objective contradictions between individual and class interest? These and similar questions did not appear on Lukács's horizon, which remained idealistically clouded by postulating an *individualistic yet uniform* moral base of social practice as an *alternative* to collective necessity. Nevertheless, he clearly spelled out not only the possibility of the proletariat turning its dictatorship against itself, but also the anguishing implications of such a state of affairs for the future when 'the legal system which the proletariat is compelled to create in this way *must be overthrown*'.

Was it this early thought, perhaps, which Lukács tried to amplify in much greater detail, in the light of subsequent developments, in an unpublished 'political testament' he wrote in 1968, following his bitter condemnation of the military intervention in Czechoslovakia? Be that as it may, the dilemma remains as acute as ever. What were those objective and subjective determinations which produced the submission of the proletariat to the political form through which it assumed power, and is it possible to overcome them? How is it possible to avoid the *potential convulsions* associated with the imperative need of changing in depth the prevailing forms of political rule? What are the conditions of transforming the existing rigid 'institutions of necessity', by means of which *dissent is suppressed and compulsion enforced,* into more flexible institutions of social involvement, foreshadowing that 'free development of individualities' which continues to elude us?

5. Individual and class

THIS is the point where we must put into relief the relevance for our problem of Marx's considerations of the relationship between individual and class. For in the absence of a proper understanding of this relationship, the transformation of the transitional political form into a dictatorship exercised also over the proletariat (notwithstanding the original democratic intent) remains deeply shrouded in mystery.

How is it possible for such a transformation to take place? The ideas of 'degeneration', 'bureaucratization', 'substitutionism' and the like not only beg the question, but also culminate in an illusory remedy, explicit or implied: namely, that the simple overthrow of this political form and the substitution of dedicated revolutionaries for party bureaucrats will reverse the process — forgetting that the blamed party bureaucrats too were in their time dedicated revolutionaries. Hypotheses of this kind idealistically transfer the problem from the plane of objective contradictions to that of individual psychology, which can explain at best only the question of why a certain type of person is best suited to mediate the objective structures of a given political form, but not the nature of those structures themselves.

Similarly, it would be very naive to accept that the new structures of political domination suddenly and automatically — and just as mysteriously — come into existence following the refusal of proletarians to accept an intensified labour-discipline and a self-sacrifice that have been dictated to them. On the contrary, the very fact that the question can be raised in this form is itself already evidence that the structures of domination are in existence before the question is even thought of.

Admonitions and threats are empty words if they do not issue out of materially sustained power. But if they do, it is an idealistic reversal of the actual state of affairs to represent *material dictates* as *moral imperatives* which, if unheeded, would be followed by material dictates and sanctions. In reality, material dictates are internalized as moral imperatives only under the exceptional circumstances of a *state of emergency*, when reality itself rules out the possibility of alternative courses of action. To identify the two — i.e. to treat material dictates as moral imperatives — would mean to lock the life-processes of society into the unbearably narrow confines of a permanent state of emergency.

WHAT are the structures of domination on the basis of which the new political form arises, which the latter must get rid of if it is not to remain a permanent obstacle to the realization of socialism? In discussions of Marx's critique of the state, what is usually forgotten is that it is not concerned simply with the determination of a specific form of class rule — the capitalist — but with a much more fundamental issue: the full emancipation of the social individual. The following quotation makes this amply clear:

> the proletarians, if they are to assert themselves as *individuals*, have to abolish the hitherto prevailing condition of their existence (which has, moreover, been that of all society up to then), namely, *labour*. Thus they find themselves directly opposed to the form in which, hitherto, the *individuals*, of which society consists, have given themselves *collective expression*, that is, the State. In order, therefore, *to assert themselves as individuals*, they must overthrow the state.[22]

Try and remove the concept of 'individuals' from this reasoning, and the whole enterprise becomes meaningless. For the need to abolish the State arises because the individuals cannot 'assert themselves as individuals', and not simply because one class is dominated by another.

The same consideration applies to the question of individual and class. Again, discussions of Marx's theory as a rule neglect this aspect, and concentrate on what he says about emancipating the proletariat from the bourgeoisie. But what would be the point of this emancipation if the individuals who constitute the proletariat remained dominated by the proletariat as a class? And it is precisely this relationship of domination which *precedes* the establishment of the dictatorship of the proletariat. There is no need to newly establish the domination of the proletarians by the proletariat, since that domination already exists, though in a different form, well before the question of taking power historically arises:

> the class in its turn assumes an *independent existence as against the individuals*, so that the latter find their conditions of life *predetermined*, and have their position in life and hence their personal development *assigned to them by their class*, thus become *subsumed* under it. This is the same phenomenon as the *subjection* of the separate individuals to

the division of labour and can only be removed by the *abolition* of private property and of *labour itself*.[23]

To be sure, this aspect of class domination holds in all forms of class society, irrespective of their specific political superstructures. Nor could it be otherwise, given the existence of irreconcilable inter-class antagonisms; indeed, the submission of the individuals to their class is a necessary concomitant of the latter.

Moreover, this condition applies just as much to advanced capitalist countries as to their more or less underdeveloped counterparts. It would, therefore, be illusory to expect that the political consequences of this objective structural contradiction could be avoided simply in virtue of some undeniable differences at the level of the legal-political superstructure. For the contradiction in question is an objective antagonism of the *socio-economic base* as structured according to a hierarchical *social division of labour*, though, of course, it also manifests itself at the political plane. Underneath any so-called 'elected dictatorship of Ministers'[24] (or, for that matter, under whatever other form of liberal democracy), there lies the 'unelected dictatorship' of the hierarchical-social division of labour. The latter structurally subordinates one class to another and at the same time subjects individuals to their own class as well, predestining them to a narrowly defined position and role in society in accordance with the material dictates of the prevailing socio-economic system, and thus unceremoniously ensures that, may Ministers come and go as the electors please, the structure of domination itself remains intact.

PARADOXICALLY, this dilemma of the structural domination of individuals by their own class becomes more rather than less acute in the aftermath of the revolution.

In the preceding form of society, the severity of inter-class antagonism gives an apparently — and to a significant extent also objectively — benevolent character to the subjection of individuals to their own class, in that the class does not champion only its own interests as a class but, simultaneously, also the interests of its individual members against the other class. Individual proletarians accept their subordination to their own class — though even that not without deep-seated conflict over objective sectional interests — since class solidarity is a *necessary prerequisite* of their emancipation from the rule of the capitalist class, even if it is at an astronomical distance from being the *sufficient condition* of their emancipation as *social individuals*. Once the capitalist class is defeated and expropriated, however, the objective structural contradiction between class and individual is activated in its full intensity, since the dampening factor of inter-class antagonism is effectively removed, or at least transferred to the international plane.

It is this contradiction between class and individual which is intensified in the aftermath of the revolution to the point that it may indeed, in the absence of adequate corrective forces and measures, endanger the very survival of the dictatorship of the proletariat and revert society to the *status quo ante*. What we witness, however, at the level of political ideology and practice is the misrepresentation of a necessary prerequisite of class emancipation as the sufficient condition of full emancipation, which is said to be hindered only by 'survivals from the past', or the 'survival of the class enemy'. Thus the rather intangible 'enemy within' becomes a mythical force whose empirical counterpart must be invented, to fill with millions of common people the emerging concentration camps.

One cannot emphasize too strongly that the ideological-political mystification does not feed on itself (if only it did, for that would be relatively easy to overcome), but on an objective contradiction of the socio-economic base. It is because 'the condition of existence of individual proletarians, namely labour'[25] is not abolished as Marx advocated — because, in other words, hierarchical social division of labour remains the fundamental regulatory force of the social metabolism — that the antagonism, deprived of its justification through the expropriation of the opposite class, intensifies, creating a new form of alienation between the individuals who constitute society on the one hand and the political power which controls their interchanges on the other.

It is because the dictatorship of the proletariat cannot remove the 'contradictions of civil society' by abolishing both sides of the social antagonism, including labour — on the contrary, it has to envisage enhancing the latter, in function of the absolutely necessary 'material foundation' — that 'the proletariat turns its dictatorship against itself'.[26] Or, to be more precise, in order to maintain its rule over society as a class, the proletariat turns its dictatorship against *all* individuals who constitute society, including the proletarians. (Indeed, including the party and state officials who have a mandate to carry out determinate functions and not others, following the imperatives of the system in existence and not their own exclusive sectional interests, even if by virtue of their privileged location with regard to the machinery of power they are in a position to appropriate a greater portion of the social product than other groups of individuals, whether or not they actually do so.)

SINCE one side of the antithesis Marx speaks of — labour — cannot be preserved on its own, under the new conditions of the post-revolutionary society, a new form of manifestation must be found for the other side as well. The expropriation of the capitalist class, and the radical disruption and alteration of the normal market conditions which characterize the functioning of commodity society, impose radically new functions on the proletarian state. It is called upon to regulate, *in toto* and in the smallest detail, the production and distribution process, directly determining the allocation of social resources, the conditions and the intensity of labour, the rate of surplus-extraction and accumulation, and the particular share of each individual in that portion of the social product which it makes available for consumption. From now on we are confronted with a system of production in which the *extraction of surplus-labour is politically determined* in the most summary form, using extra-economic criteria (ultimately the survival of the state itself) which, under determinate conditions, may in fact disrupt or even chronically retard the development of the productive forces.

Such a politically determined extraction of surplus-labour — which, under the conditions of extreme penury and in the absence of strictly economic regulatory forces and mechanisms, may indeed reach dangerously high levels, whereupon it becomes self-defeatingly counter-productive — inevitably sharpens the contradiction between individual producers and the state, with the gravest implications for the possibility of *dissent*. For under these circumstances dissent may directly endanger the extraction of surplus-labour (and everything else built upon it), thus potentially depriving the dictatorship of the proletariat of its material base and challenging its very survival.

By contrast, the liberal state, under normal conditions, has no need to regulate *directly* the extraction of surplus-value, since the complex mechanisms of commodity-production can take care of all that. All it has to do is to ensure *indirectly* the safeguard of the economic system itself. Therefore, it need not worry at all about the manifestations of political dissent, so long as the impersonal mechanisms of commodity-production carry on their functions undisturbed.

Of course, the situation significantly changes in capitalist countries at times of major crises, when the forces of opposition cannot confine themselves any longer to contesting only the *rate* of surplus-value extraction, but have to question the very *mode* of surplus-value production and appropriation. It they do this with any success, then the capitalist state may be compelled to assume very far from 'liberal' forms.

Similarly, under the conditions of present-day development, when we can witness as a trend that the whole system of global capitalism is becoming extremely 'dysfunctional', the state is forced to assume increasingly more direct regulatory functions, with potentially serious implications for dissent and opposition.

But even under such circumstances, the respective structures are fundamentally different in that the political involvement of the capitalist state applies to an all-pervasive system of commodity-production, and the ultimate aim of its interventions and emergency measures is the reconstitution of the self-regulatory function of the latter, whether it can be successfully accomplished or not.

By contrast, the post-revolutionary state combines, as a matter of *normality*, the function of overall political control with that of securing and regulating the extraction of surplus-labour as the new mode of carrying on the material life-processes of society. It is the close integration of the two which produces apparently insurmountable difficulties for dissent and opposition.

6. Breaking the rule of capital

ALL this puts sharply into relief the dilemmas we have to face when we try to envisage a socialist solution to the underlying problems. For, on the one hand, the liberal/capitalist practices of 'repressive tolerance' operate on the premise that dissent and protest may be allowed to become as loud as they please, so long as they cannot change anything at all,[28] while, on the other hand, their East European counterparts have a wider resonance in the social body, and hence the potential for contributing to real changes, but they are not allowed to voice their disagreements.

Is there a way out of this painful dilemma? If there is, it must be through the maturation of the objective conditions of development to which political movements can relate themselves, accelerating or frustrating their unfolding. In this respect, it matters very much indeed whether or not post-revolutionary societies represent some new form of capitalism ('state capitalism', for example). For if they do, with the advent of the revolution nothing has really happened: no real steps have been taken in the direction of emancipation, and the allegedly monolithic power of capitalism which prevails in all its forms makes the future look extremely gloomy.

MARX wrote his *Capital* to help break the rule of *capital*, not just *capitalism*. Yet, strangely enough, it is on the assessment of this innermost nature of his project that the misconceptions are the greatest and most damaging. The title of Book I of *Capital* (Volume One) was first translated into English, under Engels's supervision, as 'A Critical Analysis of Capitalist Production', whereas the original speaks of 'The Process of Production of Capital' *(Der Produktionsprozess des Kapitals)*, which is a radically different thing. Marx's project is concerned with the conditions of production and reproduction of *capital itself* — its genesis and expansion, as well as the inherent contradictions which foreshadow its supersession through a 'long and painful process of development' — whereas the mistranslated version speaks of a given *phase* of capital production only, conflating and confusing at the same time the concepts of 'capitalist production' and 'production of capital'.

In truth, the concept of capital is much more fundamental than that of capitalism. The latter is limited to a relatively short historical period, whereas the former embraces a great deal more. It is concerned, in addition to the mode of functioning of the given capitalist society, with the conditions of origin and development of capital production, including the phases when commodity-production is not all-pervasive and dominating as it is under capitalism. And on the other side of the radical socio-historical line of demarcation drawn by the breakdown of capitalism, it is equally concerned with the forms and modalities in which the need for capital production is bound to survive in post-capitalist societies for a long and painful historical period — until, that is, the hierarchical social division of labour itself is successfully superseded, and society is completely restructured in accordance with the free association of social individuals who consciously regulate their own life-activities.

The rule of capital, rooted in the prevailing system of division of labour (which cannot conceivably be abolished by a political act alone, no matter how radical and free from 'degeneration'), thus prevails over a significant part of the transitional period, although it must exhibit the characteristics of a *diminishing trend* if the transition is to be successful at all. But this does not mean that post-revolutionary societies remain 'capitalist', just as feudal and earlier societies cannot be rightfully characterized as capitalist on the basis of the more or less extensive use of monetary capital and the more or less advanced share which commodity-production, as a subordinate element, occupies in them.

The capitalist formation extends only over that particular phase of capital production in which:

- (1) *production for exchange* (and thus the mediation and domination of use-value by exchange-value) is *all-pervasive*;
- (2) *labour-power* itself, just as much as anything else, is treated as a *commodity*;
- (3) the drive for *profit* is the fundamental regulatory force of production;
- (4) the vital mechanism of the *extraction of surplus-value*, the radical separation of the means of production from the producers, assumes an *inherently economic form*;
- (5) the economically extracted surplus-value is *privately appropriated* by the

members of the capitalist class; and

- (6) following its own *economic imperative* of growth and expansion, capital production tends towards a *global integration*, through the intermediary of the world market, as a totally interdependent system of economic domination and subordination.

To speak of capitalism in post-revolutionary societies, when out of these essential defining characteristics only one — number four — remains, and even that in a *radically altered* form in that the extraction of surplus-labour is regulated politically and not economically, can be done only by disregarding or misrepresenting the objective conditions of development, with serious consequences for the possibility of gaining insight into the real nature of the problem at stake.

CAPITAL maintains its — by no means unrestricted — rule in post-revolutionary societies primarily through:

- (1) the material imperatives which circumscribe the possibilities of the totality of life-processes;
- (2) the inherited social division of labour which, notwithstanding its significant modifications, contradicts 'the development of free individualities';
- (3) the objective structure of the available production apparatus (including plant and machinery) and of the historically developed and restricted form of scientific knowledge, both originally produced in the framework of capital production and under the conditions of the social division of labour; and
- (4) the links and interconnections of the post-revolutionary societies with the global system of capitalism, whether these assume the form of a 'peaceful competition' (e.g., commercial and cultural exchange) or that of a potentially deadly opposition (from the arms race to more or less limited actual confrontations in contested areas).

Thus the issue is incomparably more complex and far-reaching than its conventional characterization as merely the imperative of capital accumulation, now renamed 'socialist accumulation'.

CAPITAL constitutes a highly contradictory world system, with the 'advanced' capitalist countries and the major post-revolutionary societies as its poles related to a multiplicity of gradations and stages of mixed development. It is this dynamic, contradictory totality which makes the possibilities of dissent and opposition much more hopeful than the monolithic conception of the power of capitalism would suggest. Post-revolutionary societies are also post-capitalist societies in the significant sense that their objective structures effectively resist the restoration of capitalism.

To be sure, their inner contradictions, further complicated and intensified by their interactions with capitalist countries, may produce shifts and adjustments within their structures *in favour of commodity relations*. Nevertheless, the possibility of such shifts and adjustments is fairly limited. It is circumscribed by the fact that *the political extraction of surplus-labour cannot be radically altered without profoundly affecting (indeed endangering) the political power in existence.** The system-

---

*   [A note is in order here. As we know, there were no attempts to overthrow the Soviet system from below. Moves for the restoration of capitalistic 'market society' were initiated and implemented from above by the Party hierarchy fused with the state security services.

atic frustration and prevention of dissent has its complement in the extremely limited success of recent attempts at introducing strictly economic mechanisms into the overall structure of production. Post-revolutionary societies, as yet, have no such self-regulatory mechanisms which would ensure that dissenters *'say whatever they please without changing anything at all'*. It would be a *Pyrrhic victory* if dissent developed in post-revolutionary societies parallel to the reintroduction of powerful capitalistic mechanisms and institutions.

Positive developments in this respect may be envisaged only if the system finds some way of achieving an effective, institutionally underpinned *distribution of political power* (even if very limited in the first place) which does not represent a *danger to the prevailing mode of extracting surplus-labour* as such — although of necessity it would question the particular manifestations and excesses of surplus-extraction. In other words, 'decentralization', 'diversification', 'autonomy' and the like must be implemented in post-revolutionary societies as — in the first place — *political* principles, in order to be meaningful at all.

THE dynamic, contradictory totality mentioned above is also an *interdependent* totality through and through. What happens at one place has an important bearing on the possibilities of development elsewhere. The demand for a much greater effectiveness of dissent and opposition in the West arises now under circumstances when the capitalist system exhibits severe symptoms of crisis, with potentially far-reaching consequences.

The weakening of the essential mechanisms of control of commodity society — which in their normal functioning successfully nullify dissent and opposition without the slightest need for politically suppressing them — offers more scope for the development of effective alternatives, and the debate on 'pluralism' must be situated in this problematic. At the same time, it is highly significant that virtually all forces of the left have thoroughly disengaged themselves from an earlier uncritical attitude towards the assessment of post-revolutionary developments. For the uncritical attitude in the past reflected a state of enforced *immobility*, and could not envisage more than repeatedly reasserting its ideal as a 'declaration of intent' about the future, however remote, instead of undertaking a realistic evaluation of a historical experience in relation to its own concrete tasks.

In a world of total interdependence, if lasting achievements result in this part of the world from the ongoing critical examination — which is inseparably also a critical self-examination — that will not be without positive consequences for the development of dissent and meaningful opposition in the post-revolutionary societies themselves.

Whether or not Gorbachev and his co-rulers knew it when they embarked on 'perestroika' without and against the people, their efforts to radically alter the political extraction of surplus-labour by grafting on it a capitalistic 'economic mechanism' not only 'endangered the political power in existence' but led to its overthrow by the Soviet type personifications of capital who were anxious to eternalize their rule through hereditary property rights. This is the sad meaning of the 'Pyrrhic victory' mentioned here.]

NOTES

[1] Marx, *The Poverty of Philosophy*, in Karl Marx and Frederick Engels, *Collected Works*, Lawrence and Wishart, London, 1975ff. (Henceforth referred to as MECW), Vol. 6, pp. 211-2.

[2] Marx, *The Holy Family*, in MECW, Vol. 4, p. 36.

[3] Marx, *Capital*, Penguin/NLR edition, Harmondsworth, 1976, Vol. 1, p.173.

[4] *Ibid.*

[5] Marx, *Grundrisse*, Penguin, Harmondsworth, 1973, p. 706.

[6] In a section added to the second edition of *The State and Revolution*. See Lenin, *Collected Works*, Lawrence & Wishart, London, 1960ff, Vol. 25, p.412.

[7] *Ibid.*, Vol. 26, p. 130.

[8] *Ibid.*

[9] *Ibid.*, Vol. 25, p. 412.

[10] *Ibid.*, Vol. 26, p. 89.

[11] *Ibid.*, Vol. 24, p. 49. (Lenin's emphasis).

[12] *Ibid.*, Vol. 23, p. 326. (Lenin's emphasis).

[13] *Ibid.*, Vol. 30, p. 422.

[14] *Ibid.*, Vol. 23, p. 325. (Lenin's emphasis).

[15] *Ibid.*, Vol. 30, pp. 108-9.

[16] *Ibid.*, p. 108.

[17] The extent to which the newly created state organs were structurally conditioned by the old state should not be underestimated. Lenin's analysis of this problem in his stocktaking speech on the NEP is most revealing:

> We took over the old machinery of the state, and *that was our misfortune*. Very often this machinery operates against us. In 1917, after we seized power, the government officials sabotaged us. This frightened us very much and we pleaded: 'Please come back.' They all came back but *that was our misfortune*. We now have a vast army of government employees, but lack sufficiently educated forces *to exercise real control over them*. In practice it often happens that here at the top, where we exercise political power, the machine functions somehow; but down below government employees have *arbitrary control* and they often exercise it in such a way as to *counteract our measures*. At the top, we have, I don't know how many, but at all events, I think, no more than a few thousand, at the outside several tens of thousands of our own people. Down below, however, there are hundreds of thousands of old officials whom we got from the Tsar and from bourgeois society and who, partly deliberately and partly unwittingly, work against us. (Lenin, *Collected Works*, Vol. 33, pp. 428-9.)

The new state power was constituted and consolidated through tensions and contradictions like these, which deeply affected its structural articulation at all levels. The old heritage, with its massive inertia, weighed heavily on successive stages of Soviet development. Not only in the sense that 'state officialdom placed above the people' could counteract the 'good measures' taken at the top where political power was being exercised, but even more so in that this type of decision-making — a far cry from the originally advocated alternative described in *The State and Revolution*, with reference to the principles of the Paris Commune — turned itself into an *ideal*. From now on the problem was identified as the conscious or unwitting obstruction of state authority by local officials and their allies, and the remedy as the strictest possible form of centralized control over all spheres of social life.

[18] 'Az erkölcs szerepe a komunista termelésben' (The Role of Morality in Communist

Production). The translation here is my own, but see Georg Lukács, *Political Writings: 1919-1929*, NLB, London, 1968, pp. 51-2.

[19] Lenin, *Collected Works*, Vol. 42, p. 96.

[20] 'All this syndicalist nonsense about mandatory nominations of producers must go into the wastepaper basket. To proceed on those lines would mean thrusting the Party aside and *making the dictatorship of the proletariat in Russia impossible.' Ibid.*, Vol. 32, p.62.

[21] *Ibid.*, p. 246. And again: 'The syndicalist malaise must and will be cured'. *Ibid.*, p.107.

[22] Marx and Engels, *The German Ideology*, in MECW, Vol. 5, p. 80.

[23] *Ibid.*, p. 77.

[24] To quote Lord Hailsham himself — a former Tory Minister and legal authority — who should really know.

[25] MECW, Vol. 5, p. 80.

[26] As Lukács put it in the passage quoted earlier.

[27] See in this respect Section 4. of my Isaac Deutscher Memorial Lecture, *The Necessity of Social Control*, Merlin Press, London, 1971, p.713 of the present volume.

III. THE DIVISION OF LABOUR
AND THE POSTCAPITALIST STATE*

1. Foreword

MARX formulated his basic principles with regard to the conditions of a socialist transformation well before the burden of historical experience had deeply affected the political movement of the proletariat: first through the accommodations of German Social Democracy, and then through the formation of the Leninist vanguard party after Marx's death. Understandably, therefore, the far-reaching implications of such developments had to remain beyond Marx's horizon, although the radical scepticism of his *'dixi et salvavi animam meam'* at the end of his *Critique of the Gotha Programme* bears witness to the feeling of unease with which he greeted the newly emerging trends of working class involvement in the political arena.

As is well known, Marx had great expectations of 'the social revolution of the nineteenth century.'[1] What is little known though is that the possibilities of a much longer drawn-out development also appeared on the margin of his thought, formulated as a major dilemma — implying a great many unknown factors, with all their necessary theoretical consequences — in a letter to Engels:

> The historic task of bourgeois society is the establishment of the *world market,* at least in its basic outlines, and a mode of production that rests on its basis. Since the world is round, it seems that this has been accomplished with the colonization of California and Australia and with the the the annexation of China and Japan. For us the *difficult question* is this: the revolution on the Continent is imminent and its character will be at once socialist; will it not be *necessarily crushed* in this *little corner of the world,* since on a much larger terrain the development of bourgeois society is still in its *ascendancy.*[2]

In the same letter Marx also made it clear that the collapse of bourgeois society in the foreseeable future was only a *hope,* and by no means a certainty: 'One cannot deny, bourgeois society lives its second 16th Century which, *I hope,* will take it into the grave, just as the first one brought it into life.' The world situation had to be characterized like this precisely because of what Marx underlined as the undeniable *ascendancy* of capital on that 'much larger terrain' which necessarily put the European 'little corner of the world' into perspective.

As we can see, then, some key elements of a very different assessment of the coming socialist revolution appeared in Marx's thought after the 1848-49 uprisings, and they continued to surface in various contexts up to the end of his life. Such elements did not question the necessity of the socialist revolution, but they had far-reaching implications for its *time scale* and potential *modality* of unfolding. For it made a big difference — with regard to the feasible socio-political forms of transition — *where* and under what kind of *class relations* the socialist revolution broke out and had to attempt the radical restructuring of

---

* First published in *PRAXIS Y FILOSOFIA: Ensayos en homenaje a Adolfo Sánchez Vázquez,* ed. by Juliana González, Carlos Pereyra and Gabriel Vargas Lozano, Editorial Grijalbo, México, 1985, pp.57-94.

the given social metabolism, under the more or less heavily constraining degree of development (or underdevelopment) of the inherited production forces.

In this sense, the failure of the socialist revolution to break through in the European 'little corner of the world' — while its success was meant to block the development of the bourgeois order on the incomparably larger terrain of the rest of the world — carried some weighty implications for the maturation of capital's inner contradictions. Since the establishment of the anticipated new social order was said to be possible only as the 'act of the dominant peoples "all at once" and simultaneously', on the basis of the 'universal development of the productive forces and the world intercourse bound up with them', the possibility of developing capital's productive outlets everywhere where bourgeois society was still in its *ascendancy* was synonymous with the possibility of *displacing* for the duration of the selfsame historical ascendancy capital's inner contradictions. Until, that is, 'world intercourse' as a whole would become *saturated* by the dynamics of capital's inexorable self-expansion so as to drive the whole process to a halt through an ever-deepening structural crisis of the 'universally developed productive forces', on a truly global scale.

Naturally, Marx could not be primarily concerned with elaborating the manifold implications of this long-term perspective when he *hoped* — and explicitly said so — that 'the second 16th Century of bourgeois society' would take the capitalist order into its grave, as a result of the successful socialist revolutions of the proletariat in the advanced European countries. The fact that postcapitalist societies emerged in capitalistically far less developed parts of the world presented socialist theory with some major problems to face up to. For it is often argued that the Marxian conception of socialism has no relevance — or that it *no longer* has any relevance — to advanced capitalist societies.

What is the nature of postcapitalist societies and how do they affect the perspectives of a global socialist transformation? How did it come about that the capitalist system proved to be much more resilient in displacing its contradictions than originally thought? Is it possible to reconcile the position of the working class in the societies of contemporary capitalism with the role assigned to it in the Marxian theory as the agency of emancipation? How does the experience of postcapitalist societies measure up to the Marxian expectations? Why does the hierarchical social division of labour stubbornly persist in such societies? What is the nature of the postcapitalist state and to what extent is the working class in control of it? And, finally, what happened to the anticipated development of socialist *'mass consciousness'* and how is it possible to overcome the great difficulties experienced in this regard?

These are the questions which the present essay attempts to address itself to, through a reexamination of some fundamental tenets of the Marxian theory in the light of developments since Marx's death.

2. The gaps in Marx

AS we all know today, bourgeois society was not taken to its grave by its second 16th century and by the social revolutions of the 20th, let alone by those of the 19th. The successful exploitation by capital of the gigantic potential outlets of its global ascendancy in the peasant and underdeveloped societies presented the forces aspiring to socialist revolution with a new challenge. For while the 'dominant peoples' — the main beneficiaries of capital's renewed expansion and imperialist domination — were held back by their vested interests from pursuing the road towards a socialist transformation, new types of contradiction appeared on the 'periphery' and at the 'weakest links' of the increasingly interdependent and saturated global system. At the same time, the eruption of revolutions on the underdeveloped periphery, and the successful consolidation of their (no matter how limited and problematical[3]) results, put the question of the *transition to socialism* on the historical agenda in a *hostile* global context: under conditions, that is, when even the most tentative first steps in the direction of the originally envisaged perspective of the state's *'withering away'* could not be seriously contemplated for a moment, in view of the prevailing relation of forces heavily dominated by the capitalist 'dominant peoples'.[4]

Thus, taking also 'hindsight' into account, the gaps in Marx's own approach to our problem may be described as follows:

(1) The problems of the *transition to socialism* were never discussed by Marx in any detail, apart from some brief general references to the major contrast between the 'lower' and 'higher' phases of the future society in the *Critique of the Gotha Programme,* dictated by the latter's polemical context.

Admittedly the issue itself, with all its bewildering practical dimensions, was by no means an acute historical challenge in Marx's life-time, given capital's newly won vitality on the ground of its imperialist expansion. Nevertheless, inasmuch as Marx contemplated the possibility that the 'dominant peoples' might not move 'all at once and simultaneously' in the direction of a socialist transformation, such consideration carried with it some weighty implications for future developments, especially with regard to the likely changes in the legal and political superstructure and their necessary impact on the material processes of society in general. For the fundamental requirements of the social metabolism assert themselves in very different ways under substantially different political circumstances, notwithstanding the primacy of the material base — 'in the last analysis' — in the overall structure of determinations and interchanges. This is why assessing the true significance and material inertia of the international division of labour vis-à-vis the societies of transition is inseparable from confronting the problems of the state in its global setting. (Clearly, the book Marx originally planned but never even began on the state reciprocally integrated with the international relations of production and exchange, pinpoints a crucial missing dimension of Marx's undertaking in this respect.)

This factor is all the more important once the internal and international political parameters of the social metabolism (which are vital even under the most favourable circumstances) appear historically articulated as a set of *antagonistic inter-state relations,* in the aftermath of a socialist revolution at the 'weakest link' of the imperialist chain. Given such conditions, the inertial force of politics — defined as acting in response to the moves of a *hostile* outside world, under the banner of a besieged, hence greatly *strengthened* state, and not one that begins to show the first signs of 'withering away' — becomes overpowering.

(2) The historical unfolding of the contradiction between *social production and private appropriation* was amenable to an alternative reading: one very different

from that offered by Marx. As Paul Mattick rightly stressed: 'For Marx, capitalism was private-property capitalism, and where it seemed to lose its strictly private-enterprise nature, as in state-industries, and even in the joint stock companies, he saw it as a partial abolition of the capitalist mode of production within the capitalist mode of production; a sign of the decay of the capitalist system.'[5] In reality, however, a great variety of 'hybrid' combinations — all possible permutations of the mystifying 'mixed economy' — are thoroughly compatible with the continued survival (even temporary revitalisation) of private capitalism, not to mention the ultimate limits of capital as such. Indeed, the fairly large-scale 'nationalization' of bankrupt industries which we have experienced in capitalist countries — frequently followed by the profitable practice of de-nationalization in due course: after the imposition, that is, of the necessary, and by fragmented private capital unachievable, political/economic changes (with regard to Trade Union power, for instance) — represents a very welcome way of extending the manipulative rationality of the capitalist system.

In all such developments conscious collective self-activity of individuals does not advance one single step nearer to its realization, since the control of the fundamental social/economic processes remains radically divorced from and opposed to the — far from associated — producers. The industry-wide — even transnational (misnamed as 'multi-national') — integration of the production process does not make the producers any more 'associated producers' than they were in capitalist industrial enterprises of a more limited scale. For what really decides the issue is the successful transfer — from capital to the producers — of the *effective control* of the various units of production, whatever their size. And that is equivalent to a genuine *socialization* of the process of production in all its essential characteristics, well beyond the immediate problem of ownership, as opposed to its remote hierarchical management through '*statalization*' and '*nationalisation*', — or, for that matter, through its growing transnational integration. In other words, the issue at stake is primarily political/social, requiring in the first place a qualitative political change for its realization; and the latter is by no means necessarily helped (but may, on the contrary, be actually hindered) by the unfolding of capital's centralization and concentration as an economic necessity so hopefully evaluated by Marx. For in the face of the massive power of capital's increasing concentration and centralisation, the countervailing political force of labour must be on an equally large scale if it is to have any chance of success against its adversary.

(3) Marx's optimistic evaluation of the Paris Commune as 'a Revolution not against this or that ... form of State Power [but] a Revolution against the *State itself*'[6] was coupled with an equally optimistic characterization of the Bonapartist Second Empire as 'the *last* expression of that state power', the '*last possible form* of [bourgeois] class rule' and the '*last* triumph of a State separate from and independent of society.'[7]

This view was in marked contrast to his own way of linking in the same work[8] '*political superstructures*' to determinate '*social bodies*' which sustain them, talking about the 'withering away' of certain social bodies which make the continued existence of their political superstructures a historical anachronism. Also, in another passage[9] he stressed that the social soil that corresponds to the 'superstructure of a centralized statepower' is the 'systematic and hierarchic division of labour', thereby indicating the strongest possible reciprocal determination and mutual support between the two.

The problem is, though, that the obvious and highly disturbing implications of such remarks undermine Marx's hopeful expectations about the 'last possible form' of a state power separate from and independent of society. For so long as the social soil of the systematic and hierarchic division of labour exists — and indeed successfully renews and strengthens itself in conjunction with the ongoing transformation of the relevant social bodies of 'civil society' on an ever-extending scale, in the direction of an ultimate global integration — a corresponding restructuring of state-forms in the interest of continued class rule (both internally and at the level of inter-state relations) cannot be denied to the established system. Accordingly, even today we are still very far from the 'last form' of the capitalist state and its class rule, let alone at the time when Marx wrote the lines just quoted from his defence of the Commune.

(4) The other side of the question of the state's continued domination of society and refusal to 'wither away' concerns the proletariat. For a working-class revolution — as Marx saw the Commune[10] — is only on a long-term historical scale *ipso facto* also a revolution 'against the State itself' (i.e. against the *state as such*); it is not so in terms of the really feasible impact of its inescapable immediate objectives. Such a limitation is not simply the consequence of an isolated revolution and its ensuing 'encirclement', although, of course, the latter has a great deal to do with it in the sense that the *'harmonious national and international coordination'*[11] of social intercourse anticipated by Marx cannot be even dreamed about under such circumstances. Nevertheless, the historical delay in attacking the foundations of the state as such arises primarily from the very nature of the task itself: 'to work out the *economic emancipation* of labour' through the *'political form* at last discovered'[12], so that *'free and associated labour'* should assume the form of *'united co-operative societies'* in order 'to regulate *national* production upon a common plan.'[13]

Thus, in Marx's conception, the objective and subjective *requirements* of a socialist transformation — the full emancipation of labour from the prevailing social division of labour — stipulate a *political form* (the proletarian state) under which the advocated transition from the old to the new society should be accomplished, while this transitional state itself is called upon to act simultaneously as both master and servant of the long-drawn-out process of emancipation.[14] Such a state is said to have no interest of its own to defend, despite its unquestionably strategic function — as the *specific political form* of the necessary 'national coordination' of social life — in the division of labour whose continuation is unavoidable (even if progressively diminishing) for the whole period of radical restructuring. There seems to be no contradiction whatsoever in asking the new *political form* to work out the *economic emancipation* of labour, since the working class is said to be in complete control of the political process in a social framework in which the interest of those who directly control the transitional state machinery and that of society as a whole fully coincide.

To be sure, Marx is well aware of the fact that the changes required for superseding the inherited division of labour can only result from a highly complex historical process of transformation. Indeed, he insists that the working class 'will have to pass through *long struggles,* through a series of historic processes, transforming *circumstances and men.*'[15] Yet, he has to resort to equivocation in order to reconcile the contradiction between the far from accomplished task of 'transforming circumstances and men' and assuming the necessary communist consciousness of the working class as *already given*.

Communist consciousness in *The German Ideology* was defined as 'the consciousness of the necessity of a fundamental revolution.'[16] At the same time it was also stated that 'Both for the production on a mass scale of this communist consciousness, and for the success of the cause itself, *the alteration of men on a mass scale is necessary.*'[17]

The same ideas appear in the evaluation of the Commune, but this time ascribing to the working class in the present 'the *full consciousness* of their historic mission.'[18] Furthermore, it is also claimed that the working class possess a practical determination to act in accordance with that consciousness — as well as the ability to do so without state-interference, 'in self-working and self-governing communes'[19]. Thus, beginning each sentence with: 'the working class know', or 'they know,'[20] Marx is able to turn some vital historical *imperatives* (whose realization depends on the full articulation of 'communist consciousness on a mass scale') into the 'affirmatives' of already developed and effectively self-asserting social forces.

Similarly, in *The German Ideology* Marx stated that 'Communism is for us not ... an ideal to which reality will have to adjust itself.'[21] Now the same idea is put forward in a significantly modified form, saying that: 'They [the working class] have no ideals to realize, but to set free the elements of the new society with which old collapsing bourgeois society itself is pregnant.'[22] The problem is not whether or not one should call the enterprise of 'setting free the elements of the new society' an 'ideal to realize'. What matters in the present context is the shift from *'for us'* — or from 'for the Communists' in some other writings[23] — to the *working class as a whole,* postulating, even if in an ambiguous form, the accomplished *actualization* of that communist mass consciousness whose *production* was presented in *The German Ideology* as a challenging historical task for the future.

This treatment of working class consciousness is inextricably linked to Marx's reflections on proletarian political power. Indeed, we find a similar equivocation in refusing to call the proletarian state a state, describing it, instead, as 'the political form of social emancipation'[24] and as 'the Communal form of political organization.'[25] In praising the fact that under the Commune 'the state-functions [were] reduced to a few functions for general national purposes,'[26] there is no hint that an extreme *state of emergency* — as the Paris Commune of necessity had to be — cannot be the model of the future development of the proletarian state and of its complex internal and international functions under normal circumstances. If the working class has the historic mission to work out through the 'new political form' the full emancipation of labour, and thus the emancipation of society as a whole from the social tyranny of the inherited division of labour, how could a task of such magnitude, intricacy, and long time-scale be carried out on the basis of the reduction of the state-functions to a simplified absolute minimum when, at the same time, one has to achieve also that 'harmonious national and international coordination' of production and distribution — obviously representing a problem of the highest complexity — of which Marx spoke?

To be sure, the ultimate 'withering away' of the state is inconceivable without a progressive reduction and simplification of its tasks and their transfer to the 'self-working and self-governing' social body. To suggest, however, that this process of reduction and simplification at the political level can be accomplished by immediately substituting for the state as such an unproblematical 'new political form', whereafter difficulties remain only with regard to economically emancipating society from the division of labour, is to make ideal shortcuts to the future. This is all the more problematical since the social soil of the 'systematic and hierarchic division of labour' is inseparable from the 'superstructure of a centralized statepower', even if not of the capitalist type. In reality the state can only be laboriously 'dismantled' (in the process of the political 'de-alienation' and *communalization* of society) to the extent to which the inherited social division of labour itself is correspondingly changed, and thus the social metabolism as a whole is effectively restructured.

The perspective of such shortcuts — understandable in the context of the defence of the Paris Commune — brings with it also the stipulative characterization of working class consciousness which we have just seen. Since the required social change is acknowledged to extend over a long historical process of confrontations and struggles, the power of 'communist consciousness on a mass scale' acquires particular importance in the Marxian conception. For, in virtue of its determination as *mass consciousness,* it protects the socialist forces involved in the struggle from internal divisions and from the establishment of new hierarchies, in contrast to Bakunin's elitistic vision of the rule of society after the conquest of power by the self-appointed few who claim to know better. Accordingly, if there is an identity of purpose among the vast majority of the population — an identity which, under the prevailing circumstances, only the working class's 'full consciousness of its historic mission and heroic resolve to act up to it'[27] can produce — in that case the *state* immediately becomes a fully controlled transitional 'political form' and a mere means to emancipatory action, since the difference between the rulers and the governed disappears by definition. This is why Marx can retort to Bakunin's question — 'The Germans number nearly 40 million. Will, for example, all 40 million be members of the government?' — with an emphatic *'Certainly,* for the thing *begins* with the *self-government* of the *commune'.*[28]

Another important aspect of communist mass consciousness in this perspective is that it can *bridge the gap* that separates the present conditions of hardship from the 'new historic form' aimed at. For through its orienting force it can guarantee the general direction of development that must be sustained, and minimize the danger of relapses and reversals under the pressure of the difficulties encountered. Indeed, under the historically *premature* conditions of the advocated 'social revolution' — when capitalism is acknowledged by Marx to be in its *ascendancy* on by far the greater part of the planet — only the stipulated communist mass consciousness can bridge this great historical gap and provide the desired guarantee for maintaining the impetus of the necessary struggle.

(5) The final and most complex issue to consider here concerns Marx's evaluation of the working class's position in the existing *division of labour*. It is closely connected with his views on the post-revolutionary 'political form', with major implications for the development of class consciousness and for the articulation of socialist political strategies. To anticipate the main point: in the Marxian perspective the *fragmentation* of the working class is greatly underestimated and the necessary political consequences of such fragmentation (and stratification) remain largely unexplored. The accent is on the proletariat constituting the *'universal class'*: a characterization eminently suitable to underline the qualitative change from the old to the 'new historic form', but full of ambiguities and question marks as regards the practical constraints of the immediate future.

This is all the more remarkable since Marx insisted in *The German Ideology* that: 'The division of labour implies from the outset the division of the conditions of labour, of tools and materials, and thus the fragmentation of accumulated capital among different owners, and thus, also, the fragmentation between capital and labour, and the different forms of property itself. The more the division of labour develops and accumulation grows, the further fragmentation develops. *Labour itself can only exist on the premise of this fragmentation.*'[29]

However, Marx never spells out what might be the consequences of labour existing 'on the premise of the fragmentation' engendered by the capitalistic division of labour. On the contrary, a natural progression is stipulated from occasional and partial to permanent and comprehensive trade unionism, in accordance with the development of production on a world scale:

combination has not ceased for an instant to go forward and grow with the development and growth of modern industry. It has now reached such a stage, that *the degree to which combination has developed in any country clearly marks the rank it occupies in the hierarchy of the world market.* England, whose industry has attained the highest degree of development, has the biggest and best organised combinations.[30]

At the same time it is also suggested that there is an irresistible movement from the defence of limited economic group-interests to the politically conscious assertion of the interests of universal emancipation,[31] accomplished by the united proletarian 'class for itself' through the abolition of all classes and through its own self-abolition.[32]

Significantly, Marx's early idea that the proletariat is 'victorious only by abolishing itself and its opposite'[33] is restated, again and again, throughout his life. For example, this is how Marx answers Bakunin's question, 'What is meant by the proletariat transformed into the ruling class?', in 1874:

It means that the proletariat, instead of fighting individually against the economically privileged classes, has gained sufficient strength and is sufficiently well organised to employ general means of compulsion in its struggle against these classes. It can, however, use only *economic* means designed to abolish its own distinctive trait as a wage-earner, and hence to *abolish itself as a class.* Its complete *victory* is consequently also the *end of its domination,* since its class character has disappeared.[34]

There is no hint in Marx that in addition to the fragmentation 'between capital and labour', etc., one must also face the fragmentation *within labour itself* as a major problem for the proletariat both before and after the conquest of political power. The process of emancipation in the aftermath of the revolution is conceived as an essentially *economic* problem (as we have seen on several occasions, including the last quoted passage). The proletariat's ability to act as a united force is predicated as a matter of course, in sharp contrast to the peasantry:

> The small-holding peasants form a vast mass, the members of which live in similar conditions but without entering into manifold relations with one another. Their mode of production isolates them from one another, instead of bringing them into mutual intercourse. ... In so far as millions of families live under economic conditions of existence that separate their mode of life, their interests and their culture from those of the other classes, and put them in hostile opposition to the latter, they form a class. In so far as there is merely a local interconnection among these small-holding peasants, and the identity of their interests begets no community, no national bond and no political organization among them, they do not form a class. They are consequently *incapable of enforcing their class interests in their own name,* whether through a parliament or through a convention. *They cannot represent themselves, they must be represented.* Their representative must at the same time appear ... as an authority over them, as an unlimited governmental power that *protects them against the other classes* ... The political influence of the small-holding peasants, therefore, finds its final expression in the *executive power subordinating society to itself.*[35]

The problem is, however, that a great deal of what Marx says here about the peasantry is equally valid for the working class itself. Indeed, the united action and rule of the latter cannot be taken for granted without first confronting the difficult 'premise of fragmentation' within the prevailing division of labour. For while the proletariat has the *potentiality* to overcome its own fragmentation and subordinate position in the existing division of labour, the *actualization* of this potentiality depends on the maturation of a number of objective conditions, including some major developments in the political organization and conscious collective self-determination of the individuals who constitute the class of 'freely associated producers'. Thus, to suggest that the 'degree of combination' of any particular country directly corresponds to 'the rank which it occupies in the hierarchy of the world market,'[36] is to turn a historical *requirement* into a necessary *attainment*. Equally, to anticipate the global trade unionization and political articulation of the united working class, while the capitalistic division of labour — and the fragmentation of labour necessarily entailed by such division of labour — remains intact, is merely to restate the long-term potential of the 'universal class' for emancipating society from class rule, without indicating, however, the subjective and objective as well as the internal and international obstacles that must be overcome in the course of transition towards the end advocated.

There can be no disagreement with the proposition that the proletariat is 'victorious only by abolishing itself'. Also, considering the position of labour in maintaining the normal functioning of the social metabolism, it is impossible to disagree with Marx that the proletariat, on the one hand, 'cannot emancipate itself without abolishing the conditions of its life', and that, on the other hand, 'it cannot abolish the conditions of its own life without abolishing all the inhuman conditions of life of society today which are summed up in its own situation.'[37] However, saying this we only define the necessary *conditions* of a successful 'social revolution', but not the specific *way* in which this apparently vicious circle — making the victory of the particular enterprise depend on the successful solution of the problems of the whole, and vice versa — can and will be broken.

The vicious circle in question is not a *conceptual* one. Rather, it is the suffocating practical circularity of the prevailing social division of labour. For the latter assigns to labour itself the key role in sustaining the social metabolism, structurally constraining labour thereby with regard to its feasible margin of emancipatory and self-emancipatory action. This is why the Marxian conclusion is inescapable: the proletariat is 'victorious only by abolishing itself and its opposite', and labour's self-emancipation can only be accomplished to the extent to which society as a whole is emancipated. Thus the issue at stake concerns simultaneously both the division of labour as such, and the position of the proletariat (or labour) within it. In other words, the question is how to break the stranglehold of the social division of labour over labour, without jeopardizing at the same time the vital functions of the social metabolism itself.

Inevitably, in a question of such magnitude and complexity the subjective and objective, as well as the political and socio-economic aspects are inextricably intertwined. *Subjectively,* only labour itself can accomplish the task in question 'for itself', which stipulates the necessary development of working class consciousness. On the other hand, without demonstrating the *objective* determinations which actually propel the development of totalizing — as opposed to partial and narrowly self-interested — class consciousness, the necessity of the latter is only postulated, instead of being established as a social force adequate to its 'historic task'. Furthermore, while the *political* confrontation of labour with the capitalist state formation is the necessary point of departure (for which the appropriate institutional form must be found), it can be no more than a point of departure. For the fundamental issue is the transcendence of the inherited social division of labour, which is conceivable only on the basis of the radical restructuring of the whole *socio-economic* framework. Paradoxically, however, the latter implies that full political control of society remains for the duration of the entire process of restructuring. The various constituents of the social whole — including labour — must accomodate themselves to the available margin of action, under the guidance of the new 'political form'. Only the latter is in a position to supervise the overall process, although it was supposed to constitute merely the point of departure of the ongoing socialist transformation.

This is where we can clearly see perhaps the most acute of Marx's theoretical difficulties. He cannot really acknowledge labour's fragmentation and stratification, because that would greatly complicate, indeed ultimately undermine, his conception of the transitional 'political form'. For if the objective *partial interests* of the various groups of workers — inevitably arising on the basis of labour's structural fragmentation — are asserted in the form of conflicting claims, in that case the *'common interest'* defended and imposed by the new 'political form' is not as self-evident as it would appear on the assumption of *united labour.* Such an assumption, however, unjustifiably casts aside the earlier recognised 'premise of labour's fragmentation'.

Thus, to give full weight to the necessary fragmentation of labour under the conditions of the inherited division of labour means, at the same time, to acknowledge the space left wide open for the exercise of *traditional* state functions for a whole historical epoch. That is to say, for as long as the fragmentation of labour is not effectively superseded — in material as well as in ideological and political terms — through the actual 'abolition' (*Aufhebung*/transcendence/radical restructuring) of the social division of labour. Naturally, this means that whatever might be the proletarian state's function in its *external* relations, internally it cannot be simply the defence of the proletariat against the former ruling class. Rather, the primary *internal* function of the proletarian state — after a relatively short period of time — is *arbitration* over a multiplicity of complicated, even contradictory, partial interests, on the basis of the continued social division of labour. This is why the proletariat can — and under such conditions must — 'turn its dictatorship against itself', and not because it fails to live up to the ideal dictates of some categorical moral imperative, as Lukács suggested in his essay on 'The Role of Morality in Communist Production'.

Marx's theoretical difficulties are only in part due to his original linkage of the 'universal class' to 'the *categorical imperative to overthrow all relations* in which man is a debased, enslaved, forsaken, despicable being.'[38] He is, in fact, anxious to establish the world-historic role and task which the 'socialist writers *ascribe* to the ... fully-formed proletariat'[39] on the basis of an objective socio-historical necessity. This is why he insists that what decides the issue 'is not a question of what this or that proletarian, or even the whole proletariat, at the moment *regards* as its aim. It is a question of *what the proletariat is,* and what, in accordance with this *being,* it will historically be compelled to do.'[40] However, in postulating the unfolding of a fully adequate proletarian class consciousness, in the face of the *premature* character of the social revolution under the conditions of capital's *global ascendancy,* he is forced to claim that 'a large part of the English and French proletariat is *already conscious* of its historic task and is *constantly working* to develop that consciousness into *complete clarity*.'[41] Thus, he tends to anticipate a much less problematical course of events — just as he did in projecting a global trade unionization and corresponding political militancy — than the available historical evidence would actually support.

3. The future of labour

THE consequence of all this is that, on the one hand, a number of paradoxical and rather ambiguous propositions must fill the gap between the prevailing state of affairs and the long-term historical anticipations, and that, on the other hand, some important characteristics of working class existence cannot be given their full weight in the Marxian perspective. In the first category it is enough to think of statements like 'the proletariat is victorious only by abolishing itself and its opposite', which is both incontestable in terms of its ultimate implications and full of riddles with regard to the necessary steps that must be taken towards its realization by the potentially 'universal and self-transcending' proletarian partiality. As to the second category, historical development provided us with far too abundant examples to need much discussion, from the 'social chauvinism' of working class parties during the First World War to the 'integration' of the American working class and to the exploitative relationship of the Western working classes in general to the 'Third World'.

It is, therefore, very problematical to assert that 'With labour emancipated, every man becomes a working man, and productive labour ceases to be a class attribute.'[42] For such assertion merely stipulates that emancipation implies the universal sharing of work by all members of society, without defining at the same time the meaning of 'productive work' and, more important perhaps, ignoring an issue of utmost gravity with regard to the fragmentation and internal division of labour: the necessarily and precipitously growing *scarcity of labour-opportunities* within the framework of capitalist economic and technological development.

The only context in which Marx addresses himself to this problem concerns the inherent inadequacy of capitalist accountancy to find outlets for the irresistibly growing productive potentiality of labour. He describes a process of development on the basis of 'large-scale industry' — treating it, in fact, rather ambiguously since it could never come about before a radical break with capital's constraining framework is effectively accomplished — as a result of which:

> Labour no longer appears so much to be included within the production process; rather, the human being comes to relate more as watchman and regulator to the production process itself. ... [The worker] steps to the side of the production process instead of being its chief actor. In this transformation, it is neither the direct human labour he himself performs, nor the time during which he works, but rather the appropriation of his own general productive power, his understanding of nature and his mastery over it by virtue of his presence as a social body — it is, in a word, the development of the social individual which appears as the great foundation-stone of production and of wealth.[43]

At this point, Marx emphasizes again the irreconcilable contradictions involved in the developments he is concerned with, and concludes his line of reasoning with a number of powerful imperatives:

> The theft of alien labour time, on which the present wealth is based, appears a miserable foundation in face of this new one, *created by large-scale industry itself.* As soon as labour in the direct form has ceased to be the great well-spring of wealth, labour time ceases and *must cease* to be its measure, and hence exchange value *must cease* to be the measure of use value. The surplus labour of the mass has ceased to be the condition for the development of general wealth, just as the non-labour of the few, for the development of the general powers of the human head. With that, *production based on exchange value breaks down,* and the direct, material production process is stripped of the form of penury and antithesis. ... Forces of production and social relations — two different sides of the development of the social individual — appear to capital as mere means, and are merely means for it to produce on its limited foundation. In fact, however, they are the material conditions *to blow this foundation sky high.*[44]

The difficulty here is that so long as the capitalistic determinations remain in control of society, labour — even if *ideally* it must — simply *cannot* cease to be the well-spring of wealth, nor labour time its measure. Equally, under such conditions, exchange value *cannot* cease to be the measure of use value, nor can we simply postulate that in virtue of the *ideal* implications of these relations — which turn the capitalist system into a *historical,* but by no means immediately visible and materially felt anachronism — the mode of production based on exchange value *actually* breaks down. Thus, as long as capital can find new outlets for expansion over the vast terrain of its global ascendancy, the non-realizability of the social individual remains only a *latent* contradiction of this society, instead of blowing its narrow foundations 'sky high'.

If, therefore, we consider the historically identifiable unfolding of capital's inherent tendency for the drastic reduction of necessary labour time, without postulating, *ipso facto,* the breakdown of the capitalist system (even if such breakdown is conceptually implied by the *long-term* and *full* articulation of this tendency), in that case it becomes clear that we have to face here a major *negative* force that sustains capital for a long time, rather than offering any comfort to labour in the foreseeable future. For the tendency in question in its immediate impact can only further divide and fragment labour, turning its various sections against one another, instead of positively contributing to the global 'unification' and homogenization of labour anticipated in the Marxian perspective.

4. *The fragmentation and division of labour*
THE fragmentation and hierarchical division of labour, thus, appears under the following main aspects, corresponding to significantly different objective divisions of interest:

(1) within any particular group or section of labour;

(2) among different groups of workers belonging to the same national community;

(3) between nationally different bodies of labour opposed to one another in the context of international capitalist competition, from the smallest to the most comprehensive scale, including the potential collision of interests in the form of wars;

(4) the labour force of the advanced capitalist countries — the relative beneficiaries of the global capitalist division of labour — as opposed to the differentially far more exploited labour force of the 'Third World';

(5) labour in employment, as separated from and opposed to the objectively different — and politically/organisationally in general unarticulated — interests of the 'unwaged' and unemployed, including the ever-multiplying victims of the 'second industrial revolution'.

The reason why such fragmentation and division of interests *within labour itself* matters so much is because it carries with it — both *before* and *after* the revolution — an inescapable reliance on the *state,* although in theory the latter is supposed to be the most obvious immediate target of the socialist revolution. Indeed, the bourgeois state finds its support among various groups of labour primarily on the ground of the 'protection' it provides in legally sustaining and safeguarding the objectively established framework of division of labour. It is enough to recall the great variety of measures adopted by the state in this respect, from minimum wage and social security legislation to erecting protective tariffs and other national barriers, and from internally balancing the relation of forces against 'excesses', to embarking on international enterprises which secure the greatest advantage to the national ruling class, delivering at the same time some relative advantage also to the national labour force.

Naturally, the bourgeois state can perform its 'protective' function on behalf of the fragmented and divided groups of labour only to the extent to which the exercise of that function objectively corresponds to the interests of the ruling class as a whole. This condition happens to be, of course, also the basis upon which the state can overrule various fractional interests on its own side of the more or less latent social confrontation.

Also, it cannot be stressed enough, we are not talking here about some negligible degree of shared interests, especially in the advanced capitalist countries. For precisely in view of the social division of labour that originates, reproduces and constantly reinforces labour's own fragmentation and internal division, labour itself has a major vested interest in continued *social stability* — (hence the pursuit of the 'line of least resistance') — as the vital condition of its own self-reproduction.

Thus, under normal circumstances, internally divided and fragmented labour is at the mercy not only of the ruling class and its state, but also of the objective requirements of the prevailing social division of labour. Hence we see paradoxical and problematical manifestations of the interests which labour happens to share with its adversary within the compass of the materially and institutionally enforced (and to a large extent self-enforcing) social metabolism. Only at times of quite elemental crises — when the continued functioning of the fundamental social metabolism itself is being called into question, in the midst of a massive economic collapse, or as a result of the bourgeois state's dramatic disintegration in the aftermath of a lost war, etc. — can labour temporarily extricate itself from these paralyzing constraints.

It is under the circumstances of such elemental structural crises that labour can successfully assert its claims to being the only feasible *hegemonic alternative* to the established order in all its dimensions, from the basic material conditions of life to the most intricate political and ideological aspects of social interchange. The all-important question of submitting the state itself to labour's effective control, too, can only arise under the selfsame circumstances of a *hegemonic crisis* (i.e., the crisis of bourgeois hegemony). However, while labour can successfully overthrow the bourgeois state and take over the control of the crucial political regulators of the social metabolism, thereby *initiating* the necessary process of radical *restructuring,* the 'workers' state' cannot conceivably *abolish* the inherited social division of labour, except insofar as it directly concerns the ownership of the means of production. Nor can the 'new political form' simply abolish the fragmentation and internal division of labour linked to and embedded in the inherited productive instruments and practices of society. For the required changes in question involve the whole process of restructuring itself, with all its objective and subjective constraints which escape the power of direct political intervention to a significant degree.

5. *The postrevolutionary state*

THIS is where we can see the disconcerting 'new circularity' between the *postrevolutionary* 'civil society' and its division of labour on the one hand, and the proletarian state on the other. For the various sections of fragmented and internally divided labour need the protection of the state, for a long time after the revolution, not only against the former ruling classes but also against one another as situated within the framework of the still prevailing social division of labour. Thus, paradoxically, they call into being and maintain in existence for the duration of the whole process of radical restructuring a *strong executive* over against themselves. This situation is not entirely unlike that of the French peasantry in its subjection to its own state-form under 'Napoleon le Petit' as a result of its fragmentation, since the latter enabled the Bonapartist executive power to subordinate society to itself, as we have seen in Marx's analysis.

At the same time, to complete the new vicious circle between the postrevolutionary civil society and its state, the latter is not merely the manifestation of the continuing division of labour but also the hierarchical apex of its system of decision making. Accordingly, it has a strong interest of its own to retain, indefinitely, the firmest possible grip over the ongoing process of transformation as a whole, thereby reinforcing, rather than undermining, the established social division of labour of which — in virtue of its strategic role — the postrevolutionary state itself happens to constitute the most privileged dimension. (Here, again, we can see that the much disputed issue of 'bureaucratic privileges' is not simply a matter of the personnel involved but, above all, that of the retention of *objectively* 'privileged' — i.e., strategically vital — functions by the state in the overall social metabolism. The continued exercise of these, strategically privileged, functions by a separate body is bound to find in its turn its subjective equivalent at the plane of the 'bureaucratised state personnel' too, in the absence of some alternative form of social control: one based on ever-increasing and truly active mass-involvement.)

The subordination of postrevolutionary civil society to the 'new political form' of a powerful executive in the early phases of transition is, thus, first and foremost the consequence of labour's own fragmentation and internal division as 'signed and sealed' by the inherited division of labour. This may be aggravated, of course, by some specific characteristics of structural underdevelopment — including so-called 'Asiatic backwardness' — on account of a particularly unfavourable relative position of a country's aggregate labour force in the international division of labour. However, the point to stress is that — in view of the objective structural conditions of the given social metabolism and the difficult material and institutional constraints of its restructuring — the politically 'top-heavy' conditions of development apply everywhere, even in the economically most advanced countries, with the longest historical tradition of liberal democracy. For the circumstances of more favourable economic developments and liberal democratic traditions, no matter how advantageous in some respects, do not eliminate the overwhelming negative determinant of labour's fragmentation and internal division. Consequently, on their own they do not support the anticipations of some theoreticians of the New Left, as well as of some leading politicians of the Labour Left, who see in them some sort of apriori historical guarantee with regard to the prospects of a democratic socialist transformation in advanced capitalist countries.

Furthermore, in accordance with the inherent necessities of transformations which cannot avoid attacking the foundations of the capitalist market economy, the liberal democratic measures that paradoxically arise out of the absolute material tyranny of the market, with no Court of Appeal, must be replaced by new types of political/administrative regulators, extending also over formerly 'unregulated' areas of social interaction. And in this respect it is of little comfort that the liberal democratic framework of relatively 'unregulated' regulation is feasible and affordable only because of the immense material discriminatory power of the capitalist market which minimizes the need for direct (political) interference with the everyday-life of individuals under normal circumstances. For the fact remains that the socially necessary removal of the — no matter how blind and anarchistic — self-regulatory levers of liberal 'market-democracy' creates an institutional vacuum at the political level. Consequently, also in this respect, the less the postrevolutionary civil society succeeds in institutionally articulating and safeguarding the objective interests of its various groups on a truly co-operative basis, the greater the power of the state executive and its scope for the imposition of a — *Stalinist type* — 'political autonomy'.

Understandably, therefore, but by no means without some heavy 'irony of history', in the aftermath of the Stalinist abuse of power theories of *'market socialism'* appear, illusorily suggesting that it is possible to secure *socialist democracy* by reinstating the self-regulatory mechanisms of a modified capitalist market under 'state supervision'. Even if we disregard the incompatibilities necessarily involved in this course of action — tendencies towards the inadmissible wholesale restoration of capitalism on the one hand, and the reassertion of authoritarian political counter-measures to prevent the successful consummation of those tendencies, on the other — the trouble with these theories is that nothing is really solved by the creation of such 'partially controlled markets'. Strategies of this kind can, at best, only *postpone* the all-important issue of radical *restructuring,* which is far from being only, or even primarily, an *'economic'* problem that could be tackled within the narrowly 'efficiency-orientated' parameters of the idealised market. Curiously, the advocates of 'market socialism' seem to forget that the necessity of the socialist transformation itself arises in the first place out of the inescapable crisis of the socio-economic order that brings to perfection and universal domination a structure of 'living contradictions': the self-regulatory market which they now want to rescue and use as the secure foundation of democratic socialist developments, disregarding (for the sake of a rather naive hope) the *certainty of mass unemployment* that goes with such a regulatory framework.

6. Unity and mediation: the development of socialist consciousness

THUS perhaps the greatest difficulty for socialist theory is this: how to envisage the transcendence of labour's fragmentation and internal division without reducing the problems at stake to some direct appeal to an idealised class consciousness, advocating *'unity'* as the desirable solution while neglecting the objective material basis of the existing fragmentation, inherent in the continued division of labour.

As we have seen, Marx did not indulge in a direct appeal to an idealised proletarian class consciousness, except in the polemical context imposed on him by the need to defend the Paris Commune against a hostile press. Nevertheless, he firmly expected the emergence of what he called 'communist mass consciousness' — coupled with a fully adequate institutional articulation in the form of a global trade-unionism and corresponding political militancy — through the historical development of the capitalist social order, under the impact of the inexorable unfolding of the productive potentials as well as contradictions of that social order. Yet, it is not only thanks to the benefit of hindsight that we can see, today, that such expectations were rather problematical. In fact, some of the ambiguities of Marx's own analyses already pointed in the same direction, as we have seen above.

To conclude then: given the helping hand in displacing its contradictions which capital receives from the fragmenting and divisive impact of 'uneven development' and of the international division of labour, in their inseparability from the differential rate of exploitation of labour, some of the conditions for the socialization of production and the ensuing unification of labour anticipated by Marx are most unlikely to materialise within the confines and structural constraints of the capitalist social order itself.

Naturally, this does not decrease the importance of a socialist mass consciousness. On the contrary, it puts the vital socio-historical function of such consciousness even more into relief. For the full realization of the socialist project is inconceivable without a successfully integrated and 'totalizing' (though, of course, not unmediated), conscious management of their problems by the associated producers, in a globally interlinked setting which is *'unconsciously'*[45] brought into being in the first place by the development of capital itself.

But precisely for the latter reason, one can realistically appeal to the increasing importance of a totalizing social consciousness only by calling at the same time for the necessary *material mediations* — aimed at transcending the given fragmentation of labour — through which the development of this consciousness first becomes possible.

Labour's fragmentation cannot be eliminated by the capitalistic 'socialization of production'. Neither can it be readily transcended — in view of the deeply embedded material structures of the inherited global division of labour — for a long time after the socialist political revolution. Hence the necessary material *mediations* in question, characterized by a vital capacity for bringing about a progressive reduction in the constraining role of the inherited material *determinations,* must remain the regulative framework of social life for the entire historical epoch of transition.

NOTES

[1] The term used by Marx to characterize the tasks of the socialist revolution from 1843 onwards, sharply contrasting the *'social* revolution' with the narrowly *political* horizons of the revolutions of the past.

[2] Marx, *Letter to Engels,* 8 October 1858, MEW, Vol. 29, p.360.

[3] We should recall Lenin's repeated complaints about the paralysing impact of 'Asiatic backwardness' on postrevolutionary developments.

[4] This is how Lenin tried to reinsert the revolution of *'backward Russia'* — contrasted with the potentialities of the *'advanced countries of Western Europe'* — into the original perspectives:

It would be erroneous to lose sight of the fact that, soon after the victory of the proletarian revolution in at least one of the advanced countries, a sharp change will probably come about: *Russia will cease to be the model* and will once again become a *backward country* (in the "Soviet" and socialist sense). (Lenin, *Collected Works,* Lawrence and Wishart, London 1960ff, Vol. 31., p.21.)

To be sure, the relation of forces has significantly changed since Lenin wrote these lines. Nevertheless, the still unrealized proletarian revolution 'in at least one of the advanced countries' continues to maintain the 'historical dislocation' with regard to the radical transformation and ultimate 'withering away' of the state as well as to the potentialities of 'conscious collective totalization' — i.e., the self-determined comprehensive integration and conscious collective action of the social individuals — implicit in the developments anticipated by Marx.

[5] Paul Mattick, *Critique of Marcuse: One-Dimensional Man in Class Society,* Merlin Press, London 1972, p.61. While one cannot value highly enough the genuinely Marxian perspective of Mattick's work — maintained over a period of many years, with single-minded determination and consistency, under the conditions of an almost complete isolation in the United States — the point at which one has to part company with him is where he summarily characterizes the various *postcapitalist* societies as *'state capitalist'* formations.

[6] Marx, *The Civil War in France, Op.cit.,* p.166.

[7] *Ibid.,* p.167.

[8] *Ibid.,* p.237.

[9] *Ibid.,* p.227.

[10] The Commune 'was essentially a *working-class* government'. *Ibid.,* p.72.

[11] *Ibid.,* p.172.

[12] *Ibid.,* p.72.

[13] *Ibid.,* p.73.

[14] '...to serve as a lever for uprooting the economic foundations upon which rests the existence of classes'. *(Ibid.,* p.72.), and 'to make *individual property* a truth by transforming the means of production, land and capital, now chiefly the means of enslaving and exploiting labour, into mere instruments of *free and associated labour.' (Ibid.,* p.73.)

[15] *Ibid.*

[16] MECW., Vol. 5, p.52.

[17] *Ibid.,* pp.52-3.

[18] *The Civil War in France,* p.73.

[19] *Ibid.,* p.171.

[20] *'The working class know* that they have to pass through different phases of class-struggle. *They know* that the superseding of the economic conditions of the slavery of labour by the conditions of free and associated labour can only be the progressive work of time, ...that they require not only a change of distribution, but a new organisation of production, or rather the delivery (setting free) of the social forms of production in present organised labour, (engendered by present industry), of the trammels of slavery, of their present class character, and their harmonious national and international coordination. *They know* that this work of regeneration will be again and again relented and impeded by the resistance of vested interests and class egotism. *They know* that the present "spontaneous action of the natural laws of capital and landed property" — can only be superseded by "the spontaneous action of the laws of the social economy of free and associated labour" by a long process of development of new conditions... But *they know* at the same time that great strides may be made at once through the Communal form of political organisation and that the time has come to begin that movement for themselves and mankind.' *Ibid.,* pp.172-3.

[21] MECW., Vol. 5, p.49.

[22] *The Civil War in France,* p.73.

[23] In the *Communist Manifesto,* for instance.

[24] *The Civil War in France,* p.171.

[25] *Ibid.,* p.173.

[26] *Ibid.,* p.171.

[27] *Ibid.,* p.73.

[28] Marx, 'Conspectus of Bakunin's Book: *State and Anarchy',* in Marx, Engels, Lenin, *Anarchism and Anarcho-Syndicalism,* Progress Publishers, Moscow 1972, p.151.

[29] MECW., Vol. 5, p.86.

[30] *Ibid.*, p.210.

[31] See Marx, *The Poverty of Philosophy*, MECW., Vol. 6, pp.206-212.

[32] *Ibid.*, pp.211-12.

[33] MECW., Vol. 4, p.36.

[34] Marx, 'Conspectus of Bakunin's Book: *State and Anarchy*', *Op.cit.*, p.150.

[35] Marx, 'The Eighteenth Brumaire of Louis Bonaparte', *Op.cit.*, p.334.

[36] For us, in hindsight, it is enough to think of the United States to see how problematical Marx's stipulative generalization is. The 'development and growth of modern industry' and the advancement of the international division of labour which, according to the Marxian formula, should have brought with it the highest degree of 'combination' and a correspondingly high level of organised and fully conscious political militancy, failed to achieve the anticipated results. To explain the actual trend of U.S. developments — often described as the 'integration of the working class' — together with the possibility of its reversal, it is obviously necessary to introduce a number of important qualifying conditions which do not appear at all in Marx's original framework of assessment.

[37] MECW., Vol. 4, p.37.

[38] MECW., Vol. 3, p.182. (Marx's italics.) This is how Marx defines the role of the proletariat in the context of the 'categorical imperative' here referred to: 'In France partial emancipation is the basis of universal emancipation; in Germany universal emancipation is the *conditio sine qua non* of any partial emancipation. In France it is the reality of gradual liberation, in Germany the impossibility of gradual liberation, that *must* give birth to *complete freedom.*'

Starting from such a premise, Marx proceeds to ask the question, 'Where, then, is the positive possibility of a German emancipation?', and answers it as follows: 'In the formation of a class with *radical chains*, a class of civil society which is not a class of civil society, an estate which is the dissolution of all estates, a sphere which has a *universal* character by its *universal* suffering and claims to *no particular right* because no particular wrong but wrong generally is perpetrated against it; which can no longer invoke a historical but only a human title; which does not stand in any one-sided antithesis to the consequences but in an all-round antithesis to the premises of the German state; a sphere, finally, which cannot emancipate itself without emancipating itself from all other spheres of society and *thereby emancipating all other spheres of society*, which, in a word, is the complete loss of man and hence can win itself only through the complete rewinning of man. This *dissolution* of society as a *particular* estate is the *proletariat.*'

Thus, the proletariat fits in perfectly well with the 'categorical imperative to overthrow all established relations'. While the imperatival connotations of this train of thought are later largely removed, several of its vital aspects — from explaining the development of the 'universal class' from the 'drastic dissolution of society, mainly of the middle estate', to the definition of the relationship between partiality and universality in relation to the conditions of emancipation — remain central to Marx's thought throughout his life. (Quotations from MECW., Vol. 3, pp.186-7.)

[39] MECW., Vol. 4, p.36.

[40] *Ibid.*, p.37. (Marx's italics.) Here we can see Lukács's model of class consciousness in the Marxian contrast between 'what the proletariat at the moment regards as its aim', and what is 'ascribed to the fully-formed proletariat' by the socialist writers (i.e., the 'psychological' as opposed to the 'imputed' class consciousness in Lukács's terms). However, the fundamental difference is that while Marx expects the realization of his version of 'ascribed consciousness' in the class *as a whole,* in accordance with the transformation of its being under the compulsion of history, Lukács assigns to the Party the function of being the actual 'carrier' and 'embodiment' of the proletariat's 'imputed' class consciousness.

[41] *Ibid.*

42 Marx, *The Civil War in France, Op.cit.*, p.72.

43 Marx, *Grundrisse, Op.cit.*, p.705.

44 *Ibid.*, pp.705-6.

45 Unconsciously in the sense of operating by way of atomistic totalizations — i.e., in the form of *partial* anticipations and *expectations* more or less ruthlessly overruled by a reifying *feedback* from the unwanted consequences of the *post festum aggregative* individual interactions — as implemented through the market and similar vehicles and institutional intermediaries.

IV. RADICAL POLITICS AND TRANSITION TO SOCIALISM: REFLECTIONS ON MARX'S CENTENARY*

MARX wrote his *Capital* in order to help break the rule of capital under favourable conditions; that is to say: when 'total social capital' — in its relentless drive to subdue everything to itself on a global scale — cannot displace any longer its contradictions and is pushed to its untranscendable limits, thus foreshadowing what Marx called the 'realm of the new historic form'.

Today, one hundred years after Marx's death, we are a great deal closer to the conditions of capital's global breakdown and to the real possibility of that fundamental transformation which his work was meant to identify with scientific rigour and socialist passion. Naturally, it would be rather naive to suggest that from now on there will be no more outlets for capital's further expansion and for the displacement of many of its problems with the full involvement of the state. Equally, however, no one should doubt that we are in the midst of a crisis never experienced before on anything like a comparable scale.

Accordingly, not only are the stakes getting higher and the confrontations sharper, but also the possibilities of a positive outcome are set in a new historical perspective. For precisely because the stakes are getting higher and potentially more explosive, the storehouse of compromises that formerly served so well the forces of unchallenged 'consensus politics' is also becoming more depleted, thereby blocking certain roads and opening up some others while calling for the adoption of new strategies.

Against this background of capital's structural crisis and the concomitant new historical potentialities, it is necessary to reexamine the requirements and objective conditions of going BEYOND CAPITAL in the spirit of the original socialist project. For the transition to socialism on a global scale envisaged by Marx has acquired a new and more urgent historical actuality today, in view of the intensity and severity of the unfolding crisis.

In this article I can address only a few, closely linked, problems. *First,* the question of what is really meant by going 'beyond capital': a concept that designates the necessary objective and orienting perspective of viable socialist strategies. For the chosen *goal* necessarily conditions the stages leading to its realization, and thus the misidentification of the proper target of socialist transformation inevitably carries with it serious consequences for the socialist movement, as is painfully well known from past history.

The *second* problem to discuss concerns the necessity of a socialist offensive under the conditions of its new historical actuality. This implies also the necessity to face up to the major challenge of being compelled to embark on such an *offensive* within the framework of the existing institutions of the working class, which happened to be *defensively* constituted, under very different historical

---

* First published in the Brazilian periodical *Escrita Ensaio,* Año V, No. 11-12, 1983, pp.105-124.

conditions, in the past.

Both going beyond capital and envisaging a socialist offensive are paradigm issues of a transition to socialism. They take us to the *third* problem I must briefly talk about: the need for a theory of transition, in keeping with the socioeconomic and political conditions of our own times when *objectively* the issue itself has surfaced on the historical agenda.

And *finally* — in contrast to various strategies on the left which tend to respond to the present crisis by advocating a limited 'restructuring of the economy' — I wish to consider the role *radical politics* is called upon to play in that fundamental restructuring of society as a whole without which any transition to socialism is inconceivable.

1. The meaning of 'BEYOND CAPITAL'.

AS a point of departure, it is necessary to focus on the meaning of 'BEYOND CAPITAL'. This happens to be an all-important problem, both theoretically and practically, with several clearly distinguishable aspects:

(1) Marx wrote *Capital* in order to help break the rule of capital. And he called his main work 'CAPITAL', not 'Capitalism', for a very good reason indeed, as we shall see in a moment. Similarly, he defined the object of volume one as 'Der Produktionsprozess des Kapitals', i.e. 'The Production-process of Capital', and not as the process of 'Capitalist Production' — the way it has been wrongly translated into English, under Engels's supervision — which is a radically different matter.

(2) 'Capital' is a dynamic *historical* category and the social force to which it corresponds appears — in the form of 'monetary', 'mercantile' etc. capital — many centuries before the social formation of *capitalism* as such emerges and consolidates itself. Indeed, Marx is very greatly concerned about grasping the historical specificities of the various forms of capital and their transitions into one another, until eventually *industrial capital* becomes the dominant force of the social/economic metabolism and objectively defines the classical phase of the capitalist formation.

(3) The same is true of 'commodity production', which should not be identified with *capitalist* commodity production. The former precedes the latter, again by many centuries, thus calling for a precise definition of the historical specificities of the capitalist mode of commodity production. For, as Marx insists, 'commodity production necessarily turns into *capitalist* commodity production *at a certain point*' (Marx, 'Marginal Notes on Wagner', p.228 of *Value Studies by Marx*, 1976, London: New Park Publications).

(4) The importance of (2) and (3) is not merely theoretical but more and more directly *practical* as well. For the historical dimension of capital and commodity production is not confined to the *past*, illuminating the dynamic transition from the precapitalist formations to capitalism, but asserts its necessary practical implications for the present and the future too, foreshadowing the objective constraints and unavoidable structural determinants of the *postcapitalist* phase of development. Just as capitalism itself is not intelligible without this historical dimension of its fundamental structural characteristics reaching back to a more or less distant past, in the same way the real problems of a socialist transformation cannot be grasped without fully acknowledging that capital and commod-

ity production not only *precede* but also necessarily *survive* capitalism; and they do not do so simply as a matter of 'Asiatic backwardness' (which happens to be an additional complication, under determinate sociohistorical and political circumstances) but as a matter of innermost structural determinations.

(5) All this has far-reaching implications for socialist strategies: for their necessary and feasible objectives within the setting of the prevalent structural and historical determinations. Given such parameters, the socialist project, paradoxically, cannot help defining itself in the first place as a *radical disjuncture* between its *fundamental* historical objective and its *immediately* feasible one. The former aims at the establishment of a socialist society which represents a qualitatively 'new historic form' (Marx) in that it succeeds in going *beyond capital* itself, thus effectively superseding the world of *capital as such*; whereas the latter is forced to define its target as attacking and overcoming the dominant forces of *capitalism* only, while necessarily remaining in a vitally important sense within the structural parameters of capital as such. By contrast, without a *radical restructuring* of capital's overall controlling framework as embedded not merely in the given economic mechanisms but in the inherited *social metabolism* in general — which is feasible only as a complex historical process, with all its contradictions and potential relapses or disruptions — it is inconceivable to bring the socialist project to its proper fruition.

Confounding (for no matter how urgent and burning a political/historical reason) the fundamental strategic objective of socialism — to go *beyond capital* — with the necessarily limited and immediately feasible objective of *negating capitalism*, and thereafter pretending in the name of the latter to have realised the first, produces disorientation, the loss of all objective measure and ultimately a 'going around in circles', at best, in the absence of a viable measure and direction.

The real strategic objective of all socialist transformation is and remains the radical transcendence of capital itself, in its global complexity and with the totality of its given as well as potential historical configurations, and not merely this or that particular form of more or less developed (or underdeveloped) capitalism. It is possible to envisage negating and superseding *capitalism* in a particular social setting, provided that the given conditions themselves favour such historical intervention. At the same time, though, the much debated strategy of 'socialism in one country' is feasible only as a limited *postcapitalist* — i.e., not yet *inherently socialist* — project. In other words, it is feasible as only one *step* in the direction of a global sociohistorical transformation whose objective cannot be other than going *beyond capital* in its entirety.

Furthermore, the unavoidable fact is that the *postcapitalist* phase as a whole remains — even if to a potentially diminishing degree — within the constraints and *objective* structural parameters of capital's ultimate determinations which, contrary to Stalinist practices, should not be voluntaristically conceptualised as if they were nothing more than the *subjective*, conspiratorial manipulations of the 'enemy'. Consequently, the very process of radical restructuring — the crucial condition of success of the socialist project — can only make progress if the strategy aims at the radical supersession of capital *as such*, consciously and persistently reducing capital's power of regulating the social metabolism itself, instead of hailing as the realisation of socialism some limited postcapitalist achievements. This can be accomplished by locating neutralisable and adaptable mechanisms and processes which favour the required complex transformation, in contrast to firing 'shots in the dark' through the adoption of more or less haphazard measures, on the basis of the false identification of the fundamental strategic aim of socialism with some immediately feasible but necessarily restricted objectives.

To put it more strongly, given the inherent character of the processes involved, while various forms of postcapitalist undertaking are undoubtedly feasible in no matter how limited a setting, for precisely the same reason — i.e. the necessary limitation of this setting — they also *remain under a permanent threat*. And they remain under such threat for as long as the fundamental issue of going *beyond capital* is not settled. In other words, this or that particular form of capitalism can indeed be 'abolished' in a limited historical setting, but such 'abolition' cannot provide any guarantee against its *potential revitalisation or 'restoration,'* depending on the total configuration of the social and historical circumstances as defined by capital's more or less important role in the overall social metabolism on a *global scale*.

2. Historical conditions of the socialist offensive.

THE necessity and historical actuality of the socialist offensive does not mean the advocacy of some facile, naively optimistic, immediate agitational perspective. Far from it. For, in the first place, the *historical* actuality of a process of transformation — as arising from the manifold, uneven/conflicting determinations of an objective historical *tendency* — refers to the *historical phase* in its *entirety*, with all its complications and potential relapses, and not to some sudden event that produces an unproblematical linear development. It is worth recalling here Lenin's words:

> Capitalism could have been declared — and with full justice — to be 'historically obsolete' many decades ago, but that does not at all remove the need for a very long and very persistent struggle on the basis of capitalism. Parliamentarism is "historically obsolete" from the standpoint of *world history,* i.e., the *era* of bourgeois parliamentarism is over, and the *era* of the proletarian dictatorship has *begun.* That is incontestable. But world history is counted in decades. (Lenin, *Collected Works,* vol. 31, p.56. Lenin's emphases.)

In this sense, 'historical actuality' means precisely what it says: the emergence and unfolding actualisation of a trend in all its historical complexity, embracing a whole historical era or epoch and delimiting its strategic parameters — for better or worse as the case might be under the changing circumstances — and *ultimately* asserting the fundamental tendency of the epoch in question, notwithstanding all fluctuations, unevenness, and even relapses.

Furthermore: it cannot be stressed enough that in the midst of the deepening *structural* crisis of capital we may only talk about the *historical* actuality of the socialist offensive also in the sense that major institutional changes are required so as to bring to fruition the historical tendency in question. This is because of the badly constraining fact that the existing instruments and institutions of socialist struggle have been constituted at a qualitatively different historical conjuncture, defining themselves:

(a) in opposition to *capitalism* (not to *capital* as such), and

(b) in a fundamentally *defensive* way, in keeping with their essentially negating original potential and function.

Thus, the historical actuality of the socialist offensive under the new historical phase of capital's structural crisis asserts itself as:

(1) the increasing difficulty and ultimate impossibility of obtaining *defensive gains* — on the model of the past — through the existing *defensive institutions* (and, accordingly, the end of the earlier experienced consensus politics, carrying with it the noticeably *more aggressive posture* of the dominant forces of capital vis-à-vis labour); and

(2) the objective pressure for radically restructuring the existing institutions of socialist struggle so as to be able to meet the new historical challenge on an organisational basis which proves itself adequate to the growing need for a strategic offensive.

What is at stake, then, is the constitution of an organisational framework capable not only of negating the ruling order but simultaneously also of exercising the vital positive functions of control, in the new form of *self-activity and self-management*, if the socialist forces are to break the vicious circle of capital's social control and their own negative/defensive dependency on it.

The historical novelty of the new situation is manifest in the qualitative redefinition of the conditions of success of even the most limited socioeconomic objectives. For in the past it was not only *possible* to obtain significant *partial gains* from capital by means of the existing defensive institutions — so much so, in fact, that the working classes of the dominant capitalist countries today have incomparably more to lose than their chains — but such gains were indeed a necessary and positive constituent of the *inner dynamic* of *capital's self-expansion* itself (which meant, of course, that capital never had to pay a single penny for those gains).

In sharp contrast, under the new historical conditions of capital's structural crisis even the bare maintenance of the acquired standard of living, not to mention the acquisition of meaningful additional gains, requires a major change in strategy, in accordance with the historical actuality of the socialist offensive. Capital's growing *legislative attack* on the labour movement underlines the necessity of such a change in the strategic orientation of its adversary.

3. The need for a theory of transition.

AT the time when Marx spelled out his original conception, the accent had to be on demonstrating the inner contradictions of capital, indicating only the sketchiest outline of what Marx called 'the new historic form'. The question of how to get from the negated world of capital to the realm of the merely 'intimated' new historic form, could not play any part in Marx's theoretical project. Indeed, he scorned those who engaged in such 'speculations about the future'.

Nor was the problem of transition relevant to Lenin prior to the October revolution, since he was engaged in elaborating a strategy for 'breaking the weakest link of the chain', in the hope of initiating a chain-reaction which should have resulted in a problematic very different from that which actually presented itself through the painful historical constraints of an isolated Soviet revolution.

Thus the need for a theory of transition appeared with a burning urgency 'out of the blue', in the aftermath of the October revolution and, consequently, became mixed up with the specific determinations and concerns of Soviet society. The controversy over 'socialism in one country' was itself already a bewilderingly complex, indeed confounding issue in that an underdeveloped and devastated country was supposed to make, in isolation and encirclement, the great leap forward on its own for the whole of mankind. But much worse was still to come. For with the triumph of Stalinism in the international working class movement this issue had become even more confounding, since the 'Soviet road to socialism' had been proclaimed the compulsory model of all conceivable socialist transformation. It was uncritically adopted as a model by the adherents of the Comintern including the major Western Communist Parties whose objective circumstances lacked the relative historical justification of 'Asiatic backwardness' and encirclement for advocating such a strategy.

As a result, theorising transition was hopelessly derailed soon after its first appearance, ending up in the blind alley of Stalinist voluntarism on the one hand, and of its various abstract negations on the other. There were, of course, a few individual attempts that aimed at finding a way out of this blind alley — Antonio Gramsci's both humanly and theoretically heroic achievements represent their incomparable peak — but they were condemned to remain tragically isolated under the circumstances.

Nor could the openly announced intention of 'de-Stalinisation' produce a fundamental change in this respect. While it undoubtedly reopened the possibilities of critical self-examination (especially in the Western communist movement), the stifling of criticism in the East after a short period of 'thaw' — blind to the upheavals and explosions in Germany, Poland, Hungary, Czechoslovakia and in Poland again — underlined the severity of the crisis. It became increasingly obvious that what was really at stake was not a mere ideological factor — conceptualised in wishful/subjective categories that circularly referred to, yet never really explained even the possibility of the 'personality cult', let alone provided a guarantee for its effective supersession — but the persistent power of inertia of massive objective structures and forces which could not be effectively dislodged except in the global strategic framework of socialist development and structural transformation.

IF the historical experience of Eastern Europe could not provide a sufficient ground for developing a critical and self-critical theory of transition, that was not simply due to ideological/political pressures and taboos — although, of course, they too played their part — but primarily to the sociohistorical limitations of the experience itself.

The urgent need for a theory of transition appeared on the historical agenda with the October revolution, but it asserted itself in an unavoidably *partial* form. This had to be the case, first, because of the weight of the local constraints and contradictions under which the revolution had to be carried on as a 'holding operation' (as Lenin had called it) if it was to survive. But even more so, the partiality in question was the consequence of the essentially *defensive* historical determinations to which the struggling socialist forces of the period were subjected in their unequal confrontations with capital. This defensive determination represented an overwhelming negative historical constraint which Stalin apologetically turned into a positive virtue and model, thus frustrating and paralysing even the limited dynamic potential of the international socialist movement for decades.

Today the situation is qualitatively different in that 'transition' cannot be any longer conceptualised in a *limited* sense, since the need for it arises in relation to the deepening structural crisis of capital as a global phenomenon.

IT is always difficult to pin down with precision major historical demarcation lines and the beginning of a new historical phase; both because the roots of fundamental new trends reach back into the depths of past determinations and because it takes a long time before they unfold in all their dimensions and fully assert themselves at all levels of social life. Even such gigantic historical earthquakes as 1789 and 1917 — from which we now count the origin of many subsequent historical changes — are intelligible only in terms of both their roots in the past and their long, dramatic aftermath which had to overcome forbiddingly strong resistances in order to succeed in asserting their significance as seminal historical events.

But even if one cannot locate the beginning of the new historical phase of the necessary socialist offensive around some precise date or event, we can nevertheless identify three major social confrontations that dramatically signalled the eruption of capital's structural crisis towards the end of the 1960s:

(1) the Vietnam war and the collapse of the most openly aggressive form of American interventionism;

(2) May 1968 in France (and elsewhere, more or less at the same time, in similar social situations), clamorously demonstrating in a heartland of 'advanced' capitalism the sickness of society, the fragility and hollowness of its loudly advertised achievements, and the striking alienation of a vast number of people from the 'system' denounced with words of bitter contempt; and

(3) the repression of reform attempts in Czechoslovakia and in Poland, underlining the growing contradictions of the societies of 'actual socialism' as an *integral part of the overall structural crisis.*

Significantly, everything that happened since, falls into the same three categories — which embrace:

(1) the exploitative relations of 'metropolitan' or capitalistically advanced countries with underdeveloped ones, in their reciprocal determinations;

(2) the problems and contradictions of the Western capitalist countries, taken by themselves as well as in conjunction with one another; and

(3) the various postcapitalist countries or societies of 'actual socialism' as related to (and at times even militarily confronting) one another.

Developments in the last two decades underlined with respect to all three dimensions the working of some powerful forces and tendencies which, in their interrelatedness, define the deepening structural crisis of capital. Let me merely list a few major events and signposts of these developments, as manifest in all three areas of our concern.

With regard to the first set of relations:
• the end of the colonial regime in Mozambique and Angola;
• the defeat of white racism and the transfer of power to Z.A.N.U. in

Zimbabwe;

- the collapse of the U.S. client regime run by the Colonels in Greece and the subsequent victory of Andreas Papandreou's PASOK forces;
- the disintegration of Somosa's lifelong, U.S.-backed rule in Nicaragua and the striking victory of the Sandinista Front;
- armed liberation struggles in El Salvador and elsewhere in Central America and the end of the erstwhile easy control of the region by U.S. imperialism;
- the total bankruptcy — not only figuratively but also in a literal sense — of 'metropolitan' inspired and dominated 'developmental strategies' all over the 'Third World' and the eruption of massive structural contradictions in all three principal industrial powers in Latin America: Argentina, Brazil and even oil rich Mexico;
- the dramatic and total disintegration of the Shah's regime in Iran and with it a major defeat of long established U.S. strategies in the region, calling into existence *desperately dangerous substitute strategies* — to be implemented *directly or by proxy* — ever since.

As to the second:

- the U.S. debt crisis and the growing resentment of American economic domination;
- conflicts with industrially successful Japan and increasing signs of a potentially devastating trade war;
- the eruption of major contradictions within the European Economic Community, at times to the point of threatening it with break-up;
- the failure of postwar Keynesianism and its replacement by equally unviable 'monetarist' strategies aimed at revitalising capital in crisis;
- massive and still growing 'structural unemployment' and the corresponding eruption of major social disturbances on the ruins of the 'welfare state', following the collapse of the postwar strategy which confidently announced the realization of 'full employment in a free society';
- the failure of the postwar strategy of 'neo-colonialism' — with its ideology of 'modernization' and with its self-serving 'transfer of technology' — and the slipping control of the advanced capitalist countries over the 'Third World' (illustrated by the spread of debt-defaults, for instance), with potentially far-reaching consequences.

And, finally, as regards the major contradictions that surfaced in the internal and external relations of the so-called societies of 'actual socialism':

- the collapse of the Chinese cultural revolution and the rapprochement between China and the West, carrying with it at times quite devastating consequences for socialist aspirations;
- the undescribable tragedy of the people of Cambodia;
- armed confrontation between China and Vietnam, and between Vietnam and Cambodia;
- Soviet occupation of Afghanistan and the ensuing armed conflict;
- renewed crises in Czechoslovakia;
- increasing indebtedness of several East European countries to Western bankers, to the point of bankruptcy politely/capitalistically rebaptised as 'debt rescheduling';
- massive economic crisis in Poland and the emergence as well as the military repression of the grass root 'Solidarity' movement.

CONSIDERED against such a background of ubiquitous and perilously multiplying contradictions which amount to a veritable structural crisis, it is impossible to raise the problem of transition as one of only partial significance and thus applying to no more than the specific circumstances of a historically limited conjuncture. It is no longer possible to conceive the objective of postcapitalist strategies as some kind of a 'holding operation' whose meaning is strictly defensive, hoping for a significant improvement in the overall historical conditions and in the relation of forces which might later on favour the chances of a genuine socialist transformation.

The 'force of circumstance' tragically constraining and determining the character of a transitional effort as a 'holding operation' is one thing; the necessity of a radical social transformation on a global scale is quite another. In this sense, today the need for a comprehensive theory of transition appears on the historical agenda in the perspective of the socialist offensive, on the ground of its general historical actuality, in response to the growing structural crisis of capital which threatens the very survival of humanity.

4. 'Restructuring the economy' and its political preconditions.
4.1 The Dynamics of Postwar Developments

THERE is today a growing concern about the need for 'restructuring the economy', and understandably so. For while the postwar years, for well over two decades, saw the unprecedented expansion and revitalisation of capital — by bringing into its orbit for the first time in history the totality of global productive forces, as well as by successfully restructuring the economy so as to meet the insatiable requirements of the 'military/industrial complex' — now the whole dynamic has come to a halt and the system cannot any longer 'deliver the goods' on which its undisturbed development depends.

However, the aim of 'restructuring the economy' appears problematical in more ways than one, no matter how justifiable the concern behind it. For in view of the fact that the present state of affairs is the direct result of the postwar period's dramatic restructuring of capital's productive outlets, it is by no means obvious that switching resources today from some areas to others would produce the expected economic results, not to mention the overwhelming political complications involved in such an undertaking.

Considered under its principal aspects, any effort at 'restructuring the economy' is bound to meet with great resistance, since the leverage with which it operates remains within the confines of capital's objective determinations and mechanisms of control favouring itself and nothing else. To single out three main dimensions, it is not too difficult to perceive the irreconcilable contradictions inherent

- (1) in the problem of productivity itself (i.e., in the ultimately self-destructive productivity of capital which we shall consider presently);
- (2) in the growing demands of the military/industrial complex confronting the rest of the economy; and
- (3) in the emergence of the industrialised parts of the 'Third World' — under

the irrepressible dynamic of capital's self-expansion — as direct competitors to Western capital.

Let us briefly look at them one by one.

(1) The postwar period of development was undoubtedly fuelled, above all else, by capital's ability to activate immense, formerly repressed or latent, human and material resources for its purposes of self-expansion. It significantly extended and intensified productive economic activity by increasing both the absolute size of the labour force and of its relative productivity all over the world. So long as such process of productive self-expansion could go on unhindered, there could be no problems which capital could not, in principle, overcome.

Things had to change dramatically, however, when increasing productivity itself started to conflict with the requirement of enlarging (or even just maintaining stationary) the labour force. Under such conditions of 'structural unemployment', the necessary mode of functioning and the very *raison d'être* of capital is called into question as a matter of objective historical imperative, even if this is not immediately conceptualised as such by the actors involved.

Nor is it feasible to envisage a solution to this structural problem by simply 'creating more jobs' through 'restructuring the economy'. For what is at stake is not really capital's *efficiency* that might be improved by a more or less drastic reallocation of the economic resources, but, on the contrary, the very nature of its *productivity:* a productivity that necessarily defines itself through the imperative of its relentless, alienated self-expansion as *destructive productivity* in that it unceremoniously demolishes everything that happens to stand in its way.

Furthermore — due to the inherently contradictory nature of capital — in periods of recession the heavily *overproduced* (and at the same time grossly *under-utilised*) quantity of capital absurdly asserts itself as an extreme *scarcity of capital*, thus constraining all further productive advance and adding an *adventurist financial dimension* (as well as its Quixotic counterpart, in the form of monetarism) to all the other problems. It is therefore impossible to see how could the massive resources required for the envisaged 'economic restructuring' be found within the confines of capital's inner determinations as manifest both in its devastating 'productivity' and chronic 'scarcity' at times of economic troubles.

(2) The second major factor of capital's dynamic postwar expansion: the staggering development of the military/industrial complex, turned equally sour, despite the state's determined efforts to extend its power, or at least to keep it intact under the circumstances of 'hardship' and cuts.

Ironically, the very fact that today the problem can be formulated in this way — namely: as a call to increase or maintain military expenditure *at the expense* of social services and of the economic activity that sustains them — indicates that we are facing here a fundamental structural contradiction. For in the past the much advertised 'technological fall-out' from military developments and their claimed beneficial effects on the consumer-industry served as a self-evident ideological/economic justification of military waste, in addition to the military/industrial complex's ability to stimulate economic development all round by its huge demand on the available — and at first sight apparently limitless — material and human resources which it originally helped multiplying.

That the time might come when the multiplication of such wasteful demand cannot be sustained any longer and therefore choices must be made between military and 'consumer' expenditure, this never crossed the mind of the strategists of postwar capital-expansion. Given some inner laws and contradictions of 'advanced' capital, the road opened up by the saturation-proof, self-consuming military/industrial complex had to be pursued, irrespective of the potential complications which, in fact, seemed to be non-existent so long as the unhindered self-expansion of capital could be taken for granted.

The changes that occurred under these circumstances amounted, beyond any doubt, to a 'restructuring of the economy' so powerful, deep-seated, far-reaching and all-encompassing in character that its intensity and impact finds no parallel in the history of capital since the industrial revolution itself. To envisage, therefore, a new 'restructuring of the economy' by simply reversing this trend and transferring resources from the military/industrial complex to socially productive use, seems to be greatly underestimating the difficulties even in strictly economic terms. Not to mention the political/military complications involved in attempting to curtail in the required drastic form, as well as to keep under control ever after, the might of such a powerful adversary.

(3) The industrialisation of the 'Third World', notwithstanding its obvious subordination to the requirements and interests of Western capital, reached significant proportions in the global configuration of capital during the postwar years, especially in the last two decades.

To be sure, this industrialization was never meant to meet the needs of the starving and socially deprived people of the countries concerned, but to provide unrestrained outlets for capital-export and to generate formerly unimaginable levels of super-profit, under the ideology of 'modernisation' and the elimination of 'underdevelopment'. Nevertheless, due to the sheer size of the material and human resources thus activated by capital, the overall impact of such developments could not be other than phenomenal as far as the total production of profit in the global framework of capital was concerned. For despite all one-sided talk about 'dependency', not to mention the obscenely hypocritical talk about 'developmental aid', Western capital had become far more dependent on the 'Third World' — for raw materials, energy, capital-outlets and eagerly repatriated super-profit — than the other way round.

Naturally, in this context no less than in any other, the underlying process can only be characterised as capital's leapfrogging from one contradiction to another, in keeping with the insoluble contradictoriness of its innermost nature. For capital derives its original dynamic from the inner determination of its nature to overcome the encountered obstacles, however great, *displacing* at the same time some major contradictions. But it can do this only to end up with the *regeneration of its contradictions with a vengeance,* on an incomparably larger scale than that which had brought into being in the first place the displacing process in question.

Accordingly, no matter how bastardised and cynically manipulated the neo-capitalist industrialisation of the 'Third World' had to be in its inception and execution, inevitably it also acquired its own dynamic and local momentum, leading to an ultimately irreconcilable contradiction between the *local dynamic* and the original *'metropolitan' intent*. This took the form of establishing powerful production units whose very existence enhances the prospects of an uncontrollable trade-war, in addition to causing the structural bankruptcy and close-down of entire branches of labour-intensive industries in the advanced 'mother countries', in the explosively contradictory — unemployment generating — overall interest of Western expatriate capital.

This is not the place to enter into the details of such developments. However, it must be emphasised in the present context that the competitive complications arising out of this dynamic, with their potentially most destructive repercussions on the core of 'advanced capital', do not represent by any means the sum total of the difficulties and contradictions of these sets of relations. We must add to them the growing internal contradictions of the 'developing economies' themselves: the by now all too obvious collapse of the much advertised 'developmental strategies' and the corresponding driving to a halt of the originally quite spectacular local rates of expansion. (As in Brazil and Mexico, for instance.)

All these factors cannot but underline the insuperable difficulties facing any effort aimed at 'restructuring the economy' as they present themselves under this crucial dimension of global capital. For the problem of restructuring cannot be considered other than a comprehensive one, in every sense of the word. This is because in the contemporary world we are confronted with a bewilderingly complex and contradictory network of *reciprocal dependencies* on a global scale, with multiplying and ever-intensifying troubles and demands in every particular area, by now well beyond the control of any single 'centre', no matter how powerful and 'advanced'.

4.2 Alternatives to the dominant 'economic imperatives'

THUS — viewed in relation to its main internal and international dimensions — the question of 'restructuring the economy' defines itself as:

(1) The necessity of generating a *new type of productivity* on the ruins of capital's wasteful and destructive subordination of the productive forces and energies of society to its own perverse needs of self-expansion. In the same context this requirement also implies generating an adequately expandable supply of funds and resources, in harmony with the new type of productivity, instead of one that constrains and potentially cripples it, since the absurd overproduction/scarcity of capital today necessarily straitjackets the given mode of productivity.

(2) The challenge of instituting a viable alternative to the military/industrial complex. This presents itself as

(a) the necessity of finding an economic solution to the most destructive law of capital which brought it into being in the first place: the *decreasing rate of utilization*, tending towards the zero rate; and

(b) the creation of the political conditions of collective security and world disarmament, parallel to the establishment of a new institutional framework of inter-state relations under which the military/industrial complex loses its self-serving justification and legitimation.

(3) The institution of a radically new and truly equitable relationship with the 'Third World', on the basis of a positive recognition of the reciprocal dependencies and necessary interdeterminations in a world whose social/economic constituents can no longer be kept either isolated from or structurally

subordinated to one another if we are to see a sustainable global development. A problem of which, not surprisingly, efforts like the 'Brandt Commission's Report' do not even scratch the surface (not to mention the derision with which they are greeted and swept aside by the governing establishment to which their authors themselves once belonged). Yet, here we have to face a problem of the greatest importance to which, sadly and rather less understandably, Western socialists dedicate far too little attention.

CONSIDERED in these terms, the task of 'restructuring the economy' turns out to be primarily *political/social* and not *economic*.

To be sure, all sociopolitical objectives have their necessary *economic implications:* a rule to which fulfilling the aim of 'restructuring the economy' without a major economic intervention at the appropriate level would represent a very odd exception indeed. However, things are decidedly not the other way round — i.e., we are not facing a primarily economic challenge, with some more or less serious *political implications*, as it is often conceptualised — when the issue is: how to break the vicious circle of capital's 'iron determinations' to which no known economic mechanism can provide an answer.

If, therefore, 'restructuring the economy' is meant to equal 'restructuring society' as a whole — 'from top to bottom', as Marx once suggested — there can be no disagreement with that aim. But it cannot be stressed enough that the resistance and obstacles to be overcome in the course of realising such an aim are bound to remain primarily political/social for the entire historical period of transition whose objective is to go *beyond capital* in order to create the social/ economic structures of the 'new historic form'.

TIMES of major economic crises always open up a sizeable breach in the established order which no longer succeeds in delivering the goods that served as its unquestioned justification. Such breaches may be enlarged, in the service of social restructuring, or indeed filled in for shorter or longer duration, in the interest of capital's continued survival, depending on the general historical circumstances and on the relation of forces in the political and social arena. Given the temporal dimension of the problem — i.e., the relatively long time-scale of producing significant economic results, under the extreme urgency of the crisis — only a radical *political* initiative can move into the breach: a fact that greatly enhances the power of political action under such conditions. (Theories which exaggerate the 'autonomy' of politics — to the point of unrealistically predicating or implying its effective *independence* — tend to generalise characteristics valid for the initial phase of a major crisis, but not under normal circumstances.)

However, since the *immediate* manifestations of the crisis are *economic* — from inflation to unemployment, and from the bankruptcy of local industrial and commercial enterprises to a general trade-war and the potential collapse of the international financial system — the pressure emanating from the given social base inevitably tends to define the task at hand in terms of finding urgent *economic* answers at the level of the crisis-manifestations themselves, while leaving their *social causes* intact.

Thus, the economic definition of what *needs* to be done as well as what *can* be done under the circumstances of the acknowledged 'economic emergency'

— from 'tightening the belt' and 'accepting the necessary sacrifices' to 'creating real jobs', 'injecting new investment funds', 'increasing productivity and competitiveness', etc. — imposes the *social premises* of the established order (in the name of purely *economic* imperatives) on the socialist political initiative potentially favoured by the crisis prior to its unwitting readoption of capital's social/economic horizon. As a result, the restructuring potential of revolutionary politics is nullified as it is dissipated in the course of struggling with narrowly defined economic tasks — invariably at the expense of its own supporters — within the framework of the old social premises and structural determinations, thereby, as a matter of bitter irony, ending up with the revitalization of capital against the original intentions.

4.3 The historical moment of radical politics

THE difficulty is that the 'moment' of radical politics is strictly limited by the nature of the crises in question and the temporal determinations of their unfolding. The breach opened up at times of crisis cannot be left open forever and the measures adopted to fill it, from the earliest steps onwards, have their own logic and cumulative impact on subsequent interventions. Furthermore, both the existing socioeconomic structures and their corresponding framework of political institutions tend to act against radical initiatives by their very inertia as soon as the worst moment of the crisis is over and thus it becomes possible to contemplate again 'the line of least resistance'. And no one can consider 'radical restructuring' the line of least resistance, since by its very nature it necessarily involves upheaval and the disconcerting prospect of the unknown.

No immediate economic achievement can offer a way out of this dilemma so as to prolong the life-span of revolutionary politics, since such limited economic achievements — made within the confines of the old premises — act in the opposite direction by relieving the most pressing crisis symptoms and, as a result, reinforcing the old reproductive mechanism shaken by the crisis.

As history amply testifies, at the first sign of 'recovery', politics is pushed back into its traditional role of helping to sustain and enforce the given socio-economic determinations. The claimed 'recovery' itself, reached on the basis of the 'well tried economic motivations', acts as the self-evident ideological justification for reverting to the subservient, routine role of politics, in harmony with the dominant institutional framework. Thus, radical politics can only accelerate its own demise (and thereby shorten, instead of extending as it should, the favourable 'moment' of major political intervention) if it consents to define its own scope in terms of limited economic targets which are in fact necessarily dictated by the established socioeconomic structure in crisis.

Paradoxical as it may sound, only a radical self-determination of politics can prolong the moment of radical politics. If that 'moment' is not to be dissipated under the weight of immediate economic pressures, a way must be found to extend its influence well beyond the peak of the crisis itself (the peak, that is, when radical politics tends to assert its effectiveness as a rule). And since the temporal duration of the crisis as such cannot be prolonged at will — nor should it be, since voluntarist politics, with its artificially manipulated 'state of emergency', may only attempt to do so at its own peril, thereby alienating the masses of people instead of securing their support — the solution can only arise from successfully turning 'fleeting time' into *enduring space* by means of restructuring the powers and institutions of decision-making.

To put it in another way, radical politics is only *temporarily* favoured by the crisis which can just as easily turn against it beyond a certain point. That is to say, beyond the point when either its economic success revitalizes capital, or its failure to deliver the anticipated economic improvement dramatically undermines its own mandate and claim to legitimacy.

Thus, to succeed in its original aim, radical politics must transfer at the height of the crisis its aspirations — in the form of effective powers of decision making at all levels and in all areas, including the economy — to the social body itself from which subsequent material and political demands would emanate. This is the only way in which radical politics could sustain its own line of strategy, instead of militating against it.

SUCH transfer of political power, together with its embedding into the socio-economic structure itself, is only feasible at times of major structural crises: when, that is, the traditional premisses of the dominant social/economic metabolism not only *can* but also *must* be questioned.

Given the existing social division of labour, this questioning in the first place cannot arise anywhere else but in the 'political arena properly so called' (Marx). If, however, the questioning remains trapped within the confines of the strictly institutional forms of political action, it is bound to be defeated by the necessary reemergence of the past economic and political/institutional inertia.

The alternative to being trapped in this way is to use the critical/liberating potentials inherent in the historically favourable moment of socialist politics so as to turn its radical aims into an enduring dimension of the social body as a whole. And to do this by asserting and diffusing its own transient power through an effective transfer of power to the sphere of *mass self-activity.*

The failure to consciously pursue such course of action can only turn defeat from a more or less real possibility into a self-imposed certainty. This is why the aim of 'restructuring the economy' badly needs qualifications. For in our present context its inner truth reveals itself as the need for a *radical restructuring of politics itself* through which the realisation of socialist economic aims first becomes feasible at all. (Hence the urgency of complementing parliamentary/ institutionalized politics by growing areas and forms of *extra-parliamentary action.)*

The socialist offensive cannot be carried to its positive conclusion unless radical politics succeeds in prolonging its moment, so as to be able to implement the policies required by the magnitude of its tasks. The only way, however, in which the historical moment of radical politics can be prolonged and extended — without, that is, resorting to dictatorial solutions, against the original intentions — is to fuse the power of political decision making with the social base from which it has been alienated for so long.

To achieve this end requires creating a new mode of political action and a new structure of — genuinely mass-oriented and determined — social/economic and political interchanges. This is why a truly socialist 'restructuring of the economy' can only proceed in the closest conjunction with a *mass-oriented restructuring of politics* as its necessary precondition.

V. THE PRESENT CRISIS*

1. Surprising admissions

AS a point of departure, let us see three, rather surprising, recent statements, made by some well known Britsh public figures. The first asserted that:

> we are on the brink of economic crisis — a crisis with social and political consequences we have barely begun to contemplate. [We are facing] continuing decline — and in its wake social and political decay and perhaps even democracy itself struggling for survival.[1]

The second warned that the immense amount of money which the U.S. annually spent on defence 'created major problems', adding that:

> It is spent largely within one market, which is perhaps the most protected market in the alliance — by technology transfer regulations, by American protection laws, by extraterritorial controls ... co-ordinated through the Pentagon and protected by Congress. It is channelled into the largest and richest companies on earth. It is irresistible and if unchecked it will ... buy its way through sector after sector of the world's advanced technologies. ... The way in which the reconstruction of the Westland PLC has been handled has raised profound issues about defence procurement and Britain's future as a technologically advanced country.'[2]

The third statement was no less dramatic. With reference to President Reagan's so-called 'Strategic Defence Initiative' (SDI) it protested against the negative implications of SDI for British industry, declaring that:

> We are being tempted by crumbs from the table. Europe should be careful that participation in the U.S. Star Wars research programme will not amount to taking in a Trojan horse.[3]

What is surprising in all this is not that such statements have been made at all, but the social and political allegiances of the people who made them. For the first warning came from Sir Edwin Nixon, Chairman of IBM in the United Kingdom. Nor was the second admonition voiced by a 'flaming revolutionary', or even by someone committed to the cause of the 'soft left'.

On the contrary, it was made by none other than the Tory Party's former Secretary of State for Defence in Britain, Michael Heseltine, in his attempt to explain why he had to resign and create a major political scandal on account of the government's pretended neutrality (and actual support) for the American transnational corporations against the European Consortium. And finally, the third statement came from Paddy Ashdown, Liberal Party Member of Parliament for Yeovil: the same man who vociferously defended the successful American takeover bid for the Westland helicopter company, against which Heseltine protested.

The point is that capitalism today is experiencing a profound crisis that could no longer be denied even by its spokesmen and beneficiaries. Nor should one imagine that U.S. capital is less affected by it than Britain and Europe. IBM's

---

* Written in August 1987, published in the Brazilian periodical *Ensaio,* No. 17-18, Numero Especial, 1989, pp.159-71.

Vice Chairman for research asserted recently, with a heavy touch of irony, that the much prophesied *'technological spin-off'* — in the name of which the prohibitively expensive and corruptly overcharged defence contracts have been enthusiastically advocated by many and approved by Parliaments and governments in the past — turned out to be no more than a mere *'drip-off'*.[4] Indeed, the overall situation is in reality much more serious than the non-materialization of the promised technological side-benefits of military waste could suggest on its own. I have argued nearly two decades ago that the necessary result of the — no matter how generously funded — state interventions in the service of capital-expansion was bound to be:

> not only the cancerous growth of the non-productive branches of industry within the total framework of capital production but — equally important — also the grave distortion of the whole structure of *capitalist cost-accounting* under the impact of contracts carried out with the ideological justification that they are 'vital to the national interest'. And since present-day capitalism constitutes a closely *interlocking system,* the devastating results of this structural distortion come to the fore in numerous fields and branches of industry, not only in those which are *directly* involved in the execution of defence contracts. The well known facts that original cost-estimates as a rule madly 'escalate', and that the committees set up by governments to scrutinize them fail to produce results (that is, results other than the white-washing of past operations, coupled with generous justifications of future outlays), find their explanation in the immanent necessities of this changed structure of capitalist production and accountancy, with the gravest implications for the future.[5]

Recent reports have amply confirmed that instead of the much advertised technologically generated commercial bonanza, a significant worsening of competitiveness had resulted from the military-orientated distortion of capitalist cost-accountancy both in Europe and in the United States. For 'as military technology has become more and more complex, expensive, clever and arcane, it has increasingly diverged from possible civilian applications.'[6]

Accordingly, among the major disadvantages underlined by a recent report on information technology Research and Development (issued by the U.S. Congress Office of Technology Assessment) we find: 'security classifications which tend to slow advancement in technology; rigid technical specifications for military procurement which have limited utility for commercial applications; and the "consumption" of limited, valuable scientific and engineering resources for military purposes, which may inhibit commercial developments.'[7]

In other words, direct state intervention in the capitalist reproduction process ultimately misfires in every way, constraining the course of civilian economic development by no means only with its secretive political/administrative rules. Also, it produces major problems in tangible economic terms by generating absurd technical specifications (e.g. the nuclear-blast-proof toilet seat that survives the incineration of its occupier) and the commercially useless productive/ engineering practices corresponding to them. At the same time, moreover, we are also confronted with the extreme *technologization of science* that strait-jackets its productive potentialities even in strictly capitalist consumer-economic terms, in the service of utterly wasteful military purposes.

2. The assertion of U.S. hegemony

THE negative consequences of such worsening of competitiveness are unavoidable. They are already noticeable in the intensification of the contradictions of international trade relations and in the measures adopted by the most powerful capitalist country to reassert in an openly aggressive fashion the long unchallenged U.S. dominance within the Western alliance. To give some instances of major importance:

2.1 'Extra-territoriality'.

This issue came to light in parliamentary debates during the summer of 1985. Since it negatively affected various sections of British capital, it could be taken up by all shades of opinion in the parliamentary spectrum.

Liberal MP, Paddy Ashdown, claimed that 'U.S. attempts to control the export of high technology systems could destroy the U.K. computer industry.' He also claimed that the U.S. Export of Goods Control Order would introduce 'a series of potentially fatal export constraints, imposed at the behest of the Pentagon and without adequate consultation with any of the industries affected in the U.K.' Furthermore, Ashdown also asserted that the U.S. was turning the law in question to its commercial gain, to quash competition from U.K. companies, alleging that 500,000 jobs have been already lost in Europe as a result.

In reply to Ashdown's representations, the Conservative British Attorney General, Sir Michael Havers, described the U.S. control attempts as an 'unwarranted encroachment of U.K. jurisdiction and *contrary to international law*.'[8] Ironically, however, by the beginning of 1987 the British Government had capitulated on the issue in a humiliating way, accepting the earlier rhetorically condemned 'unwarranted ecroachment of U.K. jurisdiction'. It conferred on U.S. trade inspectors the right to examine the books of British manufacturing companies which use American high technology components, despite the protests of U.K. firms which fear that information thus obtained from their company records could damage them.

Plessey's director of strategic planning, John Saunders, commented that the company's books contained information that could be useful to U.S. competitors. At the same time Liberal MP, Michael Meadowcroft, protested that U.K. sovereignty was breached by the move. 'It is a *monstrous interference*', he said.[9]

Naturally, the Labour Party had also joined in the debates. Labour MP, Michael Meacher, claimed that the Government sacrificed U.K. interests 'in its total failure to protect British companies who find themselves the prey of unfair American domination and interference.' He also suggested that the issue of sovereignty should be a key issue at the 1987 general election.[10]

2.2 Industrial advantage from military secrecy.

Two issues stand out in this respect.

The first, under the organization of COCOM — masterminded by Pentagon 'hawk' Richard Pearl — is concerned with the imposition of severe export restrictions on Western European countries, to the clear advantage of U.S. firms.

The second was highlighted more recently, in connection with the so-called

Strategic Defence Initiative (SDI). Many British scientists and computer experts protested against the whole initiative and the way in which it was handled by the Government. Richard Ennals, of Imperial College, the former research director of the Alvey project (named after the author of a government-sponsored report), was the first U.K. scientist to resign over the issue. He commented forcefully: 'SDI is sucking in British technology for U.S. industrial exploitation.'[11] Thus, it came as no great surprise that his book — in which he developed his criticisms at length — was suppressed a few days before its publication by his own publishers. (One can quite easily guess which quarters the pressure for suppressing his book had come from.)

Moreover, the attitude to SDI was a matter of serious concern even in some European governmental circles. It has been reported that:

> The Europen Commission is warning Common Market governments that European participation in the American Star wars programme could damage the health of pan-European research programmes like Esprit and domestic projects like Alvey. The commission has sent a confidential letter to the 10 member governments ahead of the Common Market summit in Milan later this month, warning that participation in the space defence initiative can be very damaging to high technology industry. The letter warns that European participation in Star Wars research would divert European research efforts. Apart from threatening Alvey and Esprit it would seriously diminish overall European research then boost the constraints which are already being unilaterally imposed by the United States on European hi-tech trade.[12]

Irrespective of what might or might not be done eventually about such concerns by the particular European governments, it is impossible to ignore the severity of the underlying contradictions.

2.3 Direct trade pressures applied by the U.S. legislative and executive.

Some recent examples include the *agricultural tariffs war* threatened by the Reagan Administration — over which the Governments of the European Economic Community in the end capitulated — and the *European Air Bus project* over which they refused to capitulate so far. Conflict with Japan too intensifies, as recently underlined by the unanimous vote of the U.S. Senate, calling for strong protectionist measures against Japan, duly followed by the application of some punitive tariffs.

But well beyond such particular confrontations (which happen to be quite significant even by themselves), there is the prospect of abandoning altogether the framework of GATT as the institutional regulator of tariff agreements between the U.S. and Europe. We can now witness in the U.S. a growing pressure to switch from such *multilateral* regulators of commercial interchange to strictly *bilateral* trade agreements through which the incomparably more powerful American side could dictate the conditions to the much smaller and weaker European competitors, taken separately. For bilateral trade relations — by their very nature — always favour the considerably stronger party involved in such contracts, enhancing its relative advantage in more ways than one.

Whether or not the growing pressures for undermining or leaving GATT — as well as similar moves directed at other mechanisms of regulation — will prevail in the not too distant future, is at this point an open question. What is nevertheless highly significant is that the need for a drastic restructuring of

American trade relations with the rest of the world on a *bilateral* basis is being seriously contemplated at all.

2.4 *The real debt problem.*

There is a great deal of discussion concerning the severe and by now obviously unmanageable indebtedness of Latin American countries, as well as the dangerous implications of such indebtedness for the world financial system as a whole. While no one should wish to deny the importance of this issue, it must be stressed that it is quite astonishing how little attention is paid to the need to put it in perspective. For the *entire* Latin American debt, amounting to less than $350 billion at the time of writing this article (which had been collectively accumulated by the countries concerned over a period of *several decades*) pales into total insignificance if set against U.S. indebtedness — both internal and external — which must be counted in *trillions* of dollars; i.e. in magnitudes that quite simply defy the imagination.

Characteristically, however, this matter is kept most of the time out of sight, thanks to the conspiracy of silence of the interested parties. As if such astronomical debts could be 'written into the chimney breast, so as to let the soot take care of it', as a Hungarian adage puts it (about small debts, incurred among close friends who can easily cope with such 'write-offs'). Yet, to imagine that this practice of chimney-breast debt-management, involving trillions of dollars, could go on indefinitely, goes well beyond the limits of all credulity.

Admittedly, the partners to such practices — the European countries no less than Japan — are locked into a system of heavy dependency on U.S. markets and on the concomitant debt-generated 'liquidity'. Thus, they are in a very precarious position when it comes to devising effective measures for bringing under control the real debt problem. Indeed, they are sucked deeper and deeper into the whirlpool of those contradictory determinations whereby they 'voluntarily' increase their own dependence on the escalating American debt, with all its dangers for themselves, while helping to promote and finance it.

However, from the fact that this vicious circle exists it does not follow that the global capitalist system can escape from the perilous implications of the U.S. trillions mounting on the wrong side of the balance-sheet. In fact the limits of how long such practices can be maintained should not be too difficult to identify.

To be sure, the Western capitalist countries — partly due to the internal contradictions of their own economies and partly because of their heavy dependence on American commodity and financial markets — will continue to participate with their financial assets in safeguarding the relative stability of the U.S. economy, and thereby of the global system. For the adventurist dominance of *finance capital* in general is rather the *manifestation* of deep-seated economic crises than their *cause,* even if in its turn it greatly contributes to their subsequent aggravation. Thus, the tendency to destroy certain industries and to transfer much of the financial assets thus generated to the U.S., is by no means accidental. (Though, of course, it is utterly grotesque that Britain, for instance, which leads the capitalist world in such process of 'de-industrialization', should be also one of the principal *creditor* countries today.) Nor should it be surprising that once the assets of a country are deployed in this way, the pressure for protecting them against the danger of a disastrous financial chain-reaction and ultimate collapse

— by transferring further funds, supporting the dollar through the manipulative intervention of central banks, etc. — becomes quite irresistible.

Nevertheless, only fools and blind apologists could deny that the ongoing U.S. practice of debt-management is built on very shaky ground. It will become totally untenable when the rest of the world (including the 'third world' from which massive transfers are still successfully extracted in one way or another every year) is no longer in a position to *produce* the resources which the American economy requires in order to maintain itself in existence as the today still often idealized 'engine' of the capitalist world-economy.

2.5 Political antagonism arising from U.S. economic penetration.

In the midst of a recent political scandal, following the exposure of secret government negotiations with U.S. giant firms, the Leader of the British Labour Party talked of 'a *further act of colonization* in the British economy'.[13] He received the full approval of the liberal press. An Editorial of *The Guardian* protested:

> First there was United Technologies, negotiating to take a stake in Westland [and succeeding, through governmental manipulation and suspect share dealings, under the cloak of secrecy]. Then General Motors with Lotus; then a threat to take the contract for airborne radar away from GEC [which, also, later turned into an accomplished fact] and lob it into the hands of Boeing. Now, Ford may buy BL, all that remains of a British-owned motor industry. One or two of these deals might have been excusable. But so many, so close, give the impression that Mrs Thatcher has such little faith in U.K. manufacturers that she wants to turn the country into a *Third World assembler of multinational products.*[14]

Ironically, it was not the Labour leadership but the same Editorial article of *The Guardian* that pointed out the grave implications of such economic take-overs for the position of labour. It reminded its readers of the direct threat of increasing unemployment as a matter of transnational industrial policy, — cynically spelled out by the management of one of the principal U.S. companies — adding to its critical concern also a warning about the consequences of U.S. penetration into the British economy for the balance of payments and for the future of British industry in general:

> Mr Bob Lutz, chairman of Ford of Europe, recently told the *Financial Times*: 'If we find we have major assembly facilities regardless of the country involved, which for one reason or another — perhaps *uneducated government* action (giving *longer holidays, a shorter working week*) or *union intransigence* — cannot be competitive, *we would not shy away from a decision to close them.*'
>
> Ford U.K. ... is also a substantial drain on the balance of payments, amounting to £1.3 billion in 1983 as it (quite properly from its own self-interest) sourced from the cheaper imports.
>
> The Government claims not to have an industrial strategy. In fact, of course, it has one. Privatise everything that moves and sell what you can to foreign buyers. You don't have to be a *Little Englander* to realise that this is an abdication of responsibility which could make the *terminal decline of industry* in this country a self-fulfilling prophecy.[15]

But, of course, the heaviest irony arises from the peculiar circumstance that all this is happening against the background of massive American indebtedness.

Senator McGovern at the time of his Presidential campaign pointed out that the U.S. was running the Vietnam war on credit card. Since then U.S. capital has graduated to pursue much bigger stakes in financial terms. Its deep penetration not only into the 'Third World' but also into the heart-lands of Western 'advanced capitalism', through the relentless pursuit of its *credit-card imperialism*, points to a major contradiction that cannot be hidden away indefinitely even by the most servile 'friendly Governments' (like Mrs Thatcher's Conservative one currently in office in Britain), as the growing number of protests coming from the adversely affected capitalist circles testify.

The most important, and potentially most harmful, dimension of this economic penetration is that it is being pursued — with the full complicity of the most powerful sections of capital in the Western countries concerned — on the basis of an already astronomical, and inexorably growing, U.S. indebtedness that foreshadows an *ultimate default* of quite unimaginable magnitude.

But even with regard to the modality of the financial operations involved, it is rather revealing that the major U.S. take-overs of foreign companies are often financed from credit raised internally, in the affected countries themselves, diverting much needed resources from alternative investments to financing American credit-card imperialism.

Furthermore, there is frequently also a direct connection with the interests of the military/industrial complex and with the lucrative military contracts — often constituting the hidden motivation behind take-over deals — which happen to be vital to maintaining the profitability of the dominant capitalist corporations.

A characteristic example came to light in the debates over the secret deal between the British Government and General Motors — foiled as a result of the political scandal that followed its revelation — concerning British Leyland's truck division as well as Land-Rover. In the parliamentary debate over this affair:

> Alan Williams MP, a Labour industry spokesman, said that the defence implications of a U.S. takeover of Land-Rover had not been considered. A subsidiary of Land-Rover called Self-Change Gear supplied components to the British-made battle tank and was in contention for a £ *200 million contract* for the American battle tank. Its major competitor was General Motors, to whom the Government was now considering selling it.[16]

Here the issue was that had the secret deal materialized — i.e. simply presented to Parliament and to the public by the British Government, at an opportune moment, in the usual way, as an accomplished fact to which 'there is no alternative' — General Motors not only would have acquired, *for absolutely nothing*, British Leyland's truck division as well as (more importantly) its Land-Rover division, but at the same time it would have also pocketed a very handsome profit on top of its free acquisitions, as a 'side-benefit'.

Such practices, however, can only generate conflicts even in formerly unsuspected quarters, intensifying the pressure for protectionist measures. A pressure which not so long ago — at the time of the postwar expansionary phase of capitalist development and its concomitant consensus — inasmuch as it existed at all, could be safely ignored in view of its limited extent and only subterranian character. Ominously, however, under the present conjuncture the protectionist pressure tends to erupt into the open in all important areas of the global capitalist economic and inter-state relations, aggravating thereby the various contradictions of the system on which it has a direct or indirect bearing.

3. *Wishful thinking about 'the decline of the U.S. as hegemonic power.'*

IT might be tempting to overstate the gravity and immediacy of the present crisis, jumping to the kind of conclusion which we were offered five years ago in a book co-authored by four highly respected left-wing intellectuals who prematurely announced 'the decline of the United States as a hegemonic power'.[17]

Such a view directly contradicted Baran's characterization of the radically altered postwar international power relationships in the capitalist world which spoke of 'the unabated rivalry among the imperialist countries as well as the growing inability of the old imperialist nations to hold their own in face of the American quest for expanded influence and power',[18] insisting that 'the assertion of American supremacy in the "free" world implies the reduction of Britain and France (not to speak of Belgium, Holland, and Portugal) to the status of junior partners of American imperialism'.[19]

In reality it is Baran's more than three decades old diagnosis which stood the test of time as against others, including the much more recent one quoted above. In fact there is as yet no serious sign of the wishfully anticipated 'decline of the United States as a hegemonic power', notwithstanding the appearance of numerous crisis symptoms in the global system. For the contradictions which we can identify concern the *whole* of the interlocking system of global capital in which American capital occupies, maintains, and indeed continues to strengthen its dominant position in every way, paradoxically even through its — on the face of it quite vulnerable, yet up to the present time without too much opposition successfully enforced — practices of credit-card imperialism.

People who speak of, and attach so much significance to, the alleged decline of the U.S. as a hegemonic power seem to forget that such possibilities — i.e. the many ways of imposing astronomical U.S. indebtedness on the rest of the world, disregarding its unavoidable negative implications for the other capitalistically advanced societies as well — are available only to one single country, in virtue of its practically undisputed (and short of a major socioeconomic earthquake undisputable) hegemonic power within the capitalist world.

One set of rules of 'good house-keeping' reserved for one single member of the club of 'advanced capitalism', and a very different set imposed on all the others, including Japan and West Germany: what is that if not evidence for the continued hegemonic supremacy of the United States? Besides, even on the terrain of *ideology* we could observe in the postwar period, and particularly in the last decade, a remarkable *strengthening* of American hegemony, rather than its *weakening,* as postulated by the 'end of U.S. hegemony' thesis. And the fact that this ideological domination is — to a far from negligible extent — materially sustained by the credit-card financed *'brain drain'* in which European 'jet-set-socialist intellectuals' participate on a permanent or part-time basis (no less than their natural science research colleagues in the domain of technology), and as a feed-back from such participation they actively help to diffuse on this side of the Atlantic, not only in academic circles but also among the leadership of Western working class parties and trade unions, the dominant American liberal/bourgeois discourse on so-called 'feasible socialism,' only underlines the sobering truth that economic supremacy can produce most unexpected forms of ideological mystification.

4. The official view of 'healthy expansion'.

ALL the same, it could be hardly denied that something significantly new is happening to the system as a whole. Its nature cannot be explained, as often attempted, simply in terms of a traditional *cyclic* crisis, since both the *scope* and the *duration* of the crisis which we have been subjected to in the last two decades, by now has well overreached the historically known limits of cyclic crises. Nor is it really plausible to ascribe the identifiable crisis symptoms to the so-called *'long wave'*: an idea which, as a somewhat mysterious explanatory hypothesis, has been naively or apologetically injected into more recent debates.

As the crisis symptoms multiply and their severity is aggravated, it looks much more likely that the system as a whole is approaching certain *structural limits* of capital, even though it would be far too optimistic to suggest that the capitalist mode of production has already reached the point of no return leading to its collapse. Nevertheless, we must face up to the prospect of very serious complications when the U.S. debt default reverberates over the global economy with all its might in the not too distant future. After all, we should not forget that the U.S. Government has defaulted already — under Richard Nixon's Presidency — on its solemn pledge concerning the gold-convertibility of the dollar, without the slightest regard for the interests of those directly affected by its decision, and indeed without any concern whatsoever for the severe implications of its unilateral action for the future of the international monetary system. Recently we came a considerable step nearer to the U.S. debt default with the record April-June 1987 trade deficit, amounting to $39.53 billions, of which $15.71 billions represented the month of June alone: yet another all-time record. For even the April-June figure (constituting an annual sum of nearly $160 billions) well exceeds the *total* accumulated debt of Argentina and Brazil put together; not to speak of the annual $188.52 billions trade deficit which we are heading for on the basis of the June 1987 figure. At the same time, as if he wanted to underline the total unreality of the adopted remedial measures:

> Mr Robert Heller, Federal Reserve Governor, said yesterday that the U.S. economy was becoming more balanced, noting that 'what we are seeing is a healthy continuation of the current economic expansion.'[20]

If $188.52 billions annual balance of trade deficit, coupled with astronomical budgetary deficits, can be considered 'the healthy continuation of economic expansion', one shudders to think what will the *unhealthy* condition of the economy look like when we reach it.

Postscript 1995: The Meaning of Black Mondays (and Wednesdays)

A few weeks after the completion of this article — to be precise: on Monday 21, 1987 — we were entertained to the spectacle of a big tumble on the world's stock exchanges. This must have been still part of the 'healthy continuation of economic expansion', since it happened so soon after the reassuring statement made by the U.S. Federal Reserve Governor. The aftermath of this event was also very interesting, and to the world of big business no doubt also reassuring. For the governments of the capitalistically advanced countries instituted some binding regulations and the corresponding computer mechanisms, with a view to call a temporary halt to all stock market activity in the event of 'excessive speculative transactions', in order to prevent the repetition of *'Black Monday'*, as October 21, 1987 came to be known.\

Strangely, however, all this had very little effect on the events leading to *'Black Wednesday'* in 1993, and the (pretended) 'forced abandonment' of the European 'Exchange Mechanism' by the British Government. For the Bank of England always had the resources to eat speculative Fund Managers, like George Soros, for breakfast by the dozen; on this occasion, however, it was decided, instead, to reward his enterprise with $1billion in exchange for the convenient excuse that Britain was 'forced out' of the European system of monetary regulation, and therefore could not help breaking its treaty obligations. Naturally, the result of this move was an almost 30 percent devaluation of the Pound Sterling and with it the acquisition of a significant competitive advantage against the country's European partners — precisely what the Exchange Mechanism was designed to prevent — and an 'export-led recovery' which has been hailed ever since by the British government. For the greatly devalued currency's competitive advantage helps a great deal — even if by no means forever — in the field of exports, although it refuses to deliver the frequently announced 'full recovery' and 'healthy expansion' for the economy as a whole.

Three years before *Black Monday* the sorrowful but for the financial world happy-ending tale of *'Black Sunday'* had hit the headlines. At that time

the Bank of England was called into action to save an important institution when Johnson Matthey Bankers (JMB), the bullion trader, collapsed and had to be rescued by a Bank-organized lifeboat. That crisis broke on a Sunday and after holding a council of war with City elders, the Bank took JMB into *public ownership*.[21]

Unhappily for another important financial force, 'Barings Securities' — one of the oldest banking institution in Britain, founded in 1772, and once described as the sixth great power of Europe, after Britain, France, Austria, Russia and Prussia — its disastrous collapse unfolded in February 1995 on a *'Black Saturday'*, followed by another *Black Sunday*.

The crisis stunned senior City figures. Sir Michael Richardson, one of the Square Mile's [the London City's] most respected bankers, said last night: 'This is the most devastating news, and one of the most serious things I have heard in ages'.[22]

Barings, alas, could not be rescued. For the customary way of dealing with large-scale failures — by taking the enterprises concerned into 'public ownership' (so much despised by the champions of 'privatization' and market-idolatry), thereby 'nationalizing' private capitalist bankruptcy whenever that suits the system's convenience — cannot always do the trick, in the absence of a bottomless public purse. There was more than a touch of irony in the collapse of Barings, in that before its fate was sealed on the Singapore stock exchange 'it had been weakened by heavy losses on its South American business, following the collapse of the Mexican peso'.[23] Thus, what was supposed to be one of the great historical advances of present-day capitalism — 'modernizing globalization' — had gone sour not only in Mexico, with the most painful consequences for its people. It contributed at the same time also to the ignominious liquidation of one of the most venerable and bluest of blue City institutions.

'Black Tuesday', by contrast, happened in the most unexpected place, even if

it was fully in tune with the logic of capital. The dramatic day in question was everywhere described as *Black Tuesday* when only after a few years of enjoying the blessings of 'marketization' and monetary 'convertibility' the Russian economy suffered a major shock — on 11 October 1994 — through a catastrophic fall of the (already absurdly undervalued) Rouble against the Dollar. Thus, by now we are not only witnessing the same kind of crises erupt, with discomforting frequency, even in the once financially sheltered corners of the world, but also seem to be running out of days of the week to be blackened, as befits the system.

THE day after *Black Monday* a group of high-powered bankers and leading economists discussed the crisis on BBC television. One of them argued that the root cause of the disaster was the American debt and the failure to do something about it. Yet, the most cynical of the City bankers hit the nail on the head when he rebutted that the one thing much more disastrous than not doing anything about the American debt would be to attempt to do something about it.

It is only right and proper that an economic system riddled with contradictions should find its guiding principles in the topsy-turvy world of apologetic economic wisdom. In a world of utmost financial *insecurity* nothing suits better the practice of gambling with astronomical and criminally unsecured sums on the world's stock exchanges — foreshadowing an earthquake of magnitude 9 or 10 on the Financial 'Richter Scale' — than to call the enterprises which engage in such gambling *'Securities* Management'; a fact highlighted by the demise of 'Barings Securities'. In the same vein in which reckless gambling is served up as 'security', one of the recent discoveries of 'economic science' is called the *'confidence coefficient'*, which is supposed to measure and depict on a 'scientific graph' — on the basis of the most fanciful hearsay and wishful thinking — the health and future prospects of the capitalist economy. An even more recent rejoinder of equal explanatory value is the much talked about *'feel-good factor'*, which is supposed to demonstrate by its non-arrival that everything is all right with the economy, when to every sane person matters are visibly and painfully wrong. Some high-flown and respectably sounding economic categories fully match the apologetic intent. Thus we are mystified by the notions of *'negative growth'* — meaning *recession* — and *'sustained negative growth'*, equivalent to *depression*. In accord with these concepts even in dire trouble there can be nothing to worry about. In the meantime, the Japanese Nikkei average, which fell from its peak of 40,000 to around the perilous 14,000 level at the present — not in a single 'Black Day', but over five years of 'sustained negative growth' — is very near to precipitating a global financial crisis. For below 14,000 'many of the shares held by Japan's banks and insurers will be worth less than the institutions paid for them'.[24] And that is where yet another 'economic category' is supposed to help. It is called *'negative equity'*, which translates into human language as being in the immediate vicinity of bankruptcy. Many millions of mortgage holders all over the world share the privilege of 'negative equity' with Japan's banks and other economic institutions; but they are most unlikely to derive any reassurance from such an exalted financial status. For already hundreds of thousands of them have lost their homes, and many more are being *repossessed* — for which there seems to be no soothing category in contemporary 'economic science' — and refuse to 'feel good' about it. As to Japan itself, the astronomical amount of 'negative equity' possessed by its financial institutions has potentially disastrous economic consequences on account of the necessity to withdraw huge external capital funds, primarily from the U.S. The repercussions of such a move would affect the whole of the global financial market.

The American hegemony discussed in this article was clamorously underlined also with the implosion of the Soviet system, and, even if far from uncontested, remains a major determining factor for world economic development in the foreseeable future. When exactly and in what form — of which there can be several, more or less directly brutal, varieties — the U.S. will default on its astronomical debt, cannot be seen at this point in time. There can be only two certainties in this regard. The first is that the inevitability of the American default will deeply affect everyone on this planet. And the second, that the preponderant hegemonic power position of the U.S. will continue to be asserted in every way, so as to make the rest of the world pay for the American debt for as long as it is capable of doing.

Two brief passages should illustrate the continued assertion of American hegemony. The first concerns the Newly Industrialized Countries (NICs).

> Not facing a debt crisis, the NICs have been able to avoid Structural Adjustment Programs [ruthlessly imposed on indebted 'developing countries' by the U.S.]. They have not, however, been able to avoid the pressure of rollback. *Dark Victory*[25] shows how the U.S. government has repeatedly used the threat of trade war to force NIC states to reduce their economic activity and open up their economies to U.S. imports and investment. The new GATT agreement is an important part of the U.S. offensive. Although promoted as a generalized free trade agreement, it is primarily designed to restrict state direction of economic activity.[26]

The second quotation reminds us of the constant pressure applied by the U.S. even on one of the economic giants of advanced capitalism, Germany, the same way as on Japan. As we learn from an article of *The Financial Times:*

> calls from Washington for smaller fiscal deficits must be intensely irritating to the Germans. U.S. policymakers have, after all, called for a fiscal boost by Germany almost every year since the G7 was formed. More irritating still, the U.S. has itself followed the most consistently profligate fiscal policy of the three major economies. If global interest rates are to fall — as, indeed, they must — the U.S. must put its own fiscal house in order.[27]

However, there is a limit to everything, even to U.S. profligacy. The limit in this respect is that the average gross public debt of the OECD economies has grown in just two decades — between 1974 and 1994 — from *35 percent* to *71 percent*. Given the same trend of development, it will not take many decades before it will be unavoidable to actually 'do something about' these intractable problems, disregarding the views of City bankers and other vested interests.

NOTES

[1] *Computer Weekly,* 19 December 1985.

[2] Michael Heseltine's resignation statement, 9 January 1986.

[3] *Computer Weekly,* 13 June 1985.

[4] Quoted in Mary Kaldor, 'Towards a High-Tech Europe?', *New Socialist,* No. 35, February 1986, p. 10.

[5] Mészáros, *The Necessity of Social Control,* p. 50.

[6] Mary Kaldor, *Ibid.* The author gives some revealing examples in her article:

Electrical industries are interesting to look at because this sector has both military and commercial markets. You can, for example, compare the share of government-funded R&D (predominantly defence-related, except in West Germany) in the electrical industries as a whole, and competitiveness in office machinery and computers, electronic components, and electrical machinery. Apart from office machinery and computers, where the large military market makes the U.S. competitive, the inverse relation between defence R&D and competitiveness is quite marked. Another interesting example is chemicals. The only high technology sector in which the U.K. is very competitive, as defined by the OECD, is drugs and medicine. This is one area where military R&D — and its influence — is negligible.

Concern about declining competitiveness in manufacturing has prompted a series of official reports in both Britain and the United States. In Britain, two reports — one by the House of Lords Select Committee on Science and Technology, the other by Sir Ieuan Maddocks, on behalf of the National Economic Development Council — argued that the high level of defence R&D is a major reason for the failure of Britain to exploit science and technology effectively enough to increase the competitiveness of British manufacturing. *Ibid.*, p. 11.

[7] *Ibid.*

[8] *Computer Weekly*, 18 July 1985.

[9] *Ibid.*, 19 February 1987.

[10] See Editorial article in *Computer Weekly*, entitled 'Blame Reagan, not U.S. Trade'. The congenital illusions of the liberal position are well illustrated by this editorial title itself. As if the actions of the U.S. administration could be separated from, and opposed to, the interests of U.S. trade.

[11] *Ibid.*, 16 January 1986.

[12] *Ibid.*, 13 June 1985.

[13] Parliamentary debates, 4 February 1986.

[14] 'Selling off, and shrugging yet again', *The Guardian,* 5 February 1986.

[15] *Ibid.*

[16] As reported in *The Guardian,* 5 February 1986.

[17] See the collective volume by Samir Amin, Giovanni Arrighi, André Gunder Frank and Immanuel Wallerstein, *Dynamics of Global Crisis,* Macmillan, London, 1982.

[18] Paul Baran, *The Political Economy of Growth,* Monthly Review Press, New York, 1957, p. vii.

[19] *Ibid.* Baran quotes on the same page also another passage from the bitterly realist words of the London *Economist* [17 November 1957]:

We must learn that we are not the Americans' equals now, and cannot be. We have a right to state our minimum national interests and expect the Americans to respect them. But this done, we must look for their lead.

[20] 'U.S. trade deficit hits quarterly record', *Financial Times,* 27 Aug. 1987.

[21] Andrew Lorenz and Frank Kane, 'Barings seeks rescue buyer', *The Sunday Times,* 26 February 1995.

[22] *Ibid.*

[23] *Ibid.*

[24] 'Where a slump might start', *The Economist,* 17 June 1995.

[25] Walter Bello, Shea Cunningham and Bill Rau, *Dark Victory: The United States, Structural Adjusment, and Global Poverty,* Institute for Food and Development Policy, Oakland, 1994.

[26] Martin Hart-Landsberg, 'Dark Victory: Capitalism Unchecked;, *Monthly Review,* March 1995, p.55.

VI. 'SOCIALISMO HOY DIA'*

1. The quickening pace of history.
IN July 1989 we could witness a curious event: the gathering in Paris of the heads of the conservative establishment from all over the world, treated to a frivolous showbiz spectacle on the Champs Elisées by their 'socialist' host. They had to be brought together and suitably entertained, brushing aside all criticism of the extravagant financial waste incurred in order to celebrate the ritualized burial of even the faint memory of the French Revolution, on the occasion of its Bicentenary. In the course of this odd 'happening' the assembled dignitaries went on reassuring and congratulating themselves that thanks to their firm hold on the levers of power the possibility of revolutionary upheavals irretrievably belongs to the past. And since the guardians of the established order always find great delight in the theoretical eternalization of their rule, later on in the year they conferred world prominence on the bizarre fantasies of a middle-ranking State Department official, Fukuyama, who announced nothing less than the capitalistically triumphant 'end of history'.

However, unruly history not only refused to oblige and lie down with grace in its freshly dug grave but actually quickened its pace beyond recognition. So much so, in fact, that the same establishment organs which a few months earlier still exalted the irreversible happy ending of history had to say farewell to the outgoing year with page-wide headlines like this: *'1989 — The Year of The Revolutions'*.

Indeed, there can be no doubt that in the twentieth century no single year saw the same quickening of the pace of historical change as 1989, ever since the '9 days that changed the world' in 1917. Moreover, anybody who thinks that the possibility of the kind of dramatic intensification of historical time which we have recently witnessed must be confined to the East by virtue of some neo-Hegelian metaphysical predetermination is bound to be confronted with some big surprises in the not too distant future. For major historical events and upheavals cannot be kept in artificially isolated compartments in our globally intertwined contemporary world.

The British Prime Minister, Margaret Thatcher, greeted the opening of the Berlin wall as 'a great day for freedom'. The same day she hastened to make her own contribution to freedom, contemptuously disregarding even the 80 percent democratic popular support on the side of her targeted adversaries, by sending in the troops — with their ill-equipped Landrovers and medically under-qualified personnel, responsible as a result for many unnecessary deaths in the weeks that followed — in order to beat the ambulance workers into submission in their five-months old industrial dispute; just as she used in 1984-85 the full economic

---

* Written in December 1989 - January 1990 for an inquest of the Venezuelan periodical: *El ojo del huracán,* published in its No. 2 issue, Febrero/Marzo/Abril 1990, pp.i-vi.

might and repressive power of the capitalist state against the British miners engaged in a one-year long strike.

Thus social antagonisms to which only socialism could bring a lasting solution continue to erupt on a significant scale even in the most privileged capitalist countries, despite the latest variants of 'bipartisan politics'. Yet, we are expected to believe in the convenient fairy-tale according to which the ideological triumph of 'liberal democracy' has put a happy end to history and its conflicts.

President Bush, too, made his contribution recently to our quickening historical time. Only a few days after his summit meeting in Malta with Mikhail Gorbachev, he ordered the invasion of Panama and the violation of the territorial integrity of the Nicaraguan Embassy in that country. Naturally, he did all this (and more) in the name of restoring and safeguarding democracy and freedom. Nor are indeed actions like the invasion of Panama out of character with the strategies pursued by the most powerful Western democracy. As we all know, after the 'Irangate Contra Affair' the U.S. Congressional Investigation came to the sombre conclusion that President Reagan was 'guilty of undermining the Law and subverting the Constitution'. Yet, despite the severity of this indictment, nothing happened to rectify matters in order to ensure that such grave violations of the openly professed democratic rule of the law should not occur in the future. On the contrary, the voices advocating and justifying the use of naked force — including political assassinations and military interventions — as 'legitimate instruments of U. S. foreign policy' have been gathering momentum in Washington D.C. One wonders, therefore, which particular Latin American country might be the next one on President Bush's list — Nicaragua or Columbia, or perhaps even Venezuela in a situation of major internal crisis? — destined to be the beneficiary of the recently seen U.S. liberal-democratic action in Panama.

Unhappily, this is the sobering global context in which the difficult problems of contemporary socialism can and must be assessed, in contrast to the self-complacent euphoria with which all those who are only too happy to overlook the gross violation of even the most elementary conditions of freedom and democracy in the capitalistically advanced countries of the West greeted the dramatic events in the East as the concluding act in the realization of the liberal-democratic millennium.

Once, on a visit to the capital of the British Empire, Mahatma Gandhi — described by Sir Winston Churchill as 'that half-naked Indian fakir' — was asked what he thought of Western Civilization. Gandhiji answered that in his humble opinion 'that would be a very good idea indeed'. Facing the sharp contradiction between the ideal and the reality, one is strongly tempted to give the same answer when one is expected to indulge in the glorification of Western democracy. For democracy was never in greater danger than in our own times, under growing assaults from the far from liberal forces of monopoly-based corporatism.

It is in fact one of the salient characteristics of life in the capitalistically advanced societies of the West that while the mythology of 'individual freedom' is retained as the dominant ideology, the once institutionally safeguarded freedoms — which had arisen on the ground of an earlier prevailing relation of social forces — are violated in reality every day and in all spheres. This dangerous trend is evident wherever we look, from the liquidation of the last relics of local political decision making power to the central legislative enaction of repressive anti-trade-union laws, in accord with the relentless concentration and centralization of economic power in every major capitalist country. Only the fruition of mass-oriented socialist strategies can offer the hope of rescuing democracy from its precarious predicament in this period of quickening historical transformations.

2. The premature burial of socialism.

IN the immediate aftermath of the recently unfolding events the spokesmen of the capitalist establishment never even bothered to consider how the 'Third World', with all its burning problems, might fit into their triumphalist calculations concerning the East. The question that despite the serious troubles of 'actual socialism' the need for a genuinely socialist alternative in the 'Third World' might be as great as ever, if not greater, could not be allowed to disturb the self-congratulatory celebrations.

Equally, in voicing their 'disinterested' expectations in response to what was happening in the societies of 'actual socialism', the trusted 'personifications of capital' used a coded language at first. They were speaking only of 'free market' (as if it could exist anywhere on earth in the age of ever-more dominant monopolies) and of pure 'democracy', leaving the key term — *capitalist* — diplomatically unmentioned when the conditions of 'economic aid' and 'co-operation' with the East were stipulated.

Later on, however, it became quite clear that the real expectation was the complete restoration of capitalism in all postrevolutionary societies. By the time of drawing the balance-sheet of 1989 it was boldly stated that

Western capitalism defeated Soviet communism. ... Communist economies now lie in ruins. Capitalist forces have been called in to help their postwar reconstruction.[1]

The future was sketched in the same vein, confidently projecting that

As East Europe and the Soviet Union establish market economies, they will inevitably be drawn into the European Community's sphere of influence. By 2000, a Greater European Economic Community should be in sight. In the 21st century, Europe could once again become the dominant economic superpower.[2]

Alternative views to such wishful thinking only entered the horizon when the world's Stock Exchanges took a sudden (even if not dramatic) tumble, hardly four days after the just quoted euphoric prognostication, following the news that Gorbachev had cancelled his appointments with some foreign visitors.

The ease with which theories and strategic expectations like the 700 million strong *'Europe poised for world dominance'* (the sonorous title of the article quoted above) can be unhinged speaks eloquently enough for their soundness. Their vacuity becomes even more striking when we recall that a few days earlier the end of socialism was predicated not only in relation to the historically contingent (and in principle alterable) conditions of the East but aprioristically for all places, as well as for all times ahead of us.

YET, despite everything, the profound structural crisis of the societies of 'actual socialism' — which, in order to be made intelligible, needs a somewhat better explanatory framework than the wishful thinking of neo-capitalist euphoria —

has at least two important positive aspects to it, with far-reaching implications for the prospects of socialism as a global historical enterprise.

First, recent developments in the East brought with them an amply clear demonstration that socialism can represent only an *internal* challenge to the capitalist order.

For a long time in the past the people in the West who were convinced that only the socialist alternative can provide a way out of the destructive antagonisms and inhumanities of the global capital system were greatly handicapped by the mystification of the ruling ideology which could successfully misrepresent the *internal challenge* of socialism as an *external confrontation:* a 'subversion' directed from abroad by a 'monolithic' enemy (Reagan's 'Evil Empire', under whatever name). In the light of the changes that have been taking place in Gorbachev's Russia, exposing at the same time to public view also the long persistent weakness of the Soviet economy, even the most extreme cold warriors must find it difficult to carry on singing to a receptive audience their old 'Evil Empire' song.

The direct consequences of this change are fairly obvious as far as the West European members of the Nato Alliance — above all Germany whose still occupied soil represents the primary stake as the front line of the hypostatized war — are concerned. However, the implications of the new perspective in which the once cherished idea of the Soviet domination of the world has lost its credibility are far greater than that. For from now on the forces which strive for their emancipation from capitalist exploitation and neo-imperialist oppression — whether in Latin America or in Africa and South-East Asia — cannot be so easily discredited and even outlawed in the future as they were in the past, in the name of a holy crusade against 'communist world domination'. The problems arising from the internal antagonisms of the capitalist system will have to be faced everywhere at the plane where they continue to arise. Thus the socialist alternative not only cannot be buried forever, as we are expected to believe, but, on the contrary, acquires a much greater urgency and relevance today as the solution of the internally generated problems.

The *second* positive aspect of the recent changes is of an equally great importance. It concerns the — direct or indirect — acknowledgement that 'socialism in one country' had been, and can only be, a myth, and a most damaging one at that.

In truth, Marx unequivocally stated that each nation is 'dependent on the revolutions of the others' and, therefore

communism is only possible as the act of the dominant peoples 'all at once' and simultaneously, which presupposes the universal development of productive forces and the world intercourse bound up with them.[3]

Many years later — in fact as late as 1892 — Engels reiterated essentially the same position by saying that 'the triumph of the European working class ... can only be secured by the cooperation of at least England, France and Germany'.[4]

Under the impact of painful historical contingencies, culminating in the unchallenged rule of Stalinism, this line of approach was completely abandoned in the 1920s. In its place, not only the possibility but the full realization of socialism was voluntaristically decreed in the Soviet Union in the 1930s, elevating an extremely problematical sociohistorical development to the status of a — for a long time in the international movement compulsory — *model.*

The consequences were quite devastating not only in the U.S.S.R. but for socialist aspirations everywhere. The critical reassessment of 'actual socialism' from a socialist perspective could only begin after Stalin's death, and it took no less than three and a half decades — as well as several major explosions, from Germany to Poland and from Hungary to Czechoslovakia — to produce the necessary break with Stalinist strategies and institutional practices.

Thus, the abandoning of the pretences that the difficult task of building socialism had been accomplished in the Soviet Union a long time ago has a liberating significance well beyond the boundaries of that country. The realistic acknowledgement of the global requirements and constraints within which the socialist historical project can be brought to its realization in due course carries with it a sobering implication. Namely, that in every single country, including those which were the first to embark on the road to 'break the weakest links of the chain' in Lenin's words, one can only talk of a variety of *transitional* — and by their very nature inevitably *endangered* — formations, until the overall relation of forces (which even today still greatly favours the international capitalist system) is radically changed. Only under the circumstances of a significant weakening of Western capital's strangle-hold on the rest of the world can the progressively accomplished 'universal development of the productive forces and the world intercourse bound up with them' facilitate an irreversible breakthrough towards the inherently global 'new historic form' which alone may be rightfully characterized as socialism.

Naturally, this does not mean standing idly by until the fully ripe fruit falls into one's lap. On the contrary. Only a truthful historical perspective, freed from the self-interested mythologies of the Stalinist past, can offer the chance of an effective intervention in the historical process, in accordance with the prevailing conditions and objective possibilities of the existing national communities.

The realization of the complex and multifaceted historic task of building socialism in an inextricably intertwined global system of material, political, and cultural interchanges is feasible only through the specific *material and institutional mediations* appropriate to the particular national communities in which the need for a transition towards a socialist mode of societal interchange arises out of the antagonisms of the established order. Only the ultimate historical coalescence of a multiplicity of such transitional forms, whatever their limitations and contradictions in the first place, can lead to the realization of the socialist project under favourable circumstances. The long overdue rejection of the false perspective of 'socialism in one country' represents a most important step in that direction.

3. The dramatic reappearance of the national question.

UNDERLINING that the recently proclaimed death of socialism as a global project belongs to the realm of wishful thinking does not mean that we can afford to close our eyes to the great difficulties and contradictions manifest in the societies of 'actual socialism'. Many things have been shaken to their very foundation in the countries concerned in the last few years, and in particular during the closing months of '1989: The Year of The Revolutions'. The strategic framework of their development — the road they are likely to follow in the foreseeable future — has become wide open, clamorously refuting the not so long ago widely held tenet according to which the social and political foundations of the postrevolutionary system are absolutely irreversible.

One of the most painful problems recently highlighted in the East concerns the *national* question. Historically it goes back to the tragic circumstance that the first successful anti-capitalist revolution took place — in October 1917 — in a country which was not only greatly underdeveloped but also happened to be a *multinational empire guilty of oppressing its ethnic minorities.*

Within a few years after the revolution the attempts to rectify the authoritarian subjection of the various ethnic communities had been cast aside, and the originally proclaimed principle of national sovereignty and autonomy, including the right to secession, was turned into a mockery. Already in 1920 Stalin defined 'Soviet autonomy' as the

> ensuring of a revolutionary *union between the centre and the border regions.* ... We are against the secession of the border regions from Russia, because secession in that case would mean a weakening of the revolutionary might of Russia.

Thus the various national communities — including the Ukraine — had been degraded to the status of 'border regions' to which others could be added later (the Baltic states) as historical circumstances allowed, heaping up enormous problems for the future.

As it was publicly acknowledged at the time of the 20th Congress of the Soviet Party, Lenin in his last letters and articles took a grave view of the national problem and of Stalin's fateful responsibility in the matter. He stressed the disastrous role of the bureaucratic state apparatus which

> we took over from tsarism and slightly anointed with Soviet oil. The apparatus we call our own is, in fact, still quite alien to us. ... It is quite natural that in such circumstances the 'freedom to secede from the union' by which we justify ourselves will be a mere scrap of paper, unable to defend the non-Russians from the onslaught of that really Russian man, the Great-Russian chauvinist, in substance a rascal and a tyrant, such as the typical Russian bureaucrat is.

Just like Gorbachev today, Lenin was convinced that if the right to secession was genuinely conceded, there would be no need to make use of it. At the same time he warned against the failure to live up to the socialist principle of real national equality. He put into relief the consequences of Stalinist policy on the national issue for socialist development in general in no uncertain fashion:

> The Georgian [Stalin] who is neglectful of this aspect of the question, or who carelessly flings about accusations of 'nationalist socialism' (whereas he himself is a real and true 'nationalist-socialist', and even a Great-Russian bully), violates, in substance, the interests of proletarian class solidarity, for nothing holds up the development and strengthening of proletarian class solidarity so much as national injustice.

It was a great tragedy for subsequent developments that Lenin soon after writing these pages (in which he also requested Stalin's replacement: a request which the Central Committee significantly preferred to ignore) died, and thus could not follow through the implications of his grave analysis by means of effective practical measures. For there was much to be practically reassessed in the light of his severe diagnosis: above all how to deal with the contradictions of the multinational state inherited from tsarism. This was by no means simply a matter of the state apparatus but in general, the profoundly iniquitous nature of the social relations which constitute that structure of dependency and domination of which the Russian postrevolutionary state inherited from tsarism is only one variant.

It was this fundamental — structurally entrenched — inequality as a major practical challenge which Lenin briefly hinted at in the same writing, insisting that

> internationalism on the part of oppressors or 'great' nations, as they are called (though they are great only in their violence, only great as bullies), must consist not only in the observance of the formal equality of nations but even in an inequality of the oppressor nation, the great nation, that must make up for the inequality which obtains in actual practice. Anybody who does not understand this has not grasped the real proletarian attitude to the national question.

WHAT were the social interests and forces which, despite such warnings as these, myopically crossed the path of understanding and produced that *blocked development* which, after the original positive impact of the October revolution, negatively affected — and still continues so to affect — socialist aspirations all over the world? Is there a way out of the contradictions soberly identified by Lenin but wishfully repressed and, against their own design, greatly intensified by his successors?

Clearly, the 'Brezhnev doctrine' represented the direct continuation of Stalin's policies which, in the name of socialism, cynically degraded also the nations of Eastern Europe after the Second World War to the status of 'border regions', imposing on them at the same time — absurdly, again, in the name of 'building socialism' as a forced enterprise — the contradictions of the selfsame blocked development which plagues Soviet society even today. Thus, Gorbachev's rejection of the 'Brezhnev doctrine' represents a historic advance in this respect, even if the closely related socioeconomic and political problems are far from resolved with the removal of direct Soviet interference in the internal affairs of East European nations.

Ever since its first formulation, Marxist theory insisted that a nation which oppresses and dominates other nations simultaneously deprives itself of its own freedom: a dictum which Lenin never ceased to reiterate. It is not difficult to see why this should be so. For any form of inter-state domination presupposes a strictly regulated framework of social interchange in which the exercise of control is expropriated by the relatively few. A national state which is constituted in such a way that it should be able to dominate other nationalities, or the so-called 'peripheral' and 'border regions', presupposes the complicity of its politically active citizenry in the exercise of domination, thus mystifying and weakening the working masses in the aspiration to emancipate themselves. This is so notwithstanding the fact that the hierarchically structured state apparatus assigns very different effective power to the various social groups. Thus, how could the postrevolutionary state treat its own citizens on the basis of true equality when it reserves to itself the power to carry out acts of domination toward other nationalities? For the same power — as deposited in the organs of the state, in separation from the social body as a whole — can be used just as easily for the purposes of internal oppression as against national minorities or outside forces. Besides, a multi-national state which is built on the inherited structure of domination of its national minorities will find it very difficult to establish inter-state relations of equality, especially with smaller nations. Understandably therefore, socialist theory, from the very beginning, advocated the principle of *self-activity* (or real self-determination) at all levels of social life, from the everyday decisions of individuals to the highest and most complex forms of social decision making.

As of today, despite the first historic steps taken in the right direction, the challenging issues of instituting genuine socialist inter-state relations stay unresolved. The establishment of socialist confederations of sovereign nations — perhaps, after learning the lessons of the present crisis, in Eastern Europe as well, not only in the Soviet Union — which regulate their interchanges on the basis of genuine equality remains only an ideal. For the precondition of its realization is the articulation and successful functioning of a social reproductive system managed on the basis of *substantive democracy,* i.e. one that progressively supersedes the existing hierarchies, together with their unavoidable antagonisms. This is so because the latter always find their destructive equivalents — no matter how sincere might be the 'good intentions' with which the road to Dante's hell is paved — also on the plane of international and inter-state relations.

4. The 'marketization' of postrevolutionary societies: some limits and incompatibilities.

EVEN the most liberal wing of the bourgeois press has a great predilection for presenting causal relations upside-down, so that the historical dimension of the process leading to the present should disappear, eternalizing thereby the established order of things. In this spirit, the political editor of the *Financial Times* trumpets in the headline of an article: 'IMF plunges into East European economic maelstrom'[5], diametrically overturning the causal relationship whereby the IMF (and similar institutions) in fact 'plunged Eastern Europe into an economic maelstrom', in full conformity to their habitual role of safeguarding and enforcing the interests of U.S. hegemony in the 'Third World'.

In the same way, in the characteristic misrepresentation of recent developments in Eastern Europe, the party line of the bourgeois press happens to be that the economies of the countries concerned simply 'collapsed', without any involvement of Western capitalism in the process leading to the present crisis. They hail their own side as the 'saviour' that generously comes to the rescue of the East, so that we may all live happily ever after.

The truth of the matter is, of course, quite different. For in the severe crisis and 'economic collapse' of East European societies the ties of economic dependency which they 'enjoyed' for a long time with Western capital played a very significant role in their present-day predicament. Indeed the negative, potentially even disastrous, consequences of such dependency have been visible now for a decade. I have argued in a study first published in the Spring of 1982 that

> *while the aggressive fantasies of a military 'roll-back' of 'actual socialism' proved to be an utter failure, the success of neo-capitalist penetration through its growing economic tentacles represents a much more serious danger also in this respect.*

To understand the relative importance of the latter trend, we have to bear in mind that the indebtedness of several East European countries — especially Poland and Hungary — to Western capitalism is quite phenomenal. Hungary, for instance, is in debt to the tune of approximately 2,000 dollars per head of population. (Given the lower level of income in these countries in comparison to their Western counterparts, the per capita debt is thus much higher than it appears at first sight.) Naturally, such debts must be serviced, and the sheer magnitude of interest payments alone may impose enormous strains — as the 'rescheduled' bankruptcy of the Polish economy testifies — on the countries concerned. Not to mention the ironical consequences of *importing inflation* into the 'planned economy' with the blessing of Western capital. And this is only one of the many ways in which the growing network of economic relations functions in favour of the capitalist countries. Others include:

— disproportionately one-sided trade relations;

— exporting, for the sake of Western currency, goods in which there is a shortage at home (including food, disregarding even the danger of food riots, as we have seen in the case of Poland);

— developing certain sectors of the economy primarily for the sake of Western markets;

— producing finished products on behalf of capitalist concerns, for sale abroad;

— subcontracting to Western firms for the supply of components;

— production under capitalist licence and disbursing the concomitant royalty payments;

— purchasing entire capitalist plants which involves, again, substantial royalty payments, often for antiquated products and processes;

— highly inflated 'unofficial' conversion rates for Western currency, in the context of the tourist trade and elsewhere;

— constructing luxury hotels and even gambling casinos (economic 'no-go areas' for the local population) and leasing them to Western capitalist enterprises on terms highly advantageous to the latter.

One could go on, but there is no need to do so. For the trends and measures already listed are more than sufficient to illustrate that such developments are quite serious as regards their weight and impact on the societies of 'actual socialism' even as things stand today, not to mention their implications for the future.'[6]

The dangerous implications of the past are the explosive reality of today. For the original advocacy of 'market socialism' in some countries of Eastern Europe quickly turned into the acceptance of the most ruthless capitalistic practices, with devastating consequences for the labour force.

The truth of *'market socialism'* — which was supposed to remedy the ills of 'actual socialism' — turned out to be in no time at all the prosaic actuality of *dependent capitalism,* rationalized and justified in the name of 'market-efficiency'. As a result, the workers are now subjected to the more or less immediate prospect of *mass unemployment,* in addition to enormous price increases dictated by the IMF and other Western agencies and capitalistic concerns. No wonder, therefore, that

The IMF regards as 'very courageous' — a euphemism for draconian — an economic reform programme which has just been submitted to the Hungarian Parliament. Talks with Hungary are 'well advanced and should be concluded soon, though there are still some difficulties'.[7]

The full implementation of the conditions imposed by Western capital will indeed create more difficulties even in Hungary and Poland than the production of the now requested and readily supplied 'declarations of intent'. The real difficulties are much greater than what could be remedied by the cooperation of the state bureaucracy whose members have now seen the light on the 'road to Damascus', after many years of imposing on the people the authoritarian rules of the 'command economy'.

For one thing, Western capital is not in the least interested in giving away its own markets, supplying at the same time also a generous 'Marshall aid' to the societies of 'actual socialism' (in accordance with the fantasies of former 'market socialists') in order to acquire for itself in exchange some forcefully revitalized competitors. What it needs and is determined to get are new markets and super-profits for itself, together with the economic and political domination of Eastern Europe (as well as of the Soviet Union and China in due course). Western capital needs such new outlets and areas of domination in order to help remedy the structural defects and contradictions of its own system, including the literally *astronomical* internal and external deficits of the U.S. — counted in *trillions* of dollars — which represent the real debt problem today (and even more so tomorrow).

In the pecking order of global capital the place assigned to the East is in no way better than the one into which the 'Third World' had been forced. Now that the political obstacles towards the restoration of capitalism have been removed in the East European countries, the real expectations can be cynically spelled out by the editorial writers of the capitalist press who talk about

the likely realities of *inflation, debt and continued shortages* ... more like *Latin America* than south-east Asia.[8]

The socioeconomic and political framework of the postrevolutionary societies and the inner dynamics of their development present an even greater obstacle to solving their contradictions through the wishful strategy of straightforward marketization than the constraints of dependency on Western capital. For the uncomfortable truth is that there can be no such thing as 'straightforward marketization'.

The inherent logic of the market as the *economic* regulator of society's reproductive metabolism — which cannot *tolerate* political constraints interfering with its mode of operation, only *generate* them in its own favour — tends toward the restoration of unadulterated capitalism. Consequently, in countries where such restoration is not a readily feasible option (e.g. the Soviet Union and China), the conversion of the given reproductive metabolism to a market-regulated variety is not very realistic. The point is that in postrevolutionary societies the *politically regulated extraction of surplus-labour* is not simply a bureaucratic imposition. On the contrary, it represents the way in which *postcapitalist* societies must define themselves in the first place in their effort to break the rule of capital — the inherited hierarchical social division of labour — in due course.

Thus, it comes as no surprise that when the Chairman of the Soviet Party's Ideological Commission (a Member of Gorbachev's Politburo) tells us that *'Socialism is only one possible choice among many other multi-coloured and various forms'*,[9] he must keep the secret to himself: which are the 'many other' historical alternatives to socialism beside capitalism? By contrast, the people in the Soviet Union who have 'turned emphatically against such entrepreneurial activities as cooperatives evolving outside the state sector, suspecting them of bringing capitalism into the Soviet economy by the back door',[10] seem to be much more realistic in their assessment of the ongoing developments.

In reality the 'free market' operates on the basis of a twofold tyrannical determination: the legally sanctioned and protected *authoritarianism of the particular workshops* (in which the capitalist owners and managers enjoy the absolute power to 'hire and fire' etc.), and the *tyranny of the totalizing market* (which subsumes under its own imperatives the particular units of production and distribution, favouring the strong while ruthlessly 'weeding out' the weak). To treat the market as a 'neutral mechanism' which could be transplanted into any system, expecting that it could abandon its own logic and inner dynamics, in a happy submission to a 'benevolent' political ('market socialist') regulator, is rather far-fetched. For there is an unavoidable *structural mismatch* — a veritable contradiction — between the socioeconomic and political framework of post-capitalist societies (which, not by caprice but by necessity, operate on the basis of the *political* extraction of surplus-labour, inasmuch as they represent an alternative to capitalism at all) and the *necessary* mode of operation of the self-asserting/self-imposing market.

Even in countries like Poland and Hungary the successful restoration of capitalism in the name of market-efficiency might turn out to be unrealizable, as the latent antagonisms break out into the open and assume the form of frustrating underdevelopment, mass unemployment, and even major social upheavals. As to the Soviet Union and China, where the anti-capitalist revolution was indigenous (and not forcibly imposed by a foreign power), setting as a result deep roots, whatever the concomitant contradictions, one could envisage the restoration of capitalism only through *the most devastating convulsions.* The tragic events of Tiananman Square in the Summer of 1989, following a period of what is now called 'excessive modernization', might be indicative in this respect.

In any case, the record of *5 years of Perestroika,* if nothing else, should give ample food for thought concerning the objective incompatibilities between the socioeconomic and political structures of postcapitalist societies and the market-propelled solution of the long persistent — potentially explosive — contradictions of the postrevolutionary order.

Naturally, no social system can function successfully, to the satisfaction of its individual members, without its own system of *incentives.* It would be, however, the greatest and most damaging fallacy to equate the *capitalist market* with the necessary — and by the Stalinist system under all its forms neglected — *incentives* capable of activating the creative energies of the individuals. In other words, the real issue at stake is not how to embrace the 'market mechanism', but how to turn into reality the socialist project of genuine *self-management.*

5. Conclusion.

IT may come as a surprise to many that Marx linked the eventual success of socialism to the question of how far in time capital's 'global ascendancy' will extend, adding that

> For us the difficult question is this: the revolution on the Continent [of Europe] is imminent and its character will be at once socialist; will it not be *necessarily crushed in this little corner of the world,* since on a much larger terrain the development of bourgeois society is still in the *ascendant.*[11]

It is indeed the reversal of such global ascendancy that ultimately decides the issue, by activating the structural contradictions of capital's iniquitous and wasteful productive system and dehumanizing mode of social control. In the meantime, one cannot ignore the necessity of reciprocal adjustments in the actions of the major contending forces in their actual sociohistorical confrontations.

The inescapable constraints of such adjustments are determined by the prevailing historical circumstances and by the changing relation of forces. Given certain overriding pressures, such as the perilous state of the arms race, or extreme difficulties in securing the material conditions of 'original accumulation' (be it called 'capital-accumulation' or 'socialist accummulation') on the required scale, it is in principle possible that the Marxian approach, with its radically uncompromising attitude as regards the genuinely socialist *solution* to the structural antagonisms of society, has to be *cast aside* for a considerable historical period even in countries which claim to be involved in building socialism.

However, to see *permanent* solutions in such contingent temporary adjustments, no matter how necessary they might be considered under the prevailing circumstances, would be as naive as to imagine that the modernizing intent of the Chinese leadership can transform the whole of China into a king-size Hong Kong. One should not confuse the necessarily varied *time-scale and modalities* of socialist transformation in *particular* areas with the *terminus ad quem* — the overall direction and outcome — of the *globally* unfolding social process. For 'historical compromises' do not *eliminate* the underlying contradictions, only modify their conditions of eruption and eventual resolution.

In the end there can be no 'half-way house' between the rule of capital and the socialist transformation of society on a global scale. And that in its own turn necessarily implies that capital's inherent antagonisms must be ultimately 'fought out' to a truly irreversible, structurally safeguarded conclusion.

NOTES

[1] Brian Reading, 'Europe Poised for World Dominance', *The Sunday Times,* 31 Dec. 1989, Section C, p.5)
[2] *Ibid.*
[3] *The German Ideology,* MECW, Vol. 5, p.49.
[4] Engels, Introduction to the English edition of *Socialism: Utopian and Scientific.* In Marx and Engels, *Selected Works,* Vol. 2, p.105.
[5] Peter Riddell, 'IMF plunges into East European economic maelstrom', *Financial Times,* 6 January 1990, p.2.
[6] 'Il rinnovamento del marxismo e l'attualità storica dell'offensiva socialista', special issue of *Problemi del Socialismo* ed. by Furio Cerutti, anno xxiii, No. 23, January-April 1982, pp.5-141. Quoted from the English edition, 'The Cunning of History in Reverse Gear', pp.7-8 of *Radical Philosophy,* No. 42, Winter/Spring 1986.
[7] From the article quoted in note 5.
[8] 'New Year euphoria', Editorial article in the *Financial Times* (6 January 1990), announcing the new party line after the unexpected fall on the Stock Exchange.
[9] Vadim A. Medvedev, 'The Ideology of Perestroika', in *Perestroika Annual,* Vol. 2, edited by Abel G. Aganbegyan, Futura Publications (Macdonald & Co. Ltd.), London, 1990, p.36.
[10] 'Economic crisis, Soviet style', *New Statesman supplement on Soviet Spring,* 12 January 1990, p.18.
[11] Marx, Letter to Engels, 8 October 1858.

APPENDIX

MARXISM TODAY*

Sartre's alternative

RP: You met Sartre in 1957. Why did you decide to write a book on him?

I always felt that Marxists owed a great debt to Sartre because we live in an age in which the power of capital is overbearing, where, significantly, the common-place platitude of politicians is that 'there is no alternative', whether you think of Mrs. Thatcher, or Gorbachev, who endlessly repeated the same until he had to find out, like Mrs. Thatcher, that after all there had to be an alternative to both of them. But it goes on an on, and if you look around and think of how Conservative or Labour politicians talk, they always talk about 'there is no alternative', and the underlying pressures are felt everywhere. Sartre was a man who always preached the diametrical opposite: there is an alternative, there must be an alternative; you as an individual have to rebel against this power, this monstrous power of capital. Marxists on the whole failed to voice that side. I don't say that you have to become therefore an existentialist or a politically committed existentialist in order to face it, but there is no one in the last fifty years of philosphy and literature who tried to hammer it home with such single-mindedness and determination as Sartre did: the necessity that there has to be a rebellion against the wisdom of 'there is no alternative' and there has to be an individual participation in it. I don't embrace his ideas but I embrace the aim. How you realize that aim is up to you in the context of your own approach, but the aim is something without which we won't get anywhere. Sartre today in France is a very embarrassing person even to mention. Why? Because what happended is that in the name of privatism and individualism they have totally sold out to the powers of repression, a capitulation to the forces of 'there is no alternative', and that's why Sartre is a terrible reminder. When you also look into the background of the people we are talking about, 'post-modernists' of a great variety, they very often were politically engaged people. But their engage-ment was skin-deep. Some of these people, around 1968, were more Maoist than the extreme Maoists in China, and now they have embraced the right in a most enthusiastic way; or they were in the 'Socialism or Barbarism' group and have become the peddlers of the most stupid platitudes of 'post-modernity'. What these people have lost is their frame of reference. In France intellectual life used to be dominated in one way or another by the Communist Party. That goes also for Sartre who tried criticizing it from outside and pushing it in a

*   An interview published in the British journal *Radical Philosophy* (No. 62, Autumn 1992) and later in a somewhat abbreviated version in *Monthly Review* (Vol. 44, No. 11, April 1993). The interview was conducted by Chris Arthur and Joseph McCarney in April 1992. The text printed below is the same as published in *Monthly Review*.

direction which he embraced until he had to come to the conclusion that work in collaboration with the Communist Party is both necessary and impossible, which is a terrible, bitter dilemma. He said this at the time of the Algerian war when the role of the Communist Party was absolutely disgraceful. Thtat's what made it necessary, because you need a movement to oppose the repressive force of the state; and impossible, because look what that movement is like.. What happened, of course, was the disintegration of the French Communist Party like several other parties of the Third International in the last two decades. And with the sinking of this big ship in relation to which the French intellectuals defined themselves in one way or another, here are these intellectuals left behind: the ship has disappeared and they find themselves in their self-inflated rubber dinghies throwing little darts at each other. Not a very reassuring sight: and they are not going to get out of it by simply fantasizing about some individuality which doesn't exist; because true individuality is inconceivable without a community with which your relate yourself and define yourself.

Marxism Today

RP: You have lived in various countries. Why did you settle in England? Surely English culture is not very congenial to your kind of thought?

Well, I beg to differ because I had actually quite a long relationship to English-speaking culture way before I left Hungary. I had been a great admirer of a certain line of thought from Hobbes to the great figures of the English and Scottish Enlightenment and these really meant a hell of a lot to me, because they had a great message for the future and have to be an integral part of your own work. Another reason was that I was always a great admirer of English and Scottish poetry from Shakespeare to the present. And the third reason which I found equally important is that I always thought of England as the country of the Industrial Revolution which went with a working class with tremendously deep roots, and that remains despite everything. I think your have to relate yourself to something: political and social commitment cannot be in thin air or in a vacuum. I am deeply committed to the working class, and that is how I think of the future intellectually. Theoretically there must be points of reference: there cannot be social transformation without an agency and the only agency conceivable under the present conditions to take us out of this mess is labour — labour in the sense Marx was talking about and which we have to rediscover for ourselves under our present conditions.

RP: Your most recent book is The Power Of Ideology. *The last part has some interesting criticisms of Marx. What do we have to rethink in Marx's legacy?*

Well, we have to relate him to his time which does not mean we have to in any way abandon the framework of his theory. The framework of Marxian theory remains the overall horizon also of our activity, our orientation, because it embraces the whole epoch, this epoch of capital in crisis and the necessity of finding a way out of it. However, historical circumstances change and some of the things about which I wrote in *The Power of Ideology* show that he had to take short-cuts. For well over ten years I have tried to draw attention to the passage in which Marx talks about this 'little corner of the world', Europe. Europe is after all only a little corner of the world. What is it for us socialists, what is the meaning of it, that capital on a much larger terrain, the rest of the world, not this little corner of the world, is in the ascendant? He decided to put that on the side and proceed from the horizon and perspective of the little corner of the world which Europe was. And that was a conscious choice for him.

RP: In recent papers on socialist transformation, your have introduced an important distinction between capital and capitalism. Can you explain this distinction and its significance for socialist struggle?

In fact this distinction goes back to Marx himself. I pointed out several times that Marx didn't entitle his main work *'Capitalism'* but *'Capital'*, and I also underlined that the subtitle of Volume One was mistranslated under Engels' supervision as 'the capitalist production process', when in fact it is 'the production process of capital', which has a radically different meaning. What is at stake of course here is that the object, the target, of socialist transformation is overcoming the power of capital. Capitalism is a relatively easy object in this enterprise because you can in a sense abolish capitalism through revolutionary upheaval and intervention at the level of politics, the expropriation of the capitalist. You have put an end to capitalism but you have not even touched the power of capital when you have done it. Capital is not dependent on the power of capitalism and this is important also in the sense that capital precedes capitalism by thousands of years. Capital can survive capitalism, hopefully not by throusands of years, but when capitalism is overthrown in a limited area, the power of capital continues even if it is in a hybrid form.

The Soviet Union was not capitalist, not even state capitalist. But the Soviet system was very much dominated by the power of capital: the division of labour remained intact, the hierarchical command structure of capital remained. Capital is a command system whose mode of functioning is accumulation-oriented, and the accumulation can be secured in a number of different ways. In the Soviet Union surplus labour was extracted in a political way and this is what came into crisis in recent years. The politically regulated extraction of surplus labour became untenable for a variety of reasons. The political control of labour power is not what you might consider an ideal or optimal way of controlling the labour process. Under capitalism in the West what we have is an economically regulated extraction of surplus labour and surplus value. In the Soviet system this was done in a very improper fashion from the point of view of productivity because labour retained a hell of a lot of power in the form of negative acts, defiance, sabotage, moonlighting, etc., through which one could not even dream of achieving the kind of productivity which is feasible elsewhere, and which underminded the *raison d'être* of this system under Stalin and his successors, politically forced accumulation. The accumulation part of it became stuck and that is why the whole system had to collapse. I published in Italy a long essay in Spring 1982, in which I explicitly stated that, whereas the old U.S. policies for the military-political rollback of communism were not likely to succeed, what was happening in Eastern Europe was likely to lead to the restoration of capitalism. I also found for the same reason the idea of 'market socialism' a contradiction in terms, because it would, in a wishful concept, want to wed the two modalities: of the economic extraction of surplus labour with the politically regulated extraction — so that was why it was always a non-starter really.

What is absolutely crucial is to recognize that capital is a metabolic system, a social-economic metabolic system of control. You can overthrown the capitalist but the factory system remains, the division of labour remains, nothing has changed in the metabolic functions of society. Indeed, sooner or later you find the need for reassigning those forms of control to personalities, and that's how the bureaucracy comes into existence. The bureaucracy is a function of this command structure under the changed circumstances where in the absence of the private capitalist you have to find an equivalent to that control. I think this is a very important conclusion, because very often the notion of bureaucracy is pushed forward as a kind of mythical explanatory framework, and it doesn't explain anything. The bureaucracy itself needs explanation. How come this bureaucracy arises? When you use it as a kind of *deus ex machina* that explains everything in terms of bureaucracy, if you get rid of bureaucracy then everything will be all right. But you don't get rid of bureaucracy unless you attack the social economic foundation and devise an alternative way of regulating the metabolic process of society in such a way that the power of capital at first is curtailed and is of course in the end done away with altogether. Capital is a controlling force, you cannot control capital, you can do away with it only through the transformation of the whole complex of metabolic relationships of society, you cannot just fiddle with it. It either controls you or you do away with it, there is no half-way house between, and that's why the idea of market socialism could not conceivably function from the very beginning. The real need is not for the restoration of the capitalist market under the name of an utterly fictitious social market, but for the adoption of a proper system of incentives. There is no social production system which can function without incentives, and who are the people to whom these incentives have to be related? Not abstract collective entitites but individuals. So if people as individuals are not interested, not involved in the production process, then sooner or later they assume a negative or even actively hostile attitude towards it.

RP: Are we talking about material incentives?

It can be both. The opposition between moral and material incentives is often a very rhetorical one, an abstract and rhetorical one, because if the result of this intervention and participation in the social processes is a better production, an increasing productivity, activation of the potentialities of the individuals involved, then it becomes a material incentive. But in as much as they are in control of their own life processes, it is also a moral incentive, so the two go hand-in-hand. Material and moral incentives have to go hand-in-hand. It is a question of the control of the processes of this social economic system in which the activation of the repressed potential of the people is also an incentive. Material incentives in our society as presented to us always divide people against one another. You can see this everywhere, in every profession, teaching, university, every walk of life: the incentives work on the presumption that we can divide people against one another in order to control them better; that's the whole process. Now if you then reverse this relationship and say that people are in control of what they are involved in, then the divisiveness doesn't work any longer because they are not the suffering subjects of that sort of system. So material incentives and moral incentives can also be egalitarian in character. That is the tragedy of the Soviet-type of development. When they talk about the collapse of socialism in relation to that, it's a grotesque misrepresentation of the facts, because socialism was not even started, not even the first steps have been taken in the direction of a socialist transformation whose target can only be to overcome the power of capital and to overcome the social division of labour, to overcome the power of the state which is also a command structure regulating the lives of the people from above.

Mickey Mouse Socialism

RP: You talk about challenging the power of capital and I wondered if you could say a bit more about the practical implications, the implications for socialist struggle of your distinction between capital and capitalism.

First of all, the strategy which you have to envisage has to be spelled out in those terms. Socialists cannot carry on with the illusion that all you have to do is abolish private capitalism — because the real problem remains. We are really in a profound historical crisis. This process of the expansion of capital embracing the globe itself has been more or less accomplished. What we have witnessed in the last couple of decades is the structural crisis of capital. I always maintained that there is a big difference from the time when Marx talked about crisis in terms of the crisis that discharges itself in the form of great thunderstorms. Now it doesn't have to discharge itself in thunderstorms. What is characteristic in the crisis of our time is precipitations of varying intensity, tending towards a depressed continuum. Recently we started to talk about double-dip recession, soon we will talk about triple-dip recession. What I am saying is that this tendency towards a depressed continuum, where one recession follows another, is not a condition which can be maintained indefinitely because at the end it reactivates capital's internal explosive contradictions with a vengeance, and there are also some absolute limits which one has to consider in that respect.

Remember, I am talking about the structural crisis of capital, which is a much more serious problem than the crisis of capitalism; because one way to get out of the crisis of capitalism in principle was a state regulation of the economy, and in some respects on the outer horizon of the Western capitalist system you can allow for its possibility. State capitalism can arise when the Western capitalist system is in deepest trouble, but again I would say it's not a tenable solution in the long run because the same kinds of contradictions are reactivated, namely the contradiction between the political and the economic extraction of surplus labour. I am not talking about fictitious future events. Think of fascism, think of the Nazi system which attempted this kind of corporatist state regulation of the system in order to get out of the crisis of German capitalism at that given time of history. Therefore what we are considering here is that all those ways of displacing temporarily the internal contradictions of capital are being exhausted. The world as a whole is very insecure. The overwhelming majority of humanity lives in the most abominable conditions. Whatever happened to the modernization of these countries? It has taken such forms of robbery and extraction and mindless refusal to consider even the implications for the survival of humanity — the way in which these territories have been treated — that the whole thing has been totally undermined, and today you find a situation in which nobody believes any more in the modernization of the so-called 'Third World'. And that is why that depressed continuum is, in the long run, an untenable situation and for that reason a social transformation must be feasible. But it is not feasible through the revitalization of capital. It can only be done on the basis of a radical departure from the logic of this accumulation-oriented mindless destructive control.

The tremendous crisis I am talking about saw not only the virtual extinction of the Communist parties, the parties of the Third International, but also the extinction of the parties of the Second International. For about a hundred years those who believed in the virtues of evolutionary socialism and reform were talking about the transformation of society which leads towards socialist relations of humanity. This has gone totally out of the window even in terms of their own programs and perspectives. You have seen recently that the socialist parties of the Second International, and their various associates, have suffered quite devastating setbacks and defeats in every single country: in France, in Italy, in Germany, in Belgium and the Scandinavian countries, and now recently also in England, the fourth successive defeat for the Labour Party. It was quite appropriate that this serial defeat in all these countries coincided with the celebratory opening of Euro-Disneyland, because what these parties themselves have adopted in this historical period, in their response to the crisis, is some kind of Mickey Mouse socialism and this Mickey Mouse socialism is totally incapable of intervening in the social process. That is why it is not accidental that these parties adopt the wisdom of capital as an irreplaceable sytem. The leader of the Labour Party once declared that the task of socialists is the better management of capitalism. Now this kind of preposterous nonsense is in itself a contradiction. It is a contradiction in terms because it is extremely presumptious to think that the capitalist system would work better with a Labourite government. The problems continue to become more severe, and the political system is incapable of responding because the political system operates under the ever narrowing constraints of capital. Capital as such doesn't allow any more margin for manoeuvre. The margin of manoeuvre for political movements and parliamentary forces was incomparably greater in the nineteenth century or in the first third of the twentieth century. Britain is already part of Europe and there is no way in which you can unwind that process, in the sense that little England will be capable of solving these problems.

But that immediately also raises the question, how do we relate ourselves to the rest of the world? With what happened in the East, in the Soviet Union? A new fundamental problem has arisen on the horizon. In the case of Russia I read recently that, in addition to the $25 billion which exist in the form of promises from the West, Russia will need this year alone another $20 billion. Where are we going to find these billions which Russia needs for this process when the American debt is itself quite astronomical? The problems of this world are becoming so intertwined, so enmeshed with one another, that you can't think of partial resolution to them. Fundamental structural changes are needed. The two and a half decades of expansion after the Second World War was followed by deepening malaise, the collapse of the earlier cherished strategies, the end of Keynesianism, the appearance of monetarism, etc., and all of them leading nowhere. When self-complacent people like Prime Minister John Major say 'socialism is dead, capitalism works', we must ask: capitalism works for whom and for how long? I read recently that the directors of Merrill Lynch received, one $16.5 million, another $14 million, and another ten or fifteen of them $5.5 million each, as annual remuneration. Capitalism works very well indeed for them, but how does it work for the people in Africa, where you see them every day on on your television screen? Or in vast areas of Latin America, or in India, or in Pakistan, or in Bangladesh? I could continue and name the countries where you are talking about thousands of millions of people who can hardly survive.

RP: The agent of change in this situation, the revolutionary subject, is still in your view the working class?

Undoubtedly, there cannot be any other. I remember there was a time when Herbert Marcuse was dreaming about new social agents, the intellectuals and the outcasts, but neither of them had the power to implement change. The intellectuals can play an important role in defining strategies, but it cannot be that the outcasts are the force which implements this change. The only force which can introduce this change and make it work is society's producers, who have the repressed energies and potentialities through which all those problems and contradictions can be solved. The only agency which can rectify this situation, which can assert itself, and find fulfilment in the process of asserting itself, is the working class.

The Problem of Organization

What about its form of organization? Do you think new forms of organization are needed? Some people say the old-style political party is irrelevant.

Yes, I would completely agree with that. The old-style political party is integrated into the parliamentary system which itself has outlived its historical relevance. It was in existence well before the working class appeared on the historical horizon as a social agency. The working class had to accommodate itself and constrain itself in accordance with whatever possibilities that framework provided and consequently it could produce only defensive organizations. All organizations of the working class which have been historically constituted — its political parties and trade unions have been the most important of them — all of them were defensive organizations. They worked up to a point, and that was why the reformist perspective of evolutionary socialism was successful for so many years, because partial improvements could be gained. The working-class

INDEX

Bracke, Wilhelm 514, 515, 863
Brandt, Willie 575, 693, 698, 949
Braverman, Harry 268, 846
Bray, J. F. 616
Brecht, Bertolt 496
Brezhnev, Leonid 98, 282, 646, 662, 663, 670, 971
Bridges, Amy 846
Bromlei, Julian 655, 861
Braun, Werner von 875
Brus, Wlodimierz 827-9, 830, 869, 970
Buchanan, James 857
Bukharin, Nicolai 312, 501
Buonarroti, Philippe 277
Burnham, James 73, 93, 264
Burrell, Ian 280
Bush, George 270, 654, 776, 966
Butler, Rab 244

Camara, Dom Elder 123
Carey, Henry Charles 855
Carillo, Santiago 622, 857
Castle, Barbara 263, 885, 897
Cerutti, Furio 499, 500, 976
Chávez Frias, Hugo 770,771, 864
Chomsky, Noam 726, 865
Churchill, Lord Randolph 436
Churchill, Sir Winston 136, 243, 272, 688, 712, 966
Clausewitz, Karl Marie von 152, 656
Claussen, D. 499
Clinton, Bill 154 257
Cohen, Peter 280
Cole, H. S. D. 273
Collison Black, R. D. 262
Colvil, Marie 276
Comte, Auguste 120, 533
Condorcet, Marquis de 224
Constantino, Renato 155, 163, 271
Craxi, Bettino 731
Crosland, Anthony 448
Cunningham, Shea 964

Daiches, David 895
Danielson, N. F. 863
Daumer, Georg Friedrich 113
Davidson, James Dale 721, 865
de Gaulle, Charles 342

Debray, Régis 785, 857
Denman, Sir Roy 699, 700
Descartes, René 120, 501
Deutscher, Isaac 256, 508, 637, 859, 872, 894, 916, 986
Diderot, Denis 110, 111, 117, 199, 268
Dilthey, Wilhelm 330
Dobb, Maurice 508, 869
Dorfman, Joseph 261
Drummond, Victor A. Wellington 440, 441
Dubcek, Alexander 646
Duncan, Alan 857
Durie, John xx
Dutschke, Rudi 884

Edgeworth, F. Y. 80, 81, 86, 88, 197, 261, 262, 263
Ehrenreich, Barbara 846
Ehrenreich, John 846
Einstein, Albert 120, 123, 857
Eisner, Kurt 339
Engels, Friedrich xii, xxi, 2, 23, 34, 36, 84, 162, 189-90,195, 254, 256, 269, 272, 274, 275, 341, 360, 363, 435, 436-7, 445, 449, 450, 456, 479, 484, 503, 505, 506, 514,515, 516,518, 519, 520, 614, 622, 694, 697, 713, 714, 724, 846, 856, 863, 866, 870, 912, 915, 916, 917, 933, 934, 968, 976, 980
Ennals, Richard 955
Enzensberger, Hans Magnus 896
Ewen, Elizabeth 846

Fagan, Gus 859
Fedorenko, N. 649
Ferguson, Adam 553, 849
Feuerbach, Ludwig 445, 505, 515, 519, 520, 876
Fichte, J. G. 56, 291, 299
Flew, A. G. N. 123, 269
Foà, Lisa 860
Foot, Michael 721
Forbes, Duncan 849
Ford, Henry 118
Forrester, Jay 270